Java Programming:
Program Design Including Data Structures

D.S. Malik

COURSE TECHNOLOGY
CENGAGE Learning™

Australia • Brazil • Japan • Korea • Mexico • Singapore • Spain • United Kingdom • United States

**Java Programming: Program Design
Including Data Structures**
D.S. Malik

Senior Product Manager: Alyssa Pratt

Managing Editor: Mary Franz

Associate Production Manager: Aimee
Poirier

Senior Marketing Manager: Karen Seitz

Associate Product Manager: Jennifer Smith

Editorial Assistant: Allison Murphy

Senior Manufacturing Coordinator: Justin
Palmeiro

Cover Designer: Abby Scholz

Compositor: GEX Publishing Services

For product information and technology assistance, contact us at
Cengage Learning Customer & Sales Support, 1-800-354-9706

For permission to use material from this text or product, submit all
requests online at **cengage.com/permissions**
Further permissions questions can be emailed to
permissionrequest@cengage.com

ISBN-13: 978-1-4188-3540-8

ISBN-10: 1-4188-3540-4

Course Technology
25 Thomson Place
Boston, Massachusetts 02210
USA

Cengage Learning is a leading provider of customized learning solutions
with office locations around the globe, including Singapore, the United
Kingdom, Australia, Mexico, Brazil, and Japan. Locate your local office at:
international.cengage.com/region

Cengage Learning products are represented in Canada by Nelson
Education, Ltd.

For your lifelong learning solutions, visit **course.cengage.com**

Purchase any of our products at your local college store or at our preferred
online store **www.ichapters.com**

The programs in this book are for instructional purposes only. They have
been tested with care but are not guaranteed for any particular intent
beyond educational purposes. The author and the publisher do not offer
any warranties or representations, nor do they accept any liabilities with
respect to the programs.

Sun, Sun Microsystems, the Sun logo, Java, Forte for Java and all Java-based
marks are trademarks or registered trademarks of Sun Microsystems, Inc. in
the United States and other countries. Pentium® is a registered trademark
of Intel Corporation; IBM® is a registered trademark of Industrial Business
Machines; Windows XP is a registered trademark of Microsoft Corporation.

Printed in China by China Translation & Printing Services Limited
4 5 6 7 8 9 09

TO

My Daughter

Shelly Malik

TABLE OF
Contents

APPENDIX E Java Classes

Preface

Welcome to *Java Programming: Program Design Including Data Structures*. Designed for a two semester (CS1 and CS2) Java course, this text will provide a breath of fresh air to you and your students. The CS1 and CS2 courses serve as the cornerstone of the computer science curriculum. My primary goal is to motivate and excite all programming students, regardless of their level. Motivation breeds excitement for learning. Motivation and excitement are critical factors that lead to the success of the programming student. This text is a culmination and development of my classroom notes throughout more than fifty semesters of teaching successful programming.

Java Programming: Program Design Including Data Structures started as a collection of brief examples, exercises, and lengthy programming examples. It soon turned into a collection large enough to develop into a text. *The approach taken in this book to present the material is, in fact, driven by the students' demand for clarity and readability*. Most of the examples in this book resulted from student interaction in the classroom.

As with any profession, practice is essential. Cooking students practice their recipes. Budding violinists practice their scales. New programmers must practice solving problems and writing code. This is not a Java cookbook. We do not simply list the Java syntax followed by an example; we dissect the "why" behind all concepts. The crucial question of "Why?" is answered for every topic when first introduced. This technique offers a bridge to learning Java. Students must understand the "Why?" in order to be motivated to learn.

Traditionally, a Java programming neophyte needed a working knowledge of another programming language. This book assumes no prior programming experience. However, some adequate mathematics background such as college algebra is required.

APPROACH

Once conceived as a Web programming language, Java is steadily finding its way into classrooms in the computer science curriculum. Numerous colleges and universities now teach their first programming language course (CS1) using Java. As remarked earlier, this book is intended for a two-semester course covering CS1 and CS2 topics in a Computer Science department. The first eleven or twelve chapters can be covered in the first course, while the remaining chapters can be handled in the second course.

Java is a combination of traditional style programming—programming with a nongraphical user interface—and modern style programming with a graphical user interface (GUI). This book introduces you to both styles of programming. After giving a brief description of each chapter, we discuss how to read this book.

Chapter 1 briefly reviews the history of computers and programming languages. The reader can quickly skim and become familiar with some of the hardware and software components of the computer. This chapter also gives an example of a Java program and describes how a Java program is processed. The two basic problem-solving techniques, structured programming and object-oriented design, are also presented.

After completing Chapter 2, students become familiar with the basics of Java and are ready to write programs that are complicated enough to do some computations. Moreover, this chapter introduces the **class Scanner** (available in J2SE 5.0 (JDK 5.0), for inputting data into a program.

Three terms that you will encounter throughout the book are primitive type variables, reference variables, and objects. Chapter 3 makes clear distinctions between these terms and sets the tone for the rest of the book. An object is a fundamental entity in an object-oriented programming language. This chapter further explains how an object works. The **class String** is one of the most important classes in Java. This chapter introduces this class and explains how various methods of this class can be used to manipulate strings. Because input/output is fundamental to any programming language, it is introduced early, and is covered in detail in Chapter 3.

Chapters 4 and 5 introduce control structures used to alter the sequential flow of execution.

Java is equipped with powerful yet easy-to-use graphical user interface (GUI) components to create user-friendly graphical programs. Chapter 6 introduces various GUI components and gives examples of how to use these components in Java application programs. Because Java is an object-oriented programming language, the second part of Chapter 6 discusses and gives examples of how to solve various problems using object-oriented design methodology. J2SE 5.0 (JDK 5.0) introduces autoboxing and unboxing of primitive types. This chapter explains autoboxing and unboxing of primitive types in some details and gives examples to clarify this new concept.

Chapter 7 discusses user-defined methods. Parameter passing is a fundamental concept in any programming language. Several examples, including visual diagrams, help readers understand this concept. To pass primitive type values as objects, we use several classes introduced in Chapter 6. (Appendix D, available on the CD accompanying the text, gives more detail about these classes and how to use them in Java programs. Because Chapter 6 is not a prerequisite for Chapter 7, you can review these classes in Appendix D if necessary.) It is recommended that readers with no prior programming background spend extra time on this material.

Chapter 8 discusses user-defined classes. In Java, a class is an important and widely used element. It is used to create Java programs, group related operations, and it allows users to create their own data types. This chapter uses extensive visual diagrams to illustrate how objects of classes manipulate data.

Chapter 9 describes arrays. This chapter also introduces variable length formal parameter lists, a new feature of Java. In addition, this chapter introduces foreach loops, another new feature of Java, and explains how this loop can be used to process the elements of an array. Chapter 10 discusses the `class Vector`, additional features of the `class String`, as well as covering `enum` type.

Inheritance is an important principle of object-oriented design. It encourages code reuse. Chapter 11 discusses inheritance, and gives various examples to illustrate how classes are derived from existing classes. In addition, this chapter also discusses polymorphism, abstract classes, inner classes, and composition.

An occurrence of an undesirable situation that can be detected during program execution is called an exception. For example, division by zero is an exception. Java provides extensive support for handing exceptions. Chapter 12 shows how to handle exceptions in a program. Chapter 12 also discusses event handling, which was introduced in Chapter 6.

Chapter 13 picks up the discussion of GUI components started in Chapter 6. This chapter introduces additional GUI components and discusses how to create applets.

Chapter 14 introduces recursion. Several examples illustrate how recursive methods execute.

To create generic code, with the release of J2SE 5.0 (JDK 5.0) Java introduces generic classes and methods. Chapter 15 explains how to create and work with generic classes and methods. Moreover, this chapter explains in some detail how Java `interface`s `Cloneable` and `Comparable` work. The concepts introduced in the first half of the chapter are then used to create generic array-based lists.

After discussing generic array-based lists in Chapter 15, Chapters 16 and 17 are devoted to the study of additional data structures. Discussed in detail are linked lists in Chapter 16, and stacks and queues in Chapter 17. The programming code developed in these chapters is generic. These chapters effectively use the fundamentals of OOD.

Chapter 18 discusses various searching and sorting algorithms. In addition to showing how these algorithms work, the chapter also provides relevant analysis and results concerning the performance of the algorithms. The algorithm analysis allows the user to decide which algorithm to use in a particular application. This chapter also includes several sorting algorithms. The instructor can decide which algorithms to cover.

Chapter 19 provides an introduction to binary trees. Various traversal algorithms, as well as the basic properties of binary trees, are discussed and illustrated. Special binary trees, called binary search trees, are introduced. Searching, as well as item insertion and deletion from a binary search tree, are described and illustrated. A common way to traverse a binary tree is to use recursion. However, there are situations when nonrecursive traversal algorithms are more effective and well-suited. For example, to create an iterator to a binary tree, which is also discussed in this chapter, nonrecursive traversal algorithms are easy to use and work with. Therefore, nonrecursive binary tree traversal algorithms are introduced and discussed. This chapter also introduces and discusses in some detail height-balanced trees, also known as AVL trees.

Graph algorithms are discussed in Chapter 20. After introducing the basic graph theory terminology, the representation of graphs in computer memory is discussed. This chapter also discusses graph traversal algorithms, the shortest path algorithm, the minimal spanning tree algorithm, and topological sorting.

Java is equipped with a powerful library—called Collections—of data structures and algorithms that can be used effectively in a wide variety of applications. Chapter 21 describes various features of Collections. After discussing the Java `class LinkedList`, this chapter describes the `interface Collection` and some of its subclasses. Commonly used algorithms are packaged in the `class Collections`. Therefore, the latter half of this chapter shows how various `Collections` algorithms can be used in a program.

Appendix A lists the reserved words in Java. Appendix B shows the precedence and associativity of the Java operators. Appendix C lists the ASCII (American Standard Code for Information Interchange) portion of the Unicode character set as well as the EBCDIC (Extended Binary Code Decimal Interchange) character set.

Appendix D contains additional topics in Java. The topics covered are converting a base 10 number to binary (base 2) number and vice versa, and how to compile and execute a Java program using command line statements. Appendix E describes the Java classes used in this book. Appendix F gives a list of references for further study. Appendix G provides answers to all the odd numbered exercises in the text. Note that all the appendices are on the CD that accompanies this book.

How to Use This Book

Java is a complex and very powerful language. In addition to traditional (non-GUI) programming, Java provides extensive support for creating programs that use a graphical user interface (GUI). Chapter 3 introduces graphical input and output dialog boxes. Chapter 6 introduces most commonly used GUI components such as labels, buttons, and text fields. More extensive coverage of GUI components is provided in Chapter 13.

This book can be used in two ways. One is an integrated approach in which readers learn how to write both non-GUI and GUI programs as they learn basic programming concepts and skills. The other approach focuses on illustrating fundamental programming concepts with non-GUI programming first, and later incorporating GUI components. The recommended chapter sequence for each of these approaches is as follows:

- **Integrated approach:** Study all chapters in sequence.

- **Non-GUI first, then GUI:** Study Chapters 1–5 in sequence. Then study Chapters 7–12 and Chapter 14–21. This approach initially skips Chapters 6 and 13, the primary GUI chapters. After studying Chapters 1–5, 7–12, and 14–21, the reader can come back to study Chapters 6 and 13, the GUI chapters.

If you choose the second approach, it should also be noted that the Programming Examples in Chapters 8 and 11 are developed first without any GUI components, and then the programs are extended to incorporate GUI components. Also, if Chapter 6 is skipped, the reader can skip the event handling part of Chapter 12. Chapter 14 (recursion) contains two Programming Examples: one creates a non-GUI application program, while the other creates a program that uses GUI. If you skip Chapters 6 and 13, you can skip the GUI part of the Programming Examples in Chapters 8, 11, 12, 14, and 17. Once you have studied Chapter 6 and 13, you can study the GUI part of the Programming Examples of Chapters 8, 11, 12, 14, and 17.

Figure 1 shows a chapter dependency diagram for this book. Solid arrows indicate that the chapter at the beginning of the arrow is required before studying the chapter at the end of the arrow. A dotted arrow indicates that the chapter at the beginning of the arrow is not essential to studying the chapter at the end of the dotted arrow.

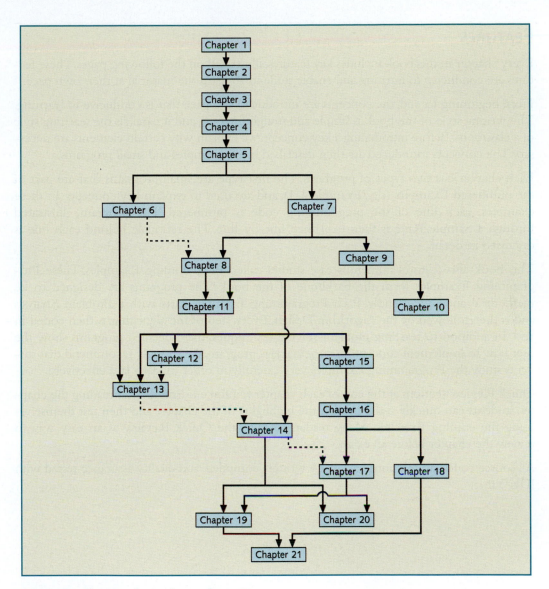

Figure 1 Chapter dependency diagram

FEATURES

Every chapter in this book includes key features, illustrated on the following pages. These features are conducive to learning and enable students to learn the material at their own pace.

From beginning to end, the concepts are introduced at a pace that is conducive to learning. The writing style of this book is simple and straightforward, and it parallels the teaching style of a classroom. Before introducing a key concept, we explain why certain elements are necessary. The concepts introduced are then described using examples and small programs.

Each chapter has two types of programs. The first type are small programs that are part of the numbered Examples (*e.g.*, Example 4-1), and are used to explain key concepts. In these examples, each line of the programming code is numbered. The program, illustrated through a Sample Run, is then explained line-by-line. The rationale behind each line is discussed in detail.

This book also features numerous case studies called Programming Examples. These Programming Examples form the backbone of the book. The programs are designed to be methodical and user-friendly. Each Programming Example starts with a Problem Analysis and is then followed by the Algorithm Design. Every step of the algorithm is then coded in Java. In addition to teaching problem-solving techniques, these detailed programs show the user how to implement concepts in an actual Java program. We strongly recommend that students study the Programming Examples very carefully in order to learn Java effectively.

Quick Review sections at the end of each chapter reinforce learning. After reading the chapter, students can quickly walk through the highlights of the chapter and then test themselves using the ensuing Exercises. Many readers refer to the Quick Review as an easy way to review the chapter before an exam.

All source code and solutions have been written, compiled, and quality assurance tested with JDK 5.0.

For example, the string `"Air"` is less than the string `"Big"` because the first character `'A'` of `"Air"` is less than the first character `'B'` of `"Big"`. The string `"Air"` is less than the string `"An"` because the first characters of `"Air"` and `"An"` are the same, but the second character `'i'` of `"Air"` is less than the second character `'n'` of `"An"`. Moreover, the string `"Hello"` is less than the string `"hello"` because the first character `'H'` of `"Hello"` is less than the first character `'h'` of `"hello"`.

If two strings of different lengths are compared and the character-by-character comparison is equal until it reaches the last character of the shorter string, the shorter string is evaluated as less than the larger string. For example, the string `"Bill"` is less than the string `"Billy"` and the string `"Sun"` is less than the string `"Sunny"`.

4

The **class** `String` provides the method `compareTo`, to compare objects of the **class** `String`. The syntax to use the method `compareTo` is:

```
str1.compareTo(str2)
```

where `str1` and `str2` are `String` variables. Moreover, `str2` can also be a `String` constant. This expression returns an integer value as follows:

$$str1.compareTo(str2)=\begin{cases} \text{an integer value less than 0 if string } str1 \text{ is less than string } str2 \\ 0 \text{ if string } str1 \text{ is equal to string } str2 \\ \text{an integer value greater than 0 if string } str1 \text{ is greater than string } str2 \end{cases}$$

Consider the following statements:

```
String str1 = "Hello";
String str2 = "Hi";
String str3 = "Air";
String str4 = "Bill";
String str5 = "Bigger";
```

Using these variable declarations, Table 4–3 shows how the method `compareTo` works.

Four-color interior design shows accurate Java code and related comments.

Features of the book

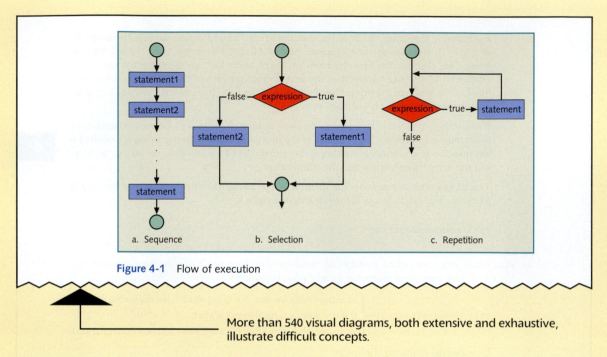

Figure 4-1 Flow of execution

More than 540 visual diagrams, both extensive and exhaustive, illustrate difficult concepts.

NOTE

In Java, the symbol ==, which consists of two equal signs, is called the **equality operator**. Recall that the symbol = is called the assignment operator. Remember that the equality operator, ==, determines whether two expressions are equal, whereas the assignment operator, =, assigns the value of an expression to a variable.

Notes highlight important facts about the concepts introduced in the chapter.

Features of the book

```java
//The String method compareTo

public class StringComparison
{
    public static void main(String[] args)
    {
        String str1 = "Hello";                          //Line 1
        String str2 = "Hi";                             //Line 2
        String str3 = "Air";                            //Line 3
        String str4 = "Bill";                           //Line 4
        String str5 = "Bigger";                         //Line 5

        System.out.println("Line 6: " +
                    "str1.compareTo(str2) evaluates to "
                + str1.compareTo(str2));                 //Line 6
```

Numbered Examples illustrate the key concepts with their relevant code. The programming code in these examples is numbered for easy reference, and is followed by a Sample Run. An explanation then follows that describes what each line in the code does.

PROGRAMMING EXAMPLE: CABLE COMPANY BILLING

This programming example demonstrates a program that calculates a customer's bill for a local cable company. There are two types of customers: residential and business. There are two rates for calculating a cable bill: one for residential customers and one for business customers.

For residential customers, the following rates apply:

- Bill-processing fee: $4.50
- Basic service fee: $20.50
- Premium channel: $7.50 per channel

Programming Examples are complete programs featured in each chapter. These examples include the accurate, concrete stages of Input, Output, Problem Analysis and Algorithm Design, and a Complete Program Listing.

Features of the book

EXERCISES

1. Mark the following statements as true or false.

a. The result of a logical expression cannot be assigned to an **int** variable.

b. In a one-way selection, if a semicolon is placed after the expression in an **if** statement, the expression in the **if** statement is always **true**.

c. Every **if** statement must have a corresponding **else**.

d. The expression:

```
(ch >= 'A' && ch <= 'Z')
```

evaluates to **false** if either ch < 'A' or ch >= 'Z'.

e. Suppose the input is 5. (Assume that all variables are properly declared.) The output of the code:

```
num = console.nextInt();
if (num > 5)
    System.out.println(num);
    num = 0;
else
    System.out.println("Num is zero");

is:

Num is zero.
```

Exercises further reinforce learning and ensure that students have, in fact, learned the material.

PROGRAMMING EXERCISES

1. Write a program that prompts the user to input a number. The program should then output the number and a message saying whether the number is positive, negative, or zero.

2. Write a program that prompts the user to input three numbers. The program should then output the numbers in ascending order.

3. Write a program that prompts the user to input an integer between 0 and 35. If the number is less than or equal to 9, the program should output the number; otherwise, it should output A for 10, B for 11, C for 12, ..., and Z for 35. (*Hint:* Use the cast operator (**char**) for numbers >= 10.)

Programming Exercises challenge students to write Java programs with a specified outcome.

SUPPLEMENTAL RESOURCES

The following supplemental materials are available when this book is used in a classroom setting. All of the teaching tools available with this book are provided to the instructor on a single CD-ROM and on the book's website at www.course.com.

Electronic Instructor's Manual. The Instructor's Manual that accompanies this textbook includes:

- Additional instructional material to assist in class preparation, including suggestions for lecture topics.

- Solutions to all the end-of-chapter materials, including the Programming Exercises.

ExamView®. This textbook is accompanied by ExamView, a powerful testing software package that allows instructors to create and administer printed, computer (LAN-based), and Internet exams. ExamView includes hundreds of questions that correspond to the topics covered in this text, enabling students to generate detailed study guides that include page references for further review. These computer-based and Internet testing components allow students to take exams at their computers, and save the instructor time because each exam is graded automatically.

PowerPoint Presentations. This book comes with Microsoft PowerPoint slides for each chapter. These are included as a teaching aid for classroom presentations, either to make available to students on the network for chapter review, or to be printed for classroom distribution. Instructors can add their own slides for additional topics that they introduce to the class.

Distance Learning. Course Technology is proud to offer online courses in WebCT and Blackboard, as well as at MyCourse.com, Course Technology's own course enhancement tool, to provide the most complete and dynamic learning experience possible. When you add online content to one of your courses, you're adding a lot: self-tests, links, glossaries, and—most of all—a gateway to the 21st century's most important information resource. We hope that you will make the most of your course, both online and offline. For more information on how to bring distance learning to your course, contact your local Course Technology sales representative.

Source Code. The source code is available at www.course.com, and is also available on the Teaching Tools CD-ROM. The input files needed to run some of the programs are also included with the source code. However, the input files should first be stored on a floppy disk in drive A:.

Solution files. The solution files for all programming exercises are available at www.course.com and are also available on the Teaching Tools CD-ROM. The input files needed to run some of the programming exercises are also included with the solution files. However, the input files should first be stored on a floppy disk in drive A:.

ACKNOWLEDGMENTS

There are many people that I must thank who, one way or another, contributed to the success of this book. First, I would like to thank Dr. Timothy Austin, Dean, Creighton College of Arts and Science, for encouraging, recognizing, and supporting this project. I am thankful to Professors S.C. Cheng, Randall L. Crist, John Mordeson, and Vasant Raval for constantly supporting this project. I must thank Lee I. Fenicle, Director, Office of Technology Transfer, Creighton University, for his involvement, support, and for providing encouraging words whenever I need them. Special thanks to Mike McCloskey of Sun Microsystems for clarifying various things regarding J2SE 5.0 (JDK 5.0) and its beta versions. I am also very grateful to the reviewers who reviewed earlier versions of this book and offered many critical suggestions on how to improve it.

I owe a great deal to the following reviewers who patiently read each page of every chapter of the current version and made critical comments to improve on the book: Oliver Grillmeyer: University of San Francisco; Mary Horstman: Western Illinois University; and Blayne Mayfield: Oklahoma State University. The reviewers will recognize that their criticisms have not been overlooked and, in fact, made this a better book. All this would not have been possible without the careful planning of Senior Product Manager Alyssa Pratt. I extend my sincere thanks to Alyssa, as well as to Associate Production Manager, Aimee Poirier, and also to the QA department of Course Technology for carefully testing the code.

I am thankful to my parents for their blessings.

Finally, I am thankful to the support of my wife Sadhana and especially my daughter Shelly, to whom this book is dedicated. They cheered me up whenever I was overwhelmed during the writing of this book.

I welcome any comments concerning the text. Comments may be forwarded to the following e-mail addresses: malik@creighton.edu.

D.S. Malik

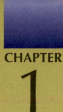

AN OVERVIEW OF COMPUTERS AND PROGRAMMING LANGUAGES

In this chapter, you will:

- ◆ Learn about different types of computers
- ◆ Explore the hardware and software components of a computer system
- ◆ Learn about the language of a computer
- ◆ Learn about the evolution of programming languages
- ◆ Examine high-level programming languages
- ◆ Discover what a compiler is and what it does
- ◆ Examine a Java program
- ◆ Examine how a Java program is processed
- ◆ Become aware of the Internet and World Wide Web
- ◆ Learn what an algorithm is and explore problem-solving techniques
- ◆ Become aware of structured and object-oriented programming design methodologies

INTRODUCTION

We live in an era where information is processed almost at the speed of light. Through computers, the technological revolution is drastically changing the way we live and communicate with one another. Terms such as "the Internet," which was unfamiliar just a few years ago, are now common. With the help of computers you can send letters to, and receive letters from, loved ones within seconds. You no longer need to send a résumé by mail to apply for a job; in many cases you can simply submit your job application via the Internet. You can watch how stocks perform in real time, and instantly buy and sell them. Students in elementary school regularly "surf" the Internet and use computers to design their classroom projects. Students no longer type their papers on typewriters or write them by hand. Instead, they use powerful word-processing software to complete their term papers. Many people maintain and balance their checkbooks on computers.

These are some of the ways that computers have greatly affected our daily lives. They are all made possible by the availability of different software, which are computer programs. For example, word-processing software is a program that enables you to write term papers, create impressive-looking résumés, and even write a book. This book, for example, was created with the help of a powerful word processor. Without software a computer is useless. Software is developed with the help of programming languages. The programming language Java is especially well suited for developing software to accomplish a specific task.

Until the early 1990s, at the beginning of a programming language course, instructors spent the first few weeks just teaching their students how to use computers. Today, by the time students graduate from high school, they know very well how to work with a computer. This book is not concerned with explaining how to use computers. Rather, it teaches you how to write programs in the Java programming language. It is useful, however, to understand some of the basic terminology and different components of a computer before you begin programming. This chapter briefly describes the main components of a computer system, the history and evolution of computer languages, and some fundamental ideas about how to solve problems with computer programming.

AN OVERVIEW OF THE HISTORY OF COMPUTERS

In the 1950s, computers were large devices accessible to only a very few people. All work—surgery, accounting, word processing, and calculations, among other tasks—was done without the aid of computers. In the 1960s, multimillion-dollar computers emerged, and only large companies could afford them. These computers were very large in size, and only computer experts were allowed to use them. During the mid-1970s, computers became cheaper and smaller. By the mid-1990s, people from all walks of life were able to afford them. During the late 1990s, small computers became even less expensive and much faster. Although there are several categories of computers, such as mainframe, midsize, and micro, all computers share some basic elements.

ELEMENTS OF A COMPUTER SYSTEM

A computer is an electronic device capable of performing commands. The basic commands that a computer performs are input (get data), output (display results), storage, and performance of arithmetic and logical operations.

In today's market, personal computers are sold with descriptions such as Pentium 4 Processor 2.8 GHz, 1 GB RAM, 80 GB HD, 19-inch SVGA monitor, and come with preloaded software such as operating systems, games, encyclopedias, and application software such as word processors or money-management programs. These descriptions represent two categories: hardware and software. Items such as "Pentium 4 Processor 2.8 GHz, 1 GB RAM, 80 GB HD, 19-inch SVGA monitor" fall into the hardware category. Items such as "operating systems, games, encyclopedias, and application software" fall into the software category. Let's look at the hardware first.

Hardware

Major hardware components include the following: central processing unit (CPU); main memory (MM), also called random access memory (RAM); input/output devices; and secondary storage. Some examples of input devices are the keyboard, mouse, and secondary storage. Examples of output devices are the monitor, printer, and secondary storage. Let's examine these components in more detail.

Central Processing Unit

The **central processing unit (CPU)** is the brain of the computer and the single most expensive piece of hardware in your personal computer. The more powerful the CPU, the faster the computer. The main components of the CPU are the control unit (CU), arithmetic logic unit (ALU), and registers. Figure 1-1 shows how certain components of the CPU fit together.

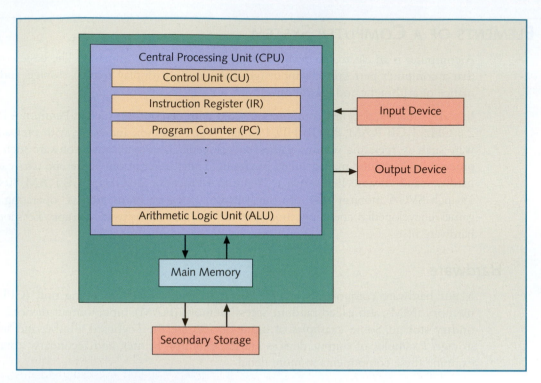

Figure 1-1   Hardware components of a computer

The CPU components shown in Figure 1-1 work as follows:

- The **control unit (CU)** has three main functions: fetch and decode the instructions; control the flow of information (instructions or data) between the CPU and main memory; and control the operation of the CPU's internal components.

- The **arithmetic logic unit (ALU)** carries out all arithmetic and logical operations.

- The CPU contains various registers. Some are special-purpose registers. For example, the **instruction register (IR)** holds the instruction currently being executed, and the **program counter (PC)** points to the next instruction to be executed. Other, general-purpose, registers provide temporary storage.

Main Memory

Main memory is directly connected to the CPU. All programs must be loaded into main memory before they can be executed. Similarly, all data must be brought into main memory before a program can manipulate it. When the computer is turned off, everything in main memory is lost for good.

Main memory is an ordered sequence of cells, called **memory cells**. Each cell has a unique location in main memory, called the **address** of the cell. These addresses help you access the information stored in the cell. Figure 1-2 shows main memory with 100 storage cells.

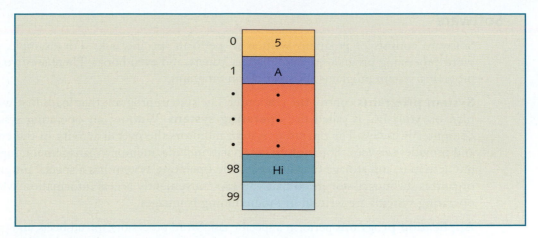

Figure 1-2   Main memory with 100 storage cells

Today's computers come with main memory consisting of millions to billions of cells. Although Figure 1-2 shows data stored in cells, the content of a cell can be either a programming instruction or data. Moreover, this figure shows the data as numbers and letters. However, as explained in the next section, Language of a Computer, in main memory everything is stored as sequences of 0s and 1s. The memory addresses are also expressed as sequences of 0s and 1s.

Secondary Storage

Because programs and data must be stored in main memory before processing and because everything in main memory is lost when the computer is turned off, information stored in main memory must be transferred to some other device for permanent storage. The device that stores information permanently (unless the device becomes unusable or you change the information by rewriting it) is called **secondary storage**. To be able to transfer information from main memory to secondary storage, these components must be directly connected to each other. Examples of secondary storage are hard disks, floppy disks, ZIP disks, CD-ROMs, and tapes.

Input/Output Devices

For a computer to perform a useful task, it must be able to take in data and programs and display the results of calculations. The devices that feed data and programs into computers are called **input devices**. The keyboard, mouse, and secondary storage are examples of input devices. The devices that the computer uses to display results are called **output devices**. A monitor, printer, and secondary storage are examples of output devices.

Software

Software consists of programs written to perform specific tasks. For example, you use word-processing programs to write letters, papers, and even books. There are two types of programs: system programs and application programs.

System programs control the computer. The system program that loads first when you turn on your PC is called the **operating system**. Without an operating system, the computer is useless. The operating system monitors the overall activity of the computer and provides services. Some of these services include: memory management, input/output activities, and storage management. The operating system has a special program that organizes secondary storage so that you can conveniently access information. Moreover, operating systems are written in programming languages.

Application programs perform a specific task. Word processors, spreadsheets, and games are examples of application programs. All application programs are written using computer programming languages. The operating system is the program that runs the application programs.

LANGUAGE OF A COMPUTER

When you press A on your keyboard, the computer displays A on the screen, but what is actually stored inside the computer's main memory? What is the language of the computer? How does it store whatever you type on the keyboard?

Remember that a computer is an electronic device. Electrical signals move along channels inside the computer. There are two types of electrical signals: analog and digital. **Analog signals** are continuous waveforms used to represent things such as sound. Audio tapes, for example, store data in analog signals. **Digital signals** represent information with a sequence of 0s and 1s. A 0 represents a low voltage, and a 1 represents a high voltage. Digital signals are more reliable carriers of information than are analog signals and can be copied from one device to another with exact precision. You might have noticed that when you make a copy of an audio tape, the sound quality of the copy is not as good as that on the original tape. Therefore, of the two signals, the computer uses digital signals.

Because digital signals are processed inside a computer, the language of a computer, called **machine language**, is a sequence of 0s and 1s. The digit 0 or 1 is called a **binary digit**, or **bit**. Sometimes a sequence of 0s and 1s is referred to as a **binary code** or a **binary number**.

Bit: A binary digit 0 or 1.

A sequence of eight bits is called a **byte**. Moreover, $2^{10} = 1024$ bytes is called a **kilobyte (KB)**. Table 1-1 summarizes the terms used to describe the various numbers of bytes.

Table 1-1   **Binary Units**

Unit	Symbol	Bits/Bytes
Byte		8 bits
Kilobyte	KB	$2^{10} = 1024$ bytes
Megabyte	MB	$2^{10} = 1024$ KB $= 2^{20} = 1, 048,576$ bytes
Gigabyte	GB	$2^{10} = 1024$ MB $= 2^{30} = 1, 073,741,824$ bytes
Terabyte	TB	$2^{10} = 1024$ GB $= 2^{40} = 1, 099,511,627,776$ bytes

Every letter, number, or special symbol (such as * or {) on your keyboard is encoded as a sequence of bits, each having a unique representation. The most commonly used encoding scheme on personal computers is the seven-bit **American Standard Code for Information Interchange (ASCII)**. The ASCII data set consists of 128 characters numbered 0 through 127. That is, in the ASCII data set, the position of the first character is 0, the position of the second character is 1, and so on. In this scheme, **A** is encoded as **1000001**. In fact, **A** is the 66th character in the ASCII character code, but its position is 65 because the position of the first character is 0. Furthermore, **1000001** is the binary representation of **65**. The character 3 is encoded as **0110011**. For a complete list of the printable ASCII character set, refer to Appendix C.

The number system that we use in our daily life is called the **decimal system** or **base 10**. Because everything inside a computer is represented as a sequence of 0s and 1s, that is, binary numbers, the number system that a computer uses is called binary or **base 2**. We indicated in the preceding paragraph that the number 1000001 is the binary representation of 65. Appendix D describes how to convert a number from base 10 to base 2 and vice versa.

Inside the computer, every character is represented as a sequence of eight bits, that is, as a byte. Because ASCII is a seven-bit code, you must add **0** to the left of the ASCII encoding of a character. Hence, inside the computer, the character **A** is represented as **01000001**, and the character 3 is represented as **00110011**.

There are other encoding schemes, such as EBCDIC (used by IBM) and Unicode, which is a more recent development. EBCDIC consists of 256 characters; **Unicode** consists of 65,536 characters. To store a Unicode character, you need two bytes. Java uses the Unicode character set. Therefore, in Java, every character is represented as a sequence of 16 bits, that is, 2 bytes. In Unicode, the character **A** is represented as **0000000001000001**.

The ASCII character set is a subset of Unicode; the first 128 characters of Unicode are the same as the characters in ASCII. If you are dealing with only the English language, then the ASCII character set is sufficient to write Java programs. The advantage of the Unicode character set is that symbols from languages other than English can be easily handled.

EVOLUTION OF PROGRAMMING LANGUAGES

The most basic computer language, machine language, provides program instructions in bits. Even though most computers perform the same kinds of operations, the designers of different CPUs sometimes choose different sets of binary codes to perform those operations. Therefore, the machine language of one computer is not necessarily the same as the machine language of another computer. The only consistency among computers is that in any computer, all data are stored and manipulated as a binary code.

Early computers were programmed in machine language. To see how instructions are written in machine language, suppose you want to use the equation:

```
wages = rate · hours
```

to calculate weekly wages. Assume that the memory locations of `rate`, `hours`, and `wages` are `010001`, `010010`, and `010011`, respectively. Further suppose that the binary code `100100` stands for load, `100110` stands for multiplication, and `100010` stands for store. In machine language, you might need the following sequence of instructions to calculate the weekly wages:

```
100100    010001
100110    010010
100010    010011
```

To represent the weekly wages equation in machine language, the programmer had to remember the machine language codes for various operations. Also, to manipulate data, the programmer had to remember the locations of the data in main memory. Remembering specific codes made programming difficult and error-prone.

Assembly languages were developed to make the programmer's job easier. In **assembly language**, an instruction is an easy-to-remember form called a **mnemonic**. Table 1-2 shows some examples of instructions in assembly language and their corresponding machine language code.

Table 1-2 Examples of Instructions in Assembly Language and Machine Language

Assembly Language	Machine Language
LOAD	100100
STOR	100010
MULT	100110
ADD	100101
SUB	100011

Using assembly language instructions, you can write the equation to calculate the weekly wages as follows:

```
LOAD    rate
MULT    hours
STOR    wages
```

As you can see, it is much easier to write instructions in assembly language. However, a computer cannot execute assembly language instructions directly. The instructions first have to be translated into machine language. A program called an **assembler** translates the assembly language instructions into machine language.

Assembler: A program that translates a program written in assembly language into an equivalent program in machine language.

Moving from machine language to assembly language made programming easier, but a programmer was still forced to think in terms of individual machine instructions. The next step toward making programming easier was to devise **high-level languages** that were closer to spoken languages, such as English, French, German, and Spanish. Basic, FORTRAN, COBOL, Pascal, C, C++, and Java are all high-level languages. You will learn the high-level language Java in this book.

In Java, you write the weekly wages equation as follows:

```
wages = rate * hours;
```

The instruction written in Java is much easier to understand and is self-explanatory to a novice user who is familiar with basic arithmetic. As in the case of assembly language, however, the computer cannot directly execute instructions written in a high-level language. To run on a computer, these Java instructions first need to be translated into an intermediate language called **bytecode** and then interpreted into a particular machine language. A program called a **compiler** translates instructions written in Java into bytecode.

Compiler: A program that translates a program written in a high-level language into the equivalent machine language. (In the case of Java, this machine language is the bytecode.)

Recall that the computer understands only the machine language. Moreover, different types of CPUs use different machine languages. To make Java programs **machine independent**, that is, able to run on many different types of computer platforms, the designers of Java introduced a hypothetical computer called the **Java Virtual Machine (JVM)**. In fact, bytecode is the machine language for the JVM.

In languages such as C and C++, the compiler directly translates the source code into the machine language of your computer's CPU. For such languages, a different compiler is needed for each type of CPU. Therefore, programs in these languages are not easily portable from one type of machine to another type of machine. The source code must be recompiled for each type of CPU. To make Java programs machine independent and easily portable, as well as run on a Web browser, the designers of the Java language introduced the Java Virtual Machine (JVM) and bytecode as the (machine) language of this machine. It is easier to translate a bytecode into a particular type of CPU. We elaborate on this in the section, Processing a Java Program, later in this chapter.

A JAVA PROGRAM

In Chapter 2, you will learn the basic elements and concepts of the Java programming language to create a Java program. In addition to giving examples to illustrate various concepts, we also include Java programs to help clarify them. This section gives an example of a Java program. At this point you need not be too concerned with the details of this program. You need to know only the effect of an *output* statement, which is introduced in this program.

Consider the following Java (application) program:

```java
public class ASimpleJavaProgram
{
    public static void main(String[] args)
    {
        System.out.println("My first Java program.");
        System.out.println("The sum of 2 and 3 = " + 5);
        System.out.println("7 + 8 = " + (7 + 8));
    }
}
```

Sample Run: (When you compile and execute this program, the following three lines are displayed on the screen.)

```
My first Java program.
The sum of 2 and 3 = 5
7 + 8 = 15
```

These lines are displayed on the screen after the following three lines (in the preceding program) are executed:

```java
System.out.println("My first Java program.");
System.out.println("The sum of 2 and 3 = " + 5);
System.out.println("7 + 8 = " + (7 + 8));
```

Next, we explain how this happens. Let us first consider the following statement:

```java
System.out.println("My first Java program.");
```

This is an example of a Java *output* statement. It causes the program to evaluate whatever is in the parentheses and display the result on the screen. Typically, anything in double quotation marks, called a *string*, evaluates to itself. Therefore, the statement causes the system to display the following line on the screen:

```
My first Java program.
```

Let us now consider the following statement:

```
System.out.println("The sum of 2 and 3 = " + 5);
```

In this output statement, the parentheses consist of the string `"The sum of 2 and 3 = "`, + (the plus sign), and the number 5. Here the symbol + is used to concatenate (join) the strings. In this case, the system automatically converts the number 5 into a string, joins that string with the first string, and displays the following line on the screen:

```
The sum of 2 and 3 = 5
```

Let us now consider the following statement:

```
System.out.println("7 + 8 = " + (7 + 8));
```

In this output statement, the parentheses consist of the string `"7 + 8 = "`, + (the plus sign), and the expression `(7 + 8)`. In the expression `(7 + 8)`, notice the parentheses around 7 + 8. This causes the system to add the numbers 7 and 8, resulting in 15. The number 15 is then converted to the string 15 and then joined with the string `"7 + 8 = "`. Therefore, the output of this statement is:

```
7 + 8 = 15
```

In the next chapter, until we explain how to properly construct a Java program, we will use output statements such as the preceding ones to explain various concepts. After Chapter 2, you should be able to write Java programs well enough to do some computations and show results.

Before leaving this chapter, let us note the following about the preceding Java program. The basic unit of a Java program is a **class**. Typically, every Java **class** consists of one or more methods. Roughly speaking, a method is set of statements or instructions whose objective is to accomplish something. In the first line of the program, that is:

```
public class ASimpleJavaProgram
```

`ASimpleJavaProgram` is the name of the Java **class**. The second line of the program consists of the left brace, which is matched with the second right brace (the very last brace). These braces together mark the beginning and end of (the body of) the **class** `ASimpleJavaProgram`. The third line consists of the following line:

```
public static void main(String[] args)
```

This is the heading of the method `main`. A Java **class** can have at most one method `main`. Moreover, if a Java **class** contains an application program, such as the preceding program, it must contain the method `main`. When you execute a Java (application) program, execution always begins with the method `main`.

The fourth line consists of a left brace (the second left brace of the program). This marks the beginning of (the body of) the method **main**. The first right brace (on the eighth line of the program) matches this left brace and marks the end of (the body of) the method **main**. Chapter 2 explains the meaning of the other words such as the ones shown in blue.

PROCESSING A JAVA PROGRAM

Java has two types of programs—applications and applets. The Java program given in the preceding section is an example of an application program. In the preceding sections, we discussed the machine language high-level languages, and showed a Java application program. Because a computer can understand only the machine language, next we review the steps required to execute programs written in Java.

You must carry out the following steps, as shown in Figure 1-3, to execute a program written in Java.

1. You use an editor, such as Notepad, to create (that is, type) a program in Java following the rules, or syntax, of the language. This program is called the **source program**. The program must be saved in a text file named **ClassName.java** where **ClassName** is the name of the Java class contained in the file. For example, in the preceding section, A Java Program, the name of the (**public**) class containing the Java program is **ASimpleJavaProgram**. Therefore, this program must be saved in the text file named **ASimpleJavaProgram.java**. Otherwise an error will occur.

Source program: A program written in a high-level language.

2. You must verify that the program obeys the rules of the programming language—that is, the program must be syntactically correct—and translate the program into the equivalent bytecode. The compiler checks for the correctness of the syntax and translates the program into bytecode. That is, the compiler checks the source program for syntax errors and, if no error is found, translates the program into bytecode. The bytecode is saved in the file with the **.class** extension. For example, the bytecode for **ASimpleJavaProgram.java** is stored in the **ASimpleJavaProgram.class** file by the compiler.

3. To run a Java application program, the **.class** file must be loaded into computer memory. To run a Java applet, you must use either a Web browser or an applet viewer, a stripped-down Web browser for running applets. The programs that you write in the Java language are typically developed using a **software development kit (SDK)**. The SDK contains many programs that are useful in creating your program. For example, it contains the necessary code to display the results of the program and several mathematical functions to make the programmer's job somewhat easier. Therefore, if certain code is already available to you, you can use the available code rather than writing your own code. Moreover, you can develop your own libraries (also called packages in Java), which are described in Chapter 8. Therefore, in general, a Java program is divided into various parts, called **classes**. Typically, each

class is contained in a separate file and is separately compiled. Therefore, to success-fully run a Java program, the bytecode for the classes used in the program must be connected. The program that automatically does this in Java is known as the **loader**.

4. The next step is to execute the Java program. In addition to connecting the bytecode from various classes, in Java, the loader also loads your Java program's bytecode into main memory. As the classes are loaded into main memory, the *bytecode verifier* verifies that the bytecode for the classes is valid and does not violate Java's security restrictions. Finally, a program called an **interpreter** translates each bytecode instruction into your computer's machine language, and then executes it.

Interpreter: A program that reads and translates each bytecode instruction into your computer's machine language, and then executes it.

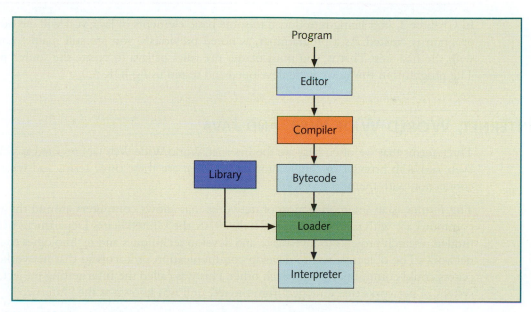

Figure 1-3   Processing a Java program

Note that the Java interpreter translates and executes one bytecode instruction at a time. It does not first translate the entire bytecode into your computer's machine language. As indi-cated earlier, in languages such as C++, a different compiler is needed for each type of CPU. On the other hand, a Java compiler translates a Java source program into bytecode, the machine language of JVM, which is independent of any particular type of CPU. The Java interpreter translates each bytecode instruction into a particular type of CPU and then exe-cutes the instruction. Thus, in the case of the Java language, a different type of interpreter is needed for a particular type of CPU. However, interpreters are programs that are simpler than compilers. Because the Java interpreter translates one bytecode instruction at a time, Java programs run more slowly.

As a programmer, your primary concern is with Step 1. That is, you must learn, understand, and master the rules of the programming language to create source programs. As noted earlier, programs are developed using an SDK. Well-known SDKs used to create programs in the high-level language Java include Forte (from Sun), JBuilder (from Borland), CodeWarrior (from Metrowerks), and jGrasp. These SDKs contain an editor to create the program, a compiler to check the program for syntax errors, a program to load the object codes of the resources used from the SDK, and a program to execute the program. These SDKs also are quite user friendly. When you compile your program, the compiler not only identifies the syntax errors, but also typically suggests how to correct them.

 Other software that can be used to develop Java programs include TextPad, JCreator, and BlueJ.

In Chapter 2, after being introduced to some basic elements of Java, you will see how a Java program is created. As a programmer, as noted previously, you are still mainly concerned with the first step. That is, you must master the rules of Java to create the source program. The programs in this book were developed and tested using JDK 5.0.

INTERNET, WORLD WIDE WEB, AND JAVA

Three terms that we often hear are the Internet, World Wide Web (abbreviated as WWW) or Web, and Web browser or simply browser. So what are these three terms and what is Java's connection with them?

The *Internet* is an interconnection of networks that allows computers around the world to communicate with each other. In the early 1970s, the United States Department of Defense funded research projects to investigate and develop techniques and technologies to interlink networks. The objective was to develop communication protocols so that networked computers could communicate with each other. This was called the Internetting project, and the system of networks that emerged from the research was known as the "Internet."

Over the last four decades the Internet has grown manyfold. In 1973, approximately 23 computers were connected via the Internet. This number grew to 700,000 computers by 1991, and to over 10,000,000 by 2000. Each day more and more computers are getting connected via the Internet.

The Internet allows computers to be connected and communicate with each other. On the other hand, the *World Wide Web* (abbreviated as WWW) or Web uses software programs that enable computer users to view documents on almost any subject over the Internet with the click of a mouse. Undoubtedly, the Internet has become one of the world's leading communication mechanisms. The terms Internet and World Wide Web are often used interchangeably. However, as the preceding discussion notes, there is a difference between the two. Computers around the world communicate via the Internet; the World Wide Web makes that communication a fun activity.

The primary language for the Web is known as *Hypertext Markup Language* (HTML). It is a simple language for laying out and linking documents, as well as for viewing images and listening to sound. However, HTML is not capable of interacting with the user except to collect information via simple forms. Therefore, Web pages are essentially static. As remarked previously, Java has two types of programs—applications and applets. In terms of programming, both types of programs are similar. Application programs are stand-alone programs that can run on your computer. Java applets are programs that run from a *Web browser* or simply *browser* and make the Web responsive and interactive. The two well-known browsers are Netscape and Internet Explorer. Java applets can run in either browser. Moreover, through applets the Web becomes responsive, interactive, and fun to use.

PROGRAMMING WITH THE PROBLEM ANALYSIS–CODING–EXECUTION CYCLE

Programming is a process of problem solving. Different people use different techniques to solve problems. Some techniques are nicely outlined and easy to follow; they solve the problem and give insight into how the solution was reached. Such problem-solving techniques can be easily modified if the domain of the problem changes.

To be a skillful problem solver and hence to become a skillful programmer, you must use good problem-solving techniques. One common problem-solving technique includes analyzing a problem, outlining the problem requirements, and designing steps, called an **algorithm**, to solve the problem.

Algorithm: A step-by-step problem-solving process in which a solution is arrived at in a finite amount of time.

In the programming environment, the problem-solving process involves the following steps:

1. Analyze the problem, outline the problem and its solution requirements, and design an algorithm to solve the problem.

2. Implement the algorithm in a programming language, such as Java, and verify that the algorithm works.

3. Maintain the program by using and modifying it if the problem domain changes.

Figure 1-4 summarizes this programming process. This figure shows only the main components of the problem analysis–coding–execution cycle. This figure does not show the loading stage, shown earlier in Figure 1-3, which takes place automatically.

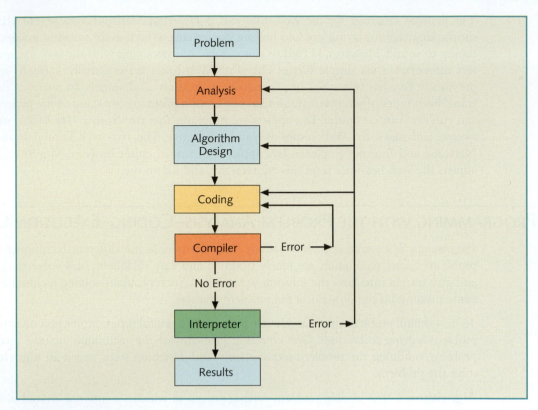

Figure 1-4   Problem analysis–coding–execution cycle

To develop a program to solve a problem, you start by analyzing the problem. You then design the algorithm; you write the program instructions in a high-level language, or code the program; and you enter the program into a computer system. *Analyzing the problem is the first and most important step.* This step requires that you do the following:

- Thoroughly understand the problem.

- Understand the problem requirements. Requirements can include whether the program requires interaction with the user, whether it manipulates data, whether it produces output, and what the output looks like. If the program manipulates data, the programmer must know what the data are and how they are represented. That is, you need to look at sample data.

- If the program produces output, you should know how the results should be generated and formatted. If the problem is complex, divide the problem into sub-problems and repeat Steps 1 and 2. That is, for complex problems, you need to analyze each subproblem and understand each subproblem's requirements.

After you carefully analyze the problem, the next step is to design an algorithm to solve the problem. If you broke the problem into subproblems, you need to design an algorithm for each subproblem. Once you design an algorithm, you need to check it for correctness. You can sometimes test an algorithm's correctness by using sample data. At other times, you might need to perform some mathematical analysis to test the algorithm's correctness.

Once you have designed the algorithm and verified its correctness, the next step is to convert the equivalent code into a high-level language. You use a text editor to enter the program into a computer. You must then make sure that the program follows the language's syntax. To verify the correctness of the syntax, you run the code through a compiler. If the compiler generates error messages, you must identify the errors in the code, remove them, and then run the code through the compiler again. When all the syntax errors are removed, the compiler generates the machine code (bytecode in Java).

The final step is to execute the program. The compiler guarantees only that the program follows the language's syntax; it does not guarantee that the program will run correctly. During execution the program might terminate abnormally due to logical errors, such as division by zero. Even if the program terminates normally, it may still generate erroneous results. Under these circumstances, you may have to reexamine the code, the algorithm, or even the problem analysis.

Your overall programming experience will *benefit* if you spend enough time to thoroughly complete the problem analysis before attempting to write the programming instructions. Usually, you do this work on paper using a pen or pencil. Taking this careful approach to programming has a number of advantages. It is much easier to discover errors in a program that is well analyzed and well designed. Furthermore, a thoroughly analyzed and carefully designed program is much easier to follow and modify. Even the most experienced programmers spend a considerable amount of time analyzing a problem and designing an algorithm.

Throughout this book, you will learn not only the rules of writing programs in Java, but also problem-solving techniques. Each chapter discusses several programming problems, each of which is clearly marked as a Programming Example. These Programming Examples teach techniques to analyze and solve the problems and also help you understand the concepts discussed in the chapter. To gain the full benefit of this book, we recommend that you work through the Programming Examples at the end of each chapter.

Example 1-1

In this example, we design an algorithm to find the perimeter and area of a rectangle.

To find the perimeter and area of a rectangle, you need to know the rectangle's length and width. The perimeter and area of the rectangle are then given by the following formulas:

```
perimeter = 2 · (length + width)
```

```
area = length · width
```

The algorithm to find the perimeter and area of the rectangle can be written as follows:

1. Get the length of the rectangle.

2. Get the width of the rectangle.

3. Find the perimeter using the following equation:

```
perimeter = 2 · (length + width)
```

4. Find the area using the following equation:

```
area = length · width
```

Example 1-2

In this example, we design an algorithm that calculates the sales tax and price of an item sold in a particular state.

The sales tax is calculated as follows: The state's portion of the sales tax is 4% and the city's portion of the sales tax is 1.5%. If the item is a luxury item, such as a car over $50,000, then there is a 10% luxury tax.

To calculate the item's price, we need to calculate both the state's portion of the sales tax and the city's portion of the sales tax. Moreover, if it is a luxury item, we need to calculate the luxury tax. Suppose `salePrice` denotes the item's selling price, `stateSalesTax` denotes the state's sales tax, `citySalesTax` denotes the city's sales tax, `luxuryTax` denotes the luxury tax, `salesTax` denotes the total sales tax, and `amountDue` the item's final price.

To calculate the sales tax, we must know the item's selling price and whether it is a luxury item.

The `stateSalesTax` and `citySalesTax` can be calculated using the following formulas:

```
stateSalesTax = salePrice · 0.04
```

```
citySalesTax = salePrice · 0.015
```

Next, you can determine `luxuryTax` as follows:

```
if (item is a luxury item)
   luxuryTax = salePrice · 0.1
otherwise
   luxuryTax = 0
```

Next, you can determine `salesTax` as follows:

```
        salesTax = stateSalesTax + citySalesTax
                 + luxuryTax
```

Finally, you can calculate `amountDue` as follows:

```
amountDue = salePrice + salesTax
```

The algorithm to determine `salesTax` and `amountDue` is, therefore:

1. Get the item's selling price.

2. Get, that is, determine whether the item is a luxury item.

3. Find the state's portion of the sales tax using the formula:

```
stateSalesTax = salePrice · 0.04
```

4. Find the city's portion of the sales tax using the formula:

```
citySalesTax = salePrice · 0.015
```

5. Find the luxury tax using the formula:

```
if (item is a luxury item)
    luxuryTax = salePrice · 0.1
otherwise
    luxuryTax = 0
```

6. Find **salesTax** using the formula:

```
salesTax = stateSalesTax + citySalesTax
            + luxuryTax
```

7. Find **amountDue** using the formula:

```
amountDue = salePrice + salesTax
```

Example 1-3

In this example, we design an algorithm that calculates the monthly paycheck of a salesperson at a local department store.

Every salesperson has a base salary. The salesperson also receives a bonus at the end of each month based on the following criteria: If the salesperson has been with the store for five or fewer years, the bonus is $10 for each year that he or she has worked there. If the salesperson has been with the store for more than five years, the bonus is $20 for each year that he or she has worked there. The salesperson can earn an additional bonus as follows: If the salesperson's total sales for the month are more than $5000 but less than $10000, he or she receives a 3% commission on sales. If the salesperson's total sales for the month are at least $10000, he or she receives a 6% commission on sales.

To calculate a salesperson's monthly paycheck, you need to know the base salary, the number of years that the salesperson has been with the company, and the total sales made by the salesperson for that month. Suppose **baseSalary** denotes the base salary, **noOfServiceYears** denotes the number of years that the salesperson has been with the store, **bonus** denotes the bonus, **totalSale** denotes the salesperson's total sales for the month, and **additionalBonus** denotes the additional bonus.

You can determine the bonus as follows:

```
if (noOfServiceYears is less than or equal to five)
     bonus = 10 · noOfServiceYears
otherwise
     bonus = 20 · noOfServiceYears
```

Next, you can determine the additional bonus of the salesperson as follows:

```
if (totalSale is less than 5000)
    additionalBonus = 0
otherwise
    if (totalSale is greater than or equal to 5000 and
                totalSale is less than 10000)
        additionalBonus = totalSale · (0.03)


    otherwise
        additionalBonus = totalSale · (0.06)
```

Using the preceding information, you can now design the algorithm to calculate a salesperson's monthly paycheck.

1. Get `baseSalary`.

2. Get `noOfServiceYears`.

3. Calculate `bonus` using the following formula:

   ```
   if (noOfServiceYears is less than or equal to five)
       bonus = 10 · noOfServiceYears
   otherwise
       bonus = 20 · noOfServiceYears
   ```

4. Get `totalSale`.

5. Calculate `additionalBonus` using the following formula:

   ```
   if (totalSale is less than 5000)
       additionalBonus = 0
   otherwise
           if (totalSale is greater than or equal to 5000 and
                       totalSale is less than 10000)
               additionalBonus = totalSale · (0.03)
           otherwise
               additionalBonus = totalSale · (0.06)
   ```

6. Calculate `payCheck` using the equation:

   ```
   payCheck = baseSalary + bonus + additionalBonus
   ```

The type of coding used in Examples 1–1, 1–2, and 1-3 is called **pseudocode**, which is an "outline" of a program that could be translated into actual code. Pseudocode is not written in a particular language, nor does it have syntax rules; it is mainly a technique to show the programming steps.

PROGRAMMING METHODOLOGIES

Two popular approaches to programming design are the structured approach and the object-oriented approach, which are outlined below.

Structured Programming

Dividing a problem into smaller subproblems is called **structured design**. Each subproblem is then analyzed, and a solution for the subproblem is obtained. The solutions to all the subproblems are then combined to solve the overall problem. This process of implementing a structured design is called **structured programming**. The structured design approach is also known as **top-down design**, **stepwise refinement**, and **modular programming**.

Object-Oriented Programming

The previous section discussed the structured design programming methodology. This section briefly describes a widely used programming methodology called **object-oriented design (OOD)**.

In OOD, the first step in the problem-solving process is to identify the components called **objects**, which form the basis of the solution, and determine how these objects interact with one another. For example, suppose you want to write a program that automates the video rental process for a local video store. The two main objects in this problem are the video and the customer.

After identifying the objects, the next step is to specify the relevant data for each object and possible operations to be performed on that data. For example, for a video object, the data might include the movie name, starring actors, producer, production company, and number of copies in stock. Some of the operations on a video object might include checking the name of the movie, reducing the number of copies in stock by one after a copy is rented, and incrementing the number of copies in stock by one after a customer returns a particular video.

This illustrates that each **object** consists of data and the operations on those data. An object combines data and operations on that data into a single unit. In OOD, the final program is a collection of interacting objects. A programming language that implements OOD is called an **object-oriented programming (OOP)** language. You will learn about the many advantages of OOD in later chapters.

Because an object consists of data and operations on those data, before you can design and use objects, you need to learn how to represent data in computer memory, how to manipulate data, and how to implement operations. In Chapter 2, you will learn the basic data types of Java and discover how to represent and manipulate data in computer memory. Chapter 3 discusses how to input data into a Java program and output the results generated by a Java program.

To create operations, you write algorithms and implement them in a programming language. Because a data element in a complex program usually has many operations, to separate operations from each other and to use them effectively and in a convenient manner, you use **methods** to implement algorithms. After a brief introduction in Chapters 2 and 3, you will learn the details of methods in Chapter 7. Certain algorithms require that a program make decisions, a process called selection. Other algorithms might require that certain statements be repeated until certain conditions are met, a process called repetition. Still other algorithms might require both selection and repetition. You will learn about selection and repetition mechanisms, called control structures, in Chapters 4 and 5.

Finally, to work with objects, you need to know how to combine data and operations on that data into a single unit. In Java, the mechanism that allows you to combine data and operations on the data into a single unit is called a **class**. In Chapter 8, you will learn how to create your own classes.

In Chapter 9, using a mechanism called an array, you will learn how to manipulate data when data items are of the same type, such as the items in a list of sales figures. As you can see, you need to learn quite a few things before working with the OOD methodology.

For some problems, the structured approach to program design is very effective. Other problems are better addressed by OOD. For example, if a problem requires manipulating sets of numbers with mathematical functions, you might use the structured design approach and outline the steps required to obtain the solution. The Java library supplies a wealth of functions that you can use to effectively manipulate numbers. On the other hand, if you want to write a program that would make a candy machine operational, the OOD approach is more effective. Java was designed especially to implement OOD. Furthermore, OOD works well and is used in conjunction with structured design. Chapter 6 explains how to use an existing class to create a Graphical User Interface (GUI), and then gives several examples explaining how to solve problems using OOD concepts.

Both the structured design and OOD approaches require that you master the basic components of a programming language to be an effective programmer. In the next few chapters, you will learn the basic components of Java required by either approach to programming.

QUICK REVIEW

1. A computer is an electronic device capable of performing arithmetic and logical operations.

2. A computer system has two components: hardware and software.

3. The central processing unit (CPU) and the main memory are examples of hardware components.

4. Some of the components of the CPU are the control unit (CU), instruction register (IR), and program counter (PC).

1

5. The control unit (CU) controls a program's overall execution. It is one of several components of the CPU.

6. The arithmetic logic unit (ALU) is the CPU component that performs arithmetic and logical operations.

7. The instruction register (IR) holds the instruction currently being executed.

8. The program counter (PC) points to the next instruction to be executed.

9. All programs must be brought into main memory before they can be executed.

10. When the power is switched off, everything in main memory is lost.

11. Secondary storage provides permanent storage for information. Hard disks, floppy disks, ZIP disks, CD-ROMs, and tapes are examples of secondary storage.

12. Input to the computer is done via an input device. Two common input devices are the keyboard and the mouse.

13. The computer sends its output to an output device such as the computer monitor.

14. Software are programs run by the computer.

15. The operating system monitors the overall activity of the computer and provides services.

16. Application programs perform a specific task.

17. The most basic language of a computer is a sequence of 0s and 1s called machine language. Every computer directly understands its own machine language.

18. A bit is a binary digit, 0 or 1.

19. A sequence of 0s and 1s is called a binary code or a binary number.

20. A byte is a sequence of eight bits.

21. One kilobyte (KB) is $2^{10} = 1024$ bytes; one megabyte (MB) is $2^{20} = 1,048,576$ bytes; one gigabyte (GB) is $2^{30} = 1,073,741,824$ bytes; and one terabyte (TB) is $2^{40} = 1,099,511,627,776$ bytes.

22. Assembly language uses easy-to-remember instructions called mnemonics.

23. Assemblers are programs that translate a program written in assembly language into machine language.

24. To run a Java program on a computer, the Java program must first be translated into an intermediate language called bytecode and then interpreted into a particular machine language.

25. To make Java programs machine independent, the designers of the Java language introduced a hypothetical computer called the Java Virtual Machine (JVM).

26. Bytecode is the machine language for the JVM.

27. Compilers are programs that translate a program written in a high-level language into an equivalent machine language. In the case of Java, this machine language is the bytecode.

28. In Java, the necessary steps to execute a program are: edit, compile, load, and execute.

29. A Java loader transfers the bytecode of the classes needed to execute the program into main memory.

30. An interpreter is a program that reads, translates each bytecode instruction into the machine language of your computer, and then executes it.

31. The Internet is a network of networks through which computers around the world are connected.

32. The World Wide Web, or Web, uses software programs that allow computer users to view documents on almost any subject over the Internet with the click of a mouse.

33. Java application programs are stand-alone programs that can run on your computer. Java applets are programs that run from a Web browser, or simply browser.

34. Programming is a process of problem solving.

35. A problem-solving process has three steps: analyze the problem and design an algorithm, implement the algorithm in a programming language, and maintain the program.

36. An algorithm is a step-by-step problem-solving process in which a solution is arrived at in a finite amount of time.

37. There are two basic approaches to programming design: structured design and object-oriented design.

38. In structured design, a problem is divided into smaller subproblems. Each subproblem is solved, and the solutions to all the subproblems are then combined to solve the problem.

39. In object-oriented design (OOD), the programmer identifies components called objects, which form the basis of the solution, and determines how these objects interact with one another. In OOD, a program is a collection of interacting objects.

40. An object consists of data and the operations on those data.

EXERCISES

1. Mark the following statements as true or false.

   a. Assembly language is the language that uses mnemonics for its instructions.

   b. The arithmetic logic unit performs arithmetic operations and, if an error is found, it outputs the logical errors.

   c. A Java compiler is a program that translates a Java program into bytecode.

   d. Bytecode is the machine language of the JVM.

   e. The CPU functions under the control of the control unit.

   f. RAM stands for readily available memory.

   g. A program written in a high-level programming language is called a source program.

   h. The operating system is the first program loaded into the computer when the power is turned on.

   i. The first step in the problem-solving process is to analyze the problem.

2. Name some components of the central processing unit.

3. What is the function of the control unit?

4. Name two input devices.

5. Name two output devices.

6. Why is secondary storage needed?

7. Why do you need to translate a program written in a high-level language into machine language?

8. Why would you prefer to write a program in a high-level language rather than a machine language?

9. What are the advantages of problem analysis and algorithm design over directly writing a program in a high-level language?

10. What is the output of the following Java program?

```java
public class Exercise_10
{
    public static void main(String[] args)
    {
        System.out.println("This is exercise 10.");
        System.out.println("In Java, the multiplication symbol is *.");
        System.out.println("2 + 3 * 5 = " + (2 + 3 * 5));
    }
}
```

11. Design an algorithm to find the weighted average of four test scores. The four test scores and their respective weights are given in the following format:

```
testscore1 weight1
...
```

For example, a sample data is as follows:

```
75 0.20
95 0.35
85 0.15
65 0.30
```

12. A salesperson leaves his home every Monday and returns every Friday. He travels by company car. Each day on the road, the salesperson records the amount of gasoline put in the car. Given the starting odometer reading (the odometer reading before he leaves on Monday) and the ending odometer reading (the odometer reading after he returns home on Friday), design an algorithm to find the average miles per gallon.

Data is given in the following format:

```
startOdometerReading endOdometerReading gUsedD1 gUsedD2 gUsedD3
gUsedD4 gUsedD5
```

(Here **gUsedD1** means gas used on Day 1, and so on.) A sample data is as follows:

68723 71289 15.75 16.30 10.95 20.65 30.00

13. To make a profit, prices of the items sold in a furniture store are marked up 60%. Design an algorithm to find the selling price of an item sold at the furniture store. What information do you need to find the selling price?

14. Suppose a, b, and c denote the lengths of the sides of a triangle. Then, the area of the triangle can be calculated using the formula:

$$\sqrt{s(s-a)(s-b)(s-c)},$$

where $s = (1/2)(a + b + c)$. Design an algorithm that uses this formula to find the area of a triangle. What information do you need to find the area?

2

BASIC ELEMENTS OF JAVA

In this chapter, you will:

♦ Become familiar with the basic components of a Java program, including methods, special symbols, and identifiers

♦ Explore primitive data types

♦ Discover how to use arithmetic operators

♦ Examine how a program evaluates arithmetic expressions

♦ Explore how mixed expressions are evaluated

♦ Learn about type casting

♦ Become familiar with the `String` type

♦ Learn what an assignment statement is and what it does

♦ Discover how to input data into memory by using input statements

♦ Become familiar with the use of increment and decrement operators

♦ Examine ways to output results using output statements

♦ Learn how to import packages and why they are necessary

♦ Discover how to create a Java application program

♦ Explore how to properly structure a program, including using comments to document a program

In this chapter, you will learn the basics of Java. As you begin to learn the Java programming language, two questions naturally arise: First, what is a computer program? Second, what is programming? A **computer program**, or a program, is a sequence of statements whose objective is to accomplish a task. **Programming** is a process of planning and creating a program. These two definitions tell the truth, but not the whole truth, about programming. It might take an entire book to give a satisfactory definition of programming. An analogy might help you gain a better grasp of the nature of programming, so we'll use a topic on which almost everyone has some knowledge—cooking. A recipe is also a program, and everyone with some cooking experience can agree on the following:

1. It is usually easier to follow a recipe than to create one.

2. There are good recipes and there are bad recipes.

3. Some recipes are easy to follow and some are difficult to follow.

4. Some recipes produce reliable results and some do not.

5. You must have some knowledge of how to use cooking tools to follow a recipe to completion.

6. To create good new recipes, you must have much knowledge and understanding of cooking.

These same six points can also be applied to programming. Let us take the cooking analogy one step further. Suppose you need to teach someone how to become a chef. How would you go about it? Would you introduce the person to good food, hoping the person develops a taste for good food? Would you have the person follow recipe after recipe in the hope that some of it rubs off? Or, would you first teach the use of the tools, the nature of ingredients and foods and spices, and then explain how these subjects fit together?

Just as there are many ways to teach cooking, there are also different ways to teach programming. However, some fundamentals apply to programming, just as they do to cooking or music.

Learning a programming language is like learning to become a chef or learning to play a musical instrument. All three skills require direct interaction with the tools. You cannot become a good chef just by reading recipes. Similarly, you cannot become a musician by reading books about musical instruments. The same is true of programming. You must have a fundamental knowledge of the language, and you must test your programs on the computer to make sure that each program does what it is supposed to do.

BASICS OF A JAVA PROGRAM

There are two types of Java programs—Java applets and Java application programs. Java applets are programs designed to run on a Web browser. Java application programs are stand-alone programs. To introduce the basic Java components, in the next few chapters we develop Java application programs. Java applets are discussed in Chapter 13.

The program in Example 2-1 demonstrates a Java application program. At this point you need not be concerned with the details of the program.

Example 2-1

The following is a sample Java application program:

```java
public class Welcome
{
    public static void main(String[] args)
    {
        System.out.println("Welcome to Java Programming.");
    }
}
```

If you execute this program, it will print the following line on the screen:

```
Welcome to Java Programming.
```

If you have never seen a program written in a programming language, the Java program in Example 2-1 may look like a foreign language. To make meaningful sentences in any foreign language, you must learn its alphabet, words, and grammar. The same is true of a programming language. To write meaningful programs, you must learn the programming language's special symbols, words, and syntax rules. The **syntax rules** tell you which statements (instructions) are legal, or accepted by the programming language, and which are not. You must also learn the **semantic rules**, which determine the meaning of the instructions. The programming language's rules, symbols, and special words enable you to write programs to solve problems. The syntax rules determine which instructions are valid.

Programming language: A set of rules, symbols, and special words used to construct programs.

In the remainder of this section, you will learn about some of the special symbols of a Java program. Other special symbols are introduced as other concepts are encountered in later chapters. Similarly, syntax and semantic rules are introduced and discussed throughout the book.

The smallest individual unit of a program written in any programming language is called a **token**. Java's tokens are divided into special symbols, word symbols, and identifiers.

Special Symbols

Following are some of the special symbols:

```
+         -         *         /
.         ;         ?         ,
<=        !=        ==        >=
```

The first row includes mathematical symbols for addition, subtraction, multiplication, and division. The second row consists of punctuation marks taken from English grammar. Note that the comma is a special symbol. In Java, commas are used to separate items in a list. Semicolons are used to end a Java statement. Note that a blank, which is not shown above, is also a special symbol. You create a blank symbol by pressing the spacebar (only once) on the keyboard. The third row consists of tokens made up of two characters, but which are regarded as single symbols. No character can come between the two characters, not even a blank.

Word Symbols

A second category of tokens is word symbols. Some word symbols include the following:

int, float, double, char, void, public, static, throws, return

Word symbols are also called **reserved words**, or **keywords**. The letters in a reserved word are always lowercase. Like the special symbols, each word symbol is considered a single symbol. Furthermore, word symbols cannot be redefined within any program; that is, they cannot be used for anything other than their intended use. For a complete list of reserved words in Java, see Appendix A.

 Throughout this book, the reserved words are shown in **blue**.

Identifiers

A third category of tokens is identifiers. **Identifiers** are names of things, such as variables, constants, and methods, that appear in programs. Some identifiers are predefined; others are defined by the user. All identifiers must obey Java's rules for identifiers.

Identifier: A Java identifier consists of letters, digits, the underscore character (_), and the dollar sign ($), and must begin with a letter, underscore, or the dollar sign.

Identifiers can be made of only letters, digits, the underscore character (_), and the dollar sign ($); no other symbols are permitted to form an identifier.

 Java is case sensitive—uppercase and lowercase letters are considered different. Thus, the identifier NUMBER is not the same as the identifier number. Similarly, the identifiers X and x are different.

In Java, identifiers can be any length. Some predefined identifiers that you will encounter frequently are `print`, `println`, and `printf`, which are used when generating output, and `nextInt`, `nextDouble`, `next`, and `nextLine`, which are used to input data. Unlike reserved words, predefined identifiers can be redefined, but it would not be wise to do so.

Example 2-2

The following are legal identifiers in Java:

```
first
conversion
payRate
counter1
$Amount
```

Table 2-1 shows some illegal identifiers and explains why they are illegal.

Table 2-1 Examples of Illegal Identifiers

Identifier	Description
`employee Salary`	There can be no space between `employee` and `Salary`.
`Hello!`	The exclamation mark cannot be used in an identifier.
`one+two`	The symbol + cannot be used in an identifier.
`2nd`	An identifier cannot begin with a digit.

DATA TYPES

The objective of a Java program is to manipulate data. Different programs manipulate different data. A program designed to calculate an employee's paycheck will add, subtract, multiply, and divide numbers; some of the numbers might represent hours worked and pay rate. Similarly, a program designed to alphabetize a class list will manipulate names. You wouldn't expect a cherry pie recipe to help you bake cookies. Similarly, you wouldn't manipulate alphabetic characters with a program designed to perform arithmetic calculations. Furthermore, you wouldn't multiply or subtract names. Reflecting such underlying differences, Java categorizes data into different types, and only certain operations can be performed on a particular type of data. At first it may seem confusing, but by being so type conscious, Java has built-in checks to guard against errors.

Data type: A set of values together with a set of operations.

Primitive Data Types

The primitive data types are the fundamental data types in Java. There are three categories of primitive data types:

- **Integral**, which is a data type that deals with integers, or numbers without a decimal part
- **Floating-point**, which is a data type that deals with decimal numbers
- **Boolean**, which is a data type that deals with logical values

Figure 2-1 illustrates these three data types.

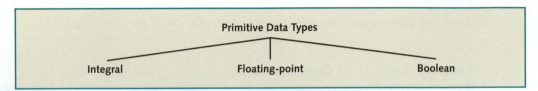

Figure 2-1 Primitive Data Types

Integral data types are further classified into five categories, as shown in Figure 2-2.

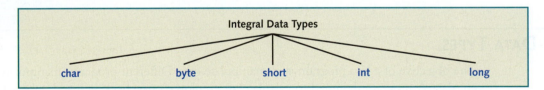

Figure 2-2 Integral Data Types

Why are there so many categories of integral data types? Every data type has a different set of values associated with it. For example, the **int** data type is used to represent integers between –2147483648 and 2147483647. The data type **short** is used to represent integers between –32768 and 32767.

Which data type you use depends on how big a number your program needs to deal with. In the early days of programming, computers and main memory were very expensive. Only a small amount of memory was available to execute programs and manipulate data. As a result, programmers had to optimize the use of memory. Because writing and making a program work is already a complicated process, not having to worry about the size of the memory makes for one less thing to think about. To effectively use memory, a programmer can look at the type of data used in a program and figure out which data type to use.

Table 2-2 gives the range of possible values associated with the five integral data types and the size of memory allocated to manipulate these values.

Table 2-2 Values and Memory Allocation for Integral Data Types

Data Type	Values	Storage (in bytes)
char	0 to 65535	2 (16 bits)
byte	−128 to 127	1 (8 bits)
short	−32768 to 32767	2 (16 bits)
int	−2147483648 to 2147483647	4 (32 bits)
long	−9223372036854775808 to 9223372036854775807	8 (64 bits)

The most commonly used integral data type is **int** and is described next. Note that the discussion of the **int** data type also applies to the integral types **byte**, **short**, and **long**.

int Data Type

This section describes the **int** data type, but this discussion also applies to other integral data types. Integers in Java, as in mathematics, are numbers such as the following:

−6728,   −67,   0,   78,   36782,   +763

Note the following two rules from these examples:

- Positive integers do not have to have a + sign in front of them.

- No commas are used within an integer. Recall that in Java, commas are used for separating items in a list. Thus, 36,782 is interpreted as two integers: 36 and 782.

char Data Type

As indicated in Table 2-2, the **char** data type has 65536 values, 0 to 65535. However, the main purpose of this data type is to represent single characters—that is, letters, digits, and special symbols. Therefore, the **char** data type can represent any key on your keyboard. When using the **char** data type, you enclose each character represented within single quotation marks. Examples of values belonging to the **char** data type include the following:

'A', 'a', '0', '*', '+', '$', '&', ' '

Note that a blank space is a character and is written as ' ', with a space between the single quotation marks.

The data type **char** allows only one symbol to be placed between the single quotation marks. Thus, the value 'abc' is not of the type **char**. Furthermore, even though != and similar special symbols are considered to be one symbol, they are not regarded as possible values of the data type **char** when enclosed in single quotation marks. All the individual symbols located on the keyboard that are printable are considered possible values of the `char` data type.

As stated in Chapter 1, each character has a specific representation in computer memory and there are several different coding schemes. Java uses the Unicode character set, which contains 65536 values numbered 0 to 65535. The position of the first character is 0, the position of the second character is 1, and so on. Other commonly used character data sets are the American Standard Code for Information Interchange (ASCII) and Extended Binary-Coded Decimal Interchange Code (EBCDIC). The ASCII character set has 128 values. ASCII is a subset of Unicode. That is, the first 128 characters of Unicode are the same as the characters in ASCII. The EBCDIC character set has 256 values and was created by IBM. Both character sets are described in Appendix C.

Each of the 65536 values of the Unicode character set represents a different character. For example, the value `65` represents `'A'`, and the value `43` represents `'+'`. Thus, each character has a predefined ordering, which is called a **collating sequence**, in the set. The collating sequence is used when you compare characters. For example, the value representing `'B'` is `66`, so `'A'` is smaller than `'B'`. Similarly, `'+'` is smaller than `'A'` since `43` is smaller than `65`.

The 14th character in the Unicode (and ASCII) character set is called the newline character and is represented as `'\n'`. (Note that the position of the newline character in the Unicode and ASCII character sets is 13 because the position of the first character is 0.) Even though the newline character is a combination of two characters, it is treated as one character. Similarly, the horizontal tab character is represented in Java as `'\t'`, and the null character is represented as `'\0'` (a backslash followed by zero). (Later in this chapter, we elaborate on these special characters.) Furthermore, the first 32 characters in the Unicode and ASCII character sets are nonprintable. (See Appendix C for a list of these characters.)

`boolean` Data Type

The data type `boolean` has only two values: `true` and `false`. Also, `true` and `false` are called the **logical (Boolean) values**. The central purpose of this data type is to manipulate logical (Boolean) expressions. An expression that evaluates to `true` or `false` is called a **logical (Boolean) expression**. Logical (Boolean) expressions are formally defined and discussed in detail in Chapter 4. In Java, `boolean`, `true`, and `false` are reserved words. The memory allocated for the `boolean` data type is 1 bit.

Floating-Point Data Types

To deal with decimal numbers, Java provides the floating-point data type, which we discuss in this section. To facilitate the discussion, we will review a concept from a high school or college algebra course.

You may be familiar with scientific notation. For example:

43872918 = 4.3872918 * 10^7   {10 to the power of seven}

.0000265 = 2.65 * 10^{-5}   {10 to the power of minus five}

47.9832 = 4.79832 * 10^1   {10 to the power of one}

To represent real numbers, Java uses a form of scientific notation called **floating-point notation**. Table 2-3 shows how Java might print a set of real numbers. In the Java floating-point notation, the letter **E** stands for the exponent.

Table 2-3 Examples of Real Numbers Printed in Java Floating-Point Notation

Real Number	Java Floating-Point Notation
75.924	7.592400E1
0.18	1.800000E-1
0.0000453	4.530000E-5
-1.482	-1.482000E0
7800.0	7.800000E3

Java provides two data types to manipulate decimal numbers: **float** and **double**. As in the case of integral data types, the data types **float** and **double** differ in the set of values. Figure 2-3 illustrates these data types.

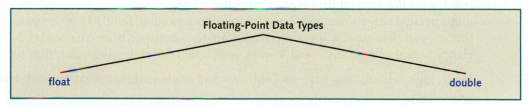

Figure 2-3 Floating-point data types

float: The data type **float** is used in Java to represent any real number between -3.4E+38 and 3.4E+38. The memory allocated for the **float** data type is 4 bytes.

double: The data type **double** is used in Java to represent any real number between -1.7E+308 and 1.7E+308. The memory allocated for the **double** data type is 8 bytes.

Other than the set of values, there is one more difference between the data types **float** and **double**. The maximum number of significant digits—that is, the number of decimal places—in `float` values is 6 or 7. Typically, the maximum number of significant digits in values belonging to the `double` type is 15. The maximum number of significant digits is called the **precision**. Sometimes `float` values are called **single precision**, and values of the type `double` are called **double precision**.

 In Java, by default, floating-point numbers are considered of the type `double`. Therefore, if you use the data type `float` to manipulate floating-point numbers in a program, you might get a warning or an error message such as "truncation from double to float" or "possible loss of data". To avoid such messages, you should use the `double` data type. For illustration purposes and to avoid such messages in programming examples, this book mostly uses the data type `double` to manipulate floating-point numbers.

ARITHMETIC OPERATORS AND OPERATOR PRECEDENCE

One of the most important features of a computer is its ability to calculate. You can use the standard arithmetic operators to manipulate integral and floating-point data types. There are five arithmetic operators:

+ addition

– subtraction

* multiplication

/ division

% mod (modulus) operator

You can use these operators with both integral and floating-point data types. When you use / with the integral data type, it gives the quotient in integer division. That is, integral division truncates any fractional part; there is no rounding. Similarly, when you use % with the integral data type, it gives the remainder in integer division. (Examples 2-3 and 2-4 clarify how the operators / and % work with integral and floating–point data types.)

Since high school, you have probably worked with arithmetic expressions such as the following:

(i)   –5
(ii) 8 – 7
(iii) 3 + 4
(iv) 2 + 3 * 5
(v)   5.6 + 6.2 * 3
(vi) x + 2 * 5 + 6 / y

In expression (vi), x and y are some unknown numbers. Formally, an **arithmetic expression** is constructed by using arithmetic operators and numbers. The numbers in the expression are called **operands**. Moreover, the numbers used to evaluate an operator are called the operands for that operator.

In expression (i), the operator – (subtraction) is used to specify that the number 5 is negative. Moreover, this expression, –5, has only one operand. Operators that have only one operand are called **unary operators**.

In expression (ii), the symbol – is used to subtract 7 from 8. In this expression, – has two operands, 8 and 7. Operators that have two operands are called **binary operators**.

Unary operator: An operator that has only one operand.

Binary operator: An operator that has two operands.

In expression (iii), 3 and 4 are the operands for the operator +. Because the operator + has two operands, in this expression, + is a binary operator. Now consider the following expression:

+27

In this expression, the operator + is used to indicate that the number 27 is positive. Here, because + has only one operand, it acts as a unary operator.

From the preceding discussion, it follows that – and + can be unary or binary arithmetic operators. However, the arithmetic operators *, /, and % are binary and must have two operands.

The following examples show how arithmetic operators—especially / and %—work with integral data types. As you can see from these examples, the operator / represents the quotient in ordinary division when used with integral data types.

Example 2-3

Arithmetic Expression	Result	Description
2 + 5	7	
13 + 89	102	
34 – 20	14	
45 – 90	–45	
2 * 7	14	
5 / 2	2	In the division 5 / 2, the quotient is 2 and the remainder is 1. Therefore, 5 / 2 with the integral operands evaluates to the quotient, which is 2.
14 / 7	2	
34 % 5	4	In the division 34 / 5, the quotient is 6 and the remainder is 4. Therefore, 34 % 5 evaluates to the remainder, which is 4.

-34 % 5	-4	In the division -34 / 5, the quotient is -6 and the remainder is -4. Therefore, -34 % 5 evaluates to the remainder, which is -4.
34 % -5	4	In the division 34 / -5, the quotient is -6 and the remainder is 4. Therefore, 34 % -5 evaluates to the remainder, which is 4.
-34 % -5	-4	In the division -34 / -5, the quotient is 6 and the remainder is -4. Therefore, -34 % -5 evaluates to the remainder, which is -4.
4 % 6	4	In the division 4 / 6, the quotient is 0 and the remainder is 4. Therefore, 4 % 6 evaluates to the remainder, which is 4.

Note that in the divisions 34 / 5 and -34 / -5, the quotients, which are 6, are the same, but the remainders are different. In the division 34 / 5, the remainder is 4; in the division -34 / -5, the remainder is -4.

The following Java program evaluates the preceding expressions:

```java
public class Example2_3
{
    public static void main(String[] args)
    {
        System.out.println("2 + 5 = " + (2 + 5));
        System.out.println("13 + 89 = " + (13 + 89));
        System.out.println("34 - 20 = " + (34 - 20));
        System.out.println("45 - 90 = " + (45 - 90));
        System.out.println("2 * 7 = " + (2 * 7));
        System.out.println("5 / 2 = " + (5 / 2));
        System.out.println("14 / 7 = " + (14 / 7));
        System.out.println("34 % 5 = " + (34 % 5));
        System.out.println("-34 % 5 = " + (-34 % 5));
        System.out.println("34 % -5 = " + (34 % -5));
        System.out.println("-34 % -5 = " + (-34 % -5));
        System.out.println("4 % 6 = " + (4 % 6));
    }
}
```

Sample Run:
```
2 + 5 = 7
13 + 89 = 102
34 - 20 = 14
45 - 90 = -45
2 * 7 = 14
5 / 2 = 2
14 / 7 = 2
```

```
34 % 5 = 4
-34 % 5 = -4
34 % -5 = 4
-34 % -5 = -4
4 % 6 = 4
```

The following expressions show how arithmetic operators work with floating-point numbers.

Example 2-4

The following Java program evaluates various floating-point expressions. (The details are left as an exercise for you.)

```java
public class Example2_4
{
    public static void main(String[] args)
    {
        System.out.println("5.0 + 3.5 = " + (5.0 + 3.5));
        System.out.println("3.0 + 9.4 = " + (3.0 + 9.4));
        System.out.println("16.4 - 5.2 = " + (16.4 - 5.2));
        System.out.println("4.2 * 2.5 = " + (4.2 * 2.5));
        System.out.println("5.0 / 2.0 = " + (5.0 / 2.0));
        System.out.println("5.0 % 2.0 = " + (5.0 % 2.0));
        System.out.println("34.5 / 6.0 = " + (34.5 / 6.0));
        System.out.println("34.5 % 6.0 = " + (34.5 % 6.0));
        System.out.println("34.5 / 6.5 = " + (34.5 / 6.5));
        System.out.println("34.5 % 6.5 = " + (34.5 % 6.5));
    }
}
```

Sample Run:

```
5.0 + 3.5 = 8.5
3.0 + 9.4 = 12.4
16.4 - 5.2 = 11.2
4.2 * 2.5 = 10.5
5.0 / 2.0 = 2.5
5.0 % 2.0 = 1.0
34.5 / 6.0 = 5.75
34.5 % 6.0 = 4.5
34.5 / 6.5 = 5.3076923076923075
34.5 % 6.5 = 2.0
```

Order of Precedence

Consider the following expression:

```
3 + 4 * 5
```

Recall from a high school or college algebra course that, in this expression, the operator `*` is evaluated first, and then the operator `+`. In other words, the operator `*` has higher **precedence** than the operator `+`.

When more than one arithmetic operator is used in an expression, Java uses the operator precedence rules to determine the order in which the operations are performed to evaluate the expression. According to the order of precedence rules for arithmetic operators,

```
*,     /,   %
```

have a higher level of precedence than:

```
+,    -
```

Note that the operators `*`, `/`, and `%` have the same level of precedence. Similarly, the operators `+` and `−` have the same level of precedence.

When operators have the same level of precedence, operations are performed from left to right. To avoid confusion, you can use parentheses to group arithmetic expressions. For example, using the order of precedence rules,

```
3 * 7 - 6 + 2 * 5 / 4 + 6
```

means the following:

```
  (((3 * 7) - 6) + (( 2 * 5) / 4 )) + 6
= ((21 - 6) + (10 / 4)) + 6          (Evaluate *)
= ((21 - 6) + 2) + 6                 (Evaluate /)
= (15 + 2) + 6                       (Evaluate -)
= 17 + 6                             (Evaluate first +)
= 23                                 (Evaluate +)
```

Note that using parentheses in the preceding expression clarifies the order of precedence. You can also use parentheses to override the order of precedence rules (see Example 2-5).

Example 2-5

In the expression:

```
3 + 4 * 5
```

`*` is evaluated before `+`. Therefore, the result of this expression is `23`. On the other hand, in the expression:

```
(3 + 4) * 5
```

`+` is evaluated before `*` and the result of this expression is `35`.

Because arithmetic operators are evaluated from left to right, unless parentheses are present, the **associativity** of arithmetic operators is said to be from left to right.

Character arithmetic: Since the `char` data type is also an integral data type, Java allows you to perform arithmetic operations on `char` data. You should use this ability carefully. There is a difference between the character `'8'` and the integer 8. The integer value of 8 is 8. The integer value of `'8'` is 56, which is the Unicode collating sequence of the character `'8'`.

When evaluating arithmetic expressions, 8 + 7 = 15, `'8'` + `'7'` = 56 + 55, yields 111, and `'8'` + 7 = 56 + 7, yields 63. Furthermore, `'8'` * `'7'` = 56 * 55 = 3080.

These examples illustrate that many things can go wrong when you perform character arithmetic. If you must use arithmetic operations on the `char` type data, do so with caution.

EXPRESSIONS

To this point, we have discussed only arithmetic operators. In this section, we discuss arithmetic expressions in detail. (Arithmetic expressions were introduced in the last section.)

If all operands (that is, numbers) in an expression are integers, the expression is called an **integral expression**. If all operands in an expression are floating-point numbers, the expression is called a **floating-point** or **decimal expression**. An integral expression yields an integral result; a floating-point expression yields a floating-point result. Looking at some examples will help clarify these definitions.

Example 2-6

Consider the following Java integral expressions:

```
2 + 3 * 5
3 + x - y / 7
x + 2 * (y - z) + 18
```

In these expressions, **x**, **y**, and **z** represent variables of the integral type; that is, they can hold integer values. (Variables are discussed later in this chapter.)

Example 2-7

Consider the following Java floating-point expressions:

```
12.8 * 17.5 - 34.50
x * 10.5 + y - 16.2
```

Here, **x** and **y** represent variables of the floating-point type; that is, they can hold floating-point values. (Variables are discussed later in this chapter.)

Evaluating an integral or a floating-point expression is straightforward. As already noted, when operators have the same precedence, the expression is evaluated from left to right. To avoid confusion you can always use parentheses to group operands and operators.

Mixed Expressions

An expression that has operands of different data types is called a **mixed expression**. A mixed expression contains both integers and floating-point numbers. The following expressions are examples of mixed expressions:

```
2 + 3.5
6 / 4 + 3.9
5.4 * 2 - 13.6 + 18 / 2
```

In the first expression, the operand + has one integer operand and one floating-point operand. In the second expression, both operands for the operator / are integers; the first operand of + is the result of 6 / 4, and the second operand of + is a floating-point number. The third example is a more complicated mix of integers and floating-point numbers. How does Java evaluate such mixed expressions?

Two rules apply when evaluating a mixed expression:

1. When evaluating an operator in a mixed expression:

   a. If the operator has the same types of operands (that is, both are integers or both are floating-point numbers), the operator is evaluated according to the type of the operand. Integer operands yield an integer result; floating-point numbers yield a floating-point number result.

   b. If the operator has both types of operands (that is, one is an integer and the other is a floating-point number), during calculation the integer is changed to a floating-point number with the decimal part of zero, and then the operator is evaluated. The result is a floating-point number.

2. The entire expression is evaluated according to the precedence rules. The multiplication, division, and modulus operators are evaluated before the addition and subtraction operators. Operators having the same level of precedence are evaluated from left to right. Grouping is allowed for clarity.

Following these rules, when you evaluate a mixed expression, you concentrate on one operator at a time, using the rules of precedence. If the operator to be evaluated has operands of the same data type, evaluate the operator using Rule 1(a). That is, an operator with integer operands yields an integer result, and an operator with floating-point operands yields a floating-point result. If the operator to be evaluated has one integer operand and one floating-point operand, before evaluating this operator you convert the integer operand to a floating-point number with a decimal part of zero. Example 2-8 shows how to evaluate mixed expressions.

Example 2-8

Mixed Expression	Evaluation	Rule Applied
3 / 2 + 5.0	= 1 + 5.0 = 6.0	3 / 2 = 1 (integer division; Rule 1(a)) (1 + 5.0 = 1.0 + 5.0 (Rule 1(b)) = 6.0)

15.6 / 2 + 5	= 7.8 + 5
	
	= 12.8
		15.6 / 2 = 15.6 / 2.0 (Rule 1(b))
		     = 7.8
		7.8 + 5 = 7.8 + 5.0 (Rule 1(b))
		     = 12.8

4 + 5 / 2.0	= 4 + 2.5
	
	= 6.5
		5 / 2.0 = 5.0 / 2.0 (Rule 1(b))
		     = 2.5
		4 + 2.5 = 4.0 + 2.5 (Rule 1(b))
		     = 6.5

4 * 3 + 7 / 5 − 25.5	= 12 + 7 / 5 − 25.5 = 12 + 1 − 25.5 = 13 − 25.5 = −12.5	4 * 3 = 12; (Rule 1(a)) 7 / 5 = 1 (integer division; Rule 1(a)) 12 + 1 = 13; (Rule 1(a)) 13 − 25.5 = 13.0 − 25.5 (Rule 1(b)) = −12.5

The following Java program evaluates the preceding expressions:

```java
public class Example2_8
{
    public static void main(String[] args)
    {
        System.out.println("3 / 2 + 5.0 = " + (3 / 2 + 5.0));
        System.out.println("15.6 / 2 + 5 = " + (15.6 / 2 + 5));
        System.out.println("4 + 5 / 2.0 = " + (4 + 5 / 2.0));
        System.out.println("4 * 3 + 7 / 5 − 25.5 = "
                        + (4 * 3 + 7 / 5 − 25.5));
    }
}
```

Sample Run:
```
3 / 2 + 5.0 = 6.0
15.6 / 2 + 5 = 12.8
4 + 5 / 2.0 = 6.5
4 * 3 + 7 / 5 − 25.5 = −12.5
```

These examples illustrate that an integer is not converted to a floating-point number unless the operator to be evaluated has one integer and one floating-point operand.

TYPE CONVERSION (CASTING)

In the previous section, you learned that when evaluating an arithmetic expression if the operator has mixed operands, the integer value is changed to a floating-point value with the zero decimal part. When a value of one data type is automatically changed to another data type, an **implicit type coercion** has occurred. As the examples in the preceding section illustrate, if you are not careful about data types, implicit type coercion can generate unexpected results.

To avoid implicit type coercion, Java provides for explicit type conversion through the use of a cast operator. The **cast operator**, also called **type conversion** or **type casting**, takes the following form:

```
(dataTypeName) expression
```

First, the `expression` is evaluated. Its value is then converted to a value of the type specified by `dataTypeName`.

When using the cast operator to convert a floating-point (decimal) number to an integer, you simply drop the decimal part of the floating-point number. That is, the floating-point number is truncated. The following examples show how cast operators work. Be sure you understand why the last two expressions evaluate as they do.

Example 2-9

Expression	Evaluates to
`(int)(7.9)`	7
`(int)(3.3)`	3
`(double)(25)`	25.0
`(double)(5 + 3)`	= `(double)(8)` = 8.0
`(double)(15)/ 2`	= 15.0 / 2 (since `(double)(15)` = 15.0)
	= 15.0 / 2.0 = 7.5
`(double)(15 / 2)`	= `(double)(7)` (since 15 / 2 = 7)
	= 7.0
`(int)(7.8 + (double)(15)/ 2)`	= `(int)(7.8 + 7.5)`
	= `(int)(15.3)`
	= 15
`(int)(7.8 + (double)(15/ 2))`	= `(int)(7.8 + 7.0)`
	= `(int)(14.8)`
	= 14

The following Java program evaluates the preceding expressions:

```
public class Example2_9
{
    public static void main(String[] args)
    {
        System.out.println("(int)(7.9) = " + (int)(7.9));
        System.out.println("(int)(3.3) = " + (int)(3.3));
        System.out.println("(double)(25) = " + (double)(25));
        System.out.println("(double)(5 + 3) = "
                            + (double)(5 + 3));
        System.out.println("(double)(15) / 2 = "
                            + ((double)(15) / 2));
        System.out.println("(double)(15 / 2) = "
                            + ((double)(15 / 2)));
        System.out.println("(int)(7.8 + (double)(15) / 2) = "
                            + ((int)(7.8 + (double)(15) / 2)));
        System.out.println("(int)(7.8 + (double)(15 / 2)) = "
                            + ((int)(7.8 + (double)(15 / 2))));
    }
}
```

Sample Run:
```
(int)(7.9) = 7
(int)(3.3) = 3
(double)(25) = 25.0
(double)(5 + 3) = 8.0
(double)(15) / 2 = 7.5
(double)(15 / 2) = 7.0
(int)(7.8 + (double)(15) / 2) = 15
(int)(7.8 + (double)(15 / 2)) = 14
```

Consider another series of examples. For these examples, x = 15, y = 23, and z = 3.75. A Java program similar to the preceding one generated the output of the following expressions. (The Web site accompanying this book contains that Java program. The program is named Example2_9B.)

Expression	Value
(int)(7.9 + 6.7)	14
(int)(7.9) + (int)(6.7)	13
(double)(y / x) + z	4.75
(double)(y) / x + z	5.283333333333333

You can also use cast operators to explicitly convert **char** data values into **int** data values, and **int** data values into **char** data values. To convert **char** data values into **int** data values, you use a collating sequence. For example, in the Unicode character set, (**int**)('A') is 65 and (**int**)('8') is 56. Similarly, (**char**)(65) is 'A' and (**char**)(56) is '8'.

In this and the previous sections of this chapter, you learned how arithmetic expressions are formed and evaluated in Java. If you want to use the value of one expression in another expression, you must first save the value of the expression. There are many reasons to save the value of an expression. Some expressions are complex and may require a considerable amount of computer time to evaluate. By calculating the values once and saving them for further use, you save computer time and create a program that executes more quickly, and you also avoid possible typographical errors. In Java, expressions are evaluated and if the value is not saved, it is lost. That is, to use the value of an expression in later calculations, it must be saved. In the section Saving and Using the Value of an Expression, later in this chapter, you will learn how to save the value of an expression and use it in subsequent calculations.

class String

In the preceding sections, we discussed primitive types to deal with data consisting of numbers and characters. What about data values such as a person's name? A person's name contains more than one character. Such values are called strings. More formally, a **string** is a sequence of zero or more characters. Strings in Java are enclosed in double quotation marks (not in single quotation marks, as are the `char` data types).

Most often we process strings as a single unit. To process strings effectively, Java provides the **class** `String`. The **class** `String` contains various operations to manipulate a string. You will see this class used throughout the book. Chapter 3 discusses various operations provided by the **class** `String`. Moreover, technically speaking, the **class** `String` is not a primitive type.

A string that contains no characters is called a **null** or **empty** string. The following are examples of strings. Note that `""` is the empty string.

```
"William Jacob"
"Mickey"
""
```

Every character in a string has a relative position in the string. The position of the first character is 0, the position of the second character is 1, and so on. The **length** of a string is the number of characters in it.

Example 2-10

String	Position of a Character in the String	Length of the String
"William Jacob"	Position of 'W' is 0. Position of the first 'i' is 1. Position of ' ' (the space) is 7. Position of 'J' is 8. Position of 'b' is 12.	13

String	Position of a Character in the String	Length of the String
"Mickey"	Position of 'M' is 0.	6
	Position of 'i' is 1.	
	Position of 'c' is 2.	
	Position of 'k' is 3.	
	Position of 'e' is 4.	
	Position of 'y' is 5.	

When determining the length of a string, you must also count the spaces if the string contains any spaces. For example, the length of the following string is 22.

```
"It is a beautiful day."
```

INPUT

As noted earlier, the main objective of Java programs is to perform calculations and manipulate data. Recall that the data must be loaded into main memory before it can be manipulated. In this section, you learn how to put data into the computer's memory. Storing data in the computer's memory is a two–step process:

1. Instruct the computer to allocate memory.

2. Include statements in the program to put the data into the allocated memory.

Allocating Memory with Named Constants and Variables

When you instruct the computer to allocate memory, you tell it what names to use for each memory location, and what type of data to store in those memory locations. Knowing the location of the data is essential because data stored in one memory location might be needed at several places in the program. As you learned earlier, knowing what data type you have is crucial for performing accurate calculations. It is also critical to know whether your data must remain fixed throughout program execution or whether it should change.

Some data must not be changed. For example, the pay rate might be the same for all part-time employees. The value in a conversion formula that converts inches into centimeters is fixed because 1 inch is always equal to 2.54 centimeters. When stored in memory, this type of data must be protected from accidental changes during program execution. In Java, you can use a **named constant** to instruct a program to mark those memory locations in which data is fixed throughout program execution.

Named constant: A memory location whose content is not allowed to change during program execution.

To allocate memory, we use Java's declaration statements. The syntax to declare a named constant is:

```
static final dataType IDENTIFIER = value;
```

In Java, **static** and **final** are reserved words. The reserved word **final** specifies that the value stored in the identifier is fixed and cannot be changed.

 In syntax, the shading indicates the part of the definition that is optional.

Because the reserved word **static** is shaded, it may or may not appear when a named constant is declared. The section, Creating a Java Application Program, later in this chapter, explains when this reserved word might be required. Also, notice that the identifier for a named constant is in uppercase letters. This is because Java programmers typically use uppercase letters to name a named constant. (If the name of a named constant is a combination of more than one word, called a *run-together-word*, then the words are separated using an underscore; see the next example.)

Example 2-11

Consider the following Java statements:

```
final double CENTIMETERS_PER_INCH = 2.54;
final int NO_OF_STUDENTS = 20;
final char BLANK = ' ';
final double PAY_RATE = 15.75;
```

The first statement tells the compiler to allocate enough memory to store a value of the type **double**, call this memory space CENTIMETERS_PER_INCH, and store the value **2.54** in it. Throughout a program that uses this statement, whenever the conversion formula is needed, the memory space CENTIMETERS_PER_INCH can be accessed. The other statements have similar meanings.

 As remarked earlier, the default type of floating-point numbers is **double**. Therefore, if you declare a named constant of the type **float**, then you must specify that the value is of the type **float** as follows:

```
final float PAY_RATE = 15.75f;
```

otherwise, the compiler will generate an error message. Notice that in 15.75f, the letter f at the end specifies that 15.75 is a **float** value. Recall that the memory size for **float** values is 4 bytes; for **double** values, 8 bytes. Because (these days) memory size is of little concern, as indicated earlier, we will mostly use the type **double** to work with floating-point values.

Using a named constant to store fixed data, rather than using the data value itself, has one major advantage. If the fixed data changes, you do not need to edit the entire program and change the old value to the new value. Instead, you can make the change at just one place, recompile the program, and execute it using the new value throughout. In addition, by storing a value and referring to that memory location whenever the value is needed, you avoid typing the same value again and again and you prevent typos. If you misspell the name of the location, the computer might warn you through an error message, but it will not warn you if the value is mistyped.

Certain data must be modified during program execution. For example, after each test, a student's average test score and the number of tests taken change. Similarly, after each pay increase, an employee's salary changes. This type of data must be stored in memory cells whose contents can be modified during program execution. In Java, memory cells whose contents can be modified during program execution are called **variables**.

Variable: A memory location whose content may change during program execution.

The syntax for declaring one variable or multiple variables is:

```
dataType identifier1, identifier2, . . ., identifierN;
```

Example 2-12

Consider the following statements:

```
double amountDue;
int    counter;
char   ch;
int    x, y;
```

The first statement tells the compiler to allocate enough memory to store a value of the type **double** and call it **amountDue**. Statements 2 and 3 have similar conventions. The fourth statement tells the compiler to allocate two different memory spaces, each large enough to store a value of the type **int**; name the first memory space **x**; and name the second memory space **y**.

 Java programmers typically use lowercase letters to declare variables. If a variable name is a combination of more than one word, then the first letter of each word, except the first word, is uppercase. (For example, see the variable amountDue in the preceding example.)

From now on, when we say "variable," we mean a variable memory location.

 In Java (within a method), you must declare all identifiers before you can use them. If you refer to an identifier without declaring it, the compiler will generate an error message indicating that the identifier is not declared.

Putting Data into Variables

Now that you know how to declare variables, the next question is: How do you put data into those variables? The two common ways to place data into a variable are:

1. Use an assignment statement.

2. Use input (read) statements.

Assignment Statement

The assignment statement takes the following form:

```
variable = expression;
```

In an assignment statement, the value of the **expression** should match the data type of the **variable**. The expression on the right side is evaluated, and its value is assigned to the variable (and thus to a memory location) on the left side.

A variable is said to be **initialized** the first time a value is placed in the variable.

In Java, = (the equals sign) is called the **assignment operator**.

Example 2-13

Suppose you have the following variable declarations:

```
int i, j;
double sale;
char first;
String str;
```

Now consider the following assignment statements:

```
i = 4;
j = 4 * 5 - 11;
sale = 0.02 * 1000;
first = 'D';
str = "It is a sunny day.";
```

For each of these statements, the computer first evaluates the expression on the right and then stores that value in a memory location named by the identifier on the left. The first statement stores the value 4 in i, the second statement stores 9 in j, the third statement stores 20.00 in sale, and the fourth statement stores the character D in first. The fifth statement assigns the string "It is a sunny day." to the variable str.

The following Java program shows the effect of the preceding statements:

```
public class Example2_13
{
    public static void main(String[] args)
    {
```

```
    int i, j;
    double sale;
    char first;
    String str;

    i = 4;
    System.out.println("i = " + i);

    j = 4 * 5 - 11;
    System.out.println("j = " + j);

    sale = 0.02 * 1000;
    System.out.println("sale = " + sale);

    first = 'D';
    System.out.println("first = " + first);

    str = "It is a sunny day.";
    System.out.println("str = " + str);
  }
}
```

Sample Run:

```
i = 4
j = 9
sale = 20.0
first = D
str = It is a sunny day.
```

For the most part, the preceding program is straightforward. Let us take a look at the output statement:

```
System.out.println("i = " + i);
```

This output statement consists of the string `"i = "`, `+`, and the variable `i`. Here the value of `i` is concatenated with the string `"i = "`, resulting in the string `"i = 4"`, which is then output. The meaning of the other output statements is similar.

A Java statement such as:

```
i = i + 2;
```

means "evaluate whatever is in `i`, add 2 to it, and assign the new value to the memory location `i`." The expression on the right side must be evaluated first; that value is then assigned to the memory location specified by the variable on the left side. Thus, the sequence of Java statements:

```
i = 6;
i = i + 2;
```

and the statement:

```
i = 8;
```

both assign 8 to i. Note that the statement i = i + 2 is meaningless if i has not been initialized.

The statement i = 5; is read as "i becomes 5" or "i gets 5" or "i is assigned the value 5."

Suppose that i, j, and k are **int** variables. The sequence of statements:

```
i = 12;
i = i + 6;
j = i;
k = j / 2;
k = k / 3;
```

result in storing 18 in i, 18 in j, and 3 in k.

 The Java language is strongly typed, which means that you cannot assign a value to a variable that is not compatible with its data type. For example, a string cannot be stored in an **int** variable. If you try to store an incompatible value in a variable, an error is generated when you compile the program or during program execution. Therefore, in an assignment statement, the expression on the right side must evaluate to a value compatible with the data type of the variable on the left side.

Suppose that x, y, and z are **int** variables. The following is a legal statement in Java:

```
x = y = z;
```

In this statement, first the value of z is assigned to y, and then the new value of y is assigned to x. Because the assignment operator = is evaluated from right to left, the **associativity** of the **assignment operator** is said to be from right to left.

Saving and Using the Value of an Expression

Now that you know how to declare variables and put data into them, you can learn how to save the value of an expression. You can then use this value in a later expression without using the expression itself. To save the value of an expression and use it in a later expression, do the following:

1. Declare a variable of the appropriate data type. For example, if the result of the expression is an integer, declare an **int** variable.

2. Use the assignment statement to assign the value of the expression to the variable that was declared. This action saves the value of the expression into the variable.

3. Wherever the value of the expression is needed, use the variable holding the value.

Example 2-14 illustrates this concept.

Example 2-14

Suppose that you have the following declaration:

```
int a, b, c, d;
int x, y;
```

Further suppose that you want to evaluate the expressions:

$$-b + (b^2 - 4ac)$$

and:

$$-b - (b^2 - 4ac)$$

and assign the values of these expressions to **x** and **y**, respectively. Because the expression $b^2 - 4ac$ appears in both expressions, you can first calculate the value of this expression and save its value in **d**. You can then use the value of **d** to evaluate the expressions, as shown in the following statements:

```
d = b * b - 4 * a * c;
x = -b + d;
y = -b - d;
```

Earlier, you learned that if a variable is used in an expression, the expression yields a meaningful value only if the variable has first been initialized. You also learned that after declaring a variable, you can use an assignment statement to initialize it. It is possible to initialize and declare variables simultaneously. Before we discuss how to use an input (read) statement, we address this important issue.

Declaring and Initializing Variables

When a variable is declared, Java might not automatically put a meaningful value into it. In other words, Java might not automatically initialize all the variables you declare. For example, the **int** and **double** variables might not be initialized to **0**, as happens in some programming languages.

If you declare a variable and then use it in an expression without first initializing it, when you compile the program you are likely to get an error. To avoid these pitfalls, Java allows you to initialize variables while they are being declared. Consider the following Java statements in which variables are first declared and then initialized:

```
int first, second;
char ch;
double x, y;

first = 13;
second = 10;
ch = ' ';
x = 12.6;
y = 123.456;
```

You can declare and initialize these variables at the same time using the following Java statements:

```
int first = 13, second = 10;
char ch = ' ';
double x = 12.6, y = 123.456;
```

The first Java statement declares two **int** variables, **first** and **second**, and stores 13 in **first** and 10 in **second**. The other statements have similar meanings. Declaring and initializing variables simultaneously is another way to place meaningful data into a variable.

 Not all variables are initialized during declaration. The nature of the program or the programmer's choice dictates which variables should be initialized during declaration.

Input (Read) Statement

In an earlier section, you learned how to put data into variables using the assignment statement. In this section, you learn how to put data into variables from the standard input device using Java's input (or read) statements.

 In most cases, the standard input device is the keyboard.

When the computer gets the data from the keyboard, the user is said to be acting interactively.

To put data into variables from the standard input device, we first create an input stream object and associate it with the standard input device. The following statement accomplishes this:

```
static Scanner console = new Scanner(System.in);
```

This statement creates the input stream object **console** and associates it with the standard input device. (Note that **Scanner** is a (predefined) Java class and the preceding statement creates **console** to be an object of this class.) The object **console** reads the next input as follows:

a. If the next input can be interpreted as an integer, then the expression:

```
console.nextInt()
```

retrieves that integer; that is, the value of this expression is that integer.

b. If the next input can be interpreted as a floating-point number, then the expression:

```
console.nextDouble()
```

retrieves that floating-point number; that is, the value of this expression is that floating-point number.

c. The expression:

```
console.next()
```

retrieves the next input as a string; that is, the value of this expression is the next input string. (Notice that if the next input is a number, this expression interprets that number as a string.)

d. The expression:

```
console.nextLine()
```

retrieves the next input as a string until the end of the line; that is, the value of this expression is the next input line. (Notice that this expression also reads the newline character, but the newline character is not stored as part of the string.)

While scanning for the next input, the expressions `console.nextInt()`, `console.nextDouble()`, and `console.next()` skip any whitespace characters. Whitespace characters are blanks and certain nonprintable characters such as newline and tab.

`System.in` is called a **standard input stream object** and is designed to input data from the standard input device. However, the object `System.in` extracts data in the form of bytes from the input stream. Therefore, using `System.in`, we first create a `Scanner` object, such as `console`, as shown previously so that the data can be extracted in a desired form. Moreover, Chapter 3 explains the meaning of the word `new`.

The **class** Scanner is added to the Java library in JDK version 5.0. Therefore, this class is *not* available in JDK versions lower than 5.0.

Example 2-15

Suppose that `miles` is a variable of the data type **double**. Further suppose that the input is `73.65`. Consider the following statements:

```
miles = console.nextDouble();
```

This statement causes the computer to get the input, which is `73.65`, from the standard input device, and stores it in the variable `miles`. That is, after this statement executes, the value of the variable `miles` is `73.65`.

Example 2-16 further explains how to input numeric data into a program.

Example 2-16

Suppose we have the following declaration:

```
static Scanner console = new Scanner(System.in);
```

Consider the following statements:

```
int feet;
int inches;
```

Suppose the input is:

```
23 7
```

Next, consider the following statements:

```
feet = console.nextInt();    //Line 1
inches = console.nextInt(); //Line 2
```

The statement in Line 1 stores the number 23 into the variable feet. The statement in Line 2 stores the number 7 into the variable inches. Notice that when these numbers are entered via the keyboard, they are separated with a blank. In fact, they can be separated with one or more blanks or lines or even the tab character.

The following Java program shows the effect of the preceding input statements:

```
import java.util.*;
public class Example2_16
{
    static Scanner console = new Scanner(System.in);
    public static void main(String[] args)
    {
        int feet;
        int inches;

        System.out.println("Enter two integers separated by spaces.");
        feet = console.nextInt();
        inches = console.nextInt();

        System.out.println("Feet = " + Feet);
        System.out.println("Inches = " + Inches);
    }
}
```

Sample Run: (In this sample run, the user input is shaded.)
```
Enter two integers separated by spaces.
23 7
Feet = 23
Inches = 7
```

In the preceding program, notice the first line:

```
import java.util.*;
```

This line is required to use the **class** Scanner.

If the next input cannot be expressed as an appropriate number, then the expressions `console.nextInt()` and `console.nextDouble()` will cause the program to terminate with an error message (unless some care is taken in the program), indicating an input mismatch. For example, if the next input cannot be expressed as an integer, then the expression `console.nextInt()` will cause the program to terminate with the error message indicating an input mismatch. Examples of invalid integers are `24w5` and `12.50`. Chapter 12 explains why the program terminates with the error message indicating an input mismatch and how to include the necessary code to handle this problem. Until then we assume that the user enters valid numbers.

The Java program in Example 2-17 illustrates how to read strings and numeric data.

Example 2-17

```java
import java.util.*;
public class Example2_17
{
    static Scanner console = new Scanner(System.in);
    public static void main(String[] args)
    {
        String firstName;                               //Line 1
        String lastName;                                //Line 2
        int age;                                        //Line 3
        double weight;                                  //Line 4

        System.out.println("Enter first name, last name, "
                        + "age, and weight separated "
                        + "by spaces.");                //Line 5
        firstName = console.next();                     //Line 6
        lastName = console.next();                      //Line 7
        age = console.nextInt();                        //Line 8
        weight = console.nextDouble();                  //Line 9

        System.out.println("Name: " + firstName
                        + " " + lastName);              //Line 10
        System.out.println("Age: " + age);             //Line 11
        System.out.println("Weight: " + weight);       //Line 12
    }
}
```

Sample Run: (In this sample run, the user input is shaded.)
```
Enter first name, last name, age, and weight separated by spaces.
Sheila Mann 23 120.5
Name: Sheila Mann
Age: 23
Weight: 120.5
```

Before explaining how the preceding program works, let us note the following. Each statement in the body of the method **main** contains **//Line** and a number. These are called single line comments. More formally, single line comments in Java begin with **//**. Comments are typically used to document a program. Here we use them so that we can easily refer to a specific statement in the program and explain what the statement does. When a Java program is complied, the compiler ignores the comments. Moreover, notice that the comments are shown in green. Various SDK's show the comments in green.

The preceding program works as follows: The statements in Lines 1 to 4 declare the variables **firstName** and **lastName** of the type **String**, **age** of the type **int**, and **weight** of the type **double**. The statement in Line 5 is an output statement and tells the user what to do. (Such output statements are called prompt lines.) As shown in the sample run, the input to the program is:

```
Sheila Mann 23 120.5
```

The statement in Line 6 reads and assigns the string **Sheila** to the variable **firstName**; the statement in Line 7 skips the space after **Sheila** and reads and assigns the string **Mann** to the variable **lastName**. Next, the statement in Line 8 skips the blank after **Mann** and reads and stores **23** into the variable **age**. Similarly, the statement in Line 9 skips the blank after **23** and reads and stores **120.5** into the variable **weight**.

The statements in Lines 10, 11, and 12 produce the third, fourth, and fifth lines of the sample run.

Variable Initialization

Consider the following declaration:

```
int feet;
```

You can initialize the variable **feet** to a value of **35** either by using the assignment statement:

```
feet = 35;
```

or by executing the following statement and entering **35** during program execution:

```
feet = console.nextInt();
```

If you use the assignment statement to initialize **feet**, then you are stuck with the same value each time the program runs unless you edit the source code, change the value, recompile, and run. By using an input statement, each time the program runs, you are prompted to enter a value, and the value entered is stored in **feet**. Therefore, a read statement is much more versatile than an assignment statement.

Sometimes it is necessary to initialize a variable by using an assignment statement. This is especially true if the variable is used only for internal calculation and not for reading and storing data.

Recall that Java might not automatically initialize all the variables when they are declared. Some variables can be initialized when they are declared, whereas others must be initialized using either an assignment statement or a read statement. (Variable initialization is covered in more detail in Chapter 8.)

Suppose you want to store a character into a **char** variable using an input statement. During program execution, when you input the character, you do not include the single quotation marks. Suppose that ch is a **char** variable. Consider the following input statement:

```
ch = console.next().charAt(0);
```

If you want to store K in ch using this statement, during program execution you type K without the single quotation marks. Similarly, if you want to store a string in a **String** variable using an input statement, during program execution you enter only the string without the double quotation marks.

Reading a Single Character

Suppose the next input is a single printable character, say A. Further suppose that ch is a **char** variable. To input A into ch, you can use the following statement:

```
ch = console.next().charAt(0);
```

where **console** is as declared before.

When something goes wrong in a program and the results it generates are not what you expect, you should do a walk-through of the statements that assign values to your variables. Example 2-18 illustrates how to do a walk-through of your program. The walk-through is a very effective debugging technique.

Example 2-18

This example further illustrates how assignment statements and input statements manipulate variables. Consider the following declarations:

```
static Scanner console = new Scanner(System.in);
int firstNum, secondNum;
char ch;
double z;
```

Also suppose that the following statements execute in the order given:

1. firstNum = 4;

2. secondNum = 2 * firstNum + 6;

3. z = (firstNum + 1) / 2.0;

```
4. ch = 'A';

5. secondNum = console.nextInt();

6. z = console.nextDouble();

7. firstNum = 2 * secondNum + (int)(z);

8. secondNum = secondNum + 1;

9. ch = console.next().charAt(0);

10. firstNum = firstNum + (int)(ch);

11. z = firstNum - z;
```

In addition, suppose the input is:

```
8 16.3 D
```

Let's now determine the values of the declared variables after the last statement executes. To explicitly show how a particular statement changes the value of a variable, the values of the variables after each statement executes are shown. (In Figures 2-4 through 2-7, a question mark (?) in a box indicates that the value in the box is unknown.)

Before Statement 1 executes, all variables are uninitialized, as shown in Figure 2-4.

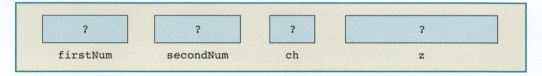

Figure 2-4   Variables before Statement 1 executes

Statement 1 stores 4 in the variable `firstNum`. After Statement 1 executes, the values of the variables are as shown in Figure 2-5.

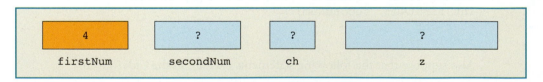

Figure 2-5   Values of `firstNum`, `secondNum`, `ch`, and `z` after Statement 1 executes

Statement 2 first evaluates the expression 2 * firstNum + 6 (which evaluates to 14) and then stores the value of the expression in secondNum. After Statement 2 executes, the values of the variables are as shown in Figure 2-6.

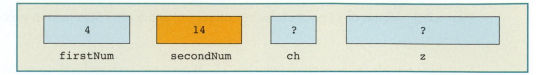

Figure 2-6   Values of firstNum, secondNum, ch, and z after Statement 2 executes

Statement 3 first evaluates the expression (firstNum + 1) / 2.0 (which evaluates to 2.5) and then stores the value of the expression in z. After Statement 3 executes, the values of the variables are as shown in Figure 2-7.

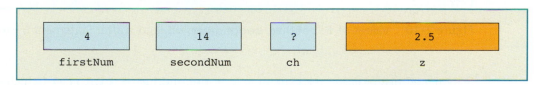

Figure 2-7   Values of firstNum, secondNum, ch, and z after Statement 3 executes

Statement 4 stores the character 'A' into ch. After Statement 4 executes, the values of the variables are as shown in Figure 2-8.

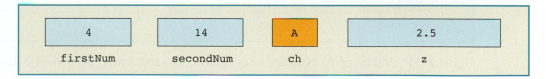

Figure 2-8   Values of firstNum, secondNum, ch, and z after Statement 4 executes

Statement 5 reads the next input (which is 8) from the keyboard and stores the number 8 in secondNum. This statement replaces the old value of secondNum with this new value. After Statement 5 executes, the values of the variables are as shown in Figure 2-9.

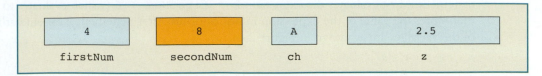

Figure 2-9   Values of `firstNum`, `secondNum`, `ch`, and `z` after Statement 5 executes

Statement 6 reads the next input (which is **16.3**) from the keyboard and stores the number in **z**. This statement replaces the old value of **z** with this new value. After Statement 6 executes, the values of the variables are as shown in Figure 2-10.

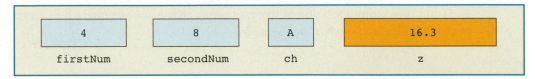

Figure 2-10   Values of `firstNum`, `secondNum`, `ch`, and `z` after Statement 6 executes

Statement 7 first evaluates the expression 2 * secondNum + (int)(z) (which evaluates to 32), and then stores the value of the expression in firstNum. This statement replaces the old value of firstNum with the new value. After Statement 7 executes, the values of the variables are as shown in Figure 2-11.

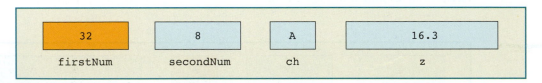

Figure 2-11   Values of `firstNum`, `secondNum`, `ch`, and `z` after Statement 7 executes

Statement 8 first evaluates the expression **secondNum + 1** (which evaluates to **9**) and stores the value of this expression in **secondNum**. This statement updates the value of **secondNum** by incrementing the old value by **1**. After Statement 8 executes, the values of the variables are as shown in Figure 2-12.

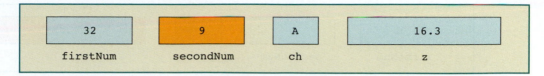

Figure 2-12   Values of `firstNum`, `secondNum`, `ch`, and `z` after Statement 8 executes

Statement 9 reads the next input (which is D) from the keyboard and stores it in `ch`. This statement replaces the old value of `ch` with the new value. After Statement 9 executes, the values of the variables are as shown in Figure 2-13.

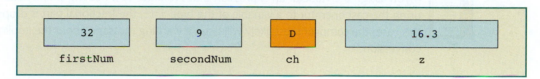

Figure 2-13   Values of `firstNum`, `secondNum`, `ch`, and `z` after Statement 9 executes

Statement 10 first evaluates the expression `firstNum + (int)(ch)`, which is `32 + (int)('D')`, which equals `32 + 68 = 100`. Here `(int)('D')` gives the collating sequence of the character D in the Unicode character data set, which is `68`. Statement 10 then stores the value of this expression in `firstNum`. This statement replaces the old value of `firstNum` with the new value. After Statement 10 executes, the values of the variables are as shown in Figure 2-14.

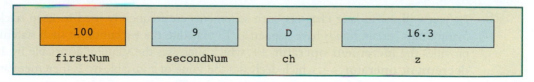

Figure 2-14   Values of `firstNum`, `secondNum`, `ch`, and `z` after Statement 10 executes

Finally, Statement 11 first evaluates the expression `firstNum - z` (which equals `100 - 16.3 = 100.0 - 16.3 = 83.7`) and then stores the value of this expression in `z`. The values of the variables after the last statement executes are shown in Figure 2-15.

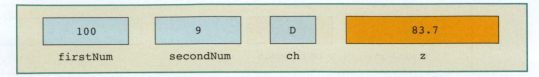

Figure 2-15   Values of `firstNum`, `secondNum`, `ch`, and `z` after Statement 11 executes

 The Web site accompanying this book contains a Java program that shows the effect of the 11 statements listed at the beginning of Example 2-18. The program is named `Example2_18.java`.

 If you assign the value of an expression that evaluates to a floating-point value without using the cast operator to a variable of the type `int`, the fractional part is dropped. In this case, the compiler most likely will issue a warning message about the implicit type conversion.

INCREMENT AND DECREMENT OPERATORS

Now that you know how to declare a variable and enter data into a variable, in this section you learn about two more operators: the increment and decrement operators. These operators are used frequently by Java programmers and are useful programming tools.

Suppose `count` is an `int` variable. The statement:

```
count = count + 1;
```

increments the value of `count` by 1. To execute this assignment statement, the computer first evaluates the expression on the right, which is `count + 1`. It then assigns this value to the variable on the left, which is `count`.

As you will see in later chapters, such statements are frequently used to keep track of how many times certain things have happened. To expedite the execution of such statements, Java provides the **increment operator**, `++`, which increases the value of a variable by 1, and the **decrement operator**, `--`, which decreases the value of a variable by 1. Increment and decrement operators each have two forms, pre and post. The syntax of the increment operator is:

```
Pre-increment:      ++variable
Post-increment:     variable++
```

The syntax of the decrement operator is:

```
Pre-decrement:      --variable
Post-decrement:     variable--
```

Let's look at some examples. The statement:

```
++count;
```

or:

```
count++;
```

increments the value of `count` by 1. Similarly, the statement:

```
--count;
```

or:

```
count--;
```

decrements the value of `count` by 1.

Because increment and decrement operators are built into Java, the value of a variable is quickly incremented or decremented without having to use the form of an assignment statement.

As you can see from these examples, both the pre- and post-increment operators increment the value of the variable by 1. Similarly, the pre- and post-decrement operators decrement the value of the variable by 1. What is the difference between the pre and post forms of these operators? The difference becomes apparent when the variable using these operators is used in an expression.

Suppose that `x` is a variable of the type `int`. If `++x` is used in an expression, first the value of `x` is incremented by 1, and then the new value of `x` is used to evaluate the expression. On the other hand, if `x++` is used in an expression, first the current value of `x` is used in the expression, and then the value of `x` is incremented by 1. The following example clarifies the difference between the pre- and post-increment operators.

Suppose that `x` and `y` are `int` variables. Consider the following statements:

```
x = 5;
y = ++x;
```

The first statement assigns the value 5 to `x`. To evaluate the second statement, which uses the pre-increment operator, first the value of `x` is incremented to 6, and then this value, 6, is assigned to `y`. After the second statement executes, both `x` and `y` have the value 6.

Now consider the following statements:

```
x = 5;
y = x++;
```

As before, the first statement assigns 5 to `x`. In the second statement, the post-increment operator is applied to `x`. To execute the second statement, first the value of `x`, which is 5, is used to evaluate the expression, and then the value of `x` is incremented to 6. Finally, the value of the expression, which is 5, is stored in `y`. After the second statement executes, the value of `x` is 6, and the value of `y` is 5.

The following example further illustrates how the pre- and post- increment operators work.

Example 2-19

Suppose a and b are **int** variables and:

```
a = 5;
b = 2 + (++a);
```

The first statement assigns 5 to a. To execute the second statement, first the expression 2 + (++a) is evaluated. Because the pre-increment operator is applied to a, first the value of a is incremented to 6. Then 2 is added to 6 to get 8, which is then assigned to b. Therefore, after the second statement executes, a is 6 and b is 8. On the other hand, after the execution of:

```
a = 5;
b = 2 + (a++);
```

the value of a is 6 while the value of b is 7.

 This book most often uses the increment and decrement operators with a variable in a stand-alone statement. That is, the variable using the increment or decrement operator will not be part of any expression.

STRINGS AND THE OPERATOR +

One of the most common operations performed on strings is the concatenate operation, which allows a string to be appended at the end of another string. The operator + can be used to concatenate two strings, as well as a string and a numeric value or a character.

Consider the following statements, which illustrate how the operator + works with strings:

```
String str;

str = "Sunny";                    //Line 1
str = str + " Day";               //Line 2
```

After the statement in Line 2 executes, the string assigned to str is:

```
"Sunny Day"
```

Now consider the following statements:

```
str = "Amount Due = $" + 576.35;      //Line 3
```

When the operator + evaluates in Line 3, the numeric value 576.35 is converted to the string "576.35", which is then concatenated with the string:

```
"Amount Due = $"
```

Therefore, after the statement in Line 3 executes, the string assigned to `str` is:

```
"Amount Due = $576.35"
```

Example 2-20 further explains how the operator + works with the `String` data type.

Example 2-20

Consider the following statements:

```
String str;
int num1, num2;

num1 = 12;
num2 = 26;

"The sum = " + num1 + num2;
```

After this statement executes, the string assigned to `str` is:

```
"The sum = 1226";
```

The string assigned to `str` is not what you might have expected. Rather than adding the values of `num1` and `num2`, the values of `num1` and `num2` are concatenated. This is because the associativity of the operator + is from left to right—the operator + is evaluated from left to right. The expression:

```
"The sum = " + num1 + num2
```

is evaluated as follows:

```
"The sum = " + num1 + num2      = ("The sum = " + num1) + num2
                                = ("The sum = " + 12) + num2
                                = "The sum = 12" + num2
                                = "The sum = 12" + 26
                                = "The sum = 1226"
```

Now consider the following statement:

```
"The sum = " + (num1 + num2);
```

In this statement, because of the parentheses, you first evaluate `num1 + num2`. Because `num1` and `num2` are both **int** variables, `num1 + num2 = 12 + 26 = 38`. After this statement executes, the string assigned to `str` is:

```
"The sum = 38";
```

First the expression `(num1 + num2)` is evaluated, which results in 38. Therefore,

```
"The sum = " + 38
```

evaluates to:

```
"The sum = 38"
```

Consider the statement:

```
str = num1 + num2 + " is the sum";
```

After this statement executes, the string assigned to `str` is `"38  is  the  sum"`. First `num1 + num2` is evaluated, which results in 38; then 38 is converted to `"38"`, which is then concatenated with the string `" is the sum"`.

For another example, consider the following statement:

```
str = "The sum of " + num1 + " and " + num2 + " = " + (num1 + num2);
```

Notice the parentheses around `num1 + num2`. After this statement executes, the string assigned to `str` is:

```
"The sum of 12 and 26 = 38";
```

The following Java program shows the effect of the preceding statements:

```
public class Example2_20
{
    public static void main(String[] args)
    {
        String str;
        int num1, num2;

        num1 = 12;                                              //Line 1
        num2 = 26;                                              //Line 2
        str = "The sum = " + num1 + num2;                       //Line 3
        System.out.println("Line 4: str: " + str);             //Line 4

        str = "The sum = " + (num1 + num2);                     //Line 5
        System.out.println("Line 6: str: " + str);             //Line 6

        str = num1 + num2 + " is the sum";                      //Line 7
        System.out.println("Line 8: str: " + str);             //Line 8

        str = "The sum of " + num1 + " and " + num2 + " = "
                + (num1 + num2);                                //Line 9
        System.out.println("Line 10: str: " + str);            //Line 10
    }
}
```

Sample Run:

```
Line 4: str: The sum = 1226
Line 6: str: The sum = 38
Line 8: str: 38 is the sum
Line 10: str: The sum of 12 and 26 = 38
```

OUTPUT

In the preceding sections, you have seen how to put data into the computer's memory and how to manipulate that data. We also used certain output statements to show the results. This section explains in some detail how to further use output statements to generate the desired results.

 The standard output device is usually the monitor.

In Java, output on the standard output device is accomplished by using the **standard output object** `System.out`. The object `System.out` has access to two methods, `print` and `println`, to output a string on the standard output device.

 As of Java 5.0, you can also use the method `printf` to generate the output of a program. Chapter 3 discusses this method in detail.

The syntax to use the object `System.out` and the methods `print` and `println` is:

```
System.out.print(expression);
System.out.println(expression);
System.out.println();
```

These are **output statements**. The `expression` is evaluated, and its value is printed at the current insertion point on the output device. After outputting the value of `expression`, the method `print` leaves the insertion point after the last character of the value of `expression`, while the method `println` positions the insertion point at the beginning of the next line. Moreover, the statement:

```
System.out.println();
```

only positions the insertion point at the beginning of the next line. In this statement, notice the empty parentheses after `println`. They are still needed even though there is no expression between them.

 On the screen, the insertion point is where the cursor is.

In an output statement, if `expression` consists of only one string or a single constant value, then `expression` evaluates to itself. If `expression` consists of only one variable, then `expression` evaluates to the value of the variable. Also see, as explained in the preceding section, how the operator + works with strings and numeric values. Examples 2-21 and 2-22 illustrate how the output statements work as well as give examples of **expression**s.

When an output statement outputs **char** values, it outputs the character without the single quotation marks (unless the single quotation marks are part of the output statement). For example, suppose ch is a **char** variable and ch = 'A';. The statement:

```
System.out.println(ch);
```

or:

```
System.out.println('A');
```

outputs:

```
A
```

Similarly, when an output statement outputs the value of a string, it outputs the string without the double quotation marks (unless you include double quotation marks as part of the string).

Example 2-21

Consider the following statements. The output is shown to the right of each statement.

Statement	Output
1 `System.out.println(29 / 4);`	7
2 `System.out.println("Hello there.");`	Hello there.
3 `System.out.println(12);`	12
4 `System.out.println("4 + 7");`	4 + 7
5 `System.out.println(4 + 7);`	11
6 `System.out.println('A');`	A
7 `System.out.println("4 + 7 = " + (4 + 7));`	4 + 7 = 11
8 `System.out.println(2 + 3 * 5);`	17
9 `System.out.println("Hello \nthere.");`	Hello there.

Look at the output of Statement 9. Recall that in Java, the newline character is '\n'; it causes the insertion point to move to the beginning of the next line before printing. Therefore, when \n appears in a string in an output statement, it moves the insertion point to the beginning of the next line on the output device. This explains why **Hello** and **there.** are printed on separate lines.

In Java, \ is called the **escape character** and \n is called the **newline escape sequence**.

Example 2-22

Consider the following Java program.

```java
public class Example2_22
{
    public static void main(String[] args)
    {
        int a = 65;                                 //Line 1
        int b = 78;                                 //Line 2

        System.out.println(29 / 4);                 //Line 3
        System.out.println(3.0 / 2);                //Line 4
        System.out.print("Hello there.\n");         //Line 5
        System.out.println(7);                      //Line 6
        System.out.println(3 + 5);                  //Line 7
        System.out.print("3 + 5");                  //Line 8
        System.out.println();                       //Line 9
        System.out.println(2 - 28 / 7);             //Line 10
        System.out.println("a");                    //Line 11
        System.out.println("a = " + a);             //Line 12
        System.out.println("b = " + b);             //Line 13
        System.out.println("a + b = " + (a + b));   //Line 14
    }
}
```

Sample Run: (Note that the column marked "**Output of Statement at**" and the line numbers are not part of the output. The line numbers are shown in this column to make it easy to see which output corresponds to which statement.)

	Output of Statement at
7	Line 3
1.5	Line 4
Hello there.	Line 5
7	Line 6
8	Line 7
3 + 5	Line 8
-2	Line 10
a	Line 11
a = 65	Line 12
b = 78	Line 13
a + b = 143	Line 14

For the most part, the output is straightforward. Look at the output of the statements in Lines 7, 8, 9, and 10. The statement in Line 7 outputs the result of 3 + 5, which is 8, and moves the cursor to the beginning of the next line. The statement in Line 8 outputs the string 3 + 5. Note that the statement in Line 8 uses the method **print** and consists of only the string 3 + 5. Therefore, after printing 3 + 5, the insertion point stays positioned after 5; it does not move to the beginning of the next line.

The output statement in Line 9 contains the method `println` with empty parentheses, which moves the insertion point to the beginning of the next line. Therefore, when the statement in Line 10 executes, the output starts at the beginning of the line. Note that in this output, the column "**Output of Statement at**" does not contain Line 9. This is because the statement in Line 9 does not produce any printable output; it simply moves the insertion point to the beginning of the next line. Next, the statement in Line 10 outputs the result of the expression 2 - 28 / 7, which is -2.

Let's take a closer look at the newline character, `'\n'`. Consider the following Java statements:

```
System.out.print("Hello there. ");
System.out.print("My name is James.");
```

If these statements are executed in sequence, the output is:

```
Hello there. My name is James.
```

Consider the following `Java` statements:

```
System.out.print("Hello there.\n");
System.out.print("My name is James.");
```

The output of these Java statements is:

```
Hello there.
My name is James.
```

When \n is encountered in the string, the insertion point is positioned at the beginning of the next line. Note also that \n may appear anywhere in the string. For example, the output of the statement:

```
System.out.print("Hello \nthere. \nMy name is James.");
```

is:

```
Hello
there.
My name is James.
```

Also note that the output of the statement:

```
System.out.print("\n");
```

is the same as the output of the statement:

```
System.out.println();
```

Thus, the output of the sequence of statements:

```
System.out.print("Hello there.\n");
System.out.print("My name is James.");
```

is equivalent to the output of the sequence of statements:

```
System.out.println("Hello there.");
System.out.print("My name is James.");
```

Example 2-23

Consider the following Java statements:

```
System.out.print("Hello there.\nMy name is James.");
```

or:

```
System.out.print("Hello there.");
System.out.print("\nMy name is James.");
```

or:

```
System.out.println("Hello there.");
System.out.print("My name is James.");
```

In each case, the output of the statements is:

```
Hello there.
My name is James.
```

Example 2-24

Suppose you want to output the following sentence in one line as part of a message:

```
It is sunny, warm, and not a windy day. Let us go golfing.
```

Obviously, you will use the methods `print` and/or `println` to produce this output. However, in the programming code, this statement may not fit in one line as part of the output statement. Of course, you can use more than one output statement, as follows:

```
System.out.print("It is sunny, warm, and not a windy day. ");
System.out.println("Let us go golfing.");
```

Two output statements are used to output the sentence in one line. You can also use the following statement to output this sentence:

```
System.out.println("It is sunny, warm, and not a windy day. " +
                   "Let us go golfing.");
```

In this statement, note that because there is no semicolon at the end of the first line, this output statement continues at the second line. Also, note that the first line is followed by the operator +, and there is a double quotation mark at the beginning of the second line. The string is broken into two strings, but both strings are part of the same output statement.

If a string appearing in an output statement is long and you want to output the string in one line, you can break the string by using either of the above two ways. However, the following statement using the **Enter** (or return) key would be incorrect:

```
System.out.println("It is sunny, warm, and not a windy day.
                    Let us go golfing.")
```

The **Enter** (or return) key on your keyboard cannot be part of the string—in programming code, a string *cannot* be broken into more than one line by using the **Enter** (return) key.

Recall that the newline character is \n, which moves the insertion point to the beginning of the next line. In Java, there are many other escape sequences that allow you to control the output. Table 2-4 lists some of the commonly used escape sequences.

Table 2-4 Commonly Used Escape Sequences

	Escape Sequence	Description
\n	Newline	Insertion point moves to the beginning of the next line
\t	Tab	Insertion point moves to the next tab stop
\b	Backspace	Insertion point moves one space to the left
\r	Return	Insertion point moves to the beginning of the current line (*not* the next line)
\\	Backslash	Backslash is printed
\'	Single quotation	Single quotation mark is printed
\"	Double quotation	Double quotation mark is printed

Example 2-25 shows the effect of some of these escape sequences.

Example 2-25

The output of the statement:

```
System.out.println("The newline escape sequence is \\n");
```

is:

```
The new line escape sequence is \n
```

The output of the statement:

```
System.out.println("The tab character is represented as \'\\t\'");
```

is:

```
The tab character is represented as '\t'
```

Note that the single quote can also be printed without using the escape sequence. Therefore, the preceding statement is equivalent to the following output statement:

```
System.out.println("The tab character is represented as '\\t'");
```

The output of the statement:

```
System.out.println("The string \"Sunny\" contains five characters");
```

is:

```
The string "Sunny" contains five characters
```

 The Web site accompanying this book contains the Java program that shows the effect of the statements in Example 2-25. (The program is named `Example2_25.java`.)

Method `flush`

In the preceding section, you learned how to use the methods **print** and **println** for outputting data. Recall that **println**, after outputting data, positions the insertion point at the beginning of the next line. Consider the following statement:

```
System.out.print("Enter a number: ");
```

When the computer executes this statement, you would expect to see the following line on the screen with the insertion point one space after the colon, as in the following:

```
Enter a number:
```

This might not happen because the output generated by the methods **print** and **println** first goes into an area in the computer called a buffer. When the buffer is full, the output is sent to the output device.

You can use the method **flush** associated with **System.out** to empty the buffer even if it is not full. Note that the method **flush** does not position the insertion point at the beginning of the next line; it simply empties the buffer and the output is sent to the output device. The preceding output statement can be written as follows:

```
System.out.print("Enter a number: ");
System.out.flush();
```

PACKAGES, CLASSES, METHODS, AND THE import STATEMENT

Only a small number of operations, such as arithmetic and assignment operations, are explicitly defined in Java. Many of the methods and identifiers needed to run a Java program are provided as a collection of libraries, called packages. A **package** is a collection of related classes. Moreover, every package has a name.

In Java, *class* is a broadly used term. The term **class** is used to create Java programs—either application or applet; it is used to group a set of related operations; and it is used to allow users to create their own data types. For example, there are various mathematical operations, such as determining the absolute value of a number, determining one number raised to the power of another number, and determining the logarithm of a number. Each of these operations is implemented using the Java mechanism of *methods*. Think of a **method** as a set of instructions designed to accomplish a specific task. For example, the name of the method implementing the operation of one number raised to the power of another number is **pow**. This and other mathematical methods are contained in the **class** Math. The name of the package containing the **class** Math is java.lang.

The package java.util contains the **class** Scanner and the methods nextInt, nextDouble, next, and nextLine for inputting data into a program. In the next section, you learn how class(es) are used to create a Java application program.

 To see the complete definitions of the (predefined) Java classes such as String, Math, and Scanner, as well as the class hierarchy, you can visit the Web site *www.sun.com*. Appendix E describes various predefined Java classes and their methods used in this book.

In the next section, you learn how class(es) are used to create a Java application program.

To make use of the existing classes, methods, and identifiers, you must tell the program which package contains the appropriate information. The **import** statement helps you do this.

The general syntax to import the contents of a package in a Java program is:

```
import packageName.*;
```

In Java, **import** is a reserved word. For example, the following statement imports the necessary classes from the package java.util:

```
import java.util.*;
```

To import a specific class from a package, you can specify the name of the class in place of the *. The following statement imports the **class** Scanner from the package java.util:

```
import java.util.Scanner;
```

If you use the character * in the `import` statement, as in the statement:

`import java.util.*;`

then the compiler determines the relevant class(es) used in the program.

 The primitive data types are directly part of the Java language, and do not require that any package be imported into the program. Also, the **class** `String` is contained in the package `java.lang`. You do not need to import classes from the package `java.lang`. The system automatically does it for you.

CREATING A JAVA APPLICATION PROGRAM

In previous sections, you learned enough Java concepts to write meaningful programs. In this section, you learn how to create a complete Java application program.

The basic unit of a Java program is called a class. A Java application program is, therefore, a collection of one or more classes. Roughly speaking, a class is a collection of methods and data members. As described in the previous section, a method is a set of instructions designed to accomplish a specific task. Some **predefined** or **standard** methods such as `nextInt`, `print`, and `println` are already written and are provided as part of the system. But to accomplish most tasks, programmers must learn to write their own methods.

One of the classes in a Java application program must have the method called `main`. Moreover, there can be only one method `main` in a Java class. If a Java application program has only one class, it *must* contain the method `main`. Until Chapter 6, other than using some predefined methods, you will mainly deal with Java application programs that have only one class.

Statements to declare memory spaces (named constants and variables), statements to create input stream objects, statements to manipulate data (such as assignments), and statements to input and output data will be placed within the class.

Statements to declare named constants and input stream objects are usually placed outside the method `main`, and statements to declare variables are usually placed within the method `main`. Statements to manipulate data, and input and output statements are placed within the method `main`.

The syntax of a class to create a Java application program is:

```
public class ClassName
{
    classMembers
}
```

where `ClassName` is a user-defined Java identifier; `classMembers` consists of the data members and methods (such as the method `main`). In Java, **public** and **class** are reserved words.

A typical syntax of the method `main` is:

```
public static void main (String[] args)
{
    statement1
         .
         .
         .
    statementn
}
```

Recall that in a syntax example, the shading indicates the part of the definition that is optional.

A Java application program might be using the resources provided by the SDK such as the necessary code to input data, which require your program to import certain packages. You can therefore, divide a Java application program into two parts: import statements and the program itself. The import statements tell the compiler which packages are used in the program. The program contains statements (placed in a class) that accomplish some meaningful results. Together, the import statements and the program statements constitute the Java **source code**. To be useful, this source code must be saved in a file, called a **source file**, that has the file extension `.java`. Moreover, the name of the class and the name of the file containing the Java program must be the same. For example, if the name of the class to create the Java program is `Welcome`, then the name of the source file must be `Welcome.java`.

Because the programming instructions are placed in the method `main`, let us elaborate on the method `main` a bit more.

The basic parts of the method `main` are the heading and the body. The first line of the method `main`,

```
public static void main(String[] args)
```

is called the **heading** of the method `main`.

The statements enclosed between curly braces (`{` and `}`) form the **body** of the method `main`. The body of the method `main` contains two types of statements:

- Declaration statements
- Executable statements

Declaration statements are used to declare things such as variables.

Executable statements perform calculations, manipulate data, create output, accept input, and so on.

In Java, variables or identifiers can be declared anywhere within a method, but they must be declared before they can be used.

Example 2-26

The following statements are examples of variable declarations:

```
int   a, b, c;
double  x, y;
```

Example 2-27

Some executable statements that you have encountered so far are the assignment, input, and output statements.

The following statements are examples of executable statements:

```
a = 4;                              //assignment statement
b = console.nextInt();              //input and
                                    //assignment statement

System.out.println(a + " " + b);    //output statement
```

In skeleton form, a Java application program looks like the following:

```
import statements if any

public class ClassName
{
    declare named constants and/or stream objects

        public static void main(String[] args)
        {
          variable declaration

          executable statements
        }
}
```

 Notice that the heading of the method `main` contains the reserved word `static`. The statements to declare the named constants and the input stream objects are placed outside the definition of the method `main`. Therefore, Java requires that you declare the named constants and the input stream objects with the reserved word `static`. Example 2-28 illustrates this concept.

Example 2-28

The following is a simple Java application program showing where in a Java program import statements, the method **main**, and statements such as named constants, declarations, assignment statements, and input and output statements typically appear.

```
import java.util.*;                                          //Line 1

public class FirstJavaProgram                               //Line 2
{                                                           //Line 3

    static final int NUMBER = 12;                           //Line 4

    static Scanner console = new Scanner(System.in);        //Line 5

    public static void main(String[] args)                  //Line 6
    {                                                       //Line 7

        int firstNum;                                       //Line 8
        int secondNum;                                      //Line 9

        firstNum = 18;                                      //Line 10
        System.out.println("Line 11: firstNum = "
                          + firstNum);                      //Line 11

        System.out.print("Line 12: Enter an integer: ");    //Line 12
        secondNum = console.nextInt();                      //Line 13
        System.out.println();                               //Line 14

        System.out.println("Line 15: secondNum = "
                          + secondNum);                     //Line 15

        firstNum = firstNum + NUMBER + 2 * secondNum;       //Line 16

        System.out.println("Line 17: The new value of " +
                          "firstNum = " + firstNum);        //Line 17
    }                                                       //Line 18
}                                                           //Line 19
```

Sample Run: In this sample run, the user input is shaded.
```
Line 11: firstNum = 18
Line 12: Enter an integer: 15

Line 15: secondNum = 15
Line 17: The new value of firstNum = 60
```

The preceding program works as follows: The statement in Line 1 imports the **class** Scanner. The statement in Line 2 names the **class** containing statements of the program as FirstJavaProgram. The left brace in Line 3 marks the beginning of the **class** FirstJavaProgram. The statement in Line 4 declares the named constant NUMBER and sets its value to 12. The statement in Line 5 declares and initializes the object **console** to input the data from the keyboard. The statement in Line 6 contains the heading of the method `main`, and the left brace in Line 7 marks the beginning of the method `main`. The statements in Lines 8 and 9 declare the variables `firstNum` and `secondNum`.

The statement in Line 10 sets the value of `firstNum` to `18`, and the statement in Line 11 outputs the value of `firstNum`. Next, the statement in Line 12 prompts the user to enter an integer. The statement in Line 13 reads and stores the integer into the variable `secondNum`, which is `15` in the sample run. The statement in Line 14 positions the insertion point on the screen at the beginning of the next line. The statement in Line 15 outputs the value of `secondNum`. The statement in Line 16 evaluates the expression:

```
firstNum + NUMBER + 2 * secondNum
```

and assigns the value of this expression to the variable `firstNum`, which is `60` in the sample run. The statement in Line 17 outputs the new value of `firstNum`. The right brace in Line 18 marks the end of the method `main`, and the right brace in Line 19 marks the end of the `class` `FirstJavaProgram`.

PROGRAMMING STYLE AND FORM

In previous sections you learned how to create a Java application program. Here we describe the proper structure of a program. Using the proper structure makes a Java program easier to understand and modify. It is frustrating trying to follow, and perhaps modify, a program that is syntactically correct, but has no structure.

Every Java application program must satisfy certain language rules. It must also satisfy the syntax rules, which, like grammar rules, tell what is correct and what is incorrect, and what is legal and what is illegal in the language. Other rules give precise meaning to the language; that is, they support the language's semantics. The sections that follow are designed to help you learn how to put together the Java programming elements you have learned so far and create a functioning program. These sections cover syntax; the use of blanks; the use of semi-colons, brackets, and commas; semantics; prompt lines; documentation, including comments and naming identifiers; and form and style.

Syntax

The syntax rules of a language tell what is legal and what is illegal. Errors in syntax are detected during compilation. Consider the following Java statements:

```
int x;              //Line 1
int y               //Line 2
double z;           //Line 3

y = w + x;          //Line 4
```

When these statements are compiled, a compilation error will occur at Line 2 because there is no semicolon after the declaration of the variable **y**. A second compilation error will occur at Line 4 because the identifier **w** is used but has not been declared.

As discussed in Chapter 1, you enter a program into the computer by using an editor. When a program is typed, errors are almost unavoidable. Therefore, when the program is compiled, you most likely will see syntax errors. It is possible that a syntax error at a particular place might lead to syntax errors in several subsequent statements. It is common for the omission of a single character to cause four or five error messages. However, when the first syntax error is removed and the program is recompiled, subsequent syntax errors caused by the first syntax error may disappear. Therefore, you should correct syntax errors in the order in which the compiler lists them. As you become more experienced with Java, you will learn how to quickly spot and fix syntax errors. Note that compilers not only discover syntax errors, but also provide hints and sometimes tell the user where the syntax errors are and how to fix them.

Use of Blanks

In Java, you use one or more blanks to separate numbers when data is input. Blanks are also used to separate reserved words and identifiers from each other and from other symbols. Blanks must never appear within a reserved word or identifier.

Use of Semicolons, Braces, and Commas

All Java statements must end with a semicolon. The semicolon is also called a **statement terminator**.

Note that braces, { and }, are not Java statements even though they often appear on a line with no other code. You might regard braces as delimiters because they enclose the body of a method and set it off from other parts of the program. (Braces have other uses, which will be explained in Chapter 4.)

Recall that commas are used to separate items in a list. For example, you use commas when you declare more than one variable following a data type.

Semantics

The set of rules that gives meaning to a language is called **semantics**. For example, the order-of-precedence rules for arithmetic operators are semantic rules.

If a program contains syntax errors, the compiler will warn you. What happens when a program contains semantic errors? It is quite possible to eradicate all syntax errors in a program and still not have it run. And if it runs, it may not do what you meant it to do. For example, the following two lines of code are both syntactically correct expressions, but they have different meanings:

```
2 + 3 * 5
```

and:

```
(2 + 3) * 5
```

If you substitute one of these lines of code for the other in a program, you will not get the same results—even though the numbers are the same, the semantics are different. You will learn about semantics throughout this book.

Naming Identifiers

Consider the following two sets of statements:

```
final double A = 2.54;    //conversion constant
double x;                 //variable to hold centimeters
double y;                 //variable to hold inches

x = y * A;
```

and:

```
final double CENTIMETERS_PER_INCH = 2.54;
double centimeters;
double inches;

centimeters = inches * CENTIMETERS_PER_INCH;
```

The identifiers in the second set of statements, such as `CENTIMETERS_PER_INCH`, are usually called **self-documenting** identifiers. As you can see, self-documenting identifiers can make comments less necessary.

Consider the self-documenting identifier `monthlypaycheck`. This identifier is called a **run-together-word**. When using self-documenting identifiers, you may inadvertently include run-together-words, which may lessen your documentation's clarity. You can make run-together-words easier to understand by either capitalizing the beginning of each new word or by inserting an underscore just before a new word. For example, you could use either `monthlyPaycheck` or `monthly_paycheck` to create a clearer identifier.

Earlier in this chapter, we specified the rules that Java programmers traditionally follow to name named constants and variables. Next, we summarize these rules as well give the rules to name a class.

1. An identifier used to name a named constant is all uppercase. If the identifier is a run-together-word, then the words are separated with the underscore character. For example:

```
final double CENTIMETERS_PER_INCH = 2.54;
final int INCHES_PER_FOOT = 12;
```

2. An identifier used to name a variable is lowercase. If the identifier is a run-together-word, then the first letter of each word, except the first word, is uppercase. For example:

```
double salary;
int firstNumber;
```

3. An identifier used to name a class is all lowercase with the first letter of each word in uppercase. For example, `Welcome` and `MakeChange`.

Prompt Lines

Part of good documentation is the use of clearly written prompts so that users will know what to do when they interact with a program. It is frustrating for a user to sit in front of a running program and not have the foggiest notion of whether to enter something, and if so, what to enter. **Prompt lines** are executable statements that inform the user what to do. Consider the following Java statements, in which `num` is an `int` variable:

```
System.out.println("Please enter a number between 1 and 10 and "
                   + "press Enter");
num = console.nextInt();
```

When these two statements execute in the order given, first the output statement causes the following line of text to appear on the screen:

```
Please enter a number between 1 and 10 and press Enter
```

After seeing this line, an example of a prompt line, users know that they must enter a number and press the `Enter` key. If the program contained only the second statement, users would not know that they must enter a number, and the computer would wait indefinitely for the input. The preceding output statement is an example of a prompt line.

In a program, whenever users must provide input, you must include the necessary prompt lines. Furthermore, these prompt lines should include as much information as possible about what input is acceptable. For example, the preceding prompt line not only tells the user to input a number, but also informs the user that the number should be between 1 and 10.

Documentation

The programs that you write should be clear not only to you, but also to anyone else. Therefore, you must properly document your programs. A well-documented program is easier to understand and modify, even a long time after you originally write it. You use comments to document programs. Comments should appear in a program to explain the purpose of the program, identify who wrote it, and explain the purpose of particular statements.

Comments

The two most commonly used types of comments in Java are: single line comments and multiple line comments. **Single line comments** begin with `//` and can be placed anywhere in the line. Everything encountered in that line after `//` is ignored by the compiler. **Multiple line comments** are enclosed between `/*` and `*/`. The compiler ignores anything that appears between `/*` and `*/`.

You can insert certain comments at the top of a program to briefly explain the program and give information about the programmer. You can also include comments before each key step to briefly describe what that step does.

In this book, in the programming code, comments are shown in **green**.

Form and Style

You might think that Java has too many rules. However, in practice, the rules give Java a great degree of freedom. For example, consider the following two ways of declaring variables:

```
int feet, inch;
double x, y;
```

and:

```
int feet,inches;double x,y;
```

The computer has no difficulty understanding either of these formats, but the first form is easier to read and follow.

What about blank spaces? Where are they significant and where are they meaningless?

Consider the following two statements:

```
int a,b,c;
```

and

```
int    a,    b,    c;
```

Both of these declarations mean the same thing. Here the blanks between the identifiers in the second statement are meaningless. On the other hand, consider the following statement:

```
inta,b,c;
```

This statement contains a syntax error. The lack of a blank between the t in **int** and the identifier a changes the reserved word **int** and the identifier a into a new identifier, `inta`.

The clarity of the rules of syntax and semantics frees you to adopt formats that are pleasing to you and easier to understand.

The following example further elaborates on form and style.

Example 2-29

Consider the following Java program:

```java
//An improperly formatted Java program.

import java.util.*;

public class Example2_29A
{
        static Scanner console = new Scanner(System.in);
public static void main(String[] args)
{
int num; double height;
String name;
System.out.print("Enter an integer: "); System.out.flush();
num=console.nextInt(); System.out.println();
    System.out.println("num: "+num);
System.out.print("Enter the first name: "); System.out.flush();
name=console.next();
    System.out.println();System.out.print("Enter the height: ");
System.out.flush();
height = console.nextDouble(); System.out.println();

System.out.println("Name: "+name);System.out.println("Height: "
+height);
}}
```

This program is syntactically correct; the Java compiler would have no difficulty reading and compiling this program. However, this program is very hard to read. The program that you write should be properly indented and formatted. Next, we rewrite the preceding program and properly format it.

```java
//A properly formatted Java program.

import java.util.*;

public class Example2_29B
{
    static Scanner console = new Scanner(System.in);

    public static void main(String[] args)
    {
        int num;
        double height;
        String name;

        System.out.print("Enter an integer: ");
        System.out.flush();
        num = console.nextInt();
        System.out.println();

        System.out.println("num: " + num);
```

2

```
        System.out.print("Enter the first name: ");
        System.out.flush();
        name = console.next();
        System.out.println();

        System.out.print("Enter the height: ");
        System.out.flush();
        height = console.nextDouble();
        System.out.println();

        System.out.println("Name: " + name);
        System.out.println("Height: " + height);
    }
}
```

As you can see, this program is easier to read. Your programs should be properly indented and formatted. To document the variables, programmers typically declare one variable per line. Also, always put a space before and after an operator.

MORE ON ASSIGNMENT STATEMENTS

The assignment statements you have seen so far are called **simple assignment statements**. In certain cases, you can use special assignment statements called **compound assignment statements** to write simple assignment statements using more concise notation.

Corresponding to the five arithmetic operators +, -, *, /, and %, Java provides five compound operators +=, -=, *=, /=, and %=, respectively. Consider the following simple assignment statement, where x and y are int variables:

```
x = x * y;
```

Using the compound operator *=, this statement can be written as:

```
x *= y;
```

In general, using the compound operator *=, you can rewrite the simple assignment statement:

```
variable = variable * (expression);
```

as:

```
variable *= expression;
```

Similar conventions apply to the other arithmetic compound operators. For example, using the compound operator +=, you can rewrite the simple assignment statement:

```
variable = variable + (expression);
```

as:

```
variable += expression;
```

Thus, the compound assignment statement lets you write simple assignment statements in a concise fashion by combining an arithmetic operator with an assignment operator.

Example 2-30

This example shows several compound assignment statements that are equivalent to simple assignment statements.

Simple Assignment Statement

```
i = i + 5;
counter = counter + 1;
sum = sum + number;
amount = amount*(interest + 1);
x = x / ( y + 5);
```

Compound Assignment Statement

```
i += 5;
counter += 1;
sum += number;
amount *= interest + 1;
x /= y + 5;
```

 Any compound assignment statement can be converted into a simple assignment statement. However, a simple assignment statement may not be (easily) converted into a compound assignment statement. Consider the following simple assignment statement:

```
x = x * y + z - 5;
```

To write this statement as a compound assignment statement, the variable x must be a common factor in the right side, which is not the case. Therefore, you cannot immediately convert this statement into a compound assignment statement. In fact, the equivalent compound assignment statement is:

```
x *= y + (z - 5)/x;
```

which is more complicated than the simple assignment statement. Furthermore, in the preceding compound statement x cannot be zero. We recommend avoiding such compound expressions.

 In programming code, this book typically uses only the compound operator +=. That is, statements such as a = a + b; are written as a += b; .

PROGRAMMING EXAMPLE: CONVERT LENGTH

Write a program that takes as input given lengths expressed in feet and inches. The program should then convert and output the lengths in centimeters. Assume that the given lengths in feet and inches are integers.

Input   Length in feet and inches

Output   Equivalent length in centimeters

Problem Analysis and Algorithm Design

The lengths are given in feet and inches, and you need to find the equivalent length in centimeters. One inch is equal to 2.54 centimeters. The first thing the program needs to do is convert the length given in feet and inches to all inches. Then you can use the conversion formula, 1 inch $= 2.54$ centimeters, to find the equivalent length in centimeters. To convert the length from feet and inches to inches, you multiply the number of feet by 12 (1 foot is equal to 12 inches), and add your answer to the given inches.

Suppose the input is 5 feet and 7 inches. You find the total inches as follows:

```
totalInches = (12 * feet) + inches
            = 12 * 5 + 7
            = 67
```

You can then apply the conversion formula, 1 inch $= 2.54$ centimeters, to find the length in centimeters.

```
centimeters = totalInches * 2.54
            = 67 * 2.54
            = 170.18
```

Based on this analysis, you can design an algorithm as follows:

1. Get the length in feet and inches.
2. Convert the length into total inches.
3. Convert total inches into centimeters.
4. Output centimeters.

Variables

The input for the program is two numbers: one for feet and one for inches. Thus, you need two variables: one to store feet and the other to store inches. Because the program will first convert the given length into inches, you need a third variable to store the total inches. You need a fourth variable to store the equivalent length in centimeters. In summary, you need the following variables:

```java
int feet;          //variable to store feet
int inches;        //variable to store inches
int totalInches;   //variable to store the total inches
double centimeters; //variable to store the length in centimeters
```

Named Constant

Recall that to calculate the equivalent length in centimeters, you need to multiply the total inches by **2.54**. Instead of using the value **2.54** directly in the program, you will declare this value as a named constant. Similarly, to find the total inches, you need to multiply the feet by **12** and add the inches. Instead of using **12** directly in the program, you will also declare this value as a named constant. Using named constants makes it easier to modify the program later. Because the named constants will be placed before the method **main**, you must use the modifier **static** to declare these named constants (see the section, Creating a Java Application Program).

```java
static final double CENTIMETERS_PER_INCH = 2.54;
static final int INCHES_PER_FOOT = 12;
```

Main Algorithm

In the preceding sections, we analyzed the problem and determined the formulas to perform the calculations. We also determined the necessary variables and named constants. We can now expand the algorithm given in the section Problem Analysis and Algorithm Design to solve the problem given at the beginning of this programming example (converting feet and inches to centimeters).

1. Prompt the user for the input. (Without a prompt line, the user will stare at a blank screen and not know what to do.)
2. Get **feet**.
3. Prompt the user to enter a value for **inches**.
4. Get **inches**.
5. Echo the input—output what the program read as input. (Without this step, after the program has executed, you will not know what the input was.)
6. Find the length in inches.
7. Output the length in inches.
8. Convert the length to centimeters.
9. Output the length in centimeters.

Putting It Together

Now that the problem has been analyzed and the algorithm has been designed, the next step is to translate the algorithm into Java code. Because this is the first complete Java program you are writing, let's review the necessary steps in sequence.

The program will begin with comments that document its purpose and functionality. Because there is both input to this program (the length in feet and inches) and output (the equivalent length in centimeters), you will use the system resources for input/output. In other words, the program will use input statements to get the data into the program and output statements to print the results. Because the data will be entered from the keyboard, the program must import the **class** Scanner from the package java.util. Thus, the first statement of the program, after the comments as described previously, will be the **import** statement to import the **class** Scanner from the package java.util.

This program requires two types of memory locations for data manipulation: named constants and variables. Recall that named constants are usually placed before the method main so that they can be used throughout the program.

This program has only one class, which contains the method main. The method main will contain all of the programming instructions in its body. In addition, the program needs variables to manipulate the data, and these variables will be declared in the body of the method main. (The reasons for declaring variables in the body of the method main are explained in Chapter 7.) The body of the method main will also contain the Java statements that implement the algorithm. Moreover, the program will use an input stream object, as described in this chapter, for inputting data, and the method main will not handle any I/O exceptions. Therefore, for this program, the definition of the method main has the following form:

```java
public static void main(String[] args)
{
    declare variables
    statements
}
```

To write the complete length conversion program, follow these steps:

1. Begin the program with comments for documentation.
2. Use **import** statements to import the classes required by the program.
3. Declare the named constants, if any.
4. Write the definition of the method main.

Complete Program Listing

```java
//*****************************************************
//    Program Convert: This program converts measurements
// in feet and inches into centimeters using the
// formula that 1 inch is equal to 2.54 centimeters.
//*****************************************************

import java.util.*;

public class Conversion
{
    static Scanner console = new Scanner(System.in);

    static final double CENTIMETERS_PER_INCH = 2.54;
    static final int INCHES_PER_FOOT = 12;

    public static void main (String[] args)
    {
            //declare variables
        int feet;
        int inches;
        int totalInches;
        double centimeters;

        System.out.print("Enter feet: ");                      //Step 1
        System.out.flush();
        feet = console.nextInt();                              //Step 2
        System.out.println();

        System.out.print("Enter inches: ");                    //Step 3
        System.out.flush();
        inches = console.nextInt();                            //Step 4
        System.out.println();

        System.out.println("The numbers you entered are "
                        + feet + " for feet and "
                        + inches + " for inches.");            //Step 5

        totalInches = INCHES_PER_FOOT * feet + inches;         //Step 6

        System.out.println();
        System.out.println("The total number of inches = "
                        + totalInches);                        //Step 7

        centimeters = totalInches * CENTIMETERS_PER_INCH;      //Step 8
```

```
        System.out.println("The number of centimeters = "
                        + centimeters);                      //Step 9
    }
}
```

Sample Run: In this sample run, the user input is shaded.
Enter feet: 15

Enter inches: 7

The numbers you entered are 15 for feet and 7 for inches.

The total number of inches = 187
The number of centimeters = 474.98

> The programming code of this program must be saved in the file
> Conversion.java because we named the class containing the method
> main Conversion.

PROGRAMMING EXAMPLE: MAKE CHANGE

Write a program that takes as input any change expressed in cents. It should then compute the number of half-dollars, quarters, dimes, nickels, and pennies to be returned, using as many half-dollars as possible, then quarters, dimes, nickels, and pennies, in that order. For example, 483 cents would be returned as 9 half-dollars, 1 quarter, 1 nickel, and 3 pennies.

Input Change in cents

Output Equivalent change in half-dollars, quarters, dimes, nickels, and pennies

Problem Analysis and Algorithm Design

Suppose the given change is 646 cents. To find the number of half-dollars, you divide 646 by 50, the value of a half-dollar, and find the quotient, which is 12, and the remainder, which is 46. The quotient, 12, is the number of half-dollars, and the remainder, 46, is the remaining change.

Next, divide the remaining change by 25, to find the number of quarters. The remaining change is 46, so division by 25 gives the quotient 1, which is the number of quarters, and a remainder of 21, which is the remaining change. This process continues for dimes and nickels. To calculate the remainder (pennies) in integer division, you use the mod operator, %.

Applying this discussion to 646 cents yields the following calculations:

1. Change = 646
2. Number of half-dollars = 646 / 50 = 12
3. Remaining change = 646 % 50 = 46
4. Number of quarters = 46 / 25 = 1
5. Remaining change = 46 % 25 = 21
6. Number of dimes = 21 / 10 = 2
7. Remaining change = 21 % 10 = 1
8. Number of nickels = 1 / 5 = 0
9. Number of pennies = remaining change = 1 % 5 = 1

This discussion translates into the following algorithm:

1. Get the change in cents.
2. Find the number of half-dollars.
3. Calculate the remaining change.
4. Find the number of quarters.
5. Calculate the remaining change.
6. Find the number of dimes.
7. Calculate the remaining change.
8. Find the number of nickels.
9. Calculate the remaining change.
10. The remaining change is the number of pennies.

Variables

From the previous discussion and algorithm, it appears that the program needs variables to hold the number of half-dollars, quarters, and so on. However, the numbers of half-dollars, quarters, and so on are not used in later calculations, so the program can simply output these values without saving them in variables. The only thing that keeps changing is the change, so the program needs only one variable:

```java
int change;
```

Named Constants

The program performs calculations using the values of a half-dollar, 50; a quarter, 25; a dime, 10; and a nickel, 5. Because these data are special and the program uses these values more than once, it makes sense to declare them as named constants. (Using named constants also simplifies later modification of the program.)

```java
static final int HALFDOLLAR = 50;
static final int QUARTER  = 25;
static final int DIME = 10;
static final int NICKEL = 5;
```

Main Algorithm

In the preceding sections, we analyzed the problem and determined the formulas to do the calculations. We also determined the necessary variables and named constants. We can now expand the algorithm given in the section Problem Analysis and Algorithm Design to solve the problem given at the beginning of this programming example (expressing change in cents).

1. Prompt the user for the input.
2. Get the input.
3. Echo the input by displaying the entered change on the screen.
4. Compute and print the number of half-dollars.
5. Calculate the remaining change.
6. Compute and print the number of quarters.
7. Calculate the remaining change.
8. Compute and print the number of dimes.
9. Calculate the remaining change.
10. Compute and print the number of nickels.
11. Calculate the remaining change.
12. Print the remaining change.

Complete Program Listing

```
// ************************************************
// Program Make Change: Given any amount of change
// expressed in cents, this program computes the number
// of half-dollars, quarters, dimes, nickels, and
// pennies to be returned, returning as many
// half-dollars as possible, then quarters, dimes,
// nickels, and pennies, in that order.
//************************************************

import java.util.*;

public class MakeChange
{
    static Scanner console = new Scanner(System.in);

    static final int HALFDOLLAR = 50;
    static final int QUARTER  = 25;
    static final int DIME = 10;
    static final int NICKEL = 5;

    public static void main (String[] args)
    {
         //declare variables
        int change;
```

```
    //Statements: Step 1 - Step 12
System.out.print("Enter the change in cents: ");    //Step 1
System.out.flush();

change = console.nextInt();                          //Step 2
System.out.println();
System.out.println("The change you entered is "
                    + change);                       //Step 3

System.out.println("The number of half dollars "
                + "to be returned is "
                + change / HALFDOLLAR);              //Step 4

change = change % HALFDOLLAR;                        //Step 5

System.out.println("The number of quarters to be "
                + "returned is "
                + change / QUARTER);                 //Step 6

change = change % QUARTER;                           //Step 7

System.out.println("The number of dimes to be "
                + "returned is "
                + change / DIME);                    //Step 8

change = change % DIME;                              //Step 9

System.out.println("The number of nickels to be "
                + "returned is "
                + change / NICKEL);                  //Step 10

change = change % NICKEL;                            //Step 11

System.out.println("The number of pennies to be "
                + "returned is " + change);          //Step 12
    }
}
```

Sample Run: In this sample run, the user input is shaded.
```
Enter the change in cents: 583

The change you entered is 583
The number of half dollars to be returned is 11
The number of quarters to be returned is 1
The number of dimes to be returned is 0
The number of nickels to be returned is 1
The number of pennies to be returned is 3
```

QUICK REVIEW

1. A Java program is a collection of classes.

2. Every Java application program has a method called `main`.

3. In Java, identifiers are names of things.

4. A Java identifier consists of letters, digits, the underscore character (_), and the dollar sign ($), and must begin with a letter, underscore, or the dollar sign.

5. Reserved words cannot be used as identifiers in a program.

6. All reserved words in Java consist of lowercase letters (see Appendix A).

7. Java is case-sensitive.

8. A data type is a set of values with a set of operations.

9. The primitive data types are the fundamental data types in Java.

10. The three categories of primitive data types are integral, floating-point, and Boolean.

11. Integral data types are used to deal with integers.

12. There are five categories of integral data types—`char`, `byte`, `short`, `int`, and `long`.

13. The `int` data type is used to represent integers between −2147483648 and 2147483647. The memory allocated for the `int` data type is 4 bytes.

14. The data type `short` is used to represent integers between −32768 and 32767. The memory allocated for the `short` data type is 2 bytes.

15. Java uses the Unicode character set, which is a set of 65536 characters. The ASCII character set, which has 128 values, is a subset of Unicode. The first 128 characters of Unicode, 0–127, are the same as those of ASCII.

16. The collating sequence of a character is its preset number in the character data set.

17. The data types `float` and `double` are used to deal with floating-point numbers.

18. The data type `float` is used in Java to represent any real number between −3.4E+38 and 3.4E+38. The memory allocated for the `float` data type is 4 bytes.

19. The data type `double` is used in Java to represent any real number between −1.7E+308 and 1.7E+308. The memory allocated for the `double` data type is 8 bytes.

20. The maximum number of significant digits—that is, the number of decimal places—in `float` values is 6 or 7. Typically, the maximum number of significant digits in values belonging to the `double` type is 15. The maximum number of significant digits is called the precision.

21. Values of the type `float` are called single precision, and values of the type `double` are called double precision.

22. The arithmetic operators in Java are addition (+), subtraction (−), multiplication (*), division (/), and mod (%).

23. The mod operator, %, gives the remainder.

24. Arithmetic expressions are evaluated using the precedence rules and the associativity of the arithmetic operators.

25. All operands in an integral expression, or integer expression, are integers, and all operands in a floating-point expression are decimal numbers.

26. A mixed expression is an expression that consists of both integers and decimal numbers.

27. When evaluating an operator in an expression, an integer is converted to a floating-point number, with a decimal part of zero, only if the operator has mixed operands.

28. You can use the cast operator to explicitly convert values from one data type to another.

29. The **class** `String` is used to manipulate strings.

30. A string is a sequence of zero or more characters.

31. Strings in Java are enclosed in double quotation marks.

32. A string containing no characters is called a null or empty string.

33. During program execution, the contents of a named constant cannot be changed.

34. A named constant is declared by using the reserved word **final**.

35. A named constant is initialized when it is declared.

36. All variables must be declared before they can be used.

37. Java may not automatically initialize all the variables you declare.

38. Every variable has a name, a value, a data type, and a size.

39. When a new value is assigned to a variable, the old value is destroyed.

40. Only an assignment statement or an input (read) statement can change the value of a variable.

41. Input from the standard input device is accomplished using a `Scanner` object initialized to the standard input device.

42. If `console` is a `Scanner` object initialized to the standard input device, then the expression `console.nextInt()` retrieves the next integer from the standard input device. Similarly, the expression `console.nextDouble()` retrieves the next floating number, and the expression `console.next()` retrieves the next string from the standard input device.

43. When data is input into a program, the data items, such as numbers, are usually separated by blanks, lines, or tabs.

44. The increment operator, ++, increments the value of its operand by 1.

45. The decrement operator, --, decrements the value of its operand by 1.

46. The operator + can be used to concatenate two strings.

47. Output of the program to the standard output device is accomplished by using the standard output object `System.out` and the methods `print` and `println`.

48. The character \ is called the escape character.

49. The sequence \n is called the newline escape sequence.

50. A package is a collection of related classes. A class consists of methods, and a method is designed to accomplish a specific task.

51. The **import** statement is used to import the components of a package into a program. For example, the statement:

   import java.util.*;

   imports the (components of the) **package** java.util into the program.

52. In Java, **import** is a reserved word.

53. Because the primitive data types and the **class** String are directly part of the Java language, they do not require any import statements to use them.

54. All Java statements end with a semicolon. The semicolon in Java is called the statement terminator.

55. A file containing a Java program usually ends with the extension .java.

56. The compiler skips comments.

57. A single line comment starts with the pair of symbols //anywhere in the line.

58. Multiple line comments are enclosed between /* and */.

59. Prompt lines are executable statements that tell the user what to do.

60. Corresponding to the five arithmetic operators +, -, *, /, and %, Java provides the five compound operators +=, -=, *=, /=, and %=, respectively.

61. Using the compound operator *=, you can rewrite the simple assignment statement:

   variable = variable * (expression);

   as:

   variable *= expression;

   Similar conventions apply for the other arithmetic compound operators.

EXERCISES

1. Mark the following statements as true or false.

   a. An identifier can be any sequence of digits and letters.

   b. In Java, there is no difference between a reserved word and a predefined identifier.

   c. A Java identifier can start with a digit.

   d. The operands of the modulus operator must be integers.

   e. If the value of a is 4 and the value of b is 3, then after the statement a = b; executes, the value of b is still 3.

   f. In an output statement, the newline character can be a part of the string.

g. The following is a legal Java program:

```
public class JavaProgram
{
    public static void main(String[] args)
    {
    }
}
```

h. In a mixed expression, all the operands are converted to floating-point numbers.

i. Suppose `x = 5`. After the statement `y = x++;` executes, `y` is 5 and `x` is 6.

j. Suppose `a = 5`. After the statement `++a;` executes, the value of `a` is still 5 because the value of the expression is not saved in another variable.

2. Which of the following are valid Java identifiers?

a. `RS6S6`

b. `MIX-UP`

c. `STOP!`

d. `exam1`

e. `September1Lecture`

f. `2May`

g. `Mike's`

h. `First Exam`

i. `J`

j. `Three`

3. Which of the following is a reserved word in Java?

a. `int`

b. `INT`

c. `Char`

d. `CHAR`

4. Circle the best answer.

a. The value of `15 / 2` is:
    (i) `7`   (ii) `7.5`   (iii) $7^1/_2$ (iv) `0.75`   (v) none of these

b. The value of `18 / 3` is:
    (i) `6`   (ii) `0.167`   (iii) `6.0`   (iv) none of these

c. The value of `22 % 7` is:
    (i) `3`   (ii) `1`   (iii) `3.142`   (iv) `22/7`

d. The value of `5 % 7` is:
    (i) `0`   (ii) `2`   (iii) `5`   (iv) undefined

2

e. The value of `17.0 % 4` is:

(i) 4   (ii) `4.25`   (iii) 4¼   (iv) undefined

f. The value of `5 - 3.0 + 2` is:

(i) 0   (ii) `0.0`   (iii) 4   (iv) `4.0`

g. The value of `7 - 5 * 2 + 1` is:

(i) `-2`   (ii) 5   (iii) 6   (iv) none of these

h. The value of `15.0 / 3.0 + 2.0` is:

(i) 3   (ii) `3.0`   (iii) 5   (iv) none of these

5. If `x = 5, y = 6, z = 4`, and `w = 3.5`, evaluate each of the following expressions, if possible. If it is not possible, state the reason.

a. `(x + z) % y`

b. `(x + y) % w`

c. `(y + w) % x`

d. `(x + y ) * w`

e. `(x % y) % z`

f. `(y % z) % x`

g. `(x * z) % y`

h. `((x * y) * w) * z`

6. Given:

```
int n, m, l;
double x, y;
```

which of the following assignments are valid? If an assignment is not valid, state the reason. When not noted, assume that each variable is declared.

a. `n = m = 5;`

b. `m = l = 2 * n;`

c. `n = 5; m = 2 + 6; n = 6 / 3;`

d. `m + n = l;`

e. `x = 2 * n + 5.3;`

f. `l + 1 = n;`

g. `x / y = x * y;`

h. `m = n % l;`

i. `n = x % 5;`

j. `x = x + 5;`

k. `n = 3 + 4.6`

7. Do a walk-through to find the value assigned to **e**. Assume that all variables are properly declared.

```
a = 3;
b = 4;
c = (a % b) * 6;
d = c / b;
e = (a + b + c + d)/ 4;
```

8. Which of the following variable declarations are correct? If a variable declaration is not correct, give the reason(s) and provide the correct variable declaration.

```
n = 12;                    //Line 1
char letter = ;            //Line 2
int one = 5, two;          //Line 3
double x, y, z;            //Line 4
```

9. Which of the following are valid Java assignment statements? Assume that **i**, **x**, and **percent** are **double** variables.

a. `i = i + 5;`

b. `x + 2 = x;`

c. `x = 2.5 * x;`

d. `percent = 10%`

10. Write Java statements that accomplish the following.

a. Declare the **int** variables **x** and **y**.

b. Initialize an **int** variable **x** to 10 and a **char** variable **ch** to **'B'**.

c. Update the value of an **int** variable **x** by adding **5** to it.

d. Set the value of a **double** variable **z** to **25.3**.

e. Copy the content of an **int** variable **y** into an **int** variable **z**.

f. Swap the contents of the **int** variables **x** and **y**. (Declare additional variables, if necessary.)

g. Output the content of a variable **x** and an expression **2 * x + 5 - y**, where **x** and **y** are **double** variables.

h. Declare a **char** variable **grade** and sets the value of **grade** to **'A'**.

i. Declare **int** variables to store four integers.

j. Copy the value of a **double** variable **z** to the nearest integer into an **int** variable **x**.

11. Write each of the following as a Java expression.

a. −10 times **a**

b. The character that represents 8

c. $(b^2 - 4ac)/ 2a$

d. $(-b + (b^2 - 4ac)) / 2a$

12. Suppose x, y, z, and w are **int** variables. What value is assigned to each variable after the last statement executes?

```
x = 5; z = 3;
y = x - z;
z = 2 * y + 3;
w = x - 2 * y + z;
z = w - x;
w++;
```

13. Suppose x, y, and z are **int** variables and w and t are **double** variables. What value is assigned to each variable after the last statement executes?

```
x = 17;
y = 15;
x = x + y / 4;
z = x % 3 + 4;
w = 17 / 3 + 6.5;
t = x / 4.0 + 15 % 4 - 3.5;
```

14. Suppose x and y are **int** variables and x = 25 and y = 35. What is the output of each of the following statements?

a. `System.out.println(x + ' ' + y);`

b. `System.out.println(x + " " + y);`

15. Suppose x, y, and z are **int** variables and x = 2, y = 5, and z = 6. What is the output of each of the following statements?

a. `System.out.println("x = " + x + ", y = " + y + ", z = " + z);`

b. `System.out.println("x + y = " + (x + y));`

c. `System.out.println("Sum of " + x + " and " + z + " is " +`
   `                     (x + z));`

d. `System.out.println("z / x = " + (z / x));`

e. `System.out.println("2 times " + x + " = " + (2 * x));`

16. What is the output of the following statements? Suppose a and b are **int** variables, c is a **double** variable, and a = 13, b = 5, and c = 17.5.

Output

a. `System.out.println(a + b - c);`   _____

b. `System.out.println(15 / 2 + c);`   _____

c. `System.out.println(a / (double)(b) + 2 * c);`   _____

d. `System.out.println(14 % 3 + 6.3 + b / a);`   _____

e. `System.out.println((int)(c)% 5 + a - b);`   _____

f. `System.out.println(13.5 / 2 + 4.0 * 3.5 + 18);` _____

17. How do you print the carriage return?

18. Which of the following are correct Java statements?

    a. `System.out.println("Hello There!");`

    b. `System.out.println("Hello");`
       `                    (" There!");`

    c. `System.out.println("Hello" +`
       `                    " There!");`

    d. `System.out.println('Hello There!');`

19. The following two programs have syntax mistakes. Correct them. On each successive line, assume that any preceding error has been corrected. After you have corrected the syntax errors, type these programs to check if all errors have been found.

    a.

    ```java
    public class ProgWithErrorsA
    {
        static final int  PRIME = 11,213;
        static final RATE = 15.6;
        public void main(String[] arg)
        {
            int i, x, y, w;
            x = 7;
            y = 3;
            x = x + w;
            PRIME = x + PRIME;
            System.out.println(PRIME);
            wages = rate * 36.75;
            System.out.println("Wages = "  wages);
        }
    }
    ```

    b.

    ```java
    public class ProgWithErrorsB
    {
        static final char = BLANK = ' ';
        static final int  ONE 5;

        public static void main(String[] arg)
        {
            int a, b, cc;

            a = one + 5;
            b = a + BLANK;
            cc := a + ONE * 2;
            a + cc = b;
            ONE = b + c;
            System.out.println("a = " + a
                            + ", b = " + b
                            + ", cc = " + cc);
        }
    }
    ```

20. Write equivalent compound statements if possible.

    a. `x = 2 * x;`

    b. `x = x + y - 2;`

    c. `sum = sum + num;`

    d. `z = z * x + 2 * z;`

    e. `y = y / (x + 5);`

21. Write the following compound statements as equivalent simple statements.

    a. `x += 5 - z;`

    b. `y *= 2 * x + 5 - z;`

    c. `w += 2 * z + 4;`

    d. `x -= z + y - t;`

    e. `sum += num;`

    f. `x /= y - 2;`

22. Suppose a, b, and c are **int** variables and a = 5 and b = 6. What value is assigned to each variable after each statement executes? If a variable is undefined at a particular statement, report UND (undefined).

	a	b	c
`a = (b++) + 3;`	____	____	____
`c = 2 * a + (++b);`	____	____	____
`b = 2 * (++c) - (a++);`	____	____	____

23. Suppose a, b, and sum are **int** variables and c is a **double** variable. What value is assigned to each variable after each statement executes? Suppose a = 3, b = 5, and c = 14.1.

	a	b	c	sum
`sum = a + b + (int)c;`	____	____	____	____
`c /= a;`	____	____	____	____
`b += (int)c - a;`	____	____	____	____
`a *= 2 * b + (int)c;`	____	____	____	____

24. What is printed by the following program? Suppose the input is:

`20 15`

```java
import java.util.*;

public class Mystery
{
    static Scanner console = new Scanner(System.in);

    static final int NUM = 10;
    static final double X = 20.5;
```

```java
public static void main(String[] arg)
{
    int a, b;
    double z;
    char grade;
    a = 25;
    System.out.println("a = " + a);
    System.out.print("Enter the first integers: ");
    System.out.flush();
    a = console.nextInt();
    System.out.println();
    System.out.print("Enter the second integers: ");
    System.out.flush();
    b = console.nextInt();
    System.out.println();
    System.out.println("The numbers you entered are "
                       + a + " and " + b);
    z = X + 2 * a - b;
    System.out.println("z = " + z);
    grade = 'A';
    System.out.println("Your grade is " + grade);

    a = 2 * NUM + (int) z;
    System.out.println("The value of a = " + a);
}
}
```

25. What type of input does the following program require, and in what order must the input be provided?

```java
import java.util.*;

public class Strange
{
    static Scanner console = new Scanner(System.in);

    public static void main(String[] arg)
    {
        int x, y;
        String name;

        x = console.nextInt();
        name = console.nextLine();
        y = console.nextInt();
    }
}
```

PROGRAMMING EXERCISES

2

1. Write a program that produces the following output:

```
************************************
*      Programming Assignment 1     *
*        Computer Programming I      *
*          Author: Duffy Ducky       *
*      Due Date: Thursday, Jan. 24   *
************************************
```

2. Write a program that prints the following pattern:

```
    *
  *   *
 *   *   *
```

3. Write a program that prints the following banner:

```
***************************
***************************
********* WELCOME *********
===========================
===========================
*********   HOME   *********
***************************
***************************
```

4. Consider the following program segment:

```
//import classes

public class Exercise
{
    public static void main(String[] args)
    {
        //variable declaration

        //executable statements
    }
}
```

a. Write a Java statement that imports the **class** Scanner.

b. Write a Java statement that declares **console** to be a **Scanner** object for inputting data from the standard input device.

c. Write Java statements that declare and initialize the following named constants: **SECRET** of the type **int** initialized to **11**, and **RATE** of the type **double** initialized to **12.50**.

d. Write Java statements that declare the following variables: `num1`, `num2`, and `newNum` of the type `int`; `name` of the type `String`; and `hoursWorked` and `wages` of the type `double`.

e. Write Java statements that prompt the user to input two integers and store the first number in `num1` and the second number in `num2`.

f. Write a Java statement(s) that outputs the values of `num1` and `num2`, indicating which is `num1` and which is `num2`. For example, if `num1` is 8 and `num2` is 5, then the output is:

```
The value of num1 = 8 and the value of num2 = 5.
```

g. Write a Java statement that multiplies the value of `num1` by 2, adds the value of `num2` to it, and then stores the result in `newNum`. Then write a Java statement that outputs the value of `newNum`.

h. Write a Java statement that updates the value of `newNum` by adding the value of the named constant `SECRET`. Then write a Java statement that outputs the value of `newNum` with an appropriate message.

i. Write Java statements that prompt the user to enter a person's last name and then store the last name into the variable `name`.

j. Write Java statements that prompt the user to enter a decimal number between 0 and `70` and then store the number entered into `hoursWorked`.

k. Write a Java statement that multiplies the value of the named constant `RATE` with the value of `hoursWorked`, and then stores the result into the variable `wages`.

l. Write Java statements that produce the following output:

```
Name:              //output the value of the variable name
Pay Rate: $        //output the value of the variable rate
Hours Worked:      //output the value of the variable hoursWorked
Salary: $          //output the value of the variable wages
```

For example, if the value of `name` is `"Rainbow"` and `hoursWorked` is `45.50`, then the output is:

```
Name: Rainbow
Pay Rate: $12.5
Hours Worked: 45.5
Salary: $568.75
```

m. Write a Java program that tests each of the Java statements that you wrote in parts a through l. Place the statements at the appropriate places in the previous Java program segment. Test run your program (twice) on the following input data:

a. `num1 = 13, num2 = 28; name = "Jacobson"; hoursWorked = 48.30.`

b. `num1 = 32, num2 = 15; name = "Crawford"; hoursWorked = 58.45.`

2

5. Write a program that prompts the user to input a decimal number and outputs the number rounded to the nearest integer.

6. Write a program that prompts the user to input the length and width of a rectangle and then prints the rectangle's area and perimeter.

7. Write a program that prompts the user to enter five test scores and then prints the average test score.

8. Write a program that prompts the user to input five decimal numbers. The program should then add the five decimal numbers, convert the sum to the nearest integer, and print the result.

9. Write a program that does the following:

   a. Prompts the user to input five decimal numbers

   b. Prints the five decimal numbers

   c. Converts each decimal number to the nearest integer

   d. Adds the five integers

   e. Prints the sum and average of the five integers

10. Write a program that prompts the user to input a four-digit positive integer. The program then outputs the digits of the number, one digit per line. For example, if the input is 3245, the output is:

    3
    2
    4
    5

11. Write a Java program that prompts the user to input the elapsed time for an event in seconds. The program then outputs the elapsed time in hours, minutes, and seconds. (For example, if the elapsed time is 9630 seconds, the output is 2:40:30.)

12. Write a Java program that prompts the user to input the elapsed time for an event in hours, minutes, and seconds. The program then outputs the elapsed time in seconds.

13. To make profit, a local store marks up the prices of its items by a certain percentage. Write a Java program that reads the original price of the item sold, the percentage of the marked-up price, and the sales tax rate. The program then outputs the original price of the item, the marked-up percentage of the item, the store's selling price of the item, the sales tax rate, the sales tax, and the final price of the item. (The final price of the item is the selling price plus the sales tax.)

14. Write a program that prompts the user to input a length expressed in centimeters. The program should convert the length to inches, to the nearest inch, and then output the length expressed in yards, feet, and inches, in that order. For example, 123 inches would be output as:

    3 yard(s), 1 feet (foot), and 3 inch(es)

It should not be output as:

```
2 yard(s) 4 feet (foot) 3 inch(es)
```

or

```
10 feet (foot) 3 inch(es)
```

or

```
10.25 feet (foot)
```

3

INTRODUCTION TO OBJECTS AND INPUT/OUTPUT

In this chapter, you will:

- ♦ Learn about objects and reference variables
- ♦ Explore how to use predefined methods in a program
- ♦ Become familiar with the `class String`
- ♦ Explore how to format output using the method `printf`
- ♦ Learn how to use input and output dialog boxes in a program
- ♦ Become familiar with the `String` method `format`
- ♦ Become familiar with file input and output

Chapter 2 introduced you to the basic elements of Java programs, including special symbols and identifiers, primitive data types, arithmetic operators, and the order of precedence of operators. You were briefly introduced to the `class String` for manipulating strings, the `class Scanner` for inputting data into a program, and general rules on programming style. In this chapter, you learn more about input and output and how to use predefined methods in your programs. You also learn, in some detail, how to use the `class String` to manipulate strings.

OBJECTS AND REFERENCE VARIABLES

Three terms that you will repeatedly encounter throughout this book are variables, reference variables, and objects. This section defines these terms early in the book so you will be familiar with them.

In Chapter 2, you learned the primitive data types such as **int**, **double**, **char**, and also worked with strings. We used **String** variables to manipulate or process strings.

Consider the following statement:

```
int x;          //Line 1
```

This statement declares **x** to be an **int** variable. Now consider the statement:

```
String str;     //Line 2
```

This statement declares **str** to be a **String** variable.

The statement in Line 1 allocates memory space to store an **int** value and calls this memory space **x**. The variable **x** can store an **int** value in its memory space. For example, the following statement stores **45** in **x**, as shown in Figure 3-1:

```
x = 45;         //Line 3
```

Figure 3-1   Variable x and its data

Next, let us see what happens with the statement in Line 2. The statement in Line 2 allocates memory space for the variable **str**. However, unlike the variable x, the variable **str** *cannot* directly store data in its memory space. The variable **str** stores the memory location, that is, the address of the memory space where the actual data is stored. For example, the effect of the statement:

```
str = "Java Programming";    //Line 4
```

is shown in Figure 3-2.

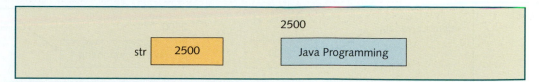

Figure 3-2   Variable `str` and the data it points to

3

For the `String` variable `str`, the statement in Line 4 causes the system to allocate memory space starting at, say location `2500`, stores the string `"Java Programming"` in this memory space, and then stores the address `2500` in the memory space of `str`.

The next obvious question is: How does this happen? In reality, the statement in Line 4 is equivalent to the following statement:

```
str = new String("Java Programming");    //Line 5
```

Now the obvious question is: What is `new`? In Java, `new` is an operator. It causes the system to allocate memory space of a specific type, store specific data in that memory space, and return the address of that memory space. Therefore, the statement in Line 4 causes the system to allocate memory space large enough to store the string `"Java Programming"` and return the address of the allocated memory space. The assignment operator stores the address of that memory space into the variable `str`.

`String` is not a primitive data type. In Java terminology, the data type `String` is called the **class** `String`. In this and subsequent chapters, you will encounter some other classes provided by the Java system. In Chapter 8, you will learn how to create your own classes.

In Java, variables such as `str` are called **reference variables**. More formally, reference variables are variables that store the address of a memory space. In Java, any variable declared using a **class** (such as the variable `str`) is a reference variable. Because `str` is a reference variable declared using the **class** `String`, we say that `str` is a reference variable of the `String` type.

The memory space `2500`, where the string `"Java Programming"` is stored, is called a **String object**. Moreover, we call `String` objects **instances** of the **class** `String`.

Because `str` is a reference variable of the `String` type, `str` can store the address of any `String` object. In other words, `str` can point to or refer to any `String` object. Moreover, it follows that we are dealing with two different things—the reference variable `str` and the `String` object that `str` points to. We call the `String` object that `str` points to, which is at memory space `2500` in Figure 3-2, the object `str`.

To emphasize that the `String` object at memory space `2500` is the object `str`, we can redraw Figure 3-2 as Figure 3-3.

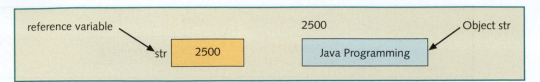

Figure 3-3 Variable `str` and the object `str`

Using the operator **new** to create a **class** object is called an **instantiation** of that **class**.

Let us summarize the Java terminology used in the preceding paragraphs, especially the use of the terms *variable* and *object*. While working with classes, we declare a reference variable of a **class** type and then, typically, using the operator **new** we instantiate an object of that **class** type and store the address of the object into the reference variable. For example, suppose that `refVar` is a reference variable of a **class** type. When we use the term *variable* `refVar`, we mean the value of `refVar`, that is, the address stored in `refVar`. When we use the term *object* `refVar`, we mean the object whose address is stored in `refVar`. The object that `refVar` points to can be accessed via the variable `refVar`.

The next obvious question is: How can you change the value of the object from `"Java Programming"` to, say, `"Hello there!"` in Figure 3–3? To do so, you must look at the **class** `String` and see if it provides a method that allows you to change the value of the (*existing*) object from `"Java Programming"` to `"Hello there!"`. (The next section briefly describes what a method is.) Unfortunately, the **class** `String` does not provide any such method. (The **class** `String` is discussed later in this chapter.) In other words, the value of the `String` object at memory space `2500` cannot be altered. It thus follows that `String` objects are *immutable*; that is, once they are created they cannot be changed.

You could execute another statement, similar to the statement in Line 4, with the value `"Hello there!"`. Suppose that the following statement is executed:

```
str = "Hello there!";
```

This statement would again cause the system to allocate memory space to store the string `"Hello there!"` and the address of the allocated memory space would be stored in `str`. However, the address of the allocated memory space will be different than that in the first statement. To be specific, suppose that the address of the allocated memory space is `3850`. Figure 3-4 illustrates the result.

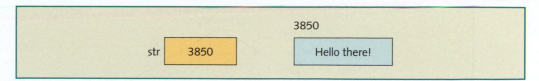

Figure 3-4   Variable `str`, its value, and the object `str`

This is an important property of reference variables of the `String` type and `String` objects, and must be recognized and understood. Furthermore, it is especially important to know this property when we start comparing strings.

To simplify Figure 3-4, we usually use the format in Figure 3-5.

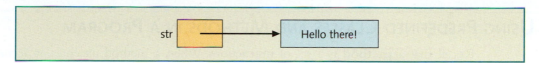

Figure 3-5   Variable `str` and the object `str`

In Figure 3-5, the arrow originating in the box `str` means that `str` contains an address. The arrow pointing to the memory space containing the value `"Hello there!"` means that the variable `str` contains the address of the object containing the value `"Hello there!"`. We will use this arrow notation to explain various examples.

You might ask: What happened to memory space `2500` and the string `"Java Programming"` stored in it? If no other `String` variable refers to it, then sometimes during program execution, the Java system reclaims this memory space for later use. This is called **garbage collection**. If you do not want to depend on the system for garbage collection, then you can include the statement:

```
System.gc();
```

in your program to instruct the computer to run the garbage collector.

We can now summarize the discussion of the preceding sections. You can declare two types of variables in Java—primitive type variables and reference variables, as shown in Figure 3-6. Primitive type variables store data *directly* into their own memory spaces. Reference variables store the address of the object containing the data. An object is an instance of a **class** and the operator **new** is used to instantiate an object.

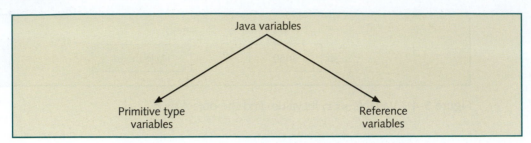

Figure 3-6   Java variables

Before discussing the **class** String, we first discuss how to use predefined methods in a program.

USING PREDEFINED CLASSES AND METHODS IN A PROGRAM

Recall that a **method** is a set of instructions. When a method executes, it accomplishes something. The method main, with which you worked in Chapter 2, executes automatically when you run a Java program. Other methods execute only when they are activated—that is, called. Java comes with a wealth of classes called **predefined classes**. In addition, every predefined **class** contains many useful **predefined methods**, which accomplish very useful results. In this section, you do not learn how to write your own methods, but you do learn how to use some of the predefined classes and methods provided by the Java system.

Recall from Chapter 2 that predefined classes are organized as a collection of packages, called **class libraries**. A particular **package** can contain several classes and each **class** can contain several methods. Therefore, to use a predefined **class** and/or a method, you need to know the name of the **package**, the name of the **class**, and the name of the method. To use a method, you also need to know a few other things, which are described shortly.

There are two types of methods in a **class**: **static** and non-**static**. A **static** method can be used, that is, called, using the name of the **class** containing the method. (Chapter 8 describes these methods in detail. At this point, you need to know only how to use predefined methods, which may be **static** or non-**static**.)

The Java system contains the **class** Math, which in turn contains powerful and useful mathematical functions. The **class** Math is contained in the **package** java.lang. Every method of the **class** Math is a **static** method. Therefore, you can use every method of the **class** Math using the name of the **class**, which is Math.

import java.lang.Math;

x = Math.PI;

The **class** Math contains a very useful method, pow, called the method **power**, which is used to calculate x^y in a program, that is, Math.pow(x, y) = x^y. For example, Math.pow(2, 3) = 2^3 = 8 and Math.pow(4, 0.5) = $4^{0.5}$ = $\sqrt{4}$ = 2. The numbers x and y used in the method pow are called the **arguments** or **parameters** of the method pow. For example, in Math.pow(2, 3), the parameters are 2 and 3.

An expression such as Math.pow(2, 3) is called a **method call**, and causes the code attached to the method pow to execute and, in this case, computes 2^3. The method pow computes a value of the type **double**. Therefore, we say that the return type of the method pow is **double** or the method pow is of the type **double**.

In general, to use a predefined method in a program:

1. You need to know the name of the **class** containing the method.

2. You need to know the name of the **package** containing the **class**, and import this **class** from the **package** in the program.

3. You need to know the name of the method. In addition, you need to know the number of parameters the method takes and the type of each parameter. You must also be aware of what the return type of the method is or, loosely speaking, what the method does.

For example, to use the method nextInt, you include the **package** java.util.

As noted in Chapter 2, the Java system automatically imports methods and **class**es from the **package** java.lang. Therefore, you do not need to explicitly import any contents of the **package** java.lang. Because the **class** Math is contained in the **package** java.lang, to use the method pow, you need to know that the name of the method is pow, the method pow has two parameters, both of which are numbers, and the method calculates the first parameter to the power of the second parameter.

Dot Between Class (Object) Name and Class Member: A Precaution

In Chapter 2, you learned how to use the method nextInt of the **class** Scanner to input the next token, which can be expressed as an integer. In the preceding section, you learned how to use the method pow of the **class** Math.

Consider the following statement:

```
x = console.nextInt();
```

where x is a variable of the type **int**. Notice the dot between console and nextInt; the name of the object console and the name of the method nextInt are separated by the dot.

In Java, the dot (.) is an operator called the **member access operator**.

Omitting the dot between console and nextInt results in a syntax error. In the statement:

```
x = consolenextInt();
```

`consolenextInt` becomes a new identifier. If you used `consolenextInt` in a program, the compiler would try to resolve the undeclared identifier syntax error. Similarly, omitting the parentheses, as in `console.nextInt`, also results in a syntax error.

Usually, several methods and/or variables are associated with a particular **class**, each doing a specific job. In **dot notation**, the dot separates the **class** variable name, that is, the object name from the member, or method, name. *It is also worth noting that methods are distinguished from (reference) variables by the presence of parentheses, and that methods that have no parameters must have empty parentheses* (like in `nextInt()`). For example, `console` is the name of a (reference) variable, and `nextInt` is the name of a method.

class String

This section explains how to use **String** methods to manipulate strings. However, first we fix some terminology that we typically use while working with strings and the **class** String.

Consider the following statements:

```
String name;             //Line 1
name = "Lisa Johnson";   //Line 2
```

The statement in Line 1 declares **name** to be a **String** variable. The statement in Line 2 creates the string **"Lisa Johnson"** and assigns it to **name**.

Some notes on terminology:

1. In the statement in Line 2, that is:

   ```
   name = "Lisa Johnson"; //Line 2
   ```

   we usually say that the `String` object, or the string `"Lisa Johnson"`, is assigned to the `String` variable or the variable name. In reality, as explained before, a `String` *object* with the value "`Lisa Johnson`" is instantiated and the address of the object is stored in name. However, if no confusion arises, we will use the phrase, "the `String` object or the string '`Lisa Johnson`' is assigned to the `String` variable or the variable name" to explain statements such as in Line 2.

2. Whenever we use the term "the string name", we are referring to the object containing the string `"Lisa Johnson"`. Similarly, when we use the terms (reference) variable name or `String` variable name, we simply mean name, whose value is an address.

Suppose `str` is a `String` variable. Earlier, we indicated that statements such as:

```
str = "Java Programming";
```

are equivalent to the statement:

```
str = new String("Java Programming");
```

You might wonder why we used the assignment operator to assign a string to a `String` variable. This is because the **class** `String` is so important in Java that it has defined the assignment operator for the **class** `String`. Therefore, while working with `String` variables and objects, we typically use the assignment operator to instantiate a `String` object.

The remainder of this section describes various features of the **class** `String`. In Chapter 2, you learned that two strings can be joined using the operator +. The **class** `String` provides various methods that allow us to manipulate strings in various ways. For example, we can find the length of a string, extract part of a string, convert a string into uppercase or lowercase letters, find the position of a particular string in another string, convert a number into a string, and convert a numeric string into a number.

Each method associated with the **class** `String` implements a specific operation and has a specific name. For example, the method for determining the length of a string is named `length`, and the method for extracting a string from within another string is named `substring`.

As explained in the earlier section, Using Predefined Classes and Methods in a Program, in general, to use a method you must know the name of the **class** containing the method, the name of the **package** containing the **class**, you must import the **class**, and you must know the method name, its parameters, and what the method does.

Because the Java system automatically makes the **class** `String` available, you do not need to import this **class**. Therefore, in order to use a `String` method you need to know its name, parameters, and what the method does.

Recall that a string is a sequence of 0 or more characters, and strings are enclosed in double quotation marks. The **index** (position) of the first character is 0, the index of the second character is 1, and so on. The length of a string is the number of characters in it.

Suppose that `str` is a `String` variable and we need to determine a substring in the string `str`. For the method `substring` to work, it must know the following:

1. The position of the first character of the substring being determined in the string `str`

2. The position of the last character of the substring being determined in the string `str`

That is, to use the method substring, you must know the starting and ending position of the substring. The general statement to use the method substring is:

`StringVariable.substring(startIndex, endIndex)`

This statement determines the substring in the string specified by **StringVariable** starting at the position indicated by **startIndex** until **endIndex-1**. For example, the statement:

`str.substring(3, 8)`

determines the substring in the string `str`, starting at position 3 until the position, 8 − 1, that is, 7.

Example 3-1 illustrates how to use the method `substring`.

Example 3-1

Consider the following statements:

```
String sentence;
String str1;
String str2;

sentence = "It is cloudy and warm.";
```

Now consider the following expression:

```
sentence.substring(0, 12)
```

This expression says, in the string **sentence**, determine the substring starting at position 0 and ending at position 12 − 1, that is, position 11. The character at position 0 is **I** and the character at position 11 is **y**. Therefore, the preceding expression returns the string `"It is cloudy"`. Similarly, the expression:

```
sentence.substring(3, 5)
```

returns the string `"is"` because the character at position 3 is **i** and the character at position 5 − 1, that is, position 4, is **s**.

Example 3-2

Assume the declaration of Example 3–1, that is,

```
String sentence;
String str1;
String str2;

sentence = "It is cloudy and warm.";
```

The following statements show the effect of the method `substring`:

Statement	Effect
`System.out.println(sentence.substring(0, 5));`	Outputs the string: `"It is"`
`System.out.println(sentence.substring(6, 12));`	Outputs the string: `"cloudy"`
`System.out.println(sentence.substring(6, 22));`	Outputs the string: `"cloudy and warm"`
`System.out.println(sentence.substring(3, 9));`	Outputs the string: `"is clo"`
`str1 = sentence.substring(0, 8);`	`str1 = "It is cl"`
`str2 = sentence.substring(2, 12);`	`str2 = " is cloudy"`

Recall that when a string is output, the double quotation marks (unless they are part of the string) are not output. Therefore, the string `"It is"` is output as:

```
It is
```

The program in Example 3-3 tests the preceding statements.

Example 3-3

```java
//The substring function

public class SubstringMethod
{
    public static void main(String[] args)
    {
        String  sentence;
        String  str1;
        String  str2;

        sentence = "It is cloudy and warm.";                    //Line 1

        System.out.println("Line 2: "
                        + sentence.substring(0, 5));            //Line 2
        System.out.println("Line 3: "
                        + sentence.substring(6, 12));           //Line 3
        System.out.println("Line 4: "
                        + sentence.substring(6, 22));           //Line 4
        System.out.println("Line 5: "
                        + sentence.substring(3, 9));            //Line 5

        str1 = sentence.substring(0, 8);                        //Line 6
        System.out.println("Line 7: str1 = \"" + str1 + "\""); //Line 7

        str2 = sentence.substring(2, 12);                       //Line 8
        System.out.println("Line 9: str2 = \"" + str2 + "\""); //Line 9
    }
}
```

Sample Run:
```
Line 2: It is
Line 3: cloudy
Line 4: cloudy and warm.
Line 5: is clo
Line 7: str1 = "It is cl"
Line 9: str2 = " is cloudy"
```

Like the method `substring`, the **class** `String` contains various methods to manipulate a string. The methods associated with the **class** `String` are called the **members** of the **class** `String`.

Table 3-1 lists some commonly used `String` methods. It shows the method heading, the method name in bold, and any parameters. Comments explain the purpose of the method, show the return type, and give examples. Examples in Table 3-1 use the following statements:

```
String sentence;
sentence = "Programming with Java";
```

Table 3-1 Some Commonly Used String Methods

```
String(String str)
  //Constructor: Creates a string object and initializes the string
  //object with characters specified by str.
  //Example:
  //String myStr = new String(sentence);
  //       myStr is a String variable initialized using sentence
char charAt(int index)
  //Returns the character at the position specified by index.
  //Example: sentence.charAt(3) returns 'g'
int indexOf(char ch)
  //Returns the index of the first occurrence of the character
  //specified by ch; if the character specified by ch does not
  //appear in the string, it returns -1.
  //Example: sentence.indexOf('J') returns 17
  //         sentence.indexOf('a') returns 5
int indexOf(char ch, int pos)
  //Returns the index of the first occurrence of the character
  //specified by ch. The parameter pos specifies from where to begin
  //the search; if the character specified by ch does not
  //appear in the string, it returns -1.
  //Example: sentence.indexOf('a', 10) returns 18
int indexOf(String str)
  //Returns the index of the first occurrence of the string
  //specified by str; if the string specified by str does not
  //appear in the string, it returns -1.
  //Example: sentence.indexOf("with") returns 12
  //         sentence.indexOf("ing") returns 8
int indexOf(String str, int pos)
  //Returns the index of the first occurrence of the string
  //specified by str. The parameter pos specifies from where to begin
  //the search; if the string specified by str does not appear
  //in the string, it returns -1.
```

Table 3-1 Commonly Used String Methods (continued)

```
String concat(String str)
  //Returns the string that is this string concatenated with str
  //Example: The expression
  //        sentence.concat(" is fun.")
  //        returns the string "Programming with Java is fun."
int length()
  //Returns the length of the string
  //Example: sentence.length() returns 21, the number of characters in
  //        "Programming with Java"
String replace(char charToBeReplaced, char charReplacedWith)
  //Returns the string in which every occurrence of
  //charToBeReplaced is replaced with charReplacedWith
  //Example: sentence.replace('a', '*') returns the string
  //        "Progr*mming with J*v*"
  //        Each occurrence of a is replaced with *
String substring(int startIndex, int endIndex)
  //Returns the string which is a substring of this string
  //starting at startIndex until endIndex - 1.
String toLowerCase()
  //Returns the string that is same as this string except that
  //all uppercase letters of this string are replaced with
  //their equivalent lowercase letters.
  //Example: sentence.toLowerCase() returns "programming with java"
String toUpperCase()
  //Returns the string that is same as this string except
  //that all lowercase letters of this string are replaced with
  //their equivalent uppercase letters.
  //Example: sentence.toUpperCase() returns "PROGRAMMING WITH JAVA"
```

 Table 3-1 lists only some of the methods for string manipulation. Moreover, the table gives only the name of the method, the number of parameters, and the type of the method. See Appendix E for the complete heading of each method.

The general expression to use a **String** method, listed in Table 3-1, on a **String** variable is:

StringVariable.StringMethodName(parameters)

In this statement, the variable name and the method name are separated with the dot (**.**).

The program in Example 3-4 illustrates how to use some of the **String** methods shown in Table 3-1.

Example 3-4

```
//Program to illustrate the effect of various String methods.

public class VariousStringMethods
{
    public static void main(String[] args)
    {
        String sentence;
        String str1;
        String str2;
        String str3;
        int index;

        sentence = "Now is the time for the birthday party";    //Line 1

        System.out.println("Line 2: sentence = \""
                            + sentence + "\"");                  //Line 2
        System.out.println("Line 3: The length of sentence = "
                            + sentence.length());                //Line 3

        System.out.println("Line 4: The character at index 16 in "
                            + "sentence = "
                            + sentence.charAt(16));              //Line 4

        System.out.println("Line 5: The index of the first t in "
                            + "sentence = "
                            + sentence.indexOf('t'));            //Line 5

        System.out.println("Line 6: The index of for in sentence "
                            + "= "
                            + sentence.indexOf("for"));          //Line 6

        System.out.println("Line 7: sentence in uppercase = \""
                            + sentence.toUpperCase() + "\"");    //Line 7

        index = sentence.indexOf("birthday");                    //Line 8
        str1 = sentence.substring(index, index + 14);            //Line 9
        System.out.println("Line 10: str1 = \"" + str1 + "\""); //Line 10

        str2 = "Super " + str1;                                  //Line 11
        System.out.println("Line 12: str2 = \"" + str2 + "\""); //Line 12

        str3 = sentence.replace('t', 'T');                       //Line 13
        System.out.println("Line 14: str3 = \"" + str3 + "\""); //Line 14
    }
}
```

Sample Run:

```
Line 2: sentence = "Now is the time for the birthday party"
Line 3: The length of sentence = 38
Line 4: The character at index 16 in sentence = f
Line 5: The index of first t in sentence = 7
Line 6: The index of for in sentence = 16
Line 7: sentence in uppercase = "NOW IS THE TIME FOR THE BIRTHDAY PARTY"
Line 10: str1 = "birthday party"
Line 12: str2 = "Super birthday party"
Line 14: str3 = "Now is The Time for The birThday parTy"
```

The preceding program works as follows: The statement in Line 1 initializes the `String` object `sentence` to the string:

`"Now is the time for the birthday party"`

The statement in Line 2 outputs the string `sentence`, and the statement in Line 3 outputs the length of the string `sentence`. Note that the output of the statement in Line 2 contains double quotation marks around the string because the print statement in Line 2 contains double quotation marks.

The statement in Line 4 outputs the character at index 16, which is `f` in the string `sentence`. The statement in Line 5 outputs the first position (index) of the character `t` in the string `sentence`. Similarly, the statement in Line 6 outputs the index of the string `"for"` in the string `sentence`.

The statement in Line 7 uses the method `toUpperCase` to output `sentence` in uppercase letters. The statement in Line 8 determines and stores the index of the string `"birthday"` in the string `sentence`. The statement in Line 9 determines the substring starting at the index specified by `index` until the index given by `index + 14 - 1`. The substring is assigned to the variable `str1`. The statement in Line 10 outputs `Str1`.

The statement in Line 11 concatenates the string `"Super"` with the string `str1`. Note that the string assigned to `str2` is `"Super birthday party"`. The statement in Line 12 outputs `str2`.

The statement in Line 13 assigns to `str3` the same string in `sentence` except that the lowercase `t` is replaced with an uppercase `T`. The statement in Line 14 outputs `str3`.

To summarize the preceding discussion of the **class** `String`:

1. `String` variables are reference variables.

2. A string object is an instance of the **class** `String`.

3. The **class** String contains various methods to manipulate `strings`.

4. A `String` variable invokes a `String` method using the dot operator, the method name, and the set of arguments (if any) required by the method.

INPUT/OUTPUT

A program performs three basic operations: it gets data into the program, it manipulates the data, and it outputs the results. In Chapter 2, you learned how to manipulate numeric data using arithmetic operations. Because writing programs for input/output (I/O) is quite complex, Java offers extensive support for I/O operations by providing a substantial number of I/O classes such as the **class** `Scanner`. In the remainder of this chapter, you will:

- Learn how to format output using the method `printf`.

- Learn other ways to input data and output results in Java.

- Learn how to format the output of decimal numbers to a specific number of decimal places.

- Learn how to instruct the program to read data from or write output to a file. If there is a large amount of data, inputting data from the keyboard every time you execute your program is not practical. Similarly, if the output is large or you want to save the output for later use, you must be able to save a program's output to a file.

Formatting Output with `printf`

In Chapter 2, you learned how to show the output of a program on the standard output device using the standard output object `System.out` and the methods `print` and `println`. More specifically, to output the results, you used statements such as `System.out.print(expression)` and/or `System.out.println(expression)`, where `expression` is evaluated and its value is output. However, the methods `print` and `println` cannot *directly* format certain outputs in a specific manner. For example, the default output of floating-point numbers is typically up to 6 decimal places for **float** values and up to 15 decimal places for **double** values. Moreover, sometimes we would like to align the output in certain columns. To format the output in a specific manner, you use the method `printf`.

A syntax to use the method `printf` to produce the output on the standard output device is:

```
System.out.printf(formatString);
```

or:

```
System.out.printf(formatString, argumentList);
```

where `formatString` is a string specifying the format of the output and `argumentList` is a list of arguments. The `argumentList` is a list of arguments that consists of constant values, variables, or expressions. If `argumentList` has more than one argument, then the arguments are separated with commas.

For example, the statement:

```
System.out.printf("Hello there!");                        //Line 1
```

consists of only the format string, and the statement:

```
System.out.printf("There are %.2f inches in %d centimeters.%n",

              centimeters / 2.54, centimeters);      //Line 2
```

3

consists of both the format string and `argumentList`, where `centimeters` is a variable of the `int` type. Notice that the argument list consists of the expression `centimeters / 2.54` and the variable `centimeters`. Also notice that the format string consists of the two expressions, `%.2f` and `%d`; these are called **format specifiers**. By default, format specifiers and the arguments in `argumentList` have a one-to-one correspondence. Here, the first format specifier `%.2f` is matched with the first argument, which is the expression `centimeters / 2.54`. It says to output the value of the expression `centimeters / 2.54` to two decimal places. The second format specifier `%d` is matched with the second argument, which is `centimeters`. It says to output the value of `centimeters` as a (decimal) integer. (The format specifier `%n` positions the insertion point at the beginning of the next line.)

The output of the statement in Line 1 is:

```
Hello there!
```

Suppose that the value of `centimeters` is 150. Now (to 14 decimal places):

```
centimeters / 2.54 = 150 / 2.54 = 59.05511811023622
```

Therefore, the output of the statement in Line 2 is:

```
There are 59.06 inches in 150 centimeters.
```

Notice that the value of the expression `centimeters / 2.54` is rounded and printed to two decimal places.

It follows that when outputting the format string, the format specifiers are replaced with the formatted values of the corresponding arguments.

A format specifier for general, character, and numeric types has the following syntax:

```
%[argument_index$][flags][width][.precision]conversion
```

The expressions in square brackets are optional. That is, they may or may not appear in a format specifier.

The optional *argument_index* is a (decimal) integer indicating the position of the argument in the argument list. The first argument is referenced by `"1$"`, the second by `"2$"`, and so on.

The optional *flags* is a set of characters that modifies the output format. The set of valid flags depends on the conversion.

The optional *width* is a (decimal) integer indicating the minimum number of characters to be written to the output.

The optional *precision* is a (decimal) integer usually used to restrict the number of characters. The specific behavior depends on the conversion.

The required *conversion* is a character indicating how the argument should be formatted. The set of valid conversions for a given argument depends on the argument's data type. Table 3-2 summarizes some of the supported conversions.

Table 3-2 Some of the Supported Conversions

	Conversion	The result is
's'	general	a string
'c'	character	a Unicode character
'd'	integral	formatted as a (decimal) integer
'e'	floating point	formatted as a decimal number in computerized scientific notation
'f'	floating point	formatted as a decimal number
'%'	percent	'%'
'n'	line separator	the platform-specific line separator

The method `printf` is available in JDK 5.0 and higher versions.

Example 3-5

The following program illustrates how to format the output of decimal numbers using the method `printf`.

```
//Program to illustrate how to format the output of
//decimal numbers.

public class FormattingDecimalNum
{
    public static void main (String[] args)
    {
        double x = 15.674;                                        //Line 1
        double y = 235.73;                                        //Line 2
        double z = 9525.9864;                                     //Line 3

        System.out.println("Line 4: Outputting the values of "
                        + "x, y, and z with two decimal "
                        + "places.");                             //Line 4
        System.out.printf("Line 5: x = %.2f %n", x);             //Line 5
        System.out.printf("Line 6: y = %.2f %n", y);             //Line 6
        System.out.printf("Line 7: z = %.2f %n", z);             //Line 7
```

```
        System.out.println("Line 8: Outputting the values of "
                         + "x, y, and z with three decimal "
                         + "places.");                        //Line 8
        System.out.printf("Line 9: x = %.3f %n", x);         //Line 9
        System.out.printf("Line 10: y = %.3f %n", y);        //Line 10
        System.out.printf("Line 11: z = %.3f %n", z);        //Line 11
    }
}
```

3

Sample Run:
```
Line 4: Outputting the values of x, y, and z with two decimal places.
Line 5: x = 15.67
Line 6: y = 235.73
Line 7: z = 9525.99
Line 8: Outputting the values of x, y, and z with three decimal places.
Line 9: x = 15.674
Line 10: y = 235.730
Line 11: z = 9525.986
```

Notice that in Lines 5, 6, and 7, the format specifier is `%.2f`, which causes the values of **x**, **y**, and **z** to be output to two decimal places. Also notice that the values of **x** and **z** are rounded. Moreover, the format specifier `%n` positions the insertion point at the beginning of the next line.

In Lines 9, 10, and 11, the format specifier is `%.3f`, which causes the values of **x**, **y**, and **z** to be output to three decimal places. Notice that the given value of **y** has only two decimal places. Therefore, to output the value of **y** to three decimal places, 0 is shown at the thousandth place.

In a format specifier, by using the option *width* you can also specify the number of columns to be used to output the value of an expression. For example, suppose **num** is an **int** variable and **rate** is a **double** variable. Furthermore, suppose that:

```
num = 96;
rate = 15.50;
```

Consider the following statements:

```
System.out.println("123456789012345");              //Line 1
System.out.printf("%5d %n", num);                    //Line 2
System.out.printf("%5.2f %n", rate);                 //Line 3
System.out.printf("%5d%6.2f %n", num, rate);         //Line 4
System.out.printf("%5d %6.2f %n", num, rate);        //Line 5
```

The output of the statement in Line 1 shows the column positions. The statement in Line 2 outputs the value of **num** in five columns. Because the value of **num** is **96**, we need only two columns to output the value of **num**. The (*default*) output is right justified, so the first three columns are left blank.

The statement in Line 3 outputs the value of **rate** in five columns with two decimal places. Note that the decimal point also requires a column. That is, the width specifiers for floating-point values also include a column for the decimal point.

The statements in Lines 4 and 5 output the values of **num** in five columns followed by the value of **rate** in 6 columns with two decimal places. The output of these statements is:

```
123456789012345
   96
15.50
   96 15.50
   96  15.50
```

Let us take a close look at the output of the statements in Lines 4 and 5. First, consider the statement in Line 4, that is:

```
System.out.printf("%5d%6.2f %n", num, rate);
```

In this statement, the format string is `"%5d%6.2f %n"`. Notice that there is no space between the format specifiers `%5d` and `%6.2f`. Therefore, after outputting the value of **num** in the first five columns, the value of **rate** is output starting at column 6 (see the fourth line of output). Because only five columns are needed to output the value of **rate** and the output is right justified, column 6 is left blank.

Now consider the statement in Line 5. Here the format string is `"%5d %6.2f %n"`. Notice that there is a space between the format specifiers `%5d` and `%6.2f`. Therefore, after outputting the value of **num** in the first five columns, the sixth column is left blank. The value of **rate** is output starting at column 7 (see the fifth line of output). Because only five columns are needed to output the value of **rate** and the output is right justified, column 7 is (also) left blank.

 In a format specifier, if the number of columns in the option *width* is less than the number of columns required to output the value of the expression, the output is expanded to the required number of columns. That is, the output is not truncated. For example, the output of the statement:

```
System.out.printf("%2d", 8756);
```

is:

```
8756
```

even though only two columns are specified to output 8756, which requires four columns.

Example 3-6 further illustrates the use of the method **printf**.

Example 3-6

The following program illustrates how to format output using the `printf` method and format specifier.

```java
public class FormattingOutputWithprintf
{
    public static void main (String[] args)
    {
        int num = 763;                                          //Line 1
        double x = 658.75;                                      //Line 2
        String str = "Java Program.";                           //Line 3

        System.out.println("123456789012345678901234567890");//Line 4
        System.out.printf("%5d%7.2f%15s%n", num, x, str);    //Line 5
        System.out.printf("%15s%6d%9.2f%n", str, num, x);    //Line 6
        System.out.printf("%8.2f%7d%15s%n", x, num, str);    //Line 7

        System.out.printf("num = %5d%n", num);                //Line 8
        System.out.printf("x = %10.2f%n", x);                 //Line 9
        System.out.printf("str = %15s%n", str);               //Line 10
        System.out.printf("%10s%7d%n", "Program No.", 4);     //Line 11
    }
}
```

Sample Run:
```
123456789012345678901234567890
  763 658.75   Java Program.
  Java Program.    763    658.75
  658.75     763   Java Program.
num =    763
x =       658.75
str =    Java Program.
Program No.      4
```

For the most part, the preceding output is self-explanatory. Let us consider some of these statements. Notice that for each output statement, the output is right justified.

The statement in Line 4 outputs the first line of the sample run, which shows the column positions. The statements in Lines 5 through 11 produce the remaining lines of output. Let us consider the statement in Line 5, that is:

```java
System.out.printf("%5d%7.2f%15s%n", num, x, str);
```

In this statement, the format string is `"%5d%7.2f%15s%n"` and the argument list is `num, x, str`. The value of `num` is output in five columns, the value of `x` is output in seven columns with two decimal places, and the value of `str` is output in 15 columns. Because only three columns are needed to output the value of **num**, the first two columns are left blank. There is no space between the format specifiers **%5d** and **%7.2f**; therefore, the output of **x** begins at column 6. Because only six columns are needed to output the value of **x** and the format specifier **%7.2f** specifies seven columns, column 6 is left blank. Once again, there is no space between the format specifiers **%7.2f** and **%15s**. The output of the object's value that **str** points to begins at column 13. The reference variable **str** refers to the **String** object with the value **"Java Program."**. Because the format specifier **%15s** specifies 15 columns and only 13 columns are needed to output the string **"Java Program."**, the first two columns, columns 13 and 14, are left blank. The format specifier **%n** positions the insertion point at the beginning of the next line. The statements in Lines 6 and 7 work similarly.

Let us consider the statement in Line 8, that is:

```
System.out.printf("num = %5d%n", num);
```

Notice that in this statement, the format string, **"num = %5d%n"**, consists of a string and the format specifier. This statement first outputs the string **"num = "**, which requires six columns. Then, starting at column 7, the value of **num** is output in five columns. Because only three columns are needed to output the value of **num**, columns 7 and 8 are left blank.

If the number of columns specified in a format specifier is more than the number of columns needed to output the result, then the (default) output is right justified. However, strings such as names are typically left justified. To force the output to be left justified, you can use the format specifier flag. If the flag is set to **'-'**, then the output of the result is left justified.

For example, consider the following statements:

```
System.out.println("123456789012345678901234567890");    //Line 1
System.out.printf("%-15s ***%n", "Java Program.");        //Line 2
```

The output of these statements is:

```
123456789012345678901234567890
Java Program.    ***
```

Notice that the string **"Java Program."** is printed in 15 columns and the output is left justified. Because in Line 2, in the format specifier, there is a space between **s** and *******, the sixteenth column is left blank. Then ******* is printed.

The following example further clarifies this.

Example 3-7

```java
public class Example3_7
{
    public static void main (String[] args)
    {
        int num = 763;                                              //Line 1
        double x = 658.75;                                          //Line 2
        String str = "Java Program.";                              //Line 3

        System.out.println("123456789012345678901234567890"); //Line 4
        System.out.printf("%-5d%-7.2f%-15s ***%n",
                            num, x, str);                          //Line 5
        System.out.printf("%-15s%-6d%-9.2f ***%n",
                            str, num, x);                          //Line 6
        System.out.printf("%-8.2f%-7d%-15s ***%n",
                            x, num, str);                          //Line 7

        System.out.printf("num = %-5d ***%n", num);                //Line 8
        System.out.printf("x = %-10.2f ***%n", x);                 //Line 9
        System.out.printf("str = %-15s ***%n", str);               //Line 10
        System.out.printf("%-10s%-7d ***%n",
                            "Program No.", 4);                     //Line 11
    }
}
```

Sample Run:
```
123456789012345678901234567890
763  658.75 Java Program.    ***
Java Program.   763   658.75      ***
658.75  763      Java Program.   ***
num = 763    ***
x = 658.75      ***
str = Java Program.   ***
Program No.4        ***
```

The output of this program is similar to the output of the program in Example 3-6. Here the output is left justified. Notice that in the Sample Run, Lines 2 through 8 contain ***. This is to show how the value of the last argument is printed. The details are left as an exercise for you.

Next, we explain how to use input/output dialog boxes to input data into a program and then display the output of the program. However, input to a program using input dialog boxes is in string format. Even numeric data is input as strings. Therefore, you first need to learn how to convert numeric strings, called parsing numeric strings, into numeric form.

Parsing Numeric Strings

A string consisting of only an integer or a decimal number is called a **numeric string**. For example, the following are numeric strings:

```
"6723"
"-823"
"345.78"
"-782.873"
```

To process these strings as numbers for addition or multiplication, we first must convert them into numeric form. Java provides special methods to convert numeric strings into their equivalent numeric form.

1. To convert a string consisting of an integer to a value of the type `int`, we use the following expression:

   ```
   Integer.parseInt(strExpression)
   ```

   For example:

   ```
   Integer.parseInt("6723") = 6723
   Integer.parseInt("-823") = -823
   ```

2. To convert a string consisting of a decimal number to a value of the type `float`, we use the following expression:

   ```
   Float.parseFloat(strExpression)
   ```

   For example:

   ```
   Float.parseFloat("34.56") = 34.56
   Float.parseFloat("-542.97") = -542.97
   ```

3. To convert a string consisting of a decimal number to a value of the type `double`, we use the following expression:

   ```
   Double.parseDouble(strExpression)
   ```

   For example:

   ```
   Double.parseDouble("345.78") = 345.78
   Double.parseDouble("-782.873") = -782.873
   ```

Note that `Integer`, `Float`, and `Double` are classes that contain methods to convert a numeric string into a number. These classes are called **wrapper** classes. Moreover, `parseInt` is a method of the **class** `Integer`, which converts a numeric integer string into a value of the type `int`. Similarly, `parseFloat` is a method of the **class** `Float` and is used to convert a numeric decimal string into an equivalent value of the type `float`, and the method `parseDouble` is a method of the **class** `Double`, which is used to convert a numeric decimal string into an equivalent value of the type `double`. At this time do not be overly concerned with the details of these classes and methods; just continue to use them as shown previously whenever you need them. (Chapter 6 discusses these wrapper classes in some detail.)

3

Example 3-8

The following expressions show how numeric strings are converted to their equivalent numeric form.

1.

`Integer.parseInt("34")`	`= 34`
`Integer.parseInt("-456")`	`= -456`
`Double.parseDouble("754.89")`	`= 754.89`

2.

`Integer.parseInt("34") + Integer.parseInt("75")`	`= 34 + 75 = 109`
`Integer.parseInt("87") + Integer.parseInt("-67")`	`= 87 - 67 = 20`

3.

	`Double.parseDouble("754.89") - Double.parseDouble("87.34")`
`=`	`754.89 - 87.34`
`=`	`667.55`

Using Dialog Boxes for Input/Output

Recall that you have already used the **class** `Scanner` to input data into a program from the keyboard and you used the object `System.out` to output the results.

Another way to gather input and output results is to use a graphical user interface (GUI). Java provides the **class** `JOptionPane`, which allows the programmer to use GUI components for I/O. This section describes how to use these facilities to make I/O more efficient and the program more attractive.

The **class** `JOptionPane` is contained in the **package** `javax.swing`. This **class** has two methods that we use here—`showInputDialog` and `showMessageDialog`. The method `showInputDialog` allows the user to input a string from the keyboard; the method `showMessageDialog` allows the programmer to display the results.

The syntax to use the method `showInputDialog` is:

```
str = JOptionPane.showInputDialog(stringExpression);
```

where `str` is a `String` variable and `stringExpression` is an expression evaluating to a string. When this statement executes, a dialog box containing `stringExpression` appears on the screen prompting the user to enter the data. The data entered is returned as a string and assigned to the variable `str`.

The `stringExpression` usually informs the user what to do.

Consider the following statement (suppose that `name` is a `String` variable):

```
name = JOptionPane.showInputDialog("Enter your name and press OK");
```

When this statement executes, the dialog box shown in Figure 3-7 appears on the screen. (Note that the arrow and the words Text Field are not part of the dialog box.)

Figure 3-7   Input dialog box prompting the user to input name

The user enters the name in the white area, called a **text field**, as shown in Figure 3-8.

Figure 3-8   Input dialog box with user input

After you enter a name and press the OK button, the dialog box disappears and the entered name is assigned to the variable `name`. In this case, the string `"Ashley Mann"` is assigned to `name`.

Now that you know how to use an input dialog box, let's turn to the method `showMessageDialog` for output.

The syntax to use the method `showMessageDialog` is:

```
JOptionPane.showMessageDialog(parentComponent,
                             messageStringExpression,
                             boxTitleString, messageType);
```

The method `showMessageDialog` has four parameters, which are described in Table 3–3.

Table 3-3 Parameters for the Method `showMessageDialog`

Parameter	Description
parentComponent	An object that represents the parent of the dialog box. For now, we will specify the `parentComponent` to be `null`, in which case the program uses a default component that causes the dialog box to appear in the middle of the screen. Note that `null` is a reserved word in Java.
messageStringExpression	The `messageStringExpression` is evaluated and its value appears in the dialog box.
boxTitleString	The `boxTitleString` represents the title of the dialog box.
messageType	An `int` value representing the type of icon that will appear in the dialog box. Alternately, you can use certain `JOptionPane` options described below.

Table 3–4 describes the options of the **class** JOptionPane that can be used with the parameter **messageType**. The option name is shown in bold. Moreover, Examples 3–9 through 3–11 illustrate these options.

Table 3-4 `JOptionPane` Options for the Parameter `messageType`

messageType	Description
JOptionPane.**ERROR_MESSAGE**	The error icon, , is displayed in the dialog box.
JOptionPane.**INFORMATION_MESSAGE**	The information icon, , is displayed in the dialog box.
JOptionPane.**PLAIN_MESSAGE**	No icon appears in the dialog box.
JOptionPane.**QUESTION_MESSAGE**	The question icon, , is displayed in the dialog box.
JOptionPane.**WARNING_MESSAGE**	The warning icon, , is displayed in the dialog box.

Example 3-9

The output of the statement:

```
JOptionPane.showMessageDialog(null, "Hello World!", "Greetings",
                         JOptionPane.INFORMATION_MESSAGE);
```

is shown in Figure 3-9.

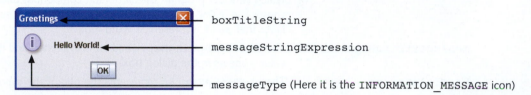

Figure 3-9   Message dialog box showing its various components

After you press the OK button, the dialog box disappears. Notice the `INFORMATION_MESSAGE` icon to the left of `Hello World!` and the word `Greetings` in the title bar.

Example 3-10

Figure 3-10 shows the output of the statement:

```
JOptionPane.showMessageDialog(null, "Amount Due = $" + 500.45,
                         "Invoice", JOptionPane.PLAIN_MESSAGE);
```

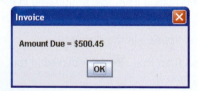

Figure 3-10   Message dialog box without any icon

In the message dialog box in Figure 3-10, no icon appears to the left of the `messageStringExpression`. This is because the `messageType` is `JOptionPane.PLAIN_MESSAGE`.

3

Example 3-11

Consider the following statements:

```
String str;
int num1 = 45;
int num2 = 56;
int sum;

str = "The two numbers are: " + num1 + " and " + num2 + "\n";
sum = num1 + num2;

str = str + "The sum of the numbers is: " + sum  + "\n";
str = str + "That is all for now!";
```

Figure 3-11 shows the output of the statement:

```
JOptionPane.showMessageDialog(null, str, "Summing Numbers",
                        JOptionPane.ERROR_MESSAGE);
```

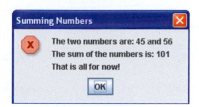

Figure 3-11   Message dialog box showing the output of the string `str`

The **class** JOptionPane is contained in the **package** javax.swing. Therefore, to use this **class** in a program, the program must import this **class** from the **package** javax.swing. The following statement illustrates how to import the **class** JOptionPane. (You can use either of the following statements.)

```
import javax.swing.JOptionPane;
```

or:

```
import javax.swing.*;
```

Statement `System.exit`

In order to use the input/output dialog boxes and properly terminate program execution, the program must include the following statement:

```
System.exit(0);
```

Note that this statement is needed only for programs that have GUI components such as input/output dialog boxes.

Example 3-12 shows a program that calculates the area and circumference of a circle and uses input/output dialog boxes.

Example 3-12 (Area and Circumference of a Circle)

The following program prompts the user to enter the radius of a circle. The program then outputs the circle's radius, area, and circumference.

```java
//Program to determine the area and circumference of a circle.

import javax.swing.JOptionPane;

public class AreaAndCircumferenceProgram
{
    public static final double PI = 3.14;                       //Line 1

    public static void main(String[] args)                      //Line 2
    {
        double radius;                                          //Line 3
        double area;                                            //Line 4
        double circumference;                                   //Line 5
        String radiusString;                                    //Line 6
        String outputStr;                                       //Line 7

        radiusString =
            JOptionPane.showInputDialog("Enter the radius: ");  //Line 8

        radius = Double.parseDouble(radiusString);              //Line 9

        area = PI * radius * radius;                            //Line 10
        circumference = 2 * PI * radius;                        //Line 11

        outputStr = "Radius: " + radius + "\n" +
                    "Area: " + area + " square units\n" +
                    "Circumference: " + circumference +
                    " units";                                   //Line 12

        JOptionPane.showMessageDialog(null, outputStr, "Circle",
                        JOptionPane.INFORMATION_MESSAGE);       //Line 13

        System.exit(0);                                         //Line 14
    }
}
```

Sample Run Figure 3–12 shows a sample run of this program. The input screen is shown first, then the output screen.

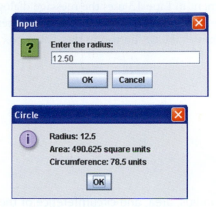

Figure 3-12   Sample run of the program to calculate a circle's area and circumference

The preceding program works as follows. The statement in Line 1 declares and initializes the named constant **PI** to **3.14**. The statements in Lines 3 through 7 declare the appropriate variables to manipulate the data.

The statement in Line 8 displays the input dialog box with the message **Enter the radius:** (in Figure 3–13, the entered value is 12.50).

Figure 3-13   Input dialog box to enter the radius

The string containing the input data is assigned to the **String** variable **radiusString**. The statement in Line 9 converts the string containing the radius into a value of the type **double** and stores it in the variable **radius**.

The statements in Lines 10 and 11 calculate the area and circumference of the circle and store them in the variables `area` and `circumference`, respectively. The statement in Line 12 constructs the string containing the radius, area, and circumference of the circle. The string is assigned to the variable `outputStr`. The statement in Line 13 uses the message dialog box to display the circle's radius, area, and circumference, as shown in Figure 3-14. The statement in Line 14 terminates the program after the user presses the OK button in the dialog box.

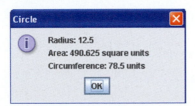

Figure 3-14   Output dialog box showing the radius, area, and circumference of the circle

  If the amount of input data is small and the output is small, dialog boxes are an effective and attractive way to build your application.

Formatting the Output Using the `String` Method `format`

Earlier in this chapter, you learned how to format the output on the standard output device using the stream method `printf`. However, the method `printf` cannot be used with output dialog boxes. So the obvious question is: How do we format the output in an output dialog box, particularly decimal numbers? This can be done two ways. One way is to use the `String` method `format`; the other is to use the **class** `DecimalFormat`. Next, we describe how to use the `String` method `format`. Appendix D describes the **class** `DecimalFormat`.

An expression to use the `String` method `format` is:

`String.format(formatString, argumentList)`

where the meaning of the parameters `formatString` and `argumentList` is the same as with the method `printf`. The value of the expression is a formatted string. The following example shows how the method `format` works.

Example 3-13

Suppose we have the following declarations and initializations:

```
double x = 15.674;
double y = 235.73;
double z = 9525.9864;
int num = 83;
String str;
```

Expression	Value
String.format("%.2f", x)	"15.67"
String.format("%.3f", y)	"235.730"
String.format("%.2f", z)	"9525.99"
String.format("%7s", "Hello")	" Hello"
String.format("%5d%7.2f", num, x)	" 83 15.67"
String.format("The value of num = %5d", num)	"The value of num = 83"
str = String.format("%.2f", z)	str = "9525.99"

Because the value of the **String** method **format** is a string, the method **format** can also be used as an argument to the methods **print**, **println**, or **printf**. Example 3-14 illustrates this concept.

Example 3-14

```
public class StringMethodformat
{
    public static void main (String[] args)
    {
        double x = 15.674;
        double y = 235.73;
        double z = 9525.9864;
        int num = 83;
        String str;

        System.out.println("123456789012345678901234567890");
        System.out.println(String.format("%.2f", x));
        System.out.println(String.format("%.3f", y));
        System.out.println(String.format("%.2f", z));

        System.out.println(String.format("%7s", "Hello"));
        System.out.println(String.format("%5d%7.2f", num, x));
```

```
        System.out.println(String.format("The value of num = %5d", num));

        str = String.format("%.2f", z);

        System.out.println(str);
    }
}
```

Sample Run:
```
12345678901234567890123456789 0
15.67
235.730
9525.99
  Hello
   83  15.67
The value of num =       83
9525.99
```

The preceding sample run is self-explanatory. The details are left as an exercise for you.

The following example illustrates how the **String** method **format** can be used to format the output in an output dialog box.

Example 3-15

```
import javax.swing.JOptionPane;

public class Example3_15
{
    public static void main(String[] args)
    {
        double x = 15.674;
        double y = 235.73;
        double z = 9525.9864;
        String str;

        str = String.format("The value of x with two decimal places = %.2f%n", x)
            + String.format("The value of y with two decimal places = %.2f%n", y)
            + String.format("The value of z with two decimal places = %.2f%n", z);

        JOptionPane.showMessageDialog(null, str,
                        "Formatting with the String Method format",
                        JOptionPane.INFORMATION_MESSAGE);

        System.exit(0);
    }
}
```

Sample Run:

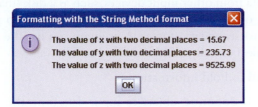

Figure 3-15   Output dialog box showing the values of x, y, and z with two decimal places

Note that in the preceding program, first we constructed `str` using the `String` method `format` and then used `str` in the output dialog box. However, you could have used the `String` method `format` directly in the output dialog box. That is, you can replace the statement:

```
JOptionPane.showMessageDialog(null, str,
                    "Formatting with the String Method format",
                    JOptionPane.INFORMATION_MESSAGE);
```

with the following statement:

```
JOptionPane.showMessageDialog(null,
        String.format("The value of x with two decimal places = %.2f%n", x)
        + String.format("The value of y with two decimal places = %.2f%n", y)
        + String.format("The value of z with two decimal places = %.2f%n", z),
        "Formatting with the String Method format",
        JOptionPane.INFORMATION_MESSAGE);
```

FILE INPUT/OUTPUT

The previous sections discussed in some detail how to get input from the keyboard (standard input device) and send output to the screen (standard output device). However, getting input from the keyboard and sending output to the screen has limitations. If the amount of input data is large, it is inefficient to type it at the keyboard each time you run a program. In addition to the inconvenience of typing large amounts of data, typing can generate errors, and unintentional typos cause erroneous results. Sending output to the screen works well if the amount of data is small (no larger than the size of the screen), but suppose you want to distribute the output in a printed format? The solution to these problems is to use an alternate form of input and output: files. By using a file as a source of input data, you can prepare the data before running a program, and the program can access the data each time it runs. Saving output to a file allows the output to be saved and distributed to others, and the output produced by one program can be used as input to other programs.

This section discusses how to obtain data from other input devices, such as a disk (that is, secondary storage), and how to save the output to a disk. Java allows a program to get data directly from, and save output directly to, secondary storage. A program can use the file I/O and read data from or write data to a file. Formally, a **file** is defined as follows:

File: An area in secondary storage used to hold information.

In Chapter 2, you learned how to use a `Scanner` object to input data from the standard input device. Recall that the following statement creates the `Scanner` object `console` and initializes it to the standard input device:

```
Scanner console = new Scanner(System.in);
```

You can also initialize a `Scanner` object to input sources other than the standard input device by passing an appropriate argument in place of the object `System.in`. To do this, we use the **class** `FileReader` as follows. Suppose that the input data is stored in a file, say `prog.dat`, and this file is on floppy disk `A`. The following statement creates the `Scanner` object `inFile` and initializes it to the file `prog.dat`:

```
Scanner inFile = new Scanner(new FileReader("a:\\prog.dat")); //Line 1
```

Next, you use the object `inFile` to input the data from the file `prog.dat`, just the way you used the object `console` to input the data from the standard input device using the methods `next`, `nextInt`, `nextDouble`, and so on.

Notice that there are two \ after `a:` in Line 1. Recall from Chapter 2 that in Java \ is the escape character. Therefore, to produce a \ within a string you need \\. (Moreover, to be absolutely sure about specifying the source, such as the floppy disk `a:\\`, where the input file is stored, check your system's documentation.)

If your Java program and the input file reside in the same directory, then you do not need to include a:\\ before the filename in statements such as in Line 1.

To send the output to a file, you use the **class**es `PrintWriter` and `FileWriter`. These classes are both contained in the **package** `java.io`.

To summarize, Java file I/O is a four-step process:

1. Import the necessary classes from the **package**s `java.util` and `java.io` into the program.

2. Create and associate the appropriate objects with the input/output sources.

3. Use the appropriate methods associated with the variables created in Step 2 to input/output the data.

4. Close the files.

We now describe these four steps and then provide a skeleton program that shows how the steps might appear in a program.

Step 1 requires that the necessary classes be imported from the **package**s java.util and java.io. The following statements accomplish this task:

```
import java.util.*;
import java.io.*;
```

Step 2 requires that you create and associate appropriate **class** variables with the input/output sources. We already discussed how to declare and associate **Scanner** objects for inputting the data from a file. The next section describes how to create the appropriate objects to send the output to a file.

Step 3 requires us to read the data from the input file using the variables created in Step 2. Example 3-16 describes how to the read data from a file.

In Step 4, you close the input and output files. To do so, you use the method **close** as described later in this section.

Example 3-16

Suppose an input file, say employeeData.txt, consists of the following data:

```
Emily Johnson 45 13.50
```

The file consists of an employee's name, the number of hours the employee worked, and the pay rate. (Assume that the file is stored on floppy disk A.) The following statements declare the appropriate variables to read and store the data into the variables:

```
    //Create and associate the Scanner object with the input source.
Scanner inFile = new Scanner(new FileReader("a:\\employeeData.txt"));

String firstName;    //variable to store the first name
String lastName;     //variable to store the last name

double hoursWorked;  //variable to store the hours worked
double payRate;      //variable to store the pay rate
double wages;        //variable to store the wages

firstName = inFile.next();   //get the first name
lastName = inFile.next();    //get the last name

hoursWorked = inFile.nextDouble(); //get the hours worked
payRate = inFile.nextDouble();     //get the pay rate

wages = hoursWorked * payRate;
```

The following statement closes the input file to which inFile is associated:

```
inFile.close();   //close the input file
```

Storing (Writing) Output to a File

To store the output of a program in a file, you use the **class** `PrintWriter`. You declare a `PrintWriter` variable and associate this variable with the destination, that is, the file where the output will be stored. Suppose the output is to be stored in the file `prog.out` on floppy disk `A`. Consider the following statement:

```
PrintWriter outFile = new PrintWriter("a:\\prog.out");
```

This statement creates the `PrintWriter` object `outFile` and associates it with the file `prog.out` on floppy disk `A`.

You can now use the methods `print`, `println`, `printf`, and `flush` with `outFile` just the same way they have been used with the object `System.out`.

For example, the statement:

```
outFile.println("The paycheck is: $" + pay);
```

stores the output—The paycheck is: $565.78—in the file `prog.out`. This statement assumes that the value of the variable `pay` is `565.78`.

Once the output is completed, Step 4 requires closing the file. You close the input and output files by using the method `close`. For example, assuming that `inFile` and `outFile` are as declared before, the statements to close these files are:

```
inFile.close();
outFile.close();
```

Closing the output file ensures that the buffer holding the output will be emptied, that is, the entire output generated by the program will be sent to the output file.

Step 3 requires that you create appropriate objects for file I/O. In the case of an input file, the file must exist before the program executes. If the input file does not exist, then the statement to associate the object with the input file fails and it **throws** a `FileNotFoundException` exception. At this time, we will not require the program to handle this exception, so the method **main** will also throw this exception. Therefore, the heading of the method **main** will contain an appropriate command to throw a `FileNotFoundException`.

An output file does not have to exist before it is opened; if the output file does not exist, the computer prepares an empty file for output. *If the designated output file already exists, by default the old contents are erased when the file is opened.* Note that if the program is not able to create or access the output file, it throws a `FileNotFoundException`.

(`throws` **clause**) During program execution, various things can happen; for example, division by zero or inputting a letter for a number. If such things happen, the system would not tolerate it. In such cases, we say that an exception has occurred. If an exception occurs in a method, then the method should either handle the exception or *throw* it for the calling environment to handle. If an input file does not exist, the program throws a `FileNotFoundException`. Similarly, if an output file cannot be created or accessed, the program throws a `FileNotFoundException`. For the next few chapters, we will not be concerned with the handling of the exceptions; we will simply throw the exceptions. Because we do not need the method **main** to handle the `FileNotFoundException` exception, we will include a command in the heading of the method **main** to throw the `FileNotFoundException` exception. Chapter 12 describes exception handling.

In skeleton form, a program that uses file I/O is usually of the following form:

```java
import java.io.*;
import java.util.*;

//Add additional packages as needed.

public class ClassName
{
    //Declare the appropriate variables.
    public static void main(String[] args)
                        throws FileNotFoundException
    {
        //Create and associate the stream objects.
        Scanner inFile =
            new Scanner(new FileReader("a:\\prog.dat"));

        PrintWriter outFile = new PrintWriter("a:\\prog.out");

        //code for data manipulation


        //Close the file.
        inFile.close();
        outFile.close();
    }
}
```

The remainder of this chapter gives two programming examples—one illustrates dialog boxes for input/output; the other illustrates file input/output.

PROGRAMMING EXAMPLE: MOVIE TICKET SALE AND DONATION TO CHARITY

A movie in a local theater is in great demand. The theater owner has decided to donate to a local charity a portion of the gross amount generated from the movie. This example designs and implements a program that prompts the user to input the movie name, adult ticket price, child ticket price, number of adult tickets sold, number of child tickets sold, and percentage of the gross amount to be donated to the charity. The output of the program is shown in Figure 3-16.

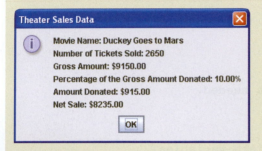

Figure 3-16   Output of the movie ticket sales program

Note that the decimal numbers are output with two decimal places.

Input   The input to the program consists of the movie name, adult ticket price, child ticket price, number of adult tickets sold, number of child tickets sold, and percentage of the gross amount to be donated to the charity.

Output   The output is as shown in Figure 3-16.

Problem Analysis and Algorithm Design

To calculate the amount donated to the local charity and the net sale, you first need to determine the gross amount. To calculate the gross amount, you multiply the number of adult tickets sold by the price of an adult ticket, multiply the number of child tickets sold by the price of a child ticket, and then add these two numbers:

```
grossAmount = adultTicketPrice * noOfAdultTicketsSold
            + childTicketPrice * noOfChildTicketsSold;
```

Next, you determine the percentage of the amount donated to the charity, and then calculate the net sale amount by subtracting the amount donated from the gross amount. The formulas to calculate the amount donated and the net sale amount are given below. This analysis leads to the following algorithm:

1. Get the movie name.
2. Get the price of an adult ticket.
3. Get the price of a child ticket.
4. Get the number of adult tickets sold.
5. Get the number of child tickets sold.
6. Get the percentage of the gross amount donated to the charity.
7. Calculate the gross amount using the following formula:

```
grossAmount = adultTicketPrice * noOfAdultTicketsSold
            + childTicketPrice * noOfChildTicketsSold;
```

8. Calculate the amount donated to the charity using the following formula:

```
amountDonated = grossAmount * percentDonation / 100;
```

9. Calculate the net sale amount using the following formula:

```
netSaleAmount = grossAmount - amountDonated;
```

Variables

From the preceding discussion, it follows that you need variables to store the movie name, adult ticket price, child ticket price, number of adult tickets sold, number of child tickets sold, percentage of the gross amount donated to the charity, gross amount, amount donated, and net sale amount. You also need a variable to get the string containing the sales data and a string to format the output. Therefore, the following variables are needed:

```
String  movieName;
String  inputStr;
String  outputStr;
double  adultTicketPrice;
double  childTicketPrice;
int     noOfAdultTicketsSold;
int     noOfChildTicketsSold;
double  percentDonation;
double  grossAmount;
double  amountDonated;
double  netSaleAmount;
```

Formatting the Output

To show the desired output, you first create the string consisting of the strings and the values required. The following string accomplishes this:

```
outputStr = "Movie Name: " + movieName + "\n"
          + "Number of Tickets Sold: "
          + (noOfAdultTicketsSold +
             noOfChildTicketsSold) + "\n"
          + "Gross Amount: $"
          + String.format("%.2f", grossAmount) + "\n"
          + "Percentage of the Gross Amount Donated: "
          + String.format("%.2f%%", percentDonation) + "\n"
          + "Amount Donated: $"
          + String.format("%.2f", amountDonated) + "\n"
          + "Net Sale: $"
          + String.format("%.2f", netSaleAmount);
```

Notice that we have used the method `format` of the **class** `String` to output decimal numbers to two decimal places.

Main Algorithm

In the preceding sections, we analyzed the problem and determined the formulas to do the calculations. We also determined the necessary variables and the output string. We can now expand the algorithm given in the section Problem Analysis and Algorithm Design to solve the problem given at the beginning of this programming example.

1. Declare the variables.
2. Display the input dialog box to enter a movie name and retrieve the movie name.
3. Display the input dialog box to enter the price of an adult ticket.
4. Retrieve the price of an adult ticket.
5. Display the input dialog box to enter the price of a child ticket.
6. Retrieve the price of a child ticket.
7. Display the input dialog box to enter the number of adult tickets sold.
8. Retrieve the number of adult tickets sold.
9. Display the input dialog box to enter the number of child tickets sold.
10. Retrieve the number of child tickets sold.
11. Display the input dialog box to enter the percentage of the gross amount donated.
12. Retrieve the percentage of the gross amount donated.
13. Calculate the gross amount.
14. Calculate the amount donated.
15. Calculate the net sale amount.
16. Format the output string.
17. Display the message dialog box to show the output.
18. Terminate the program.

Complete Program Listing

```java
//Program: Movie Ticket Sale and Donation to Charity.

import javax.swing.JOptionPane;

public class MovieTicketSale
{
    public static void main(String[] args)
    {
            //Step 1
        String movieName;
        String inputStr;
        String outputStr;
        double adultTicketPrice;
        double childTicketPrice;
        int noOfAdultTicketsSold;
        int noOfChildTicketsSold;
        double percentDonation;
        double grossAmount;
        double amountDonated;
        double netSaleAmount;

        movieName = JOptionPane.showInputDialog
                    ("Enter the movie name");                   //Step 2

        inputStr = JOptionPane.showInputDialog
                    ("Enter the price of an adult ticket");   //Step 3
        adultTicketPrice = Double.parseDouble(inputStr);      //Step 4

        inputStr = JOptionPane.showInputDialog
                    ("Enter the price of a child ticket");    //Step 5
        childTicketPrice = Double.parseDouble(inputStr);      //Step 6

        inputStr = JOptionPane.showInputDialog
                ("Enter the number of adult tickets sold"); //Step 7
        noOfAdultTicketsSold = Integer.parseInt(inputStr);    //Step 8

        inputStr = JOptionPane.showInputDialog
                ("Enter the number of child tickets sold"); //Step 9
        noOfChildTicketsSold = Integer.parseInt(inputStr);    //Step 10

        inputStr = JOptionPane.showInputDialog
                ("Enter the percentage of the donation");   //Step 11
        percentDonation = Double.parseDouble(inputStr);       //Step 12

        grossAmount = adultTicketPrice * noOfAdultTicketsSold +
                childTicketPrice * noOfChildTicketsSold;    //Step 13
```

```
       amountDonated = grossAmount * percentDonation / 100; //Step 14
       netSaleAmount = grossAmount - amountDonated;          //Step 15


     outputStr = "Movie Name: " + movieName + "\n"
               + "Number of Tickets Sold: "
               + (noOfAdultTicketsSold +
                 noOfChildTicketsSold) + "\n"
               + "Gross Amount: $"
               + String.format("%.2f", grossAmount) + "\n"
               + "Percentage of the Gross Amount Donated: "
               + String.format("%.2f%%", percentDonation) + "\n"
               + "Amount Donated: $"
               + String.format("%.2f", amountDonated) + "\n"
               + "Net Sale: $"
               + String.format("%.2f", netSaleAmount);    //Step 16

     JOptionPane.showMessageDialog(null, outputStr,
                    "Theater Sales Data",
                    JOptionPane.INFORMATION_MESSAGE); //Step 17
     System.exit(0);                                       //Step 18
  }
}
```

Sample Run   In this sample run, the user input is in the input dialog boxes.

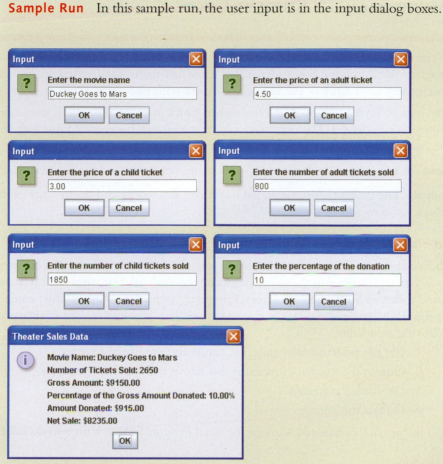

Figure 3-17   Sample run of the movie sales program

In this output, the first six dialog boxes (from left to right) get the necessary data to generate the Theater Sales Data dialog box.

Programming Example: Student Grade

Write a program that reads a student's first and last name followed by five test scores. The program should output the student's first name, last name, the five test scores, and the average test score. Output the average test score with two decimal places.

The data to be read is stored in a file named `test.txt`, and the file is stored on a floppy disk in drive A. The output should be stored in a file named `testavg.out`, and the output file should be stored on the floppy disk in drive A.

Input   A file containing the student's first name, last name, and the five test scores

Output   The student's first name, last name, five test scores, and the average of the five test scores, saved to a file

Problem Analysis and Algorithm Design

To find the average of the five test scores, you add the five test scores and divide the sum by 5. The input data is in the following form: the student's first name, followed by the last name, followed by the five test scores. Therefore, we read the student's first name, followed by the last name, followed by the five test scores. This problem analysis translates into the following algorithm:

1. Get the student's first name, last name, and the five test scores.
2. Output the student's first name, last name, and the five test scores.
3. Calculate the average.
4. Output the average.

You output the average test score in the fixed decimal format with two decimal places.

Variables

The program needs to read a student's first name, last name, and five test scores. Therefore, you need two variables to store the student's first name and last name, and five variables to store the five test scores. To find the average, you must add the five test scores and then divide the sum by 5. Thus, you also need a variable to store the average test score. Furthermore, because the input data is in a file and the output is to be stored in a file, you must declare and initialize the appropriate variables. The program needs at least the following variables:

```
double test1, test2, test3, test4, test5; //variables to
                              //store the five test scores
double average;      //variable to store the average test score
String firstName;    //variable to store the first name
String lastName;     //variable to store the last name
```

```
Scanner inFile = new Scanner(new FileReader("a:\\test.txt"));

PrintWriter outFile = new PrintWriter("a:\\testavg.out");
```

Main Algorithm

In the preceding sections, we analyzed the problem and determined the formulas to perform the calculations. We also determined the necessary variables. Now we can expand the algorithm given in the Problem Analysis and Algorithm Design section to solve the Student Grade problem given at the beginning of this programming example.

1. Declare the variables.
2. Create a `Scanner` object and associate it with the input source.
3. Create a `PrintWriter` object and associate it with the output source.
4. Get the student's first name and last name.
5. Output the student's first name and last name.
6. Read the five test scores.
7. Output the five test scores.
8. Find the average test score.
9. Output the average test score.
10. Close the files.

This program reads the data from a file and outputs the data to a file, so it must import the necessary classes from the **package**s `java.io` and `java.util`.

Complete Program Listing

```java
//Program to calculate the average test score.

import java.io.*;
import java.util.*;

public class StudentGrade
{
    public static void main(String[] args) throws
                                        FileNotFoundException
    {

        //declare and initialize the variables          //Step 1
        double test1, test2, test3, test4, test5;
        double average;
        String firstName;
        String lastName;
```

```
            Scanner inFile =
               new Scanner(new FileReader("a:\\test.txt"));        //Step 2

            PrintWriter outFile = new
                         PrintWriter("a:\\testavg.out");           //Step 3

            firstName = inFile.next();                             //Step 4
            lastName = inFile.next();                              //Step 4

            outFile.println("Student Name: "
                         + firstName + " " + lastName);            //Step 5

               //Step 6 - retrieve the five test scores
            test1 = inFile.nextDouble();
            test2 = inFile.nextDouble();
            test3 = inFile.nextDouble();
            test4 = inFile.nextDouble();
            test5 = inFile.nextDouble();


            outFile.printf("Test scores: %5.2f %5.2f %5.2f "
                         + "%5.2f %5.2f %n", test1, test2,
                           test3, test4, test5);                   //Step 7

            average = (test1 + test2 + test3 + test4
                     + test5) / 5.0;                               //Step 8
            outFile.printf("Average test score: %5.2f %n",
                           average);                               //Step 9

            inFile.close();                                        //Step 10
            outFile.close();                                       //Step 10
      }
}
```

Sample Run

Input File (contents of the file `test.txt`):

Don Johnson 87.5 89.00 65 37.5 98.0

Output File (contents of the file `testavg.out`) :

```
Student Name: Don Johnson
Test scores: 87.50 89.00 65.00 37.50 98.00
Average test score: 75.40
```

The preceding program uses five variables—**test1**, **test2**, **test3**, **test4**, and **test5**—to read the five test scores and then find the average test score. The Web site accompanying this book contains a modified version of this program that uses only one variable, **testscore**, to read the test scores and another variable, **sum**, to find the sum of the test scores. The program is named **StudentGradeVersion2.java**.

QUICK REVIEW

1. A reference variable is a variable that stores the address of a memory space.

2. In Java, all variables declared using a **class** are reference variables.

3. A reference variable does not directly store data in its memory space. It stores the address of the memory space where the actual data is stored.

4. Class objects are instances of that **class**.

5. Using the operator **new** to create a **class** object is called an instantiation of that **class**.

6. To use a predefined method in a program, you must know the name of the **class** containing the method, the name of the **package** containing the **class**, and import the **package** into the program. In addition, you need to know the name of the method, the number of parameters the method takes, and the type of each parameter. You must also be aware of what the return type of the method is or, loosely speaking, what the method does.

7. In Java, the dot (.) is called the member access operator. The dot separates the **class** name from the member, or method, name. Dot notation is also used when a reference variable of a **class** type accesses a certain member of that **class**.

8. The **class** String is used to manipulate strings.

9. The assignment operator is defined for the **class** String and it works the same way as the operator **new**.

10. The method **substring** of the **class** String returns a substring from another string.

11. The **class** String contains many other useful methods such as: **charAt**, **indexOf**, **concat**, **length**, **replace**, **toLowerCase**, and **toUpperCase**.

12. You can use the method **printf** to format the output in a specific manner.

13. A format specifier for general, character, and numeric types has the following syntax:

    `%[argument_index$][flags][width][.precision]conversion`

    The expressions in square brackets are optional. The required **conversion** is a character indicating how the argument should be formatted.

14. The method **printf** is available in JDK 5.0 and its higher versions.

15. In a format specifier, using the option `width` you can also specify the number of columns to be used to output the value of an expression. The (*default*) output is right justified.

16. In a format specifier, if the number of columns in the option `width` is less than the number of columns required to output the value of the expression, the output is expanded to the required number of columns. That is, the output is not truncated.

17. To force the output to be *left* justified, you use the format specifier flag. If the flag is set to `'-'`, then the output of the result is left justified.

18. A numeric string consists of an integer or a decimal number.

19. To convert a numeric integer string into an integer, you use the expression:

    `Integer.parseInt(strExpression)`

    where `strExpression` is an expression containing a numeric integer string.

20. To convert a numeric decimal string into a **double** value, you use the expression:

    `Double.parseDouble(strExpression)`

    where `strExpression` is an expression containing a numeric string.

21. The method `showInputDialog` of the **class** `JOptionPane` is used to create an input dialog box.

22. The method `showMessageDialog` of the **class** `JOptionPane` is used to create an output message dialog box.

23. The **class** `JOptionPane` is contained in the **package** `javax.swing`.

24. If a program uses input and output dialog boxes, it must also use the statement `System.exit(0)`.

25. To format a floating-point number to a specific number of decimal places, you can use the `String` method `format`.

26. To input data from a file, you use the **class**es `Scanner` and `FileReader`; to send output to a file, you use the **class**es `FileWriter` and `PrintWriter`.

27. File I/O is a four-step process: (i) import the necessary classes from the **package**s `java.util` and `java.io` into the program; (ii) create and associate the appropriate objects with the input/output sources; (iii) use the appropriate methods associated with the objects created in (ii) to input/output the data; and (iv) close the files.

EXERCISES

1. Mark the following statements as true or false.

   a. A variable declared using a **class** is called an object.

   b. In the statement **x = console.nextInt();**, x must be a variable.

   c. You generate the newline character by pressing the Enter (return) key on the keyboard.

   d. To format a decimal number to a specific number of decimal places, you use the methods **printf** and **format**.

2. How does a variable of a primitive type differ from a reference variable?

3. What is an object?

4. What does the operator **new** do?

5. Suppose that **str** is a **String** variable. Write a Java statement that uses the operator **new** to instantiate the object **str** and assign the string **"Java Programming"** to **str**.

6. Consider the following statements:

```
String str = "Going to the amusement park.";
char ch;
int len;
int position;
```

   a. What value is stored in **ch** by the following statement?

   ```
   ch = str.charAt(0);
   ```

   b. What value is stored in **ch** by the following statement?

   ```
   ch = str.charAt(10);
   ```

   c. What value is stored in **len** by the following statement?

   ```
   len = str.length();
   ```

   d. What value is stored in **position** by the following statement?

   ```
   position = str.indexOf('t');
   ```

   e. What value is stored in **position** by the following statement?

   ```
   position = str.indexOf("park");
   ```

7. Assume the declaration in Exercise 6. What is the output of the following statements?

   a. `System.out.println(str.substring(0, 5));`

   b. `System.out.println(str.substring(13, 22));`

   c. `System.out.println(str.toUpperCase());`

   d. `System.out.println(str.toLowerCase());`

   e. `System.out.println(str.replace('t', '*'));`

8. a. What method is used to create an input dialog box?

   b. What method is used to create an output dialog box?

   c. What is the name of the **class** that contains the methods to create the input and output dialog boxes?

   d. What is the name of the **package** that contains the **class** described in c?

9. What does the following statement do? (Assume that **scoreStr** is a **String** variable.)

   ```
   scoreStr = JOptionPane.showInputDialog("Enter the score:");
   ```

10. Write a Java statement that creates the output dialog box in Figure 3-18.

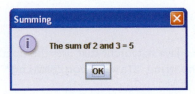

Figure 3-18   Figure for Exercise 10, Chapter 3

11. Write a Java statement that creates the output dialog box in Figure 3-19.

Figure 3-19   Figure for Exercise 11, Chapter 3

12. Consider the following statements:

    ```
    double x = 75.3987;
    double y = 982.89764;
    ```

    What is the output of the following statements?

    a. `System.out.printf("%.2f %n", x);`

    b. `System.out.printf("%.2f %n", y);`

    c. `System.out.printf("%.3f %n", x);`

    d. `System.out.printf("%.3f %n", y);`

13. Consider the statements:

```
int x, y;
char ch;
```

and the input:
```
46 A 49
```

Write Java statements that store **46** in **x**, **A** in **ch**, and **49** in **y**. (Assume that **console** is a **Scanner** object initialized to the input source.)

14. The following program is supposed to read two numbers from a file named **Ex14Input.txt**, and write the sum of the numbers to a file named **Ex14Output.dat**. However, it fails to do so. Rewrite the program so that it performs correctly. (You may assume that the input and output files are on floppy disk **A**.)

```
import java.util.*;

public class Ch3Ex14
{
    public static void main(String[] args)
    {
        Scanner inFile =
            new Scanner(new FileReader("a:\\Ex14Input.txt"));

        int num1, num2;

        num1 = inFile.nextInt();
        num2 = inFile.nextInt();
        outFile.println("Sum = " + (num1 + num2));

        outFile.close();
    }
}
```

15. A program reads data from a file called **inputFile.dat** and, after doing some calculations, writes the results to a file called **outFile.dat**. Answer the following questions:

a. After the program executes, what are the contents of the file **inputFile.dat**?

b. After the program executes, what are the contents of the file **outFile.dat** if this file was empty before the program executed?

c. After the program executes, what are the contents of the file **outFile.dat** if this file contained **100** numbers before the program executed?

d. What would happen if the file **outFile.dat** did not exist before the program executed?

PROGRAMMING EXERCISES

1. Consider the following incomplete Java program:

```java
public class Ch3_PrExercise1
{
    public static void main(String[] args)
    {
        ...
    }
}
```

a. Write Java statements that import the **class**es Scanner, FileReader, Print-Writer, and FileWriter from the **package**s java.util and java.io.

b. Write statements that declare inFile to be a reference variable of the type Scanner and outFile to be a reference variable of the type PrintWriter.

c. The program will read the data from the file inData.txt and write the output to the file outData.dat. Write statements to open both these files, associating inFile with inData.txt, and associating outFile with outData.dat.

d. Suppose that the file inData.txt contains the following data:

```
56 38
A
7 8
```

Write statements so that after the program executes, the contents of the file outData.dat are as shown below. If necessary, declare additional variables. Your statements should be general enough so that if the content of the input file changes and the program is run again (without editing and recompiling), it outputs the appropriate results.

```
The sum of 56 and 38 = 94.
The character that comes after A in the Unicode set is B.
The product of 7 and 8 = 56.
```

e. Write the statement that closes the output file.

f. Write a Java program that tests the Java statements you wrote in parts a through e.

2. Write a program that prompts the user to enter a decimal number and then outputs this number rounded to two decimal places.

3. The manager of a football stadium wants you to write a program that calculates the total ticket sales after each game. There are four types of tickets—box, sideline, premium, and general admission. After each game, the data is stored in a file in the following form:

```
ticketPrice    numberOfTicketsSold
...
```

Sample data are shown below:

```
250 5750
100 28000
50 35750
25 18750
```

The first line indicates that the box ticket price is $250 and that 5750 tickets were sold at that price. Output the number of tickets sold and the total sale amount. Format your output with two decimal places.

4. Write a program to calculate the property tax. Property tax is calculated on 92% of the assessed value of the property. For example, if the assessed value is $100000, the property tax is on $92000. Assume that the property tax rate is $1.05 for each $100 of the assessed value. Your program should prompt the user to enter the assessed value of the property. Store the output in a file in the following sample format:

```
Assessed Value:                   $ 100000.00
Taxable Amount:                   $  92000.00
Tax Rate for each $100.00:  $       1.05
Property Tax:                     $     966.00
```

Format your output to two decimal places.

5. Write a program that converts a temperature from degrees Fahrenheit to degrees Celsius. The formula for converting the temperature from degrees Fahrenheit to degrees Celsius is:

```
C = (5/9) (F - 32)
```

Your program should prompt the user to enter a temperature given in degrees Fahrenheit. The program should then output the temperature in both degrees Fahrenheit and degrees Celsius. Format your output to two decimal places.

6. Write a program that calculates and prints the monthly paycheck for an employee. The net pay is calculated after taking the following deductions:

Federal Income Tax:	15%
State Tax:	3.5%
Social Security Tax:	5.75%
Medicare/Medicaid Tax:	2.75%
Pension Plan:	5%
Health Insurance:	$75.00

Your program should prompt the user to input the employee name and the gross amount. The output will be stored in a file. Format your output to two decimal places. A sample output follows:

```
Allison Nields
Gross Amount:            $ 3575.00
Federal Tax:             $  536.25
State Tax:               $  125.13
Social Security Tax:     $  205.56
Medicare/Medicaid Tax: $   98.31
Pension Plan:            $  178.75
Health Insurance:        $   75.00
Net Pay:                 $ 2356.00
```

4

CONTROL STRUCTURES I

Selection

> **In this chapter, you will:**
>
> ♦ Learn about control structures
> ♦ Examine relational and logical operators
> ♦ Explore how to form and evaluate logical (Boolean) expressions
> ♦ Learn how to use the selection control structures `if`, `if...else`, and `switch` in a program

Chapter 2 defined a program as a sequence of statements whose objective is to accomplish some task. The programs you have examined so far have been simple and straightforward. In executing programs, the computer starts at the first executable statement and executes the statements in order until it comes to the end. In this chapter and in Chapter 5, you will learn how to tell a computer that it does not have to follow a simple sequential order of statements; it can also make decisions and/or repeat certain statements over and over until certain conditions are met.

CONTROL STRUCTURES

A computer can process a program in one of three ways: in **sequence**; by making a selection or a choice, which is also called a **branch**; or by repetition, executing a statement over and over using a structure called a **loop**. These three kinds of program flow are shown in Figure 4-1. The programming examples in Chapters 2 and 3 include simple sequential programs. With such a program, the computer starts at the beginning and follows the statements in order. No choices are made; there is no repetition. Control structures provide alternatives to sequential program execution and are used to alter the flow of execution. The two most common control structures are selection and repetition. In **selection**, the program executes particular statements depending on some condition(s). In **repetition**, the program repeats particular statements a certain number of times depending on some condition(s). This chapter introduces selection (branching), and Chapter 5 introduces repetition (looping).

Branch: Altering the flow of program execution by making a selection or choice.

Loop: Altering the flow of program execution by the repetition of statement(s).

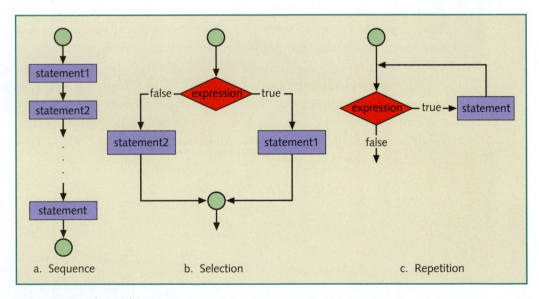

Figure 4-1 Flow of execution

Before you can learn about selection and repetition, you must understand the nature of conditional statements and how to use them. Consider the following three statements (notice that these are not Java statements):

```
1. if (score is greater than or equal to 90)
      grade is A
```

2. **if** (hours worked are less than or equal to 40)
    wages = rate * hours
  otherwise
    wages = (rate * 40) + 1.5 * (rate * (hours - 40))

3. **if** (temperature is greater than 50 degrees and it is not raining)
    recommended activity is golfing

These statements are examples of conditional statements. You can see that these statements are to be executed only if certain conditions are met. A condition is met if it evaluates to **true**. For example, in statement 1,

score is greater than or equal to 90

is **true** if the value of score is greater than or equal to 90; it is **false** otherwise. For example, if the value of score is 95, the statement evaluates to **true**. Similarly, if the value of score is 86, the statement evaluates to **false**.

It would be useful if the computer could recognize these types of statements to be **true** for appropriate values. Furthermore, in certain situations, the truth or falsity of a statement could depend on more than one condition. For example, in statement 3, both temperature is greater than 50 degrees and it is not raining must be **true** for the recommended activity to be golfing.

As you can see from these examples, to make decisions, the computer must be able to react to conditions that exist when the program executes. The next few sections discuss how to represent and evaluate conditional statements in Java.

RELATIONAL OPERATORS

To make decisions, you must be able to express conditions and make comparisons. For example, the interest rate and service charges on a checking account might depend on the balance at the end of the month. If the balance is less than some minimum balance, not only is the interest rate lower, but there is also usually a service charge. Therefore, to determine the interest rate, you must be able to state the minimum balance (a condition) and compare the account balance with the minimum balance. The premium on an insurance policy is also determined by stating conditions and making comparisons. For example, to determine an insurance premium, you must be able to check the smoking status of the policyholder. Nonsmokers (the condition) receive lower premiums than smokers. Both of these examples involve comparing items. Certain items are compared for equality against a particular condition; others are compared for inequality—greater than or less than—against a particular condition.

An expression that has a value of either **true** or **false** is called a **logical (Boolean) expression**. The values **true** and **false** are called **logical (Boolean) values**. In Java, a condition is represented by a logical (Boolean) expression.

Logical (Boolean) expression: An expression that has a value of either **true** or **false**.

Suppose i and j are integers. Consider the expression:

i > j

If this expression is a logical expression, it will have the value **true** if the value of i is greater than the value of j; otherwise, it will have the value **false**. You can think of the symbol > as an operator that (in this case) takes integer operands and yields a logical value. Here, the symbol > is similar to the operators + and − that yield integer or real results. In fact, the symbol > is called a **relational operator** because the value of i > j is **true** only when the relationship "greater than" holds between i and j.

Relational operator: An operator that allows you to make comparisons in a program.

Java includes six relational operators that enable you to state conditions and make comparisons. Table 4-1 lists the relational operators.

Table 4-1 Relational Operators in Java

Operator	Description
==	equal to
!=	not equal to
<	less than
<=	less than or equal to
>	greater than
>=	greater than or equal to

 In Java, the symbol ==, which consists of two equal signs, is called the **equality operator**. Recall that the symbol = is called the assignment operator. Remember that the equality operator, ==, determines whether two expressions are equal, whereas the assignment operator, =, assigns the value of an expression to a variable.

Each of the relational operators is a binary operator; that is, it requires two operands. Because the result of a comparison is **true** or **false**, expressions using these operators evaluate to **true** or **false**.

RELATIONAL OPERATORS AND PRIMITIVE DATA TYPES

You can use the relational operators with integral and floating-point primitive data types. For example, the following expressions use both integers and floating-point numbers:

Expression	Meaning	Value
8 < 15	8 is less than 15	true
6 != 6	6 is not equal to 6	false
2.5 > 5.8	2.5 is greater than 5.8	false
5.9 <= 7.5	5.9 is less than or equal to 7.5	true

4

 It is important to remember that the comparison of floating-point numbers for equality may not behave as you would expect; see Example 4-1.

Example 4-1

Consider the following program:

```
public class FloatingPointNumbers
{
    public static void main(String[] args)
    {
        System.out.println("3.0 / 7.0 = " + (3.0 / 7.0));
        System.out.println("2.0 / 7.0 = " + (2.0 / 7.0));
        System.out.println("3.0 / 7.0 + 2.0 / 7.0 + 2.0 / 7.0 = "
                           + (3.0 / 7.0 + 2.0 / 7.0 + 2.0 / 7.0));
    }
}
```

Sample Run
```
3.0 / 7.0 = 0.42857142857142855
2.0 / 7.0 = 0.2857142857142857
3.0 / 7.0 + 2.0 / 7.0 + 2.0 / 7.0 = 0.9999999999999999
```

From the output, it follows that the following equality evaluates to **false**:

```
1.0 == 3.0 / 7.0 + 2.0 / 7.0 + 2.0 / 7.0
```

 The preceding program and its output show that you should be careful when comparing floating-point numbers for equality. One way to check whether two floating-point numbers are equal is to check whether the absolute value of their difference is less than a certain tolerance. For example, suppose x and y are floating-point numbers and the tolerance is 0.000001. Then x and y are equal if the absolute value of (x - y) is less than 0.000001. To find the absolute value you can use the method abs of the **class** Math. For example, the expression Math.abs(x - y) gives the absolute value of x - y. Therefore, the expression Math.abs(x - y) < 0.000001 determines whether the absolute value of (x - y) is less than 0.000001.

For **char** values, whether an expression, using relational operators, evaluates to **true** or **false** depends on the collating sequence of the Unicode character set. Table 4-2 shows how expressions using the Unicode character set are evaluated.

Table 4-2 Evaluating Expressions Using Relational Operators and the Unicode (ASCII) Collating Sequence

Expression	Value of the Expression	Explanation
`' ' < 'a'`	true	The Unicode value of `' '` is 32, and the Unicode value of `'a'` is 97. Because 32 < 97 is **true**, it follows that `' ' < 'a'` is **true**.
`'R' > 'T'`	false	The Unicode value of `'R'` is 82, and the Unicode value of `'T'` is 84. Because 82 > 84 is **false**, it follows that `'R' > 'T'` is **false**.
`'+' < '*'`	false	The Unicode value of `'+'` is 43, and the Unicode value of `'*'` is 42. Because 43 < 42 is **false**, it follows that `'+' < '*'` is **false**.
`'6' <= '>'`	true	The Unicode value of `'6'` is 54, and the Unicode value of `'>'` is 62. Because 54 <= 62 is **true**, it follows that `'6' <= '>'` is **true**.

Consider the following expression:

`8 < '5'`

You might think that 8 is being compared with 5. This is not the case. Here the integer 8 is being compared with the character 5. That is, 8 is being compared with the collating sequence of `'5'`, which is 53. The Java system uses implicit type conversion, changes `'5'` to 53, and compares 8 with 53. Therefore, the expression `8 < '5'` always evaluates to **true**. However, the expression `8 < 5` always evaluates to **false**.

Expressions such as 4 < 6 and `'R' > 'T'` are examples of logical (Boolean) expressions. When Java evaluates a logical expression, it returns the **boolean** value **true** if the logical expression evaluates to **true**; it returns the **boolean** value **false** otherwise.

COMPARING STRINGS

In Java, strings are compared character by character, starting with the first character and using the collating sequence. The character-by-character comparison continues until one of three conditions is met: a mismatch is found, the last characters have been compared and are equal, or one string is exhausted.

For example, the string `"Air"` is less than the string `"Big"` because the first character `'A'` of `"Air"` is less than the first character `'B'` of `"Big"`. The string `"Air"` is less than the string `"An"` because the first characters of `"Air"` and `"An"` are the same, but the second character `'i'` of `"Air"` is less than the second character `'n'` of `"An"`. Moreover, the string `"Hello"` is less than the string `"hello"` because the first character `'H'` of `"Hello"` is less than the first character `'h'` of `"hello"`.

If two strings of different lengths are compared and the character-by-character comparison is equal until it reaches the last character of the shorter string, the shorter string is evaluated as less than the larger string. For example, the string `"Bill"` is less than the string `"Billy"` and the string `"Sun"` is less than the string `"Sunny"`.

The **class** `String` provides the method `compareTo`, to compare objects of the **class** `String`. The syntax to use the method `compareTo` is:

> `str1.compareTo(str2)`

where `str1` and `str2` are `String` variables. Moreover, `str2` can also be a `String` constant. This expression returns an integer value as follows:

$$str1.compareTo(str2) = \begin{cases} \text{an integer value less than 0 if string } str1 \text{ is less than string } str2 \\ \text{0 if string } str1 \text{ is equal to string } str2 \\ \text{an integer value greater than 0 if string } str1 \text{ is greater than string } str2 \end{cases}$$

Consider the following statements:

```
String str1 = "Hello";
String str2 = "Hi";
String str3 = "Air";
String str4 = "Bill";
String str5 = "Bigger";
```

Using these variable declarations, Table 4–3 shows how the method `compareTo` works.

Table 4-3 Comparing Strings with the Method `compareTo`

Expression	Value	Explanation
`str1.compareTo(str2)`	< 0	`str1 = "Hello"` and `str2 = "Hi"`. The first character of `str1` and `str2` are the same, but the second character `'e'` of `str1` is less than the second character `'i'` of `str2`. Therefore, `str1.compareTo(str2)< 0`.
`str1.compareTo("Hen")`	< 0	`str1 = "Hello"`. The first two characters of `str1` and `"Hen"` are the same, but the third character `'l'` of `str1` is less than the third character `'n'` of `"Hen"`. Therefore, `str1.compareTo("Hen") < 0`.

Table 4-3 Comparing Strings with the Method `compareTo` (continued)

Expression	Value	Explanation
`str4.compareTo(str3)`	`> 0`	`str4 = "Bill"` and `str3 = "Air"`. The first character `'B'` of `str4` is greater than the first character `'A'` of `str3`. Therefore, `str4.compareTo(str3) > 0`.
`str1.compareTo("hello")`	`< 0`	`str1 = "Hello"`. The first character `'H'` of `str1` is less than the first character `'h'` of `"hello"` because the Unicode value of `'H'` is 72, and the Unicode value of `'h'` is 104. Therefore, `str1.compareTo("hello") < 0`.
`str2.compareTo("Hi")`	`= 0`	`str2 = "Hi"`. The strings `str2` and `"Hi"` are of the same length and their corresponding characters are the same. Therefore, `str2.compareTo("Hi") = 0`.
`str4.compareTo("Billy")`	`< 0`	`str4 = "Bill"` has four characters and `"Billy"` has five characters. Therefore, `str4` is the shorter string. All four characters of `str4` are the same as the corresponding first four characters of `"Billy"` and `"Billy"` is the larger string. Therefore, `str4.compareTo("Billy") < 0`.
`str5.compareTo("Big")`	`> 0`	`str5 = "Bigger"` has six characters and `"Big"` has three characters. Therefore, `str5` is the larger string. The first three characters of `str5` are the same as the corresponding first three characters of `"Big"`. Therefore, `str5.compareTo("Big") > 0`.

The program in Example 4–2 evaluates the expressions in Table 4–3.

Example 4-2

```java
//The String method compareTo

public class StringComparison
{
    public static void main(String[] args)
    {
        String str1 = "Hello";                          //Line 1
        String str2 = "Hi";                             //Line 2
        String str3 = "Air";                            //Line 3
        String str4 = "Bill";                           //Line 4
        String str5 = "Bigger";                         //Line 5

        System.out.println("Line 6: " +
                    "str1.compareTo(str2) evaluates to "
                  + str1.compareTo(str2));              //Line 6
```

```
        System.out.println("Line 7: " +
                        "str1.compareTo(\"Hen\") evaluates to "
                   +  str1.compareTo("Hen"));              //Line 7

        System.out.println("Line 8: " +
                        "str4.compareTo(str3) evaluates to "
                   +  str4.compareTo(str3));               //Line 8

        System.out.println("Line 9: " +
                        "str1.compareTo(\"hello\") evaluates to "
                   +  str1.compareTo("hello"));            //Line 9

        System.out.println("Line 10: " +
                        "str2.compareTo(\"Hi\") evaluates to "
                   +  str2.compareTo("Hi"));               //Line 10

        System.out.println("Line 11: " +
                        "str4.compareTo(\"Billy\") evaluates to "
                   +  str4.compareTo("Billy"));            //Line 11

        System.out.println("Line 12: " +
                        "str5.compareTo(\"Big\") evaluates to "
                   +  str5.compareTo("Big"));              //Line 12
    }
}
```

Sample Run
```
Line 6: str1.compareTo(str2) evaluates to -4
Line 7: str1.compareTo("Hen") evaluates to -2
Line 8: str4.compareTo(str3) evaluates to 1
Line 9: str1.compareTo("hello") evaluates to -32
Line 10: str2.compareTo("Hi") evaluates to 0
Line 11: str4.compareTo("Billy") evaluates to -1
Line 12: str5.compareTo("Big") evaluates to 3
```

Notice that the values, such as −4, −2, 1, and so on, printed in Lines 6 through 12, are the differences of the collating sequences of the first unmatched characters of the strings. The only thing we need to know is whether the value is positive, negative, or zero. The output is self-explanatory.

In addition to the method `compareTo`, you can also use the method `equals` of the **class** `String` to determine whether two `String` objects contain the same value. However, the method `equals` returns the value **true** or **false**. For example, the expression:

```
str1.equals("Hello")
```

evaluates to **true**, while the expression:

```
str1.equals(str2)
```

evaluates to **false**, where `str1` and `str2` are as defined in Example 4-2.

You can apply the relational operators == and != to variables of the `String` type, such as the variables `str1` and `str2`. However, when these operators are applied to these variables they compare the values of these variables, not the values of the `String` objects they point to. For example, suppose, as in Figure 4-2:

```
str1 = "Hello";
str2 = "Hi";
```

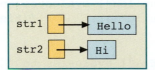

Figure 4-2   Variables `str1`, `str2`, and the objects they point to

The expression (`str1` == `str2`) determines whether the values of `str1` and `str2` are the same, that is, if `str1` and `str2` point to the same `String` object. Similarly, the expression (`str1` != `str2`) determines whether the values of `str1` and `str2` are *not* the same, that is, if `str1` and `str2` do not point to the same `String` object.

Consider the statement:

```
String str = "Sunny";
```

As explained in Chapter 3, when this statement executes, memory is allocated to store the string `"Sunny"` and the address of the allocated memory is stored in the variable `str`. In reality, the computer checks whether there already is a `String` object with the value `"Sunny"`; if so, then the address of that object is stored in `str`. The following further explains this concept. Consider the following statements:

```
String str1 = "Hello";
String str2 = "Hello";
```

When the first statement executes, a `String` object with the value `"Hello"` is created and its address is assigned to `str1`. When the second statement executes, because there already exists a `String` object with the value `"Hello"`, the address of this `String` object is stored in `str2`. (See Figure 4-3.)

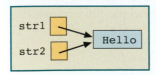

Figure 4-3   Variables `str1`, `str2`, and the objects they point to

Therefore, if you evaluate the expression (`str1 == str2`) after these statements, this expression evaluates to **true**. Moreover, here the expression `str1.equals(str2)` also evaluates to **true**.

If you later assigned a different string, say the string `"Cloudy"`, to `str2`, then if no `String` object exists with the value `"Cloudy"`, a `String` object with this value is created and its address is stored in `str2`. However, `str1` would still point to the string `"Hello"`. In other words, changing the value of the string `str2` does not change the value of the string `str1`.

LOGICAL (BOOLEAN) OPERATORS AND LOGICAL EXPRESSIONS

This section describes how to form and evaluate logical expressions that are combinations of other logical expressions. **Logical (Boolean) operators** enable you to combine logical expressions. Java has three logical (Boolean) operators, as shown in Table 4-4.

Table 4-4   Logical (Boolean) Operators in Java

Operator	Description
!	not
&&	and
||	or

Logical operators take only logical values as operands and yield only logical values as results. The operator ! is unary, so it has only one operand. The operators && and || are binary.

Table 4–5 shows that when you use the ! operator, !**true** is **false** and !**false** is **true**. Putting ! in front of a logical expression reverses the value of that logical expression. Moreover, Table 4–5 is called the **truth table** of the operator !. Example 4–3 gives examples of the ! operator.

Table 4-5   ! (not) Operator

Expression	!(Expression)
true	false
false	true

Example 4-3

Expression	Value	Explanation
!('A' > 'B')	true	Because 'A' > 'B' is **false**, !('A' > 'B') is **true**.
!(6 <= 7)	false	Because 6 <= 7 is **true**, !(6 <= 7) is **false**.

Table 4-6 defines the operator `&&` (and). From this table, it follows that `Expression1 && Expression2` is **true** if and only if both `Expression1` and `Expression2` are **true**; otherwise `Expression1 && Expression2` evaluates to **false**. Moreover, Table 4-6 is called the **truth table** of the operator `&&`. Example 4-4 gives examples of the `&&` operator.

Table 4-6 `&&` (and) Operator

Expression1	Expression2	Expression1 && Expression2
true	true	true
true	false	false
false	true	false
false	false	false

Example 4-4

Expression	Value	Explanation
(14 >= 5) && ('A' < 'B')	true	Because (14 >= 5) is **true**, ('A' < 'B') is **true**, and **true** && **true** is **true**, the expression evaluates to **true**.
(24 >= 35) && ('A' < 'B')	false	Because (24 >= 35) is **false**, ('A' < 'B') is **true**, and **false** && **true** is **false**, the expression evaluates to **false**.

Table 4-7 defines the operator `||` (or). From this table, it follows that `Expression1 || Expression2` is **true** if and only if at least one of the expressions, `Expression1` or `Expression2`, is **true**; otherwise, `Expression1 || Expression2` evaluates to **false**. Moreover, Table 4-7 is called the **truth table** of the operator `||`. Example 4-5 gives examples of the `||` operator.

Table 4-7 || (or) Operator

Expression1	Expression2	Expression1 || Expression2
true	true	true
true	false	true
false	true	true
false	false	false

4

Example 4-5

Expression	Value	Explanation
(14 >= 5) || ('A' > 'B')	true	Because (14 >= 5) is **true**, ('A' > 'B') is **false**, and **true** || **false** is **true**, the expression evaluates to **true**.
(24 >= 35) || ('A' > 'B')	false	Because (24 >= 35) is **false**, ('A' > 'B') is **false**, and **false** || **false** is **false**, the expression evaluates to **false**.
('A' <= 'a') || (7 != 7)	true	Because ('A' <= 'a') is **true**, (7 != 7) is **false**, and **true** || **false** is **true**, the expression evaluates to **true**.

ORDER OF PRECEDENCE

Complex logical expressions can be difficult to evaluate. Consider the following logical expression:

```
11 > 5 || 6 < 15 && 7 >= 8
```

This logical expression yields different results depending on whether || or && is evaluated first. If || is evaluated first, it evaluates to **false**; if && is evaluated first, it evaluates to **true**.

To work with complex logical expressions, there must be some priority scheme for determining which operators to evaluate first. Because an expression might contain arithmetic, relational, and logical operators, as in the expression 5 + 3 <= 9 && 2 > 3, an order of precedence for all Java operators must be established. Table 4–8 shows the order of precedence of some Java operators, including the arithmetic, relational, and logical operators. (See Appendix B for the precedence of all Java operators.)

Table 4-8 Precedence of Operators

Operators	Precedence
!, +, – (unary operators)	first
*, /, %	second
+, –	third
<, <=, >=, >	fourth
==, !=	fifth
&&	sixth
||	seventh
= (assignment operator)	last

Using the precedence rules given in Table 4-8, in an expression, relational and logical opera-tors are evaluated from left to right. Because relational and logical operators are evaluated from left to right, the **associativity** of these operators is said to be from left to right.

You can insert parentheses into an expression to clarify its meaning. Using the standard order of precedence, the expression:

11 > 5 || 6 < 15 && 7 >= 8

is equivalent to:

11 > 5 || (6 < 15 && 7 >= 8)

In this expression:

11 > 5 is **true**,
6 < 15 is **true**,

and:

7 >= 8 is **false**.

Substitute these values in the expression:

11 > 5 || (6 < 15 && 7 >= 8)

to get:

true || (**true** && **false**) = **true** || **false** = **true**.

Therefore, the expression 11 > 5 || (6 < 15 && 7 >= 8) evaluates to **true**.

Example 4-6

Evaluate the following expression:

```
(17 < 4 * 3 + 5) || (8 * 2 == 4 * 4) && !(3 + 3 == 6)
```

Now,

```
  (17 < 4 * 3 + 5) || (8 * 2 == 4 * 4) && !(3 + 3 == 6)
= (17 < 12 + 5) || (16 == 16) && !(6 == 6)
= (17 < 17) || true && !(true)
= false || true && false
= false || false (Because true && false is false)
= false
```

Therefore, the value of the original logical expression is **false**.

You can also use parentheses to override the precedence of operators. For example, in the expression:

```
(7 >= 8 || 'A' < 'B') && 5 * 4 == 20
```

the operator **||** evaluates before the operator **&&**; whereas, in the expression:

```
7 >= 8 || 'A' < 'B' && 5 * 4 == 20
```

the operator **&&** evaluates before the operator **||**.

Example 4-7 illustrates how logical expressions consisting of variables are evaluated.

Example 4-7

Suppose you have the following declarations:

```
boolean found = true;
boolean flag = false;
double x = 5.2;
double y = 3.4;
int a = 5, b = 8;
int n = 20;
char ch = 'B';
```

Consider the following expressions:

Expression	Value	Explanation
!found	false	Because found is **true**, !found is **false**.
x > 4.0	true	Because x is 5.2 and 5.2 > 4.0 is **true**, the expression x > 4.0 evaluates to **true**.

`!found && (x >= 0)`	false	In this expression, `!found` is **false**. Also, because x is **5.2** and **5.2 >= 0** is **true**, **x >= 0** is **true**. Therefore, the value of the expression `!found && (x >= 0)` is **false && true**, which evaluates to **false**.
`!(found && (x >= 0))`	false	In this expression, `found && (x >= 0)` is **true && true**, which evaluates to **true**. Therefore, the value of the expression `!(found && (x >= 0))` is `!`**true**, which evaluates to **false**.
`x + y <= 20.5`	true	Because **x + y = 5.2 + 3.4 = 8.6** and **8.6 <= 20.5**, it follows that **x + y <= 20.5** evaluates to **true**.
`(n >= 0) && (n <= 100)`	true	Here n is **20**. Because **20 >= 0** is **true**, **n >= 0** is **true**. Also, because **20 <= 100** is **true**, **n <= 100** is **true**. Therefore, the value of the expression `(n >= 0) && (n <= 100)` is **true && true**, which evaluates to **true**.
`('A' <= ch && ch <= 'Z')`	true	In this expression, the value of ch is **'B'**. Because **'A' <= 'B'** is **true**, **'A' <= ch** evaluates to **true**. Also, because **'B' <= 'Z'** is **true**, **ch <= 'Z'** evaluates to **true**. Therefore, the value of the expression `('A' <= ch && ch <= 'Z')` is **true && true**, which evaluates to **true**.
`(a + 2 <= b) && !flag`	true	Here **a + 2 = 5 + 2 = 7** and b is **8**. Because **7 < 8** is **true**, the expression **a + 2 < b** evaluates to **true**. Also, because flag is **false**, `!flag` is **true**. Therefore, the value of the expression `(a + 2 <= b) && !flag` is **true && true**, which evaluates to **true**.

You can also write a Java program to evaluate the logical expressions given in Example 4-7, as shown in Example 4-8.

Example 4-8

The following program evaluates and outputs the values of the logical expressions given in Example 4–7.

```java
//Chapter 4: Logical operators

public class LogicalOperators
{
    public static void main(String[] args)
    {
        boolean found = true;
        boolean flag = false;
        double x = 5.2;
        double y = 3.4;
        int a = 5, b = 8;
        int n = 20;
        char ch = 'B';

        System.out.println("Line 1: !found evaluates to "
                         + !found);                               //Line 1
        System.out.println("Line 2: x > 4.0 evaluates to "
                         + (x > 4.0));                            //Line 2
        System.out.println("Line 3: !found && (x >= 0) "
                         + "evaluates to "
                         + (!found && (x >= 0)));                 //Line 3
        System.out.println("Line 4: !(found && (x >= 0)) "
                         + "evaluates to "
                         + !(found && (x >= 0)));                 //Line 4
        System.out.println("Line 5: x + y <= 20.5 evaluates to "
                         + (x + y <= 20.5));                      //Line 5
        System.out.println("Line 6: (n >= 0) && (n <= 100) "
                         + "evaluates to "
                         + ((n >= 0) && (n <= 100)));             //Line 6
        System.out.println("Line 7: ('A' <= ch && ch <= 'Z') "
                         + "evaluates to "
                         + ('A' <= ch && ch <= 'Z'));             //Line 7
        System.out.println("Line 8: (a + 2 <= b) && !flag "
                         + "evaluates to "
                         + ((a + 2 <= b) && !flag));              //Line 8
    }
}
```

Sample Run
```
Line 1: !found evaluates to false
Line 2: x > 4.0 evaluates to true
Line 3: !found && (x >= 0) evaluates to false
Line 4: !(found && (x >= 0)) evaluates to false
```

```
Line 5: x + y <= 20.5 evaluates to true
Line 6: (n >= 0) && (n <= 100) evaluates to true
Line 7: ('A' <= ch && ch <= 'Z') evaluates to true
Line 8: (a + 2 <= b) && !flag evaluates to true
```

 Be careful when forming logical expressions. Some beginners make the following common mistake: Suppose that num is an **int** variable. Further suppose that you want to write a logical expression that evaluates to **true** if the value of num is between 0 and 10, including 0 and 10, and that evaluates to **false** otherwise. The following expression appears to represent a comparison of 0, num, and 10 that will yield the desired result:

```
0 <= num <= 10
```

This statement is *not* legal in Java and you will get a syntax error. This is because the associativity of the operator <= is from left to right. Therefore, the preceding expression is equivalent to:

```
(0 <= num) <= 10
```

The value of the expression (0 <= num) is either **true** or **false**. Because you cannot compare the **boolean** values **true** and **false** with other data types, the expression would result in a syntax error. One of the correct ways to write this expression in Java is:

```
0 <= num && num <= 10
```

When creating a complex logical expression, take care to use the proper logical operators.

Short-Circuit Evaluation

Logical expressions in Java are evaluated using a highly efficient algorithm. This algorithm is illustrated with the help of the following statements:

```
(x > y) || (x == 5)
(a == b) && (x >= 7)
```

In the first statement, the two operands of the operator || are the expressions (x > y) and (x == 5). This expression evaluates to **true** if either the operand (x > y) is **true** or the operand (x == 5) is **true**. With **short-circuit evaluation**, the computer evaluates the logical expression from left to right. As soon as the value of the entire logical expression is known, the evaluation stops. For example, in the first statement, if the operand (x > y) evaluates to **true**, then the entire expression evaluates to **true** because **true** || **true** is **true** and **true** || **false** is **true**. Therefore, the value of the operand (x == 5) has no bearing on the final outcome.

Similarly, in the second statement, the two operands of the operator && are (a == b) and (x >= 7). Now, if the operand (a == b) evaluates to **false**, then the entire expression evaluates to **false** because **false** && **true** is **false** and **false** && **false** is **false**.

Short-circuit evaluation (of a logical expression): A process in which the computer evaluates a logical expression from left to right and stops as soon as the value of the expression is known.

Example 4-9

Consider the following expressions:

```
(age >= 21) || (x == 5)          //Line 1
(grade == 'A') && (x >= 7)       //Line 2
```

For the expression in Line 1, suppose that the value of `age` is 25. Because (`25 >= 21`) is **true** and the logical operator used in the expression is `||`, the expression evaluates to **true**. Due to short–circuit evaluation, the computer does not evaluate the expression (`x == 5`). Similarly, for the expression in Line 2, suppose that the value of `grade` is `'B'`. Because (`'A' == 'B'`) is **false** and the logical operator used in the expression is `&&`, the expression evaluates to **false**. The computer does not evaluate (`x >= 7`).

 In Java, `&` and `|` are also operators. You can use the operator `&` in place of the operator `&&` in a logical expression. Similarly, you can use the operator `|` in place of the operator `||` in a logical expression. However, there is no short-circuit evaluation of the logical expressions if `&` is used in place of `&&` or `|` is used in place of `||`.

`boolean` Data Type and Logical (Boolean) Expressions

Recall that Java contains the built–in data type **boolean**, which has the logical (Boolean) values **true** and **false**. Therefore, you can manipulate logical (Boolean) expressions using the **boolean** data type. Also, recall that in Java, **boolean**, **true**, and **false** are reserved words.

Suppose that you have the following statements:

```
boolean legalAge;
int age;
```

The statement:

```
legalAge = true;
```

sets the value of the variable `legalAge` to **true**. The statement:

```
legalAge = (age >= 21);
```

assigns the value **true** to `legalAge` if the value of `age` is greater than or equal to 21. This statement assigns the value **false** to `legalAge` if the value of `age` is less than 21. For example, if the value of `age` is 25, the value assigned to `legalAge` is **true**. Similarly, if the value of `age` is 16, the value assigned to `legalAge` is **false**.

SELECTION: `if` AND `if...else`

Although there are only two logical values, **`true`** and **`false`**, they are extremely useful because they permit programs to incorporate decision making that alters the processing flow. The remainder of this chapter discusses ways to incorporate decisions into a program. Java has two selection or branch control structures: **`if`** statements and the **`switch`** structure. This section discusses how **`if`** and **`if...else`** statements can be used to create one-way selection, two-way selection, and multiple selections. The **`switch`** structure is discussed later in this chapter.

One-Way Selection

A bank wants to send a notice to a customer if her or his checking account balance falls below the required minimum balance. That is, if the checking account balance is below the required minimum balance, the bank should send a notice to the customer; otherwise, it should do nothing. Similarly, if the policyholder of an insurance policy is a nonsmoker, the company wants to apply a 10% discount to the policy premium. Both of these examples involve one-way selection. In Java, one-way selections are incorporated using the **`if`** statement. The syntax of one-way selection is:

```
if (expression)
    statement
```

Note the elements of this syntax. It begins with the reserved word **`if`**, followed by an **`expression`** contained within parentheses, followed by a **`statement`**. The **`expression`** is sometimes called a **decision maker** because it decides whether to execute the **`statement`** that follows it. The **`expression`** is a logical expression. If the value of the **`expression`** is **`true`**, the **`statement`** executes. If the value is **`false`**, the **`statement`** does not execute and the computer goes on to the next statement in the program. The **`statement`** following the **`expression`** is sometimes called the **action statement**. Figure 4-4 shows the flow of execution of the **`if`** statement (one-way selection).

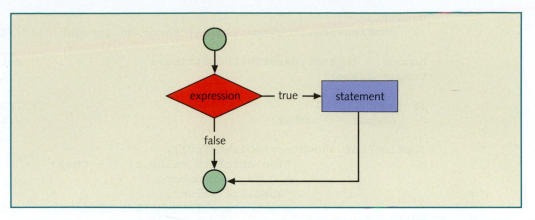

Figure 4-4 One-way selection

Next, we give various examples to show how an **if** statement works as well as some common syntax and/or semantic errors that beginning programmers often make.

Example 4-10

```
if (score >= 90)
    grade = 'A';
```

In this code, if the expression (**score >= 90**) evaluates to **true**, the assignment statement, **grade = 'A';**, executes. If the expression evaluates to **false**, the assignment statement, **grade = 'A';**, is skipped. For example, if the value of **score** is **95**, the value assigned to the variable **grade** is **A**.

Example 4-11

The following Java program finds the absolute value of an integer.

```
//Determine the absolute value of an integer

import javax.swing.JOptionPane;

public class AbsoluteValue
{
    public static void main(String[] args)
    {
        int number;
        int temp;
        String numString;
```

```
        numString =
            JOptionPane.showInputDialog("Enter an integer:"); //Line 1

        number = Integer.parseInt(numString);                 //Line 2
        temp = number;                                        //Line 3

        if (number < 0)                                       //Line 4
            number = -number;                                 //Line 5

        JOptionPane.showMessageDialog(null,
                        "The absolute value of " + temp
                        + " is " + number,
                        "Absolute Value",
                        JOptionPane.INFORMATION_MESSAGE);     //Line 6
        System.exit(0);
    }
}
```

Sample Run: Figure 4–5 shows a sample run.

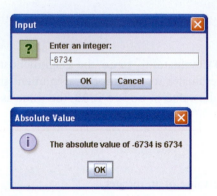

Figure 4-5   Sample run for Example 4-11

The statement in Line 1 displays the input dialog box and prompts the user to enter an integer. The entered number is stored as a string in `numString`. The statement in Line 2 uses the method `parseInt` of the **class** `Integer`, converts the value of `numString` into the number, and stores the number in the variable `number`. The statement in Line 3 copies the value of `number` into `temp`. The statement in Line 4 checks whether `number` is negative. If `number` is negative, the statement in Line 5 changes `number` to a positive number. The statement in Line 6 displays the message dialog box and shows the original number, stored in `temp`, and the absolute value of the number stored in `number`.

Example 4-12

Consider the following statement:

```
if score >= 90
    grade = 'A';
```

This statement illustrates an incorrect version of an **if** statement. The parentheses around the logical expression are missing, which is a syntax error.

Putting a semicolon after the parentheses following the expression in an **if** statement (that is, before the statement) is a semantic error. If the semicolon immediately follows the closing parenthesis, the **if** statement will operate on the empty statement.

Example 4-13

Consider the following Java statements:

```
if (score >= 90);          //Line 1
    grade = 'A';           //Line 2
```

This statement represents a one-way selection. Because there is a semicolon at the end of the expression in Line 1, the **if** statement terminates at Line 1, the action of the **if** statement is null, and the statement in Line 2 is not part of the **if** statement. The statement in Line 2 executes regardless of how the **if** statement evaluates.

Two-Way Selection

In the previous section, you learned how to implement one-way selections in a program. There are many situations in which you must choose between two alternatives. For example, if a part-time employee works overtime, the paycheck is calculated using the overtime payment formula; otherwise, the paycheck is calculated using the regular formula. This is an example of two-way selection. To choose between two alternatives—that is, to implement two-way selections—Java provides the **if...else** statement. Two-way selection uses the following syntax:

```
if (expression)
    statement1
else
    statement2
```

Take a moment to examine this syntax. It begins with the reserved word **if**, followed by a logical expression contained within parentheses, followed by a statement, followed by the reserved word **else**, followed by a second statement. Statements 1 and 2 can be any valid Java statements. In a two-way selection, if the value of the **expression** is **true**, then **statement1** executes. If the value of the **expression** is **false**, then **statement2** executes. Figure 4-6 shows the flow of execution of the **if...else** statement (two-way selection).

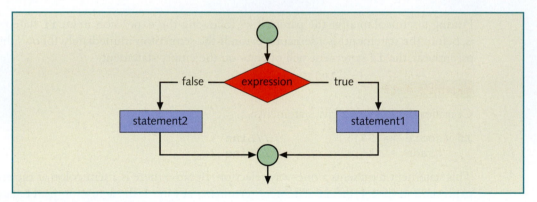

Figure 4-6   Two-way selection

Example 4-14

Consider the following statements:

```
if (hours > 40.0)                                    //Line 1
    wages = 40.0 * rate +
            1.5 * rate * (hours - 40.0);             //Line 2
else                                                 //Line 3
    wages = hours * rate;                            //Line 4
```

If the value of the variable **hours** is greater than **40.0**, then the **wages** include overtime payment. Suppose that **hours** is **50**. The expression in the **if** statement in Line 1 evaluates to **true**, so the statement in Line 2 executes. On the other hand, if **hours** is **30**, or any number less than or equal to 40, the expression in the if statement in Line 1 evaluates to false. In this case, the program skips the statement in Line 2 and executes the statement in Line 4—that is, the statement following the reserved word else executes.

In a two-way selection statement, putting a semicolon after the right parenthesis and before statement1 creates a syntax error. If the if statement ends with a semicolon, statement1 is no longer part of the if statement, and the else part of the if...else statement stands by itself. There is no stand-alone else statement in Java; that is, the else statement cannot be separated from the if statement.

4

Example 4-15

The following statements show an example of a syntax error:

```
if (hours > 40.0);                                     //Line 1
    wages = 40.0 * rate +
            1.5 * rate * (hours - 40.0);               //Line 2
else                                                   //Line 3
    wages = hours * rate;                              //Line 4
```

Because a semicolon follows the closing parenthesis of the if statement (Line 1), the else statement stands alone. The semicolon at the end of the if statement (see Line 1) ends the if statement, so the statement in Line 2 separates the else clause from the if statement. That is, else is by itself. Because there is no separate else statement in Java, this code generates a syntax error.

Example 4-16

The following program determines an employee's weekly wages. If the hours worked exceed 40, then wages include overtime payment.

```
//Chapter 4: Weekly Wages

import java.util.*;

public class WeeklyWages
{
    static Scanner console = new Scanner(System.in);

    public static void main(String[] args)
    {
```

```
        double wages, rate, hours;                    //Line 1

        System.out.print("Line 2: Enter the working "
                         + "hours: ");                 //Line 2
        hours = console.nextDouble();                 //Line 3
        System.out.println();                         //Line 4

        System.out.print("Line 5: Enter the pay "
                         + "rate: ");                  //Line 5
        rate = console.nextDouble();                  //Line 6
        System.out.println();                         //Line 7

        if (hours > 40.0)                             //Line 8
            wages = 40.0 * rate +
                    1.5 * rate * (hours - 40.0);       //Line 9
        else                                          //Line 10
            wages = hours * rate;                     //Line 11

        System.out.printf("Line 12: The wages are $%.2f %n",
                           wages);                    //Line 12
        System.out.println();                         //Line 13
    }
}
```

Sample Run: In this sample run, the user input is shaded:
Line 2: Enter the working hours: 75.5

Line 5: Enter the pay rate: 12.50

Line 12: The wages are $1165.62

The statement in Line 1 declares the appropriate variables. The statement in Line 2 prompts the user to input the number of hours worked. The statement in Line 3 inputs and stores the working hours in the variable **hours**. The statement in Line 5 prompts the user to input the pay rate. The statement in Line 6 inputs and stores the pay rate into the variable **rate**. The statement in Line 8 checks whether the value of the variable **hours** is greater than **40.0**. If **hours** is greater than **40.0**, then the wages are calculated by the statement in Line 9, which includes overtime payment; otherwise, the wages are calculated by the statement in Line 11. The statement in Line 12 outputs the wages.

Let's now consider more examples of **if** statements and examine some of the common errors made by beginning programmers.

Example 4-17

Consider the following statements:

```
if (score >= 90)                                        //Line 1
    grade = 'A';                                        //Line 2
    System.out.println("The grade is " + grade);        //Line 3
```

Here you might think that just because the statements in Lines 2 and 3 are aligned, both these statements are the action statements of the **if** statement. However, this is not the case. The **if** statement acts on only one statement, which is `grade = 'A';`. The output statement executes regardless of whether (`score >= 90`) is **true** or **false**.

Example 4-18 illustrates another common mistake.

Example 4-18

Consider the following statements:

```
if (score >= 60)
    System.out.println("Passing");
    System.out.println("Failing");
```

If the expression (`score >= 60`) evaluates to **false**, the output would be `Failing`. That is, this set of statements performs the same action as an **else** statement. It will execute the second output statement rather than the first. For example, if the value of `score` is `50`, these statements will output the following line:

```
Failing
```

However, if the expression `score >= 60` evaluates to **true**, the program will write both statements, giving an unsatisfactory result. For example, if the value of `score` is `70`, these statements will output the following lines:

```
Passing
Failing
```

The correct code to print `Passing` or `Failing`, depending on the value of `score`, is:

```
if (score >= 60)
    System.out.println("Passing");
else
    System.out.println("Failing");
```

Compound (Block of) Statements

The **if** and **if...else** structures control only one statement at a time. Suppose, however, that you want to execute more than one statement if the **expression** in an **if** or **if...else** statement evaluates to **true**. To permit more complex statements, Java provides a structure called a **compound statement** or a **block** of statements. A compound statement takes the following form:

```
{
    statement1
    statement2
       .
       .
       .
    statementn
}
```

That is, a compound statement or block consists of a sequence of statements enclosed in curly braces, { and }. In an **if** or **if...else** structure, a compound statement functions as if it were a single statement. Thus, instead of having a simple two-way selection similar to the following code:

```
if (age > 18)
    System.out.println("Eligible to vote.");
else
    System.out.println("Not eligible to vote.");
```

you could include compound statements, similar to the following code:

```
if (age > 18)
{
    System.out.println("Eligible to vote.");
    System.out.println("No longer a minor.");
}
else
{
    System.out.println("Not eligible to vote.");
    System.out.println("Still a minor.");
}
```

The compound statement is very useful and will be used in most of the ensuing structured statements in this chapter.

Multiple Selections: Nested if

In the previous sections, you learned how to implement one-way and two-way selections in a program. However, some problems require the implementation of more than two alternatives. For example, suppose that if the checking account balance is greater than or equal to $50000, the interest rate is 7%; if the balance is greater than or equal to $25000 and less than $50000, the interest rate is 5%; if the balance is greater than or equal to $1000 and less than $25000, the interest rate is 3%; otherwise, the interest rate is 0%. This particular problem has four alternatives—that is, multiple selection paths. You can include multiple selection paths in a program by using an if...else structure, if the action statement itself is an if or if...else statement. When one control statement is located within another, it is said to be **nested**.

Example 4-19

Suppose that balance and interestRate are variables of the type double. The following statements determine the interestRate depending on the value of balance:

```
if (balance >= 50000.00)                      //Line 1
    interestRate = 0.07;                      //Line 2
else                                          //Line 3
    if (balance >= 25000.00)                  //Line 4
        interestRate = 0.05;                  //Line 5
    else                                      //Line 6
        if (balance >= 1000.00)               //Line 7
            interestRate = 0.03;              //Line 8
        else                                  //Line 9
            interestRate = 0.00;              //Line 10
```

Suppose that the value of balance is 60000.00. Then the expression balance >= 50000.00 in Line 1 evaluates to **true** and the statement in Line 2 executes. Now suppose the value of balance is 40000.00. Then the expression balance >= 50000.00 in Line 1 evaluates to **false**. So the **else** part in Line 3 executes. The statement part of this **else** is an if...else statement. Therefore, the expression balance >= 25000.00 is evaluated, which evaluates to **true** and the statement in Line 5 executes. Note that the expression in Line 4 is evaluated only when the expression in Line 1 evaluates to **false**. The expression in Line 1 evaluates to **false** if balance < 50000.00 and then the expression in Line 4 is evaluated. It follows that the expression in Line 4 determines whether the value of balance is greater than or equal to 25000 and less than 50000. In other words, the expression in Line 4 is equivalent to the expression (balance >= 25000.00 && balance < 500000.00). The expression in Line 7 works the same way.

The statements in Example 4-19 illustrate how to incorporate multiple selections using a nested if...else structure.

A nested **if...else** structure demands the answer to an important question: How do you know which **else** is paired with which **if**? Recall that in Java there is no stand-alone **else** statement. Every **else** must be paired with an **if**. The rule to pair an **else** with an **if** is as follows:

Pairing an else with an if: In a nested **if** statement, Java associates an **else** with the most recent incomplete **if**—that is, the most recent **if** that has not been paired with an **else**.

Using this rule, in Example 4-19, the **else** in Line 3 is paired with the **if** in Line 1. The **else** in Line 6 is paired with the **if** in Line 4, and the **else** in Line 9 is paired with the **if** in Line 7.

To avoid excessive indentation, the code in Example 4-19 can be rewritten as follows:

```
if (balance >= 50000.00)                          //Line 1
    interestRate = 0.07;                          //Line 2
else if (balance >= 25000.00)                     //Line 3
        interestRate = 0.05;                      //Line 4
else if (balance >= 1000.00)                      //Line 5
        interestRate = 0.03;                      //Line 6
else                                              //Line 7
    interestRate = 0.00;                          //Line 8
```

Example 4-20

Assume that **score** is a variable of the type **int**. Based on the value of **score**, the following code determines the grade:

```
if (score >= 90)
    System.out.println("The grade is A");
else if (score >= 80)
        System.out.println("The grade is B");
else if (score >= 70)
        System.out.println("The grade is C");
else if (score >= 60)
        System.out.println("The grade is D");
else
    System.out.println("The grade is F");
```

The following examples will further help you see the various ways in which you can use nested **if** structures to implement multiple selection.

Example 4-21

Assume that all variables are properly declared, and consider the following statements:

```
if (temperature >= 50)                                      //Line 1
    if (temperature >= 80)                                  //Line 2
        System.out.println("Good day for swimming."); //Line 3
    else                                                    //Line 4
        System.out.println("Good day for golfing.");   //Line 5
else                                                        //Line 6
    System.out.println("Good day to play tennis.");    //Line 7
```

In this Java code, the **else** in Line 4 is paired with the **if** in Line 2, and the **else** in Line 6 is paired with the **if** in Line 1. Note that the **else** in Line 4 cannot be paired with the **if** in Line 1. If you pair the **else** in Line 4 with the **if** in Line 1, the **if** in Line 2 becomes the action statement part of the **if** in Line 1, leaving the **else** in Line 6 dangling. Also, the statements in Lines 2 though 5 form the statement part of the **if** in Line 1.

Example 4-22

Assume that all variables are properly declared, and consider the following statements:

```
if (temperature >= 50)                                      //Line 1
    if (temperature >= 80)                                  //Line 2
        System.out.println("Good day for swimming.");  //Line 3
    else                                                    //Line 4
        System.out.println("Good day for golfing.");   //Line 5
```

In this code, the **else** in Line 4 is paired with the **if** in Line 2. Note that for the **else** in Line 4, the most recent incomplete **if** is the **if** in Line 2. In this code, the **if** in Line 1 has no **else** and is a one-way selection.

Example 4-23

Assume that all variables are properly declared, and consider the following statements:

```
if (GPA >= 2.0)                                             //Line 1
    if (GPA >= 3.9)                                         //Line 2
        System.out.println("Dean\'s Honor List.");     //Line 3
else                                                        //Line 4
    System.out.println("Current GPA below graduation "
                    + "requirement."  +
                    "\nSee your academic advisor.");   //Line 5
```

This code won't work the way we want it to work. Let us explore why. Following the rule of pairing an **else** with an **if**, the **else** in Line 4 is paired with the **if** in Line 2. However, this pairing produces an unsatisfactory result. Suppose that the GPA is **3.8**. The **expression** in the **if** at Line 1 evaluates to **true**, and the statement part of the **if**, which is an **if...else** structure, executes. Because GPA is **3.8**, the **expression** in the **if** in Line 2 evaluates to **false**, and the **else** associated with this **if** executes, producing the following output:

```
Current GPA below graduation requirement.
See your academic advisor.
```

However, a student with a GPA of **3.8** would graduate with some type of honor. In fact, we intended for the code to print the message:

```
Current GPA below graduation requirement.
See your academic advisor.
```

only if the GPA is less than **2.0**, and the message:

```
Dean's Honor List.
```

if the GPA is greater than or equal to **3.9**. To achieve that result, the **else** in Line 4 must be paired with the **if** in Line 1. To pair the **else** in Line 4 with the **if** in Line 1, you must use a compound statement, as follows:

```
if (GPA >= 2.0)                                                    //Line 1
{
    if (GPA >= 3.9)                                                //Line 2
        System.out.println("Dean\'s Honor List.");                //Line 3
}
else                                                              //Line 4
    System.out.println("Current GPA below graduation "
                    + "requirement."  +
                    "\nSee your academic advisor.");              //Line 5
```

In cases such as this one, the general rule is that you cannot look inside a block (that is, inside the braces) to pair an **else** with an **if**. The **else** in Line 4 cannot be paired with the **if** in Line 2 because the **if** statement in Line 2 is enclosed within braces, and the **else** in Line 4 cannot look inside those braces. Therefore, the **else** in Line 4 is paired with the **if** in Line 1.

Comparing **if...else** Statements with a Series of **if** Statements

Consider the following Java program segments, both of which accomplish the same task:

(a)

```
if (month == 1)                          //Line 1
    System.out.println("January");       //Line 2
else if (month == 2)                     //Line 3
        System.out.println("February");  //Line 4
```

4

```java
else if (month == 3)                          //Line 5
        System.out.println("March");          //Line 6
else if (month == 4)                          //Line 7
        System.out.println("April");          //Line 8
else if (month == 5)                          //Line 9
        System.out.println("May");            //Line 10
else if (month == 6)                          //Line 11
        System.out.println("June");           //Line 12
```
(b)

```java
if (month == 1)
    System.out.println("January");
if (month == 2)
    System.out.println("February");
if (month == 3)
    System.out.println("March");
if (month == 4)
    System.out.println("April");
if (month == 5)
    System.out.println("May");
if (month == 6)
    System.out.println("June");
```

Program segment (a) is written as a sequence of if...else statements; program segment (b) is written as a series of if statements. Both program segments accomplish the same thing. If month is 3, then both program segments output March. If month is 1, then in program segment (a), the expression in the if statement in Line 1 evaluates to **true**. The statement (in Line 2) associated with this **if** then executes; the rest of the structure, which is the **else** of this **if** statement, is skipped, and the remaining **if** statements are not evaluated. In program segment (b), the computer has to evaluate the expression in each **if** statement because there is no **else** statement. As a consequence, program segment (b) executes more slowly than does program segment (a).

Conditional Operator (? :)

 The reader can skip this section without any discontinuation.

Certain if...else statements can be written more concisely by using Java's conditional operator. The **conditional operator**, written as ?:, is a **ternary operator**, which means that it takes three arguments. The syntax for using the conditional operator is:

expression1 ? expression2 : expression3

This type of statement is called a **conditional expression**. The conditional expression is evaluated as follows: If `expression1` evaluates to `true`, the result of the conditional expression is `expression2`; otherwise, the result of the conditional expression is `expression3`.

Consider the following statements:

```java
if (a >= b)
    max = a;
else
    max = b;
```

You can use the conditional operator to simplify the writing of this `if...else` statement as follows:

```java
max = (a >= b) ? a : b;
```

switch STRUCTURES

Recall that there are two selection, or branch, structures in Java. The first selection structure, which is implemented with `if` and `if...else` statements, usually requires the evaluation of a (logical) expression. The second selection structure, which does not require the evaluation of a logical expression, is called a **switch** structure. Java's **switch** structure gives the computer the power to choose from many alternatives.

The general syntax of a **switch** statement is:

```java
switch (expression)
{
case value1: statements1
             break;
case value2: statements2
             break;
    ...
case valuen: statementsn
             break;
default: statements
}
```

In Java, **switch**, **case**, **break**, and **default** are reserved words. In a **switch** structure, the `expression` is evaluated first. The value of the `expression` is then used to perform the actions specified in the statements that follow the reserved word **case**. (Recall that, in a syntax template, the shading indicates an optional part of the definition.)

Although it need not be, the `expression` is usually an identifier. Whether it is an identifier or an expression, the value of the identifier or the expression can be only *integral*, that is, an integer. The `expression` is sometimes called the **selector**. Its value determines which statement is selected for execution. A particular **case** value must appear only once. One or more statements may follow a **case** label, so you do not need to use braces to turn multiple statements into a single compound statement. The **break** statement may or may not appear after each `statements1`, `statements2`, ..., `statementsn`. Figure 4-7 shows the flow of execution of a **switch** statement.

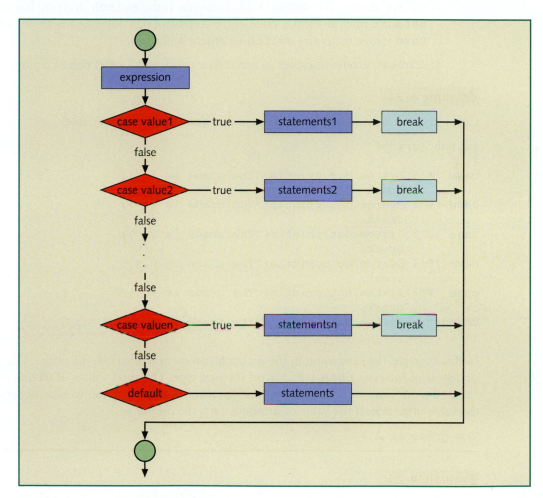

Figure 4-7   **switch** statement

A **switch** statement executes according to the following rules:

1. When the value of the **expression** is matched against a **case** value (also called a label), the statements execute until either a **break** statement is found or the end of the **switch** structure is reached.

2. If the value of the **expression** does not match any of the **case** values, the statements following the **default** label execute. If the **switch** structure has no **default** label, and if the value of the **expression** does not match any of the **case** values, the entire **switch** statement is skipped.

3. A **break** statement causes an immediate exit from the **switch** structure.

Example 4-24

Consider the following statements (assume that **grade** is a **char** variable):

```
switch (grade)
{
case 'A': System.out.println("The grade is A.");
          break;
case 'B': System.out.println("The grade is B.");
          break;
case 'C': System.out.println("The grade is C.");
          break;
case 'D': System.out.println("The grade is D.");
          break;
case 'F': System.out.println("The grade is F.");
          break;
default:  System.out.println("The grade is invalid.");
}
```

In this example, the expression in the **switch** statement is a variable identifier. The variable **grade** is of the type **char**, which is an integral type. The valid values of **grade** are **'A'**, **'B'**, **'C'**, **'D'**, and **'F'**. Each **case** label specifies a different action to take, depending on the value of **grade**. If the value of **grade** is **'A'**, the output is:

```
The grade is A.
```

Example 4-25

The following program illustrates the effect of the **break** statement. It asks the user to input a number between **0** and **10**.

```
//Effect of break statements in a switch structure

import java.util.*;

public class BreakStatementsInSwitch
{
    static Scanner console = new Scanner(System.in);
```

```
public static void main(String[] args)
{
    int num;

    System.out.print("Enter an integer between "
                     + "0 and 10: ");                       //Line 1
    num = console.nextInt();                                //Line 2
    System.out.println();                                   //Line 3

    System.out.println("The number you entered is "
                       + num);                              //Line 4

    switch (num)                                            //Line 5
    {
    case 0:                                                 //Line 6
    case 1: System.out.print("Hello ");                     //Line 7
    case 2: System.out.print("there. ");                    //Line 8
    case 3: System.out.print("I am ");                      //Line 9
    case 4: System.out.println("Mickey.");                  //Line 10
            break;                                          //Line 11
    case 5: System.out.print("How ");                       //Line 12
    case 6:                                                 //Line 13
    case 7:                                                 //Line 14
    case 8: System.out.println("are you?");                 //Line 15
            break;                                          //Line 16
    case 9: break;                                          //Line 17
    case 10: System.out.println("Have a nice day.");        //Line 18
             break;                                         //Line 19
    default: System.out.println("Sorry the number is "
                                + "out of range.");         //Line 20
    }

    System.out.println("Out of the switch "
                       + "structure.");                     //Line 21
}
}
```

Sample Runs

These outputs were obtained by executing the preceding program several times. In each of these outputs, the user input is shaded.

Sample Run 1:
```
Enter an integer between 0 and 10: 0

The number you entered is 0
Hello there. I am Mickey.
Out of the switch the structure.
```

Sample Run 2:
Enter an integer between 0 and 10: 1

The number you entered is 1
Hello there. I am Mickey.
Out of the switch structure.

Sample Run 3:
Enter an integer between 0 and 10: 3

The number you entered is 3
I am Mickey.
Out of the switch structure.

Sample Run 4:
Enter an integer between 0 and 10: 4

The number you entered is 4
Mickey.
Out of the switch structure.

Sample Run 5:
Enter an integer between 0 and 10: 5

The number you entered is 5
How are you?
Out of the switch structure.

Sample Run 6:
Enter an integer between 0 and 10: 7

The number you entered is 7
are you?
Out of the switch structure.

Sample Run 7:
Enter an integer between 0 and 10: 9

The number you entered is 9
Out of the switch structure.

Sample Run 8:
Enter an integer between 0 and 10: 10

The number you entered is 10
Have a nice day.
Out of the switch structure.

Sample Run 9:
```
Enter an integer between 0 and 10: 11

The number you entered is 11
Sorry the number is out of range.
Out of the switch structure.
```

A walk-through of this program, using certain values of the **switch** expression, num, can help you understand how the **break** statement functions. If the value of num is 0, the value of the **switch** expression matches the **case** value 0. All statements following **case** 0: execute until a **break** statement appears.

The first **break** statement appears in Line 11, just before the **case** value of 5. Even though the value of the **switch** expression does not match any of the **case** values (1, 2, 3, or 4), the statements following these values execute.

When the value of the **switch** expression matches a **case** value, *all* statements execute until a **break** is encountered, and the program skips all **case** labels in between. Similarly, if the value of num is 3, it matches the **case** value of 3 and the statements following this label execute until the **break** statement is encountered in Line 11. If the value of num is 9, it matches the **case** value of 9. In this situation, the action is empty, because only the **break** statement, in Line 17, follows the **case** value of 9.

4

Example 4-26

Although a **switch** structure's **case** values (labels) are limited, the **switch** statement **expression** can be as complex as necessary. Consider the following **switch** statement:

```
switch (score / 10)
{
case 0: case 1: case 2:
case 3: case 4: case 5: grade = 'F';
                        break;
case 6: grade = 'D';
        break;
case 7: grade = 'C';
        break;
case 8: grade = 'B';
        break;
case 9: case 10: grade = 'A';
                 break;
default: System.out.println("Invalid test score.");
}
```

Assume that **score** is an **int** variable with values between 0 and 100. If **score** is 75, then score / 10 = 75 / 10 = 7 and the grade assigned is **'C'**. If the value of **score** is between 0 and 59, then the grade is **'F'**. If **score** is between 0 and 59, score / 10 is 0, 1, 2, 3, 4, or 5; each of these values corresponds to the grade **'F'**.

Therefore, in this **switch** structure, the action statements of **case** 0, **case** 1, **case** 2, **case** 3, **case** 4, and **case** 5 are all the same. Rather than write the statement **grade = 'F';** followed by the **break** statement for each of the **case** values of 0, 1, 2, 3, 4, and 5, you can simplify the programming code by first specifying all of the case values (as shown in the preceding code) and then specifying the desired action statement. The **case** values of 9 and 10 follow similar conventions.

Choosing Between an **if...else** and a **switch** Structure

As you can see from the preceding examples, the **switch** statement is an elegant way to implement multiple selections. You will see a **switch** statement used in the programming example in this chapter. No fixed rules exist that can be applied to decide whether to use an **if...else** structure or a **switch** structure to implement multiple selections, but you should remember the following considerations: If multiple selections involve a range of values, you should use either an **if...else** structure or a **switch** structure, wherein you convert each range to a finite set of values.

For instance, in Example 4–26, the value of **grade** depends on the value of **score**. If **score** is between 0 and 59, **grade** is **'F'**. Because **score** is an **int** variable, 60 values correspond to the grade of **'F'**. If you list all 60 values as **case** values, the **switch** statement could be very long. However, dividing by 10 reduces these 60 values to only 6 values: 0, 1, 2, 3, 4, and 5.

If the range of values is infinite and you cannot reduce them to a set containing a finite number of values, you must use the **if...else** structure. For example, if **score** is a **double** variable, the number of values between 0 and 60 is infinite. However, you can use the expression **(int)(score) / 10** and reduce this infinite number of values to just six values.

PROGRAMMING EXAMPLE: CABLE COMPANY BILLING

This programming example demonstrates a program that calculates a customer's bill for a local cable company. There are two types of customers: residential and business. There are two rates for calculating a cable bill: one for residential customers and one for business customers.

For residential customers, the following rates apply:

- Bill-processing fee: **$4.50**
- Basic service fee: **$20.50**
- Premium channel: **$7.50** per channel

For business customers, the following rates apply:

- Bill-processing fee: $15.00
- Basic service fee: $75.00 for the first 10 connections; $5.00 for each additional connection
- Premium channel: $50.00 per channel for any number of connections

The program should ask the user for an account number (an integer) and a customer code. Assume that R or r stands for a residential customer, and B or b stands for a business customer.

Input   Input to the program is the customer's account number, customer code, number of premium channels to which the customer subscribes and, in the case of business customers, the number of basic service connections.

Output   Customer's account number and the billing amount.

Problem Analysis and Algorithm Design

The purpose of this program is to calculate and print the billing amount. To calculate the billing amount, you need to know the customer for whom the billing amount is calculated (whether the customer is residential or business) and the number of premium channels to which the customer subscribes. In the case of a business customer, you need to know the number of basic service connections and the number of premium channels. Other data needed to calculate the bill, such as bill-processing fees and the cost of a premium channel, are known quantities. The program should print the billing amount to two decimal places, which is standard for monetary amounts. This problem analysis translates into the following algorithm:

1. Prompt the user for the account number and customer type.
2. Determine the number of premium channels and basic service connections, compute the bill, and print the bill based on the customer type:
   a. If the customer type is R or r,
      (i)   Prompt the user for the number of premium channels.
      (ii) Compute the bill.
      (iii) Print the bill.
   b. If the customer type is B or b,
      (i)   Prompt the user for the number of basic service connections and number of premium channels.
      (ii) Compute the bill.
      (iii) Print the bill.

Variables

Because the program will ask the user to input the customer account number, customer code, number of premium channels, and number of basic service connections, you need variables to store all of this information. Also, because the program will calculate the billing amount, you need a variable to store the billing amount. Thus, the program needs at least the following variables to compute and print the bill:

```
int    accountNumber;     //variable to store the customer's
                          //account number
char   customerType;      //variable to store the customer code
int    numberOfPremiumChannels;  //variable to store the number
                                 //of premium channels to which the
                                 //customer subscribes
int    numberOfBasicServiceConnections;  //variable to store
                     //the number of basic service connections
                     //to which the customer subscribes
double amountDue;     //variable to store the billing amount
```

Named Constants

As you can see, the bill-processing fees, the cost of a basic service connection, and the cost of a premium channel are fixed; these values are needed to compute the bill. Although these values are constants in the program, they can change with little warning. To simplify the process of modifying the program later, instead of using these values directly in the program, you should declare them as named constants. Based on the problem analysis, you need to declare the following named constants:

```
        //Named constants - residential customers
static final double R_BILL_PROC_FEE = 4.50;
static final double R_BASIC_SERV_COST = 20.50;
static final double R_COST_PREM_CHANNEL = 7.50;

        //Named constants - business customers
static final double B_BILL_PROC_FEE = 15.00;
static final double B_BASIC_SERV_COST = 75.00;
static final double B_BASIC_CONN_COST = 5.00;
static final double B_COST_PREM_CHANNEL = 50.00;
```

Formulas

The program uses a number of formulas to compute the billing amount. To compute the residential bill, you need to know only the number of premium channels to which the user subscribes. The following statement calculates the billing amount for a residential customer:

```
amountDue = R_BILL_PROC_FEE + R_BASIC_SERV_COST +
            numberOfPremiumChannels * R_COST_PREM_CHANNEL;
```

To compute the business bill, you need to know the number of basic service connections and the number of premium channels to which the user subscribes. If the number of basic service connections is less than or equal to 10, the cost of the basic service connections is fixed. If the number of basic service connections exceeds 10, you must add the cost for each connection over 10. The following statement calculates the business billing amount:

```
if (numberOfBasicServiceConnections <= 10)
    amountDue =   B_BILL_PROC_FEE + B_BASIC_SERV_COST +
                  numberOfPremiumChannels * B_COST_PREM_CHANNEL;
else
    amountDue =   B_BILL_PROC_FEE + B_BASIC_SERV_COST +
                  (numberOfBasicServiceConnections - 10) *
                  B_BASIC_CONN_COST +
                  numberOfPremiumChannels * B_COST_PREM_CHANNEL;
```

Main Algorithm

Based on the preceding discussion, you can now write the main algorithm.

1. Prompt the user to enter the account number.
2. Get the customer account number.
3. Prompt the user to enter the customer code.
4. Get the customer code.
5. If the customer code is r or R:
   a. Prompt the user to enter the number of premium channels.
   b. Get the number of premium channels.
   c. Calculate the billing amount.
   d. Print the account number.
   e. Print the billing amount.
6. If the customer code is b or B:
   a. Prompt the user to enter the number of basic service connections.
   b. Get the number of basic service connections.
   c. Prompt the user to enter the number of premium channels.
   d. Get the number of premium channels.
   e. Calculate the billing amount.
   f. Print the account number.
   g. Print the billing amount.
7. If the customer code is something other than r, R, b, or B, output an error message.

For Steps 5 and 6, the program uses a **switch** statement to calculate the bill for the desired customer. (You can also use an **if...else** statement to implement Steps 5 and 6.)

Complete Program Listing

```java
//Chapter 4: Cable Company Billing

import java.util.*;

public class CableCompanyBilling
{
    static Scanner console = new Scanner(System.in);

        //Named constants - residential customers
    static final double R_BILL_PROC_FEE = 4.50;
    static final double R_BASIC_SERV_COST = 20.50;
    static final double R_COST_PREM_CHANNEL = 7.50;

      //Named constants - business customers
    static final double B_BILL_PROC_FEE = 15.00;
    static final double B_BASIC_SERV_COST = 75.00;
    static final double B_BASIC_CONN_COST = 5.00;
    static final double B_COST_PREM_CHANNEL = 50.00;

    public static void main(String[] args)
    {
            //Variable declaration
        int    accountNumber;
        char   customerType;
        int    numberOfPremiumChannels;
        int    numberOfBasicServiceConnections;
        double amountDue;

        System.out.println("This program computes a cable bill.");

        System.out.print("Enter the account number: ");        //Step 1
        accountNumber = console.nextInt();                     //Step 2
        System.out.println();

        System.out.print("Enter the customer type: "
                        + "R or r (Residential), "
                        + "B or b (Business): ");               //Step 3
        customerType = console.next().charAt(0);                //Step 4
        System.out.println();

        switch (customerType)
        {
        case 'r':                                               //Step 5
        case 'R': System.out.print("Enter the number "
                                + "of premium channels: ");     //Step 5a
```

```java
                    numberOfPremiumChannels =
                              console.nextInt();              //Step 5b
               System.out.println();

               amountDue = R_BILL_PROC_FEE +                  //Step 5c
                        R_BASIC_SERV_COST +
                        numberOfPremiumChannels *
                        R_COST_PREM_CHANNEL;

               System.out.println("Account number = "
                              + accountNumber);               //Step 5d
               System.out.printf("Amount due = $%.2f %n",
                              amountDue);                     //Step 5e
               break;
   case 'b':                                                  //Step 6
   case 'B': System.out.print("Enter the number of basic "
                              + "service connections: ");     //Step 6a
               numberOfBasicServiceConnections =
                              console.nextInt();              //Step 6b
               System.out.println();
               System.out.print("Enter the number "
                              + "of premium channels: ");     //Step 6c
               numberOfPremiumChannels =
                              console.nextInt();              //Step 6d
               System.out.println();

               if (numberOfBasicServiceConnections <= 10)     //Step 6e
                   amountDue = B_BILL_PROC_FEE +
                            B_BASIC_SERV_COST +
                            numberOfPremiumChannels *
                            B_COST_PREM_CHANNEL;
               else
                   amountDue = B_BILL_PROC_FEE +
                            B_BASIC_SERV_COST +
                            (numberOfBasicServiceConnections - 10)
                            * B_BASIC_CONN_COST +
                            numberOfPremiumChannels *
                            B_COST_PREM_CHANNEL;

               System.out.println("Account number = "
                              + accountNumber);               //Step 6f
               System.out.printf("Amount due = $%.2f %n",
                              amountDue);                     //Step 6g
               break;
   default: System.out.println("Invalid customer type.");  //Step 7
   }//end switch
   }
}
```

Sample Run: In this sample run, the user input is shaded:

```
This program computes a cable bill.
Enter the account number: 12345

Enter the customer type: R or r (Residential), B or b (Business): b

Enter the number of basic service connections: 16

Enter the number of premium channels: 8

Account number = 12345
Amount due = $520.00
```

QUICK REVIEW

1. Control structures alter the normal flow of control.

2. The two most common control structures are selection and repetition.

3. Selection structures incorporate decisions in a program.

4. The Java relational operators are == (equality), < (less than), <= (less than or equal to), > (greater than), >= (greater than or equal to), and != (not equal to).

5. Including a space within the relational operators ==, <=, >=, and != creates a syntax error. (For example, = = will create a syntax error.)

6. Characters are compared using the collating sequence of the Unicode character set.

7. To compare strings, you use the method `compareTo` of the **class** String.

8. To use the method `compareTo`, you use the expression:

   ```
   str1.compareTo(str2)
   ```

   where `str1` and `str2` are String variables. Moreover, `str2` can also be a String constant. The expression `str1.compareTo(str2)` evaluates as follows:

   $$str1.compareTo(str2) = \begin{cases} \text{an integer value less than 0 if string } str1 \text{ is less than string } str2 \\ 0 \text{ if string } str1 \text{ is equal to string } str2 \\ \text{an integer value greater than 0 if string } str1 \text{ is greater than string } str2 \end{cases}$$

9. Logical (Boolean) expressions evaluate to **true** or **false**.

10. In Java, **boolean** variables are used to store the value of a logical expression.

11. In Java, the logical operators are ! (not), && (and), and || (or).

12. In Java, there are two selection structures.

13. One-way selection takes the following form:

```
if (expression)
    statement
```

If `expression` is **true**, then the `statement` executes; otherwise, the computer executes the statement following the **if** statement.

14. Two-way selection takes the following form:

```
if (expression)
    statement1
else
    statement2
```

If `expression` is **true**, then `statement1` executes; otherwise, `statement2` executes.

15. The expression in an **if** or **if...else** structure is a logical expression.

16. Including a semicolon before the `statement` in a one-way selection creates a semantic error. In this case, the action of the **if** statement is empty.

17. Including a semicolon before `statement1` in a two-way selection creates a syntax error.

18. There is no stand-alone **else** statement in Java. Every **else** has a related **if**.

19. An **else** is paired with the most recent **if** that has not been paired with any other **else**.

20. A sequence of statements enclosed between braces, **{** and **}**, is called a compound statement or block of statements. A compound statement is treated as a single statement.

21. A **switch** structure is used to handle multiple selections.

22. The **expression** in a **switch** statement must evaluate to an integer.

23. A **switch** statement executes according to the following rules:

1. When the value of the **expression** is matched against a **case** value, the statements execute until either a **break** statement is found or the end of the **switch** structure is reached.

2. If the value of the **expression** does not match any of the **case** values, the statements following the **default** label execute. If the **switch** structure has no **default** label, and if the value of the **expression** does not match any of the **case** values, the entire **switch** statement is skipped.

3. A **break** statement causes an immediate exit from the **switch** structure.

EXERCISES

1. Mark the following statements as true or false.

   a. The result of a logical expression cannot be assigned to an **int** variable.

   b. In a one-way selection, if a semicolon is placed after the expression in an **if** statement, the expression in the **if** statement is always **true**.

   c. Every **if** statement must have a corresponding **else**.

   d. The expression:

      ```
      (ch >= 'A' && ch <= 'Z')
      ```

      evaluates to **false** if either ch < 'A' or ch >= 'Z'.

   e. Suppose the input is 5. (Assume that all variables are properly declared.) The output of the code:

      ```
      num = console.nextInt();
      if (num > 5)
          System.out.println(num);
          num = 0;
      else
          System.out.println("Num is zero");
      ```

      is:

      ```
      Num is zero.
      ```

   f. The expression in a **switch** statement should evaluate to a value of a primitive data type.

   g. The expression !(x > 0) is true only if x is a negative number.

   h. In Java, both ! and != are logical operators.

   i. The order in which statements execute in a program is called the flow of control.

2. Circle the best answer.

   a.

      ```
      if (6 < 2 * 5)
          System.out.print("Hello");
          System.out.print(" There");
      ```

      outputs the following:

      (i) Hello There   (ii) Hello   (iii) Hello   (iv) There
                                                    There

b.

```java
if ('a' > 'b' || 66 > (int)('A'))
    System.out.println("#*#");
```

outputs the following:

(i) `#*#`   (ii) `#`   (iii) `*`   (iv) none of these

           `*`

           `#`

c.

```java
if (7 <= 7)
    System.out.println(6 - 9 * 2 / 6);
```

outputs the following:

(i) `-1`   (ii) `3`   (iii) `3.0`   (iv) none of these

d.

```java
if (7 < 8)
{
    System.out.println("2 4 6 8");
    System.out.println("1 3 5 7);
}
```

outputs the following:

(i) `2 4 6 8`   (ii) `1 3 5 7`   (iii) none of these

    `1 3 5 7`

e.

```java
if (5 < 3)
    System.out.println("*");
else
    if (7 == 8)
        System.out.println("&");
    else
        System.out.println("$");
```

outputs the following:

(i) `*`   (ii) `&`   (iii) `$`   (iv) none of these

3. What is the output of the following Java code?

```java
x = 100;
y = 200;

if (x > 100 && y <= 200)
    System.out.println(x + " " + y + " " + (x + y));
else
    System.out.println(x + " " + y + " " + (2 * x - y));
```

4. Write Java statements that output `Male` if the gender is `'M'`, `Female` if the gender is `'F'`, and `invalid gender` otherwise.

5. Correct the following code so that it prints the correct message.

```java
if (score >= 60)
    System.out.println("You pass.");
else;
    System.out.println("You fail.");
```

6. Suppose that you have the following declaration:

```java
int j = 0;
```

The output of the statement:

```java
if ((8 > 4) || (j++ == 7))
    System.out.println("j = " + j);
```

is:

```
j = 0
```

while the output of the statement:

```java
if ((8 > 4) | (j++ == 7))
    System.out.println("j = " + j);
```

is:

```
j = 1
```

Explain why.

7. State whether the following are valid **switch** statements. If not, explain why. Assume that n and `digit` are **int** variables.

a.

```java
switch (n <= 2)
{
case 0: System.out.println("Draw.");
        break;
case 1: System.out.println("Win.");
        break;
case 2: System.out.println("Lose.");
        break;
}
```

b.

```java
switch (digit / 4)
{
case 0: case 1: System.out.println("low.");
                break;
case 1: case 2: System.out.println("middle.");
                break;
case 3: System.out.println("high.");
}
```

c.

```
switch (n % 6)
{
case 1: case 2: case 3: case 4: case 5: System.out.println(n);
                                         break;
case 0: System.out.println();
        break;
 }
```

d.

```
switch (n % 10)
{
case 0: case 2: case 4: case 6:
case 8: System.out.println("Even");
        break;
case 1: case 3: case 5: case 7: System.out.println("Odd");
                                break;
 }
```

8. Suppose the input is 5. What is the value of `alpha` after the following Java code executes? (Assume that `alpha` is an `int` variable and `console` is a `Scanner` object initialized to the keyboard.)

```
alpha = console.nextInt();

switch (alpha)
{
case 1:
case 2: alpha = alpha + 2;
        break;
case 4: alpha++;
case 5: alpha = 2 * alpha;
case 6: alpha = alpha + 5;
        break;
default: alpha--;
}
```

9. Suppose the input is 3. What is the value of `beta` after the following Java code executes? (Assume that all variables are properly declared.)

```
beta = console.nextInt();

switch (beta)
{
case 3: beta = beta + 3;
case 1: beta++;  break;
case 5: beta = beta + 5;
case 4: beta = beta + 4;
}
```

10. Suppose the input is 6. What is the value of a after the following Java code executes? (Assume that all variables are properly declared.)

```java
a = console.nextInt();

if (a > 0)
    switch (a)
    {
    case 1: a = a + 3;
    case 3: a++;
            break;
    case 6: a = a + 6;
    case 8: a = a * 8;
            break;
    default: a--;
    }
else
        a = a + 2;
```

11. In the following code, correct any errors that would prevent the program from compiling or running.

```java
public class Errors
{
    public static void main(String[] args)
    {
        int a, b;
        boolean found;

        System.out.print("Enter the first integer: ");
        a = console.nextInt();;
        System.out.println();

        System.out.print("Enter the second integer: ");
        b = console.nextInt();;

        if a > a * b && 10 < b
            found = 2 * a > b;
        else
        {
            found = 2 * a < b;
            if found
                a = 3;
                c = 15;
            if b
            {
                b = 0;
                a = 1;
            }
        }
    }
}
```

12. The following program contains errors. Correct them so that the program will run and output w = 21.

```
public class Mystery
{
    static final int ONE = 5;

    public static void main(String[] args)
    {
        int  x, y, w, z;
        z = 9;

        if z > 10
            x = 12;  y = 5,    w = x + y + one;
        else
            x = 12;  y = 4,    w = x + y + one;

        System.out.println("w = " + w);
    }
}
```

4

PROGRAMMING EXERCISES

1. Write a program that prompts the user to input a number. The program should then output the number and a message saying whether the number is positive, negative, or zero.

2. Write a program that prompts the user to input three numbers. The program should then output the numbers in ascending order.

3. Write a program that prompts the user to input an integer between 0 and 35. If the number is less than or equal to 9, the program should output the number; otherwise, it should output A for 10, B for 11, C for 12, ..., and Z for 35. (*Hint:* Use the cast operator (**char**) for numbers >= 10.)

4. The cost of an international call from New York to New Delhi is calculated as follows: connection fee, $1.99; $2.00 for the first three minutes; and $0.45 for each additional minute. Write a program that prompts the user to enter the number of minutes the call lasted and outputs the amount due. Format your output with two decimal places.

5. In a right triangle, the square of the length of the longest side is equal to the sum of the squares of the lengths of the other two sides. Write a program that prompts the user to enter the lengths of three sides of a triangle, and then outputs a message indicating whether the triangle is a right triangle.

6. The roots of the quadratic equation $ax^2 + bx + c = 0$, where a, b, and c are real numbers, and $a \neq 0$, are given by the following formula:

$$\frac{-b \pm \sqrt{b^2 - 4ac}}{2a}$$

In this formula, the term $b^2 - 4ac$ is called the discriminant. If $b^2 - 4ac = 0$, then the equation has a single (repeated) root. If $b^2 - 4ac > 0$, the equation has two real roots. If $b^2 - 4ac < 0$, the equation has two complex roots. Write a program that prompts the user to input the value of a (the coefficient of x^2), b (the coefficient of x), and c (the constant term), and outputs the type of roots of the equation. Furthermore, if $b^2 - 4ac > 0$, the program should output the roots of the quadratic equation. (*Hint:* Use the method **sqrt** from the **class** Math to calculate the square root. **Math.sqrt(x)** is the square root of **x**, where **x** $\geq$ **0**.)

7. Write a program that prompts the user to input the x-y coordinate of a point in a Cartesian plane. The program should then output a message indicating whether the point is the origin, is located on the x (or y) axis, or appears in a particular quadrant.

   For example:

   ```
   (0, 0) is the origin
   (4, 0) is on the x-axis
   (0, -3) is on the y-axis
   (-2, 3) is in the second quadrant
   ```

8. Write a program that mimics a calculator. The program should take as input two integers and the operation to be performed. It should then output the numbers, the operator, and the result. (For division, if the denominator is zero, output an appropriate message.) Some sample output follows:

   ```
   3 + 4 = 7
   13 * 5 = 65
   ```

9. Redo Exercise 8 to handle floating-point numbers. (Format your output to two decimal places.)

10. A bank in your town updates its customers' accounts at the end of each month. The bank offers two types of accounts: savings and checking. Every customer must maintain a minimum balance. If a customer's balance falls below the minimum, there is a service charge of $10.00 for savings accounts and $25.00 for checking accounts. If the balance at the end of the month is at least the minimum balance, the account receives interest as follows:

    - Savings accounts receive 4% interest.

    - Checking accounts with balances of up to $5000 more than the minimum balance receive 3% interest; otherwise, the interest is 5%.

    Write a program that reads a customer's account number (**int** type), account type (**char**; s for savings, c for checking), minimum balance that the account should maintain, and the current balance. The program should then output the account number, account type, current balance, and an appropriate message. Test your program by running it five times, using the following data:

    ```
    46728 S 1000 2700
    87324 C 1500 7689
    79873 S 1000 800
    89832 C 2000 3000
    98322 C 1000 750
    ```

11. Write a program that implements the algorithm given in Example 1-2 (Chapter 1), which determines the monthly wages of a salesperson.

12. Write a program that calculates and prints the bill for a cellular telephone company. The company offers two types of service: regular and premium. Its rates vary depending on the type of service. The rates are computed as follows:

Regular service: $10.00 plus first 50 minutes are free. Charges for over 50 minutes are $0.20 per minute.

Premium service: $25.00 plus:

    a. For calls made from 6:00 A.M. to 6:00 P.M., the first 75 minutes are free; charges for over 75 minutes are $0.10 per minute.

    b. For calls made from 6:00 P.M. to 6:00 A.M., the first 100 minutes are free; charges for over 100 minutes are $0.05 per minute.

Your program should prompt the user to enter an account number, a service code (type **char**), and the number of minutes the service was used. A service code of r or R means regular service; a service code of p or P means premium service. Treat any other character as an error. Your program should output the account number, type of service, number of minutes the telephone service was used, and the amount due from the user.

For the premium service, the customer may be using the service both during the day and at night. Therefore, to calculate the bill, you must ask the user to input the number of minutes the service was used during the day and the number of minutes the service was used at night.

4

CONTROL STRUCTURES II

Repetition

In this chapter, you will:

♦ Learn about repetition (looping) control structures

♦ Explore how to construct and use counter-controlled, sentinel-controlled, flag-controlled, and EOF-controlled repetition structures

♦ Examine **break** and **continue** statements

♦ Discover how to form and use nested control structures

In Chapter 4, you learned how decisions are incorporated in programs. In this chapter, you learn how repetitions are incorporated in programs.

WHY IS REPETITION NEEDED?

Suppose you want to add five integers to find their average. From what you have learned so far, you know that you could proceed as follows (assume that all the variables are properly declared):

```
num1 = console.nextInt();    //get the first number
num2 = console.nextInt();    //get the second number
num3 = console.nextInt();    //get the third number
num4 = console.nextInt();    //get the fourth number
num5 = console.nextInt();    //get the fifth number

sum = num1 + num2 + num3 + num4 + num5;    //add the numbers
average = sum / 5;                         //find the average
```

But suppose you want to add and average 1000 or more numbers. You would have to declare that many variables, and list them again in the input statements, and perhaps again in the output statements. This would take an exorbitant amount of typing as well as time. Also, if you wanted to run this program again with different values, or with a different number of values, you would have to rewrite the program.

Suppose you want to add the following numbers:

5 3 7 9 4

Assume that the input is these five numbers. Consider the following statements, in which sum and num are variables of the type **int**:

```
sum = 0;                     //Line 1
num = console.nextInt();     //Line 2
sum = sum + num;             //Line 3
```

The statement in Line 1 initializes **sum** to 0. Let's execute the statements in Lines 2 and 3. The statement in Line 2 stores 5 in num; the statement in Line 3 updates the value of **sum** by adding num to it. After Line 3 executes, the value of **sum** is 5.

Let's repeat the statements in Lines 2 and 3. After the statement in Line 2 executes (after the programming code reads the next number),

num = 3

After the statement in Line 3 executes,

sum = sum + num = 5 + 3 = 8

At this point, **sum** contains the sum of the first two numbers. Let's repeat the statements in Lines 2 and 3 a third time. After the statement in Line 2 executes (after the programming code reads the next number),

num = 7

After the statement in Line 3 executes,

```
sum = sum + num = 8 + 7 = 15
```

Now **sum** contains the sum of the first three numbers. If you repeat the statements in Lines 2 and 3 two more times, **sum** will contain the sum of all five numbers.

If you want to add 10 integers, you can repeat the statements in Lines 2 and 3 ten times. And if you want to add 100 numbers, you can repeat the statements one hundred times. In either case, you do not have to declare any additional variables as you did in the first code in this chapter. By repeating the statements in Lines 2 and 3 you can add any set of integers, whereas the earlier code requires that you drastically change the code.

There are many situations in which it is necessary to repeat a set of statements. For example, for each student in a class, the formula to determine the course grade is the same. Java has three repetition, or looping, structures that let you repeat statements over and over until certain conditions are met: **while**, **for**, and **do...while**. The following sections discuss these three looping (repetition) structures.

while LOOPING (REPETITION) STRUCTURE

In the previous section, you saw that sometimes it is necessary to repeat a set of statements several times. One way to repeat a set of statements is to type the set of statements in the program over and over. For example, if you want to repeat a set of statements 100 times, you type the set of statements 100 times in the program. However, this way of repeating a set of statements is impractical, if not impossible. Fortunately, there is a better way to repeat a set of statements. As noted earlier, Java has three repetition, or looping, structures that allow you to repeat a set of statements until certain conditions are met. This section discusses the first looping structure, a **while** loop.

The general form of the **while** statement is:

```
while (expression)
    statement
```

In Java, **while** is a reserved word. The **expression**, called a **loop condition**, acts as a *decision-maker* and is a logical expression. The **statement** is called the body of the loop. Moreover, the **statement** can be either a simple or compound statement. Also note that the parentheses around the **expression** are part of the syntax. Figure 5-1 shows the flow of execution of a **while** loop.

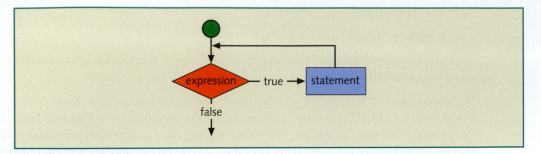

Figure 5-1   `while` loop

The `expression` provides an entry condition. If it initially evaluates to **true**, the `statement` executes. The loop condition—the `expression`—is then reevaluated. If it again evaluates to **true**, the `statement` executes again. The `statement` (body of the loop) continues to execute until the `expression` is no longer **true**. A loop that continues to execute endlessly is called an **infinite loop**. To avoid an infinite loop, make sure that the loop's body contains one or more statements that ensure that the loop condition—the `expression` in the `while` statement—will eventually be **false**.

Example 5-1

Consider the following Java program segment:

```
i = 0;                                     //Line 1

while (i <= 20)                            //Line 2
{
    System.out.print(i + " ");             //Line 3
    i = i + 5;                             //Line 4
}

System.out.println();                      //Line 5
```

Sample Run:
0 5 10 15 20

In Line 1, the variable i is set to 0. The `expression` in the `while` statement (in Line 2), i <= 20, is then evaluated. Because the expression i <= 20 evaluates to **true**, the body of the `while` loop executes next. The body of the `while` loop consists of the statements in Lines 3 and 4. The statement in Line 3 outputs the value of i, which is 0; the statement in Line 4 changes the value of i to 5. After executing the statements in Lines 3 and 4, the `expression` in the `while` loop (Line 2) is evaluated again. Because i is 5, the expression i <= 20 evaluates to **true** and the body of the `while` loop executes again. This process of evaluating the `expression` and executing the body of the `while` loop continues until the `expression` i <= 20 (Line 2) no longer evaluates to **true**.

The variable `i` (Line 2) in the expression is called the **loop control variable**.

Note the following from the preceding example:

1. Eventually, within the loop, `i` becomes `25`, but is not printed because the entry condition is **false**.

2. If you omit the statement:

   ```
   i = i + 5;
   ```

   from the body of the loop, you will have an infinite loop, continually printing rows of zeros.

3. You must initialize the loop control variable `i` before you execute the loop. If the statement:

   ```
   i = 0;
   ```

   (in Line 1) is omitted, either the loop might not execute at all or the compiler will generate an error. (Recall that not all variables in Java are automatically initialized.)

4. In the previous program segment, if the two statements in the body of the loop are interchanged, the result may be drastically altered. For example, consider the following statements:

   ```
   i = 0;

   while (i <= 20)
   {
       i = i + 5;
       System.out.print(i + " ");
   }

   System.out.println();
   ```

   Here the output is:

   ```
   5 10 15 20 25
   ```

   Typically, this would be a semantic error because you rarely want a condition to be **true** for `i <= 20`, and yet produce results for `i > 20`.

 (Designing while loops) As shown in Example 5-1, the body of a `while` loop executes only when the `expression`, in the `while` statement, evaluates to **true**. Typically, the `expression` checks whether a variable(s), called the loop control variable (LCV), satisfies certain conditions. For example, in Example 5-1, the `expression` in the `while` statement checks whether `i <= 20`. (Recall that in Java, when variables are declared, they are not automatically initialized.) The LCV must be properly initialized before the `while` loop, and it should eventually make the `expression` evaluate to `false`. We do this by updating the LCV in the body of the `while` loop. Therefore, `while` loops are typically written in the following form:

```
//initialize the loop control variable(s)

while (expression)        //expression tests the LCV
{
    .
    .
    .
    //update the loop control variable(s)
    .
    .
    .
}
```

For instance, in Example 5-1, the statement in Line 1 initializes the LCV `i` to 0. The expression `i <= 20` in Line 2 checks whether `i` is less than or equal to 20, and the statement in Line 4 updates the value of `i`.

Example 5-2

Consider the following Java program segment:

```
i = 20;                             //Line 1
while (i < 20)                      //Line 2
{
    System.out.print(i + " ");      //Line 3
    i  =  i + 5;                     //Line 4
}

System.out.println();               //Line 5
```

It is easy to overlook the difference between this example and Example 5-1. Here, in Line 1, `i` is set to 20. Because `i` is 20, the expression `i < 20` in the `while` statement (Line 2) evaluates to `false`. Initially the loop entry condition, `i < 20`, is `false`, so the body of the `while` loop never executes. Hence, no values are output and the value of `i` remains 20.

The next few sections describe the various forms of `while` loops.

Counter-Controlled while Loops

Suppose you know exactly how many times certain statements need to be executed. For example, suppose you know exactly how many pieces of data (or entries) need to be read. In such cases, the while loop assumes the form of a **counter-controlled while loop**. Suppose that a set of statements needs to be executed N times. You can set up a counter (initialized to 0 before the while statement) to track how many items have been read. Before executing the body of the while statement, the counter is compared with N. If counter < N, the body of the while statement executes. The body of the loop continues to execute until the value of counter >= N. Thus, inside the body of the while statement, the value of counter increments after it reads a new item. In this case, the while loop might look like the following:

```
counter = 0;        //initialize the loop control variable

while (counter < N) //test the loop control variable
{
      .
      .
      .
      counter++;    //update the loop control variable
      .
      .
      .
}
```

If N represents the number of data items in a file, then the value of N can be determined several ways: The program can prompt you to specify the number of items in the file; an input statement can read the value; or you can specify the first item in the file as the number of items in the file, so that you need not remember the number of input values (items). This is useful if someone other than the programmer enters the data. Consider Example 5-3.

Example 5-3

Suppose the input is:

12 8 9 2 3 90 38 56 8 23 89 7 2 8 3 8

The first number, 12, specifies the number of values in the data set. Suppose you want to add these numbers and find their average. Note that only 12 values are read; the others are discarded. The complete program is as follows:

```java
//Counter-controlled while loop

import java.util.*;

public class CounterControlledWhileLoop
{
    static Scanner console = new Scanner(System.in);

    public static void main (String[] args)
    {
        int limit;      //store the number of items
                        //in the list
        int number;     //variable to store the number
        int sum;        //variable to store the sum
        int counter;    //loop control variable

        System.out.println("Line 1: Enter the data for "
                        + "processing.");               //Line 1

        limit = console.nextInt();                      //Line 2

        sum = 0;                                        //Line 3
        counter = 0;                                    //Line 4

        while (counter < limit)                         //Line 5
        {
            number = console.nextInt();                 //Line 6
            sum = sum + number;                         //Line 7
            counter++;                                  //Line 8
        }

        System.out.printf("Line 9: The sum of the %d " +
                    "numbers = %d%n", limit, sum);      //Line 9

        if (counter != 0)                               //Line 10
            System.out.printf("Line 11: The average = %d%n",
                            (sum / counter));            //Line 11
        else                                            //Line 12
            System.out.println("Line 13: No input.");   //Line 13
    }
}
```

Sample Run: In this sample run, the user input is shaded.

```
Line 1: Enter the data for processing.
12 8 9 2 3 90 38 56 8 23 89 7 2 8 3 8
Line 9: The sum of the 12 numbers = 335
Line 11: The average = 27
```

The preceding program works as follows: The statement in Line 1 prompts the user to input the data for processing. The statement in Line 2 reads the next input line and stores it in the variable `limit`. The value of `limit` indicates the number of items to be read. The statements in Lines 3 and 4 initialize the variables `sum` and `counter` to 0. The **while** statement in Line 5 checks the value of `counter` to determine how many items have been read. If

counter is less than **limit**, the **while** loop proceeds for the next iteration. The statement in Line 6 stores the next number in the variable **number**. The statement in Line 7 updates the value of **sum** by adding the value of **number** to the previous value. The statement in Line 8 increments the value of **counter** by 1. The statement in Line 9 outputs the sum of the numbers. The statements in Lines 10 through 13 output either the average or the text: **Line 13: No input.**

Note that in this program, in Line 3, **sum** is initialized to 0. In Line 7, after storing the next number in **number** in Line 6, the program adds the next number to the sum of all the numbers scanned before the current number. The first number read is added to zero (because **sum** is initialized to 0), giving the correct sum of the first number. To find the average, divide **sum** by **counter**. If **counter** is 0, then dividing by 0 terminates the program and you get an error message. Therefore, before dividing **sum** by **counter**, you must check whether or not **counter** is 0.

Notice that in this program, the statement in Line 4 initializes the LCV **counter** to 0. The expression **counter < limit** in Line 5 evaluates whether **counter** is less than **limit**. The statement in Line 8 updates the value of **counter**. Note that in this program, the **while** loop can also be written without using the variable **number** as follows:

```
while (counter < limit)
{
    sum = sum + console.nextInt();
    counter++;
}
```

Sentinel-Controlled while Loops

You might not know exactly how many times a set of statements needs to be executed, but you do know that the statements need to be executed until a special value is met. This special value is called a **sentinel**. For example, while processing data, you might not know how many pieces of data (or entries) need to be read, but you do know that the last entry is a special value. In such cases, you read the first item before entering the **while** statement. If this item does not equal the sentinel, the body of the **while** statement executes. The **while** loop continues to execute as long as the program has not read the sentinel. Such a **while** loop is called a **sentinel-controlled while loop**. In this case, a **while** loop might look like the following:

```
input the first data item into variable //initialize the
                                         //loop control variable

while (variable != sentinel)    //test the loop control variable
{
    .
    .
    .
```

```
input a data item into variable   //update the loop
                                  //control variable
    .
    .
    .
}
```

Example 5-4

Suppose you want to read some positive integers and average them, but you do not have a preset number of data items in mind. Suppose the number **–999** marks the end of the data. You can proceed as follows:

```java
//Sentinel-controlled while loop

import java.util.*;

public class SentinelControlledWhileLoop
{
    static Scanner console = new Scanner(System.in);

    static final int SENTINEL = -999;

    public static void main (String[] args)
    {
        int number;            //variable to store the number
        int sum = 0;           //variable to store the sum
        int count = 0;         //variable to store the total
                               //numbers read

        System.out.println("Line 1: Enter positive integers "
                    + "ending with " + SENTINEL);    //Line 1

        number = console.nextInt();                  //Line 2

        while (number != SENTINEL)                   //Line 3
        {
            sum = sum + number;                      //Line 4
            count++;                                 //Line 5
            number = console.nextInt();              //Line 6
        }

        System.out.printf("Line 7: The sum of the %d " +
                    "numbers = %d%n", count, sum);   //Line 7

        if (count != 0)                              //Line 8
            System.out.printf("Line 9: The average = %d%n",
                            (sum / count));          //Line 9
        else                                         //Line 10
            System.out.println("Line 11: No input.");  //Line 11
    }
}
```

Sample Run: In this sample run, the user input is shaded.
```
Line 1: Enter positive integers ending with -999
34 23 9 45 78 0 77 8 3 5 -999
Line 7: The sum of the 10 numbers = 282
Line 9: The average = 28
```

This program works as follows: The statement in Line 1 prompts the user to enter numbers ending with **-999**. The statement in Line 2 reads the first number and stores it in the variable **number**. The **while** statement in Line 3 checks whether **number** is not equal to **SENTINEL**. If **number** is not equal to **SENTINEL**, the body of the **while** loop executes. The statement in Line 4 updates the value of **sum** by adding **number** to it. The statement in Line 5 increments the value of **count** by 1. The statement in Line 6 stores the next number in the variable **number**. The statements in Lines 4 through 6 repeat until the program reads **-999**. The statement in Line 7 outputs the sum of the numbers, and the statements in Lines 8 through 11 output the average of the numbers.

Notice that the statement in Line 2 initializes the LCV **number**. The expression **number != SENTINEL** in Line 3 checks whether the value of **number** is not equal to **SENTINEL**. The statement in Line 6 updates the LCV **number**. Also, note that the program continues to read data as long as the user has not entered **-999**.

Next, consider another example of a sentinel-controlled **while** loop. In this example, the user is prompted to enter the value to be processed. If the user wants to stop the program, he or she can enter the sentinel.

Example 5-5 Telephone Digits

The following program reads the letter codes **'A'** through **'Z'** and prints the corresponding telephone digit. This program uses a sentinel-controlled **while** loop. To stop the program, the user is prompted for the sentinel, which is **'#'**. This is also an example of a nested control structure, where **if... else**, **switch**, and the **while** loop are nested.

```java
//*****************************************************
// Program: Telephone Digits
// This is an example of a sentinel-controlled while loop.
// This program converts uppercase letters to their
// corresponding telephone digits.
//*****************************************************

import javax.swing.JOptionPane;

public class TelephoneDigitProgram
{
    public static void main (String[] args)
    {
```

5

```java
char letter;                                          //Line 1
String inputMessage;                                  //Line 2
String inputString;                                   //Line 3
String outputMessage;                                 //Line 4

inputMessage = "Program to convert uppercase "
             + "letters to their corresponding "
             + "telephone digits.\n"
             + "To stop the program enter #.\n"
             + "Enter a letter:";                     //Line 5
inputString =
    JOptionPane.showInputDialog(inputMessage);        //Line 6
letter = inputString.charAt(0);                       //Line 7

while (letter != '#' )                                //Line 8
{
    outputMessage = "The letter you entered is: "
                  + letter + "\n"
                  + "The corresponding telephone "
                  + "digit is: ";                     //Line 9
    if (letter >= 'A' && letter <= 'Z')               //Line 10
    {
        switch (letter)                               //Line 11
        {
        case 'A': case 'B':
        case 'C': outputMessage = outputMessage
                                + "2";                //Line 12
                  break;                              //Line 13
        case 'D': case 'E':
        case 'F': outputMessage = outputMessage
                                + "3";                //Line 14
                  break;                              //Line 15
        case 'G': case 'H':
        case 'I': outputMessage = outputMessage
                                + "4";                //Line 16
                  break;                              //Line 17
        case 'J': case 'K':
        case 'L': outputMessage = outputMessage
                                + "5";                //Line 18
                  break;                              //Line 19
        case 'M': case 'N':
        case 'O': outputMessage = outputMessage
                                + "6";                //Line 20
                  break;                              //Line 21
        case 'P': case 'Q': case 'R':
        case 'S': outputMessage = outputMessage
                                + "7";                //Line 22
```

```
                        break;                          //Line 23
          case 'T': case 'U':
          case 'V': outputMessage = outputMessage
                                    + "8";              //Line 24
                        break;                          //Line 25
          case 'W': case 'X': case 'Y':
          case 'Z': outputMessage = outputMessage
                                    + "9";              //Line 26

          }
       }
       else                                             //Line 27
           outputMessage = outputMessage
                        + "Invalid input";              //Line 28

       JOptionPane.showMessageDialog(null, outputMessage,
                     "Telephone Digit",
                     JOptionPane.PLAIN_MESSAGE); //Line 29
       inputMessage = "Enter another uppercase letter "
                   + "to find its corresponding "
                   + "telephone digit.\n"
                   + "To stop the program enter #.\n"
                   + "Enter a letter:";          //Line 30

       inputString =
          JOptionPane.showInputDialog(inputMessage); //Line 31
       letter = inputString.charAt(0);              //Line 32
     }//end while

     System.exit(0);                                //Line 33
   }
 }
```

Sample Run: Figure 5-2 shows the sample run.

5

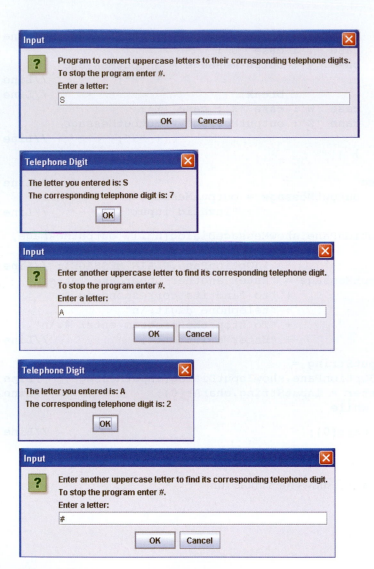

Figure 5-2   Sample run of `telephone digit program`

The program in Example 5-5 works as follows: The statements in Lines 1 through 4 declare the appropriate variables. The statement in Line 5 creates the appropriate string to be included in the input dialog box. The statement in Line 6 displays the input dialog box informing the user what to do. This statement also retrieves the string entered by the user and assigns this string to the `inputString`. (Notice that even though the user enters a single letter, it is still considered a string.) The statement in Line 7 retrieves the letter from `inputString` and stores it in `letter`. The expression in the **while** statement in Line 8 checks that the letter is not #. If the letter entered by the user is not #, the body of the **while** loop executes. The statement in Line 9 creates the appropriate string to be displayed in the output dialog box.

The **if** statement in Line 10 checks whether the letter entered by the user is uppercase. If the letter entered by the user is uppercase, the **expression** in the **if** statement (in Line 10) evaluates to **true** and the **switch** statement executes, which determines the appropriate telephone digit and appends the telephone digit to **outputMessage**. (See the statements in Lines 11 through 26.) If the letter entered by the user is not uppercase, the **else** statement (in Line 27) executes and the statement in Line 28 appends the string **"Invalid input"** to **outputMessage**. The statement in Line 29 displays the output dialog box showing the result of the input.

Once the current letter is processed, the statement in Line 30 creates the message string, and the statement in Line 31 displays the input dialog box informing the user what to do next. The statement in Line 32 copies the letter entered by the user into **letter**. (Note that the statement in Line 30 is similar to the statement in Line 5, and that the statements in Lines 31 and 32 are the same as the statements in Lines 6 and 7.) After the statement in Line 32 (at the end of the **while** loop) executes, the control goes back to the top of the **while** loop and the same process begins again. When the user enters #, the program terminates.

In the program in Example 5-5, you can write the statements between Lines 10 and 28 using just a **switch** structure, that is, without the **if** in Line 10 and the **else** in Line 27. (See Programming Exercise 3 at the end of this chapter.)

Flag-Controlled while Loops

A **flag-controlled while loop** uses a **boolean** variable to control the loop. Suppose found is a **boolean** variable. The flag-controlled **while** loop takes the following form:

```
found = false;        //initialize the loop control variable

while (!found)         //test the loop control variable
{
    .
    .
    .

    if (expression)
        found = true; //update the loop control variable
    .
    .
    .
}
```

The variable, such as `found`, which is used to control the execution of the `while` loop, is called a **flag variable**.

Example 5-6 further illustrates the use of a flag-controlled `while` loop.

Example 5-6 Guessing the Number Game

The following program randomly generates an integer greater than or equal to 0 and less than 100. The program then prompts the user to guess the number. If the user guesses the number correctly, the program outputs an appropriate message. Otherwise, the program checks whether the guessed number is less than the random number. If the guessed number is less than the random the number generated by the program, the program outputs the message, "Your guess is lower than the number"; otherwise, the program outputs the message, "Your guess is higher than the number". The program then prompts the user to enter another number. The user is prompted to guess the random number until the user enters the correct number.

The program uses the method `random` of the **class** `Math` to generate a random number. To be specific, the expression:

```
Math.random()
```

returns a value of type **double** greater than or equal to 0.0 and less than 1.0. To convert it to an integer greater than or equal to 0 and less than 100, we use the following expression:

```
(int) (Math.random() * 100);
```

Furthermore, the program uses the **boolean** variable `done` to control the loop. The **boolean** variable `done` is initialized to **false**. It is set to **true** when the user guesses the correct number.

```
//Flag-controlled while loop.
//Guessing the number game.

import java.util.*;

public class FlagControlledLoop
{
    static Scanner console = new Scanner(System.in);

    public static void main (String[] args)
    {
            //declare the variables
        int num;        //variable to store the random
                        //number
        int guess;      //variable to store the number
                        //guessed by the user
```

```
    boolean done;   //boolean variable to control
                    //the loop

    num = (int) (Math.random() * 100);            //Line 1

    done = false;                                 //Line 2

    while (!done)                                 //Line 3
    {                                             //Line 4
        System.out.print ("Enter an integer greater"
                    + " than or equal to 0 and "
                    + "less than 100: ");         //Line 5
        guess = console.nextInt();                //Line 6
        System.out.println();                     //Line 7

        if (guess == num)                         //Line 8
        {                                         //Line 9
            System.out.println("You guessed the "
                        + "correct number.");     //Line 10
            done = true;                          //Line 11
        }                                         //Line 12
        else                                      //Line 13
            if (guess < num)                      //Line 14
                System.out.println("Your guess is "
                            + "lower than "
                            + "the number.\n"
                            + "Guess again!");     //Line 15
            else                                  //Line 16
                System.out.println("Your guess is "
                            + "higher than "
                            + "the number.\n"
                            + "Guess again!");     //Line 17
    } //end while                                 //Line 18
}                                                 //Line 19
}
```

Sample Run: In this sample run, the user input is shaded.

Sample Run 1:

Enter an integer greater than or equal to 0 and less than 100: 25

Your guess is higher than the number.
Guess again!
Enter an integer greater than or equal to 0 and less than 100: 5

Your guess is lower than the number.
Guess again!
Enter an integer greater than or equal to 0 and less than 100: 10

Your guess is higher than the number.
Guess again!
Enter an integer greater than or equal to 0 and less than 100: 8

```
Your guess is higher than the number.
Guess again!
Enter an integer greater than or equal to 0 and less than 100: 6

Your guess is lower than the number.
Guess again!
Enter an integer greater than or equal to 0 and less than 100: 7

You guessed the correct number.
```

Sample Run 2:

```
Enter an integer greater than or equal to 0 and less than 100: 80

Your guess is higher than the number.
Guess again!
Enter an integer greater than or equal to 0 and less than 100: 40

Your guess is lower than the number.
Guess again!
Enter an integer greater than or equal to 0 and less than 100: 60

Your guess is higher than the number.
Guess again!
Enter an integer greater than or equal to 0 and less than 100: 50

Your guess is higher than the number.
Guess again!
Enter an integer greater than or equal to 0 and less than 100: 45

Your guess is lower than the number.
Guess again!
Enter an integer greater than or equal to 0 and less than 100: 48

Your guess is higher than the number.
Guess again!
Enter an integer greater than or equal to 0 and less than 100: 47

You guessed the correct number.
```

The preceding program works as follows: The statement in Line 1 creates an integer greater than or equal to 0 and less than 100 and stores this number in the variable num. The statement in Line 2 sets the **boolean** variable done to **false**. The **while** loop starts at Line 3 and ends at Line 18. The expression in the **while** loop at Line 3 evaluates the expression !done. If done is **false**, then !done is **true** and the body of the **while** loop executes; if done is **true**, then !done is **false**, so the **while** loop terminates.

The statement in Line 5 prompts the user to enter an integer greater than or equal to 0 and less than 100. The statement in Line 6 stores the number entered by the user in the variable guess. The expression in the **if** statement in Line 8 determines whether the value of guess is the same as num, that is, if the user guessed the number correctly. If the value of

guess is the same as **num**, then the statements in Lines 10 and 11 execute. The statement in Line 10 outputs the message:

```
You guessed the correct number.
```

The statement in Line 11 sets the variable **done** to **true**. The control then goes back to Line 3. Because **done** is **true**, **!done** is **false** and the **while** loop terminates.

If the expression in Line 8 evaluates to **false**, then the **else** statement in Line 13 executes. The statement part of this **else** is an **if...else** statement, starting at Line 14 and ending at Line 17. The **if** statement in Line 14 determines whether the value of **guess** is less than **num**. In this case, the statement in Line 15 outputs the message:

```
Your guess is lower than the number.
Guess again!
```

If the expression in the **if** statement in Line 14 evaluates to **false**, then the statement in Line 17 executes, which outputs the message:

```
Your guess is higher than the number.
Guess again!
```

The program then prompts the user to enter an integer greater than or equal to 0 and less than **100**.

EOF-Controlled **while** Loops

If the data file is frequently altered (for example, if data is frequently added or deleted), it's best not to read the data with a sentinel value. Someone might accidentally erase the sentinel value or add data past the sentinel, especially if the programmer and data entry person are different people. Also, the programmer sometimes does not know what the sentinel is. In such situations, you can use an **EOF (End Of File)-controlled while** loop.

In Java, the form of the EOF-controlled **while** loop depends on the type of stream object used to input data into a program. Because we have been using the **Scanner** object to input data into a program, next we describe the EOF-controlled **while** loop that uses a **Scanner** object to input data.

Recall that the following statement creates the **Scanner** object **console** and initializes it to the standard input device:

```
static Scanner console = new Scanner(System.in);    //Line 1
```

This statement is equivalent to the following statements:

```
static Scanner console;               //Line 2
console = new Scanner(System.in);   //Line 3
```

The statement in Line 2 declares **console** to be the **Scanner** variable; the statement in Line 3 initializes **console** to the standard input device. On the other hand, the statement in Line 1 both declares and initializes the **Scanner** variable **console**.

In an EOF-controlled **while** loop that uses the **Scanner** object **console** to input data, **console** acts at the loop control variable. The statement in Line 3 initializes the loop control variable. The method **hasNext**, of the **class** Scanner, returns **true** if there is an input in the input stream, otherwise it returns **false**. In other words, the expression **console.hasNext()** evaluates to **true** if there is an input in the input stream, otherwise it returns **false**. Therefore, the expression **console.hasNext()** acts as the loop condition. Moreover, expressions such as **console.nextInt()** update the value of the loop control variable **console**.

It now follows that a general form of the EOF-controlled **while** loop that uses the **Scanner** object **console** to input data is of the following form (we assume that **console** has been created and initialized using either the statement in Line 1 or the statements in Lines 2 and 3):

```
while (console.hasNext())
{
    //Get the next input (token) and store it in an
    //appropriate variable.
    //Process the data.
}
```

 In the Windows console environment, the end-of-file marker is entered using `Ctrl+z`. (Hold the `Ctrl` key and press z.) In the UNIX environment, the end-of-file marker is entered using `Ctrl+d`. (Hold the `Ctrl` key and press d.)

Suppose that **inFile** is a **Scanner** object initialized to the input file. In this case, the EOF-controlled **while** loop takes the following form:

```
while (inFile.hasNext())
{
    //Get the next input (token) and store it in an
    //appropriate variable.
    //Process the data.
}
```

Example 5-7

The following code uses an EOF-controlled **while** loop to find the sum of a set of numbers:

```
static Scanner console = new Scanner(System.in);

int sum = 0;
int num;

while (console.hasNext())
{
    num = console.nextInt();    //Get the next number
    sum = sum + num;            //Add the number to sum
}
System.out.printf("Sum = %d%n", sum);
```

The Programming Example Checking Account Balance, located later in this chapter, further illustrates how to use an EOF-controlled **while** loop in a program.

More on Expressions in **while** Statements

In the examples in the previous sections, the expression in the **while** statement is quite simple. In other words, the **while** loop is controlled by a single variable. However, there are situations where the expression in the **while** statement may be more complex.

For example, the program in Example 5-6 uses a flag-controlled **while** loop to implement the Guessing the Number game. However, the program gives as many tries as the user needs to guess the number. Suppose you want to give the user, for example, at most five tries to guess the number. If the user does not guess the number correctly within five tries, then the program outputs the random number generated by the program, as well as a message that you lost the game. In this case, you can write the **while** loop as follows. (Assume that noOfGuesses is an **int** variable initialized to 0.)

```java
while ((noOfGuesses < 5) && (!done))
{
    System.out.print ("Enter an integer greater "
                    + "than or equal to 0 and "
                    + "less than 100: ");
    guess = console.nextInt();
    System.out.println();
    noOfGuesses++;

    if (guess == num)
    {
        System.out.println("Winner!. You guessed the "
                        + "correct number.");
        done = true;
    }
    else
        if (guess < num)
            System.out.println("Your guess is "
                            + "lower than "
                            + "the number.\n"
                            + "Guess again!");

        else
            System.out.println("Your guess is "
                            + "higher than "
                            + "the number.\n"
                            + "Guess again!");
}//end while
```

5

You also need the following code, to be included after the **while** loop, in case the user cannot guess the correct number in five tries.

```
if (!done)
    System.out.println("You lose! The correct "
                        + "number is " + num);
```

We leave it as an exercise for you to write a complete Java program to implement the Guessing the Number game in which the user has at most five tries to guess the number. (See Programming Exercise 14 at the end of this chapter).

As you can see from the preceding **while** loop, the expression in a **while** statement can be complex. The main objective of a **while** loop is to repeat certain statement(s) until certain conditions are met.

PROGRAMMING EXAMPLE: CHECKING ACCOUNT BALANCE

A local bank in your town is looking for someone to write a program that calculates a customer's checking account balance at the end of each month. The data is stored in a file in the following form:

```
467343 23750.40
W 250.00
D 1200
W 75.00
I 120.74
    .
    .
    .
```

The first line of data shows the account number, followed by the account balance at the beginning of the month. Thereafter, each line has two entries: the transaction code and the transaction amount. The transaction code **W** or **w** means withdrawal, **D** or **d** means deposit, and **I** or **i** means interest paid by the bank. The program updates the balance after each transaction. If at any time during the month the balance goes below $1000.00, a $25.00 service fee is charged. The program prints the following information: account number, balance at the beginning of the month, balance at the end of the month, interest paid by the bank, total amount of deposit, number of deposits, total amount of withdrawal, number of withdrawals, and service charge if any.

Input   A file consisting of data in the above format

Output   The output is of the following form:

```
Account Number: 467343
Beginning Balance: $23750.40
Ending Balance: $24611.49
Interest Paid: $366.24

Amount Deposited: $2230.50
Number of Deposits: 3

Amount Withdrawn: $1735.65
Number of Withdrawals: 6
```

Note that the output is to be sent to a file.

Problem Analysis and Algorithm Design

The first entries in the input file are the account number and the beginning balance. There-fore, the program first reads the account number and the beginning balance. Thereafter, each entry in the file is of the following form:

```
transactionCode transactionAmount
```

To determine the account balance at the end of the month, you need to process each entry that contains the transaction code and the transaction amount. Begin with the starting balance and then update the account balance after processing each entry. If the transaction code is D, d, I, or i, the transaction amount is added to the account bal-ance; if the transaction code is W or w, the transaction amount is subtracted from the balance. Because the program also outputs the number of withdrawals and deposits, you need to keep separate counts of the withdrawals and deposits. This discussion translates into the following algorithm:

1. Declare the necessary variables and objects.
2. Initialize the variables.
3. Get the account number and beginning balance.
4. Get the transaction code and transaction amount.
5. Analyze the transaction code and update the appropriate variables.
6. Repeat Steps 4 and 5 until there is no more data.
7. Print the result.

Variables and Objects

The program outputs the account number, beginning balance, balance at the end of the month, interest paid, amount deposited, number of deposits, amount withdrawn, number of withdrawals, and service charge if any. So far, you need the following variables to store all this information:

```
acctNumber          //variable to store the account number
beginningBalance    //variable to store the beginning balance
accountBalance      //variable to store the account balance at the
                    //end of the month
amountDeposited     //variable to store the total amount deposited
numberOfDeposits    //variable to store the number of deposits
amountWithdrawn     //variable to store the total amount withdrawn
numberOfWithdrawals //variable to store the number of withdrawals
interestPaid        //variable to store the interest amount paid
```

Because the program reads the data from a file and the output is stored in a file, the program needs both input and output stream objects. After the first line, the data in each line is the transaction code and the transaction amount; the program needs a variable to store this information.

Whenever the account balance goes below the minimum balance, a service charge for that month is applied. After each withdrawal, you need to check the account balance. If the balance goes below the minimum after a withdrawal, a service charge is applied. You can potentially have several withdrawals in a month; once the account balance goes below the minimum, a subsequent deposit might bring the balance above the minimum, and another withdrawal might again reduce it below the minimum. However, the service charge is applied only once.

To implement this idea, the program uses a **boolean** variable, isServiceCharged, that is initialized to **false** and set to **true** whenever the account balance goes below the minimum. Before applying a service charge, the program checks the value of the variable isServiceCharged. If the account balance is less than the minimum and isServiceCharged is **false**, a service charge is applied. The program needs the following variables:

```
int       acctNumber;
double    beginningBalance;
double    accountBalance;

double    amountDeposited;
int       numberOfDeposits;

double    amountWithdrawn;
int       numberOfWithdrawals;

double    interestPaid;
char      transactionCode;
double    transactionAmount;

boolean   isServiceCharged;
```

Suppose the input data is in the file `money.txt` on a floppy disk in drive A:. Also suppose that the output will be stored in the file `money.out` on a floppy disk in drive A:. The following statements create the appropriate input and output stream objects:

```
Scanner inFile =
         new Scanner(new FileReader("a:\\money.txt"));
PrintWriter outFile = new PrintWriter("a:\\money.out");
```

Named Constants

The minimum account balance and the service charge amount are fixed, so the program uses two named constants to store them:

```
static final double MINIMUM_BALANCE = 1000.00;
static final double SERVICE_CHARGE = 25.00;
```

Because this program is more complex than previous ones, before writing the main algorithm, the preceding seven steps are described more fully here:

1. **Declare the variables and objects:** Declare the variables and objects as discussed previously.
2. **Initialization:** After each deposit, the total amount deposited is updated and the number of deposits is incremented by one. Before the first deposit, the total amount deposited is 0 and the number of withdrawals is 0. Therefore, the variables `amountDeposited` and `numberOfDeposits` must be initialized to 0. Similarly, the variables `amountWithdrawn`, `numberOfWithdrawals`, and `interestPaid` must be initialized to 0. Also, as discussed earlier, the variable `isServicedCharged` is initialized to **false**. Of course, you can initialize these variables when you declare them.

   Before the first deposit, withdrawal, or interest paid, the account balance is the same as the beginning balance. Therefore, after reading the beginning balance in the variable `beginningBalance` from the file, you need to initialize the variable `accountBalance` to the value of the variable `beginningBalance`.
3. **Get the account number and starting balance:** This is accomplished by the following statements:

   ```
   acctNumber = inFile.nextInt();
   beginningBalance = inFile.nextDouble();
   ```
4. **Get the transaction code and transaction amount:** This is accomplished by the following input statement:

   ```
   transactionCode = inFile.next().charAt(0);
   transactionAmount = inFile.nextDouble();
   ```
5. **Analyze the transaction code and update the appropriate variables:** If `transactionCode` is `'D'` or `'d'`, update `accountBalance` by adding `transactionAmount`, update `amountDeposited` by adding `transactionAmount`, and increment `numberOfDeposits`. If

transactionCode is 'I' or 'i', update accountBalance by adding
transactionAmount and update interestPaid by adding
transactionAmount. If transactionCode is 'W' or 'w', update
accountBalance by subtracting transactionAmount, update
amountWithdrawn by adding transactionAmount, increment
numberOfWithdrawals, and if the account balance is below the minimum
and service charges have not been applied, subtract the service charge from
the account balance and mark the service charge as having been applied. The
following **switch** statement does this:

```java
switch (transactionCode)
{
case 'D':
case 'd': accountBalance = accountBalance
                          + transactionAmount;
         amountDeposited = amountDeposited
                          + transactionAmount;
         numberOfDeposits++;
         break;
case 'I':
case 'i': accountBalance = accountBalance
                          + transactionAmount;
         interestPaid = interestPaid
                          + transactionAmount;
         break;
case 'W':
case 'w': accountBalance = accountBalance
                          - transactionAmount;
         amountWithdrawn = amountWithdrawn
                          + transactionAmount;
         numberOfWithdrawals++;

         if ((accountBalance < MINIMUM_BALANCE)
             && (!isServiceCharged))
         {
             accountBalance = accountBalance
                             - SERVICE_CHARGE;
             isServiceCharged = true;
         }
         break;

default: System.out.println("Invalid transaction code.");
}//end switch
```

6. **Repeat Steps 4 and 5 until there is no more data:** Because the number of
   entries in the input file is not known, the program needs an EOF-controlled
   while loop.

7. **Print the result:** This is accomplished by using output statements.

The preceding discussion translates into the following algorithm:

Main Algorithm

1. Declare and initialize the variables and the input and output stream objects.
2. Get `accountNumber` and `beginningBalance`.
3. Set `accountBalance` to `beginningBalance`.
4. While (not end of input file):
   a. Get `transactionCode`.
   b. Get `transactionAmount`.
   c. If `transactionCode` is `'D'` or `'d'`:
      i.   Add `transactionAmount` to `accountBalance`.
      ii. Add `transactionAmount` to `amountDeposited`.
      iii. Increment `numberOfDeposits`.
   d. If `transactionCode` is `'I'` or `'i'`:
      i.   Add `transactionAmount` to `accountBalance`.
      ii. Add `transactionAmount` to `interestPaid`.
   e. If `transactionCode` is `'W'` or `'w'`:
      i.   Subtract `transactionAmount` from `accountBalance`.
      ii. Add `transactionAmount` to `amountWithdrawn`.
      iii. Increment `numberOfWithDrawals`.
      iv. If (`accountBalance < MINIMUM_BALANCE`
           `&& !isServicedCharged`)
           1. Subtract `SERVICE_CHARGE` from `accountBalance`.
           2. Set `isServiceCharged` to `true`.
   f. If `transactionCode` is other than `'D'`, `'d'`, `'I'`, `'i'`, `'W'`, or `'w'`,
      output an error message.
5. Output the results.

Complete Program Listing

```java
//*****************************************************
// Program: Checking Account Balance
// This program calculates a customer's checking account
// balance at the end of the month.
//*****************************************************

import java.io.*;
import java.util.*;

public class CheckingAccountBalance
{
    static final double MINIMUM_BALANCE = 1000.00;
    static final double SERVICE_CHARGE = 25.00;
```

```java
public static void main(String[] args)
                    throws FileNotFoundException
{
    //Declare and initialize the variables        //Step 1
    int acctNumber;
    double beginningBalance;
    double accountBalance;

    double amountDeposited = 0.0;
    int numberOfDeposits = 0;

    double amountWithdrawn = 0.0;
    int numberOfWithdrawals = 0;

    double interestPaid = 0.0;

    char transactionCode;
    double transactionAmount;

    boolean isServiceCharged = false;

    Scanner inFile =
         new Scanner(new FileReader("a:\\money.txt"));

    PrintWriter outFile =
         new PrintWriter("a:\\money.out");

    acctNumber = inFile.nextInt();                     //Step 2
    beginningBalance = inFile.nextDouble();            //Step 2

    accountBalance = beginningBalance;                 //Step 3

    while (inFile.hasNext())                            //Step 4
    {
        transactionCode = inFile.next().charAt(0);     //Step 4a
        transactionAmount = inFile.nextDouble();       //Step 4b

        switch (transactionCode)
        {
        case 'D':                                      //Step 4c
        case 'd': accountBalance = accountBalance
                            + transactionAmount;
                  amountDeposited = amountDeposited
                             + transactionAmount;
                  numberOfDeposits++;
                  break;
        case 'I':                                      //Step 4d
        case 'i': accountBalance = accountBalance
                            + transactionAmount;
```

```java
                    interestPaid = interestPaid
                                 + transactionAmount;
                break;
        case 'W':                                           //Step 4e
        case 'w': accountBalance = accountBalance
                                 - transactionAmount;
                amountWithdrawn = amountWithdrawn
                                 + transactionAmount;
                numberOfWithdrawals++;

                if ((accountBalance < MINIMUM_BALANCE)
                             && (!isServiceCharged))
                {
                    accountBalance = accountBalance
                                   - SERVICE_CHARGE;
                    isServiceCharged = true;
                }
                break;

        default: System.out.println("Invalid transaction "
                                  + "code.");              //Step 4f
    }//end switch

}//end while

        //Output the results    //Step 5
outFile.printf("Account Number: %d%n", acctNumber);
outFile.printf("Beginning Balance: $%.2f %n",
                beginningBalance);
outFile.printf("Ending Balance: $%.2f %n",
                accountBalance);           .
outFile.println();
outFile.printf("Interest Paid: $%.2f %n",
                interestPaid);
outFile.println();
outFile.printf("Amount Deposited: $%.2f %n",
                amountDeposited);
outFile.printf("Number of Deposits: %d%n",
                numberOfDeposits);
outFile.println();
outFile.printf("Amount Withdrawn: $%.2f %n",
                amountWithdrawn);
outFile.printf("Number of Withdrawals: %d%n",
                numberOfWithdrawals);
outFile.println();
```

```
        if (isServiceCharged)
            outFile.printf("Service Charge: $%.2f %n",
                            SERVICE_CHARGE);

        outFile.close();
    }
}
```

Sample Run: Contents of the output file `money.out`:
```
Account Number: 467343
Beginning Balance: $23750.40
Ending Balance: $24611.49

Interest Paid: $366.24

Amount Deposited: $2230.50
Number of Deposits: 3

Amount Withdrawn: $1735.65
Number of Withdrawals: 6
```

Input File: `money.txt`

```
467343 23750.40
W 250.00
D 1200.00
W 75.00
I 120.74
W 375.00
D 580.00
I 245.50
W 400.00
W 600.00
D 450.50
W 35.65
```

PROGRAMMING EXAMPLE: FIBONACCI NUMBER

So far, you have seen several examples of loops. Recall that in Java, `while` loops are used when a certain statement(s) must be executed repeatedly until certain conditions are met. The following program uses a `while` loop to find a **Fibonacci number**.

Consider the following sequence of numbers:

```
1, 1, 2, 3, 5, 8, 13, 21, 34, ....
```

Given the first two numbers of the sequence (say a_1 and a_2), the nth number a_n, n >= 3, of this sequence is given by the formula:

$$a_n = a_{n-1} + a_{n-2}$$

Thus,

```
a₃ = a₂ + a₁
   = 1 + 1
   = 2,
a₄ = a₃ + a₂
   = 2 + 1
   = 3,
```

and so on.

Such a sequence is called a **Fibonacci sequence**. In the preceding sequence, $a_2 = 1$ and $a_1 = 1$. However, given any first two numbers of the sequence, using this process you can determine the nth number, a_n, n >= 3, of the sequence. The number determined this way is called the **nth Fibonacci number**. Suppose $a_2 = 6$ and $a_1 = 3$. Then:

$$a_3 = a_2 + a_1 = 6 + 3 = 9; \quad a_4 = a_3 + a_2 = 9 + 6 = 15.$$

Next, we write a program that determines the nth Fibonacci number of a Fibonacci sequence, given the first two numbers of that sequence.

Input   The first two numbers of the Fibonacci sequence and the position of the desired Fibonacci number in the Fibonacci sequence

Output   The nth Fibonacci number

Problem Analysis and Algorithm Design

To find a_{10}, the tenth Fibonacci number of a sequence, you must first find a_9 and a_8, which requires you to find a_7 and a_6, and so on. Therefore, to find a_{10}, you must first find $a_3, a_4, a_5, \ldots, a_9$. This discussion translates into the following algorithm:

1. Get the first two Fibonacci numbers.
2. Get the position of the desired number in the Fibonacci sequence. That is, get the position, n, of the number in the Fibonacci sequence.

3. Calculate the next Fibonacci number by adding the previous two elements of the Fibonacci sequence.

4. Repeat Step 2 until the nth Fibonacci number is found.

5. Output the nth Fibonacci number.

Note that the program assumes that the first number of the Fibonacci sequence is less than or equal to the second number of the Fibonacci sequence, and both numbers are nonnegative. Moreover, the program also assumes that the user enters a valid value for the position of the desired number in the Fibonacci sequence; that is, it is a positive integer. (See Programming Exercise 12 at the end of this chapter.)

Variables

Because you must know the last two numbers to find the current Fibonacci number, you need the following variables: two variables—say, `previous1` and `previous2`—to hold the previous two numbers of the Fibonacci sequence, and one variable—say, `current`—to hold the current Fibonacci number. The number of times that Step 2 of the algorithm repeats depends on the position of the Fibonacci number you are calculating. For example, if you want to calculate the 10th Fibonacci number, you must execute Step 3 eight times. (Remember, the user gives the first two numbers of the Fibonacci sequence.) Therefore, you need a variable to store the number of times that Step 3 should execute. You also need a variable—the loop control variable—to track the number of times that Step 3 has executed. Therefore, you need five variables for the data manipulation:

```
int previous1;     //variable to store the first
                   //Fibonacci number
int previous2,     //variable to store the second
                   //Fibonacci number
int current;       //variable to store the current
                   //Fibonacci number
int counter;       //loop control variable
int nthFibonacci;  //variable to store the desired
                   //Fibonacci number
```

To calculate the third Fibonacci number, add the value of `previous1` and `previous2` and store the result in `current`. To calculate the fourth Fibonacci number, add the value of the second Fibonacci number (that is, `previous2`) and the value of the third Fibonacci number (that is, `current`). Thus, when the fourth Fibonacci number is calculated, you no longer need the first Fibonacci number. Instead of declaring additional variables, which could be several, after calculating a Fibonacci number to determine the next Fibonacci number, `current` becomes `previous2` and `previous2` becomes `previous1`. Therefore, you can again use the variable `current` to store the next Fibonacci number. This process is repeated until the desired Fibonacci number is calculated. Initially, `previous1` and `previous2` are the first two elements of the sequence, supplied by the user. From the preceding discussion, it follows that you need five variables.

Main Algorithm

1. Display the input dialog box to prompt the user for the first Fibonacci number—that is, `previous1`. Store the string representing `previous1` into `inputString`.

2. Retrieve the string from `inputString`, and store the first Fibonacci number into `previous1`.

3. Display the input dialog box to prompt the user for the second Fibonacci number—that is, `previous2`. Store the string representing `previous2` into `inputString`.

4. Retrieve the string from `inputString`, and store the second Fibonacci number into `previous2`.

5. Create the `outputString` and append `previous1` and `previous2`.

6. Display the input dialog box to prompt the user for the desired Fibonacci number, that is, `nthFibonacci`. Store the string representing `nthFibonacci` into `inputString`.

7. Retrieve the string from `inputString`, and store the desired *n*th Fibonacci number into `nthFibonacci`.

8. a. `if (nthFibonacci == 1)`

   the desired Fibonacci number is the first Fibonacci number. Copy the value of `previous1` into `current`.

   b. `else if (nthFibonacci == 2)`

   the desired Fibonacci number is the second Fibonacci number. Copy the value of `previous2` into `current`.

   c. `else` calculate the desired Fibonacci number as follows:

   Since you already know the first two Fibonacci numbers of the sequence, start by determining the third Fibonacci number.

   c.1. Initialize `counter` to 3, to keep track of the calculated Fibonacci numbers.

   c.2. Calculate the next Fibonacci number, as follows:

   ```
   current = previous2 + previous1;
   ```

   c.3. Assign the value of `previous2` to `previous1`.

   c.4. Assign the value of `current` to `previous2`.

   c.5. Increment `counter`.

   Repeat Steps 8c.2 through 8c.5 until the Fibonacci number you want is calculated. The following `while` loop executes Steps 8c.2 through c.5 and determines the *n*th Fibonacci number:

   ```
   while (counter <= nthFibonacci)
   {
       current = previous2 + previous1;
       previous1 = previous2;
       previous2 = current;
       counter++;
   }
   ```

9. Append the nth Fibonacci number to `outputString`. Notice that the nth Fibonacci number is stored in `current`.

10. Display the output dialog box showing the first two and the nth Fibonacci numbers.

Complete Program Listing

```java
//Program: nth Fibonacci number

import javax.swing.JOptionPane;

public class FibonacciNumber
{
    public static void main (String[] args)
    {
                    //Declare the variables
        String inputString;
        String outputString;
        int previous1;
        int previous2;
        int current = 0;
        int counter;
        int nthFibonacci;

        inputString =
            JOptionPane.showInputDialog("Enter the first "
                            + "Fibonacci number: ");   //Step 1
        previous1 = Integer.parseInt(inputString);       //Step 2

        inputString =
            JOptionPane.showInputDialog("Enter the second "
                            + "Fibonacci number: "); //Step 3
        previous2 = Integer.parseInt(inputString);       //Step 4

        outputString = "The first two numbers of the "
                        + "Fibonacci sequence are: "
                        + previous1 + " and " + previous2;  //Step 5
```

```
        inputString =
            JOptionPane.showInputDialog("Enter the position "
                        + "of the desired number in "
                        + "the Fibonacci sequence: ");   //Step 6
        nthFibonacci = Integer.parseInt(inputString);    //Step 7

        if (nthFibonacci == 1)                           //Step 8.a
            current = previous1;
        else if (nthFibonacci == 2)                      //Step 8.b
                current = previous2;
        else                                             //Step 8.c
        {
            counter = 3;                                 //Step 8.c.1

                //Steps 8.c.2 - 8.c.5
            while (counter <= nthFibonacci)
            {
                current = previous2 + previous1;         //Step 8.c.2
                previous1 = previous2;                   //Step 8.c.3
                previous2 = current;                     //Step 8.c.4
                counter++;                               //Step 8.c.5
            }
        }

        outputString = outputString + "\nThe "
                        + nthFibonacci
                        + "th Fibonacci number of "
                        + "the sequence is: "
                        + current;                       //Step 9
        JOptionPane.showMessageDialog(null, outputString,
                        "Fibonacci Number",
                    JOptionPane.INFORMATION_MESSAGE);     //Step 10
        System.exit(0);
    }
}
```

Sample Run: Figure 5-3 shows the sample run.

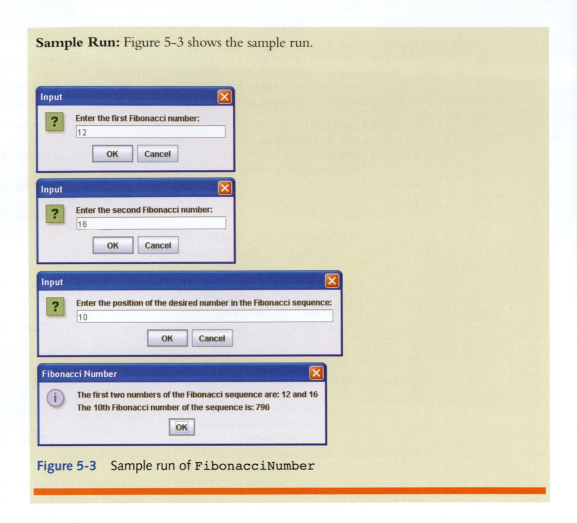

Figure 5-3   Sample run of `FibonacciNumber`

`for` LOOPING (REPETITION) STRUCTURE

The **while** loop discussed in the previous section is general enough to implement all forms of repetitions. The Java **for** looping structure is a specialized form of the **while** loop. Its primary purpose is to simplify the writing of counter-controlled loops. For this reason, the **for** loop is typically called a **counted** or **indexed** **for** loop.

The general form of the **for** statement is:

```
for (initial statement; loop condition; update statement)
    statement
```

In Java, **for** is a reserved word. The `initial statement`, `loop condition`, and `update statement` (called **for** loop **control statements**) are enclosed within parentheses and control the body (`statement`) of the **for** statement. Note that the **for** loop control statements are separated by semicolons, and that the body of a **for** loop can have either a simple or compound statement. Figure 5-4 shows the flow of execution of a **for** loop.

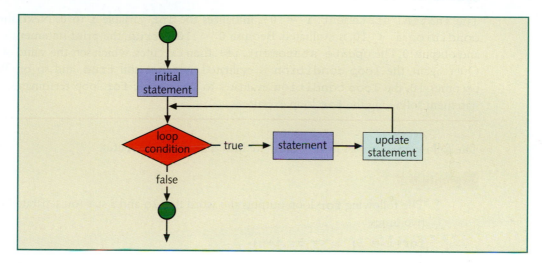

Figure 5-4   **for** loop

The **for** loop executes as follows:

1. The `initial statement` executes.

2. The `loop condition` is evaluated. If the `loop condition` evaluates to **true**:

   a. Execute the **for** loop `statement`.

   b. Execute the `update statement` (the third expression in the parentheses).

3. Repeat Step 2 until the `loop condition` evaluates to **false**.

The `initial statement` usually initializes a variable (called the **for** loop control, or indexed, variable).

 As the name implies, the `initial statement` in the **for** loop is the first statement to execute; it executes only once.

Example 5-8

The following **for** loop prints the first 10 nonnegative integers:

```
for (i = 0; i < 10; i++)
    System.out.print(i + " ");

System.out.println();
```

The **initial statement**, i = 0;, initializes the **int** variable i to 0. Next, the **loop condition**, i < 10, is evaluated. Because 0 < 10 is **true**, the print statement executes and outputs 0. The **update statement**, i++, then executes, which sets the value of i to 1. Once again, the **loop condition** is evaluated, which is still **true**, and so on. When i becomes 10, the **loop condition** evaluates to **false**, the **for** loop terminates, and the statement following the **for** loop executes.

The following examples further illustrate how a **for** loop executes.

Example 5-9

1. The following **for** loop outputs the word **Hello** and a star (on separate lines) five times:

   ```
   for(i = 1; i <= 5; i++)
   {
       System.out.println("Hello");
       System.out.println("*");
   }
   ```

2. Now consider the following **for** loop:

   ```
   for(i = 1; i <= 5; i++)
       System.out.println("Hello");
       System.out.println("*");
   ```

   This loop outputs the word **Hello** five times and the star only once. In this case, the **for** loop controls only the first output statement because the two output statements are not made into a compound statement using curly braces. Therefore, the first output statement executes five times because the **for** loop executes five times. After the **for** loop executes, the second output statement executes only once.

Example 5-10

The following **for** loop executes five empty statements:

```
for (i = 0; i < 5; i++);          //Line 1
    System.out.println("*");      //Line 2
```

The semicolon at the end of the **for** statement (before the output statement in Line 2) terminates the **for** loop. The action of this **for** loop is empty.

The preceding examples show that care is required to get a **for** loop to perform the desired action.

Some additional comments on **for** loops follow:

- If the loop condition is initially **false**, the loop body does not execute.

- The update expression, when executed, changes the value of the loop control variable (initialized by the initial expression), which eventually sets the value of the loop condition to **false**. The **for** loop executes indefinitely if the loop condition is always **true**.

- If you put a semicolon at the end of a **for** statement (just before the body of the loop), the action of the **for** loop is empty.

- In a **for** statement, if the `loop condition` is omitted, it is assumed to be **true**.

- In a **for** statement, you can omit all three statements—`initial statement`, `loop condition`, and `update statement`. The following is a legal **for** loop:

```
for (;;)
    System.out.println("Hello");
```

This is an infinite **for** loop, continuously printing the world `Hello`.

More examples of **for** loops follow.

Example 5-11

1. You can count backward using a **for** loop if the **for** loop control expressions are set correctly. For example, consider the following **for** loop:

```
for (i = 10; i >= 1; i--)
    System.out.print(i + " ");

System.out.println();
```

The output is:

```
10 9 8 7 6 5 4 3 2 1
```

In this **for** loop, the variable i is initialized to 10. After each iteration of the loop, i is decremented by 1. The loop continues to execute as long as i >= 1.

2. You can increment (or decrement) the loop control variable by any fixed number. In the following **for** loop, the variable is initialized to 0; at the end of the **for** loop, i is incremented by 2. This **for** loop outputs the first 10 nonnegative integers 0 through 18:

```
for (i = 0; i < 20; i = i + 2)
    System.out.print(i + " ");

System.out.println();
```

Example 5-12

Consider the following examples, where i is an **int** variable.

1.

```
for (i = 10; i <= 9; i++)
    System.out.print(i + " ");

System.out.println();
```

In this **for** loop, the initial statement sets i to 10. Because initially the loop condition (i <= 9) is **false**, the body of the **for** loop does not execute.

2.

```
for (i = 9; i >= 10; i--)
    System.out.print(i + " ");

System.out.println();
```

In this **for** loop, the initial statement sets i to 9. Because initially the loop condition (i >= 10) is **false**, the body of the **for** loop does not execute.

3.

```
for (i = 10; i <= 10; i++)          //Line 1
    System.out.print(i + " ");      //Line 2

System.out.println();               //Line 3
```

In this **for** loop, the output statement in Line 2 executes once.

4.

```
for (i = 1; i <= 10; i++);
    System.out.print(i + " ");

System.out.println();
```

This **for** loop has no effect on the output statement. The semicolon at the end of the **for** statement terminates the **for** loop; the action of the **for** loop is thus empty. Both output statements are outside the scope of the **for** loop, so the **for** loop has no effect on them. Note that this code will output 11.

5.

```
for (i = 1; ; i++)
    System.out.print(i + " ");

System.out.println();
```

In this **for** loop, because the loop condition is omitted from the **for** statement, the loop condition is always **true**. This is an infinite loop.

Example 5-13

In this example, a **for** loop reads five integers and finds their sum and average. Consider the following programming code, in which i, newNum, sum, and average are **int** variables.

```
sum = 0;

for (i = 0; i < 5; i++)
{
    newNum = console.nextInt();
    sum = sum + newNum;
}

average = sum / 5;
System.out.println("The sum is " + sum);
System.out.println("The average is " + average);
```

In the preceding **for** loop, after getting a newNum, this value is added to the previously cal-culated (partial) sum of all the numbers read before the current number. The variable sum is initialized to 0 before the **for** loop. Thus, after the program gets the first number and adds it to the value of sum, the variable sum holds the correct sum of the first number.

Example 5-14

The following Java program finds the sum of the first n positive integers.

```
//*************************************************************
//Program: Sum the first n positive integers
//This program finds the sum of the first n positive integers.
//*************************************************************

import java.util.*;

public class SumFirstNNumbers
{
    static Scanner console = new Scanner(System.in);

    public static void main (String[] args)
    {
        int counter;    //loop control variable
        int sum;        //variable to store the sum of the numbers
        int n;          //variable to store the number of
                        //first positive integers to be added

        System.out.print("Line 1: Enter the number of positive "
                         + "integers to be added: ");        //Line 1
        System.out.flush();                                  //Line 2
        n = console.nextInt();                               //Line 3
        System.out.println();                                //Line 4

        sum = 0;                                             //Line 5
```

```
    for (counter = 1; counter <= n; counter++)      //Line 6
        sum = sum + counter;                        //Line 7

    System.out.println("Line 8: The sum of the first "
                       + n + " positive integers is "
                       + sum);                       //Line 8
    }
}
```

Sample Run: In this sample run, the user input is shaded.
`Line 1: Enter the number of positive integers to be added: 100`

`Line 8: The sum of the first 100 positive integers is 5050`

The statement in Line 1 prompts the user to enter the number of first positive integers to be added. The statement in Line 3 stores the number entered by the user in n and the statement in Line 5 initializes sum to 0. The **for** loop in Line 6 executes n times. (In the sample run, n is 100.) In the **for** loop, counter is initialized to 1 and is incremented by 1 after each iteration of the loop. Therefore, counter ranges from 1 to n. Each time through the loop, the value of counter is added to sum. Because sum was initialized to 0, counter ranges from 1 to n, and the current value of counter is added to the value of sum. After the **for** loop executes, sum contains the sum of the first n positive integers, which in the sample run is 100 positive integers. Notice that the program assumes that the user enters a positive value for n.

Recall that putting one control structure statement inside another is called **nesting**. The following programming example demonstrates a simple instance of nesting, and also nicely demonstrates counting.

PROGRAMMING EXAMPLE: CLASSIFY NUMBERS

This program reads a given set of integers and then prints the number of odd and even integers. It also outputs the number of zeros.

The program reads 20 integers, but you can easily modify it to read any set of numbers. In fact, you can modify the program so that it first prompts the user to specify how many integers are to be read.

Input 20 integers—positive, negative, or zeros

Output The number of zeros, even numbers, and odd numbers

Problem Analysis and Algorithm Design

After reading a number, you need to check whether it is even or odd. Suppose the value is stored in the variable **number**. Divide **number** by 2 and check the remainder. If the remainder is zero, **number** is even. Increment the even count and then check whether **number** is zero. If it is, increment the zero count. If the remainder is not zero, increment the odd count.

The program uses a **switch** statement to decide whether **number** is odd or even. Suppose that **number** is odd. Dividing by 2 gives the remainder 1 if **number** is positive, and the remainder −1 if negative. If **number** is even, dividing by 2 gives the remainder 0 whether **number** is positive or negative. You can use the mod operator, **%**, to find the remainder. For example:

```
6 % 2 = 0, −4 % 2 = 0, −7 % 2 = −1, 15 % 2 = 1
```

Repeat the preceding process of analyzing a number for each number in the list.

This discussion translates into the following algorithm:

1. For each number in the list:
   a. Get the number.
   b. Analyze the number.
   c. Increment the appropriate count.
2. Print the results.

Variables

Because you want to count the number of zeros, even numbers, and odd numbers, you need three variables of the type **int**—say **zeros**, **evens**, and **odds**, to track the counts. You also need a variable—say, **number**—to read and store the number to be analyzed, and another variable—say, **counter**—to count the numbers analyzed. Your program thus needs the following variables:

```
int counter;    //loop control variable
int number;     //variable to store the number read
int zeros;      //variable to store the zero count
int evens;      //variable to store the even count
int odds;       //variable to store the odd count
```

Clearly, you must initialize the variables **zeros**, **evens**, and **odds** to zero. You can initialize these variables when you declare them.

Main Algorithm

1. Initialize the variables.
2. Prompt the user to enter 20 numbers.
3. For each number in the list:
   a. Get the next number.
   b. Output the number (echo input).
   c. If the number is even:

   {

      i.   Increment the even count.

     ii.   If the number is zero, increment the zero count.

   }

   otherwise

       Increment the odd count.
4. Print the results.

Before writing the Java program, let's describe Steps 1 through 4 in more detail. It will be much easier for you to then write the instructions in Java.

1. Initialize the variables. You can initialize the variables **zeros**, **evens**, and **odds** when you declare them.
2. Use an output statement to prompt the user to enter 20 numbers.
3. For Step 3, you can use a **for** loop to process and analyze the 20 numbers. In pseudocode, this step is written as follows:

```
for (counter = 1; counter <= 20; counter++)
{
    a.   get the number;
    b.   output the number;
    c.   switch (number % 2)      //check the remainder
         {
         case 0:   increment the even count;
                   if (number == 0)
                        increment the zero count;
                   break;
         case 1: case -1: increment the odd count;
         }//end switch
}//end for
```

4. Print the result. Output the values of the variables **zeros**, **evens**, and **odds**.

Complete Program Listing

```java
//*********************************************************
// Program: Classify Numbers
// This program counts the number of odd and even numbers.
// The program also counts the number of zeros.
//*********************************************************

import java.util.*;

public class ClassifyNumbers
{
    static Scanner console = new Scanner(System.in);

    static final int N = 20;

    public static void main (String[] args)
    {
            //Declare the variables
        int counter;      //loop control variable
        int number;       //variable to store the new number

        int zeros = 0;                              //Step 1
        int odds = 0;                               //Step 1
        int evens = 0;                              //Step 1

        System.out.println("Please enter " + N
                        + " integers, positive, "
                        + "negative, or zeros.");   //Step 2

        for (counter = 1; counter <= N; counter++)  //Step 3
        {
            number = console.nextInt();             //Step 3a
            System.out.print(number + " ");         //Step 3b

                //Step 3c
            switch (number % 2)
            {
            case 0: evens++;
                    if (number == 0)
                        zeros++;
                    break;
            case 1:
            case -1: odds++;
            }//end switch

        }//end for loop

        System.out.println();
```

```
            //Step 4
    System.out.println("There are " + evens + " evens, "
                     + "which also includes "
                     + zeros + " zeros");
    System.out.println("Total number of odds is: " + odds);
  }
}
```

Sample Run: In this sample run, the user input is shaded.
```
Please enter 20 integers, positive, negative, or zeros.
0 0 -2 -3 -5 6 7 8 0 3 0 -23 -8 0 2 9 0 12 67 54
0 0 -2 -3 -5 6 7 8 0 3 0 -23 -8 0 2 9 0 12 67 54
There are 13 evens, which also includes 6 zeros
Total number of odds is: 7
```

We recommend that you do a walk-through of this program using the above sample input.

do...while LOOPING (REPETITION) STRUCTURE

This section describes the third type of looping or repetition structure—a **do...while** loop. The general form of a **do...while** statement is:

```
do
   statement
while (expression);
```

In Java, **do** is a reserved word. As with the other repetition structures, the **do...while statement** can be either a simple or compound statement. If it is a compound statement, enclose it between curly braces. The **expression** is called the **loop condition**. Figure 5-5 shows the flow of execution of a **do...while** loop.

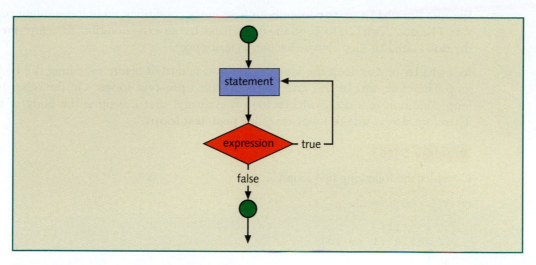

Figure 5-5 do...while loop

The **statement** executes first, and then the **expression** is evaluated. If the **expression** evaluates to **true**, the **statement** executes again. As long as the **expression** in a **do...while** statement is **true**, the **statement** executes. To avoid an infinite loop, you must, once again, make sure that the body of the loop contains a statement that ultimately makes the **expression** evaluate to **false** and assures that it exits properly.

Example 5-15

```
i = 0;
do
{
    System.out.print(i + " ");
    i = i + 5;
}
while (i <= 20);
```

The output of this code is:

```
0 5 10 15 20
```

After the value **20** is output, the statement:

```
i = i + 5;
```

changes the value of **i** to **25**, so **i <= 20** becomes **false**, which halts the loop.

Because the `while` or `for` loops both have entry conditions, these loops might never acti-vate. The `do...while` loop, on the other hand, has an exit condition; therefore, the body of the `do...while` loop always executes at least once.

In a `while` or `for` loop, the loop condition is evaluated before executing the body of the loop. Therefore, `while` and `for` loops are called **pre-test loops**. On the other hand, the loop condition in a `do...while` loop is evaluated after executing the body of the loop. Therefore, `do...while` loops are called **post-test loops**.

Example 5-16

Consider the following two loops:

(a)

```
i = 11;
while (i <= 10)
{
        System.out.print(i + " ");
        i = i + 5;
}

System.out.println();
```

(b)

```
i = 11;
do
{
    System.out.print(i + " ");
    i = i + 5;
}
while (i <= 10);

System.out.println();
```

In (a), the `while` loop produces nothing. In (b), the `do...while` loop outputs the number 11 and also changes the value of `i` to `16`.

The `do...while` loop is useful when it does not make sense to check a condition until after the action occurs. The following program illustrates this idea.

Example 5-17 Divisibility Test by 3 and 9

Suppose that m and n are integers and m is nonzero. Then m is called a **divisor** of n if $n = mt$ for some integer t; that is, when m divides n, the remainder is 0.

Let $n = a_k a_{k-1} a_{k-2} \ldots a_1 a_0$ be an integer. Let $s = a_k + a_{k-1} + a_{k-2} + \ldots + a_1 + a_0$ be the sum of the digits of n. It is known that n is divisible by 3 and 9 if s is divisible by 3 and 9. In other words, an integer is divisible by 3 and 9 if and only if the sum of its digits is divisible by 3 and 9.

For example, suppose $n = 27193257$. Then $s = 2 + 7 + 1 + 9 + 3 + 2 + 5 + 7 = 36$. Because 36 is divisible by both 3 and 9, it follows that 27193257 is divisible by both 3 and 9.

Next, we write a program that determines whether a positive integer is divisible by 3 and 9 by first finding the sum of its digits and then checking whether the sum is divisible by 3 and 9.

To find the sum of the digits of a positive integer, we need to extract each digit of the number. Consider the number 951372. Note that 951372 % 10 = 2, which is the last digit of 951372. Also note that 951372 / 10 = 95137, that is, when the number is divided by 10, it removes the last digit. Next, we repeat this process on the number 95137. Of course, we need to add the extracted digits.

Suppose that sum and num are int variables and the positive integer is stored in num. We thus have the following algorithm to find the sum of the digits:

```java
sum = 0;
do
{
    sum = sum + num % 10;  //extract the last digit
                           //and add it to sum
    num = num / 10;        //remove the last digit
} while (num > 0);
```

Using this algorithm, we can write the following program that uses a **do...while** loop to implement the preceding divisibility test algorithm.

```java
//Program: Divisibility test by 3 and 9

import java.util.*;

public class DivisibilityTest
{
    static Scanner console = new Scanner(System.in);

    public static void main(String[] args)
    {
        int num, temp, sum;

        System.out.print("Enter a positive integer: ");
        num = console.nextInt();
        System.out.println();

        temp = num;

        sum = 0;
        do
        {
            sum = sum + num % 10;  //extract the last digit
                                   //and add it to sum
            num = num / 10;        //remove the last digit
        } while (num > 0);
```

```
        System.out.println("The sum of the digits = " + sum);

        if (sum % 3 == 0)
            System.out.println(temp + " is divisible by 3");
        else
            System.out.println(temp + " is not divisible by 3");

        if (sum % 9 == 0)
            System.out.println(temp + " is divisible by 9");
        else
            System.out.println(temp + " is not divisible by 9");
    }
}
```

Sample Run: In these sample runs, the user input is shaded.

Sample Run 1
```
Enter a positive integer: 27193257

The sum of the digits = 36
27193257 is divisible by 3
27193257 is divisible by 9
```

Sample Run 2
```
Enter a positive integer: 609321

The sum of the digits = 21
609321 is divisible by 3
609321 is not divisible by 9
```

Sample Run 3
```
Enter a positive integer: 161905102

The sum of the digits = 25
161905102 is not divisible by 3
161905102 is not divisible by 9
```

All three loops have their place in Java. You can usually replace one with another, but it's often awkward. For example, you can rewrite the **while** loop in the program `SentinelControlledWhileLoop` (see Example 5-4) as a **do...while** loop. To do so, however, takes the awkward form:

```
if (number != -999)
    do
    {
        sum = sum + number;
        count++;
        number = console.nextInt();
    } while (number != -999);
```

That is,

```
if (expression)
    do
        action
    while (expression);
```

replaces the simpler:

```
while (expression)
        action
```

break AND continue STATEMENTS

The **break** and **continue** statements alter the flow of control in a program. As you have seen, the **break** statement, when executed in a **switch** structure, provides an immediate exit from the **switch** structure. Similarly, you can use the **break** statement in **while**, **for**, and **do...while** loops to immediately exit from these structures. The **break** statement is typically used for two purposes:

- To exit early from a loop

- To skip the remainder of the **switch** structure

After the **break** statement executes, the program continues to execute starting at the first statement after the structure.

Suppose that you have the following declaration:

```
static Scanner console = new Scanner(System.in);

int sum;
int num;
boolean isNegative;
```

The use of a **break** statement in a loop can eliminate the use of certain **boolean** variables. The following Java code segment helps illustrate this idea:

```
sum = 0;
isNegative = false;

while (console.hasNext() && !isNegative)
{
    num = console.nextInt();
    if (num < 0)  //if the number is negative, terminate the
                  //loop after this iteration
    {
        System.out.println("Negative number found in the data.");
        isNegative = true;
    }
    else
        sum = sum + num;
}
```

This **while** loop is supposed to find the sum of a set of positive numbers. If the data set contains a negative number, the loop terminates with an appropriate error message. This **while** loop uses the flag variable **isNegative** to accomplish the desired result. The variable **isNegative** is initialized to **false** before the **while** loop. Before adding **num** to **sum**, the code checks whether **num** is negative. If **num** is negative, an error message appears on the screen and **isNegative** is set to **true**. In the next iteration, when the expression in the **while** statement is evaluated, it evaluates to **false** because **!isNegative** is **false**. (Note that because **isNegative** is **true**, **!isNegative** is **false**.)

The following **while** loop is written without using the variable **isNegative**:

```
sum = 0;

while (console.hasNext())
{
    num = console.nextInt();
    if (num < 0)    //if the number is negative, terminate the loop
    {
        System.out.println("Negative number found in the data.");
        break;
    }

    sum = sum + num;
}
```

In this form of the **while** loop, when a negative number is found, the expression in the **if** statement evaluates to **true**; after printing an appropriate message, the **break** statement terminates the loop. (After executing the **break** statement in a loop, the remaining statements in the loop are skipped.)

The **continue** statement is used in **while**, **for**, and **do...while** structures. When the **continue** statement is executed in a loop, it skips the remaining statements in the loop and proceeds with the next iteration of the loop. In a **while** or **do...while** structure, the **expression** (that is, the loop-continue test) is evaluated immediately after the **continue** statement. In a **for** structure, the **update statement** is executed after the **continue** statement, and then the **loop condition** (that is, the loop-continue test) executes.

If the previous program segment encounters a negative number, the **while** loop terminates. If you want to ignore the negative number and read the next number rather than terminate the loop, replace the **break** statement with the **continue** statement, as shown in the following example:

```
sum = 0;

while (console.hasNext())
{
    num = console.nextInt();

    if (num < 0) //if the number is negative, go to the
                 //next iteration
    {
        System.out.println("Negative number found in the data.");
        continue;
    }

    sum = sum + num;
}
```

5

 As stated earlier, all three loops have their place in Java and one loop can often replace another. The execution of a **continue** statement, however, is where a **while** structure differs from a **for** structure. In a **while** loop, when the **continue** statement is executed, if the `update statement` appears after the **continue** statement, the `update statement` is not executed. In a **for** loop, the `update statement` always executes.

NESTED CONTROL STRUCTURES

This section briefly reviews the control structures discussed so far in this chapter and in Chapter 4. You have seen that by placing one control structure within another, you can achieve dramatic and fruitful results; nesting of control structures provides new power, subtlety, and complexity. Consider the following program that reads students' IDs and their test scores. For each student, the program outputs the student's ID, test score, and grade. The program also outputs the number of students in the class.

```
import java.util.*;

public class NestedControlStructure
{
    static Scanner console = new Scanner(System.in);

    public static void main(String[] args)
    {
        String studentId;
        int    testScore;
        int    count = 0;

        System.out.print("Enter the student ID "
                    + "(Enter ZZZ to end): ");
        System.out.flush();
        studentId = console.next();
        System.out.println();
```

```
        while (!studentId.equals("ZZZ"))
        {
            count++;

            System.out.print("Enter the test score: ");
            System.out.flush();
            testScore = console.nextInt();
            System.out.println();

            System.out.print("Student Id = " + studentId
                            + ", test score = "
                            + testScore + ", and grade = ");

            if (testScore >= 90)
                System.out.println("A.");
            else if (testScore >= 80)
                    System.out.println("B.");
            else if (testScore >= 70)
                    System.out.println("C.");
            else if (testScore >= 60)
                    System.out.println("D.");
            else
                System.out.println("F.");

            System.out.print("Enter the student ID "
                            + "(Enter ZZZ to end): ");

            System.out.flush();
            studentId = console.next();
            System.out.println();
        }//end while

        System.out.println("\nStudents in class = " + count);
    }
}
```

How would this program look if you wrote it as a sequence of **if...** statements (with no **else** or as a **switch** structure) within the **while** loop?

The remainder of this section gives examples that illustrate how to use nested loops to achieve amazing results as well as process data.

Example 5-18

Suppose you want to create the following pattern:

```
*
**
***
****
*****
```

Clearly, you want to print five lines of stars. In the first line you want to print one star, in the second line two stars, and so on. Because five lines will be printed, start with the following **for** statement:

```
for (i = 1; i <= 5; i++)
```

The value of i in the first iteration is 1, in the second iteration it is 2, and so on. You can use the value of i as the limiting condition in another **for** loop nested within this loop to control the number of stars in a line. A little more thought produces the following code:

```
for (i = 1; i <= 5; i++)          //Line 1
{                                 //Line 2
    for (j = 1; j <= i; j++)      //Line 3
        System.out.print("*");    //Line 4
    System.out.println();         //Line 5
}                                 //Line 6
```

A walk-through of this code shows that the **for** loop, in Line 1, starts with i = 1. When i is 1, the inner **for** loop, in Line 3, outputs one star and the insertion point moves to the next line. Then i becomes 2, the inner **for** loop outputs two stars, and the output statement in Line 5 moves the insertion point to the next line, and so on. This process continues until i becomes 6 and the loop stops.

What pattern does this code produce if you replace the **for** statement, in Line 1, with the following?

```
for (i = 5; i >= 1; i--)
```

Example 5-19

Suppose you want to create the following grid of numbers:

```
1 2 3 4 5
2 3 4 5 6
3 4 5 6 7
4 5 6 7 8
5 6 7 8 9
```

This grid has five lines. Therefore, as in Example 5-18, we use a **for** statement to output these lines as follows:

```
for (i = 1; i <= 5; i++)
    //output a line of numbers
```

In the first line, we want to print the numbers 1 through 5, in the second line we want to print the numbers 2 through 6, and so on. Notice that the first line starts with 1 and when this line is printed, i is 1. Similarly, the second line starts with 2 and when this line is printed, the value of i is 2, and so on. If i is 1, i + 4 is 5; if i is 2, i + 4 is 6; and so on.

Therefore, to print a line of numbers we can use the value of `i` as the starting number and the value of `i + 4` as the limiting value. That is, consider the following **for** loop:

```
for (j = i; j <= i + 4; j++)
    System.out.print(j + " ");
```

Let us take a look at this **for** loop. Suppose `i` is 1. Then we are printing the first line of the grid. Also, `j` goes from 1 to 5 and so this **for** loop outputs the numbers 1 through 5, which is the first line of the grid. Similarly, if `i` is 2, we are printing the second line of the grid. Also, `j` goes from 2 to 6, and so this **for** loop outputs the numbers 2 through 6, which is the second line of the grid, and so on.

A little more thought produces the following nested loops to output the desired grid:

```
for (i = 1; i <= 5; i++)              //Line 1
{                                     //Line 2
    for (j = i; j <= i + 4; j++)      //Line 3
        System.out.print(j + " ");    //Line 4
    System.out.println();             //Line 5
}                                     //Line 6
```

Notice that you can also write the inner **for** loop, Lines 3 and 4, as follows:

```
for (j = 0; j < 5; j++)               //Line 3
    System.out.print((i + j) + " ");  //Line 4
```

Example 5-20

Consider the following data:

```
65 78 65 89 25 98 -999
87 34 89 99 26 78 64 34 -999
23 99 98 97 26 78 100 63 87 23 -999
62 35 78 99 12 93 19 -999
```

The number **-999** at the end of each line acts as a sentinel and therefore it is not part of the data. Our objective is to find the sum of the numbers in each line and output the sum. Moreover, assume that this data is to be read from a file, say **Exp_5_20.txt**. We assume that the input file has been opened using the input file stream variable **inFile**.

This particular data set has four lines of input. So we can use a **for** loop or a counter-controlled **while** loop to process each line of data. Let us use a **for** loop to process these four lines. The **for** loop takes the following form:

```
for (counter = 0; counter < 4; counter++;)   //Line 1
{                                            //Line 2
    //process the line
    //output the sum
}
```

Let us now concentrate on processing a line. Each line has a varying number of data items. For example, the first line has 6 numbers, the second line has 8 numbers, and so on. Because each line ends with −999, we can use a sentinel-controlled **while** loop to find the sum of the numbers in each line. Remember how a sentinel-controlled loop works. Consider the following **while** loop:

```
sum = 0;                           //Line 3
num = inFile.nextInt();            //Line 4
while (num != -999)                //Line 5
{                                  //Line 6
    sum = sum + num;               //Line 7
    num = inFile.nextInt();        //Line 8
}                                  //Line 9
```

The statement in Line 3 initializes **sum** to 0, and the statement in Line 4 reads and stores the first number of the line into **num**. The **boolean** expression, **num != -999**, in Line 5, checks whether the number is −999. If **num** is not −999, the statements in Lines 7 and 8 execute. The statement in Line 7 updates the value of **sum**; the statement in Line 8 reads and stores the next number into **num**. The loop continues to execute as long as **num** is not −999.

It now follows that the nested loop to process the data is as follows (assume that all variables are properly declared):

```
for (counter = 0; counter < 4; counter++;)      //Line 1
{                                               //Line 2
    sum = 0;                                    //Line 3
    num = inFile.nextInt();                     //Line 4
    while (num != -999)                         //Line 5
    {                                           //Line 6
        sum = sum + num;                        //Line 7
        num = inFile.nextInt();                 //Line 8
    }                                           //Line 9

    System.out.println("Line " + (counter + 1)
                  + ": Sum = " + sum);          //Line 10
}                                               //Line 11
```

Example 5-21

Suppose that we want to process data similar to the data in Example 5-20, but the input file is of an unspecified length. That is, each line contains the same data as the data in each line in Example 5-20, but we do not know the number of input lines.

Because we do not know the number of input lines, we must use an EOF-controlled **while** loop to process the data. In this case, the required code is as follows (assume that all variables are properly declared and the input file has been opened using the **Scanner** variable **inFile**):

```
counter = 0;                                    //Line 1

while (inFile.hasNextInt())                      //Line 2
{                                                //Line 3
```

```
    sum = 0;                                          //Line 4
    num = inFile.nextInt();                           //Line 5

    while (num != -999)                               //Line 6
    {                                                 //Line 7
        sum = sum + num;                              //Line 8
        num = inFile.nextInt();                       //Line 9
    }                                                 //Line 10

    System.out.println("Line " + (counter + 1)
                    + ": Sum = " + sum);              //Line 11
    counter++;                                        //Line 12
}                                                     //Line 13
```

Notice that we have again used the variable **counter**. The only reason to do so is because we want to print the line number with the sum of each line.

Example 5-22

Consider the following data:

```
Lance 65 78 65 89 25 98 -999
Cynthia 87 34 89 99 26 78 64 34 -999
Sheila 23 99 98 97 26 78 100 63 87 23 -999
David 62 35 78 99 12 93 19 -999
...
```

The number **-999** at the end of each line acts as a sentinel and therefore it is not part of the data. The objective is to find the sum of the numbers in each line and output the sum and average of the numbers. Moreover, assume that this data is to be read from a file, say **Exp_5_22.txt**, of unknown size. We assume that the input file has been opened using the **Scanner** variable **inFile**.

As in Example 5-21, because the input file is of an unspecified length, we use an EOF-controlled **while** loop. The first data item in each line is a string, and the remaining data items are numbers. Therefore, for each line, first we read and store the name in a **String** variable, say **name**. We then process the numbers in each line. The necessary **while** loop takes the following form:

```
while (inFile.hasNext())        //Line 1
{
    name = inFile.next();       //Line 2; read the name in the line

    //process the numbers in each line
    //output the name and average
}
```

In this example, we want to find the average of the numbers in each line. Therefore, we must both add the numbers and count the numbers. The required `while` loop is:

```
sum = 0;                         //Line 3
count = 0;                        //Line 4

num = inFile.nextInt();          //Line 5; read the first number

while (num != -999)              //Line 6
{                                 //Line 7
    sum = sum + num;             //Line 8; update sum
    count++;                      //Line 9; update count
    num = inFile.nextInt();      //Line 10; read the next number
}
```

We can now write the following nested loop to process the data:

```
while (inFile.hasNext())            //Line 1
{
    name = inFile.next();           //Line 2; read the name

    sum = 0;                        //Line 3
    count = 0;                       //Line 4

    num = inFile.nextInt();         //Line 5; read the first number

    while (num != -999)             //Line 6
    {                                //Line 7
        sum = sum + num;            //Line 8; update sum
        count++;                     //Line 9; update count
        num = inFile.nextInt();     //Line 10; read the next number
    }

        //find the average
    if (count != 0)                 //Line 11
        average = sum / count;      //Line 12
    else                             //Line 13
        average = 0;                 //Line 14

    System.out.println("Name: " + name
                  + ", Sum: " + sum
                  + ", Average: "
                  + average);   //Line 15

}
```

Example 5-23

Consider the following data:

```
101
Lance Smith
65 78 65 89 25 98 -999
102
```

```
Cynthia Marker
87 34 89 99 26 78 64 34 -999
103
Sheila Mann
23 99 98 97 26 78 100 63 87 23 -999
104
David Arora
62 35 78 99 12 93 19 -999
...
```

The number **-999** at the end of a line acts as a sentinel and therefore is not part of the data.

Assume that this is the data of certain candidates seeking the student council's presidential seat. For each candidate the data is in the following form:

```
ID
Name
Votes
```

The objective is to find the total number of votes received by each candidate.

We assume that the data is input from the file, **Exp_5_23.txt**, of unknown size. We also assume that the input file has been opened using the **Scanner** variable **inFile**.

As in Example 5-22, because the input file is of an unspecified length, we use an EOF-controlled **while** loop. For each candidate, the first data item is the **ID** of the type, say **int**, on a line by itself; the second data item is the name, which may consist of more than one word; and the third line contains the votes received from the various departments.

To read the **ID** we use the method **nextInt**; to read the name we use the method **nextLine**. Notice that after reading the **ID**, the reading marker is after the **ID** and the character after the **ID** is the newline character. Therefore, after reading the **ID**, the reading marker is after the **ID** and at the newline character (of the line containing the **ID**).

The method **nextLine** reads until the end of the line. Therefore, if we read the name immediately after reading the **ID**, then what is stored in the variable **name** is the newline character after the **ID**. It follows that to read the name, we must read and discard the newline character after the **ID**, which we can do using the method **nextLine**. (Assume that **discard** is a variable of the type **String**.) Therefore, the statements to read the **ID** and name are as follows:

```
ID = inFile.nextInt();       //read the ID
discard = inFile.nextLine(); //read the newline character
                             //after the ID
name = inFile.nextLine();    //read the name
```

The general loop to process the data is:

```
while (inFile.hasNext())                 //Line 1
{                                        //Line 2
    ID = inFile.nextInt();               //Line 3
```

```
    discard = inFile.nextLine();          //Line 4
    name = inFile.nextLine();             //Line 5

    //process the numbers in each line
}
```

The code to read and sum up the voting data is the same as in Example 5-20. That is, the required **while** loop is:

```
sum = 0;                        //Line 6

num = inFile.nextInt();         //Line 7; read the first number

while (num != -999)             //Line 8
{                               //Line 9
    sum = sum + num;            //Line 10; update sum
    num = inFile.nextInt();     //Line 11; read the next number
}                               //Line 12
```

We can now write the following nested loop to process the data:

```
while (inFile.hasNext())          //Line 1
{                                 //Line 2
    ID = inFile.nextInt();        //Line 3
    discard = inFile.nextLine();  //Line 4
    name = inFile.nextLine();     //Line 5

    sum = 0;                      //Line 6

    num = inFile.nextInt();       //Line 7; read the first number

    while (num != -999)           //Line 8
    {                             //Line 9
        sum = sum + num;          //Line 10; update sum
        num = inFile.nextInt();   //Line 11; read the next number
    }                             //Line 12

    System.out.println("Name: " + name
                   + ", Votes: " + sum);  //Line 13

}                                         //Line 14
```

To learn more about the nesting of **for** loops, see Exercise 30 at the end of this chapter.

QUICK REVIEW

1. Java has three looping (repetition) structures: **while**, **for**, and **do...while**.
2. The syntax of the **while** statement is:

```
while (expression)
    statement
```

3. In Java, **while** is a reserved word.

4. In a **while** statement, the parentheses around the **expression**, the decision maker, are required; they mark the beginning and end of the expression.

5. The **statement** is called the body of the loop.

6. The body of the **while** loop typically contains statement(s) that eventually set the expression to **false** to terminate the loop.

7. A counter-controlled **while** loop uses a counter to control the loop.

8. In a counter-controlled **while** loop, you must initialize the counter before the loop, and the body of the loop must contain a statement that changes the value of the counter variable.

9. A sentinel is a special value that marks the end of the input data. The sentinel must be similar, yet different, from all the data items.

10. A sentinel-controlled **while** loop uses a sentinel to control the **while** loop. The **while** loop continues to execute until the sentinel is read.

11. An EOF-controlled **while** loop continues to execute until the program detects the end-of-file marker.

12. The method **hasNext** returns the value **true** if there is an input (token) in the input stream, otherwise it returns **false**.

13. In the Windows console environment, the end-of-file marker is entered using **Ctrl+z**. (Hold the **Ctrl** key and press **z**.) In the UNIX environment, the end-of-file marker is entered using **Ctrl+d**. (Hold the **Ctrl** key and press **d**.)

14. In Java, **for** is a reserved word.

15. A **for** loop simplifies the writing of a counter-controlled **while** loop.

16. The syntax of the **for** loop is:

```
for (initialize statement; loop condition; update statement)
    statement
```

The **statement** is called the body of the **for** loop.

17. If you put a semicolon at the end of the **for** loop (before the body of the **for** loop), the action of the **for** loop is empty.

18. The syntax of the **do...while** statement is:

```
do
   statement
while (expression);
```

19. The **statement** is called the body of the **do...while** loop.

20. The body of the **while** and **for** loops might not execute at all, but the body of a **do...while** loop always executes at least once.

21. Executing a **break** statement in the body of a loop immediately terminates the loop.

22. Executing a **continue** statement in the body of a loop skips the loop's remaining statements and proceeds with the next iteration.

23. When a **continue** statement executes in a **while** or **do...while** loop, the update statement in the body of the loop might not execute.

24. After a **continue** statement executes in a **for** loop, the update statement is the next statement executed.

25. In a **while** or **for** loop, the loop condition is evaluated before executing the body of the loop. Therefore, **while** and **for** loops are called pre-test loops.

26. In a **do...while** loop, the loop condition is evaluated after executing the body of the loop. Therefore, **do...while** loops are called post-test loops.

5

EXERCISES

1. Mark the following statements as true or false.

    a. In a counter-controlled **while** loop, it is not necessary to initialize the loop control variable.

    b. It is possible that the body of a **while** loop might not execute at all.

    c. In an infinite **while** loop, the loop condition is initially false, but after the first iteration it is always true.

    d. The **while** loop:

       ```
       j = 0;
       while (j <= 10)
               j++;
       ```
       terminates when j > 10.

    e. A sentinel-controlled **while** loop is an event-controlled **while** loop whose termination depends on a special value.

    f. A loop is a control structure that causes certain statements to execute over and over.

    g. To read data from a file of an unspecified length, an EOF-controlled loop is a good choice.

    h. When a **while** loop terminates, the control first goes back to the statement just before the **while** statement, and then the control goes to the statement immediately following the **while** loop.

2. What is the output of the following Java code?

    ```
    count = 1;
    y = 100;
    while (count < 100)
    {
        y = y - 1;
        count++;
    }
    System.out.println("y = " + y + " and count = " + count);
    ```

3. What is the output of the following Java code?

```java
num = 5;
while (num > 5)
      num = num + 2;
System.out.println(num);
```

4. What is the output of the following Java code?

```java
num = 1;
while (num < 10)
{
      System.out.print(num + " ");
      num = num + 2;
}
System.out.println();
```

5. When does the following **while** loop terminate?

```java
ch = 'D';
while ('A' <= ch && ch <= 'Z')
      ch = (char)((int)(ch) + 1));
```

6. Suppose that the input is:

```
38 45 71 4 −1
```

What is the output of the following code? Assume all variables are properly declared.

```java
sum = console.nextInt();
num = console.nextInt();

for (j = 1; j <= 3; j++)
{
      num = console.nextInt();
      sum = sum + num;
}
System.out.println("Sum = " + sum);
```

7. Suppose that the input is:

```
38 45 71 4 −1
```

What is the output of the following code? Assume all variables are properly declared.

```java
sum = console.nextInt();
num = console.nextInt();

while (num != -1)
{
   sum = sum + num;
   num = console.nextInt();
}
System.out.println("Sum = " + sum);
```

8. Suppose that the input is:

```
38 45 71 4 −1
```

What is the output of the following code? Assume all variables are properly declared.

```
num = console.nextInt();
sum = num;

while (num != -1)
{
    num = console.nextInt();
    sum = sum + num;
}

System.out.println("Sum = " + sum);
```

9. Suppose that the input is:

```
38 45 71 4 -1
```

What is the output of the following code? Assume all variables are properly declared.

```
sum = 0;
num = console.nextInt();

while (num != -1)
{
    sum = sum + num;
    num = console.nextInt();
}

System.out.println("Sum = " + sum);
```

10. Correct the following code so that it finds the sum of 10 numbers.

```
sum = 0;
while (count < 10)
        num = console.nextInt();
        sum = sum + num;
        count++;
```

11. What is the output of the following program?

```
public class WhatIsTheOutput
{
    public static void main(String[] args)
    {
        int x, y, z;

        x = 4;
        y = 5;
        z = y + 6;

        while (((z - x) % 4) != 0)
        {
            System.out.print(z + " ");
            z = z + 7;
        }
        System.out.println();
    }
}
```

5

12. Suppose that the input is:

58   23   46   75   98   150   12   176   145 –999

What is the output of the following program?

```java
import java.util.*;

public class FindTheOutput
{
    static Scanner console = new Scanner(System.in);
    public static void main(String[] args)
    {
        int num;

        num = console.nextInt();

        while (num != -999)
        {
            System.out.print(num % 25 + "  ");
            num = console.nextInt();
        }

        System.out.println();
    }
}
```

13. Given the following code:

```java
for (i = 12; i <= 25; i++)
    System.out.println(i);
System.out.println();
```

Answer the following questions:

a. The seventh integer printed is _____.

b. The **for** loop produces _____ lines of output.

c. If i++ were changed to i--, a compilation error would result. True or False?

14. Given that the following code is correctly inserted into a program, state its entire output as to content and form.

```java
num = 0;
for (i = 1; i <= 4; i++)
{
    num = num + 10 * (i - 1);
    System.out.print(num + " ");
}
System.out.println();
```

15. Given that the following code is correctly inserted into a program, state its entire output as to content and form.

```
j = 2;
for (i = 0; i <= 5; i++)
{
    System.out.print(j + " ");
    j = 2 * j + 3;
}
System.out.println();
```

16. Assume that the following code is correctly inserted into a program:

```
s = 0;
for (i = 0; i < 5; i++)
{
    s = 2 * s + i;
    System.out.print(s + " ");
}

System.out.println();
```

a. What is the final value of s?

(i) 11   (ii) 4   (iii) 26   (iv) none of these

b. If a semicolon is inserted after the right parentheses in the **for** loop control expression, what is the final value of s?

(i) 0   (ii) 1   (iii) 2   (iv) 5   (v) none of these

c. If the 5 is replaced with a 0 in the **for** loop control expression, what is the final value of s?

(i) 0   (ii) 1   (iii) 2   (iv) none of these

17. State what output, if any, results in each of the following statements:

a. ```
for (i = 1; i <= 1; i++)
        System.out.print("*");
System.out.println();
```

b. ```
for (i = 2; i >= 1; i++)
        System.out.print("*");
System.out.println();
```

c. ```
for (i = 1; i <= 1; i--)
        System.out.print("*");
System.out.println();
```

d. ```
for (i = 12; i >= 9; i--)
        System.out.print("*");
System.out.println();
```

e. ```
for (i = 0; i <= 5; i++)
        System.out.print("*");
System.out.println();
```
```

f.
```
for (i = 1; i <= 5; i++)
{
    System.out.print("*");
    i = i + 1;
}
System.out.println();
```

18. Write a **for** statement to add all the multiples of 3 between 1 and 100.

19. What is the exact output of the following program?

```
public class Mystery
{
    public static void main (String[] args)
    {
        int counter;

        for (counter = 7; counter <= 16; counter++)
            switch (counter % 10)
            {
            case 0: System.out.print(", ");
                    break;
            case 1: System.out.print("OFTEN ");
                    break;
            case 2: case 8: System.out.print("IS ");
                            break;
            case 3: System.out.print("NOT ");
                    break;
            case 4: case 9: System.out.print("DONE ");
                            break;
            case 5: System.out.print("WELL");
                    break;
            case 6: System.out.print(".");
                    break;
            case 7: System.out.print("WHAT ");
                    break;
            default: System.out.print("Bad number. ");
            }

        System.out.println();
    }
}
```

20. Suppose that the input is:

5 3 8

What is the output of the following code? Assume all variables are properly declared.

```
a = console.nextInt();
b = console.nextInt();
c = console.nextInt();
```

```
for (j = 1; j < a; j++)
{
    d = b + c;
    b = c;
    c = d;
    System.out.print(c + "   ");
}
System.out.println();
```

21. What is the output of the following Java program segment? Assume all variables are properly declared.

```
for (j = 0; j < 8; j++)
{
    System.out.print(j * 25 + " - ");
    if (j != 7)
        System.out.println((j + 1) * 25 - 1);
    else
        System.out.println((j + 1) * 25);
}
```

22. The following program has more than five mistakes that prevent it from compiling and/or running. Correct all such mistakes.

```
public class Exercise22
{
    final int N = 2,137;

    public static main(String[] args)
    {
        int a, b, c, d:

        a := 3;
        b = 5;
        c = c + d;
        N = a + n;
        for (i = 3; i <= N; i++)
        {
            System.out.print(" " + i);
            i = i + 1;
        }

        System.out.println();
    }
}
```

23. Which of the following apply to the **while** loop only? To the **do...while** loop only? To both?
    a. It is considered a conditional loop.
    b. The body of the loop executes at least once.
    c. The logical expression controlling the loop is evaluated before the loop is entered.
    d. The body of the loop might not execute at all.

24. How many times will each of the following loops execute? What is the output in each case?

a.

```
x = 5; y = 50;
do
    x = x + 10;
while (x < y);

System.out.println(x + " " + y);
```

b.

```
x = 5; y = 80;
do
   x = x * 2;
while (x < y);

System.out.println(x + " " + y);
```

c.

```
x = 5; y = 20;
do
    x = x + 2;
while (x >= y);

System.out.println(x + " " + y);
```

d.

```
x = 5; y = 35;
while (x < y)
      x = x + 10;

System.out.println(x + " " + y);
```

e.

```
x = 5; y = 30;
while (x <= y)
      x = x * 2;

System.out.println(x + " " + y);
```

f.

```
x = 5; y = 30;
while (x > y)
      x = x + 2;

System.out.println(x + " " + y);
```

25. The **do...while** loop in the following program is supposed to read some numbers until it reaches a sentinel (in this case, −1). It is supposed to add all of the numbers except for the sentinel. If the data looks like:

```
12 5 30 48 −1
```

the program fails to do what it is purported to do. Make any necessary corrections.

```java
import java.util.*;
public class Strange
{
    static Scanner console = new Scanner(System.in);
    public static void main(String[] args)
    {
        int total = 0,
            number;
        do
        {
            number = console.nextInt();
            total = total + number;
        }
        while (number != -1);
        System.out.println("The sum of the numbers entered is: "
                           + total);
    }
}
```

26. Using the data from Exercise 25, the following two loops also fail. Correct them.

    a.

    ```java
    number = console.nextInt();

    while (number != -1)
        total = total + number;
        number = console.nextInt();
    ```

    b.

    ```java
    number = console.nextInt();

    while (number != -1)
    {
        number = console.nextInt();
        total = total + number;
    }
    ```

27. Given the following program segment:

    ```java
    for (number = 1; number <= 10; number++)
        System.out.print(number + " ");
    System.out.println();
    ```

    write a **while** and a **do...while** loop that have the same output.

28. Given the following program segment:

```
j = 2;
for (i = 1; i <= 5; i++)
{
    System.out.print(j + " ");
    j = j + 5;
}
System.out.println();
```

write a **while** and a **do...while** loop that have the same output.

29. What is the output of the following program?

```
public class Mystery
{
    public static void main(String[] args)
    {
        int x, y, z;

        x = 4;
        y = 5;
        z = y + 6;
        do
        {
            System.out.print(z + " ");
            z = z + 7;
        }
        while (((z - x) % 4) != 0);

        System.out.println();
    }
}
```

30. To further learn how nested **for** loops work, do a walk-through of the following program segments and, in each case, determine the exact output.

a.

```
int i, j;
for (i = 1; i <= 5; i++)
{
    for (j = 1; j <= 5; j++)
        System.out.printf("%3d", i);
    System.out.println();
}
```

b.

```
int i, j;
for (i = 1; i <= 5; i++)
{
    for (j = 1; j <= i; j++)
```

```
            System.out.printf("%3d", j);
         System.out.println();
    }
```

c.

```
    int i, j;

    for (i = 1; i <= 5; i++)
    {
        for (j = 1; j <= 5; j++)
            System.out.printf("%3d", i * j);
        System.out.println();
    }
```

d.

```
    int i, j;

    for (i = 1; i <= 5; i++)
    {
        for (j = (i + 1); j <= 5; j++)
            System.out.printf("%5d", j);
        System.out.println();
    }
```

e.

```
    final int m = 10;
    final int n = 10;
    int i, j;

    for (i = 1; i <= m; i++)
    {
        for (j = 1; j <= n; j++)
            System.out.printf("%4d", (m * (i - 1) + j));
        System.out.println();
    }
```

f.

```
    int i, j;

    for (i = 1; i <= 9; i++)
    {
        for (j = 1; j <= (9 - i); j++)
            System.out.print(" ");
        for (j = 1; j <= i; j++)
            System.out.print(j);
        for (j = (i - 1); j >= 1; j--)
            System.out.print(j);
        System.out.println();
    }
```

PROGRAMMING EXERCISES

1. Write a program that prompts the user to input an integer and then outputs both the individual digits of the number and the sum of the digits. For example, the program should: output the individual digits of 3456 as 3 4 5 6; output the individual digits of 8030 as 8 0 3 0; and output the individual digits of 2345526 as 2 3 4 5 5 2 6; output the individual digits of 4000 as 4 0 0 0; and output the individual digits of –2345 as 2 3 4 5.

2. Write a program that prompts the user to input an integer and then outputs the number with the digits reversed. For example, if the input is 12345, the output should be 54321. Your program must also output 5000 as 0005 and 980 as 089.

3. Rewrite the program of Example 5-5, Telephone Digits. Replace the statements from Line 10 to Line 28 so that the program uses only a **switch** structure to find the digit that corresponds to an uppercase letter.

4. The program Telephone Digits outputs only telephone digits that correspond to uppercase letters. Rewrite the program so that it processes both uppercase and lowercase letters and outputs the corresponding telephone digit. If the input is other than an uppercase or lowercase letter, the program must output an appropriate error message.

5. To make telephone numbers easier to remember, some companies user letters to show their telephone number. For example, using letters, the telephone number 438-5626 can be shown as GET LOAN. In some cases, to make a telephone number meaningful, companies might use more than seven letters. For example, 225-5466 can be displayed as CALL HOME, which uses eight letters. Write a program that prompts the user to enter a telephone number expressed in letters and outputs the corresponding telephone number in digits. If the user enters more than 8 letters, then process only the first seven letters. Also output the – (hyphen) after the third digit. Allow the user to use uppercase and lowercase letters, as well as spaces between words. Moreover, your program should process as many telephone numbers as the user wants. (*Hint*: You can read the entered telephone number as a string and then use the **charAt** method of the **class** String to extract each character. For example, if **str** refers to a string, then the expression **str.charAt(i)** returns the character at the ith position. Recall that in a string, the position of the first character is 0.)

6. Write a program that reads a set of integers, and then finds and prints the sum of the even and odd integers.

7. Write a program that prompts the user to input a positive integer. It should then output a message indicating whether the number is a prime number. (*Note*: An even number is prime if it is 2. An odd integer is prime if it is not divisible by any odd integer less than or equal to the square root of the number.)

8. Let $n = a_k a_{k-1} a_{k-2} \ldots a_1 a_0$ be an integer. Let $t = a_0 - a_1 + a_2 - \ldots + (-1)^k a_k$. It is known that n is divisible by 11 if and only if t is divisible by 11. For example, suppose that $n = 8784204$. Then $t = 4 - 0 + 2 - 4 + 8 - 7 + 8 = 11$. Because 11 is divisible by 11, it follows that 8784204 is divisible by 11. If $n = 54063297$, then $t = 7 - 9 + 2 - 3 + 6 - 0 + 4 - 5 = 2$. Because 2 is not divisible by 11, 54063297 is not divisible by 11.

Write a program that prompts the user to enter a positive integer and then uses this criterion to determine whether the number is divisible by 11.

9. Write a program that uses `while` loops to perform the following steps:

   a. Prompt the user to input two integers: `firstNum` and `secondNum`. (`firstNum` must be less than `secondNum`.)

   b. Output all the odd numbers between `firstNum` and `secondNum`.

   c. Output the sum of all the even numbers between `firstNum` and `secondNum`.

   d. Output all the numbers and their squares between 1 and 10.

   e. Output the sum of the squares of all the odd numbers between `firstNum` and `secondNum`.

   f. Output all the uppercase letters.

10. Redo Exercise 9 using `for` loops.

11. Redo Exercise 9 using `do...while` loops.

12. The program in the Programming Example Fibonacci Number does not check whether the first number entered by the user is less than or equal to the second number and both the numbers are nonnegative. Also, the program does not check whether the user entered a valid value for the position of the desired number in the Fibonacci sequence. Rewrite that program so that it checks for these things.

13. Suppose that m and n are integers and m is nonzero. Recall that m is called a *divisor* of n if $n = mt$ for some integer t; that is, when m divides n, the remainder is 0. Moreover, m is called a **proper divisor** of n if $m < n$ and m divides n. A positive integer is called **perfect** if it is the sum of its positive proper divisors. For example, the positive proper divisors of 28 are 1, 2, 4, 7, and 14, and $1 + 2 + 4 + 7 + 14 = 28$. Therefore, 28 is perfect. Write a program that does the following:

   a. Outputs the first four perfect integers.

   b. Takes as input a positive integer and then outputs whether the integer is perfect.

14. The program in Example 5-6 implements the Guessing the Number game. However, in that program the user is given as many tries as needed to guess the correct number. Rewrite that program so that the user has at most five tries to guess the correct number. Your program should print an appropriate message such as "You win!" or "You lose!"

15. Example 5-6 implements the Guessing the Number game program. If the guessed number is not correct, the program outputs a message indicating whether the guess is low or high. Modify the program as follows: Suppose that the variables `num` and `guess` are as declared in Example 5-6 and `diff` is an `int` variable. Let `diff` = the absolute value of (`num` - `guess`). If `diff` is 0, then `guess` is correct and the program outputs a message indicating that the user guessed the correct number. Suppose `diff` is not 0. Then the program outputs the message as follows:

   a. If `diff` is greater than or equal to `50`, the program outputs the message indicating that the guess is very high (if `guess` is greater than `num`) or very low (if `guess` is less than `num`).

5

b. If `diff` is greater than or equal to `30` and less than `50`, the program outputs the message indicating that the guess is high (if `guess` is greater than `num`) or low (if `guess` is less than `num`).

c. If `diff` is greater than or equal to `15` and less than `30`, the program outputs the message indicating that the guess is moderately high (if `guess` is greater than `num`) or moderately low (if `guess` is less than `num`).

d. If `diff` is greater than `0` and less than `15`, the program outputs the message indicating that the guess is somewhat high (if `guess` is greater than `num`) or somewhat low (if `guess` is less than `num`).

As in Programming Exercise 14, give the user at most five tries to guess the number. (To find the absolute value of `num - guess`, use the expression `Math.abs(num - guess)`.)

16. A high school has 1000 students and 1000 lockers, one locker for each student. On the first day of school, the principal plays the following game: She asks the first student to go and open all the lockers. She then asks the second student to go and close all the even numbered lockers. The third student is asked to check every third locker. If it is open, the student closes it; if it is closed, the student opens it. The fourth student is asked to check every fourth locker. If it is open, the student closes it; if it is closed, the student opens it. The remaining students continue this game. In general, the nth student checks every nth locker. If the locker is open, the student closes it; if it is closed, the student opens it. After all the students have taken their turn, some of the lockers are open and some are closed. Write a program that prompts the user to enter the number of lockers in a school. After the game is over, the program outputs the number of lockers that are open. Test run your program for the following inputs: 1000, 5000, 10000. Do you see any pattern developing for the locker numbers that are open in the output?

(*Hint*: Consider locker number 100. This locker is visited by student numbers 1, 2, 4, 5, 10, 20, 25, 50, and 100. These are the positive divisors of 100. Similarly, locker number 30 is visited by student numbers 1, 2, 3, 5, 6, 10, 15, and 30. Notice that if the number of positive divisors of a locker number is odd, then at the end of the game the locker is open. If the number of positive divisors of a locker number is even, then at the end of the game the locker is closed.)

17. For research purposes and to assist students, the admissions office of your local university wants to know how well female and male students perform in certain courses. You receive a file that contains female and male students' GPAs for certain courses. Due to confidentiality, the letter code `f` is used for female students; `m` is used for male students. Every file entry consists of a letter code followed by a GPA. Each line has one entry. The number of entries in the file is unknown. Write a program that computes and outputs the average GPA for both female and male students. Format your results to two decimal places.

18. If interest is compounded annually, it grows as follows. Suppose `P0` is the initial amount and `INT` is the interest rate per year. If `P1`, `P2`, and `P3` represent the balance at the end of the first, second, and third year, respectively, then:

```
P1 = P0 + P0 * INT = P0 * (1 + INT)
P2 = P1 + P1 * INT = P1 * (1 + INT) = P0 * (1 + INT) * (1 + INT)
   = P0 * (1 + INT)²
```

```
P3 = P2 + P2 * INT = P2 * (1 + INT)
   = P0 * (1 + INT) * (1 + INT) * (1 + INT)
   = P0 * (1 + INT)³
```

and so on.

When money is deposited in an IRA, it is usually sheltered from taxes until the money is withdrawn after the age of 59. Suppose that someone dear to you opened such an account for you on your 16th birthday at 10% interest, and then he or she forgot about it (so no money was added or withdrawn). On your 60th birthday, some fortune hunters notify you about this account. The money has been compounded annually at the 10% rate. Write a program that reads an initial amount and computes the total in the account on your 60th birthday.

You decide to leave the money in the IRA for another year. Starting from your 61st birthday, you decide to withdraw each year's interest income. In other words, you withdraw the interest and leave the rest of the money untouched. How much income would you have per month for the rest of your life?

Design your program to accept any integer input. Test it with initial investments of $1700, $3600, and $8500. (*Note*: Use a loop to compute the amount at your 60th birthday. Do *not* use the predefined method **pow**.) The program should do all the computing needed, and output all the relevant data as follows:

```
The initial investment was $_____. The total amount
accumulated after _____ years, if $_____ is
allowed to compound with an interest rate of 10.00%, comes to
$_____.

The total amount accumulated after _____ (years + 1)
years, if $ _____ is allowed to compound with an
interest rate of 10%, comes to $_____.

The interest earned during this year is $_____. If
interest is withdrawn each year thereafter, my income is
$_____ per month.
```

19. Write a complete program to generate the pattern given in Example 5-18.

20. Write a complete program to generate the grid of numbers given in Example 5-19.

21. Write a complete program to process the data given in Example 5-20.

22. Write a complete program to process the data given in Example 5-21.

23. Write a complete program to process the data given in Example 5-22.

24. Write a complete program to process the data given in Example 5-23.

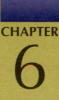
GRAPHICAL USER INTERFACE (GUI) AND OBJECT-ORIENTED DESIGN (OOD)

In this chapter, you will:

♦ Learn about basic GUI components

♦ Explore how the GUI components **JFrame**, **JLabel**, **JTextField**, and **JButton** work

♦ Become familiar with the concept of event-driven programming

♦ Discover events and event handlers

♦ Explore object-oriented design

♦ Learn how to identify objects, classes, and members of a class

♦ Learn about wrapper classes

♦ Become aware of the autoboxing and unboxing of primitive data types

Java is equipped with many powerful, yet easy-to-use graphical user interface (GUI) components, such as the input and output dialog boxes you learned about in Chapter 3. You can use these to make your programs attractive and user friendly. The first half of this chapter introduces you to some basic Java GUI components.

In Chapter 1, you were introduced to the object-oriented design (OOD) problem-solving methodology. The second half of this chapter outlines a general approach to solving problems using OOD, and provides several examples to clarify this problem-solving methodology.

GRAPHICAL USER INTERFACE (GUI) COMPONENTS

In Chapter 3, you learned how to use input and output dialog boxes to input data into a program and show the output of a program. Before introducing the various GUI components, we will use input and output dialog boxes to write a program to determine the area and perimeter of a rectangle. We will then discuss how to use different GUI components to create a different graphical user interface to determine the area and perimeter of a rectangle.

The program in Example 6-1 prompts the user to input the length and width of a rectangle and then displays its area and perimeter. We will use the method `showInputDialog` to create an input dialog box and the method `showMessageDialog` to create an output dialog box. Recall that these methods are contained in the **class** `JOptionPane` and this class is contained in the package `javax.swing`.

Example 6-1: (Area and Perimeter of a Rectangle)

```java
//This Java program determines the area and
//perimeter of a rectangle.

import javax.swing.JOptionPane;

public class Rectangle
{
    public static void main(String[] args)
    {
        double width, length, area, perimeter;              //Line 1

        String lengthStr, widthStr, outputStr;              //Line 2

        lengthStr =
            JOptionPane.showInputDialog("Enter the length: "); //Line 3
        length = Double.parseDouble(lengthStr);             //Line 4

        widthStr =
            JOptionPane.showInputDialog("Enter the width: ");  //Line 5
        width = Double.parseDouble(widthStr);               //Line 6

        area = length * width;                              //Line 7
        perimeter = 2 * (length + width);                   //Line 8

        outputStr = "Length: " + length + "\n" +
                    "Width: " + width + "\n" +
                    "Area: " + area + " square units\n" +
                    "Perimeter: " + perimeter + " units\n";   //Line 9

        JOptionPane.showMessageDialog(null, outputStr,
                                    "Rectangle",
                          JOptionPane.INFORMATION_MESSAGE);   //Line 10
```

```
        System.exit(0);                                              //Line 11
    }
}
```

Sample Run: Figure 6-1 shows the sample run.

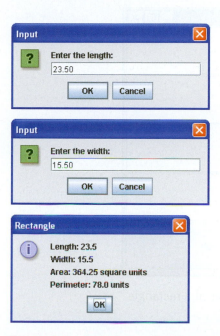

Figure 6-1   Sample run for `Rectangle`

The program in Example 6-1 works as follows: The statements in Lines 1 and 2 declare various variables to manipulate the data. The statement in Line 3 displays the first dialog box of the sample run and prompts the user to enter the length of the rectangle. The entered length is assigned as a string to `lengthStr`. The statement in Line 4 retrieves the length and stores it in the variable `length`.

The statement in Line 5 displays the second dialog box of the sample run and prompts the user to enter the width of the rectangle. The entered width is assigned as a string to `widthStr`. The statement in Line 6 retrieves the width and stores it in the variable `width`.

The statement in Line 7 determines the area, and the statement in Line 8 determines the perimeter of the rectangle. The statement in Line 9 creates the string containing the desired output and assigns this string to `outputStr`. The statement in Line 10 uses the output dialog box to display the desired output, which is shown in the third dialog box of the sample run. Finally, the statement in Line 11 terminates the program.

The program in Example 6-1 uses input and output dialog boxes to accomplish its job. When you run this program, you see only one dialog box at a time.

However, suppose that you want the program to display all the input and output in one dialog box, as shown in Figure 6-2.

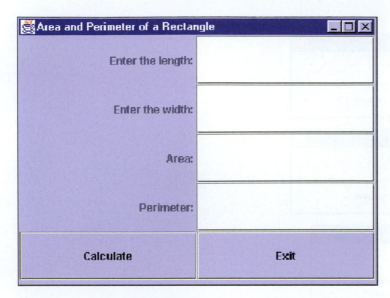

Figure 6-2   GUI to find the area and perimeter of a rectangle

In Java terminology, such a dialog box is called a GUI, or simply a user interface. In this GUI, the user enters the length and width in the top two white boxes. When the user clicks the `Calculate` button, the program displays the area and the perimeter in their respective locations. When the user clicks the `Exit` button, the program terminates.

In this interface, the user can:

- See the entire input and output simultaneously

- Input values for length and width, in any order the user prefers

- Input values that can be corrected after entering them and before clicking the `Calculate` button

- Enter another set of input values and click the `Calculate` button to obtain the area and perimeter of another rectangle

The interface shown in Figure 6-2 contains various Java GUI components that are labeled in Figure 6-3.

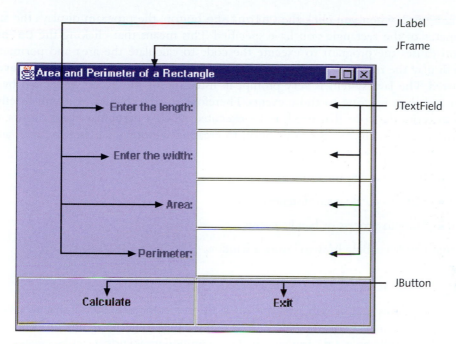

Figure 6-3   Java GUI components

As you can see in Figure 6-3, the white areas used to get the input and show the results are called `JTextField`s. The labels for these text fields, such as `Enter the length:`, are called `JLabel`s; the buttons `Calculate` and `Exit` are each called a `JButton`. All these components are placed in a window, called `JFrame`.

Creating this type of user interface is not difficult. Java has done all the work; you need to learn only how to use the tools provided by Java to create such an interface. For example, to create an interface like the one shown in Figures 6-2 and 6-3 that contains labels, text areas, buttons, and windows, you need to learn how to write the statements that create these components. In the following sections you will learn how to create the following GUI components:

- Windows
- Labels
- Text areas
- Buttons

The GUI components, such as labels, are placed in an area called the **content pane** of the window. You can think of a content pane as the inner area of the window, below the title bar and inside the border. You will also learn how to place these GUI components in the content pane of a window.

In Figure 6-2, when you click the `Calculate` button, the program displays the area and perimeter of the rectangle you have specified. This means that clicking the `Calculate` button causes the program to execute the code to calculate the area and perimeter and then display the results. When the `Calculate` button is clicked, we say that an **event** has occurred. The Java system is very prompt in listening for the events generated by a program and then reacting to those events. Therefore, in this chapter, you will briefly learn how to write the code that needs to be executed when a particular event occurs, such as when a button is clicked. So, in addition to creating windows, labels, text areas, and buttons, in the next few sections, you will learn:

- How to access the content pane
- How to create event listeners
- How to process or handle events

We begin by describing how to create a window.

Creating a Window

GUI components such as windows and labels are, in fact, objects. Recall that an object is an instance of a particular class. Therefore, these components (objects) are instances of a particular class type. `JFrame` is a **class** and the GUI component `window` can be created by using a `JFrame` object. Various attributes are associated with a window. For example:

- Every window has a title.
- Every window has width and height.

JFrame

The **class** `JFrame` provides various methods to control the attributes of a window. For example, it has methods to set the window title and methods to specify the height and width of the window. Table 6-1 describes some of the methods provided by the **class** `JFrame`.

Table 6-1 Some Methods Provided by the **class** JFrame

Method / Description / Example
| ```java
public JFrame()
   //This is used when an object of the type JFrame is
   //instantiated and the window is created without any title.
   //Example: JFrame myWindow = new JFrame();
   //          myWindow is a window with no title
``` |
| ```java
public JFrame(String s)
   //This is used when an object of the type JFrame is
   //instantiated and the title of the window is also specified.
   //Example: The statement
   //          JFrame myWindow = new JFrame("Rectangle");
   //          myWindow is a window with the title Rectangle
``` |
| ```java
public void setSize(int w, int h)
   //Method to set the size of the window.
   //Example: The statement
   //          myWindow.setSize(400, 300);
   //          sets the width of the window to 400 pixels and
   //          the height to 300 pixels.
``` |
| ```java
public void setTitle(String s)
   //Method to set the title of the window.
   //Example: myWindow.setTitle("Rectangle");
   //          sets the title of the window to Rectangle.
``` |
| ```java
public void setVisible(boolean b)
   //Method to display the window in the program. If the value of b is
   //true, the window will be displayed on the screen.
   //Example: myWindow.setVisible(true);
   //   After this statement executes, the window will be shown
   //   during program execution.
``` |
| ```java
public void setDefaultCloseOperation(int operation)
   //Method to determine the action to be taken when the user clicks
   //on the window closing button, ×, to close the window.
   //Choices for the parameter operation are the named constants —
   //EXIT_ON_CLOSE, HIDE_ON_CLOSE, DISPOSE_ON_CLOSE, and
   //DO_NOTHING_ON_CLOSE. The named constant EXIT_ON_CLOSE is defined
   //in the class JFrame. The last three named constants are defined in
   //javax.swing.WindowConstants.
   //Example: The statement
   //          setDefaultCloseOperation(EXIT_ON_CLOSE);
   //sets the default close option of the window closing to close the
   //window and terminate the program when the user clicks the
   //window closing button, ×.
``` |
| ```java
public void addWindowListener(WindowEvent e)
   //Method to register a window listener object to a JFrame.
``` |

 The **class** JFrame also contains methods to set the color of a window. Chapter 13 describes these methods.

6
```

There are two ways to make an application program create a window. The first way is to declare an object of the type **JFrame**, instantiate the object, and then use various methods to manipulate the window. In this case, the object created can use the various applicable methods of the class.

The second way is to create the class containing the application program by *extending* the definition of the **class** JFrame; that is, the class containing the application program is built "on top of" the **class** JFrame. In Java, this way of creating a class uses the mechanism of **inheritance**. Inheritance means that a new class can be derived from or based on an already existing class. The new class "inherits" features such as methods from the existing class, which saves a lot of time for programmers. For example, we could define a new **class** RectangleProgram that would extend the definition of JFrame. The class RectangleProgram would be able to use the variables and methods from JFrame, and also add some functionality of its own (such as the ability to calculate the area and perimeter of a rectangle).

When you use inheritance, the class containing your application program will have more than one method. In addition to the method **main**, you will have at least one other method that will be used to create a window object containing the required GUI components (such as labels and text fields). This additional method is a special type of method called a **constructor**. A constructor is a method of a class that is automatically executed when an object of the class is created. Typically, a constructor is used to initialize an object. The name of the constructor is always the same as the name of the class. For example, the constructor for the **class** RectangleProgram would be named **RectangleProgram**.

 Chapter 11 discusses the principles of inheritance in detail. Constructors are covered in detail in Chapter 8.

Because inheritance is an important concept in programming languages such as Java, we will use the second way of creating a window. We will extend the definition of the **class** JFrame by using the modifier **extends**. For example, the definition of the **class** RectangleProgram, containing the application program to calculate the area and perimeter of a rectangle, is as follows:

```
public class RectangleProgram extends JFrame
{
    public RectangleProgram()        //constructor
    {
        //Necessary code
    }

    public static void main(String[] args)
    {
        //Code for the method main
    }
}
```

In Java, **extends** is a reserved word. The remainder of this section describes the necessary code to create a window.

An important property of inheritance is that the class—called a **subclass**—that extends the definition of an existing class—called a **superclass**—inherits all the properties of the superclass. For example, all **public** methods of the superclass can be *directly* accessed in the subclass. In our example, the **class** RectangleProgram is a subclass of the **class** JFrame, so it can access the **public** methods of the **class** JFrame. Therefore, to set the title of the window to Area and Perimeter of a Rectangle, you use the method setTitle of the **class** JFrame as follows:

```
setTitle("Area and Perimeter of a Rectangle");        //Line 1
```

Similarly, the statement:

```
setSize(400, 300);                                    //Line 2
```

sets the window's width to 400 pixels and its height to 300 pixels. (A **pixel** is the smallest unit of space on your screen. The term pixel stands for *picture element*.) Note that since the pixel size depends on the current monitor setting, it is impossible to predict the exact width and height of a window in centimeters or inches.

Next, to display the window, you must invoke the method setVisible. The following statement accomplishes this:

```
setVisible(true);                                     //Line 3
```

To terminate the application program when the user closes the window, use the following statement (as described in Table 6-1):

```
setDefaultCloseOperation(EXIT_ON_CLOSE);              //Line 4
```

The statements in Lines 1, 2, 3, and 4 will be placed in the constructor (that is, in the method whose heading is **public** RectangleProgram()). Thus, you can write the constructor as follows:

```
public RectangleProgram()
{
    setTitle("Area and Perimeter of a Rectangle");
    setSize(400, 300);
    setVisible(true);
    setDefaultCloseOperation(EXIT_ON_CLOSE);
}
```

You could create a window by using an object of the type JFrame. However, for our program, if we do so, then the window created will not have a title or the required size unless we specify the necessary statements similar to the ones in the preceding code. Because RectangleProgram is also a **class**, we can create objects of the type

RectangleProgram. Because the **class** RectangleProgram **extends** the definition of the **class** JFrame, it inherits the properties of the **class** JFrame. If we create an object of the type RectangleProgram, not only do we create a window, but the created window will also have a title and a specific size, and the window will be displayed when the program executes.

Consider the following statement:

```
RectangleProgram rectObject = new RectangleProgram();   //Line 5
```

This statement creates the object rectObject of the type RectangleProgram.

The statement in Line 5 causes the window shown in Figure 6-4 to appear on the screen.

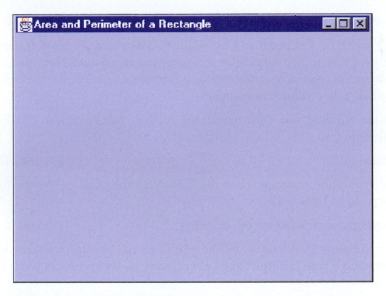

Figure 6-4   Window with the title Area and Perimeter of a Rectangle

You can close the window in Figure 6-4 by clicking the "close" button, the button containing the ✕, in the upper-right corner. The window in Figure 6-4 is empty because we have not yet created labels, text fields, and so on.

The program to create the window shown in Figure 6-4 uses the **class** JFrame and this class is contained in the package javax.swing. Therefore, the program must include either of the following two statements:

```
import javax.swing.*;
```

or:

```
import javax.swing.JFrame;
```

After making the minor changes in the statements described in this section, the program to create the window shown in Figure 6-4 is as follows:

```java
//Java program to create a window

import javax.swing.*;

public class RectangleProgram extends JFrame
{
    private static final int WIDTH = 400;
    private static final int HEIGHT = 300;

    public RectangleProgram()
    {
        setTitle("Area and Perimeter of a Rectangle");
        setSize(WIDTH, HEIGHT);
        setVisible(true);
        setDefaultCloseOperation(EXIT_ON_CLOSE);
    }

    public static void main(String[] args)
    {
        RectangleProgram rectProg = new RectangleProgram();

    }

}
```

Notice that the named constants WIDTH and HEIGHT are declared with the modifier private. This is because we want these named constants to be used only within the class RectangleProgram. In general, if a named constant, variable, or method is to be used only within the specified class, then it is declared with the modifier private. Also note that private is a reserved word in Java. (Chapter 8 discusses the modifier private in detail.)

Let's review the important points introduced in this section:

- The preceding program has exactly one class: RectangleProgram.

- The class RectangleProgram contains the constructor RectangleProgram and the main method.

- You created the new class RectangleProgram by extending the existing class, JFrame. Therefore, JFrame is the superclass of RectangleProgram, and RectangleProgram is a subclass of JFrame.

- Whenever there is a superclass–subclass relationship, the subclass inherits all the data members and methods of the superclass. The methods setTitle, setSize, setVisible, and setDefaultCloseOperation are methods of the class JFrame, and these methods can be inherited by its subclasses.

The next few sections describe how to create GUI labels, text fields, and buttons, which can all be placed in the content pane of a window. Before you can place GUI components in the content pane, you must learn how to access the content pane.

Getting Access to the Content Pane

If you can visualize `JFrame` as a window, think of the content pane as the inner area of the window (below the title bar and inside the border). The **class** `JFrame` has the method `getContentPane` that you can use to access the content pane of the window. However, the **class** `JFrame` does not have the necessary tools to manage the components of the content pane. The components of the content pane are managed by declaring a reference variable of the `Container` type and then using the method `getContentPane` as shown next.

Consider the following statements:

```
Container pane;                          //Line 1
pane = getContentPane();                 //Line 2
```

The statement in Line 1 declares **pane** to be a reference variable of the `Container` type. The statement in Line 2 gets the content pane of the window as a container, that is, the reference variable **pane** now points to the content pane. You can now access the content pane to add GUI components to it by using the reference variable **pane**.

The statements in Lines 1 and 2 can be combined into one statement:

```
Container pane = getContentPane();       //Line 3
```

If you look back at Figure 6-2, you will see that the labels, text areas, and buttons are laid out, that is, arranged, in 5 rows and 2 columns. To control the layout—where to place the GUI components in the content pane—you set the layout of the content pane. The layout used in Figure 6-2 is called the grid layout. The **class** `Container` provides the method `setLayout`, as described in Table 6-2, to set the layout of the content pane. To add components such as labels and text fields to the content pane, you use the method **add** of the **class** `Container`, which is also described in Table 6-2.

Table 6-2 Some Methods of the **class** `Container`

Method / Description
`public void add(Object obj)`   `//Method to add an object to the pane`
`public void setLayout(Object obj)`   `//Method to set the layout of the pane`

The **class** `Container` is contained in the package `java.awt`. To use this **class** in your program, you need to include either the statement:

```
import java.awt.*;
```

or:

```
import java.awt.Container;
```

As noted earlier, the method `setLayout` is used to set the layout of the content pane, `pane`. To set the layout of the container to a grid, you use the **class** `GridLayout`. Consider the following statement:

```
pane.setLayout(new GridLayout(5, 2));
```

This statement creates an object belonging to the **class** `GridLayout` and assigns that object as the layout of the content pane, `pane`, by invoking the `setLayout` method. Moreover, this statement sets the layout of the content pane, `pane`, to 5 rows and 2 columns. This allows you to add 10 components arranged in 5 rows and 2 columns.

If you do not specify a layout, Java uses a default layout. If you specify a layout, you must set the layout before adding any components. Once the layout is set, you can use the method **add** to add the components to the pane; this process is described in the next section.

JLabel

Now you will learn how to create labels and add them to the pane. We assume the following statements:

```
Container pane = getContentPane();

pane.setLayout(new GridLayout(4, 1));
```

Labels are objects of a particular **class** type. The Java **class** that you use to create labels is `JLabel`. Therefore, to create labels, you instantiate objects of the type `JLabel`. The **class** `JLabel` is contained in the package `javax.swing`.

Just like a window, various attributes are associated with a label. For example, every label has a title, width, and height. The **class** `JLabel` contains various methods to control the display of labels. Table 6-3 describes some of the methods provided by the **class** `JLabel`.

Table 6-3 Some Methods Provided by the **class** `JLabel`

Method / Description/ Example

`public JLabel(String str)`
　　`//Constructor to create a label with left-aligned text specified`
　　`//by str.`
　　`//Example: JLabel lengthL;`
　　`//　　　lengthL = new JLabel("Enter the length:")`
　　`//　Creates the label lengthL with the title Enter the length:`

`public JLabel(String str, int align)`
　　`//Constructor to create a label with the text specified by str.`
　　`//　　The value of align can be any one of the following:`
　　`//　　SwingConstants.LEFT, SwingConstants.RIGHT,`
　　`//　　SwingConstants.CENTER`
　　`//Example:`
　　`//　JLabel lengthL;`
　　`//　lengthL = new JLabel("Enter the length:",`
　　`//　　　　　　SwingConstants.RIGHT);`
　　`//　The label lengthL is right aligned.`

Table 6-3 Some Methods Provided by the **class** JLabel (continued)

Method / Description/ Example

public JLabel(String t, Icon icon, **int** align)
   //Constructs a JLabel with both text and an icon.
   //The icon is to the left of the text.

public JLabel(Icon icon)   //Constructs a JLabel with an icon.

 In Table 6-3, SwingConstants.LEFT, SwingConstants.RIGHT, and SwingConstants.CENTER are constants defined in the **class** SwingConstants. They specify whether to set the string describing the label as left-justified, right-justified, or centered.

Consider the statements:

```
JLabel lengthL;
lengthL = new JLabel("Enter the length:", SwingConstants.RIGHT);
```

After these statements execute, the label in Figure 6-5 is created.

Enter the length:

Figure 6-5 JLabel with the text Enter the length:

Now consider the following statements:

```
private JLabel lengthL, widthL, areaL, perimeterL;            //Line 1

lengthL =
    new JLabel("Enter the length: ", SwingConstants.RIGHT); //Line 2
widthL =
    new JLabel("Enter the width: ", SwingConstants.RIGHT);  //Line 3
areaL = new JLabel("Area: ", SwingConstants.RIGHT);          //Line 4
perimeterL =
    new JLabel("Perimeter: ", SwingConstants.RIGHT);        //Line 5
```

The statement in Line 1 declares four reference variables, lengthL, widthL, areaL, and perimeterL, of the JLabel type. The statement in Line 2 instantiates the object lengthL, assigns it the title `Enter the length:`, and sets the title alignment to right-justified. The statements in Lines 3 through 5 instantiate the objects `widthL`, `areaL`, and `perimeterL` with appropriate titles and text alignment.

Next, we add these labels to the `pane` declared at the beginning of this section. The following statements accomplish this. (Recall from the preceding section that we use the method `add` to add components to a `pane`.)

```
pane.add(lengthL);
pane.add(widthL);
pane.add(areaL);
pane.add(perimeterL);
```

Because we have specified a grid layout for the `pane` with four rows and one column, the label `lengthL` is added to the first row, the label `widthL` is added to the second row, and so on.

Now that you know how to add the components to the `pane`, you can put together the program to create these labels. `RectangleProgramTwo` builds on the `RectangleProgram` of the preceding section and, like `RectangleProgram`, is a subclass of `JFrame`.

```
//Java program to create a window and place four labels

import javax.swing.*;
import java.awt.*;

public class RectangleProgramTwo extends JFrame
{
    private static final int WIDTH = 400;
    private static final int HEIGHT = 300;

    private JLabel lengthL, widthL, areaL, perimeterL;

    public RectangleProgramTwo()
    {
        setTitle("Area and Perimeter of a Rectangle");

        lengthL =
            new JLabel("Enter the length: ", SwingConstants.RIGHT);
        widthL =
            new JLabel("Enter the width: ", SwingConstants.RIGHT);
        areaL = new JLabel("Area: ", SwingConstants.RIGHT);
        perimeterL =
            new JLabel("Perimeter: ", SwingConstants.RIGHT);

        Container pane = getContentPane();
        pane.setLayout(new GridLayout(4, 1));
```

6

```
        pane.add(lengthL);
        pane.add(widthL);
        pane.add(areaL);
        pane.add(perimeterL);

        setSize(WIDTH, HEIGHT);
        setVisible(true);
        setDefaultCloseOperation(EXIT_ON_CLOSE);
    }

    public static void main(String[] args)
    {
        RectangleProgramTwo rectObject = new RectangleProgramTwo();
    }
}
```

Sample Run: Figure 6-6 shows a sample run.

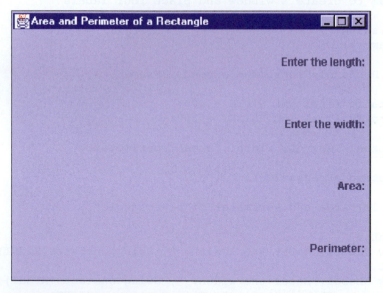

Figure 6-6 Sample run for `RectangleProgramTwo`

Now you are ready to create and place the text fields and buttons. The good news is that the techniques for creating and placing components such as **JTextField** and **JButton** in a container are similar to the ones used for **JLabel**, and are described in the next two sections.

JTextField

As you may recall, text fields are objects belonging to the **class** JTextField. Therefore, you can create a text field by declaring a reference variable of the type JTextField followed by an instantiation of the object.

Table 6-4 describes some of the methods of the **class** JTextField.

Table 6-4   Some Methods of the **class** JTextField

Method / Description
public JTextField(int columns)   //Constructor to set the size of the text field.

public JTextField(String str)
   //Constructor to initialize the object with the text specified
   //by str.

public JTextField(String str, int columns)
   //Constructor to initialize the object with the text specified
   //by str and to set the size of the text field.

public void setText(String str)
   //Method to set the text of the text field to the string specified
   //by str.

public String getText()   //Method to return the text contained in the text field.

public void setEditable(Boolean b)
   //If the value of the Boolean variable b is false, the user cannot
   //type in the text field.
   //In this case, the text field is used as a tool to display
   //the result.

public void addActionListener(ActionListener obj)   //Method to register a listener object to a JTextField.

Consider the following statements:

```
private JTextField lengthTF, widthTF, areaTF,
                   perimeterTF;                  //Line 1
lengthTF = new JTextField(10);                   //Line 2
widthTF = new JTextField(10);                    //Line 3
areaTF = new JTextField(10);                     //Line 4
perimeterTF = new JTextField(10);                //Line 5
```

The statement in Line 1 declares four reference variables, lengthTF, widthTF, areaTF, and perimeterTF, of the type JTextField. The statement in Line 2 instantiates the object lengthTF and sets the width of this text field to 10 characters. That is, this text field can display no more than 10 characters. The meaning of the other statements is similar.

Placing these objects involves using the **add** method of the **class Container** as described in the previous section. The following statements add these components to the container:

```
pane.add(lengthTF);
pane.add(widthTF);
pane.add(areaTF);
pane.add(perimeterTF);
```

The container **pane** now would contain eight objects—four labels and four text fields. We want to place the object **lengthTF** adjacent to the label **lengthL** in the same row, and use similar placements for the other objects. So we need to expand the grid layout to 4 rows and 2 columns. The following statements create the required grid layout and the necessary objects:

```
pane.setLayout(new GridLayout(4, 2));
pane.add(lengthL);
pane.add(lengthTF);
pane.add(widthL);
pane.add(widthTF);
pane.add(areaL);
pane.add(areaTF);
pane.add(perimeterL);
pane.add(perimeterTF);
```

The following program, **RectangleProgramThree**, summarizes our discussion so far:

```java
//Java program to create a window
//and place four labels and four text fields

import javax.swing.*;
import java.awt.*;

public class RectangleProgramThree extends JFrame
{
    private static final int WIDTH = 400;
    private static final int HEIGHT = 300;

    private JLabel lengthL, widthL, areaL, perimeterL;
    private JTextField lengthTF, widthTF, areaTF,
                        perimeterTF;

    public RectangleProgramThree()
    {
        setTitle("Area and Perimeter of a Rectangle");
```

```
    lengthL =
        new JLabel("Enter the length: ", SwingConstants.RIGHT);
    widthL =
        new JLabel("Enter the width: ", SwingConstants.RIGHT);
    areaL =
        new JLabel("Area: ", SwingConstants.RIGHT);
    perimeterL =
        new JLabel("Perimeter: ", SwingConstants.RIGHT);

    lengthTF = new JTextField(10);
    widthTF = new JTextField(10);
    areaTF = new JTextField(10);
    perimeterTF = new JTextField(10);

    Container pane = getContentPane();
    pane.setLayout(new GridLayout(4, 2));

    pane.add(lengthL);
    pane.add(lengthTF);
    pane.add(widthL);
    pane.add(widthTF);
    pane.add(areaL);
    pane.add(areaTF);
    pane.add(perimeterL);
    pane.add(perimeterTF);

    setSize(WIDTH, HEIGHT);
    setVisible(true);
    setDefaultCloseOperation(EXIT_ON_CLOSE);
    }

    public static void main(String[] args)
    {
        RectangleProgramThree rectObject =
                        new RectangleProgramThree();
    }
}
```

Sample Run: Figure 6-7 shows the sample run.

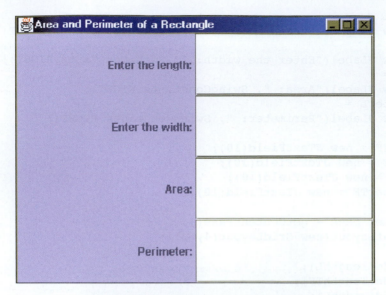

Figure 6-7 Sample run for `RectangleProgramThree`

To complete the design of the user interface, you now learn how to create buttons.

JButton

To create a button, Java provides the **class** `JButton`. Thus, to create objects belonging to the **class** `JButton`, we use a technique similar to the one we used to create instances of `JLabel` and `JTextField`. Table 6-5 shows some methods of the **class** `JButton`.

Table 6-5 Commonly Used Methods of the **class** `JButton`

Method / Description

`public JButton(Icon ic)`
`//Constructor to initialize the button object with the icon`
`//specified by ic.`

`public JButton(String str)`
`//Constructor to initialize the button object to the text specified`
`//by str.`

`public JButton(String str, Icon ic)`
`//Constructor to initialize the button object to the text specified`
`//by str and the icon specified by ic.`

`public void setText(String str)` `//Method to set the text of the button to the string specified by str.`

Table 6-5 Commonly Used Methods of the **class** JButton (continued)

Method / Description
`public String getText()`   `//Method to return the text contained in the button.`
`public void addActionListener(ActionListener obj)`   `//Method to register a listener object to the button object.`

The following three lines will create two buttons, Calculate and Exit, shown earlier in Figure 6-2.

```
JButton calculateB, exitB;                  //Line 1
calculateB = new JButton("Calculate");      //Line 2
exitB = new JButton("Exit");                //Line 3
```

The statement in Line 1 declares calculateB and exitB to be reference variables of the type JButton. The statement in Line 2 instantiates the button object calculateB and sets the text for the button to the string Calculate. Similarly, the statement in Line 3 instantiates the button object exitB and sets the text for exitB to the string Exit.

The buttons calculateB and exitB can be placed into the container pane by using the method add. The following statements add these buttons to the pane:

```
pane.add(calculateB);
pane.add(exitB);
```

Now you have two more objects in the container, so you need to modify the GridLayout to accommodate 5 rows and 2 columns, and then add all the components. The following statements create the required grid layout and add the labels, text fields, and buttons to the container pane.

```
pane.setLayout(new GridLayout(5,2));//specify the layout
pane.add(lengthL);                      //add the label lengthL
pane.add(lengthTF);                     //add the text field lengthTF
pane.add(widthL);                       //add the label widthL
pane.add(widthTF);                      //add the text field widthTF
pane.add(areaL);                        //add the label areaL
pane.add(areaTF);                       //add the text field areaTF
pane.add(perimeterL);                   //add the label perimeterL
pane.add(perimeterTF);                  //add the text field perimeterTF
pane.add(calculateB);                   //add the button calculateB
pane.add(exitB);                        //add the button exitB
```

Notice that the preceding add statements place the components from left to right and from top to bottom.

Handling an Event

You have now learned how to create a window, how to create a container, and how to create labels, text fields, and buttons.

Now that you can create a button, such as `calculateB`, you need to specify how such a button should behave when you click it. For example, when you click the button `calculateB`, you want the program to calculate the area and perimeter of the rectangle and display these values in their respective text fields. Similarly, when you click the button `exitB`, the program should terminate.

When you click a `JButton` an event is created, known as an **action event**, which sends a message to another object, known as an **action listener**. When the listener receives the message, it performs some action. Sending a message or an event to a listener object simply means that some method in the listener object is invoked with the event as the argument. This invocation happens automatically; you will not see the code corresponding to the method invocation. However, you must specify two things:

- For each `JButton`, you must specify the corresponding listener object. In Java, this is known as **registering** the listener.

- You must define the methods that will be invoked when the event is sent to the listener. Normally, you will write these methods and you will never write the code for invocation.

Java provides various classes to handle different kinds of events. The action event is handled by the **class** `ActionListener`, which contains only the method `actionPerformed`. In the method `actionPerformed`, you include the code that you want the system to execute when an action event is generated.

The **class** `ActionListener` that handles the action event is a special type of class called an **interface**. In Java, **interface** is a reserved word. Roughly speaking, an **interface** is a class that contains only the method headings, and each method heading is terminated with a semicolon. For example, the definition of the **interface** `ActionListener` containing the method `actionPerformed` is:

```
public interface ActionListener
{
    public void actionPerformed(ActionEvent e);
}
```

Because the method `actionPerformed` does not contain a body, Java does not allow you to instantiate an object of the type `ActionListener`. So how do you register an action listener with the object `calculateB`?

One way is as follows (there are other ways not discussed here): Because you cannot instantiate an object of the type `ActionListener`, first you need to create a class on top of `ActionListener` so that the required object can be instantiated. The class created must provide the necessary code for the method `actionPerformed`. You will create the **class** `CalculateButtonHandler` to handle the event generated by clicking the button `calculateB`.

The **class** `CalculateButtonHandler` is created on top of the **interface** `ActionListener`. The definition of the **class** `CalculateButtonHandler` is:

```
private class CalculateButtonHandler implements
                                        ActionListener   //Line 1
{
    public void actionPerformed(ActionEvent e)          //Line 2
    {
        //The code for calculating the area and the perimeter
        //and displaying these quantities goes here
    }
}
```

Notice the following:

- The **class** `CalculateButtonHandler` starts with the modifier **private**. This is because you want this class to be used only within your `RectangleProgram`.

- This class uses another modifier, **implements**. This is how you build classes on top of classes that are interfaces. Notice that you have not yet provided the code for the method `actionPerformed`. You will do that shortly.

In Java, **implements** is a reserved word.

Next, we illustrate how to create a listener object of the type `CalculateButtonHandler`. Consider the following statements:

```
CalculateButtonHandler cbHandler;
cbHandler = new CalculateButtonHandler();   //instantiate the object
```

As described, these statements create the listener object. Having created a listener, you next must associate (or in Java terminology, register) this handler with the corresponding JButton. The following line of code registers `cbHandler` as the listener object of `calculateB`:

```
calculateB.addActionListener(cbHandler);
```

The complete definition of the **class** `CalculateButtonHandler` including the code for the method `actionPerformed` is:

```
private class CalculateButtonHandler implements
                                        ActionListener   //Line 1
{
    public void actionPerformed(ActionEvent e)          //Line 2
    {
        double width, length, area, perimeter;          //Line 3

        length
            = Double.parseDouble(lengthTF.getText());   //Line 4
```

6

```
width
         = Double.parseDouble(widthTF.getText());    //Line 5
area = length * width;                               //Line 6
perimeter = 2 * (length + width);                    //Line 7

areaTF.setText("" + area);                           //Line 8
perimeterTF.setText("" + perimeter);                 //Line 9
    }
}
```

In the preceding program segment, Line 1 declares the **class** CalculateButtonHandler and makes it an action listener by including the phrase **implements** ActionListener. Note that all of this code is just a new class definition. This class has one method and Line 2 is the first statement of that method. Let us look at the statement in Line 4:

```
length = Double.parseDouble(lengthTF.getText());
```

The length of the rectangle is stored in the text field lengthTF. We use the method getText to retrieve the string from this text field, specifying the length. Now the value of the expression lengthTF.getText() is the length, but it is in a string form. So we need to use the method parseDouble to convert the length string into an equivalent decimal number. The length is then stored in the variable length. The statement in Line 5 works similarly for the width.

The statements in Lines 6 and 7 compute the area and the perimeter, respectively. The statement in Line 8 uses the method setText of the **class** JTextField to display the area. Because setText requires that the argument be a string, you need to convert the value of the variable area into a string. The easiest way to do this is to concatenate the value of area to an empty string. Similar conventions apply for the statement in Line 9.

It follows that the method actionPerformed displays the area and perimeter in the corresponding JTextFields.

Before creating an action listener for the JButton exitB, let us summarize what we've done so far to create and register an action event listener:

1. Created a class that implements the **interface** ActionListener. For example, for the JButton calculateB we created the **class** CalculateButtonHandler.

2. Provided the definition of the method actionPerformed within the class that you created in Step 1. The method actionPerformed contains the code that the program executes when a specific event is generated. For example, when you click the JButton calculateB, the program should calculate and display the area and perimeter of the rectangle.

3. Created and instantiated an object of the class type created in Step 1. For example, for the JButton calculateB we created the object cbHandler.

4. Registered the event handler created in Step 3 with the object that generates an action event using the method `addActionListener`. For example, for `JButton calculateB` the following statement registers the object `cbHandler` to listen and register the action event:

```
calculateB.addActionListener(cbHandler);
```

We can now repeat these four steps to create and register the action listener with the `JButton exitB`.

```java
private class ExitButtonHandler implements ActionListener
{
    public void actionPerformed(ActionEvent e)
    {
        System.exit(0);
    }
}
```

The following statements create the action listener object for the button `exitB`:

```java
ExitButtonHandler ebHandler;
ebHandler = new ExitButtonHandler();
exitB.addActionListener(ebHandler);
```

The `interface` ActionListener is contained in the package `java.awt.event`. Therefore, to use this interface to handle events, your program must include the statement:

```java
import java.awt.event.*;
```

or:

```java
import java.awt.event.ActionListener;
```

The complete program to calculate the perimeter and area of a rectangle is:

```java
//Given the length and width of a rectangle, this Java
//program determines its area and perimeter.

import javax.swing.*;
import java.awt.*;
import java.awt.event.*;

public class RectangleProgram extends JFrame
{
    private JLabel lengthL, widthL, areaL, perimeterL;

    private JTextField lengthTF, widthTF, areaTF, perimeterTF;

    private JButton calculateB, exitB;

    private CalculateButtonHandler cbHandler;
    private ExitButtonHandler ebHandler;
```

6

```java
    private static final int WIDTH = 400;
    private static final int HEIGHT = 300;

    public RectangleProgram()
    {
            //Create the four labels
        lengthL = new JLabel("Enter the length: ",
                                    SwingConstants.RIGHT);
        widthL = new JLabel("Enter the width: ",
                                    SwingConstants.RIGHT);
        areaL = new JLabel("Area: ", SwingConstants.RIGHT);
        perimeterL = new JLabel("Perimeter: ",
                                    SwingConstants.RIGHT);

            //Create the four text fields
        lengthTF = new JTextField(10);
        widthTF = new JTextField(10);
        areaTF = new JTextField(10);
        perimeterTF = new JTextField(10);

            //Create Calculate Button
        calculateB = new JButton("Calculate");
        cbHandler = new CalculateButtonHandler();
        calculateB.addActionListener(cbHandler);

            //Create Exit Button
        exitB = new JButton("Exit");
        ebHandler = new ExitButtonHandler();
        exitB.addActionListener(ebHandler);

            //Set the title of the window
        setTitle("Area and Perimeter of a Rectangle");

            //Get the container
        Container pane = getContentPane();

            //Set the layout
        pane.setLayout(new GridLayout(5, 2));

            //Place the components in the pane
        pane.add(lengthL);
        pane.add(lengthTF);
        pane.add(widthL);
        pane.add(widthTF);
        pane.add(areaL);
        pane.add(areaTF);
        pane.add(perimeterL);
```

```java
            pane.add(perimeterTF);
            pane.add(calculateB);
            pane.add(exitB);

                    //Set the size of the window and display it
            setSize(WIDTH, HEIGHT);
            setVisible(true);
            setDefaultCloseOperation(EXIT_ON_CLOSE);
        }

        private class CalculateButtonHandler implements ActionListener
        {
            public void actionPerformed(ActionEvent e)
            {
                double width, length, area, perimeter;

                length = Double.parseDouble(lengthTF.getText());
                width = Double.parseDouble(widthTF.getText());
                area = length * width;
                perimeter = 2 * (length + width);

                areaTF.setText("" + area);
                perimeterTF.setText("" + perimeter);
            }
        }

        private class ExitButtonHandler implements ActionListener
        {
            public void actionPerformed(ActionEvent e)
            {
                System.exit(0);
            }
        }

        public static void main(String[] args)
        {
            RectangleProgram rectObject = new RectangleProgram();
        }
    }
```

Sample Run: Figure 6-8 shows the sample run.

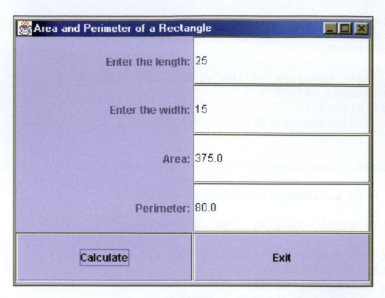

Figure 6-8 Sample run for the final `RectangleProgram`

PROGRAMMING EXAMPLE: TEMPERATURE CONVERSION

Write a program that creates the GUI shown in Figure 6-9, to convert the temperature from Fahrenheit to Celsius and from Celsius to Fahrenheit.

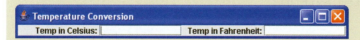

Figure 6-9 GUI for the temperature conversion program

When the user enters the temperature in the text field adjacent to the label `Temp in Celsius` and presses the `Enter` key, the program displays the equivalent temperature in the text field adjacent to the label `Temp in Fahrenheit`. Similarly, when the user enters the temperature in Fahrenheit and presses the `Enter` key, the program displays the equivalent temperature in Celsius.

Input   Temperature in Fahrenheit or Celsius

Output   Temperature in Celsius if the input is Fahrenheit; the temperature in Fahrenheit if the input is Celsius

Problem Analysis, GUI Design, and Algorithm Design

Suppose that the variable `celsius` represents the temperature in Celsius and the variable `fahrenheit` represents the temperature in Fahrenheit. If the user enters the temperature in Fahrenheit, the formula for calculating the equivalent temperature in Celsius is:

```
celsius = (5.0 / 9.0) * (fahrenheit - 32)
```

For example, if `fahrenheit` is `98.6`, then:

```
celsius = 5.0 / 9.0 * (98.6 - 32) = 37.00
```

Similarly, if the user enters the temperature in Celsius, then the formula for calculating the equivalent temperature in Fahrenheit is:

```
fahrenheit = 9.0 / 5.0 * celsius + 32
```

For example, if `celsius` is `20`, then:

```
fahrenheit = 9.0 / 5.0 * 20 + 32 = 68.0
```

The GUI in Figure 6-9 contains a window, a container, two labels, and two text fields. The labels and text fields are placed in the container of the window. As we did in the rectangle program earlier in this chapter, we can create the window by making the application extend the **class** `JFrame`. To get access to the container, we will use a reference variable of the `Container` type. To create labels, we use objects of the type `JLabel`; to create text fields, we use objects of the type `JTextField`. Suppose that we have the following declarations:

```
JLabel celsiusLabel;          //label Celsius
JLabel fahrenheitLabel;       //label Fahrenheit

JTextField celsiusTF;         //text field Celsius
JTextField fahrenheitTF;      //text field Fahrenheit
```

When the user enters the temperature in the text field `celsiusTF` and presses the **Enter** key, we want the program to show the equivalent temperature in the text field `fahrenheitTF` and vice versa.

Recall that when you click a `JButton`, it generates an action event. Moreover, the action event is handled by the method `actionPerformed` of the **interface** `ActionListener`. Similarly, when you press the **Enter** key in a text field, it generates an action event. Therefore, we can register an action event listener with the text fields `celsiusTF` and `fahrenheitTF` to take the appropriate action.

Based on this analysis and the GUI shown in Figure 6-9, you can design an event-driven algorithm as follows:

1. Have a listener in each text field.
2. Register an event handler with each text field.

3. Let the event handler registered with a text field do the following:

   a. Get the data from the text field once the user presses the ENTER key.

   b. Apply the corresponding formula to perform the conversion.

   c. Set the value of the other text field.

This process of adding an event listener and then registering the event listener to a text field is similar to the process we used to register an event listener to a JButton earlier in the chapter. (This process will be described later in this programming example.)

Variables, Objects, and Named Constants

The input to the program is either the temperature in Celsius or the temperature in Fahrenheit. If the input is a value for Celsius, then the program calculates the equivalent temperature in Fahrenheit. Similarly, if the input is a value for Fahrenheit, then the program calculates the equivalent temperature in Celsius. Therefore, the program needs the following variables:

```
double celsius;            //variable to hold Celsius
double fahrenheit;         //variable to hold Fahrenheit
```

Notice that these variables are needed in each event handler.

The formulas to convert the temperature from Fahrenheit to Celsius and vice versa use the special values 32, 9.0/5.0, and 5.0/9.0, which we will declare as named constants as follows:

```
private static final double FTOC = 5.0 / 9.0;
private static final double CTOF = 9.0 / 5.0;
private static final int OFFSET = 32;
```

As in the GUI, you need two labels—one to label the text field corresponding to the Celsius value and another to label the text field corresponding to the Fahrenheit value. Therefore, the following statements are needed:

```
JLabel celsiusLabel;                    //label Celsius
JLabel fahrenheitLabel;                 //label Fahrenheit

celsiusLabel = new JLabel("Temp in Celsius: ",
                    SwingConstants.RIGHT);//object instantiation
fahrenheitLabel = new JLabel("Temp in Fahrenheit: ",
                    SwingConstants.RIGHT);//object instantiation
```

You also need two JTextField objects. The necessary Java code is:

```
JTextField celsiusTF;                   //text field Celsius
JTextField fahrenheitTF;                //text field Fahrenheit

celsiusTF = new JTextField(7);          //object instantiation
fahrenheitTF = new JTextField(7);       //object instantiation
```

Now you need a window to display the labels and the text fields. Because a window is an object of the type `JFrame`, the class containing the application program that we create will extend the definition of the **class** `JFrame`. We will set the width of the window to 500 pixels and the height to 50 pixels. We'll call the class containing the application program `TempConversion`. The application will look like this:

```java
//Java program to convert the temperature from Celsius to
//Fahrenheit and vice versa.

import javax.swing.*;

public class TempConversion extends JFrame
{
    private static final int WIDTH = 500;
    private static final int HEIGHT = 50;

    private static final double FTOC = 5.0 / 9.0;
    private static final double CTOF = 9.0 / 5.0;
    private static final int OFFSET = 32;

    public TempConversion()
    {
        setTitle("Temperature Conversion");
        setSize(WIDTH, HEIGHT);
        setVisible(true);
        setDefaultCloseOperation(EXIT_ON_CLOSE);
    }

    public static void main(String[] args)
    {
        TempConversion tempConv = new TempConversion();
    }
}
```

Now you need to access the container content pane to place the GUI components and set the required layout of the pane. Therefore, as before, you need the following statements:

```java
Container c = getContentPane();     //get the container
c.setLayout(new GridLayout(1, 4)); //create a new layout

c.add(celsiusLabel);                //add the label celsiusLabel
                                    //to the container
c.add(celsiusTF);                   //add the text field celsiusTF
                                    //to the container
c.add(fahrenheitLabel);             //add the label fahrenheitLabel
                                    //to the container
c.add(fahrenheitTF);                //add the text field fahrenheitTF
                                    //to the container
```

You want your program to respond to the events generated by `JTextField`s. Just as when you click a `JButton` an action event is generated, when you press the `Enter` key in a `JTextField`, it generates an action event. Therefore, to register event listeners with `JTextField`s, we use the four steps outlined in the section Handling an Event earlier in this chapter: (1) create a class that implements the **interface** `ActionListener`; (2) provide the definition of the method `actionPerformed` within the class that you created in Step 1; (3) create and instantiate an object of the class created in Step 1; and (4) register the event handler created in Step 3 with the object that generates an action event using the method `addActionListener`.

Next, we create and register an action listener with the `JTextField celsiusTF`.

First we create the **class** `CelsHandler`, implementing the **interface** `ActionListener`. Then we provide the definition of the method `actionPerformed` of the **class** `CelsHandler`. When the user enters the temperature in the `JTextField celsiusTF` and presses the `Enter` key, the program needs to calculate and display the equivalent temperature in the `JTextField fahrenheitTF`. The necessary code is placed within the body of the method `actionPerformed`.

We now describe the steps of the method `actionPerformed`. The temperature in Celsius is contained in the `JTextField celsiusTF`. We use the method `getText` of the **class** `JTextField` to retrieve the temperature in `celsiusTF`. However, the value returned by the method `getText` is in string form, so we use the method `parseDouble` of the **class** `Double` to convert the numeric string into a decimal value. It follows that we need a variable of the type **double**, say `celsius`, to store the temperature in Celsius. We accomplish this with the following statement:

```
celsius = Double.parseDouble(celsiusTF.getText());
```

We also need a variable of the type **double**, say `fahrenheit`, to store the equivalent temperature in Fahrenheit. Because we want to display the temperature to two decimal places, we use the method `format` of the **class** `String`.

We can now write the definition of the **class** `CelsHandler` as follows:

```
private class CelsHandler implements ActionListener
{
    public void actionPerformed(ActionEvent e)
    {
        double celsius, fahrenheit;

        celsius =
                Double.parseDouble(celsiusTF.getText());
        fahrenheit = celsius * CTOF + OFFSET;
        fahrenheitTF.setText(String.format("%.2f",
                                            fahrenheit));
    }
}
```

We can now create an object of the type `CelsHandler` as follows:

```java
CelsHandler celsiusHandler;
celsiusHandler = new CelsHandler();
```

Having created a listener, you must associate this handler with the corresponding `JTextField celsiusTF`. The following code does this:

```java
celsiusTF.addActionListener(celsiusHandler);
```

Similarly, we can create and register an action listener with the text field `fahrenheitTF`. The necessary code is:

```java
private class FahrHandler implements ActionListener
{
    public void actionPerformed(ActionEvent e)
    {
        double celsius, fahrenheit;

        fahrenheit =
            Double.parseDouble(fahrenheitTF.getText());
        celsius = (fahrenheit - OFFSET) * FTOC;
        celsiusTF.setText(String.format("%.2f",
                                        celsius));

    }
}

FahrHandler fahrenheitHandler;
fahrenheitHandler = new FahrHandler(); //instantiate the object

fahrenheitTF.addActionListener(fahrenheitHandler);
                                //add the action listener
```

Now that we have created the necessary GUI components and the programming code, in the next section we put everything together to create the complete program.

Putting It Together

You can start with the window creation program and then add all the components, handlers, and classes developed. You also need the necessary **import** statements. In this case they are:

```java
import java.awt.*;              //due to the class Container
import java.awt.event.*;        //due to events
import javax.swing.*;           //due to JLabel and JTextField
```

Thus, you have the following Java program:

```java
//Java program to convert the temperature between Celsius and
//Fahrenheit.

import java.awt.*;
import java.awt.event.*;
import javax.swing.*;

public class TempConversion extends JFrame
{
    private JLabel celsiusLabel;
    private JLabel fahrenheitLabel;
    private JTextField celsiusTF;
    private JTextField fahrenheitTF;
    private CelsHandler celsiusHandler;
    private FahrHandler fahrenheitHandler;

    private static final int WIDTH = 500;
    private static final int HEIGHT = 50;
    private static final double FTOC = 5.0 / 9.0;
    private static final double CTOF = 9.0 / 5.0;
    private static final int OFFSET = 32;

    public TempConversion()
    {
        setTitle("Temperature Conversion");
        Container c = getContentPane();
        c.setLayout(new GridLayout(1, 4));

        celsiusLabel = new JLabel("Temp in Celsius: ",
                                  SwingConstants.RIGHT);
        fahrenheitLabel = new JLabel("Temp in Fahrenheit: ",
                                     SwingConstants.RIGHT);

        celsiusTF = new JTextField(7);
        fahrenheitTF = new JTextField(7);

        c.add(celsiusLabel);
        c.add(celsiusTF);
        c.add(fahrenheitLabel);
        c.add(fahrenheitTF);

        celsiusHandler = new CelsHandler();
        fahrenheitHandler = new FahrHandler();

        celsiusTF.addActionListener(celsiusHandler);
        fahrenheitTF.addActionListener(fahrenheitHandler);

        setSize(WIDTH, HEIGHT);
        setDefaultCloseOperation(EXIT_ON_CLOSE);
```

```java
        setVisible(true);
    }

    private class CelsHandler implements ActionListener
    {
        public void actionPerformed(ActionEvent e)
        {
            double celsius, fahrenheit;

            celsius =
                Double.parseDouble(celsiusTF.getText());
            fahrenheit = celsius * CTOF + OFFSET;
            fahrenheitTF.setText(String.format("%.2f",
                                            fahrenheit));
        }
    }

    private class FahrHandler implements ActionListener
    {
        public void actionPerformed(ActionEvent e)
        {
            double celsius, fahrenheit;

            fahrenheit =
                Double.parseDouble(fahrenheitTF.getText());
            celsius = (fahrenheit - OFFSET) * FTOC;
            celsiusTF.setText(String.format("%.2f",
                                            celsius));
        }
    }

    public static void main(String[] args)
    {
        TempConversion tempConv = new TempConversion();
    }
}
```

Sample Run: Figure 6-10 shows the display after the user typed **98.60** and pressed the **Enter** key in the text field **Temp in Fahrenheit**.

Figure 6-10 Sample run for TempConversion

OBJECT-ORIENTED DESIGN

Chapter 3 discussed the **class** `String` in detail. Using the **class** `String` you can create various `String` objects. Moreover, using the methods of the **class** `String`, you can manipulate the string stored in a `String` object. Recall that `String` objects are instances of the **class** `String`. Similarly, a Java program that uses GUI components also uses various objects. For example, in the first part of this chapter you used the `JFrame`, `JLabel`, `JTextField`, and `JButton` objects. Note that labels are instances of the **class** `JLabel`, buttons are instances of the **class** `JButton`, and so on. In general, objects are instances of a particular class.

In this section, we delve a little deeper into the general concept of objects and how they are used in object-oriented design (OOD). OOD is a major field of study in its own right; most likely your university offers courses on the topic. This section by no means presents an in-depth treatise on OOD. Rather, we review its general concepts and give a simplified methodology for using the OOD approach to problem solving.

Since Chapter 2, you have used `String` objects. Moreover, in the first part of this chapter you used objects belonging to various classes such as `JFrame`, `JLabel`, `JTextField`, `JButton`, and `String`. In fact, in your daily life you use objects such as a VCR, CD player, and so on without realizing how they might be conceptualized as objects or classes. For example, regarding a VCR, note the following facts:

- To use a VCR, you do not need to know how the VCR is made. You do not need to know the internal parts of a VCR or how they work. These are hidden from you.

- To use a VCR, you do need to know the functions of various buttons and how to use them.

- Once you know how to use a VCR, you can use it either as a stand-alone device or you can combine it with other devices to create an entertainment system.

- You cannot modify the functions of a VCR. The Record button will always function as a Record button.

Any Java objects, such as `String` objects, that you have encountered also have the properties mentioned above. You can use the objects and their methods, but you don't need to know how they work.

The aim of OOD is to build software from components called classes so that if someone wants to use a class, all they need to know is the various methods provided by that class.

Recall that in OOD, an object combines data and operations on that data in a single unit, a feature called **encapsulation**. In OOD, we first identify the object, then identify the relevant data, and then identify the operations needed to manipulate the object.

For example, the relevant data for a `String` object is the actual string and the length of the string, that is, the number of characters in the string. Every `String` object must have memory space to store the relevant data, that is, the string and its length. Next, we must identify the type of operations performed on a string. Some of the operations on a string might be to replace a particular character of a string, extract part of a string, change a string from uppercase to lowercase, and so on. The **class** `String` provides the necessary operations to be performed on a string.

As another example of how an object contains both data and operations on that data, consider objects of the type `JButton`. Because every button has a label, which is a string, every button must have memory space to store its label. Some of the operations on a button that you have encountered are to set the label of the button and add a listener object to a button. Other operations that can be performed on a button are to set its size and location. These operations are the methods of a class. Thus the **class** `JButton` provides the methods to set a button's size and location.

A Simplified OOD Methodology

Now that you have an overview of objects and the essential components of OOD, you may be eager to learn how to solve a particular problem using OOD methodology. The best way to learn is by practice. A simplified OOD methodology can be expressed in the following steps:

1. Write down a detailed description of the problem.

2. Identify all the (relevant) nouns and verbs.

3. From the list of nouns, select the objects. Identify the data components of each object.

4. From the list of verbs, select the operations.

In Step 3, after identifying the objects or classes, usually you will realize that several objects function in the same way. That is, they have the same data components and same operations. In other words, they will lead to the construction of the same class.

Remember that objects are nothing but instances of a particular class. Therefore, to create objects you have to learn how to create classes. In other words, to create objects you first need to create classes; to know what type of classes to create, you need to know what an object stores and what operations are needed to manipulate an object's data. You can see that objects and classes are closely related. Because an object consists of data and operations on the data in a single unit, in Java we use the mechanism of classes to combine data and its operations in a single unit. In OOD methodology, we therefore identify classes, data members of classes, and operations. In Java, data members are also known as **fields**.

The remainder of this section gives various examples to illustrate how objects, data components of objects, and operations of data are identified. In these examples, nouns (objects) are in bold type, and verbs (operations) are in italics.

Example 6-2

Consider the problem presented in Example 6-1. In simple terms, the problem can be stated as follows:

"Write a **program** to *input* the **length** and **width** of a **rectangle** and *calculate* and *print* the **perimeter** and **area** of the **rectangle**."

Step 1: Identify all the (relevant) nouns.

Length

Width

Perimeter

Area

Rectangle

Step 2: Identify the class(es).

Considering all five nouns, it is clear that:

- Length is the length of a rectangle.

- Width is the width of a rectangle.

- Perimeter is the perimeter of a rectangle.

- Area is the area of a rectangle.

Notice that four of the five nouns are related to the fifth one, namely, `rectangle`. Therefore, choose `Rectangle` as a class. From the **class** `Rectangle`, you can instantiate rectangles of various dimensions. The **class** `Rectangle` can be graphically represented as in Figure 6-11.

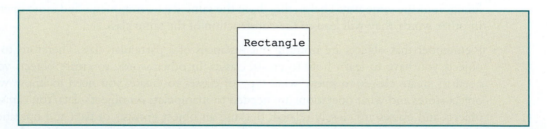

Figure 6-11   class `Rectangle`

Step 3: Identify the data members for each of the classes.

In this step, you evaluate the remaining nouns and determine the information essential to fully describe each class. Therefore, consider each noun—length, width, perimeter, area, and rectangle—and ask: "Is each of these nouns essential for describing the rectangle?"

- Perimeter is not needed, because it can be computed from length and width. Perimeter is not a data member.

- Area is not needed, because it can be computed from length and width. Area is not a data member.

- Length is required. Length is a data member.

- Width is required. Width is a data member.

Having made these choices, the **class** `Rectangle` can be represented with data members, as shown in Figure 6-12.

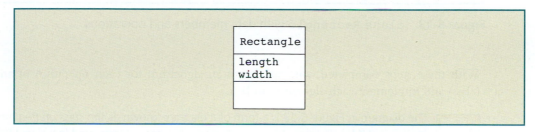

Figure 6-12 **class** `Rectangle` with data members

Step 4: Identify the operations for each of the classes.

Many operations for a class or an object can be determined by looking at the list of verbs. Let us consider the verbs *input*, *calculate*, and *print*. The possible operations on a rectangle object are *input* the length and width, *calculate* the perimeter and area, and *print* the perimeter and area. In this step, we focus on the functionalities of the class(es) involved. By carefully reading the problem statement, you may conclude that you need at least the following operations:

- `setLength`: Set the length of the rectangle.
- `setWidth`: Set the width of the rectangle.
- `computePerimeter`: Calculate the perimeter of the rectangle.
- `computeArea`: Calculate the area of the rectangle.
- `print`: Print the perimeter and area of the rectangle.

It is customary to include operations to retrieve the values of the data members of an object. Therefore, you also need the following operations:

- `getLength`: Retrieve the length of the rectangle.
- `getWidth`: Retrieve the width of the rectangle.

Figure 6-13 shows the **class** `Rectangle` with data members and operations.

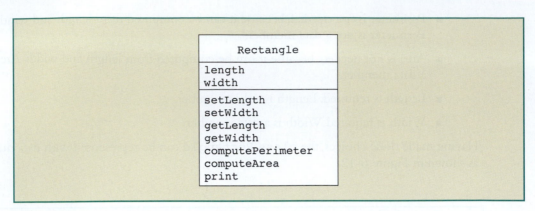

Figure 6-13 `class Rectangle` with data members and operations

With these steps completed, you can design an algorithm for each operation of an object (class) and implement each algorithm in Java.

 The diagram in Figure 6-13 is a form of a diagram known as the *class unified modeling language (UML) diagram*. After introducing a few more terms used in a class UML diagram, we formally introduce the class UML diagram in Chapter 8, when we discuss classes in general.

Example 6-3

Consider the following problem:

A **place** to buy **candy** is from a **candy machine**. A new candy machine is bought for the **gym**, but it is not working properly. The candy machine has four **dispensers** to hold and release **items** sold by the candy machine and a **cash register**. The machine sells four products—**candies**, **chips**, **gum**, and **cookies**—each stored in a separate dispenser. You have been asked to write a program for this candy machine so that it can be put into operation.

The program should do the following:

- *Show* the **customer** the different **products** sold by the **candy machine**.
- Let the **customer** *make* the selection.
- *Show* the **customer** the **cost of the item** selected.
- *Accept* the **money** from the **customer**.
- *Return* the **change**.
- *Release* the **item**, that is, *make* the sale.

The OOD solution to this problem proceeds as follows:

Step 1: Identify all the nouns.

- place
- candy
- candy machine
- gym
- dispenser
- items
- cash register
- chips
- gum
- cookies
- customer
- products
- cost of the item
- money
- change

In this description of the problem, products stand for items such as candy, chips, gum, and cookies. In fact, the actual product in the machine is not that important. What *is* important is to note that there are four dispensers, each capable of dispensing one product. Further, there is one cash register. Thus, the candy machine consists of four dispensers and one cash register. Graphically, this can be represented as in Figure 6-14.

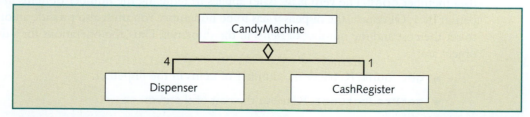

Figure 6-14 CandyMachine and its components

In Figure 6-14, the number 4 on top of the box `Dispenser` indicates that there are 4 dispensers in the candy machine. Similarly, the number 1 on top of the box `CashRegister` indicates that the candy machine has 1 cash register.

Step 2: Identify the class(es).

You can see that the program you are about to write is supposed to deal with dispensers and cash registers. That is, the main objects are four dispensers and a cash register. Because all the dispensers are of the same type, you need to create a class, say `Dispenser`, to create the dispensers. Similarly, you need to create a class, say `CashRegister`, to create a cash register. We will create the **class** `CandyMachine` containing the four dispensers, a cash register, and the application program.

Step 3: Identify the data members for each of the class(es).

Dispenser   To make the sale, at least one item must be in the dispenser and the customer must know the cost of the product. Therefore, the data members of a dispenser are:

- Product cost
- Number of items in the dispenser

Cash Register   The cash register accepts money and returns change. Therefore, the cash register has only one data member, which we call `cashOnHand`.

Candy Machine   The **class** `CandyMachine` has four dispensers and a cash register. You can name the four dispensers by the items they store. Therefore, the candy machine has five data members—four dispensers and a cash register.

Step 4: Identify the operations for each of the objects (classes).

The relevant verbs are *show* (selection), *make* (selection), *show* (cost), *accept* (money), *return* (change), and *make* (sale).

The verbs *show* (selection) and *make* (selection) relate to the candy machine. The verbs *show* (cost) and *make* (sale) relate to the dispenser. Similarly, the verbs *accept* (money) and *return* (change) relate to the cash register.

Dispenser   The verb *show* (cost) applies to either printing or retrieving the value of the data member `cost`. The verb *make* (sale) applies to reducing the number of items in the dispenser by 1. Of course, the dispenser has to be nonempty. You must also provide an operation to set the cost and the number of items in the dispenser. Thus, the operations for a dispenser object are:

- `getCount`: Retrieve the number of items in the dispenser.
- `getProductCost`: Retrieve the cost of the item.
- `makeSale`: Reduce the number of items in the dispenser by 1.
- `setCost`: Set the cost of the product.
- `setNumberOfItems`: Set the number of items in the dispenser.

Cash Register   The verb *accept* (money) applies to updating the money in the cash register by adding the money deposited by the customer. Similarly, the verb *return* (change) applies to reducing the money in the cash register by returning the overpaid amount (by the customer) to the customer. You also need to (initially) set the money in the cash register and also retrieve the money from the cash register. Thus, the possible operations on a cash register are:

- `acceptAmount`: Update the amount in the cash register.

- `returnChange`: Return the change.

- `getCashOnHand`: Retrieve the amount in the cash register.

- `setCashOnHand`: Set the amount in the cash register.

Candy Machine   The verbs *show* (selection) and *make* (selection) apply to the candy machine. Thus, the two possible operations are:

- `showSelection`: Show the number of products sold by the candy machine.

- `makeSelection`: Allow the customer to select the product.

The result of the OOD for this problem is shown in Figure 6-15.

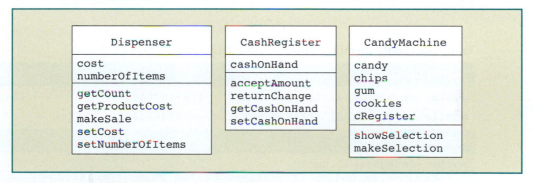

Figure 6-15   Classes `Dispenser`, `CashRegister`, `CandyMachine`, and their members

IMPLEMENTING CLASSES AND OPERATIONS

From the preceding examples, it is clear that once the relevant classes, data members of each class, and relevant operations for each class are identified, the next step is to implement these things in Java. Because objects are nothing but instances of classes, we need to learn how to implement classes in Java. Implementing data members, that is, fields, of classes is simple because you need variables to store the data.

What about operations? In Java, to implement operations we write algorithms. Because there is usually more than one operation on an object, each algorithm is implemented with the help of Java's methods. In Chapter 3 we briefly introduced methods and described some pre-defined methods. However, Java does not provide all the methods that you will ever need. Therefore, to learn how to design and implement classes, you first must learn how to construct and implement your own methods. Because methods are an essential part of Java (or any programming language), Chapter 7 is devoted to teaching you how to create methods.

Primitive Data Types and the Wrapper Classes

Chapter 3 discussed how to use the method **parseInt** of the **class** Integer to convert an integer string into an integer. Moreover, you learned that the **class** Integer is called a **wrapper** class, or simply a wrapper. It is used to wrap **int** values into Integer objects so that **int** values can be regarded objects. Similarly, the **class** Long is used to wrap **long** values into Long objects, the **class** Double is used to wrap **double** values into Double objects, and the **class** Float is used to wrap **float** values into Float objects. In fact, Java provides a wrapper class corresponding to each primitive data type. For example, the wrapper class corresponding to the type **int** is Integer. Therefore, an **int** value can be wrapped into an Integer object.

Next, we briefly discuss the **class** Integer. Table 6-6 describes some members of the **class** Integer. (For additional members of this class, see Appendix E.)

Table 6-6 Some members of the class Integer

Named Constants
`public static final int MAX_VALUE = 2147483647;`
`public static final int MIN_VALUE = -2147483648;`

Constructors

`public Integer(int num)`
`  //Creates an object initialized to the value specified`
`  //by num.`

`public Integer(String str)`
`  //Creates an object initialized to the value specified`
`  //by the num contained in str.`

Table 6-6 Some members of the `class` Integer (continued)

Methods

`int compareTo(Integer anotherInteger)`
`//Compares two Integer objects numerically.`
`//Returns the value 0 if the value of this Integer object is`
`//equal to the value of anotherInteger object, a value less`
`//than 0 if the value of this Integer is less than the value of`
`//anotherInteger object, and a value greater than 0 if the value`
`//of this Integer object is greater than the value of`
`//anotherInteger object.`

`public int intValue()` `//Returns the value of the object as an int value.`
`public double doubleValue()` `//Returns the value of the object as a double value.`

`public boolean equals(Object obj)`
`//Returns true if the value of this object is equal`
`//to the value of the object specified by obj;`
`//otherwise returns false.`

`public static int parseInt(String str)` `//Returns the value of the number contained in str.`
`public String toString()` `//Returns the int value, of the object, as a string.`
`public static String toString(int num)` `//Returns the value of num as a string.`

`public static Integer valueOf(String str)`
`//Returns an Integer object initialized to the value`
`//specified by str.`

Consider the following statements:

```
Integer num;              //Line 1
num = new Integer(86)     //Line 2
```

The statement in Line 1 declares **num** to be a reference variable of the type **Integer**. The statement in Line 2 creates an **Integer** object, stores the value **86** in it, and then stores the address of this object into **num**. (See Figure 6-16. Suppose that the address of the **Integer** object is **1350**.)

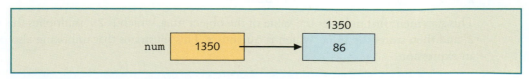

Figure 6-16   Reference variable num and the object it points to

As you can see, the `int` value 86 is wrapped into an `Integer` object. Just like the **class** `String`, the **class** `Integer` does not provide any method to change the value of an existing `Integer` object. That is, `Integer` objects are **immutable**. (In fact, wrapper class objects are immutable.)

As of JDK 5.0, Java has simplified the wrapping and unwrapping of primitive type values, called the **autoboxing** and **auto-unboxing** of primitive types. For example, consider the following statements:

```
int x;         //Line 3
Integer num;   //Line 4
```

The statement in Line 3 declares the `int` variable x; the statement in Line 4 declares `num` to be a reference variable of the type `Integer`.

Consider the statement:

```
num = 25;               //Line 5
```

This statement is equivalent to the statement:

```
num = new Integer(25);   //Line 6
```

That is, either of these statements creates an `Integer` object, stores `25` into that object, and the reference of that object is stored in `num`. In other words, `num` refers to or points to an `Integer` object with the value `25`. The expression in Line 5 is referred to as *autoboxing* of the `int` type.

Now consider the statement:

```
x = num;                //Line 7
```

This statement is equivalent to the statement:

```
x = num.intValue();     //Line 8
```

After the statement in either Line 7 or Line 8 executes, the value of x is `25`. The statement in Line 7 is referred to as the *auto-unboxing* of the `int` type.

 Autoboxing and unboxing of primitive data types are features of JDK 5.0 and are *not* available in JDK versions lower than 5.0, such as JDK 1.4.0.

Next, consider the following statement:

```
x = 2 * num;            //Line 9
```

This statement first unboxes the value of the object `num`, which is `25`, multiplies this value by 2, and then stores the value, which is `50`, into x. This illustrates that unboxing also occurs in an expression.

To compare the values of two `Integer` objects, you can use the method `compareTo`, described in Table 6-6. If you want to compare the values of two `Integer` objects only for equality, then you can use the method `equals`.

 Suppose you have the following statements:

```
Integer num1 = 24;
Integer num2 = 35;

int x = 23;
int y = 15;
```

Now consider the following statements:

```
if (num1.equals(num2))
    System.out.println("The values of the "
                     + "objects num1 and num2 "
                     + "are the same.");
else
    System.out.println("The values of the "
                     + "objects num1 and num2 "
                     + "are not the same.");
```

The expression in the `if` statement determines whether the value of object num1, which is 24, is the same as the value of the object num2, which is 35. Next, consider the following statements:

```
if (num1 == num2)
    System.out.println("Both num1 and num2 "
                     + "point to the same "
                     + "object.");
else
    System.out.println("num1 and num2 "
                     + "do not point to the "
                     + "same object.");
```

The expression in the `if` statement determines whether the values of num1 and num2 are the same, that is, whether num1 and num2 point to the same object.

It follows that when the operator == is used with reference variables of the `Integer` type, it compares whether the two objects point to the same object. Therefore, if you want to compare the values of two `Integer` objects, then you should use the method `equal` of the **class** `Integer`. On the other hand, if you want to determine whether two reference variables of the `Integer` type point to the same `Integer` object, then you should use the operator ==.

The preceding discussion also applies to other wrapper classes.

Auto boxing and unboxing of primitive data types is a new feature of Java and is available in JDK 5.0 and higher versions. It automatically boxes and unboxes primitive type values into appropriate objects. For example, as explained previously, `int` values can be automatically boxed and unboxed into `Integer` objects. Example 6-4 further illustrates the autoboxing and auto-unboxing of `Integer` objects.

6

Example 6-4

```java
//Program that illustrates the autoboxing and unboxing
//of Integer objects.

public class IntegerClassExample
{
    public static void main(String[] args)
    {
        int x, y;                                            //Line 1
        Integer num1, num2;                                  //Line 2

        num1 = 8;      //Autobox 8                           //Line 3
        num2 = 16;     //Autobox 16                          //Line 4

        System.out.println("Line 5: num1 = " + num1
                        + ", num2 = " + num2);               //Line 5

        x = num1 + 4;                                        //Line 6

        System.out.println("Line 7: x = " + x);             //Line 7

        y = num1 + num2;                                     //Line 8

        System.out.println("Line 9: y = " + y);             //Line 9

        System.out.println("Line 10: The value of "
                        + "2 * num1 + num2 = "
                        + (2 * num1 + num2));                //Line 10

        System.out.println("Line 11: The value of "
                        + "x * num2 - num1 = "
                        + (x * num2 - num1));                //Line 11

        System.out.println("Line 12: The value of "
                        + "num1 <= num2 is "
                        + (num1 <= num2));                   //Line 12

        System.out.println("Line 13: The value of "
                        + "2 * num1 <= x is "
                        + (2 * num1 <= x));                  //Line 13

        System.out.println("Line 14: The value of "
                        + "2 * num1 > num2 is "
                        + (2 * num1 >= num2));               //Line 14
    }
}
```

Sample Run:
```
Line 5: num1 = 8, num2 = 16
Line 7: x = 12
Line 9: y = 24
Line 10: The value of 2 * num1 + num2 = 32
Line 11: The value of x * num2 - num1 = 184
Line 12: The value of num1 <= num2 is true
Line 13: The value of 2 * num1 <= x is false
Line 14: The value of 2 * num1 > num2 is true
```

For the most part, the preceding sample run is self-explanatory. Let us look at some of the statements. The statement in Line 3 autoboxes the value 8 into an **Integer** object and stores the address of that object into the reference variable **num1**. The meaning of the statement in Line 4 is similar.

The statement in Line 6 unboxes the value of the object to which **num1** points, adds 4 to that value, and stores the result in **x**. Similarly, the statement in Line 8 unboxes the values of the objects pointed to by **num1** and **num2**, adds the values, and stores the result in **y**.

The statement in Line 12 unboxes the values of the objects pointed to by **num1** and **num2**, and then compares these values using the relational operator **<=**. (Note that because we are not using the operator **==**, autoboxing occurs here.)

The **class Double** also has methods similar to the methods given in Table 6-6. (See Appendix E for further details.) The Web site accompanying this book has a program, named **DoubleClassExample.java**, that illustrates the autoboxing and unboxing of **double** values into **Double** objects. However, you should use the method **equals** to compare the values, for equality, of the wrapper class objects. Using the method **equals** is illustrated in the following example:

Example 6-5

```
//Program that shows how the operator == and the method equals
//work with Double objects.

public class DoubleClassMethodEquals
{
    public static void main(String[] args)
    {
        Double num1, num2;                              //Line 1

        num1 = 2567.58;                                 //Line 2
        num2 = 2567.58;                                 //Line 3

        System.out.println("Line 4: num1 = " + num1
                    + ", num2 = " + num2);              //Line 4
```

6

```
        System.out.println("Line 5: The value of "
                    + "num1.equals(num2) is "
                    + num1.equals(num2));        //Line 5

        System.out.println("Line 6: The value of "
                    + "num1 == num2 is "
                    + (num1 == num2));           //Line 6
    }
}
```

Sample Run:

```
Line 4: num1 = 2567.58, num2 = 2567.58
Line 5: The value of num1.equals(num2) is true
Line 6: The value of num1 == num2 is false
```

In the preceding program, the statements in Lines 2 and 3 create two objects, each with the value **2567.58** and make **num1** and **num2**, respectively, point to these objects. The expression, **num1.equals(num2)**, in Line 5 compares the values stored in the objects to which **num1** and **num2** point. Because both objects contain the same value, this expression evaluates to **true**; see the output of the statement in Line 5. On the other hand the expression, **num1 == num2**, in Line 6 determines whether **num1** and **num2** point to the same object.

class IntClass

Chapter 3 showed you how to use certain mathematical functions and how to pass numbers as parameters. In this chapter, we also passed objects as parameters to methods such as adding a button and labels to a container and registering a listener to a button and a text field. You can also pass **String** objects and **Integer** objects as parameters. Java provides the classes **Integer**, **Double**, **Character**, **Long**, and **Float** so that the values of the primitive data types can be treated as objects. As remarked in the preceding section, these classes are called wrapper classes. They wrap primitive type values. However, these classes have limitations. You can create objects of the type, say **Integer**, to store **int** values, but (as previously noted) you cannot change the values stored in the objects. Parameter passing, as you will see, is a fundamental concept in any programming language. Therefore, we have created the classes **IntClass** and **DoubleClass**, which are similar to the classes **Integer** and **Double**, respectively. You can create objects of the type **IntClass** and/or **DoubleClass**, store, and/or change the values of the objects. Table 6-7 describes the data member and methods of the **class IntClass**. (See also Appendix D.)

Table 6-7 The **class** IntClass

data member: **int** x; //variable to store the number

public IntClass()
  //constructor
  //When the object is instantiated, the value of x is initialized
  //to 0.

public IntClass(**int** num)
  //constructor
  //When the object is instantiated, the value of x is initialized
  //to num.

public void setNum(**int** num)
  //Method to set the data member x.
  //The value of num is copied into x.

public int getNum()
  //Method to retrieve the value of x.
  //The value of x is returned.

public void addToNum(**int** num)
  //Method to update the value of x by adding the value of num.
  //x = x + num;

public void multiplyToNum(**int** num)
  //Method to update the value of x by multiplying by the value
  //of num.
  //x = x * num;

public int compareTo(**int** num)
  //Method to compare the value of x with the value of num.
  //Returns a value < 0 if x < num.
  //Returns 0 if x == num.
  //Returns a value > 0 if x > num.

public boolean equals(**int** num)
  //Method to compare x with num for equality.
  //Returns true if x == num; otherwise it returns false.

public String toString()   //Method to return the value of x as a string.

Consider the following statements:

```
IntClass firstNum = new IntClass();        //Line 1
IntClass secondNum = new IntClass(5);      //Line 2
int num;                                   //Line 3
```

The statement in Line 1 creates the object `firstNum` and initializes it to 0. The statement in Line 2 creates the object `secondNum` and initializes it to 5. The statement in Line 3 declares `num` to be an `int` variable. Now consider the following statements:

```
firstNum.setNum(24);              //Line 4
secondNum.addToNum(6);            //Line 5
num = firstNum.getNum();          //Line 6
```

The statement in Line 4 sets the value of `firstNum` (in fact, the value of the data member `x` of `firstNum`) to 24. The statement in Line 5 updates the value of `secondNum` to 11 (the previous value 5 is updated by adding 6 to it). The statement in Line 6 retrieves the value of the object `firstNum` (the value of the data member `x`), and assigns it to `num`. After this statement executes, the value of `num` is 24.

The following statements output the values of `firstNum` and `secondNum` (in fact, the values of their data members):

```
System.out.println("firstNum = " + firstNum);
System.out.println("secondNum = " + secondNum);
```

 The **class** DoubleClass is similar to the **class** IntClass. In other words, the **class** DoubleClass has one data member of the type **double** and similar methods with the same name. (See Appendix D.)

QUICK REVIEW

1. GUI stands for graphical user interface.

2. Every GUI program requires a window.

3. Various components are added to the content pane of the window and not to the window itself.

4. You must create a layout before you can add a component to the content pane.

5. Pixel stands for picture element. Windows are measured in pixels of height and width.

6. `JFrame` is a class and the GUI component `window` can be created as an instance of `JFrame`.

7. `JLabel` is used to label other GUI components as well as to display information to the user.

8. A `JTextField` can be used for both input and output.

9. A `JButton` generates an event.

10. An event handler is a Java method that determines the action to be performed as the event happens.

11. When you click a button, an action event is created and sent to another object known as an action listener.

12. An action listener must have a method called `actionPerformed`.

13. A **class** is a collection of data members and methods associated with those data members.

14. OOD starts with a problem statement and tries to identify the classes required by identifying the nouns appearing in the problem statement.

15. Methods of a class are identified with the help of verbs appearing in the problem specification.

16. To wrap values of primitive data types into objects corresponding to each primitive type, Java provides a **class**, called a wrapper class. For example, to wrap an **int** value into an object, the corresponding wrapper **class** is `Integer`. Similarly, to wrap a **double** value into an object, the corresponding wrapper **class** is `Double`.

17. JDK 5.0 simplifies the wrapping and unwrapping of primitive type values, called the autoboxing and auto-unboxing of primitive data types.

18. `Integer` objects are immutable. (In fact, wrapper classes' objects are immutable.)

19. To compare the values of two `Integer` objects, you can use the method `compareTo`. If you want to compare the values of two `Integer` objects only for equality, then you can use the method `equal`.

EXERCISES

1. Mark the following statements as true or false.

   a. Every window has a width and height.

   b. In Java, `JFrame` is a class.

   c. To display the window you need not invoke a method such as `setVisible`.

   d. In Java, the reserved word **extends** allows you to create a new class from an existing one.

   e. The window you see displayed on your screen is a class.

   f. Labels are used to display the output of a program.

   g. Every GUI component you need has to be created and added to a container.

   h. In Java, **implements** is a keyword.

   i. Clicking a button is an example of an action event.

   j. In a problem statement, every verb is a possible class.

   k. In a problem statement, every noun is a possible method.

   l. To use an object, you must know how it is implemented.

2. Name some commonly used GUI components and their uses.

3. Name a GUI component that can be used for both input and output.

4. Name two input GUI components.

5. Why do you need labels in a GUI program?

6. Why would you prefer a GUI program over a non–GUI version?

7. What are the advantages of problem analysis, GUI design, and algorithm design over directly writing a program?

8. Modify the temperature conversion program to convert centimeters to inches, and vice versa.

9. Modify the program to compute the area and perimeter of a rectangle so that your new program will compute the sum and product of two numbers.

10. Fill in the blanks in each of the following:

    a. A(n) _____ places GUI components in a container.

    b. Clicking a button is a(n) _____.

    c. The method _____ is invoked when a button is pressed and a(n) _____ is registered to handle the event.

    d. _____ operator is needed to instantiate an object.

    e. A class has two types of members: _____ and _____.

    f. To create a window, you extend the _____ class.

    g. Every GUI program is a(n) _____ program.

    h. The method _____ gets the string in the **JTextField** and the method _____ changes the string displayed in a **JTextField**.

    i. If **Student** is a class and you create a new **class GradStudent** by extending **Student**, then **Student** is a(n) _____ and **GradStudent** is a(n) _____.

    j. Event and event listener classes are contained in the package _____.

    k. The unit of measure of length in a window is _____.

11. Write necessary statements to create the following GUI components:

    a. A **JLabel** with the text string **"Enter the number of courses"**

    b. A **JButton** with the text string **"Run"**

    c. A **JTextField** that can display 15 characters

    d. A window with the title **"Welcome Home!"**

    e. A window with a width of 200 pixels and a height of 400 pixels

    f. A **JTextField** that displays the string **"Apple tree"**

12. Correct the syntax errors in the following program and add any additional statements necessary to make the program work:

```
import javax.jswing.*;

public class ROne extends JFrame
{
        static private final int WIDTH = 400;
        static private final int HEIGHT = 300;

        public RectangleProgramOne()
        {
            setTitle("Welcome");
            setSize(WIDTH,HEIGHT);
            SetVisible(true);
            setDefaultCloseOperation(EXIT_ON_CLOSE);
        }

        public static void main(String[] args)
        {
                ROne r1 = r1();
        }
}
```

13. Correct the syntax errors in the following program:

```
public class RTwo extends JFrame
{
        public RTwoProgram()
        {
            private JLabel length, width, area;

            setTitle("Good day area");

            length =  JLabel("Enter the length);
            width = JLabel("Enter the width);
            area = JLabel("Area: ");
            containerPane  = ContentPane();
            pane.setLayout(GridLayout(4, 1));
            setSize(WIDTH,HEIGHT);
            setVisible();
            setDefaultCloseOperation(EXIT_ON_CLOSE);
        }

        public static void main( String args[] )
        {
                RTwoProgram R2 = new RTwoProgram ();
        }
}
```

14. Consider a common VCR. What are the methods of a VCR?

15. What are the methods of an ATM?

16. Do an OOD analysis of the following problem: Write a program to input the dimensions of a cylinder, and calculate and print the surface area and volume.

17. Lead County Credit Union (LCCU) has recently upgraded its software systems to an OOD design. List at least five classes that you think should be included in this design. For each class, identify some of the data members and methods.

18. Your local public library wants to design new software to keep track of patrons, books, and lending activity. List at least three classes you think should be in the design. For each class, identify some data members and methods.

19. The Custom Consulting Company (CCC) places temporary computer professionals in companies that request such employees. CCC's business can be explained as follows:

CCC keeps a list of professionals willing to work or currently working on a temporary assignment. A professional may have up to three qualifications, including programmer, senior programmer, analyst, tester, designer, and so on. A company always requests a professional with a single specific qualification. CCC keeps a list of all its clients (that is, a list of other companies) and their current needs. If CCC can find a match, a professional with the required qualification is assigned to a specific opening at one of CCC's clients.

Identify at least five classes and, for each class, list possible data members and methods.

PROGRAMMING EXERCISES

1. Design a GUI program to find the weighted average of four test scores. The four test scores and their respective weights are given in the following format:

```
testscore1 weight1
...
```

For example, the sample data is as follows:

```
75 0.20
95 0.35
85 0.15
65 0.30
```

The user is supposed to enter the data and press a Calculate button. The program must display the weighted average.

2. Write a GUI program that converts seconds to years, weeks, days, hours, and minutes. For this problem, assume 1 year is 365 days.

3. Design and implement a GUI program to compare two strings and display the larger one.

4. Write a GUI program to convert a character to a corresponding integer, and vice versa.

5. Write a GUI program to convert all letters in a string to uppercase letters. For example, `Alb34ert` will be converted to `ALB34ERT`.

6. Write a GUI program to convert all lowercase letters in a string to uppercase letters, and vice versa. For example, `Alb34eRt` will be converted to `aLB34ErT`.

7. Write a GUI program to compute the amount of a certificate of deposit on maturity. The sample data follows:

```
Amount deposited: 80000.00
Years: 15
Interest rate: 7.75
```

Hint: To solve this problem, compute `80000.00 (1 + 7.75 / 100)`^{15}.

8. Write a GUI program that will accept three (integer) input values, say `x`, `y`, and `z`, and then verify whether or not `x * x + y * y = z * z`.

9. Design and implement a GUI program to convert a positive number given in one base to another base. For this problem, assume that both bases are less than or equal to 10. Consider the sample data:

```
number = 2010, base = 3, and new base = 4.
```

In this case, first convert `2010` in base `3` into the equivalent number in base `10` as follows:

```
2 * 3³ + 0 * 3² + 1 * 3 + 0 = 54 + 0 + 3 + 0  = 57
```

To convert `57` to base `4`, you need to find the remainders obtained by dividing by `4`, as shown in the following:

```
57 % 4 = 1, quotient = 14
14 % 4 = 2, quotient = 3
3 % 4 = 3, quotient = 0.
```

Therefore, `57` in base `4` is `321`.

6

7

USER-DEFINED METHODS

In this chapter, you will:

♦ Understand how methods are used in Java programming

♦ Learn about predefined methods and how to use them in a program

♦ Learn about user-defined methods

♦ Examine value-returning methods, including actual and formal parameters

♦ Explore how to construct and use a value-returning, user-defined method in a program

♦ Learn how to construct and use user-defined void methods in a program

♦ Explore variables as parameters

♦ Learn about the scope of an identifier

♦ Become aware of method overloading

In Chapter 2, you learned that a Java application program is a collection of classes, and that a class is a collection of methods and data members. One such method is `main`. The programs in Chapters 2 through 5 use only the method `main`; all the programming instructions are packed into one method. This technique, however, is good only for short programs. For large programs, it is not practical (although it is possible) to put the entire programming instructions into one method, as you will soon discover. You must learn to break the problem into manageable pieces. This chapter first discusses previously defined methods and then user–defined methods.

Let's imagine an automobile factory. When an automobile is manufactured, it is not made from basic raw materials; it is put together from previously manufactured parts. Some parts are made by the company itself, others are manufactured by different companies.

Methods in Java are like automobile parts; they are building blocks. Methods are used to divide complicated programs into manageable pieces. There are both **predefined methods**, methods that are already written and provided by Java, and **user-defined methods**, methods that you create.

Using methods has several advantages:

- While working on one method, you can focus on just that part of the program and construct it, debug it, and perfect it.

- Different people can work on different methods simultaneously.

- If a method is needed in more than one place in a program, or in different programs, you can write it once and use it many times.

- Using methods greatly enhances the program's readability because it reduces the complexity of the method `main`.

Methods are often called *modules*. They are like miniature programs; you can put them together to form a larger program. When user-defined methods are discussed, you will see that this is the case. This ability is less apparent with predefined methods because their programming code is not available to us. However, because predefined methods are already written for us, you will learn these first so that you can use them when needed. To use a predefined method in your program(s), you need to know only how to use it.

PREDEFINED METHODS

Before formally discussing Java's predefined methods, let's review a concept from college algebra. In algebra, a function can be considered a rule or correspondence between values, called the function's arguments, and the unique value of the function associated with the arguments. Thus, if `f(x) = 2x + 5`, then `f(1) = 7`, `f(2) = 9`, and `f(3) = 11`, where 1, 2, and 3 are arguments of `f`, and 7, 9, and 11 are the corresponding values of the function `f`.

In Java, the concept of a method, predefined or user-defined, is similar to that of a function in algebra. For example, every method has a name and, depending on the values specified by the user, it does some computation. This section discusses various predefined methods.

Some of the predefined mathematical methods are `pow(x, y)` and `sqrt(x)`.

The *power* method, `pow(x, y)`, calculates x^y; that is, the value of `pow(x, y)` is x^y. For example, `pow(2, 3)` is `8.0` and `pow(2.5, 3)` is `15.625`. Because the value of `pow(x, y)` is of the type **double**, we say that the method `pow` is of the type **double** or that the method `pow` returns a value of the type **double**. Moreover, `x` and `y` are called the **parameters** (or **arguments**) of the method `pow`. The method `pow` has two parameters.

The *square root* method, `sqrt(x)`, calculates the non-negative square root of `x` for `x >= 0.0`. For example, `sqrt(2.25)` is `1.5`. The method `sqrt` is of the type **double** and has only one parameter.

In Java, predefined methods are organized as a collection of classes, called **class libraries**. For example, the **class** Math contains mathematical methods. Table 7–1 lists some of Java's predefined mathematical methods. The table gives the name of the method, number of parameters, the data type of the parameters, and the method type. The **method type** is the data type of the value returned by the method. The name of the method is shown in bold. The table also shows how a method works. The **class** Math is contained in the package java.lang. (For a list of additional classes and their associated methods, see Appendix E.)

Table 7-1 Some Predefined Mathematical Methods and Named Constants

class Math (Package: java.lang)	
Named Constants	
double E;	E = 2.718281828459045
double PI;	PI = 3.141592653589793
Methods	
Expression	**Description**
abs(x)	Returns the absolute value of x. If x is of the type int, it returns a value of the type int; if x is of the type long, it returns a value of the type long; if x is of the type float, it returns a value of the type float; if x is of the type double, it returns a value of the type double. **Example:** abs(-67) returns the value 67. abs(35) returns the value 35. abs(-75.38) returns the value 75.38.
ceil(x)	x is of the type double. Returns a value of the type double, which is the smallest integer value that is not less than x. **Example:** ceil(56.34) returns the value 57.0.
exp(x)	x is of the type double. Returns e^x, a value of the type double, where e is approximately 2.7182818284590455. **Example:** exp(3) returns the value 20.085536923187668.
floor(x)	x is of the type double. Returns a value of the type double, which is the largest integer value less than x. **Example:** floor(65.78) returns the value 65.0.
log(x)	x is of the type double. Returns a value of the type double, which is the natural logarithm (base e) of x. **Example:** log(2) returns the value 0.6931471805599453.

7

Table 7-1 Some Predefined Mathematical Methods and Named Constants (continued)

Expression	Description
`log10(x)`	x is of the type `double`. Returns a value of the type `double`, which is the common logarithm (base 10) of x. **Example:** `log10(2)` returns the value `0.3010299956639812`.
`max(x, y)`	Returns the larger of x and y. If x and y are of the type `int`, it returns a value of the type `int`; if x and y are of the type `long`, it returns a value of the type `long`; if x and y are of the type `float`, it returns a value of the type `float`; if x and y are of the type `double`, it returns a value of the type `double`. **Example:** `max(15, 25)` returns the value `25`. `max(23.67, 14.28)` returns the value `23.67`. `max(45, 23.78)` returns the value `45.00`.
`min(x, y)`	Returns the smaller of x and y. If x and y are of the type `int`, it returns a value of the type `int`; if x and y are of the type `long`, it returns a value of the type `long`; if x and y are of the type `float`, it returns a value of the type `float`; if x and y are of the type `double`, it returns a value of the type `double`. **Example:** `min(15, 25)` returns the value `15`. `min(23.67, 14.28)` returns the value `14.28`. `min(12, 34.78)` returns the value `12.00`.
`pow(x, y)`	x and y are of the type `double`. Returns a value of the type `double`, which is x^y. **Example:** `pow(2.0, 3.0)` returns the value `8.0`. `pow(4, 0.5)` returns the value `2.0`.
`round(x)`	Returns a value that is the integer closest to x. If x is of the type `float`, it returns a value of the type `int`; if x is of the type `double`, it returns a value of the type `long`. **Example:** `round(24.56)` returns the value `25`. `round(18.35)` returns the value `18`.
`sqrt(x)`	x is of the type `double`. Returns a value of the type `double`, which is the square root of x. **Example:** `sqrt(4.0)` returns the value `2.0`. `sqrt(2.25)` returns the value `1.5`.
`cos(x)`	x is of the type `double`. Returns the cosine of x measured in radians. **Example:** `cos(0)` returns the value `1.0`. `cos(PI / 3)` returns the value `0.5000000000000001`
`sin(x)`	x is of the type `double`. Returns the sine of x measured in radians. **Example:** `sin(0)` returns the value `0.0`. `sin(PI / 2)` returns the value `1.0`
`tan(x)`	x is of the type `double`. Returns the tangent of x measured in radians. **Example:** `tan(0)` returns the value `0.0`.

The method `log10` is not available in JDK versions lower than 5.0.

Java also provides methods, contained in the **class** `Character`, to manipulate characters. Table 7-2 describes some of the methods of the **class** `Character` contained in the package `java.lang`. As in Table 7-1, Table 7-2 shows the name of the method in bold, and gives examples of how the methods work.

Table 7-2 Some Predefined Methods for Character Manipulation

class Character (Package: java.lang)	
Expression	**Description**
isDigit(ch)	ch is of the type **char**. Returns **true** if ch is a digit; **false** otherwise. **Example:** isDigit('8') returns the value **true**. isDigit('*') returns the value **false**.
isLetter(ch)	ch is of the type **char**. Returns **true** if ch is a letter; **false** otherwise. **Example:** isLetter('a') returns the value **true**. isLetter('*') returns the value **false**.
isLowerCase(ch)	ch is of the type **char**. Returns **true** if ch is a lowercase letter; **false** otherwise. **Example:** isLowerCase('a') returns the value **true**. isLowerCase('A') returns the value **false**.
isUpperCase(ch)	ch is of the type **char**. Returns **true** if ch is an uppercase letter; **false** otherwise. **Example:** isUpperCase('B') returns the value **true**. isUpperCase('k') returns the value **false**.
isSpaceChar(ch)	ch is of the type **char**. Returns **true** if ch is the space character; **false** otherwise. **Example:** isSpaceChar(' ') returns the value **true**. isSpaceChar('*') returns the value **false**.

7

Table 7-2 Some Predefined Methods for Character Manipulation (continued)

Expression	Description
`isWhitespace(ch)`	ch is of the type `char`. Returns `true` if ch is a white-space character; `false` otherwise. **Example:** `isWhitespace('\n')` returns the value `true`. `isWhitespace('\t')` returns the value `true`. `isWhitespace('\r')` returns the value `true`. `isWhitespace(' ')` returns the value `true`. `isWhitespace('*')` returns the value `false`.
`toLowerCase(ch)`	ch is of the type `char`. Returns the character that is the lowercase equivalent of ch. If ch does not have a corresponding lowercase letter, it returns ch. **Example:** `toLowerCase('D')` returns the value d. `toLowerCase('*')` returns the value *.
`toUpperCase(ch)`	ch is of the type `char`. Returns the character that is the uppercase equivalent of ch. If ch does not have a corresponding uppercase letter, it returns ch. **Example:** `toUpperCase('j')` returns the value J. `toUpperCase('8')` returns the value 8.

Using Predefined Methods in a Program

In general, to use the predefined methods of a class in a program, you must import the **class** from the package containing the class. For example, to use the method `nextInt` of the **class** Scanner contained in the **package** java.util, we imported this **class** from the **package** java.util. However, as stated in Chapter 2, if a **class** is contained in the **package** java.lang and you want to use a (**public**) method of this **class**, Java does not require you to explicitly include an **import** statement to import that **class**. For example, to use any (**public**) method of the **class** String contained in the **package** java.lang, in a program we do not need an **import** statement. By default, Java automatically imports classes from the package java.lang.

A method of a class may contain the reserved word **static** (in its heading). For example, the method **main** contains the reserved word **static** in its heading. If (the heading of) a method contains the reserved word **static**, it is called a **static** method; otherwise, it is called a **nonstatic** method. Similarly, the heading of a method may contain the reserved word **public**. If the heading of a method contains the reserved word **public**, it is called a **public** method. An important property of a **public** and **static** method is that (in a program) it can be used (called) using the name of the class, the dot operator, the method name, and the appropriate parameters. For example, all the methods of the **class** Math are **public** and **static**. Therefore, the general syntax to use a method of the **class** Math is:

```
Math.methodName(parameters)
```

For example, the following expression determines $2.5^{3.5}$:

```
Math.pow(2.5, 3.5)
```

Similarly, if a method of the **class** Character is **public** and **static**, you can use the name of the **class**, which is Character, the dot operator, the method name, and the appropriate parameters. The methods of the **class** Character listed in Table 7-2 are **public** and **static**.

To simplify the use of (**public**) **static** methods of a class, JDK 5.0 introduces the following import statements:

```
import static packageName.ClassName.*;  //to use any (public) static
                                        //method of the class

import static packageName.ClassName.methodName; //to use a specific
                                                //method of the class
```

These are called **static import** **statements**. After including such statements in your program, when you use a (**public**) **static** method (or any other **public static** member) of a **class**, you can omit the name of the class and the dot operator.

For example, after including the **import** statement:

```
import static java.lang.Math.*;
```

you can determine $2.5^{3.5}$ by using the expression:

```
pow(2.5, 3.5)
```

After including the **static import** statement, in reality, you have a choice. When you use a (**public**) **static** method of a **class**, you can either use the name of the class and the dot operator or omit them. For example, after including the **static import** statement:

```
import static java.lang.Math.*;
```

in a program, you can determine $2.5^{3.5}$ by using either the expression Math.pow(2.5, 3.5) or the expression pow(2.5, 3.5).

The **static import** statement is *not* available in versions of Java lower than 5.0, such as 1.4.0. Therefore, if you are using, say Java 1.4.0, then you must use a **static** method of the **class** Math using the name of the class and the dot operator.

The (**public**) **static** methods of the **class** Character have similar conventions.

Example 7-1 illustrates how to use predefined methods.

Example 7-1

This example shows you how to use some of the predefined methods:

```java
//How to use predefined methods

import static java.lang.Math.*;
import static java.lang.Character.*;

public class PredefinedMethods
{
    public static void main(String[] args)
    {
        int x;
        double u, v;

        System.out.println("Line 1: Uppercase a is "
                            + toUpperCase('a'));              //Line 1
        u = 4.2;                                             //Line 2
        v = 3.0;                                             //Line 3
        System.out.printf("Line 4: %.1f to the power of "
                    + "%.1f = %.2f%n", u, v, pow(u, v));     //Line 4

        System.out.printf("Line 5: 5 to the power of 4 = "
                    + "%.2f%n", pow(5, 4));                  //Line 5

        u = u + Math.pow(3, 3);                              //Line 6
        System.out.printf("Line 7: u = %.2f%n", u);          //Line 7

        x = -15;                                             //Line 8
        System.out.printf("Line 9: The absolute value of %d = "
                    + "%d%n", x, abs(x));                    //Line 9
    }
}
```

Sample Run:
```
Line 1: Uppercase a is A
Line 4: 4.2 to the power of 3.0 = 74.09
Line 5: 5 to the power of 4 = 625.00
Line 7: u = 31.20
Line 9: The absolute value of -15 = 15
```

This program works as follows: The statement in Line 1 outputs the uppercase letter that corresponds to 'a', which is 'A'. In the statement in Line 4, the method **pow** (of the **class** Math) is used to output u^v. In Java terminology, it is said that the method **pow** is called with the parameters u and v. In this case, the values of u and v are passed to the method **pow**. The statement in Line 5 uses the method **pow** to output 5^4. The statement in Line 6 uses the method **pow** to determine 3^3, adds this value to the value of u, and then stores the new value into u. Notice that in this statement, the method **pow** is called using the name of the **class**, which is `Math`, and the dot operator. The statement in Line 7 outputs the value of `u`. The statement in Line 8 stores `-15` into `x`, and the statement in Line 9 outputs the absolute value of `x`.

 The Web site accompanying this book contains additional programming examples that show how to use some of the other methods of the **class**es `Math` and `Character`.

USER-DEFINED METHODS

Because Java does not provide every method that you will ever need, and designers cannot possibly know a user's specific needs, you must learn to write your own methods.

User-defined methods in Java are classified into two categories:

- **Value-returning methods**—methods that have a return type.
- **Void methods**—methods that do not have a return type.

The next section discusses value-returning methods. Many concepts regarding value-returning methods also apply to void methods. Void methods are discussed later in this chapter.

Value-Returning Methods

The section Predefined Methods introduced some predefined Java methods such as `pow`, `sqrt`, `isLowerCase`, and `toUpperCase`. These are examples of value-returning methods, that is, methods that calculate and return a value. To use these methods in your programs, you must know:

1. The name of the method.
2. The number of **parameters**, if any.
3. The data type of each parameter.
4. The data type of the value computed (that is, the value returned) by the method, called the type of the method.

Because the value returned by a value-returning method is unique, it is natural for you to use the value in one of three ways:

- Save the value for further calculation.
- Use the value in some calculation.
- Print the value.

This suggests that a value-returning method is used in either an assignment statement or an output statement. That is, a value-returning method is used in an expression.

In addition to the four properties just described, one more thing is associated with methods (both value-returning and void):

5. The code required to accomplish the task.

Before we look at the syntax of a user-defined value-returning method, let's review the things associated with such methods. The first four properties become part of what is called the **heading** of the method; the fifth property is called the **body** of the method. Together, these five properties form what is called the **definition** of the method.

 For predefined methods, you need to be concerned only with the first four properties. Software companies do not give out the actual source code, which is the body of the method.

For example, for the method **abs** (*absolute*), the heading might look like:

```
public static int abs(int number)
```

Similarly, the method **abs** might have the following definition:

```
public static int abs(int number)
{
    if (number < 0)
        number = -number;

    return number;
}
```

The variable declared in the heading, within the parentheses, of the method **abs** is called the **formal parameter** of the method **abs**. Thus, the formal parameter of **abs** is **number**.

The program in Example 7-1 contains several statements that use the method **pow**. In Java terminology, we say that the method **pow** is *called* several times. Later in this chapter, we discuss what happens when a method is called.

Suppose that the heading of the method **pow** is:

```
public static double pow(double base, double exponent)
```

In this heading, you can see that the formal parameters of **pow** are **base** and **exponent**. Consider the following statements:

```
double u = 2.5;
double v = 3.0;
double x, y, w;

x = pow(u, v);          //Line 1
y = pow(2.0, 3.2);      //Line 2
w = pow(u, 7);          //Line 3
```

In Line 1, the method **pow** is called with the parameters u and v. In this case, the values of u and v are passed to the method **pow**. In fact, the value of u is copied into **base** and the value of v is copied into **exponent**. The variables u and v that appear in the call to the method **pow** in Line 1 are called **actual parameters** of that call. In Line 2, the method **pow** is called with the parameters **2.0** and **3.2**. In this call, the value **2.0** is copied into **base** and **3.2** is copied into **exponent**. In this call to the method **pow**, the actual parameters are **2.0** and

3.2, respectively. Similarly, in Line 3, the actual parameters of the method pow are u and 7. The value of u is copied into base, and 7.0 is copied into exponent.

We can now formally present the following two definitions:

Formal parameter: A variable declared in the method heading.

Actual parameter: A variable or expression listed in a call to a method.

Syntax: Value-Returning Method

The syntax of a value-returning method is:

```
modifier(s) returnType methodName(formal parameter list)
{
        statements
}
```

In this syntax:

- **modifier(s)** indicates the visibility of the method, that is, where in a program the method can be used (called). Some of the modifiers are **public**, **private**, **protected**, **static**, **abstract**, and **final**. If you include more than one modifier, they must be separated with spaces. You can select one modifier among **public**, **protected**, and **private**. The modifier **public** specifies that the method can be called outside the class; the modifier **private** specifies that the method cannot be used outside the class. Similarly, you can choose one of the modifiers **static** or **abstract**. More information about these modifiers is provided when we discuss classes in general in Chapter 8. Meanwhile, we will use the modifiers **public** and/or **static**, as used in the method main.

- **returnType** is the type of value that the method returns. This type is also called the type of the value-returning method.

- **methodName** is a Java identifier, giving a name to the method.

- Statements enclosed between curly braces form the body of the method.

In Java, **public**, **protected**, **private**, **static**, and **abstract** are reserved words.

 Abstract methods are covered in Chapter 11. Chapter 8 describes, in detail, the meaning of the modifiers **public**, **private**, and **static**.

Syntax: Formal Parameter List

The syntax of a formal parameter list is:

```
dataType identifier, dataType identifier,...
```

Method Call

The syntax to call a value-returning method is:

```
methodName(actual parameter list)
```

Syntax: Actual Parameter List

The syntax of an actual parameter list is:

```
expression or variable, expression or variable, ...
```

Thus, to call a value-returning method, you use its name, with the actual parameters (if any) in parentheses.

A method's formal parameter list can be empty, but the parentheses are still needed. If the formal parameter list is empty, the method heading of the value-returning method takes the following form:

```
modifiers(s) returnType methodName()
```

If the formal parameter list is empty in a method call, the actual parameter list is also empty. In the case of an empty formal parameter list, in a method call the empty parentheses are still needed. Thus, a call to a value-returning method with an empty formal parameter list is:

```
methodName()
```

In a method call, the number of actual parameters, together with their data types, must match the formal parameters in the order given. That is, actual and formal parameters have a one-to-one correspondence.

As stated previously, a value-returning method is called in an expression. The expression can be part of an assignment statement, or an output statement, or a parameter in a method call. A method call in a program causes the body of the called method to execute.

Recall that the heading of the method `main` contains the modifier `static`. The main objective of this chapter is to learn how to write your own methods and use them in a Java application program. Therefore, the methods that you will lean to write in this chapter will be called (used) within the method `main` and/or in other methods of the `class` containing the application program. Because a `static` method cannot call another nonstatic method of the `class`, the heading of the methods that you will learn to write in this chapter will contain the modifier `static`. Chapter 8 discusses the `static` methods (members) of a `class` in detail.

Next, we describe how a value-returning method returns its value.

return Statement

A value-returning method uses a **return**(s) statement to return its value; that is, it passes a value outside the method.

Syntax: return Statement

The **return** statement has the following syntax:

```
return expr;
```

where **expr** is a variable, constant value, or expression. The **expr** is evaluated and its value is returned. The data type of the value that **expr** computes should be compatible with the return type of the method.

In Java, **return** is a reserved word.

When a **return** statement executes in a method, the method immediately terminates and control goes back to the caller.

To put the ideas of this section to work, we'll write a method that determines the larger of two numbers. Because the method compares two numbers, it follows that this method has two parameters and that both parameters are numbers. Assume that the data type of these numbers is floating-point (decimal)—say **double**. Because the larger number is of the type **double**, the method's data type is also **double**. Let's name this method **larger**. The only thing you need to complete this method is the body of the method. Thus, following the syntax of a method, you can write this method as follows:

7

```
public static double larger(double x, double y)
{
    double max;

    if (x >= y)
        max = x;
    else
        max = y;

    return max;
}
```

You can also write this method as follows:

```
public static double larger(double x, double y)
{
    if (x >= y)
        return x;
    else
        return y;
}
```

Because the execution of a **return** statement in a method terminates the function, the preceding definition of the method **larger** can also be written (without the word **else**) as:

```
public static double larger(double x, double y)
{
    if (x >= y)
        return x;

    return y;
}
```

The first form of the method **larger** requires that you use an additional variable **max** (called a **local declaration**, where **max** is a variable local to the method **larger**); the second form does not.

1. In the method definition, x and y are formal parameters.
2. The **return** statement can appear anywhere in the method. Recall that once a **return** statement executes, all subsequent statements are skipped. Thus, it's a good idea to return the value as soon as it is computed.

Example 7-2

Suppose that you have the following declaration:

```java
static Scanner console = new Scanner(System.in);
```

The following Java code illustrates how to use the method `larger` in the method `main`:

```java
public static void main(String[] args)
{
    double one, two, maxNum;                            //Line 1

    System.out.println("The larger of 5 and 6 is "
                    + larger(5, 6));                    //Line 2

    System.out.print("Enter two numbers: ");            //Line 3
    one = console.nextDouble();                         //Line 4
    two = console.nextDouble();                         //Line 5
    System.out.println();                               //Line 6

    System.out.println("The larger of " + one
                    + " and " + two + " is "
                    + larger(one, two));                //Line 7
    System.out.println("The larger of " + one
                    + " and 29 is "
                    + larger(one, 29));                 //Line 8
    maxNum = larger(38.45, 56.78);                      //Line 9
    System.out.println("maxNum = " + maxNum);           //Line 10
}
```

Note the following in Example 7-2:

1. The expression `larger(5, 6)` in Line 2 is a method call, and 5 and 6 are the actual parameters.
2. The expression `larger(one, two)` in Line 7 is a method call. Here, one and two are the actual parameters.
3. The expression `larger(one, 29)` in Line 8 is also a method call. Here, one and 29 are the actual parameters.
4. The expression `larger(38.45, 56.78)` in Line 9 is a method call. In this call, the actual parameters are 38.45 and 56.78. In this statement, the value returned by the method `larger` is assigned to the variable `maxNum`.

In a method call, you specify only the actual parameter, not its data type. For example, notice that in Example 7-2 the statements in Lines 2, 7, 8, and 9 show how to call the method `larger` with the actual parameters. However, the following statements contain incorrect calls to the method `larger` and would result in syntax errors. (Assume that all variables are properly declared.)

```java
x = larger(int one, 29); //illegal
y = larger(int one, int 29); //illegal
System.out.println(larger(int one, int two)); //illegal
```

Once a method is written, you can use it anywhere it is "visible" in the program (the rules for visibility within a class, called the *scope*, are discussed later in this chapter). The method `larger` compares two numbers and returns the larger of the two. Let's now write another method that uses this method to determine the largest of three numbers. We call this method `compareThree`.

```
public static double compareThree(double x, double y, double z)
{
    return larger(x, larger(y, z));
}
```

In the definition of the method `compareThree`, first the larger of `y` and `z` is determined, which is then compared with `x`. Finally, the `return` statement returns the largest number. In the method heading, `x`, `y`, and `z` are formal parameters.

Final Program

You now know enough to write the entire program, compile it, and run it. The following program uses the functions `larger`, `compareThree`, and `main` to determine the larger/largest of two or three numbers.

```
//Program: Largest of three numbers

import java.util.*;

public class LargerNumber
{
    static Scanner console = new Scanner(System.in);

    public static void main(String[] args)
    {
        double num1, num2;                                      //Line 1

        System.out.println("The Line 2: The larger of 5.6 "
                        + "and 10.8 is "
                        + larger(5.6, 10.8));                   //Line 2
        System.out.print("Line 3: Enter two numbers: ");       //Line 3
        num1 = console.nextDouble();                           //Line 4
        num2 = console.nextDouble();                           //Line 5
        System.out.println();                                  //Line 6

        System.out.println("Line 7: The larger of "
                        + num1 + " and " + num2 + " is "
                        + larger (num1, num2));                //Line 7
```

```
        System.out.println("Line 8: The largest of 23.5, "
                         + "34.6, and 12 is "
                         + compareThree(23.5, 34.6, 12));   //Line 8
    }

    public static double larger(double x, double y)
    {
        if (x >= y)
            return x;
        else
            return y;
    }

    public static double compareThree(double x, double y, double z)
    {
        return larger(x, larger(y, z));
    }
}
```

Sample Run: In this sample run, the user input is shaded.
```
Line 2: The larger of 5.6 and 10.8 is 10.8
Line 3: Enter two numbers: 34 43

Line 7: The larger of 34.0 and 43.0 is 43.0
Line 8: The largest of 23.5, 34.6, and 12 is 34.6
```

 You can put methods within a class in any order.

 A value-returning method must return a value. Consider the following method, secret, that takes as a parameter an **int** value. If the value of the parameter, x, is greater than 5, it should return twice the value of x; otherwise, it should return the value of x.

```
public static int secret(int x)
{
    if (x > 5)            //Line 1
        return 2 * x;     //Line 2
}
```

Because this is a value-returning method of the type **int**, it must return a value of the type **int**. Suppose the value of x is 10. Then the expression, x > 5, in Line 1, evaluates to **true**. So the **return** statement in Line 2 returns the value 20. Now suppose that x is 3. The expression, x > 5, in Line 1, now evaluates to **false**. The **if** statement therefore fails and the **return** statement in Line 2 *does not* execute. However, the body of the method has no more statements to be executed. It thus follows that if the value of **x** is less than or equal to 5, the method does not contain any valid **return** statements to return the value of **x**. In this case, in fact, the compiler generates an error message such as **missing return statement**.

The correct definition of the function **secret** is:

```
public static int secret(int x)
{
    if (x > 5)              //Line 1
        return 2 * x;       //Line 2

    return x;               //Line 3
}
```

Here, if the value of **x** is less than or equal to 5, the **return** statement in Line 3 executes, which returns the value of **x**. On the other hand, if the value of **x** is, say 10, the **return** statement in Line 2 executes, which returns the value 20 and also terminates the method.

Following is an example of a method that returns a Boolean value.

PROGRAMMING EXAMPLE: PALINDROME NUMBER

In this example, we write a program that determines whether an integer is a palindrome. An integer is a **palindrome** if it reads forward and backward in the same way. For example, the integers 5, 44, 434, -1881, and 789656987 are all palindromes.

Input   An integer (positive or negative)

Output   A message indicating whether the integer is a palindrome

Problem Analysis and Algorithm Design

The first thing the program does is read the integer. Because the input to the program is a string, the string containing the integer is converted into the integer. If the integer is negative, the program changes it to positive. The next step is to convert the integer back to a string and then determine whether the string is a palindrome.

1. Read the string containing the integer.
2. Convert the string into the integer.
3. If the integer is negative, change it to positive.
4. Convert the integer into a string.
5. Determine whether the string is a palindrome.

Next, we design the method `isPalindrome` that returns **true** if a string is a palindrome and **false** otherwise.

Method `isPalindrome`   The method `isPalindrome` takes a string as a parameter and returns **true** if the string is a palindrome, **false** otherwise. Suppose that the `String` variable `str` refers to the string. To be specific, suppose that `str` refers to the string `"845548"`. The length of this string is 6. Recall that the position of the first character of a string is 0, the position of the second character is 1, and so on.

To determine whether the string `str`, `"845548"` is a palindrome, first we compare the character at position 0 with the character at position 5. If these two characters are the same, then we compare the character at position 1 with the character at position 4; if these two characters are the same, then we compare the characters at position 2 and 3. If we find mismatched characters, the string `str` is not a palindrome, and the method returns **false**. It follows that we need two variables, `i` and `j`; `i` is initialized to 0 and `j` is initialized to the last character of the string. We then compare the characters at positions `i` and `j`. If the characters at positions `i` and `j` are the same, we then increment `i` and decrement `j`, and continue this process. If the characters at positions `i` and `j` are not the same, then the method returns **false**. Note that we need to compare only the characters in the first half of the string with the characters in the second half of the string in the order described above. This discussion translates into the following algorithm:

1. Find the length of the string. Because `str` is a `String` variable, we can use the method `length` of the **class** `String` to find the length of the string. Suppose `len = str.length();`.

2. Set `j = len - 1`. (Recall that in a string, the position of the first character is 0, the position of the second character is 1, and so on. Therefore, the position of the last character in the string `str` is `len - 1`.)

3. Use a **for** loop to compare the characters in the first half of the string with those in the second half. Now `len` specifies the length of the string, so `len - 1` specifies the position of the last character in the string. Therefore, `(len - 1) / 2` gives the position of the character at the mid position in the string. Initially `j` is set to `len - 1` and we will use a variable, `i` (**for** loop control variable), initialized to 0. After each iteration, `i` is incremented by 1 and `j` is decremented by 1. Therefore, when `i` is `(len - 1) / 2`, the value of `i` gives the position of the character at the mid position in the string. Moreover, notice that when `i` is at the last character of the first half of the string, `j` is at the first character of the second half of the string. The required **for** loop is:

```
for (i = 0; i <= (len - 1)/2; i++)
{
  a. if (str.charAt(i) is not equal to str.charAt(j))
       return false;
  b. j--;
}
```

4. Return **true**.

The following method implements this algorithm:

```java
public static boolean isPalindrome(String str)
{
    int len = str.length();                      //Step 1
    int i, j;

    j = len - 1;                                 //Step 2

    for (i = 0; i <= (len - 1)/2; i++)           //Step 3
    {
        if (str.charAt(i) !=  str.charAt(j))     //Step 3.a
            return false;
        j--;                                     //Step 3.b
    }

    return true;                                 //Step 4
}
```

Complete Program Listing

```java
//Program Palindrome

import javax.swing.JOptionPane;

public class Palindrome
{
    public static void main(String[] args)
    {
        long num, temp;
        String inputStr, outputStr;

        inputStr =
            JOptionPane.showInputDialog("Enter an integer, "
                                    + "positive or negative");

        num = Long.parseLong(inputStr);
        temp = num;

        if (num <= 0)
        {
            num = -num;
            inputStr = inputStr.valueOf(num);
        }

        if (isPalindrome(inputStr))
            outputStr = temp + " is a palindrome";
```

```java
        else
            outputStr = temp + " is not a palindrome";

        JOptionPane.showMessageDialog(null, outputStr,
                            "Palindrome Program",
                            JOptionPane.INFORMATION_MESSAGE);
        System.exit(0);
    }

    public static boolean isPalindrome(String str)
    {
        int len = str.length();                       //Step 1
        int i, j;

        j = len - 1;                                  //Step 2

        for (i = 0; i <= (len - 1)/2; i++)            //Step 3
        {
            if (str.charAt(i) !=  str.charAt(j))      //Step 3.a
                return false;
            j--;                                      //Step 3.b
        }

        return true;                                  //Step 4
    }
}
```

Sample Run 1: Figure 7-1 shows Sample Run 1.

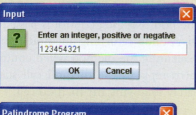

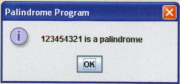

Figure 7-1   Sample Run 1 of the Palindrome program

Sample Run 2: Figure 7-2 shows Sample Run 2.

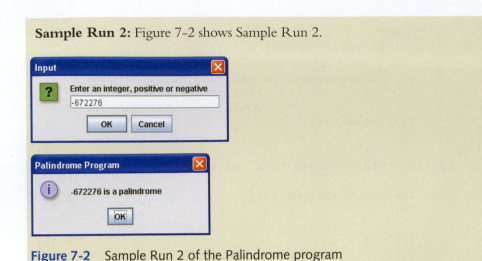

Figure 7-2 Sample Run 2 of the Palindrome program

FLOW OF EXECUTION

As you know, a Java application program is a collection of classes, and a class is a collection of methods and data members. In a Java program, methods can appear in any order. However, when the program executes, the first statement in the method `main` always executes first, regardless of where in the program the method `main` is placed. Other methods execute only when they are called.

A method call statement transfers control to the first statement in the body of the method. In general, after the last statement of the called method executes, control is passed back to the point immediately following the method call. A value-returning method returns a value. Therefore, for value-returning methods, after executing the method when control goes back to the caller, the value that the method returns replaces the method call statement. The execution then continues at the point immediately following the method call.

PROGRAMMING EXAMPLE: LARGEST NUMBER

In this programming example, the method `larger` is used to determine the largest number from a set of numbers, in this case the largest number from a set of 10 numbers. You can easily modify this program to accommodate any set of numbers.

Input   A set of 10 numbers

Output   The largest of 10 numbers

Problem Analysis and Algorithm Design

Suppose that the input data is:

```
15 20 7 8 28 21 43 12 35 3
```

Read the first number of the data set. Because this is the only number read to this point, you can assume that it is the largest number and call it `max`. Next, read the second number and call it `num`. Now compare `max` and `num`, and store the larger number into `max`. Now `max` contains the larger of the first two numbers. Next, read the third number. Compare it with `max` and store the larger number into `max`. At this point, `max` contains the largest of the first three numbers. Read the next number, compare it with `max`, and store the larger into `max`. Repeat this process for each remaining number in the data set. Eventually, `max` will contain the largest number in the data set. This discussion translates into the following algorithm:

1. Get the first number. Because this is the only number that you have read so far, it is the largest number so far. Save it in a variable called `max`.
2. For each remaining number in the list:
   a. Get the next number. Store it in a variable called `num`.
   b. Compare `num` and `max`. If `max < num`, then `num` is the new largest number; update the value of `max` by copying `num` into `max`. If `max >= num`, discard `num`; that is, do nothing.
3. Because `max` now contains the largest number, print it.

To find the larger of two numbers, the program uses the method `larger`.

Complete Program Listing

```java
//Program: Largest number

import java.util.*;

public class LargestNumber
{
    static Scanner console = new Scanner(System.in);
```

```java
public static void main(String[] args)
{
    double num;          //variable to hold the current number
    double max;          //variable to hold the larger number
    int count;           //loop control variable

    System.out.println("Enter 10 numbers:");

    num = console.nextDouble();                          //Step 1
    max = num;                                           //Step 1

    for (count = 1; count < 10; count++)                 //Step 2
    {
        num = console.nextDouble();                      //Step 2a
        max = larger(max, num);                          //Step 2b
    }

    System.out.println("The largest number is "
                        + max);                          //Step 3
}

public static double larger(double x, double y)
{
    if (x >= y)
        return x;
    else
        return y;
}
}
```

Sample Run: In this sample run, the user input is shaded.
```
Enter 10 numbers:
10.5 56.34 73.3 42 22 67 88.55 26 62 11
The largest number is 88.55
```

VOID METHODS

Void methods (methods that do not have a **return** type) and value-returning methods have similar structures. Both have a heading part and a statement part. You can place user-defined void methods either before or after the method **main**. However, program execution always begins with the first statement in the method **main**. Because a void method does not have a data type, **returnType** in the heading part and the **return** statement in the body of the void method are meaningless. However, in a void method, you can use the **return** statement without any value; it is typically used to exit the method early. Like value-returning methods, void methods may or may not have formal parameters.

Because void methods do not have a data type, they are not used (that is, called) in an expression. A call to a void method is a stand-alone statement. Thus, to call a void method, you use the method name together with the actual parameters (if any) in a stand-alone statement. Moreover, when a void method exits, control goes back to the calling environment at the statement immediately following the point where it was called.

Void Methods without Parameters

This section discusses void methods that do not have formal parameters.

Method Definition

The general form (syntax) of a void method without parameters is as follows:

```
modifier(s) void methodName()
{
      statements
}
```

where `modifier(s)` are as previously described. (Until we discuss classes in general, we will use the modifiers **public** and/or **static**.)

Method Call (Within the Class)

A method call has the following syntax:

```
methodName();
```

Because these methods do not have parameters, within a class such methods are usually good for displaying information about the program or for printing statements. Consider the program in Example 7-3.

Example 7-3

Suppose you want to print the following banner to announce the annual spring sale. (See a similar program in Chapter 2, Programming Exercise 3.)

```
*****************************
*****************************
********* Annual  **********
*****************************
*****************************
******* Spring Sale **********
*****************************
*****************************
```

The banner starts with two lines of stars. After printing the line containing the text `Annual`, you need to print another two lines of stars. After printing the line containing the text `Spring Sale`, you need to print two more lines of stars. You can write a method that prints two lines of stars and call it whenever you need it. The complete program looks like this:

```
public class Banner
{
    public static void main (String[] args)
    {
        printStars();                                           //Line 1
        System.out.println("********** Annual   ***********");//Line 2
        printStars();                                           //Line 3
        System.out.println("******* Spring Sale **********");//Line 4
        printStars();                                           //Line 5

    }

    public static void printStars()
    {
        System.out.println("******************************");
        System.out.println("******************************");
    }
}
```

Sample Run:

```
******************************
******************************
********** Annual   **********
******************************
******************************
******* Spring Sale **********
******************************
******************************
```

In Line 1, the method `printStars` is called and it outputs the first two lines of the output. The statement in Line 2 outputs the line of stars containing the text `Annual`, which is the third line of the output. In Line 3, the method `printStars` is called again and it outputs the next two lines of the output. The statement in Line 4 then outputs the line of stars containing the text `Spring Sale`, which is the sixth line of the output. In Line 5, the method `printStars` is called again and it outputs the last two lines of the output.

The statement `printStars();` in the method `main` is a method call.

In the previous program, you can replace the method `printStars` with the following method:

```
public static void printStars()
{
    int stars, lines;

    for (lines = 1; lines <= 2; lines++)          //Line 1
    {
        for (stars = 1; stars <= 30; stars++)     //Line 2
            System.out.print("*");                //Line 3

        System.out.println();                     //Line 4
    }
}
```

In this method definition, the outer **for** loop (Line 1) executes twice. For each iteration of the outer **for** loop (Line 1), the inner **for** loop (Line 2) executes 30 times, each time printing 30 stars in a line. The statement in Line 3 prints each star. The output statement in Line 4 positions the insertion point at the beginning of the next line on the standard output device. Because the outer **for** loop executes twice, this method outputs two lines of stars with 30 stars in each line.

You would agree that the definition of the method `printStars` using **for** loops to output 2 lines of stars with 30 stars in each line is much easier to modify than the definition of `printStars` given in Example 7-3. If you need to output 5 lines of stars instead of 2 lines, for instance, you can replace the number 2 (in the first **for** loop, Line 1) with the number 5. Similarly, if you need to output 40 stars instead of 30 stars in each line, you can replace the number 30 (in the second **for** loop, Line 2) with the number 40. As you will soon discover, the definition of the method `printStars` using **for** loops is much easier to modify to establish the communication links with the calling method (such as the method `main`) and to do different things each time the method `printStars` is called.

Void Methods with Parameters

In the previous program, the method `printStars` always prints two lines of stars, with 30 stars in each line. Suppose that you want to print the following pattern (a triangle of stars):

```
   *
  * *
 * * *
* * * *
```

You could write a method similar to the method `printStars`. However, if you need to extend this pattern to 20 lines, the method `printStars` will have to be edited and modified. Moreover, every time you call the method `printStars`, it prints the same number of lines; the method `printStars` is inflexible. However, if you can somehow tell the method `printStars` how many lines to print, you can considerably enhance its flexibility. A communication link must exist between the calling method and the called method. Parameters provide this link between the calling method (such as `main`) and the called method. They enable methods to manipulate different data each time they are called.

Method Definition

The definition of a void method with parameters has the following syntax:

```
modifier(s) void methodName(formal parameter list)
{
    statements
}
```

Formal Parameter List

A formal parameter list has the following syntax:

```
dataType variable, dataType variable, ...
```

Method Call

A method call has the following syntax:

```
methodName(actual parameter list);
```

Actual Parameter List

An actual parameter list has the following syntax:

```
expression or variable, expression or variable, ...
```

As with value-returning methods, in a method call the number of actual parameters, together with their data types, must match the formal parameters in the order given. Actual and formal parameters have a one-to-one correspondence. A method call causes the body of the called method to execute. Two examples of void methods with parameters follow:

Example 7-4

Consider the following method heading:

```
public static void funexp(int a, double b, char c, String name)
```

The method `funexp` has four formal parameters: (1) `a`, a parameter of the type `int`;, (2) `b`, a parameter of the type `double`;, (3) `c`, a parameter of the type `char`, and (4) `name`, a parameter of the type `String`.

Example 7-5

Consider the following method heading:

```
public static void expfun(int one, DoubleClass two, char three,
                        String four)
```

The method **expfun** has four formal parameters: (1) **one**, a parameter of the type **int**;, (2) **two**, a parameter of the **DoubleClass**; type, (3) **three**, a parameter of the type **char**, and (4) **four**, a parameter of the type **String**.

Let's now write the Java program to print the pattern (triangle of stars) given at the beginning of this section.

Example 7-6

The following Java program prints a triangle of stars:

```
//Program: Print a triangle of stars

import java.util.*;

public class TriangleOfStars
{
    static Scanner console = new Scanner(System.in);

    public static void main (String[] args)
    {
        int numberOfLines;
        int counter;
        int numberOfBlanks;

        System.out.print("Enter the number of star lines "
                    + "(1 to 20) to be printed: ");        //Line 1
        numberOfLines = console.nextInt();                 //Line 2
        System.out.println();                              //Line 3

        while (numberOfLines < 0 || numberOfLines > 20)    //Line 4
        {
            System.out.println("The number of star "
                        + "lines should be between "
                        + "1 and 20");                      //Line 5
            System.out.print("Enter the number of star "
                        + "lines (1 to 20) to be "
                        + "printed: ");                     //Line 6
```

```
            numberOfLines = console.nextInt();              //Line 7
            System.out.println();                           //Line 8
        }

        numberOfBlanks = 30;                                //Line 9

        for (counter = 1; counter <= numberOfLines;
                          counter++)                        //Line 10
        {
            printStars(numberOfBlanks, counter);            //Line 11
            numberOfBlanks--;                               //Line 12
        }
    }

    public static void printStars(int blanks, int starsInLine)
    {
        int count;

        for (count = 1; count <= blanks; count++)           //Line 13
            System.out.print(" ");                          //Line 14
        for (count = 1; count <= starsInLine; count++)      //Line 15
            System.out.print(" *");                         //Line 16
        System.out.println();                               //Line 17
    }
}
```

Sample Run: In this sample run, the user input is shaded.
Enter the number of star lines (1 to 20) to be printed: 15

In this program, the statement (see Line 11):

`printStars(numberOfBlanks, counter);`

in the method **main** is a method call. The variables **numberOfBlanks** and **counter** are actual parameters.

The method **printStars** works as follows. The method **printStars** has two parameters. Whenever the method **printStars** executes, it outputs a line of stars with a certain number of blanks before the stars. The number of blanks and the number of stars in a line are passed as parameters to the method **printStars**. The first parameter, **blanks**, tells how many blanks to print; the second parameter, **starsInLine**, tells how many stars to print in a line. If the value of the parameter **blanks** is 30, for instance, then the first **for** loop (Line 13) in the method **printStars** executes 30 times and prints 30 blanks. Also, because you want to print spaces between the stars, every iteration of the second **for** loop (Line 15) in the method **printStars** prints the string " *" (Line 16)—a blank followed by a star.

In the method **main**, the user is first asked to specify how many lines of stars to print (Line 1). (In this program, the user is restricted to 20 lines because a triangular grid of up to 20 lines fits nicely on the screen.) Because the program is restricted to only 20 lines, the **while** loop in Lines 4 through 8 ensures that the program prints the triangular grid of stars only if the number of lines is between 1 and 20.

The **for** loop (Line 10) in the method **main** calls the method **printStars** (Line 11). Every iteration of this **for** loop specifies the number of blanks followed by the number of stars to print in a line, using the variables **numberOfBlanks** and **counter**. Every call of the method **printStars** receives one fewer blank and one more star than the previous call. For example, the first iteration of the **for** loop in the method **main** specifies 30 blanks and 1 star (which are passed as the parameters, **numberOfBlanks** and **counter**, to the method **printStars**). The **for** loop then:

1. Decrements the number of blanks by 1. This is done by executing the following statement in Line 12:

   ```
   numberOfBlanks--;
   ```

2. At the end of the **for** loop, the number of stars is incremented by 1 for the next iteration. This is done by executing the update statement, **counter++** (Line 10), in the **for** statement, which increments the value of the variable **counter** by 1.

In other words, the second call of the method **printStars** receives 29 blanks and 2 stars as parameters.

PRIMITIVE DATA TYPE VARIABLES AS PARAMETERS

In Chapter 3 you learned that Java has two categories of variables—primitive type variables and reference variables. Before considering examples of void methods with parameters, let's make the following observation about variables of primitive types and reference variables. When a method is called, the value of the actual parameter is copied into the corresponding formal parameter. If a formal parameter is a variable of a primitive data type, then after copying the value of the actual parameter, there is no connection between the formal parameter and the actual parameter. That is, the formal parameter has its own copy of the data. Therefore, during program execution, the formal parameter manipulates the data stored in its own memory space. The program in Example 7-7 further illustrates how a primitive data type formal parameter works.

Example 7-7

The following program shows how a formal parameter of a primitive data type works:

```java
//Example 7-7
//Program illustrating how a formal parameter of a
//primitive data type works.

public class PrimitiveTypeParameters
{
    public static void main(String[] args)
    {
        int number = 6;                                     //Line 1

        System.out.println("Line 2: Before calling the "
                        + "method funcPrimFormalParam, "
                        + "number = " + number);            //Line 2

        funcPrimFormalParam(number);                        //Line 3

        System.out.println("Line 4: After calling the "
                        + "method funcPrimFormalParam, "
                        + "number = " + number);            //Line 4
    }

    public static void funcPrimFormalParam(int num)
    {
        System.out.println("Line 5: In the method "
                        + "funcPrimFormalParam, before "
                        + "changing, num = " + num);        //Line 5

        num = 15;                                           //Line 6

        System.out.println("Line 7: In the method "
                        + "funcPrimFormalParam, after "
                        + "changing, num = " + num);        //Line 7
    }
}
```

Sample Run:
```
Line 2: Before calling the method funcPrimFormalParam, number = 6
Line 5: In the method funcPrimFormalParam, before changing, num = 6
Line 7: In the method funcPrimFormalParam, after changing, num = 15
Line 4: After calling the method funcPrimFormalParam, number = 6
```

The preceding program works as follows. The execution begins at the method `main`. The statement in Line 1 declares and initializes the `int` variable `number`. The statement in Line 2 outputs the value of `number` before calling the method `funcPrimFormalParam`. The statement in Line 3 calls the method `funcPrimFormalParam`. The value of the variable `number` is passed to the formal parameter `num`. Control now transfers to the method `funcPrimFormalParam`. The statement in Line 5 outputs the value of `num` before changing its value. The statement in Line 6 changes the value of `num` to `15`, and the statement in Line 7 outputs the value of `num`. After this statement executes, the method `funcPrimFormalParam` exits and control goes back to the method `main` at Line 4. The statement in Line 4 outputs the value of `number` after calling the method `funcPrimFormalParam`. As you can see from the output, the value of `number`, as shown by the output of the statements in Lines 2 and 4, remains the same even though the value of its corresponding formal parameter `num` was changed within the method `funcPrimFormalParam`.

After copying data, a formal parameter of the primitive data type has no connection with the actual parameter, so a formal parameter of the primitive data type cannot pass any result back to the calling method. When the method executes, any changes made to the formal parameters do not in any way affect the actual parameters. The actual parameter has no knowledge of what is happening to the formal parameter. Thus, formal parameters of the primitive data types cannot pass information outside the method; formal parameters of the primitive data types provide only a one-way link between the actual parameters and formal parameters.

REFERENCE VARIABLES AS PARAMETERS

The program in Example 7-7 illustrates how a formal parameter of a primitive data type works. Now suppose that a formal parameter is a reference variable. Here, also, the value of the actual parameter is copied into the corresponding formal parameter, but there is a slight difference. Recall that a reference variable does not store data directly in its own memory space. We use the operator **new** to allocate memory for an object belonging to a specific class, and a reference variable of that class type contains the address of the allocated memory space. Therefore, when we pass the value of the actual parameter to the corresponding formal parameter, after copying the value of the actual parameter, both the actual and the formal parameters refer to the same memory space, that is, the same object. Therefore, if the formal parameter changes the value of the object, it also changes the value of the object of the actual parameter.

Because a reference variable contains the address (that is, memory location) of the actual data, both the formal and the value parameters refer to the same object. Therefore, reference variables can pass one or more values from a method and can change the value of the actual parameter.

Reference variables as parameters are useful in three situations:

- When you want to return more than one value from a method

- When the value of the actual object needs to be changed

- When passing the address would save memory space and time, relative to copying a large amount of data

As illustrated by the program in Example 7-7, if a formal parameter is of the primitive data type and the corresponding actual parameter is a variable, then the formal parameter cannot change the value of the actual parameter. In other words, changing the value of a formal parameter of the primitive data type has no effect on the actual parameter. So, how do we pass the values of primitive data types outside the method? As described in the preceding paragraph, only reference variables can pass values outside the method. Corresponding to each primitive data type, Java provides a class so that the values of primitive data types can be considered objects. For example, you can use the **class** Integer to treat **int** values as objects, the **class** Double to treat **double** values as objects, and so on. These wrapper classes were introduced in Chapter 3 and described in some detail in Chapter 6. As discussed in Chapter 6, even though you can uses the **class** Integer to treat **int** values as objects, the **class** Integer does not provide any method to change the value of an existing Integer object. The same is true of other wrapper classes. Chapter 6 introduced the **class** IntClass so that values of the **int** type could be wrapped in an object. The **class** IntClass also provides methods to change the value of an IntClass object. You can review these classes in Chapter 6 and Appendix D. Appendix D also shows how to use these classes in a program.

Example 7-8: Calculate Grade

Consider the following program. Given a course score (a value between 0 and 100), it determines a student's course grade. This program to determine the course grade based on the course score has three methods: main, getScore, and printGrade. These three methods are described as follows:

1. main

    a. Get the course score.

    b. Print the course grade.

2. getScore

    a. Prompt the user for the input.

    b. Get the input.

    c. Print the course score.

3. printGrade

    a. Calculate the course grade.

    b. Print the course grade.

The complete program is as follows:

```java
//Program: Compute the grade
//This program reads a course score and prints the
//associated course grade.

import java.util.*;

public class Example7_8
{
    static Scanner console = new Scanner(System.in);

    public static void main (String[] args)
    {
        DoubleClass courseScore = new DoubleClass();

        System.out.println("Line 1: Based on the course "
                         + "score, this program "
                         + "computes the course grade.");   //Line 1

        getScore(courseScore);                              //Line 2
        printGrade(courseScore.getNum());                   //Line 3
    }

    public static void getScore(DoubleClass score)
    {
        double s;                                           //Line 4

        System.out.print("Line 5: Enter the "
                        + "course score: ");                //Line 5
        s = console.nextDouble();                           //Line 6
        System.out.println();                               //Line 7

        score.setNum(s);                                    //Line 8

        System.out.println("Line 9: The course "
                         + "score is " + s);                //Line 9
    }

    public static void printGrade(double testScore)
    {
        System.out.print("Line 10: Your grade for "
                        + "the course is ");                //Line 10
```

7

```
        if (testScore >= 90)                                    //Line 11
            System.out.println("A");
        else if (testScore >= 80)
                System.out.println("B");
        else if (testScore >= 70)
                System.out.println("C");
        else if (testScore >= 60)
                System.out.println("D");
        else
            System.out.println("F");
    }
}
```

Sample Run: In this sample run, the user input is shaded.

```
Line 1: Based on the course score, this program computes the course grade.
Line 5: Enter course score: 90.50

Line 9: The course score is 90.5
Line 10: Your grade for the course is A
```

This program works as follows: The statement in Line 1 prints the first line of the output. (See the Sample Run.) The statement in Line 2 calls the method `getScore` with the actual parameter `courseScore` (a reference variable of the `DoubleClass` type declared in `main`). The formal parameter `score`, of the method `getScore`, is a reference variable of the `DoubleClass` type, which receives the value of `courseScore`. Thus, both `score` and `courseScore` point to the same object. (See Figure 7-3.) Note that the method `getScore` also has a local variable, `s`, declared in Line 4, of the type **double**.

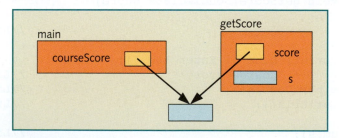

Figure 7-3   Variable `courseScore` and the parameter `score`

Any changes that `score` makes to the object immediately change the value of the object to which `courseScore` points.

Control is then transferred to the method `getScore`. The statement in Line 4 declares the variable `s` of the type **double**. The statement in Line 5 prints the second line of output (see the Sample Run). This statement prompts the user to enter the course `score`. The statement in Line 7 reads and stores the value entered by the user (`90.50` in the Sample Run) in `s`.

The statement in Line 8 copies the value of **s** into the object to which **score** points. Thus, at this point, the value of the object to which **score** and **courseScore** point is 90.50. (See Figure 7-4.)

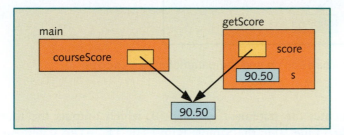

Figure 7-4   Variable **courseScore** and the parameter **score** after the statement in Line 8 executes

Next the statement in Line 9 outputs the value of **s** as shown by the third line of the Sample Run. After the statement in Line 9 executes, control goes back to the method **main**. (See Figure 7-5.)

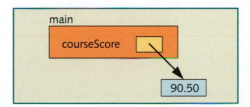

Figure 7-5   Variable **courseScore** after the statement in Line 9 executes and control goes back to **main**

The statement in Line 3 executes next. It is a method call to the method **printGrade** with the actual parameter **courseScore.getNum()**. In the expression **courseScore.getNum()**, the method **getNum** of the **class** DoubleClass returns the value of the object to which **courseScore** points, the course score. Because the formal parameter **testScore** of the method **printScore** is of a primitive data type, the parameter **testScore** receives the course score. Thus, the value of **testScore** is 90.50. (See Figure 7-6.)

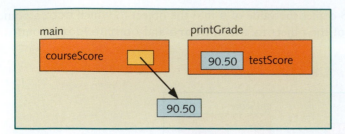

Figure 7-6   Variable `courseScore` and the parameter `testscore`

Next, the program executes the statement in Line 10, which outputs the fourth line. (See the statement marked Line 10 in the Sample Run.) The **if...else** statement in Line 11 determines and outputs the grade for the course. Notice that the output of the **if...else** statement is part of the fourth line of the output. (See the Sample Run.) After the **if...else** statement executes, control goes back to the method **main**. Because there are no more statements in the method **main**, the program terminates.

In this program, the method **main** first calls the method **getScore** to get the course score from the user. The method **main** then calls the method **printGrade** to calculate and print the grade based on the course score. The course score is returned by the method **getScore**; later this course score is used by the method **printGrade**. Because the value retrieved by the **getScore** method is used later in the program, the method **getScore** must pass this value to the calling environment. Thus, the formal parameter that holds this value must be an object.

Parameters and Memory Allocation

When a method is called, memory for its formal parameters and variables declared in the body of the method, called **local variables**, is allocated in the method data area. The value of the actual parameter is copied into the memory cell of its corresponding formal parameter. If the parameter is an object (of a class type), both the actual parameter and the formal parameter refer to the same memory space.

Reference Variables of the `String` Type as Parameters: A Precaution

Recall that reference variables do not directly contain the data. Reference variables contain the address of the memory space where the data is stored. Moreover, we use the operator **new** to allocate memory space of a specific type. However, in the case of reference variables of the type **String**, we can use the assignment operator to allocate memory space to store a string and assign the string to a **String** variable. Consider the following statements:

```
String str;                    //Line 1
```

The statement:

```
str = "Hello";                 //Line 2
```

is equivalent to the statement:

```
str = new String("Hello");     //Line 3
```

Figure 7-7 illustrates this concept.

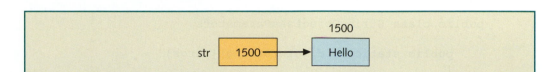

Figure 7-7   Variable `str` and the string object

We assume that the address of the memory space where the string `"Hello"` is stored is 1500. Now suppose that you execute either the statement:

```
str = "Hello There";
```

or the statement:

```
str = str + " There";
```

Figure 7-8 illustrates the effect of either of these statements.

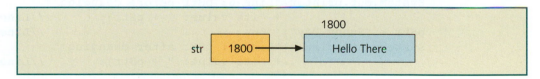

Figure 7-8   `str` after the statement `str = "Hello There";` or
              `str = str + " There";` executes

Note that the string `"Hello There"` is stored at a different location. It is now clear that any time you use the assignment operator (or the operator **new**) to assign a string to a `String` variable, the computer allocates a different memory space large enough to store the string. In other words, when a string is created and assigned to a `String` variable, the *string cannot be changed*. Moreover, the **class** `String` does not contain any method that allows you to change an existing string.

If you pass a `String` variable, that is, a reference variable of the `String` type, as a parameter to a method, and within the method you use the assignment operator to change the string, you might think that you have changed the string assigned to the actual parameter. But this does not happen. The string of the actual parameter remains unchanged; a new string is assigned to the formal parameter. The following example further illustrates this concept.

Example 7-9: String objects as parameters

Consider the following program:

```java
//Program: String Objects as Parameters

public class StringObjectsAsParameters
{
    public static void main(String[] args)
    {
        String str = "Hello";                                    //Line 1

        System.out.println("Line 2: str before calling "
                           + "the method stringParameter: "
                           + str);                               //Line 2
        stringParameter(str);                                    //Line 3
        System.out.println("Line 4: str after calling "
                           + "the method stringParameter: "
                           + str);                               //Line 4
    }

    public static void stringParameter(String pStr)
    {
        System.out.println("Line 5: In the method "
                           + "stringParameter");                 //Line 5
        System.out.println("Line 6: pStr before changing "
                           + "its value: " + pStr);              //Line 6
        pStr = "Sunny Day";                                      //Line 7
        System.out.println("Line 8: pStr after changing "
                           + "its value: " + pStr);              //Line 8
    }
}
```

Sample Run:
```
Line 2: str before calling the method stringParameter: Hello
Line 5: In the method stringParameter
Line 6: pStr before changing its value: Hello
Line 8: pStr after changing its value: Sunny Day
Line 4: str after calling the method stringParameter: Hello
```

The preceding program works as follows: The statement in Line 1 declares `str` to be a `String` variable and assigns the string `"Hello"` to it. (See Figure 7-9.)

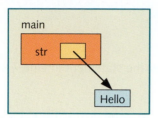

Figure 7-9   Variable `str` after the statement in Line 1 executes

The statement in Line 2 outputs the first line of output. The statement in Line 3 calls the method `stringParameter`. The actual parameter is `str` and the formal parameter is `pStr`, so the value of `str` is copied into `pStr`. Because both these parameters are reference variables, `str` and `pStr` point to the same string, which is `"Hello"`. (See Figure 7-10.)

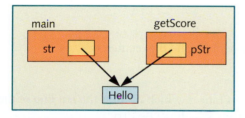

Figure 7-10 Variable `str` and the parameter `pStr` before the statement in Line 5 executes

Control is then transferred to the method `stringParameter`. The next statement executed is in Line 5, which outputs the second line of the output. The statement in Line 6 outputs the third line of the output. Notice that this statement also outputs the string referenced by `pStr` and the printed value is the string `"Hello"`. The next statement executed is in Line 7. This statement uses the assignment operator and assigns the string `"Sunny Day"` to `pStr`. After the statement in Line 7 executes, `str` no longer refers to the same string as does `pStr`. The statement in Line 7, in fact, uses the operator **new** to allocate memory space, stores the string in it, and assigns this string to `pStr`. (See Figure 7-11.)

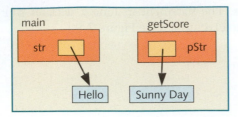

Figure 7-11 Variable `str` and the parameter `pStr` after the statement in Line 7 executes

The statement in Line 8 outputs the fourth line. Notice that the printed value is the string `"Sunny Day"`. After this statement executes, control goes back to the method `main` at Line 4. (See Figure 7-12).

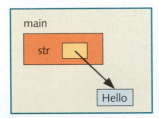

Figure 7-12 Variable `str` after the statement in Line 8 executes

Therefore, the next statement executed is in Line 4, which outputs the last line of the output. Notice that `str` still refers to the same string, which is `"Hello"`.

 The preceding example shows that you should be careful when passing `String` variables as parameters.

class StringBuffer

If you want to pass strings as parameters to a method and want to change the actual parameters, you can use the **class** `StringBuffer`. The **class** `StringBuffer` is similar to the **class** `String`. However, strings assigned to `StringBuffer` variables can be altered.

The **class** `StringBuffer` contains the method `append`, which allows you to append a string to an existing string, and the method `delete`, which allows you to delete all the characters of the string. It also contains other methods to manipulate a string. (See Appendix E for various methods associated with the **class** `StringBuffer`.)

The assignment operator *cannot* be used with `StringBuffer` variables. You must use the operator **new** to (*initially*) allocate memory space for a string.

The following example illustrates how objects of the type `StringBuffer` are passed as parameters.

Example 7-10

```java
//Program: StringBuffer Objects as Parameters

public class StringBufferObjectsAsParameters
{
    public static void main(String[] args)
    {
        StringBuffer str = new StringBuffer("Hello");          //Line 1

        System.out.println("Line 2: str before calling "
                            + "the method stringParameter: "
                            + str);                            //Line 2
        stringParameter(str);                                  //Line 3
        System.out.println("Line 4: str after calling "
                            + "the method stringParameter: "
                            + str);                            //Line 4
    }

    public static void stringParameter(StringBuffer pStr)
    {
        System.out.println("Line 5: In the method "
                            + "stringParameter");              //Line 5
        System.out.println("Line 6: pStr before changing "
                            + "its value: " + pStr);           //Line 6
        pStr.append(" There");                                 //Line 7
        System.out.println("Line 8: pStr after changing "
                            + "its value: " + pStr);           //Line 8
    }
}
```

Sample Run:
```
Line 2: str before calling the method stringParameter: Hello
Line 5: In the method stringParameter
Line 6: pStr before changing its value: Hello
Line 8: pStr after changing its value: Hello There
Line 4: str after calling the method stringParameter: Hello There
```

The preceding program works as follows: The statement in Line 1 declares `str` to be a reference variable of the `StringBuffer` type and assigns the string `"Hello"` to it. The statement in Line 2 outputs the first line of output. The statement in Line 3 calls the method `stringParameter`. The actual parameter is `str` and the formal parameter is `pStr`. The value of `str` is copied into `pStr`. Because both of these parameters are reference variables, `str` and `pStr` point to the same string, which is `"Hello"`.

Control is then transferred to the method `stringParameter`. The next statement executed is in Line 5, which outputs the second line of the output. The statement in Line 6 outputs the third line of the output. Notice that this statement also outputs the string to which `pStr` points, and the printed value is that string. The next statement executed is in Line 7. This statement uses the method `append` to append the string `" There"` to the string referenced by `pStr`. After this statement executes, `pStr` refers to the string `"Hello There"`. However, this also changes the string that was assigned to the variable `str`. After the statement in Line 7 executes, `str` points to the same string as does `pStr`.

The statement in Line 8 outputs the fourth line of output. Notice that the printed value is the string `"Hello There"`, which is the string referenced by `pStr`. After this statement executes, control goes back to the method `main` at Line 4. Therefore, the next statement executed is in Line 4, which outputs the last line of the output. Notice that `str` refers to the string `"Hello There"`.

Because parameter passing is fundamental to any programming language, Example 7-11 further illustrates this concept.

Example 7-11

```java
//Example 7-11

public class Example7_11
{
    public static void main(String[] args)
    {
        int num1;                               //Line 1
        IntClass num2 = new IntClass();         //Line 2
        char ch;                                //Line 3
        StringBuffer str;                       //Line 4

        num1 = 10;                              //Line 5
        num2.setNum(15);                        //Line 6
        ch = 'A';                               //Line 7
        str = new StringBuffer("Sunny");        //Line 8

        System.out.println("Line 9: Inside main: "
                          + "num1 = " + num1
                          + ", num2 = " + num2.getNum()
                          + ", ch = " + ch
```

```
                      + ", and str = "
                      + str);                           //Line 9

        funcOne(num1, num2, ch, str);                   //Line 10

        System.out.println("Line 11: After funcOne: "
                      + "num1 = " + num1
                      + ", num2 = " + num2.getNum()
                      + ", ch = " + ch
                      + ", and str = "
                      + str);                           //Line 11
    }

    public static void funcOne(int a, IntClass b,
                               char v, StringBuffer pStr)
    {
        int num;                                        //Line 12
        int len;                                        //Line 13

        num = b.getNum();                               //Line 14
        a++;                                            //Line 15
        b.addtoNum(12);                                 //Line 16
        v = 'B';                                        //Line 17
        len = pStr.length();                            //Line 18
        pStr.delete(0, len);                            //Line 19
        pStr.append("Warm");                            //Line 20

        System.out.println("Line 21: Inside funcOne: \n"
                      + "            a = " + a
                      + ", b = " + b.getNum()
                      + ", v = " + v
                      + ", pStr = " + pStr
                      + ", len = " + len
                      + ", and num = " + num);  //Line 21
    }
}
```

Sample Run:
```
Line 9: Inside main: num1 = 10, num2 = 15, ch = A, and str = Sunny
Line 21: Inside funcOne:
        a = 11, b = 27, v = B, pStr = Warm, len = 5, and num = 15
Line 11: After funcOne: num1 = 10, num2 = 27, ch = A, and str = Warm
```

Let's walk through this program. The lines are numbered for easy reference, and the values of the variables are shown before and/or after each statement executes.

Just before the statement in Line 5 executes, memory is allocated only for the variables and objects of the method `main`. Moreover, `num1`, `ch`, and `str` are not initialized. The variable num2 in Line 2 is declared, and memory for the data is also allocated and initialized to 0. This is because num2 is a reference variable of the `IntClass` type and the **class** `IntClass` automatically initializes the allocated memory space of the object to 0. Just before the statement in Line 5 executes, the variables and objects are as shown in Figure 7-13.

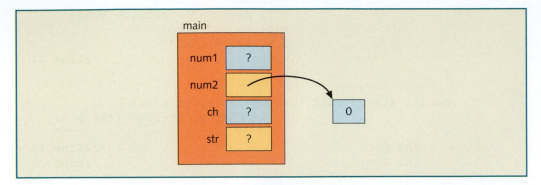

Figure 7-13 Variables and objects just before the statement, (num1 = 10;), in Line 5 executes

The statement in Line 5 stores 10 into num1, the statement in Line 6 stores 15 into the object to which num2 points, the statement in Line 7 stores the character 'A' into ch, and the statement in Line 8 allocates memory space to store the string "Sunny" into it and assigns this string to str. After the statement in Line 8 executes, the variables and objects of the method main are as shown in Figure 7-14.

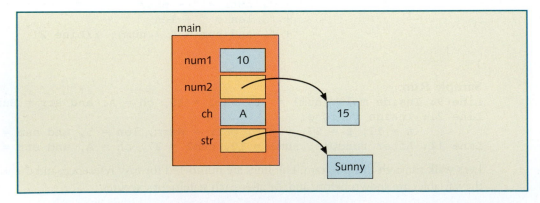

Figure 7-14 Variables and objects after the statement, str = **new** StringBuffer("Sunny");, in Line 8 executes

Line 9 produces the following output:

```
Line 9: Inside main: num1 = 10, num2 = 15, ch = A, and str = Sunny
```

The statement in Line 10 calls the method `funcOne`. The method `funcOne` has four parameters and two local variables. Memory for the parameters and the local variables of the method `funcOne` is allocated. The values of the actual parameters are copied into the corresponding formal parameters. Therefore, the value of `num1` is copied into `a`, the value of `num2` is copied into `b`, the value of `ch` is copied into `v`, and the value of `str` is copied into `pStr`. Both the formal parameters `b` and `pStr` are reference variables, so they point to the objects to which their corresponding actual parameters refer.

Just before the statement in Line 14 executes, the variables and objects are as shown in Figure 7-15.

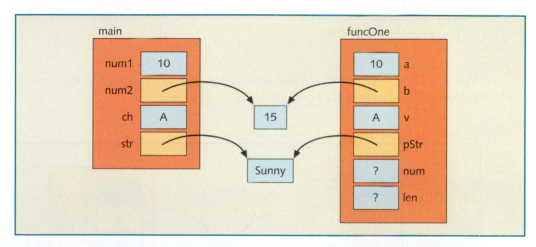

Figure 7-15 Variables and objects just before the statement, num = `b.getnum();`, in Line 14 executes

The statement in Line 14 retrieves the value of `b` and stores it into `num`. After the statement in Line 14 executes, the variables and objects are as shown in Figure 7-16.

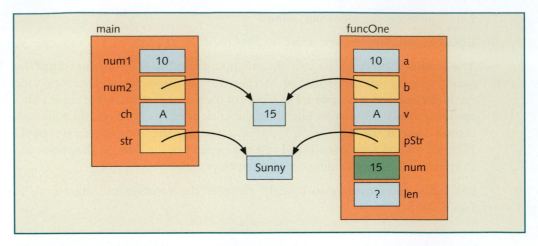

Figure 7-16 Variables and objects after the statement, `num = b.getNum();`, in Line 14 executes

The statement in Line 15 increments the value of **a** by **1**. After the statement in Line 15 executes, the variables and objects are as shown in Figure 7-17.

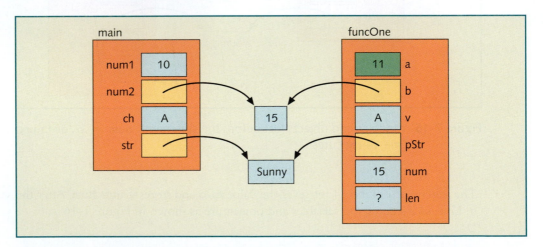

Figure 7-17 Variables and objects after the statement, `a++;`, in Line 15 executes

The statement in Line 16 adds **12** to the previous value of the object referred to by **b**. After the statement in Line 16 executes, the variables and objects are as shown in Figure 7-18.

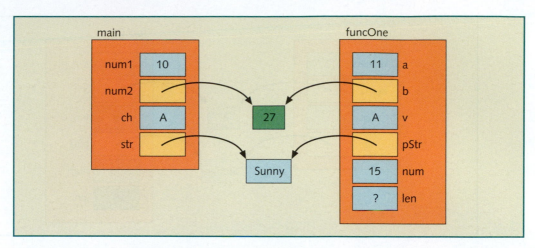

Figure 7-18   Variables and objects after the statement, `b.addtoNum(12);`, in
                   Line 16 executes

The statement in Line 17 stores the character `'B'` into `v`. After the statement in Line 17
executes, the variables and objects are as shown in Figure 7-19.

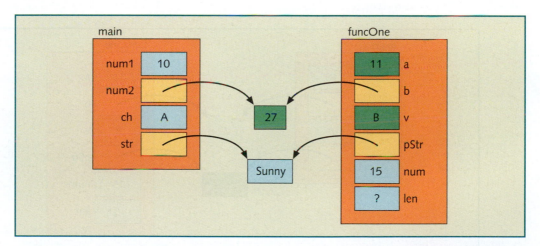

Figure 7-19   Variables and objects after the statement, `v = 'B';`, in Line 17 executes

The statement in Line 18 stores the length of the string to which `pStr` refers into `len`. After
the statement in Line 18 executes, the variables and objects are as shown in Figure 7-20.
(Notice that the length of the string `"Sunny"` is 5.)

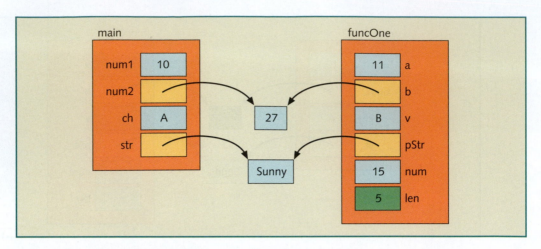

Figure 7-20 Variables and objects after the statement, `len = pStr.length();`, in Line 18 executes

The statement in Line 19 uses the method **delete** of the **class StringBuffer** and deletes the string **"Sunny"**. After the statement in Line 19 executes, the variables and objects are as shown in Figure 7-21.

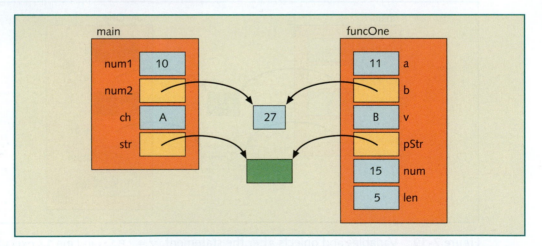

Figure 7-21 Variables and objects after the statement, `pStr.delete(0, len);`, in Line 19 executes

The statement in Line 20 uses the method **append** of the **class StringBuffer** and appends the string **"Warm"** to the string referred to by **pStr**. After the statement in Line 20 executes, the variables and objects are as shown in Figure 7–22.

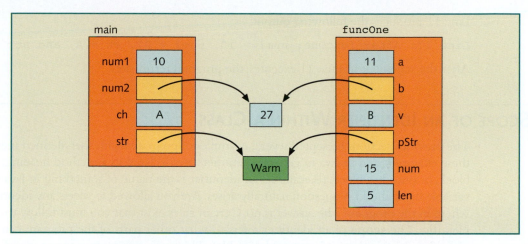

Figure 7-22 Variables and objects after the statement, `pStr.append("Warm");`, in Line 20 executes

The statement in Line 21 produces the following output:

```
Line 21: Inside funcOne:
         a = 11, b = 27, v = B, pStr = Warm, len = 5, and num = 15
```

After the statement in Line 21 executes, control goes to Line 11. The memory allocated for the variables of the method `funcOne` is deallocated. The values of the variables of the method `main` are as shown in Figure 7-23.

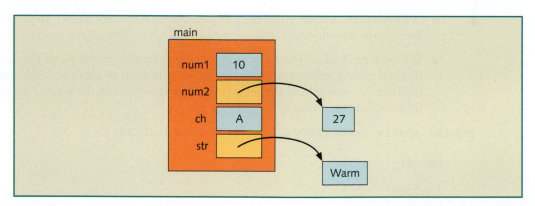

Figure 7-23 Variables and objects of `main` when control goes back to `main`

Line 11 produces the following output:

```
Line 11: After funcOne: num1 = 10, num2 = 27, ch = A, and str = Warm
```

After the statement in Line 11 executes, the program terminates.

SCOPE OF AN IDENTIFIER WITHIN A CLASS

The previous sections presented several examples of programs with user-defined methods. In these examples, and in Java in general, identifiers are declared in a method heading, within a block, or outside a block. (Recall that an identifier is the name of something in Java such as a variable or method.) A question naturally arises: Are you allowed to access any identifier anywhere in the program? The answer is no. Certain rules exist that you must follow to access an identifier. The **scope** of an identifier refers to what other parts of the program can "see" an identifier, that is, where it is accessible (visible). This section examines the scope of an identifier. Let's first define the following widely used term:

Local identifier: An identifier declared within a method or block and that is visible only within that method or block.

Before giving the scope rules of an identifier, let us note the following:

- Java does not allow the nesting of methods. That is, you cannot include the definition of one method in the body of another method.

- Within a method or a block, an identifier must be declared before it can be used. Note that a block is a set of statements enclosed within braces. A method's definition can contain several blocks. The body of a loop or an **if** statement also forms a block.

- Within a class, outside every method definition (and every block), an identifier can be declared anywhere.

- Within a method, an identifier used to name a variable in the outer block of the method cannot be used to name any other variable in an inner block of the method. For example, in the following method definition, the second declaration of the variable **x** is illegal:

```
public static void illegalIdentifierDeclaration()
{
    int x;

    //block
    {
        double x;    //illegal declaration, x is already declared
        ...
    }
}
```

Next, we describe the scope rules of an identifier declared within a class and accessed within a method (block) of the class. (In Chapter 8, we describe the rules for an *object* to access the identifiers of its class.)

- An identifier, say **x**, declared within a method (block) is accessible:
  - Only within the block from the point at which it is declared until the end of the block.
  - By those blocks that are nested within that block.
- Suppose **x** is an identifier declared within a class and outside every method's definition (block).
  - If **x** is declared *without* the reserved word **static** (such as a named constant or a method name), then it *cannot* be accessed within a **static** method.
  - If **x** is declared *with* the reserved word **static** (such as a named constant or a method name), then it *can* be accessed within a method (block), provided the method (block) does not have any other identifier named **x**.

Before considering an example that explains these scope rules, first note the scope of the identifier declared in the **for** statement. Java allows the programmer to declare a variable in the initialization statement of the **for** statement. For example, the following **for** statement:

```java
for (int count = 1; count < 10; count++)
    System.out.println(count);
```

declares the variable **count** and initializes it to 1. The scope of the variable **count** is limited only to the body of the **for** loop.

Example 7-12 illustrates the scope rules.

Example 7-12

Consider the following Java program.

```java
public class ScopeRules
{
    static final double rate = 10.50;
    static int z;
    static double t;

    public static void main(String[] args)
    {
        int num;
        double x, z;
        char ch;

        //...
    }
```

```java
public static void one(int x, char y)
{
    //...
}

public static int w;

public static void two(int one, int z)
{
    char ch;
    int a;

        //block three
    {
        int x = 12;

        //...
    }//end block three
    //...
}
}
```

Table 7-3 summarizes the scope (visibility) of the identifiers in Example 7–12.

Table 7-3 Scope (Visibility) of the Identifiers

Identifier	Visibility in one	Visibility in two	Visibility in block three	Visibility in main
rate (before main)	Y	Y	Y	Y
z (before main)	Y	N	N	N
t (before main)	Y	Y	Y	Y
main	Y	Y	Y	Y
local variables of main	N	N	N	Y
one (method name)	Y	Y	Y	Y
x (one's formal parameter)	Y	N	N	N
y (one's formal parameter)	Y	N	N	N
w (before method two)	Y	Y	Y	Y
two (method name)	Y	Y	Y	Y
one (two's formal parameter)	N	Y	Y	N
z (two's formal parameter)	N	Y	Y	N
local variables of two	N	Y	Y	N
x (block three's local variable)	N	N	Y	N

Before we look at some programming examples, we will explore the concept of method overloading.

METHOD OVERLOADING: AN INTRODUCTION

In Java, within a `class`, several methods can have the same name. This is called **method overloading** or **overloading a method name**. Before we give the rules to overload a method, let us define the following:

Two methods are said to have **different formal parameter lists** if both methods have:

- A different number of formal parameters, or

- If the number of formal parameters is the same, then the data type of the formal parameters, in the order you list, must differ in at least one position.

For example, consider the following method headings:

```java
public void methodOne(int x)
public void methodTwo(int x, double y)
public void methodThree(double y, int x)
public int methodFour(char ch, int x, double y)
public int methodFive(char ch, int x, String name)
```

These methods all have different formal parameter lists.

Now consider the following headings:

```java
public void methodSix(int x, double y, char ch)
public void methodSeven(int one, double u, char firstCh)
```

The methods `methodSix` and `methodSeven` both have three formal parameters and the data type of the corresponding parameters is the same. Therefore, these methods have the same formal parameter list.

To overload a method name, within a `class`, any two definitions of the method must have different formal parameter lists.

Method overloading: Creating several methods, within a `class`, with the same name.

The **signature** of a method consists of the method name and its formal parameter list. Two methods have different signatures if they have either different names or different formal parameter lists. (Note that the signature of a method does not include the return type of the method.)

If a method's name is overloaded, then all the methods in the set have the same name. Therefore, all the methods in the set have different signatures, if they have different formal parameter lists. Thus, the following method headings correctly overload the method `methodXYZ`:

```java
public void methodXYZ()
public void methodXYZ(int x, double y)
```

```
public void methodXYZ(double one, int y)
public void methodXYZ(int x, double y, char ch)
```

Consider the following method headings to overload the method `methodABC`:

```
public void methodABC(int x, double y)
public int methodABC(int x, double y)
```

Both these method headings have the same name and same formal parameter list. Therefore, these method headings to overload the method `methodABC` are incorrect. In this case, the compiler will generate a syntax error. (Notice that the return types of these method headings are different.)

If a method is overloaded, then in a call to that method the signature, that is, the formal parameter list of the method, determines which method to execute.

 Some authors define the signature of a method as the formal parameter list; other authors consider the entire heading of the method as its signature. However, in this book, the signature of a method consists of the method's heading and its formal parameter list. If the method names are different, then, of course, the compiler would have no problem identifying which method is called and correctly translating the code. However, if a method name is overloaded, then as noted, the method's formal parameter list determines which method's body executes.

Suppose you need to write a method that determines the larger of two items. Both items can be integers, floating-point numbers, characters, or strings. You could write several methods as follows (we give only the method heading):

```
int largerInt(int x, int y)
char largerChar(char first, char second)
double largerDouble(double u, double v)
String largerString(String first, String second)
```

The method `largerInt` determines the larger of two integers, the method `largerChar` determines the larger of two characters, and so on. All of these methods perform similar operations. Instead of giving different names to these methods, you can use the same name—say, `larger`—for each method; that is, you can overload the method `larger` as follows:

```
int larger(int x, int y)
char larger(char first, char second)
double larger(double u, double v)
String larger(String first, String second)
```

If the call is `larger(5, 3)`, for example, the first method executes because the actual parameters match the formal parameters of the first method. If the call is `larger('A', '9')`, the second method executes, and so on.

Method overloading is used when you have the same action for different sets of data. Of course, for method overloading to work, you must give the definition of each method.

PROGRAMMING EXAMPLE: DATA COMPARISON

This programming example illustrates:

1. How to read data from more than one file in the same program.
2. How to send the output to a file.
3. How to generate bar graphs.
4. With the help of methods and parameter passing, how to use the same program segment on different (but similar) sets of data.
5. How to use structured design to solve a problem and how to perform parameter passing.

This program is broken into two parts. First, you learn how to read data from more than one file. Second, you learn how to generate bar graphs.

Two groups of students at a local university are enrolled in certain special courses during the summer semester. The courses are offered for the first time and are taught by different teachers. At the end of the semester, both groups are given the same tests for the same courses and their scores are recorded in separate files. The data in each file is in the following form:

```
courseID   score1, score2, ..., scoreN -999
courseID   score1, score2, ..., scoreM -999
.
.
.
```

Let's write a program that finds the average course score for each course for each group. The output is of the following form:

```
Course ID    Group No     Course Average
  CSC           1            83.71
                2            80.82

  ENG           1            82.00
                2            78.20
.
.
.
Avg for group 1: 82.04
Avg for group 2: 82.01
```

Input Because the data for the two groups is recorded in separate files, the input data appears in two separate files

Output As shown above

Problem Analysis and Algorithm Design

Reading the input data from both files is straightforward. Suppose the data is stored in the file `group1.txt` for group 1 and in the file `group2.txt` for group 2, and these files are on floppy disk A. After processing the data for one group, we can process the data for the second group for the same course, and continue until we run out of data. Processing the data for each course is similar and uses the following process:

   a. Sum the scores for the course.

   b. Count the number of students in the course.

   c. Divide the total score by the number of students to find the course average.

   d. Output the results.

We are comparing only the averages of the corresponding courses in each group. The data in each file is ordered according to course ID. To ensure that only the averages of the corresponding courses are compared, we compare the course IDs for each group. If the corresponding course IDs are not the same, we output an error message and terminate the program.

This discussion suggests that we should write a method, `calculateAverage`, to find the course average. We should also write another method, `printResult`, to output the data in the form given. By passing the appropriate parameters, we can use the same methods, `calculateAverage` and `printResult`, to process each course's data for both groups. (In the second part of the program, we modify the method `printResult`.)

The preceding discussion translates into the following algorithm:

   1. Initialize the variables.

   2. Get the course IDs for group 1 and group 2.

   3. If the course IDs are different, print an error message and exit the program.

   4. Calculate the course average for group 1 and group 2.

   5. Print the results in the form given earlier.

   6. Repeat Steps 2 through 6 for each course.

   7. Print the final results.

Variables (Method `main`)

The preceding discussion suggests that the program needs the following variables for data manipulation in the method `main`:

```
String courseId1;                        //course ID for group 1
String courseId2;                        //course ID for group 2
int numberOfCourses;
DoubleClass avg1 = new DoubleClass(); //average for a course
                                         //in group 1
DoubleClass avg2 = new DoubleClass(); //average for a course
                                         //in group 2
```

```
double avgGroup1;                    //average of group 1
double avgGroup2;                    //average of group 2

Scanner group1 =
        new Scanner(new FileReader("a:\\group1.txt"));
Scanner group2 =
        new Scanner(new FileReader("a:\\group2.txt"));

PrintWriter outfile = new PrintWriter("a:\\student.out");
```

Next, we discuss the methods `calculateAverage` and `printResult`. Then we will put the method `main` together.

Method `calculateAverage`

This method calculates the average for a course. Because the input is stored in a file and the input file is opened in the method `main`, we must pass the variable associated with the input file to this method. Furthermore, after calculating the course average, this method must pass the course average to the method `main`. Therefore, this method has two parameters.

To find the course average, we must first find the sum of all the scores for the course and the number of students who took the course; we then divide the sum by the number of students. Thus, we need a variable to find the sum of the scores, a variable to find the number of students, and a variable to read and store a score. Of course, we must initialize to zero the variables to find the sum and the number of students.

Local Variables (Method `calculateAverage`)

In the previous discussion of data manipulation, we identified three variables for the method `calculateAverage`:

```
double totalScore;     //to store the sum of the scores
int numberOfStudents;  //to store the number of students
int score;             //to read and store a course score
```

The above discussion translates into the following algorithm for the method `calculateAverage`:

    a. Declare the variables.

    b. Initialize `totalScore` to `0.0`.

    c. Initialize `numberOfStudents` to `0`.

    d. Get the (next) course score.

    e. `while` (`score != -999`):

        i. Update `totalScore` by adding the course score read in Step d.

        ii. Increment `numberOfStudents` by `1`.

        iii. Get the next course score.

    f. `courseAvg.setNum(totalScore / numberOfStudents);`

A `while` loop is used to repeat Steps d, e, and f.

We are now ready to write the definition of the method `calculateAverage`.

```java
public static void calculateAverage(Scanner inp,
                                    DoubleClass courseAvg)
{
    double totalScore = 0.0;
    int numberOfStudents = 0;
    int score = 0;

    score = inp.nextInt();

    while (score != -999)
    {
        totalScore = totalScore + score;
        numberOfStudents++;
        score = inp.nextInt();
    }//end while

    courseAvg.setNum(totalScore / numberOfStudents);
}//end calculate Average
```

Method `printResult`

The method `printResult` prints the group's course ID, group number, and course average. The output is stored in a file. We must pass four parameters to this method: the variable associated with the output file, the group number, the course ID, and the course average for the group. Also, from the output, it is clear that we print the course ID only before group 1. In pseudocode, the algorithm is:

```
if (group number == 1)
    print course ID
else
    print a blank

print group number and course average
```

The definition of the method `printResult` follows:

```java
public static void printResult(PrintWriter outp,
                               String courseId,
                               int groupNo, DoubleClass avg)
{
    if (groupNo == 1)
        outp.print("  " + courseId + "    ");
    else
        outp.print("        ");

    outp.println("%9d %15.2f%n", groupNo, avg.getNum());
}
```

Now that we have designed and defined the methods `calculateAverage` and `printResults`, we can describe the algorithm for the method `main`. Before outlining the algorithm, however, note the following: It is quite possible that in both input files the data is ordered according to the course IDs, but one file might have fewer courses than the other. We discover this error only after we have processed both files and discover that one file has unprocessed data. Make sure to check for this error before printing the final answer—that is, the average for group 1 and group 2.

Main Algorithm: Method `main`

1. Declare the variables (local declaration).
2. Create and initialize the variables to open the input and output files.
3. Initialize the course average for group 1 to `0.0`.
4. Initialize the course average for group 2 to `0.0`.
5. Initialize the number of courses to `0`.
6. Print the heading.
7. For each course in group 1 and group 2:

   a. Get `courseId1` for group 1.

   b. Get `courseId2` for group 2.

   c.
   ```
   if (courseId1 != courseId2)
   {
       System.out.println("Data error: Course IDs do not match");
       return;
   }
   ```

   d.
   ```
   else
   {
   ```
   i.   Calculate the course average for group 1 (call the method `calculateAverage` and pass the appropriate parameters).

   ii. Calculate the course average for group 2 (call the method `calculateAverage` and pass the appropriate parameters).

   iii. Print the results for group 1 (call the method `printResult` and pass the appropriate parameters).

   iv. Print the results for group 2 (call the method `printResult` and pass the appropriate parameters).

   v.   Update the average for group 1.

   vi. Update the average for group 2.

   vii. Increment the number of courses.
   ```
   }
   ```

8. a. if not_end_of_file on group 1 and end_of_file on group 2

    print "Ran out of data for group 2 before group 1"

 b. else

    if end_of_file on group 1 and not_end_of_file on group 2

    print "Ran out of data for group 1 before group 2"

 c. else

    print the average of group 1 and group 2.

9. Close the files.

Complete Program Listing

```java
//Program: Comparison of Class Averages

import java.io.*;
import java.util.*;

public class DataComparison
{
    public static void main(String[] args)
                        throws FileNotFoundException
    {
              //Step 1
        String courseId1;                       //course ID for group 1
        String courseId2;                       //course ID for group 2
        int numberOfCourses;
        DoubleClass avg1 = new DoubleClass();//average for a course
                                        //in group 1
        DoubleClass avg2 = new DoubleClass();//average for a course
                                        //in group 2
        double avgGroup1;           //average of group 1
        double avgGroup2;           //average of group 2

              //Step 2 Open the input and output files
        Scanner group1 = new Scanner(new FileReader("a:\\group1.txt"));
        Scanner group2 = new Scanner(new FileReader("a:\\group2.txt"));

        PrintWriter outfile = new PrintWriter("a:\\student.out");

        avgGroup1 = 0.0;                                    //Step 3
        avgGroup2 = 0.0;                                    //Step 4

        numberOfCourses = 0;                               //Step 5
              //print heading: Step 6
        outfile.println("Course ID    Group No     Course Average");
```

```java
while (group1.hasNext() && group2.hasNext())          //Step 7
{
    courseId1 = group1.next();                        //Step 7a
    courseId2 = group2.next();                        //Step 7b

    if (!courseId1.equals(courseId2))                 //Step 7c
    {
        System.out.println("Data error: Course IDs "
                    + "do not match.");
        System.out.println("Program terminates.");
        outfile.println("Data error: Course IDs "
                    + "do not match.");
        outfile.println("Program terminates.");
        outfile.close();
        return;
    }
    else                                              //Step 7d
    {
        calculateAverage(group1, avg1);               //Step 7d.i
        calculateAverage(group2, avg2);               //Step 7d.ii
        printResult(outfile, courseId1, 1, avg1);     //Step 7d.iii
        printResult(outfile, courseId2, 2, avg2);     //Step 7d.iv
        avgGroup1 = avgGroup1 + avg1.getNum();        //Step 7d.v
        avgGroup2 = avgGroup2 + avg2.getNum();        //Step 7d.vi
        outfile.println();
        numberOfCourses++;                            //Step 7d.vii
    }
}//end while

if (group1.hasNext() && !group2.hasNext())            //Step 8a
    System.out.println("Ran out of data for group 2 "
                + "before group 1.");
else                                                  //Step 8b
    if (!group1.hasNext() && group2.hasNext())
        System.out.println("Ran out of data for "
                    + "group 1 before group 2.");
    else                                              //Step 8c
    {
        outfile.printf("Avg for group 1: %.2f %n",
                    (avgGroup1 / numberOfCourses));
        outfile.printf("Avg for group 2: %.2f %n",
                    (avgGroup2 / numberOfCourses));
    }
```

```java
        group1.close();                                      //Step 9
        group2.close();                                      //Step 9
        outfile.close();                                     //Step 9
    }

    public static void calculateAverage(Scanner inp,
                                        DoubleClass courseAvg)
    {
        double totalScore = 0.0;
        int numberOfStudents = 0;
        int score = 0;

        score = inp.nextInt();

        while (score != -999)
        {
            totalScore = totalScore + score;
            numberOfStudents++;
            score = inp.nextInt();
        }//end while

        courseAvg.setNum(totalScore / numberOfStudents);
    }//end calculate Average

    public static void printResult(PrintWriter outp,
                                   String courseId,
                                   int groupNo, DoubleClass avg)
    {
        if (groupNo == 1)
            outp.print("  " + courseId + "    ");
        else
            outp.print("            ");

        outp.println("%9d %15.2f%n", groupNo, avg.getNum());
    }
}
```

Sample Run:

Course ID	Group No	Course Average
CSC	1	83.71
	2	80.82
ENG	1	82.00
	2	78.20

```
      HIS              1           77.69
                       2           84.15

      MTH              1           83.57
                       2           84.29

      PHY              1           83.22
                       2           82.60

Avg for group 1: 82.04
Avg for group 2: 82.01
```

Input Data Group 1

```
CSC 80 100 70 80 72 90 89 100 83 70 90 73 85 90 -999
ENG 80 90 80 94 90 74 78 63 83 80 90 -999
HIS 90 70 80 70 90 50 89 83 90 68 90 60 80  -999
MTH 74 80 75 89 90 73 90 82 74 90 84 100 90 79 -999
PHY 100 83 93 80 63 78 88 89 75 -999
```

Input Data Group 2

```
CSC 90 75 90 75 80 89 100 60 80 70 80 -999
ENG 80 80 70 68 70 78 80 90 90 76 -999
HIS 100 80 80 70 90 76 88 90 90 75 90 85 80 -999
MTH 80 85 85 92 90 90 74 90 83 65 72 90 84 100 -999
PHY 90 93 73 85 68 75 67 100 87 88 -999
```

Bar Graphs

In the business world, company executives often like to see results in a visual form, such as bar graphs. Many currently available software packages can analyze data in several forms and then display the results in such visual forms as bar graphs or pie charts. The second part of this program displays the earlier results in the form of bar graphs, as shown below:

```
Course          Course Average
  ID     0   10   20   30   40   50   60   70   80   90   100
         |....|....|....|....|....|....|....|....|....|....|
  CSC    ******************************************
         ########################################

  ENG    ********************************************
         ########################################


Group 1 -- ****
Group 1 -- ####

Avg for group 1: 82.04
Avg for group 2: 82.01
```

Each symbol (* or #) in the bar graph represents 2 points. If a course average is less than 2, no symbol is printed.

Because the output is in the form of a bar graph, we need to modify the method `printResult`.

Method `printResult`

The method `printResult` prints the course ID and the bar graph representing the average for a course. The output is stored in a file. So we must pass four parameters to this method: the variable associated with the output file, the group number (to print * or #), the course ID, and the course average for the department.

To print the bar graph, we can use a loop to print a symbol for each two points. If the average is `78.45`, for example, we must print `39` symbols to represent this average. To find the number of symbols to print, we can use integer division as follows:

```
numberOfSymbols = (int)(average) / 2;
```

For example, `(int)(78.45) / 2 = 78 / 2 = 39`.

Following this outline, the definition of the method `printResult` is:

```
public static void printResult(PrintWriter outp, String courseId,
                               int groupNo, DoubleClass avg)
{
    int noOfSymbols;
    int count;

    if (groupNo == 1)
        outp.print(" " + courseId + "      ");
    else
        outp.print("           ");

    noOfSymbols = (int)(avg.getNum())/2;

    if (groupNo == 1)
        for (count = 1; count <= noOfSymbols; count++)
            outp.print("*");
    else
        for (count = 1; count <= noOfSymbols; count++)
            outp.print("#");

    outp.println();
}//end printResults
```

We also include a method, `printHeading`, to print the first two lines of the output. The definition of this method is:

```
public static void printHeading(PrintWriter outp)
{
    outp.println("Course            Course Average");
    outp.println("  ID    0    10   20   30   40   50   60   70"
              + "   80   90   100");
    outp.println("          |....|....|....|....|....|....|....|"
              + "....|....|....|");
}//end printHeading
```

If you replace the method `printResult` in the preceding program, include the method `printHeading`, include the statements to output—Group 1 -- **** and Group 2 -- ####—and rerun the program, then the output for the previous data is as follows:

Sample Output:

```
Course            Course Average
  ID    0    10   20   30   40   50   60   70   80   90   100
          |....|....|....|....|....|....|....|....|....|....|
  CSC   ****************************************
        ######################################

  ENG   *****************************************
        #####################################

  HIS   ***************************************
        ########################################

  MTH   ******************************************
        #########################################

  PHY   *****************************************
        #########################################

Group 1 -- ****
Group 2 -- ####
Avg for group 1: 82.04
Avg for group 2: 82.01
```

Compare both outputs. Which one do you think is better?

QUICK REVIEW

1. Methods enable you to divide a program into manageable tasks.

2. The Java system provides standard (predefined) methods.

3. In general, to use a predefined method, you must:

   a. Know the name of the class containing the method, and the name of the package containing the class that contains the method.

   b. Import the class into the program.

   c. Know the name and type of the method, and the number and types of the parameters (arguments).

4. To use a method of a class contained in the package **java.lang** in a program, you do not need to explicitly import these classes into your program.

5. To simplify the use of **static** methods (members) of a class, JDK 5.0 provides the **static import** statement.

6. There are two types of user-defined methods: value-returning methods and void methods.

7. Variables defined in a method heading are called formal parameters.

8. Expressions, variables, or constant values used in a method call are called actual parameters.

9. In a method call, the number of actual parameters and their types must match the formal parameters in the order given.

10. To call a method, use its name together with the actual parameter list.

11. A value-returning method returns a value. Therefore, a value-returning method is typically used (called) in either an expression or an output statement, or as a parameter in a method call.

12. The general syntax of a value-returning method is:

```
modifier(s) returnType  methodName(formal parameter list)
{
    statements
}
```

13. The line:

```
modifier(s) returnType methodName(formal parameter list)
```

is called the method heading (or method header). Statements enclosed between curly braces, { and }, are called the body of the method.

14. The method heading and the body of the method are called the definition of the method.

15. If a method has no parameters, you still need the empty parentheses in both the method heading and the method call.

16. A value-returning method returns its value via the **return** statement.

17. A method can have more than one **return** statement. However, whenever a **return** statement executes in a method, the remaining statements are skipped and the method exits.

18. When a program executes, the execution always begins with the first statement in the method **main**.

19. User-defined methods execute only when they are called.

20. A call to a method transfers control from the caller to the called method.

21. In a method call statement, you specify only the actual parameters, not their data type or the method type.

22. When a method exits, control goes back to the caller.

23. A method that does not have a return type is called a **void** method.

24. A return statement without any value can be used in a **void** method.

25. If a return statement is used in a **void** method, it is typically used to exit the method early.

26. In Java, **void** is a reserved word.

27. A **void** method may or may not have parameters.

28. To call a **void** method, you use the method name together with the actual parameters in a stand-alone statement.

29. A formal parameter receives a copy of its corresponding actual parameter.

30. If a formal parameter is of the primitive data type, it directly stores the value of the actual parameter.

31. If a formal parameter is a reference variable, it copies the value of its corresponding actual parameter, which is the address of the object where the actual data is stored. Therefore, if a formal parameter is a reference variable, both the formal and actual parameters refer to the same object.

32. The scope of an identifier refers to those parts of the program where it is accessible.

33. Java does not allow the nesting of methods. That is, you cannot include the definition of one method in the body of another method.

34. Within a method or a block, an identifier must be declared before it can be used. Note that a block is a set of statements enclosed within braces. A method's definition can contain several blocks. The body of a loop or an **if** statement also forms a block.

35. Within a class, outside every method definition (and every block), an identifier can be declared anywhere.

36. Within a method, an identifier used to name a variable in the outer block of the method cannot be used to name any other variable in an inner block of the method.

7

37. The scope rules of an identifier declared within a class and accessed within a method (block) of the class are as follows:

   ■ An identifier, say **x**, declared within a method (block) is accessible:

   ■ Only within the block from the point at which it is declared until the end of the block.

   ■ By those blocks that are nested within that block.

   ■ Suppose **x** is an identifier declared within a class and outside every method's definition (block).

   ■ If **x** is declared without the reserved word **static** (such as a named constant or a method name), then it cannot be accessed within a **static** method.

   ■ If **x** is declared with the reserved word **static** (such as a named constant or a method name), then it can be accessed within a method (block), provided the method (block) does not have any other identifier named **x**.

38. Two methods are said to have different formal parameter lists if both methods have:

   ■ A different number of formal parameters, or

   ■ If the number of formal parameters is the same, then the data type of the formal parameters, in the order you list, must differ in at least one position.

39. The signature of a method consists of the method name and its formal parameter list. Two methods have different signatures if they have either different names or different formal parameter lists.

40. If a method is overloaded, then in a call to that method the signature, that is, the formal parameter list of the method, determines which method to execute.

EXERCISES

1. Mark the following statements as true or false.

   a. To use a predefined method of a **class** contained in the package **java.lang** in a program, you need to know only what the name of the method is and how to use it.

   b. A value-returning method returns only one value via the return statement.

   c. Parameters allow you to use different values each time the method is called.

   d. When a **return** statement executes in a user-defined method, the method immediately exits.

   e. A value-returning method returns only integer values.

   f. If a Java method does not use parameters, parentheses around the empty parameter list are still needed.

   g. In Java, the names of the corresponding formal and actual parameters must be the same.

   h. In Java, method definitions can be nested; that is, the definition of one method can be enclosed in the body of another method.

2. What is the output of the following Java program?

```java
import static java.lang.Math.*;

public class Exercise2
{
    public static void main(String[] args)
    {
        int counter;

        for (counter = 1; counter <= 100; counter++)
            if (pow(floor(sqrt(counter)), 2) == counter)
                System.out.print(counter + " ");
        System.out.println();
    }
}
```

3. Which of the following method headings are valid? If they are invalid, explain why.

```java
public static one(int a, int b)
public static int thisone(char x)
public static char another(int a, b)
public static double yetanother
```

4. Consider the following statements:

```java
double num1, num2, num3;
int int1, int2, int3;
double value;
```

```java
num1 = 5.0; num2 = 6.0; num3 = 3.0;
int1 = 4; int2 = 7; int3 = 8;
```

and the method heading:

```java
public static double cube(double a, double b, double c)
```

Which of the following statements are valid? If they are invalid, explain why.

a. `value = cube (num1, 15.0, num3);`

b. `System.out.println(cube(num1, num3, num2));`

c. `System.out.println(cube(6.0, 8.0, 10.5));`

d. `System.out.println(num1 + " " + num3);`

e. `System.out.println(cube(num1, num3));`

f. `value = cube(num1, int2, num3);`

g. `value = cube(7, 8, 9);`

5. Consider the following methods:

```java
public static int secret(int x)
{
    int i, j;

    i = 2 * x;

    if (i > 10)
        j = x / 2;
    else
        j = x / 3;

    return j - 1;
}

public static int another(int a, int b)
{
    int i, j;

    j = 0;

    for (i = a; i <= b; i++)
        j = j + i;

    return j;
}
```

What is the output of each of the following program segments?

a. ```java
x = 10;
System.out.println(secret(x));
```

b. ```java
x = 5; y = 8;
System.out.println(another(x, y));
```

c. ```java
x = 10; k = secret(x);
System.out.println(x + " " + k + " "
                    + another(x, k));
```

d. ```java
x = 5; y = 8;
System.out.println(another(y, x));
```

6. Consider the following method headings:

```java
public static int test(int x, char ch, double d, int y)
public static double two(double d1, double d2)
public static char three(int x, int y, char ch, double d)
```

Answer the following questions.

a. How many parameters does the method **test** have? What is the type of the method **test**?

b. How many parameters does method **two** have? What is the type of method **two**?

c. How many parameters does method **three** have? What is the type of method **three**?

d. How many actual parameters are needed to call the method **test**? What is the type of each parameter, and in what order should you use these parameters in a call to the method **test**?

e. Write a Java statement that prints the value returned by the method **test** with the actual parameters **5, 5, 7.3,** and **'z'**.

f. Write a Java statement that prints the value returned by method **two** with the actual parameters **17.5** and **18.3**, respectively.

g. Write a Java statement that prints the next character returned by method **three**. (Use your own actual parameters.)

7. Consider the following method:

```
public static int mystery(int x, double y, char ch)
{
    int u;

    if ('A' <= ch && ch <= 'R')
        return(2 * x + (int)(y));
    else
        return((int)(2 * y) - x);
}
```

What is the output of the following Java statements?

a. `System.out.println(mystery(5, 4.3, 'B'));`

b. `System.out.println(mystery(4, 9.7, 'v'));`

c. `System.out.println(2 * mystery(6, 3.9, 'D'));`

8. Consider the following method:

```
public static int secret(int one)
{
    int i;
    int prod = 1;

    for (i = 1; i <= 3; i++)
        prod = prod * one;
    return prod;
}
```

a. What is the output of the following Java statements?

i. `System.out.println(secret(5));`

ii. `System.out.println(2 * secret(6));`

b. What does the method **secret** do?

9. Show the output of the following program.

```java
public class MysteryClass
{
    public static void main(String[] args)
    {
        int n;

        for (n = 1; n <= 5; n++)
            System.out.println(mystery(n));
    }

    public static int mystery(int k)
    {
        int x, y;

        y = k;

        for (x = 1; x <= (k - 1); x++)
            y = y * (k - x);

        return y;
    }
}
```

10. Show the output of the following program.

```java
public class StrangeClass
{
    public static void main(String[] args)
    {
        int num = 0;

        while (num <= 29)
        {
            if (strange(num))
                System.out.println("True");
            else
                System.out.println("False");

            num = num + 4;
        }
    }
}
```

```java
public static boolean strange(int n)
{
        if (n % 2 == 0 && n % 3 == 0)
            return true;
        else
            return false;
}
}
```

11. In the program fragment shown below, identify the following items: method heading, method body, method definition, formal parameters, actual parameters, method call, and local variables.

```java
public class Exercise11                       //Line 1
{                                             //Line 2
    public static void main(String[] args)    //Line 3
    {                                         //Line 4
        int x;                                //Line 5
        double y;                             //Line 6
        char z;                               //Line 7
        //...                                 //Line 8
        hello(x, y, z);                       //Line 9
        //...                                 //Line 10
        hello(x + 2, y - 3.5, 'S');           //Line 11
        //...                                 //Line 12
    }                                         //Line 13

    public static void hello(int first, double second, //Line 14
                              char ch)        //Line 15
    {                                         //Line 16
        int num;                              //Line 17
        double y;                             //Line 18
        //...                                 //Line 19
    }                                         //Line 20
}
```

12. For the program in Exercise 11, fill in the blanks below with variable names to show the matching that occurs between the actual and the formal parameter list in each of the two calls.

First Call to `hello`   Second Call to `hello`

	Formal	Actual		Formal	Actual
1.	_____	_____	1.	_____	_____
2.	_____	_____	2.	_____	_____
3.	_____	_____	3.	_____	_____

13. What is the output of the following program?

```java
public class Exercise13
{
    public static void main(String[] args)
    {
        int num1;
        IntClass num2;

        num1 = 5;
        num2 = new IntClass(10);
        test(24, num2);
        test(num1, num2);
        test(num1 * num1, num2);
        test(num1 + num1, num2);
    }

    public static void test(int first, IntClass second)
    {
        int third;

        third = first + second.getNum() * second.getNum() + 2;
        first = second.getNum() - first;
        second.setNum(2 * second.getNum());
        System.out.println(first + " " + second + " "
                           + third);
    }
}
```

14. Assume the following input values:

```
7 3 6 4
2 6 3 5
```

Show the output of the following program:

```java
import java.util.*;

public class Exercise14
{
    static Scanner console = new Scanner(System.in);

    public static void main(String[] args)
    {
        int first, third;
        IntClass second, fourth;

        first = 3;
        second = new IntClass(4);
        third = 6;
        fourth = new IntClass(7);
```

```
            System.out.println(first + "   " + second.getNum()
                                + " " + third + "   "
                                + fourth.getNum());
            getData(first, second, third, fourth);
            System.out.println(first + "   " + second.getNum()
                                + "   " + third + "   "
                                + fourth.getNum());
            fourth.setNum(first * second.getNum() + third +
                          fourth.getNum());
            getData(third, fourth, first, second);
            System.out.println(first + "   " + second.getNum()
                                + "   " + third + "   "
                                + fourth.getNum());
        }

        public static void getData(int a, IntClass b, int c,
                            IntClass d)
        {
            a = console.nextInt();
            b.setNum(console.nextInt());
            c = console.nextInt();
            d.setNum(console.nextInt());

            b.setNum(a * b.getNum() - c);
            d.setNum(b.getNum() + d.getNum());
        }
    }
```

7

15. In the following program, number the marked statements to show the order in which they will execute (the logical order of execution).

```
import java.util.*;

public class Exercise15
{
    static Scanner console = new Scanner(System.in);

    public static void main(String[] args)
    {
        int num1, num2;
        System.out.println("Please enter two integers "
                            + "on separate lines");
_____ num1 = console.nextInt();
_____ num2 = console.nextInt();
_____ func (num1, num2);
_____ System.out.println("The two integers are " + num1
                            + ", " + num2);
    }
```

```
    public static void func(int val1, int val2)
    {
        int val3, val4;
_____   val3 = val1 + val2;
_____   val4 = val1 * val2;
_____   System.out.println("The sum and product are " + val3
                        + " and " + val4);
    }
```

16. Consider the following program. What is its exact output? Show the values of the variables after each line executes, as in Example 7-11.

```
public class Exercise16
{
    public static void main(String[] args)
    {
        int num1;
        IntClass num2;

        num1 = 10;                                              //Line 1
        num2 = new IntClass(20);                                //Line 2

        System.out.println("Line 3: In main: num1 = "
                        + num1 + ", num2 = "
                        + num2.getNum());                       //Line 3
        funcOne(num1, num2);                                    //Line 4
        System.out.println("Line 5: In main after funcOne: "
                        + "num1 = " + num1 + ", num2 = "
                        + num2.getNum());                       //Line 5
    }

    public static void funcOne(int a, IntClass b)
    {
        int x;
        int z;

        x = b.getNum();                                         //Line 6
        z = a + x;                                              //Line 7

        System.out.println("Line 8: In funcOne: a = " + a
                        + ", b = " + b.getNum()
                        + ", x = " + x
                        + ", and z = " + z);                    //Line 8

        x = x + 5;                                              //Line 9

        System.out.println("Line 10: In funcOne: a = " + a
                        + ", b = " + b.getNum()
                        + ", x = " + x
                        + ", and z = " + z);                    //Line 10
```

```
        a = a + 8;                                      //Line 11
        b.setNum(a + x + z);                            //Line 12

        System.out.println("Line 13: In funcOne: a = " + a
                          + ", b = " + b.getNum()
                          + ", x = " + x
                          + ", and z = " + z);          //Line 13
    }
}
```

PROGRAMMING EXERCISES

1. Write a value-returning method, isVowel, that returns the value **true** if a given character is a vowel, and otherwise returns **false**.

2. Write a program that prompts the user to input a sequence of characters and outputs the number of vowels. (Use the method isVowel written in Programming Exercise 1.)

3. Consider the following program segment:

```
public class Ch7Ex3
{
    public static void main(String[] args)
    {
        int num;
        double dec;
        .
        .
        .
    }

    public static int one(int x, int y)
    {
        .
        .
        .
    }

    public static double two(int x, double a)
    {
        int first;
        double z;
        .
        .
        .
    }
}
```

a. Write the definition of method **one** so that it returns the sum of **x** and **y** if **x** is greater than **y**; otherwise, it should return **x** minus 2 times **y**.

b. Write the definition of method **two** as follows:

　　i. Read a number and store it in **z**.

　　ii. Update the value of **z** by adding the value of **a** to its previous value.

　　iii. Assign the variable **first** the value returned by method **one** with the parameters 6 and 8.

　　iv. Update the value of **first** by adding the value of **x** to its previous value.

　　v. If the value of **z** is more than twice the value of **first**, return **z**; otherwise, return 2 times **first** minus **z**.

c. Write a Java program that tests parts a and b. (Declare additional variables in the method **main**, if necessary.)

4. Write a method, **reverseDigit**, that takes an integer as a parameter and returns the number with its digits reversed. For example, the value of **reverseDigit(12345)** is **54321**. Also, write a program to test your method.

5. The following formula gives the distance between two points (x_1, y_1) and (x_2, y_2) in the Cartesian plane:

$$\sqrt{(x_2-x_1)^2+(y_2-y_1)^2}$$

Given the center and a point on a circle, you can use this formula to find the radius of the circle. Write a program that prompts the user to enter the center and a point on the circle. The program should then output the circle's radius, diameter, circumference, and area. Your program must have at least the following methods:

a. **distance**: This method takes as its parameters four numbers that represent two points in the plane and returns the distance between them.

b. **radius**: This method takes as its parameters four numbers that represent the center and a point on the circle, calls the method **distance** to find the radius of the circle, and returns the circle's radius.

c. **circumference**: This method takes as its parameter a number that represents the radius of the circle and returns the circle's circumference. (If r is the radius, the circumference is $2\pi r$.)

d. **area**: This method takes as its parameter a number that represents the radius of the circle and returns the circle's area. (If r is the radius, the area is πr^2.)

e. Assume that $\pi = 3.1416$.

6. If P is the population on the first day of the year, B is the birth rate, and D is the death rate, the estimated population at the end of the year is given by the formula:

$$P + \frac{B*P}{100} - \frac{D*P}{100}$$

The population growth rate is given by the formula:

$$B - D$$

Write a program that prompts the user to enter the starting population, birth and death rates, and n, the number of years. The program should then calculate and print the estimated population after n years. Your program must consist of the following methods:

a. `growthRate`: This method takes as its parameters the birth and death rates, and it returns the population growth rate.

b. `estimatedPopulation`: This method takes as its parameters the current population, population growth rate, and n, the number of years. It returns the estimated population after n years.

Your program should not accept a negative birth rate, negative death rate, or a population less than 2.

7. Rewrite the Programming Example Cable Company Billing (from Chapter 4) so that it uses the following methods to calculate the billing amount:

a. `residentialCustomer`: This method calculates and returns the billing amount for the residential customer.

b. `businessCustomer`: This method calculates and returns the billing amount for the service business customer.

8. Rewrite the program in Programming Exercise 12 from Chapter 4 (cell phone company) so that it uses the following methods to calculate the billing amount. (In this programming exercise, do not output the number of minutes during which the service is used.)

a. `regularBill`: This method calculates and returns the billing amount for regular service.

b. `premiumBill`: This method calculates and returns the billing amount for premium service.

9. Consider the following program segment (with the method `main`):

```
public class Ch7Ex9
{
    public static void main(String[] arg)
    {
        IntClass x, y;
        CharClass z;
        double rate, hours;
        double amount;
            .
            .
            .

    }
}
```

Write the following definitions:

a. Write the definition of the method `initialize` that initializes `x` and `y` to `0` and `z` to the blank character.

b. Write the definition of the method `getHoursRate` that prompts the user to input the hours worked and rate per hour to initialize the variables `hours` and `rate` of the method `main`.

c. Write the definition of the value-returning method `payCheck` that calculates and returns the amount to be paid to an employee, based on the hours worked and rate per hour. The hours worked and rate per hour are stored in the variables `hours` and `rate`, respectively, of the method `main`. The formula for calculating the amount to be paid is as follows: for the first 40 hours, the rate is the given rate; for hours over 40, the rate is 1.5 times the given rate.

d. Write the definition of the method `printCheck` that prints the hours worked, rate per hour, and the amount due.

e. Write the definition of the method `funcOne` that prompts the user to input a number. The method then changes the value of `x` to 2 times the old value of `x` plus the value of `y` minus the value entered by the user.

f. Write the definition of the method `nextChar` that sets the value of `z` to the next character stored in `z`.

g. Write the definition of a method `main` that tests each of these methods. Also, write a complete program to test the methods of (a) through (e).

10. The method `printGrade` of this chapter's Example 7–8 is written as a **void** method to compute and output the course grade. The course score is passed as a parameter to the method `printGrade`. Rewrite the method `printGrade` as a value-returning method so that it computes and returns the course grade. (The course grade must be output in the method `main`.) Also, change the name of the method to `calculateGrade`.

11. In this exercise, you are to rewrite the Programming Example Classify Numbers (from Chapter 5). As written, the program inputs the data from the standard input device (keyboard) and outputs the results on the standard output device (screen). The program can process only 20 numbers. Rewrite the program to incorporate the following requirements:

a. Data to the program is input from a file of an unspecified length; that is, the program does not know in advance how many numbers are in the file.

b. Save the output of the program in a file.

c. Write the method `getNumber` so that it reads a number from the input file (opened in the method `main`), outputs the number to the output file (opened in the method `main`), and sends the number read to the method `main`. Print only 10 numbers per line.

d. Have the program find the sum and average of the numbers.

e. Write the method `printResults` so that it outputs the final results to the output file (opened in the method `main`). Other than outputting the appropriate counts, the definition of the method `printResults` should also output the sum and average of the numbers.

12. Rewrite the program developed in Programming Exercise 11 in Chapter 5, so that the method `main` is merely a collection of method calls. Your program should use the following methods:

a. Method `initialize`: This method initializes variables such as `countFemale`, `countMale`, `sumFemaleGPA`, and `sumMaleGPA`.

b. Method `sumGrades`: This method finds the sum of female and male students' GPAs.

c. Method `averageGrade`: This method finds the average GPA for female and male students.

d. Method `printResults`: This method outputs the relevant results.

Use the appropriate parameters to pass the information in and out of the methods.

13. Write a program that prints the day number of the year, given the date is in the form month day year. For example, if the input is 1 1 05, the day number is 1; if the input is 12 25 05, the day number is 359. The program should check for a leap year. A year is a leap year if it is divisible by 4 but not divisible by 100. For example, 1992 and 2008 are divisible by 4, but not by 100. A year that is divisible by 100 is a leap year if it is also divisible by 400. For example, 1600 and 2000 are divisible by 400. However, 1800 is not a leap year because 1800 is not divisible by 400.

14. Write a program that reads a student's name together with his or her test scores. The program should then compute the average test score for each student and assign the appropriate grade. The grade scale is as follows: `90-100, A; 80-89, B; 70-79, C; 60-69, D; 0-59, F`.

Your program must use the following methods:

a. A void method, `calculateAverage`, to determine the average of the five test scores for each student. Use a loop to read and sum the five test scores. (This method does not output the average test score. That task must be done in the method `main`.)

b. A value-returning method, `calculateGrade`, to determine and return each student's grade. (This method does not output the grade. That task must be done in the method `main`.)

7

Test your program on the following data. Read the data from a file and send the output to a file. Use the appropriate parameters to pass the values in and out of the methods.

```
Johnson 85 83 77 91 76
Aniston 80 90 95 93 48
Cooper 78 81 11 90 73
Gupta 92 83 30 69 87
Blair 23 45 96 38 59
Clark 60 85 45 39 67
Kennedy 77 31 52 74 83
Bronson 93 94 89 77 97
Sunny 79 85 28 93 82
Smith 85 72 49 75 63
```

Sample Output: The output should be of the following form. Fill the last two columns and the last line showing the class average.

(Output the test average and class average with two decimal places.)

Student	Test1	Test2	Test3	Test4	Test5	Average	Grade
Johnson	85	83	77	91	76		
Aniston	80	90	95	93	48		
Cooper	78	81	11	90	73		
Gupta	92	83	30	69	87		
Blair	23	45	96	38	59		
Clark	60	85	45	39	67		
Kennedy	77	31	52	74	83		
Bronson	93	94	89	77	97		
Sunny	79	85	28	93	82		
Smith	85	72	49	75	63		

```
Class Average =
```

15. Write a program to process text files. The program should read a text file and output the data in the file as is. The program should also output the number of words, number of lines, and number of paragraphs.

You must write and use the following methods:

a. `initialize`: This method initializes all the variables of the method `main`.

b. `processBlank`: This method reads and writes the blanks. Whenever it hits a non-blank (except whitespace characters), it increments the number of words in a line (this number is set back to zero in the method `updateCount`). The method exits after processing blanks.

c. `processText`: This method reads and writes nonblank characters. Whenever it hits a blank, it exits.

d. `updateCount`: This method takes place at the end of each line. It increments the number of lines and sets the number of words on a line back to zero. If there are no words in a line, it increments the number of paragraphs. One blank line (between paragraphs) is used to distinguish paragraphs and should not be counted with the number of lines. This method also updates the total word count.

e. `printTotal`: This method outputs the number of words, number of lines, and number of paragraphs.

Your program should read the data from a file and send the output to a file. Use the appropriate parameters to pass the values in and out of the methods. Test your program using the method `main` that looks like:

```
public static void main(String[] args)
{
    variable declarations
    open the files

    read a character
    while (not end of file)
    {
        while(not end of line)
        {
            processBlank(parameters);
            processText(parameters);
        }
        updateCount(parameters);
        read a character;
        ...
    }
    printTotal(parameters);
    close the files;
}
```

Because the program needs to do a character count, the program should read the input file character-by-character. Moreover, the program should also count the number of lines. Therefore, while reading the data from the input file, the program must capture the newline character. The `Scanner` **class** does not contain any method that can read only the next character in the input stream, unless the character is delimited by whitespace characters such as blanks. Moreover, using the `Scanner` **class**, the program should read the entire line, or the newline character will be ignored.

To simplify the reading of the input file character-by-character, you can use the Java **class** `FileReader`. (In Chapter 3, we introduced this class to create and initialize a `Scanner` object to the input source.) The **class** `FileReader` contains the method `read` that returns the integer value of the next character. For example, if the next input character is A, then the method `read` returns `65`. We can use the cast operator to change the value `65` to the character A. Notice that the method `read` *does not* skip any whitespace characters. Moreover, the method `read` returns `-1` when the end of the input file is reached. You can, therefore, use the value returned by the method **read** to determine whether the end of the input file is reached.

Consider the following statement:

```
FileReader inputStream = new FileReader("a:\\text.txt");
```

This statement creates the **FileReader** object **inputStream** and initializes it to the input file **text.txt**. (We assume that this file is on floppy drive A.) If **nextChar** is a **char** variable, then the following statement reads and stores the next character, from the input file, into **nextChar**:

```
ch = (char) inputStream.read();
```

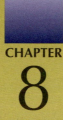

8

USER-DEFINED CLASSES
AND ADTs

In this chapter, you will:

♦ Learn about classes
♦ Learn about **private**, **protected**, **public**, and **static** members of a class
♦ Explore how classes are implemented
♦ Learn about the various operations on classes
♦ Examine constructors
♦ Examine the method `toString`
♦ Became aware of accessors and mutator methods
♦ Learn how to create your own packages
♦ Become aware of the reference **this**
♦ Learn about the abstract data type (ADT)

In the preceding chapters, you learned how to use various classes and their methods to manipulate data. Java does not provide all the classes that you will ever need. Therefore, you must learn how to create your own classes. This chapter discusses how to create classes and objects.

CLASSES

As you learned in earlier chapters, the first step in problem-solving with object-oriented design (OOD) is to identify the components called objects. An object combines data and the operations on that data in a single unit; the mechanism in Java that allows you to combine data and the operations on that data in a single unit is called a *class*. (Moreover, combining data and operations on that data is called *encapsulation*—the first principle of OOD.) Now that you know how to store and manipulate data in computer memory and how to construct your own methods, you are ready to learn how objects are constructed.

A **class** is a collection of a fixed number of components. The components of a **class** are called the **members** of the **class**.

The general syntax for defining a **class** is:

```
modifier(s) class ClassIdentifier modifier(s)
{
     classMembers
}
```

where **modifier(s)** are used to alter the behavior of the class and, usually, **classMembers** consist of named constants, variable declarations, and/or methods. That is, usually a member of a **class** can be either a variable (to store data) or a method. Some of the modifiers that we have encountered are **public**, **private**, and **static**.

- If a member of a class is a named constant, you declare it just like any other named constant.

- If a member of a class is a variable, you declare it just like any other variable.

- If a member of a class is a method, you define it just like any other method.

- If a member of a class is a method, it can (directly) access any member of the class—data members and methods. Therefore, when you write the definition of a method, you can directly access any data member of the class (without passing it as a parameter).

In Java, **class** is a reserved word, and it defines only a data type; no memory is allocated. It announces the declaration of a class. In Java, the data members of a **class** are also called **fields**.

The members of a **class** are usually classified into three categories: **private**, **public**, and **protected**. This chapter discusses the first two categories: **private** and **public**. Chapter 11 discusses **protected** members.

Following are some facts about **private** and **public** members of a class:

- If a member of a class is **private**, you *cannot* access it outside the class.

- If a member of a class is **public**, you *can* access it outside the class.

Recall that a package is collection of related classes. Later in this chapter, you will learn how to create your own packages. If a class member is declared/defined without any modifiers, then that class member can be accessed from anywhere in the package.

In Java, **private**, **protected**, and **public** are reserved words.

Suppose that we want to define the **class Clock** to implement the time of day in a program. Further suppose that the time is represented as a set of three integers: one to represent the hours, one to represent the minutes, and one to represent the seconds. We also want to perform the following operations on the time:

1. Set the time.

2. Return the hours.

3. Return the minutes.

4. Return the seconds.

5. Print the time.

6. Increment the time by one second.

7. Increment the time by one minute.

8. Increment the time by one hour.

9. Compare the two times for equality.

10. Copy the time.

11. Return a copy of the time.

To implement these 11 operations, we write algorithms, which we implement as methods— 11 methods to implement these 11 operations. So far, the **class Clock** has 14 members: 3 data members and 11 methods. Suppose that the 3 data members are **hr**, **min**, and **sec**, each of the type **int**.

Some members of the **class Clock** will be **private**, others will be **public**. Deciding which members to make **private** and which to make **public** depends on the nature of each member. The general rule is that any member that needs to be accessed from outside the class is declared **public**; any member that should not be accessed directly by the user should be declared **private**. For example, the user should be able to set the time and print the time. Therefore, the methods that set the time and print the time should be declared **public**.

Similarly, the method to increment the time and compare the times for equality should be declared **public**. On the other hand, users should not control the *direct* manipulation of the data members **hr**, **min**, and **sec**, so we will declare them **private**. Note that if the user has direct access to the data members, methods such as **setTime** are not needed.

The data members for the **class** Clock are:

```
private int hr;   //store the hours
private int min;  //store the minutes
private int sec;  //store the seconds
```

The (non-**static**) data members, variables declared without using the modifier (reserved word) **static**, of a **class** are called **instance variables**. Therefore, the variables hr, min, and sec are the instance variables of the **class** Clock.

Suppose the 11 methods to implement the 11 operations are as follows (we also specify the headings of the methods):

1. setTime sets the time to the time specified by the user. The method heading is:

   public void setTime(**int** hours, **int** minutes, **int** seconds)

2. getHours returns the hours. The method heading is:

   public int getHours()

3. getMinutes returns the minutes. The method heading is:

   public int getMinutes()

4. getSeconds returns the seconds. The method heading is:

   public int getSeconds()

5. printTime prints the time in the form hh:mm:ss. The method heading is:

   public void printTime()

6. incrementHours increments the time by one hour. The method heading is:

   public void incrementHours()

7. incrementMinutes increments the time by one minute. The method heading is:

   public void incrementMinutes()

8. incrementSeconds increments the time by one second. The method heading is:

   public void incrementSeconds()

9. equals compares two times to determine whether they are equal. The method heading is:

   public boolean equals(Clock otherClock)

10. makeCopy copies the time of one object into another object. The method heading is:

    public void makeCopy(Clock otherClock)

11. getCopy returns a copy of the time. A copy of the object's time is created and a reference to the copy is returned. The method heading is:

    public Clock getCopy()

The objective of the method `setTime` is to set the values of the instance variables. In other words, it changes the values of the instance variables. Such methods are called *mutator* methods. On the other hand, the method `getTime` only accesses the value of an instance variable; that is, it does not change the value of the instance variable. Such methods are called *accessor* methods. These methods are described in detail later in this chapter.

The methods of a class are called the **instance methods** of the class.

 In the definition of the **class** `Clock`, all the data members are **private** and all the method members are **public**. However, a method can also be **private**. For example, if a method is used only to implement other methods of the class, and the user does not need to access this method, you make it **private**. Similarly, a data member of a **class** can also be **public**.

Notice that we have not yet written the definitions of the methods of the **class** `Clock`. (You will learn how to write them in the section Definitions of the Constructors and Methods of the **class** `Clock`.) Also notice that the method `equals` has only one parameter, although you need two things to make a comparison. Similarly, the method `makeCopy` has only one parameter. An example later in this chapter will help explain this concept.

Before giving the definition of the **class** `Clock`, we first introduce another important concept related to classes—constructors.

Constructors

In addition to the methods necessary to implement operations, every class has *special* types of methods called constructors. A **constructor** has the same name as the class, and it executes automatically when an object of that class is created. Constructors are used to guarantee that the instance variables of the class initialize to specific values.

There are two types of constructors: with parameters and without parameters. The constructor without parameters is called the **default constructor**.

Constructors have the following properties:

- The name of a constructor is the same as the name of the class.

- A constructor, even though it is a method, has no type. That is, it is neither a value-returning method nor a **void** method.

- A class can have more than one constructor. However, all constructors of a class have the same name. That is, the constructors of a class can be overloaded.

- If a class has more than one constructor, the constructors have a different number of formal parameters. However, if the number of formal parameters is the same, then the data types of the formal parameters, in the order you list, must differ in at least one position. In other words, any two constructors must have different *signatures*.

8

- Constructors execute automatically when class objects are instantiated. Because they have no types, they cannot be called like other methods.

- If there are multiple constructors, the constructor that executes depends on the type of values passed to the class object when the class object is instantiated.

For the **class** Clock, we will include two constructors: the default constructor and a constructor with parameters. The default constructor initializes the instance variables to store the hours, minutes, and seconds, each to 0. Similarly, the constructor with parameters initializes the instance variables to the values specified by the user. We will illustrate shortly how constructors are invoked.

The heading of the default constructor is:

public Clock()

The heading of the constructor with parameters is:

public Clock(**int** hours, **int** minutes, **int** seconds)

It now follows that the definition of the **class** Clock has 16 members: 11 methods to implement the 11 operations, 2 constructors, and 3 instance variables to store the hours, minutes, and seconds.

 If you do not include any constructor in a class, then Java *automatically* provides the default constructor. Therefore, when you create an object, the instance variables are initialized to their default values. For example, **int** variables are initialized to 0. If you provide at least one constructor and do not include the default constructor, then Java *will not automatically* provide the default constructor. Generally, if a class includes constructors, you also include the default constructor.

Unified Modeling Language Class Diagrams

A class and its members can be described graphically using **Unified Modeling Language (UML)** notation. For example, Figure 8-1 shows the UML diagram of the **class** Clock. Moreover, what appears in the figure is called the **UML class diagram** of the class.

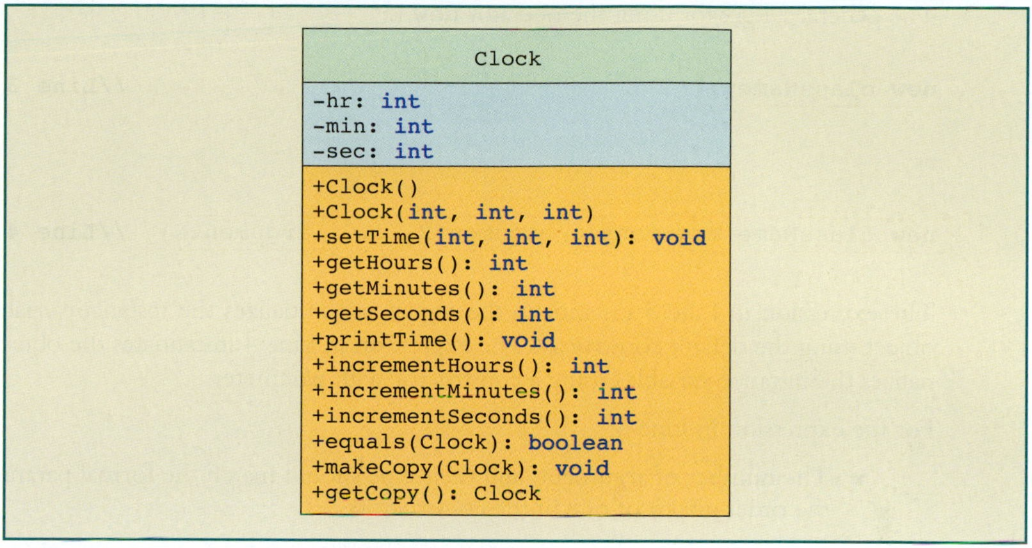

```
                          Clock

        -hr:  int
        -min: int
        -sec: int

        +Clock()
        +Clock(int, int, int)
        +setTime(int, int, int): void
        +getHours(): int
        +getMinutes(): int
        +getSeconds(): int
        +printTime(): void
        +incrementHours(): int
        +incrementMinutes(): int
        +incrementSeconds(): int
        +equals(Clock): boolean
        +makeCopy(Clock): void
        +getCopy(): Clock
```

Figure 8-1   UML class diagram of the **class** `Clock`

8

The top box in the UML diagram contains the name of the class. The middle box contains the data members and their data types. The last box contains the method names, parameter list, and return types. The + (plus) sign in front of a member indicates that it is a **public** member; the – (minus) sign indicates that it is a **private** member. The # symbol before a member name indicates that it is a **protected** member.

Variable Declaration and Object Instantiation

Once a **class** is defined, you can declare reference variables of that **class** type. For example, the following statements declare `myClock` and `yourClock` to be reference variables of the type `Clock`:

```
Clock myClock;           //Line 1
Clock yourClock;         //Line 2
```

These statements *do not* allocate memory spaces to store the hours, minutes, and seconds. Next, we explain how to allocate memory space to store the hours, minutes, and seconds, and how to access that memory space using the variables `myClock` and `yourClock`.

The **class** `Clock` has three instance variables. To store the hours, minutes, and seconds, we need to create a `Clock` object, which is accomplished by using the operator **new**.

The general syntax for using the operator **new** is:

```
new className()                                            //Line 3
```

or:

```
new className(argument1, argument2, ..., argumentN)  //Line 4
```

The expression in Line 3 instantiates the object and initializes the instance variables of the object using the default constructor. The expression in Line 4 instantiates the object and initializes the instance variables using a constructor with parameters.

For the expression in Line 4:

- The number of arguments and their type should match the formal parameters (in the order given) of one of the constructors.

- If the type of the arguments does not match the formal parameters of any constructor (in the order given), Java uses type conversion and looks for the best match. For example, an integer value might be converted to a floating-point value with a zero decimal part. Any ambiguity will result in a compile-time error.

Consider the following statements (notice that **myClock** and **yourClock** are as declared in Lines 1 and 2):

```
myClock = new Clock();                                    //Line 5
yourClock = new Clock(9, 35, 15);                         //Line 6
```

The statement in Line 5 allocates memory space for a **Clock** object, initializes each instance variable of the object to **0**, and stores the address of the object into **myClock**. The statement in Line 6 allocates memory space for a **Clock** object; initializes the instance variables **hr**, **min**, and **sec** of the object to **9**, **35**, and **15**, respectively; and stores the address of the object into **yourClock**. See Figure 8-2.

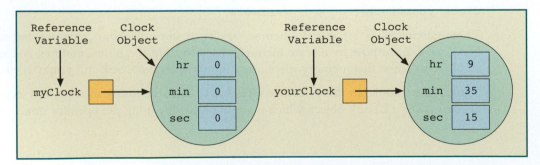

Figure 8-2 Variables **myClock** and **yourClock** and **Clock** objects

To be specific, we call the object to which `myClock` points the object `myClock` and the object to which `yourClock` points the object `yourClock`. See Figure 8-3.

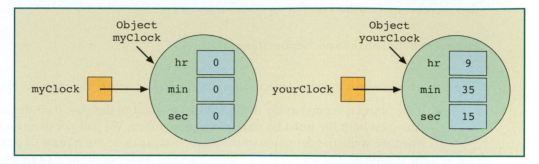

Figure 8-3   Objects `myClock` and `yourClock`

Of course, you can combine the statements to declare the variable and instantiate the object into one statement. For example, the statements in Lines 1 and 5 can be combined as:

```
Clock myClock = new Clock();    //declare and instantiate myClock
```

That is, the preceding statement declares `myClock` to be a reference variable of the type `Clock`, and instantiates the object `myClock` to store the hours, minutes, and seconds. Each instance variable of the object `myClock` is initialized to 0 by the default constructor.

Similarly, the statements in Lines 2 and 6 can be combined as:

```
Clock yourClock = new Clock(9, 35, 15);   //declare and
                                          //instantiate yourClock
```

That is, the preceding statement declares `yourClock` to be a reference variable of the type `Clock`, and instantiates the object `yourClock` to store the hours, minutes, and seconds. The instance variables `hr`, `min`, and `sec` of the object `yourClock` are initialized to 9, 35, and 15, respectively, by the constructor with parameters.

 When we use phrases such as "create an object of a **class** type," we mean to: (i) declare a reference variable of the **class** type; (ii) instantiate the **class** object; and (iii) store the address of the object into the reference variable declared. For example, the following statements create the object `tempClock` of the `Clock` type:

```
Clock tempClock = new Clock();
```

The object `tempClock` is accessed via the reference variable `tempClock`.

Recall from Chapter 3 that a **class** object is called an **instance** of that **class**.

Accessing Class Members

Once an object of a class is created, the object can access the members (as explained in the next paragraph, after the syntax) of the **class**. The general syntax for an object to access a data member or a method is:

referenceVariableName.memberName

The class members that the class object can access depend on where the object is created.

- If the object is created in the definition of a method of the class, then the object can access both the **public** and **private** members. We will elaborate on this when we write the definition of the method **equals** of the **class** Clock (in the section, Definitions of the Constructors and Methods of the **class** Clock, later in this chapter).

- If the object is created elsewhere (for example, in a user's program), then the object can access *only* the **public** members of the class.

Recall that in Java, the dot **.** (period) is called the **member access operator**.

Example 8-1 illustrates how to access the members of a class.

Example 8-1

Suppose that the objects **myClock** and **yourClock** have been created as before. Consider the following statements:

```
myClock.setTime(5, 2, 30);
myClock.printTime();
yourClock.setTime(x, y, z);   //Assume x, y, and z are
                              //variables of the type int
                              //and they have been initialized.

if (myClock.equals(yourClock))
 .
 .
 .
```

These statements are legal; that is, they are syntactically correct. Note the following:

- In the first statement, myClock.setTime(5, 2, 30);, the method setTime is executed. The values 5, 2, and 30 are passed as parameters to the method setTime, and the method uses these values to set the values of hr, min, and sec of the object myClock to 5, 2, and 30, respectively.

- Similarly, the second statement executes the method printTime and outputs the values of hr, min, and sec of the object myClock.

- In the third statement, the values of the variables **x**, **y**, and **z** are used to set the values of **hr**, **min**, and **sec** of the object **yourClock**.

- In the fourth statement, the method **equals** executes and compares the instance variables of the object **myClock** with the corresponding instance variables of the object **yourClock**. Because in this statement the method **equals** is invoked by the variable **myClock**, it has direct access to the instance variables of the object **myClock**. So it needs one more object, which in this case is the object **yourClock**, to compare. This explains why the method **equals** has only one parameter.

The objects **myClock** and **yourClock** can access only **public** members of the class. The following statements are illegal because **hr** and **min** are **private** members of the **class Clock** and, therefore, cannot be accessed by **myClock** and **yourClock**:

```
myClock.hr = 10;                    //illegal
myClock.min = yourClock.min;        //illegal
```

Built-in Operations on Classes

Most of Java's built-in operations do not apply to classes. You cannot perform arithmetic operations on class objects. For example, you cannot use the operator + to add the values of two **Clock** objects. Also, you cannot use relational operators to compare two class objects.

The built-in operation that is valid for classes is the dot operator (**.**). A reference variable uses the dot operator to access **public** members; classes can use the dot operator to access **public static** members.

Assignment Operator and Classes: A Precaution

This section discusses how the assignment operator works with reference variables and objects.

Suppose that the objects **myClock** and **yourClock** are as shown in Figure 8-4.

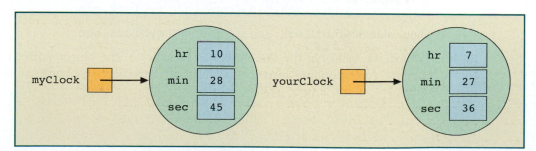

Figure 8-4   Objects **myClock** and **yourClock**

The statement:

```
myClock = yourClock;
```

copies the value of the reference variable `yourClock` into the reference variable `myClock`. After this statement executes, both `yourClock` and `myClock` refer to the same object. Figure 8-5 illustrates this situation.

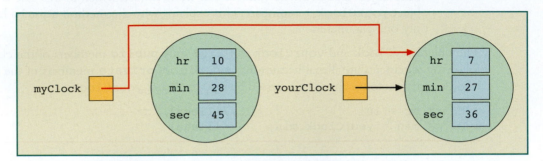

Figure 8-5 `myClock` and `yourClock` after the statement `myClock = yourClock;` executes

This is called the shallow copying of data. In **shallow copying** two or more reference variables of the same type point to the same object.

To copy the instance variables of the object `yourClock` into the corresponding instance variables of the object `myClock`, you need to use the method **makeCopy**. This is accomplished by the following statement:

```
myClock.makeCopy(yourClock);
```

After this statement executes:

1. The value of `yourClock.hr` is copied into `myClock.hr`.

2. The value of `yourClock.min` is copied into `myClock.min`.

3. The value of `yourClock.sec` is copied into `myClock.sec`.

In other words, the values of the three instance variables of the object `yourClock` are copied into the corresponding instance variables of the object `myClock`, as shown in Figure 8-6.

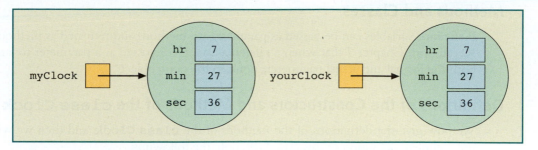

Figure 8-6   Objects `myClock` and `yourClock` after the statement `myClock.makeCopy(yourClock);` executes

This is called the deep copying of data. In **deep copying**, each reference variable refers to its *own* object, as in Figure 8-6, *not* the same object, as in Figure 8-5.

Another way to avoid the shallow copying of data is to have the object being copied create a copy of itself, and then return a reference to the copy. This is accomplished by the method `getCopy`. Consider the following statement:

```
myClock = yourClock.getCopy();
```

In this statement, the expression `yourClock.getCopy()` makes a copy of the object `yourClock` and returns the address, that is, the reference, of the copy. The assignment statement stores this address into `myClock`.

 The methods `makeCopy` and `getCopy` are both used to avoid the shallow copying of data. The main difference between these two methods is: To use the method `makeCopy`, both objects—the object whose data is being copied and the object that is copying the data—must be instantiated before invoking this method. To use the method `getCopy`, the object whose data is being copied must be instantiated before invoking this method, while the object of the reference variable receiving a copy of the data need not be instantiated. Moreover, note that `makeCopy` and `getCopy` are *user-defined* methods.

 It is important to understand the difference between the shallow and deep copying of data and when to use which. Shallow copying is a common mistake, especially by beginning Java programmers.

Class Scope

A reference variable has the same scope as other variables. A member of a class is local to the class. You access a **public class** member outside the **class** through the reference variable name or the **class** name (for **static** members) and the member access operator (**.**).

Methods and Classes

Reference variables can be passed as parameters to methods and returned as method values. Recall from Chapter 7 that when a reference variable is passed as a parameter to a method, both the formal and actual parameters point to the same object.

Definitions of the Constructors and Methods of the **class** Clock

We now give the definitions of the methods of the **class** Clock, and then we will write the complete definition of this class. First, note the following:

1. The **class** Clock has 11 methods: setTime, getHours, getMinutes, getSeconds, printTime, incrementHours, incrementMinutes, incrementSeconds, equals, makeCopy, and getCopy. It has two constructors and three instance variables: hr, min, and sec.

2. The three instance variables—hr, min, and sec—are **private** to the **class** and cannot be accessed outside the **class**.

3. The 11 methods—setTime, getHours, getMinutes, getSeconds, printTime, incrementHours, incrementMinutes, incrementSeconds, equals, makeCopy, and getCopy—can directly access the instance variables (hr, min, and sec). In other words, we do not pass instance variables or data members as parameters to these methods. Similarly, constructors directly access the instance variables.

Let's first write the definition of the method setTime. The method setTime has three parameters of the type **int**. This method sets the instance variables to the values specified by the user, which are passed as parameters to this function. The definition of the method setTime follows:

```java
public void setTime(int hours, int minutes, int seconds)
{
    if (0 <= hours && hours < 24)
        hr = hours;
    else
        hr = 0;

    if (0 <= minutes && minutes < 60)
        min = minutes;
    else
        min = 0;

    if (0 <= seconds && seconds < 60)
        sec = seconds;
    else
        sec = 0;
}
```

Note that the definition of the method `setTime` checks for the valid values of `hours`, `minutes`, and `seconds`. If any of these values are out of range, the corresponding instance variable is initialized to `0`. Now let's look at how the method `setTime` works.

The method `setTime` is a **void** method and has three parameters. Therefore:

- A call to this method is a stand–alone statement.

- We must use three parameters in a call to this method.

Furthermore, recall that because `setTime` is a member of the **class** `Clock`, it can directly access the instance variables `hr`, `min`, and `sec`, as shown in the definition of `setTime`.

Suppose that the object `myClock` is as shown in Figure 8-7.

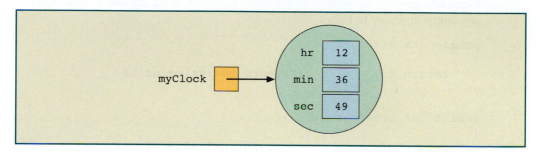

Figure 8-7   Object `myClock`

Consider the following statement:

```
myClock.setTime(3, 48, 52);
```

The variable `myClock` accesses the member `setTime`. In the statement `myClock.setTime(3, 48, 52);`, `setTime` is accessed by the variable `myClock`. Therefore, the three variables—`hr`, `min`, and `sec`—referred to in the body of the method `setTime` are the three instance variables of the object `myClock`. Thus, the values `3`, `48`, and `52`, which are passed as parameters in the preceding statement, are assigned to the three instance variables of the object `myClock` by the method `setTime` (see the body of the method `setTime`). After the previous statement executes, `myClock` is as shown in Figure 8–8.

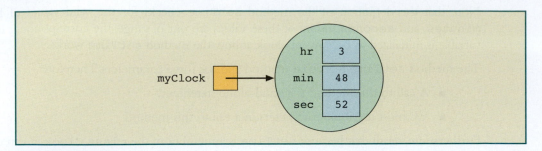

Figure 8-8   `myClock` after the statement `myClock.setTime(3, 48, 52);` executes

Next, let's give the definitions of the other methods of the **class** Clock. These definitions are simple and easy to follow.

```
public int getHours()
{
    return hr;          //return the value of hr
}

public int getMinutes()
{
    return min;         //return the value of min
}

public int getSeconds()
{
    return sec;         //return the value of sec
}

public void printTime()
{
    if (hr < 10)
        System.out.print("0");
    System.out.print(hr + ":");

    if (min < 10)
        System.out.print("0");
    System.out.print(min + ":");

    if (sec < 10)
        System.out.print("0");
    System.out.print(sec);
}
```

```
public void incrementHours()
{
    hr++;              //increment the value of hr by 1
    if (hr > 23)       //if hr is greater than 23,
        hr = 0;        //set hr to 0
}

public void incrementMinutes()
{
    min++;                 //increment the value of min by 1
    if (min > 59)          //if min is greater than 59
    {
        min = 0;               //set min to 0
        incrementHours();      //increment hr
    }
}

public void incrementSeconds()
{
    sec++;                 //increment the value of sec by 1
    if (sec > 59)          //if sec is greater than 59
    {
        sec = 0;                   //set sec to 0
        incrementMinutes();        //increment min
    }
}
```

From the definitions of the methods **incrementMinutes** and **incrementSeconds**, you can see that a method of a **class** can call other methods of the **class**.

The method **equals** has the following definition:

```
public boolean equals(Clock otherClock)
{
    return(hr == otherClock.hr
           && min == otherClock.min
           && sec == otherClock.sec);
}
```

Let's see how the method **equals** works.

Suppose that **myClock** and **yourClock** are as shown in Figure 8-9.

8

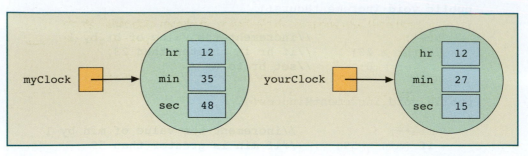

Figure 8-9   Objects `myClock` and `yourClock`

Consider the following statement:

```
if (myClock.equals(yourClock))
.
.
.
```

In the expression:

```
myClock.equals(yourClock)
```

`myClock` accesses the method `equals`. The value of the parameter `yourClock` is passed to the formal parameter `otherClock`, as shown in Figure 8–10.

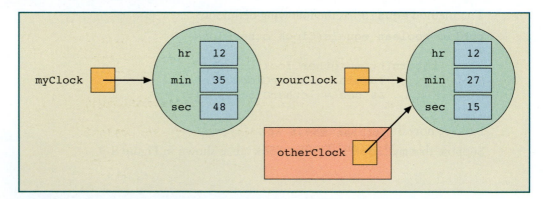

Figure 8-10   Object `myClock` and the parameter `otherClock`

Note that `otherClock` and `yourClock` refer to the same object. The instance variables `hr`, `min`, and `sec` of the object `otherClock` have the values 12, 27, and 15, respectively. In other words, when the body of the method `equals` executes, the value of `otherClock.hr` is 12, the value of `otherClock.min` is 27, and the value of `otherClock.sec` is 15. The method `equals` is a member of `myClock`. When the method `equals` executes, the variables `hr`, `min`, and `sec` in the body of the method `equals` are the instance variables of the object `myClock`. Therefore, the instance variable `hr` of the object `myClock` is compared with `otherClock.hr`, the instance variable `min` of the object `myClock` is compared with `otherClock.min`, and the instance variable `sec` of the object `myClock` is compared with `otherClock.sec`.

Once again, in the expression:

`myClock.equals(yourClock)`

the method `equals` is invoked by `myClock` and compares the object `myClock` with the object `yourClock`. It follows that the method `equals` needs only one parameter.

Let us again take a look at the definitions of the method `equals`. Notice that within the definition of this method, the object `otherClock` accesses the data members `hr`, `min`, and `sec`. However, these data members are **private**. So is there any violation? The answer is no. The method `equals` is a member of the **class** `Clock` and `hr`, `min`, and `sec` are the data members. Moreover, `otherClock` is an object of the **class** `Clock`. Therefore, the object `otherClock` can access its **private** data members within the definition of the method `equals`. The same is, in fact, true for any method of a class.

That is, in general, when you write the definition of a method, say `dummyMethod`, of a **class**, say `DummyClass`, and the method uses an object, `dummyObject` of the **class** `DummyClass`, then within the definition of `dummyMethod` the object `dummyObject` can access its **private** data members (in fact, any **private** member of the class.)

The method `makeCopy` copies the instance variables of its parameter, `otherClock`, into the corresponding instance variables of the object referenced by the variable using this method. Its definition is:

```
public void makeCopy(Clock otherClock)
{
    hr = otherClock.hr;
    min = otherClock.min;
    sec = otherClock.sec;
}
```

Consider the following statement:

`myClock.makeCopy(yourClock);`

In this statement, the method `makeCopy` is invoked by `myClock`. The three instance variables `hr`, `min`, and `sec` in the body of the method `makeCopy` are the instance variables of the object `myClock`. The variable `yourClock` is passed as a parameter to `makeCopy`. Therefore, `yourClock` and `otherClock` refer to the same object, which is the object `yourClock`. Thus, after the preceding statement executes, the instance variables of the object `yourClock` are copied into the corresponding instance variables of the object `myClock`.

8

The method `getCopy` creates a copy of an object's `hr`, `min`, and `sec` and returns the address of the copy of the object. That is, the method `getCopy` creates a new `Clock` object, initializes the instance variables of this object, and returns the object's address. The definition of the method `getCopy` is:

```
public Clock getCopy()
{
    Clock temp = new Clock();    //Line 1

    temp.hr = hr;                //Line 2
    temp.min = min;              //Line 3
    temp.sec = sec;              //Line 4

    return temp;                 //Line 5
}
```

The following discussion illustrates how the method `getCopy` works. Suppose that `yourClock` is as shown in Figure 8-11.

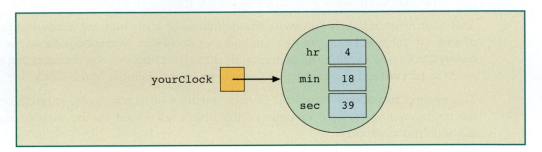

Figure 8-11   Object `yourClock`

Consider the following statement:

```
myClock = yourClock.getCopy();        //Line A
```

In this statement, because the method `getCopy` is invoked by `yourClock`, the three variables `hr`, `min`, and `sec` in the body of the method `getCopy` are the instance variables of the object `yourClock`. The body of the method `getCopy` executes as follows: The statement in Line 1 creates the `Clock` object `temp`. The statements in Lines 2 through 4 copy the instance variables of the object `yourClock` into the corresponding instance variables of `temp`. In other words, the object referenced by `temp` is a copy of the object `yourClock`. (See Figure 8-12.)

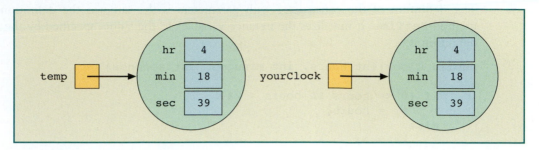

Figure 8-12   Objects `temp` and `yourClock`

The statement in Line 5 returns the value of `temp`, which is the address of the object holding a copy of the data. The value returned by the method `getCopy` is copied into `myClock`. Therefore, after the statement in Line A executes, `myClock` and `yourClock` are as shown in Figure 8–13.

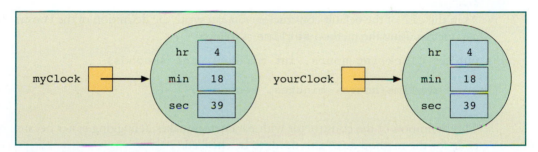

Figure 8-13   Objects `myClock` and `yourClock`

Next, we give the definitions of the constructors. The default constructor initializes each instance variable to 0. Its definition is:

```
public Clock()
{
    hr = 0;
    min = 0;
    sec = 0;
}
```

You can also write the definition of the default constructor using the method `setTime` as follows:

```
public Clock()
{
    setTime(0, 0, 0);
}
```

The definition of the constructor with parameters is the same as the definition of the method `setTime`. It initializes the instance variables to the values specified by the user. Its definition is:

```java
public Clock(int hours, int minutes, int seconds)
{
    if (0 <= hours && hours < 24)
        hr = hours;
    else
        hr = 0;

    if (0 <= minutes && minutes < 60)
        min = minutes;
    else
        min = 0;

    if (0 <= seconds && seconds < 60)
        sec = seconds;
    else
        sec = 0;
}
```

As in the case of the default constructor, you can write the definition of the constructor with parameters using the method `setTime` as follows:

```java
public Clock(int hours, int minutes, int seconds)
{
    setTime(hours, minutes, seconds);
}
```

This definition of the constructor with parameters makes debugging easier because only the code for the method `setTime` needs to be checked.

Definition of the `class` Clock

Now that you have defined the methods of the **class** Clock, we can give the complete definition of the **class** Clock. Before the definition of a method, we include comments specifying the preconditions and/or postconditions.

Precondition: A statement specifying the condition(s) that must be true before the function is called.

Postcondition: A statement specifying what is true after the function call is completed:

The definition of the **class** Clock is:

```java
public class Clock
{
    private int hr;  //store hours
    private int min; //store minutes
    private int sec; //store seconds

        //Default constructor
        //Postcondition: hr = 0; min = 0; sec = 0;
```

```
public Clock()
{
    setTime(0, 0, 0);
}

    //Constructor with parameters, to set the time
    //The time is set according to the parameters.
    //Postcondition: hr = hours; min = minutes; sec = seconds;
public Clock(int hours, int minutes, int seconds)
{
    setTime(hours, minutes, seconds);
}


    //Method to set the time
    //The time is set according to the parameters.
    //Postcondition: hr = hours; min = minutes; sec = seconds;
public void setTime(int hours, int minutes, int seconds)
{
    if (0 <= hours && hours < 24)
        hr = hours;
    else
        hr = 0;

    if (0 <= minutes && minutes < 60)
        min = minutes;
    else
        min = 0;

    if (0 <= seconds && seconds < 60)
        sec = seconds;
    else
        sec = 0;
}


    //Method to return the hours
    //Postcondition: The value of hr is returned.
public int getHours()
{
    return hr;
}


    //Method to return the minutes
    //Postcondition: The value of min is returned.
public int getMinutes()
{
    return min;
}
```

8

```java
        //Method to return the seconds
        //Postcondition: The value of sec is returned.
public int getSeconds()
{
    return sec;
}

        //Method to print the time
        //Postcondition: The time is printed in the form hh:mm:ss.
public void printTime()
{
    if (hr < 10)
        System.out.print("0");
    System.out.print(hr + ":");

    if (min < 10)
        System.out.print("0");
    System.out.print(min + ":");

    if (sec < 10)
        System.out.print("0");
    System.out.print(sec);
}

        //Method to increment the time by one second
        //Postcondition: The time is incremented by one second.
        //If the before-increment time is 23:59:59, the time
        //is reset to 00:00:00.
public void incrementSeconds()
{
    sec++;
    if (sec > 59)
    {
        sec = 0;
        incrementMinutes(); //increment min
    }
}

        //Method to increment the time by one minute
        //Postcondition: The time is incremented by one minute.
        //If the before-increment time is 23:59:53, the time
        //is reset to 00:00:53.
public void incrementMinutes()
{
    min++;
    if (min > 59)
    {
        min = 0;
        incrementHours(); //increment hr
    }
}
```

```java
    //Method to increment the time by one hour
    //Postcondition: The time is incremented by one hour.
    //If the before-increment time is 23:45:53, the time
    //is reset to 00:45:53.
public void incrementHours()
{
    hr++;
    if (hr > 23)
        hr = 0;
}


    //Method to compare the two times
    //Postcondition: Returns true if this time is equal to
    //               otherClock; otherwise returns false.
public boolean equals(Clock otherClock)
{
    return(hr == otherClock.hr
            && min == otherClock.min
            && sec == otherClock.sec);
}
    //Method to copy the time
    //Postcondition: The instance variables of otherClock are
    //               copied into the corresponding data
//               members of this time.
    //               hr = otherClock.hr; min = otherClock.min;
    //               sec = otherClock.sec
public void makeCopy(Clock otherClock)
{
    hr = otherClock.hr;
    min = otherClock.min;
    sec = otherClock.sec;
}


    //Method to return a copy of the time
    //Postcondition: A copy of the object is created and
    //               a reference of the copy is returned.
public Clock getCopy()
{
    Clock temp = new Clock();

    temp.hr = hr;
    temp.min = min;
    temp.sec = sec;

    return temp;
}
}
```

8

In a class definition, it is a common practice to list all the instance variables, named constants, other data members, or variable declarations first, then the constructors, and then the methods.

Once a class is properly defined and implemented, it can be used in a program. A program or software that uses and manipulates the objects of a class is called a **client** of that class.

Example 8-2

```java
//Program to test the various operations of the class Clock

import java.util.*;

public class TestProgClock
{
    static Scanner console = new Scanner(System.in);
    public static void main(String[] args)
    {
        Clock myClock = new Clock(5, 4, 30);           //Line 1
        Clock yourClock = new Clock();                 //Line 2

        int hours;                                     //Line 3
        int minutes;                                   //Line 4
        int seconds;                                   //Line 5

        System.out.print("Line 6: myClock: ");         //Line 6
        myClock.printTime();                           //Line 7
        System.out.println();                          //Line 8

        System.out.print("Line 9: yourClock: ");       //Line 9
        yourClock.printTime();                         //Line 10
        System.out.println();                          //Line 11

        yourClock.setTime(5, 45, 16);                  //Line 12

        System.out.print("Line 13: After setting "
                    + "the time, yourClock: ");         //Line 13
        yourClock.printTime();                         //Line 14
        System.out.println();                          //Line 15

        if (myClock.equals(yourClock))                 //Line 16
            System.out.println("Line 17: Both the "
                        + "times are equal.");          //Line 17
        else                                           //Line 18
            System.out.println("Line 19: The two "
                        + "times are not "
                        + "equal.");                    //Line 19
```

```
        System.out.print("Line 20: Enter the hours, "
                        + "minutes, and seconds: ");     //Line 20
        hours = console.nextInt();                       //Line 21
        minutes = console.nextInt();                     //Line 22
        seconds = console.nextInt();                     //Line 23
        System.out.println();                            //Line 24

        myClock.setTime(hours, minutes, seconds);        //Line 25

        System.out.print("Line 26: New time of "
                        + "myClock: ");                   //Line 26
        myClock.printTime();                             //Line 27
        System.out.println();                            //Line 28

        myClock.incrementSeconds();                      //Line 29

        System.out.print("Line 30: After "
                        + "incrementing the time by "
                        + "one second, myClock: ");       //Line 30
        myClock.printTime();                             //Line 31
        System.out.println();                            //Line 32

        yourClock.makeCopy(myClock);                     //Line 33
        System.out.print("Line 34: After copying "
                        + "myClock into yourClock, "
                        + "yourClock: ");                 //Line 34
        yourClock.printTime();                           //Line 35
        System.out.println();                            //Line 36
    }//end main
}
```

Sample Run: In this sample run, the user input is shaded.
```
Line 6: myClock: 05:04:30
Line 9: yourClock: 00:00:00
Line 13: After setting the time, yourClock: 05:45:16
Line 19: The two times are not equal.
Line 20: Enter the hours, minutes, and seconds: 11 22 59

Line 26: New time of myClock: 11:22:59
Line 30: After incrementing the time by one second, myClock: 11:23:00
Line 34: After copying myClock into yourClock, yourClock: 11:23:00
```

As an exercise, it is recommended that you do a walk-through of the preceding program.

COPY CONSTRUCTOR

Suppose that you have the following statement:

```
Clock myClock = new Clock(8, 45, 22);          //Line 1
```

You can use the object `myClock` to declare and instantiate another `Clock` object. Consider the following statement:

```
Clock aClock = new Clock(myClock);          //Line 2
```

This statement declares `aClock` to be a reference variable of the type `Clock`, instantiates the object `aClock`, and initializes the instance variables of the object `aClock` using the values of the corresponding instance variables of the object `myClock`. However, to successfully execute the statement in Line 2, you need to include a special constructor, called a **copy constructor**, in the **class** `Clock`. The copy constructor executes when an object is instantiated and initialized using an existing object.

The syntax of the heading of the copy constructor is:

```
public ClassName(ClassName otherObject)
```

For example, the heading of the copy constructor for the **class** `Clock` is:

```
public Clock(Clock otherClock)
```

The definition of the copy constructor for the **class** `Clock` is:

```
public Clock(Clock otherClock)
{
    hr = otherClock.hr;
    min = otherClock.min;
    sec = otherClock.sec;
}
```

If you include this definition of the copy constructor in the **class** `Clock`, then the statement in Line 2 declares `aClock` to be a reference variable of the type `Clock`, instantiates the object `aClock`, and initializes the instance variables of the object `aClock` using the values of the instance variables of the object `myClock`.

The copy constructor is very useful and will be included in most of the classes.

CLASSES AND THE METHOD toString

Suppose that **x** is an **int** variable and the value of **x** is 25. The statement:

```
System.out.println(x);
```

outputs:

```
25
```

However, the output of the statement:

```
System.out.println(myClock);
```

is:

```
Clock@11b86e7
```

which looks strange. This is because whenever you create a **class**, the Java system provides the method **toString** to the **class**. The method **toString** is used to convert an object to a **String** object. The methods **print**, **println**, and **printf** output the string created by the method **toString**.

The default definition of the method **toString** creates a string that is the name of the object's **class**, followed by the hash code of the object. For example, in the preceding statement, **Clock** is the name of the object **myClock**'s **class** and the hash code for the object referenced by **myClock** is **@11b86e7**.

The method **toString** is a **public** value-returning method. It does not take any parameters and returns the address of a **String** object. The heading of the method **toString** is:

```
public String toString()
```

You can *override* the default definition of the method **toString** to convert an object to a desired string. Suppose that for the objects of the **class** Clock you want the method **toString** to create the string hh:mm:ss—the string consists of the object's hour, minutes, seconds, and the colons as shown. The string created by the method **toString** is the same as the string output by the method **print** of the **class** Clock. This is easily accomplished by providing the following definition of the method **toString**:

8

```
public String toString()
{
    String str = "";
    if (hr < 10)
        str = "0";
    str = str + hr + ":";

    if (min < 10)
        str = str + "0" ;
    str = str + min + ":";

    if (sec < 10)
        str = str + "0";
    str = str + sec;

    return str;
}
```

In the preceding code, `str` is a `String` variable used to create the required string.

The preceding definition of the method `toString` must be included in the **class** Clock. In fact, after including the method `toString` in the **class** Clock, we can remove the method `print`. If the values of the instance variables `hr`, `min`, and `sec` of `myClock` are 8, 25, and 56, respectively, then the output of the statement:

```
System.out.println(myClock)
```

is:

```
08:25:56
```

You can see that the method `toString` is quite useful for outputting the values of the instance variables. Note that the method `toString` only returns the (formatted) string; the methods `print`, `println`, or `printf` output the string.

STATIC MEMBERS OF A CLASS

In Chapter 7, we described the **class**es Math and Character. In Example 7-1 (of Chapter 7), we used several methods of the **class**es Math and Character; however, we did not need to create any objects to use these methods. We simply used the import statement:

```
import static java.lang.Math.*;
```

and then called the method with an appropriate actual parameter list. For example, to use the method `pow` of the **class** Math, we used expressions such as:

```
pow(5, 3)
```

Recall from Chapter 7 that if you are using versions of JDK lower than JDK 5.0 or you do not include the preceding statement, then you call the method pow as follows:

```
Math.pow(5,f3)
```

That is, we can simply call the method using the name of the class and the dot operator.

Can we do the same with the **class** Clock? The answer is no. Although the methods of the **class**es Math and Character are **public**, they also are defined using the modifier **static**. For example, the heading of the method pow of the **class** Math is:

```
public static double pow(double base, double exponent)
```

The modifier **static** in the heading specifies that the method can be invoked by using the name of the **class**. Similarly, if a data member of a **class** is declared using the modifier **static**, it can be accessed by using the name of the **class**.

The following example clarifies the effect of the modifier **static**.

Example 8-3

Consider the following definition of the class Illustrate:

```
public class Illustrate
{
    private int x;
    private static int y;
    public static int count;

        //Default constructor
        //Postcondition: x = 0;
    public Illustrate()
    {
        x = 0;
    }

        //Constructor with parameters
        //Postcondition: x = a;
    public Illustrate(int a)
    {
        x = a;
    }

        //Method to set x.
        //Postcondition: x = a;
    void setX(int a)
    {
        x = a;
    }
```

8

```
            //Method to return the values of the instance
            //and static variables as a string.
            //The string returned is used by the methods
            //print, println, or printf, to print the values
            //of the instance and static variables.
            //Postcondition: The values of x, y, and count
            //are returned as a string.
        public String toString()
        {
            return("x = " + x + ", y = " + y
                + ", count = " + count);
        }


            //Method to increment the value of the private
            //static member y.
            //Postcondition: y is incremented by 1.
        public static void incrementY()
        {
            y++;
        }
}
```

Further, suppose that you have the following declaration:

```
Illustrate illusObject = new Illustrate();
```

The reference variable **illusObject** can access any **public** member of the **class** **Illustrate**. Because the method **incrementY** is **static** and **public**, the following statement is legal:

```
Illustrate.incrementY();
```

Similarly, because the data member **count** is **static** and **public**, the following statement is legal:

```
Illustrate.count++;
```

In essence, **public static** members of a **class** can be accessed either by an object, that is, by using a reference variable of the **class** type, or using the **class** name and the dot operator.

static **Variables (Data Members) of a Class**

Suppose that you have a **class**, say **MyClass**, with data members (**static** and non-**static**). When you instantiate the objects of the type **MyClass**, only the non-**static** data members of the **class** **MyClass** become the data members of each object. What about the memory for the **static** data members of **MyClass**? For each **static** data member of the

class, Java allocates only one memory space. All **MyClass** objects refer to the same memory space. In fact, **static** data members of a **class** *exist* even when no object of the **class** type is instantiated. Moreover, **static** variables are initialized to their default values. You can access the **public static** data members outside the **class**, as explained in the previous section.

The following example further clarifies how memory space is allocated for **static** and non-**static** data members of a class.

Suppose that you have the **class Illustrate**, as given in Example 8-3. Then memory space exists for the **static** data members **y** and **count**.

Consider the following statements:

```
Illustrate illusObject1 = new Illustrate(3);        //Line 1
Illustrate illusObject2 = new Illustrate(5);        //Line 2
```

The statements in Line 1 and Line 2 declare **illusObject1** and **illusObject2** to be reference variables of the **Illustrate** type and instantiate these objects. (See Figure 8-14.)

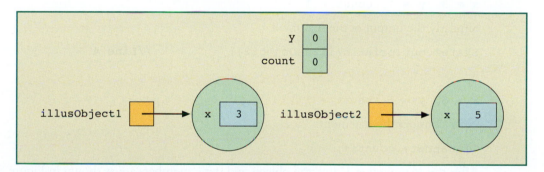

Figure 8-14   **illusObject1** and **illusObject2**

Consider the following statements:

```
Illustrate.incrementY();
Illustrate.count++;
```

After these statements execute, the objects and static members are as shown in Figure 8-15.

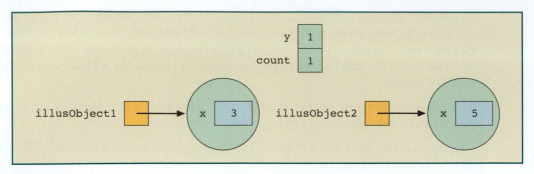

Figure 8-15   `illusObject1` and `illusObject2` after the statements
                 `Illustrate.incrementY();` and `Illustrate.count++;` execute

The output of the statement:

```
System.out.println(illusObject1);          //Line 3
```

is:

```
x = 3, y = 1, count = 1
```

Similarly, the output of the statement:

```
System.out.println(illusObject2);          //Line 4
```

is:

```
x = 5, y = 1, count = 1
```

Now consider the statement:

```
Illustrate.count++;
```

After this statement executes, the objects and static members are as shown in Figure 8-16.

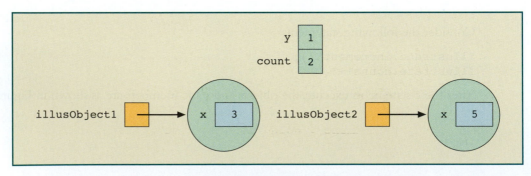

Figure 8-16   `illusObject1` and `illusObject2` after the statement
                 `Illustrate.count++;` executes

The output of the statements:

```
System.out.println(illusObject1);
System.out.println(illusObject2);
```

is:

```
x = 3, y = 1, count = 2
x = 5, y = 1, count = 2
```

The program in Example 8-4 further illustrates how **static** members of a class work.

Example 8-4

```java
public class StaticMembers
{
    public static void main(String[] args)
    {
        Illustrate illusObject1 = new Illustrate(3);      //Line 1
        Illustrate illusObject2 = new Illustrate(5);      //Line 2

        Illustrate.incrementY();                          //Line 3
        Illustrate.count++;                               //Line 4
        System.out.println(illusObject1);                 //Line 5
        System.out.println(illusObject2);                 //Line 6

        System.out.println("Line 7: ***Increment y "
                        + "using illusObject1***");        //Line 7
        illusObject1.incrementY();                        //Line 8
        illusObject1.setX(8);                             //Line 9
        System.out.println(illusObject1);                 //Line 10
        System.out.println(illusObject2);                 //Line 11

        System.out.println("Line 12: ***Increment y "
                        + "using illusObject2***");        //Line 12
        illusObject2.incrementY();                        //Line 13
        illusObject2.setX(23);                            //Line 14
        System.out.println(illusObject1);                 //Line 15
        System.out.println(illusObject2);                 //Line 16
    }
}
```

Sample Run:

```
x = 3, y = 1, count = 1
x = 5, y = 1, count = 1
Line 7: ***Increment y using illusObject1***
x = 8, y = 2, count = 1
x = 5, y = 2, count = 1
Line 12: ***Increment y using illusObject2***
x = 8, y = 3, count = 1
x = 23, y = 3, count = 1
```

8

The preceding program works as follows: The **static** data members **y** and **count** are initialized to **0**. The statements in Lines 1 and 2 create the **Illustrate** objects **illusObject1** and **illusObject2**. The instance variable **x** of **illusObject1** is initialized to **3**; the instance variable **x** of **illusObject2** is initialized to **5**.

The statement in Line 3 uses the name of the **class Illustrate** and the method **incrementY** to increment **y**. Because **count** is a **public static** member of the **class Illustrate**, the statement in Line 4 uses the name of the **class Illustrate** to directly access **count**, and increments it by 1. The statements in Lines 5 and 6 output the data stored in the objects **illusObject1** and **illusObject2**. Notice that the value of **y** for both objects is the same. Similarly, the value of **count** for both objects is the same.

The statement in Line 7 is an output statement. The statement in Line 8 uses the object **illusObject1** and the method **incrementY** to increment **y**. The statement in Line 9 sets the value of the instance variable **x** of **illusObject1** to **8**. Lines 10 and 11 output the data stored in the objects **illusObject1** and **illusObject2**. Notice that the value of **y** for both objects is the same. Similarly, the value of **count** for both objects is the same. Moreover, notice that the statement in Line 9 changes only the value of the instance variable **x** of **illusObject1** because **x** is *not* a **static** member of the **class Illustrate**.

The statement in Line 13 uses the object **illusObject2** and the method **incrementY** to increment **y**. The statement in Line 14 sets the value of the instance variable **x** of **illusObject2** to **23**. Lines 15 and 16 output the data stored in the objects **illusObject1** and **illusObject2**. Notice that the value of **y** for both objects is the same. Similarly, the value of **count** for both objects is the same. Moreover, notice that the statement in Line 14 changes only the value of the instance variable **x** of **illusObject2** because **x** is *not* a **static** member of the **class Illustrate**.

 Here are some additional comments on **static** members of a class. As you have seen in this section, a **static** method of a class does not need any object to be invoked. It can be called using the name of the class and the dot operator. Therefore, a **static** method cannot use anything that depends on a calling object. In other words, in the definition of a **static** method, you cannot use a non-**static** data member or a non-**static** method, unless there is a locally declared object that accesses the non-**static** data member or the non-**static** method.

FINALIZERS

Like constructors, **finalizers** are also special types of methods. However, a finalizer is a **void** method. Moreover, a **class** can have only one finalizer, and the finalizer cannot have any parameters. The name of the finalizer is **finalize**. The method **finalize** automatically executes when the class object goes out of scope.

ACCESSOR AND MUTATOR METHODS

Earlier in this chapter, we defined the terms mutator and accessor methods. This section discusses these terms in detail and explains why such methods are needed to construct a class.

Let us look at the methods of the **class** Clock. The method setTime sets the values of the data members to the values specified by the user. In other words, it alters or modifies the values of the instance variables. Similarly, the methods incrementHours, incrementMinutes, and incrementSeconds also modify the instance variables. However, methods such as getHours, getMinutes, getSeconds, printTime, and equals only access the values of the data members; they *do not* modify the data members. We can, therefore, divide the methods of the **class** Clock into two categories: methods that modify the data members, and methods that only access, and so do not modify, the data members.

This is typically true for any class. That is, every class has methods that only access and do not modify the data members, called **accessor methods**, and methods that modify the data members, called **mutator methods**.

Accessor Method: A method of a class that only accesses (that is, does not modify) the value(s) of the data member(s).

Mutator Method: A method of a class that modifies the value(s) of the data member(s).

Typically, the instance variables of a class are declared **private** so that the user of a class does not have direct access to them. In general, every class has a set of mutator and accessor methods to work with the instance variables. Typically, mutator methods begin with the word set and accessor methods begin with the word get. You might wonder why we need both mutator and accessor methods when we can simply make the instance variables **public**. However, look closely, for example, at the mutator method setTime of the **class** Clock. Before setting the time, it validates the time. On the other hand, if the instance variables are all **public**, then the user of the class can put any values in the instance variables. Similarly, the accessor methods only return the value(s) of an instance variable(s); that is, they do not modify the values. A well-designed class uses **private** instance variables and mutator and accessor methods to implement the OOD principle of encapsulation.

Example 8-5 further illustrates how classes are designed and implemented. The **class** Person that we create in this example is very useful; we will use this **class** in subsequent chapters.

Example 8-5

Two common attributes of a person are the person's first name and last name. The typical operations on a person's name are to set the name and print the name. The following statements define a **class** with these properties. (See Figure 8-17.)

```
public class Person
{
    private String firstName; //store the first name
    private String lastName;  //store the last name
```

```java
        //Default constructor
        //Initialize firstName and lastName to an empty string.
        //Postcondition: firstName = ""; lastName = "";
    public Person()
    {
        firstName = "";
        lastName = "";

    }

        //Constructor with parameters
        //Set firstName and lastName according to the parameters.
        //Postcondition: firstName = first; lastName = last;
    public Person(String first, String last)
    {
        setName(first, last);
    }

        //Method to output the first name and last name
        //in the form firstName lastName.
    public String toString()
    {
        return (firstName + " " + lastName);
    }

        //Method to set firstName and lastName according to
        //the parameters.
        //Postcondition: firstName = first; lastName = last;
    public void setName(String first, String last)
    {
        firstName = first;
        lastName = last;
    }

        //Method to return the firstName.
        //Postcondition: The value of firstName is returned.
    public String getFirstName()
    {
        return firstName;
    }

        //Method to return the lastName.
        //Postcondition: The value of lastName is returned.
    public String getLastName()
    {
        return lastName;
    }
}
```

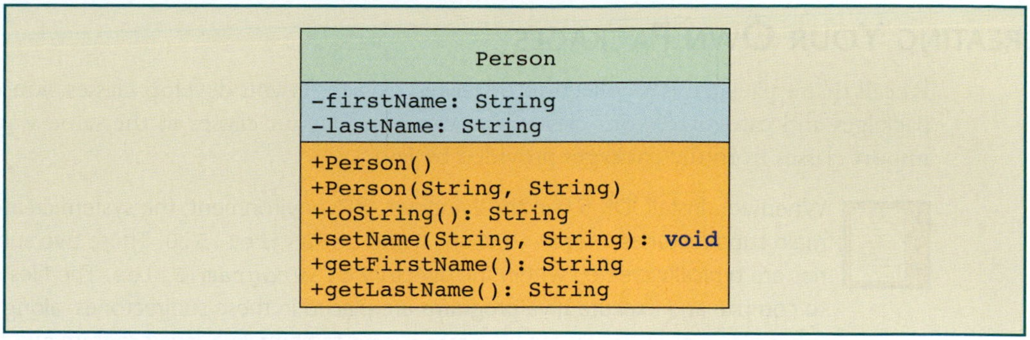

Figure 8-17 UML diagram of the **class** Person

The following program tests the **class** Person:

```
public class TestProgPerson
{
    public static void main(String[] args)
    {
        Person name = new Person();                        //Line 1

        Person emp = new Person("Donald", "Jackson");      //Line 2

        System.out.println("Line 3: name: " + name);       //Line 3

        name.setName("Ashley", "Blair");                   //Line 4
        System.out.println("Line 5: name: " + name);       //Line 5

        System.out.println("Line 6: emp: " + emp);         //Line 6

        emp.setName("Sandy", "Smith");                     //Line 7
        System.out.println("Line 8: emp: " + emp);         //Line 8
    }//end main
}
```

Sample Run:
```
Line 3: name:
Line 5: name: Ashley Blair
Line 6: emp: Donald Jackson
Line 8: emp: Sandy Smith
```

CREATING YOUR OWN PACKAGES

Recall that a package is a collection of related classes. As you develop classes, you can create packages and categorize your classes. You can import your classes in the same way that you import classes from the packages provided by Java.

 When you install JDK 5.0 in the Windows (XP) environment, the system creates two main subdirectories: `Java\jdk1.5.0` and `Java\jre1.5.0`. These two subdirectories are typically created within the directory `c:\Program Files`. The files necessary to compile and execute Java programs are placed in these sudirectories, along with other files. For example, the file `javac.exe` to compile a Java program and the file `java.exe` to execute a Java application program are placed within the subdirectory `Java\jdk1.5.0\bin`. As explained in Appendix D, you can set (or alter) the Windows system environment variable `Path` to add the path where the files `javac.exe` and `java.exe` are located. This allows you to conveniently compile a Java program from within any subdirectory. When you compile a Java program using the command line compiler, you can instruct the system, as explained below, to store the compiled code of the program in any subdirectory you want. In the Windows (XP) environment, you can set the environment variable CLASSPATH so that when you execute a Java program, the system can find the compiled code of the program. Check your operating system's documentation to learn how to set the environment variables.

To create a package and add a class to the package so that the class can be used in a program, you do the following:

1. Define the class to be **public**. If the class is not **public**, it can be used only within the package.

2. Choose a name for the package. To organize your package, you can create subdirectories within the directory that contains the compiled code of the classes. For example, you could create a directory for the classes you create in this book. Because the title of this book is *Java Programming: From Problem Analysis to Program Design*, you could create a directory named `jpfpatpd`. You could then make subdirectories for the classes used in each chapter, such as the subdirectory `ch08` within the directory `jpfpatpd`.

Suppose that you want to create a **package** to group the classes related to time. You could call this **package** clockPackage. To add the **class** Clock to this package and to place the package clockPackage within the subdirectory ch08 of the directory jpfpatpd, you include the following package statement with the file containing the **class** Clock:

package jpfpatpd.ch08.clockPackage;

We put this statement before the definition of the **class**, like this:

```
package jpfpatpd.ch08.clockPackage;

public class Clock
{
    //put the instance variables and methods, as before, here
}
```

The name of the file containing the **package** statement and the definition of the **class** Clock is Clock.java. The next step is to compile the file Clock.java using the compile command in the SDK you are using.

The following discussion assumes that you have set the Path so that the files javac.exe and java.exe can be executed from within any subdirectory. Suppose that the file Clock.java is in the subdirectory c:\jpfpatpd. We assume that you have switched to the subdirectory c:\jpfpatpd.

If you are using JDK 5.0, which contains a command-line compiler, you include the option –d to place the compiled code of the program Clock.java in a specific directory. For example, the command:

```
javac –d "c:\Program Files\Java\jre1.5.0\lib\classes" Clock.java
```

places the compiled code of the program Clock.java in the subdirectory:

```
c:\Program Files\Java\jre1.5.0\lib\classes\jpfpatpd\ch08\clockPackage
```

Similarly, the following command places the compiled code of the program Clock.java in the subdirectory c:\jpfpatpd\ch08\clockPackage:

```
javac –d c:\ Clock.java
```

If the directories jpfpatpd, ch08, and clockPackage do not exist, then the compiler automatically creates these directories. Note that for the earlier command to execute successfully, the subdirectory c:\Program Files\Java\jre1.5.0\lib\classes must exist. If this subdirectory does not exist, you must first create it. Also, to be absolutely sure about the correct directory path, check your system's documentation. Moreover, if you do not use the –d option with the path of the subdirectory to specify the subdirectory to store the compiled code, then the compiled code is, typically, stored in the current subdirectory.

Once the **package** is created, you can use the appropriate **import** command in your program to make use of the **class**. For example, to use the **class** Clock, as created in the preceding code, you use the following **import** statement in your program:

```
import jpfpatpd.ch08.clockPackage.Clock;
```

In Java, **package** is a reserved word.

Example 8-6 further explains how to use a package in a program. We assume that the **class** Clock has been compiled and placed in the subdirectory c:\jpfpatpd\ch08\clockPackage.

Example 8-6

The following program uses the **class** Clock.

```java
import jpfpatpd.ch08.clockPackage.Clock;

public class TestClock
{
    public static void main(String[] args)
    {
        Clock myClock = new Clock(12, 30, 45);

        System.out.println("myClock: " + myClock);
    }
}
```

Because this program uses the **class** Clock, when you compile this program using the complier command, you use the option **–classpath** to specify where to find the compiled code of the **class** Clock. Suppose that the file **TestClock.java** is in the subdirectory **c:\jpfpatpd**. Consider the following command:

```
javac -classpath c:\ TestClock.java
```

This command finds Clock.class in the subdirectory c:\jpfpatpd\ ch08\clockPackage. The compiled code TestClock.class of the program TestClock.java is placed in the current subdirectory. On the other hand, the following command places the compiled code, TestClock.class, in the subdirectory c:\jpfpatpd:

```
javac -d c:\jpfpatpd -classpath c:\ TestClock.java
```

Suppose the file TestClock.class is in the subdirectory c:\jpfpatpd. The following command executes the program TestClock.class:

```
java TestClass
```

If the compiled code of the classes is in the subdirectory, say c:\jpfpatpd, then you can set the system variable CLASSPATH to c:\jpfpatpd. If the system variable CLASSPATH already exists, then you can add the path c:\jpfpatpd to it. To be absolutely sure how to set CLASSPATH in the Windows environment check your operating system's documentation. Moreover, if you are using other operating systems such as UNIX, check you operating system's documentation to set the variables so that you can conveniently compile and execute a Java program.

If you are using an SDK to create Java programs, then you need to be familiar with the commands to compile and execute them. Typically, an SDK automatically stores the compiled code of the classes in an appropriate subdirectory.

Multiple File Programs

In the preceding section, you learned how to create a **package**. Creating a **package** to group related **class**(es) is very useful if the classes are to be used again and again. On the other hand, if a **class** is to be used in only one program, or if you have divided your program so that it uses more than one **class**, rather than create a **package**, you can directly add the file(s) containing the **class**(es) to the program.

The Java SDKs—Forte for Java, J++ Builder, and CodeWarrior—put the editor, compiler, and loader all into one program. With one command, a program is compiled. These SDKs also manage multiple-file programs in the form of a project. A **project** consists of several files, called the project files. These SDKs include a command that allows you to add several files to a project. Also, these SDKs usually have commands such as **build**, **rebuild**, or **make** (check your software's documentation) to automatically compile all the files required. When one or more files in the project change, you can use these commands to recompile the files.

REFERENCE this

 This section can be omitted without any discontinuation.

8

In this chapter, we defined the **class** Clock. Suppose that myClock is a reference variable of the type Clock. Moreover, assume that the object myClock has been created. Consider the following statements:

```
myClock.setTime(5, 6, 59);        //Line 1
myClock.incrementSeconds();       //Line 2
```

The statement in Line 1 uses the method setTime to set the instance variables hr, min, and sec of the object myClock to 5, 6, and 59, respectively. The statement in Line 2 uses the method incrementSeconds to increment the time of the object myClock by one second. The statement in Line 2 also results in a call to the method incrementMinutes because after incrementing the value of sec by 1, the value of sec becomes 60, which then is reset to 0, and the method incrementMinutes is invoked.

How do you think Java makes sure that the statement in Line 1 sets the instance variables of the object myClock and not of another Clock object? How does Java make sure that when the method incrementSeconds calls the method incrementMinutes, the method incrementMinutes increments the value of the instance variable min of the object myClock and not of another Clock object?

The answer is that every object has access to a reference of itself. The name of this reference is **this**. In Java, **this** is a reserved word.

Java implicitly uses the reference **this** to refer to both the instance variables and the methods of a class. Recall that the definition of the method **setTime** is:

```
public void setTime(int hours, int minutes, int seconds)
{
    if (0 <= hours && hours < 24)
        hr = hours;
    else
        hr = 0;

    if (0 <= minutes && minutes < 60)
        min = minutes;
    else
        min = 0;

    if (0 <= seconds && seconds < 60)
        sec = seconds;
    else
        sec = 0;
}
```

In the method **setTime**, the statement:

```
hr = hours;
```

is in fact, equivalent to the statement:

```
this.hr = hours;
```

In this statement, the reference **this** is explicitly used. You can explicitly use the reference **this** and write the equivalent definition of the method **setTime** as follows:

```
public void setTime(int hr, int min, int sec)
{
    if (0 <= hr && hr < 24)
        this.hr = hr;
    else
        this.hr = 0;

    if (0 <= min && min < 60)
        this.min = min;
    else
        this.min = 0;

    if (0 <= sec && sec < 60)
        this.sec = sec;
    else
        this.sec = 0;
}
```

Notice that in the preceding definition of the method `setTime`, the name of the formal parameters and the name of the instance variables are the same. In this definition of the method `setTime`, the expression `this.hr` means the instance variable `hr`, not the formal parameter `hr`, and so on. Because the code explicitly uses the reference `this`, the compiler can distinguish between the instance variables and the formal parameters. Of course, you could have kept the name of the formal parameters as before and still used the reference `this` as shown in the code.

Similarly, explicitly using the reference `this`, you can write the definition of the method `incrementSeconds` as follows:

```
public void incrementSeconds()
{
    this.sec++;
    if (this.sec > 59)
    {
        this.sec = 0;
        this.incrementMinutes(); //increment min
    }
}
```

Cascaded Method Calls

 This section can be omitted without any discontinuation.

In addition to explicitly referring to the instance variables and methods of an object, the reference `this` has another use. It can be used to implement cascaded method calls. We explain this with the help of an example.

Example 8-5 shows a class we designed to implement a person's name in a program. Here, we extend the definition of the **class** Person to individually set a person's first name and last name, and then return a reference to the object. The following code is the extended definition of the **class** Person. (The methods `setFirstName` and `setLastName` are added to this definition of the **class** Person.)

```
public class Person
{
    private String firstName; //store the first name
    private String lastName;  //store the last name

        //Default constructor
        //Initialize firstName and lastName to an empty string.
        //Postcondition: firstName = ""; lastName = "";
    public Person()
    {
        firstName = "";
        lastName = "";
    }
```

8

```java
    //Constructor with parameters
    //Set firstName and lastName according to the parameters.
    //Postcondition: firstName = first; lastName = last;
public Person(String first, String last)
{
    SetName(first, last);
}


    //Method to return the first name and last name
    //in the form firstName lastName
public String toString()
{
    return (firstName + " " + lastName);
}


    //Method to set firstName and lastName according to
    //the parameters
    //Postcondition: firstName = first; lastName = last;
public void setName(String first, String last)
{
    firstName = first;
    lastName = last;
}


    //Method to set the last name
    //Postcondition: lastName = last;
    //        After setting the last name, a reference
    //        to the object is returned.
public Person setLastName(String last)
{
    lastName = last;

    return this;
}


    //Method to set the first name
    //Postcondition: firstName = first;
    //        After setting the first name, a reference
    //        to the object is returned.
public Person setFirstName(String first)
{
    firstName = first;

    return this;
}

    //Method to return firstName
    //Postcondition: The value of firstName is returned.
```

```java
    public String getFirstName()
    {
        return firstName;
    }

        //Function to return lastName
        //Postcondition: The value of lastName is returned.
    public String getLastName()
    {
        return lastName;
    }
}
```

Consider the following function `main`.

```java
public class CascadedMethodCalls
{
    public static void main(String[] args)
    {
        Person student1 =
                    new Person("Angela", "Clodfelter");    //Line 1

        Person student2 = new Person();                    //Line 2

        Person student3 = new Person();                    //Line 3

        System.out.println("Line 4 -- Student 1: "
                    + student1);                           //Line 4

        student2.setFirstName("Shelly").setLastName("Malik");//Line 5

        System.out.println("Line 6 -- Student 2: "
                    + student2);                           //Line 6

        student3.setFirstName("Chelsea");                  //Line 7

        System.out.println("Line 8 -- Student 3: "
                    + student3);                           //Line 8

        student3.setLastName("Tomek");                     //Line 9

        System.out.println("Line 10 -- Student 3: "
                    + student3);                           //Line 10

    }
}
```

Sample Run:
```
Line 4 -- Student 1: Angela Clodfelter
Line 6 -- Student 2: Shelly Malik
Line 8 -- Student 3: Chelsea
Line 10 -- Student 3: Chelsea Tomek
```

The statements in Lines 1, 2, and 3 declare the variables `student1`, `student2`, and `student3` and also instantiate the objects. The instance variables of the objects `student2` and `student3` are initialized to empty strings. The statement in Line 4 outputs the value of `student1`. The statement in Line 5 works as follows. In the statement:

```
student2.setFirstName("Shelly").setLastName("Malik");
```

first the expression:

```
student2.setFirstName("Shelly")
```

is executed because the associativity of the dot operator is from left to right. This expression sets the first name to `"Shelly"` and returns a reference to the object, which is the object `student2`. Thus, the next expression executed is:

```
student2.setLastName("Malik")
```

which sets the last name of the object `student2` to `"Malik"`. The statement in Line 6 outputs the value of `student2`. The statement in Line 7 sets the first name of `student3` to `"Chelsea"`, and the statement in Line 8 outputs `student3`. Notice the output in Line 8. The output shows only the first name, not the last name, because we have not yet set the last name of the object `student3`. The last name of the object `student3` is still empty, which was set by the statement in Line 3 when `student3` was declared. Next, the statement in Line 9 sets the last name of the object `student3`, and the statement in Line 10 outputs `student3`.

INNER CLASSES

The classes defined thus far in this chapter are said to have file scope, that is, they are contained within a file, but not within another class. In Chapter 6, while designing the **class** `RectangleProgram`, we defined the **class** `CalculateButtonHandler` to handle an action event. The definition of the **class** `CalculateButtonHandler` is contained within the **class** `RectangleProgram`. Classes that are defined within other classes are called **inner classes**.

An inner class can be either a complete class definition, such as the **class** `CalculateButtonHandler`, or an anonymous inner class definition. Anonymous classes are classes with no name.

One of the main uses of inner classes is to handle events—as we did in Chapter 6.

ABSTRACT DATA TYPES

To help you understand an abstract data type (ADT), and how it might be used, we'll provide an analogy. The following items seem unrelated:

- A deck of playing cards
- A set of index cards containing contact information
- Telephone numbers stored in your cellular phone

All three of these items share the following structural properties:

- Each one is a collection of elements.

- There is a first element.

- There is a second element, third element, and so on.

- There is a last element.

- Given an element other than the last element, there is a "next" element.

- Given an element other than the first element, there is a "previous" element.

- An element can be removed from the collection.

- An element can be added to the collection.

- A specified element can be located in the collection by systematically going through the collection.

In your programs, you may want to keep a collection of various elements such as addresses, students, employees, departments, and projects. Thus, this structure commonly appears in various applications, and it is worth studying in its own right. We call this organization a *list* and a list is an example of an ADT.

8

There is a data type called **Vector** (discussed in Chapter 10) with basic operations such as:

- Insert an item.

- Delete an item.

- Find an item.

You can use a **Vector** object to create an address book. You would not need to write a program to insert an address, delete an address, or find an item in your address book. Java also allows you to create your own abstract data types through classes.

An ADT is an abstraction of a commonly appearing data structure, along with a set of defined operations on the data structure.

Abstract data type (ADT): A data type that specifies the logical properties without the implementation details.

Historically, the concept of ADT in computer programming developed as a way of abstracting the common data structure and the associated operations. Along the way, ADT provided **information hiding**. That is, ADT *hides* the implementation details of the operations and the data from the users of the ADT. Users can use the operations of an ADT without knowing how the operation is implemented.

PROGRAMMING EXAMPLE: CANDY MACHINE

A new candy machine is bought for the gym and a program is needed to make the machine function properly. The machine sells candies, chips, gum, and cookies. In this programming example, we write a program to create a Java application program for this candy machine so that it can be put into operation.

We divide this program in two parts. In the first part we design a non-GUI application program. In the second part we design an application program that will create a GUI as described in the second part.

The non-GUI application program should do the following:

1. Show the customer the different products sold by the candy machine.
2. Let the customer make the selection.
3. Show the customer the cost of the item selected.
4. Accept the money from the customer.
5. Release the item.

Input   The item selection and the cost of the item

Output   The selected item

In the next section, we design the candy machine's basic components, which are required by either type of application program—GUI or non-GUI. The difference between the two types is evident when we write the main program to put the candy machine into operation.

Problem Analysis and Algorithm Design

A candy machine has three main components: a built-in cash register, several dispensers to hold and release the products, and the candy machine itself. Therefore, we need to define a class to implement the cash register, a class to implement the dispenser, and a class to implement the candy machine. First we describe the classes to implement the cash register and dispenser, and then we use these classes to describe the candy machine.

Cash Register   Let's first discuss the properties of a cash register. The register has some cash on hand, it accepts the amount from the customer, and if the amount entered is more than the cost of the item, then—if possible—it returns the change. For simplicity, we assume that the user enters the exact amount for the product. The cash register should also be able to show the candy machine's owner the amount of money in the register at any given time. Let's call the class implementing the cash register **CashRegister**.

The members of the **class** **CashRegister** are listed next and shown in Figure 8-18.

Instance Variables

```java
private int cashOnHand;
```

Constructors and Methods

```java
public CashRegister()
    //Default constructor to set the cash
    //in the register to 500 cents
    //Postcondition: cashOnHand = 500;

public CashRegister(int cashIn)
    //Constructor with parameters
    //Postcondition: cashOnHand = cashIn;

public int currentBalance()
    //Method to show the current amount in the cash register
    //Postcondition: The value of the instance variable
    //               cashOnHand is returned.

public void acceptAmount(int amountIn)
    //Method to receive the amount deposited by
    //the customer and update the amount in the register.
    //Postcondition: cashOnHand = cashOnHand + amountIn;
```

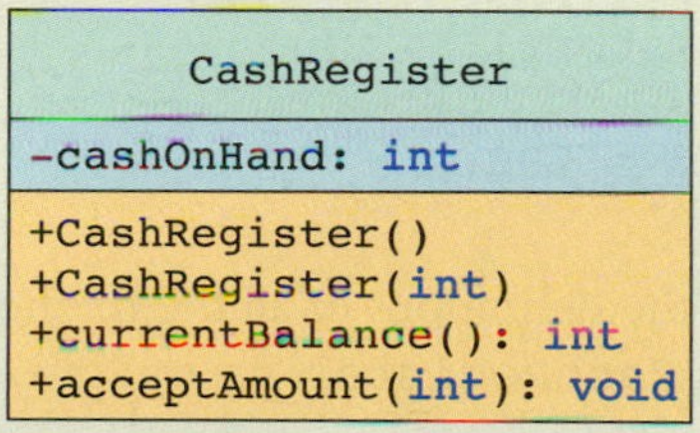

CashRegister
-cashOnHand: **int**
+CashRegister() +CashRegister(int) +currentBalance(): int +acceptAmount(int): void

Figure 8-18   UML class diagram of the **class** CashRegister

Next, we give the definitions of the methods to implement the operations of the **class** CashRegister. The definitions of these methods are simple and easy to follow.

The method **currentBalance** shows the current amount in the cash register. The amount stored in the cash register is in cents. Its definition is:

```java
public int currentBalance()
{
    return cashOnHand;
}
```

The method **acceptAmount** accepts the amount entered by the customer. It updates the cash in the register by adding the amount entered by the customer to the previous amount in the cash register. The definition of this method is:

```java
public void acceptAmount(int amountIn)
{
    cashOnHand = cashOnHand + amountIn;
}
```

The constructor with the parameter sets the value of the instance variable to the value specified by the user. The value is passed as a parameter to the constructor. The definition of the constructor with the parameter is:

```java
public CashRegister(int cashIn)
{
    if (cashIn >= 0)
        cashOnHand = cashIn;
    else
        cashOnHand = 500;
}
```

Note that the definition of the constructor checks for valid values of the parameter **cashIn**. If the value of **cashIn** is less than 0, the value assigned to the instance variable **cashOnHand** is 500.

The default constructor sets the value of the instance variable **cashOnHand** to 500 cents. Its definition is:

```java
public CashRegister()
{
    cashOnHand = 500;
}
```

Now that we have the definitions of all the methods necessary to implement the operations of the **class CashRegister**, we can give the definition of **CashRegister**. Its definition is:

```java
//class CashRegister

public class CashRegister
{
    private int cashOnHand;    //variable to store the cash
                               //in the register

        //Default constructor to set the cash in
        //the register to 500 cents
        //Postcondition: cashOnHand = 500;
    public CashRegister()
    {
        cashOnHand = 500;
    }
```

```
        //Constructor with parameters to set the cash
        //in the register to a specific amount
        //Postcondition: cashOnHand = cashIn;
    public CashRegister(int cashIn)
    {
        if (cashIn >= 0)
           cashOnHand = cashIn;
        else
           cashOnHand = 500;
    }


        //Method to show the current amount in the cash register
        //Postcondition: The value of the instance variable
        //                  cashOnHand is returned.
    public int currentBalance()
    {
        return cashOnHand;
    }


        //Method to receive the amount deposited by
        //the customer and update the amount in the register
        //Postcondition: cashOnHand = cashOnHand + amountIn;
    public void acceptAmount(int amountIn)
    {
        cashOnHand = cashOnHand + amountIn;
    }
}
```

Dispenser   The dispenser releases the selected item if it is not empty. It should show the number of items in the dispenser and the cost of the item. Let's call the class implementing a dispenser `Dispenser`. The members necessary to implement the **class** `Dispenser` are listed next and shown in Figure 8-19.

Instance Variables

```
private int numberOfItems;  //variable to store the number of
                            //items in the dispenser
private int cost;           //variable to store the cost of an item
```

Constructors and Methods

```
public Dispenser()
   //Default constructor to set the cost and
   //number of items to the default values
   //Postcondition: numberOfItems = 50; cost = 50;
```

```
public Dispenser(int setNoOfItems, int setCost)
   //Constructor with parameters to set the cost and number
   //of items in the dispenser specified by the user
   //Postcondition: numberOfItems = setNoOfItems;
   //               cost = setCost;
public int getCount()
   //Method to show the number of items in the machine
   //Postcondition: The value of the instance variable
   //               numberOfItems is returned.

public int getProductCost()
   //Method to show the cost of the item
   //Postcondition: The value of the instance
   //               variable cost is returned.

public void makeSale()
   //Method to reduce the number of items by 1
   //Postcondition: numberOfItems = numberOfItems - 1;
```

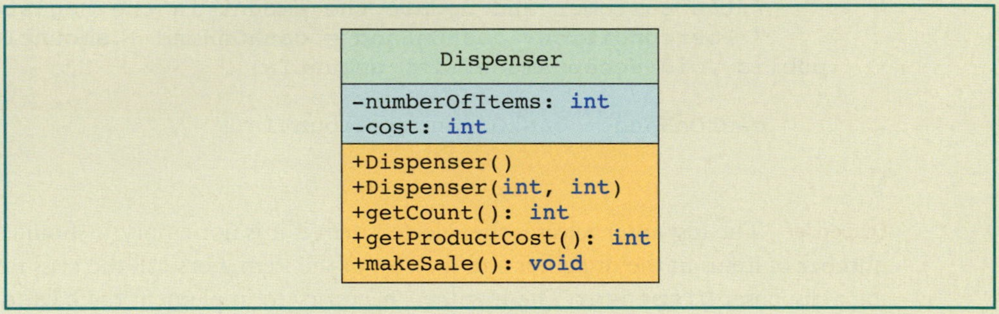

Figure 8-19   UML class diagram of the **class** Dispenser

Because the candy machine sells four types of items, we will create four objects of the type **Dispenser**. The statement:

```
Dispenser chips = new Dispenser(100, 65);
```

creates the object **chips**, sets the number of chip bags in this dispenser to **100**, and sets the cost of each chip bag to **65** cents. (See Figure 8-20.)

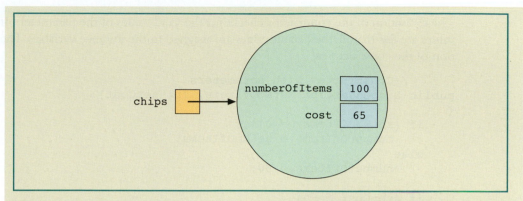

Figure 8-20 Object chips

Next, we discuss the definitions of the methods to implement the operations of the `class Dispenser`.

The method `getCount` returns the number of items of a particular product. Because the number of items currently in the dispenser is stored in the instance variable `numberOfItems`, the method `getCount` returns the value of the instance variable `numberOfItems`. The definition of this method is:

```
public int getCount()
{
    return numberOfItems;
}
```

The method `getProductCost` returns the cost of a product. Because the cost of a product is stored in the instance variable `cost`, it returns the value of the instance variable `cost`. The definition of this method is:

```
public int getProductCost()
{
    return cost;
}
```

When a product is sold, the number of items in that dispenser is reduced by 1. Therefore, the method `makeSale` reduces the number of items in the dispenser by 1. That is, it decrements the value of the instance variable `numberOfItems` by 1. The definition of this method is:

```
public void makeSale()
{
    numberOfItems--;
}
```

The definition of the constructor checks for the valid values of the parameters. If these values are less than 0, the default values are assigned to the instance variables. The definition of the constructor is:

```
    //Constructor with parameters
public Dispenser(int setNoOfItems, int setCost)
{
    if (setNoOfItems >= 0)
        numberOfItems = setNoOfItems;
    else
        numberOfItems = 50;

    if (setCost >= 0)
        cost = setCost;
    else
        cost = 50;
}
```

The default constructor assigns the default values to the instance variables:

```
public Dispenser()
{
    numberOfItems = 50;
    cost = 50;
}
```

The definition of the **class** Dispenser is:

```
//class Dispenser

public class Dispenser
{
    private int numberOfItems;   //variable to store the number of
                                 //items in the dispenser
    private int cost;      //variable to store the cost of an item

        //Default constructor to set the cost and number
        //of items to the default values
        //Postcondition: numberOfItems = 50;
        //               cost = 50;
    public Dispenser()
    {
        numberOfItems = 50;
        cost = 50;
    }

        //Constructor with parameters to set the cost and number
        //of items in the dispenser specified by the user
        //Postcondition: numberOfItems = setNoOfItems;
        //               cost = setCost;
```

```
    public Dispenser(int setNoOfItems, int setCost)
    {
        if (setNoOfItems >= 0)
            numberOfItems = setNoOfItems;
        else
            numberOfItems = 50;

        if (setCost >= 0)
            cost = setCost;
        else
            cost = 50;
    }

        //Method to show the number of items in the machine
        //Postcondition: The value of the instance variable
        //               numberOfItems is returned.
    public int getCount()
    {
        return numberOfItems;
    }


        //Method to show the cost of the item
        //Postcondition: The value of the instance variable
        //               cost is returned.
    public int getProductCost()
    {
        return cost;
    }


        //Method to reduce the number of items by 1
        //Postcondition: numberOfItems = numberOfItems - 1
    public void makeSale()
    {
        numberOfItems--;
    }
}
```

Main Program

When the program executes, it must do the following:

1. Show the different products sold by the candy machine.
2. Show how to select a particular product.
3. Show how to terminate the program.

Furthermore, these instructions must be displayed after processing each selection (except exiting the program), so that the user need not remember what to do if he or she wants to buy additional items. Once the user makes the appropriate selection, the candy machine must act accordingly. If the user opts to buy an available product, the candy machine should show the cost of the product and ask the user to deposit the money. If the money deposited is at least the cost of the item, the candy machine should sell the item and display an appropriate message.

This discussion translates into the following algorithm:

1. Show the selection to the customer.

2. Get the selection.

3. If the selection is valid and the dispenser corresponding to the selection is not empty, sell the product.

We divide this program into three functions—showSelection, sellProduct, and main.

Method showSelection This method displays the necessary information to help the user select and buy a product. Essentially, it contains the following output statements (we assume that the candy machine sells four types of products):

```
*** Welcome to Shelly's Candy Shop ***"
To select an item, enter
1 for Candy
2 for Chips
3 for Gum
4 for Cookies
9 to exit
```

The definition of the function showSelection is:

```
public static void showSelection()
{
    System.out.println("*** Welcome to Shelly's "
                     + "Candy Shop ***");
    System.out.println("To select an item, enter ");
    System.out.println("1 for Candy");
    System.out.println("2 for Chips");
    System.out.println("3 for Gum");
    System.out.println("4 for Cookies");
    System.out.println("9 to exit");
}//end showSelection
```

Next, we describe the method sellProduct.

Method sellProduct This method attempts to sell a particular product selected by the customer. The candy machine contains four dispensers, which correspond to the four products. The first thing this method does is check whether the dispenser holding the product is empty. If the dispenser is empty, the method informs the customer that this product is sold out. If the dispenser is nonempty, it tells the user to deposit the necessary amount to buy the product. For simplicity, we assume that this program does not return the extra money deposited by the customer. Therefore, the cash register is updated by adding the money entered by the user.

From this discussion, it follows that the method `sellProduct` must have access to the dispenser holding the product (to decrement the number of items in the dispenser by 1 and to show the cost of the item) as well as access to the cash register (to update the cash). Therefore, this method has two parameters: one corresponding to the dispenser, and the other corresponding to the cash register.

In pseudocode, the algorithm for this method is:

1. If the dispenser is nonempty
   a. Get the product cost.
   b. Set the variable `coinsRequired` to the price of the product.
   c. Set the variable `coinsInserted` to 0.
   d. While `coinsRequired` is greater than 0
      i.   Show and prompt the customer to enter the additional amount.
      ii. Calculate the total amount entered by the customer.
      iii. Determine the amount needed.
   e. Update the amount in the cash register.
   f. Sell the product—that is, decrement the number of items in the dispenser by 1.
   g. Display an appropriate message.
2. If the dispenser is empty, tell the user that this product is sold out.

This definition of the method `sellProduct` is:

```java
public static void sellProduct(Dispenser product,
                               CashRegister cRegister)
{
    int price;          //variable to hold the product price
    int coinsInserted;  //variable to hold the amount entered
    int coinsRequired;  //variable to show the extra amount
                        //needed

    if (product.getCount() > 0)                      //Step 1
    {
        price = product.getProductCost();            //Step 1a
        coinsRequired = price;                       //Step 1b
        coinsInserted = 0;                           //Step 1c

        while (coinsRequired > 0)                     //Step 1d
        {
            System.out.print("Please deposit "
                        + coinsRequired
                        + " cents: ");               //Step 1d.i
```

```
            coinsInserted = coinsInserted
                          + console.nextInt();      //Step 1d.ii

            coinsRequired = price
                          - coinsInserted;          //Step 1d.iii
        }

        System.out.println();

        cRegister.acceptAmount(coinsInserted);      //Step 1e
        product.makeSale();                         //Step 1f

        System.out.println("Collect your item "
                         + "at the bottom and "
                         + "enjoy.\n");              //Step 1g
    }
    else
        System.out.println("Sorry this item "
                         + "is sold out.\n");        //Step 2
}//end sellProduct
```

Method main The algorithm for the method **main** follows:

1. Create the cash register—that is, create and initialize a **CashRegister** object.
2. Create four dispensers—that is, create and initialize four objects of the type **Dispenser**. For example, the statement:

```
Dispenser candy = new Dispenser(100, 50);
```

creates a dispenser object, **candy**, to hold the candies. The number of items in the dispenser is **100**, and the cost of an item is **50** cents.

3. Declare additional variables as necessary.
4. Show the selection; call the method **showSelection**.
5. Get the selection.
6. While not done (a selection of **9** exits the program):
    a. Sell the product; call the method **sellProduct**.
    b. Show the selection; call the method **showSelection**.
    c. Get the selection.

The definition of the method **main** follows:

```
public static void main(String[] args)
{
    CashRegister cashRegister = new CashRegister();  //Step 1
    Dispenser candy = new Dispenser(100, 50);        //Step 2
    Dispenser chips = new Dispenser(100, 65);        //Step 2
    Dispenser gum = new Dispenser(75, 45);           //Step 2
    Dispenser cookies = new Dispenser(100, 85);      //Step 2
```

```
    int choice;   //variable to hold the selection      //Step 3

    showSelection();                                     //Step 4
    choice = console.nextInt();                          //Step 5

    while (choice != 9)                                  //Step 6
    {
        switch (choice)                                  //Step 6a
        {
        case 1: sellProduct(candy, cashRegister);
                break;
        case 2: sellProduct(chips, cashRegister);
                break;
        case 3: sellProduct(gum, cashRegister);
                break;
        case 4: sellProduct(cookies, cashRegister);
                break;
        default: System.out.println("Invalid Selection");
        }//end switch

        showSelection();                                 //Step 6b
        choice = console.nextInt();                      //Step 6c
    }//end while
}//end main
```

Main Program Listing

```
//Program: Candy Machine

import java.util.*;

public class CandyMachine
{
    static Scanner console = new Scanner(System.in);

    //Place the definition of the method main as given above here.

    //Place the definition of the method showSelection as
    //given above here.

    //Place the definition of the method sellProduct as
    //given above here.
}
```

Sample Run: In this sample run, the user input is shaded.

```
*** Welcome to Shelly's Candy Shop ***
To select an item, enter
1 for Candy
2 for Chips
3 for Gum
4 for Cookies
9 to exit
1
Please deposit 50 cents: 50

Collect your item at the bottom and enjoy.

*** Welcome to Shelly's Candy Shop ***
To select an item, enter
1 for Candy
2 for Chips
3 for Gum
4 for Cookies
9 to exit
3
Please deposit 45 cents: 45

Collect your item at the bottom and enjoy.

*** Welcome to Shelly's Candy Shop ***
To select an item, enter
1 for Candy
2 for Chips
3 for Gum
4 for Cookies
9 to exit
9
```

Candy Machine: Creating a GUI

 If you skipped the GUI part of Chapter 6, you can skip this section.

We will now design an application program that creates the GUI shown in Figure 8-21.

Figure 8-21 GUI for the candy machine

The program should do the following:

1. Show the customer the above GUI.
2. Let the customer make the selection.
3. When the user clicks on a product, show the customer its cost, and prompt the customer to enter the money for the product using an input dialog box as shown in Figure 8-22.

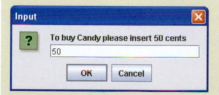

Figure 8-22 Input dialog box to enter money for the candy machine

4. Accept the money from the customer.
5. Make the sale and display a dialog box as shown in Figure 8-23.

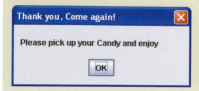

Figure 8-23 Output dialog box to show the output of the candy machine

In the first part of this programming example, we designed and implemented the **class**es CashRegister and Dispenser. Our final step is to revise the main program of the first part to create a GUI.

Main Program

We now describe how to create the candy machine using the **class**es CashRegister and Dispenser and the GUI components. When the program executes, it must display the GUI shown earlier in Figure 8-21.

The GUI contains a window, two labels, and five buttons. The labels and buttons are placed in the content pane of the window. As you learned in Chapter 6, to create the window, the application program is created by extending the definition of the **class** JFrame. Thus, we need the following GUI components:

```java
private JLabel headingMainL;    //label for the first line
private JLabel selectionL;      //label for the second line

private JButton exitB, candyB, chipsB, gumB, cookiesB;
```

The following statements create and instantiate these labels and button objects:

```java
headingMainL = new JLabel("WELCOME TO SHELLY'S CANDY SHOP",
                        SwingConstants.CENTER);
selectionL = new JLabel("To Make a Selection, "
                    + "Click on the Product Button",
                    SwingConstants.CENTER);

candyB = new JButton("Candy");

chipsB = new JButton("Chips");

gumB = new JButton("Gum");

cookiesB = new JButton("Cookies");

exitB = new JButton("Exit");
```

These components are to be placed in the content pane of the window. The seven components—labels and buttons—are arranged in seven rows. Therefore, the content pane layout will be a grid of 7 rows and 1 column. The following statements get the content pane and add these components to the content pane:

```java
Container pane = getContentPane();
setSize(300, 300);

pane.setLayout(new GridLayout(7, 1));
```

```
pane.add(headingMainL);
pane.add(selectionL);
pane.add(candyB);
pane.add(chipsB);
pane.add(gumB);
pane.add(cookiesB);
pane.add(exitB);
```

Event Handling

When the user clicks on a product button, it generates an action event. There are five buttons, each generating an action event. To handle these action events, we use the same process that we used in Chapter 6. That is:

1. Create a class implementing the **interface** `ActionListener`.
2. Provide the definition of the method `actionPerformed`.
3. Create and instantiate an object, action listener, of the class type created in Step 1.
4. Register the listener of Step 3 to each button.

In Chapter 6, we created a separate class for each of the buttons and then created a separate listener for each button. In this new program, rather than create a separate class for each button, we create only one class. Recall that the heading of the method `actionPerformed` is:

```
public void actionPerformed(ActionEvent e)
```

In Chapter 6, while providing the definition of this method, we ignored the formal parameter `e`. The formal parameter `e` is a reference variable of the `ActionEvent` type. The **class** `ActionEvent` contains `getActionCommand` (a method without parameters), which can be used to identify which button generated the event. For example, the expression:

```
e.getActionCommand()
```

returns the string containing the label of the component generating the event. We can now use the appropriate `String` method to determine the button generating the event.

If the user clicks on one of the product buttons, then the candy machine attempts to sell the product. Therefore, the action of clicking on a product button is to sell. For this, we write the method `sellProduct` (discussed later in this programming example). If the user clicks on the `Exit` button, the program should terminate. Let's call the class to handle these events `ButtonHandler`. Its definition is:

```
private class ButtonHandler implements ActionListener
{
    public void actionPerformed(ActionEvent e)
    {
        if (e.getActionCommand().equals("Exit"))
            System.exit(0);
```

```
        else if (e.getActionCommand().equals("Candy"))
                sellProduct(candy, "Candy");
        else if (e.getActionCommand().equals("Chips"))
                sellProduct(chips, "Chips");
        else if (e.getActionCommand().equals("Gum"))
                sellProduct(gum, "Gum");
        else if (e.getActionCommand().equals("Cookies"))
                sellProduct(cookies, "Cookies");
    }
}
```

You can now declare, instantiate, and register the listener as follows:

```
private ButtonHandler pbHandler;   //declare the listener

pbHandler = new ButtonHandler();   //instantiate the object

    //register the listener with each button
candyB.addActionListener(pbHandler);
chipsB.addActionListener(pbHandler);
gumB.addActionListener(pbHandler);
cookiesB.addActionListener(pbHandler);
exitB.addActionListener(pbHandler);
```

Next, we describe the method `sellProduct`.

Method `sellProduct`   The definition of this method is similar to the one we designed for the non–GUI program. (We give its definition for the sake of completeness.) This method attempts to sell a particular product selected by the customer. The candy machine contains four dispensers which correspond to the four products. These dispensers will be declared as instance variables. Therefore, the dispenser of the product to be sold and the name of the product are passed as parameters to this method. Because the cash register will be declared as an instance variable, this method can directly access the cash register.

This definition of the method `sellProduct` is:

```
private void sellProduct(Dispenser product, String productName)
{
    int coinsInserted = 0;
    int price, coinsRequired;
    String str;

    if (product.getCount() > 0)
    {
        price = product.getProductCost();
        coinsRequired = price - coinsInserted;
```

```java
while (coinsRequired > 0)
    {
        str = JOptionPane.showInputDialog("To buy "
                        + productName
                        + " please insert "
                        + coinsRequired + " cents");
        coinsInserted = coinsInserted
                        + Integer.parseInt(str);
        coinsRequired = price - coinsInserted;
    }

    cashRegister.acceptAmount(coinsInserted);
    product.makeSale();

    JOptionPane.showMessageDialog(null,"Please pick up your "
                        + productName + " and enjoy",
                        "Thank you, Come again!",
                        JOptionPane.PLAIN_MESSAGE);
    }
    else                     //the dispenser is empty
        JOptionPane.showMessageDialog(null,"Sorry "
                        + productName
                        + " is sold out\n" +
                        "Make another selection",
                        "Thank you, Come again!",
                        JOptionPane.PLAIN_MESSAGE);
}//end sellProduct
```

We have described the method `sellProduct` and the other necessary components, so next we write the Java application program for the candy machine.

The algorithm is as follows:

1. Create the cash register—that is, declare a reference variable of the type `CashRegister` and instantiate the object.
2. Create four dispensers—that is, declare four reference variables of the type `Dispenser` and instantiate the appropriate `Dispenser` objects. For example, the statement:

   `Dispenser candy = new Dispenser(100, 50);`

   declares `candy` to be a reference variable of the `Dispenser` type and instantiates the object `candy` to hold the candies. The number of items in the object `candy` is `100`, and the cost of a candy is `50` cents.
3. Create the other objects, such as labels and buttons, as previously described.
4. Display the GUI showing the candy machine as described at the beginning of this programming example.
5. Get and process the selection.

The complete list of the class containing the application program is:

```java
//Candy Machine Program

import javax.swing.*;
import java.awt.*;
import java.awt.event.*;

public class CandyMachine extends JFrame
{
    private static final int WIDTH = 300;
    private static final int HEIGHT = 300;

        //Instance variables
    private CashRegister cashRegister = new CashRegister();
    private Dispenser candy = new Dispenser(100, 50);
    private Dispenser chips = new Dispenser(100, 65);
    private Dispenser gum = new Dispenser(75, 45);
    private Dispenser cookies = new Dispenser(100, 85);

    private JLabel headingMainL;
    private JLabel selectionL;

    private JButton exitB, candyB, chipsB, gumB, cookiesB;
    private ButtonHandler pbHandler;

    public CandyMachine()
    {
        setTitle("Candy Machine");        //set the window title
        setSize(WIDTH, HEIGHT);           //set the window size

        Container pane = getContentPane();     //get the container
        pane.setLayout(new GridLayout(7, 1)); //set the pane layout

        pbHandler = new ButtonHandler();  //instantiate the listener
                                          //object

        headingMainL = new JLabel("WELCOME TO SHELLY'S CANDY SHOP",
                        SwingConstants.CENTER); //instantiate
                                                //the first label
        selectionL = new JLabel("To Make a Selection, "
                          + "Click on the Product Button",
                        SwingConstants.CENTER);  //instantiate
                                                 //the second label

        pane.add(headingMainL);   //add the first label to the pane
        pane.add(selectionL);     //add the second label to the pane
```

```java
        candyB = new JButton("Candy");   //instantiate the candy
                                         //button
        candyB.addActionListener(pbHandler);   //register the
                                               //listener to the
                                               //candy button
        chipsB = new JButton("Chips");   //instantiate the chips
                                         //button
        chipsB.addActionListener(pbHandler);   //register the
                                               //listener to the
                                               //chips button
        gumB = new JButton("Gum");       //instantiate the gum button
        gumB.addActionListener(pbHandler);   //register the listener
                                             //to the gum button

        cookiesB = new JButton("Cookies");   //instantiate the
                                             //cookies button
        cookiesB.addActionListener(pbHandler); //register the
                                    //listener to the cookies button

        exitB = new JButton("Exit");   //instantiate the exit button
        exitB.addActionListener(pbHandler); //register the listener
                                            //to the exit button

        pane.add(candyB);      //add the candy button to the pane
        pane.add(chipsB);      //add the chips button to the pane
        pane.add(gumB);        //add the gum button to the pane
        pane.add(cookiesB);    //add the cookies button to the pane
        pane.add(exitB);       //add the exit button to the pane

        setVisible(true);      //show the window and its contents
        setDefaultCloseOperation(EXIT_ON_CLOSE);

    }//end constructor

        //class to handle the button events
    private class ButtonHandler implements ActionListener
    {
        public void actionPerformed (ActionEvent e)
        {
            if (e.getActionCommand().equals("Exit"))
                System.exit(0);
            else if (e.getActionCommand().equals("Candy"))
                    sellProduct(candy, "Candy");
            else if (e.getActionCommand().equals("Chips"))
                    sellProduct(chips, "Chips");
            else if (e.getActionCommand().equals("Gum"))
                    sellProduct(gum, "Gum");
```

```java
                else if (e.getActionCommand().equals("Cookies"))
                        sellProduct(cookies, "Cookies");
        }
    }

        //Method to sell a product
    private void sellProduct(Dispenser product, String productName)
    {
        int coinsInserted = 0;
        int price, coinsRequired;
        String str;

        if (product.getCount() > 0)
        {
            price = product.getProductCost();
            coinsRequired = price - coinsInserted;

            while (coinsRequired > 0)
            {
                str = JOptionPane.showInputDialog("To buy "
                                    + productName
                                    + " please insert "
                                    + coinsRequired + " cents");
                coinsInserted = coinsInserted
                                + Integer.parseInt(str);
                coinsRequired = price - coinsInserted;
            }

            cashRegister.acceptAmount(coinsInserted);
            product.makeSale();

            JOptionPane.showMessageDialog(null,"Please pick up your "
                                + productName + " and enjoy",
                                "Thank you, Come again!",
                                JOptionPane.PLAIN_MESSAGE);
        }
        else            //the dispenser is empty
            JOptionPane.showMessageDialog(null,"Sorry "
                                + productName
                                + " is sold out\n" +
                                "Make another selection",
                                "Thank you, Come again!",
                                JOptionPane.PLAIN_MESSAGE);
    }//end sellProduct
    public static void main(String[] args)
    {
        CandyMachine candyShop = new CandyMachine();
    }
}
```

Sample Run: Figure 8-24 shows the sample run.

Figure 8-24   Sample run for `CandyMachine`

QUICK REVIEW

1. A **class** is a collection of a fixed number of components.
2. Components of a **class** are called the members of the class.
3. Members of a **class** are accessed by name.
4. In Java, **class** is a reserved word, and it defines only a data type; no memory is allocated.
5. Members of a class are classified into one of three categories: **private**, **protected**, or **public**.

6. The **private** members of a class are not accessible outside the class.

7. The **public** members of a class are accessible outside the class.

8. The **public** members are declared using the modifier **public**.

9. The **private** members are declared using the modifier **private**.

10. A member of a class can be a method or a variable.

11. If any member of a class is a variable, it is declared like any other variable.

12. In Java, a **class** is a definition.

13. Non-**static** variables of a **class** are called instance variables of that **class**.

14. Methods of a class are called instance methods.

15. Constructors guarantee that the data members are initialized when an object is declared.

16. The name of a constructor is the same as the name of the class.

17. A class can have more than one constructor.

18. A constructor without parameters is called the default constructor.

19. Constructors automatically execute when a class object is created.

20. In a UML class diagram, the top box contains the name of the class. The middle box contains the data members and their data types. The bottom box contains the methods' names, parameter list, and return type. A + (plus) sign in front of a member indicates that the member is a **public** member; a – (minus) sign indicates that this is a **private** member. The # symbol before a member name indicates that the member is a **protected** member.

21. In shallow copying, two or more reference variables of the same type refer to the same object.

22. In deep copying, each reference variable refers to its own object.

23. A reference variable has the same scope as other variables.

24. A member of a class is local to the class.

25. You access a **public class** member outside the **class** through the reference variable name or the **class** name (for **static** members) and the member access operator (**.**).

26. The copy constructor executes when an object is instantiated and initialized using an existing object.

27. The method **toString** is a **public** value-returning method. It does not take any parameters and returns the address of a **String** object.

28. The methods **print**, **println**, and **printf** output the string created by the method **toString**.

29. The default definition of the method **toString** creates a **String** that is the name of the object's **class** name followed by the object's hash code.

30. The modifier **static** in the heading of the method of a class specifies that the method can be invoked by using the name of the class.

31. If a data member of a class is declared using the modifier **static**, that data member can be invoked by using the name of the class.

32. **static** data members of a **class** *exist* even when no object of the **class** type is instantiated. Moreover, **static** variables are initialized to their default values.

33. Finalizers automatically execute when a class object goes out of scope.

34. A **class** can have only one finalizer, and the finalizer has no parameters.

35. The name of the finalizer is **finalize**.

36. A method of a class that only accesses (that is, does not modify) the value(s) of the data member(s) is called an accessor method.

37. A method of a class that modifies the value(s) of the data member(s) is called a mutator method.

38. You can create your own packages using the **package** statement.

39. Java implicitly uses the reference **this** to refer to both the instance variables and the methods of a class.

40. Classes that are defined within another class are called inner classes.

41. A data type that specifies the logical properties without the implementation details is called an abstract data type (ADT).

8

EXERCISES

1. Mark the following statements as true or false:

   a. The instance variables of a class must be of the same type.

   b. The methods of a class must be **public**.

   c. A class can have more than one constructor.

   d. A constructor can return a value of the **int** type.

   e. An accessor method of a class accesses and modifies the data members of the class.

2. Find the syntax errors in the definitions of the following classes:

   a.
   ```
   public class AA
   {
       private int x;
       private int y;
   ```

```java
        public void print()
        {
            System.out.println(x + " " + y);
        }

        public int sum()
        {
            return x + y;
        }

        public AA()
        {
            x = 0;
            y = 0;
        }

        public int AA(int a, int b)
        {
            x = a;
            y = b;
        }
    }
```

b.
```java
    public class BB
    {
        private int one;
        private int two;

        public boolean equal()
        {
            return (one == two);
        }

        public print()
        {
            System.out.println(one + " " + two);
        }

        public BB(int a, int b)
        {
            one = a;
            two = b;
        }
    }
```

3. Consider the definition of the following class:

```
class CC
{
    private int u;
    private int v;
    private double w;

    public CC()                          //Line 1
    {
    }

    public CC(int a)                     //Line 2
    {
    }

    public CC(int a, int b)              //Line 3
    {
    }

    public CC(int a, int b, double d)    //Line 4
    {
    }
}
```

a. Give the line number containing the constructor that is executed in each of the following declarations:

(i) `CC one = new CC();`

(ii) `CC two = new CC(5, 6);`

(iii) `CC three = new CC(2, 8, 3.5);`

b. Write the definition of the constructor in Line 1 so that the instance variables are initialized to 0.

c. Write the definition of the constructor in Line 2 so that the instance variable u is initialized according to the value of the parameter, and the instance variables v and w are initialized to 0.

d. Write the definition of the constructor in Line 3 so that the instance variables u and v are initialized according to the values of the parameters a and b, respectively, and the instance variable w is initialized to 0.0.

e. Write the definitions of the constructors in Line 4 so that the instance variables u, v, and w are initialized according to the values of the parameters a, b, and d, respectively.

4. Write a Java statement that creates the object mysteryClock of the Clock type, and initializes the instance variables hr, min, and sec of mysteryClock to 7, 18, and 39, respectively.

5. Given the statements:

```
Clock firstClock = new Clock(2, 6, 35);
Clock secondClock = new Clock(6, 23, 17);

firstClock = secondClock;
```

what is the output of the following statements?

```
firstClock.print();
System.out.println();
secondClock.print();
System.out.println();
```

6. Consider the following declarations:

```
public class XClass
{
    private int u;
    private double w;

    public XClass()
    {
    }

    public XClass(int a, double b)
    {
    }

    public void func()
    {

    }

    public void print()
    {
    }
}

XClass x = new XClass(10, 20.75);
```

a. How many members does **class** XClass have?

b. How many **private** members does **class** XClass have?

c. How many constructors does **class** XClass have?

d. Write the definition of the member **func** so that u is set to 10 and w is set to 15.3.

e. Write the definition of the member **print** that prints the contents of u and w.

f. Write the definition of the default constructor of the **class** XClass so that the instance variables are initialized to 0.

g. Write the definition of the constructor with parameters of the **class** XClass so that the instance variable u is initialized to the value of a and the instance variable w is initialized to the value of b.

h. Write a Java statement that prints the values of the instance variables of x.

i. Write a Java statement that creates the XClass object t and initializes the instance variables of t to 20 and 35.0, respectively.

7. Explain shallow copying.

8. Explain deep copying.

9. Suppose that two reference variables, say aa and bb, of the same type point to two different objects. What happens when you use the assignment operator to copy the value of aa into bb?

10. Assume that the method toString is defined for the **class** Clock as given in this chapter. What is the output of the following statements?

```
Clock firstClock;
Clock secondClock = new Clock(6, 23, 17);

firstClock = secondClock.getCopy();

System.out.println(firstClock);
```

11. What is the purpose of the copy constructor?

12. How does Java use the reference **this**?

13. Suppose that you have created the **class** Mystery. Write the Java statement that would put this class into the **package** strangeClasses in the subdirectory ch08 of the directory jpfpatpd.

14. Can you use the relational operator == to determine whether two different objects of the same **class** type contain the same data?

15. Consider the definition of the following **class**:

```
class TestClass
{
    private int x;
    private int y;

        //Default constructor to initialize
        //the instance variables to 0
    public TestClass()
    {
    }

        //Constructors with parameters to initialize the
        //instance variables to the values specified by
```

8

```
        //the parameters
        //Postcondition: x = a; y = b;
    TestClass(int a, int b)
    {
    }

        //return the sum of the instance variables
    public int sum()
    {
    }
        //print the values of the instance variables
    public void print()
    {
    }
}
```

a. Write the definitions of the methods as described in the definition of the **class** TestClass.

b. Write a test program to test the various operations of the **class** TestClass.

16. Write the definition of a class that has the following properties:

a. The name of the class is Secret.

b. The **class** Secret has four instance variables: name of the type string, age and weight of the type int, and height of the type double.

c. The **class** Secret has the following methods:

print—outputs the data stored in the data members with the appropriate titles.

setName—method to set the name.

setAge—method to set the age.

setWeight—method to set the weight.

setHeight—method to set the height.

getName—value-returning method to return the name.

getAge—value-returning method to return the age.

getWeight—value-returning method to return the weight.

getHeight—value-returning method to return the height.

default constructor—the default value of name is the empty string " "; the default values of age, weight, and height are 0.

constructor with parameters—sets the values of the instance variables name, age, weight, and height to the values specified by the user

d. Write the definitions of the method members of the **class** Secret as described in part c.

17. Consider the following definition of the **class** myClass:

```
class MyClass
{
    private int x;
    private static int count;

        //Default constructor
        //Postcondition: x = 0;
    public MyClass()
    {
        //write the definition
    }

        //Constructor with a parameter
        //Postcondition: x = a;
    public MyClass(int a)
    {
        //write the definition
    }

        //Method to set the value of x
        //Postcondition: x = a;
    public void setX(int a)
    {
        //write the definition
    }

        //Method to output x
    public void printX()
    {
        //write the definition
    }

        //Method to output count
    public static void printCount()
    {
        //write the definition
    }

        //Method to increment count
        //Postcondition: count++;
    public static void incrementCount()
    {
        //write the definition
    }
}
```

8

a.   Write a Java statement that increments the value of `count` by 1.

b.   Write a Java statement that outputs the value of `count`.

c.   Write the definitions of the methods and the constructors of the **class** `MyClass` as described in its definition.

d.   Write a Java statement that declares `myObject1` to be a `MyClass` object and initializes its instance variable `x` to 5.

e.   Write a Java statement that declares `myObject2` to be a `MyClass` object and initializes its instance variable `x` to 7.

f.   Which of the following statements are valid? (Assume that `myObject1` and `myObject2` are as declared in parts d and e.)

```
myObject1.printCount();     //Line 1
myObject1.printX();         //Line 2
MyClass.printCount();       //Line 3
MyClass.printX();           //Line 4
MyClass.count++;            //Line 5
```

g.   Assume that `myObject1` and `myObject2` are as declared in parts d and e. After you have written the definition of the methods of the **class** `MyClass`, what is the output of the following Java code?

```
myObject1.printX();
myObject1.incrementCount();
MyClass.incrementCount();
myObject1.printCount();
myObject2.printCount();
myObject2.printX();
myObject1.setX(14);
myObject1.incrementCount();
myObject1.printX();
myObject1.printCount();
myObject2.printCount();
```

PROGRAMMING EXERCISES

1.   Write a program that converts a number entered in Roman numerals to decimal. Your program should consist of a **class**, say `Roman`. An object of the type `Roman` should do the following:

a.   Store the number as a Roman numeral.

b.   Convert and store the number into decimal.

c.   Print the number as a Roman numeral or decimal number as requested by the user.

The decimal values of the Roman numerals are:

```
M    1000
D     500
C     100
```

```
L        50
X        10
V         5
I         1
```

   d. Test your program using the following Roman numerals: MCXIV, CCCLIX, and MDCLXVI.

2. Design and implement the **class** Day that implements the day of the week in a program. The **class** Day should store the day, such as Sun for Sunday. The program should be able to perform the following operations on an object of the type Day:

   a. Set the day.

   b. Print the day.

   c. Return the day.

   d. Return the next day.

   e. Return the previous day.

   f. Calculate and return the day by adding certain days to the current day. For example, if the current day is Monday and we add 4 days, the day to be returned is Friday. Similarly, if today is Tuesday and we add 13 days, the day to be returned is Monday.

   g. Add the appropriate constructors.

   h. Write the definitions of the methods to implement the operations for the **class** Day as defined in a through g.

   i. Write a program to test various operations on the **class** Day.

3. a. Example 8-4 defined the **class** Person to store the name of a person. The methods that we included merely set the name and print the name of a person. Redefine the **class** Person so that, in addition to what the existing **class** does, you can:

   i. Set the last name only.

   ii. Set the first name only.

   iii. Set the middle name.

   iv. Check whether a given last name is the same as the last name of this person.

   v. Check whether a given first name is the same as the first name of this person.

   vi. Check whether a given middle name is the same as the middle name of this person.

   b. Add the method **equals** that returns true if two objects contain the same first and last name.

   c. Add the method **makeCopy** that copies the instance variables of a **Person** object into another **Person** object.

   d. Add the method **getCopy** that creates and returns the address of the object, which is a copy of another **Person** object.

   e. Add the copy constructor.

8

f. Write the definitions of the methods of the **class** Person to implement the operations for this **class**.

g. Write a program that tests various operations of the **class** Person.

4. a. Some of the characteristics of a book are the title, author(s), publisher, ISBN, price, and year of publication. Design the **class** Book that defines the book as an ADT.

Each object of the **class** Book can hold the following information about a book: title, up to four authors, publisher, ISBN, price, and number of copies in stock. To keep track of the number of authors, add another instance variable.

Include the methods to perform various operations on the objects of Book. For example, the usual operations that can be performed on the title are to show the title, set the title, and check whether a title is the actual title of the book. Similarly, the typical operations that can be performed on the number of copies in stock are to show the number of copies in stock, set the number of copies in stock, update the number of copies in stock, and return the number of copies in stock. Add similar operations for the publisher, ISBN, book price, and authors. Add the appropriate constructors and a finalizer (if one is needed).

b. Write the definitions of the methods of the **class** Book.

c. Write a program that uses the **class** Book and tests various operations on the objects of **class** Book. Declare an array of 100 components of the type Book. Some of the operations that you should perform are to search for a book by its title, search by ISBN, and update the number of copies of a book.

5. In this exercise, you will design the **class** Member.

a. Each object of Member can hold the name of a person, member ID, number of books bought, and amount spent.

b. Include the methods to perform the various operations on the objects of the **class** Member—for example, modify, set, and show a person's name. Similarly, update, modify, and show the number of books bought and the amount spent.

c. Add the appropriate constructors and a finalizer (if one is needed).

d. Write the definitions of the methods of the **class** Member.

6. Using the classes designed in Programming Exercises 4 and 5, write a program to simulate a bookstore. The bookstore has two types of customers: those who are members of the bookstore and those who buy books from the bookstore only occasionally. Each member has to pay a $10 yearly membership fee and receives a 5% discount on each book bought.

For each member, the bookstore keeps track of the number of books bought and the total amount spent. For every eleventh book that a member buys, the bookstore takes the average of the total amount of the last 10 books bought, applies this amount as a discount, and then resets the total amount spent to 0.

Write a program that can process up to 1000 book titles and 500 members. Your program should contain a menu that gives the user different choices to effectively run the program; in other words, your program should be menu-driven.

7. Rational fractions are of the form a / b, where a and b are integers and $b \neq 0$. In this exercise, by "fractions" we mean rational fractions. Suppose a / b and c / d are fractions. Arithmetic operations on fractions are defined by the following rules:

$a / b + c / d = (ad + bc) / bd$

$a / b - c / d = (ad - bc) / bd$

$a / b \times c / d = ac / bd$

$(a / b) / (c / d) = ad / bc$, where $c / d \neq 0$

Fractions are compared as follows: a / b *op* c / d if ad *op* bc, where *op* is any of the relational operations. For example, $a / b < c / d$ if $ad < bc$.

Design the **class** Fraction that can be used to manipulate fractions in a program. Among others, the **class** Fraction must include methods to add, subtract, multiply, and divide fractions. When you add, subtract, multiply, or divide fractions, your answer need not be in the lowest terms. Also, override the method **toString** so that the fractions can be output using the output statement.

Write a Java program that, using the **class** Fraction, performs operations on fractions.

8

9

ARRAYS

In this chapter, you will:

- ◆ Learn about arrays
- ◆ Explore how to declare and manipulate data into arrays
- ◆ Learn about the instance variable `length`
- ◆ Understand the meaning of "array index out of bounds"
- ◆ Become aware of how the assignment and relational operators work with array names
- ◆ Discover how to pass an array as a parameter to a method
- ◆ Discover how to manipulate data in a two-dimensional array
- ◆ Learn about multidimensional arrays

In previous chapters, you worked with primitive data types and learned how to construct your own classes. Recall that a variable of a primitive data type can store only one value at a time; on the other hand, a **class** can be defined so that its objects can store more than one value at a time. This chapter introduces a special data structure called arrays, which allow the user to group data items of the same type and process them in a convenient way.

WHY DO WE NEED ARRAYS?

Before we formally define an array, let's consider the following problem. We want to write a Java program that reads five numbers, finds their sum, and prints the numbers in reverse order.

In Chapter 5, you learned how to read numbers, print them, and find their sum. What's different here is that we want to print the numbers in reverse order. We cannot print the first four numbers until we have printed the fifth, and so on. This means that we need to store all the numbers before we can print them in reverse order. From what we have learned so far, the following program accomplishes this task.

```java
//Program to read five numbers, find their sum, and print the
//numbers in reverse order.

import java.util.*;

public class ReversePrintI
{
    static Scanner console = new Scanner(System.in);

    public static void main(String[] args)
    {
        int item0, item1, item2, item3, item4;
        int sum;

        System.out.println("Enter five integers: ");
        item0 = console.nextInt();
        item1 = console.nextInt();
        item2 = console.nextInt();
        item3 = console.nextInt();
        item4 = console.nextInt();

        sum = item0 + item1 + item2 + item3 + item4;

        System.out.println("The sum of the numbers = " + sum);
        System.out.print("The numbers in reverse order are: ");
        System.out.println(item4 + " " + item3 + " " + item2
                           + " " + item1 + " " + item0);
    }
}
```

This program works fine. However, to read 100 (or more) numbers and print them in reverse order, you would have to declare 100 or more variables and write many input and output statements. Thus, for large amounts of data, this type of program is not desirable.

Note the following in the preceding program:

1. Five variables must be declared because the numbers are to be printed in reverse order.

2. All variables are of the type **int**—that is, of the same data type.

3. The way in which these variables are declared indicates that the variables to store these numbers have the same name except for the last character, which is a number.

From 1, it follows that you have to declare five variables. From 3, it follows that it would be convenient if you could somehow put the last character, which is a number, into a counter variable and use one **for** loop to count from 0 to 4 for reading, and use another **for** loop to count from 4 to 0 for printing. Finally, because all the variables are of the same type, you should be able to specify how many variables must be declared—and their data type—with a simpler statement than the one used earlier.

The data structure that lets you do all of these things in Java is called an array.

ARRAYS

An **array** is a collection of a fixed number of components, wherein all the components are of the same data type. A **one-dimensional array** is an array in which the components are arranged in a list form. The remainder of this section discusses one-dimensional arrays. Arrays of two or more dimensions are discussed later in this chapter.

The general form to declare a one-dimensional array is:

```
dataType[] arrayName;     //Line 1
```

where **dataType** is the component type.

In Java, an array is an object, just like the objects discussed in Chapter 8. Because an array is an object, **arrayName** is a reference variable. Therefore, the preceding statement only declares a reference variable. To store the data we must instantiate the array object.

The general syntax to instantiate an array object is:

```
arrayName = new dataType[intExp];     //Line 2
```

where **intExp** is any expression that evaluates to a positive integer. Also, the value of **intExp** specifies the number of components in the array.

You can combine the statements in Lines 1 and 2 into one statement as follows:

```
dataType[] arrayName = new dataType[intExp];     //Line 3
```

We typically use statements similar to the statement in Line 3 to create arrays to manipulate data.

 When an array is instantiated, Java automatically initializes its components to their default values. For example, numeric arrays are initialized to 0.

Example 9-1

The statement:

```java
int[] num = new int[5];
```

declares and creates the array `num` of 5 components. Each component is of the type `int`. The components are accessed as `num[0]`, `num[1]`, `num[2]`, `num[3]`, and `num[4]`. Figure 9-1 illustrates the array `num`.

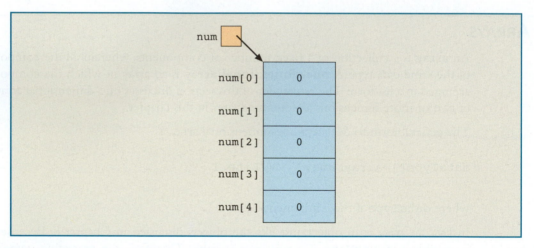

Figure 9-1 Array num

Alternate Ways to Declare an Array

Java allows you to declare arrays as follows:

```java
int list[];              //Line 1
```

Here the operator `[ ]` appears after the identifier `list`, not after the data type `int`.

You should be careful when declaring arrays as in Line 1. Consider the following statements:

```java
int alpha[], beta;     //Line 2
int[] gamma, delta;    //Line 3
```

The statement in Line 2 declares the variables `alpha` and `beta`. Similarly, the statement in Line 3 declares the variables `gamma` and `delta`. However, the statement in Line 2 declares only `alpha` to be an array reference variable, while the variable `beta` is an `int` variable. On the other hand, the statement in Line 3 declares both `gamma` and `delta` to be array reference variables.

Traditionally, Java programmers declare arrays as shown in Line 3. We recommend that you also declare arrays as in Line 3.

Accessing Array Components

The general form (syntax) used to access an array component is:

```
arrayName[indexExp]
```

where `indexExp`, called the **index**, is an expression whose value is a non-negative integer less than the size of the array. The index value specifies the position of the component in the array. In Java, the array index starts at `0`.

In Java, `[ ]` is an operator called the **array subscripting operator**.

Consider the following statement:

```java
int[] list = new int[10];
```

This statement declares an array `list` of `10` components. The components are `list[0]`, `list[1]`, ..., `list[9]`. In other words, we have declared 10 variables of the type `int`. See Figure 9-2.

9

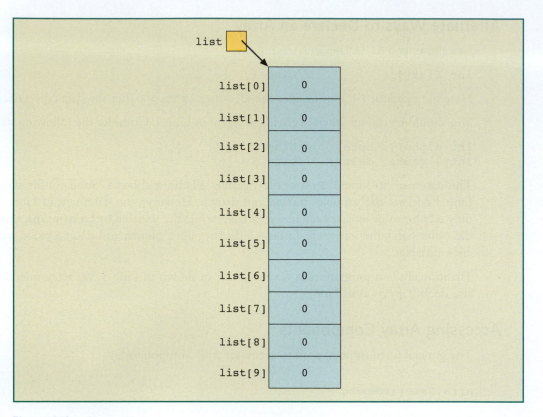

Figure 9-2   Array `list`

The assignment statement:

`list[5] = 34;`

stores 34 into `list[5]`, which is the sixth component of the array `list`. See Figure 9-3.

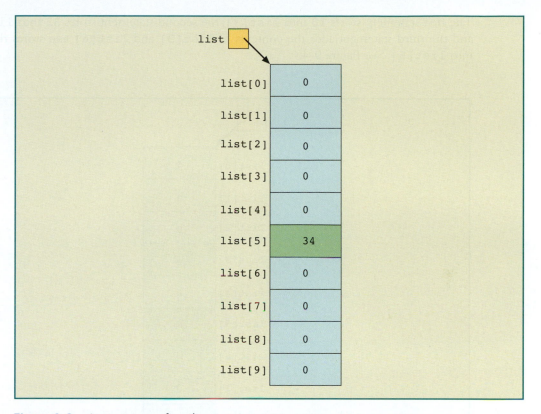

Figure 9-3   Array `list` after the statement `list[5]= 34;` executes

Suppose `i` is an **int** variable. Then the assignment statement:

```
list[3] = 63;
```

is equivalent to the assignment statements:

```
i = 3;
list[i] = 63;
```

If `i` is 4, then the assignment statement:

```
list[2 * i - 3] = 58;
```

stores 58 into `list[5]`, because `2 * i - 3` evaluates to 5. The index expression is evaluated first, giving the position of the component in the array.

Next, consider the following statements:

```
list[3] = 10;
list[6] = 35;
list[5] = list[3] + list[6];
```

The first statement stores 10 into list[3], the second statement stores 35 into list[6], and the third statement adds the contents of list[3] and list[6] and stores the result into list[5]. See Figure 9-4.

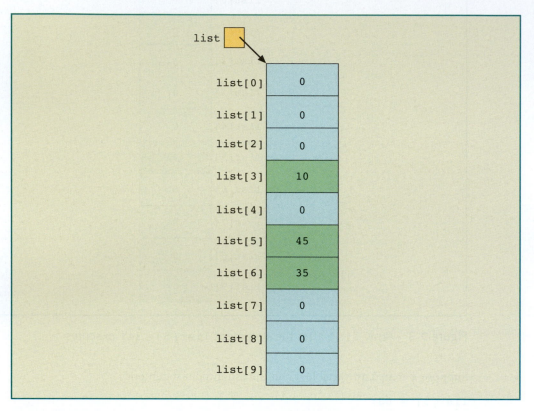

Figure 9-4   Array list after the statements list[3]= 10;, list[6]= 35;, and list[5] = list[3] + list[6]; execute

Example 9-2

You can also declare arrays as follows:

```
final int ARRAY_SIZE = 10;
int[] list = new int[ARRAY_SIZE];
```

That is, you can first declare a named constant of an integral type such as **int** and then use the value of the named constant to specify the size of the array.

Specifying Array Size During Program Execution

When you include a statement in a program to instantiate an array object, it is not necessary to know the size of the array at compile time. During program execution, you can first prompt the user to specify the size of the array and then instantiate the object. The following statements illustrate this concept (suppose that `console` is a `Scanner` object initialized to the standard input device):

```
int arraySize;                                          //Line 1

System.out.print("Enter the size of the array: ");      //Line 2
arraySize = console.nextInt();                          //Line 3
System.out.println();                                   //Line 4

int[] list = new int[arraySize];                        //Line 5
```

The statement in Line 2 asks the user to enter the size of the array when the program executes. The statement in Line 3 inputs the size of the array into `arraySize`. During program execution, the system uses the value of the variable `arraySize` to instantiate the object `list`. For example, if the value of `arraySize` is 15, `list` is an array of size 15. Arrays that are created, that is, instantiated, during program execution are called **dynamic arrays**.

Array Initialization During Declaration

Like any other primitive data type variable, an array can also be initialized to specific values when it is declared. For example, the following Java statement declares an array, `sales`, of five components and initializes those components to specific values:

```
double[] sales = {12.25, 32.50, 16.90, 23, 45.68};
```

The values, called **initial values**, are placed between braces and separated by commas. Here, `sales[0]` = 12.25, `sales[1]` = 32.50, `sales[2]` = 16.90, `sales[3]` = 23.00, and `sales[4]` = 45.68.

Note the following about declaring and initializing arrays:

- When declaring and initializing arrays, the size of the array is determined by the number of initial values within the braces.

- If an array is declared and initialized simultaneously, we *do not* use the operator `new` to instantiate the array object.

Arrays and the Instance Variable `length`

Recall that an array is an object; therefore, to store data, the array object must be instantiated. Associated with each array that has been instantiated (that is, memory has been allocated to store data), there is a **public** instance variable `length`. The variable `length` contains the size of the array. Because `length` is a **public** member, it can be directly accessed in a program using the array name and the dot operator.

Consider the following declaration:

```
int[] list = {10, 20, 30, 40, 50, 60};
```

This statement creates the array `list` of six components and initializes the components using the values given. Here `list.length` is 6.

Consider the following statement:

```
int[] numList = new int[10];
```

This statement creates the array `numList` of 10 components and initializes each component to 0. Because the number of components of `numList` is 10, the value of `numList.length` is 10. Now consider the following statements:

```
numList[0] = 5;
numList[1] = 10;
numList[2] = 15;
numList[3] = 20;
```

These statements store 5, 10, 15, and 20, respectively, in the first four components of `numList`. Even though we put data into only the first four components, the value of `numList.length` is 10, the total number of array components.

You can store the number of filled elements, that is, the actual number of elements, in the array, in a variable, say `noOfElements`. Programs commonly keep track of the number of filled elements in an array.

Processing One-Dimensional Arrays

Some of the basic operations performed on a one-dimensional array are to initialize the array, input data, output data stored in the array, and find the largest and/or smallest element in the array. If the data type of an array component is numeric, a common operation is to find the sum and average of the elements of the array. Each of these operations requires the ability to step through the elements of the array. Stepping through the elements of an array is easily accomplished by using a loop. Suppose that we have the following statements:

```
int[] list = new int[100];       //list is an array of size 100
int i;
```

The following **for** loop steps through each element of the array `list`, starting at the first element of `list`:

```
for (i = 0; i < list.length; i++)                          //Line 1
    //process list[i], the (i + 1)th element of list //Line 2
```

If processing `list` requires inputting data into `list`, the statement in Line 2 takes the form of an input statement, such as in the following code. The following statements read 100 numbers from the keyboard and store the numbers into `list`:

```
for (i = 0; i < list.length; i++)    //Line 1
    list[i] = console.nextInt();     //Line 2
```

Similarly, if processing `list` requires outputting data, then the statement in Line 2 takes the form of an output statement. The following `for` loop outputs the elements of `list`.

```
for (i = 0; i < list.length; i++)        //Line 1
    System.out.print(list[i] + " ");     //Line 2
```

Example 9-3 further illustrates how to process one-dimensional arrays.

Example 9-3

This example shows how loops are used to process arrays. The following declaration is used throughout this example:

```
double[] sales = new double[10];
int index;
double largestSale, sum, average;
```

The first statement creates the array `sales` of 10 components, with each component of the type `double`. The meaning of the other statements is clear. Also, notice that the value of `sales.length` is 10.

Loops can be used to process arrays in several ways:

1. **Initializing an array to a specific value:** To initialize every component of the array `sales` to a specific value, say `10.00`, you can use the following loop.

```
for (index = 0; index < sales.length; index++)
    sales[index] = 10.00;
```

2. **Reading data into an array:** The following loop inputs data into the array `sales`. For simplicity, we assume that the data is entered at the keyboard one number per line.

```
for (index = 0; index < sales.length; index++)
    sales[index] = console.nextDouble();
```

3. **Printing an array:** The following loop outputs the array `sales`. For simplicity, we assume that the output goes to the screen.

```
for (index = 0; index < sales.length; index++)
    System.out.print(sales[index] + " ");
```

4. **Finding the sum and average of an array:** Because the array `sales`, as its name implies, represents certain sales data, it is natural to find the total sale and average sale amounts. The following Java code finds the sum of the elements of the array `sales` (total sales) and the average sale amount.

```
sum = 0;
for (index = 0; index < sales.length; index++)
    sum = sum + sales[index];
```

9

```
if (sales.length != 0)
    average = sum / sales.length;
else
    average = 0.0;
```

5. **Determining the largest element in the array:** We now discuss the algorithm to find the largest element in an array—that is, the array component with the largest value. However, the user is typically more interested in determining the location of the largest element in the array. Of course, if you know the location (the index of the largest element in the array), you can easily determine the value of the largest element in the array. So let's describe the algorithm to determine the index of the largest element in an array—in particular, the index of the largest sale amount in the array `sales`.

We assume that `maxIndex` will contain the index of the largest element in the array `sales`. The general algorithm is as follows. Initially, we assume that the first element in the list is the largest element, so `maxIndex` is initialized to 0. We then compare the element to which `maxIndex` points with every element in the list. Whenever we find an element in the array larger than the element to which `maxIndex` points, we update `maxIndex` so that it points to the new larger element. The code to implement this algorithm is as follows:

```
maxIndex = 0;
for (index = 1; index < sales.length; index++)
    if (sales[maxIndex] < sales[index])
        maxIndex = index;

largestSale = sales[maxIndex];
```

The way this code works can be demonstrated with an example. Suppose the array `sales` is as given in Figure 9-5, and we want to determine the largest element in the array.

	[0]	[1]	[2]	[3]	[4]	[5]	[6]	[7]	[8]	[9]
sales	12.50	8.35	19.60	25.00	14.00	39.43	35.90	98.23	66.65	35.64

Figure 9-5 Array `sales`

Before the **for** loop begins, `maxIndex` is initialized to 0 and the **for** loop initializes `index` to 1. In Table 9-1, we show the values of `maxIndex`, `index`, and certain array elements during each iteration of the **for** loop:

Table 9-1 Values of `sales` Array Elements During `for` Loop Iterations

index	maxIndex	sales[maxIndex]	sales[index]	sales[maxIndex]< sales[index]
1	0	12.50	8.35	12.50 < 8.35 is false
2	0	12.50	19.60	12.50 < 19.60 is true; maxIndex = 2
3	2	19.60	25.00	19.60 < 25.00 is true; maxIndex = 3
4	3	25.00	14.00	25.00 < 14.00 is false
5	3	25.00	39.43	25.00 < 39.43 is true; maxIndex = 5
6	5	39.43	35.90	39.43 < 35.90 is false
7	5	39.43	98.23	39.43 < 98.23 is true; maxIndex = 7
8	7	98.23	66.65	98.23 < 66.65 is false
9	7	98.23	35.64	98.23 < 35.64 is false

After the `for` loop executes, `maxIndex = 7`, giving the index of the largest element in the array `sales`. Thus, `largestSale = sales[maxIndex] = 98.23`.

 The algorithm to find the smallest element in an array is similar to the algorithm for finding the largest element in an array. (See Programming Exercise 2 at the end of this chapter.)

Now that we know how to declare and process arrays, let's rewrite the program that we discussed in the beginning of this chapter. Recall that this program reads five numbers, finds the sum, and prints the numbers in reverse order.

Example 9-4

```
//Program to read five numbers, find their sum, and
//print the numbers in reverse order.

import java.util.*;

public class ReversePrintII
{
    static Scanner console = new Scanner(System.in);

    public static void main(String[] args)
    {
```

9

```
int[] items = new int[5]; //create an array of
                          //five components
int sum;
int counter;

System.out.println("Enter five integers:");

sum = 0;

for (counter = 0; counter < items.length;
                  counter++)
{
    items[counter] = console.nextInt();
    sum = sum + items[counter];
}

System.out.println("The sum of the numbers is: "
                   + sum);
System.out.print("The numbers in reverse "
                 + "order are: ");

    //print the numbers in reverse order
for (counter = items.length - 1; counter >= 0;
                                 counter--)
    System.out.print(items[counter] + " ");

System.out.println();
    }
}
```

Sample Run: In this sample run, the user input is shaded.
```
Enter five integers:
12 76 34 52 89
The sum of the numbers is: 263
The numbers in reverse order are: 89 52 34 76 12
```

Array Index Out of Bounds Exception

Consider the following declaration:

```
double[] num = double[10];
int i;
```

The component num[i] is valid, that is, i is a valid index if i = 0, 1, 2, 3, 4, 5, 6, 7, 8, or 9.

The index—say, index—of an array is **in bounds** if index >= 0 and index <= arraySize - 1. If either index < 0 or index > arraySize - 1, then we say that the index is **out of bounds**.

In Java, if an array index goes out of bounds during program execution, it throws an `ArrayIndexOutOfBoundsException` exception. If the program does not handle this exception, the program terminates with an appropriate error message.

A loop such as the following can set the index out of bounds:

```java
for (i = 0; i <= 10; i++)
    list[i] = 0;
```

Here we assume that `list` is an array of 10 components. When `i` becomes 10, the loop test condition `i <= 10` evaluates to `true`, and the body of the loop executes, and the program tries to access `list[10]`, which does not exist.

Declaring Arrays as Formal Parameters to Methods

Just like other data types, you can declare arrays as formal parameters to methods. A general syntax to declare an array as a formal parameter is:

```
dataType[] arrayName
```

For example, consider the following method:

```java
public static void arraysAsFormalParameters(int[] listA,
                                            double[] listB,
                                            int num)
{
    //...
}
```

This method has three formal parameters. The formal parameters `listA` and `listB` are arrays, and `num` is of the type `int`.

Suppose that you have the following statements:

```java
int[] intList = new int[10];
double[] doubleNumList = new double[15];
int number;
```

The following statement calls the method `arraysAsFormalParameters` with the actual parameters `intList`, `doubleNumList`, and `number`:

```java
arraysAsFormalParameters(intList, doubleNumList, number);
```

Assignment Operator, Relational Operators, and Arrays: A Precaution

Consider the following statements:

```java
int[] listA = {5, 10, 15, 20, 25, 30, 35};   //Line 1
int[] listB = new int[listA.length];          //Line 2
```

9

The statement in Line 1 creates the array `listA` of size 7 and also initializes the array. Note that the value of `listA.length` is 7. The statement in Line 2 uses the value of `listA.length` to create the array `listB` of size 7. See Figure 9-6.

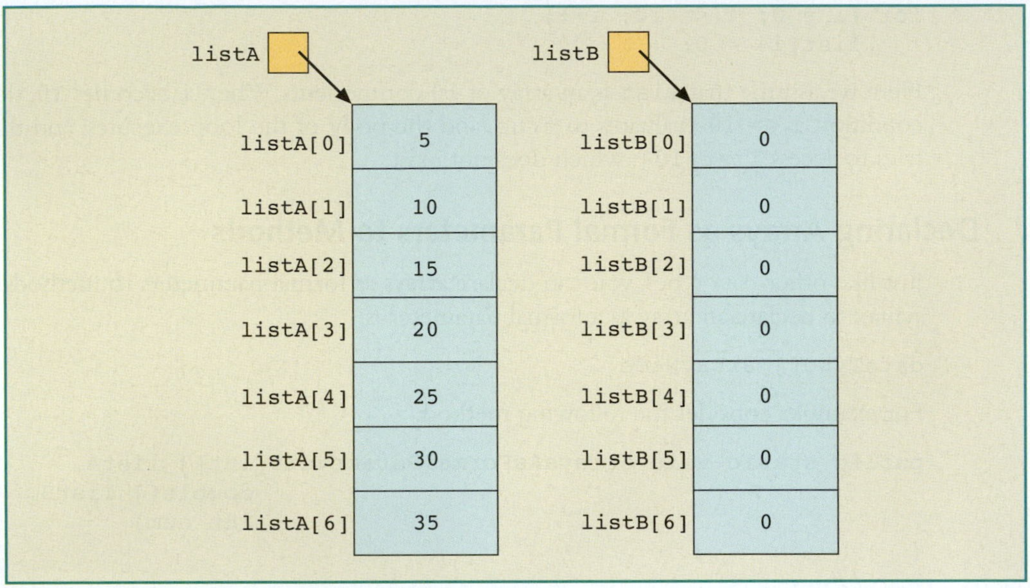

listA			listB	
listA[0]	5		listB[0]	0
listA[1]	10		listB[1]	0
listA[2]	15		listB[2]	0
listA[3]	20		listB[3]	0
listA[4]	25		listB[4]	0
listA[5]	30		listB[5]	0
listA[6]	35		listB[6]	0

Figure 9-6   Arrays `listA` and `listB`

You can use the assignment operator to assign `listA` to `listB`, and the relational operators to compare `listA` with `listB`. However, the results obtained might not be what you expect.

For example, consider the following statement:

```
listB = listA;
```

Here you might expect that the elements of `listA` are copied into the corresponding elements of `listB`. However, this is not the case. Because `listA` is a reference variable, its value is a reference, that is, a memory address. Therefore, the preceding statement copies the value of `listA` into `listB`, and so after this statement executes, both `listA` and `listB` refer to the same array. See Figure 9-7.

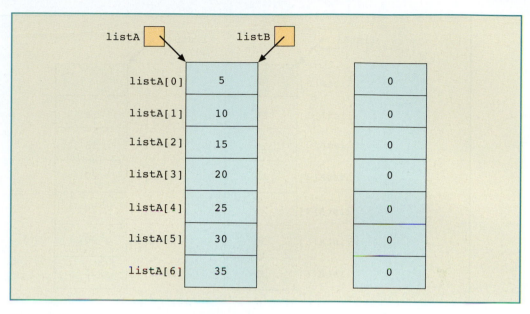

Figure 9-7   Arrays after the statement `listB = listA;` executes

Recall that this is called the *shallow copying* of data.

To copy the elements of `listA` into the corresponding elements of `listB`, you need to provide a component-by-component copy, as shown by the following loop:

```
for (int index = 0; index < listA.length; index++)
    listB[index] = listA[index];
```

After this statement executes, `listA` and `listB` still refer to their own arrays and the elements of `listA` are copied into the corresponding elements of `listB`. See Figure 9-8.

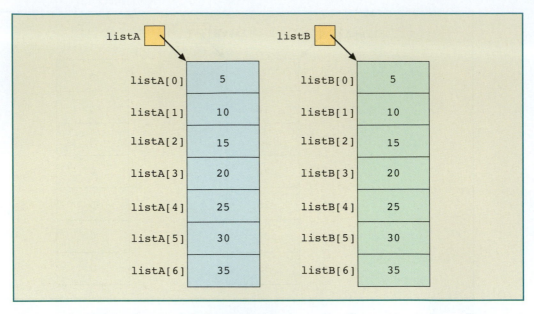

Figure 9-8 Arrays after the **for** loop executes

Recall that this is called the *deep copying* of data.

In addition to the assignment operator, you can use the relational operators == and != to compare arrays. However, you must be aware of what you are comparing. For example, in the statement:

```
if (listA == listB)
...
```

the expression listA == listB determines whether the values of listA and listB are the same and thus determines whether listA and listB refer to the same array. That is, this statement does *not* determine whether listA and listB contain the same elements.

To determine whether listA and listB contain the same elements, you need to compare them component by component. You can, in fact, write a method that returns **true** if two **int** arrays contain the same elements. For example, consider the following method:

```
boolean isEqualArrays(int[] firstArray, int[] secondArray)
{
    if (firstArray.length != secondArray.length)
        return false;
```

```
        for (int index = 0; index < firstArray.length; index++)
            if (firstArray[index] != secondArray[index]) //the
                                              //corresponding elements
                                              //are different
                return false;

        return true;
}
```

Now consider the following statement:

```
if (isEqualArrays(listA, listB))
...
```

The expression `isEqualArrays(listA, listB)` evaluates to **true** if the arrays `listA` and `listB` contain the same elements; **false** otherwise.

Arrays as Parameters to Methods

Just like other objects, arrays can be passed as parameters to methods. The following method takes as an argument any **int** array and outputs the data stored in each component:

```
public static void printArray(int[] list)
{
    int index;
    for (index = 0; index < list.length; index++)
        System.out.print(list[index] + " ");
}
```

Methods such as the preceding one process the data of an entire array. Sometimes the number of elements in the array might be less than the length of the array. For example, the number of elements in an array storing student data might increase or decrease as students drop or add courses. In situations like this, we want to process only the components of the array that hold actual data. To write methods to process such arrays, in addition to declaring an array as a formal parameter, we declare another formal parameter specifying the number of elements in the array, as in the following method:

```
public static void printArray(int[] list, int noOfElements)
{
    int index;
    for (index = 0; index < noOfElements; index++)
        System.out.print(list[index] + " ");
}
```

The first parameter of the method `printArray` is an **int** array of any size. When the method `printArray` is called, the number of elements in the actual array is passed as the second parameter of the method `printArray`.

Example 9-5

This example shows how to write methods for array processing and declare an array as a formal parameter. (Here we write general-purpose methods and so we also pass the number of elements as a parameter to the methods.) We assume that `console` is a `Scanner` object initialized to the standard input device, as declared in Example 9-6.

```java
//Method to input the data and store it in an int array.
//The array to store the data and its size are passed as
//parameters. The parameter noOfElements specifies the
//number of elements to be read.
public static void fillArray(int[] list, int noOfElements)
{
    int index;

    for (index = 0; index < noOfElements; index++)
        list[index] = console.nextInt();
}

//Method to print the elements of an int array.
//The array to be printed and the number of elements
//are passed as parameters. The parameter noOfElements
//specifies the number of elements to be printed.
public static void printArray(int[] list, int noOfElements)
{
    int index;

    for (index = 0; index < noOfElements; index++)
        System.out.print(list[index] + " ");
}

//Method to find and return the sum of the elements
//of an int array. The parameter noOfElements
//specifies the number of elements to be added.
public static int sumArray(int[] list, int noOfElements)
{
    int index;
    int sum = 0;

    for (index = 0; index < noOfElements; index++)
        sum = sum + list[index];

    return sum;
}

//Method to find and return the index of the first
//largest element in an int array. The parameter
//noOfElements specifies the number of elements in
//the array.
```

```java
public static int indexLargestElement(int[] list,
                                      int noOfElements)
{
    int index;
    int maxIndex = 0; //Assume that the first element
                      //is the largest

    for (index = 1; index < noOfElements; index++)
        if (list[maxIndex] < list[index])
            maxIndex = index;

    return maxIndex;
}


    //Method to copy one array into another array.
    //The elements of list1 are copied into list2.
    //The array list2 must be at least as large as the
    //number of elements to be copied. The parameter
    //noOfElements specifies the number of elements of
    //list1 to be copied into list2.
public static void copyArray(int[] list1, int[] list2,
                             int noOfElements)
{
    int index;

    for (index = 0; index < noOfElements; index++)
        list2[index] = list1[index];
}
```

Base Address of an Array

The **base address** of an array is the address (memory location) of the first array component. For example, if `list` is a one-dimensional array, then the base address of `list` is the address of the component `list[0]`. The value of the variable `list` is the base address of the array—the address of `list[0]`. It follows that when you pass an array as a parameter, the base address of the actual array is passed to the formal parameter.

The following program illustrates how arrays are passed as actual parameters in a method call.

Example 9-6

```java
//Arrays as parameters to methods

import java.util.*;

public class ArraysAsParameters
{
    static final int ARRAY_SIZE = 10;
    static Scanner console = new Scanner(System.in);

    public static void main(String[] args)
    {
        int[] listA = new int[ARRAY_SIZE];                      //Line 1
        int[] listB = new int[ARRAY_SIZE];                      //Line 2

        System.out.print("Line 3: listA elements: ");           //Line 3

            //output the elements of listA using
            //the method printArray
        printArray(listA, listA.length);                        //Line 4
        System.out.println();                                   //Line 5

        System.out.print("Line 6: Enter " + listA.length
                    + " integers: ");                           //Line 6

            //input the data into listA using the method fillArray
        fillArray(listA, listA.length);                         //Line 7
        System.out.println();                                   //Line 8

        System.out.print("Line 9: After filling "
                    + "listA, the elements are:"
                    + "\n           ");                          //Line 9

            //output the elements of listA
        printArray(listA, listA.length);                        //Line 10
        System.out.println();                                   //Line 11

            //find and output the sum of the elements of listA
        System.out.println("Line 12: The sum of the "
                    + "elements of listA is: "
                    + sumArray(listA, listA.length));           //Line 12

            //find and output the position of the largest
            //element in listA
        System.out.println("Line 13: The position of "
                    + "the largest element in "
                    + "listA is: "
                    + indexLargestElement(listA, listA.length));   //Line 13
```

```
                    //find and output the largest element in listA
            System.out.println("Line 14: The largest element "
                + "in listA is: "
                + listA[indexLargestElement(listA, listA.length)]); //Line 14

                    //copy the elements of listA into listB
                    //using the method copyArray
            copyArray(listA, listB, listA.length);                  //Line 15
            System.out.print("Line 16: After copying the "
                    + "elements of listA into listB,\n"
                    + "          listB elements are: ");             //Line 16

                    //output the elements of listB
            printArray(listB, listB.length);                        //Line 17
            System.out.println();                                   //Line 18
        }


        //Place the definitions of the methods fillArray and so on
        //here. Example 9-5 gives the definitions of these methods.
    }
```

Sample Run: In this sample run, the user input is shaded.
```
Line 3: listA elements: 0 0 0 0 0 0 0 0 0 0
Line 6: Enter 10 integers:  33 77 25 63 56 48 98 39 5 12

Line 9: After filling listA, the elements are:
        33 77 25 63 56 48 98 39 5 12
Line 12: The sum of the elements of listA is: 456
Line 13: The position of the largest element in listA is: 6
Line 14: The largest element in listA is: 98
Line 16: After copying the elements of listA into listB,
            listB elements are: 33 77 25 63 56 48 98 39 5 12
```

The output of this program is straightforward. The statement in Line 1 creates the array listA of 10 components and initializes each component of listA to 0. Similarly, the statement in Line 2 creates the array listB of 10 components and initializes each component of listB to 0. The statement in Line 4 calls the method printArray and outputs the values stored in listA. The statement in Line 7 calls the method fillArray to input the data into array listA. The statement in Line 12 calls the method sumArray and outputs the sum of all the elements of listA. Similarly, the statement in Line 14 outputs the value of the largest element in listA. The statement in Line 15 calls the method copyArray to copy the elements of listA into listB, and the statement in Line 17 outputs the elements of listB.

PARALLEL ARRAYS

Two (or more) arrays are called **parallel** if their corresponding components hold related information.

Suppose you need to keep track of students' course grades, together with their ID numbers, so that the grades can be posted at the end of the semester. Further suppose that there are 50 students in the class and their IDs are 5 digits long. Because there are 50 students, you need 50 variables to store the students' IDs and 50 variables to store their grades. You can declare two arrays: `studentId` of the type **int** and `courseGrade` of the type **char**. Each array has 50 components. Furthermore, `studentId[0]` and `courseGrade[0]` will store the ID and course grade of the first student, `studentId[1]` and `courseGrade[1]` will store the ID and course grade of the second student, and so on.

The statements:

```
int[] studentId = new int[50];
char[] courseGrade = new char[50];
```

declare and instantiate these two arrays.

Suppose you need to input data into these arrays and the data is provided in a file in the following form:

```
studentId courseGrade
```

For example, a sample data is:

```
23456 A
86723 B
22356 C
92733 B
11892 D
.
.
.
```

Suppose that `infile` is a `Scanner` object initialized to the input file. Because the size of each array is 50, a maximum of 50 elements can be stored into each array. Moreover, it is possible that there may be fewer than 50 students in the class. Therefore, while reading the data we also count the number of students and ensure that the array indices do not go out of bounds. The following loop reads the data into the parallel arrays `studentId` and `courseGrade`:

```
int noOfStudents = 0;

while (infile.hasNext() && noOfStudents < 50)
{
    studentId[noOfStudents] = infile.nextInt();
    courseGrade[noOfStudents] = infile.next().charAt(0);
    noOfStudents++;
}
```

ARRAYS OF OBJECTS

In the previous sections, you learned how to use an array to store and manipulate values of the primitive data types such as **int** and **double**. You can also use arrays to manipulate objects. This section explains how to create and work with arrays of objects.

Arrays of String Objects

This section discusses how to create and work with an array of **String** objects. To create an array of strings, you declare an array as follows:

```
String[] nameList = new String[5];     //Line 1
```

This statement declares and instantiates **nameList** to be an array of **5** components, wherein each component of **nameList** is a reference to a **String** object.

Next, consider the statement:

```
nameList[0] = "Amanda Green";          //Line 2
```

This statement creates a **String** object with the value **"Amanda Green"** and stores the address of the object into **nameList[0]**. Similarly, the following statements assign **String** objects, with the given values, to the other components of **nameList**.

```
nameList[1] = "Vijay Arora";           //Line 3
nameList[2] = "Sheila Mann";           //Line 4
nameList[3] = "Rohit Sharma";          //Line 5
nameList[4] = "Mandy Johnson";         //Line 6
```

After the statements in Lines 2 through 6 execute, each component of **nameList** is a reference to a **String** object, as shown in Figure 9-9.

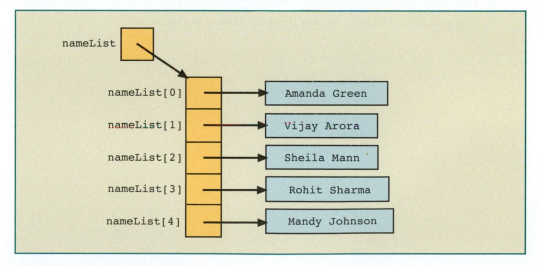

Figure 9-9   Array **nameList**

To output the names, you can use a **for** loop as follows:

```
for (int index = 0; index < namesList.length; index++)
    System.out.println(namesList[index] + " ");
```

You can use **String** methods to work with the objects of **nameList**. For example, the expression:

```
nameList[0].equals("Amanda Green")
```

evaluates to **true**, while the expression:

```
nameList[3].equals("Randy Blair")
```

evaluates to **false**.

Similarly, the expression:

```
nameList[4].substring(0, 5)
```

returns a reference to the **String** object with the string **"Mandy"**.

Arrays of Objects of Other Classes

This section discusses, in general, how to create and work with an array of objects.

Suppose that you have 100 employees who are paid on an hourly basis and you need to keep track of their arrival and departure times. In Chapter 8, we designed and implemented the **class** Clock to implement the time of day in a program. You can declare two arrays—**arrivalTimeEmp** and **departureTimeEmp**—of 100 components each, wherein each component is a reference variable of the **Clock** type. Consider the following statement:

```
Clock[] arrivalTimeEmp = new Clock[100];                //Line 1
```

The statement in Line 1 creates the array shown in Figure 9-10.

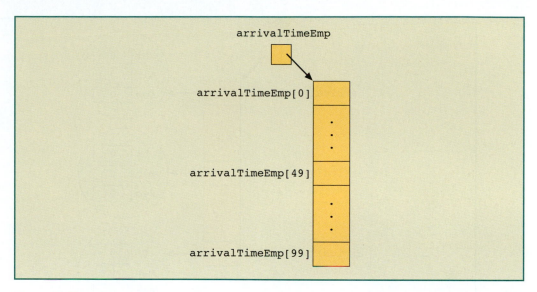

Figure 9-10 Array `arrivalTimeEmp`

The statement in Line 1 creates only the array, not the objects `arrivalTimeEmp[0]`, `arrivalTimeEmp[1]`, ..., `arrivalTimeEmp[99]`. We still need to instantiate `Clock` objects for each array component. Consider the following statements:

```
for (int j = 0; j < arrivalTimeEmp.length; j++)          //Line 2
    arrivalTimeEmp[j] = new Clock();                      //Line 3
```

The statements in Lines 2 and 3 instantiate the objects `arrivalTimeEmp[0]`, `arrivalTimeEmp[1]`, ..., `arrivalTimeEmp[99]`, as shown in Figure 9–11.

9

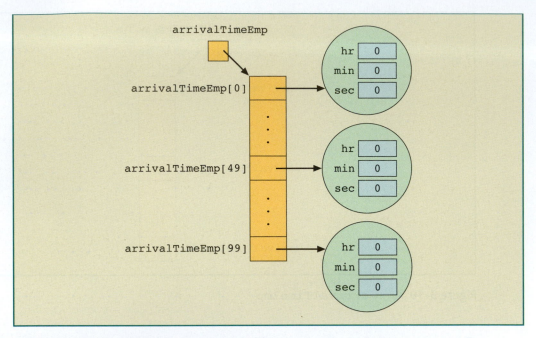

Figure 9-11 Array `arrivalTime` after instantiating the objects for each component

You can now use the methods of the **class** Clock to manipulate the time for each employee. For example, the following statement sets the arrival time—that is, hr, min, and sec—of employee 49 to 8, 5, 10, respectively. See Figure 9-12.

```
arrivalTimeEmp[49].setTime(8, 5, 10);                          //Line 4
```

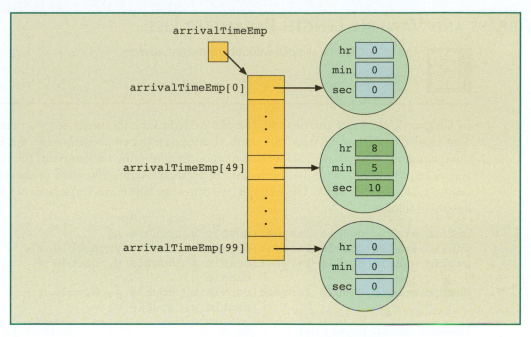

Figure 9-12   Array `arrivalTimeEmp` after setting the time of employee 49

9

To output the arrival time of each employee, you can use a loop such as the following:

```
for (int j = 0; j < arrivalTimeEmp.length; j++)          //Line 5
    System.out.println("Employee " + (j + 1)
                    + " arrival time: "
                    + arrivalTimeEmp[j]);                 //Line 6
```

The statement in Line 6 assumes that the method **toString** is defined for the **class** **Clock**, as described in Chapter 8, to return the time in the form **hr:min:sec**.

To keep track of the departure time of each employee, you can use the array **departureTimeEmp**.

Similarly, you can use arrays to manage a list of names or other objects.

ARRAYS AND VARIABLE LENGTH PARAMETER LIST

 This section can be skipped without any discontinuation.

In Chapter 7, we wrote the method `larger` to determine the larger of two numbers. We then used this method to write the method `compareThree` to determine the largest of three numbers. Similarly, we can write a method to determine the largest of four numbers, and so on. Moreover, using the mechanism of method overloading, each of these methods can be called, say, `largest`. For example, we can write several such methods with the following headings:

```
public static double largest(double x, double y)
public static double largest(double x, double y, double z)
public static double largest(double x, double y, double z,
                             double u)
public static double largest(double x, double y, double z,
                             double u, double w)
```

However, this still requires us to write the definitions of each of these methods. Java simplifies this by providing a variable length formal parameter (list). The syntax to declare a variable length formal parameter (list) is:

```
dataType ... identifier
```

where `dataType` is the name of a type such as the primitive data type or a Java class or a user-defined data type. Note the ellipsis in this syntax. This is part of the syntax. For example, consider the following formal parameter declaration:

```
double ... numList
```

This statement declares `numList` to be a variable length formal parameter. In fact, `numList` is an array wherein each component is of the type `double`, and the number of components in `list` depends on the number of arguments passed to `numList`.

Consider the following method definition:

```
public static double largest(double ... numList)
{
    double max;
    int index;

    if (numList.length != 0)
    {
        max = list[0];
```

```
        for (index = 1; index < numList.length; index++)
        {
            if (max < numList [index])
                max = numList [index];
        }

        return max;
    }

    return 0.0;
}
```

The formal parameter list of the method `largest` is of variable length. In a call to the method `largest`, you can specify either any number of actual parameters of the type **double** or an array of the type **double**. If the actual parameters of the method `largest` are of the type **double**, then the values of the actual parameters are put in the array `numList`. Because the number of actual parameters can be zero, in which case the length of `numList` is 0, before determining the largest number in `numList` we check whether the length of `numList` is 0.

Consider the following statements:

```
double num1 = largest(34, 56);                    //Line 1
double num2 = largest(12.56, 84, 92);             //Line 2
double num3 = largest(98.32, 77, 64.67, 56);      //Line 3
System.out.println(largest(22.50, 67.78,
                       92.58, 45, 34, 56));       //Line 4

double[] numberList = {18.50, 44, 56.23, 17.89,
                       92.34, 112.0, 77, 11, 22,
                       86.62);                    //Line 5

System.out.println(largest(numberList));          //Line 6
```

In Line 1, the method `largest` is called with two parameters; in Line 2 it is called with three parameters; in Line 3 it is called with four parameters; and in Line 4 it is called with six parameters. In Line 6, the actual parameter of the method `largest` is the array `numberList`.

Example 9-7 further illustrates how the method largest can be used in a program.

Example 9-7

```
//Program: Largest of a set of numbers

import java.util.*;

public class LargestNumber
{
    public static void main(String[] args)
    {
        double[] numberList = {23, 45.5, 89, 34, 92.78,
                       36, 90, 120.89, 97, 23,
                       90, 89};                   //Line 1
```

```
            System.out.println("Line 2: The larger of 5.6 "
                          + "and 10.8 is "
                          + largest(5.6, 10.8));            //Line 2

            System.out.println("Line 3: The largest of 23, "
                          + "78, and 56 is "
                          + largest(23, 78, 56));           //Line 3

            System.out.println("Line 4: The largest of 93, "
                          + "28, 83, and 66 is "
                          + largest(93, 28, 83, 66));       //Line 4

            System.out.println("Line 5: The largest of 22.5, "
                          + "12.34, 56.34, 78, "
                          + "\n        "
                          + "98.45, 25, 78, 23 and 36 is "
                          + largest(22.5, 12.34, 56.34,
                                    78, 98.45, 25, 78,
                                    23, 36));               //Line 5

            System.out.println("Line 6: The largest "
                          + "number in numList is "
                          + largest(numberList));           //Line 6

            System.out.println("Line 7: A call to the method "
                          + "largest with an empty \n"
                          + "         parameter "
                          + "list returns the value "
                          + largest());                     //Line 7
        }

        public static double largest(double ... numList)
        {
            double max;
            int index;

            if (numList.length != 0)
            {
                max = numList[0];

                for (index = 1; index < numList.length; index++)
                {
                    if (max < numList [index])
                        max = numList [index];
                }

                return max;
            }
        }
```

```
            return 0.0;
        }
}
```

Sample Run:
```
Line 2: The larger of 5.6 and 10.8 is 10.8
Line 3: The largest of 23, 78, and 56 is 78.0
Line 4: The largest of 93, 28, 83, and 66 is 93.0
Line 5: The largest of 22.5, 12.34, 56.34, 78,
        98.45, 25, 78, 23 and 36 is 98.45
Line 6: The largest number in numList is 120.89
Line 7: A call to the method largest with an empty
        parameter list returns the value 0.0
```

In the preceding program, in Line 2, the method `largest` is called with two parameters; in Line 3 it is called with three parameters; in Line 4 it is called with four parameters; and in Line 5 it is called with nine parameters. Note that in Line 6, the method `largest` is called using an array of numbers, and in Line 7 it is called with no parameters.

Just as you can create a method using the primitive data type as a variable length formal parameter, you can also create a method with objects as a variable length formal parameter (list). Examples 9-8 and 9-9 show you how to do this. First, we specify some rules to follow when using a variable length formal parameter list.

1. A method can have both a variable length formal parameter and other formal parameters. For example, consider the following method heading:

   ```
   public static void myMethod(String name, double num,
                               int ... intList)
   ```

   The formal parameter list of `myMethod` is of variable length. The formal parameter name is of the type `String`, the formal parameter `num` is of the type `double`, and the formal parameter `intList` is of variable length. The actual parameter corresponding to `intList` can be an `int` array or any number of `int` variables and/or `int` values.

2. A method can have at most one variable length formal parameter.

3. If a method has both a variable length formal parameter and other types of formal parameters, then the variable length formal parameter must be the last formal parameter of the formal parameter list.

Before giving more examples of methods with a variable length formal parameter list, let us note the following.

9

One way to process the elements of an array one-by-one, starting at the first element, is to use an index variable, initialized to `0`, and a loop. For example, to process the elements of an array, say `list`, you can a `for` loop such as the following:

```
for (int index; index < list.length; index++)
    //process list[index]
```

In fact, this chapter uses these types of loops to process the elements of an array. The most recent version of Java provides a special type of `for` loop to process the elements of an object such as an array. The syntax to use this `for` loop to process the elements of an array is:

```
for (dataType identifier : arrayName)
    statements
```

where `identifier` is a variable and the data type of `identifier` is the same as the data type of the array components. This form of the `for` loop is called a **foreach** loop.

For example, suppose `list` is an array and each component is of the type, say **double**, and `sum` is a **double** variable. The following code finds the sum of the elements of `list`:

```
sum = 0;                        //Line 1

for (double num : list)    //Line 2
    sum = sum + num;        //Line 3
```

The `for` statement in Line 2 is read: for each `num` in `list`. The identifier `num` is initialized to `list[0]`. In the next iteration, the value of `num` is `list[1]`, and so on.

Using the foreach loop, the `for` loop in the method `largest`, in Example 9-7, can be written as:

```
for (double num : numList)
{
    if (max < num)
        max = num;
}
```

(The Web site accompanying this book contains the modified program, named `LargestNumberVersionII.java`, that uses the foreach loop to determine the largest element in `list`.)

 As remarked, the foreach loop is a recent addition of Java. It processes the elements of an object, which is a collection of elements. Chapter 10 introduces the **class** `Vector`. As you will see, every `Vector` object is a collection of elements. We will show that a foreach loop can process the elements of a `Vector` object one at a time.

Example 9-8 shows that the variable length formal parameters (list) of a method can be objects. This example uses the **class** Clock designed in Chapter 8.

Example 9-8

```java
public class ObjectsAsVariableLengthParameters
{
    public static void main(String[] args)
    {

        Clock myClock = new Clock(12, 5, 10);          //Line 1
        Clock yourClock = new Clock(8, 15, 6);         //Line 2

        Clock[] arrivalTimeEmp = new Clock[10];        //Line 3

        for (int j = 0; j < arrivalTimeEmp.length;
                        j++)                           //Line 4
            arrivalTimeEmp[j] = new Clock();           //Line 5

        arrivalTimeEmp[5].setTime(8, 5, 10);           //Line 6

        printTimes(myClock, yourClock);                //Line 7

        System.out.println("\n*******************"
                        + "******* \n");               //Line 8

        printTimes(arrivalTimeEmp);                    //Line 9
    }

    public static void printTimes(Clock ... clockList)
    {
        for (int i = 0; i < clockList.length; i++)     //Line 10
            System.out.println(clockList[i]);          //Line 11
    }
}
```

Sample Run:
```
12:05:10
08:15:06


*************************


00:00:00
00:00:00
00:00:00
00:00:00
00:00:00
08:05:10
```

```
00:00:00
00:00:00
00:00:00
00:00:00
```

In this program, the statements in Lines 1 and 2 create the objects **myClock** and **yourClock**. The statement in Line 3 creates the array **arrivalTimeEmp** with ten components, wherein each component is a reference variable of the **Clock** type. The **for** loop in statements 4 and 5 instantiates the objects of the array **arrivalTimeEmp**. The statement in Line 6 sets the arrival time of employee 5, which is the sixth component of the array. The statement in Line 7 calls the method **printTimes** with two actual parameters; the statement in Line 9 calls this method with **arrivalTimeEmp** as the actual parameter, an array of ten components.

Note that the **for** loop in Lines 10 and 11 can be replaced with the following **for** loop.

```
for (Clock clockObject : clockList)      //Line 10
     System.out.println(clockObject);    //Line 11
```

Example 9-9 shows that a constructor of a class can have a variable length formal list.

Example 9-9

Consider the **class** StudentData.

```
public class StudentData
{
    private String firstName;
    private String lastName;

    private double[] testScores; //array to store
                                 //the test scores
    private char grade;

        //Default constructor
    public StudentData()
    {
        firstName = "";
        lastName = "";
        grade = '*';
        testScores = new double[5];
    }

        //Constructor with parameters
        //The parameter list is of varying length.
        //Postcondition: firstName = fName; lastName = lName;
        //               testScores = list;
        //               Calculate and assign the grade to
        //               grade.
```

```java
public StudentData(String fName, String lName,
                   double ... list)
{
    firstName = fName;
    lastName = lName;
    testScores = list;
    grade = courseGrade(list); //calculate and store
                               //the grade in grade
}

    //Method to calculate the grade
    //Postcondition: The grade is calculated and
    //               returned.
public char courseGrade(double ... list)
{
    double sum = 0;
    double average = 0;

    for (double num : list)
        sum = sum + num;     //sum the test scores

    if (list.length != 0)  //find the average
        average = sum / list.length;

    if (average >= 90)     //determine the grade
        return 'A';
    else if (average >= 80)
            return 'B';
    else if (average > 70)
            return 'C';
    else if (average > 60)
            return 'D';
    else
        return 'F';
}

    //Method to return a student's name, test scores,
    //and grade as a string
    //Postcondition: The string consisting of the first
    //               name, last name, test scores,
    //               and course grade is constructed
    //               and returned.
public String toString()
{
    String str;

    str = String.format("%-10s %-10s ", firstName,
                        lastName);
```

9

```
        for (double score : testScores)
            str = str + String.format("%7.2f", score);

        str = str + "     " + grade;

        return str;
    }
}
```

Note that the constructor with parameters of the **class** `StudentData` consists of a variable length formal parameter (list). The method `courseGrade` also consists of a variable length formal parameter (list). The following program uses the **class** `Student` to keep track of a student's name, test scores, and course grade.

```
public class TestProgStudentData
{
    public static void main(String[] args)
    {
        StudentData student1 =
                new StudentData("John", "Doe",
                           89, 78, 95, 63, 94);

        StudentData student2 =
                new StudentData("Lindsay", "Green",
                           92, 82, 90, 70, 87, 99);

        System.out.println(student1);
        System.out.println(student2);

    }
}
```

Sample Run:

John	Doe	89.00	78.00	95.00	63.00	94.00	B	
Lindsay	Green	92.00	82.00	90.00	70.00	87.00	99.00	B

We leave the details of the preceding output as an exercise for you.

To learn more about constructors with a variable length formal parameter list, see Exercise 8 at the end of this chapter.

Two-Dimensional Arrays

In the previous section, you learned how to use one-dimensional arrays to manipulate data. If the data is provided in a list form, you can use one-dimensional arrays. However, sometimes data is provided in a table form.

Suppose you want to keep track of how many cars of a particular color a local dealership has in stock. The dealership sells 6 types of cars in 5 different colors. Figure 9-13 shows a sample data table.

inStock

	[Red]	[Brown]	[Black]	[White]	[Gray]
[GM]	10	7	12	10	4
[Ford]	18	11	15	17	10
[Toyota]	12	10	9	5	12
[BMW]	16	6	13	8	3
[Nissan]	10	7	12	6	4
[Volvo]	9	4	7	12	11

Figure 9-13 Table `inStock`

You can see that the data is in a table format. The table has 30 entries, and every entry is an integer. Because all the table entries are of the same type, you can declare a one-dimensional array of 30 components of the type `int`. The first 5 components of the one-dimensional array can store the data of the first row of the table, the next 5 components of the one-dimensional array can store the data of the second row of the table, and so on. In other words, you can simulate the data given in a table format in a one-dimensional array.

If you do so, the algorithms to manipulate the data in the one-dimensional array will be somewhat complicated because you must carefully note where one row ends and another begins. You must also correctly compute the index of the particular elements. Java simplifies manipulating the data given in a table format by using **two-dimensional arrays.** This section first discusses how to declare two-dimensional arrays, and then looks at ways to manipulate the data in a two-dimensional array.

Two-dimensional array: A collection of a fixed number of components arranged in rows and columns (that is, in two dimensions), wherein all the components are of the same type.

The syntax for declaring a two-dimensional array is:

```
dataType[][] arrayName;
```

where **dataType** is the data type of the array components.

Because an array is an object, we must instantiate the object to allocate memory space to store the data. The general syntax to instantiate a two-dimensional array object is:

```
arrayName = new dataType[intExp1][intExp2];
```

where **intExp1** and **intExp2** are expressions yielding positive integer values. The two expressions, **intExp1** and **intExp2**, specify the number of rows and the number of columns, respectively, in the array.

The preceding two statements can be combined into one statement, as follows:

```
dataType[][] arrayName = new dataType[intExp1][intExp2];
```

For example, the statement:

```
double[][] sales = new double[10][5];
```

declares a two-dimensional array **sales** of **10** rows and **5** columns, wherein every component is of the type **double**. As in a one-dimensional array, the rows are numbered **0...9** and the columns are numbered **0...4**. See Figure 9-14.

	[0]	[1]	[2]	[3]	[4]
[0]	0.0	0.0	0.0	0.0	0.0
[1]	0.0	0.0	0.0	0.0	0.0
[2]	0.0	0.0	0.0	0.0	0.0
[3]	0.0	0.0	0.0	0.0	0.0
[4]	0.0	0.0	0.0	0.0	0.0
[5]	0.0	0.0	0.0	0.0	0.0
[6]	0.0	0.0	0.0	0.0	0.0
[7]	0.0	0.0	0.0	0.0	0.0
[8]	0.0	0.0	0.0	0.0	0.0
[9]	0.0	0.0	0.0	0.0	0.0

sales

Figure 9-14   Two-dimensional array `sales`

From now on in this book, whenever we instantiate a two-dimensional array and draw its diagram, we will not show all the default values as we have in Figure 9-14.

Accessing Array Components

To access the components of a two-dimensional array, you need a pair of indices: one for the row position, and one for the column position.

The syntax to access a component of a two-dimensional array is:

```
arrayName[indexExp1][indexExp2]
```

where `indexExp1` and `indexExp2` are expressions yielding non-negative integer values. `indexExp1` specifies the row position; `indexExp2` specifies the column position. Moreover, the value of `indexExp1` must be less than the number of rows, and the value of `indexExp2` must be less than the number of columns in the array.

The statement:

```
sales[5][3] = 25.75;
```

stores 25.75 into row number 5 and column number 3 (the 6th row and the 4th column) of the array sales. See Figure 9-15.

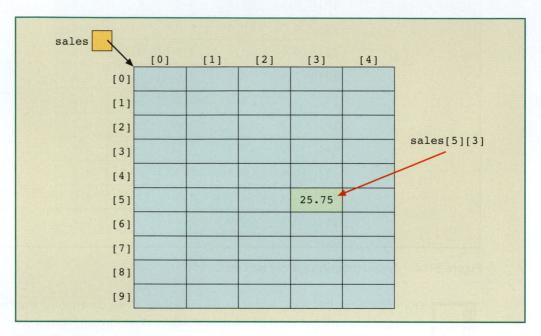

Figure 9-15   sales[5][3]

Suppose that:

```
int i = 5;
int j = 3;
```

Then the previous statement:

```
sales[5][3] = 25.75;
```

is equivalent to:

```
sales[i][j] = 25.75;
```

So the indices can also be variables.

Two-Dimensional Arrays and the Instance Variable length

Just as in one-dimensional arrays, you can use the instance variable length to determine the number of rows as well as the number of columns (in each row). Consider the following statement:

```
int[][] matrix = new int[20][15];
```

This statement declares and instantiates a two-dimensional array `matrix` of 20 rows and 15 columns. The value of the expression:

```
matrix.length
```

is 20, the number of rows.

Each row of `matrix` is a one-dimensional array and `matrix[0]`, in fact, refers to the first row. Therefore, the value of the expression:

```
matrix[0].length
```

is 15, the number of columns in the first row. Similarly, `matrix[1].length` gives the number of columns in the second row, which in this case is 15, and so on.

Two-Dimensional Arrays: Special Cases

The two-dimensional arrays created in the preceding sections are quite straightforward; each row has same number of columns. However, Java allows you to specify a different number of columns for each row. In this case, each row must be instantiated separately. Consider the following statement:

```
int[][] board;
```

Suppose that you want to create the array `board`, as shown in Figure 9-16.

9

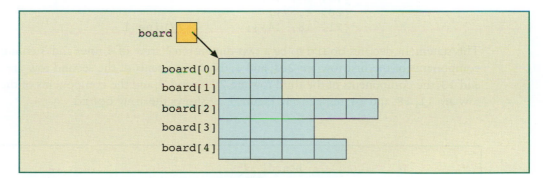

Figure 9-16   Two-dimensional array `board`

It follows from Figure 9-16 that the number of rows in `board` is 5; the number of columns in the first row is 6; the number of columns in the second row is 2; the number of columns in the third row is 5; the number of columns in the fourth row is 3; and the number of columns in the fifth row is 4. To create this two-dimensional array, first we create the one-dimensional array **board** of 5 rows. Then we instantiate each row, specifying the required number of columns, as follows:

```
board = new int[5];          //Create the number of rows
board[0] = new int[6];       //Create the columns for the first row
board[1] = new int[2];       //Create the columns for the second row
board[2] = new int[5];       //Create the columns for the third row
board[3] = new int[3];       //Create the columns for the fourth row
board[4] = new int[4];       //Create the columns for the fifth row
```

Because the number of columns in each row is not the same, such arrays are called **ragged arrays**. To process these types of two-dimensional arrays, you must know the exact number of columns for each row.

Notice that here **board.length** is 5, the number of rows in the array **board**. Similarly, **board[0].length** is 6, the number of columns in the first row; **board[1].length** is 2, the number of columns in the second row; **board[2].length** is 5, the number of columns in the third row; **board[3].length** is 3, the number of columns in the fourth row; and **board[4].length** is 4, the number of columns in the fifth row.

Two-Dimensional Array Initialization During Declaration

Like one-dimensional arrays, two-dimensional arrays can be initialized when they are declared. The example in the following statement helps illustrate this concept:

```
int[][] board = {{2, 3, 1},
                 {15, 25, 13},
                 {20, 4, 7},
                 {11, 18, 14}};        //Line 1
```

This statement declares **board** to be a two-dimensional array of 4 rows and 3 columns. The components of the first row are 2, 3, and 1; the components of the second row are 15, 25, and 13; the components of the third row are 20, 4, and 7; and the components of the fourth row are 11, 18, and 14, respectively. Figure 9-17 shows the array **board**.

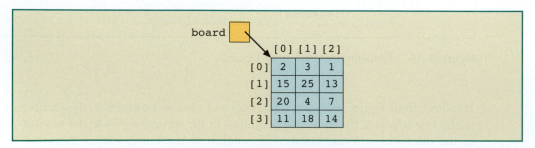

Figure 9-17 Two-dimensional array **board**

To initialize a two-dimensional array when it is declared:

- The elements of each row are enclosed within braces and separated by commas.

- All rows are enclosed within braces.

Now consider the following statement:

```
int[][] table = {{2, 1, 3, 5},
                 {15, 25},
                 {4, 23, 45}};
```

Here you see that the number of values specified for the first row of the array `table` is **4**; the number of values specified for the second row is **2**; and the number of values specified for the third row is **3**. Because the number of values specified for the first row is **4**, only four columns are assigned to the first row. Similarly, the number of columns assigned to the second and third rows are **2** and **3**, respectively. See Figure 9-18.

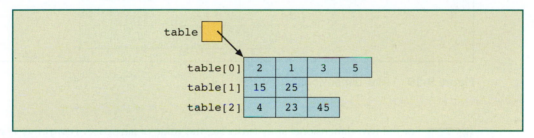

Figure 9-18   Two-dimensional array `table`

Processing Two-Dimensional Arrays

A two-dimensional array can be processed in three ways:

1. Process the entire array.

2. Process a particular row of the array, called **row processing**.

3. Process a particular column of the array, called **column processing**.

Initializing and printing the array are examples of processing the entire two-dimensional array. Finding the largest element in a row or column, or finding the sum of a row or column are examples of row (column) processing. We will use the following declarations for our discussion:

```
static final int ROWS = 7;      //this can be set to any number
static final int COLUMNS = 6;   //this can be set to any number
int[][] matrix = new int[ROWS][COLUMNS];
int row;
int col;
int sum;
```

```
int largest;
int temp;
```

Figure 9-19 shows the array `matrix`.

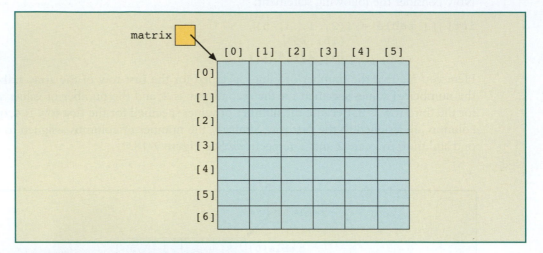

Figure 9-19   Two-dimensional array `matrix`

 For the two-dimensional array `matrix`, the value of `matrix.length` is 7, which is the same as the value of the named constant `ROWS`. Also, the values of `matrix[0].length, matrix[1].length, ..., matrix[6].length` give the number of columns in row 0, row 1, . . ., row 6, respectively. Notice that the number of columns in each row is 6.

Because all the components of a two-dimensional array are of the same type, the components of any row or column are of the same type. This means that in a two-dimensional array, each row and each column is a one-dimensional array. Therefore, when processing a particular row or column of a two-dimensional array, we use algorithms similar to those that process one-dimensional arrays. We further explain this concept with the help of the two-dimensional array `matrix`, as declared previously.

Suppose that we want to process row number 5 of `matrix` (the **sixth** row of `matrix`). The components of row number 5 of `matrix` are:

```
matrix[5][0], matrix[5][1], matrix[5][2], matrix[5][3],
matrix[5][4], matrix[5][5]
```

In these components, the first index (the row position) is fixed at 5. The second index (the column position) ranges from 0 to 5. Therefore, we can use the following **for** loop to process row number 5:

```
for (col = 0; col < matrix[5].length; col++)
    //process matrix[5][col]
```

This **for** loop is equivalent to the following **for** loop:

```
row = 5;
for (col = 0; col < matrix[row].length; col++)
    //process matrix[row][col]
```

Similarly, suppose that we want to process column number 2 of **matrix**—the third column of **matrix**. The components of this column are:

```
matrix[0][2], matrix[1][2], matrix[2][2], matrix[3][2],
matrix[4][2], matrix[5][2], matrix[6][2]
```

Here the second index (the column position) is fixed at 2. The first index (the row position) ranges from 0 to 6. In this case, we use the following **for** loop to process column 2 of **matrix**:

```
for (row = 0; row < matrix.length; row++)
    //process matrix[row][2]
```

This **for** loop is equivalent to the following **for** loop:

```
col = 2;
for (row = 0; row < matrix.length; row++)
    //process matrix[row][col]
```

Next, we discuss some specific algorithms for processing two-dimensional arrays.

Initialization

Suppose that you want to initialize row number 4 to 10, that is, the 5th row to 10. As explained earlier, the following **for** loop initializes row number 4 to 10:

```
row = 4;
for (col = 0; col < matrix[row].length; col++)
    matrix[row][col] = 10;
```

If you want to initialize the entire **matrix** to 10, you can also put the first index (the row position) in a loop. By using the following nested **for** loops, you can initialize each component of **matrix** to 10:

```
for (row = 0; row < matrix.length; row++)
    for (col = 0; col < matrix[row].length; col++)
        matrix[row][col] = 10;
```

Print

By using a nested **for** loop, you can output the components of **matrix**. The following nested **for** loops print the components of **matrix**, one row per line:

```
for (row = 0; row < matrix.length; row++)
{
    for (col = 0; col < matrix[row].length; col++)
        System.out.printf("%7d", matrix[row][col]);

    System.out.println();
}
```

Input

The following **for** loop inputs data into row number 4, that is, the 5th row of **matrix**:

```
row = 4;
for (col = 0; col < matrix[row].length; col++)
    matrix[row][col] = console.nextInt();
```

As before, by putting the row number in a loop, you can input data into each component of **matrix**. The following **for** loop inputs data into each component of **matrix**:

```
for (row = 0; row < matrix.length; row++)
    for (col = 0; col < matrix[row].length; col++)
        matrix[row][col] = console.nextInt();
```

Sum by Row

The following **for** loop finds the sum of row number 4 of **matrix**; that is, it adds the components of row number 4:

```
sum = 0;
row = 4;
for (col = 0; col < matrix[row].length; col++)
    sum = sum + matrix[row][col];
```

Once again, by putting the row number in a loop, you can find the sum of each row separately. The Java code to find the sum of each individual row follows:

```
    //Sum of each individual row
for (row = 0; row < matrix.length; row++)
{
    sum = 0;
    for (col = 0; col < matrix[row].length; col++)
        sum = sum + matrix[row][col];

    System.out.println("The sum of the elements of row "
                        + (row + 1) + " = " + sum);
}
```

Sum by Column

As in the case of sum by row, the following nested **for** loop finds the sum of each individual column. (Notice that **matrix[0].length** gives the number of columns in each row.)

```
                //Sum of each individual column
for (col = 0; col < matrix[0].length; col++)
{

    sum = 0;
    for (row = 0; row < matrix.length; row++)
        sum = sum + matrix[row][col];


    System.out.println("The sum of the elements of column "
                    + (col + 1) + " = " + sum);
}
```

(Note that the preceding code to find the sum of each column assumes that the number of columns in each row is the same. In other words, the two–dimensional array is *not* ragged.)

Largest Element in Each Row and Each Column

As stated earlier, another possible operation on a two-dimensional array is finding the largest element in each row and each column. Next, we give the Java code to perform this operation.

The following **for** loop determines the largest element in row number 4:

```
row = 4;
largest = matrix[row][0]; //assume that the first element of the
                          //row is the largest
for (col = 1; col < matrix[row].length; col++)
    if (largest < matrix[row][col])
        largest = matrix[row][col];
```

The following Java code determines the largest element in each row and each column:

```
    //The largest element of each row
for (row = 0; row < matrix.length; row++)
{

    largest = matrix[row][0]; //assume that the first element
                              //of the row is the largest
    for (col = 1; col < matrix[row].length; col++)
        if (largest < matrix[row][col])
            largest = matrix[row][col];


    System.out.println("The largest element of row "
                    + (row + 1) + " = " + largest);
}

    //The largest element of each column
for (col = 0; col < matrix[0].length; col++)
{

    largest = matrix[0][col]; //assume that the first element
                              //of the column is the largest
    for (row = 1; row < matrix.length; row++)
        if (largest < matrix[row][col])
            largest = matrix[row][col];
```

9

```
        System.out.println("The largest element of col "
                    + (col + 1) + " = " + largest);
}
```

Reversing Diagonals

Suppose that `matrix` is a square array, that is, it has the same number of rows and columns. Then `matrix` has a main diagonal and an opposite diagonal. To be specific, suppose that we have the following:

```
final int ROWS = 4;
final int COLUMNS = 4;
```

The components of the main diagonal of `matrix` are `matrix[0][0]`, `matrix[1][1]`, `matrix[2][2]`, and `matrix[3][3]`. The components of the opposite diagonal are `matrix[0][3]`, `matrix[1][2]`, `matrix[2][1]`, and `matrix[3][0]`.

We want to write a Java code to reverse both the diagonals of `matrix`. Assume that the array `matrix` is as shown in Figure 9-20.

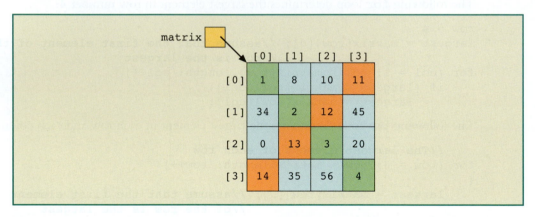

Figure 9-20   Two-dimensional array `matrix` before reversing the diagonals

After reversing both the diagonals, the array `matrix` is as shown in Figure 9-21.

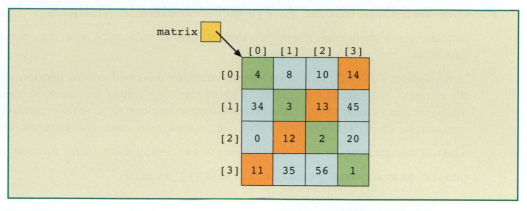

Figure 9-21 Two-dimensional array `matrix` after reversing the diagonals

To reverse the main diagonal, we do the following:

Swap `matrix[0][0]` with `matrix[3][3]`.
Swap `matrix[1][1]`ƒwithƒ`matrix[2][2]`.

To reverse the opposite diagonal, we do the following:

Swap `matrix[0][3]` with `matrix[3][0]`.
Swap `matrix[1][2]`ƒwithƒ`matrix[2][1]`.

The following **for** loops reverse the diagonals:

```
    //Reverse the main diagonal
for (row = 0; row < matrix.length / 2; row++)
{
    temp = matrix[row][row];
    matrix[row][row] =
        matrix[matrix.length - 1 - row][matrix.length - 1 - row];
    matrix[matrix.length - 1 - row][matrix.length - 1 - row] = temp;
}


    //Reverse the opposite diagonal
for (row = 0; row < matrix.length / 2; row++)
{
    temp = matrix[row][matrix.length - 1 - row];
    matrix[row][matrix.length - 1 - row] =
                matrix[matrix.length - 1 - row][row];
    matrix[matrix.length - 1 - row][row] = temp;
}
```

This Java code to reverse the diagonals works for any square two-dimensional array.

Passing Two-Dimensional Arrays as Parameters to Methods

Just like one-dimensional arrays, two-dimensional arrays can be passed as parameters to a method.

In the section, Processing Two-Dimensional Arrays, we described various algorithms to process the elements of a two-dimensional array. Using those algorithms, we can write methods that can be used in a variety of applications. In this section we write some of these methods. In these methods, for simplicity, we assume that we are processing the entire two-dimensional array.

The following method outputs the elements of a two-dimensional array, one row per line:

```java
public static void printMatrix(int[][] matrix)
{
    int row, col;

    for (row = 0; row < matrix.length; row++)
    {
        for (col = 0; col < matrix[row].length; col++)
            System.out.printf("%7d", matrix[row][col]);

        System.out.println();
    }
}
```

Similarly, the following method outputs the sum of the elements of each row of a two-dimensional array whose elements are of the type **int**:

```java
public static void sumRows(int[][] matrix)
{
    int row, col;
    int sum;

        //sum of each individual row
    for (row = 0; row < matrix.length; row++)
    {
        sum = 0;

        for (col = 0; col < matrix[row].length; col++)
            sum = sum + matrix[row][col];

        System.out.println("The sum of the elements of row "
                          + (row + 1) + " = " + sum);
    }
}
```

The following method determines the largest element in each row:

```java
public static void largestinRows(int[][] matrix)
{
```

```
int row, col;
int largest;

    //The largest element in each row
for (row = 0; row < matrix.length; row++)
{
    largest = matrix[row][0]; //assume that the first
                              //element of the row is
                              //the largest
    for (col = 1; col < matrix[row].length; col++)
        if (largest < matrix[row][col])
            largest = matrix[row][col];

    System.out.println("The largest element of row "
                      + (row + 1) + " = " + largest);

}
}
```

In a similar fashion, you can write methods to find the sum of the elements of each column, read data into a two-dimensional array, find the largest and/or smallest element in each row or each column, and so on.

Example 9-10 shows how the preceding methods are used in a program.

Example 9-10

The following program illustrates how two-dimensional arrays are passed as parameters to methods:

```
public class TwoDimArraysAsParam
{
    public static void main(String[] args)
    {
        int[][] board = {{23, 5, 6, 15, 18},
                         {4, 16, 24, 67, 10},
                         {12, 54, 23, 76, 11},
                         {1, 12, 34, 22, 8},
                         {81, 54, 32, 67, 33},
                         {12, 34, 76, 78, 9}};        //Line 1
        printMatrix(board);                           //Line 2
        System.out.println();                         //Line 3
        sumRows(board);                               //Line 4
        System.out.println();                         //Line 5
        largestinRows(board);                         //Line 6
    }

    //Place the definitions of the methods printMatrix,
    //sumRows, and largestinRows as described in this section.

}
```

Sample Run:

```
23       5       6      15      18
 4      16      24      67      10
12      54      23      76      11
 1      12      34      22       8
81      54      32      67      33
12      34      76      78       9
```

```
The sum of the elements of row 1 = 67
The sum of the elements of row 2 = 121
The sum of the elements of row 3 = 176
The sum of the elements of row 4 = 77
The sum of the elements of row 5 = 267
The sum of the elements of row 6 = 209
```

```
The largest element of row 1 = 23
The largest element of row 2 = 67
The largest element of row 3 = 76
The largest element of row 4 = 34
The largest element of row 5 = 81
The largest element of row 6 = 78
```

In the preceding program, the statement in Line 1 declares and initializes **board** to be a two-dimensional array of **6** rows and **5** columns. The statement in Line 2 uses the method **printMatrix** to output the elements of **board** (see the first six lines of the Sample Run). The statement in Line 4 uses the method **sumRows** to calculate and print the sum of each row. The statement in Line 6 uses the method **largestinRows** to find and print the largest element in each row.

When storing a two-dimensional array in computer memory, Java uses the **row order form**. That is, the first row is stored first, followed by the second row, followed by the third row, and so on.

MULTIDIMENSIONAL ARRAYS

Earlier in this chapter, we defined an array as a collection of a fixed number of elements (called components) of the same type. A one-dimensional array is an array in which the elements are arranged in a list form; in a two-dimensional array, the elements are arranged in a table form. We can also define three-dimensional or larger arrays. In Java, there is no limit on the dimensions of arrays. Following is the general definition of an array:

Array: A collection of a fixed number of elements (called components) arranged in n dimensions (n >= 1), called an **n-dimensional array**.

The general syntax for declaring and instantiating an n-dimensional array is:

```
dataType[][]...[] arrayName
                = new dataType[intExp1][intExp2] ... [intExpn];
```

where `intExp1`, `intExp2`, ..., and `intExpn` are constant expressions yielding positive integer values.

The syntax to access a component of an n-dimensional array is:

```
arrayName[indexExp1][indexExp2] ... [indexExpn]
```

where `indexExp1`, `indexExp2`, `...`, and `indexExpn` are expressions yielding non-negative integer values. Moreover, for each `i`, the value of `indexExpi` must be less than the size of the `ith` dimension. `indexExpi` gives the position of the array component in the `ith` dimension.

For example, the statement:

```
double[][][] carDealers = new double[10][5][7];
```

declares `carDealers` to be a three-dimensional array. The size of the first dimension is 10, the size of the second dimension is 5, and the size of the third dimension is 7. The first dimension ranges from 0 to 9, the second dimension ranges from 0 to 4, and the third dimension ranges from 0 to 6. The base address of the array `carDealers` is the address of the first array component—the address of `carDealers[0][0][0]`. The total number of components in the array `carDealers` is 10 * 5 * 7 = 350.

9

The statement:

```
carDealers[5][3][2] = 15564.75;
```

sets the value of the component `carDealers[5][3][2]` to `15564.75`.

You can use loops to process multidimensional arrays. For example, the nested **for** loops:

```
for (i = 0; i < 10; i++)
    for (j = 0; j < 5; j++)
        for (k = 0; k < 7; k++)
            carDealers[i][j][k] = 10.00;
```

initialize each component of the array to `10.00`.

During program execution, if an array index goes out of bounds, the program throws an `ArrayIndexOutOfBoundsException`. Exception handling is discussed in detail in Chapter 12.

PROGRAMMING EXAMPLE: CODE DETECTION

When a message is transmitted in secret code over a transmission channel, it is usually transmitted as a sequence of bits, that is, 0s and 1s. Due to noise in the transmission channel, the transmitted message may become corrupted. That is, the message received at the destination is not the same as the message transmitted; some of the bits may have been changed. There are several techniques to check the validity of the transmitted message at the destination. One technique is to transmit the same message twice. At the destination, both copies of the message are compared bit-by-bit. If the corresponding bits are the same, the message received is error-free.

Let's write a program to check whether the message received at the destination is error-free. For simplicity, assume that the secret code representing the message is a sequence of digits (0 to 9) and the maximum length of the message is 250 digits. Also, the first number in the message is the length of the message. For example, if the secret code is:

7 9 2 7 8 3 5 6

then the message is 7 digits long, and it is transmitted twice.

The above message is transmitted as:

7 9 2 7 8 3 5 6 7 9 2 7 8 3 5 6

Input A file containing the secret code and its copy.

Output The secret code, its copy, and a message—if the received code is error-free—in the following form:

```
Code Digit     Code Digit Copy
    9                9
    2                2
    7                7
    8                8
    3                3
    5                5
    6                6
Message transmitted OK.
```

The preceding output is to be stored in a file.

Problem Analysis and Algorithm Design

Because we have to compare the corresponding digits of the secret code and its copy, you first read the secret code and store it in an array. Then you read the first digit of the copy and compare it with the first digit of the secret code, and so on. If any corresponding digits are not the same, you indicate this fact by printing a message next to the digits. Because the maximum length of the message is 250, you use an array of 250 components. The first number in the secret code, and in the copy of the secret code, indicates the length of the code. This discussion translates into the following algorithm:

1. Open the input and output files.
2. Read the length of the secret code.
3. If the length of the secret code is greater than 250, terminate the program because the maximum length of the code in this program is 250.
4. Read and store the secret code into an array.
5. Read the length of the copy.
6. If the length of the secret code and its copy are the same, compare the codes; otherwise, print an error message.

We use the named constant `maxCodeSize` to store `250`, the maximum length of the secret code. Thus, we need the following statement:

```
static final int maxCodeSize = 250;
```

We need an array to store the secret code, a variable to store the length of the secret code, and variables to create the input and output stream objects. We assume that the secret code is stored in the file `SecretCode.txt` and the output is to be stored in the file `SecretCodeOut.txt`, and both files are on floppy disk A. Thus, we need the following variables:

```
int[] codeArray = new int[maxCodeSize];      //array to store the
                                             //secret code
int codeLength;   //variable to store the length
                  //of the secret code

     //Scanner object to open the input file
Scanner codeFile = new Scanner
                  (new FileReader("a:\\SecretCode.txt"));

     //PrintWriter object to open the output file
PrintWriter outFile =
                  new PrintWriter("a:\\SecretCodeOut.txt");
```

To simplify the definition of the method `main`, let us write the method `readCode` to read the secret code and another method, `compareCode`, to compare the codes. Next, we describe these two methods.

readCode The method `readCode` reads and stores the secret code into an array. Because the input is stored in a file and the file was opened in the method `main`, the variable corresponding to the input file must be passed as a parameter to this method. Also, the length of the secret code is read in the method `main`. Furthermore, after reading the secret code, the method `readCode` must pass the secret code to the method `main`. Therefore, this method has three parameters: an input file stream variable, an array to store the secret code, and the length of the secret code. The definition of the method `readCode` is as follows:

```
public static void readCode(Scanner inFile, int[] list,
                            int length)
{
    int count;

    for (count = 0; count < length; count++)
        list[count] = inFile.nextInt();
}
```

compareCode This method compares the secret code with its copy. Therefore, it must have access to the array containing the secret code and the length of the secret code. The copy of the secret code and its length are stored in the input file. Thus, the variable referring to the input file must be passed as a parameter to this method. Also, the method `compareCode` compares the secret code with the copy and prints an appropriate message. Because the output will be stored in a file, the variable referring to the output file must also be passed as a parameter to this method. Therefore, this method has four parameters: an input file stream variable, an output file stream variable, the array containing the secret code, and the length of the secret code. This discussion translates into the following algorithm for the method `compareCode`:

    a. Declare the variables.

    b. Set a **boolean** variable `codeOk` to **true**.

    c. Read the length of the copy of the secret code.

    d. If the length of the secret code and its copy are not the same, output an appropriate error message and terminate the method.

    e. Output the heading: `Code Digit    Code Digit Copy`

    f. For each digit in the input file:

        f.1. Read the next digit of the copy of the secret code.

        f.2. Output the corresponding digits from the secret code and its copy.

        f.3. If the corresponding digits are not the same, output an error message and set the **boolean** variable `codeOk` to **false**.

g. **if** the **boolean** variable **codeOk** is **true**

> Output a message indicating that the secret code was transmitted correctly.

else

> Output an error message.

Following this algorithm, the definition of the method **compareCode** is:

```java
public static void compareCode(Scanner inFile,
                               PrintWriter outP,
                               int[] list, int length)
{
        //Step a: Declare the variables
    int length2;
    int digit;
    boolean codeOk;
    int count;

    codeOk = true;                                    //Step b

    length2 = inFile.nextInt();                       //Step c

    if (length != length2)                            //Step d
    {
        System.out.println("The original code and "
                    + "its copy are not of "
                    + "the same length.");
        return;
    }

    outP.println("Code Digit    Code Digit "
            + "Copy");                                //Step e

    for (count = 0; count < length; count++)    //Step f
    {
        digit = inFile.nextInt();                     //Step f.1

        outP.printf("%5d %15d %n",
                    list[count], digit);              //Step f.2

        if (digit != list[count])                     //Step f.3
        {
            outP.println("  corresponding code "
                    + "digits are not the same");
            codeOk = false;
        }
        else
            outP.println();
    }
```

```
        if (codeOk)                              //Step g
            outP.println("Message transmitted OK.");
        else
            outP.println("Error in transmission. "
                            + "Retransmit!!");
}
```

Following is the algorithm for the method `main`.

Main Algorithm

1. Declare the variables to store the secret code and the length of the secret code.
2. Declare the variables and open the files.
3. Get the length of the secret code.
4. `if` (length of the secret code `<= 250`)

```
    {
        Call the method readCode to read the secret code.
        Call the method compareCode to compare the codes.
    }
    else
        Output an appropriate error message.
```

Complete Program Listing

```java
//Program: Code Detection

import java.io.*;
import java.util.*;

public class CodeDetection
{
    static final int maxCodeSize = 250;

    public static void main(String[] args) throws
                                        FileNotFoundException
    {
        int[] codeArray = new int[maxCodeSize];   //Step 1
        int codeLength;                            //Step 1

                //Step 2
        Scanner codeFile = new Scanner
                    (new FileReader("a:\\SecretCode.txt"));
        PrintWriter outFile =
                    new PrintWriter("a:\\SecretCodeOut.txt");

        codeLength = codeFile.nextInt();           //Step 3
```

```
            if (codeLength <= maxCodeSize)                    //Step 4
            {
                readCode(codeFile, codeArray, codeLength);
                compareCode(codeFile, outFile, codeArray,
                            codeLength);
            }
            else
                System.out.println("Length of the secret code "
                                   + "must be <= " + maxCodeSize);

            codeFile.close();
            outFile.close();
    }

    //Place the definition of the method readCode as
    //described earlier here.
    //Place the definition of the method compareCode as
    //described earlier here.

}
```

Sample Run:

Input File Data: (`SecretCode.txt`)

7 9 2 7 8 3 5 6 7 9 2 7 8 3 5 6

Output File Data: (`SecretCodeOut.txt`)

```
Code Digit   Code Digit Copy
    9                9
    2                2
    7                7
    8                8
    3                3
    5                5
    6                6
Message transmitted OK.
```

PROGRAMMING EXAMPLE: TEXT PROCESSING

Let's now write a program that reads a given text, outputs the text as is, and prints the number of lines and the number of times each letter appears in the text. An uppercase letter and a lowercase letter are treated as being the same; that is, they are tallied together.

Because there are 26 letters, we use an array of 26 components to perform the letter count. We also need a variable to store the line count.

The text is stored in a file, which we will call **text.txt**; it is on a floppy disk, which we will assume is **a**. The output will be stored in a file, which we will call **textCh.out**.

Input   A file containing the text to be processed.

Output   A file containing the text, number of lines, and the number of times a letter appears in the text.

Problem Analysis and Algorithm Design

Based on the desired output, it is clear that we must output the text as is. That is, if the text contains any whitespace characters, they must be output as well.

Let's first describe the variables that are necessary to develop the program. This will simplify the discussion that follows.

Variables   We need to store the letter count and the line count. Therefore, we need a variable to store the line count and 26 variables to perform the letter count. We will use an array of 26 components to perform the letter count. We also need a variable to read and store each character in turn, because the input file will be read character-by-character. Because the data will be read from an input file and the output will be saved in a file, we need an input stream object to open the input file and an output stream object to open the output file. Because the program needs to do a character count, the program should read the input file character-by-character. Moreover, the program should also count the number of lines. Therefore, while reading the data from the input file, the program must capture the newline character. The **Scanner class** does not contain any method that can read only the next character in the input stream, unless the character is delimited by whitespace characters such as blanks. Moreover, using the **Scanner class**, the program should read the entire line or else the newline character will be ignored.

To simplify the reading of the input file character-by-character, we use the Java **class FileReader**. (In Chapter 3, we introduced this class to create and initialize a **Scanner** object to the input source.) The **class FileReader** contains the method **read** that returns the integer value of the next character. For example, if the next input character is **A**, then the method **read** returns 65. We can use the cast operator to change the value 65 to the character **A**. Notice that the method **read** *does not* skip whitespace characters. Moreover, the method **read** returns –1 when the end of the input file has been reached. We can, therefore, use the value returned by the method **read** to determine whether the end of the input file is reached.

Consider the following statement:

```
FileReader inputStream = new FileReader("a:\\text.txt");
```

This statement creates the `FileReader` object `inputStream` and initializes it to the input file `text.txt`. (We assume that this file is on floppy drive A.) If `nextChar` is a `char` variable, then the following statement reads and stores the next character from the input file into `nextChar`:

```
ch = (char) inputStream.read();
```

It now follows that the method `main` needs (at least) the following variables:

```
int lineCount = 0;       //variable to store the line count
int[] letterCount = new int[26]; //array to store the letter count

IntClass next = new IntClass();      //variable to read a character

FileReader inputStream = new FileReader("a:\\text.txt");
PrintWriter outfile = new PrintWriter("a:\\textCh.out");
```

(Note that the method `read` throws an `IOException` when something goes wrong. At this point, we will ignore this exception by throwing it in the program. Exceptions are covered in detail in Chapter 12.)

In this declaration, `letterCount[0]` stores the `A` count, `letterCount[1]` stores the `B` count, and so on. Clearly, the variable `lineCount` and the array `letterCount` must be initialized to `0`.

The algorithm for the program is:

1. Declare and initialize the variables.
2. Create objects to open the input and output files.
3. While there is more data in the input file:
   a. For each character in a line:
      i.   Read and write the character.
      ii. Increment the appropriate letter count.
   b. Increment the line count.
4. Output the line count and letter counts.
5. Close the files.

To simplify the method `main`, we divide it into three methods:

- Method `copyText`
- Method `characterCount`
- Method `writeTotal`

The following sections describe each method in detail. Then, with the help of these methods, we describe the algorithm for the method `main`.

copyText   This method reads a line and outputs the line. Whenever a nonblank character is found, it calls the method `characterCount` to update the letter count. Clearly, this method has four parameters: an input stream object, an output stream object, a variable to read the character, and the array to update the letter count.

Note that the method `copyText` does not perform the letter count, but we still pass the array `letterCount` to it. We do this because this method calls the method `characterCount`, which needs the array `letterCount` to update the appropriate letter count. Therefore, we must pass the array `letterCount` to the `copyText` method so that it can pass the array to the method `characterCount`.

```
static void copyText(FileReader infile, PrintWriter outfile,
                IntClass next, int[] letterC) throws IOException
{
    while (next.getNum() != (int)'\n') //Process the entire line
    {
        outfile.print((char)(next.getNum())); //Output the character
        chCount((char)(next.getNum()), letterC); //Call the
                                                 //method chCount
        next.setNum(infile.read());         //Read the next character
    }
    outfile.println();                //Output the newline character
}
```

characterCount   This method increments the letter count. To increment the appropriate letter count, the method must know what the letter is. Therefore, the `characterCount` method has two parameters: a **char** variable, and the array to update the letter count. In pseudocode, this method is:

a. Convert the letter to uppercase.

b. Find the index of the array corresponding to this letter.

c. If the index is valid, increment the appropriate count. At this step, we must ensure that the character is a letter. We are counting only letters, so other characters—such as commas, hyphens, and periods—are ignored.

Following this algorithm, the definition of this method is:

```
static void chCount(char ch, int[] letterC)
{
    int index;
    int i;

    ch = Character.toUpperCase(ch);        //Step a
    index = (int) ch - 65;                 //Step b
    if (index >= 0 && index < 26)          //Step c
        letterC[index]++;
}
```

writeTotal This method outputs the line count and the letter count. It has three parameters: the output stream object, the line count, and the array to output the letter count. The definition of this method is:

```java
static void writeTotal(PrintWriter outfile, int lines,
                       int[] letters)
{
    int i;

    outfile.println();
    outfile.println("The number of lines = " + lines);

    for (i = 0; i < 26; i++)
        outfile.println((char)(i+65) + " count = " + letters[i]);
}
```

We now describe the algorithm for the method `main`.

Main Algorithm

1. Declare and initialize the variables.
2. Open the input and output files.
3. Read the first character.
4. while (not end of the input file):
   a. Process the next line; call the method `copyText`.
   b. Increment the line count. (Increment the variable `lineCount`.)
   c. Read the next character.
5. Output the line count and letter count. Call the method `writeTotal`.
6. Close the files.

Complete Program Listing

```java
//Program: Line and letter count

import java.io.*;

public class CharacterCount
{
    public static void main(String[] args)
                throws FileNotFoundException, IOException
    {
        int lineCount = 0;
        int[] letterCount = new int[26];
```

```java
IntClass next = new IntClass();

    FileReader inputStream = new FileReader("a:\\text.txt");
    PrintWriter outfile = new PrintWriter("a:\\textCh.out");

    next.setNum(inputStream.read());
    while (next.getNum() != -1)
    {
        copyText(inputStream, outfile, next, letterCount);
        lineCount++;
        next.setNum(inputStream.read());
    }//end while loop

    writeTotal(outfile, lineCount, letterCount);

    outfile.close();
}

static void copyText(FileReader infile, PrintWriter outfile,
            IntClass next, int[] letterC) throws IOException
{
    while (next.getNum() != (int)'\n')
    {
        outfile.print((char)(next.getNum()));
        chCount((char)(next.getNum()), letterC);
        next.setNum(infile.read());
    }
    outfile.println();
}

static void chCount(char ch, int[] letterC)
{
    int index;
    int i;

    ch = Character.toUpperCase(ch);            //Step a
    index = (int) ch - 65;                     //Step b
    if (index >= 0 && index < 26)              //Step c
        letterC[index]++;
}

static void writeTotal(PrintWriter outfile, int lines,
                    int[] letters)
{
    int i;
```

```
        outfile.println();
        outfile.println("The number of lines = " + lines);

        for (i = 0; i < 26; i++)
            outfile.println((char)(i+65) + " count = " + letters[i]);
    }
}
```

Sample Run:

Input file (text.txt)

Today we live in an era where information is processed
almost at the speed of light. Through computers, the
technological revolution is drastically changing the way we
live and communicate with one another. Terms such as
"the Internet," which was unfamiliar just a few years ago, are
very common today. With the help of computers you can send
letters to, and receive letters from, loved ones within
seconds. You no longer need to send a resume by mail to apply
for a job; in many cases you can simply submit your job
application via the Internet. You can watch how stocks perform
in real time, and instantly buy and sell them. Students
regularly "surf" the Internet and use computers to design
their classroom projects. They also use powerful word
processing software to complete their term papers. Many
people maintain and balance their checkbooks on computers.

Output file (textCh.txt)

Today we live in an era where information is processed
almost at the speed of light. Through computers, the
technological revolution is drastically changing the way we
live and communicate with one another. Terms such as
"the Internet," which was unfamiliar just a few years ago, are
very common today. With the help of computers you can send
letters to, and receive letters from, loved ones within
seconds. You no longer need to send a resume by mail to apply
for a job; in many cases you can simply submit your job
application via the Internet. You can watch how stocks perform
in real time, and instantly buy and sell them. Students
regularly "surf" the Internet and use computers to design
their classroom projects. They also use powerful word
processing software to complete their term papers. Many
people maintain and balance their checkbooks on computers.

```
The number of lines = 15
A count = 53
B count = 7
C count = 30
D count = 19
E count = 81
F count = 11
G count = 10
H count = 29
I count = 41
J count = 4
K count = 3
L count = 31
M count = 26
N count = 50
O count = 59
P count = 21
Q count = 0
R count = 45
S count = 48
T count = 62
U count = 24
V count = 7
W count = 15
X count = 0
Y count = 20
Z count = 0
```

QUICK REVIEW

1. An array is a structured data type with a fixed number of components. Every component is of the same type, and the components are accessed using their relative positions in the array.

2. Elements of a one-dimensional array are arranged in the form of a list.

3. An array index can be any expression that evaluates to a non-negative integer. The value of the index must always be less than the size of the array.

4. In Java, an array index starts with 0.

5. In Java, [ ] is an operator, called the array subscripting operator.

6. When an array object is instantiated, its components are initialized to their default values.

7. Arrays that are created, that is, instantiated, during program execution are called dynamic arrays.

8. Arrays can be initialized when they are created.

9. Associated with each array that has been instantiated (that is, memory has been allocated to store the data), there is a **public** instance variable **length**. The variable **length** contains the size of the array.

10. If an array index goes out of bounds, the program throws an **ArrayIndexOutOfBoundsException**.

11. The base address of an array is the address (that is, memory location) of the first array component.

12. Arrays can be passed as parameters to methods.

13. In a method call statement, when passing an array as an actual parameter, you use only its name.

14. Individual array components can be passed as parameters to methods.

15. You can create an array of objects.

16. Parallel arrays are used to hold related information.

17. The syntax to declare a variable length formal parameter is:

    dataType ... identifier

18. A method can have both a variable length formal parameter and other formal parameters.

19. A method can have at most one variable length formal parameter.

20. If a method has both a variable length formal parameter and other types of formal parameters, then the variable length formal parameter must be the last formal parameter of the formal parameter list.

21. The most recent version of Java provides a special type of **for** loop, called a foreach loop, to process the elements of an object such as an array.

22. The syntax to use a foreach loop to process the elements of an array is:

    **for (dataType identifier : arrayName)
        statements**

    where **identifier** is a variable and the data type of **identifier** is the same as the data type of the array components.

23. A two-dimensional array is an array in which the elements are arranged in a table form.

24. To access an element of a two-dimensional array, you need a pair of indices: one for the row position, and one for the column position.

25. In row processing, a two-dimensional array is processed one row at a time.

26. In column processing, a two-dimensional array is processed one column at a time.

27. Java stores two-dimensional arrays in a row order form in computer memory.

9

1. Mark the following statements as true or false.

   a. A **double** type is an example of a primitive data type.

   b. A one-dimensional array is an example of a structured data type.

   c. Arrays can be passed as parameters to a method.

   d. A method can return a value of the type array.

   e. The size of an array is determined at compile time.

   f. Given the declaration:

   ```
   int[] list = new int[10];
   ```

   the statement:

   ```
   list[5] = list[3] + list[2];
   ```

   updates the content of the fifth component of the array `list`.

   g. If an array index goes out of bounds, the program terminates in an error.

2. Write Java statements that do the following:

   a. Declare an array `alpha` of 15 components of the type **int**.

   b. Output the value of the tenth component of the array `alpha`.

   c. Set the value of the fifth component of the array `alpha` to 35.

   d. Set the value of the ninth component of the array `alpha` to the sum of the sixth and thirteenth components of the array `alpha`.

   e. Set the value of the fourth component of the array `alpha` to three times the value of the eighth component, minus 57.

   f. Output `alpha` so that five components per line are printed.

3. Consider the method headings:

   ```
   void funcOne(int[] alpha, int size)
   int funcSum(int x, int y)
   void funcTwo(int[] alpha, int[] beta)
   ```

   and the declarations:

   ```
   int[] list = new int[50];
   int[] Alist = new int[60];
   int num;
   ```

   Write Java statements that do the following:

   a. Call the method `funcOne` with the actual parameters, `list` and 50, respectively.

   b. Print the value returned by the method `funcSum` with the actual parameters, 50 and the fourth component of `list`, respectively.

c. Print the value returned by the method `funcSum` with the actual parameters, the thirtieth and tenth components of `list`, respectively.

d. Call the method `funcTwo` with the actual parameters, `list` and `Alist`, respectively.

4. Suppose `list` is an array of five components of the type `int`. What is stored in `list` after the following Java code executes?

```java
for (i = 0; i < 5; i++)
{
    list[i] = 2 * i + 5;
    if (i % 2 == 0)
        list[i] = list[i] - 3;
}
```

5. Suppose `list` is an array of six components of the type `int`. What is stored in `list` after the following Java code executes?

```java
list[0] = 5;
for (int i = 1; i < 6; i++)
{
    list[i] = i * i + 5;

    if (i > 2)
        list[i] = 2 * list[i] - list[i - 1];
}
```

6. What is the output of the following program?

```java
public class Exercise6
{
    public static void main(String[] args)
    {
        int count;
        int[] alpha = new int[5];

        alpha[0] = 5;
        for (count = 1; count < 5; count++)
        {
            alpha[count] = 5 * count + 10;
            alpha[count - 1] = alpha[count] - 4;
        }

        System.out.print("List elements: ");

        for (count = 0; count < 5; count++)
            System.out.print(alpha[count] + " ");
        System.out.println();
    }
}
```

9

7. What is the output of the following program?

```java
public class Exercise7
{
    public static void main(String[] args)
    {
        int j;
        int[] one = new int[5];
        int[] two = new int[10];

        for (j = 0; j < 5; j++)
            one[j] = 5 * j + 3;

        System.out.print("One contains: ");

        for (j = 0; j < 5; j++)
            System.out.print(one[j] + " ");

        System.out.println();

        for (j = 0; j < 5; j++)
        {
            two[j] = 2 * one[j] - 1;
            two[j + 5] = one[4 - j] + two[j];
        }

        System.out.print("Two contains: ");

        for (j = 0; j < 10; j++)
            System.out.print(two[j] + " ");

        System.out.println();
    }
}
```

8. Suppose you have the following class.

```java
public class NamesList
{
    private String[] namesList;

        //Constructor with a variable length
        //formal parameter
    public NamesList(String ... names)
    {
        namesList = names;
    }
```

```
            //Method to return namesList as a string
        public String toString()
        {
            String str = "";

            for (String name : namesList)
                str = str + name + "\n";

            return str;
        }
    }
```

What is the output of the following program?

```
public class Exercise8
{
    public static void main(String[] args)
    {
        String[] days = {"Sunday", "Monday", "Tuesday",
                         "Wednesday", "Thursday",
                         "Friday", "Saturday"};

        NamesList familyMember =
                    new NamesList("William Johnson",
                                  "Linda Johnson",
                                  "Susan Johnson",
                                  "Alex Johnson");

        NamesList friends =
                    new NamesList("Amy Miller",
                                  "Bobby Gupta",
                                  "Sheila Mann",
                                  "Chris Green",
                                  "Silvia Smith",
                                  "Randy Arora");

        NamesList seasons =
                    new NamesList("Winter", "Spring",
                                  "Summer", "Fall");

        NamesList emptyList = new NamesList();

        NamesList weekDays = new NamesList(days);

        System.out.println("*****  Family Members  "
                    + "*****");
        System.out.println(familyMember);
        System.out.println("\n*****  Friends  "
                    + "*****");
        System.out.println(friends);
        System.out.println("\n*****  Seasons  "
                    + "*****");
        System.out.println(seasons);
```

9

```
        System.out.println("\n*****  Empty Names List  "
                           + "*****");
        System.out.println(emptyList);
        System.out.println("\n*****  Week Days  "
                           + "*****");
        System.out.println(weekDays);
    }
}
```

9. Consider the following declarations:

```
const int carTypes = 5;
const int colorTypes = 6;

double[][] sales = new double [carTypes][colorTypes];
```

   a. How many components does the array **sales** have?

   b. What is the number of rows in the array **sales**?

   c. What is the number of columns in the array **sales**?

   d. To sum the sales by **carTypes**, what kind of processing is required?

   e. To sum the sales by **colorTypes**, what kind of processing is required?

10. Write Java statements that do the following:

   a. Declare an array **alpha** of 10 rows and 20 columns of the type **int**.

   b. Initialize each component of the array **alpha** to 5.

   c. Store 1 in the first row and 2 in the remaining rows.

   d. Store 5 in the first column, and the value in each remaining column is twice the value of the previous column.

   e. Print the array **alpha** one row per line.

   f. Print the array **alpha** one column per line.

11 Consider the following declaration:

```
int[][] beta = new int[3][3];
```

   What is stored in **beta** after each of the following statements executes?

   a.
```
for (i = 0; i < 3; i++)
    for (j = 0; j < 3; j++)
        beta[i][j] = 0;
```

   b.
```
for (i = 0; i < 3; i++)
    for (j = 0; j < 3; j++)
        beta[i][j] = i + j;
```

   c.
```
for (i = 0; i < 3; i++)
    for (j = 0; j < 3; j++)
        beta[i][j] = i * j;
```

   d.
```
for (i = 0; i < 3; i++)
    for (j = 0; j < 3; j++)
        beta[i][j] = 2 * (i + j) % 4;
```

PROGRAMMING EXERCISES

1. Write a Java program that declares an array `alpha` of 50 components of the type `double`. Initialize the array so that the first 25 components are equal to the square of the index variable, and the last 25 components are equal to three times the index variable. Output the array so that 10 elements per line are printed.

2. Write a Java method, `smallestIndex`, that takes as its parameters an `int` array and its size, and returns the index of the smallest element in the array. Also, write a program to test your method.

3. Write a program that reads a file consisting of students' test scores in the range 0–200. It should then determine the number of students having scores in each of the following ranges: 0–24, 25–49, 50–74, 75–99, 100–124, 125–149, 150–174, and 175–200. Output the score ranges and the number of students. Run your program with the following input data: 76, 89, 150, 135, 200, 76, 12, 100, 150, 28, 178, 189, 167, 200, 175, 150, 87, 99, 129, 149, 176, 200, 87, 35, 157, 189.

4. In a gymnastics or diving competition, each contestant's score is calculated by dropping the lowest and highest scores and then adding the remaining scores. Write a program that allows the user to enter eight judges' scores and then outputs the points received by the contestant. Format your output with two decimal places. A judge awards points between 1 and 10, with 1 being the lowest and 10 being the highest. For example, if the scores are 9.2, 9.3, 9.0, 9.9, 9.5, 9.5, 9.6, and 9.8, the contestant receives a total of 56.90 points.

5. Write a program that prompts the user to input a string and then outputs the string in uppercase letters. (Use a character array to store the string.)

6. The history teacher at your school needs help grading a True/False test. The students' IDs and test answers are stored in a file. The first entry in the file contains the answers to the test in the form:

        TFFTFFTTTTFFTFTFTFT

Every other entry in the file is the student's ID, followed by a blank, followed by the student's response. For example, the entry:

        ABC54301 TFTFTFTT TFTFTFFTTFT

indicates that the student's ID is ABC54301 and the answer to question 1 is True, the answer to question 2 is False, and so on. This student did not answer question 9. The exam has 20 questions, and the class has more than 150 students. Each correct answer is awarded two points, each wrong answer gets –1 point, and no answer gets 0 points. Write a program that processes the test data. The output should be the student's ID, followed by the answers, followed by the test score, followed by the test grade. Assume the following grade scale: 90% – 100%, A; 80% – 89.99%, B; 70% – 79.99%, C; 60% – 69.99%, D; and 0% – 59.99%, F.

9

7. Write a program that allows the user to enter the last names of five candidates in a local election and the votes received by each candidate. The program should then output each candidate's name, the votes received by that candidate, and the percentage of the total votes received by the candidate. Your program should also output the winner of the election. A sample output is:

```
Candidate    Votes Received      % of Total Votes
Johnson         5000                 25.91
Miller          4000                 20.72
Duffy           6000                 31.09
Robinson        2500                 12.95
Ashtony         1800                  9.33
Total          19300
The Winner of the Election is Duffy.
```

8. Write a program that allows the user to enter students' names followed by their test scores and outputs the following information (assume that the maximum number of students in the class is 50):

a. Class average

b. Names of all the students whose test scores are below the class average, with an appropriate message

c. Highest test score and the names of all the students having the highest score

9. Consider the following method main:

```java
public static void main(String[] args)
{
    int[][] inStock = new int[10][4];
    int[] alpha = new int[20];
    int[] beta = new int[20];
    int[] gamma = {11, 13, 15, 17};
    int[] delta = {3, 5, 2, 6, 10, 9, 7, 11, 1, 8};

        .
        .
        .

}
```

a. Write the definition of the method inputArray that prompts the user to input 20 numbers and stores the numbers in alpha.

b. Write the definition of the method doubleArray that initializes the elements of beta to two times the corresponding elements of alpha.

c. Write the definition of the method copyGamma that sets the elements of the first row of inStock to gamma and the remaining rows of inStock to three times the previous row of inStock.

d. Write the definition of the method `copyAlphaBeta` that stores `alpha` into the first five rows of `inStock` and `beta` into the last five rows of `inStock`. Make sure that you prevent the method from modifying the elements of `alpha` and `beta`.

e. Write the definition of the method `printArray` that prints any one-dimensional array of the type `int`. Print 15 elements per line.

f. Write the definition of the method `setInStock` that prompts the user to input the elements for the first column of `inStock`. The method should then set the elements in the remaining columns to two times the corresponding element in the previous column, minus the corresponding element in `delta`.

g. Write Java statements that call each of the methods in parts a through f.

h. Write a Java program that tests the method `main` and the methods discussed in parts a through f.

10. Write a program that uses a two-dimensional array to store the highest and lowest temperatures for each month of the year. The program should output the average high, average low, and highest and lowest temperatures of the year. Your program must consist of the following methods:

a. Method `getData`: This method reads and stores the data in the two-dimensional array.

b. Method `averageHigh`: This method calculates and returns the average high temperature of the year.

c. Method `averageLow`: This method calculates and returns the average low temperature of the year.

d. Method `indexHighTemp`: This method returns the index of the highest temperature in the array.

e. Method `indexLowTemp`: This method returns the index of the lowest temperature in the array.

(These methods must all have the appropriate parameters.)

9

11. Write a program that reads in a set of positive integers and outputs how many times a particular number appears in the list. You may assume that the data set has at most 100 numbers and −999 marks the end of the input data. The numbers must be output in increasing order. For example, for the data:

```
15 40 28 62 95 15 28 13 62 65 48 95 65 62 65 95 95 -999
```

the output is:

```
Number    Count
13        1
15        2
28        2
40        1
48        1
62        3
65        3
95        4
```

12. **Airplane Seating Assignment:** Write a program that can be used to assign seats for a commercial airplane. The airplane has 13 rows, with 6 seats in each row. Rows 1 and 2 are first class, the remaining rows are economy class. Rows 1 through 7 are nonsmoking. Your program must prompt the user to enter the following information:

Ticket type (first class or economy class)

For economy class, the smoking or nonsmoking section

Desired seat

Output the seating plan in the following format:

```
         A B C   D E F
Row 1    * * X   * X X
Row 2    * X *   X * X
Row 3    * * X   X * X
Row 4    X * X   * X X
Row 5    * X *   X * *
Row 6    * X *   * * X
Row 7    X * *   * X X
Row 8    * X *   X X *
Row 9    X * X   X * X
Row 10   * X *   X X X
Row 11   * * X   * X *
Row 12   * * X   X * X
Row 13   * * *   * X *
```

Here, * indicates that the seat is available; X indicates that the seat has been assigned. Make this a menu-driven program; show the user's choices and allow the user to make the appropriate choices.

13. Magic Square:

   a. Write a method `createArithmeticSeq` that prompts the user to input two numbers, `first` and `diff`. The method then creates a one-dimensional array of 16 elements ordered in an arithmetic sequence. It also outputs the arithmetic sequence. For example, if `first` = 21 and `diff` = 5, the arithmetic sequence is
21 26 31 36 41 46 51 56 61 66 71 76 81 86 91 96.

   b. Write a method `matricize` that takes a one-dimensional array of 16 elements and a two-dimensional array of 4 rows and 4 columns as parameters. This method puts the elements of the one-dimensional array into the two-dimensional array. For example, if `A` is the one-dimensional array created in part a and `B` is a two-dimensional array, then after putting the elements of `A` into `B`, the array `B` is:

```
21 26 31 36
41 46 51 56
61 66 71 76
81 86 91 96
```

   c. Write a method `reverseDiagonal` that reverses both diagonals of a two-dimensional array. For example, if the two-dimensional array is as in part b, after reversing the diagonals, the two-dimensional array is:

```
96 26 31 81
41 71 66 56
61 51 46 76
36 86 91 21
```

   d. Write a method `magicCheck` that takes a one-dimensional array of size 16, a two-dimensional array of 4 rows and 4 columns, and the sizes of the arrays as parameters. By adding all of the elements of the one-dimensional array and dividing by 4, this method determines the `magicNumber`. The method then adds each row, each column, and each diagonal of the two-dimensional array and compares each sum with the magic number. If the sum of each row, each column, and each diagonal is equal to the `magicNumber`, the method outputs "It is a magic square"; otherwise, it outputs "It is not a magic number". Do not print the sum of each row, each column, and the diagonals.

   e. Write a method `printMatrix` that outputs the elements of a two-dimensional array, one row per line. This output should be as close to a square form as possible.

   f. The methods written in parts a through e should be general enough to apply to an array of any size. (The work should be done by using loops.) The method `magicCheck` works better if it calls two separate methods: one to add the rows and columns, and one to add the diagonals. (In this case, the program compares the magic number with each sum (row, column, and diagonal) in the respective method.)

9

Test the methods you wrote in parts a through f using the following method **class** and the method `main`:

```
public class MagicSquare
{
    static final int rows = 4;
    static final int columns = 4;

    static final int listSize = 16;
    ...
    public static void main(String[] args)
    {

        int[] list = new int[listSize];
        int[][] matrix = new int[rows][columns];

        createArithmeticSeq(list);
        matricize(list, matrix);
        printMatrix(matrix);
        reverseDiagonal(matrix);
        printMatrix(matrix);
        magicCheck(list, matrix);

    }
}
```

THE CLASSES VECTOR AND STRING, AND ENUMERATION TYPES

In this chapter, you will:

♦ Become aware of the **class** Vector
♦ Learn more about manipulating strings using the **class** String
♦ Explore how to create and use **enum** types

Chapter 9 introduced arrays, a structured data type. Arrays are a convenient way to store and process data values of the same type. You learned how to effectively use loops with arrays for input/output, initialization, and other operations. However there are certain limitations to arrays. For example, once you create an array, its size remains fixed. This means that only a fixed number of elements can be stored in an array. The first section of this chapter discusses how to use Java's Vector **class** to overcome some limitations of arrays. We then revisit the **class** String to show you additional methods for manipulating strings. This chapter also discusses how to create and use **enum** types.

class Vector

Chapter 9 described how arrays can be used to implement and process lists. One of the limitations of arrays discussed so far is that once you create an array, its size remains fixed. This means that only a fixed number of elements can be stored in an array. Also, inserting an element in the array at a specific position might require that the elements of the array be shifted. Similarly, removing an element from the array also could require shifting the elements of the array, because we typically do not leave empty positions between array positions holding data. Usually, empty positions are at the end of an array.

In addition to arrays, Java provides the **class** Vector to implement a list. Unlike an array, the size of a **Vector** object can grow and shrink during program execution. Therefore, you need not be concerned about the number of data elements. Before describing how a **Vector** object is used to manage a list, Table 10-1 describes some of the members of the **class** Vector.

Table 10-1 Various Members of the class Vector

```
protected int elementCount;
protected Object[] elementData;  //Array of references
```

Constructors

```
public Vector()
  //Creates an empty vector of the default length of 10
```

```
public Vector(int size)
  //Creates an empty vector of the length specified by size
```

Methods

```
public void addElement(Object insertObj)
  //Adds the object insertObj at the end.
```

```
public void insertElementAt(Object insertObj, int index)
  //Inserts the object insertObj at the position specified by index.
  //If index is out of range, this method throws an
  //ArrayIndexOutOfBoundsException.
```

```
public Object clone()
  //Returns a copy of the vector.
```

```
public boolean contains(Object obj)
  //Returns true if this vector object contains the element specified
  //by obj; otherwise it returns false.
```

```
public void copyInto(Object[] dest)
  //Copies the elements of this vector into the array dest.
```

```
public Object elementAt(int index)
  //Returns the element of the vector at the location specified by index.
```

Table 10-1 Various Members of the **class** Vector (continued)

Methods

`public Object firstElement()`
`//Returns the first element of the vector.`
`//If the vector is empty, the method throws a`
`//NoSuchElementException.`

`public Object lastElement()`
`//Returns the last element of the vector.`
`//If the vector is empty, the method throws a`
`//NoSuchElementException.`

`public int indexOf(Object obj)`
`//Returns the position of the first occurrence of the element`
`//specified by obj in the vector.`
`//If obj is not in the vector, the method returns -1.`

`public int indexOf(Object obj, int index)`
`//Starting at index, this method returns the position of the`
`//first occurrence of the element specified by obj in the vector.`
`//If obj is not in the vector, this method returns -1.`

`public boolean isEmpty()` `//Returns true if the vector is empty; otherwise it returns false.`

`public int lastIndexOf(Object obj)`
`//Starting at the last element, using a backward search, this`
`//method returns the position of the first occurrence of the`
`//element specified by obj in the vector.`
`//If obj is not in the vector, this method returns -1.`

`public int lastIndexOf(Object obj, int index)`
`//Starting at the position specified by index and using a backward`
`//search, this method returns the position of the first occurrence`
`//of the element specified by obj in the vector.`
`//If obj is not in the vector, this method returns -1.`

`public void removeAllElements()` `//Removes all the elements of the vector.`

`public boolean removeElement(Object obj)`
`//If an element specified by obj exists in this vector, the`
`//element is removed and the value true is returned; otherwise the`
`//value false is returned.`

`public void removeElementAt(int index)`
`//If an element at the position specified by index exists, it is`
`//removed from the vector.`
`//If index is out of range, this method throws an`
`//ArrayIndexOutOfBoundsException.`

10

Table 10-1 Various Members of the **class** Vector (continued)

Methods

`public void setElementAt(Object obj, int index)`
`   //The element specified by obj is stored at the position specified by`
`   //index.`
`   //If index is out of range, this method throws an`
`   //ArrayIndexOutOfBoundsException.`

`public int size()` `   //Returns the number of elements in the vector.`
`public String toString()` `   //Returns a string representation of this vector.`

From Table 10-1, it follows that every element of a **Vector** object is a reference variable of the type **Object**. In Java, **Object** is a predefined class, and a reference variable of the **Object** type can store the address of any object. Because every component of a **Vector** object is a reference, to add an element to a **Vector** object, you must first create the appropriate object and store the data into that object. You can then store the address of the object holding the data into a **Vector** object element. Because every string in Java is considered a **String** object, we will illustrate some of the operations on a **Vector** object using string data.

Consider the following statement:

```
Vector<String> stringList = new Vector<String>();          //Line 1
```

This statement declares **stringList** to be a reference variable of the **Vector** type, instantiates an empty **Vector** object, and stores the address of this object into **stringList**. Moreover, the **Vector** object **stringList** is used to create a **Vector** of **String** objects.

 In JDK 5.0, whenever you declare a **Vector** object, you should also specify the reference type of the objects that the **Vector** object will hold. To do this, enclose the reference type of the objects in < and > after the word **Vector**. For example, in the statement in Line 1, **Vector<String>** specifies that the **Vector** object **stringList** is a **Vector** of the **String** objects. If you do not specify the reference type after the word **Vector**, the compiler will generate warning messages indicating unchecked or unsafe operations.

Next, consider the following statements:

```
stringList.addElement("Spring");
stringList.addElement("Summer");
stringList.addElement("Fall");
stringList.addElement("Winter");
```

After these statements execute, `stringList` is as shown in Figure 10-1.

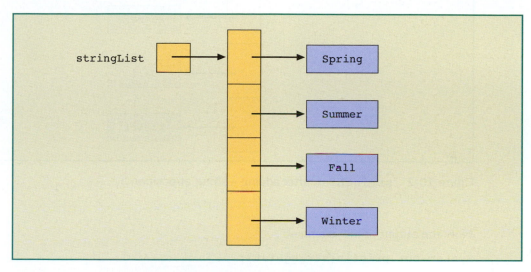

Figure 10-1   `stringList` after adding the four strings

The statement:

```
System.out.println(stringList);
```

outputs the elements of `stringList` in the following form:

```
[Spring, Summer, Fall, Winter]
```

Now consider the following statement:

```
stringList.addElement("Cool", 1);
```

This statement adds the string `"Cool"` at position 1, as shown in Figure 10-2.

10

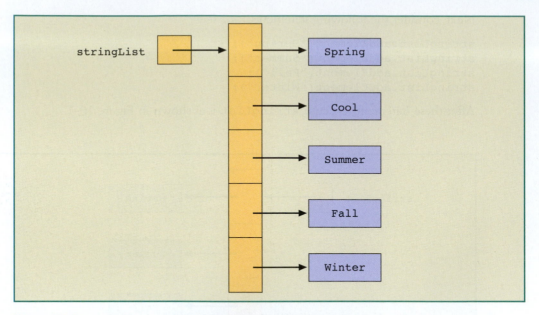

Figure 10-2   `stringList` after adding a string at position 1

Now the output of the statement:

`System.out.println(stringList);`

is:

`[Spring, Cool, Summer, Fall, Winter]`

The **class** `Vector` is contained in the package `java.util`. Therefore, to use the **class** `Vector`, your program must include either the statement:

`import java.util.*;`

or the statement:

`import java.util.Vector;`

The program in Example 10–1 further illustrates how a `Vector` object works.

Example 10-1

```java
//StringVectorExample

import java.util.Vector;

public class StringVectorExample
{
    public static void main(String[] args)
    {
        Vector<String> stringList = new Vector<String>();   //Line 1

        System.out.println("Line 2: Empty stringList?: "
                        + stringList.isEmpty());            //Line 2
        System.out.println("Line 3: Size stringList?: "
                        + stringList.size());               //Line 3
        System.out.println();                               //Line 4

        stringList.addElement("Spring");                    //Line 5
        stringList.addElement("Summer");                    //Line 6
        stringList.addElement("Fall");                      //Line 7
        stringList.addElement("Winter");                    //Line 8
        stringList.addElement("Sunny");                     //Line 9

        System.out.println("Line 10: **** After adding the "
                        + "elements to stringList ****");   //Line 10
        System.out.println("Line 11: Empty stringList?: "
                        + stringList.isEmpty());            //Line 11
        System.out.println("Line 12: Size stringList?: "
                        + stringList.size());               //Line 12
        System.out.println("Line 13: stringList: "
                        + stringList);                      //Line 13

        System.out.println("Line 14: stringList contains Fall?: "
                        + stringList.contains("Fall"));     //Line 14
        System.out.println();                               //Line 15

        stringList.insertElementAt("Cool", 1);              //Line 16
        System.out.println("Line 17: **** After adding an "
                        + "element at position 1 ****");    //Line 17
        System.out.println("Line 18: stringList: "
                        + stringList);                      //Line 18

        System.out.println();                               //Line 19

        stringList.removeElement("Fall");                   //Line 20
        stringList.removeElementAt(2);                      //Line 21
```

10

```
            System.out.println("Line 22: **** After the remove "
                         + "operations ****");                    //Line 22
            System.out.println("Line 23: stringList: "
                         + stringList);                           //Line 23
            System.out.println("Line 24: Size stringList?: "
                         + stringList.size());                    //Line 24
            System.out.println("Line 25: indexOf(\"Sunny\"): "
                         + stringList.indexOf("Sunny"));          //Line 25
    }
}
```

Sample Run:
```
Line 2: Empty stringList?: true
Line 3: Size stringList?: 0

Line 10: **** After adding the elements to stringList ****
Line 11: Empty stringList?: false
Line 12: Size stringList?: 5
Line 13: stringList: [Spring, Summer, Fall, Winter, Sunny]
Line 14: stringList contains Fall?: true

Line 17: **** After adding an element at position 1 ****
Line 18: stringList: [Spring, Cool, Summer, Fall, Winter, Sunny]

Line 22: **** After the remove operations ****
Line 23: stringList: [Spring, Cool, Winter, Sunny]
Line 24: Size stringList?: 4
Line 25: indexOf("Sunny"): 3
```

The preceding program works as follows. The statement in Line 1 creates **stringList** to be a **Vector** object to create a list of **String** object. The statement in Line 2 outputs whether **stringList** is empty and the statement in Line 3 outputs the size of **stringList**, that is, the number of **String** objects in it. Note that at this point **stringList** is empty and its size is 0.

The statements in Lines 5 to 9 use the method **addElement** of the **class** Vector to add the strings **"Spring"**, **"Summer"**, **"Fall"**, **"Winter"**, and **"Sunny"** into **stringList**. The statement in Line 11 determines whether, at this point, **stringList** is empty and the statement in Line 12 outputs the size of **stringList**. The statement in Line 13 outputs the elements currently in **stringList**.

The statement in Line 14 uses the method **contains** of the **class** Vector to determine whether **stringList** contains the string **"Fall"**. The statement in Line 16 uses the method **insertElementAt** of the **class** Vector to insert the string **"Cool"** at position 1. The statement in Line 18 outputs the elements of **stringList** after adding the string **"Cool"**.

The statement in Line 20 uses the method **removeElement** of the **class** Vector to remove the string **"Fall"** from **stringList**. The statement in Line 21 uses the method removeElementAt of the **class** Vector to remove the string currently at the position 2, which is the string "Summer", from stringList. The statement in Line 23 outputs the elements currently in stringList. The statement in Line 24 outputs the current size of stringList. The statement in Line 25 uses the method indexOf, of the **class** Vector, to find the position of the string "Sunny in stringList.

Primitive Data Types and the class Vector

As described in the preceding section, every component of a Vector object is a reference. Therefore, to create a Vector of, say, integers, the integers must be wrapped in an object. Recall that corresponding to each primitive data type, Java provides a wrapper class. For example, the wrapper class corresponding to the type int is Integer. Therefore, an int value can be wrapped in an Integer object. As explained in Chapter 6, as of JDK 5.0, Java has simplified the wrapping and unwrapping of primitive type values, called the *autoboxing* and *auto-unboxing* of primitive data types. For example, consider the following statements:

```
int x;             //Line 1
Integer num;       //Line 2
```

The statement in Line 1 declares the int variable x; the statement in Line 2 declares num to be a reference variable of the type Integer.

Consider the statement:

```
num = 25;                    //Line 3
```

This statement is equivalent to the statement:

```
num = new Integer(25);    //Line 4
```

That is, either of these statements creates an Integer object, stores 25 into that object, and the reference of that object is stored in num. In other words, num refers to or points to an Integer object with the value 25. The expression in Line 3 is called the *autoboxing* of the int type.

Now consider the statement:

```
x = num;                     //Line 5
```

This statement is equivalent to the statement:

```
x = num.intValue();        //Line 6
```

After the statement in either Line 5 or Line 6 executes, the value of x is 25. The statement in Line 5 is called the *auto-unboxing* of the int type.

Next, we illustrate how to create a Vector of Integer objects to store int values.

Suppose that you have the declaration:

```
Vector<Integer> list = new Vector<Integer>();
```

10

The following statements create `Integer` objects with the `int` values 13 and 25, and the `Integer` objects are assigned to `list`:

```
list.addElement(13);
list.addElement(25);
```

Notice that, in reality, these statements are equivalent to the following statements:

```
list.addElement(new Integer(13));
list.addElement(new Integer(25));
```

You can use other `Vector` operations to manipulate the objects of `list`.

Recall that the wrapper class corresponding to the type **char** is `Character`, the type **double** is `Double`, the type **float** is `Float`, and the type **boolean** is `Boolean`. Appendix E describes these and the other wrapper classes and their methods.

The Web site accompanying this book contains the program `IntVectorExample.java` that shows how to create and manipulate a `Vector` of `Integer` objects.

`Vector` Objects and the foreach Loop

Chapter 9 stated that a foreach loop can be used to process the elements of a collection object one at a time. Because each `Vector` object is a collection of elements, you can use a foreach loop to process the elements of a `Vector` object. The syntax to use this type of **for** loop to process the elements of a `Vector` object is:

```
for (type identifier : vectorObject)
    statements
```

where `identifier` is a (reference) variable and the data type of (the object that) `identifier` (points to) is the same as the data type of the objects that each `vectorObject` element points to. Moreover, **type** is either a primitive type or the name of a class.

For example, suppose that you have the following statements:

```
Vector<String> stringList = new Vector<String>();        //Line 1

stringList.addElement("One");                            //Line 2
stringList.addElement("Two");                            //Line 3
stringList.addElement("Three");                          //Line 4
stringList.addElement("Four");                           //Line 5
stringList.addElement("Five");                           //Line 6
stringList.addElement("Six");                            //Line 7
stringList.addElement("Seven");                          //Line 8

System.out.println("stringList: " + stringList);         //Line 9

for (String str : stringList)                            //Line 10
    System.out.println(str.toUpperCase());               //Line 11
```

The statement in Line 1 creates the `Vector` object `stringList` to create a list of `String` objects. The statements in Lines 2 through 8 add the string objects with the values `"One"`, `"Two"`, `"Three"`, `"Four"`, `"Five"`, `"Six"`, and `"Seven"`, respectively, to `stringList`. The statement in Line 9 outputs the values of the string objects of `stringList`. Note that the output of the statement in Line 9 is:

```
stringList: [One, Two, Three, Four, Five, Six, Seven]
```

The foreach loop in Lines 10 and 11 processes each element of `stringList` one at a time and outputs each string in uppercase letters. More specifically, the output is:

```
ONE
TWO
THREE
FOUR
FIVE
SIX
SEVEN
```

(The Web site that accompanies this book contains the program `StringVectorExampleII.java` that shows the effect of the statements in Lines 1 through 11. Moreover, the program `IntVectorExampleII.java` shows how a foreach loop, using the auto-unboxing feature of primitive data types, can be used to process the elements of a `Vector` object of `int` values.)

class String (REVISITED)

Chapter 3 introduced the **class** `String` and discussed how to manipulate strings using various string methods. You learned about the `String` method `substring` in detail and also how the `String` methods `length`, `charAt`, and `indexOf` work in a program. As you now know, the **class** `String` is a very important class in Java. This section introduces some other `String` methods.

Table 3-1 (in Chapter 3) described various `String` methods. This section further illustrates how the methods described in Table 3-1 work. Table 10-2 expands on Table 3-1, and shows additional `String` methods.

10

Table 10-2 Additional String Methods

```
String(String str)
  //Creates a String object and initializes the string
  //object with characters specified by str.
```

```
char charAt(int index)
  //Returns the character at the position specified by index.
```

```
int indexOf(char ch)
  //Returns the index of the first occurrence of the character
  //specified by ch; if the character specified by ch does not
  //appear in the string, it returns -1.
```

```
int indexOf(char ch, int pos)
  //Returns the index of the first occurrence of the character
  //specified by ch; the parameter pos specifies from where to begin
  //the search; if the character specified by ch does not
  //appear in the string, it returns -1.
```

```
int indexOf(String str)
  //Returns the index of the first occurrence of the string
  //specified by str; if the string specified by str does not
  //appear in the string, it returns -1.
```

```
int indexOf(String str, int pos)
  //Returns the index of the first occurrence of the string
  //specified by str; the parameter pos specifies where to begin
  //the search; if the string specified by str does not appear
  //in the string, it returns -1.
```

```
int compareTo(String str)
  //Compares two strings character-by-character.
  //Returns a negative value if this string is less than str.
  //Returns 0 if this string is the same as str.
  //Returns a positive value if this string is greater than str.
```

```
String concat(String str)
  //Returns the string that is this string concatenated with str.
```

```
boolean equals(String str)
  //Returns true if this string is the same as str.
```

```
int length()
  //Returns the length of this string.
```

```
String replace(char charToBeReplaced, char charReplacedWith)
  //Returns the string in which every occurrence of
  //charToBeReplaced is replaced with charReplacedWith.
```

```
String substring(int startIndex, int endIndex)
  //Returns the string that is a substring of this string
  //starting at startIndex until endIndex - 1.
```

Table 10-2 Additional String Methods (continued)

```
String toLowerCase()
  //Returns the string that is the same as this string except that
  //all uppercase letters of this string are replaced with
  //their equivalent lowercase letters.
```

```
String toUpperCase()
  //Returns the string that is the same as this string except
  //that all lowercase letters of this string are replaced with
  //their equivalent uppercase letters.
```

```
boolean startsWith(String str)
  //Returns true if the string begins with the string specified by
  //str; otherwise, this method returns false.
```

```
boolean endsWith(String str)
  //Returns true if the string ends with the string specified by str;
  //otherwise, this method returns false.
```

```
boolean regionMatches(int ind, String str, int strIndex, int len)
  //Returns true if the substring of str starting at strIndex and the
  //length specified by len is the same as the substring of this
  //String object starting at ind and having the same length.
```

```
boolean regionMatches(boolean ignoreCase, int ind,
                      String str, int strIndex, int len)
  //Returns true if the substring of str starting at strIndex and the
  //length specified by len is the same as the substring of this
  //String object starting at ind and having the same length. If
  //ignoreCase is true, then during character comparison the case is
  //ignored.
```

 The method substring was discussed in Chapter 3. Also, the program in Example 3-4 shows how to use the methods charAt, length, concat, replace, and toUpperCase. The methods compareTo and equals were discussed in Chapter 4.

The next example shows how the String methods startsWith, endsWith, toLowerCase, and regionMatches work.

10

Example 10-2

Consider the following statements:

```
String sentence;
String str1;
String str2;
String str3;
String str4;

sentence = "It is sunny and warm.";
str1 = "warm.";
str2 = "Programming with Java";
str3 = "sunny";
str4 = "Learning Java Programming is exciting";
```

Table 10-3 shows the effect of these statements.

Table 10-3 Effect of some `String` methods

Expression	Effect
`sentence.startsWith("It")`	Returns **true**
`sentence.startsWith(str1)`	Returns **false**
`sentence.endsWith("hot")`	Returns **false**
`sentence.endsWith(str1)`	Returns **true**
`str2.toLowerCase()`	Returns the reference to the string "programming with java"
`sentence.regionMatches(6, str3, 0, 5)`	Returns **true**
`sentence.regionMatches(true, 6, "Sunny", 0, 5)`	Returns **true**
`str4.regionMatches(9, str2, 17, 4)`	Returns **true**

For the most part, the statements are straightforward. Let's look at the last three statements, which use the method **regionMatches**:

```
sentence.regionMatches(6, str3, 0, 5)
```

In this statement, we want to determine whether **str3** appears as a substring in the string **sentence** starting at position 6. Notice that the last three arguments, **str3**, 0, and 5, specify that in **str3** the starting index is 0 and the length of the substring is 5. The substring in **sentence** starting at position 6 and of length 5 matches **str3**. So this expression returns **true**.

The expression:

```
sentence.regionMatches(true, 6, "Sunny", 0, 5)
```

is similar to the previous expression, except that when the substrings are compared, the case is ignored, that is, uppercase and lowercase letters are considered the same. Next, let's look at the expression:

```
str4.regionMatches(9, str2, 17, 4)
```

In this expression, we want to determine whether the substring in **str2** starting at position 17 and of length 4 is the same as the substring in **str4** starting at position 9 and of length 4. This expression returns **true** because these substrings are the same.

The following program evaluates the preceding expressions:

```java
//String methods - startsWith, endsWith, toLowerCase,
//                  and regionMatches

public class StringMethods
{
  public static void main(String[] args)
  {
    String sentence = "It is cloudy and warm.";           //Line 1
    String str1 = "warm.";                                 //Line 2
    String str2 = "Programming with Java";                 //Line 3
    String str3 = "cloudy";                                //Line 4
    String str4 = "Learning Java Programming is exciting"; //Line 5

    System.out.println("Line 6: sentence = \""
                       + sentence + "\"");                 //Line 6
    System.out.println("Line 7: str1 = \""
                       + str1 + "\"");                     //Line 7

    System.out.println("Line 8: sentence starts with It?: "
                       + sentence.startsWith("It"));       //Line 8
    System.out.println("Line 9: sentence starts with str1?: "
                       + sentence.startsWith(str1));       //Line 9

    System.out.println("Line 10: sentence in lowercase = \""
                       + sentence.toLowerCase() + "\"");   //Line 10

    System.out.println("Line 11: sentence ends with hot?: "
                       + sentence.endsWith("hot"));        //Line 11
    System.out.println("Line 12: sentence ends with str1?: "
                       + sentence.endsWith(str1));         //Line 12

    System.out.println("Line 13: str2 = \""
                       + str2 + "\"");                     //Line 13
    System.out.println("Line 14: str2 in lowercase: "
                       + str2.toLowerCase());              //Line 14
    System.out.println("Line 15: str3 = \""
                       + str3 + "\"");                     //Line 15
```

10

```
        System.out.println("Line 16: "
                + "sentence.regionMatches(6,str3,0,6)?: "
                + sentence.regionMatches(6,str3,0,6));        //Line 16
        System.out.println("Line 17: "
            + "sentence.regionMatches(true,6,\"Cloudy\",0,6)?: "
            + sentence.regionMatches(true,6,"Cloudy",0,6));  //Line 17

        System.out.println("Line 18: str4 = \""
                        + str4 + "\"");                       //Line 18
        System.out.println("Line 19: "
                + "str4.regionMatches(9,str2,17,4): "
                + str4.regionMatches(9,str2,17,4));           //Line 19
    }
}
```

Sample Run:
```
Line 6: sentence = "It is cloudy and warm."
Line 7: str1 = "warm."
Line 8: sentence starts with It?: true
Line 9: sentence starts with str1?: false
Line 10: sentence in lowercase = "it is cloudy and warm."
Line 11: sentence ends with hot?: false
Line 12: sentence ends with str1?: true
Line 13: str2 = "Programming with Java"
Line 14: str2 in lowercase: programming with java
Line 15: str3 = "cloudy"
Line 16: sentence.regionMatches(6,str3,0,6)?: true
Line 17: sentence.regionMatches(true,6,"Cloudy",0,6)?: true
Line 18: str4 = "Learning Java Programming is exciting"
Line 19: str4.regionMatches(9,str2,17,4): true
```

The **class** String also contains the following overloaded **static** methods:

```
public static String valueOf(boolean b)
public static String valueOf(char ch)
public static String valueOf(int num)
public static String valueOf(long num)
public static String valueOf(double decNum)
public static String valueOf(float decNum)
```

The method **valueOf** returns a string representation of its parameter. Because this is a **static** method, it can be called by using the class name, the dot operator, and the method name. For example:

```
String.valueOf(true)     returns     "true"

String.valueOf('A')      returns     "A"

String.valueOf(4567)     returns     "4567"

String.valueOf(16.78)    returns     "16.78"
```

PROGRAMMING EXAMPLE: PIG LATIN STRINGS

In this programming example, we write a program that prompts the user to input a string and then outputs the string in pig Latin form. The rules for converting a string into pig Latin form follow:

1. If the string begins with a vowel, add the string `"-way"` at the end of the string. For example, the pig Latin form of the string `"eye"` is `"eye-way"`.

2. If the string does not begin with a vowel, first add `"-"` at the end of the string. Then rotate the string one character at a time; that is, move the first character of the string to the end of the string until the first character of the string becomes a vowel. Then add the string `"ay"` at the end. For example, the pig Latin form of the string `"There"` is `"ere-Thay"`.

3. Strings such as `"by"` contain no vowels. In such cases, the letter `y` is considered a vowel. So, for this program the vowels are `a, e, i, o, u, y, A, E, I, O, U`, and `Y`. Therefore, the pig Latin form of `"by"` is `"y-bay"`.

4. Strings such as `"1234"` contain no vowels. The pig Latin form of the string `"1234"` is `"1234-way"`. That is, the pig Latin form of a string that has no vowels is the string followed by the string `"-way"`.

Input A string.

Output The string in pig Latin form.

Problem Analysis and Algorithm Design

Suppose that `str` denotes a string. To convert `str` into pig Latin form, check the first character, `str[0]`, of `str`. If `str[0]` is a vowel, add `"-way"` at the end of `str`—that is, `str = str + "-way"`.

Suppose that the first character of `str`, `str[0]`, is not a vowel. First add `"-"` at the end of the string. Then remove the first character of `str` and put it at the end of `str`. Now the second character of `str` is the first character of `str`. Checking the first character of `str` and moving it to the end of `str` if the first character of `str` is not a vowel is repeated until either the first character of `str` is a vowel or all the characters of `str` are processed, in which case `str` does not contain any vowels.

In this program, we write the method `isVowel`, to determine whether a character is a vowel; the method `rotate`, to move the first character of `str` to the end of `str`; and the method `pigLatinString`, to find the pig Latin form of `str`. The previous discussion translates into the following algorithm:

1. Get `str`.
2. Find the pig Latin form of `str` by using the method `pigLatinString`.
3. Output the pig Latin form of `str`.

Before we write the main algorithm, we describe each of these methods in detail.

Method isVowel   The method `isVowel` takes a character as a parameter and returns `true` if the character is a vowel, and `false` otherwise. The definition of the method `isVowel` is:

```
public static boolean isVowel(char ch)
{
    switch (ch)
    {
    case 'A': case 'E':
    case 'I': case 'O':
    case 'U': case 'Y':
    case 'a': case 'e':
    case 'i': case 'o':
    case 'u': case 'y': return true;
    default: return false;
    }
}
```

Method rotate   The method `rotate` takes a string as a parameter, removes the first character of the string, and places it at the end of the string. This is done by extracting the substring starting at position 1 (which is the second character) until the end of the string, and then adding the first character of the string. The new string is returned as the value of this method. Essentially, the definition of the method `rotate` is:

```
public static String rotate(String pStr)
{
    int len = pStr.length();

    String rStr;

    rStr = pStr.substring(1, len) + pStr.charAt(0);

    return rStr;
}
```

Method pigLatinString   The method `pigLatinString` takes a string, `pStr`, as a parameter and returns the pig Latin form of `pStr`. There are three possible cases: `pStr.charAt(0)` is a vowel; `pStr` contains a vowel and the first character of `pStr` is not a vowel; and `pStr` contains no vowels. Suppose that `pStr.charAt(0)` is not a vowel. Move the first character of `pStr` to the end of `pStr`. This process is repeated until either the first character of `pStr` has become a vowel or all the characters of `pStr` are checked, in which case `pStr` does not contain any vowels. This discussion translates into the following algorithm:

1. If `pStr.charAt(0)` is a vowel, add `"-way"` at the end of `pStr`.
2. Suppose `pStr.charAt(0)` is not a vowel.

3. Move the first character of `pStr` to the end of `pStr`. The second character of `pStr` becomes the first character of `pStr`. Now `pStr` may or may not contain a vowel. We use a **boolean** variable, `foundVowel`, which is set to **true** if `pStr` contains a vowel, and **false** otherwise.

   a. Suppose that `len` denotes the length of `pStr`.

   b. Initialize `foundVowel` to **false**.

   c. If `pStr.charAt(0)` is not a vowel, move `pStr.charAt(0)` to the end of `pStr` by calling the method `rotate`.

   d. Repeat Step c until either the first character of `pStr` becomes a vowel or all the characters of `pStr` have been checked.

4. Convert `pStr` into pig Latin form.

5. Return `pStr`.

The definition of the method `pigLatinString` is:

```java
public static String pigLatinString(String pStr)
{
    int len;

    boolean foundVowel;

    int counter;

    if (isVowel(pStr.charAt(0)))                       //Step 1
        pStr = pStr + "-way";
    else                                               //Step 2
    {
        pStr = pStr + "-";
        pStr = rotate(pStr);                           //Step 3

        len = pStr.length();                           //Step 3.a
        foundVowel = false;                            //Step 3.b

        for (counter = 1; counter < len - 1; counter++) //Step 3.d
            if (isVowel(pStr.charAt(0)))
            {
                foundVowel = true;
                break;
            }
            else                                       //Step 3.c
                pStr = rotate(pStr);
```

```
        if (!foundVowel)                                    //Step 4
            pStr = pStr.substring(1, len) + "-way";
        else
            pStr = pStr + "ay";
    }

    return pStr;                                            //Step 5
}
```

Main Algorithm

1. Get the string.
2. Call the method `pigLatinString` to find the pig Latin form of the string.
3. Output the pig Latin form of the string.

Complete Program Listing

```java
//Program PigLatin Strings

import java.util.*;

public class PigLatin
{
    static Scanner console = new Scanner(System.in);

    public static void main(String[] args)
    {
        String str;

        System.out.print("Enter a string: ");
        str = console.next();
        System.out.println();

        System.out.println("The pig Latin form of " + str
                        + " is: " + pigLatinString(str));
    }

    public static boolean isVowel(char ch)
    {
        switch (ch)
        {
        case 'A': case 'E':
        case 'I': case 'O':
        case 'U': case 'Y':
        case 'a': case 'e':
```

```
    case 'i': case 'o':
    case 'u': case 'y': return true;
    default: return false;
    }
}

public static String rotate(String pStr)
{
    int len = pStr.length();

    String rStr;

    rStr = pStr.substring(1, len) + pStr.charAt(0);

    return rStr;
}

public static String pigLatinString(String pStr)
{
    int len;

    boolean foundVowel;

    int counter;

    if (isVowel(pStr.charAt(0)))                //Step 1
        pStr = pStr + "-way";
    else                                        //Step 2
    {
        pStr = pStr + "-";
        pStr = rotate(pStr);                    //Step 3

        len = pStr.length();                    //Step 3.a
        foundVowel = false;                     //Step 3.b

        for (counter = 1; counter < len - 1; counter++)
                                                //Step 3.d
            if (isVowel(pStr.charAt(0)))
            {
                foundVowel = true;
                break;
            }
            else                                //Step 3.c
                pStr = rotate(pStr);
```

```
            if (!foundVowel)                        //Step 4
                pStr = pStr.substring(1, len) + "-way";
            else
                pStr = pStr + "ay";
        }

        return pStr;                                 //Step 5
    }
}
```

Sample Run 1: In this and the following sample runs, the user input is shaded.
```
Enter a string: Hello

The pig Latin form of Hello is: ello-Hay
```
Sample Run 2:
```
Enter a string: Eye

The pig Latin form of Eye is: Eye-way
```
Sample Run 3:
```
Enter a string: 123456

The pig Latin form of 123456 is: 123456-way
```

ENUMERATION TYPES

Chapter 2 defined a data type as a set of values, combined with a set of operations on those values. It then introduced the primitive data types, **int**, **char**, **double**, and **float**. Using primitive data types, Chapter 8 discussed how to design classes to create your own data types. In other words, primitive data types are the building blocks of classes.

The values belonging to primitive data types are predefined. Java allows programmers to create their own data types by specifying the values of that data type. These are called **enumeration** or **enum** types and are defined using the key word **enum**. *The values that you specify for the data types are identifiers*. For example, consider the following statement:

enum Grades {A, B, C, D, F};

This statement defines Grades to be an **enum** type; the values belonging to this type are A, B, C, D, and F. The values of an **enum** type are called **enumeration** or **enum** constants. Note that the values are enclosed in braces and separated by commas. Also, the **enum** constants within an **enum** type must be unique.

Similarly, the statement:

```
enum Sports {Baseball, Basketball, Football, Golf,
            Hockey, Soccer, Tennis};
```

defines `Sports` to be an **enum** type and the values belonging to this type, that is, the **enum** constants, are `Baseball`, `Basketball`, `Football`, `Golf`, `Hockey`, `Soccer`, and `Tennis`.

Each **enum** type is a *special type of class*, and the values belonging to the **enum** type are (special types of) objects of that class. For example, `Grades` is, in fact, a class and A, B, C, D, and F are **public static** reference variables to objects of the type `Grades`.

After an **enum** type is defined, you can declare reference variables of that type. For example, the following statement declares `myGrade` to be a reference variable of the `Grades` type:

```
Grades myGrade;
```

Because each of the variables A, B, C, D, and F is **public** and **static**, they can be accessed using the name of the class and the dot operator. Therefore, the following statement assigns the object B to `myGrade`:

```
myGrade = Grades.B;
```

The output of the statement:

```
System.out.println("myGrade: " + myGrade);
```

is

```
myGrade: B
```

Similarly, the output of the statement:

```
System.out.println("Grades.B: " + Grades.B);
```

is

```
Grades.B: B
```

Each **enum** constant in an **enum** type has a specific value, called the **ordinal value**. The ordinal value of the first **enum** constant is 0, the ordinal value of the second **enum** constant is 1, and so on. Therefore, in the **enum** type `Grades`, the ordinal value of A is 0 and the ordinal value of C is 2.

Associated with **enum** type is a set of methods that can be used to work with **enum** types. Table 10-4 describes some of those methods.

Table 10-4 Some methods associated with **enum** types

Method	Description
`ordinal()`	Returns the ordinal value of an **enum** constant
`name()`	Returns the name of the **enum** value
`values()`	Returns the values of an **enum** type as a list

10

Example 10-3 illustrates how these methods work.

Example 10-3

```java
public class EnumExample1
{
    enum Grades {A, B, C, D, F};                          //Line 1

    enum Sports {Baseball, Basketball, Football,
                 Golf, Hockey, Soccer, Tennis};           //Line 2

    public static void main(String[] args)                //Line 3
    {
        Grades myGrade;                                   //Line 4
        Sports mySport;                                   //Line 5

        myGrade = Grades.A;                               //Line 6

        mySport = Sports.Basketball;                      //Line 7

        System.out.println("Line 8: My grade: "
                           + myGrade);                    //Line 8
        System.out.println("Line 9: The ordinal "
                           + "value of myGrade is "
                           + myGrade.ordinal());          //Line 9
        System.out.println("Line 10: myGrade name: "
                           + myGrade.name());             //Line 10

        System.out.println("Line 11: My sport: "
                           + mySport);                    //Line 11
        System.out.println("Line 12: The ordinal "
                           + "value of mySport is "
                           + mySport.ordinal());          //Line 12
        System.out.println("Line 13: mySport name: "
                           + mySport.name());             //Line 13

        System.out.println("Line 14: Sports: ");          //Line 14

        for (Sports sp : Sports.values())                 //Line 15
            System.out.println(sp + "'s ordinal "
                               + "value is "
                               + sp.ordinal());           //Line 16

        System.out.println();                             //Line 17
    }
}
```

Sample Run:
```
Line 8: My grade: A
Line 9: The ordinal value of myGrade is 0
Line 10: myGrade name: A
Line 11: My sport: Basketball
Line 12: The ordinal value of mySport is 1
Line 13: mySport name: Basketball
Line 14: Sports:
Baseball's ordinal value is 0
Basketball's ordinal value is 1
Football's ordinal value is 2
Golf's ordinal value is 3
Hockey's ordinal value is 4
Soccer's ordinal value is 5
Tennis's ordinal value is 6
```

The preceding program works as follows. The statements in Lines 1 and 2 define the **enum** type Grades and Sports, respectively. The statement in Line 4 declares myGrade to be a reference variable of the type Grades and the statement in Line 5 declares mySport to be a reference variable of the type Sports. The statement in Line 6 assigns the object A to myGrade and the statement in Line 7 assigns the object Basketball to mySport.

The statement in Line 8 outputs myGrade, the statement in Line 9 uses the method ordinal to output the ordinal value of myGrade, and the statement in Line 10 uses the method name to output the name of myGrade.

The statement in Line 11 outputs mySport, the statement in Line 12 uses the method ordinal to output the ordinal value of mySport, and the statement in Line 13 uses the method name to output the name of mySport.

The foreach loop in Line 15 outputs the value of Sports and their ordinal values. Note that the method values, in the expression Sports.values(), returns the value of the **enum** type Sport as a list. The loop control variable sp ranges over those values one-by-one, starting at the first value.

10

The beginning of this section noted that an **enum** type is a special type of class and the **enum** constants are reference variables to the objects of that **enum** type. Because each **enum** type is a class, in addition to the **enum** constants, it can also contain constructors, (**private**) data members, and methods. Before describing enumeration type or **enum** in more detail, let us note the following:

1. Enumeration types are defined using the keyword **enum** rather than **class**.

2. **enum** types are implicitly **final** because **enum** constants should not be modified.

3. **enum** constants are implicitly **static**.

4. Once an **enum** type is created, you can declare reference variables of that type, but you cannot instantiate objects using the operator **new**. In fact, an attempt to instantiate an object using the operator **new** will result in compilation error.

(Because **enum** objects cannot be instantiated using the operator **new**, the constructor, if any, of an enumeration *cannot* be **public**. In fact, the constructors of an **enum** type are implicitly **private**. Moreover, if a **class** is declared **final**, you cannot create new classes from this class. Chapter 11 explains how to create new classes from existing classes.)

The **enum** type `Grades` was defined earlier in this section. Let us redefine this **enum** type by adding constructors, data members, and methods. Consider the following definition:

```
public enum Grades
{
    A ("Range 90% to 100%"),
    B ("Range 80% to 89.99%"),
    C ("Range 70% to 79.99%"),
    D ("Range 60% to 69.99%"),
    F ("Range 0% to 59.99%");

    private final String range;

    private Grades()
    {
        range = "";
    }

    private Grades(String str)
    {
        range = str;
    }

    public String getRange()
    {
        return range;
    }
}
```

This **enum** type `Grades` contains the **enum** constants A, B, C, D, and F. It has a **private** named constant `range` of the type `String`, two constructors and the method `getRange`. Note that each `Grades` object has the data member `range`. Let us consider the statement:

```
A ("Range 90% to 100%")
```

This statement creates the `Grades` object, using the constructor with parameters, with the string `"Range 90% to 100%"` and assigns that object to the reference variable A. The method `getRange` is used to return the string contained in the object.

It is not necessary to specify the modifier **private** in the heading of the constructor. Each constructor is implicitly **private**. Therefore, the two constructors of the **enum** type Grades can be written as:

```
Grades()
{
    range = "";
}

Grades(String str)
{
    range = str;
}
```

Example 10-4 illustrates how the **enum** type Grades works.

Example 10-4

```
public class EnumExample2
{
    public static void main(String[] args)
    {
        System.out.println("Grade Ranges");        //Line 1

        for (Grades gr : Grades.values())          //Line 2
            System.out.println(gr + " "
                            + gr.getRange());       //Line 3

        System.out.println();                      //Line 4
    }
}
```

Sample Run:
```
Grade Ranges
A Range 90% to 100%
B Range 80% to 89.99%
C Range 70% to 79.99%
D Range 60% to 69.99%
F Range 0% to 59.99%
```

The foreach loop in Line 2 uses the method **values** to retrieve the **enum** constants as a list. The method **getRange** in Line 3 is used to retrieve the string contained in the Grades object.

The following programming example uses an **enum** type to create a program to play the game of rock, paper, and scissors.

PROGRAMMING EXAMPLE: THE ROCK, PAPER, AND SCISSORS GAME

Everyone is familiar with the rock, paper, and scissors game. Children often play this game. This game has two players, each of whom chooses one of the three objects: rock, paper, or scissors. If player 1 chooses rock and player 2 chooses paper, player 2 wins the game because paper covers the rock. The game is played according to the following rules:

- If both players choose the same object, this play is a tie.
- If one player chooses rock and the other chooses scissors, the player choosing the rock wins this play because the rock crushes the scissors.
- If one player chooses rock and the other chooses paper, the player choosing the paper wins this play because the paper covers the rock.
- If one player chooses scissors and the other chooses paper, the player choosing the scissors wins this play because the scissors cut the paper.

We write an interactive program that allows two players to play this game.

Input   This program has two types of input:
- The players' responses to play the game
- The players' choices

Output   The players' choices and the winner of each play. After the game is over, the total number of plays and the number of times that each player won should be output as well.

Problem Analysis and Algorithm Design

Two players play this game. Players enter their choices via the keyboard. Each player enters R or r for Rock, P or p for Paper, or S or s for Scissors. While the first player enters a choice, the second player looks elsewhere. Once both entries are in, if the entries are valid, the program outputs the players' choices and declares the winner of the play. The game continues until one of the players decides to quit. After the game ends, the program outputs the total number of plays and the number of times that each player won. This discussion translates into the following algorithm:

1. Provide a brief explanation of the game and how it is played.
2. Ask the users if they want to play the game.
3. Get plays for both players.
4. If the plays are valid, output the plays and the winner.
5. Update the total game count and winner count.
6. Repeat Steps 2–5, while the users continue to play the game.
7. Output the number of plays and times that each player won.

To describe the objects `Rock`, `Paper`, and `Scissor`, we define the following **enum** type:

```
public enum RockPaperScissors
{
    Rock ("Rock crushes scissors."),
    Paper ("Paper covers rock."),
    Scissors ("Scissors cuts paper.");

    private String msg;

    private RockPaperScissors()
    {
        msg = "";
    }

    private RockPaperScissors(String str)
    {
        msg = str;
    }

    public String getMessage()
    {
        return msg;
    }
}
```

Variables (Method main)   It is clear that you need the following variables in the method `main`:

```
int gameCount;      //to count the number of
                    //games played
int winCount1;      //to count the number of
                    //games won by player 1
int winCount2;      //to count the number of
                    //games won by player 2
int gameWinner;
char response;      //to get the user's response
                    //to play the game
char selection1;
char selection2;

RockPaperScissors play1;   //player1's selection
RockPaperScissors play2;   //player2's selection
```

This program is divided into the following methods, which the ensuing sections describe in detail.

- **`displayRules`**: This method displays some brief information about the game and its rules.

- **validSelection**: This method checks whether a player's selection is valid. The only valid selections are R, r, P, p, S, and s.
- **retrievePlay**: This method uses the entered choice (R, r, P, p, S, or s) and returns the appropriate object.
- **gameResult**: This method outputs the players' choices and the winner of the game.
- **winningObject**: This method determines and returns the winning object.
- **displayResults**: After the game is over, this method displays the final results.

Method displayRules   This method has no parameters. It consists only of output statements to explain the game and rules of play. Essentially, this method's definition is:

```java
public static void displayRules()
{
    System.out.println("Welcome to the game of Rock, "
                     + "Paper, and Scissors.");
    System.out.println("This is a game for two players. "
                     + "For each game, each player \n"
                     + "selects one of the "
                     + "objects, Rock, Paper or "
                     + "Scissors.");
    System.out.println("The rules for winning the "
                     + "game are: ");
    System.out.println("1. If both players select the "
                     + "same object, it is a tie.");
    System.out.println("2. Rock crushes Scissors: So the "
                     + "player who selects Rock wins.");
    System.out.println("3. Paper covers Rock: So the "
                     + "player who selects Paper wins.");
    System.out.println("4. Scissors cuts Paper: So the "
                     + "player who selects Scissors "
                     + "wins.");
    System.out.println("Enter R or r to select Rock, "
                     + "P or p to select Paper, \n"
                     + "and S or s to select Scissors.");
}
```

Method validSelection   This method checks whether a player's selection is valid. Let's use a **switch** statement to check for the valid selection. The definition of this method is:

```java
public static boolean validSelection(char selection)
{
    switch (selection)
    {
    case 'R':
    case 'r':
    case 'P':
    case 'p':
```

```
        case 'S':
        case 's': return true;
        default: return false;
        }
}
```

Method retrievePlay This method uses the entered choice (R, r, P, p, S, or s) and returns the appropriate object. This method thus has one parameter of the type **char**. It is a value-returning method and it returns a reference to a **RockPaperScissors** object.

The definition of the method **retrievePlay** is:

```
public static RockPaperScissors retrievePlay
                                (char selection)
{
    RockPaperScissors obj = null;

    switch (selection)
    {
    case 'R':
    case 'r': obj = RockPaperScissors.Rock;
            break;
    case 'P':
    case 'p': obj = RockPaperScissors.Paper;
            break;
    case 'S':
    case 's': obj = RockPaperScissors.Scissors;
    }

    return obj;
}
```

Method gameResult This method decides whether a game is a tie or which player is the winner. It outputs the players' selections and the winner of the game. This method has two parameters: player 1's choice and player 2's choice. It returns the number (1 or 2) of the winning player.

The definition of this method is:

```
public static int gameResult(RockPaperScissors play1,
                            RockPaperScissors play2)
{
    int winner = 0;

    RockPaperScissors winnerObject;

    if (play1 == play2)
    {
```

```
            winner = 0;
            System.out.println("Both players selected "
                                + play1
                                + ". This game is a tie.");
        }
    else
    {
            winnerObject = winningObject(play1, play2);

                //Output each player's choice
            System.out.println("Player 1 selected " + play1
                                + " and player 2 selected "
                                + play2 + ".");

                //Decide the winner
            if (play1 == winnerObject)
                winner = 1;
            else
                if (play2 == winnerObject)
                    winner = 2;

                //Output winning object's message
            System.out.println(winnerObject.getMessage());

                //Output the winner
            System.out.println("Player " + winner
                                + " wins this play.");

        }

    return winner;
}
```

Method winningObject   To decide the winner of the game, you look at the players' selections and then at the rules of the game. For example, if one player chooses **Rock** and another chooses **Paper**, the player who chose **Paper** wins. In other words, the winning object is **Paper**. The method **winningObject**, given two objects, decides and returns the winning object. Clearly, this method has two parameters of the type **RockPaperScissors**, and the value returned by this method is also of the type **RockPaperScissors**. The definition of this method is:

```
public static RockPaperScissors winningObject
                            (RockPaperScissors play1,
                             RockPaperScissors play2)
{
    if ((play1 == RockPaperScissors.Rock &&
         play2 == RockPaperScissors.Scissors)
        || (play2 == RockPaperScissors.Rock &&
```

```
                        play1 == RockPaperScissors.Scissors))
            return RockPaperScissors.Rock;
    else
        if ((play1 == RockPaperScissors.Rock &&
            play2 == RockPaperScissors.Paper)
            || (play2 == RockPaperScissors.Rock &&
                play1 == RockPaperScissors.Paper))
            return RockPaperScissors.Paper;
        else
            return RockPaperScissors.Scissors;
}
```

Method `displayResults`   After the game is over, this method outputs the final results—that is, the total number of plays and the number of plays won by each player. In the method `main`, the total number of plays is stored in the variable `gameCount`, the number of plays by player 1 is stored in the variable `winCount1`, and the number of plays won by player 2 is stored in the variable `winCount2`. This method has three parameters corresponding to these three variables. Essentially, the definition of this method is as follows:

```
public static void displayResults(int gCount, int wCount1,
                                  int wCount2)
{
    System.out.println("The total number of plays: "
                    + gCount);
    System.out.println("The number of plays won by "
                    + "player 1: " + wCount1);
    System.out.println("The number of plays won by "
                    + "player 2: " + wCount2);
}
```

We are now ready to write the algorithm for the method `main`.

Main Algorithm

1. Declare the variables.
2. Initialize the variables.
3. Display the rules.
4. Prompt the users to play the game.
5. Get the users' responses to play the game.
6. `while` (response is yes)
   {
   a. Prompt player 1 to make a selection.
   b. Get the play for player 1.
   c. Prompt player 2 to make a selection.
   d. Get the play for player 2.
   e. If both the plays are legal

          {

        i.   Retrieve both plays.

        ii.   Increment the total game count.

        iii. Declare the winner of the game.

        iv. Increment the winner's game win count by 1.

        }

    f. Prompt the users to determine whether they want to play again.

    g. Get the players' response.

    }

  7. Output the game results.

Program Listing

```java
import java.util.*;

public class GameRockPaperScissors
{
    static Scanner console = new Scanner(System.in);

    public static void main(String[] args)
    {
            //Step 1
        int gameCount;  //to count the number of
                        //games played
        int winCount1;  //to count the number of
                        //games won by player 1
        int winCount2;  //to count the number of
                        //games won by player 2
        int gameWinner;
        char response;   //to get the user's response
                         //to play the game
        char selection1;
        char selection2;

        RockPaperScissors play1;   //player1's selection
        RockPaperScissors play2;   //player2's selection

            //Initialize the variables; Step 2
        gameCount = 0;
        winCount1 = 0;
        winCount2 = 0;

        displayRules();                              //Step 3
```

```java
            System.out.print("Enter Y/y to play "
                        + "the game: ");                    //Step 4
            response = console.nextLine().charAt(0);        //Step 5
            System.out.println();

            while (response == 'Y' || response == 'y')       //Step 6
            {
                System.out.print("Player 1 enter "
                            + "your choice: ");              //Step 6a
                selection1 = console.nextLine().charAt(0);   //Step 6b
                System.out.println();

                System.out.print("Player 2 enter "
                            + "your choice: ");              //Step 6c
                selection2 = console.nextLine().charAt(0);   //Step 6d
                System.out.println();

                            //Step 6e
                if (validSelection(selection1) &&
                    validSelection(selection2))
                {
                    play1 = retrievePlay(selection1);
                    play2 = retrievePlay(selection2);
                    gameCount++;
                    gameWinner = gameResult(play1, play2);
                    if (gameWinner == 1)
                        winCount1++;
                    else
                        if (gameWinner == 2)
                            winCount2++;
                }//end if

                System.out.print("Enter Y/y to play "
                            + "the game: ");                 //Step 6f
                response = console.nextLine().charAt(0);     //Step 6g
                System.out.println();
            }//end while

            displayResults(gameCount, winCount1,
                        winCount2);                          //Step 7

    }//end main

    //Place the definitions of the methods displayRules,
    //validSelection, retrievePlay, winningObject,
    //gameResult, and displayResults here.
}
```

Sample Run: (In this sample run, the user input is shaded.)
```
Welcome to the game of Rock, Paper, and Scissors.
This is a game for two players. For each game, each player
selects one of the objects, Rock, Paper or Scissors.
The rules for winning the game are:
1. If both players select the same object, it is a tie.
2. Rock crushes Scissors: So the player who selects Rock wins.
3. Paper covers Rock: So the player who selects Paper wins.
4. Scissors cuts Paper: So the player who selects Scissors wins.
Enter R or r to select Rock, P or p to select Paper,
and S or s to select Scissors.
Enter Y/y to play the game: y

Player 1 enter your choice: R

Player 2 enter your choice: S

Player 1 selected Rock and player 2 selected Scissors.
Rock crushes scissors.
Player 1 wins this play.
Enter Y/y to play the game: Y

Player 1 enter your choice: S

Player 2 enter your choice: P

Player 1 selected Scissors and player 2 selected Paper.
Scissors cuts paper.
Player 1 wins this play.
Enter Y/y to play the game: Y

Player 1 enter your choice: R

Player 2 enter your choice: P

Player 1 selected Rock and player 2 selected Paper.
Paper covers rock.
Player 2 wins this play.
Enter Y/y to play the game: n

The total number of plays: 3
The number of plays won by player 1: 2
The number of plays won by player 2: 1
```

QUICK REVIEW

1. In addition to arrays, Java provides the **class** Vector to implement a list.

2. Unlike an array, the size of a **Vector** object can grow and shrink during program execution.

3. The **class** Vector contains various methods to manipulate data in a **Vector** object.

4. Some of the methods of the **class** Vector are addElement, insertElementAt, clone, contains, copyInto, elementAt, firstElement, lastElement, indexOf, isEmpty, lastIndexOf, removeAllElements, removeElementAt, setElementAt, and size.

5. JDK 5.0 Java has simplified the wrapping and unwrapping of primitive type values, called autoboxing and autounboxing of primitive types.

6. The **class** String contains various methods to manipulate a string.

7. Some of the methods of the **class** String are charAt, indexOf, compareTo, concat, equals, length, replace, substring, toLowerCase, toUpperCase, startsWith, endsWith, and regionMatches.

8. Java allows a programmer to create their own data types by specifying the values of that data type, called enumeration or **enum**.

9. Enum types and are defined using the keyword **enum**. The values that you specify for the data types are identifiers.

10. The values of an **enum** type are called enumeration or enum constants. Moreover, the values are enclosed in braces and separated by commas.

11. The **enum** constants within an **enum** type must be unique.

12. In reality, each **enum** type is a special type of class and the values belonging to the **enum** type are (special types of) objects of that class.

13. Once an **enum** type is defined, you can declare reference variables of that type.

14. Each **enum** constant in an **enum** type has a specific value, called the ordinal value. The ordinal value of the first **enum** constant is 0, the ordinal value of the second **enum** constant is 1, and so on.

15. Associated with **enum** type is a set of methods that can be used to work with **enum** types. Some of these methods are: ordinal, name, and values.

16. The method **ordinal** returns the ordinal value of an **enum** constant.

17. The method **name** returns the name of the **enum** value.

18. The method **values** returns the values of an **enum** type as a list.

19. Each **enum** type is a class. Therefore, in addition to the **enum** constants, it can also contain constructors, (**private**) data members, and methods. Enumeration types are defined using the keyword **enum** rather than **class**.

20. **enum** types are implicitly **final** because **enum** constants should not be modified.

21. **enum** constants are implicitly **static**.

10

22. Once an **enum** type is created, you can declare reference variables of that type, but you cannot instantiate objects using the operator **new**. In fact, an attempt to instantiate an object using the operator **new** will result in a compilation error.

23. Because **enum** objects cannot be instantiated using the operator **new**, the constructor, if any, of an enumeration *cannot* be **public**. In fact, the constructors of an **enum** type are implicitly **private**.

24. It is not necessary to specify the modifier **private** in the heading of the constructor. Each constructor is implicitly **private**.

EXERCISES

1. Mark the following statements as true or false.

    a. The elements of a **Vector** object are sorted.

    b. The **String** method **regionMatches** can be used to determine whether two strings have the same substring.

    c. Because an **enum** type is a class, an **enum** type is used using the keyword **class**.

    d. The following is a legal Java **enum** type:

    ```
    enum CSCStudents{Bill, Shelly, Lisa, Ron, Cindy, Shelly};
    ```

    e. Not all **enum** constants are **static**.

    f. The method **values** of an **enum** type returns the values of the **enum** type as a list.

2. What is the effect of the following statement?

    ```
    Vector<Double> list = new Vector<Double>();
    ```

3. Suppose that you have the following **Vector** object **list**:

    ```
    list = ["One", "Two", "Three", "Four"];
    ```

    What are the elements of **list** after the following statements execute?

    ```
    list.addElement("Five");
    list.insertElementAt("Six", 1);
    ```

4. Suppose that you have the following **Vector** object **names**:

    ```
    names = ["Gwen", "Donald", "Michael", "Peter", "Susan"];
    ```

    What are the elements of **names** after the following statements execute?

    ```
    names.removeElementAt(1);
    names.removeElement("Peter");
    ```

5. What is the output of the following program?

```java
import java.util.Vector;

public class Exercise_5
{
    public static void main(String[] arg)
    {
        Vector<String> strList = new Vector<String>();
        Vector<Integer> intList = new Vector<Integer>();

        strList.addElement("Hello");
        intList.addElement(10);
        strList.addElement("Happy");
        intList.addElement(20);
        strList.addElement("Sunny");
        intList.addElement(30);

        System.out.println("strList: " + strList);
        System.out.println("intList: " + intList);

        strList.insertElementAt("Joy", 2);

        intList.removeElement(20);

        System.out.println("strList: " + strList);
        System.out.println("intList: " + intList);
    }
}
```

6. Suppose that you have the following statements:

```java
String str;
String str1 = "programming";
String str2;
String str3;
```

```java
str = "Java programming: from problem analysis to program design";
```

What is the value of the following expressions?

a. `str.indexOf("analysis")`

b. `str.substring(5, 16)`

c. `str.startsWith("Java")`

d. `str.startsWith("J")`

e. `str.endsWith(".")`

f. `str.regionMatches(6, str1, 0, str1.length())`

g. `str.regionMatches(true, 31, "Analysis", 0, 8)`

10

7. Write Java statements that do the following:

   a. Define an **enum** type, Book, with the values Math, CSC, English, History, Physics, and Philosophy.

   b. Declare a reference variable myBook of the type Book.

   c. Assign Math to the variable myBook.

   d. Output the ordinal value of the **enum** constant CSC.

   e. Output the value of the variable myBook.

8. Given:

   ```
   enum Currency {Dollar, Pound, Frank, Lira, Mark};
   Currency myCurrency;
   ```

   which of the following statements are valid?

   a. myCurrency = Dollar;

   b. System.out.println(myCurrency.ordinal());

   c. myCurrency = (Currency)(myCurrency + 1);

   d. for (Currency cr : Currency.values())
           System.out.println(cr.ordinal());

9. Suppose that you have the following statements:

   ```
   enum Crop {Wheat, Corn, Rye, Barley, Oats};
   Crop crop;
   ```

   Circle the correct answer, true or false.

   a. Crop.Wheat.ordinal() is 1   (i) true (ii) false

   b. Crop.Rye.ordinal() > Crop.Wheat.ordinal()   (i) true (ii) false

   c. Crop[] cropList = Crop.values();   (i) valid (ii) invalid

   d.
      ```
      for (int i = 0; i < Crop.values().length; i++)
              System.out.print(Crop.values()[i] + " ");
          System.out.println();
      ```
      outputs: Wheat Corn Rye Barley Oats   (i) true (ii) false

PROGRAMMING EXERCISES

1. Redo Programming Exercise 8 in Chapter 9 so that students' names and their test scores are stored in **Vector** objects. (Assume that you do not know the number of students in the class.)

2. Write a program to keep track of a hardware store's inventory. The store sells various items. For each item in the store, the following information is kept: item ID, item name, number of pieces ordered, number of pieces currently in the store, number of pieces sold, manufacturer's price of the item, and the store's selling price. At the end of each week, the store manager wants to see a report in the following form:

```
                        Friendly Hardware Store

itemID  itemName       pOrdered pInStore pSold manufPrice sellingPrice
1111    Circular Saw        150      110    40      45.00       125.00
2222    Cooking Range        50       30    20     450.00       850.00
 .
 .
 .

Total Inventory: $#########.##
Total number of items in the store: _____
```

The total inventory is the total selling value of all the items currently in the store. The total number of items is the sum of the number of pieces of all the items in the store.

Your program must be menu driven, giving the user various choices such as: Check whether an item is in the store, sell an item, and print the report. After inputting the data, sort it according to the items' names. Also, after an item is sold, update the appropriate counts.

Initially, the number of pieces (of an item) in the store is the same as the number of pieces ordered, and the number of pieces of an item sold is zero. Input to the program is a file consisting of data in the following form:

```
itemID
itemName
pOrdered manufPrice sellingPrice
```

Use seven parallel vectors to store the information. The program must contain at least the following methods—a method to input the data into the vectors, a method to display the menu, a method to sell an item, and a method to print the report for the manager. After inputting the data, sort it according to the items' names.

3. The Programming Example Pig Latin Strings converts a string into pig Latin form, but it processes only one word. Rewrite the program so that it can be used to process a text of an unspecified length. If a word ends with a punctuation mark, in pig Latin form put the punctuation at the end of the string. For example, the pig Latin form of **Hello:** is **ello-Hay:**. Assume that the text contains the following punctuation marks: **,** (comma), **.** (period), **?** (question mark), **;** (semicolon), and **:** (colon).

10

4. a. Define an enumeration type, `Triangle`, which has the values `Scalene`, `Isosceles`, `Equilateral`, and `NoTriangle`.

b. Write a method, `TriangleShape`, that takes as parameters three numbers, each of which represents the length of a side of the triangle. The method should return the shape of the triangle. (*Note*: In a triangle, the sum of the lengths of any two sides is greater than the length of the third side.)

c. Write a program that prompts the user to input the length of the sides of a triangle and outputs the shape of the triangle.

INHERITANCE AND POLYMORPHISM

Classes were introduced in Chapter 8. Using classes, you can combine data and operations on that data in a single unit, a process called *encapsulation*. Through encapsulation, an object becomes a self-contained entity. Operations can (directly) access the data, but the internal state of an object cannot be manipulated directly.

In addition to implementing encapsulation, classes have other capabilities. For instance, you can create new classes from existing classes. This important feature encourages code reuse and saves programmers an enormous amount of time. In Java, you can relate two or more classes in more than one way. This chapter examines two common ways to relate classes:

- **Inheritance** ("is–a" relationship)

- **Composition** ("has–a" relationship)

INHERITANCE

Suppose that you want to design a **class**, `PartTimeEmployee`, to implement and process the characteristics of a part-time employee. The main features associated with a part-time employee are the name, pay rate, and number of hours worked. In Example 8-4 (Chapter 8), we designed the **class** `Person` to implement a person's name. Every part-time employee is a person. Therefore, rather than design the **class** `PartTimeEmployee` from scratch, we want to be able to extend the definition of the **class** `Person` from Example 8-4 by adding additional members (data and/or methods).

Of course, we do not want to make the necessary changes directly to the **class** `Person`—that is, edit the **class** `Person`, and add and/or delete members. We want to create the **class** `PartTimeEmployee` without making any physical changes to the **class** `Person`, by adding only the members that are necessary. For example, because the **class** `Person` already has data members to store the first name and last name, we will not include any such members in the **class** `PartTimeEmployee`. In fact, these data members will be *inherited* from the **class** `Person`. (We will design the **class** `PartTimeEmployee` in Example 11-3.)

In Chapter 8, we extensively studied and designed the **class** `Clock` to implement the time of day in a program. The **class** `Clock` has three data members (instance variables) to store the hours, minutes, and seconds. Certain applications, in addition to hours, minutes, and seconds, might also require that we store the time zone. In this case, we want to *extend* the definition of the **class** `Clock` and create a **class**, `ExtClock`, to accommodate this new information. That is, we want to derive the **class** `ExtClock` by adding a data member—`timeZone`—and the necessary method members to manipulate the time.

In Java, the mechanism that allows us to extend the definition of a class without making any physical changes to the class is the principle of **inheritance**. Inheritance implies an "is-a" relationship. For example, every (part-time) employee is a person. Similarly, every extended clock, `ExtClock`, is a `clock`.

Inheritance lets you create new classes from existing classes. Any new class that you create from an existing class is called a **subclass** or **derived class**; existing classes are called **superclasses** or **base classes**. The subclass inherits the properties of the superclass. Rather than create completely new classes from scratch, you can take advantage of inheritance and reduce software complexity.

Inheritance can be viewed as a tree-like, or hierarchical, structure wherein a superclass is shown with its subclasses. Consider the diagram in Figure 11-1, which shows the relationship between various shapes.

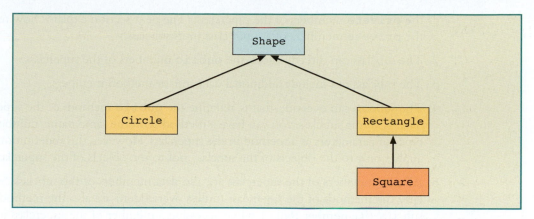

Figure 11-1 Inheritance hierarchy

In this diagram, `Shape` is the superclass. The **class**es `Circle` and `Rectangle` are derived from `Shape`, and the **class** `Square` is derived from `Rectangle`. Every `Circle` and every `Rectangle` is a `Shape`. Every `Square` is a `Rectangle`.

The general syntax to derive a class from an existing class is:

```
modifier(s) class ClassName extends ExistingClassName modifier(s)
{
    memberList
}
```

In Java, **extends** is a reserved word.

Example 11-1

Suppose that we have defined a **class** called `Shape`. The following statements specify that the **class** `Circle` is derived from `Shape`:

```
public class Circle extends Shape
{
    .
    .
    .
}
```

The following facts about superclasses and subclasses should be kept in mind:

1. The **private** members of the superclass are **private** to the superclass; hence, the members of the subclass cannot directly access them. In other words, when you write the definitions of the methods of the subclass, you cannot directly access

the **private** members of the superclass. (The next section explains how to access the **private** members of a super class in its subclass.)

2. The subclass can directly access the **public** members of the superclass.

3. The subclass can include additional data and/or method members.

4. The subclass can override, that is, redefine the **public** methods of the superclass. That is, in the subclass, you can have a method with the same name, number, and types of parameters as a method in the superclass. However, this redefinition applies only to the objects of the subclass, not to the objects of the superclass.

5. All data members of the superclass are also data members of the subclass. Similarly, the methods of the superclass (unless overridden) are also the methods of the subclass. (Remember Rule 1 when accessing a member of the superclass in the subclass.)

Each subclass, in turn, may become a superclass for a future subclass. Inheritance can be either single or multiple. In **single inheritance**, the subclass is derived from a single superclass; in **multiple inheritance**, the subclass is derived from more than one superclass. Java only supports single inheritance; that is, in Java a class can *extend* the definition of only one class.

The next sections describe two important issues related to inheritance. The first issue is using the methods of a superclass in its subclass. While discussing this issue, we will also address how to access the **private** (data) members of the superclass in the subclass. The second key inheritance issue is related to the constructor. The constructor of a subclass *cannot directly access* the **private** data members of the superclass. Thus, you must ensure that **private** data members that are inherited from the superclass are initialized when a constructor of the subclass executes.

Using Methods of the Superclass in a Subclass

Suppose that a **class** SubClass is derived from a **class** SuperClass. Further assume that both SubClass and SuperClass have some data members. It then follows that the data members of the **class** SubClass are its own data members, together with the data members of SuperClass. Similarly, in addition to its own methods, the subclass also inherits the methods of the superclass. The subclass can give some of its methods the same name as given by the superclass. For example, suppose that SuperClass contains a method, print, that prints the values of the data members of SuperClass. SubClass contains data members in addition to the data members inherited from SuperClass. Suppose that you want to include a method in SubClass that prints the data members of SubClass. You can give any name to this method. However, in the **class** SubClass, you can also name this method print (the same name used by SuperClass). This is called **overriding**, or **redefining**, the method of the superclass.

To override a **public** method of the superclass in the subclass, the corresponding method in the subclass must have the same name, the same type, and the same formal parameter list. If the corresponding method in the superclass and the subclass has the same name but different parameters, then this is method *overloading* in the subclass, which is also allowed.

Whether you override or overload a method of the superclass in the subclass, you must know how to specify a call to the method of the superclass that has the same name as used by a method of the subclass. We illustrate these concepts with the help of the following example.

Consider the definition of the following class (see Figure 11-2):

```java
public class Rectangle
{
    private double length;
    private double width;

    public Rectangle()
    {
        length = 0;
        width = 0;
    }

    public Rectangle(double l, double w)
    {
        setDimension(l, w);
    }

    public void setDimension(double l, double w)
    {
        if (l >= 0)
            length = l;
        else
            length = 0;

        if (w >= 0)
            width = w;
        else
            width = 0;
    }

    public double getLength()
    {
        return length;
    }

    public double getWidth()
    {
        return width;
    }
```

11

```java
    public double area()
    {
        return length * width;
    }

    public double perimeter()
    {
        return 2 * (length + width);
    }

    public void print()
    {
        System.out.print("Length = "  + length
                        + "; Width = " + width);
    }
}
```

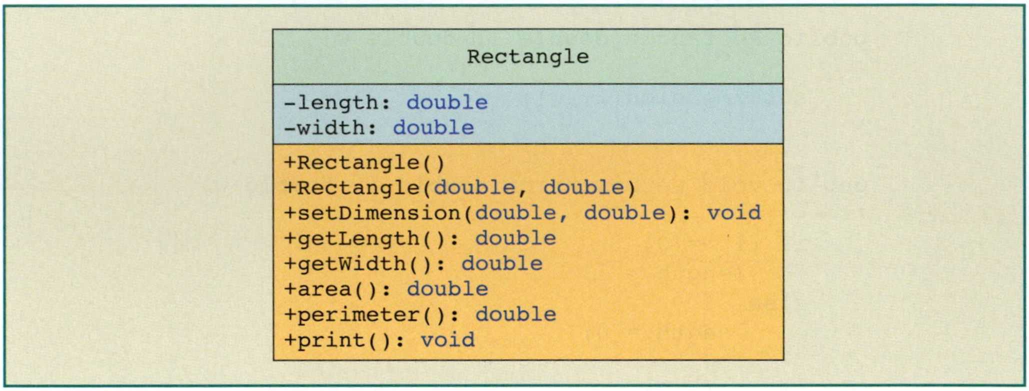

```
                    Rectangle

    -length: double
    -width: double

    +Rectangle()
    +Rectangle(double, double)
    +setDimension(double, double): void
    +getLength(): double
    +getWidth(): double
    +area(): double
    +perimeter(): double
    +print(): void
```

Figure 11-2   UML class diagram of the **class** Rectangle

The **class** Rectangle has 10 members.

Now consider the following definition of the **class** Box, derived from the **class** Rectangle (see Figure 11-3):

```java
public class Box extends Rectangle
{
    private double height;

    public Box()
    {
        //The definition is as given later in this section
    }
```

```
public Box(double l, double w, double h)
{
    //The definition is as given below
}

public void setDimension(double l, double w, double h)
{
    //Sets the length, width, and height of the box
    //The definition is as given below
}

public double getHeight()
{
    return height;
}

public double area()
{
    //Returns the surface area
    //The definition is as given below
}

public double volume()
{
    //Returns the volume
    //The definition is as given below
}

public void print()
{
    //Outputs length, width, and height of the box
    //The definition is as given below
}
}
```

11

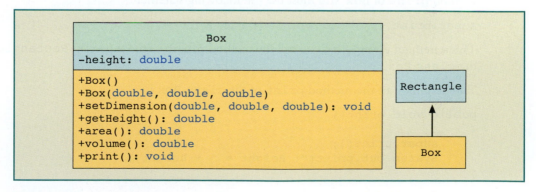

Figure 11-3   UML class diagram of the **class** Box and the inheritance hierarchy

From the definition of the **class** Box, it is clear that the **class** Box is derived from the **class** Rectangle. Therefore, all **public** members of Rectangle are **public** members of Box. The **class** Box overrides the methods print and area, and overloads the method setDimension.

In general, when writing the definitions of the methods of a subclass to specify a call to a **public** method of a superclass, you do the following:

- If the subclass overrides a **public** method of the superclass, then you specify a call to that **public** method of the superclass by using the reserved word **super** followed by the dot operator followed by the method name with an appropriate parameter list.

- If the subclass does not override a **public** method of the superclass, you can specify a call to that **public** method by using the name of the method and an appropriate parameter list.

Next, let's write the definition of the method print of the **class** Box.

The **class** Box has three data members: length, width, and height. The method print of the **class** Box prints the values of these three data members. To write the definition of the method print of the **class** Box, remember the following:

- The instance variables length and width are **private** members of the **class** Rectangle and so cannot be directly accessed in the **class** Box. Therefore, when writing the definition of the method print of the **class** Box, you cannot directly reference length and width.

- The instance variables length and width of the **class** Rectangle are accessible in the **class** Box through the **public** methods of the **class** Rectangle. Therefore, when writing the definition of the method print of the **class** Box, you first call the method print of the **class** Rectangle to print the values of length and width. After printing the values of length and width, you output the values of height.

As remarked above, to call the method print of Rectangle in the definition of the method print of Box, you must use the following statement:

```
super.print();
```

This statement ensures that you call the method print of the superclass Rectangle, not of the **class** Box.

The definition of the method print of the **class** Box is:

```
public void print()
{
    super.print();
    System.out.print("; Height = " + height);
}
```

Let's write the definitions of the remaining methods of the **class** Box.

```
public void setDimension(double l, double w, double h)
{
    super.setDimension(l, w);

    if (h >= 0)
        height = h;
    else
        height = 0;
}
```

 Notice that the **class** Box overloads the method setDimension of the **class** Rectangle. Therefore, in the preceding definition of the method setDimension of the **class** Box, you can also specify a call to the method setDimension of the **class** Rectangle without the reserved word **super** and the dot operator.

The definition of the method getHeight is:

```
public double getHeight()
{
    return height;
}
```

The method **area** of the **class** Box determines the surface area of the box. To do so, we need to access the length and width of the box, which are declared as **private** members of the **class** Rectangle. Therefore, we use the methods getLength and getWidth of the **class** Rectangle to retrieve the length and width, respectively. Because the **class** Box does not override the methods getLength and getWidth, we call these methods of the **class** Rectangle without using the reserved word **super**.

```
public double area()
{
    return 2 * (getLength() * getWidth()
             + getLength() * height
             + getWidth() * height);
}
```

The method **volume** of the **class** Box determines the volume of the box. To determine the box's volume, you multiply the length, width, and height of the box or multiply the area of the base of the box by its height. Let's write the definition of the method **volume** by using the second alternative. To do so, you can use the method **area** of the **class** Rectangle to determine the area of the base. Because the **class** Box overrides the method **area**, to spec–ify a call to the method **area** of the **class** Rectangle, we use the reserved word **super**, as shown in the following definition.

```
public double volume()
{
    return super.area() * height;
}
```

In the next section, we discuss how to specify a call to the constructor of the superclass when writing the definition of a constructor of the subclass.

 In the definitions of the **class**es Rectangle and Box you can replace the method print with the method toString. This allows you to use the object System.out and its methods print, println, or printf to output the value of an object. We included the method print in the **class**es Rectangle and Box to explicitly illustrate the redefinition of a super class method in its subclass. The Web site accompanying this book contains the modified definition of these classes.

Constructors of the Superclass and Subclass

A subclass can have its own **private** data members, so a subclass also can have its own constructors. A constructor typically serves to initialize the instance variables. When we instantiate a subclass object, this object inherits the instance variables of the superclass, but the subclass object cannot directly access the **private** instance variables of the superclass. The same is true for the methods of a subclass. That is, the methods of the subclass cannot directly access the **private** members of the superclass.

As a consequence, the constructors of the subclass can (directly) initialize only the instance variables of the subclass. Thus, when a subclass object is instantiated, to initialize the (**private**) instance variables it must also automatically execute one of the constructors of the superclass. A call to a constructor of the superclass is specified in the definition of a subclass constructor by using the reserved word **super**.

In the preceding section we defined the **class** Rectangle and derived the **class** Box from it. Moreover, we illustrated how to override a method of the **class** Rectangle. We now discuss how to write the definitions of the constructors of the **class** Box.

The **class** Rectangle has two constructors and two instance variables. The **class** Box has three instance variables: length, width, and height. The instance variables length and width are inherited from the **class** Rectangle.

To write the definitions of the constructors of the **class** Box, we first write the definition of the default constructor of the **class** Box. Recall that if a class contains the default constructor and no values are specified during object instantiation, the default constructor executes and initializes the object. Because the **class** Rectangle contains the default constructor, when we write the definition of the default constructor of the **class** Box, we use the reserved word **super** with no parameters, as shown in the following code. Moreover, a call to the (default) constructor of the superclass *must* be the first statement.

```
public Box()
{
    super();
    height = 0;
}
```

Next, we discuss how to write the definitions of the constructors with parameters.

To specify a call to a constructor with parameters of the superclass, we use the reserved word **super** with the appropriate parameters. A call to the constructor of the superclass must be the first statement.

Consider the following definition of the constructor with parameters of the **class** Box:

```
public Box(double l, double w, double h)
{
    super(l, w);
    height = h;
}
```

This definition specifies the constructor of **Rectangle** with two parameters. When this constructor of **Box** executes, it triggers the execution of the constructor with two parameters of the type **double** of the **class** Rectangle.

As an exercise, try writing the complete definition of the **class** Box.

Consider the following statements:

```
Rectangle myRectangle = new Rectangle(5, 3);              //Line 1
Box myBox = new Box(6, 5, 4);                             //Line 2
```

The statement in Line 1 creates the **Rectangle** object **myRectangle**. Thus, the object **myRectangle** has two instance variables: **length** and **width**. The statement in Line 2 creates the **Box** object **myBox**. Thus, the object **myBox** has three instance variables: **length**, **width**, and **height**. See Figure 11-4.

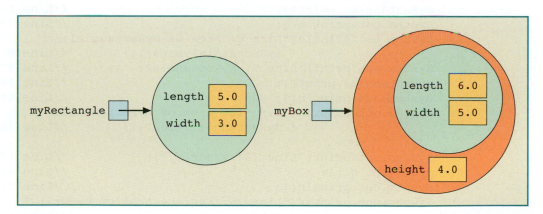

Figure 11-4   Objects **myRectangle** and **myBox**

Consider the following statements:

```
myRectangle.print();                                     //Line 3
System.out.println();                                    //Line 4
myBox.print();                                           //Line 5
System.out.println();                                    //Line 6
```

In the statement in Line 3, the method `print` of the **class** Rectangle is executed; in the statement in Line 5, the method `print` associated with the **class** Box is executed. Recall that if a subclass overrides a method of the superclass, the redefinition applies only to the objects of the subclass. Thus, the output of the statement in Line 3 is:

```
Length = 5.0; Width = 3.0
```

The output of the statement in Line 5 is:

```
Length = 6.0; Width = 5.0; Height = 4.0
```

The program in Example 11-2 shows how the objects of a superclass and a base class behave.

Example 11-2

Consider the following Java application program.

```java
public class SubClassSuperClassMethods
{
    public static void main(String[] args)
    {
        Rectangle myRectangle1 = new Rectangle();        //Line 1
        Rectangle myRectangle2 = new Rectangle(8, 6);     //Line 2

        Box myBox1 = new Box();                           //Line 3
        Box myBox2 = new Box(10, 7, 3);                   //Line 4

        System.out.print("Line 5: myRectangle1: ");        //Line 5
        myRectangle1.print();                             //Line 6
        System.out.println();                             //Line 7
        System.out.println("Line 8: Area of myRectangle1: "
                        + myRectangle1.area());            //Line 8
        System.out.print("Line 9: myRectangle2: ");        //Line 9
        myRectangle2.print();                             //Line 10
        System.out.println();                             //Line 11
        System.out.println("Line 12: Area of myRectangle2: "
                        + myRectangle2.area());            //Line 12

        System.out.print("Line 13: myBox1: ");             //Line 13
        myBox1.print();                                   //Line 14
        System.out.println();                             //Line 15
        System.out.println("Line 16: Surface Area of myBox1: "
                        + myBox1.area());                  //Line 16
        System.out.println("Line 17: Volume of myBox1: "
                        + myBox1.volume());                //Line 17

        System.out.print("Line 18: myBox2: ");             //Line 18
        myBox2.print();                                   //Line 19
        System.out.println();                             //Line 20
        System.out.println("Line 21: Surface Area of myBox2: "
                        + myBox2.area());                  //Line 21
```

```
        System.out.println("Line 22: Volume of myBox2: "
                    + myBox2.volume());                    //Line 22
    }
}
```

Sample Run:
```
Line 5: myRectangle1: Length = 0.0; Width = 0.0
Line 8: Area of myRectangle1: 0.0
Line 9: myRectangle2: Length = 8.0; Width = 6.0
Line 12: Area of myRectangle2: 48.0
Line 13: myBox1: Length = 0.0; Width = 0.0; Height = 0.0
Line 16: Surface Area of myBox1: 0.0
Line 17: Volume of myBox1: 0.0
Line 18: myBox2: Length = 10.0; Width = 7.0; Height = 3.0
Line 21: Surface Area of myBox2: 242.0
Line 22: Volume of myBox2: 210.0
```

The preceding program works as follows: The statement in Line 1 creates the **Rectangle** object **myRectangle1** and initializes its instance variables to 0. The statement in Line 2 creates the **Rectangle** object **myRectangle2** and initializes its instance variables **length** and **width** to **8.0** and **6.0**, respectively.

The statement in Line 3 creates the **Box** object **myBox1** and initializes its instance variables to 0. The statement in Line 4 creates the **Box** object **myBox2** and initializes its instance variables **length**, **width**, and **height** to **10.0**, **7.0**, and **3.0**, respectively.

The statements in Lines 5 through 8 output the length, width, and area of **myRectangle1**. Because the instance variables of **myRectangle1** are initialized to 0 by the default constructor, the area of the rectangle is **0.0** square units, as shown in the output of Line 8.

The statements in Lines 9 through 12 output the length, width, and area of **myRectangle2**. Because the instance variables **length** and **width** of **myRectangle2** are initialized to **8.0** and **6.0**, respectively, by the constructor with parameters, this rectangle's area is **48.0** square units. See the output of Line 12.

The statements in Lines 13 through 17 output the length, width, height, surface **area**, and **volume** of **myBox1**. Because the instance variables of **myBox1** are initialized to **0.0** by the default constructor, this box's surface area is **0.0** square units and the volume is **0.0** cubic units. See the output of Lines 16 and 17.

The statements in Lines 18 through 22 output the **length**, **width**, **height**, surface **area**, and **volume** of **myBox2**. Because the instance variables **length**, **width**, and **height** of **myBox2** are initialized to **10.0**, **7.0**, and **3.0**, respectively, by the constructor with parameters, this box's surface area is **242.0** square units and the volume is **210.0** cubic units. See the output of Lines 21 and 22.

From the output of this program, it follows that the redefinition of the methods **print** and **area** in the **class** Box applies only to the objects of the type **Box**.

11

The Web site accompanying this book contains the modified definitions of the `class`es `Rectangle` and `Box`, in which the method `print` is replaced by the method `toString`. The folder `Example 11_2 Modified` contains these modified definitions as well as the modified test program given in Example 11-2.

Next, we give another example illustrating how to create a subclass.

Example 11-3

Suppose that you want to define a class to group the attributes of an employee. There are full-time employees and part-time employees. Part-time employees are paid based on the number of hours worked and an hourly rate. Suppose that you want to define a class to keep track of a part-time employee's information such as the name, pay rate, and hours worked. You can then print the employee's name, together with his or her wages. Recall that Example 8-4 (Chapter 8) defined the **class** `Person` to store the first name and the last name together with the necessary operations on **name**. Because every employee is a person, we can define a **class** `PartTimeEmployee` derived from the **class** `Person`. (See Figure 11-5.) You can also override the method `toString` of the **class** `Person` to print the appropriate information.

The members of the **class** `PartTimeEmployee` are as follows:

Instance Variables:

```java
private double payRate;     //store the pay rate
private double hoursWorked; //store the hours worked
```

Instance Methods:

```java
public String toString()
        //Method to return the string consisting of the
        //first name, last name, and the wages in the form:
        //firstName lastName wages are $$$$.$$

public void setNameRateHours(String first, String last,
                              double rate, double hours)
        //Method to set the first name, last name, payRate,
        //and hoursWorked according to the parameters
        //The parameters first and last are passed to the
        //superclass.
        //Postcondition: firstName = first; lastName = last;
        //               payRate = rate; hoursWorked = hours;

public double getPayRate()
        //Method to return the pay rate
        //Postcondition: The value of payRate is returned.

public double getHoursWorked()
        //Method to return the number of hours worked
        //Postcondition: The value of hoursWorked is returned.
```

```java
public double calculatePay()
     //Method to calculate and return the wages

public PartTimeEmployee(String first, String last,
                        double rate, double hours)
     //Constructor with parameters
     //Sets the first name, last name, payRate, and
     //hoursWorked according to the parameters.
     //Parameters first and last are passed to the
     //superclass.
     //Postcondition: firstName = first; lastName = last;
     //               payRate = rate; hoursWorked = hours;

public PartTimeEmployee()
     //Default constructor
     //Sets the first name, last name, payRate, and
     //hoursWorked to the default values.
     //The first name and last name are initialized to an empty
     //string by the default constructor of the superclass.
     //Postcondition: firstName = ""; lastName = "";
     //               payRate = 0; hoursWorked = 0;
```

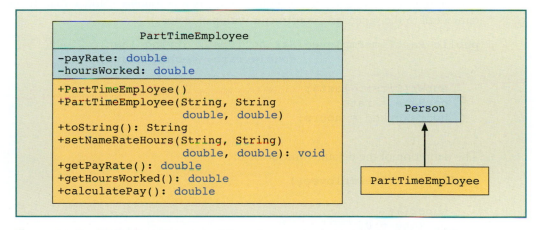

Figure 11-5   UML class diagram of the **class** PartTimeEmployee and the inheritance hierarchy

The definitions of the member methods of the **class** PartTimeEmployee are as follows:

```java
public String toString()
{
    return (super.toString() + "'s wages are: $"
        + String.format("%.2f", calculatePay()));
}
```

```java
public double getPayRate()
{
    return payRate;
}

public double getHoursWorked()
{
    return hoursWorked;
}

public double calculatePay()
{
    return (payRate * hoursWorked);
}

public void setNameRateHours(String first, String last,
                            double rate, double hours)
{
    setName(first, last);
    payRate = rate;
    hoursWorked = hours;
}
```

The definition of the constructor with parameters is as follows. (Notice that the body contains a call to the superclass's constructor with parameters.)

```java
public PartTimeEmployee(String first, String last,
                        double rate, double hours)
{
    super(first, last);
    payRate = rate;
    hoursWorked = hours;
}
```

The definition of the default constructor is:

```java
public PartTimeEmployee()
{
    super();
    payRate = 0;
    hoursWorked = 0;
}
```

The definition of the **class** PartTimeEmployee is:

```java
public class PartTimeEmployee extends Person
{
    private double payRate;      //store the pay rate
    private double hoursWorked; //store the hours worked

        //Default constructor
        //Sets the first name, last name, payRate, and
```

```
    //hoursWorked to the default values.
    //The first name and last name are initialized to an empty
    //string by the default constructor of the superclass.
    //Postcondition: firstName = ""; lastName = "";
    //                payRate = 0; hoursWorked = 0;
public PartTimeEmployee()
{
    super();
    payRate = 0;
    hoursWorked = 0;
}


    //Constructor with parameters
    //Sets the first name, last name, payRate, and
    //hoursWorked according to the parameters.
    //The parameters first and last are passed to the
    //superclass.
    //Postcondition: firstName = first; lastName = last;
    //                payRate = rate; hoursWorked = hours;
public PartTimeEmployee(String first, String last,
                        double rate, double hours)
{
    super(first, last);
    payRate = rate;
    hoursWorked = hours;
}


    //Method to return the string consisting of the
    //first name, last name, and the wages in the form:
    //firstName lastName wages are $$$$.$$
public String toString()
{
    return (super.toString() + "'s wages are: $"
        + String.format("%.2f", calculatePay()));

}


    //Method to calculate and return the wages
public double calculatePay()
{
    return (payRate * hoursWorked);
}


    //Method to set the first name, last name, payRate,
    //and hoursWorked according to the parameters.
    //The parameters first and last are passed to the
    //superclass.
    //Postcondition: firstName = first; lastName = last;
    //                payRate = rate; hoursWorked = hours;
```

11

```java
    public void setNameRateHours(String first, String last,
                                 double rate, double hours)

    {
        setName(first, last);
        payRate = rate;
        hoursWorked = hours;
    }


    //Method to return the pay rate
    //Postcondition: The value of payRate is returned.
    public double getPayRate()
    {
        return payRate;
    }


    //Method to return the number of hours worked
    //Postcondition: The value of hoursWorked is returned.
    public double getHoursWorked()
    {
        return hoursWorked;
    }
}
```

 The definition of the subclass is typically placed in a separate file. Recall that the name of the file must be the same as the name of the class, and the file extension must be `java`.

Protected Members of a Class

The **private** members of a class are **private** to the class and cannot be directly accessed outside the class. Only methods of that class can access the **private** members. As discussed previously, the subclass cannot access the **private** members of the superclass. However, it is sometimes necessary for a subclass to access a **private** member of a superclass. If you make a **private** member become **public**, then anyone can access that member. Recall that the members of a class are classified into three categories: **public**, **private**, and **protected**. So, if a member of a superclass needs to be accessed in a subclass and still prevent its direct access outside the class, you must declare that member using the modifier **protected**. Thus, the accessibility of a **protected** member of a class falls between **public** and **private**. A subclass can directly access the **protected** member of a superclass.

To summarize, if a member of a superclass needs to be accessed directly (only) by a subclass, that member is declared using the modifier **protected**.

Example 11-4 illustrates how the methods of a subclass can directly access a **protected** member of the superclass.

Example 11-4

Consider the following definitions of the **class**es BClass and DClass. (See Figures 11-6 and 11-7.)

```java
public class BClass
{
    protected char bCh;
    private double bX;

        //Default constructor
    public BClass()
    {
        bCh = '*';
        bX = 0.0;
    }

        //constructor with parameters
    public BClass(char ch, double u)
    {
        bCh = ch;
        bX = u;
    }

    public void setData(double u)
    {
        bX = u;
    }

    public void setData(char ch, double u)
    {
        bCh = ch;
        bX = u;
    }

    public String toString()
    {
        return("Superclass: bCh = " + bCh + ", bX = " + bX + '\n');
    }
}
```

11

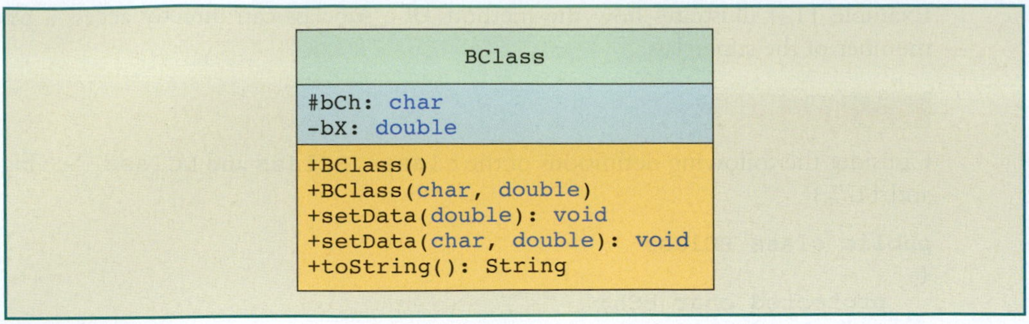

```
                    ┌─────────────────────────────────┐
                    │             BClass              │
                    ├─────────────────────────────────┤
                    │ #bCh: char                      │
                    │ -bX: double                     │
                    ├─────────────────────────────────┤
                    │ +BClass()                       │
                    │ +BClass(char, double)           │
                    │ +setData(double): void          │
                    │ +setData(char, double): void    │
                    │ +toString(): String             │
                    └─────────────────────────────────┘
```

Figure 11-6   UML class diagram of the **class** BClass

The definition of the **class** BClass contains the **protected** data member bCh of the type **char**, and the **private** data member bX of the type **double**. It also contains an overloaded method setData; one version of setData is used to set both the data members, and the other version is used to set only the **private** data members. The **class** BClass also has a constructor with default parameters.

Next, we derive a **class** DClass from the **class** BClass. The **class** DClass contains a **private** data member dA of the type **int**. It also contains a method setData, with three parameters, and the method toString.

```java
public class DClass extends BClass
{
    private int dA;

    public DClass()
    {
        //The definition as shown later in this section
    }

    public DClass(char ch, double v, int a)
    {
        //The definition as shown later in this section
    }

    public void setData(char ch, double v, int a)
    {
        //The definition as shown later in this section
    }

    public String toString()
    {
        //The definition as shown later in this section
    }
}
```

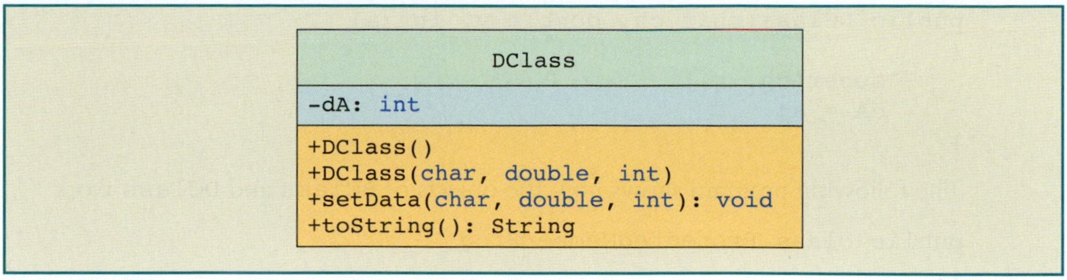

Figure 11-7   UML class diagram of the **class** DClass

Let's now write the definition of the method setData of the **class** DClass. Because bCh is a **protected** data member of the **class** BClass, it can be directly accessed in the definition of the method setData. However, because bX is a **private** data member of the **class** BClass, the method setData of the **class** DClass *cannot* directly access bX. Thus, the method setData of the **class** DClass must set bX by using the method setData of the **class** BClass. The definition of the method setData of the **class** DClass can be written as follows:

```
public void setData(char ch, double v, int a)
{
    super.setData(v);

    bCh = ch;    //initialize bCh using the assignment
                 //statement
    dA = a;
}
```

Note that the definition of the method setData contains the statement:

```
super.setData(v);
```

to call the method setData with one parameter (of the superclass), to set the data member bX, and then directly set the value of bCh.

Next, let's write the definition of the method toString (of the **class** DClass).

```
public String toString()
{
    return (super.toString() + "Subclass dA = " + dA + '\n');
}
```

The constructors' definitions are:

```
public DClass()
{
    super();
    dA = 0;
}
```

11

```java
public DClass(char ch, double v, int a)
{
    super(ch, v);
    dA = a;
}
```

The following program shows how the objects of **BClass** and **DClass** work.

```java
public class ProtectedMemberProg
{
    public static void main(String[] args)
    {
        BClass bObject = new BClass();              //Line 1

        DClass dObject = new DClass();              //Line 2

        System.out.println("Line 3: " + bObject);   //Line 3
        System.out.println("Line 4: ***   "
                            + "Subclass object ***"); //Line 4

        dObject.setData('&', 2.5, 7);               //Line 5

        System.out.println("Line 6: " + dObject);   //Line 6
    }
}
```

Sample Run:
```
Line 3: Superclass: bCh = *, bX = 0.0

Line 4: ***   Subclass object ***
Line 6: Superclass: bCh = &, bX = 2.5
Subclass dA = 7
```

When you write the definitions of the methods of the **class DClass**, the **protected** data member **bCh** can be accessed directly. However, **DClass** objects *cannot* directly access bCh. That is, the following statement is illegal (it is, in fact, a syntax error):

```java
dObject.bCh = '&';   //Illegal
```

In an inheritance hierarchy, the **public** and **protected** members of a superclass are directly accessible, in a subclass, across any number of generations, that is, at any level. To be explicit, if **class Three** is derived from **class Two** and **class Two** is derived from **class One**, then the **protected** and **public** members of **class One** are directly accessible in **class Two** as well as in **class Three**. Moreover, even though the (**public** and) **protected** data members of a super class are directly accessible in a subclass, in the inheritance hierarchy, it should be the responsibility of the superclass to properly initialize these data members.

---

class Object

In Chapter 8, we defined the **class** Clock and later included the method toString to return the time as a string. When we included the method toString, we noted that every Java class (built-in or user-defined) is automatically provided the method toString. If a user-defined class does not provide its own definition of the method toString, then the default definition of the method toString is invoked. The methods print and println use the method toString to determine what to print. As shown in Chapter 8, the default definition of the method toString returns the class name followed by the hash code of the object. You might ask, where is the method toString defined?

The method toString comes from the Java **class** Object, and is a **public** member of this class. In Java, if you define a class and do not use the reserved word **extends** to derive it from an existing class, then the class you define is automatically considered to be derived from the **class** Object. Therefore, the **class** Object directly or indirectly becomes the superclass of every class in Java. From this, it follows that the definition of the **class** Clock (previously given in Chapter 8):

```
public class Clock
{
    //Declare the instance variables as given in Chapter 8
    //The definition of the instance methods as given in Chapter 8
    //...
}
```

is, in fact, equivalent to the following:

```
public class Clock extends Object
{
    //Declare the instance variables as given in Chapter 8
    //The definition of the instance methods as given in Chapter 8
    //...
}
```

Using the mechanism of inheritance, every **public** member of the **class** Object can be overridden and/or invoked by every object of any class type. Table 11-1 describes some of the constructors and methods of the **class** Object.

11

Table 11-1 Some of the Constructors and Methods of the **class** Object

```
public Object()
  //Constructor
```

```
public String toString()
  //Method to return a string to describe the object
```

```
public boolean equals(Object obj)
  //Method to determine whether two objects are the same
  //Returns true if the object invoking the method and the object
  //specified by the parameter obj refer to the same memory space;
  //otherwise it returns false
```

```
protected Object clone()
  //Method to return a reference to a copy of the object invoking
  //this method
```

```
protected void finalize()
  //The body of this method is invoked when the object goes out
  //of scope
```

Because every Java class is directly or indirectly derived from the **class** Object, it follows from Table 11-1 that the method **toString** becomes a **public** member of every Java class. Therefore, if a class does not override this method, whenever this method is invoked, the method's default definition executes. As indicated previously, the default definition returns the class name followed by the hash code of the object as a string. Usually, every Java class overrides the method **toString**. The **class** String overrides it so that the string stored in the object is returned. The **class** Clock overrides it so that the string containing the time in the form hh:mm:ss is returned. Similarly, the **class** Person also overrides it.

The method **equals** is also a very useful method of the **class** Object. This method's definition, as given in the **class** Object, determines whether the object invoking this method and the object passed as a parameter refer to the same memory space, that is, whether they point to data in the same memory space. The method **equals** determines whether the two objects are aliases. As in the case of the method **toString**, to implement its own needs, every user-defined **class** also usually overrides the method **equals**. For example, in the **class** Clock, the method **equals** was overridden to determine whether the instance variables (hr, min, and sec) of two Clock objects contained the same value.

As usual, the default constructor is used to initialize an object. The method **clone** makes a copy of the object and returns a reference to the copy. However, the method **clone** makes only a memberwise (that is, field by field) copy of the object. In other words, the method **clone** provides a shallow copy of the data.

JAVA STREAM CLASSES

In Chapter 2, we used the **class** Scanner for inputting data from the standard input device. Chapter 3 described in detail how to perform input/output (I/O) using Java stream classes such as FileReader and PrintWriter. In Java, stream classes are implemented using the inheritance mechanism, as shown in Figure 11-8.

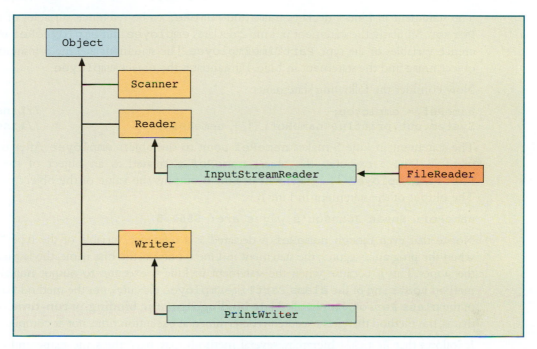

Figure 11-8   Hierarchy of Java stream classes

From Figure 11-8, it follows that the **class**es Scanner, Reader, and Writer are derived from the **class** Object. The **class** InputStreamReader is derived from the **class** Reader, and the **class** FileReader is derived from the **class** InputStreamReader. Similarly, the **class** PrintWriter is derived from the **class** Writer. A description of the methods of these classes and other Java stream classes is given in Appendix E.

POLYMORPHISM

Java allows us to treat an object of a subclass as an object of its superclass. In other words, a reference variable of a superclass type can point to an object of its subclass. There are situations when this feature of Java can be used to develop generic code for a variety of applications.

Consider the following statements. (The **class**es Person and PartTimeEmployee are as defined before.)

```
Person name, nameRef;                                        //Line 1
PartTimeEmployee employee, employeeRef;                      //Line 2

name = new Person("John", "Blair");                          //Line 3
employee = new PartTimeEmployee("Susan", "Johnson",
                                12.50, 45);                  //Line 4
```

The statement in Line 1 declares **name** and **nameRef** to be reference variables of the type **Person**. Similarly, the statement in Line 2 declares **employee** and **employeeRef** to be reference variables of the type **PartTimeEmployee**. The statement in Line 3 instantiates the object **name** and the statement in Line 4 instantiates the object **employee**.

Now consider the following statements:

```
nameRef = employee;                                          //Line 5
System.out.println("nameRef: " + nameRef);                   //Line 6
```

The statement in Line 5 makes **nameRef** point to the object **employee**. After the statement in Line 5 executes, the object **nameRef** is treated as an object of the **class** **PartTimeEmployee**. The statement in Line 6 outputs the value of the object **nameRef**. The output of the statement in Line 6 is:

```
nameRef: Susan Johnson's wages are: $562.5
```

Notice that even though **nameRef** is declared as a reference variable of the type **Person**, when the program executes, the statement in Line 6 outputs the first name, the last name, and the wages. This is because when the statement in Line 6 executes to output **nameRef**, the method **toString** of the **class** **PartTimeEmployee** executes, not the method **toString** of the **class** Person. This is called **late binding**, **dynamic binding**, or **run-time binding**; that is, the method that gets executed is determined at execution time, not at compile time.

It follows that in a class hierarchy, several methods may have the same name and the same formal parameter list. Moreover, a reference variable of a class can refer to either an object of its own class or an object of its subclass. Therefore, a reference variable can invoke, that is, execute, a method of its own class or of its subclass(es). Binding means associating a method definition with its invocation, that is, determining which method definition gets executed. In *early binding*, a method's definition is associated with its invocation when the code is compiled. In *late binding*, a method's definition is associated with the method's invocation at execution time, that is, when the method is executed. Except for a few (special) cases, (as discussed in a Note after Example 11-5 in this section), Java uses late binding for all methods. Furthermore, the term **polymorphism** means assigning multiple meanings to the same method name. In Java, polymorphism is implemented using late binding.

The reference variable **name** or **nameRef** can point to any object of the **class** Person or the **class** PartTimeEmployee. Loosely speaking, we say that these reference variables have many forms, that is, they are **polymorphic reference** variables. They can refer to either objects of their own class or objects of the subclasses inherited from their class.

The following example further illustrates polymorphism.

Example 11-5

Consider the following definitions of the **class**es RectangleFigure and BoxFigure.

```java
public class RectangleFigure
{
    private double length;
    private double width;

    public RectangleFigure()
    {
        length = 0;
        width = 0;
    }

    public RectangleFigure(double l, double w)
    {
        setDimension(l, w);
    }

    public void setDimension(double l, double w)
    {
        if (l >= 0)
            length = l;
        else
            length = 0;

        if (w >= 0)
            width = w;
        else
            width = 0;
    }

    public double getLength()
    {
        return length;
    }

    public double getWidth()
    {
        return width;
    }

    public double area()
    {
        return length * width;
    }
```

11

```java
    public double perimeter()
    {
        return 2 * (length + width);
    }

    public void print()
    {
        System.out.print("Length = " + length
                         + "; Width = " + width
                         + "\n"
                         + "Area = " + area());
    }
}
```

Note that the definition of the **class** RectangleFigure is similar to the definition of the **class** Rectangle given before. The method print of the **class** RectangleFigure, in addition to printing the length and width, also prints the area of the rectangle.

```java
public class BoxFigure extends RectangleFigure
{
    private double height;

    public BoxFigure()
    {
        super();
        height = 0;
    }

    public BoxFigure(double l, double w, double h)
    {
        super(l, w);
        height = h;
    }

    public void setDimension(double l, double w, double h)
    {
        super.setDimension(l, w);

        if (h >= 0)
            height = h;
        else
            height = 0;
    }

    public double getHeight()
    {
        return height;
    }
```

```
    public double area()
    {
        return 2 * (getLength() * getWidth()
                    + getLength() * height
                    + getWidth() * height);
    }

    public double volume()
    {
        return super.area() * height;
    }

    public void print()
    {
        System.out.print("Length = " + getLength()
                        + "; Width = " + getWidth()
                        + "; Height = " + height
                        + "\n"
                        + "Surface Area = " + area()
                        + "; Volume = " + volume());
    }
}
```

Note that the **class** BoxFigure is derived from the **class** RectangleFigure. Moreover, the definition of the **class** BoxFigure is similar to the definition of the **class** Box given before. The method print of the **class** BoxFigure, in addition to printing the length, width, and height, also prints the surface area and volume of the box.

Consider the following application program:

```
public class Polymorphism
{
    public static void main(String[] args)
    {
        RectangleFigure rec, shapeRef;            //Line 1

        BoxFigure box;                            //Line 2

        rec = new RectangleFigure(8, 5);          //Line 3
        box = new BoxFigure(10, 7, 3);            //Line 4

        shapeRef = rec;                           //Line 5
        System.out.println("Line 6: Rectangle:"); //Line 6
        shapeRef.print();                         //Line 7
        System.out.println();                     //Line 8
        System.out.println();                     //Line 9

        shapeRef = box;                           //Line 10
        System.out.println("Line 11: Box:");      //Line 11
        shapeRef.print();                         //Line 12
```

11

```
        System.out.println();                              //Line 13
    }
}
```

Sample Run:
```
Line 6: Rectangle:
Length = 8.0; Width = 5.0
Area = 40.0


Line 11: Box:
Length = 10.0; Width = 7.0; Height = 3.0
Surface Area = 242.0; Volume = 210.0
```

Note that in the preceding program, `shapeRef` is a reference variable of the `RectangleFigure` type. Because the **class** `BoxFigure` is derived from the **class** `RectangleFigure`, the reference variable `shapeRef` can point to an object of the **class** `RectangleFigure` as well as an object of the **class** `BoxFigure`.

The statement in Line 3 instantiates a `RectangleFigure` object and stores the address of this object in the reference variable `rec`. Similarly, the statement in Line 4 instantiates a `BoxFigure` object and stores the address of this object in the reference variable `box`.

After the statement in Line 5 executes, `shapeRef` points to the object `ref`. The statement in Line 7 executes the method `print`. Because `shapeRef` points to an object of the **class** `RectangleFigure`, the method `print` of the **class** `RectangleFigure` executes. Note that when the method `print` of the **class** `RectangleFigure` executes, it also executes the method `area`. In this case, the method `area` of the **class** `RectangleFigure` executes.

After the statement in Line 10 executes, `shapeRef` points to the object `box`. The statement in Line 12 executes the method `print`. Because `shapeRef` points to an object of the **class** `BoxFigure`, the method `print` of the **class** `BoxFigure` executes. Note that when the method `print` of the **class** `BoxFigure` executes, it also executes the method `area`. In this case, the method `area` of the **class** `BoxFigure` executes, which outputs the surface area of the box.

In Example 11-5, in the definitions of the **class**es `RectangleFigure` and `BoxFigure`, you can replace the method `print` with the method `toString`. This allows you to use the **object** `System.out` and its methods `print`, `println`, or `printf` to output the value of an object. We included the method `print` in the **class**es `RectangleFigure` and `BoxFigure` to explicitly illustrate polymorphism. The Web site accompanying this book contains the modified program.

You can declare a method of a class final by using the keyword `final`. For example, the following method is final:

```
public final void doSomeThing()
{
    //...
}
```

If a method of a **class** is declared **final**, it cannot be overridden with a new definition in a derived class.

Similarly, you can also declare a **class** final using the keyword **final**. If a class is declared **final**, then no other **class** can be derived from this **class**.

Java does *not* use late binding for methods that are **private**, marked **final**, or **static**.

As illustrated above, a reference variable of a superclass type can point to an object of its subclass. However, you cannot automatically consider a superclass object to be an object of a subclass. In other words, you *cannot* automatically make a reference variable of a subclass type point to an object of its superclass.

Suppose that **supRef** is a reference variable of a superclass type. Moreover, suppose that **supRef** points to an object of its subclass. You can use an appropriate cast operator on **supRef** and make a reference variable of the subclass point to the object. On the other hand, if **supRef** does not point to a subclass object and you use a cast operator on **supRef** to make a reference variable of the subclass point to the object, then Java will throw a **ClassCastException**—indicating that the **class cast** is not allowed.

Suppose name, nameRef, employee, and employeeRef are as declared in the begining of this section, that is:

```
Person name, nameRef;                          //Line 1
PartTimeEmployee employee, employeeRef;        //Line 2

name = new Person("John", "Blair");            //Line 3
employee = new PartTimeEmployee("Susan", "Johnson",
                            12.50, 45);        //Line 4
nameRef = employee;                            //Line 5
```

Now consider the following statement:

```
employeeRef = (PartTimeEmployee) name;         //Illegal
```

This statement will throw a **ClassCastException** because name points to an object of the **class** Person. It does not refer to an object of the **class** PartTimeEmployee. However, the following statement is legal:

```
employeeRef = (PartTimeEmployee) nameRef;
```

Because nameRef refers to the object employee (as set by the statement in Line 5), and employee is a reference variable of the PartTimeEmployee type, this statement would make employeeRef point to the object employee. Therefore, the output of the statement:

```
System.out.println(employeeRef);
```

is:

```
Susan Johnson's wages are: $562.50
```

11

Operator `instanceof`

As previously described, an object of a subclass type can be considered an object of the superclass type. Moreover, by using an appropriate cast operator, you can treat an object of a superclass type as an object of a subclass type. To determine whether a reference variable that points to an object is of a particular class type, Java provides the operator `instanceof`. Consider the following expression (suppose that **p** is an object of a class type):

```
p instanceof BoxShape
```

This expression evaluates to **true** if **p** points to an object of the **class** BoxShape; otherwise it evaluates to **false**. (The **class** BoxShape is defined in Example 11-6, which is given next.)

Example 11-6 further illustrates how the operator `instanceof` works.

Example 11-6

Consider the following classes. (The **class**es RectangleShape and BoxShape are the same as the **class**es Rectangle and Box given earlier in this chapter. The only difference is that the instance variables of the **class**es Rectangle and Box are **private**, while those of the **class**es RectangleShape and BoxShape are **protected**. Because the instance variables of the **class** RectangleShape are **protected**, they can be directly accessed in the **class** BoxShape. Therefore, the definitions of the methods **area** and **volume** of the **class** BoxShape directly access the instance variables **length** and **width** of the **class** RectangleShape.)

```java
public class RectangleShape
{
    protected double length;
    protected double width;

    public RectangleShape()
    {
        length = 0;
        width = 0;
    }

    public RectangleShape(double l, double w)
    {
        setDimension(l, w);
    }

    public void setDimension(double l, double w)
    {
        if (l >= 0)
            length = l;
        else
            length = 0;
```

```java
        if (w >= 0)
            width = w;
        else
            width = 0;
    }

    public double getLength()
    {
        return length;
    }

    public double getWidth()
    {
        return width;
    }

    public double area()
    {
        return length * width;
    }

    public double perimeter()
    {
        return 2 * (length + width);
    }

    public String toString()
    {
        return("Length = "  + length
              + ", Width = " + width
              + ", Perimeter = " + perimeter()
              + ", Area = " + area());
    }
}
```

The **class** BoxShape, given next, is derived from the **class** RectangleShape.

```java
public class BoxShape extends RectangleShape
{
    public BoxShape()
    {
        super();
        height = 0;
    }

    public BoxShape(double l, double w, double h)
    {
        super(l, w);
        height = h;
    }
```

```java
    public void setDimension(double l, double w, double h)
    {
        super.setDimension(l, w);

        if (h >= 0)
            height = h;
        else
            height = 0;
    }

    public double getHeight()
    {
        return height;
    }

    public double area()
    {
        return  2 * (length * width + length * height
                    + width * height);
    }

    public double volume()
    {
        return length * width * height;
    }

    public String toString()
    {
        return("Length = "   + length
            + ", Width = " + width
            + ", Height = " + height
            + ", Surface Area = " + area()
            + ", Volume = " + volume());
    }
}
```

Next, consider the following application program:

```java
public class SuperSubClassObjects
{
    public static void main(String[] args)
    {
        RectangleShape rectangle, rectRef;          //Line 1
        BoxShape box, boxRef;                       //Line 2

        rectangle = new RectangleShape(12, 4);      //Line 3
        System.out.println("Line 4: Rectangle \n"
                        + rectangle + "\n");        //Line 4
        box = new BoxShape(13, 7, 4);               //Line 5
```

```
        System.out.println("Line 6: Box\n"
                  + box + "\n");                            //Line 6
     rectRef = box;                                        //Line 7
        System.out.println("Line 8: Box via rectRef\n"
                  + rectRef + "\n");                        //Line 8

     boxRef = (BoxShape) rectRef;                          //Line 9
        System.out.println("Line 10: Box via boxRef\n"
                  + boxRef + "\n");                         //Line 10

     if (rectRef instanceof BoxShape)                      //Line 11
         System.out.println("Line 12: rectRef is "
                        + "an instance of BoxShape");       //Line 12
     else                                                  //Line 13
         System.out.println("Line 14: rectRef is not "
                        + "an instance of BoxShape");       //Line 14

     if (rectangle instanceof BoxShape)                    //Line 15
         System.out.println("Line 16: rectangle is "
                        + "an instance of BoxShape");       //Line 16
     else                                                  //Line 17
         System.out.println("Line 18: rectangle is not "
                        + "an instance of BoxShape");       //Line 18
     }
 }
```

Sample Run:

```
Line 4: Rectangle
Length = 12.0, Width = 4.0, Perimeter = 32.0, Area = 48.0

Line 6: Box
Length = 13.0, Width = 7.0, Height = 4.0, Surface Area = 342.0, Volume = 364.0

Line 8: Box via rectRef
Length = 13.0, Width = 7.0, Height = 4.0, Surface Area = 342.0, Volume = 364.0

Line 10: Box via boxRef
Length = 13.0, Width = 7.0, Height = 4.0, Surface Area = 342.0, Volume = 364.0

Line 12: rectRef is an instance of BoxShape
Line 18: rectangle is not an instance of BoxShape
```

The preceding program works as follows: The statement in Line 1 declares `rectangle` and `rectRef` to be reference variables of the `RectangleShape` type. Similarly, the statement in Line 2 declares `box` and `boxRef` to be reference variables of the `BoxShape` type.

The statement in Line 3 instantiates the object `rectangle` and initializes the instance variables `length` and `width` to `12.0` and `4.0`, respectively. The statement in Line 4 outputs the length, width, perimeter, and area of `rectangle`.

11

The statement in Line 5 instantiates the object **box** and initializes the instance variables **length**, **width**, and **height** to **13.0**, **7.0**, and **4.0**, respectively. The statement in Line 6 outputs the length, width, height, surface area, and volume of **box**.

The statement in Line 7 copies the value of **box** into **rectRef**. After this statement executes, **rectRef** points to the object **box**. Notice that **rectRef** is a reference variable of the **RectangleShape** (the superclass) type and **box** is a reference variable of the **BoxShape** (the subclass of **RectangleShape**) type.

The statement in Line 8 outputs the length, width, height, surface area, and volume of **box** via the reference variable **rectRef**. Notice that **rectRef** is a reference variable of the **RectangleShape** type. However, when the statement in Line 8 executes to output **rectRef**, the method **toString** of the **class** BoxShape executes, not the method **toString** of the **class** RectangleShape.

Because the reference variable **rectRef** points to an object of **BoxShape**, the statement in Line 9 uses the cast operator and copies the value of **rectRef** into **boxRef**. (If the reference variable **rectRef** did not point to an object of the type **BoxShape**, then the statement in Line 9 would result in an error.) The statement in Line 10 outputs the length, width, height, surface area, and volume of the object to which **boxRef** points.

The statements in Lines 11 through 14 determine whether **rectRef** is an instance of **BoxShape**, that is, if **rectRef** points to an object of the **BoxShape** type. Similarly, the statements in Lines 15 through 18 determine whether the reference variable **rectangle** is an instance of **BoxShape**.

ABSTRACT METHODS AND CLASSES

An **abstract method** is a method that has only the heading with no body. The heading of an abstract method contains the reserved word **abstract** and ends with a semicolon. The following are examples of abstract methods:

```
public void abstract print();
public abstract object larger(object, object);
void abstract insert(int insertItem);
```

An **abstract class** is a class that is declared with the reserved word **abstract** in its heading. Some facts about abstract classes follow:

- An abstract class can contain instance variables, constructors, the finalizer, and nonabstract methods.

- An abstract class can contain abstract method(s).

- If a class contains an abstract method, then the class must be declared abstract.

- You cannot instantiate an object of an abstract class. You can only declare a reference variable of an abstract class type.

- You can instantiate an object of a subclass of an abstract class, but only if the subclass gives the definitions of *all* the abstract methods of the superclass.

The following is an example of an abstract class:

```
public abstract class AbstractClassExample
{
    protected int x;

    public void abstract print();

    public void setX(int a)
    {
        x = a;
    }

    public AbstractClassExample()
    {
        x = 0;
    }
}
```

Abstract classes are used as superclasses from which other subclasses within the same context can be derived. They can be used to force subclasses to provide certain methods, as illustrated in Example 11-7.

Example 11-7

11

In Chapter 6, we introduced the **class** IntClass so that **int** values can be treated as objects. We also indicated that the **class** DoubleClass, which can be used to treat values of the type **double** as objects, has similar operations. Similarly, you can design the **class**es CharClass, LongClass, and FloatClass to treat the other values of the primitive data types as objects. The three operations that are common to all these classes, and have the same name, are equals, compareTo, and toString. To ensure that each of these classes provides these three operations, we can create the **abstract class** PrimitiveTypeClass with these operations as **abstract** methods, as follows:

```
public abstract class PrimitiveTypeClass
{
    public abstract boolean equals(PrimitiveTypeClass right);
        //Method to return true if two objects contain the same
        //data

    public abstract int compareTo(PrimitiveTypeClass right);
        //Method to compare two objects
```

```
    public abstract String toString();
        //Method to return data as a string
}
```

 In the definition of the **class** PrimitiveTypeClass, notice that the arguments of the methods equals and compareTo are objects of the type PrimitiveTypeClass.

You can derive the **class**es IntClass, DoubleClass, and so on, from the **class** PrimitiveTypeClass. For example, the definition of the **class** IntClass could be:

```
public class IntClass extends PrimitiveTypeClass
{
    private int x;

    public IntClass()
    {
        x = 0;
    }

    public IntClass(int num)
    {
        x = num;
    }

    public void setNum(int num)
    {
        x = num;
    }

    public int getNum()
    {
        return x;
    }

    public void addToNum(int num)
    {
        x = x + num;
    }

    public void multiplyToNum(int num)
    {
        x = x * num;
    }

    public int compareTo(PrimitiveTypeClass right)
    {
        IntClass temp = (IntClass) right;
```

```
            return (x - temp.getNum());
        }

        public boolean equals(PrimitiveTypeClass right)
        {
            IntClass temp = (IntClass) right;

            if (x == temp.getNum())
                return true;
            else
                return false;
        }

        public String toString()
        {
            return (String.valueOf(x));
        }
}
```

The definition of the **class** `IntClass` given here is different than the one given in Chapter 6 and used in Chapter 7. The main difference is how the methods `equals` and `compareTo` are implemented. The definition given here is derived from the abstract **class** `PrimitiveTypeClass`.

The Web site accompanying this book contains the definitions of the **class**es `PrimitiveTypeClass` and `IntClass`, as well as a program that shows how to use these classes. The folder `AbstractClasses` contains the necessary files.

INTERFACES

In Chapter 6, you learned that the **class** `ActionListener` is a special type of class called an **interface**. There are several other classes in Java that are similar to the **interface** `ActionListener`. For example, window events are handled by the **interface** `WindowListener`, and mouse events are handled by the **interface** `MouseListener`. The obvious question is: Why does Java have these interfaces? After all, they are also classes. The answer is that Java, in reality, *does not* support multiple inheritance. That is, a class can extend the definition of only one class; in other words, a class can be derived from *only* one existing class. However, a Java program might contain a variety of GUI components and thus generate a variety of events such as window events, mouse events, and action events. These events are handled by separate interfaces. Therefore, a program might need to use more than one such interface.

Until now we have handled events by using the mechanism of the inner class. For example, action events were processed by using inner classes. There are two more ways, discussed in Chapter 12, to process events in a Java program—by using anonymous classes and by making the class containing the application program implement the appropriate interface.

When we created an inner class to process an action event, the inner class was built on top of the **interface** `ActionListener` by using the mechanism of **implements**. Rather than use the inner class mechanism, the class containing the Java program can itself be created on top of an interface, just as we created the GUI program by extending the **class** JFrame. For example, for the RectangleProgram in Chapter 6, we could have defined the **class** RectangleProgram as follows:

```
public class RectangleProgram extends JFrame implements
                                        ActionListener
{
    //...
}
```

Of course, doing so would also require us to register the listener using the reference **this**, which was explained in Chapter 8.

To be able to handle a variety of events, Java allows a class to implement more than one interface. This is, in fact, how Java implements multiple inheritance, which is not true multiple inheritance. In the remainder of this section, we provide a few facts about interfaces.

You already know that an interface is a special type of class. How does an interface differ from an actual class?

Interface: An interface is a class that contains only abstract methods and/or named constants.

Interfaces are defined using the reserved word **interface** in place of the reserved word **class**. For example, the definition of the **interface** WindowListener is:

```
public interface WindowListener
{
    public void windowOpened(WindowEvent e);
    public void windowClosing(WindowEvent e);
    public void windowClosed(WindowEvent e);
    public void windowIconified(WindowEvent e);
    public void windowDeiconified(WindowEvent e);
    public void windowActivated(WindowEvent e);
    public void windowDeactivated(WindowEvent e);
}
```

The definition of the **interface** ActionListener is:

```
public interface ActionListener
{
    public void actionPerformed(ActionEvent e);
}
```

Example 11-8

The following **class** implements the **interface**s ActionListener and WindowListener:

```
public class ExampleInterfaceImp implements ActionListener,
                                        WindowListener
{
    //...
}
```

Recall that if a **class** contains an **abstract** method, it must be declared **abstract**. Moreover, you cannot instantiate an object of an **abstract class**. Therefore, if a **class** implements an **interface**, it must provide definitions for each of the methods of the **interface**; otherwise, you cannot instantiate an object of that class type.

COMPOSITION

Composition is another way to relate two classes. In **composition**, one or more members of a class are objects of another class type. Composition is a "has-a" relation; for example, "every person has a date of birth."

The **class** Person, as defined in Chapter 8, Example 8-4, stores a person's first name and last name. Suppose we want to keep track of additional information, such as a personal ID and date of birth. Because every person has a personal ID and a date of birth, we can define a new **class** PersonalInfo, in which one of the members is an object of the type Person. We can declare additional members to store the personal ID and date of birth for the **class** PersonalInfo.

First we define another **class**, Date, to store only a person's date of birth, and then construct the **class** PersonalInfo from the **class**es Person and Date. This way, we can demonstrate how to define a new class using two classes.

To define the **class** Date, we need three instance variables to store the month, day number, and year. Some of the operations that need to be performed on a date are to set the date and to print the date. The following statements define the **class** Date (see Figure 11-9):

```
public class Date
{
    private int dMonth;     //variable to store the month
    private int dDay;       //variable to store the day
    private int dYear;      //variable to store the year

        //Default constructor
        //The instance variables dMonth, dDay, and dYear are set to
        //the default values.
        //Postcondition: dMonth = 1; dDay = 1; dYear = 1900;
    public Date()
    {
        dMonth = 1;
        dDay = 1;
        dYear = 1900;
    }

        //Constructor to set the date
        //The instance variables dMonth, dDay, and dYear are set
        //according to the parameters.
        //Postcondition: dMonth = month; dDay = day;
        //                       dYear = year;
```

11

```java
    public Date(int month, int day, int year)
    {
        dMonth = month;
        dDay = day;
        dYear = year;
    }

        //Method to set the date
        //The instance variables dMonth, dDay, and dYear are set
        //according to the parameters.
        //Postcondition: dMonth = month; dDay = day;
        //                dYear = year;
    public void setDate(int month, int day, int year)
    {
        dMonth = month;
        dDay = day;
        dYear = year;
    }

        //Method to return the month
        //Postcondition: The value of dMonth is returned.
    public int getMonth()
    {
        return dMonth;
    }

        //Method to return the day
        //Postcondition: The value of dDay is returned.
    public int getDay()
    {
        return dDay;
    }
        //Method to return the year
        //Postcondition: The value of dYear is returned.
    public int getYear()
    {
        return dYear;
    }

        //Method to return the date in the form mm-dd-yyyy
    public String toString()
    {
        return (dMonth + "-" + dDay + "-" + dYear);
    }
}
```

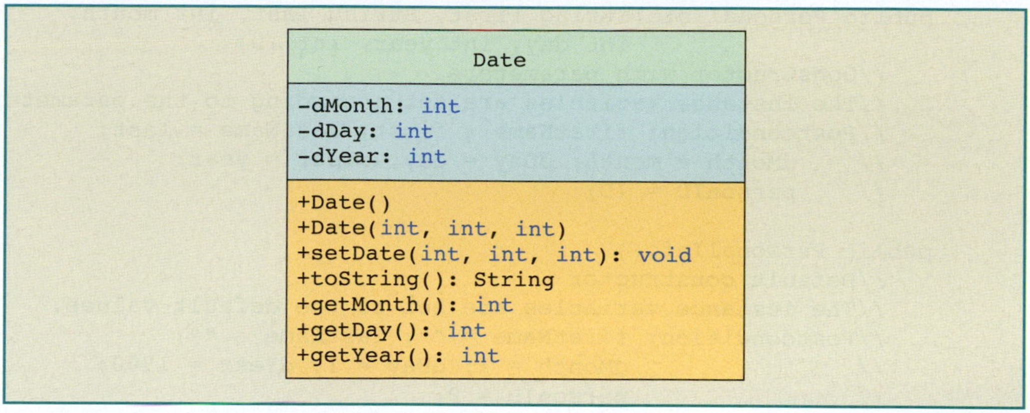

Figure 11-9   UML class diagram of the **class** Date

The definition of the method **setDate**, before storing the date into the data members, does not check whether the date is valid. That is, it does not confirm whether **month** is between 1 and 12, **year** is greater than 0, and **day** is valid (for example, for January, **day** should be between 1 and 31). In Programming Exercise 2 at the end of this chapter, you are asked to rewrite the definition of the method **setDate** so that the date is validated before storing it in the data members. Similarly, in Programming Exercise 2, you are asked to rewrite the definition of the constructor with parameters so that it checks for valid values of **month**, **day**, and **year** before storing the date into the data members.

Next, we specify the members of the **class** PersonalInfo (see Figure 11-10).

Instance Variables:

```
private Person name;
private Date bDay;
private int personID;
```

Constructors and Instance Methods:

```
public void setPersonalInfo(String first, String last, int month,
                           int day, int year, int ID)
   //Method to set the personal information
   //The instance variables are set according to the parameters.
   //Postcondition: firstName = first; lastName = last;
   //        dMonth = month; dDay = day; dYear = year;
   //        personID = ID;

public String toString()
   //Method to return the string containing the personal
   //information
```

11

```java
public PersonalInfo(String first, String last, int month,
                    int day, int year, int ID)
    //Constructor with parameters
    //The instance variables are set according to the parameters.
    //Postcondition: firstName = first; lastName = last;
    //    dMonth = month; dDay = day; dYear = year;
    //    personID = ID;

public PersonalInfo()
    //Default constructor
    //The instance variables are set to the default values.
    //Postcondition: firstName = ""; lastName = "";
    //               dMonth = 1; dDay = 1; dYear = 1900;
    //               personID = 0;
```

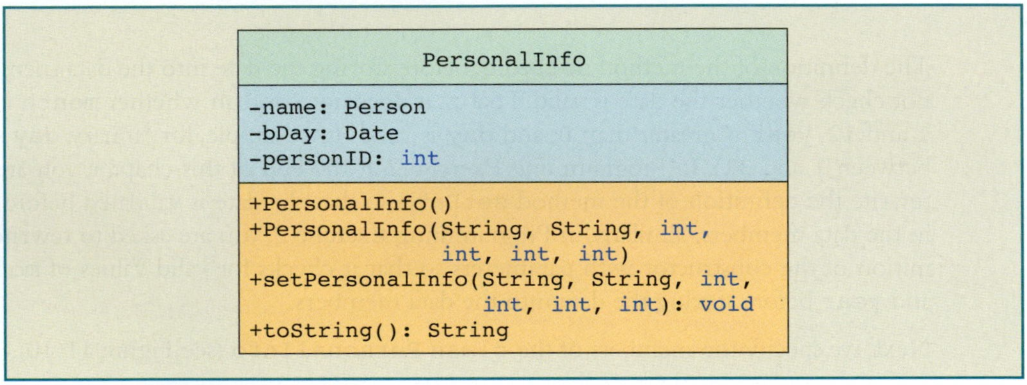

```
                    ┌─────────────────────────────────┐
                    │          PersonalInfo           │
                    ├─────────────────────────────────┤
                    │ -name: Person                   │
                    │ -bDay: Date                     │
                    │ -personID: int                  │
                    ├─────────────────────────────────┤
                    │ +PersonalInfo()                 │
                    │ +PersonalInfo(String, String, int, │
                    │            int, int, int)       │
                    │ +setPersonalInfo(String, String, int, │
                    │              int, int, int): void │
                    │ +toString(): String             │
                    └─────────────────────────────────┘
```

Figure 11-10   UML class diagram of the **class** PersonalInfo

The definitions of the methods of the **class** personalInfo follow:

```java
public void setPersonalInfo(String first, String last, int month,
                            int day, int year, int ID)
{
    name.setName(first, last);
    bDay.setDate(month, day, year);
    personID = ID;
}

public String toString()
{
    return ("Name: " + name.toString() + "\n"
            + "Date of birth: " + bDay.toString() + "\n"
            + "Personal ID: " + personID);
}
```

```
public PersonalInfo(String first, String last, int month,
                    int day, int year, int ID)
{
      name = new Person(first, last);  //instantiate and
                                       //initialize the object name
      bDay = new Date(month, day, year);//instantiate and
                                        //initialize the object bDay
      personID = ID;
}

public PersonalInfo()
{
      name = new Person();     //instantiate and initialize
                               //the object name
      bDay = new Date();       //instantiate and initialize
                               //the object bDay
      personID = 0;
}
```

Next, we give the definition of the **class** `PersonalInfo`:

```
public class PersonalInfo
{
    private Person name;
    private Date bDay;
    private int personID;

       //Default constructor
       //The instance variables are set to the default values.
       //Postcondition: firstName = ""; lastName = "";
       //                dMonth = 1; dDay = 1; dYear = 1900;
       //                personID = 0;
    public PersonalInfo()
    {
       name = new Person();
       bDay = new Date();
       personID = 0;
    }


       //Constructor with parameters
       //The instance variables are set according to the parameters.
       //Postcondition: firstName = first; lastName = last;
       //                dMonth = month; dDay = day; dYear = year;
       //                personID = ID;
    public PersonalInfo(String first, String last, int month,
                        int day, int year, int ID)
    {
        name = new Person(first, last);
        bDay = new Date(month, day, year);
        personID = ID;
    }
```

11

```
//Method to set the personal information
//The instance variables are set according to the parameters.
//Postcondition: firstName = first; lastName = last;
//                dMonth = month; dDay = day; dYear = year;
//                personID = ID;
public void setpersonalInfo(String first, String last,
                            int month, int day, int year,
                            int ID)
{
    name.setName(first, last);
    bDay.setDate(month, day, year);
    personID = ID;
}
    //Method to return the string containing the personal
    //information
public String toString()
{
    return ("Name: " + name.toString() + "\n"
          + "Date of birth: " + bDay.toString() + "\n"
          + "Personal ID: " + personID);
}
}
```

 The Web site accompanying this book contains the definitions of the **class**es `Person`, `Date`, and `PersonalInfo`, as well as a program that shows how to use these classes. The folder `Composition` contains the necessary files.

PROGRAMMING EXAMPLE: GRADE REPORT

This programming example further illustrates the concepts of inheritance and composition.

The midsemester point at your local university is approaching. The registrar's office wants to prepare the grade reports as soon as the students' grades are recorded. Some of the enrolled students have not yet paid their tuition, however.

If a student has paid the tuition, the student's grades are shown on the grade report with the grade-point average (GPA).

If a student has not paid the tuition, the grades are not printed. For these students, the grade report contains a message indicating that the grades have been held for nonpayment of the tuition. The grade report also shows the billing amount.

The registrar's office and the business office want you to help write a program that can analyze the students' data and print the appropriate grade reports.

The program is divided into two parts. In the first part, we create the application program that generates the grade report in the window's console environment, as well as stores the output in a file.

In the second part, we create a GUI to display the students' grade reports as shown in the section Student Grade Report: GUI Design.

Part I: Student Grade Report: Console Display

For this report, the data is stored in a file in the following form:

```
noOfStudents tuitionRate
studentName studentID isTuitionPaid numberOfCourses
courseName courseNumber creditHours grade
courseName courseNumber creditHours grade
.
.
.
studentName studentID isTuitionPaid numberOfCourses
courseName courseNumber creditHours grade
courseName courseNumber creditHours grade
.
.
.
```

The first line indicates the number of students enrolled and the tuition rate per credit hour. The students' data is given thereafter.

A sample input file follows:

```
3 345
Lisa Miller 890238 Y 4
Mathematics MTH345 4 A
Physics PHY357 3 B
ComputerSci CSC478 3 B
History HIS356 3 A
.
.
.
```

The first line indicates that 3 students are enrolled and the tuition rate is $345 per credit hour. Next, the course data for student **Lisa Miller** is given: Lisa Miller's ID is **890238**, she has paid the tuition, and is taking **4** courses. The course number for the mathematics class she is taking is **MTH345**, the course has **4** credit hours, her mid-semester grade is **A**, and so on. The output of the program is of the following form:

```
Student Name: Lisa Miller
Student ID: 890238
Number of courses enrolled: 4
```

```
Course No   Course Name   Credits Grade
CSC478      ComputerSci      3       B
HIS356      History          3       A
MTH345      Mathematics      4       A
PHY357      Physics          3       B

Total number of credit hours: 13
Midsemester GPA: 3.54
```

It is clear from this output that the courses must be ordered according to the course number. To calculate the GPA, we assume that the grade A is equivalent to 4 points, B is equivalent to 3 points, C is equivalent to 2 points, D is equivalent to 1 point, and F is equivalent to 0 points.

Input   A file containing the data in the form given previously. For easy reference in the rest of the discussion, let's assume that the name of the input file is `stData.txt` and this file is on floppy disk A.

Output   A file containing the output of the form given previously.

Problem Analysis and Algorithm Design

We must first identify the main components of the program. The university has students, and every student takes courses. Thus, the two main components are the student and the course.

Let's first describe the component **Course**.

Course

The main characteristics of a course are the course name, course number, and number of credit hours.

Some of the basic operations that need to be performed on an object of the course type follow:

1. Set the course information.
2. Print the course information.
3. Show the credit hours.
4. Show the course number.

Next, we define the members of the **class** Course (see Figure 11-11).

Instance Variables:

```java
private String courseName;   //object to store the course name
private String courseNo;     //object to store the course number
private int courseCredits;   //variable to store the
                             //course credits
```

Constructors and Instance Methods:

```java
public void setCourseInfo(String cName, String cNo,
                                   int credits)
   //Method to set the course information
   //The course information is set according to the
   //parameters.
   //Postcondition: courseName = cName; courseNo = cNo;
   //               courseCredits = credits;

public void setCourseName(String cName)
   //Method to set the course name
   //Postcondition: courseName = cName;

public void setCourseNumber(String cNo)
   //Method to set the course number
   //Postcondition: courseNo = cNo

public void setCourseCredits(int credits)
   //Method to set the course credits
   //Postcondition: courseCredits = credits;

public void print()
   //Method to print the course information
   //Postcondition: This method prints the course
   //               information on the screen.

public void print(PrintWriter outp)
   //Method to print the course information
   //Postcondition: This method sends the course information
   //               to a file.

public String getCourseName()
   //Method to return the course name
   //Postcondition: The value of courseName is returned.

public String getCourseNumber()
   //Method to return the course number
   //Postcondition: The value of courseNo is returned.

public int getCredits()
   //Method to return the credit hours
   //Postcondition: The value of courseCredits is returned.

public void copyCourseInfo(Course otherCourse)
   //Method to copy a course's information
   //otherCourse is copied into this course.
   //Postcondition: courseName = otherCourse.courseName;
   //               courseNo = otherCourse.courseNo;
   //               courseCredits = otherCourse.courseCredits;
```

```
public Course()
    //Default constructor
    //The object is initialized to the default values.
    //Postcondition: courseName = ""; courseNo = "";
    //                courseCredits = 0;

public Course(String cName, String cNo, int credits)
    //Constructor
    //The object is initialized according to the parameters.
    //Postcondition: courseName = cName; courseNo = cNo;
    //                courseCredits = credits;
```

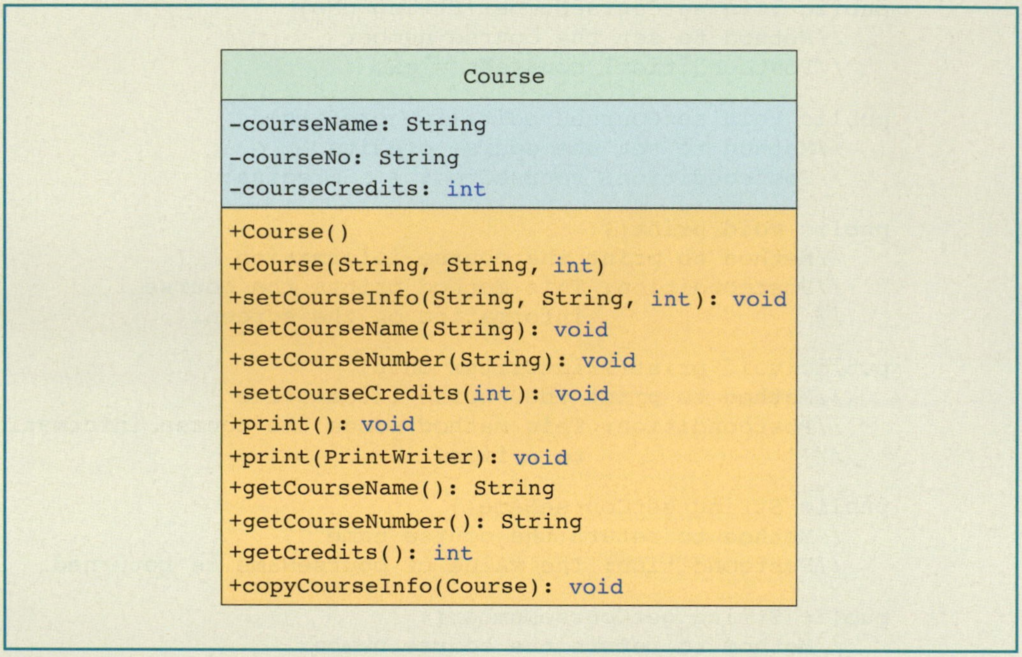

Course
-courseName: String
-courseNo: String
-courseCredits: int
+Course()
+Course(String, String, int)
+setCourseInfo(String, String, int): void
+setCourseName(String): void
+setCourseNumber(String): void
+setCourseCredits(int): void
+print(): void
+print(PrintWriter): void
+getCourseName(): String
+getCourseNumber(): String
+getCredits(): int
+copyCourseInfo(Course): void

Figure 11-11   UML class diagram of the **class** Course

Next, we discuss the definition of the methods to implement the operations of the **class** Course.

The method **setCourseInfo** sets the values of the instance variables according to the values of the parameters. Its definition is:

```
public void setCourseInfo(String cName, String cNo,
                          int credits)
{
```

```
        courseName = cName;
        courseNo = cNo;
        courseCredits = credits;
}
```

The definitions of the methods `setCourseName`, `setCourseNumber`, and `setCourseCredits` are similar to the method `setCourseInfo`. Their definitions are:

```
public void setCourseName(String cName)
{
        courseName = cName;
}
public void setCourseNumber(String cNo)
{
        courseNo = cNo;
}

public void setCourseCredits(int credits)
{
        courseCredits = credits;
}
```

The method `print` without any parameters prints the course information on the screen.

```
public void print()
{
        System.out.printf("%-12s%-15s%4s", courseNo,
                        courseName, courseCredits);
}
```

The method `print`, which has one parameter, sends the course information to a file. Other than sending the output to a file, which is passed as a parameter, this method's definition is exactly the same as the definition of the previous `print` method. The definition of this method is:

```
public void print(PrintWriter outp)
{
        outp.printf("%-12s%-15s%4s", courseNo, courseName,
                courseCredits);
}
```

The constructor with parameters uses the values specified by the formal parameters to initialize the instance variables. The default constructor uses the default values to initialize the instance variables. Their definitions are as follows:

```
public Course(String cName, String cNo, int credits)
{
```

```
    courseName = cName;
        courseNo = cNo;
        courseCredits = credits;
}
public Course()
{
        courseName = "";
        courseNo = "";
        courseCredits = 0;
}
```

The definitions of the remaining methods are as follows:

```
public String getCourseName()
{
        return courseName;
}

public String getCourseNumber()
{
        return courseNo;
}

public int getCredits()
{
        return courseCredits;
}

public void copyCourseInfo(Course otherCourse)
{
        courseName = otherCourse.courseName;
        courseNo = otherCourse.courseNo;
        courseCredits = otherCourse.courseCredits;
}
```

The definition of the **class** Course looks like the following. (You can complete the definition of this class as an exercise if you like.)

```
public class Course
{
        private String courseName;    //object to store the course name
        private String courseNo;      //object to store the course
                                      //number
        private int courseCredits;    //variable to store the course
                                      //credits

        //Place the definitions of the instance methods
        //as discussed here.
        //...
}
```

Next, we discuss the component `Student`.

The main characteristics of a student are the student name, student ID, number of courses in which the student is enrolled, courses in which the student is enrolled, and the grade for each course. Because every student must pay tuition, we also include a member to indicate whether the student has paid the tuition.

Every student is a person, and every student takes courses. We have already designed a `class Person` to process a person's first name and last name. We have also designed a class to process the course information. Thus, we see that we can derive the `class Student` to keep track of a student's information from the `class Person`, and one member of the `class Student` is of the type `Course`. We can add more members as needed.

The basic operations to be performed on an object of the type `Student` are as follows:

1. Set the student information.
2. Print the student information.
3. Calculate the number of credit hours taken.
4. Calculate the GPA.
5. Calculate the billing amount.
6. Because the grade report will print the courses in ascending order, sort the courses according to the course number.

Next, we define the members of the `class Student` (see Figure 11-12):

Instance Variables:

```
private int sId;                //variable to store the student ID
private int numberOfCourses;    //variable to store the number
                                //of courses
private boolean isTuitionPaid;     //variable to indicate whether
                                   //the tuition is paid
private Course[] coursesEnrolled; //array to store the courses
private char[] courseGrades;  //array to store the course grades
```

Constructors and Instance Methods:

```
public void setInfo(String fName, String lName, int ID,
                    int nOfCourses, boolean isTPaid,
                    Course[] courses, char[] cGrades)
   //Method to set a student's information
   //Postcondition: The instance variables are set according
   //               to the parameters.
```

```java
public void setStudentId(int ID)
   //Method to set a student's ID
   //Postcondition: sId = ID;

public void setIsTuitionPaid(boolean isTPaid)
   //Method to set whether the tuition is paid
   //Postcondition: isTuitionPaid = isTPaid;

public void setNumberOfCourses(int nOfCourses)
   //Method to set the number of courses taken
   //Postcondition: numberOfCourses = nOfCourses;

public void setCoursesEnrolled(Course[] courses,
                               char[] cGrades)
   //Method to set the courses enrolled
   //Postcondition: The array courses is copied into the
   //        array coursesEnrolled, the array cGrades is
   //        copied into the array courseGrades, and these
   //        arrays are sorted.

public void print(double tuitionRate)
   //Method to print a student's grade report
   //Postcondition: If the instance variable isTuitionPaid
   //        is true, the grades are shown; otherwise three
   //        stars are printed.

public void print(PrintWriter outp, double tuitionRate)
   //Method to print a student's grade report
   //The output is stored in a file specified by the
   //parameter outp.
   //Postcondition: If the instance variable isTuitionPaid
   //        is true, the grades are shown; otherwise three
   //        stars are printed.

public int getStudentId()
   //Method to get a student's ID
   //Postcondition: The value of sId is returned.

public boolean getIsTuitionPaid()
   //Method to return whether the tuition is paid
   //Postcondition: The value of isTuitionPaid is returned.

public int getNumberOfCourses()
   //Method to get the number of courses taken
   //Postcondition: The value of numberOfCourses is returned.
```

```
public char getGrade(int i)
    //Method to return a course grade
    //Postcondition: The value of courseGrades[i] is returned.

public Course getCourse(int i)
    //Method to get a copy of a course taken
    //Postcondition: A copy of coursesEnrolled[i]
    //                is returned.

public int getHoursEnrolled()
    //Method to return the credit hours in which a
    //student is enrolled
    //Postcondition: The total credits are calculated
    //                and returned.

public double getGpa()
    //Method to return the grade point average
    //Postcondition: The GPA is calculated and returned.

public double billingAmount(double tuitionRate)
    //Method to return the tuition fees
    //Postcondition: The billing amount is calculated
    //                and returned.

private void sortCourses()
    //Method to sort the courses
    //Postcondition: The array coursesEnrolled is sorted.
    //                The grades for each course, in the
    //                array courseGrades, are also reorganized.

public Student()
    //Default constructor
    //Postcondition: The instance variables are initialized.
```

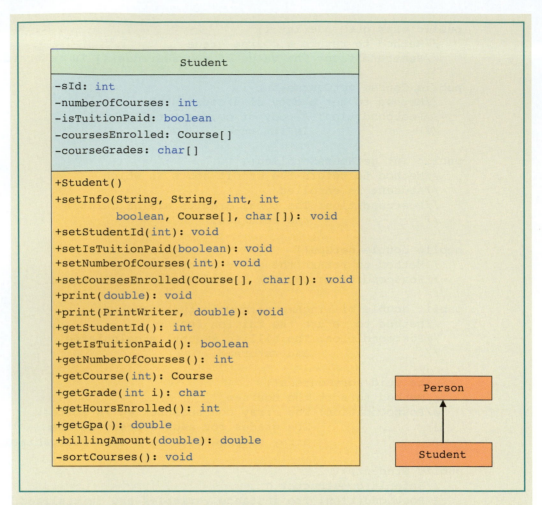

Figure 11-12   UML class diagram of the `class` `Student`

Note that the method **sortCourses** to sort the array **coursesEnrolled** is a **private** member of the **class** `Student`. This is because this method is needed for internal data manipulation and the user of the class does not need to access this member.

Next, we discuss the definitions of the methods to implement the operations of the **class** `Student`.

The method **setInfo** first initializes the **private** data members according to the incoming parameters. This method then calls the method **sortCourses** to sort the array **coursesEnrolled** by course number. The **class** `Student` is derived from the **class** `Person`, and the variables to store the first name and last name are **private** members of that class. Therefore, we call the method **setName** of the **class** `Person`, and we pass the appropriate variables to set the first and last names. The definition of the method `setInfo` is as follows:

```java
public void setInfo(String fName, String lName, int ID,
                    int nOfCourses, boolean isTPaid,
                    Course[] courses, char[] cGrades)
{
    int i;

    setName(fName, lName);          //set the name

    sId = ID;                       //set the student ID
    isTuitionPaid = isTPaid;        //set isTuitionPaid
    numberOfCourses = nOfCourses;   //set the number of courses

    for (i = 0; i < numberOfCourses; i++) //set the array
    {
        coursesEnrolled[i].copyCourseInfo(courses[i]);
        courseGrades[i] = cGrades[i];
    }

    sortCourses();          //sort the array coursesEnrolled
}
```

The definitions of the methods `setStudentId`, `setIsTuitionPaid`, `setNumberOfCourses`, and `setCoursesEnrolled` are similar to the definition of the method `setInfo`, and are given next.

```java
public void setStudentId(int ID)
{
    sId = ID;
}

public void setIsTuitionPaid(boolean isTPaid)
{
    isTuitionPaid = isTPaid;
}

public void setNumberOfCourses(int nOfCourses)
{
    numberOfCourses = nOfCourses;
}

public void setCoursesEnrolled(Course[] courses,
                               char[] cGrades)
{
    for (int i = 0; i < numberOfCourses; i++)
    {
        coursesEnrolled[i].copyCourseInfo(courses[i]);
```

```
            courseGrades[i] = cGrades[i];
        }

        sortCourses();
}
```

The default constructor initializes the instance variables to their default values.

```
public Student()
{
    super();
    numberOfCourses = 0;
    sId = 0;
    isTuitionPaid = false;

    coursesEnrolled = new Course[6];

    for (int i = 0; i < 6; i++)
        coursesEnrolled[i] = new Course();

    courseGrades = new char[6];

    for (int i = 0; i < 6; i++)
        courseGrades[i] = '*';

}
```

The method `print`, which has one parameter, prints the grade report on the screen. If the student has paid his or her tuition, the grades and the GPA are shown. Otherwise, three stars are printed in place of each grade, the GPA is not shown, a message indicates that the grades are being held for nonpayment of the tuition, and the amount due is shown. This method has the following steps:

1. Output the student's name.
2. Output the student's ID.
3. Output the number of courses in which the student is enrolled.
4. Output heading: `Course No   Course Name   Credits   Grade`
5. Print each course's information.
6. Print the total credit hours.
7. `if isTuitionPaid is true`

    Output the GPA

   `else`

    Output the billing amount and a message about withholding the grades.

The definition of the method `print` is:

```java
public void print(double tuitionRate)
{
    int i;

    System.out.println("Student Name: "
                       + super.toString());        //Step 1

    System.out.println("Student ID: " + sId);      //Step 2

    System.out.println("Number of courses enrolled: "
                       + numberOfCourses);          //Step 3
    System.out.printf("%-12s%-15s%-8s%-6s%n", "Course No",
                      "Course Name", "Credits",
                      "Grade");                     //Step 4

    for (i = 0; i < numberOfCourses; i++)           //Step 5
    {
        coursesEnrolled[i].print();

        if (isTuitionPaid)
            System.out.printf("%8s%n", courseGrades[i]);
        else
            System.out.printf("%8s%n", "***");
    }

    System.out.println();

    System.out.println("Total number of credit hours: "
                       + getHoursEnrolled());       //Step 6

    if (isTuitionPaid)                              //Step 7
        System.out.printf("Midsemester GPA: %.2f%n",
                          getGpa());
    else
    {
        System.out.println("*** Grades are being held for "
                           + "not paying the tuition. ***");
        System.out.printf("Amount Due: $%.2f%n",
                          billingAmount(tuitionRate));
    }

    System.out.println("-*-*-*-*-*-*-*-*-*-*-*-*-"
                       + "*-*-*-*-*-*-*-*-*-*-*-\n");
}
```

The method `print`, which has two parameters, sends the output to a file. The definition of this method is:

```java
public void print(PrintWriter outp, double tuitionRate)
{
    int i;

    outp.println("Student Name: "
                 + super.toString());                    //Step 1

    outp.println("Student ID: " + sId);                  //Step 2

    outp.println("Number of courses enrolled: "
                 + numberOfCourses);                     //Step 3
    outp.printf("%-12s%-15s%-8s%-6s%n", "Course No",
                 "Course Name", "Credits",
                 "Grade");                               //Step 4

    for (i = 0; i < numberOfCourses; i++)                //Step 5
    {
        coursesEnrolled[i].print(outp);

        if (isTuitionPaid)
            outp.printf("%8s%n", courseGrades[i]);
        else
            outp.printf("%8s%n", "***");
    }

    outp.println();

    outp.println("Total number of credit hours: " +
                 getHoursEnrolled());                    //Step 6

    if (isTuitionPaid)                                   //Step 7
        outp.printf("Midsemester GPA: %.2f%n",
                    getGpa());
    else
    {
        outp.println("*** Grades are being held for "
                     + "not paying the tuition. ***");
        outp.printf("Amount Due: $%.2f%n",
                    billingAmount(tuitionRate));
    }

    outp.println("-*-*-*-*-*-*-*-*-*-*-*-*-"
                 + "*-*-*-*-*-*-*-*-*-*-\n");
}
```

The definitions of the methods `getName`, `getStudentId`, `getIsTuitionPaid`, `getNumberOfCourses`, and `getCourse` are given next:

```java
public int getStudentId()
{
    return sId;
}


public boolean getIsTuitionPaid()
{
    return isTuitionPaid;
}


public int getNumberOfCourses()
{
    return numberOfCourses;
}

public char getGrade(int i)
{
    return courseGrades[i];
}

public Course getCourse(int i)
{
    Course temp = new Course();

    temp.copyCourseInfo(coursesEnrolled[i]);

    return temp;
}
```

The method `getHoursEnrolled` calculates and returns the total credit hours that a student is taking. These credit hours are needed to calculate both the GPA and the billing amount. The total credit hours are calculated by adding the credit hours of each course in which the student is enrolled. Because the credit hours for a course are in the **private** data member of an object of the type **Course**, we use the method `getCredits` of the **class** Course to retrieve the credit hours. The definition of this method is:

```java
public int getHoursEnrolled()
{
    int totalCredits = 0;
    int i;

    for (i = 0; i < numberOfCourses; i++)
        totalCredits += coursesEnrolled[i].getCredits();
```

```
        return totalCredits;
}
```

If a student has not paid the tuition, the method **billingAmount** calculates and returns the amount due, based on the number of credit hours enrolled. The definition of this method is:

```
public double billingAmount(double tuitionRate)
{
      return tuitionRate * getHoursEnrolled();
}
```

We now discuss the method **getGpa**. This method calculates a student's GPA. To find the GPA, we find the equivalent points for each grade, add the points, and then divide the sum by the total credit hours the student is taking. The definition of this method is:

```
public double getGpa()
{
    int i;
    double sum = 0.0;

    for (i = 0; i < numberOfCourses; i++)
    {
        switch (courseGrades[i])
        {
        case 'A': sum += coursesEnrolled[i].getCredits() * 4;
                  break;
        case 'B': sum += coursesEnrolled[i].getCredits() * 3;
                  break;
        case 'C': sum += coursesEnrolled[i].getCredits() * 2;
                  break;
        case 'D': sum += coursesEnrolled[i].getCredits() * 1;
                  break;
        case 'F': sum += coursesEnrolled[i].getCredits() * 0;
                  break;
        default: System.out.println("Invalid Course Grade");
        }
    }

    return sum / getHoursEnrolled();
}
```

The method **sortCourses** sorts the array **coursesEnrolled** by course number. To sort the array, we use a selection sort algorithm. Because we will compare the course numbers, which are the strings and **private** data members of the **class** Course, we first retrieve and store the course numbers in the local variables. Moreover, this method also rearranges the course grades because the course grades are stored in a separate array. The definition of this method is:

```java
private void sortCourses()
{
    int i, j;
    int minIndex;
    Course temp = new Course();   //variable to swap the data
    String course1;
    String course2;

    char tempGrade;

    for (i = 0; i < numberOfCourses - 1; i++)
    {
        minIndex = i;

        for (j = i + 1; j < numberOfCourses; j++)
        {
            //get the course numbers
            course1 =
                coursesEnrolled[minIndex].getCourseNumber();
            course2 = coursesEnrolled[j].getCourseNumber();

            if (course1.compareTo(course2) > 0)
                minIndex = j;
        }//end for

        temp.copyCourseInfo(coursesEnrolled[minIndex]);
        coursesEnrolled[minIndex].copyCourseInfo
                                (coursesEnrolled[i]);
        coursesEnrolled[i].copyCourseInfo(temp);

        tempGrade = courseGrades[minIndex];
        courseGrades[minIndex] = courseGrades[i];
        courseGrades[i] = tempGrade;
    }//end for
}//end sortCourses
```

The definition of the **class** Student looks like the following. (You can complete the definition of this class as an exercise.)

```java
import java.io.*;

public class Student extends Person
{
    private int sId;                    //variable to store the
                                        //student ID
    private int numberOfCourses;        //variable to store the number
                                        //of courses
    private boolean isTuitionPaid;      //variable to indicate whether
                                        //the tuition is paid
    private Course [] coursesEnrolled;  //array to store
                                        //the courses
    private char [] courseGrades;       //array to store the
                                        //course grades
    //Place the definitions of the instance methods
    //as discussed here.
    //...
}
```

Main Program

Now that we have designed the **class**es **Course** and **Student**, we will use these classes to complete the program.

We will restrict our program to process a maximum of 10 students. Note that this program can easily be enhanced to process any number of students.

Because the **print** method of the **class Student** does the necessary computations to print the final grade report, the main program has very little work to do. In fact, all the main program must do is create the objects to hold the students' data, load the data into these objects, and then print the grade reports. Because the input is in a file and the output will be sent to a file, we create appropriate objects to access the input and output files. Essentially, the main algorithm for the program is:

1. Declare the variables.
2. Open the input file.
3. Open the output file.
4. Get the number of students registered and the tuition rate.
5. Load the students' data.
6. Print the grade reports.

Variables   This program processes a maximum of 10 students. Therefore, we must declare an array of 10 components of the type **Student** to hold the students' data. We also need to store the number of students registered and the tuition rate. Because the data will be read from a file, and because the output is sent to a file, we need two objects to access the input and output files. Thus, we need the following variables:

```java
Student[] studentList = new Student[maxNumberOfStudents];
```

```
int noOfStudents;
double tuitionRate;
Scanner inFile =
        new Scanner(new FileReader("a:\\stData.txt"));

PrintWriter outFile = new PrintWriter("a:\\sDataOut.out");
```

To simplify the complexity of the method `main`, we write a method, `getStudentData`, to load the students' data. Note that `maxNumberOfStudents` is a named constant, which we will declare in the main program, initialized to 10.

Method `getStudentData` This method has three parameters: a parameter to access the input file, a parameter to access the array `studentList`, and a parameter to know the number of students registered. In pseudocode, the definition of this method is as follows:

For each student in the university:

1. Get the first name, last name, student ID, and `isPaid`.
2. `if isPaid` is 'Y'

      set `isTuitionPaid` to `true`

   `else`

      set `isTuitionPaid` to `false`
3. Get the number of courses the student is taking.
4. For each course:

   a. Get the course name, course number, credit hours, and grade.

   b. Load the course information into a `Course` object.
5. Load the data into a `Student` object.

We need to declare several local variables to read and store the data. The definition of the method `getStudentData` is:

```
public static void getStudentData(Scanner inpFile,
                                  Student[] sList,
                                  int numberOfStudents)
{
        //Local variables
    String fName;      //variable to store the first name
    String lName;      //variable to store the last name
    int ID;            //variable to store the student ID
    int noOfCourses;   //variable to store the number of courses
    char isPaid;       //variable to store Y/N; that is,
                       //is the tuition paid?
    boolean isTuitionPaid;  //variable to store true/false

    String cName;   //variable to store the course name
    String cNo;     //variable to store the course number
    int credits;    //variable to store the course credit hours
    char grade;     //variable to store the course grade
```

```
int count;        //loop control variable
int i;            //loop control variable

Course[] courses = new Course[6]; //array of objects to
                                  //store the course
                                  //information
char[] courseGrades = new char[6];

for (i = 0; i < 6; i++)
    courses[i] = new Course();

for (count = 0; count < numberOfStudents; count++)
{
        //Step 1
    fName = inpFile.next();
    lName = inpFile.next();
    ID = inpFile.nextInt();
    isPaid = inpFile.next().charAt(0);

    if (isPaid == 'Y')                                  //Step 2
        isTuitionPaid = true;
    else
        isTuitionPaid = false;

    noOfCourses = inpFile.nextInt();                    //Step 3

    for (i = 0; i < noOfCourses; i++)                   //Step 4
    {
        cName = inpFile.next();
        cNo = inpFile.next();
        credits = inpFile.nextInt();
        courseGrades[i] =
            inpFile.next().charAt(0);

        courses[i].setCourseInfo(cName, cNo,
                        credits);
    }

    sList[count].setInfo(fName, lName, ID,
                    noOfCourses, isTuitionPaid,
                    courses, courseGrades);  //Step 5
}//end for
}
```

Method `printGradeReports` This method prints the grade reports. For each student, it calls the method `print` of the **class** `Student` to print the grade report of each student. The definition of the method `printGradeReports` is:

```java
public static void printGradeReports(PrintWriter outfile,
                                     Student[] sList,
                                     int numberOfStudents,
                                     double tuitionRate)
{
    int count;

    for (count = 0; count < numberOfStudents; count++)
        sList[count].print(outfile, tuitionRate);
}
```

Program Listing

```java
import java.io.*;
import java.util.*;

public class GradeReportProgram
{
    static final int maxNumberOfStudents = 10;

    public static void main(String[] args) throws
                                    FileNotFoundException
    {
        Student[] studentList =
                new Student[maxNumberOfStudents];

        int noOfStudents;
        double tuitionRate;

        Scanner inFile =
                new Scanner(new FileReader("a:\\stData.txt"));
        PrintWriter outFile =
                new PrintWriter("a:\\sDataOut.out");

        for (int i = 0; i < maxNumberOfStudents; i++)
            studentList[i] = new Student();


        noOfStudents = inFile.nextInt();        //get the number
                                                //of students
        tuitionRate = inFile.nextDouble();      //get the tuition
                                                //rate
```

```
        getStudentData(inFile, studentList, noOfStudents);
        printGradeReports(outFile, studentList,
                          noOfStudents, tuitionRate);

        inFile.close();
        outFile.close();
    }

    //Place the definition of the method getStudentData as
    //described above here

    //Place the definition of the method printGradeReports as
    //described above here
}
```

Sample Run:
```
Student Name: Lisa Miller
Student ID: 890238
Number of courses enrolled: 4
Course No  Course Name  Credits Grade
CSC478     ComputerSci     3       B
HIS356     History         3       A
MTH345     Mathematics     4       A
PHY357     Physics         3       B

Total number of credit hours: 13
Midsemester GPA: 3.54
-*-*-*-*-*-*-*-*-*-*-*-*-*-*-*-*-*-*-*-*-*-

Student Name: Bill Wilton
Student ID: 798324
Number of courses enrolled: 5
Course No  Course Name  Credits Grade
BIO234     Biology         4      ***
CHM256     Chemistry       4      ***
ENG378     English         3      ***
MTH346     Mathematics     3      ***
PHL534     Philosophy      3      ***

Total number of credit hours: 17
*** Grades are being held for not paying the tuition. ***
Amount Due: 5865.00
-*-*-*-*-*-*-*-*-*-*-*-*-*-*-*-*-*-*-*-*-*-
```

```
Student Name: Dandy Goat
Student ID: 746333
Number of courses enrolled: 6
Course No    Course Name    Credits Grade
BUS128       Business          3      C
CHM348       Chemistry         4      B
CSC201       ComputerSci       3      B
ENG328       English           3      B
HIS101       History           3      A
MTH137       Mathematics       3      A

Total number of credit hours: 19
Midsemester GPA: 3.16
-*-*-*-*-*-*-*-*-*-*-*-*-*-*-*-*-*-*-*-*-*-
```

Input File

```
3 345
Lisa Miller 890238 Y 4
Mathematics MTH345 4 A
Physics PHY357 3 B
ComputerSci CSC478 3 B
History HIS356 3 A
Bill Wilton 798324 N 5
English ENG378 3 B
Philosophy PHL534 3 A
Chemistry CHM256 4 C
Biology BIO234 4 A
Mathematics MTH346 3 C
Dandy Goat 746333 Y 6
History HIS101 3 A
English ENG328 3 B
Mathematics MTH137 3 A
Chemistry CHM348 4 B
ComputerSci CSC201 3 B
Business BUS128 3 C
```

Part II: Student Grade Report: GUI Design

The first part of this programming example illustrated how to display the output in the Windows console environment. In this section, we create the GUI as shown in Figure 11-13 to show the output.

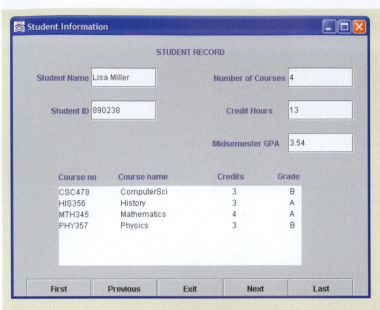

Figure 11-13   GUI to show a student's record

From the desired output, it is clear that the GUI contains various labels, text fields, and buttons. Moreover, when you click one of the buttons on the bottom row, an action event is generated. Therefore, we also need to write the code necessary to handle the events.

The students' records are stored in an array. When the user clicks the button labeled `First`, then the program must display the record of the first student in the list, that is, in the array. Similarly, when the user clicks the `Next` button, the program must display the record of the next student in the list.

 An object of the **class** `JTextField` can display only one line of text. However, the text showing the course information contains multiple lines. To display multi-line text we make use of the **class** `JTextArea`. We will create an object of the type `JTextArea` and use the appropriate methods of this class to display the courses as desired. We will introduce the methods as we need them. You can refer to Appendix E for a list of methods of the **class** `JTextArea`.

As in earlier programs, GUI components such as labels are placed in the content pane of the window. Thus, the program contains a window, a container, and various labels, text fields, a text area, and buttons. Let's first declare the reference variables to create the labels, text fields, and buttons.

```
//GUI components
//Each of the items to be displayed needs a label and text field.
//Labels end with L, text fields end with TF, and buttons end
//with B.
private JLabel headingL, stNameL, stIDL, noCoursesL,
               courseListL, creditHrsL, gpaL;

private JTextField stNameTF, stIDTF, noCoursesTF,
                   creditHrsTF, gpaTF;

private JTextArea courseListTA; //to display multiline text

private JButton exitB, nextB, prevB, firstB, lastB;
```

The following statements instantiate these objects:

```
      //instantiate the labels
headingL = new JLabel("STUDENT RECORD");
stNameL = new JLabel("Student Name ", SwingConstants.RIGHT);
stIDL = new JLabel("Student ID ", SwingConstants.RIGHT);
noCoursesL = new JLabel("Number of Courses ",
                        SwingConstants.RIGHT);
courseListL = new JLabel("Course no        Course name " +
                     "                    Credits " +
                     "                Grade");
creditHrsL = new JLabel("Credit Hours ", SwingConstants.RIGHT);
gpaL = new JLabel("Midsemester GPA ", SwingConstants.RIGHT);

      //instantiate the text fields
stNameTF = new JTextField(10);
stIDTF = new JTextField(10);
noCoursesTF = new JTextField(10);
creditHrsTF = new JTextField(10);
gpaTF = new JTextField(10);

      //instantiate the text area
courseListTA = new JTextArea(6, 20); //6 rows and 20 columns
courseListTA.setAutoscrolls(true);   //set the scroll bars to
                                     //appear

      //instantiate the buttons
exitB = new JButton("Exit");
nextB = new JButton("Next");
prevB = new JButton("Previous");
firstB = new JButton("First");
lastB = new JButton("Last");
```

We will create a class containing the application program by extending the **class** JFrame. We will also create an inner class to handle the action events.

The following statements set the title and the size of the window, and declare a reference variable that points to the content pane of the window.

```
setTitle("Student Information");   //set the title of the window
setSize(WIDTH, HEIGHT);            //set the size of the window
                                   //using the named constants
                                   //WIDTH and HEIGHT
Container pane  = getContentPane(); //get the container
```

From the GUI design it follows that GUI components are placed at a specific position in the container. To create such an interface, we set the container layout to **null**. The following statement accomplishes this:

```
pane.setLayout(null);         //set the container layout to null
```

We use the method **setSize** to specify the size of the GUI components. Recall from Chapter 6 that the heading of the method **setSize** is:

```
public void setSize(int width, int height)
```

The following statements set the size of each component:

```
headingL.setSize(200, 30);    //Label headingL is 200 pixels wide
                              //and 30 pixels high
stNameL.setSize(100, 30);
stNameTF.setSize(100, 30);
stIDL.setSize(100, 30);
stIDTF.setSize(100, 30);
noCoursesL.setSize(120, 30);
noCoursesTF.setSize(100, 30);
creditHrsL.setSize(100, 30);
creditHrsTF.setSize(100, 30);
gpaL.setSize(110, 30);
gpaTF.setSize(100, 30);
courseListL.setSize(370, 30);
courseListTA.setSize(370, 120);
firstB.setSize(100, 30);
prevB.setSize(100, 30);
exitB.setSize(100, 30);
nextB.setSize(100, 30);
lastB.setSize(100, 30);
```

Similarly, we use the method **setLocation** to specify the location of the GUI components in the container. The heading of the method **setLocation** is:

```
public void setLocation(int xCoordinate, int yCoordinate)
```

The following statements set the location of the GUI components in the container:

```
headingL.setLocation(220, 10);
```

```
stNameL.setLocation(20, 50);
stNameTF.setLocation(120, 50);
stIDL.setLocation(20, 100);
stIDTF.setLocation(120, 100);
noCoursesL.setLocation(300, 50);
noCoursesTF.setLocation(420, 50);
creditHrsL.setLocation(300, 100);
creditHrsTF.setLocation(420, 100);
gpaL.setLocation(300, 150);
gpaTF.setLocation(420, 150);
courseListL.setLocation(70, 200);
courseListTA.setLocation(70, 230);
firstB.setLocation(20, 370);
prevB.setLocation(120, 370);
exitB.setLocation(220, 370);
nextB.setLocation(320, 370);
lastB.setLocation(420, 370);
```

We will use the method **add** to put the labels, text fields, text area, and buttons into the container **pane**. The following statements accomplish this:

```
//add labels, text fields, and buttons to the pane
pane.add(headingL);
pane.add(stNameL);
pane.add(stNameTF);
pane.add(stIDL);
pane.add(stIDTF);
pane.add(noCoursesL);
pane.add(noCoursesTF);
pane.add(courseListL);
pane.add(courseListTA);
pane.add(creditHrsL);
pane.add(creditHrsTF);
pane.add(gpaL);
pane.add(gpaTF);
pane.add(firstB);
pane.add(prevB);
pane.add(exitB);
pane.add(nextB);
pane.add(lastB);
```

Method displayGradeReports Each student's record is stored in the array **studentList**. Therefore, to display a student's grade report, the relevant information is retrieved from the array **studentList** and is displayed in the respective text fields and text area. To simplify displaying a student's record, we write the method **displayGradeReports**. This method takes as its parameter an **int** variable specifying the position (index) in the array where the student's data is stored. Moreover, because the buttons `Next` and `Previous` show the data of the student preceding and following, respectively, the current student, the program must store the index of the current student, which we store in the instance variable `displayedStudentIndex`. Essentially, the definition of the method `displayGradeReports` is:

```java
public void displayGradeReports(int stNo)
{
    displayedStudentIndex = stNo;
    String CourseListing = "";

    boolean isPaid = studentList[stNo].getIsTuitionPaid();

    stNameTF.setText(studentList[stNo].getFirstName() + " "
                    + studentList[stNo].getLastName());
    stIDTF.setText("" + studentList[stNo].getStudentId());
    noCoursesTF.setText("" + studentList[stNo].getNumberOfCourses());
    creditHrsTF.setText("" + studentList[stNo].getHoursEnrolled());

    if (isPaid)
        gpaTF.setText("" + String.format("%.2f",
                        studentList[stNo].getGpa()));
    else
        gpaTF.setText("" + "****");

    for (int count = 0;
            count < studentList[stNo].getNumberOfCourses();
            count++)
    {
        String str;
        Course temp;

        temp = studentList[stNo].getCourse(count);

        str = temp.getCourseNumber() + "\t  "
            + temp.getCourseName() + "\t\t"
            + temp.getCredits() + "\t";

        if (isPaid)
            str = str + studentList[stNo].getGrade(count);
        else
            str = str + "***";

        if (count == 0)
            CourseListing = str;
        else
```

```
                    CourseListing = CourseListing + "\n" + str;
        }


        if (!isPaid)
            CourseListing = CourseListing + "\n"
                        + "*** Grades are being held for "
                        + "not paying the tuition. ***\n"
                        + "Amount Due: $"
                        + String.format("%.2f",
                    studentList[stNo].billingAmount(tuitionRate));


        courseListTA.setText(CourseListing);
}
```

Event Handling   The GUI contains five buttons, each generating a specific event. To process these events, we create the **class** ButtonHandler implementing the **interface** ActionListener. Moreover, the method getActionCommand of the **class** ActionEvent is used to identify the button generating the event. The definition of the **class** ButtonHandler and the method actionPerformed is:

```
private class ButtonHandler implements ActionListener
{
    public void actionPerformed(ActionEvent e)
    {
        if (e.getActionCommand().equals("Previous"))
            if (displayedStudentIndex > 0)
                displayGradeReports(displayedStudentIndex - 1);
            else
                displayGradeReports(displayedStudentIndex);
        else if (e.getActionCommand().equals("Next"))
            if (displayedStudentIndex + 1 < noOfStudents)
                displayGradeReports
                                (displayedStudentIndex + 1);
            else
                displayGradeReports(displayedStudentIndex);
        else if (e.getActionCommand().equals("First"))
            displayGradeReports(0);
        else if (e.getActionCommand().equals("Last"))
            displayGradeReports(noOfStudents - 1);
        else
            System.exit(0);
    }
}
```

As usual, we declare and instantiate an object of the type ButtonHandler and then register this object to each button. The following statements declare and instantiate the object handler:

```
private ButtonHandler bHandler; //declare the event handler
```

```
bHandler = new ButtonHandler(); //instantiate the event handler
```

The following statements register the listener object **bHandler** with the buttons:

```
exitB.addActionListener(bHandler);
nextB.addActionListener(bHandler);
prevB.addActionListener(bHandler);
firstB.addActionListener(bHandler);
lastB.addActionListener(bHandler);
```

Main Program

As in the first part of this program, this part also processes a maximum of 10 students. Therefore, we must declare an array of 10 components of the type **Student** to hold the students' data. We also must store the number of students registered and the tuition rate. Thus, we need the following variables:

```
Student[] studentList = new Student[maxNumberOfStudents];

int noOfStudents;
double tuitionRate;
```

Because we are creating a GUI, in order to place the data stored in **studentList** in GUI components such as the text field and text area, we declare these variables as instance variables of the class containing the application program. Moreover, because they will be declared as instance variables, these variables need not be passed as parameters to the method **getStudentData**.

The data will be read from a file, so we need the following **Scanner** object to access the input file:

```
Scanner inFile =
        new Scanner(new FileReader("a:\\stData.txt"));
```

Method getStudentData Because **studentList** and **noOfStudents** are instance variables, this method can directly access them. Therefore, this method has only one parameter: a parameter to access the input file. In pseudocode, the definition of this method is the same as the definition of this method for the non-GUI application program we designed in the first part. In fact, except for the heading of this method, the body of this method is similar to the one given in the first part of this program. Therefore, we give only the heading and leave the body as an exercise for you (see Programming Exercise 11).

```
public static void getStudentData(Scanner inFile)
{
    //Write the body of this method.
}
```

Program Listing

The preceding sections defined the necessary algorithms, methods, classes, and GUI components to complete the design of the Java program to create the GUI to display a student's data.

The program listing follows:

```java
//Main program

import java.io.*;
import java.util.*;
import javax.swing.*;
import java.awt.*;
import java.awt.event.*;

public class GradeReportProgram extends JFrame
{
    private static final int WIDTH = 550;
    private static final int HEIGHT = 430;

    private static final int maxNumberOfStudents = 10;

        //instance variables
    private Student[] studentList =
                        new Student[maxNumberOfStudents];
    private int noOfStudents;
    private double tuitionRate;
    private int displayedStudentIndex = 0;

        //GUI components
        //Each of the items to be displayed needs
        //a label and text field.
        //Labels end with L and text fields end with TF.
    private JLabel headingL, stNameL, stIDL, noCoursesL,
                courseListL, creditHrsL, gpaL;
    private JTextField stNameTF, stIDTF, noCoursesTF,
                    creditHrsTF, gpaTF;
    private JTextArea courseListTA;
    private JButton exitB, nextB, prevB, firstB, lastB;

    private ButtonHandler bHandler;

    public GradeReportProgram()
    {
      setTitle("Student Information");        //set the window title
      setSize(WIDTH, HEIGHT);                 //set the window size
```

```java
Container pane = getContentPane();   //get the container
pane.setLayout(null);   //set the container's layout to null

bHandler = new ButtonHandler();   //instantiate the button
                                  //event handler

    //instantiate the labels
headingL = new JLabel("STUDENT RECORD");
stNameL = new JLabel("Student Name ", SwingConstants.RIGHT);
stIDL = new JLabel("Student ID ", SwingConstants.RIGHT);
noCoursesL = new JLabel("Number of Courses ",
                        SwingConstants.RIGHT);
courseListL = new JLabel("Course no          Course name " +
                         "                    Credits " +
                         "              Grade");
creditHrsL = new
       JLabel("Credit Hours ", SwingConstants.RIGHT);
gpaL = new JLabel("Midsemester GPA ", SwingConstants.RIGHT);

    //instantiate the text fields
stNameTF = new JTextField(10);
stIDTF = new JTextField(10);
noCoursesTF = new JTextField(10);
creditHrsTF = new JTextField(10);
gpaTF = new JTextField(10);

  //instantiate the text area
courseListTA = new JTextArea(6, 20);
courseListTA.setAutoscrolls(true);

  //instantiate the buttons and register the listener
exitB = new JButton("Exit");
exitB.addActionListener(bHandler);

nextB = new JButton("Next");
nextB.addActionListener(bHandler);

prevB = new JButton("Previous");
prevB.addActionListener(bHandler);

firstB = new JButton("First");
firstB.addActionListener(bHandler);

lastB = new JButton("Last");
lastB.addActionListener(bHandler);
```

```java
    //set the size of the labels, text fields, and buttons
headingL.setSize(200, 30);
stNameL.setSize(100, 30);
stNameTF.setSize(100, 30);
stIDL.setSize(100, 30);
stIDTF.setSize(100, 30);
noCoursesL.setSize(120, 30);
noCoursesTF.setSize(100, 30);
creditHrsL.setSize(100, 30);
creditHrsTF.setSize(100, 30);
gpaL.setSize(110, 30);
gpaTF.setSize(100, 30);
courseListL.setSize(370, 30);
courseListTA.setSize(370, 120);
firstB.setSize(100, 30);
prevB.setSize(100, 30);
exitB.setSize(100, 30);
nextB.setSize(100, 30);
lastB.setSize(100, 30);

    //set the location of the labels, text fields, and buttons
headingL.setLocation(220, 10);
stNameL.setLocation(20, 50);
stNameTF.setLocation(120, 50);
stIDL.setLocation(20, 100);
stIDTF.setLocation(120, 100);
noCoursesL.setLocation(300, 50);
noCoursesTF.setLocation(420, 50);
creditHrsL.setLocation(300, 100);
creditHrsTF.setLocation(420, 100);
gpaL.setLocation(300, 150);
gpaTF.setLocation(420, 150);
courseListL.setLocation(70, 200);
courseListTA.setLocation(70, 230);
firstB.setLocation(20, 370);
prevB.setLocation(120, 370);
exitB.setLocation(220, 370);
nextB.setLocation(320, 370);
lastB.setLocation(420, 370);

    //add the labels, text fields, and buttons to the pane
pane.add(headingL);
pane.add(stNameL);
pane.add(stNameTF);
pane.add(stIDL);
```

```
        pane.add(stIDTF);
        pane.add(noCoursesL);
        pane.add(noCoursesTF);
        pane.add(courseListL);
        pane.add(courseListTA);
        pane.add(creditHrsL);
        pane.add(creditHrsTF);
        pane.add(gpaL);
        pane.add(gpaTF);
        pane.add(firstB);
        pane.add(prevB);
        pane.add(exitB);
        pane.add(nextB);
        pane.add(lastB);

        setVisible(true); //show the window
        setDefaultCloseOperation(EXIT_ON_CLOSE);
    }//end constructor

    public static void main(String[] args) throws
                                    FileNotFoundException
    {
        GradeReportProgram gradeProg =
                    new GradeReportProgram();

        Scanner inFile =
            new Scanner(new FileReader("a:\\stData.txt"));

        for (int i = 0; i < maxNumberOfStudents; i++)
            gradeProg.studentList[i] = new Student();

        gradeProg.noOfStudents =
                inFile.nextInt(); //get the number of students
        gradeProg.tuitionRate =
                inFile.nextDouble(); //get the tuition rate

        gradeProg.getStudentData(inFile);
        gradeProg.displayGradeReports(0);
    }

    //Write and place the definition of the method
    //getStudentData here.

    //Place the definition of the class ButtonHandler here.

    //Place the definition of the method displayGradeReports here.

}
```

Sample Output: (Programming Exercise 11, at the end of this chapter, asks you to write the definition of the method `getStudentData`. When you have completed Programming Exercise 11 and execute your program, it should produce the output shown in Figures 11-14 and 11-15.)

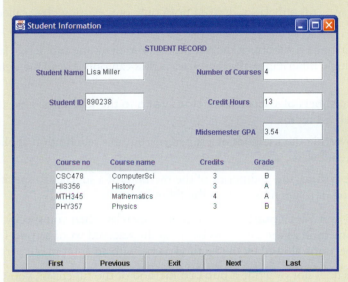

Figure 11-14   Sample GUI output of the student grade program

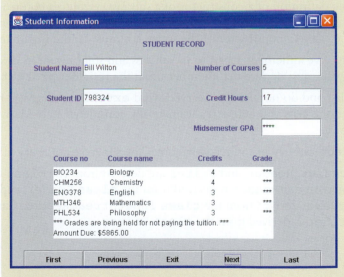

Figure 11-15   Sample output after clicking Next

QUICK REVIEW

1. Inheritance and composition are meaningful ways to relate two or more classes.

2. Inheritance is an "is-a" relationship.

3. Composition is a "has-a" relationship.

4. In single inheritance, the subclass is derived from only one existing class, called the superclass.

5. In multiple inheritance, a subclass is derived from more than one superclass. Java does not support multiple inheritance, that is, in Java a class can only *extend* the definition of one class.

6. The **private** members of a superclass are **private** to the superclass. The subclass cannot directly access them.

7. A subclass can override the methods of a superclass, but this redefinition applies only to the objects of the subclass.

8. In general, while writing the definitions of the methods of a subclass to specify a call to a **public** method of a superclass, we do the following:

   - If the subclass overrides a **public** method of a superclass, then you specify a call to that **public** method of the superclass by using the reserved word **super** followed by the dot operator followed by the method name with an appropriate parameter list.

   - If the subclass does not override a **public** method of the superclass, you can specify a call to that **public** method by using the name of the method and an appropriate parameter list.

9. While writing the definition of a constructor of a subclass, a call to a constructor of the superclass is specified using the reserved word **super** with an appropriate parameter list. Moreover, the call to a constructor of the superclass must be the first statement.

10. For a superclass to give a member access to its subclass and still prevent its direct access outside the class, you must declare that member using the modifier **protected**.

11. If you define a class and do not use the reserved word **extends** to derive it from an existing class, then the class you define is automatically considered to be derived from the **class** Object.

12. The **class** Object directly or indirectly becomes the superclass of every class in Java.

13. The **class**es Scanner, Reader, and Writer are derived from the **class** Object. The **class** InputStreamReader is derived from the **class** Reader, and the **class** FileReader is derived from the **class** InputStreamReader. Similarly, the **class** PrintWriter is derived from the **class** Writer.

14. Java allows us to treat an object of a subclass as an object of a superclass, that is, a reference variable of a superclass type can point to an object of a subclass type.

15. In a class hierarchy, several methods can have the same name and the same formal parameter list.

16. A reference variable of a class can refer to either an object of its own class or an object of its subclass.

17. In early binding, a method's definition is associated with its invocation when the code is compiled.

18. In late binding, a method's definition is associated with its invocation at execution time, that is, when the method is executed.

19. Except for a few (special) cases, Java uses late binding for all methods.

20. The term polymorphism means assigning multiple meanings to the same method. In Java, polymorphism is implemented using late binding.

21. You *cannot* automatically consider a superclass object to be an object of a subclass. In other words, you *cannot* automatically make a reference variable of a subclass type point to an object of a superclass type.

22. Suppose that `supRef` is a reference variable of a superclass type. Moreover, suppose that `supRef` points to an object of a subclass. You can use an appropriate cast operator on `supRef` and make a reference variable of the subclass point to the object. On the other hand, if `supRef` does not point to a subclass object, and you use a cast operator on `supRef` to make a reference variable of the subclass point to the object, then Java will throw a `ClassCastException`—indicating that the class cast is not allowed.

23. An abstract method is a method that has only the heading, not the body. Moreover, the heading of an abstract method is terminated with a semicolon.

24. An abstract class is a class that is declared with the reserved word `abstract` in its heading.

25. Following are some of the facts about abstract classes:

- An abstract class can contain instance variables, constructors, a finalizer, and nonabstract methods.

- An abstract class can contain abstract method(s).

- If a class contains an abstract method, then the class must be declared abstract.

- You cannot instantiate an object of an abstract class. You can only declare a reference variable of an abstract class type.

- You can instantiate an object of a subclass of an abstract class, but only if the subclass gives the definitions of *all* the abstract methods of the superclass.

26. An `interface` is a class that contains only abstract methods and/or named constants.

27. Java allows a class to implement more than one interface. This is, in fact, the way to implement multiple inheritance in Java.

28. In composition, one or more members of a class are objects of another class type.

11

EXERCISES

1. Mark the following statements as true or false.

   a. The constructor of a subclass specifies a call to the constructor of the superclass in the heading of the constructor's definition.

   b. The constructor of a subclass specifies a call to the constructor of the superclass using the name of the class.

   c. A subclass must have a constructor.

   d. In Java, polymorphism is implemented using late binding.

2. Draw a class hierarchy in which several classes are subclasses of a single superclass.

3. Suppose that a **class** Employee is derived from the **class** Person (see Example 8-4, in Chapter 8). Give examples of data and method members that can be added to the **class** Employee.

4. Explain the difference between the **private** and **protected** members of a class.

5. What is the difference between overloading a method name and overriding a method name?

6. Name two situations in which you would use the reserved word **super**.

7. Consider the following class definition:

```java
public class AClass
{
    private int u;
    private int v;

    public void print()
    {
    }

    public void set(int x, int y)
    {
    }

    public AClass()
    {
    }

    public AClass(int x, int y)
    {
    }
}
```

What is wrong with the following class definition?

```
class BClass AClass
{
    private int w;

    public void print()
    {
        System.out.println("u + v + w = " + (u + v + w));
    }

    public BClass()
    {
        super();
        w = 0;
    }

    public BClass(int x, int y, int z)
    {
        super(x, y);
        w = z;
    }
}
```

8. Consider the following statements:

```
public class YClass
{
    private int a;
    private int b;

    public void one()
    {
    }

    public void two(int x, int y)
    {
    }

    public YClass()
    {
    }
}

class XClass extends YClass
{
    private int z;
```

```
        public void one()
        {
        }

        public XClass()
        {
        }
}

YClass yObject = new YClass();
XClass xObject = new XClass();
```

a. The **private** members of **YClass** are **public** members of **XClass**. True or False?

b. Mark the following statements as valid or invalid. If a statement is invalid, explain why.

  (i) The following is a valid definition of the method **one** of **YClass**.

```
        public void one()
        {
                System.out.println(a + b);
        }
```

  (ii)

```
        yObject.a = 15;
        xObject.b = 30;
```

  (iii) The following is a valid definition of the method **one** of **XClass**.

```
        public void one()
        {
                a = 10;
                b = 15;
                z = 30;
                System.out.println(a + b + z);
        }
```

  (iv)

```
        System.out.println(yObject.a + " " + yObject.b + " "
                            + xObject.z);
```

9. Assume the declaration of Exercise 8.

  a. Write the definition of the default constructor of **YClass** so that the instance variables of **YClass** are initialized to 0.

  b. Write the definition of the default constructor of **XClass** so that the instance variables of **XClass** are initialized to 0.

  c. Write the definition of the method **two** of **YClass** so that the instance variable **a** is initialized to the value of the first parameter of **two**, and the instance variable **b** is initialized to the value of the second parameter of **two**.

10. Suppose that you have the following class:

```java
public class ClassA
{
    private int x;                              //Line 1
    protected void setX(int a)                  //Line 2
    {                                           //Line 3
        x = a;                                  //Line 4
    }
}
```

What is wrong with the following code?

```java
public class Exercise10                         //Line 5
{
    public static void main(String[] args)      //Line 6
    {
        ClassA aObject;                         //Line 7

        aObject.setX(4);                        //Line 8
    }
}
```

11. Suppose that you have the following class definition:

```java
public class One
{
    private int x;
    private int y;

    public void print()
    {
        System.out.println(x + " " + y);
    }

    protected void setData(int u, int v)
    {
        x = u;
        y = v;
    }
}
```

Consider the following class definition:

```java
public class Two extends One
{
    private int z;

    public void setData(int a, int b, int c)
    {
        //Postcondition: x = a; y = b; z = c;
    }
}
```

11

```
        public void print()
        {
            //Output the values of x, y, and z
        }
}
```

a. Write the definition of the method **setData** of the **class Two** as described in the class definition.

b. Write the definition of the method **print** of the **class Two** as described in the class definition.

12. Suppose that you have the following class definitions:

```
public class SuperClass
{
    protected int x;

    private String str;

    public void print()
    {
        System.out.println(x + " " + str);
    }

    public SuperClass()
    {
        str = "";
        x = 0;
    }

    public SuperClass(String s, int a)
    {
        str = s;
        x = a;
    }
}


public class SubClass extends SuperClass
{
    private int y;

    public void print()
    {
        System.out.println("SubClass: " + y);
        super.print();
    }
```

```
    public SubClass()
    {
        super();
        y = 0;
    }

    public SubClass(String s, int a, int b)
    {
        super("Hello Super", a + b);
        y = b;
    }
}
```

What is the output of the following Java code?

```
SuperClass superObject = new SuperClass("This is superclass", 2);
SubClass subObject = new SubClass("DDDDD", 3, 7);

superObject.print();
subObject.print();
```

13. What does the operator **instanceof** do?

14. What is an abstract method?

15. What is the difference between an abstract class and an interface?

16. Why does Java allow a class to implement more than one interface?

PROGRAMMING EXERCISES

11

1. In Chapter 8, the **class Clock** was designed to implement the time of day in a program. Certain applications, in addition to hours, minutes, and seconds, might require you to store the time zone. Derive the **class ExtClock** from the **class Clock** by adding a data member to store the time zone. Add the necessary methods and constructors to make the class functional. Also, write the definitions of the methods and the constructors. Finally, write a test program to test your class.

2. In this chapter, the **class Date** was designed to implement the date in a program, but the method **setDate** and the constructor with parameters do not check whether the date is valid before storing the date in the data members. Rewrite the definitions of the method **setDate** and the constructor with parameters so that the values of month, day, and year are checked before storing the date into the data members. Add a method **isLeapYear** to check whether a year is a leap year. Then write a test program to test your class.

3. A point in the *x-y* plane is represented by its *x*-coordinate and *y*-coordinate. Design the **class Point** that can store and process a point in the *x-y* plane. You should then perform operations on a point, such as showing the point, setting the coordinates of the point, printing the coordinates of the point, returning the *x*-coordinate, and returning the *y*-coordinate. Also write a test program to test various operations on a point.

4. Every circle has a center and a radius. Given the radius, we can determine the circle's area and circumference. Given the center, we can determine its position in the *x-y* plane. The center of a circle is a point in the *x-y* plane. Design the **class** Circle that can store the radius and center of the circle. Because the center is a point in the *x-y* plane and you designed the class to capture the properties of a point in Programming Exercise 3, you must derive the **class** Circle from the **class** Point. You should be able to perform the usual operations on a circle, such as setting the radius, printing the radius, calculating and printing the area and circumference, and carrying out the usual operations on the center.

5. Every cylinder has a base and height, where the base is a circle. Design the **class** Cylinder that can capture the properties of a cylinder and perform the usual operations on a cylinder. Derive this class from the **class** Circle designed in Programming Exercise 4. Some of the operations that can be performed on a cylinder are as follows: calculate and print the volume, calculate and print the surface area, set the height, set the radius of the base, and set the center of the base.

6. Using classes, design an online address book to keep track of the names, addresses, phone numbers, and birthdays of family members, close friends, and certain business associates. Your program should be able to handle a maximum of 500 entries.

a. Define the **class** Address that can store a street address, city, state, and ZIP code. Use the appropriate methods to print and store the address. Also, use constructors to automatically initialize the data members.

b. Define the **class** ExtPerson using the **class** Person (as defined in Example 8-4, Chapter 8), the **class** Date (as designed in this chapter's Programming Exercise 2), and the **class** Address. Add a data member to this class to classify the person as a family member, friend, or business associate. Also add a data member to store the phone number. Add (or override) methods to print and store the appropriate information. Use constructors to automatically initialize the data members.

c. Define the **class** AddressBook using previously defined classes. An object of the type AddressBook should be able to process a maximum of 500 entries.

The program should perform the following operations:

(i)   Load the data into the address book from a disk.

(ii)   Sort the address book by last name.

(iii)   Search for a person by last name.

(iv)   Print the address, phone number, and date of birth (if it exists) of a given person.

(v)   Print the names of the people whose birthdays are in a given month or between two given dates.

(vi)   Print the names of all the people between two last names.

(vii)   For special occasions, such as birthdays, print three different messages: one for family members, one for friends, and one for business associates. Your program should be able to print the names of all family members, friends, or business associates.

7. In Programming Exercise 2, the **class** Date was designed and implemented to keep track of a date, but it has very limited operations. Redefine the **class** Date so that, in addition to the operations already defined, it can perform the following operations on a date:

   a. Set the month.

   b. Set the day.

   c. Set the year.

   d. Return the month.

   e. Return the day.

   f. Return the year.

   g. Test whether the year is a leap year.

   h. Return the number of days in the month. For example, if the date is 3-12-2005, the number of days to be returned is 31 because there are 31 days in March.

   i. Return the number of days passed in the year. For example, if the date is 3-18-2005, the number of days passed in the year is 77. Note that the number of days returned also includes the current day.

   j. Return the number of days remaining in the year. For example, if the date is 3-18-2005, the number of days remaining in the year is 288.

   k. Calculate the new date by adding a fixed number of days to the date. For example, if the date is 3-18-2005 and the days to be added are 25, the new date is 4-12-2005.

   l. Return a reference to the object containing a copy of the date.

   m. Make a copy of another date. Given a reference to an object containing a date, copy the data members of the object into the corresponding data members of this object.

   n. Write the definitions of the methods to implement the operations defined for the **class** Date.

8. The **class** Date defined in Programming Exercise 7 prints the date in numerical form. Some applications might require the date to be printed in another form, such as March 24, 2005. Derive the **class** ExtDate so that the date can be printed in either form.

   Add a data member to the **class** ExtDate so that the month can also be stored in string form. Add a method to output the month in the string format followed by the year—for example, in the form March 2005.

   Write the definitions of the methods to implement the operations for the **class** ExtDate.

11

9. Using the **class**es **ExtDate** (Programming Exercise 8) and **Day** (Chapter 8, Programming Exercise 2), design the **class Calendar** so that, given the month and the year, we can print the calendar for that month. To print a monthly calendar, you must know the first day of the month and the number of days in that month. Thus, you must store the first day of the month, which is of the form **Day**, and the month and the year of the calendar. Clearly, the month and the year can be stored in an object of the form **ExtDate** by setting the day component of the date to **1**, and the month and year as specified by the user. Thus, the **class Calendar** has two data members: an object of the type **Day**, and an object of the type **ExtDate**.

Design the **class Calendar** so that the program can print a calendar for any month starting January 1, 1500. Note that the day for January 1 of the year 1500 was a Monday. To calculate the first day of a month, you can add the appropriate days to Monday of January 1, 1500.

For the **class Calendar**, include the following operations:

   a. Determine the first day of the month for which the calendar will be printed. Call this operation **firstDayOfMonth**.

   b. Set the month.

   c. Set the year.

   d. Return the month.

   e. Return the year.

   f. Print the calendar for the particular month.

   g. Add the appropriate constructors to initialize the data members.

10. a. Write the definitions of the methods of the **class Calendar** (designed in Programming Exercise 9) to implement the operations of the **class Calendar**.

   b. Write a test program to print the calendar for either a particular month or a particular year. For example, the calendar for September 2005 is

```
                    September 2005
     Sun      Mon      Tue      Wed      Thu      Fri      Sat
                                          1        2        3
      4        5        6        7        8        9       10
     11       12       13       14       15       16       17
     18       19       20       21       22       23       24
     25       26       27       28       29       30
```

11. Write the definition of the method **getStudentData** of the GUI version of the Programming Example Student Grade Report. Also complete the definition of the main program. When you execute your program, it should produce the output shown in Figures 11–14 and 11–15.

12

HANDLING EXCEPTIONS AND EVENTS

In this chapter, you will:

♦ Learn what an exception is
♦ See how a `try`/`catch` block is used to handle exceptions
♦ Become aware of the hierarchy of exception classes
♦ Learn about checked and unchecked exceptions
♦ Learn how to handle exceptions within a program
♦ Discover how to throw and rethrow an exception
♦ Learn how to handle events in a program

Chapter 3, in the section File Input/Output, when describing the syntax of the method `main`, defined an *exception* as an occurrence of an undesirable situation that can be detected during program execution. For example, division by zero and inputting invalid data are exceptions. Similarly, trying to open an input file that does not exist is an exception, as is an array index that goes out of bounds.

Until now, our programs have not included any code to handle exceptions. If exceptions occurred during program execution, the program terminated with an appropriate error message. However, there are situations when an exception occurs and you don't want the program to simply ignore the exception and terminate. For example, a program that monitors stock performance should not automatically sell if the account balance goes below a certain level. It should inform the stockholder and request an appropriate action.

This chapter provides more detail about exceptions and how they are handled in Java. You will learn about different kinds of exceptions, and the options available for programmers to deal with them. You'll also extend what you learned in Chapters 6 and 11 about event handling.

Chapter 12

HANDLING EXCEPTIONS WITHIN A PROGRAM

Chapter 2 remarked that if you try to input invalid data into a variable, the program will terminate with an error message, so an exception occurs. For example, inputting a letter or number containing a non-digit character into an **int** variable would cause an exception to occur. This section discusses how to handle exceptions. However, first we give some examples that show what can happen if an exception is not handled, as well as review some of the ways we handle exceptions.

The program in Example 12-1 shows what happens when division by zero or an invalid input occurs and this problem is not addressed.

Example 12-1

```java
import java.util.*;

public class ExceptionExample1
{
    static Scanner console = new Scanner(System.in);

    public static void main(String[] args)
    {
        int dividend, divisor, quotient;            //Line 1

        System.out.print("Line 2: Enter the "
                    + "dividend: ");                 //Line 2
        dividend = console.nextInt();               //Line 3
        System.out.println();                       //Line 4

        System.out.print("Line 5: Enter the "
                    + "divisor: ");                  //Line 5
        divisor = console.nextInt();                //Line 6
        System.out.println();                       //Line 7

        quotient = dividend / divisor;              //Line 8

        System.out.println("Line 9: Quotient = "
                    + quotient);                     //Line 9
    }
}
```

Sample Run 1:
Line 2: Enter the dividend: 12

Line 5: Enter the divisor: 5

Line 9: Quotient = 2

Sample Run 2:
```
Line 2: Enter the dividend: 24

Line 5: Enter the divisor: 0

Exception in thread "main" java.lang.ArithmeticException: / by zero
        at ExceptionExample1.main(ExceptionExample1.java:22)
```

Sample Run 3:
```
Line 2: Enter the dividend: 2e
Exception in thread "main" java.util.InputMismatchException
        at java.util.Scanner.throwFor(Unknown Source)
        at java.util.Scanner.next(Unknown Source)
        at java.util.Scanner.nextInt(Unknown Source)
        at java.util.Scanner.nextInt(Unknown Source)
        at ExceptionExample1.main(ExceptionExample1.java:14)
```

In Sample Run 1, the value of `divisor` is nonzero and so no exception occurred. The program calculated and output the quotient and terminated normally.

In Sample Run 2, the value entered for `divisor` is 0. The statement in Line 8 divides `dividend` by the divisor. However, the program does not check whether `divisor` is 0 before dividing `dividend` by `divisor`. So the program terminates with the message as shown.

In Sample Run 3, the value entered is `2e`. This input cannot be expressed as an `int` value, Therefore, the method `nextInt` in Line 3 throws an `InputMismatchException` and the program terminates with the error message as shown.

Note that on some systems, you may get the following output for Sample Run 3:

```
Line 2: Enter the dividend: 2e
Exception in thread "main" java.util.InputMismatchException
        at java.util.Scanner.throwFor(Scanner.java:819)
        at java.util.Scanner.next(Scanner.java:1431)
        at java.util.Scanner.nextInt(Scanner.java:2040)
        at java.util.Scanner.nextInt(Scanner.java:2000)
        at ExceptionExample1.main(ExceptionExample1.java:14)
```

Next, consider Example 12-2. This is the same program as in Example 12-1, except that in Line 8 the program checks whether `divisor` is zero. (We will explain, later in this chapter, how to use Java's mechanism to handle an `InputMismatchException`).

Example 12-2

```java
import java.util.*;

public class ExceptionExample2
{
    static Scanner console = new Scanner(System.in);
```

```
public static void main(String[] args)
{
    int dividend, divisor, quotient;              //Line 1

    System.out.print("Line 2: Enter the "
                      + "dividend: ");             //Line 2
    dividend = console.nextInt();                 //Line 3
    System.out.println();                         //Line 4

    System.out.print("Line 5: Enter the "
                      + "divisor: ");              //Line 5
    divisor = console.nextInt();                  //Line 6
    System.out.println();                         //Line 7

    if (divisor != 0)                             //Line 8
    {
        quotient = dividend / divisor;            //Line 9
        System.out.println("Line 10: "
                      + "Quotient = "
                      + quotient);                 //Line 10
    }
    else
        System.out.println("Line 11: Cannot "
                      + "divide by zero.");        //Line 11
}
}
```

Sample Run 1:
Line 2: Enter the dividend: 12

Line 5: Enter the divisor: 5

Line 10: Quotient = 2

Sample Run 2:
Line 2: Enter the dividend: 24

Line 5: Enter the divisor: 0

Line 11: Cannot divide by zero.

In Sample Run 1, the value of **divisor** is nonzero, so no exception occurred. The program calculated and output the quotient and terminated normally.

In Sample Run 2, the value entered for **divisor** is 0. In Line 8, the program checks whether **divisor** is 0. Because **divisor** is zero, the expression in the **if** statement fails, and the **else** part executes, which outputs the third line of the sample run.

Java's Mechanism of Exception Handling

Example 12-1 shows what happens when a division by zero or an input mismatch exception occurs in a program and is not processed. Example 12-2 shows a way to handle a division by zero exception. However, suppose that division by zero occurs in more than one place within the same block. In this case, using **if** statements may not be the most effective way to handle the exception.

Next, we describe how to effectively handle exceptions using Java's exception handling mechanism. However, first let's note the following.

When an exception occurs, an object of a particular exception **class** is created. For example, in Sample Run 2 of Example 12-1, an object of the **class ArithmeticException** is created. Java provides a number of exception classes to effectively handle certain common exceptions such as division by zero, invalid input, and file not found. For example, division by zero is an arithmetic error and is handled by the **class ArithmeticException**. Therefore, when a division by zero exception occurs, the program creates an object of the **class ArithmeticException**. Similarly, when a **Scanner** object is used to input data into a program, any invalid input errors are handled using the **class InputMismatchException**. Moreover, note that the **class Exception** (directly or indirectly) is the superclass of all the exception classes in Java.

 The section Java Exception Hierarchy, located later in this chapter, describes the hierarchy of Java's various built-in exception classes. The section Java's Exception Classes, also located later in this chapter, describes some of the built-in exception classes and their methods.

try/catch/finally Block

Statements that might generate an exception are placed in a **try** block. The **try** block might also contain statements that should not be executed if an exception occurs. The **try** block is followed by zero or more **catch** blocks. A **catch** block specifies the type of exception it can catch and contains an exception handler. The last **catch** block may or may not be followed by a **finally** block. Any code contained in a **finally** block always executes, regardless of whether an exception occurs, except when the program exits early from a **try** block by calling the method **System.exit**. If a **try** block has no **catch** block, then it *must* have the **finally** block.

Before giving the general syntax of the **try/catch/finally** block, let's observe the following: As remarked previously, when an exception occurs, Java creates an object of a specific exception class. For example, if a division by zero exception occurs, then Java creates an object of the **ArithmeticException class**.

The general syntax of the **try/catch/finally** block is:

12

```
try
{
    //statements
}
catch (ExceptionClassName1 objRef1)
{
    //exception handler code
}
catch (ExceptionClassName2 objRef2)
{
    //exception handler code
}
.
.
.
catch (ExceptionClassNameN objRefN)
{
    //exception handler code
}
finally
{
    //statements
}
```

Note the following about **try**/**catch**/**finally** blocks:

- If no exception is thrown in a **try** block, all **catch** blocks associated with the **try** block are ignored and program execution resumes after the last **catch** block.

- If an exception is thrown in a **try** block, the remaining statements in the **try** block are ignored. The program searches the **catch** blocks in the order in which they appear after the **try** block and looks for an appropriate exception handler.

- If the type of the thrown exception matches the parameter type in one of the **catch** blocks, the code of that **catch** block executes and the remaining **catch** blocks after this **catch** block are ignored.

- If there is a **finally** block after the last **catch** block, the **finally** block executes regardless of whether an exception occurs.

As noted, when an exception occurs, an object of a particular exception class type is created. The type of exception handled by a **catch** block is declared in the **catch** block heading, which is the statement between the parentheses after the keyword **catch**.

Consider the following **catch** block:

```
catch (ArithmeticException aeRef)
{
    //exception handler code
}
```

This **catch** block catches an exception of the type **ArithmeticException**. The identifier **aeRef** is a reference variable of the type **ArithmeticException**. If an exception of the type **ArithmeticException** is thrown by the **try** block associated with this **catch** block, and control reaches this **catch** block, then the reference parameter **aeRef** contains the address of the exception object thrown by the **try** block. Because **aeRef** contains the address of the exception object, you can access the exception object through the variable **aeRef**. The object **aeRef** stores a detailed description of the thrown exception. You can use the method **toString** (or the method **getMessage**) to retrieve the message containing the description of the thrown exception. Example 12-3 illustrates how to use the method **toString** to retrieve the description of the thrown exception.

Order of **catch** Blocks

A **catch** block can catch either all exceptions of a specific type or all types of exceptions. The heading of a **catch** block specifies the type of exception it handles. As discussed in Chapter 11, a reference variable of a superclass type can point to an object of its subclass. Therefore, if in the heading of a **catch** block you declare an exception using the **class Exception**, then that **catch** block can catch all types of exceptions because the **class Exception** is the superclass of all exception classes.

Suppose that an exception occurs in a **try** block and that exception is caught by a **catch** block. Then the remaining **catch** blocks associated with that **try** block are ignored. Therefore, you should be careful about the order in which you list **catch** blocks following a **try** block. For example, consider the following sequence of **try/catch** blocks:

```
try                                    //Line 1
{
    //statements
}
catch (Exception eRef)                 //Line 2
{
    //statements
}
catch (ArithmeticException aeRef)      //Line 3
{
    //statements
}
```

Suppose that an exception is thrown in the **try** block. Because the **catch** block in Line 2 can catch exceptions of all types, the **catch** block in Line 3 cannot be reached. This sequence of **try/catch** blocks would, in fact, result in a compile time error. In a sequence of **catch** blocks following a **try** block, a **catch** block declaring an exception of a subclass type should be placed before **catch** blocks declaring exceptions of a superclass type. Often it is useful to make sure that all exceptions thrown by a **try** block are caught. In this case, you should make the **catch** block that declares an exception of the **class Exception** type the last **catch** block.

12

Using `try`/`catch` Blocks in a Program

Next, we give some examples to illustrate how `try`/`catch` blocks might appear in a program.

As shown in Example 12-1, a common error that might occur while inputting numeric data is typing a nonnumeric character such as a letter. If the input is invalid, the methods `nextInt` and `nextDouble` throw an `InputMismatchException`. Similarly, another error that might occur when performing numeric calculations is division by zero with integer values. In this case, the program throws an exception of the **`class`** `ArithmeticException`. The following program shows how to handle these exceptions.

Example 12-3

```java
import java.util.*;

public class ExceptionExample3
{
    static Scanner console = new Scanner(System.in);

    public static void main(String[] args)              //Line 1
    {
        int dividend, divisor, quotient;                //Line 2

        try                                             //Line 3
        {
            System.out.print("Line 4: Enter the "
                             + "dividend: ");            //Line 4
            dividend = console.nextInt();               //Line 5
            System.out.println();                       //Line 6

            System.out.print("Line 7: Enter the "
                             + "divisor: ");             //Line 7
            divisor = console.nextInt();                //Line 8
            System.out.println();                       //Line 9

            quotient = dividend / divisor;              //Line 10
            System.out.println("Line 11: Quotient = "
                             + quotient);                //Line 11
        }
        catch (ArithmeticException aeRef)               //Line 12
        {
            System.out.println("Line 13: Exception "
                             + aeRef.toString());        //Line 13
        }
        catch (InputMismatchException imeRef)           //Line 14
        {
            System.out.println("Line 15: Exception "
                             + imeRef.toString());       //Line 15
        }
    }
}
```

Sample Run: In these sample runs, the user input is shaded.

Sample Run 1:
```
Line 4: Enter the dividend: 45

Line 7: Enter the divisor: 2

Line 11: Quotient = 22
```

Sample Run 2:
```
Line 4: Enter the dividend: 18

Line 7: Enter the divisor: 0

Line 13: Exception java.lang.ArithmeticException: / by zero
```

Sample Run 3:
```
Line 4: Enter the dividend: 2753

Line 7: Enter the divisor: 2f1
Line 15: Exception java.util.InputMismatchException
```

This program works as follows: The method **main** starts at Line 1. The statement in Line 2 declares the **int** variables dividend, divisor, and quotient. The **try** block starts at Line 3. The statement in Line 4 prompts the user to enter the value of the dividend; the statement in Line 5 stores this number in the variable dividend. The statement in Line 7 prompts the user to enter the value of divisor, and the statement in Line 8 stores this number in the variable divisor. The statement in Line 10 divides the value of dividend by the value of divisor and stores the result in quotient. The statement in Line 11 outputs the value of quotient.

The first **catch** block, which starts at Line 12, catches an ArithmeticException. The next **catch** block, which starts at Line 14, catches an InputMismatchException.

In Sample Run 1, the program did not throw any exceptions because the user entered valid data.

In Sample Run 2, the entered value of divisor is 0. Therefore, when the dividend is divided by the divisor, the statement in Line 10 throws an ArithmeticException, which is caught by the **catch** block starting at Line 12. The statement in Line 13 outputs the appropriate message.

In Sample Run 3, the value entered in Line 8 for the variable divisor contains the letter **f**, a nondigit character. Because this value cannot be converted to an integer, the statement in Line 8 throws an InputMismatchException. Notice that the InputMismatchException is thrown by the method nextInt of the **class** Scanner. The **catch** block starting at Line 14 catches this exception, and the statement in Line 15 outputs the appropriate message.

Let us again consider Sample Run 3. In this sample run, the input for the divisor is 2f1, which of course is invalid. When the expression:

```
console.nextInt()
```

in Line 8 executes, it throws an `InputMismatchException` because the input, `2f1`, cannot be expressed as an integer. Note that because `2f1` cannot be expressed as an integer it stays as the next input token in the input stream. That is, if the input token is invalid, then the method `nextInt` does not remove that input token from the input stream. To capture this invalid input as well as print it, you can read it as a string in the **catch** block, in Line 14, and then output the string. To be specific, if you replace the **catch** block starting at Line 14 with the following **catch** block:

```
catch (InputMismatchException imeRef)                //Line 14
{
    String str;                                      //Line 15

    str = console.next();                            //Line 16
    System.out.println("Line 17: Exception "
                    + imeRef.toString()
                    + " " + str );                   //Line 17
}
```

and rerun the program with the same input as in Sample Run 3, then this sample run is:

Sample Run 3 (with the modified catch block):
```
Line 4: Enter the dividend: 2753

Line 7: Enter the divisor: 2f1
Line 17: Exception java.util.InputMismatchException 2f1
```

The Web site accompanying this book contains the modified program, which is named `ExceptionExample1A.java`.

As noted, when an exception occurs in a program, the program throws an object of a specific exception class. Example 12-3 illustrates how to handle an arithmetic exception and an input mismatch exception. We also noted that the **class** Exception (directly or indirectly) becomes the superclass of the exception classes. Because Java provides many classes for handling exceptions, before giving more examples of exception handling, the next few sections describe the hierarchy of Java's exception classes as well as describe some of the exception classes in some detail.

JAVA EXCEPTION HIERARCHY

In the preceding sections, you learned ways to handle exceptions in a program. Chapter 8 discussed how to create your own classes. Every class you design can potentially cause exceptions. Java provides extensive support for exception handling by providing a number of exception classes. Java also allows users to create and implement their own exception classes to handle exceptions not covered by Java's exception classes. This section discusses the exception classes provided by Java.

The **class** `Throwable`, which is derived from the **class** `Object`, is the superclass of the **class** `Exception`, as shown in Figure 12-1.

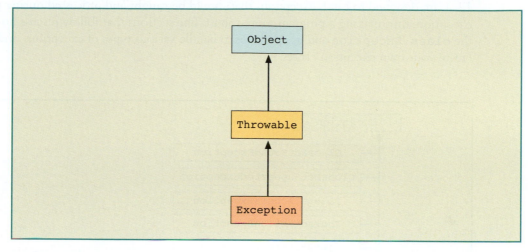

Figure 12-1 Java exception hierarchy

The **class** `Throwable` contains various constructors and methods, some of which are described in Table 12-1.

Table 12-1 Some Constructors and Methods of the **class** `Throwable`

```
public Throwable()
   //Default constructor
   //Creates an instance of Throwable with an empty message string.

public Throwable(String strMessage)
   //Constructor with parameters
   //Creates an instance of Throwable with a message string specified
   //by the parameter strMessage.

public String getMessage()
   //Returns the detailed message stored in the object.

public void printStackTrace()
   //Method to print the stack trace showing the sequence of
   //method calls when an exception occurs

public void printStackTrace(PrintWriter stream)
   //Method to print the stack trace showing the sequence of
   //method calls when an exception occurs
   //The output is sent to the stream specified by the parameter
   //stream.

public String toString()
   //Returns a string representation of the Throwable object.
```

12

The methods `getMessage`, `printStackTrace`, and `toString` are **public** and are inherited by the subclasses of the **class** `Throwable`.

The **class** `Exception` and its subclasses, some of which are shown in Figures 12-2 to 12-4, are designed to catch exceptions that should be caught and processed during program execution, thus making a program more robust. The sections that follow discuss how to use the **class** `Exception` and its subclasses to handle various types of exceptions, and how to create your own exception classes.

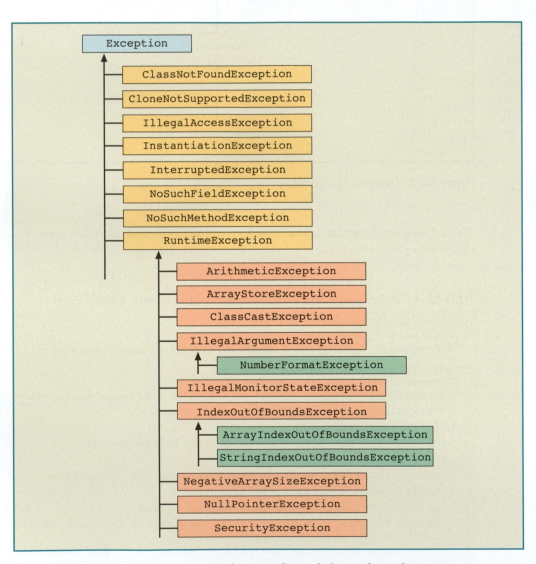

Figure 12-2 **class** `Exception` and some of its subclasses from the **package** `java.lang`

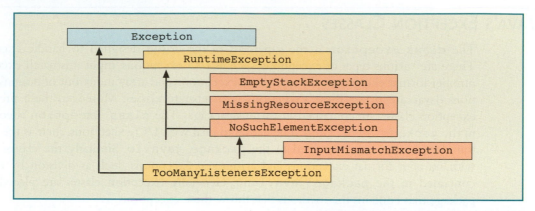

Figure 12-3 `class` Exception and some of its subclasses from the package java.util (Notice that the `class` RuntimeException is in the `package` java.lang.)

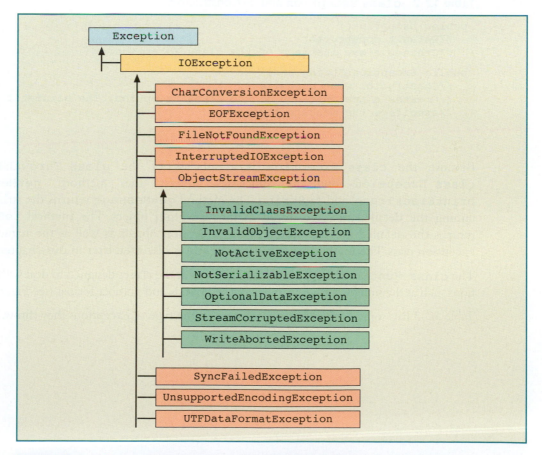

12

Figure 12-4 `class` IOException and some of its subclasses from the `package` java.io

JAVA'S EXCEPTION CLASSES

The **class** Exception is the superclass of the classes designed to handle exceptions. There are various types of exceptions, such as I/O exceptions, input mismatch exceptions, number format exceptions, file not found exceptions, and array index out of bounds exceptions. Java categorizes these exceptions into separate classes. Moreover, these predefined exception classes are contained in various packages. The **class** Exception is contained in the **package** java.lang. The classes to deal with I/O exceptions, such as the file not found exception, are contained in the **package** java.io. Similarly, the classes to deal with number format exceptions and arithmetic exceptions, such as division by zero, are contained in the **package** java.lang. Generally, exception classes are placed in the package that contains the methods that throw these exceptions.

The **class** Exception is very simple. It contains only two constructors, as shown in Table 12-2.

Table 12-2 **class** Exception and its Constructors

```
public Exception()
  //Default constructor
  //Creates a new instance of the class Exception.
public Exception(String str)
  //Constructor with parameters
  //Creates a new instance of the class Exception. The parameter str
  //specifies the message string.
```

Because the **class** Exception is a subclass of the **class** Throwable, the **class** Exception and its subclasses inherit the methods getMessage, printStackTrace, and toString. The method getMessage returns the string containing the detailed message stored in the exception object. The method toString returns the detailed message stored in the exception object as well as the name of the exception class. The method printStackTrace is discussed later in this chapter.

The **class** RuntimeException is the superclass of the classes designed to deal with exceptions such as division by zero, array index out of bounds, and number format (see Figure 12-2).

Table 12-3 lists some of the exception classes and the type of exceptions they throw.

Table 12-3 Some of Java's Exception Classes

Exception Class	Description
`ArithmeticException`	Arithmetic errors such as division by 0
`ArrayIndexOutOfBoundsException`	Array index is either less than 0 or greater than or equal to the length of the array
`FileNotFoundException`	Reference to a file that cannot be found
`IllegalArgumentException`	Calling a method with illegal arguments
`IndexOutOfBoundsException`	Array index is out of bounds
`NullPointerException`	Reference to an object that has not been instantiated
`NumberFormatException`	Use of an illegal number format
`StringIndexOutOfBoundsException`	String index is either less than 0 or greater than or equal to the length of the string
`InputMismatchException`	Input (token) retrieved does not match the pattern for the expected type, or token is out of range for the expected type

The Java application programs in the preceding chapters used the **class** Scanner and its methods `nextInt`, `nextDouble`, `next`, and `nextLine` to input data into the programs. As shown by Sample Run 3 of Example 12-1, if the user enters an invalid value, the program terminates with an error message indicating an `InputMismatchException`. This exception is thrown by the method `nextInt`. In addition to the `InputMismatchException`, the methods `nextInt` and `nextDouble` can throw other exceptions, as shown in Tables 12-4 and 12-5.

12

Table 12-4 Exceptions Thrown by the Method `nextInt`

Exception Thrown	Description
`InputMismatchException`	If the next input (token) is not an integer, or is out of range
`NoSuchElementException`	If the input is exhausted
`IllegalStateException`	If this scanner is closed

Table 12-5 Exceptions Thrown by the Method `nextDouble`

Exception Thrown	Description
InputMismatchException	If the next input (token) is not a floating-point number, or is out of range
NoSuchElementException	If the input is exhausted
IllegalStateException	If this scanner is closed

The methods `nextInt` and `nextDouble` both throw an `InputMismatchException` if the input is invalid. The **class** `InputMismatchException` is a subclass of the **class** `NoSuchElementException`, which is a subclass of the **class** `RuntimeException`. Moreover, the **class** `InputMismatchException` has only two constructors, as described in Table 12-6.

Table 12-6 **class** `InputMismatchException` and its Constructors

```
public InputMismatchException()
    //Default constructor
    //Creates a new instance of the class InputMismatchException.
    //The error message is null.

public InputMismatchException(String str)
    //Constructor with parameters
    //Creates a new instance of the class InputMismatchException.
    //The parameter str specifies the message string that is to be
    //retrieved by the method getMessage.
```

Tables 12-7 and 12-8 show the exceptions thrown by the methods `next` and `nextLine` of the **class** `Scanner`.

Table 12-7 Exceptions Thrown by the Method `next`

Exception Thrown	Description
NoSuchElementException	If there is no more input (tokens)
IllegalStateException	If this scanner is closed

Table 12-8 Exceptions Thrown by the Method `nextLine`

Exception Thrown	Description
NoSuchElementException	If the input is exhausted
IllegalStateException	If this scanner is closed

In an end-of-file (EOF)–controlled `while` loop, we use the method `hasNext` of the `class` `Scanner` to determine whether there is a token in the input stream. Table 12-9 shows the exception thrown by the method `hasNext`.

Table 12-9 Exceptions Thrown by the Method `hasNext`

Exception Thrown	Description
`IllegalStateException`	If this scanner is closed

As we have seen in the previous chapters, as an input to a dialog box or a text field, Java programs accept only strings as input. Numbers, integer or decimal, are entered as strings. We then use the method `parseInt` of the `class` `Integer` to convert an integer string into the equivalent integer. If the string containing the integer contains only digits, the method `parseInt` will return the integer. However, if the string contains a letter or any other nondigit character, the method `parseInt` throws a `NumberFormatException`. Similarly, the method `parseDouble` also throws this exception if the string does not contain a valid number. The programs that we've written up to this point ignored these exceptions. Later in this chapter we show how to handle these and other exceptions.

Tables 12-10, 12-11, and 12-12 list some of the exceptions thrown by the methods of the `class`es `Integer`, `Double`, and `String`.

Table 12-10 Exceptions Thrown by the Methods of the `class` `Integer`

Method	Exception Thrown	Description
`parseInt(String str)`	`NumberFormatException`	The string `str` does not contain an `int` value
`valueOf(String str)`	`NumberFormatException`	The string `str` does not contain an `int` value

Table 12-11 Exceptions Thrown by the Methods of the `class` `Double`

Method	Exception Thrown	Description
`parseDouble(String str)`	`NumberFormatException`	The string `str` does not contain a **double** value
`valueOf(String str)`	`NumberFormatException`	The string `str` does not contain a **double** value

12

Table 12-12   Exceptions Thrown by the Methods of the **class** String

Method	Exception Thrown	Description
String(String str)	NullPointerException	str is null
charAt(int a)	StringIndexOutOfBoundsException	The value of a is not a valid index
indexOf(String str)	NullPointerException	str is null
lastIndexOf(String str)	NullPointerException	str is null
substring(int a)	StringIndexOutOfBoundsException	The value of a is not a valid index
substring(int a, int b)	StringIndexOutOfBoundsException	The value of a and/or b is not a valid index

Appendix E describes various predefined classes as well as the exceptions thrown by the methods of these classes.

CHECKED AND UNCHECKED EXCEPTIONS

Chapter 3, while discussing file input/output, remarked that if an input file does not exist when the program executes, the program throws a `FileNotFoundException`. Similarly, if a program cannot create or access an output file, the program throws a `FileNotFoundException`. Until now, the program ignored this type of exception by including the **throws** `FileNotFoundException` clause in the heading of the method. If we did not include this **throws** clause in the heading of the method **main**, the compiler would generate a syntax error.

On the other hand, in programs that used the methods `nextInt` and `nextDouble` we neither included the code to check whether the input was valid nor included any **throws** clause (there was no need to do so), in the method heading, to ignore these exceptions, and the compiler did not generate any syntax error. So, the obvious question is: What types of exceptions need the **throws** clause in a method heading?

Moreover, we were not concerned about situations such as division by zero or even array index out of bounds. If these types of errors occurred during program execution, the program terminated with an appropriate error message. For these types of exceptions, we did not need to include a **throws** clause in the heading of any method.

Java's predefined exceptions are divided into two categories: checked exceptions and unchecked exceptions. Any exception that the compiler can recognize is called a **checked exception**. For example, `FileNotFoundException`s are checked exceptions. The constructors of the **classes** FileReader and PrintWriter that we used throw a FileNotFoundException. Therefore, these constructors throw a checked exception. When the compiler encounters the statements to open an input or output file, it checks whether the program handles FileNotFoundExceptions, or reports them by throwing them. Enabling the compiler to check for these types of exceptions reduces the number of exceptions not properly handled by the program. Because our programs so far were not required to handle FileNotFoundExceptions or other types of predefined exceptions, the programs declared the checked exceptions by throwing them. (Another common checked exception that can occur during program execution is known as IOExceptions. For example, the method **read** used in the Programming Example Text Processing, in Chapter 9, may throw an IOException.)

When a program is being compiled, the compiler may not be able to determine whether exceptions—such as division by zero, or index out of bounds, or the next input is invalid—will occur. Therefore, the compiler does not check these types of exceptions, called **unchecked exceptions**. Thus, to significantly improve the correctness of programs, programmers must check for these types of exceptions.

Because the compiler does not check for unchecked exceptions, the program does not need to either declare them using a **throws** clause or provide the code within the program to deal with them. The exceptions belonging to a subclass of the **class** RuntimeException are unchecked exceptions. Because InputMismatchException is a subclass of the **class** RuntimeException, the exceptions thrown by the methods **nextInt** and **nextDouble** are unchecked. Therefore, in all the programs that used the methods **nextInt** and **nextDouble**, we did not use the **throws** clause to throw these exceptions. If a program does not provide the code to handle an unchecked exception, then the exception is handled by Java's default exception handler.

In the method heading, the **throws** clause lists the types of exceptions thrown by the method. The syntax of the **throws** clause is:

```
throws ExceptionType1, ExceptionType2, ...
```

where **ExceptionType1**, **ExceptionType2**, and so on are the names of the exception classes.

For example, consider the following method:

```
public static void exceptionMethod()
                throws NumberFormatException, IOException
{
    //statements
}
```

The method **exceptionMethod** throws exceptions of the type NumberFormatException and IOException.

MORE EXAMPLES OF EXCEPTION HANDLING

This section gives a few more examples of exception handling.

Because Java accepts only strings as input in input dialog boxes and text fields, inputting data into a string variable won't cause any problems. However, when we use the methods parseInt, parseFloat, or parseDouble to convert a numeric string into its respective numeric form, the program may terminate with a number format error. This is because the methods parseInt, parseFloat, and parseDouble each **throw** a number format exception if the numeric string does not contain a number. For example, if the numeric string does not contain an **int** value, then when the method parseInt tries to determine the numeric form of the integer string, it throws a NumberFormatException.

Example 12-4

This example shows how to catch and handle number format and division by zero exceptions in programs that use input dialog boxes and/or text fields.

```java
import javax.swing.JOptionPane;

public class ExceptionExample4
{
    public static void main(String[] args)                    //Line 1
    {
        int dividend, divisor, quotient;                      //Line 2
        String inpStr;                                        //Line 3

        try                                                   //Line 4
        {
            inpStr =
                JOptionPane.showInputDialog
                    ("Enter the dividend: ");                 //Line 5
            dividend = Integer.parseInt(inpStr);              //Line 6

            inpStr =
                JOptionPane.showInputDialog
                    ("Enter the divisor: ");                  //Line 7
            divisor = Integer.parseInt(inpStr);               //Line 8

            quotient = dividend / divisor;                    //Line 9

            JOptionPane.showMessageDialog(null,
                    "Line 10:\nDividend = " + dividend
                + "\nDivisor = " + divisor
                + "\nQuotient =" + quotient,
                    "Quotient",
                JOptionPane.INFORMATION_MESSAGE);             //Line 10
        }
```

```
        catch (ArithmeticException aeRef)                    //Line 11
        {
            JOptionPane.showMessageDialog(null,
                    "Line 12: Exception "
                    + aeRef.toString(),
                    "ArithmeticException",
                    JOptionPane.ERROR_MESSAGE);               //Line 12
        }
        catch (NumberFormatException nfeRef)                  //Line 13
        {
            JOptionPane.showMessageDialog(null,
                    "Line 14: Exception "
                    + nfeRef.toString(),
                    "NumberFormatException",
                    JOptionPane.ERROR_MESSAGE);               //Line 14
        }

        System.exit(0);                                      //Line 15
    }
}
```

Sample Runs:

Sample Run 1:

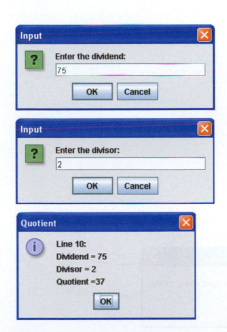

Figure 12-5   Sample Run 1 of the program `ExceptionExample4`

Sample Run 2:

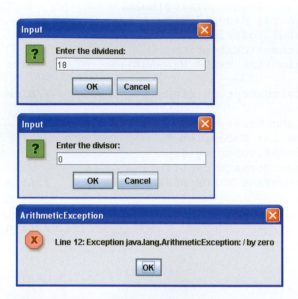

Figure 12-6   Sample Run 2 of the program `ExceptionExample4`

Sample Run 3:

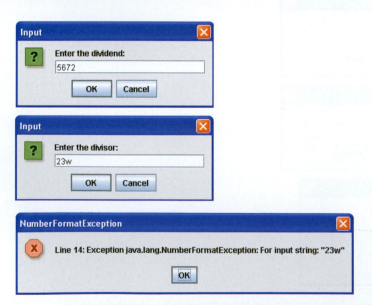

Figure 12-7   Sample Run 3 of the program `ExceptionExample4`

This program works as follows: The method **main** starts at Line 1. The statement in Line 2 declares the **int** variables dividend, divisor, and quotient. The statement in Line 3 declares the **String** variable inpStr. The **try** block starts at Line 4. The statement in Line 5 prompts the user to enter the value of the dividend; the statement in Line 6 stores this number in the variable dividend. The statement in Line 7 prompts the user to enter the value of the divisor, and the statement in Line 8 stores this number in the variable divisor. The statement in Line 9 divides the value of dividend by the value of divisor and stores the result in quotient. The statement in Line 10 outputs the values of dividend, divisor, and quotient.

The first **catch** block, which starts at Line 11, catches an **ArithmeticException**. The **catch** block that starts at Line 13 catches a **NumberFormatException**.

In Sample Run 1, the program did not throw any exceptions.

In Sample Run 2, the entered value of divisor is 0. Therefore, when the dividend is divided by the divisor, the statement in Line 9 throws an **ArithmeticException**, which is caught by the **catch** block starting at Line 11. The statement in Line 12 outputs the appropriate message.

In Sample Run 3, the value entered in Line 7 for the variable divisor contains the letter w, a nondigit character. Because this value cannot be converted to an integer, the statement in Line 8 throws a **NumberFormatException**. Note that the **NumberFormatException** is thrown by the method **parseInt** of the **class** Integer. The **catch** block starting at Line 13 catches this exception, and the statement in Line 14 outputs the appropriate message.

class Exception and the Operator instanceof

The program in Example 12-3 uses two **catch** blocks to handle two types of exceptions. Recall from Chapter 11 that a reference variable of a superclass type can point to the objects of its subclasses, and using the operator **instanceof**, you can determine whether a reference variable points to an object of a particular **class**. You can use this facility to combine the two **catch** blocks of the program in Example 12-3 into one **catch** block, as shown by the program in Example 12-5.

Example 12-5

```java
import java.util.*;

public class ExceptionExample5
{
    static Scanner console = new Scanner(System.in);

    public static void main(String[] args)          //Line 1
    {
        int dividend, divisor, quotient;            //Line 2
```

```
        try                                                    //Line 3
        {
            System.out.print("Line 4: Enter the "
                            + "dividend: ");                   //Line 4
            dividend = console.nextInt();                      //Line 5
            System.out.println();                              //Line 6

            System.out.print("Line 7: Enter the "
                            + "divisor: ");                    //Line 7
            divisor = console.nextInt();                       //Line 8
            System.out.println();                              //Line 9

            quotient = dividend / divisor;                     //Line 10
            System.out.println("Line 11: Quotient = "
                            + quotient);                       //Line 11
        }
        catch (Exception eRef)                                 //Line 12
        {
          if (eRef instanceof ArithmeticException)             //Line 13
             System.out.println("Line 14: Exception "
                            + eRef.toString());                //Line 14
          else if (eRef instanceof InputMismatchException)     //Line 15
             System.out.println("Line 16: Exception "
                            + eRef.toString());                //Line 16
        }
    }
}
```

This program works the same way as the program in Example 12-3. This program, however, has only one **catch** block, which can catch all types of exceptions. (See the statement in Line 12.) This is because, directly or indirectly, the **class** Exception is the superclass of all the exception classes, and a reference variable of a superclass can point to an object of its subclasses. The parameter, **eRef**, of the **catch** block in Line 12 is a reference variable of the Exception type. The statement in Line 13 determines whether **eRef** is an instance of the **class** ArithmeticException—that is, if it points to an object of the **class** ArithmeticException. Similarly, the statement in Line 15 determines whether **eRef** is an instance of the **class** InputMismatchException. If **eRef** is an instance of **ArithmeticException**, then the statement in Line 14 executes, and so on.

Example 12-6

The Programming Example Student Grade in Chapter 3 calculates a student's grade. It reads the data from a file and writes the output to a file. The program given in Chapter 3 throws a `FileNotFoundException` and other exceptions. Now that we know how to handle exceptions in a program, we can rewrite the program to handle the exceptions.

```java
//Program: Calculate the average test score
//This program shows how to handle a FileNotFoundException
//or any other exception.

import java.io.*;
import java.util.*;

public class StudentGrade
{
    public static void main(String[] args)
    {

        //Declare and initialize the variables          //Step 1
        double test1, test2, test3, test4, test5;
        double average;
        String firstName;
        String lastName;

        try
        {
            Scanner inFile = new Scanner
                    (new FileReader("a:\\test.txt"));   //Step 2

            PrintWriter outFile =
                    new PrintWriter("a:\\testavg.out");   //Step 3

            firstName = inFile.next();                    //Step 4
            lastName = inFile.next();                     //Step 4

            outFile.println("Student Name: "
                            + firstName + " "
                            + lastName);                  //Step 5

                //Step 6 - retrieve the five test scores
            test1 = inFile.nextDouble();
            test2 = inFile.nextDouble();
            test3 = inFile.nextDouble();
            test4 = inFile.nextDouble();
            test5 = inFile.nextDouble();
```

```
            outFile.printf("Test scores: %5.2f %5.2f %5.2f "
                    + "%5.2f %5.2f %n", test1,
                    test2, test3, test4,
                    test5);                              //Step 7

            average = (test1 + test2 + test3 + test4
                    + test5) / 5.0;                      //Step 8

            outFile.printf("Average test score: %5.2f %n",
                    average);                            //Step 9

            outFile.close();                             //Step 10

        }
        catch (FileNotFoundException fnfeRef)
        {
            System.out.println(fnfeRef.toString());
        }
        catch (Exception eRef)
        {
            System.out.println(eRef.toString());
        }
    }
}
```

Sample Run: If drive A contains a floppy disk, but no input file exists, the following message is printed:

```
java.io.FileNotFoundException: a:\test.txt (The system cannot find
the file specified.)
```

The **try** block contains statements that open both the input and output files. It also contains input and output statements. The first **catch** block catches a `FileNotFoundException`, the second **catch** block catches all types of exceptions. As shown in the Sample Run, if the input file does not exist, the statement in Step 2 in the **try** block throws a `FileNotFoundException`, which is caught and handled by the first **catch** block.

RETHROWING AND THROWING AN EXCEPTION

When an exception occurs in a **try** block, control immediately passes to one of the **catch** blocks. Typically, a **catch** block does one of the following:

- Completely handles the exception.

- Partially processes the exception. In this case, the **catch** block either rethrows the same exception or throws another exception for the calling environment to handle the exception.

- Rethrows the same exception for the calling environment to handle the exception.

The **catch** blocks in Examples 12-3 to 12-6 handled the exception. The mechanism of rethrowing or throwing an exception is quite useful in cases when a **catch** block catches the exception, but the **catch** block is unable to handle the exception, or if the **catch** block decides that the exception should be handled by the calling environment. This allows the programmer to provide the exception handling code in one place.

Rethrowing an exception or throwing an exception is accomplished by the **throw** statement. A **throw** statement can throw either a checked or an unchecked exception.

Exceptions are objects of a specific **class** type. Therefore, if you have a reference to an exception object, you can use the reference to throw the exception. In this case, the general syntax to rethrow an exception caught by a **catch** block is:

```
throw exceptionReference;
```

Example 12-7 shows how to rethrow an exception caught by a **catch** block.

Example 12-7

Consider the following Java code:

```
//RethrowExceptionExmp1

import java.util.*;

public class RethrowExceptionExmp1
{
    static Scanner console = new Scanner(System.in);

    public static void main(String[] args)          //Line 1
    {
        int number;                                 //Line 2

        try                                         //Line 3
        {
            number = getNumber();                   //Line 4
            System.out.println("Line 5: number = "
                            + number);              //Line 5
        }
        catch (InputMismatchException imeRef)       //Line 6
        {
            System.out.println("Line 7: Exception "
                            + imeRef.toString());   //Line 7
        }
    }
```

12

```
    public static int getNumber()
                throws InputMismatchException        //Line 8
    {
        int num;                                     //Line 9

        try                                          //Line 10
        {
            System.out.print("Line 11: Enter an "
                            + "integer: ");           //Line 11
            num = console.nextInt();                 //Line 12
            System.out.println();                    //Line 13

            return num;                              //Line 14
        }
        catch (InputMismatchException imeRef)        //Line 15
        {
            throw imeRef;                            //Line 16
        }
    }
}
```

Sample Runs:

Sample Run 1: In this sample run, the user input is shaded.
Line 11: Enter an integer: `56`

Line 5: number = 56

Sample Run 2: In this sample run, the user input is shaded.
Line 11: Enter an integer: `56t7`
Line 7: Exception java.util.InputMismatchException

The preceding program contains the method **getNumber**, which reads an integer and returns it to the method **main**. If the number entered by the user contains a nondigit character, the method **getNumber** throws an **InputMismatchException**. The catch block in Line 15 catches this exception. Rather than handle this exception, the method **getNumber** rethrows this exception. (See the statement in Line 16.)

The **catch** block in Line 6 of the method **main** also catches the **InputMismatchException**.

In Sample Run 1, the method **getNumber** successfully reads the number and returns the number to the method **main**. In Sample Run 2, the user enters an invalid number. The statement in Line 12 throws an **InputMismatchException**, which is caught and rethrown by the catch block starting at Line 15. After the statement in Line 16 executes, control goes back to the method **main** (Line 4), which throws an **InputMismatchException** thrown by the method getNumber. The **catch** block in Line 6 catches this exception, and the statement in Line 7 outputs the appropriate message.

Example 12-7 illustrates how to rethrow the same exception caught by a **catch** block. When an exception occurs, the system creates an object of a specific exception **class**. In fact, you can also create your own exception objects and throw them using the **throw** statement. In this case, the general syntax used for the **throw** statement is:

```
throw new ExceptionClassName(messageString);
```

Of course, you could have first created the object and then used the reference to the object in the **throw** statement.

Example 12-8 illustrates how to create and **throw** an exception object.

Example 12-8

```
//RethrowExceptionExmp2

import java.util.*;

public class RethrowExceptionExmp2
{
    static Scanner console = new Scanner(System.in);

    public static void main(String[] args)                  //Line 1
    {
        int number;                                         //Line 2

        try                                                 //Line 3
        {
            number = getNumber();                           //Line 4
            System.out.println("Line 5: number = "
                                    + number);              //Line 5
        }
        catch (InputMismatchException imeRef)               //Line 6
        {
            System.out.println("Line 7: Exception "
                                + imeRef.toString());       //Line 7
        }
    }

    public static int getNumber()
                throws InputMismatchException               //Line 8
    {
        int num;                                            //Line 9

        try                                                 //Line 10
        {
            System.out.print("Line 11: Enter an "
                        + "integer: ");                     //Line 11
```

12

```
          num = console.nextInt();                        //Line 12
          System.out.println();                           //Line 13

          return num;                                      //Line 14
      }
      catch (InputMismatchException imeRef)                //Line 15
      {
          System.out.println("Line 16: Exception "
                             + imeRef.toString()); //Line 16
          throw new InputMismatchException
                             ("getNumber");              //Line 17
      }
    }
}
```

Sample Run: In this sample run, the user input is shaded.
```
Line 11: Enter an integer: 563r9
Line 16: Exception java.util.InputMismatchException
Line 7: Exception java.util.InputMismatchException: getNumber
```

The preceding program works similarly to the program in Example 12-7. The difference is in the **catch** block starting at Line 15, in the method **getNumber**. The **catch** block in Line 15 catches an **InputMismatchException**, outputs an appropriate message in Line 16, and then in Line 17 creates an **InputMismatchException** object with the message string **"getNumber"** and throws the object. The **catch** block starting at Line 6 in the method **main** catches the thrown object. The statement in Line 7 outputs the appropriate message. Notice that the output of the statement in Line 16 (the second line of the Sample Run) does not output the string **getNumber**, whereas the statement in Line 7 (the third line of the Sample Run) outputs the string **getNumber**. This is because the statement in Line 17 creates and throws an object that is different from the **InputMismatchException** object thrown by the statement in Line 12. The message string of the object thrown by the statement in Line 12 is null; the object thrown by the statement in Line 16 contains the message string **"getNumber"**.

The programs in Examples 12-7 and 12-8 illustrate how a method can rethrow the same exception object, or create an exception object and throw it for the calling method to handle. This mechanism is quite useful; it allows a program to handle all the exceptions in one location rather than spreading exception-handling code throughout the program.

METHOD `printStackTrace`

Suppose that method A calls method B, method B calls method C, and an exception occurs in method C. Java keeps track of this sequence of method calls. Recall that the **class** **Exception** is a subclass of the **class** **Throwable**. As shown in Table 12-1, the **class**

`Throwable` contains the **public** method `printStackTrace`. Because the method `printStackTrace` is **public**, every subclass of the **class** `Throwable` inherits this method. When an exception occurs in a method, you can use the method `printStackTrace` to determine the order in which the methods were called and where the exception was handled.

Example 12-9

This example shows the use of the method `printStackTrace` to show the order in which methods are called and exceptions handled.

```java
import java.io.*;

public class PrintStackTraceExample1
{
    public static void main(String[] args)
    {
        try
        {
            methodA();
        }
        catch (Exception e)
        {
            System.out.println(e.toString() + " caught in main");
            e.printStackTrace();
        }
    }

    public static void methodA() throws Exception
    {
        methodB();
    }

    public static void methodB() throws Exception
    {
        methodC();
    }

    public static void methodC() throws Exception
    {
        throw new Exception("Exception generated in method C");
    }
}
```

Sample Run:
```
java.lang.Exception: Exception generated in method C caught in main
java.lang.Exception: Exception generated in method C
        at PrintStackTraceExample1.methodC -
        (PrintStackTraceExample1.java:31)
```

12

```
    at PrintStackTraceExample1.methodB -
    (PrintStackTraceExample1.java:26)
    at PrintStackTraceExample1.methodA -
    (PrintStackTraceExample1.java:21)
    at PrintStackTraceExample1.main -
    (PrintStackTraceExample1.java:10)
```

The preceding program contains the methods `methodA`, `methodB`, `methodC`, and the method `main`. The method `methodC` creates and throws an object of the **class** `Exception`. The method `methodB` calls `methodC`, `methodA` calls `methodB`, and the method `main` calls `methodA`. Because the methods `methodA` and `methodB` do not handle the exception thrown by `methodC`, they contain the **throws** `Exception` clause in their heading. The method `main` handles the exception thrown by `methodC`, which was propagated first by `methodB` and then by `methodA`. The **catch** block in the method `main` first outputs the message contained in the exception object and the string `" caught in main"`, then it calls the method `printStackTrace` to trace the method calls. (See the last four lines of the output.)

The program in Example 12-10 is similar to the program in Example 12-9. The main difference is that the exception thrown by `methodC` is caught and handled in `methodA`. Notice that the heading of `methodA` does not contain any **throws** clause.

Example 12-10

```java
import java.io.*;

public class PrintStackTraceExample2
{
    public static void main(String[] args)
    {
        methodA();
    }

    public static void methodA()
    {
        try
        {
            methodB();
        }
        catch (Exception e)
        {
            System.out.println(e.toString() + " caught in methodA");
            e.printStackTrace();
        }
    }
```

```
    public static void methodB() throws Exception
    {
        methodC();
    }

    public static void methodC() throws Exception
    {
        throw new Exception("Exception generated in method C");
    }
}
```

Sample Run:
```
java.lang.Exception: Exception generated in method C caught in methodA
java.lang.Exception: Exception generated in method C
        at PrintStackTraceExample2.methodC -
        (PrintStackTraceExample2.java:30)
        at PrintStackTraceExample2.methodB -
        (PrintStackTraceExample2.java:25)
        at PrintStackTraceExample2.methodA -
        (PrintStackTraceExample2.java:14)
        at PrintStackTraceExample2.main
        (PrintStackTraceExample2.java:7)
```

EXCEPTION-HANDLING TECHNIQUES

When an exception occurs in a program, usually the programmer has three choices—terminate the program, include code in the program to recover from the exception, or log the error and continue. The following sections discuss each of these situations.

Terminate the Program

In some cases, it is best to let the program terminate when an exception occurs. Suppose you have written a program that inputs data from a file. If the input file does not exist when the program executes, then there is no point in continuing with the program. In this case, the program can output an appropriate error message and terminate.

Fix the Error and Continue

In other cases, you will want to handle the exception and let the program continue. Suppose you have a program that takes as input an integer. If a user inputs a character in place of a digit, the program will throw an **InputMismatchException**. This is a situation where you can include the necessary code to keep prompting the user to input a number until the entry is valid. Example 12-11 illustrates this concept.

12

Example 12-11

The following program continues to prompt the user until the user enters a valid integer.

```java
import java.util.*;

public class FixErrorAndContinue
{
    static Scanner console = new Scanner(System.in);

    public static void main(String[] args)
    {
        int number;                                    //Line 1
        boolean done;                                  //Line 2
        String str;                                    //Line 3

        done = false;                                  //Line 4

        do                                             //Line 5
        {
            try                                        //Line 6
            {
                System.out.print("Line 7: Enter an "
                            + "integer: ");            //Line 7
                number = console.nextInt();            //Line 8
                System.out.println();                  //Line 9
                done = true;                           //Line 10

                System.out.println("Line 11: number = "
                            + number);                 //Line 11
            }
            catch (InputMismatchException imeRef)      //Line 12
            {
                str = console.next();                  //Line 13

                System.out.println("Line 14: Exception "
                            + imeRef.toString()
                            + " " + str);              //Line 14
            }
        } while (!done);                               //Line 15
    }
}
```

Sample Run: In this sample run, the user input is shaded.
```
Line 7: Enter an integer: 34t5
Line 14: Exception java.util.InputMismatchException 34t5
Line 7: Enter an integer: 398se2
Line 14: Exception java.util.InputMismatchException 398se2
```

```
Line 7: Enter an integer: r45
Line 14: Exception java.util.InputMismatchException r45
Line 7: Enter an integer: 56

Line 11: number = 56
```

In the preceding program, the statement in Line 7 prompts the user to enter an integer. The statement in Line 8 inputs the integer entered by the user into the variable `number`. If the user enters a valid integer, then that integer is stored in `number`. Then the statement in Line 10 sets the `boolean` variable `done` to `true`. After the statement in Line 11 executes, the next statement executed is the expression `!done` in Line 15. If `done` is `true`, then `!done` is `false`, so the `while` loop terminates.

Suppose that the user does not enter a valid integer. Because the next input (token) cannot be expressed as an integer, the statement in Line 8 throws an `InputMismatchException` and control is transferred to the **catch** block starting at Line 12. Notice that the invalid number entered by the user is still the next input (token) in the input stream. Therefore, the statement in Line 13 reads that invalid number and assigns that input (token) to `str`. The statement in Line 14 outputs the exception as well as the invalid input. Notice that we can output the invalid input because the program captured the invalid input at Line 13. The **do...while** loop continues to prompt the user until the user inputs a valid integer.

Notice that in the sample run, the first, second, and third inputs are `34t5`, `398se2`, and `r45`, which contain nondigit characters. The fourth input, which is `56`, is a valid integer.

The **do...while** loop continues to prompt the user until the user inputs a valid integer.

Log the Error and Continue

A program that terminates when an exception occurs usually assumes that the termination is reasonably safe. On the other hand, if your program is designed to run a nuclear reactor or continuously monitor a satellite, it cannot be terminated if an exception occurs. These programs should report the exception, but the program must continue to run.

For example, consider a program that analyzes airline-ticketing transactions. Because a large number of ticketing transactions take place each day, a program is run daily to validate that day's transactions. This type of program would take an enormous amount of time to process the transactions. Therefore, when an exception occurs, the program should write the exception into a file and continue to analyze the transactions.

12

CREATING YOUR OWN EXCEPTION CLASSES

When you create your own classes or write programs, exceptions are likely to occur. As you have seen, Java provides a substantial number of exception classes to deal with these. However, Java does not provide all the exception classes you will ever need. Therefore, Java enables programmers to create exception classes to handle the exceptions not covered by Java's exception classes or to handle their own exceptions. This section describes how to create your own exception classes.

Java's mechanism to process the exceptions you define is the same as that for built-in exceptions. However, you must throw your own exceptions using the **throw** statement.

The exception class that you define extends either the **class** Exception or one of its subclasses. Moreover, a subclass of the **class** Exception is either a predefined class or a user-defined class. In other words, if you have created an exception class, you can define other exception classes extending the definition of the exception class you created.

Typically, constructors are the only methods that you include when you define your own exception class. Because the exception class you define is a subclass of an existing exception class, built-in or user-defined, the exception class that you define inherits the members of the superclass. Therefore, objects of the exception classes can use the **public** members of the superclasses.

Because the **class** Exception is derived from the **class** Throwable, it inherits the methods **getMessage** and **toString** of the **class** Throwable. Moreover, because these methods are **public**, they are also inherited by the subclasses of the **class** Exception.

Example 12-12

This example shows how to create your own division by zero exception class.

```java
public class MyDivisionByZeroException extends Exception
{
    public MyDivisionByZeroException()
    {
        super("Cannot divide by zero");
    }

    public MyDivisionByZeroException(String strMessage)
    {
        super(strMessage);
    }
}
```

The program in Example 12-13 uses the **class** MyDivisionByZeroException designed in Example 12-12.

Example 12-13

```java
import java.util.*;

public class MyDivisionByZeroExceptionTestProg
{
    static Scanner console = new Scanner(System.in);
```

```
    public static void main(String[] args)
    {
        double numerator;                                  //Line 1
        double denominator;                                //Line 2

        try                                                //Line 3
        {
            System.out.print("Line 4: Enter the "
                            + "numerator: ");              //Line 4
            numerator = console.nextDouble();              //Line 5
            System.out.println();                          //Line 6

            System.out.print("Line 7: Enter the "
                            + "denominator: ");            //Line 7
            denominator = console.nextDouble();            //Line 8
            System.out.println();                          //Line 9

            if (denominator == 0.0)                        //Line 10
                throw new MyDivisionByZeroException();     //Line 11

            System.out.println("Line 12: Quotient = "
                        + (numerator / denominator));      //Line 12
        }
        catch (MyDivisionByZeroException mdbze)            //Line 13
        {
            System.out.println("Line 14: "
                            + mdbze.toString());           //Line 14
        }
        catch (Exception e)                                //Line 15
        {
            System.out.println("Line 16: "
                            + e.toString());               //Line 16
        }
    }
}
```

Sample Runs:

Sample Run 1: In this sample run, the user input is shaded.
```
Line 4: Enter the numerator: 25

Line 7: Enter the denominator: 4

Line 12: Quotient = 6.25
```

Sample Run 2: In this sample run, the user input is shaded.
```
Line 4: Enter the numerator: 20

Line 7: Enter the denominator: 0

Line 14: myDivisionByZeroException: Cannot divide by zero
```

If the exception class you create is a direct subclass of the **class** Exception or a direct subclass of an exception class whose exceptions are checked exceptions, then the exceptions of the class you created are checked exceptions.

EVENT HANDLING

In Chapter 6 you learned that when you click a button, it generates an action event. Similarly, when you press the Enter key in a text field, it also generates an action event. In fact, when you press a mouse button to click a button, in addition to generating an action event, a mouse event is also generated. Similarly, when you press the Enter key in a text field, in addition to the action event, it also generates a key event. Therefore, a GUI program can simultaneously generate more than one event.

As described in Chapter 6, Java provides various **interface**s to handle different events. For example, to handle action events, you use the **interface** ActionListener; to handle mouse events, you use the **interface** MouseListener; key events are handled by the **interface** KeyListener; and window events are handled by the **interface** WindowListener. These and other interfaces contain methods that are executed when a particular event occurs. For example, when an action event occurs, the method actionPerformed of the **interface** ActionListener is executed.

In order to handle an event, we create an appropriate object and register this object with the GUI component. Recall that the methods of an interface are **abstract**. That is, they only contain the headings of the methods. Therefore, you cannot instantiate an object of an interface. To create an object to handle an event, first you create a class that implements an appropriate interface.

Chapter 6 discussed in detail how to handle action events. Recall that to handle an action event, we do the following:

1. Create a class that implements the **interface** ActionListener. For example, in Chapter 6 for the JButton calculateB we created the **class** CalculateButtonHandler.

2. Provide the definition of the method actionPerformed within the class that you created in Step 1. The method actionPerformed contains the code that the program executes when the specific event is generated. For example, in Chapter 6 when you click the JButton calculateB, the program should calculate and display the area and perimeter of the rectangle.

3. Create and instantiate an object of the class created in Step 1. For example, in Chapter 6 for the JButton calculateB, we created the object cbHandler.

4. Register the event handler created in Step 3 with the object that generates an action event using the method addActionListener. For example, in Chapter 6 for the JButton calculateB, the following statement registers the object cbHandler to listen and register the action event:

```
calculateB.addActionListener(cbHandler);
```

Just as you create objects of the class that extends the **interface** `ActionListener` to handle action events, to handle window events you first create a class that implements the **interface** `WindowListener` and then create and register objects of that class. You do similar things to handle mouse events.

In Chapter 6, to terminate the program when the close window button is clicked, we used the method `setDefaultCloseOperation` with the predefined named constant `EXIT_ON_CLOSE`. If you want to provide your own code to terminate the program when the window is closed, or if you want the program to take a different action when the window closes, then you use the **interface** `WindowListener`. That is, first you create a class that implements the **interface** `WindowListener`, provide the appropriate definition of the method `windowClosed`, create an appropriate object of that class, and then register the object created with the program.

Let's look at the definition of the **interface** `WindowListener`:

```
public interface WindowListener
{
    void windowActivated(WindowEvent e);
      //This method executes when a window is activated.
    void windowClosed(WindowEvent e);
      //This method executes when a window is closed.
    void windowClosing(WindowEvent e);
      //This method executes when a window is closing, just
      //before the window is closed.
    void windowDeactivated(WindowEvent e);
      //This method executes when a window is deactivated.
    void windowIconified(WindowEvent e);
      //This method executes when a window is iconified.
    void windowDeiconified(WindowEvent e);
      //This method executes when a window is changed from
      //a minimized to a normal state.
    void windowOpened(WindowEvent e);
      //This method executes when a window is opened.
}
```

As you can see, the **interface** `WindowListener` contains several **abstract** methods. Therefore, to instantiate an object of the class that implements the **interface** `WindowListener`, that class must provide the definition of each method of the **interface** `WindowListener`, even if a method is not used. Of course, if a method is not used, you could provide an empty body for that method. Recall that if a class contains an **abstract** method, you cannot instantiate an object of that class.

In Chapter 6 we used the mechanism of the inner class to handle events. That is, the class that implemented the interface was defined within the class containing the application program. Chapter 11 noted that rather than create an inner class to implement the interface, the class containing the application program can itself implement the interface. Moreover, because a program can generate various types of events, such as action events and window events, recall from Chapter 11 that Java allows a class to implement more than one interface. However, Java does not allow a class to extend the definition of more than one class; that is, Java does not support multiple inheritance.

For interfaces such as `WindowListener` that contain more than one method, Java provides the **class** `WindowAdapter`. The **class** `WindowAdapter` implements the **interface** `WindowListener` by providing an empty body for each method of the **interface** `WindowListener`. To be specific, the definition of the **class** `WindowAdapter` is:

```
public class WindowAdapter implements WindowListener
{
    void windowActivated(WindowEvent e)
    {
    }

    void windowClosed(WindowEvent e)
    {
    }

    void windowClosing(WindowEvent e)
    {
    }

    void windowDeactivated(WindowEvent e)
    {
    }

    void windowIconified(WindowEvent e)
    {
    }

    void windowDeiconified(WindowEvent e)
    {
    }

    void windowOpened(WindowEvent e)
    {
    }
}
```

If you use the mechanism of the inner class to handle a window event, you can create the class by extending the definition of the **class** `WindowAdapter` and provide the definition of only the methods that the program needs. Similarly, to handle window events, if the class containing the application program does not extend the definition of another class, you can make that class extend the definition of the **class** `WindowAdapter`.

Chapter 6 discussed in detail how to use the mechanism of the inner class, and Chapter 11 explained how to make the class containing the application program implement more than one interface. As stated in Chapter 11, there is one more way to handle events in a program—using the mechanism of anonymous classes. This mechanism is quite useful to handle events such as window and mouse events because the corresponding interfaces contain more than one method and the program might want to use only one method.

Recall from Chapter 6 that to register an action listener object to a GUI component, you use the method **addActionListener**. To register a **WindowListener** object to a GUI component, you use the method **addWindowListener**. The **WindowListener** object being registered is passed as a parameter to the method **addWindowListener**.

Consider the following code:

```
this.addWindowListener(new WindowAdapter()
            {
                public void windowClosing(WindowEvent e)
                {
                    System.exit(0);
                }
            }
);
```

The preceding statements create an object of the anonymous class, which extends the **class** **WindowAdapter** and overrides the method **windowClosing**. The object created is passed as an argument to the method **addWindowListener**. The method **addWindowListener** is invoked by explicitly using the reference **this**.

Similarly, you can handle mouse events by using the **interface** **MouseListener**. The definition of the **interface** **MouseListener** and the **class** **MouseAdapter** is:

```
public interface MouseListener
{
    void mouseClicked(MouseEvent e);
      //This method executes when a mouse button is clicked
      //on a component.
    void mouseEntered(MouseEvent e);
      //This method executes when the mouse enters a component.
    void mouseExited(MouseEvent e);
      //This method executes when the mouse exits a component.
    void mousePressed(MouseEvent e);
      //This method executes when a mouse button is pressed
      //on a component.
    void mouseReleased(MouseEvent e);
      //This method executes when a mouse button is released
      //on a component.
}

public class MouseAdapter implements MouseListener
{
    void mouseClicked(MouseEvent e)
    {
    }
    void mouseEntered(MouseEvent e)
    {
    }
```

```
        void mouseExited(MouseEvent e)
        {
        }
        void mousePressed(MouseEvent e)
        {
        }
        void mouseReleased(MouseEvent e)
        {
        }
    }
```

To register a `MouseListener` object to a GUI component, you use the method `addMouseListener`. The `MouseListener` object being registered is passed as a parameter to the method `addMouseListener`.

In addition to the GUI components with which you have worked, Chapter 13 introduces other GUI components such as check boxes, option buttons, menu items, and lists. These GUI components also generate events. Table 12-13 summarizes the various events generated by GUI components. Table 12-13 also shows the GUI component, the listener interface, and the name of the method of the interface to handle the event.

Table 12-13 Events Generated by a GUI Component, the Listener Interface, and the Name of the Method of the Interface to Handle the Event

GUI Component	Event Generated	Listener Interface	Listener Method
JButtton	ActionEvent	ActionListener	actionPerformed
JCheckBox	ItemEvent	ItemListener	itemStateChanged
JCheckboxMenuItem	ItemEvent	ItemListener	itemStateChanged
JChoice	ItemEvent	ItemListener	itemStateChanged
JComponent	ComponentEvent	ComponentListener	componentHidden
JComponent	ComponentEvent	ComponentListener	componentMoved
JComponent	ComponentEvent	ComponentListener	componentResized
JComponent	ComponentEvent	ComponentListener	componentShown
JComponent	FocusEvent	FocusListener	focusGained
JComponent	FocusEvent	FocusListener	focusLost
Container	ContainerEvent	ContainerListener	componentAdded
Container	ContainerEvent	ContainerListener	componentRemoved
JList	ActionEvent	ActionListener	actionPerformed
JList	ItemEvent	ItemListener	itemStateChanged
JMenuItem	ActionEvent	ActionListener	actionPerformed
JScrollbar	AdjustmentEvent	AdjustmentListener	adjustmentValueChanged
JTextComponent	TextEvent	TextListener	textValueChanged
JTextField	ActionEvent	ActionListener	actionPerformed

Table 12-13 Events Generated by a GUI Component, the Listener Interface, and the Name of the Method of the Interface to Handle the Event (continued)

GUI Component	Event Generated	Listener Interface	Listener Method
Window	WindowEvent	WindowListener	windowActivated
Window	WindowEvent	WindowListener	windowClosed
Window	WindowEvent	WindowListener	windowClosing
Window	WindowEvent	WindowListener	windowDeactivated
Window	WindowEvent	WindowListener	windowDeiconified
Window	WindowEvent	WindowListener	windowIconified
Window	WindowEvent	WindowListener	windowOpened

Even though **key** and **mouse** are not GUI components, they do generate events. Table 12-14 summarizes the events generated by the **key** and **mouse** components.

Table 12-14 Events Generated by key and mouse Components

	Event Generated	Listener Interface	Listener Method
key	KeyEvent	KeyListener	keyPressed
key	KeyEvent	KeyListener	keyReleased
key	KeyEvent	KeyListener	keyTyped
mouse	MouseEvent	MouseListener	mouseClicked
mouse	MouseEvent	MouseListener	mouseEntered
mouse	MouseEvent	MouseListener	mouseExited
mouse	MouseEvent	MouseListener	mousePressed
mouse	MouseEvent	MouseListener	mouseReleased
mouse	MouseEvent	MouseMotionListener	mouseDragged
mouse	MouseEvent	MouseMotionListener	mouseMoved

The section Key and Mouse Events in Chapter 13 gives examples of how to handle key and mouse events.

PROGRAMMING EXAMPLE: CALCULATOR

In this programming example, we design a program that simulates a calculator. The program will provide the basic integer arithmetic operations +, −, *, and /. When the program executes, it displays the GUI shown in Figure 12-8.

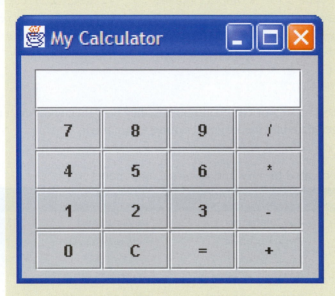

Figure 12-8   Calculator program GUI

Input   Integers via pressing various digit buttons, arithmetic operations via pressing operation buttons, the equals sign via pressing the button containing the symbol = on the calculator panel, and clearing inputs by pressing the "C" button.

Output   The result of the operation or an appropriate error message if something goes wrong.

Problem Analysis and GUI and Algorithm Design

As shown in Figure 12-8, the GUI contains 16 buttons, a text field, and a window. The buttons and the text field are placed in the content pane of the window. The user enters the input using the various buttons, and the program displays the result in the text field. To create the 16 buttons, you use 16 reference variables of the type **JButton**, and to create the text field, you use a reference variable of the type **JTextField**. You also need a reference variable to access the content pane of the window. As we did in previous GUI programs (in Chapters 6, 8, and 11), we create the class containing the application program by extending the definition of the **class JFrame**, which also allows you to create the necessary window to create the GUI. Thus, we use the following variables to create the GUI components and to access the content pane of the window:

```
private JTextField displayText = new JTextField(30);
private JButton[] button = new JButton[16];

Container pane = getContentPane(); //to access the content pane
```

As you can see from Figure 12-8, the GUI components are nicely organized. To place the GUI components as shown in Figure 12-8, we set the layout of the content pane to `null` and use the methods `setSize` and `setLocation`. The following statement instantiates the `JTextField` object `displayText` and places it in the content pane:

```
displayText.setSize(200, 30);
displayText.setLocation(10, 10);
pane.add(displayText);
```

The size of `displayText` is set to 200 pixels wide and 30 pixels high and it is placed at position (`10, 10`) in the content pane.

To assign labels to the buttons, rather than write 16 statements, we use an array of strings and a loop. Consider the following statement:

```
private String[] keys = {"7", "8", "9", "/",
                         "4", "5", "6", "*",
                         "1", "2", "3", "-",
                         "0", "C", "=", "+"};
```

Because the size of the `displayText` is 200 pixels wide and each row has four `JButtons`, we set the width of each `JButton` to 50 pixels wide. To keep the height of each `JButton` the same as the height of `displayText`, we set the height of each `JButton` to 30 pixels.

The user enters the input via the buttons. Therefore, each button can generate an action event. To respond to the events generated by a button, we will create and register an appropriate object. In Chapters 6, 8, and 11, we used the mechanism of the inner class to create and register a listener object. In this program, we make the class containing the application program implement the **interface** `ActionListener`. Therefore, we need to provide only the definition of the method `actionPerformed`, which will be described later in this section. Because the class containing the application program implements the **interface** `ActionListener`, we do not need to explicitly instantiate a listener object. We can simply use the reference **this** as an argument to the method `addActionListener` to register the listener.

The following statements instantiate the 16 `JButtons`, place them in the content pane at the proper locations, and register the listener object:

```
int x, y;

x = 10;
```

```
y = 40;
for (int ind = 0; ind < 16; ind++)
{
    button[ind] = new JButton(keys[ind]); //instantiate the
                                          //JButton and assign it
                                          //a label
    button[ind].addActionListener(this); //register the listener
                                          //object
    button[ind].setSize(50, 30);         //set the size
    button[ind].setLocation(x, y);       //set the location
    pane.add(button[ind]);               //place the button
                                          //in the content pane

        //determine the coordinates of the next JButton
    x = x + 50;
    if ((ind + 1) % 4 == 0)
    {
        x = 10;
        y = y + 30;
    }
}
```

The inputs to the program are integers, various operations, and the equals symbol. The numbers are entered via the buttons whose labels are digits, and the operations are specified via the buttons whose labels are operations. When the user presses the button with the label =, the program displays the results. The user can also press the button with the label C to clear the numbers.

Because Java accepts only strings as inputs to the program, we need two **String** variables to store the number strings. Before performing the operation, the strings will be converted to their numeric form.

To input numbers, the user presses various digit buttons, one at a time. For example, to specify that a number is **235**, the user presses the buttons labeled **2**, **3**, and **5** in sequence. After pressing each button, the number is displayed in the text field. Each number is entered as a string and therefore concatenated with the previous string. When the user presses an operation button, it indicates that the user will start entering the second number. Therefore, we use a **boolean** variable which is set to **false** after the first number is input. We will need the following variables:

```
private String numStr1 = "";
private String numStr2 = "";

private char op;
private boolean firstInput = true;
```

When an event is generated by a button, the method **actionPerformed** is executed. So when the user clicks the = button, the program must display the result. Similarly, when the user clicks an operation button, the program should prepare to receive the second number, and so on. We, therefore, see that the instructions to receive the inputs and operations and display the results will be placed in the method `actionPerformed`. Next, we describe this method.

Method `actionPerformed`   As described above, the method `actionPerformed` is executed when the user presses any button. Several things can go wrong while using the calculator. For example, the user might press an operation button without specifying the first number, or the user might press the equals button either without specifying any number or after inputting the first number. Of course, we must also take care of division by zero. Therefore, the method `actionPerformed` must appropriately respond to the errors.

Suppose that the user wants to add three numbers. After adding the first two numbers, the third number can be added to the sum of the first two numbers. In this case, when the third number is added, the first number is the sum of the first two numbers and the second number becomes the third number. Therefore, after each operation, we will set the first number as the result of the operation. The user can click the C button to start a different calculation. This discussion translates into the following algorithm:

1. Declare the appropriate variables.
2. Use the method `getActionCommand` to identify the button clicked. Retrieve the label of the button, which is a string.
3. Retrieve the character specifying the button label and store it in the variable `ch`.
4. a. If `ch` is a digit and `firstInput` is **true**, append the character at the end of the first number string; otherwise, append the character at the end of the second number string.
   b. If `ch` is an operation, set `firstInput` to **false** and set the variable `op` to `ch`.
   c. If `ch` is = and there is no error, perform the operation, display the result, and set the first number as the result of the operation. If an error occurred, display an appropriate message.
   d. If `ch` is C, set both number strings to blank and clear the `displayText`.

To perform the operation, we write the method `evaluate`, which is described in the next section.

The definition of the method `actionPerformed` is:

```java
public void actionPerformed(ActionEvent e)
{
    String resultStr;                                  //Step 1

    String str
        = String.valueOf(e.getActionCommand());  //Steps 1 and 2

    char ch = str.charAt(0);                      //Steps 1 and 3
```

```
        switch (ch)                                          //Step 4
        {
        case '0': case '1': case '2':                        //Step 4a
        case '3': case '4': case '5':
        case '6': case '7': case '8':
        case '9': if (firstInput)
                  {
                      numStr1 = numStr1 + ch;
                      displayText.setText(numStr1);
                  }
                  else
                  {
                      numStr2 = numStr2 + ch;
                      displayText.setText(numStr2);
                  }
                  break;
        case '+': case '-': case '*':                        //Step 4b
        case '/': op = ch;
                  firstInput = false;
                  break;
        case '=': resultStr = evaluate();                    //Step 4c
                  displayText.setText(resultStr);
                  numStr1 = resultStr;
                  numStr2 = "";
                  firstInput = false;
                  break;
        case 'C': displayText.setText("");                   //Step 4d
                  numStr1 = "";
                  numStr2 = "";
                  firstInput = true;

        }
    }
```

Method evaluate   The method `evaluate` performs an operation and returns the result of the operation as a string. This method also handles various exceptions such as division by zero and number format error (which occurs if one of the number strings is empty). The definition of this method is:

```
private String evaluate()
{
    final char beep = '\u0007';

    try
    {
        int num1 = Integer.parseInt(numStr1);
        int num2 = Integer.parseInt(numStr2);
        int result = 0;
```

```
        switch (op)
        {
        case '+': result = num1 + num2;
                break;
        case '-': result = num1 - num2;
                break;
        case '*': result = num1 * num2;
                break;
        case '/': result = num1 / num2;
        }

        return String.valueOf(result);
    }
    catch (ArithmeticException e)
    {
        System.out.print(beep);
        return "E R R O R: " + e.getMessage();
    }
    catch (NumberFormatException e)
    {
        System.out.print(beep);
        if (numStr1.equals(""))
            return "E R R O R: Invalid First Number" ;
        else
            return "E R R O R: Invalid Second Number" ;
    }
    catch (Exception e)
    {
        System.out.print(beep);
        return "E R R O R";
    }
}
```

Before writing the complete program, we must do one more thing. When the user clicks the window closing button, the program must terminate. Clicking the window closing button generates a window event. Therefore, we must create a `WindowListener` object and register the object of the class containing the application program because this class extends the definition of the **class** `JFrame`. The window events are handled by the **interface** `WindowListener`. To terminate the program when the user clicks the window closing button, we must provide the definition of the method `windowClosing` of the **interface** `WindowListener`. Because the **interface** `WindowListener` contains more than one method and we want to use only the method `windowClosing`, we use the mechanism of anonymous class to create and register the window event object. To do so, we make the class containing the application program use the **class** `WindowAdapter` to create and register the window event object. Creating and registering the window event object is accomplished by the following statements:

```
this.addWindowListener(new WindowAdapter()

            {
                    public void windowClosing(WindowEvent e)
                    {
                            System.exit(0);
                    }
            }
);
```

We can now outline the program listing

Program Listing

```
//GUI Calculator Program

import javax.swing.*;
import java.awt.*;
import java.awt.event.*;
import java.io.*;

public class Calculator extends JFrame implements ActionListener
{
    private JTextField displayText = new JTextField(30);
    private JButton[] button = new JButton[16];

    private String[] keys = {"7", "8", "9", "/",
                             "4", "5", "6", "*",
                             "1", "2", "3", "-",
                             "0", "C", "=", "+"};

    private String numStr1 = "";
    private String numStr2 = "";

    private char op;
    private boolean firstInput = true;

    public Calculator()
    {
        setTitle("My Calculator");
        setSize(230, 200);
        Container pane = getContentPane();
```

```
        pane.setLayout(null);

        displayText.setSize(200, 30);
        displayText.setLocation(10, 10);
        pane.add(displayText);

        int x, y;

        x = 10;
        y = 40;
        for (int ind = 0; ind < 16; ind++)
        {
            button[ind] = new JButton(keys[ind]);
            button[ind].addActionListener(this);
            button[ind].setSize(50, 30);
            button[ind].setLocation(x, y);
            pane.add(button[ind]);
            x = x + 50;
            if ((ind + 1) % 4 == 0)
            {
                x = 10;
                y = y + 30;
            }
        }

        this.addWindowListener(new WindowAdapter()
                {
                    public void windowClosing(WindowEvent e)
                    {
                        System.exit(0);
                    }
                }
        );

        setVisible(true);
        setDefaultCloseOperation(EXIT_ON_CLOSE);
    }

//Place the definition of the method actionPerformed
//as described here

//Place the definition of the method evaluate
//as described here
```

```
    public static void main(String[] args)
    {
        Calculator C = new Calculator();
    }
}
```

Sample Run 1: In this sample run (see Figure 12-9), the user entered the numbers **34** and **25** and the operation **+**. The result is shown in the bottom screen.

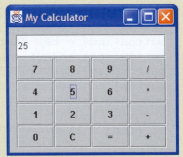

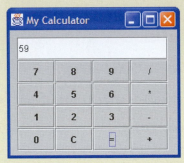

Figure 12-9   Adding the numbers 34 and 25

Sample Run 2: In this sample run (see Figure 12-10), the user attempted to divide by 0, resulting in an error message.

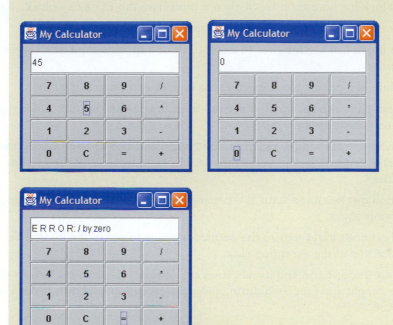

Figure 12-10 An attempt to divide by 0

QUICK REVIEW

1. An exception is an object of a specific exception class. Java provides extensive support for exception handling by providing a number of exception classes. Java also allows users to create and implement their own exception classes.

2. The `try`/`catch`/`finally` block is used to handle exceptions within a program.

3. Statements that may generate an exception are placed in a `try` block. The `try` block also contains statements that should not be executed if an exception occurs.

4. A `try` block is followed by zero or more `catch` blocks.

5. A `catch` block specifies the type of exception it can catch and contains an exception handler.

6. The last `catch` block may or may not be followed by a `finally` block.

7. The code contained in the **finally** block always executes, regardless of whether an exception occurs, except when the program exits early from a **try** block by calling the method **System.exit**.

8. If a **try** block has no **catch** block, then it must have the **finally** block.

9. When an exception occurs, an object of a specific exception class is created.

10. A **catch** block can catch either all exceptions of a specific type or all types of exceptions.

11. The heading of a **catch** block specifies the type of exception it handles.

12. The **class** **Throwable**, which is derived from the **class** **object**, is the superclass of the **class** **Exception**.

13. The methods **getMessage**, **printStackTrace**, and **toString** of the **class** **Throwable** are **public** and so are inherited by the subclasses of the **class** **Throwable**.

14. The method **getMessage** returns the string containing the detailed message stored in the exception object.

15. The method **toString** returns the detailed message stored in the exception object as well as the name of the exception class.

16. The **class** **Exception** and its subclasses are designed to catch exceptions that should be caught and processed during program execution, and thus make a program more robust.

17. The **class** **Exception** is the superclass of the classes designed to handle exceptions.

18. The **class** **Exception** is contained in the package **java.lang**.

19. The classes to deal with I/O exceptions, such as the file not found exception, are contained in the **package** **java.io**.

20. The **class** **InputMismatchException** is contained in the package **java.util**.

21. The classes to deal with number format exceptions and arithmetic exceptions, such as division by zero, are contained in the **package** **java.lang**.

22. Generally, exception classes are placed in the package that contains the methods that throw these exceptions.

23. Java's predefined exceptions are divided into two categories—checked exceptions and unchecked exceptions.

24. Any exception that can be recognized by the compiler is called a checked exception.

25. Unchecked exceptions are exceptions that are not checked by the compiler.

26. Typically, a **catch** block does one of the following:

    - Completely handles the exception.

    - Partially processes the exception. In this case, the **catch** block either rethrows the same exception or throws another exception for the calling environment to handle the exception.

    - Rethrows the same exception for the calling environment to handle the exception.

27. The general syntax to rethrow an exception caught by a **catch** block is:

    ```
    throw exceptionReference;
    ```

28. The general syntax to throw your own exception object is:

    ```
    throw new ExceptionClassName(messageString);
    ```

29. The method **printStackTrace** is used to determine the order in which the methods were called and where the exception was handled.

30. The exception class that you define extends the **class** Exception or one of its subclasses.

31. Action events are handled by appropriately implementing the **interface** **ActionListener**.

32. Window events are handled by appropriately implementing the **interface** **WindowListener**.

33. The **class** WindowAdapter implements the **interface** WindowListener by providing empty bodies to the methods.

34. To register a window listener object to a GUI component, you use the method **addWindowListener**. The window listener object being registered is passed as a parameter to the method **addWindowListener**.

35. Mouse events are handled by appropriately implementing the **interface** **MouseListener**.

36. The **class** MouseAdapter implements the **interface** MouseListener by providing empty bodies to the methods.

37. To register a mouse listener object to a GUI component, you use the method **addMouseListener**. The mouse listener object being registered is passed as a parameter to the method **addMouseListener**.

38. Key events are handled by appropriately implementing the **interface** **KeyListener**.

12

EXERCISES

1. Mark the following statements as true or false.

   a. The block **finally** is always executed.

   b. Division by zero is a checked exception.

   c. File not found is an unchecked exception.

   d. Exceptions are thrown either in a **try** block in a method or from a method called directly or indirectly from a **try** block.

   e. The order in which **catch** blocks are listed is not important.

   f. An exception can be caught either in the method where it occurred or in any one of the methods that led to the invocation of this method.

g. One way to handle an exception is to print an error message and exit the program.

h. All exceptions must be reported to avoid compilation errors.

i. An event handler is a method.

j. A GUI component can generate only one type of event.

2. Consider the following Java code:

```java
int lowerLimit;

   .
   .
   .

try
{
   System.out.println("Entering the try block.");
   if (lowerLimit < 100)
       throw new Exception("Lower limit violation.");
   System.out.println("Exiting the try block.");
}
catch (Exception e)
{
   System.out.println("Exception: " + e.getMessage());
}
System.out.println("After the catch block");
```

What is the output if:

a. The value of `lowerLimit` is 50?

b. The value of `lowerLimit` is 150?

3. Consider the following Java code:

```java
int lowerLimit;
int divisor;
int result;

try
{
   System.out.println("Entering the try block.");
   result = lowerLimit / divisor;
   if (lowerLimit < 100)
       throw new Exception("Lower limit violation.");
   System.out.println("Exiting the try block.");
}
catch (ArithmeticException e)
{
   System.out.println("Exception: " + e.getMessage());
   result = 110;
}
catch (Exception e)
{
```

```
        System.out.println("Exception: " + e.getMessage());
    }
    System.out.println("After the catch block");
```

What is the output if:

a. The value of `lowerLimit` is 50 and the value of `divisor` is 10?

b. The value of `lowerLimit` is 50 and the value of `divisor` is 0?

c. The value of `lowerLimit` is 150 and the value of `divisor` is 10?

d. The value of `lowerLimit` is 150 and the value of `divisor` is 0?

4. Rewrite the Java code given in Exercise 3 so that the new equivalent code has exactly one `catch` block.

5. Correct any compile time errors in the following code:

```java
import java.util.*;

public class SAverage
{
    public static void main(String[] args)
    {
        double test1, test2, test3, test4;
        double average;

        try
        {
            Scanner inFile = new
                    Scanner(new FileReader("a:\\test.txt"));
            PrintWriter outFile = new
                    PrintWriter("a:\\testavg.out");

            test1 = inFile.nextDouble();
            test2 = inFile.nextDouble();
            test3 = inFile.nextDouble();
            test4 = inFile.nextDouble();

            outFile.printf("Test scores: %.2f %.2f %.2f %.2f %n",
                    test1, test2, test3, test4);

            average = (test1 + test2 + test3 + test4) / 4.0;

            outFile.println("Average test score: %.2f",
                    average);

            outFile.close();

        }
        catch (Exception e)
        {
```

12

```
              System.out.println(e.toString());
        }
        catch (FileNotFoundException e)
        {
            System.out.println(e.toString());
        }
    }
}
```

6. Define the exception **class** `TornadoException`. The class should have two constructors, including one default constructor. If the exception is thrown with the default constructor, the method `getMessage` should return:

   `"Tornado: Take cover immediately!"`

   The other constructor has a single parameter, say `m`, of the **int** type. If the exception is thrown with this constructor, the method `getMessage` should return:

   `"Tornado: m miles away; and approaching!"`

7. Write a Java program to test the **class** `TornadoException` specified in Exercise 6.

8. Suppose the exception **class** `MyException` is defined as follows:

   ```
   public class MyException extends Exception
   {
       public MyException()
       {
           super("MyException thrown!");
           System.out.println("Immediate attention required!");
       }
       public MyException(String msg)
       {
           super(msg);
           System.out.println("Attention required!");
       }
   }
   ```

   What output will be produced if the exception is thrown with the default constructor? What output will be produced if the exception is thrown with the constructor with parameter and the actual parameter `"May Day, May Day"`?

9. What are the three different ways you can implement an interface?

PROGRAMMING EXERCISES

1. Write a program that prompts the user to enter the length in feet and inches and outputs the equivalent length in centimeters. If the user enters a negative number or a nondigit number, throw and handle an appropriate exception and prompt the user to enter another set of numbers.

2. Redo Programming Exercise 11 of Chapter 5 so that if the input file does not exist, the program handles the `FileNotFoundException`, outputs an appropriate message, and terminates normally.

3. Redo the Text Processing Programming Example in Chapter 9 so that if the array index goes out of bounds when the program accesses the array `letterCount`, it throws and handles the `ArrayIndexOutOfBoundsException`.

4. Redo Programming Exercise 7 of Chapter 8 so that your program handles exceptions such as division by zero.

5. Extend the Programming Example Calculator of this chapter by adding three buttons with the labels `M`, `R`, and `E` as follows: If the user clicks the button `M`, the number currently in the `displayText` field is stored in the variable, say `memory`; if the user clicks the button `R`, the number stored in memory is displayed and also becomes the first number (so that another number can be added, subtracted, multiplied, or divided); and if the user clicks the button `E`, the program terminates.

6. The Programming Example Calculator of this chapter is designed to perform operations on integers. Write a similar program that can be used to perform operations on decimal numbers. (*Note*: If division by zero occurs with values of the **int** data type, the program throws a division by zero exception. However, if you divide a decimal number by zero, Java does not throw the division by zero exception; it returns the answer as `infinity`. However, if division by zero occurs, your calculator program must output the message `ERROR: / by zero`.)

7. In Programming Exercise 7 in Chapter 8, we defined a **class** `Roman` to implement Roman numerals in a program. In that exercise, we also implemented the method `romanToDecimal` to convert a Roman numeral into its equivalent decimal number.

a. Modify the definition of the **class** `Roman` so that the data members are declared as **protected**. Also include the method `decimalToRoman`, which converts the decimal number (the decimal number must be a positive integer) to an equivalent Roman numeral format. Write the definition of the method `decimalToRoman`. Your definition of the **class** `Roman` must contain the method `toString`, which returns the string containing the number in Roman format. For simplicity, we assume that only the letter `I` can appear in front of another letter and that it appears only in front of the letters `V` and `X`. For example, 4 is represented as `IV`, 9 is represented as `IX`, 39 is represented as `XXXIX`, and 49 is represented as `XXXXIX`. Also, 40 is represented as `XXXX`, 190 is represented as `CLXXXX`, and so on.

b. Derive the **class** `ExtendedRoman` from the **class** `Roman` to do the following. In the **class** `ExtendedRoman`, add the methods `add`, `subtract`, `multiply`, and `divide` so that arithmetic operations can be performed on Roman numerals.

To add (subtract, multiply, or divide) Roman numerals, add (subtract, multiply, or divide, respectively) their decimal representations and then convert the result to the Roman numeral format. For subtraction, if the first number is smaller than the second number, throw the exception, "`Because the first number is smaller than the second, the numbers cannot be subtracted`". Similarly, for division, the numerator must be larger than the denominator.

12

c. Write the definitions of the methods `add`, `subtract`, `multiply`, and `divide` as described in Part b. Also, your definition of the **class** ExtendedRoman must contain the method `toString` that returns the string containing the number in Roman format.

d. Write a program to test various operations on your **class** ExtendedRoman.

13

ADVANCED GUIS AND GRAPHICS

In this chapter, you will:

♦ Learn about applets

♦ Explore the **class** Graphics

♦ Learn about the **class** Font

♦ Explore the **class** Color

♦ Learn how to use additional Layout managers

♦ Become familiar with more GUI components

♦ Learn how to create menu-based programs

♦ Explore how to handle key and mouse events

There are two types of Java programs—applications and applets. Up to this point, we have created only application programs. Even the programs we've created that use GUI components are application programs. Java **applets** are small applications that can be embedded in an HTML page. In this chapter, you learn how to create an applet. You also learn how to convert a GUI application to a Java applet. This chapter also shows you how to use different fonts, colors, and geometric shapes to enhance the output of your programs.

In Chapter 6, you learned how to use GUI components, such as `JFrame`, `JLabel`, `JTextField`, and `JButton`, to make your programs attractive and user friendly. In this chapter, you learn about other commonly used GUI components. The **class** `JComponent` is the superclass of the classes used to create various GUI components. Figure 13-1 shows the inheritance hierarchy of the GUI classes that you have used in previous chapters, plus the ones you encounter in this chapter. The package containing the definition of the class is also shown.

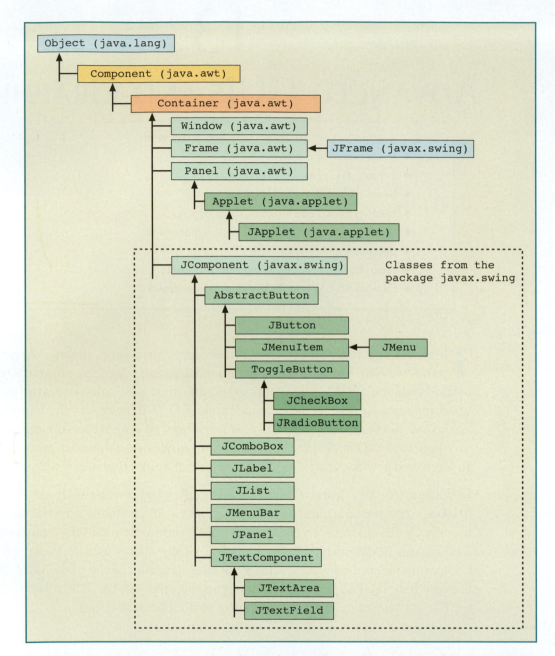

Figure 13-1 Inheritance hierarchy of GUI classes (classes shown in the dotted rectangle are from the **package** `javax.swing`)

As shown in Figure 13-1, the **class** Container, which is a subclass of the **class** Component, is the superclass of all the classes designed to provide a GUI. Therefore, all **public** members of these classes are inherited by their subclasses, as shown in Figure 13-1. Moreover, both the Container and Component classes are **abstract**.

The **class** Component contains many methods that are inherited by its subclasses. You have used methods such as setSize and setLocation in various GUI programs. Table 13-1 describes some of the constructors and methods of the **class** Component.

Table 13-1 Some Constructors and Methods of the **class** Component

```
protected Component()
   //Constructor
   //Creates a new instance of a component.

public void addComponentListener(ComponentListener lis)
   //Adds the component listener specified by lis.

public void addFocusListener(FocusListener lis)
   //Adds the focus listener specified by lis.

public void addKeyListener(KeyListener lis)
   //Adds the key listener specified by lis.

public void addMouseListener(MouseListener lis)
   //Adds the mouse listener specified by lis.

public void addMouseMotionListener(MouseMotionListener lis)
   //Adds the mouse motion listener specified by lis.

public void removeComponentListener(ComponentListener lis)
   //Removes the component listener specified by lis.

public void removeFocusListener(FocusListener lis)
   //Removes the focus listener specified by lis.

public void removeKeyListener(KeyListener lis)
   //Removes the key listener specified by lis.

public void removeMouseListener(MouseListener lis)
   //Removes the mouse listener specified by lis.

public void removeMouseMotionListener(MouseMotionListener lis)
   //Removes the mouse motion listener specified by lis.

public Color getBackground()
   //Returns the background color of this component.

public Color getForeground()
   //Returns the foreground color of this component.

public void setBackground(Color c)
   //Sets the background color of this component to color c.

public void setForeground(Color c)
   //Sets the foreground color of this component to color c.

public Font getFont()
   //Returns the font of this component.
```

13

Table 13-1 Some Constructors and Methods of the `class` Component (continued)

```
public void setFont(Font ft)
   //Sets the font of this component to ft.
```

```
public void setSize(int w, int h)
   //Sets the size of this component to width w and height h.
```

```
public boolean isVisible()
   //Returns true if the component is visible; false otherwise.
```

```
public void setVisible(boolean tog)
   //If tog is true, sets the component to visible;
   //if tog is false, the component is not shown.
```

```
public void paint(Graphics g)
   //Paints the component with the graphic component specified by g.
```

```
public void repaint()
   //Repaints the component.
```

```
public void repaint(int x, int y, int wid, int ht)
   //Repaints the rectangular portion of the component from (x, y)
   //to (x + wid, y + ht).
```

```
public void setLocation(int x, int y)
   //Sets the component at the location (x, y).
```

```
public String toString()
   //Returns a string representation of this component.
```

```
public void update(Graphics g)
   //Invokes the paint method.
```

```
public void validate()
   //Validates this container and all of its subcomponents. The
   //method validate is used to cause a container to lay out its
   //subcomponents once more. Typically called after the components
   //it contains have been added to or modified.
```

The **class** Container inherits all the methods of the **class** Component. In addition to the methods given in Table 13-1, Table 13-2 shows some commonly used methods of the **class** Container.

Table 13-2 Some Methods of the `class` Container

```
public Component add(Component comp)
   //Appends the specified component to the end of this container.
```

```
public Component add(Component comp, int index)
   //Adds the specified component to this container at the
   //position specified by index.
```

```
public void paint(Graphics g)
   //Paints the container with the graphics component specified by g.
```

Table 13-2 Some Methods of the **class** Container (continued)

```
public void update(Graphics g)
  //Invokes the paint method.
public void validate()
  //Validates this container and all of its subcomponents. The
  //method validate is used to cause a container to lay out its
  //subcomponents once more. Typically called after the components
  //it contains have been added to or modified.
```

In the remainder of this chapter, whenever we list the methods of a class, we will not show the methods that are inherited from the **class**es Component and Container.

Next, we discuss how to create a Java applet. For the most part, the programs in this chapter are Java applets.

APPLETS

The term *applet* refers to a little application. In Java, an **applet** is a Java program that is embedded within a Web page and executed by a Web browser. You create an applet by extending the **class** JApplet, which is contained in the **package** javax.swing.

Table 13-3 describes some commonly used methods of the **class** JApplet.

Table 13-3 Some Members of the **class** JApplet (**package** javax.swing)

```
public void init()
  //Called by the browser or applet viewer to inform this applet
  //that it has been loaded into the system.
public void start()
  //Called by the browser or applet viewer to inform this applet
  //that it should start its execution. It is called after the init
  //method and each time the applet is revisited in a Web page.
public void stop()
  //Called by the browser or applet viewer to inform this applet
  //that it should stop its execution. It is called before the
  //method destroy.
public void destroy()
  //Called by the browser or applet viewer. Informs this applet that
  //it is being reclaimed and that it should destroy any resources
  //that it has allocated. The method stop is called before destroy.
public void showStatus(String msg)
  //Displays the string msg in the status bar.
public Container getContentPane()
  //Returns the ContentPane object for this applet.
```

13

Table 13-3 Some Members of the **class** JApplet (**package** javax.swing) (continued)

```
public JMenuBar getJMenuBar()
  //Returns the JMenuBar object for this applet.
public URL getDocumentBase()
  //Returns the URL of the document that contains this applet.
public URL getCodeBase()
  //Returns the URL of this applet.
public void update(Graphics g)
  //Calls the paint() method.
protected String paramString()
  //Returns a string representation of this JApplet; mainly used
  //for debugging.
```

Unlike Java application programs, Java applets do not have the method **main**. Instead, when a browser runs an applet, the methods **init**, **start**, and **paint** are guaranteed to be invoked in sequence. Therefore, as a programmer, to develop an applet, all you have to do is override one or all of the methods **init**, **start**, and **paint**. Of these three methods, the **paint** method has one argument, which is a **Graphics** object. This allows you to use the **class** Graphics without actually creating a **Graphics** object. Later in this chapter, when you see the **class** Graphics in detail, you will notice that the **class** Graphics is an **abstract** class; therefore, you cannot create an instance of this class. For now, all you need to do is import the **package** java.awt so that you can use various methods of the **class** Graphics in the paint method. To do so, you need the following two **import** statements:

```
import java.awt.Graphics;
import javax.swing.JApplet;
```

Because you create an applet by extending the **class** JApplet, in skeleton form a Java applet looks something like this:

```
import java.awt.Graphics;
import javax.swing.JApplet;

public class WelcomeApplet extends JApplet
{

}
```

As a general rule, you keep all statements to be executed only once in the **init** method. The **paint** method is used to draw various items, including strings, in the content pane of the applet. Thus, in the applets presented in this chapter, we use **init** to:

- Initialize variables
- Get data from the user
- Place various GUI components

The **paint** method is used to create the output. The **init** and **paint** methods need to share common data items, so these common data items are the data members of the applet.

Let's now create an applet that will display a welcome message. Because no initialization is required, all you need to do is override the method **paint** so that it draws the welcome message. Whenever you override a method, it is a good idea to invoke the corresponding method of the parent **class**. Thus, whenever you override the **paint** method, the first Java statement is:

super.paint(g);

where g is a **Graphics** object. Recall that **super** is a reserved word in Java and refers to the instance of the parent class.

To display the string containing the welcome message, we use the method **drawString** of the **class** Graphics. The method **drawString** is an overloaded method. One of the headings of the method **drawString** is:

public abstract void drawString(String str, int x, int y)

The method **drawString** displays the string specified by **str** at the horizontal position **x** pixels away from the upper-left corner of the applet, and the vertical position **y** pixels away from the upper-left corner of the applet. In other words, the applet has a coordinate system xy, with x = 0, y = 0 at the upper-left corner; the x value increases from left to right and the y value increases from top to bottom. Thus, the method **drawString** as given previously draws the string **str** starting at the position (x, y).

The following Java applet displays a welcome message:

```java
//Welcome Applet

import java.awt.Graphics;
import javax.swing.JApplet;

public class WelcomeApplet extends JApplet
{
    public void paint(Graphics g)
    {
        super.paint(g);                              //Line 1
        g.drawString("Welcome to Java Programming",
                30, 30);                             //Line 2
    }
}
```

In the preceding applet, the statement in Line 1 invokes the **paint** method of the **class** JApplet. Notice that the method **paint** uses a **Graphics** object g as the argument. Recall that the **class** Graphics is an **abstract** class, and for this reason, you cannot create an instance of the **class** Graphics. The system will create a **Graphics** object for you; you need not be concerned about it. The statement in Line 2 draws the string **"Welcome to Java Programming"** at the coordinate position (30, 30).

13

Until now, when we created a GUI application program, we used methods such as `setTitle` and `setSize`. As you can see in the preceding applet, such methods are not used in an applet. Note the following about applets:

- The method `setTitle` is not used in applets because applets do not have titles. An applet is embedded in an HTML document, and the applet itself does not have a title. The HTML document may have a title, which is set by the document.

- The method `setSize` is not used in applets because the applet's size is determined in the HTML document, not by the applet. You do not need to set the size of the applet.

- You need not invoke the method `setVisible`.

- You need not close the applet. When the HTML document containing the applet is closed, the applet is destroyed.

- There is no method `main`.

As with an application, you compile an applet and produce a `.class` file. Once the `.class` file is created, you need to place it in a Web page to run the applet. For example, you can create a file with the `.html` extension, say `WelcomeApplet.html`, with the following lines in the same folder where the `WelcomeApplet.class` file resides:

```
<!DOCTYPE HTML PUBLIC "-//W3C//DTD HTML 4.01 Transitional//EN">

<HTML>
  <HEAD>
    <TITLE>WELCOME APPLET</TITLE>
  </HEAD>
  <BODY>
    <OBJECT code = "WelcomeApplet.class" width = "240" height = "60">
    </OBJECT>
  </BODY>
</HTML>
```

Once the HTML file is created, you can run your applet either by opening `Welcome.html` with a Web browser, or you can enter:

```
appletviewer WelcomeApplet.html
```

at a command-line prompt, if you are using the Java Development Kit (JDK).

Sample Run: Figure 13-2 shows the output of the `WelcomeApplet` produced by the Applet Viewer in Windows XP.

Figure 13-2 Output of the `WelcomeApplet`

You terminate the applet by clicking the close button in the upper-right corner of the Applet Viewer, or by closing the HTML document in which the applet is embedded.

Two ways to make your applets more attractive are to vary the type font and color. Next, we introduce the **class**es `Font` and `Color`, contained in the **package** `java.awt`.

class Font

The GUI programs we have created so far have used only the default font. To show text in different fonts when the program executes, Java provides the **class** `Font`. The **class** `Font` is contained in the **package** `java.awt`, so you need to use the following **import** statement in your program:

```
import java.awt.*;
```

The **class** `Font` contains various constructors, methods, and constants, some of which are described in Table 13-4.

13

Table 13-4 Some Constructors and Methods of the **class** `Font`

Method

`public Font(String name, int style, int size)`
`  //Constructor`
`  //Creates a new Font from the specified name, style, and point`
`  //size.`

`public String getFamily()` `  //Returns the family name of this Font.`
`public String getFontName()` `  //Returns the font face name of this Font.`

Typically, you use only the constructor of the **class** Font. As shown in Table 13-4, the constructor of the **class** Font takes the following three arguments:

- A string specifying the font face name (or font name for short)
- An **int** value specifying the font style
- An **int** value specifying the font size expressed in points, where 72 points equal one inch

Fonts available on a particular system vary widely. However, using the JDK guarantees the following fonts:

- Serif
- SanSerif
- Monospaced
- Dialog
- DialogInput

If you want to know which fonts are available on your system, you can run the program given next. (This program uses a graphics environment, which is covered later in this chapter.)

```java
import java.awt.*;

public class FontNames
{
    public static void main(String[] args)
    {
        String[] listOfFontNames =
                GraphicsEnvironment.getLocalGraphicsEnvironment()
                    .getAvailableFontFamilyNames();

        for (int i = 0; i < listOfFontNames.length; i++)
            System.out.println(listOfFontNames[i]);
    }
}
```

The **class** Font contains the constants Font.PLAIN, Font.ITALIC, and Font.BOLD, which you can apply to change the style of a font. For example, the Java statement:

```java
new Font("Serif", Font.ITALIC, 12)
```

creates a 12-point Serif italic font. Likewise, the statement:

```java
new Font("Dialog", Font.ITALIC + Font.BOLD, 36)
```

creates a 36-point Dialog italic and bold font.

The applet given in Example 13-1 illustrates how to change fonts in text.

Example 13-1

```java
//FontsDisplayed Applet

import java.awt.*;
import javax.swing.JApplet;

public class FontsDisplayed extends JApplet
{
    public void paint(Graphics g)
    {
        super.paint(g);
        g.setFont(new Font("Courier", Font.BOLD, 24));
        g.drawString("Courier bold 24pt font", 30, 36);

        g.setFont(new Font("Arial", Font.PLAIN, 30));
        g.drawString("Arial plain 30pt font", 30, 70);

        g.setFont(new Font("Dialog", Font.BOLD + Font.ITALIC, 36));
        g.drawString("Dialog italic bold 36pt font", 30, 110);

        g.setFont(new Font("Serif", Font.ITALIC, 30));
        g.drawString("Serif italic 42pt font", 30, 156);
    }
}
```

The HTML file that invokes this applet contains the following code:

```html
<!DOCTYPE HTML PUBLIC "-//W3C//DTD HTML 4.01 Transitional//EN">

<HTML>
  <HEAD>
    <TITLE>Four Fonts</TITLE>
  </HEAD>
  <BODY>
    <OBJECT code = "FontsDisplayed.class" width = "500" height = "190">
    </OBJECT>
  </BODY>
</HTML>
```

13

Sample Run: Figure 13-3 shows the output of the **FontsDisplayed** applet in Applet Viewer.

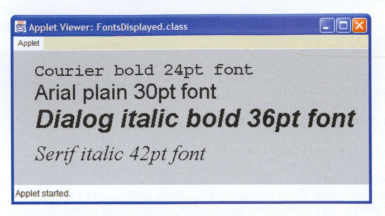

Figure 13-3   Output of the `FontsDisplayed` applet

class Color

So far, we have used only the default colors in our GUI programs. For example, the text always appeared as black. You may want to show the text in different colors or change the background color of a component. Java provides the **class** `Color` to accomplish this. Because the **class** `Color` is contained in the **package** `java.awt`, you need to use the following **import** statement:

`import java.awt.*;`

Table 13-5 shows various constructors and methods of the **class** `Color`.

Table 13-5   Some Constructors and Methods of the **class** `Color`

```
Color(int r, int g, int b)
   //Constructor
   //Creates a Color object with the red value r, green value g,
   //and blue value b. In this case, r, g, and b can be
   //between 0 and 255.
   //Example: new  Color(0, 255, 0)
   //      creates a color with no red or blue component.

Color(int rgb)
   //Constructor
   //Creates a Color object with the red value r, green value g,
   //and blue value b; RGB value consisting of the red component
   //in bits 16-23, the green component in bits 8-15, and the
   //blue component in bits 0-7.
   //Example: new  Color(255)
   //      creates a color with no red or green component.
```

Table 13-5 Some Constructors and Methods of the **class** Color (continued)

```
Color(float r, float g, float b)
  //Constructor
  //Creates a Color object with the red value r, green value g,
  //and blue value b. In this case, r, g, and b can be between 0
  //and 1.0.
  //Example: new  Color(1.0, 0, 0)
  //       creates a color with no green or blue component.
```

```
public Color brighter()
  //Returns a Color that is brighter.
```

```
public Color darker()
  //Returns a Color that is darker.
```

```
public boolean equals(Object o)
  //Returns true if the color of this object is the same as the
  //color of the object o; false otherwise.
```

```
public int getBlue()
  //Returns the value of the blue component.
```

```
public int getGreen()
  //Returns the value of the green component.
```

```
public int getRed()
  //Returns the value of the red component.
```

```
public int getRGB()
  //Returns the RGB value.
```

```
public String toString()
  //Returns a string with the information about the color.
```

You can use the methods `setBackground` and `setForeground`, described in Table 13-1, to set the background and foreground color of a component.

Java uses the color scheme known as RGB, where R stands for red, G for green, and B for blue, respectively. You create instances of `Color` by mixing red, green, and blue hues in various proportions. The **class** `Color` contains three constructors, as shown in Table 13-5. In the first constructor, an RGB value is represented as three **int** values. The second constructor specifies an RGB value as a single integer. In either form, the closer an r, g, or b value is to 255, the more hue is mixed into the color. For example, if you use the first constructor, pure red is produced by mixing red 255, green 0, and blue 0 parts each. To produce the color red, you use the first constructor as follows:

```
Color redColor = new Color(255, 0, 0);
```

Various shades of black, white, and gray can be created by mixing all three colors in the same proportion. For example, the color white has the RGB values 255, 255, 255, and black has the RGB values 0, 0, 0. An RGB value of 100, 100, 100 creates a gray color darker than one with an RGB value of 200, 200, 200.

13

In addition to the methods shown in Table 13-5, the **class** Color defines a number of standard colors as constants. Table 13-6 shows the color name in bold and its values for easy reference.

Table 13-6 Constants Defined in the **class** Color

Color.black: (0, 0, 0)	Color.magenta: (255, 0, 255)
Color.blue: (0, 0, 255)	Color.orange: (255, 200, 0)
Color.cyan: (0, 255, 255)	Color.pink: (255, 175, 175)
Color.darkGray: (64, 64, 64)	Color.red: (255, 0, 0)
Color.gray: (128, 128, 128)	Color.white: (255, 255, 255)
Color.green: (0, 255, 0)	Color.yellow: (255, 255, 0)
Color.lightGray: (192, 192, 192)	

A simple applet to illustrate the use of the **class** Color is given in Example 13-2. In Example 13-2, we use the **class** GridLayout, described in Chapter 6, to place the GUI components. Recall that GridLayout divides the container into a grid of rows and columns, and so allows you to place the components in rows and columns. Every component placed in a GridLayout will have the same width and height. The components are placed from left to right in the first row, followed by left to right in the second row, and so on.

The **class** GridLayout is contained in the **package** java.awt. Appendix E describes various methods of this class. Most often we use the following constructor of the **class** GridLayout:

GridLayout(**int** row, **int** col)

where row specifies the number of rows and col specifies the number of columns in the grid, respectively. For example, to create a grid with 10 rows and 5 columns, and set it as the layout of the container c, you use the following Java statement:

c.setLayout(**new** GridLayout(10, 5));

In our next applet, we use a grid with 2 rows and 2 columns. Therefore, we use the statement:

c.setLayout(**new** GridLayout(2, 2));

Example 13-2 uses the method **random** of the **class** Math that returns a random value between 0 and 1. For example, the statement:

Math.random();

returns a random **double** value between 0 and 1. Note that the third constructor of the Color **class** (see Table 13-5) takes three **float** values, each between 0 and 1, as parameters. Therefore, we use the explicit cast operator (**float**) to convert the **double** value

returned by the **random** method. Thus, we use the following statements to randomly generate a value for the colors red, green, and blue:

```
red = (float) Math.random();
green = (float) Math.random();
blue = (float) Math.random();
```

These statements assign random **float** values between 0 and 1 to the **float** variables **red**,
green, and **blue**. Suppose that **bottomrightJL** is a **JLabel**. The statement:

```
bottomrightJL.setForeground(new Color(red, green, blue));
```

creates a color and assigns it as the foreground color of the label **bottomrightJL**.

Example 13-2

This example gives the complete program listing and a sample run that shows how to set the
colors of a text and GUI components.

```java
//ColorsDisplayed Applet

import java.awt.*;
import javax.swing.*;

public class ColorsDisplayed extends JApplet
{
    JLabel topleftJL, toprightJL, bottomleftJL, bottomrightJL;

    int i;
    float red, green, blue;

    public void init()
    {
        Container c = getContentPane();
        c.setLayout(new GridLayout(2, 2));
        c.setBackground(Color.white);
        topleftJL = new JLabel("Red", SwingConstants.CENTER);
        toprightJL = new JLabel("Green", SwingConstants.CENTER);
        bottomleftJL = new JLabel("Blue", SwingConstants.CENTER);
        bottomrightJL = new JLabel("Random", SwingConstants.CENTER);

        topleftJL.setForeground(Color.red);
        toprightJL.setForeground(Color.green);
        bottomleftJL.setForeground(Color.blue);
        red = (float) Math.random();
        green = (float) Math.random();
        blue = (float) Math.random();
        bottomrightJL.setForeground(new Color(red, green, blue));
```

13

```
        c.add(topleftJL);
        c.add(toprightJL);
        c.add(bottomleftJL);
        c.add(bottomrightJL);
    }
}
```

The HTML file that invokes this applet contains the following code:

```
<!DOCTYPE HTML PUBLIC "-//W3C//DTD HTML 4.01 Transitional//EN">

<HTML>
  <HEAD>
    <TITLE>Four Colors</TITLE>
  </HEAD>
  <BODY>
    <OBJECT code = "ColorsDisplayed.class" width = "200" height = "200">
    </OBJECT>
  </BODY>
</HTML>
```

Sample Run: Figure 13-4 shows the output of the `ColorsDisplayed` applet.

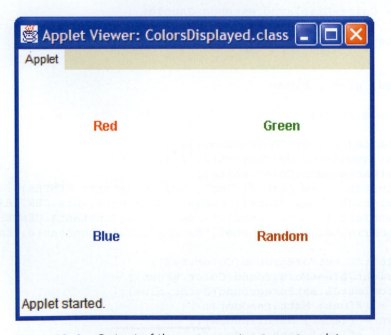

Figure 13-4   Output of the `ColorsDisplayed` applet

You can use both the **class** Font and the **class** Color to enhance your presentation of an applet. For example, consider the GrandWelcome applet given in Example 13-3. Because no new ideas are introduced, we give the complete listing followed by the sample run.

Example 13-3

```java
//GrandWelcome Applet

import java.awt.*;
import javax.swing.JApplet;

public class GrandWelcome extends JApplet
{
    public void paint(Graphics g)
    {
        super.paint(g);
        g.setColor(Color.red);
        g.setFont(new Font("Courier", Font.BOLD, 24));
        g.drawString("Welcome to Java Programming", 30, 30);
    }
}
```

The HTML file for this program contains the following code:

```html
<!DOCTYPE HTML PUBLIC "-//W3C//DTD HTML 4.01 Transitional//EN">
<HTML>
  <HEAD>
    <TITLE>WELCOME</TITLE>
  </HEAD>
  <BODY>
    <OBJECT code = "GrandWelcome.class" width = "440" height = "50">
    </OBJECT>
  </BODY>
</HTML>
```

Sample Run: Figure 13-5 shows the output of the GrandWelcome applet.

13

Figure 13-5 Output of the GrandWelcome applet

class Graphics

This section presents a glimpse of the **class** Graphics, which is contained in the **package** java.awt. The **class** Graphics provides methods for drawing items such as lines, ovals, and rectangles on the screen. Some methods of the **class** Graphics draw shapes; others draw bitmap images. This class also contains methods to set the properties of graphic elements including the clipping area, fonts, and colors. Table 13-7 shows some of the constructors and methods of the **class** Graphics.

Table 13-7 Some Constructors and Methods of the **class** Graphics

```
protected Graphics()
    //Constructs a Graphics object that defines a context in which the
    //user can draw. This constructor cannot be called directly.

public void draw3DRect(int x, int y, int w, int h, boolean t)
    //Draws a 3D rectangle at (x, y) of the width w and height h. If t is
    //true, the rectangle will appear raised.

public abstract void drawArc(int x, int y, int w, int h,
                             int sangle, int aangle)
    //Draws an arc in the rectangle at the position (x, y) of width w
    //and height h. The arc starts at the angle sangle with an arc angle
    //aangle. Both angles are measured in degrees.

public abstract boolean drawImage(Image img, int xs1, int ys1,
                  int xs2, int ys2, int xd1, int yd1,
                  int xd2, int yd2, Color c, ImageObserver ob)
    //Draws the image specified by img from the area defined by the
    //bounding rectangle, (xs1, ys1) to (xs2, ys2), in the area defined
    //by the rectangle (xd1, yd1) to (xd2, yd2). Any transparent color
    //pixels are drawn in the color c. The ob monitors the progress of
    //the image.

public abstract void drawLine(int xs, int ys, int xd, int yd)
    //Draws a line from (xs, ys) to (xd, yd).

public abstract void drawOval(int x, int y, int w, int h)
    //Draws an oval at the position (x, y) of width w and height h.

public abstract void drawPolygon(int[] x, int[] y, int num)
    //Draws a polygon with the points (x[0], y[0]), ...,
    //(x[num - 1], y[num - 1]). Here num is the number of points in
    //the polygon.

public abstract void drawPolygon(Polygon poly)
    //Draws a polygon as defined by the object poly.

public abstract void drawRect(int x, int y, int w, int h)
    //Draws a rectangle at the position (x, y) the width w and the
    //height h.
```

Table 13-7 Some Constructors and Methods of the **class** `Graphics` (continued)

```
public abstract void drawRoundRect(int x, int y, int w, int h,
                                   int arcw, int arch)
    //Draws a round-cornered rectangle at the position (x, y) having a
    //width w and height h. The shape of the rounded corners is
    //determined by the arc with the width arcw and the height arch.

public abstract void drawString(String s, int x, int y)
    //Draws the string s at (x, y).

public void fill3DRect(int x, int y, int w, int h, boolean t)
    //Draws a 3D filled rectangle at (x, y) the width w and height h.
    //If t is true, the rectangle will appear raised. The rectangle is
    //filled with the current color.

public abstract void fillArc(int x, int y, int w, int h,
                             int sangle, int aangle)
    //Draws a filled arc in the rectangle at the position (x, y) of
    //width w and height h starting at angle sangle with the arc
    //angle aangle. Both angles are measured in degrees. The arc is
    //filled with the current color.

public abstract void fillOval(int x, int y, int w, int h)
    //Draws a filled oval at the position (x, y) having a width w and
    //height h. The oval is filled with the current color.

public abstract void fillPolygon(int[] x, int[] y, int num)
    //Draws a filled polygon with the points (x[0], y[0]), ...,
    //(x[num - 1], y[num - 1]). Here num is the number of points in
    //the polygon. The polygon is filled with the current color.

public abstract void fillPolygon(Polygon poly)
    //Draws a filled polygon as defined by the object poly. The polygon
    //is filled with the current color.

public abstract void fillRect(int x, int y, int w, int h)
    //Draws a filled rectangle at the position (x, y) of width w
    //and height h. The rectangle is filled with the current color.

public abstract void fillRoundRect(int x, int y, int w, int h,
                                   int arcw, int arch)
    //Draws a filled, round-cornered rectangle at the position (x, y)
    //of width w and height h. The shape of the rounded corners
    //is determined by the arc with the width arcw and the height arch.
    //The rectangle is filled with the current color.

public abstract Color getColor()
    //Returns the current color for this graphics context.

public abstract void setColor(Color c)
    //Sets the current color for this graphics context to c.

public abstract Font getFont()
    //Returns the current font for this graphics context.

public abstract void setFont(Font f)
    //Sets the current font for this graphics context to f.
```

13

Table 13-7 Some Constructors and Methods of the **class** Graphics (continued)

```
public FontMetrics getFontMetrics()
  //Returns the font metrics associated with this graphics context.
public FontMetrics getFontMetrics(Font f)
  //Returns the font metrics associated with font f.
public void String toString()
  //Returns a string representation of this graphics context.
```

You have already used the **drawString** method to output a string. Other draw methods are used in a similar manner. For example, to draw a line from (10, 10) to (10, 40) you use the method **drawLine** as follows:

```
g.drawLine(10, 10, 10, 40);
```

where **g** is a **Graphics** object. Let's draw three more lines, so that our welcome message is inside a box.

```
g.drawLine(10, 40, 430, 40);    //bottom line
g.drawLine(430, 40, 430, 10);   //right line
g.drawLine(430, 10, 10, 10);    //top line
```

Placing these lines in our **GrandWelcome** applet of Example 13-3, we have the program shown in Example 13-4.

Example 13-4

```
//GrandWelcomeLine Applet

import java.awt.*;
import javax.swing.JApplet;

public class GrandWelcomeLine extends JApplet
{
    public void paint(Graphics g)
    {
        super.paint(g);
        g.setColor(Color.red);
        g.setFont(new Font("Courier", Font.BOLD, 24));
        g.drawString("Welcome to Java Programming", 30, 30);

        g.drawLine(10, 10, 10, 40);     //left line
        g.drawLine(10, 40, 430, 40);    //bottom line
        g.drawLine(430, 40, 430, 10);   //right line
        g.drawLine(430, 10, 10, 10);    //top line
    }
}
```

The HTML file for this program contains the following code:

```
<!DOCTYPE HTML PUBLIC "-//W3C//DTD HTML 4.01 Transitional//EN">

<HTML>
  <HEAD>
    <TITLE>WELCOME</TITLE>
  </HEAD>
  <BODY>
    <OBJECT code = "GrandWelcomeLine.class" width = "440" height = "50">
    </OBJECT>
  </BODY>
</HTML>
```

Sample Run: Figure 13-6 shows the output of the `GrandWelcomeLine` applet.

Figure 13-6   Output of the `GrandWelcomeLine` applet

In the applet of Example 13-4, you could have used the method **drawRect** to draw a rectangle rather than four lines. In that case, you could use the following statement:

```
g.drawRect(10, 10, 430, 40);    //draw rectangle
```

The program in Example 13-5 further illustrates how to use various methods of the **Graphics class**. In Example 13-5 we create a random collection of geometric shapes. The program uses the method **random** of the **class** Math to randomly determine the number of figures. We want to have at least 5 and at most 14 figures. Therefore, we declare an **int** variable and initialize it as follows:

```
int noOfFigures;

noOfFigures = 5 + (int)(Math.random() * 10); //determine the
                                             //number of figures
```

For each figure, we want a random color, random anchor point, random width, and random height. Further, we want a random shape from a set of possible options. This applies to all figures. Therefore, we need to have a loop similar to the following:

```
for (i = 0; i < noOfFigures; i++)
{
    //...
}
```

Inside the preceding loop, we determine a random color. We can use the method **random** of the **class** Math to get red, green, and blue values between 0 and 255 and use them to create a random color. Therefore, we need the following statements (assume that g is a reference variable of the Graphics type):

```
int red;
int green;
int blue;

red = (int)(Math.random() * 256);     //red component
green = (int)(Math.random() * 256);   //green component
blue = (int)(Math.random() * 256);    //blue component

g.setColor(new Color(red, green, blue));   //color for
                                           //this figure
```

We also need to compute four more values for **x**, **y**, and the width and height between, say, 0 and 200. Further, to make the program easier to modify, we use the named constant SIZE, initialized to 200. Thus, we need the following Java statements:

```
private final int SIZE = 200;
int x;
int y;
int width;
int height;
int red;

x = (int)(Math.random() * SIZE);          //x value
y = (int)(Math.random() * SIZE);          //y value
width = (int)(Math.random() * SIZE);      //width
height = (int)(Math.random() * SIZE);     //height
```

Now all that is left is to randomly select a shape among, say, rectangle, filled rectangle, oval, and filled oval. So let's assign the values:

- 0 for rectangle

- 1 for filled rectangle

- 2 for oval

- 3 for filled oval

respectively. A **switch** statement can be used to invoke the appropriate method, as shown in the following:

```
shape = (int)(Math.random() * 4);

switch (shape)
{
case 0 : g.drawRect(x, y, width, height);
         break;
case 1 : g.fillRect(x, y, width, height);
         break;
case 2 : g.drawOval(x, y, width, height);
         break;
case 3 : g.fillOval(x, y, width, height);
         break;
}
```

Putting it all together, we have the Java applet given in Example 13-5.

Example 13-5

```java
//Java applet to draw ovals and rectangles

import java.awt.*;
import javax.swing.*;

public class OvalRectApplet extends JApplet
{
    private final int SIZE = 200;

    public void paint(Graphics g)
    {
        int shape;
        int noOfFigures;
        int x;
        int y;
        int width;
        int height;
        int red;
        int green;
        int blue;

        int i;

                //determines the number of figures
        noOfFigures = 5 + (int)(Math.random() * 10);

        for (i = 0; i < noOfFigures; i++)
        {
            red = (int)(Math.random() * 256);      //red component
            green = (int)(Math.random() * 256);    //green component
            blue = (int)(Math.random() * 256);     //blue component
```

13

```java
            g.setColor(new Color(red, green, blue));    //color for
                                                         //this figure

            x = (int)(Math.random() * SIZE);        //x value
            y = (int)(Math.random() * SIZE);        //y value
            width = (int)(Math.random() * SIZE);    //width
            height = (int)(Math.random() * SIZE);   //height

            shape = (int)(Math.random() * 4);

            /**
             *      0 : Rectangle
             *      1 : Filled Rectangle
             *      2 : Oval
             *      3 : Filled Oval
             *
             **/

            switch (shape)
            {
            case 0: g.drawRect(x, y, width, height);
                    break;
            case 1: g.fillRect(x, y, width, height);
                    break;
            case 2: g.drawOval(x, y, width, height);
                    break;
            case 3: g.fillOval(x, y, width, height);
                    break;
            }//end switch
        }//end for
    }
}
```

The HTML file for this program contains the following code:

```html
<!DOCTYPE HTML PUBLIC "-//W3C//DTD HTML 4.01 Transitional//EN">

<HTML>
  <HEAD>
    <TITLE>OVAL APPLET</TITLE>
  </HEAD>
  <BODY>
    <OBJECT code = "OvalRectApplet.class" width = "500" height = "500">
    </OBJECT>
  </BODY>
</HTML>
```

Sample Run: Figure 13-7 shows a sample run of `OvalRectApplet`.

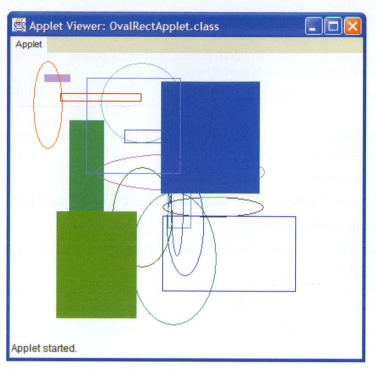

Figure 13-7　Sample Run of `OvalRectApplet`

Converting an Application Program to an Applet

At this point you might wonder whether there is a simple scheme to convert GUI applications to applets. An applet class shares many features of a GUI application. The main differences are:

- An applet class is derived from the **class** `JApplet`, whereas a GUI application class is created by extending the **class** `JFrame`.

- Applets do not have the method `main`. Instead, an applet invokes the `init`, `start`, `paint`, `stop`, and `destroy` methods in sequence. Quite often, you the place initialization code in `init` and the output is produced by the method `paint`.

- Applets do not use constructors. Instead, they use the method `init` to initialize various GUI components and data members.

- Applets do not require methods such as `setVisible`. Applets are embedded in HTML documents, and it is the HTML document that displays the applet.

- Applets do not use the method `setTitle`; the HTML document sets the title.

13

- Applets do not use the method `setSize`; the HTML document specifies the size of the applet.

- Applets do not have to be closed. In particular, there is no `Exit` button. The applet closes when the HTML document closes.

Therefore, in most cases, you perform the following five steps to convert a GUI application to an applet:

1. Make your **class** extend the definition of the **class** JApplet. In other words, change JFrame to JApplet.

2. Change the constructor to the method `init`.

3. Remove method calls such as `setVisible`, `setTitle`, and `setSize`.

4. Remove the method `main`.

5. Remove the `Exit` button, if you have one, and all code associated with it, such as the action listener and so on.

As an example, we modify the temperature conversion program presented in Chapter 6 as a GUI application. The statements changed to create an applet are shown as comments.

```
//Java program to convert the temperature between
//Celsius and Fahrenheit.

import java.awt.*;
import java.awt.event.*;
import javax.swing.*;

    //public class TempConversion extends JFrame
    //
    //Replace JFrame with JApplet
    //
public class TempConvertApplet extends JApplet
{
    private JLabel celsiusLabel;
    private JLabel fahrenheitLabel;
    private JTextField celsiusTF;
    private JTextField fahrenheitTF;
    private CelsHandler celsiusHandler;
    private FahrHandler fahrenheitHandler;

    private static final int WIDTH = 500;
    private static final int HEIGHT = 50;
    private static final double FTOC = 5.0 / 9.0;
    private static final double CTOF = 1.8;     // 9 / 5
    private static final int OFFSET = 32;

    //public TempConversion()
    //
    //Replace this constructor with the init method
    //
```

```java
public void init()
{
      //setTitle("Temperature Conversion");
      //
      //delete setTitle("Temperature Conversion");
      //

   Container c = getContentPane();
   c.setLayout(new GridLayout(1, 4));

   celsiusLabel = new JLabel("Enter Celsius",
                             SwingConstants.RIGHT);
   fahrenheitLabel = new JLabel("Enter Fahrenheit ",
                                SwingConstants.RIGHT);

   celsiusTF = new JTextField(7);
   fahrenheitTF = new JTextField(7);

   c.add(celsiusLabel);
   c.add(celsiusTF);
   c.add(fahrenheitLabel);
   c.add(fahrenheitTF);

   celsiusHandler = new CelsHandler();
   fahrenheitHandler = new FahrHandler();
   celsiusTF.addActionListener(celsiusHandler);
   fahrenheitTF.addActionListener(fahrenheitHandler);

      //setSize(WIDTH, HEIGHT);
      //Delete: setSize(WIDTH, HEIGHT)

      //setDefaultCloseOperation(EXIT_ON_CLOSE);
      //Delete: setDefaultCloseOperation(EXIT_ON_CLOSE);

      //setVisible(true);
      //Delete: setVisible(true)
}

private class CelsHandler implements ActionListener
{
    public void actionPerformed(ActionEvent e)
    {
      double celsius, fahrenheit;

      celsius = Double.parseDouble(celsiusTF.getText());
      fahrenheit =  celsius * CTOF + OFFSET;
      fahrenheitTF.setText(""+ String.format("%.2f",
                                      fahrenheit));
    }
}
```

13

```java
    private class FahrHandler implements ActionListener
    {
        public void actionPerformed(ActionEvent e)
        {
            double celsius, fahrenheit;

            fahrenheit = Double.parseDouble(fahrenheitTF.getText());
            celsius = (fahrenheit - OFFSET) * FTOC;
            celsiusTF.setText(""+ String.format("%.2f", celsius));
        }
    }

    //public static void main(String[] args)
    //{
    //    TempConversion tempConv = new TempConversion();
    //}
    //
    //Delete the method main
    //
}//end TempConvertApplet
```

The HTML file for this program contains the following code:

```html
<!DOCTYPE HTML PUBLIC "-//W3C//DTD HTML 4.01 Transitional//EN">

<HTML>
  <HEAD>
    <TITLE>TEMPERATURE APPLET</TITLE>
  </HEAD>
  <BODY>
    <OBJECT code = "TempConvertApplet.class" width = "500" height = "50">
    </OBJECT>
  </BODY>
</HTML>
```

ADDITIONAL GUI COMPONENTS

The remainder of this chapter introduces GUI components other than those introduced in Chapter 6. For the most part, these additional GUI components are used in the same way as the ones introduced earlier. For example, you create an instance (or object) using the opera-tor **new**. If the program needs to respond to an event occurring in a GUI component such as JTextField or JButton, you must add an event listener and provide the associated method that needs to be invoked, commonly called the event handler. We will also illustrate the use of various methods of the **class** Graphics.

JTextArea

The GUI programs in previous chapters extensively used the **class** JTextField to display a line of text. However, there are situations when the program must display multiple lines of text. For example, an employee's address is shown in three or more lines. Because an object of the **class** JTextField can display only one line of text, you cannot use an object of this class to display multiple lines of text. Java provides the **class** JTextArea to either collect multiple lines of input from the user or to display multiple lines of output. Using an object of this class, the user can type multiple lines of text, which are separated by pressing the Enter key. In Java, each line ends with the newline character '\n'.

The GUI part of the Programming Example Student Grade Report in Chapter 11 uses a JTextArea to display multiple lines of text to show the various courses taken by a student and the grade in each course. This section discusses the capabilities of the **class** JTextArea in some detail.

Both JTextField and JTextArea are derived from the **class** JTextComponent and, as such, share many common methods. However, you cannot create an instance of the **class** JTextComponent because it is an **abstract** class. Table 13-8 lists some of the constructors and methods of the **class** JTextArea.

Table 13-8 Commonly Used Constructors and Methods of the **class** JTextArea

```
public JTextArea(int r, int c)
  //Constructor
  //Creates a new JTextArea with r number of rows and
  //c number of columns.

public JTextArea(String t, int r, int c)
  //Constructor
  //Creates a new JTextArea with r number of rows, c number
  //of columns, and the initial text t.

public void setColumns(int c)
  //Sets the number of columns to c.

public void setRows(int r)
  //Sets the number of rows to r.

public void append(String t)
  //Concatenates the text already in the JTextArea with t.

public void setLineWrap(boolean b)
  //If b is true, the lines are wrapped.

public void setWrapStyleWord(boolean b)
  //If b is true, the lines are wrapped at the word boundaries.
  //If b is false, the word boundaries are not considered.

public void setTabSize(int c)
  //Sets tab stops every c columns.
```

13

Table 13-9 shows the methods, which you have used with a **JTextField** object, that are inherited by the **class JTextArea** from the parent **class JTextComponent**.

Table 13-9 Methods Inherited by the **class** JTextArea from the Parent **class**
              JTextComponent

```
public void setText(String t)
   //Changes the text of the text area to t.

public String getText()
   //Returns the text contained in the text area.

public void setEditable(boolean b)
   //If b is false, the user cannot type in the text area. In this case,
   //the text area is used as a tool to display the result.
```

Example 13-6

The program in this example illustrates the use of **JTextArea**. It creates the GUI shown in Figure 13-8.

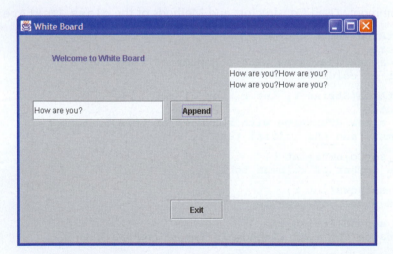

Figure 13-8   White Board GUI

As shown in Figure 13-8, the GUI contains a **JLabel**, two **JButtons**, a text field, and a text area. The user can type a line of text in the text field, and when the user clicks the **Exit** button, the program terminates. Similarly, if the user clicks the **Append** button, the text in the text field is appended to the text in the text area.

In this example, we write this program as a GUI application. A corresponding applet is left as an exercise for you; see Programming Exercise 8 at the end of this chapter.

As in the previous GUI application program, we create the necessary labels, text fields, and text areas, and place them in the content pane. We also create and place two buttons, `exitB` and `appendB`, in the content pane. The following statements access the content pane, create the GUI components, and place the GUI components in the content pane:

```java
private JLabel headingL;
headingL = new JLabel("Welcome to White Board");

private JTextField lineTF;
lineTF = new JTextField(20);

private JTextArea whiteBoardTA;
whiteBoardTA = new JTextArea(10, 20);

private JButton exitB, appendB;
exitB = new JButton("Exit");
appendB = new JButton("Append");

Container pane = getContentPane();

pane.add(headingL);
pane.add(lineTF);
pane.add(whiteBoardTA);
pane.add(appendB);
pane.add(exitB);
```

We will specify the sizes and locations of the GUI components when we write the complete program.

In Chapter 6, action listener interfaces are implemented through inner classes. As explained in Chapter 11, any class containing the application can directly implement the **interface** `ActionListener`. The GUI programs of this chapter directly implement the interfaces to handle events. Suppose `WhiteBoard` is the name of the class to implement the application to create the preceding GUI. Then, the heading of this class is:

```java
public class WhiteBoard extends JFrame implements ActionListener
```

The method `actionPerformed` is included as a member of the **class** `WhiteBoard`. To register the action listener with `exitB`, all you need to do is include the following statement in the program:

```java
exitB.addActionListener(this);
```

Of course, the necessary code is placed in the method `actionPerformed`.

Because action events are generated by the two buttons, the method `actionPerformed` uses the methods `getActionCommand` and `equals` to identify the source of the event. The definition of this method is:

```
public void actionPerformed(ActionEvent e)
{
    if (e.getActionCommand().equals("Append"))        //Line 1
        whiteBoardTA.append(lineTF.getText());        //Line 2
    else if (e.getActionCommand().equals("Exit"))     //Line 3
            System.exit(0);                           //Line 4
}
```

If the user clicks the `Append` button, the `if` statement in Line 1 evaluates to `true`. In this case, the statement in Line 2 retrieves the line of text from the text field object `lineTF` and appends it to the text in the text area object `whiteBoardTA`. When the user clicks the `Exit` button, the `if` statement in Line 3 evaluates to `true` and the statement in Line 4 terminates the program.

The complete program listing follows:

```
import javax.swing.*;
import java.awt.*;
import java.awt.event.*;

public class WhiteBoard extends JFrame implements ActionListener
{
    private static int WIDTH = 550;
    private static int HEIGHT = 350;

    private int row = 10;
    private int col = 20;

        //GUI components
    private JLabel headingL;
    private JTextField lineTF;
    private JTextArea whiteBoardTA;
    private JButton exitB, appendB;

    public WhiteBoard()
    {
        setTitle("White Board");
        Container pane = getContentPane();
        setSize(WIDTH, HEIGHT);

        headingL = new JLabel("Welcome to White Board");
        lineTF = new JTextField(20);
```

```
        whiteBoardTA = new JTextArea(row, col);
        exitB = new JButton("Exit");
        exitB.addActionListener(this);

        appendB = new JButton("Append");
        appendB.addActionListener(this);

        pane.setLayout(null);

        headingL.setLocation(50, 20);
        lineTF.setLocation(20, 100);
        whiteBoardTA.setLocation(320, 50);
        appendB.setLocation(230, 100);
        exitB.setLocation(230, 250);

        headingL.setSize(200, 30);
        lineTF.setSize(200, 30);
        whiteBoardTA.setSize(200, 200);
        appendB.setSize(80, 30);
        exitB.setSize(80, 30);

        pane.add(headingL);
        pane.add(lineTF);
        pane.add(whiteBoardTA);
        pane.add(appendB);
        pane.add(exitB);

        setVisible(true);
        setDefaultCloseOperation(EXIT_ON_CLOSE);

    } //end of the constructor

    public static void main(String[] args)
    {
        WhiteBoard board = new WhiteBoard();
    }

    public void actionPerformed(ActionEvent e)
    {
        if (e.getActionCommand().equals("Append"))
            whiteBoardTA.append(lineTF.getText());
        else if (e.getActionCommand().equals("Exit"))
                System.exit(0);
    }
}
```

13

Sample Run: Figure 13-9 shows a sample run of this program. (Note that to get the new line in the text area, click the mouse to position the insertion point in the text area, and then press the Enter key. The next append should now be in the next line.)

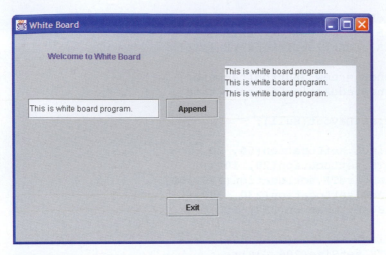

Figure 13-9 Sample run of the White Board program

JCheckBox

In the previous section you learned how to use text fields and text areas to collect input from the user. When you use a text field or a text area to input data, users can type anything they want. However, sometimes you want the user to select from a set of predefined values. For example, to specify gender, the user would select either male or female; similarly, a student would select either undergraduate or graduate. In addition to freeing the user from typing in such values, to get precise input, you want the user to select a value from a set of given values.

The `JCheckBox` and `JRadioButton` classes allow a user to select a value from a set of given values. These classes are both subclasses of the **abstract class** `ToggleButton`. The **class** `JCheckBox` is described in this section; the **class** `JRadioButton` is discussed in the next section.

Table 13-10 shows some of the constructors and methods of the **class** `JCheckBox`.

Table 13-10 Some Constructors and Methods of the **class** `JCheckBox`

```
public JCheckBox()
  //Creates an initially unselected check box button
  //with no label and no icon.
  //Example: JCheckBox myJCheckBox = new JCheckBox()
  //         myJCheckBox points to the check box with no label and no
  //         icon.
public JCheckBox(Icon icon)
  //Creates an initially unselected check box button with
  //the specified icon and no label.
  //Example: JCheckBox myJCheckBox = new JCheckBox(anIcon);
  //         myJCheckBox points to the check box with the icon "anIcon".
```

Table 13-10 Some Constructors and Methods of the **class** JCheckBox (continued)

```
public JCheckBox(Icon icon, boolean selected)
  //Creates a check box with the specified
  //image and selection state, but with no label.
  //Example: JCheckBox myJCheckBox = new JCheckBox(anIcon, true);
  //      myJCheckBox points to the selected check box with
  //      anIcon as the icon.
```

```
public JCheckBox(String text)
  //Creates an unselected check box with
  //the specified label.
  //Example: JCheckBox myJCheckBox = new JCheckBox("Box");
  //      myJCheckBox points to the unselected check box with the
  //      label "Box".
```

```
public JCheckBox(String text, boolean selected)
  //Creates a check box with the specified
  //label and selection state.
  //Example: JCheckBox myJCheckBox = new JCheckBox("Box", false);
  //      myJCheckBox points to the unselected check box with the
  //      label "Box".
```

```
public JCheckBox(String text, Icon icon)
  //Creates a check box with the specified image
  //and specified label.
  //Example: JCheckBox myJCheckBox = new JCheckBox("Box", anIcon,);
  //      myJCheckBox points to the unselected check box with the label
  //      "Box" and anIcon as the icon.
```

```
public JCheckBox(String text, Icon icon, boolean selected)
  //Creates a check box with the specified image
  //and selection state, and with the specified text.
  //Example: JCheckBox myJCheckBox =
  //                      new JCheckBox("Box", anIcon, true);
  //      myJCheckBox points to the selected check box with the label
  //      "Box" and anIcon as the icon.
```

```
public boolean isSelected()
  //This method is inherited from the AbstractButton class and is
  //used to retrieve the state of a button.
  //Example: if(myJCheckBox.isSelected() == true)
  //      The "if" block will be executed provided myJCheckBox
  //      is checked.
```

```
public boolean setSelected(boolean b)
  //This method is inherited from the AbstractButton class and is
  //used to set the state of a button.
  //Example: myJCheckBox.setSelected(true);
  //      myJcheckBox gets checked.
```

13

Similar to buttons, check boxes also come with their own identifying labels. Consider the following statements:

```
JCheckBox italicCB;                            //Line 1
italicCB = new JCheckBox("Italic");            //Line 2
```

The statement in Line 1 declares `italicCB` to be a reference variable of the `JCheckBox` type. The statement in Line 2 creates the object `italicCB` and assigns it the label `Italic`. After the statement in Line 2 executes, the figure shown in Figure 13-10 results.

Figure 13-10   Check box with label

In Figure 13-10, the box to the left of the label `Italic` is a check box. The user clicks it to select or deselect it. For example, clicking the check box in Figure 13-10 produces the result shown in Figure 13-11.

Figure 13-11   Result of clicking the check box

If you click the check box shown in Figure 13-11, the checkmark disappears. A check box is an example of a toggle button. If it is not selected and you click it, then the box is selected and a checkmark appears. If it is selected and you click it, the checkmark disappears.

When you click a `JCheckBox`, it generates an **item event**. Item events are handled by the **interface** `ItemListener`. The **interface** `ItemListener` contains only the **abstract** method `itemStateChanged`. The heading of the method is:

```
public void itemStateChanged(ItemEvent e)
```

To make the program respond to the event generated by clicking a check box, you write the code that needs to be executed in the body of the method `itemStateChanged`, and register an item listener object to the check box.

Next, we write an applet that has two check boxes and also displays a line of text. The first check box is used to indicate the selection of bold style and the second to indicate the selection of italic style. The user can click the check boxes to change the font and style of the text.

We create two check boxes with the labels **"Bold"** and **"Italic"** and place them in the content pane of the applet. The method **init** contains the statements needed for these initializations. Therefore, the **init** method can be written as follows:

```
public void init()
{
    Container c = getContentPane();    //get the container
    c.setLayout(null);                 //set the layout to null

        //create the check boxes with the appropriate labels
    boldCB = new JCheckBox("Bold");
    italicCB = new JCheckBox("Italic");

        //set the sizes of the check boxes
    boldCB.setSize(100, 30);
    italicCB.setSize(100, 30);

        //set the location of the check boxes
    boldCB.setLocation(100, 100);
    italicCB.setLocation(300, 100);

        //register the item listener to the check boxes
    boldCB.addItemListener(this);
    italicCB.addItemListener(this);

        //add the check boxes to the pane
    c.add(boldCB);
    c.add(italicCB);
}
```

To specify the font and style of the text, we use two **int** variables, **intBold** and **intItalic**. These variables are set to **Font.PLAIN** when the check boxes are not checked. They are set to **Font.BOLD** and **Font.ITALIC**, respectively, if the corresponding check boxes are checked. To create bold and italic fonts, you simply add the values of the variables **bold** and **italic**. In other words, you can create desired fonts by just using **intBold + intItalic** as the style value. Note that because **Font.PLAIN** has a value of zero, **Font.PLAIN + Font.PLAIN** remains **Font.PLAIN**. The **paint** method can be used to set the color and font, and to display the welcome message. The definition of the method **paint** can be written as follows:

```
public void paint(Graphics g)
{
    super.paint(g);
    g.setColor(Color.red);
    g.setFont(new Font("Courier", intBold + intItalic, 24));
    g.drawString("Welcome to Java Programming", 30, 30);
}
```

To make the program respond to the events generated by the check boxes, next we write the definition of the method **itemStateChanged**. As shown earlier, the method **itemStateChanged** has one parameter, **e**, of the type **ItemEvent**. Because there are two check boxes, we use the method **getSource** to identify the box generating the event.

13

The expression:

```
e.getSource() == boldCB
```

is **true** if the check box associated with **boldCB** generated the event. Similarly, the expression:

```
e.getSource() == italicCB
```

is **true** if the check box associated with **italicCB** generated the event.

After identifying the check box that generated the event, we determine whether the user selected or deselected the check box. For this, we use the method **getStateChange** of the **class ItemEvent** that returns either the constant **ItemEvent.SELECTED** or the constant **ItemEvent.DESELECTED**, which are defined in the **class** ItemEvent. For example, the expression:

```
e.getStateChange() == ItemEvent.SELECTED
```

is **true** if the event **e** corresponds to selecting the check box.

Finally, every time an event happens, you want to change the font accordingly. This can be achieved by invoking the **paint** method. To call the **paint** method, you need a **Graphics** object. So, you invoke the **repaint** method, which in turn invokes the **paint** method. Therefore, you need to call the **repaint** method before leaving the event handler method.

The definition of the method **itemStateChanged** is:

```java
public void itemStateChanged(ItemEvent e)
{
    if (e.getSource() == boldCB)
    {
        if (e.getStateChange() == ItemEvent.SELECTED)
            intBold = Font.BOLD;
        if (e.getStateChange() == ItemEvent.DESELECTED)
            intBold = Font.PLAIN;
    }

    if (e.getSource() == italicCB)
    {
        if (e.getStateChange() == ItemEvent.SELECTED)
            intItalic = Font.ITALIC;
        if (e.getStateChange() == ItemEvent.DESELECTED)
            intItalic = Font.PLAIN;
    }

    repaint();
}
```

Now that the necessary components are written, we can write the complete program.

```java
//Welcome Applet with check boxes

import java.awt.*;
import java.awt.event.*;
import javax.swing.*;

public class GrandWelcomeCheckBox extends JApplet implements
                                            ItemListener
{
    private int intBold = Font.PLAIN;
    private int intItalic = Font.PLAIN;
    private JCheckBox boldCB, italicCB;

    public void init()
    {
        Container c = getContentPane();
        c.setLayout(null);
        boldCB = new JCheckBox("Bold");
        italicCB = new JCheckBox("Italic");

        boldCB.setSize(100, 30);
        italicCB.setSize(100, 30);

        boldCB.setLocation(100, 100);
        italicCB.setLocation(300, 100);

        boldCB.addItemListener(this);
        italicCB.addItemListener(this);

        c.add(boldCB);
        c.add(italicCB);
    }

    public void paint(Graphics g)
    {
        super.paint(g);
        g.setColor(Color.red);
        g.setFont(new Font("Courier", intBold + intItalic, 24));
        g.drawString("Welcome to Java Programming", 30, 30);
    }

    public void itemStateChanged(ItemEvent e)
    {
        if (e.getSource() == boldCB)
        {
            if (e.getStateChange() == ItemEvent.SELECTED)
                intBold = Font.BOLD;
```

13

```
            if (e.getStateChange() == ItemEvent.DESELECTED)
                intBold = Font.PLAIN;
        }

        if (e.getSource() == italicCB)
        {
            if (e.getStateChange() == ItemEvent.SELECTED)
                intItalic = Font.ITALIC;
            if (e.getStateChange() == ItemEvent.DESELECTED)
                intItalic = Font.PLAIN;
        }

        repaint();
    }
}
```

The HTML file for this program contains the following code:

```
<!DOCTYPE HTML PUBLIC "-//W3C//DTD HTML 4.01 Transitional//EN">

<HTML>
  <HEAD>
    <TITLE>WELCOME</TITLE>
  </HEAD>
  <BODY>
    <OBJECT code = "GrandWelcomeCheckBox.class" width = "440" height = "200">
    </OBJECT>
  </BODY>
</HTML>
```

Sample Run: Figure 13-12 shows a sample run of the applet with check boxes.

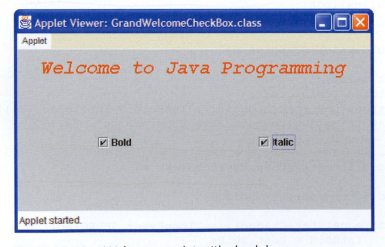

Figure 13-12   Welcome applet with check boxes

JRadioButton

Check boxes allow the user to select a value from a set of values. The program in the previous section used two check boxes. The user could select or deselect one or both check boxes. However, there are situations in which you want the user to make only one selection from a set of values. For example, if the user needs to select the gender of a person, the user selects either female or male, but not both. If you want the user to select exactly one, and only one, of the options presented, you use radio buttons. To make such selections possible, Java provides the **class** JRadioButton.

Table 13-11 shows some of the constructors and methods of the **class** JRadioButton.

Table 13-11 Some Constructors and Methods of the **class** JRadioButton

```
public JRadioButton()
   //Creates an initially unselected radio button
   //with no label and no icon.
   //Example: JRadioButton myJRadioButton = new JRadioButton();
   //    myJRadioButton points to the radio button with no label
   //    and no icon.
```

```
public JRadioButton(Icon icon)
   //Creates an initially unselected radio button
   //with the specified icon and no label.
   //Example: JRadioButton myJRadioButton = new JRadioButton(anIcon);
   //    myJRadioButton points to the radio button with the icon "anIcon".
```

```
public JRadioButton(Icon icon, boolean selected)
   //Creates a radio button with the specified
   //icon and selection state, but with no label.
   //Example:JRadioButton myJRadioButton =
   //                      new JRadioButton(anIcon, true);
   //    myJRadioButton points to the selected radio button with the
   //    icon "anIcon".
```

```
public JRadioButton(String text)
   //Creates an unselected radio button with the
   //specified text as the label.
   //Example: JRadioButton myJRadioButton = new JRadioButton("Box");
   //    myJRadioButton points to the unselected radio button
   //    with the label "Box".
```

```
public JRadioButton(String text, boolean selected)
   //Creates a radio button with the specified
   //text as the label and selection state.
   //Example:
   //    JRadioButton myJRadioButton = new JRadioButton("Box", false);
   //       myJRadioButton points to the unselected radio button
   //       with the label "Box".
```

13

Table 13-11 Some Constructors and Methods of the **class** JRadioButton (continued)

```
public JRadioButton(String text, Icon icon)
   //Creates a radio button with the specified
   //icon and the specified text as the label.
   //Example:
   //   JRadioButton myJRadioButton = new JRadioButton("Box", anIcon);
   //      myJRadioButton points to the unselected radio button
   //      with the label "Box" and the icon "anIcon".

public JRadioButton(String text, Icon icon, boolean selected)
   //Creates a radio button with the specified icon
   //and selection state, and with the specified text as the label.
   //Example: JRadioButton myJRadioButton =
   //                  new JRadioButton("Box", anIcon, true);
   //      myJRadioButton points to the selected radio button with the
   //      label "Box" and the icon "anIcon".

public boolean isSelected()
   //This method is inherited from the AbstractButton class and is
   //used to retrieve the state of a button.
   //Example: if (myJRadioButton.isSelected() == true)
   //         The "if" block will be executed provided myJRadioButton
   //         is checked.

public boolean setSelected(boolean b)
   //This method is inherited from the AbstractButton class and is
   //used to set the state of a button.
   //Example: myJRadioButton.setSelected(true);
   //         myJRadioButton gets checked.
```

Radio buttons are created the same way check boxes are created. Consider the following statements:

```
private JRadioButton redRB, greenRB, blueRB;        //Line 1
redRB = new JRadioButton("Red");                    //Line 2
greenRB = new JRadioButton("Green");                //Line 3
blueRB = new JRadioButton("Blue");                  //Line 4
```

The statement in Line 1 declares **redRB**, **greenRB**, and **blueRB** to be reference variables of the **JRadioButton** type. The statement in Line 2 instantiates the object **redRB** and assigns it the label **"Red"**. Similarly, the statements in Lines 3 and 4 instantiate the objects **greenRB** and **blueRB** and with the labels **"Green"** and **"Blue"**, respectively.

As with check boxes, we create and place radio buttons in the content pane of the applet. However, in this case, to force the user to select only one radion button at a time, we create a button group and group these radio buttons. Consider the following statements:

```
private ButtonGroup ColorSelectBGroup;              //Line 5

ColorSelectBGroup = new ButtonGroup();              //Line 6
ColorSelectBGroup.add(redRB);                       //Line 7
```

```
ColorSelectBGroup.add(greenRB);                    //Line 8
ColorSelectBGroup.add(blueRB);                     //Line 9
```

The statements in Lines 5 and 6 create the object `ColorSelectBGroup`, and the statements in Lines 7, 8, and 9 add the radio buttons `redRB`, `greenRB`, and `blueRB` to this object. The statements in Lines 1 through 9 create and group the radio buttons shown in Figure 13-13.

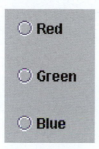

Figure 13-13 Radio buttons

Because the radio buttons `redRB`, `greenRB`, and `blueRB` are grouped, the user can select only one of these buttons. Similarly to `JCheckBox`, `JRadioButton` also generates an `ItemEvent`. So we use the **interface** `ItemListener` and its method `itemStateChanged` to handle the events.

In the following example, we start with the applet we created in the section `JCheckBox` and add three radio buttons so that the text color can be selected from the list: red, green, blue.

Grouping buttons enforces the constraint that only one radio button can be selected at any time. This also affects how you write the event handler. Because only one button can be selected, once you know the source of the event, you can conclude that the associated radio button is selected. Thus, the relevant code for handling the events generated by these radio buttons can be written as follows:

```
if (e.getSource() == redRB)
    currentColor = Color.red;
else if (e.getSource() == greenRB)
        currentColor = Color.green;
else if (e.getSource() == blueRB)
        currentColor = Color.blue;
```

13

The complete program, along with the sample run, follows:

```java
import java.awt.*;
import java.awt.event.*;
import javax.swing.*;

public class GrandWelcomeRButton extends JApplet implements
                                                   ItemListener
{
    private int intBold = Font.PLAIN;
    private int intItalic = Font.PLAIN;
    private Color currentColor = Color.black;
    private JCheckBox boldCB, italicCB;
    private JRadioButton redRB, greenRB, blueRB;
    private ButtonGroup ColorSelectBGroup;

    public void init()
    {
        Container c = getContentPane();
        c.setLayout(null);
        boldCB = new JCheckBox("Bold");
        italicCB = new JCheckBox("Italic");
        redRB = new JRadioButton("Red");
        greenRB = new JRadioButton("Green");
        blueRB = new JRadioButton("Blue");

        boldCB.setSize(100, 30);
        italicCB.setSize(100, 30);
        redRB.setSize(100, 30);
        greenRB.setSize(100, 30);
        blueRB.setSize(100, 30);

        boldCB.setLocation(100, 70);
        italicCB.setLocation(100, 150);
        redRB.setLocation(300, 70);
        greenRB.setLocation(300, 110);
        blueRB.setLocation(300, 150);

        boldCB.addItemListener(this);
        italicCB.addItemListener(this);
        redRB.addItemListener(this);
        greenRB.addItemListener(this);
        blueRB.addItemListener(this);

        c.add(boldCB);
        c.add(italicCB);
        c.add(redRB);
        c.add(greenRB);
        c.add(blueRB);
```

```java
        ColorSelectBGroup = new ButtonGroup();
        ColorSelectBGroup.add(redRB);
        ColorSelectBGroup.add(greenRB);
        ColorSelectBGroup.add(blueRB);
    }

    public void paint(Graphics g)
    {
        super.paint(g);
        g.setColor(Color.orange);
        g.drawRoundRect(75, 50, 125, 140, 10, 10);
        g.drawRoundRect(275, 50, 125, 140, 10, 10);
        g.setColor(currentColor);
        g.setFont(new Font("Courier", intBold + intItalic, 24));
        g.drawString("Welcome to Java Programming", 30, 30);
    }

    public void itemStateChanged(ItemEvent e)
    {
        if (e.getSource() == boldCB)
        {
            if (e.getStateChange() == ItemEvent.SELECTED)
                intBold = Font.BOLD;
            if (e.getStateChange() == ItemEvent.DESELECTED)
                intBold = Font.PLAIN;
        }

        if (e.getSource() == italicCB)
        {
            if (e.getStateChange() == ItemEvent.SELECTED)
                intItalic = Font.ITALIC;
            if (e.getStateChange() == ItemEvent.DESELECTED)
                intItalic = Font.PLAIN;
        }

        if (e.getSource() == redRB)
            currentColor = Color.red;
        else if (e.getSource() == greenRB)
                currentColor = Color.green;
        else if (e.getSource() == blueRB)
                currentColor = Color.blue;

        repaint();
    }
}
```

13

The HTML file for this program contains the following code:

```
<!DOCTYPE HTML PUBLIC "-//W3C//DTD HTML 4.01 Transitional//EN">

<HTML>
  <HEAD>
    <TITLE>WELCOME</TITLE>
  </HEAD>
  <BODY>
    <OBJECT code = "GrandWelcomeRButton.class" width = "440" height = "200">
    </OBJECT>
  </BODY>
</HTML>
```

Sample Run: Figure 13-14 is a sample run showing check boxes and radio buttons.

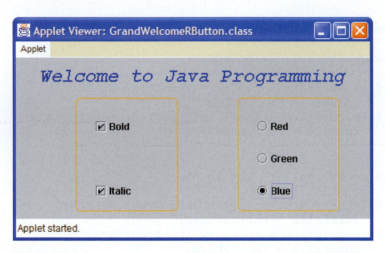

Figure 13-14   Sample run showing check boxes and radio buttons

JComboBox

A **combo box**, commonly known as a drop-down list, is used to select an item from a list of possibilities. A JComboBox generates an ItemEvent monitored by an ItemListener, which invokes the method itemStateChanged exactly as in JCheckBox or in JRadioButton.

Table 13-12 lists some constructors of the **class** JComboBox.

Table 13-12 Some Constructors of the **class** JComboBox

```
public JComboBox()
  //Creates a JComboBox with no items to select.
  //Example: JComboBox selectionList = new JComboBox();
  //         selectionList is created but has no selectable items.

public JComboBox(Vector v)
  //Creates a JComboBox to display the elements
  //in the vector provided as an input parameter.
  //Example: JComboBox selectionList = new JComboBox(v);
  //         selectionList points to the combo box that lists the
  //         elements contained in Vector v.

public JComboBox(Object[] o)
  //Constructor:  Creates a JComboBox that displays the
  //elements in the object array provided as an input parameter.
  //Example: JComboBox selectionList = new JComboBox(o);
  //         creates the new combo box called selectionList and
  //         displays the selections. For an object list, would
  //         display o.toString() values.
```

In the previous two sections, we created an applet that uses check boxes and radio buttons to change the font and style of the text. In this section, we add a **JComboBox** to the program so that the user can select a font from a list of font names, and apply that font to the text.

To create a combo box, we first declare a reference variable as follows:

```
private JComboBox fontFaceDD;                              //Line 1
```

Next, we create an array of strings and initialize it with the list of font names. The corresponding Java statement is:

```
private String fontNames[] = {"Dialog", "Century Gothic",
                              "Courier", "Serif"};        //Line 2
```

Next, we use the variable **fontFaceDD**, declared in Line 1, and the array of strings **fontNames**, created in Line 2, to create a combo box. Consider the following statement:

```
fontFaceDD = new JComboBox(fontNames);                    //Line 3
```

This statement creates the object **fontFaceDD** and initializes this object using the strings in the array **fontNames**.

The object **fontFaceDD** has four items. When you click the combo box, it shows you these four choices. You can control the number of choices shown by using the method **setMaximumRowCount**. For example, the statement:

```
fontFaceDD.setMaximumRowCount(3);
```

sets the number of choices to be shown to 3. Because there are four choices in the combo box **fontFaceDD** and only three choices are shown, a vertical scroll bar appears to the right of the box. You can scroll this bar to see and select the other choices.

13

When you click an item in the combo box, it generates an item event. To process item events, we use the interface ItemListener. As described in the previous section, the item event handler code is placed in the body of the method itemStateChanged.

When the user selects an item from a combo box, the index of the selected item can be obtained by using the method getSelectedIndex(). For example, the statement:

```
currentFontName = fontNames[fontFaceDD.getSelectedIndex()];
```

assigns the current font name to the string variable currentFontName.

Example 13-7 gives the complete program listing for this JComboBox example.

Example 13-7

```java
//Welcome program with check boxes, radio buttons, and combo box

import java.awt.*;
import java.awt.event.*;
import javax.swing.*;

public class GrandWelcomeFinal extends JApplet implements
                                                    ItemListener
{
    private int intBold = Font.PLAIN;
    private int intItalic = Font.PLAIN;
    private Color currentColor = Color.black;
    private String currentFontName = "Courier";
    private JCheckBox boldCB, italicCB;
    private JRadioButton redRB, greenRB, blueRB;
    private ButtonGroup ColorSelectBGroup;
    private JComboBox fontFaceDD;
    private String[] fontNames
                = {"Dialog", "Century Gothic", "Courier", "Serif"};

    public void init()
    {
        Container c = getContentPane();
        c.setLayout(null);
        boldCB = new JCheckBox("Bold");
        italicCB = new JCheckBox("Italic");
        redRB = new JRadioButton("Red");
        greenRB = new JRadioButton("Green");
        blueRB = new JRadioButton("Blue");
        fontFaceDD = new JComboBox(fontNames);
        fontFaceDD.setMaximumRowCount(3);
```

```java
        boldCB.setSize(80, 30);
        italicCB.setSize(80, 30);
        redRB.setSize(80, 30);
        greenRB.setSize(80, 30);
        blueRB.setSize(80, 30);
        fontFaceDD.setSize(80, 30);

        boldCB.setLocation(100, 70);
        italicCB.setLocation(100, 150);
        redRB.setLocation(300, 70);
        greenRB.setLocation(300, 110);
        blueRB.setLocation(300, 150);
        fontFaceDD.setLocation(200, 70);

        boldCB.addItemListener(this);
        italicCB.addItemListener(this);
        redRB.addItemListener(this);
        greenRB.addItemListener(this);
        blueRB.addItemListener(this);
        fontFaceDD.addItemListener(this);

        c.add(boldCB);
        c.add(italicCB);
        c.add(redRB);
        c.add(greenRB);
        c.add(blueRB);
        c.add(fontFaceDD);
        ColorSelectBGroup = new ButtonGroup();
        ColorSelectBGroup.add(redRB);
        ColorSelectBGroup.add(greenRB);
        ColorSelectBGroup.add(blueRB);
    }

    public void paint(Graphics g)
    {
        super.paint(g);
        g.setColor(Color.orange);
        g.drawRoundRect(75, 50, 324, 140, 10, 10);
        g.drawLine(183, 50, 183, 190);
        g.drawLine(291, 50, 291, 190);

        g.setColor(currentColor);
        g.setFont(new Font(currentFontName, intBold + intItalic, 24));
        g.drawString("Welcome to Java Programming", 30, 30);
    }
```

13

```java
public void itemStateChanged(ItemEvent e)
{
    if (e.getSource() == boldCB)
    {
        if (e.getStateChange() == ItemEvent.SELECTED)
            intBold = Font.BOLD;
        if (e.getStateChange() == ItemEvent.DESELECTED)
            intBold = Font.PLAIN;
    }

    if (e.getSource() == italicCB)
    {
        if (e.getStateChange() == ItemEvent.SELECTED)
            intItalic = Font.ITALIC;
        if (e.getStateChange() == ItemEvent.DESELECTED)
            intItalic = Font.PLAIN;
    }

    if (e.getSource() == redRB)
        currentColor = Color.red;
    else if (e.getSource() == greenRB)
            currentColor = Color.green;
    else if (e.getSource() == blueRB)
            currentColor = Color.blue;

    if (e.getSource() == fontFaceDD)
        currentFontName =
                    fontNames[fontFaceDD.getSelectedIndex()];

    repaint();
    }
}
```

The HTML file for this program contains the following code:

```html
<!DOCTYPE HTML PUBLIC "-//W3C//DTD HTML 4.01 Transitional//EN">

<HTML>
  <HEAD>
    <TITLE>WELCOME</TITLE>
  </HEAD>
  <BODY>
    <OBJECT code = "GrandWelcomeFinal.class" width = "440" height = "200">
    </OBJECT>
  </BODY>
</HTML>
```

Sample Run: Figure 13-15 shows a sample run of the Welcome applet with check boxes, combo box, and radio buttons.

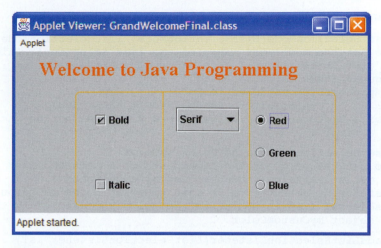

Figure 13-15   Welcome applet with check boxes, combo box, and radio buttons

JList

A **list** displays a number of items from which the user can select one or more items. This section illustrates the use of a single selection list. The programming example at the end of this chapter uses a multiple selection list. Table 13-13 shows some constructors and methods of the **class** JList.

Table 13-13 Some Constructors and Methods of the **class** JList

```
public JList()
   //Creates a JList with no items to select.
   //Example: JList selectionList = new JList();
   //         selectionList is created but has no selectable items.
public JList(Vector v)
   //Creates a JList to display the elements in the
   //vector provided as an input parameter.
   //Example: JList selectionList = new JList(v);
   //         selectionList is a new list that lists the elements
   //         contained in Vector v.
public JList(Object[] o)
   //Creates a JList that displays the elements in the object
   //array provided as an input parameter.
   //Example: JList selectionList = new JList(o);
   //      creates the new list called selectionList and displays
   //      the selections. For an object list, would
   //      display o.toString() values.
```

13

Table 13-13 Some Constructors and Methods of the **class** JList (continued)

```
public void setSelectionMode(ListSelectionModel listselectionmodel)
  //Method to set the model for managing the list selections. Allows
  //only one item to be selected or a range of contiguous or
  //noncontiguous items to be selected.
  //Example: pictureList.setSelectionMode
  //                  (ListSelectionModel.SINGLE_SELECTION);
  //          limits pictureList to allow only a single selection
  //          at a time.
```

```
public void setSelectionBackground(Color sbColor)
  //Method to set the color of the background of a selected item
  //Example: myList.setSelectionBackground(myCustomColor);
  //    This statement sets the color that appears in the background
  //    of a selected item in myList to the color represented by the
  //    Color object myCustomColor.
```

```
public void addListSelectionListener(ListSelectionListener lsl)
  //Method to add a listener class to take action when an item
  //in the list is selected.
  //Example: pictureList.addListSelectionListener(handler);
  //    This statement adds a new ListSelectionListener object,
  //    named handler, to pictureList to process the events related to
  //    the selection of a list item.
```

```
public int getSelectedIndex()
  //When an item in the list is selected, this method returns the
  //index of that item (0 to the number of items - 1). Returns -1 if
  //nothing is selected.
  //Example: myLabel.setIcon
  //                  (pictures[ pictureList.getSelectedIndex() ]);
  //    This statement sets an icon for a label to the item in an
  //    array of image icons specified by the index of the selected
  //    item in the list.
```

Let's write a program that uses a **JList** and **JLabels** to create the GUI as shown in Figure 13-16.

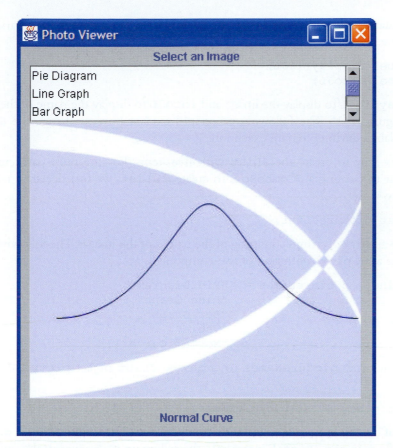

Figure 13-16   GUI using `JList` and `JLabel`

The GUI in Figure 13-16 contains four GUI components—a `JList` and three `JLabel`s. The `JList` object contains the list of items, such as `Pie Diagram`, `Line Graph`, and `Bar Graph`. The first `JLabel` contains the string `"Select an Image"`. Below this label is the `JList` object, and below the `JList` object is a `JLabel` that displays an image. For example, if the user selects Normal Curve, this `JLabel` object shows the image of a normal curve. Below the label showing an image is a `JLabel` that displays the name of the image. For example, in Figure 13-16, this label displays the text `Normal Curve`.

The top and the bottom labels display a line of text, so they are manipulated using strings as labels. The label showing an image is manipulated using images. For this program we include five JPEG images. The following statement creates the `JLabel` object `promptJL` with `Select an Image` as its label and sets the justification of the label to center:

```
private JLabel promptJL = new JLabel("Select an Image",
                              SwingConstants.CENTER);
```

13

The following statements declare `displayPicJL` and `infoJL` to be reference variables of the `JLabel` type:

```
private JLabel displayPicJL;
private JLabel infoJL;
```

We use `displayPicJL` to display the image and `infoJL` to display the name of the image, as shown in Figure 13-16. The following paragraphs explain how to change the text and image of these labels during program execution.

We now discuss how to create the `JList` with five items. For the most part, creating a `JList` is similar to creating a `JComboBox`. To create a `JList`, we first declare a reference variable as follows:

```
private JList pictureJList;
```

Next, we create an array of strings consisting of the names of the images. The following statement creates the array `pictureNames` of five components:

```
private String[] pictureNames = {"Pie Diagram",
                                 "Line Graph",
                                 "Bar Graph",
                                 "Table",
                                 "Normal Curve"};
```

Next, we use the array `pictureNames` to create the `JList` object `pictureJList` as follows:

```
pictureJList = new JList(pictureNames);
```

As in the case of combo boxes, you can use the method `setVisibleRowCount` to set the number of visible rows of a `JList`. For example, the following statement sets the number of visible rows of `pictureJList` to 3:

```
pictureJList.setVisibleRowCount(3);
```

In the program we are writing, we want the user to select only one item at a time from `pictureJList`, so we set `pictureJList` to the single selection mode by using the method `setSelectionMode` together with the constant `ListSelectionModel.SINGLE_SELECTION` as follows:

```
pictureJList.setSelectionMode(ListSelectionModel.SINGLE_SELECTION);
```

When the user selects an image from `pictureJList`, the program displays the corresponding image using the `JLabel` object `displayPicJL`. We use the **class** `ImageIcon` and create an array of images as follows:

```
private ImageIcon[] pictures = {new ImageIcon("pieDiagram.jpg"),
                                new ImageIcon("lineGraph.jpg"),
                                new ImageIcon("barGraph.jpg"),
                                new ImageIcon("table.jpg"),
                                new ImageIcon("normalCurve.jpg")};
```

When the user clicks to select an item from the `JList` object `pictureJList`, `ListSelectionEvent` is generated. To process `ListSelectionEvent`, we use the **interface** `ListSelectionListener`. This **interface** has the method `valueChanged`, which executes when a `ListSelectionEvent` occurs. The heading of this method is:

```java
public void valueChanged(ListSelectionEvent e)
```

We can put the code to display the required image and its name in this method. When the user clicks an item in the `JList`, we can determine the index of the selected item by using the method `getSelectedIndex`. We then use this index to select the corresponding image from the array `pictures` and the name of the image from the array `pictureNames`. We can now use the method `repaint` to repaint the pane. The definition of the method `valueChanged` is:

```java
public void valueChanged(ListSelectionEvent e)
{
    displayPicJL.setIcon(
            pictures[pictureJList.getSelectedIndex()]);
    infoJL.setText(
            pictureNames[pictureJList.getSelectedIndex()]);
    repaint();
}
```

Of course, we must register the list selection listener to the `JList`. The following statement accomplishes this:

```java
pictureJList.addListSelectionListener(this);
```

There are five items in `pictureJList`. When the program executes, it displays only three of these items in the list at a time. Therefore, we want to attach a vertical scroll bar to `pictureJList`, so that the user can scroll to select an item not currently shown in the list. To do so, we use the **class** `JScrollPane` as follows. First we create the `JScrollPane` object `selectionJS` and initialize this object using the object `pictureJList`. We then add the object to the pane `selectionJS`. The following statements illustrate this concept:

```java
selectionJS = new JScrollPane(pictureJList);
pane.add(selectionJS);
```

We will set the pane layout to **null** and specify the size and the location of the GUI components. The complete program listing, given next, contains these statements:

```java
//Program to demonstrate JLIST

import java.awt.*;
import javax.swing.*;
import javax.swing.event.*;

public class JListPictureViewer extends JFrame implements
                                ListSelectionListener
```

13

```java
{
    private String[] pictureNames = {"Pie Diagram",
                                     "Line Graph",
                                     "Bar Graph",
                                     "Table",
                                     "Normal Curve"};

    private ImageIcon[] pictures =
                {new ImageIcon("pieDiagram.jpg"),
                 new ImageIcon("lineGraph.jpg"),
                 new ImageIcon("barGraph.jpg"),
                 new ImageIcon("table.jpg"),
                 new ImageIcon("normalCurve.jpg")};

    private BorderLayout layoutBL;
    private JList pictureJList;
    private JScrollPane selectionJS;
    private JLabel promptJL;
    private JLabel displayPicJL;
    private JLabel infoJL;

    public JListPictureViewer()
    {
        super("Photo Viewer");

        Container pane = getContentPane();
        pane.setLayout(null);

        promptJL = new JLabel("Select an Image",
                              SwingConstants.CENTER);
        promptJL.setSize(350, 20);
        promptJL.setLocation(10, 0);
        pane.add(promptJL);

        pictureJList = new JList(pictureNames);
        pictureJList.setVisibleRowCount(3);
        pictureJList.setSelectionMode
                    (ListSelectionModel.SINGLE_SELECTION);
        pictureJList.addListSelectionListener(this);

        selectionJS = new JScrollPane(pictureJList);
        selectionJS.setSize(350, 60);
        selectionJS.setLocation(10, 20);
        pane.add(selectionJS);

        displayPicJL = new JLabel(pictures[4]);
        displayPicJL.setSize(350, 350);
        displayPicJL.setLocation(10, 50);
```

```
      pane.add(displayPicJL);

      infoJL = new JLabel(pictureNames[4],
                          SwingConstants.CENTER);
      infoJL.setSize(350, 20);
      infoJL.setLocation(10, 380);
      pane.add(infoJL);

      setSize(380, 440);
      setVisible(true);
      setDefaultCloseOperation(EXIT_ON_CLOSE);
   }

   public static void main(String args[])
   {
      JListPictureViewer picViewer = new JListPictureViewer();
   }

   public void valueChanged(ListSelectionEvent e)
   {
      displayPicJL.setIcon(
            pictures[pictureJList.getSelectedIndex() ]);
      infoJL.setText(
            pictureNames[pictureJList.getSelectedIndex() ]);
      repaint();
   }
}
```

Sample Run: Figure 13-17 shows a sample run of the `JListPictureViewer` program.

13

Figure 13-17   Sample run of the `JListPictureViewer` program

LAYOUT MANAGERS

In earlier chapters, you saw two layout managers, `GridLayout` and `null`. For `GridLayout`, you specify the number of rows and columns you want, and you can place your components from left to right, row-by-row, from top to bottom. If you choose the `null` layout, you have to specify the size and location of each component. Java provides many layout managers. This section briefly introduces two more layout managers.

FlowLayout

`FlowLayout` is the default layout manager for a Java application. Creating a `FlowLayout` manager is similar to creating a `GridLayout` manager. For example, suppose that you have the following declaration:

```
Container pane = getContentPane();
```

The statement(s):

```
pane.setLayout(new FlowLayout());
```

or:

```
FlowLayout flowLayoutMgr = new FlowLayout();
pane.setLayout(flowLayoutMgr);
```

set(s) the layout of the container pane to `FlowLayout`. `FlowLayout` places the components from left to right until no more items can be placed. The next item will be placed in the second line. Thus, a `FlowLayout` manager works similarly to a `GridLayout` manager. The main difference between these two layouts is that in a `GridLayout`, all rows (columns) have the same number of components and all components have the same size. However, in a `FlowLayout`, there is no such guarantee. Moreover, in a `FlowLayout`, you can align each line left, center, or right using a statement such as:

```
flowLayoutMgr.setAlignment(FlowLayout.RIGHT);
```

Note that the default alignment is `LEFT`.

The following Java application program illustrates the use of the `FlowLayout` manager:

```
//Program to illustrate FlowLayout

import javax.swing.*;
import java.awt.*;

public class FlowLayoutExample extends JFrame
{
    private static int WIDTH = 350;
    private static int HEIGHT = 350;

        //Variables to create the GUI components
    private JLabel labelJL;
    private JTextField textFieldTF;
    private JButton buttonJB;
    private JCheckBox checkboxCB;
    private JRadioButton radioButtonRB;
    private JTextArea textAreaTA;

    private FlowLayout flowLayoutMgr;

    public FlowLayoutExample()
    {
        setTitle("FlowLayout Manager");                 //Line 1
        Container pane = getContentPane();              //Line 2
        setSize(WIDTH, HEIGHT);                         //Line 3

        flowLayoutMgr = new FlowLayout();               //Line 4
        pane.setLayout(flowLayoutMgr);                  //Line 5
```

13

```
        flowLayoutMgr.setAlignment(FlowLayout.CENTER);  //Line 6

        labelJL = new JLabel("First Component");        //Line 7
        textFieldTF = new JTextField(15);               //Line 8
        textFieldTF.setText("Second Component");        //Line 9
        buttonJB = new JButton("Third Component");      //Line 10

        checkboxCB = new JCheckBox("Fourth Component"); //Line 11

        radioButtonRB =
             new JRadioButton("Fifth Component");       //Line 12

        textAreaTA = new JTextArea(10, 20);             //Line 13

        textAreaTA.setText("Sixth Component.\n");       //Line 14

        textAreaTA.append(
            "Use the mouse to resize the window.");     //Line 15

            //place the GUI components into the pane
        pane.add(labelJL);                              //Line 16
        pane.add(textFieldTF);                          //Line 17
        pane.add(buttonJB);                             //Line 18
        pane.add(checkboxCB);                           //Line 19
        pane.add(radioButtonRB);                        //Line 20
        pane.add(textAreaTA);                           //Line 21

        setVisible(true);                               //Line 22
        setDefaultCloseOperation(EXIT_ON_CLOSE);        //Line 23
    }

    public static void main(String[] args)              //Line 24
    {
        FlowLayoutExample flow =
                    new FlowLayoutExample();             //Line 25
    }
}
```

Sample Run: Figure 13-18 shows a sample run of the **FlowLayoutExample** program.

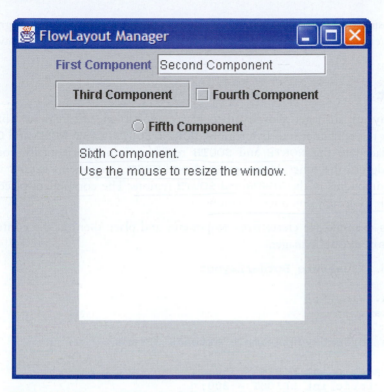

Figure 13-18 Sample run of the `FlowLayoutExample` program

The preceding program works as follows: The statement in Line 1 sets the title of the window, and the statement in Line 2 accesses the content pane. The statement in Line 3 sets the size of the window. The statement in Line 4 creates the `FlowLayout` object `flowLayoutMgr`; the statement in Line 5 uses this object to set the layout of the pane to `FlowLayout`. The statement in Line 6 sets the GUI alignment to centered. The statement in Line 7 instantiates the `JLabel` object `labelJL`. The statement in Line 8 instantiates the `JTextField` object `textFieldTF`, and the statement in Line 9 sets the text of the object `textFieldTF`. The statement in Line 10 instantiates the `JButton` object `buttonJB`, and the statement in Line 11 instantiates the `JCheckBox` object `checkboxCB`. The statement in Line 12 instantiates the `JRadioButton` object `radioButtonRB`. The statement in Line 13 instantiates the `JTextArea` object `textAreaTA` with 10 rows and 20 columns. The statement in Line 14 places the text `Sixth Component` into the text area, and the statement in Line 15 appends the text:

`Use the mouse to resize the window.`

The statements in Lines 16 through 21 place the GUI components in the pane. The statement in Line 22 sets the visibility of the window to **true**, and the statement in Line 23 sets

13

the window closing option to close when the program terminates. When the program executes, the statement in Line 25 creates the window with the GUI components shown in the sample run.

BorderLayout

The `BorderLayout` manager allows you to place items in specific regions. This layout manager divides the container into five regions: NORTH, SOUTH, EAST, WEST, and CENTER. Components placed in the NORTH and SOUTH regions extend horizontally, completely spanning one edge to the other. However, EAST and WEST components extend vertically between the components in the NORTH and SOUTH regions. The component placed at the CENTER expands to occupy any unused regions.

In the following example, we create five components and place them in the content pane using the `BorderLayout` manager.

```java
//Program to illustrate BorderLayout

import javax.swing.*;
import java.awt.*;

public class BorderLayoutExample extends JFrame
{
    private static int WIDTH = 350;
    private static int HEIGHT = 300;

        //GUI components
    private JLabel labelJL;
    private JTextField textFieldTF;
    private JButton buttonJB;
    private JCheckBox checkboxCB;
    private JRadioButton radioButtonRB;
    private JTextArea textAreaTA;

    private BorderLayout borderLayoutMgr;

    public BorderLayoutExample()
    {
        setTitle("BorderLayout Manager");
        Container pane = getContentPane();
        setSize(WIDTH, HEIGHT);

        borderLayoutMgr = new BorderLayout(10, 10);
        pane.setLayout(borderLayoutMgr);
        labelJL = new JLabel("North Component");
        textAreaTA = new JTextArea(10, 20);
        textAreaTA.setText("South Component.\n");
```

```
        textAreaTA.append(
            "Use the mouse to change the size of the window.");
        buttonJB = new JButton("West Component");
        checkboxCB = new JCheckBox("East Component");
        radioButtonRB = new JRadioButton("Center Component");

        pane.add(labelJL, BorderLayout.NORTH);
        pane.add(textAreaTA, BorderLayout.SOUTH);
        pane.add(buttonJB, BorderLayout.EAST);
        pane.add(checkboxCB, BorderLayout.WEST);
        pane.add(radioButtonRB, BorderLayout.CENTER);

        setVisible(true);
        setDefaultCloseOperation(EXIT_ON_CLOSE);
    }

    public static void main(String[] args)
    {
        BorderLayoutExample flow = new BorderLayoutExample();
    }
}
```

Sample Run: A sample run of the `BorderLayoutExample` program is shown in Figure 13-19.

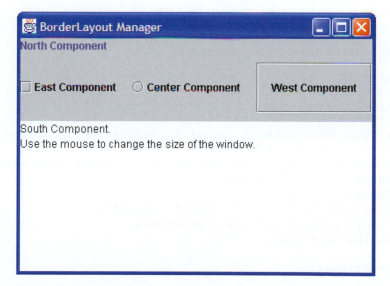

Figure 13-19   Sample run of the `BorderLayoutExample` program

MENUS

Menus allow you to provide various functions without cluttering the GUI with too many components. Menus can be attached to objects such as `JFrame` and `JApplet`.

The **class**es JFrame and JApplet both have the method `setJMenuBar` that allows you to set a menu bar. To set a menu bar, say `menuMB`, you need statements such as the following:

```
private JMenuBar menuMB = new JMenuBar();  //creates a menu bar

setJMenuBar(menuMB);                        //sets the menu bar
```

Once you have created a menu bar, you can add menus, and in each menu you can add menu items. For instance, to create an `Edit` menu and add it to the menu bar created above, you need the following two statements:

```
JMenu editM = new JMenu("Edit");   //creates a menu "Edit"
menuMB.add(editM);                 //adds the menu to menu bar
                                   //menuMB created above
```

Likewise, if you need to create a `File` menu, you may do so by adding the following lines of code:

```
JMenu fileM = new JMenu("File");

menuMB.add(fileM);
```

Notice that the order in which you add menus to the menu bar determines the order in which they appear. For example, if you want the `File` menu to appear first, you must add it first.

The following program illustrates the use of menus:

```java
import java.awt.*;
import java.awt.event.*;
import javax.swing.*;

public class TextEditor extends JFrame implements ActionListener
{
    private JMenuBar menuMB = new JMenuBar(); //creates the menu bar
    private JMenu fileM, editM, optionM;
    private JMenuItem exitI;
    private JMenuItem cutI, copyI, pasteI, selectI;
    private JTextArea pageTA = new JTextArea();
    private String scratchpad = "";

    public TextEditor()
    {
        setTitle("Simple Text Editor");
        Container pane = getContentPane();
        pane.setLayout(new BorderLayout());
        pane.add(pageTA, BorderLayout.CENTER);
        pane.add(new JScrollPane(pageTA));
```

```
        pageTA.setLineWrap(true);
        setJMenuBar(menuMB);
        setFileMenu();
        setEditMenu();
        setSize(300, 200);
        setVisible(true);
        setDefaultCloseOperation(EXIT_ON_CLOSE);
    }

    private void setFileMenu()
    {
        fileM = new JMenu("File");
        menuMB.add(fileM);
        exitI = new JMenuItem("Exit");
        fileM.add(exitI);
        exitI.addActionListener(this);
    }

    private void setEditMenu()
    {
        editM = new JMenu("Edit");
        menuMB.add(editM);
        cutI = new JMenuItem("Cut");
        editM.add(cutI);
        cutI.addActionListener(this);
        copyI = new JMenuItem("Copy");
        editM.add(copyI);
        copyI.addActionListener(this);
        pasteI = new JMenuItem("Paste");
        editM.add(pasteI);
        pasteI.addActionListener(this);
        selectI = new JMenuItem("Select All");
        editM.add(selectI);
        selectI.addActionListener(this);
    }

    public void actionPerformed(ActionEvent e)
    {
        JMenuItem mItem = (JMenuItem) e.getSource();

        if (mItem == exitI)
        {
            System.exit(0);
        }
        else if (mItem == cutI)
        {
                scratchpad = pageTA.getSelectedText();
                pageTA.replaceRange("",
                            pageTA.getSelectionStart(),
                            pageTA.getSelectionEnd());
        }
```

13

```
        else if (mItem == copyI)
        {
                scratchpad = pageTA.getSelectedText();
        }
        else if (mItem == pasteI)
        {
                pageTA.insert(scratchpad, pageTA.getCaretPosition());
        }
        else if (mItem == selectI)
        {
                pageTA.selectAll();
        }
    }

    public static void main(String args[])
    {
        TextEditor texted = new TextEditor();
    }
}
```

Sample Run: A sample run of the program with menus is shown in Figure 13–20.

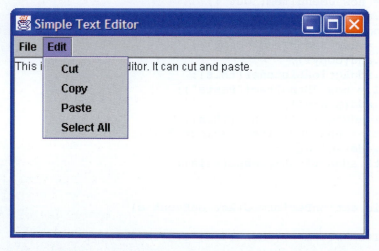

Figure 13-20 Sample run of the `TextEditor` program

KEY AND MOUSE EVENTS

In this and the preceding chapters, you learned how to handle action events when you click a button. Moreover, Chapter 12 noted that when you press the **Enter** key in a text field, an action event is generated. Also recall that when you press a mouse button to click a button, in addition to generating an action event, a mouse event is generated. Likewise, when you press the `Enter` key in a text field, in addition to the action event, a key event is generated. Therefore, a GUI program can simultaneously generate more than one event. This section gives various programs to show how to handle key and mouse events.

Recall from Chapter 12 that key events are handled by the **interface** `KeyListener`, and mouse events are handled by the **interface**s `MouseListener` and `MouseMotionListener`. The key and mouse events and the corresponding event handlers were shown in Table 12-9, which is reproduced in Table 13-14.

Table 13-14 Events Generated by the Keyboard and Mouse

	Event Generated	Listener Interface	Listener Method
key	KeyEvent	KeyListener	keyPressed
key	KeyEvent	KeyListener	keyReleased
key	KeyEvent	KeyListener	keyTyped
mouse	MouseEvent	MouseListener	mouseClicked
mouse	MouseEvent	MouseListener	mouseEntered
mouse	MouseEvent	MouseListener	mouseExited
mouse	MouseEvent	MouseListener	mousePressed
mouse	MouseEvent	MouseListener	mouseReleased
mouse	MouseEvent	MouseMotionListener	mouseDragged
mouse	MouseEvent	MouseMotionListener	mouseMoved

Key Events

This section describes how to handle key events. As shown in Table 13-14, there are three types of key events. The **interface** `KeyListener` contains the methods—`keyPressed`, `keyReleased`, and `keyTyped`—that correspond to these events. These methods specify the action that needs to be taken when a key event occurs. When you press a meta key (such as Control, Shift, or Alt), the method `keyPressed` is executed; when you type a regular alphanumeric key, the method `keyTyped` is executed. When you release any key, the method `keyReleased` is executed. The program in Example 13-8 shows how to handle key events.

Example 13-8

This program displays the character that corresponds to the key typed by the user. For example, if the user presses the key `A`, the program displays `A`. We use a `JTextField` object to display the character.

When you type an alphanumeric key, a key event is generated. The key event is handled by the method `keyTyped`. The necessary code to display the key is placed in the body of the method `keyTyped`. Before displaying the key typed by the user, the previous character is removed from the `JTextField` object. In other words, the program displays only one character at a time, corresponding to the key typed. In this program, the font of the character is set to `Courier` and the color of the character is randomly selected.

Because the interface `keyListener` contains three methods and we want to implement only one of these methods, we use the anonymous class mechanism to register a listener object. The complete program listing follows. (Notice that the program uses a message dialog box to inform the user what to do.)

```java
//Key Event

import java.awt.*;
import java.awt.event.*;
import javax.swing.*;

public class OneChar extends JApplet
{
    JTextField oneLetter = new JTextField(1);

    public void init()
    {
        Container c = getContentPane();

        //register the listener object
        oneLetter.addKeyListener(new KeyAdapter()
        {
            public void keyTyped(KeyEvent e)
            {
                float red, green, blue;
                Color fg, bg;

                oneLetter.setText(" ");
                red = (float) Math.random();
                green = (float) Math.random();
                blue = (float) Math.random();
                fg = new Color(red, green, blue);
                bg = Color.white;
                oneLetter.setForeground(fg);
                oneLetter.setBackground(bg);
                oneLetter.setCaretColor(bg);
                oneLetter.setFont(new Font("Courier", Font.BOLD, 200));
            }
        });

        c.setLayout(new GridLayout(1, 1));
        c.setBackground(Color.white);
        c.add(oneLetter);
        JOptionPane.showMessageDialog
```

```
                    (null, "Click on the applet, then type a key ",
                    "Information", JOptionPane.PLAIN_MESSAGE );
        }
}
```

The HTML file for this program contains the following code:

```
<!DOCTYPE HTML PUBLIC "-//W3C//DTD HTML 4.01 Transitional//EN">

<HTML>
  <HEAD>
    <TITLE>ONECHAR APPLET</TITLE>
  </HEAD>
  <BODY>
    <OBJECT code = "OneChar.class" width = "350" height = "300">
    </OBJECT>
  </BODY>
</HTML>
```

Sample Run: Figure 13-21 shows a sample run of the OneChar applet. (Notice that Figure 13-21 does not show the message dialog box. However, when you execute this program, it first shows the message dialog box.)

Figure 13-21   Sample run of the OneChar applet

Mouse Events

This section describes how to handle mouse events. A mouse can generate seven different types of events, as shown earlier in Table 13-14. As you see in Table 13-14, some mouse events are handled by the **interface** MouseListener and others are handled by the **interface** MouseMotionListener. Table 13-14 also shows which listener method is executed when a particular mouse event occurs. Example 13-9 illustrates how to handle mouse events.

Example 13-9

This example shows how to handle the following mouse events: mouse clicked, mouse entered, mouse exited, mouse pressed, and mouse released. To handle these events, we use the methods of the **interface** MouseListener. The MouseExample program contains six labels corresponding to the five mouse events and one label to display the mouse location. When you run this program and use the mouse, the foreground color of the label corresponding to the generated mouse event changes, and the mouse location where the event occurred is displayed.

```
//Program to illustrate mouse events

import javax.swing.*;
import java.awt.*;
import java.awt.event.*;

public class MouseExample extends JFrame
                          implements MouseListener
{
    private static int WIDTH = 350;
    private static int HEIGHT = 250;

        //GUI components
    private JLabel[] labelJL;

    public MouseExample()
    {
        setTitle("Mouse Events");
        Container pane  = getContentPane();
        setSize(WIDTH, HEIGHT);

        GridLayout gridMgr = new GridLayout(6, 1, 10, 10);
        pane.setLayout(gridMgr);

        labelJL = new JLabel[6];

        labelJL[0] = new JLabel("Mouse Clicked",
                            SwingConstants.CENTER);
        labelJL[1] = new JLabel("Mouse Entered",
                            SwingConstants.CENTER);
```

```java
        labelJL[2] = new JLabel("Mouse Exited",
                                SwingConstants.CENTER);
        labelJL[3] = new JLabel("Mouse Pressed",
                                SwingConstants.CENTER);
        labelJL[4] = new JLabel("Mouse Released",
                                SwingConstants.CENTER);
        labelJL[5] = new JLabel("", SwingConstants.CENTER);

        for (int i = 0; i < labelJL.length; i++)
        {
            labelJL[i].setForeground(Color.gray);
            pane.add(labelJL[i]);
        }

        pane.addMouseListener(this);

        setVisible(true);
        setDefaultCloseOperation(EXIT_ON_CLOSE);
    }

    public void mouseClicked(MouseEvent event)
    {
        for (int i = 0; i < labelJL.length; i++)
        {
            if (i == 0)
                labelJL[i].setForeground(Color.yellow);
            else
                labelJL[i].setForeground(Color.gray);
        }

        labelJL[5].setText("[" + event.getX() + ","
                        + event.getY() + "]");

    }

    public void mouseEntered(MouseEvent event)
    {
        for (int i = 0; i < labelJL.length; i++)
        {
            if (i == 1)
                labelJL[i].setForeground(Color.green);
            else
                labelJL[i].setForeground(Color.gray);
        }

        labelJL[5].setText("[" + event.getX() + ","
                        + event.getY() + "]");
    }
```

13

```java
    public void mouseExited(MouseEvent event)
    {
        for (int i = 0; i < labelJL.length; i++)
        {
            if (i == 2)
                labelJL[i].setForeground(Color.red);
            else
                labelJL[i].setForeground(Color.gray);
        }

        labelJL[5].setText("[" + event.getX() + ","
                            + event.getY() + "]");
    }

    public void mousePressed(MouseEvent event)
    {
        for (int i = 0; i < labelJL.length; i++)
        {
            if (i == 3)
                labelJL[i].setForeground(Color.blue);
            else
                labelJL[i].setForeground(Color.gray);
        }

        labelJL[5].setText("[" + event.getX() + ","
                            + event.getY() + "]");
    }

    public void mouseReleased(MouseEvent event)
    {
        for (int i = 0; i < labelJL.length; i++)
        {
            if (i == 4)
                labelJL[i].setForeground(Color.pink);
            else
                labelJL[i].setForeground(Color.gray);
        }

        labelJL[5].setText("[" + event.getX() + ","
                            + event.getY() + "]");
    }

    public static void main(String[] args)
    {
        MouseExample flow = new MouseExample();
    }
}
```

Sample Run: Figure 13-22 shows a sample run of the MouseExample program.

Figure 13-22   Sample run of the `MouseExample` program

Example 13-10

The program in this example shows how to handle the mouse dragged event. You can handle the mouse moved event similarly. These events are handled by the **interface** `MouseMotionListener`, which contains the methods `mouseDragged` and `mouseMoved`, which, in turn, are used to handle the mouse dragged and mouse moved events, respectively.

The program starts with some colored dots. If you drag a dot using the mouse, the dot turns into a line. This way, you can "freehand draw" different pictures. What is really happening is that we created small circle objects. The program contains the method `selected` to check whether or not the mouse is on a circle. If you drag a circle, the method `mouseDragged` is invoked and it paints a new circle. The sequence of circles gives the impression of drawing a line. The complete program listing follows:

```java
//MouseMotionListener applet

import javax.swing.*;
import java.awt.event.*;
import java.applet.*;
import java.awt.*;

public class FreeDrawApplet extends JApplet implements
                                        MouseMotionListener
{
```

13

```java
    //instance variables
ColorCircle[] myGraph;

final int NUM_CIRCLES = 7;
final int WIDTH = 400;
final int HEIGHT = 400;

public class ColorCircle
{
    private int x;
    private int y;

    public void setX(int iNewX)
    {
        x = iNewX;
    }

    public void setY(int iNewY)
    {
        y = iNewY;
    }

    public void paint (Graphics g)
    {
        g.fillOval(x - 10, y - 10, 20, 20);
    }

    public boolean selected(int iXcoord, int iYcoord)
    {
        if ((iXcoord >= x - 10) && (iXcoord <= x + 10)
            && (iYcoord >= y - 10) && (iYcoord <= y + 10))
            return true;
        else
            return false;
    }
}

public void init()
{
    addMouseMotionListener(this);
    myGraph = new ColorCircle[NUM_CIRCLES];

    for (int i = 0; i < NUM_CIRCLES; i++)
    {
        ColorCircle myVertex = new ColorCircle();
        myVertex.setX((int) (Math.random() * (WIDTH - 50)));
        myVertex.setY((int) (Math.random() * (HEIGHT - 100)));
        myGraph[i] = myVertex;
    }
```

```
          JOptionPane.showMessageDialog(null,
                  "Try to drag any one of the colored circles ",
                  "Information", JOptionPane.PLAIN_MESSAGE );

    }

    public void paint(Graphics g)
    {
        Color[] myColor = {Color.black, Color.red, Color.blue,
                           Color.green, Color.cyan,
                           Color.orange, Color.yellow};

        if (NUM_CIRCLES > 0)
            for (int i = 0; i < NUM_CIRCLES; i++)
            {
                g.setColor(myColor[i]);
                myGraph[i].paint(g);
            }
    }

    public void mouseDragged(MouseEvent event)
    {
        int iX = event.getX();
        int iY = event.getY();

        for (int i = 0; i < NUM_CIRCLES; i++)
            if (myGraph[i].selected(iX, iY))
            {
                myGraph[i].setX(iX);
                myGraph[i].setY(iY);
                break;
            }

        repaint();
    }

    public void mouseMoved(MouseEvent p1)
    {
    }
}
```

The HTML file for this program contains the following code:

```
<!DOCTYPE HTML PUBLIC "-//W3C//DTD HTML 4.01 Transitional//EN">

<HTML>
  <HEAD>
    <TITLE>Drawing Board</TITLE>
  </HEAD>
  <BODY>
```

13

```
      <OBJECT code = "FreeDrawApplet.class" width = "400" height = "400">
      </OBJECT>
   </BODY>
</HTML>
```

Sample Run: Figure 13-23 shows a sample run of the `FreeDrawApplet`.

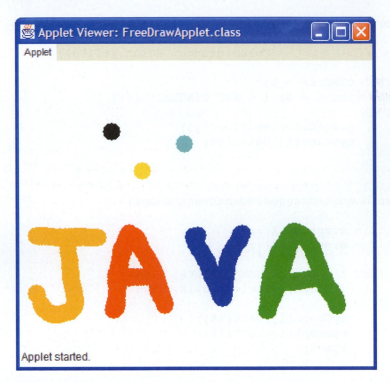

Figure 13-23   Sample run of the `FreeDrawApplet`

The program `FreeDrawApplet` uses small circles to draw lines. Because there is no GUI component we can use, we created the **class** `ColorCircle`. This class has two **private** members: `x` and `y` of the type **int**. The point (`x, y`) specifies the center of the circle, and the radius of the circle is fixed at 10 pixels. In addition to the methods to set the values of `x` and `y`, the **class** `ColorCircle` has only two other methods, `paint` and `isSelected`. The `paint` method draws a filled circle of radius 10 at the point (`x, y`). The method `isSelected` returns **true** if and only if (`iXcoord, iYcoord`) lies inside a 20-by-20 square with the point (`x, y`) as the center. We use this method to check whether the mouse is at, say, (`iXcoord, iYcoord`) on the circle with the center (`x, y`). Note that because `ColorCircle` is not a GUI component, it can generate any event. Therefore, any time a `mouseDragged` event is generated, we must check whether the mouse is on any of the circles. We do so using the following **for** loop:

```
for (int i = 0; i < NUM_CIRCLES; i++)
    if (myGraph[i].selected(iX, iY))
    {
        myGraph[i].setX(iX);
        myGraph[i].setY(iY);
        break;
    }
```

Note that if a **mouseDragged** event occurs on a **ColorCircle** object, the preceding **for** loop sets the current mouse position as the new center of the **ColorCircle** object. This, in effect, moves the **ColorCircle** object. By continually moving a **ColorCircle** object, we create a line.

PROGRAMMING EXAMPLE: JAVA KIOSK

In this programming example, we design a program that simulates a fast food kiosk. The program displays a menu similar to one you might find in a fast food restaurant. The user makes a selection and then presses a **JButton** to mark the end of the selection process. The program then calculates and displays the bill. A sample output is shown in Figure 13-24.

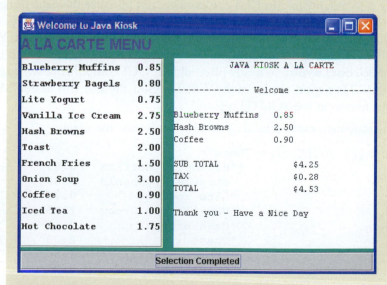

Figure 13-24   Sample output of the Java Kiosk program

Input   A list of selected items from the menu shown on the left in Figure 13-24.

Output   The bill shown on the right in Figure 13-24.

Problem Analysis and GUI and Algorithm Design

As shown in Figure 13-24, there are five GUI components: a frame, a label, a list, a text area, and a button. All components other than the frame are placed into the content pane of the window. The user selects various list items and then presses the `Selection Completed` button. Recall that when you click a button it generates an action event, which is processed by using the **interface** `ActionListener`. Therefore, we will create and register an action listener object with the button.

When the event is generated, the event handler computes the subtotal, tax, and total. The program then displays the result in the text area. To create the label, list, text area, and button, you use reference variables of the types `JLabel`, `JList`, `JTextArea`, and `JButton`, respectively. You also need a reference variable to access the content pane of the window. As in the GUI programs in previous chapters, we create the class containing the application program by extending the definition of the **class** `JFrame`; this also allows you to create the necessary window to create the GUI. Thus, we use the following reference variables to create the GUI components and to access the content pane of the window:

```
private JList yourChoices;
private JTextArea bill;

private Container pane;
JLabel yourChoicesJLabel;
JButton button;
```

The next step is to instantiate four GUI components and initialize the pane using the method `getContentPane`. Recall that, to create a list, you first create an array of strings, and then use the array as the argument in the constructor of the `JList`. You can instantiate other GUI components the same way you have done previously. This program uses the `BorderLayout` to neatly place all four GUI components. We place the label in the NORTH region, the list in the WEST region, the text area in the EAST region, and the button in the SOUTH region.

The following statement creates the array of strings to create the menu:

```
static String[] yourChoicesItems =
                    {"Blueberry Muffins    0.85",
                     "Strawberry Bagels    0.80",
                     "Lite Yogurt          0.75",
                     "Vanilla Ice Cream    2.75",
                     "Hash Browns          2.50",
                     "Toast                2.00",
                     "French Fries         1.50",
                     "Onion Soup           3.00",
```

```
                              "Coffee              0.90",
                              "Iced Tea            1.00",
                              "Hot Chocolate       1.75"};
```

The following statements create the necessary GUI components and place them in the container:

```
private JList yourChoices;
private JTextArea bill;

private Container pane;

pane = getContentPane();
pane.setBackground(new Color(0, 200, 200));
pane.setLayout(new BorderLayout(5, 5));

        //Create a label and place it in the NORTH region
        //and set the font of this label
JLabel yourChoicesJLabel = new JLabel("A LA CARTE MENU");
pane.add(yourChoicesJLabel, BorderLayout.NORTH);
yourChoicesJLabel.setFont(new Font("Dialog", Font.BOLD, 20));

        //Create a list and place it in the WEST region
        //and set the font of this list
yourChoices = new JList(yourChoicesItems);
pane.add(new JScrollPane (yourChoices),BorderLayout.WEST);
yourChoices.setFont(new Font("Courier", Font.BOLD, 14));

        //Create a text area and place it in the EAST region
        //and set the font of this text area
bill = new JTextArea();
pane.add(bill, BorderLayout.EAST);
bill.setFont(new Font("Courier", Font.PLAIN, 10));

        //Create a button and place it in the SOUTH region and
        //add an action listener.
JButton button = new JButton("Selection Completed");
pane.add(button, BorderLayout.SOUTH);
button.addActionListener(this);
```

You need another array to keep track of the prices of the various items.

```
static double[] yourChoicesPrices = {0.85, 0.80, 0.75, 2.75,
                                     2.50, 2.00, 1.50, 3.00,
                                     0.90, 1.00, 1.75};
```

The following statements set the size of the window and set its visibility to **true**:

```
setSize(500, 360);
setVisible(true);
```

Recall that when an action event is generated by a button, the method `actionPerformed` is invoked. When the user clicks the button, the program must compute the subtotal, tax, and total, and display the result in the text area. The instructions to perform these tasks are placed in the method `actionPerformed`, which is described next.

Method `actionPerformed`   As noted previously, the method `actionPerformed` is executed when the user clicks the button. The method `actionPerformed` calculates and displays the bill. We write the method `displayBill` that computes the bill and displays it using the text area. The method `actionPerformed` invokes the method `displayBill` to display the bill. The definition of the method `actionPerformed` is:

```java
public void actionPerformed(ActionEvent event)
{
    if (event.getActionCommand().equals("Selection Completed"))
    {
        displayBill();
    }
}
```

Method `displayBill`   The method `displayBill` first needs to identify the items selected by the user. The method `getSelectedIndices` of the `JList` will return an array of indices. Because you need an integer array to hold these indices, you might need the following Java statements:

```java
int[] listArray = yourChoices.getSelectedIndices();
double localTax = 0.065;
double tax;
double subtotal = 0;
double total;
```

Note that `listArray[0]`, `listArray[1]`,..., `listArray[listArray.length - 1]` contains the indices of the items selected from the menu list. Therefore, the following **for** loop computes the total cost of the items selected from the menu:

```java
for (int index = 0; index < listArray.length; index++)
    subTotal = subTotal + yourChoicesPrices[listArray[index]];
```

Next, we compute the tax and add it to `subTotal` to get the billing amount.

```java
tax = localTax * subTotal;
total = subTotal + tax;
```

To display the bill, we append the necessary statements to the **JTextArea** and invoke the **repaint** method to redraw the GUI components. To place another order, we unselect the selected items. The definition of the method **displayBill** is:

```java
    // method to display the order and total cost
private void displayBill()
{
    int[] listArray = yourChoices.getSelectedIndices();
    double localTax = 0.065;
    double tax;
    double subtotal = 0;
    double total;

        //set the text area to non-edit mode
        //and start with an empty string
    bill.setEditable(false);
    bill.setText("");

        //calculate the cost of the items ordered
    for (int index = 0; index < listArray.length; index++)
        subTotal = subTotal + yourChoicesPrices[listArray[index]];

    tax = localTax * subTotal;
    total = subTotal + tax;

        //display costs
    bill.append("            JAVA KIOSK A LA CARTE\n\n");
    bill.append("--------------- Welcome ----------------\n\n");
    for (int index = 0; index < listArray.length; index++)
    {
        bill.append(yourChoicesItems[listArray[index]] + "\n");
    }

    bill.append("\n");
    bill.append("SUB TOTAL\t\t$"
            + String.format("%.2f", subTotal) + "\n");
    bill.append("TAX        \t\t$"
            + String.format("%.2f", tax) + "\n");
    bill.append("TOTAL    \t\t$"
            + String.format("%.2f", total) + "\n\n");
    bill.append("Thank you - Have a Nice Day\n\n");

        //reset the list array
    yourChoices.clearSelection();

    repaint();
}
```

The program listing is as follows.

Program Listing

```java
//A la Carte

import java.awt.*;
import java.awt.event.*;
import javax.swing.*;
import javax.swing.event.*;

public class AlaCarte extends JFrame implements ActionListener
{
    static String[] yourChoicesItems =
                        {"Blueberry Muffins    0.85",
                         "Strawberry Bagels    0.80",
                         "Lite Yogurt          0.75",
                         "Vanilla Ice Cream    2.75",
                         "Hash Browns          2.50",
                         "Toast                2.00",
                         "French Fries         1.50",
                         "Onion Soup           3.00",
                         "Coffee               0.90",
                         "Iced Tea             1.00",
                         "Hot Chocolate        1.75"};

    static double[] yourChoicesPrices = {0.85, 0.80, 0.75, 2.75,
                         2.50, 2.00, 1.50, 3.00,
                         0.90, 1.00, 1.75};

    private JList yourChoices;
    private JTextArea bill;

    private Container pane;

    public AlaCarte()
    {
        super("Welcome to Java Kiosk");

        //Get the content pane and set its background color
        //and layout manager.
        pane = getContentPane();
        pane.setBackground(new Color(0, 200, 200));
        pane.setLayout(new BorderLayout(5, 5));
```

```java
        //Create a label and place it at NORTH. Also
        //set the font of this label.
   JLabel yourChoicesJLabel = new JLabel("A LA CARTE MENU");
   pane.add(yourChoicesJLabel, BorderLayout.NORTH);
   yourChoicesJLabel.setFont(new Font("Dialog", Font.BOLD,20));

        //Create a list and place it at WEST. Also
        //set the font of this list.
   yourChoices = new JList(yourChoicesItems);
   pane.add(new JScrollPane (yourChoices), BorderLayout.WEST);
   yourChoices.setFont(new Font("Courier", Font.BOLD, 14));

        //Create a text area and place it at EAST. Also
        //set the font of this text area.
   bill = new JTextArea();
   pane.add(bill, BorderLayout.EAST);
   bill.setFont(new Font("Courier", Font.PLAIN, 12));

        //Create a button and place it in the SOUTH region and
        //add an action listener.
   JButton button = new JButton("Selection Completed");
   pane.add(button, BorderLayout.SOUTH);
   button.addActionListener(this);

   setSize(500, 360);
   setVisible(true);
   setDefaultCloseOperation(EXIT_ON_CLOSE);
}

        //Method to display the order and the total cost
private void displayBill()
{
   int[] listArray = yourChoices.getSelectedIndices();
   double localTax = 0.065;
   double tax;
   double subTotal = 0;
   double total;

      //Set the text area to non-edit mode and start
      //with an empty string.
   bill.setEditable(false);
   bill.setText("");

      //Calculate cost of the items ordered.
   for (int index = 0; index < listArray.length; index++)
      subTotal = subTotal
                   + yourChoicesPrices[listArray[index]];
```

```java
        tax = localTax * subTotal;
        total = subTotal + tax;

            //Display the costs.
        bill.append("            JAVA KIOSK A LA CARTE\n\n");
        bill.append("--------------- Welcome ---------------\n\n");

        for (int index = 0; index < listArray.length; index++)
        {
            bill.append(yourChoicesItems[listArray[index]] + "\n");
        }

        bill.append("\n");
        bill.append("SUB TOTAL\t\t$"
                    + String.format("%.2f", subTotal) + "\n");
        bill.append("TAX        \t\t$"
                    + String.format("%.2f", tax) + "\n");
        bill.append("TOTAL     \t\t$"
                    + String.format("%.2f", total) + "\n\n");
        bill.append("Thank you - Have a Nice Day\n\n");

            //Reset the list array.
        yourChoices.clearSelection();

        repaint();
    }

    public void actionPerformed(ActionEvent event)
    {
        if (event.getActionCommand().equals("Selection Completed"))
            displayBill();
    }

    public static void main(String[] args)
    {
        AlaCarte alc = new AlaCarte();
    }
}
```

Sample Run: Figure 13-25 shows a sample run of the program. (To make more than one selection, click the first selection, hold the Ctrl key, and then click the left mouse button on the other selections. To make contiguous selections, click the first item, hold the Shift key, and then click the last item you want to select.)

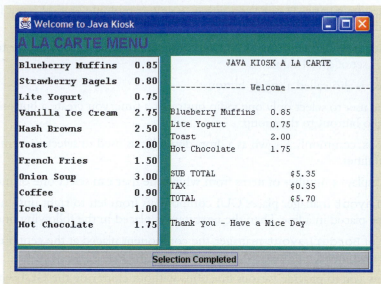

Figure 13-25   Sample run of the Java Kiosk program

QUICK REVIEW

1. The term applet means a little application.

2. An applet is a Java program that is embedded within a Web page and executed by a Web browser.

3. You create an applet by extending the **class** `JApplet`, which is contained in the **package** `javax.swing`.

4. Unlike a Java application program, Java applets do not have the **main** method.

5. When a browser runs an applet, the methods `init`, `start`, and `paint` are guaranteed to be invoked in sequence.

6. All statements to be executed only once are kept in the `init` method of an applet.

7. An applet does not have a title.

8. The **class**es `Font` and `Color` are contained in the **package** `java.awt`.

9. Java uses the color scheme known as `RGB`, where `R` stands for red, `G` for green, and `B` for blue, respectively.

10. You create instances of the **class** `Color` by mixing red, green, and blue hues in various proportions.

11. An applet class is derived from the **class** `JApplet`, whereas a GUI application class is created by extending the **class** `JFrame`.

12. Applets do not use constructors.

13. Java provides the **class** JTextArea either to collect multiple lines of input from the user or to display multiple lines of output.

14. Java provides the **class**es JCheckBox and JRadioButton to allow a user to select a value from a set of given values.

15. A check box is also called a toggle button.

16. To force the user to select only one radio button at a time, you create a button group and add radio buttons to the group.

17. A combo box, commonly known as a drop-down list, is used to select an item from a list of possibilities.

18. A JList displays a number of items from which the user can select one or more items.

19. The FlowLayout manager places GUI components from left to right until no more items can be placed in a line. Then the next item is placed in the following line.

20. In the case of BorderLayout manager, the component placed at the center expands to occupy any unused regions.

21. Menus allow you to provide various functions without cluttering the GUI with components.

22. Menus can be attached to objects such as JFrame and JApplet.

23. Key events are handled by the **interface** KeyListener; mouse events are handled by the **interface**s MouseListener and MouseMotionListener.

EXERCISES

1. Mark the following statements as true or false.

   T a. An applet's width and height are specified in the HTML file.

   T b. In Java, JApplet is a class.

   T c. To display an applet, you need not invoke a method such as setVisible().

   F d. You must include an exit button in all Java applets.

   F e. When an applet is loaded, the method start is invoked ~~before~~ *after* the method init.

   F f. Check boxes are used to display the output of a program.

   T g. A radio button comes with a label.

   F h. You use JList to create a combo box.

   F i. JTextField can be used to output multiple lines of text.

2. Name four GUI components that can be used for input only.

3. Name two GUI components that can be used for both input and output.
   JTextField   JTextArea

4. Name a GUI component that can be used for output only.

5. Why do you need check boxes in a GUI program?
   to allow user selection from predefined list

6. Fill in the blanks in each of the following:

a. The ___*drawRect*___ method of the **class** Graphics draws a rectangle.

b. RGB is short for ___*red*___, ___*green*___, and ___*blue*___.

c. The method _____ is invoked when an item is selected from a combo box and a(n) _____ is registered to handle an event.

d. The _____ method of the **class** Graphics can be used to draw a circle.

e. Font sizes are specified in units called ___*points*___.

f. Both **JTextField** and **JTextArea** inherit directly from the **class** _____.

g. The method **Random** returns a value between ___*0*___ and ___*1*___.

h. The method ___*getText()*___ gets the string in the **JTextArea**, and the method ___*setText(String t)*___ changes the string displayed in a **JTextArea**.

i. The **BorderLayout** manager divides the container into five regions: ___*N*___, ___*S*___, ___*E*___, ___*W*___, and ___*center*___.

j. The _____ class is used to create a slider for _____.

k. You cannot use **System.out.println** inside a(n) _____ method.

7. Write the necessary statements to create the following:

a. A **JList** with the list items **orange**, **apple**, **banana**, **grape**, and **pineapple**

b. A check box with the label **draft**

c. A group of three radio buttons with the labels **home**, **visitor**, and **neutral**

d. A menu bar

e. A Courier bold 32-point font

f. A new color that is not already defined in the **class** Color

8. Correct any syntax errors in the following program:

```
//Grand Welcome Problem Applet

import java.awt.*;
import javax.swing.JApplet;

public class GrandWelcomeProblem extends JApplet
{
    public int()
    {
            JLabel myLabel = new JLabel("");
    }
```

```java
public void paint( Graphics g)
{
    super.paint(g);
    Container pane = g.getContentPane();
    pane.setLayout(BORDER_LAYOUT);
    pane.add(BORDER_LAYOUT.CENTER);

    myLabel.setText("A Grand Welcome to Java Programming!");
}
}
```

PROGRAMMING EXERCISES

1. Create an applet to draw a digit using the method **drawLine** of the **class** Graphics. For instance, if the input is 4, the applet will display the digit 4 as shown in Figure 13–26.

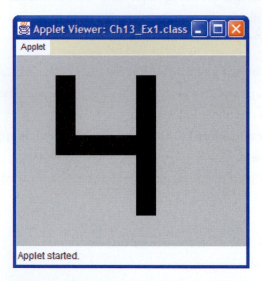

Figure 13-26   Figure for Programming Exercise 1

2. Modify the applet created in Programming Exercise 1 by adding eight radio buttons so the user can change the color of the digit drawn.

3. Modify the applet created in Programming Exercise 1 by adding a color menu to change the color of the digit drawn.

4. Modify the applet created in Programming Exercise 1 by adding a `JList` of eight items so the user can change the background color of the applet.

5. Create an applet that will draw a set of ovals similar to that shown in Figure 13-27. The user can specify the number of ovals.

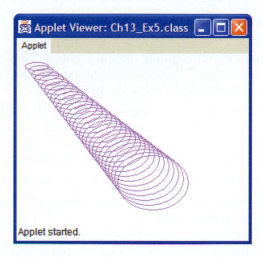

Figure 13-27   Figure for Programming Exercise 5

6. Modify the applet in Programming Exercise 5 by adding three different types of GUI components so the user can select from the following:

   a. Number of figures: 1, 2, 4, 8, 16, or various combinations of these numbers

   b. Type of figures: circle, oval, rectangle, or square

   c. Color: red, blue, green, yellow, pink, black, cyan, or magenta

13

7. Modify the applet in Programming Exercise 5 by adding the necessary menus so the user can select from the following:

   a. Number of figures: 1, 10, 20, 30, or 40

   b. Type of figures: circle, oval, rectangle, or square

   c. Color: red, blue, green, yellow, pink, black, cyan, or magenta

8. Convert the `WhiteBoard` program (given earlier in this chapter) from an application to an applet.

9. Redo `JListPictureViewer` (given earlier in this chapter) using one of the layout managers. For this exercise, just use a `JList` and one `JLabel` to display the image.

10. Create an applet to draw lines. The user can choose the start and end points of the line to be drawn by clicking the mouse.

11. Create an application to illustrate mouse events, mouse motion events, and keyboard events. Figure 13-28 shows the user interface. The key code corresponding to a key event or the position of the mouse is displayed just above the text field.

12. Create an applet to draw lines, rectangles, squares, circles, and ovals. The user can select any one of these through a menu. The user also can choose the start and end points of the line to be drawn by clicking the mouse. For other geometric figures, the user chooses the upper-left corner and lower-right corner by clicking the mouse.

13. Convert the Java Kiosk Programming Example from an application to an applet.

14. Create an applet that starts with displaying several colored circles that can be moved to different places in the applet by dragging the mouse.

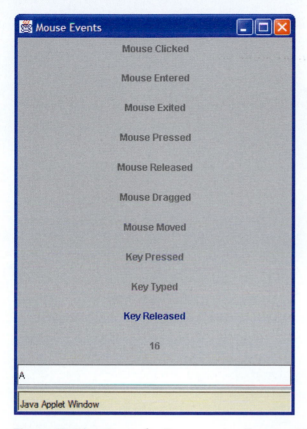

Figure 13-28 Figure for Programming Exercise 11

RECURSION

In this chapter, you will:

♦ Learn about recursive definitions

♦ Explore the base case and general case of a recursive definition

♦ Learn about recursive algorithms

♦ Learn about recursive methods

♦ Become aware of direct and indirect recursion

♦ Explore how to use recursive methods to implement recursive algorithms

In previous chapters, to devise problem solutions we used the most common technique, called iteration. For certain problems, however, using the iterative technique to obtain the solution is quite complicated. This chapter introduces another problem-solving technique, called recursion, and provides several examples demonstrating how recursion works.

RECURSIVE DEFINITIONS

The process of solving a problem by reducing it to smaller versions of itself is called **recursion**. Recursion is a powerful way to solve certain problems for which the solution would otherwise be very complicated. Let's consider a familiar problem.

In mathematics, the factorial of an integer is defined as follows:

$$0! = 1 \qquad\qquad\qquad\qquad\qquad (14\text{-}1)$$
$$n! = n \times (n-1)! \ \ \text{if} \ \ n > 0 \qquad (14\text{-}2)$$

In this definition, 0! is defined to be 1, and if n is an integer greater than 0, first we find $(n-1)!$ and then multiply it by n. To find $(n-1)!$, we apply the definition again. If $(n-1) > 0$, then we use Equation 14-2; otherwise, we use Equation 14-1. Thus, for an integer n greater than 0, $n!$ is obtained by first finding $(n-1)!$ (that is, $n!$ is reduced to a smaller version of itself) and then multiplying $(n-1)!$ by n.

Let's apply this definition to find 3!. Here $n = 3$. Because $n > 0$, we use Equation 14-2 to obtain:

$$3! = 3 \times 2!$$

Next we find 2!. Here $n = 2$. Because $n > 0$, we use Equation 14-2 to obtain:

$$2! = 2 \times 1!$$

Now to find 1!, we again use Equation 14-2 because $n = 1 > 0$. Thus:

$$1! = 1 \times 0!$$

Finally, we use Equation 14-1 to find 0!, which is 1. Substituting 0! into 1! gives 1! = 1. This gives 2! = 2 $\times$ 1! = 2 $\times$ 1 = 2, which in turn gives 3! = 3 $\times$ 2! = 3 $\times$ 2 = 6.

Note that the solution in Equation 14-1 is direct—that is, the right side of the equation contains no factorial notation. The solution in Equation 14-2 is given in terms of a smaller version of itself. The definition of the factorial as given in Equations 14-1 and 14-2 is called a **recursive definition**. Equation 14-1 is called the **base case**, the case for which the solution is obtained directly; Equation 14-2 is called the **general case** or **recursive case**.

Recursive definition: A definition in which something is defined in terms of a smaller version of itself.

From the previous example, it is clear that:

    1. Every recursive definition must have one (or more) base cases.

    2. The general case must eventually be reduced to a base case.

    3. The base case stops the recursion.

The concept of recursion in computer science works similarly. Here we talk about recursive algorithms and recursive methods. An algorithm that finds the solution to a given problem by reducing the problem to smaller versions of itself is called a **recursive algorithm**. The recursive algorithm must have one or more base cases, and the general solution must eventually be reduced to a base case.

A method that calls itself is called a **recursive method**. That is, the body of the recursive method contains a statement that causes the same method to execute before completing the current call. Recursive algorithms are implemented using recursive methods.

Next, let's write the recursive method that implements the factorial definition.

```java
public static int fact(int num)
{
    if (num == 0)
        return 1;
    else
        return num * fact(num - 1);
}
```

Figure 14-1 traces the execution of the following statement:

```java
System.out.println(fact(4));
```

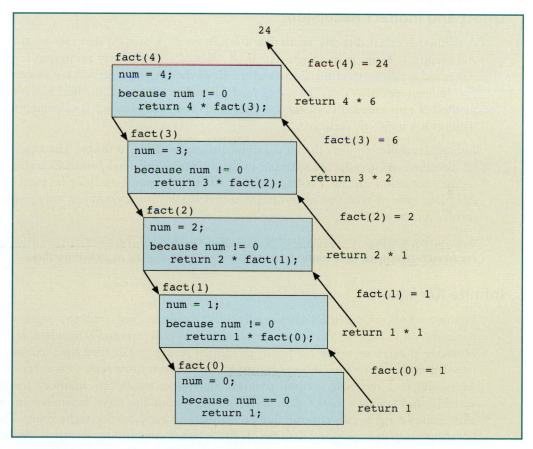

Figure 14-1   Execution of the expression `fact(4)`

The output of the preceding statement is:

24

In Figure 14-1, the downward arrows represent the successive calls to the method `fact`, and the upward arrows represent the values returned to the caller, that is, the calling method.

While tracing the execution of the recursive method `fact`, note the following:

- Logically, you can think of a recursive method as having unlimited copies of itself.

- Every call to a recursive method—that is, every recursive call—has its own code and its own set of parameters and local variables.

- After completing a particular recursive call, control goes back to the calling environment, which is the previous call. The current (recursive) call must execute completely before control goes back to the previous call. The execution in the previous call begins from the point immediately following the recursive call.

Direct and Indirect Recursion

A method is called **directly recursive** if it calls itself. A method that calls another method and eventually results in the original method call is called **indirectly recursive**. For example, if method A calls method B and method B calls method A, then method A is indirectly recursive. Indirect recursion could be several layers deep. For example, if method A calls method B, method B calls method C, method C calls method D, and method D calls method A, then method A is indirectly recursive.

Indirect recursion requires the same careful analysis as direct recursion. The base cases must be identified and appropriate solutions to them must be provided. However, tracing through indirect recursion can be a tedious process. Therefore, extra care must be exercised when designing indirect recursive methods. For simplicity, this book considers only problems that involve direct recursion.

A recursive method in which the last statement executed is the recursive call is called a **tail recursive method**. The method `fact` is an example of a tail recursive method.

Infinite Recursion

Figure 14-1 shows that the sequence of recursive calls reached a call that made no further recursive calls. That is, the sequence of recursive calls eventually reached a base case. However, if every recursive call results in another recursive call, then the recursive method (algorithm) is said to have infinite recursion. In theory, infinite recursion executes forever. Every call to a recursive method requires the system to allocate memory for the local variables and formal parameters. In addition, the system also saves the information so that after completing a call, control can be transferred back to the right caller. Therefore, because computer memory is finite, if you execute an infinite recursive method on a computer, the method will execute until the system runs out of memory, which results in an abnormal termination of the program.

Recursive methods (algorithms) must be carefully designed and analyzed. You must make sure that every recursive call eventually reduces to a base case. The following sections give various examples illustrating how to design and implement recursive algorithms.

To design a recursive method, you must:

1. Understand the problem requirements.

2. Determine the limiting conditions. For example, for a list, the limiting condition is determined by the number of elements in the list.

3. Identify the base cases and provide a direct solution to each base case.

4. Identify the general cases and provide a solution to each general case in terms of a smaller version of itself.

PROBLEM SOLVING USING RECURSION

Examples 14-1 through 14-3 illustrate how recursive algorithms are developed and implemented in Java using recursive methods.

Example 14-1: Largest Element in the Array

In Chapter 9, we used a loop to find the largest element in an array. This example uses a recursive algorithm to find the largest element in an array. Consider the list given in Figure 14-2.

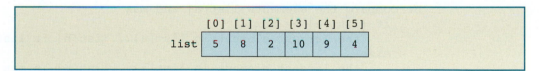

Figure 14-2   List with six elements

The largest element in the list given in Figure 14-2 is 10.

Suppose `list` is the name of the array containing the list elements. Also suppose that `list[a]...list[b]` stands for the array elements `list[a]`, `list[a + 1]`, ..., `list[b]`. For example, `list[0]...list[5]` represents the array elements `list[0]`, `list[1]`, `list[2]`, `list[3]`, `list[4]`, and `list[5]`. Similarly, `list[1]...list[5]` represents the array elements `list[1]`, `list[2]`, `list[3]`, `list[4]`, and `list[5]`. To write a recursive algorithm to find the largest element in `list`, let's think in terms of recursion.

If `list` is of length 1, then `list` has only one element, which is the largest element. Suppose the length of `list` is greater than 1. To find the largest element in `list[a]...list[b]`, we first find the largest element in `list[a + 1]...list[b]` and then compare this largest element with `list[a]`. That is, the largest element in `list[a]...list[b]` is given by:

`maximum(list[a], largest(list[a + 1]...list[b]))`

Let's apply this formula to find the largest element in the list shown in Figure 14-2. This list has six elements, given by `list[0]...list[5]`. Now the largest element in `list` is:

`maximum(list[0], largest(list[1]...list[5]))`

That is, the largest element in `list` is the maximum of `list[0]` and the largest element in `list[1]...list[5]`. To find the largest element in `list[1]...list[5]`, we use the same formula again because the length of this list is greater than 1. The largest element in `list[1]...list[5]` is then:

`maximum(list[1], largest(list[2]...list[5]))`

and so on. Note that every time we use the preceding formula to find the largest element in a sublist, the length of the sublist in the next call is reduced by one. Eventually, the sublist is of length 1, in which case the sublist contains only one element, which in turn is the largest element in the sublist. From this point onward, we backtrack through the recursive calls. This discussion translates into the following recursive algorithm, which is presented in pseudocode:

```
if the size of the list is 1
   the only element in the list is the largest element
else
   to find the largest element in list[a]...list[b]
       a. find the largest element in list[a + 1]...list[b] and call
          it max
       b. compare the elements list[a] and max
          if (list[a] >= max)
              the largest element in list[a]...list[b] is list[a]
          else
              the largest element in list[a]...list[b] is max
```

This algorithm translates into the following Java method to find the largest element in an array:

```
public static int largest(int[] list,
                          int lowerIndex, int upperIndex)
{
    int max;

    if (lowerIndex == upperIndex)    //the size of the sublist is 1
        return list[lowerIndex];
    else
    {
        max = largest(list, lowerIndex + 1, upperIndex);
        if (list[lowerIndex] >= max)
            return list[lowerIndex];
        else
            return max;
    }
}
```

Consider the list given in Figure 14-3.

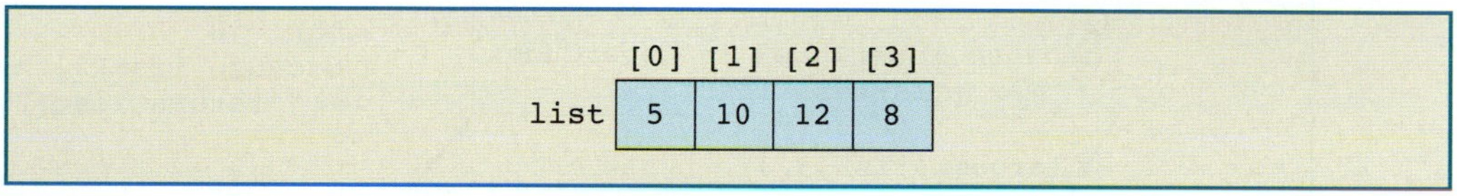

Figure 14-3   List with four elements

Let's trace the execution of the following statement:

```
System.out.println(largest(list, 0, 3));
```

Here **upperIndex** = 3 and the list has four elements. Figure 14-4 traces the execution of `largest(list, 0, 3)`.

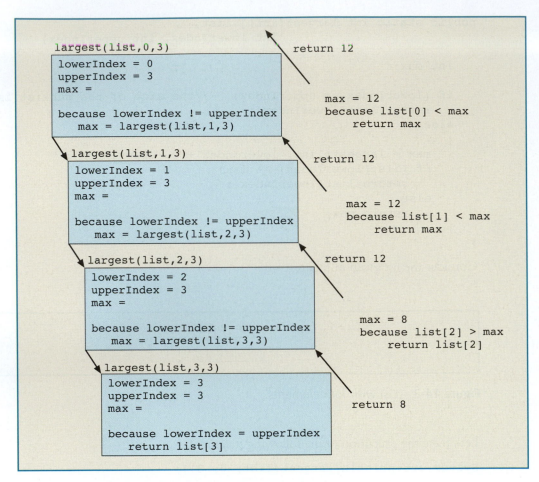

Figure 14-4 Execution of the expression `largest(list, 0, 3)`

The value returned by the expression `largest(list, 0, 3)` is 12, which is the largest element in `list`.

The following Java program uses the method `largest` to determine the largest element in the list:

```
//Recursion: Largest Element in an Array

import java.io.*;

public class largestElementInAnArray
{
```

```
public static void main(String[] args)
{
    int[] intArray = {23, 43, 35, 38, 67, 12, 76, 10, 34, 8};

    System.out.println("The largest element in intArray: "
                + largest(intArray, 0, intArray.length - 1));
}

public static int largest(int[] list,
                          int lowerIndex, int upperIndex)
{
    int max;

    if (lowerIndex == upperIndex)    //the size of the sublist is 1
        return list[lowerIndex];
    else
    {
        max = largest(list, lowerIndex + 1, upperIndex);
        if (list[lowerIndex] >= max)
            return list[lowerIndex];
        else
            return max;
    }
}
}
```

Sample Run:
```
The largest element in intArray: 76
```

Example 14-2: Fibonacci Number

In Chapter 5, we designed a program to determine the desired Fibonacci number. In this example, we write a recursive method, rFibNum, to determine the desired Fibonacci number. The method rFibNum takes as parameters three numbers representing the first two numbers of the Fibonacci sequence and a number n, the desired nth Fibonacci number. The method rFibNum returns the nth Fibonacci number in the sequence.

Recall that the third Fibonacci number is the sum of the first two Fibonacci numbers. The fourth Fibonacci number in a sequence is the sum of the second and third Fibonacci numbers. Therefore, to calculate the fourth Fibonacci number, we add the second Fibonacci number and the third Fibonacci number (which itself is the sum of the first two Fibonacci numbers). The following recursive algorithm calculates the nth Fibonacci number, where a denotes the first Fibonacci number, b the second Fibonacci number, and n the nth Fibonacci number:

$$\text{rFibNum}(a,b,n) = \begin{cases} a & \text{if } n = 1 \\ b & \text{if } n = 2 \\ \text{rFibNum}(a,b,n-1) + \text{rFibNum}(a,b,n-2) & \text{if } n > 2. \end{cases} \quad (14\text{-}3)$$

14

Suppose that we want to determine:

    1. `rFibNum(2, 5, 4)`

Here a = 2, b = 5, and n = 4. That is, we want to determine the fourth Fibonacci number of the sequence whose first number is 2 and whose second number is 5. Because n is 4 > 2,

`rFibNum(2, 5, 4) = rFibNum(2, 5, 3) + rFibNum(2, 5, 2)`

Next, we determine `rFibNum(2, 5, 3)` and `rFibNum(2, 5, 2)`. Let's first determine `rFibNum(2, 5, 3)`. Here, a = 2, b = 5, and n is 3. Because n is 3,

    1.a `rFibNum(2, 5, 3) = rFibNum(2, 5, 2) + rFibNum(2, 5, 1)`

This statement requires that we determine `rFibNum(2, 5, 2)` and `rFibNum(2, 5, 1)`. In `rFibNum(2, 5, 2)`, a = 2, b = 5, and n = 2. Therefore, from the definition given in Equation 14-3, it follows that:

    1.a.1 `rFibNum(2, 5, 2) = 5`

To find `rFibNum(2, 5, 1)`, note that a = 2, b = 5, and n = 1. Therefore, by the definition given in Equation 14-3:

    1.a.2 `rFibNum(2, 5, 1) = 2`

We substitute the values of `rFibNum(2, 5, 2)` and `rFibNum(2, 5, 1)` into (1.a) to get:

`rFibNum(2, 5, 3) = 5 + 2 = 7`

Next we determine `rFibNum(2, 5, 2)`. As in (1.a.1), `rFibNum(2, 5, 2) = 5`. We can substitute the values of `rFibNum(2, 5, 3)` and `rFibNum(2, 5, 2)` into (1) to get:

`rFibNum(2, 5, 4) = 7 + 5 = 12`

The following recursive method implements this algorithm:

```java
public static int rFibNum(int a, int b, int n)
{
    if (n == 1)
        return a;
    else if (n == 2)
            return b;
    else
        return rFibNum(a, b, n - 1) + rFibNum(a, b, n - 2);
}
```

Let's trace the execution of the following statement:

`System.out.println(rFibNum(2, 3, 5));`

In this statement, the first number is 2, the second number is 3, and we want to determine the 5th Fibonacci number of the sequence. Figure 14-5 traces the execution of the expression `rFibNum(2, 3, 5)`. The value returned is 13, which is the 5th Fibonacci number of the sequence whose first number is 2 and whose second number is 3.

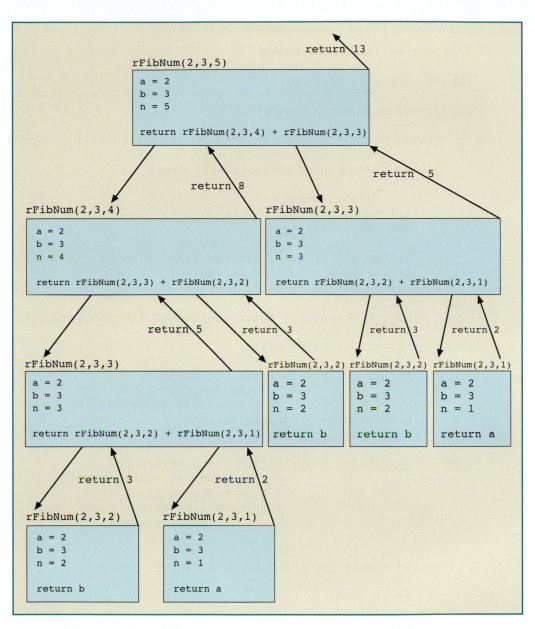

Figure 14-5   Execution of the expression `rFibNum(2, 3, 5)`

14

The following Java program uses the method `rFibNum`:

```java
//Recursion: Fibonacci Number

import java.util.*;

public class FibonacciNumber
{
    static Scanner console = new Scanner(System.in);

    public static void main(String[] args)
    {
        int firstFibNum;
        int secondFibNum;
        int nthFibonacci;

        System.out.print("Enter the first Fibonacci number: ");
        firstFibNum = console.nextInt();
        System.out.println();

        System.out.print("Enter the second Fibonacci number: ");
        secondFibNum = console.nextInt();
        System.out.println();

        System.out.print("Enter the position "
                        + "of the desired number in "
                        + "the Fibonacci sequence: ");
        nthFibonacci = console.nextInt();
        System.out.println();

        System.out.println("The " + nthFibonacci
                        + "th Fibonacci number of "
                        + "the sequence is: "
                        + rFibNum(firstFibNum, secondFibNum,
                                    nthFibonacci));
    }

    public static int rFibNum(int a, int b, int n)
    {
        if (n == 1)
            return a;
        else if (n == 2)
                return b;
        else
            return rFibNum(a, b, n - 1) + rFibNum(a, b, n - 2);
    }
}
```

Sample Run: In these sample runs, the user input is shaded.

Sample Run 1:
```
Enter the first Fibonacci number: 2

Enter the second Fibonacci number: 5

Enter the position of the desired number in the Fibonacci sequence: 6

The 6th Fibonacci number of the sequence is: 31
```

Sample Run 2:
```
Enter the first Fibonacci number: 3

Enter the second Fibonacci number: 4

Enter the position of the desired number in the Fibonacci sequence: 6

The 6th Fibonacci number of the sequence is: 29
```

Sample Run 3:
```
Enter the first Fibonacci number: 12

Enter the second Fibonacci number: 18

Enter the position of the desired number in the Fibonacci sequence: 15

The 15th Fibonacci number of the sequence is: 9582
```

Example 14-3: Tower of Hanoi

In the nineteenth century, a game called the Tower of Hanoi was popular in Europe. This game is based on a legend regarding the construction of the temple of Brahma. According to this legend, at the creation of the universe, priests in the temple of Brahma were given three diamond needles, with one needle containing 64 golden disks. Each golden disk is slightly smaller than the disk below it. The priests' task was to move all 64 disks from the first needle to the third needle. The rules for moving the disks are as follows:

1. Only one disk can be moved at a time.

2. The removed disk must be placed on one of the needles.

3. A larger disk cannot be placed on top of a smaller disk.

14

The priests were told that once they had moved all the disks from the first needle to the third needle, the universe would come to an end.

Our objective is to write a program that prints the sequence of moves needed to transfer the disks from the first needle to the third needle. Figure 14-6 shows the Tower of Hanoi problem with three disks.

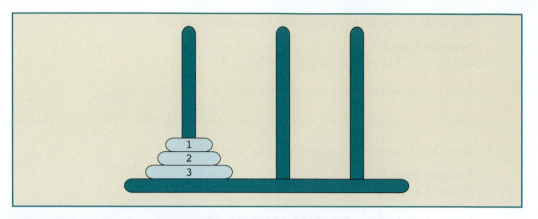

Figure 14-6   Tower of Hanoi problem with three disks

As before, we think in terms of recursion. Let's first consider the case where the first needle contains only one disk. In this case, the disk can be moved directly from needle 1 to needle 3. Now let's consider the case when the first needle contains only two disks. In this case, first we move the first disk from needle 1 to needle 2, and then we move the second disk from needle 1 to needle 3. Finally, we move the first disk from needle 2 to needle 3. Next, we consider the case where the first needle contains three disks, and then generalize this to the case of 64 disks (in fact, to an arbitrary number of disks).

Suppose that needle 1 contains three disks. To move disk number 3 to needle 3, the top two disks must first be moved to needle 2. Disk number 3 can then be moved from needle 1 to needle 3. To move the top two disks from needle 2 to needle 3, we use the same strategy as before. This time we use needle 1 as the intermediate needle. Figure 14-7 shows a solution to the Tower of Hanoi problem with three disks.

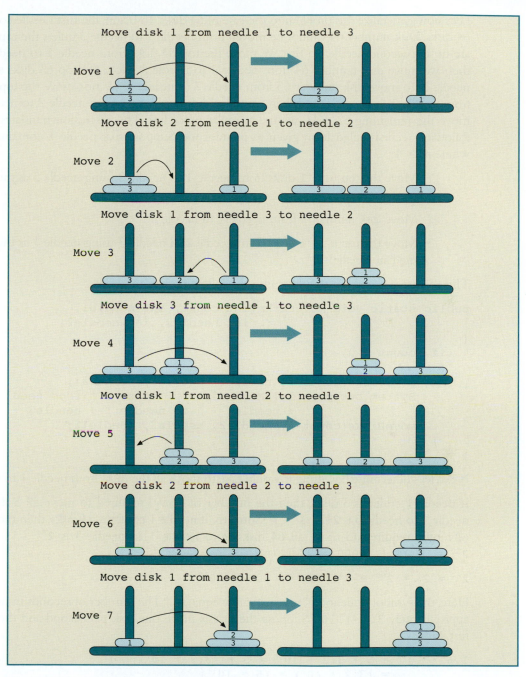

Figure 14-7   Solution to the Tower of Hanoi problem with three disks

Let's now generalize this problem to the case of 64 disks. To begin, the first needle contains all 64 disks. Disk number 64 cannot be moved from needle 1 to needle 3 unless the top 63 disks are on the second needle. So first we move the top 63 disks from needle 1 to needle 2, and then we move disk number 64 from needle 1 to needle 3. Now the top 63 disks are all on needle 2. To move disk number 63 from needle 2 to needle 3, we first move the top 62 disks from needle 2 to needle 1, and then we move disk number 63 from needle 2 to needle 3. To move the remaining 62 disks, we use a similar procedure. This discussion translates into the following recursive algorithm given in pseudocode. Suppose that needle 1 contains n disks, where $n \geq 1$.

1. Move the top $n - 1$ disks from needle 1 to needle 2 using needle 3 as the intermediate needle.

2. Move disk number n from needle 1 to needle 3.

3. Move the top $n - 1$ disks from needle 2 to needle 3 using needle 1 as the intermediate needle.

This recursive algorithm translates into the following Java method:

```java
public static void moveDisks(int count, int needle1,
                             int needle3, int needle2)
{
    if (count > 0)
    {
        moveDisks(count-1, needle1, needle2, needle3);
        System.out.println("Move disk " + count + " from needle "
                           + needle1 + " to needle " + needle3 + ".");
        moveDisks(count-1, needle2, needle3, needle1);
    }
}
```

Next, let's determine how long it would take to move all the disks from needle 1 to needle 2.

If needle 1 contains 3 disks, then the number of moves required to move all 3 disks from needle 1 to needle 3 is $2^3 - 1 = 7$. Similarly, if needle 1 contains 64 disks, then the number of moves required to move all 64 disks from needle 1 to needle 3 is $2^{64} - 1$. Because $2^{10} = 1024 \approx 1000 = 10^3$,

$$2^{64} = 2^4 * 2^{60} \approx 2^4 * 10^{18} = 1.6 * 10^{19}$$

Here, the symbol $\approx$ denotes "approximately equal to." The number of seconds in one year is approximately $3.2 * 10^7$. Suppose the priests move one disk per second and they do not rest. Now,

$$1.6 * 10^{19} = 5 * 3.2 * 10^{18} = 5 * (3.2 * 10^7) * 10^{11}$$
$$= (3.2 * 10^7) * (5 * 10^{11})$$

Thus, the time required to move all 64 disks from needle 1 to needle 3 is roughly $5 * 10^{11}$ years. It is estimated that our universe is about 15 billion $= 1.5 * 10^{10}$ years old.

Also, $5 * 10^{11} = 50 * 10^{10} \approx 33 * (1.5 * 10^{10})$. This calculation shows that our universe would last about 33 times as long as it already has.

Assume that a computer can generate 1 billion or 10^9 moves per second. Then the number of moves that the computer can generate in one year is:

$(3.2 * 10^7) * 10^9 = 3.2 * 10^{16}$

So the computer time required to generate 2^{64} moves is:

$2^{64} \approx 1.6 * 10^{19} = 1.6 * 10^{16} * 10^3 = (3.2 * 10^{16}) * 500$

Thus, it would take about 500 years for the computer to generate 2^{64} moves at the rate of 1 billion moves per second.

RECURSION OR ITERATION?

In Chapter 5, we designed a program to determine a desired Fibonacci number. That program used a loop to perform the calculation. In other words, the programs in Chapter 5 used an iterative control structure to repeat a set of statements. More formally, **iterative control structures** use a looping structure, such as **while**, **for**, or **do...while**, to repeat a set of statements. In Example 14-2, we designed a recursive method to calculate a Fibonacci number. From the examples in this chapter, it follows that in recursion, a set of statements is repeated by having the method call itself. Moreover, a selection control structure is used to control the repeated calls in recursion.

Similarly, in Chapter 9, we used an iterative control structure (a **for** loop) to determine the largest element in a list. In this chapter, we use recursion to determine the largest element in a list. In addition, this chapter began by designing a recursive method to find the factorial of a non-negative integer. Using an iterative control structure, we can also write an algorithm to find the factorial of a non-negative integer. The only reason we gave a recursive solution to a factorial problem is to illustrate how recursion works.

We thus see that there are usually two ways to solve a particular problem—recursion and iteration. The obvious question is, which method is better—recursion or iteration? There is no simple answer. In addition to the nature of the problem, the other key factor in determining the best solution method is efficiency.

When we traced the execution of the program in Example 7-11 (Chapter 7), we saw that whenever a method is called, memory space for its formal parameters and (automatic) local variables is allocated. When the method terminates, that memory space is then deallocated.

In this chapter, while tracing the execution of recursive methods, we see that every (recursive) call also has its own set of parameters and local variables. That is, every (recursive) call requires that the system allocate memory space for its formal parameters and local variables, and then deallocate the memory space when the method exits. Thus, overhead is associated with executing a (recursive) method, both in terms of memory space and computer time.

14

Therefore, a recursive method executes more slowly than its iterative counterpart. On slower computers, especially those with limited memory space, the (slow) execution of a recursive method would be noticeable.

Today's computers, however, are fast and have inexpensive memory. Therefore, the execution of a recursive method is not so noticeable. Keeping in mind the power of today's computers, the choice between iteration or recursion depends on the nature of the problem. Of course, for problems such as mission control systems, efficiency is absolutely critical and, therefore, the efficiency factor dictates the solution method.

As a general rule, if you think an iterative solution is more obvious and easier to understand than a recursive solution, use the iterative solution, which is more efficient. On the other hand, problems exist for which the recursive solution is more obvious or easier to construct, such as the Tower of Hanoi problem. (In fact, it turns out that it is difficult to construct an iterative solution for the Tower of Hanoi problem.) Keeping in mind the power of recursion, if the definition of a problem is inherently recursive, then you should consider a recursive solution.

PROGRAMMING EXAMPLE: CONVERTING A NUMBER FROM DECIMAL TO BINARY

This programming example discusses and designs a program that uses recursion to convert a non-negative integer in decimal format—that is, base 10—into the equivalent binary number—that is, base 2. First we define some terms.

Let **x** be a non-negative integer. We call the remainder of **x** after division by 2 the **rightmost bit** of **x**.

Thus, the rightmost bit of 33 is 1 because 33 % 2 is 1, and the rightmost bit of 28 is 0 because 28 % 2 is 0.

We first use an example to illustrate the algorithm to convert an integer in base 10 to the equivalent number in binary format.

Suppose we want to find the binary representation of 35. First, we divide 35 by 2. The quotient is 17 and the remainder—that is, the rightmost bit of 35—is 1. Next we divide 17 by 2. The quotient is 8 and the remainder—that is, the rightmost bit of 17—is 1. Next we divide 8 by 2. The quotient is 4 and the remainder—that is, the rightmost bit of 8—is 0. We continue this process until the quotient becomes 0.

The rightmost bit of 35 cannot be printed until we have printed the rightmost bit of 17. The rightmost bit of 17 cannot be printed until we have printed the rightmost bit of 8, and so on. Thus, the binary representation of 35 is the binary representation of 17 (that is, the quotient of 35 after division by 2), followed by the rightmost bit of 35.

Thus, to convert a non–negative integer num in base 10 into the equivalent binary number, we first convert the quotient num / 2 into an equivalent binary number, and then append the rightmost bit of num to the binary representation of num / 2.

This discussion translates into the following recursive algorithm, where binary(num) denotes the binary representation of num:

    1. binary(num) = num if num = 0.

    2. binary(num) = binary(num / 2) followed by num % 2 if num > 0.

The following recursive method implements this algorithm:

```java
public static void decToBin(int num, int base)
{
    if (num > 0)
    {
        decToBin(num / base, base);
        System.out.print(num % base);
    }
}
```

Figure 14-8 traces the execution of the following statement:

```java
decToBin(13, 2);
```

where num is 13 and base is 2.

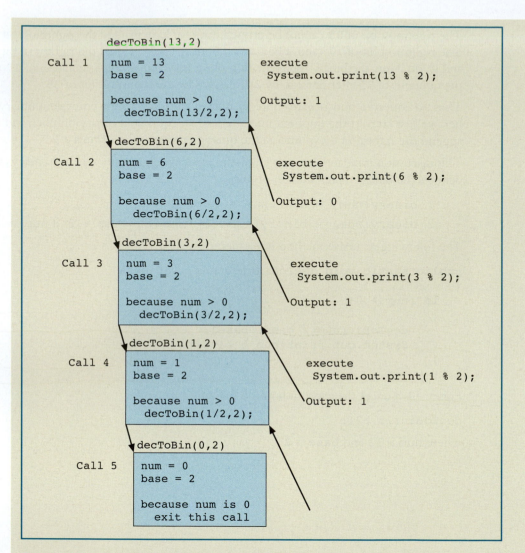

Figure 14-8   Execution of the statement `decToBin(13, 2);`

Because the **if** statement in Call 5 fails, this call does not print anything. The first out-put is produced by Call 4, which prints 1; the second output is produced by Call 3, which prints 1; the third output is produced by Call 2, which prints 0; and the fourth output is produced by Call 1, which prints 1. Thus, the output of the statement:

`decToBin(13, 2);`

is:

1101

The following Java program tests the method `decToBin`:

```
//Recursion: Program - Decimal to Binary

import java.util.*;

public class DecimalToBinary
{
    static Scanner console = new Scanner(System.in);

    public static void main(String[] args)
    {
        int decimalNum;
        int base;

        base = 2;

        System.out.print("Enter a positive integer in decimal: ");
        decimalNum = console.nextInt();
        System.out.println();

        System.out.print("Decimal " + decimalNum + " = ");
        decToBin(decimalNum, base);
        System.out.println(" binary");
    }

    public static void decToBin(int num, int base)
    {
        if (num > 0)
        {
            decToBin(num / base, base);
            System.out.print(num % base);
        }
    }
}
```

Sample Run: In this sample run, the user input is shaded.
```
Enter a positive integer in decimal: 57

Decimal 57 = 111001 binary
```

PROGRAMMING EXAMPLE: SIERPINSKI GASKET

To draw the shapes of natural scenes such as mountains, trees, and clouds, graphic programmers typically use special mathematical tools, called **fractals**, related to fractal geometry. Fractal geometry is a major area of research in mathematics in its own right. The term fractal was introduced by the mathematician Benoit Mandelbrot in the late 1970s. Roughly speaking, a fractal is a geometric shape in which certain patterns repeat, perhaps at a different scale and orientation. Mandelbrot is credited to be the first person to demonstrate that fractals occur in various places in mathematics and nature.

Because in a fractal certain patterns occur at various places, a convenient and effective way to write programs to draw fractals is to use recursion. This section describes a special type of fractal called a **Sierpinski gasket**.

Suppose that you have the triangle *ABC* as given in Figure 14-9(a). Now determine the midpoints *P*, *Q*, and *R* of the sides *AB*, *AC*, and *BC*, respectively. Next, draw the lines *PQ*, *QR*, and *PR*. This creates three triangles, *APQ*, *BPR*, and *CRQ*, as shown in Figure 14-9(b), that have similar shapes as in the triangle *ABC*. The process of finding the midpoints of the sides and then drawing lines through those midpoints is now repeated on each of the triangles *APQ*, *BPR*, and *CRQ*, as shown in Figure 14-9(c). Figure 14-9(a) is called a Sierpinski gasket of order (or level) 0; Figure 14-9(b) is called a Sierpinski gasket of order (or level) 1; Figure 14-9(c) is called a Sierpinski gasket of order (or level) 2; and Figure14-9(d) shows a Sierpinski gasket of order (or level) 3.

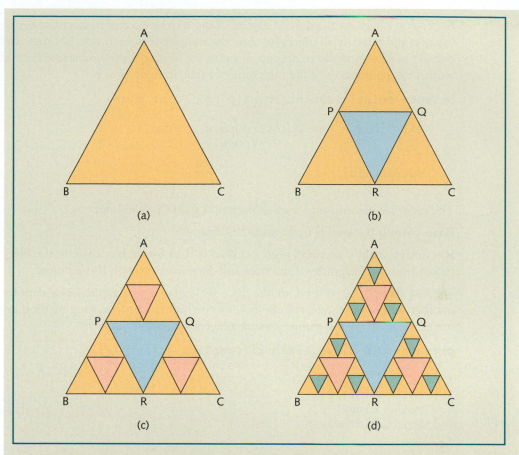

Figure 14-9   Sierpinski gaskets of various orders (levels)

Input   A non-negative integer indicating the level of the Sierpinski gasket.

Output   A triangle shape displaying a Sierpinski gasket of the given order.

Problem Analysis and Algorithm Design

The problem is as described previously. Initially, we specify the coordinates of the first triangle and then draw the triangle. We use the **class** Point, as described in Appendix E, to store the *x-y* coordinates of a point. We also use the method drawLine, as described in Chapter 13, to draw a line between two points.

For each triangle, we need three objects of the **class** Point to store the vertices of the triangle, and three more objects to store the midpoints of each side. Because we frequently need to find the midpoints of a line, we write the method midPoint, which returns the coordinates of the midpoint of a line. Its definition is:

```
private Point midPoint(Point pOne, Point pTwo)
{
    Point mid = new Point((pOne.x + pTwo.x) / 2,
                          (pOne.y + pTwo.y) / 2 );

    return mid;
}
```

The recursive algorithm to draw a Sierpinski gasket is as follows:

Base case: If the level is 0, draw the first triangle.

Recursive case: If the level is greater than 0, then for each triangle in the Sierpinski gasket, find the midpoints of the sides and draw lines through those points.

Suppose that p1, p2, and p3 are the three vertices of a triangle, and lev denotes the number of levels of the Sierpinski gasket to be drawn. The following method implements the recursive algorithm to draw a Sierpinski gasket:

```
private void drawSierpinski(Graphics g, int lev,
                            Point p1, Point p2, Point p3)
{
    Point midP1P2;
    Point midP2P3;
    Point midP3P1;

    if (lev > 0)
    {
        g.drawLine(p1.x, p1.y, p2.x, p2.y);
        g.drawLine(p2.x, p2.y, p3.x, p3.y);
        g.drawLine(p3.x, p3.y, p1.x, p1.y);

        midP1P2 = midPoint(p1, p2);
        midP2P3 = midPoint(p2, p3);
        midP3P1 = midPoint(p3, p1);

        drawSierpinski(g, lev - 1, p1, midP1P2, midP3P1);
        drawSierpinski(g, lev - 1, p2, midP2P3, midP1P2);
        drawSierpinski(g, lev - 1, p3, midP3P1, midP2P3);
    }
}
```

The following program listing provides the complete algorithm to draw a Sierpinski gasket of a given order. Notice that the program uses an input dialog box to get the user's input.

Complete Program Listing

```java
//Java program to draw a SierpinskiGasket

import java.awt.*;
import javax.swing.*;

public class SierpinskiGasket extends JApplet
{
    int level = 0;

    public void init()
    {
        String levelStr = JOptionPane.showInputDialog
                          ("Enter the recursion depth: ");

        level = Integer.parseInt(levelStr);
    }

    public void paint(Graphics g)
    {
        Point pointOne = new Point(60, 160);
        Point pointTwo = new Point(220, 160);
        Point pointThree = new Point(140, 20);

        drawSierpinski(g, level, pointOne, pointTwo, pointThree);
    }

    private void drawSierpinski(Graphics g, int lev,
                                Point p1, Point p2, Point p3)
    {
        Point midP1P2;
        Point midP2P3;
        Point midP3P1;

        if (lev > 0)
        {
            g.drawLine(p1.x, p1.y, p2.x, p2.y);
            g.drawLine(p2.x, p2.y, p3.x, p3.y);
            g.drawLine(p3.x, p3.y, p1.x, p1.y);

            midP1P2 = midPoint(p1, p2);
            midP2P3 = midPoint(p2, p3);
            midP3P1 = midPoint(p3, p1);

            drawSierpinski(g, lev - 1, p1, midP1P2, midP3P1);
            drawSierpinski(g, lev - 1, p2, midP2P3, midP1P2);
```

```
                        drawSierpinski(g, lev - 1, p3, midP3P1, midP2P3);
                }
        }

        private Point midPoint(Point pOne, Point pTwo)
        {
                Point mid = new Point((pOne.x + pTwo.x) / 2,
                                       (pOne.y + pTwo.y) / 2 );

                return mid;
        }
}
```

Sample Run: In these sample runs, the user input is entered in input dialog boxes.

Sample Run 1: Figure 14-10 shows Sample Run 1.

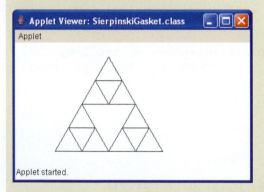

Figure 14-10   Recursion depth of 3 produces a Sierpinski gasket of order 2

Sample Run 2: Figure 14-11 shows Sample Run 2.

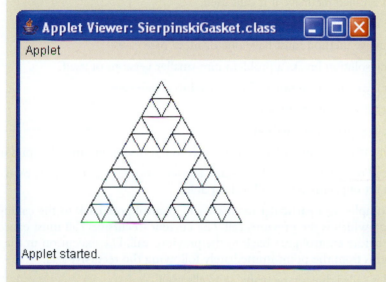

Figure 14-11   Recursion depth of 4 produces a Sierpinski gasket of order 3

QUICK REVIEW

1. The process of solving a problem by reducing it to smaller versions of itself is called recursion.

2. A recursive definition defines the problem in terms of smaller versions of itself.

3. Every recursive definition has one or more base cases.

4. A recursive algorithm solves a problem by reducing it to smaller versions of itself.

5. Every recursive algorithm has one or more base cases.

6. The solution to a problem in a base case is obtained directly.

7. A method is called recursive if it calls itself.

8. Recursive algorithms are implemented using recursive methods.

9. Every recursive method must have one or more base cases.

10. The general solution breaks a problem into smaller versions of itself.

11. The general case must eventually be reduced to a base case.

12. The base case stops the recursion.

13. While tracing a recursive method:

    a. Logically, you can think of a recursive method as having unlimited copies of itself.

    b. Every call to a recursive method—that is, every recursive call—has its own code and its own set of parameters and local variables.

    c. After completing a particular recursive call, control goes back to the calling environment, which is the previous call. The current (recursive) call must execute completely before control goes back to the previous call. The execution in the previous call begins from the point immediately following the recursive call.

14. A method is called directly recursive if it calls itself.

15. A method that calls another method and eventually results in the original method call is said to be indirectly recursive.

16. A recursive method in which the last statement executed is the recursive call is called a tail recursive method.

17. To design a recursive method, you must do the following:

    a. Understand the problem requirements.

    b. Determine the limiting conditions. For example, for a list, the limiting condition is determined by the number of elements in the list.

    c. Identify the base cases and provide a direct solution to each base case.

    d. Identify the general case(s) and provide a solution to each general case in terms of smaller versions of itself.

EXERCISES

1. Mark the following statements as true or false.

   a. Every recursive definition must have one or more base cases.

   b. Every recursive method must have one or more base cases.

   c. The general case stops the recursion.

   d. In the general case, the solution to the problem is obtained directly.

   e. A recursive method always returns a value.

2. What is a base case?

3. What is a recursive case?

4. What is direct recursion?

5. What is indirect recursion?

6. What is tail recursion?

7. Consider the following recursive method:

```
public static int mystery(int number)        //Line 1
{
    if (number == 0)                          //Line 2
        return number;                        //Line 3
    else                                      //Line 4
        return(number + mystery(number - 1)); //Line 5
}
```

   a. Identify the base case.

   b. Identify the general case.

   c. What valid values can be passed as parameters to the method `mystery`?

   d. If `mystery(0)` is a valid call, what is its value? If not, explain why.

   e. If `mystery(5)` is a valid call, what is its value? If not, explain why.

   f. If `mystery(-3)` is a valid call, what is its value? If not, explain why.

8. Consider the following recursive method:

```
public static void funcRec(int u, char v)               //Line 1
{
    if (u == 0)                                         //Line 2
        System.out.print(v);                           //Line 3
    else if (u == 1)                                   //Line 4
            System.out.print((char)((int)(v) + 1));    //Line 5
    else                                               //Line 6
        funcRec(u - 1, v);                             //Line 7
}
```

14

Answer the following questions:

a. Identify the base case.

b. Identify the general case.

c. What is the output of the following statement?

```
funcRec(5,'A');
```

9. Consider the following recursive method:

```java
public static void exercise(int x)
{
    if (x > 0 && x < 10)
    {
        System.out.print(x + " ");
        exercise(x + 1);
    }
}
```

What is the output of the following statements?

a. `exercise(0);`

b. `exercise(5);`

c. `exercise(10);`

d. `exercise(-5);`

10. Consider the following method:

```java
public static int test(int x, int y)
{
    if (x == y)
        return x;
    else if (x > y)
            return (x + y);
    else
        return test(x + 1, y - 1);
}
```

What is the output of the following statements?

a. `System.out.println(test(5, 10));`

b. `System.out.println(test(3, 9));`

11. Consider the following method:

```java
public static int Func(int x)
{
    if (x == 0)
        return 2;
    else if (x == 1)
            return 3;
    else
        return (Func(x - 1) + Func(x - 2));
}
```

What is the output of the following statements?

a. `System.out.println(Func(0));`

b. `System.out.println(Func(1));`

c. `System.out.println(Func(2));`

d. `System.out.println(Func(5));`

12. Suppose that `intArray` is an array of integers and `length` specifies the number of elements in `intArray`. Also, suppose that `low` and `high` are two integers such that `0 <= low < length, 0 <= high < length` and `low < high`. That is, `low` and `high` are two indices in `intArray`. Write a recursive definition that reverses the elements in `intArray` between `low` and `high`.

13. Write a recursive definition to multiply two positive integers m and n using repeated addition.

PROGRAMMING EXERCISES

1. Write a recursive method that takes as a parameter a non-negative integer and generates the following pattern of stars. If the non-negative integer is 4, then the pattern generated is:

```
****
***
**
*
*
**
***
****
```

Also, write a program that prompts the user to enter the number of lines in the pattern and uses the recursive method to generate the pattern. For example, specifying the number of lines to be 4 generates the preceding pattern.

2. Write a recursive method to generate a pattern of stars such as the following:

```
*
**
***
****
****
***
**
*
```

Also, write a program that prompts the user to enter the number of lines in the pattern and uses the recursive method to generate the pattern. For example, specifying the number of lines to be 4 generates the preceding pattern.

14

3. Write a recursive method to generate the following pattern of stars:

Also, write a program that prompts the user to enter the number of lines in the pattern and uses the recursive method to generate the pattern. For example, specifying the number of lines to be 4 generates the preceding pattern.

4. Write a recursive method, **vowels**, that returns the number of vowels in a string. Also, write a program to test your method.

5. Write a recursive method that finds and returns the sum of the elements of an **int** array. Also, write a program to test your method.

6. A palindrome is a string that reads the same both forward and backward. For example, the string "**madam**" is a palindrome. Write a program that uses a recursive method to check whether a string is a palindrome. Your program must contain a value-returning recursive method that returns **true** if the string is a palindrome and **false** otherwise. Use appropriate parameters in your method.

7. Write a program that uses a recursive method to print a string backward. Your program must contain a recursive method that prints the string backward. Use appropriate parameters in your method.

8. Write a recursive method, **reverseDigits**, that takes an integer as a parameter and returns the number with the digits reversed. Also, write a program to test your method.

9. Write a recursive method, **power**, that takes as parameters two integers x and y such that x is nonzero and returns x^y. You can use the following recursive definition to calculate x^y. If $y \geq 0$,

$$power(x, y) = \begin{cases} 1 & \text{if } y = 0 \\ x & \text{if } y = 1 \\ x * power(x, y-1) & \text{if } y > 1. \end{cases}$$

If $y < 0$,

$$power(x, y) = \frac{1}{power(x, -y)}.$$

Also, write a program to test your method.

10. **Greatest Common Divisor.** Given two integers x and y, the following recursive definition determines the greatest common divisor of x and y, written $gcd(x,y)$:

$$gcd(x, y) = \begin{cases} x & \text{if } y = 0 \\ gcd(y, x\%y) & \text{if } y \neq 0 \end{cases}$$

(*Note*: In this definition, % is the mod operator.)

Write a recursive method, **gcd**, that takes as parameters two integers and returns the greatest common divisor of the numbers. Also, write a program to test your method.

11. Write a recursive method to implement the recursive definition of Exercise 12 (reversing the elements of an array between two indices). Also, write a program to test your method.

12. Write a recursive method to implement the recursive definition of Exercise 13 (multiply two positive integers using repeated addition). Also, write a program to test your method.

13. In the Programming Example, Converting a Number from Decimal to Binary, given in this chapter, you learned how to convert a decimal number into its equivalent binary number. Two more number systems, octal (base 8) and hexadecimal (base 16), are of interest to computer scientists.

The digits in the octal number system are 0, 1, 2, 3, 4, 5, 6, and 7. The digits in the hexadecimal number system are 0, 1, 2, 3, 4, 5, 6, 7, 8, 9, A, B, C, D, E, and F. So A in hexadecimal is 10 in decimal, B in hexadecimal is 11 in decimal, and so on.

The algorithm to convert a positive decimal number into an equivalent number in octal (or hexadecimal) is the same as that discussed for binary numbers. Here we divide the decimal number by 8 (for octal) and by 16 (for hexadecimal). Suppose a_b represents the number a to the base b. For example, 75_{10} means 75 to the base 10 (that is decimal), and 83_{16} means 83 to the base 16 (that is, hexadecimal). Then:

$753_{10} = 1361_8$
$753_{10} = 2F1_{16}$

The method of converting a decimal number to base 2, or 8, or 16 can be extended to any arbitrary base. Suppose you want to convert a decimal number n into an equivalent number in base b, where b is between 2 and 36. You then divide the decimal number n by b as in the algorithm for converting decimal to binary.

Note that the digits in, say base 20, are 0, 1, 2, 3, 4, 5, 6, 7, 8, 9, A, B, C, D, E, F, G, H, I, and J.

Write a program that uses a recursive method to convert a number in decimal to a given base b, where b is between 2 and 36. Your program should prompt the user to enter the number in decimal and in the desired base.

Test your program on the following data:

9098 and base 20

692 and base 2

753 and base 16

14

14. **Converting a Number from Binary to Decimal.** The language of a computer, called machine language, is a sequence of 0s and 1s. When you press the A key on the keyboard, `01000001` is stored in the computer. Note that the collating sequence of A in the Unicode character set is `65`. In fact, the binary representation of A is 01000001 and the decimal representation of A is 65.

   The numbering system we use is called the decimal system, or base 10 system. The numbering system that the computer uses is called the binary system, or base 2 system. This chapter described how to convert a decimal number into an equivalent binary number. The purpose of this exercise is to write a program to convert a number from base 2 to base 10.

   To convert a number from base 2 to base 10, we first find the weight of each bit in the binary number. The weight of each bit in the binary number is assigned from right to left. The weight of the rightmost bit is 0. The weight of the bit immediately to the left of the rightmost bit is 1, the weight of the bit immediately to the left of it is 2, and so on. Consider the binary number `1001101`. The weight of each bit is as follows:

   ```
   weight    6  5  4  3  2  1  0
             1  0  0  1  1  0  1
   ```

   We use the weight of each bit to find the equivalent decimal number. For each bit, we multiply the bit by 2 to the power of its weight and then add all of the numbers. For the above binary number, the equivalent decimal number is:

   $$1 * 2^6 + 0 * 2^5 + 0 * 2^4 + 1 * 2^3 + 1 * 2^2 + 0 * 2^1 + 1 * 2^0$$

   $$= 64 + 0 + 0 + 8 + 4 + 0 + 1$$

   $$= 77$$

   To write a program that converts a binary number into the equivalent decimal number, we note two things: (1) the weight of each bit in the binary number must be known; and (2) the weight is assigned from right to left. Because we do not know in advance how many bits are in the binary number, we must process the bits from right to left. After processing a bit, we can add 1 to its weight, giving the weight of the bit immediately to its left. Also, each bit must be extracted from the binary number and multiplied by 2 to the power of its weight. To extract a bit, you can use the mod operator. Write a method that converts a binary number into an equivalent decimal number. Moreover, write a program and test your method for the following values: `11000101`, `10101010`, `11111111`, `10000000`, and `1111100000`.

15. Write a program that uses recursion to draw a Koch snowflake fractal of any given order. A Koch snowflake of order 0 is an equilateral triangle. To create the next-higher-order fractal, each line segment in the shape is modified by replacing its middle third with a sharp protrusion made of two line segments, each having the same length as the replaced one, as shown in Figure 14-12.

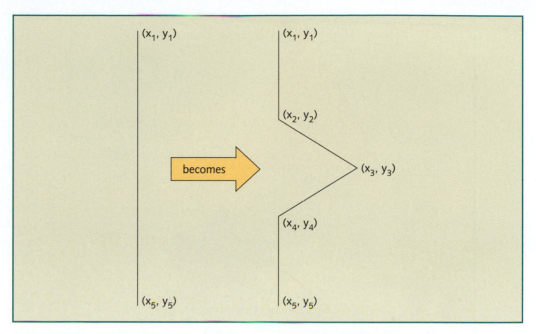

Figure 14-12   Line segments for Koch snowflakes

Here is the necessary information to compute the three new points (x_2, y_2), (x_3, y_3), and (x_4, y_4) in terms of (x_1, y_1) and (x_5, y_5).

Let:

```
deltaX = x₅ - x₁
deltaY = y₅ - y₁
```

Then:

```
x₂ = x₁ + deltaX / 3,
y₂ = y₁ + deltaY / 3,

x₃ = 0.5 * (x₁ + x₅) + √3 * (y₁ - y₅) / 6,
y₃ = 0.5 * (y₁ + y₅) + √3 * (x₅ - x₁) / 6,

x₄ = x₁ + 2 * deltaX / 3,
y₄ = y₁ + 2 * deltaY / 3,
```

The first three Koch snowflakes produced by the program might look like Figure 14–13.

14

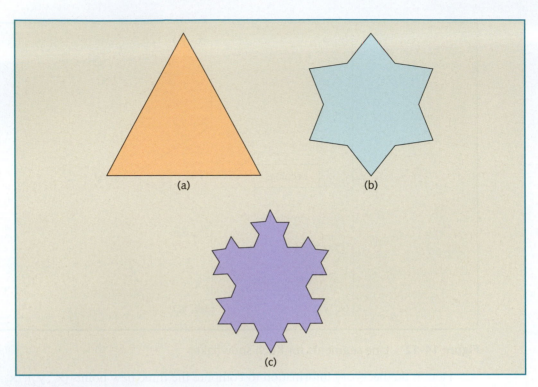

Figure 14-13 First three Koch snowflakes

15

GENERIC METHODS, CLASSES, AND ARRAY-BASED LISTS

In this chapter, you will:

- Learn about the **interface**s Cloneable and Comparable and how to implement them
- Learn about generic methods and classes
- Learn how to implement generic array-based lists
- Explore how various operations, such as search, insert, and remove, are implemented on lists

In the next few chapters, we discuss and create various data structures, such as array-based lists, linked lists, and binary trees. Rather than create the data structures for a specific application, we'll create generic data structures. This allows us to create the data structure without concern for the type of data to be manipulated. Therefore, before describing array-based lists, we discuss generic methods and generic classes. In addition, to create generic data structures, we also discuss sorting and searching algorithms. One of the common operations performed on a set of data is to search the data for a specific item. This means that we must be able to compare data items. Moreover, sometimes to improve the efficiency of algorithms, such as search, the data items must be in a specific order, such as ascending or descending. Primitive type data can be compared using relational operators, and wrapper and **String** classes provide the method **compareTo** to compare objects of the same class. The data structures that we design not only manipulate data composed of built-in types but also user-defined types. The built-in types that we use to create data have the necessary methods to process data. To force user-defined classes to provide certain methods, such as the method **compareTo**, that are necessary to manipulate data, in the first part of this chapter we describe the two interfaces **Cloneable** and **Comparable**.

THE `interface Cloneable`

In Chapter 11, we discussed the **class** Object and its methods. Among others, one of the methods discussed is `clone`. This is a **protected** method. So it is inherited, but it cannot be invoked by an object outside the definition of its class. For example, in a user program, an object cannot invoke the method `clone` of the **class** Object. The default definition of the `clone` method provides a bit-by-bit copy of the object's data in storage. In other words, it provides a shallow copy of object's data. Therefore, to meet with the specific requirement, every class provides its own definition of the `clone` method. Until now we have avoided the direct implementation of the `clone` method within a class. However, to make a deep copy of an object's data, we included the methods `getCopy` and `makeCopy`. In this section, we discuss how to override the default definition of the method `clone` in a class.

To force a class to provide an appropriate definition of the method `clone`, that class must implement the **interface** Cloneable. In reality, the **interface** Cloneable has no method headings that need to be implemented. Moreover, it has no defined constant. So what is the purpose of this **interface**? When you define a class that implements the **interface** Cloneable, you must redefine the `clone` method (inherited from the super class or the **class** Object) in a particular way.

As mentioned previously, the method `clone` (of the **class** Object) does a bit-by-bit copy of an object's data in storage. If the object's data is composed only of primitive type data or data of immutable objects, such as Integer or String objects, then the bit-by-bit copy works as required and has no unintended side effects. However, if the data in the object being cloned contains instance variables that refer to mutable objects, such as Clock objects, then the bit-by-bit copy would cause shallow copying of mutable objects data, because the instance variables of two different objects would refer to the same mutable object. (When we discuss the method `clone` of the **class** PersonalInfo later in this section, we show how to explicitly clone objects of such instance variables. Moreover, shallow and deep copy are discussed in detail in Chapter 8.)

When a **class** implements the Cloneable **interface**, that **class** must override the definition of the `clone` method of its super class or the **class** Object. When writing the definition of the method `clone` in a class, first we invoke the `clone` method of the **class** Object (or whatever the super class is). If the class has instance variables whose type is a mutable class, then we change the values of those instance variables. (We will illustrate this when we include the method `clone` in the **class** PersonalInfo described later in this section.) Moreover, the method `clone` of the **class** Object throws CloneNotSupportedException, which must be handled. We explain this with the help of an example.

In Chapter 8, we defined the **class** Clock. Suppose we want to include the method `clone` in that class. We start by indicating that the **class** Clock implements the **interface**

Cloneable and include the method **clone** as a **public** member of the **class** Clock. Therefore, the heading of the **class** Clock is:

```
public class Clock implements Cloneable
```

Next we provide the definition of the method **clone**. Because the instance variables **hr**, **min**, and **sec** of the **class** Clock are of the primitive type **int**, a bit-by-bit copy of object's data in storage is enough. This is accomplished by invoking the method **clone** of the super class—in this case the **class** Object. Because the method **clone** of the **class** Object throws CloneNotSupportedException, this exception must be handled appropriately. The complete definition of the method **clone** for the **class** Clock is:

```
public Object clone()
{
    try
    {
        return super.clone();   //Invoke the method clone of
                                //the super class

    }
    catch (CloneNotSupportedException e)
    {
        return null;
    }
}
```

Note that the method **clone** returns a reference of the type **Object** or the value **null**.

Next consider the following statements:

```
Clock myClock = new Clock(5, 4, 30);    //Line 1
Clock tempClock;                         //Line 2
```

The statement in Line 1 creates the **Clock** object **myClock** and sets the hours, minutes, and seconds to **5**, **4**, and **30**, respectively. The statement in Line 2 declares the **Clock** reference variable **tempClock**. Next consider the following statement:

```
tempClock = (Clock) myClock.clone();
```

This statement creates a clone of the object **myClock** and assigns the reference of the clone object to the variable **tempClock**. Note that the expression **myClock.clone()** returns a reference of the **Object** type. Therefore, we must type cast the returned reference to a reference of the **Clock** type. Next we give the complete definition of the **class** Clock.

Because we have now included the method **clone** in the **class** Clock, we no longer need the methods **getCopy** and **makeCopy**. The modified definition of the **class** Clock is:

15

```
//class Clock

public class Clock implements Cloneable
{
    private int hr;  //store hours
    private int min; //store minutes
    private int sec; //store seconds

        //Default constructor
        //Postcondition: hr = 0; min = 0; sec = 0
    public Clock()
    {
        setTime(0, 0, 0);
    }

        //Constructor with parameters
        //The time is set according to the parameters
        //Postcondition: hr = hours; min = minutes; sec = seconds
    public Clock(int hours, int minutes, int seconds)
    {
        setTime(hours, minutes, seconds);
    }

        //Copy constructor
        //The time is set according to the time of otherClock
        //Postcondition: hr = otherClock.hr;
        //               min = otherClock.min;
        //               sec = otherClock.sec
    public Clock(Clock otherClock)
    {
        setTime(otherClock.hr, otherClock.min, otherClock.sec);
    }

        //Method clone
        //Postcondition: Returns a reference of the copy of
        //               object's data.
    public Object clone()
    {
        try
        {
            return super.clone();
        }
        catch (CloneNotSupportedException e)
        {
            return null;
        }
    }
```

```java
    //Method to set the time
    //The time is set according to the parameters
    //Postcondition: hr = hours; min = minutes;
    //                   sec = seconds
    public void setTime(int hours, int minutes, int seconds)
    {
        if (0 <= hours && hours < 24)
            hr = hours;
        else
            hr = 0;

        if (0 <= minutes && minutes < 60)
            min = minutes;
        else
            min = 0;

        if (0 <= seconds && seconds < 60)
            sec = seconds;
        else
            sec = 0;
    }


    //Method to return the hours
    //Postcondition: The value of hr is returned.
    public int getHours()
    {
        return hr;
    }


    //Method to return the minutes
    //Postcondition: The value of min is returned.
    public int getMinutes()
    {
        return min;
    }


    //Method to return the seconds
    //Postcondition: The value of sec is returned.
    public int getSeconds()
    {
        return sec;
    }
```

15

```java
    //Method to increment the time by one second
    //Postcondition: The time is incremented by one second.
    //If the before-increment time is 23:59:59, the time
    //is reset to 00:00:00.
public void incrementSeconds()
{
    sec++;

    if (sec > 59)
    {
        sec = 0;
        incrementMinutes(); //increment minutes
    }
}

    //Method to increment the time by one minute
    //Postcondition: The time is incremented by one minute.
    //If the before-increment time is 23:59:53, the time
    //is reset to 00:00:53.
public void incrementMinutes()
{
    min++;

    if (min > 59)
    {
        min = 0;
        incrementHours(); //increment hours
    }
}

    //Method to increment the time by one hour
    //Postcondition: The time is incremented by one hour.
    //If the before-increment time is 23:45:53, the time
    //is reset to 00:45:53.
public void incrementHours()
{
    hr++;

    if (hr > 23)
        hr = 0;
}

    //Method to compare the two times
    //Postcondition: Returns true if this time is equal to
    //               otherClock; otherwise returns false
public boolean equals(Clock otherClock)
{
    return (hr == otherClock.hr
            && min == otherClock.min
```

```
                   && sec == otherClock.sec);
    }

    public String toString()
    {
        String str = "";

        if (hr < 10)
            str = "0";
        str = str + hr + ":";

        if (min < 10)
            str = str + "0" ;
        str = str + min + ":";

        if (sec < 10)
            str = str + "0";
        str = str + sec;

        return str;
    }
}
```

The program in Example 15-1 shows how the method `clone` of the **class** `Clock` works.

Example 15-1

```
public class ClockCloneTestProg
{
    public static void main(String[] args)
    {
        Clock myClock = new Clock(5, 4, 30);           //Line 1

        System.out.println("Line 2: myClock: "
                           + myClock);                 //Line 2

        Clock tempClock = (Clock) myClock.clone();     //Line 3

        System.out.println("Line 4: tempClock: "
                           + tempClock);               //Line 4

        if (myClock == tempClock)                      //Line 5
            System.out.println("Line 6: myClock "
                               + "and tempClock "
                               + "refer to the "
                               + "same object.");      //Line 6
        else                                           //Line 7
            System.out.println("Line 8: myClock "
```

15

```
                                + "and tempClock do "
                                + "not refer to the "
                                + "same object.");        //Line 8

        myClock.setTime(12, 28, 33);                      //Line 9

        System.out.println("Line 10: After "
                            + "changing the time, "
                            + "myClock: "
                            + myClock);                   //Line 10

        System.out.println("Line 11: tempClock: "
                            + tempClock);                 //Line 11
    }//end main
}
```

Sample Run:
```
Line 2: myClock: 05:04:30
Line 4: tempClock: 05:04:30
Line 8: myClock and tempClock do not refer to the same object.
Line 10: After changing the time, myClock: 12:28:33
Line 11: tempClock: 05:04:30
```

The preceding program works as follows. The statement in Line 1 creates the **Clock** object **myClock** and sets the hours, minutes, and seconds to **5**, **4**, and **30**, respectively. The statement in Line 2 outputs the time of **myClock**.

The statement in Line 3 creates a clone of **myClock** and stores the reference of the clone in **tempClock**. The statement in Line 4 outputs the time of **tempClock**.

The statement in Line 5 determines whether **myClock** and **tempClock** refer to the same **Clock** object. The output of the statement in Line 8 shows that they do not refer to the same **Clock** object. The statement in Line 9 sets the time of **myClock** to **12:28:33**. The statement in Line 10 outputs the time of **myClock**. The statement in Line 11 outputs the value of **tempClock**.

From the output of Lines 10 and 11 it is clear that the statement in Line 9 only sets the time of **myClock**.

Just as we can include the method **clone** in the **class** **Clock**, we can also include the method **clone** in the **class**es **Person**, defined in Chapter 8, and the **class** **Date**, defined in Chapter 11. Because we will refer to these **class**es in the next example, we provide their definitions for easy references:

```
public class Person implements Cloneable
{
    private String firstName; //store the first name
    private String lastName;  //store the last name
```

```java
    //Default constructor;
    //Initialize firstName and lastName to empty string
    //Postcondition: firstName = ""; lastName = "";
public Person()
{
    firstName = "";
    lastName = "";
}

    //Constructor with parameters
    //Set firstName and lastName according to the parameters
    //Postcondition: firstName = first; lastName = last;
public Person(String first, String last)
{
    firstName = first;
    lastName = last;
}

    //Method clone
    //Postcondition: Returns a reference of the copy of
    //               object's data.
public Object clone()
{
    try
    {
        return super.clone();
    }
    catch (CloneNotSupportedException e)
    {
        return null;
    }
}

    //Method to return the first name and last name
    //as a string in the form firstName lastName
public String toString()
{
    return (firstName + " " + lastName);
}

    //Method to set firstName and lastName according to
    //the parameters
    //Postcondition: firstName = first; lastName = last;
public void setName(String first, String last)
{
    firstName = first;
    lastName = last;
}
```

15

```java
    //Method to return the firstName
    //Postcondition: the value of firstName is returned
public String getFirstName()
{
    return firstName;
}

    //Method to return the lastName
    //Postcondition: the value of lastName is returned
public String getLastName()
{
    return lastName;
}
}
```

The definition of the **class** Date is:

```java
public class Date implements Cloneable
{
    private int dMonth;        //variable to store the month
    private int dDay;          //variable to store the day
    private int dYear;         //variable to store the year


        //Default constructor
        //The instance variables dMonth, dDay, and dYear are
        //set to the default values.
        //Postcondition: dMonth = 1; dDay = 1; dYear = 1900;
    public Date()
    {
        dMonth = 1;
        dDay = 1;
        dYear = 1900;
    }

        //Constructor with parameters
        //The instance variables dMonth, dDay, and dYear are
        //set according to the parameters.
        //Postcondition: dMonth = month; dDay = day;
        //                    dYear = year;
    public Date(int month, int day, int year)
    {
        dMonth = month;
        dDay = day;
        dYear = year;
    }
```

```java
    //Method clone
    //Postcondition: Returns a reference of the copy of
    //               object's data.
public Object clone()
{
    try
    {
        return super.clone();
    }
    catch (CloneNotSupportedException e)
    {
        return null;
    }
}


    //Method to set the date
    //The instance variables dMonth, dDay, and dYear are
    //set according to the parameters.
    //Postcondition: dMonth = month; dDay = day;
    //               dYear = year;
public void setDate(int month, int day, int year)
{
    dMonth = month;
    dDay = day;
    dYear = year;
}


    //Method to return the month
    //Postcondition: The value of dMonth is returned.
public int getMonth()
{
    return dMonth;
}


    //Method to return the day
    //Postcondition: The value of dDay is returned.
public int getDay()
{
    return dDay;
}


    //Method to return the year
    //Postcondition: The value of dYear is returned.
public int getYear()
{
    return dYear;
}
```

15

```
    //Method to return the date in the form mm-dd-yyyy
public String toString()
{
    return (dMonth + "-" + dDay + "-" + dYear);
}
}
```

Next we illustrate how to write the definition of the method `clone` in a class that has instance variables that are references to mutable objects.

In Chapter 11, we defined the **class** `PersonalInfo` to keep track of a person's name, date of birth, and ID. The instance variables of the **class** `PersonalInfo` are:

```
private Person name;
private Date bDay;
private int personID;
```

The instance variable `name` is a reference variable of the type `Person` whose objects are mutable. Similarly, the instance variable `bDay` is a reference to a mutable object. Therefore, when we write the definition of the method `clone` for the **class** `PersonalInfo`, after making a bit-by-bit copy of object's data in storage, we need to explicitly clone the objects `name` and `bDay`. Therefore, the definition of the method `clone` for the **class** `PersonalInfo` is:

```
public Object clone()
{
    try
    {
        PersonalInfo copy = (PersonalInfo) super.clone();

        copy.bDay = (Date) bDay.clone();      //explicitly clone
                                              //the object bDay
        copy.name = (Person) name.clone();    //explicitly clone
                                              //the object name

        return copy;
    }
    catch (CloneNotSupportedException e)
    {
        return null;
    }
}
```

The complete definition of the **class** `PersonalInfo` is:

```
public class PersonalInfo implements Cloneable
{
    private Person name;
    private Date bDay;
    private int personID;
```

```java
    //Default constructor
    //Instance variables are set to the default values
    //Postcondition: firstName = ""; lastName = "";
    //                dMonth = 1; dDay = 1; dYear = 1900;
    //                personID = 0;
public PersonalInfo()
{
    name = new Person();
    bDay = new Date();
    personID = 0;
}


    //Constructor with parameters
    //Instance variables are set according to the parameters
    //Postcondition: firstName = first; lastName = last;
    //                dMonth = month; dDay = day;
    //                dYear = year; personID = ID;
public PersonalInfo(String first, String last, int month,
                    int day, int year, int ID)
{
    name = new Person(first, last);
    bDay = new Date(month, day, year);
    personID = ID;
}


    //Method clone
    //Postcondition: Returns a reference of the copy of
    //                object's data.
public Object clone()
{
    try
    {
        PersonalInfo copy = (PersonalInfo) super.clone();

        copy.bDay = (Date) bDay.clone(); //explicitly clone
                                         //the object bDay
        copy.name = (Person) name.clone(); //explicitly
                                           //clone the object name

        return copy;
    }
    catch (CloneNotSupportedException e)
    {
        return null;
    }
}
```

15

```
        //Method to set the personal information
        //Instance variables are set according to the parameters
        //Postcondition: firstName = first; lastName = last;
        //                dMonth = month; dDay = day; dYear = year;
        //                personID = ID;
    public void setpersonalInfo(String first, String last,
                                int month, int day,
                                int year, int ID)
    {
        name.setName(first, last);
        bDay.setDate(month, day, year);
        personID = ID;
    }

        //Method to return the string containing
        //personal information
    public String toString()
    {
        return ("Name: " + name.toString() + "\n"
              + "Date of birth: " + bDay.toString() + "\n"
              + "Personal ID: " + personID);
    }
}
```

The program in Example 15-2 shows how the method **clone** of the **class** PersonalInfo works.

Example 15-2

```
public class TestProgPersonalInfo
{
    public static void main(String[] args)
    {
        PersonalInfo student =
                new PersonalInfo("William", "Jordan",
                                 8, 24, 1963,
                                 555238911);        //Line 1

        System.out.println("Line 2: student: "
                          + student);                //Line 2
        System.out.println();                        //Line 3

        PersonalInfo temp =
                (PersonalInfo) student.clone(); //Line 4

        System.out.println("Line 5: temp: "
                          + temp);                   //Line 5
```

```
        System.out.println();                        //Line 6

        student.setpersonalInfo("Mary", "Smith",
                            11, 22, 1953,
                            888434343);               //Line 7

        System.out.println("Line 8: student: "
                        + student);                   //Line 8
        System.out.println();                         //Line 9

        System.out.println("Line 10: temp: "
                        + temp);                      //Line 10
    }
}
```

Sample Run:
```
Line 2: student: Name: William Jordan
Date of birth: 8-24-1963
Personal ID: 555238911

Line 5: temp: Name: William Jordan
Date of birth: 8-24-1963
Personal ID: 555238911

Line 8: student: Name: Mary Smith
Date of birth: 11-22-1953
Personal ID: 888434343

Line 10: temp: Name: William Jordan
Date of birth: 8-24-1963
Personal ID: 555238911
```

The preceding program works as follows. The statement in Line 1 creates the **PersonalInfo** object **student**. The statement in Line 2 outputs the value of the object to which **student** points.

The statement in Line 4 declares **temp** to be a **PersonalInfo** reference variable and assigns the reference of a clone of **student**. The statement in Line 5 outputs the value of the object to which **temp** points.

The statement in Line 7 changes the value of the object to which **student** points. The statements in Lines 8 and 10 output the values of the objects to which **student** and **temp** point, respectively. Note that the statement in Line 7 changes only the value of the object to which **student** points, not the object to which **temp** points. It follows that the statement in Line 4 creates a true clone of the object to which **student** points.

15

THE interface Comparable

The preceding section described the **interface** Cloneable and discussed how to implement the method clone. Recall that when a **class** implements the **interface** Cloneable, it must provide an appropriate definition of the method clone to override the method clone of its super class. Another **interface** of our interest is Comparable. The **interface** Comparable has only one method heading, which is compareTo.

The **interface** Comparable is used to force a **class** to provide an appropriate definition of the method compareTo so that the values of two objects of that **class** can be properly compared. To do so, we make that **class** implement the **interface** Comparable. For example, to force the **class** Clock, defined in Chapter 8, to provide an appropriate definition of the method compareTo, we make this class implement the **interface** Comparable. Therefore, the heading of the **class** Clock is:

```
public class Clock implements Comparable
```

Next we include the following method compareTo in the definition of the **class** Clock:

```
public int compareTo(Object otherClock)
{
    Clock temp = (Clock) otherClock;

    int hrDiff = hr - temp.hr;

    if (hrDiff != 0)
        return hrDiff;

    int minDiff = min - temp.min;

    if (minDiff != 0)
        return minDiff;

    return sec - temp.sec;
}
```

The complete definition of the **class** Clock, that implements the **interfaces** Cloneable and Comparable, is available at the Web site accompanying this book. Note that in this definition of the **class** Clock we have slightly changed the definition of the method equals to be compatible with the method equals of the **class** Object. To be specific, the definition of the method equals is:

```
public boolean equals(Object otherClock)
{
    Clock temp = (Clock) otherClock;

    return (hr == temp.hr
            && min == temp.min
            && sec == temp.sec);
}
```

The program in Example 15-3 illustrates how the method `compareTo` of the **class** Clock works.

Example 15-3

```java
public class TestProgClockCompareToMethod
{
    public static void main(String[] args)
    {
        Clock myClock = new Clock(3, 8, 22);         //Line 1
        Clock yourClock = new Clock(13, 5, 18);      //Line 2
        Clock tempClock = new Clock(3, 8, 22);       //Line 3

        System.out.println("Line 4: myClock: "
                           + myClock);               //Line 4
        System.out.println("Line 5: yourClock: "
                           + yourClock);             //Line 5
        System.out.println("Line 6: tempClock: "
                           + tempClock);             //Line 6

        if (myClock.compareTo(yourClock) == 0)       //Line 7
            System.out.println("Line 8: the time "
                              + "of myClock is "
                              + "the same as the "
                              + "time of "
                              + "yourClock.");        //Line 8
        else if (myClock.compareTo(yourClock) < 0)   //Line 9
            System.out.println("Line 10: the time "
                              + "of myClock is "
                              + "less than the "
                              + "time of "
                              + "yourClock.");        //Line 10
        else                                          //Line 11
            System.out.println("Line 12: the time "
                              + "of myClock is "
                              + "greater than the "
                              + "time of "
                              + "yourClock.");        //Line 12

        if (myClock.compareTo(tempClock) == 0)       //Line 13
            System.out.println("Line 14: the time "
                              + "of myClock is "
                              + "the same as the "
                              + "time of "
                              + "tempClock.");        //Line 14
        else if (myClock.compareTo(tempClock) < 0)   //Line 15
            System.out.println("Line 16: the time "
                              + "of myClock is "
                              + "less than the "
```

15

```
                                     + "time of "
                                     + "tempClock.");        //Line 16
                        else                                 //Line 17
                           System.out.println("Line 18: the time "
                                     + "of myClock is "
                                     + "greater than the "
                                     + "time of "
                                     + "tempClock.");        //Line 18

        }
    }
}
```

Sample Run:
```
Line 4: myClock: 03:08:22
Line 5: yourClock: 13:05:18
Line 6: tempClock: 03:08:22
Line 10: the time of myClock is less than the time of yourClock.
Line 14: the time of myClock is the same as the time of tempClock.
```

The preceding program works as follows. The statements in Lines 1, 2, and 3 create the
Clock objects myClock, yourClock, and tempClock, respectively. The statements in
Lines 4, 5, and 6 output the values of the Clock objects to which myClock, yourClock,
and tempClock, respectively, point.

The statements in Lines 7 to 12 compare the time of myClock and yourClock and output
the appropriate message.

The statements in Lines 13 to 18 compare the time of myClock and tempClock and output the appropriate message.

 If the **class** Clock implements both the **interface**s Cloneable and
Comparable, then its heading is:

public class Clock **implements** Cloneable, Comparable

In this case, the **class** Clock must provide appropriate definitions of the methods
clone and compareTo. The complete definition of the **class** Clock that implements both the **interface**s Cloneable and Comparable is available at the
Web site accompanying this book.

Just as the **class** Clock implements the **interface** Comparable, the **class**es Person,
Date, and PersonalInfo can also implement this interface. Next we give only the definitions of the method compareTo for each of these classes. The complete definitions of these
classes, including the definition of the method equals, can be found at the Web site accompanying this book.

The definition of the method compareTo of the **class** Person is:

```
public int compareTo(Object otherPerson)
{
    Person temp = (Person) otherPerson;

    if (firstName.equals(temp.firstName)
        && lastName.equals(temp.lastName))
        return 0;
    else if ((lastName.compareTo(temp.lastName) < 0) ||
            ((lastName.equals(temp.lastName) &&
             (firstName.compareTo(temp.firstName) < 0))))
        return -1;
    else
        return 1;
}
```

> **NOTE**
>
> The definition of the method compareTo of the **class** Person can also be written as:
>
> ```
> public int compareTo(Object otherPerson)
> {
>     Person temp = (Person) otherPerson;
>     int retValue;
>
>     retValue = lastName.compareTo(temp.lastName);
>
>     if (retValue == 0)
>         retValue = firstName.compareTo(temp.firstName);
>
>     return retValue;
> }
> ```

The definition of the method compareTo of the **class** Date is:

```
public int compareTo(Object otherDate)
{
    Date temp = (Date) otherDate;

    int yrDiff = dYear - temp.dYear;

    if (yrDiff != 0)
        return yrDiff;
```

15

```
    int monthDiff = dMonth - temp.dMonth;

    if (monthDiff != 0)
        return monthDiff;

    return dDay - temp.dDay;
}
```

The definition of the method compareTo of the **class** PersonalInfo is:

```
public int compareTo(Object other)
{
    PersonalInfo temp = (PersonalInfo) other;

    if (personID == temp.personID
        && name.equals(temp.name)
        && bDay.equals(temp.bDay))
        return 0;
    else if ((name.compareTo(temp.name) < 0) ||
            (name.equals(temp.name) &&
             (bDay.compareTo(temp.bDay) < 0)) ||
            (name.equals(temp.name) && bDay.equals(temp.bDay)
                && personID < temp.personID))
        return -1;
    else
        return 1;
}
```

> **NOTE**
>
> The definition of the method compareTo of the **class** PersonalInfo can also be written as:
>
> ```
> public int compareTo(Object other)
> {
>     PersonalInfo temp = (PersonalInfo) other;
>     int retValue;
>
>     retValue = personID - temp.personID;
>
>     if (retValue == 0)
>         retValue = name.compareTo(temp.name);
>
>     if (retValue == 0)
>         retValue = bDay.compareTo(temp.bDay);
>
>
>     return retValue;
> }
> ```

In the preceding sections, we described the purpose of the **interface**s Cloneable and Comparable and how to implement them. We will refer to the **class**es Clock, Person, Date, and PersonalInfo, when we discuss sorting and searching algorithms as well as when we illustrate how to make a deep copy of a list later in this chapter.

GENERIC METHODS

Suppose that you are working with a program that deals with lists of integers, decimal numbers, and strings. Furthermore, suppose that you frequently need to print the data stored in a list. In this case, we can write three (overloaded) methods: one to print a list of integers, one to print a list of decimal numbers, and one to print a list of strings. For example, you could write the three methods as follows:

```java
public static void print(int ... list)
{
    for (int elem : list)
        System.out.print(elem + " ");
    System.out.println();
}

public static void print(double ... list)
{
    for (double elem : list)
        System.out.print(elem + " ");
    System.out.println();
}

public static void print(String ... list)
{
    for (String elem : list)
        System.out.print(elem + " ");
    System.out.println();
}
```

First note that the formal parameter of the method **print**, in each case, is a variable length parameter. We used a variable length formal parameter so that the actual parameter in a call to the method **print** can be either an array or a list of individual values. Next note that the definition of the method **print** in each case is the same except the type of the formal parameter and the type of the foreach loop control variable.

Because the definition of the method **print** in each case is identical, we can use Java's mechanism of generic methods and write only one definition rather than write three different definitions. Before we give the definition of a generic method **print**, we describe the rules for defining a generic method.

Generic methods are defined using type parameters. Every generic method has a type parameters section that precedes the return type of the method; the type parameters are separated by commas and enclosed in angular brackets, < and >. **Type parameters**, also known as **type variables**, are identifiers that specify generic type names. In a generic method, typically, type parameters are used to do the following:

1. Declare the return type of the method.

2. Declare formal parameters.

3. Declare local variables.

Note that type parameters can represent only reference parameters, *not* primitive types. A skeleton form of a generic method is:

```
modifier(s) <T> methodType methodName(formal parameter list)
{
    //method body
}
```

Here `T` is referred as the type parameter.

 You can declare a reference variable using the type parameter `T`. However, you cannot instantiate objects using the type parameter. For example, if `T` is a type parameter in a generic method, then the statement

```
T ref;
```

is correct. But the statement

```
ref = new T();    //illegal
```

is illegal.

Next let us write the definition of the generic method `print`. However, let us first note the following: Because a type parameter can represent only reference parameters, the type parameter can refer only to **class**es. However, the method `print` prints a list of **int** values as well as a list of **double** values. In Chapter 6, we introduced the wrapper classes to wrap primitive type values into objects and also discussed the autoboxing and auto-unboxing mechanism. Therefore, we can wrap primitive type variables into their respective classes and use the wrapper **class**es objects as actual parameters. We will elaborate on this shortly.

The generic definition of the method `print` is as follows:

```
public static <T> void print(T ... list)      //Line 1
{
    for (T elem : list)                        //Line 2
        System.out.print(elem + " ");          //Line 3
    System.out.println();                      //Line 4
}
```

In Line 1, the type parameter `T` is enclosed between `<` and `>`. Next `T` is used to declare the (variable length) formal parameter `list`. In Line 2, `T` is used to declare the reference variable `elem`.

Suppose that you have the following statements:

```
Integer[] intList = {2, 3, 32, 56};
Double[] numList = {14.56, 32.78, 11.98};
String[] strList = {"Java", "C++", "Basic", "Perl"};
```

Consider the statement:

```
print(intList);
```

In this statement, the actual parameter is `intList`, which is an array wherein each component is an object of the **class Integer**. The output of this statement is:

```
2 3 32 56
```

Similarly, the output of the statement

```
print(numList);
```

is

```
14.56 32.78 11.98
```

The output of the statement

```
print(strList);
```

is

```
Java C++ Basic Perl
```

The program in Example 15–4 further illustrates how the generic method `print` works.

Example 15-4

```
//Generic method print

public class GenericMethodPrint
{
    public static void main(String[] args)
    {
```

15

```
        Integer[] intList = {2, 13, 4, 18, 21,
                             11, 5, 10};              //Line 1

        System.out.print("Line 2: intList: ");       //Line 2
        print(intList);                              //Line 3
        System.out.println();                        //Line 4

        Double[] numList = {12.0, 23.5, 4.6,
                            28.3, 11.25};             //Line 5

        System.out.print("Line 6: numList: ");       //Line 6
        print(numList);                              //Line 7
        System.out.println();                        //Line 8

        String[] strList = {"Java", "C++",
                            "Basic", "Perl"};         //Line 9

        System.out.print("Line 10: strList: ");      //Line 10
        print(strList);                              //Line 11
        System.out.println();                        //Line 12

        Clock[] clockList = new Clock[5];             //Line 13

        clockList[0] = new Clock(12, 5, 12);         //Line 14
        clockList[1] = new Clock(5, 8, 22);          //Line 15
        clockList[2] = new Clock(12, 35, 52);        //Line 16
        clockList[3] = new Clock(2, 16, 42);         //Line 17
        clockList[4] = new Clock(21, 33, 18);        //Line 18

        System.out.print("Line 19: clockList: ");    //Line 19
        print(clockList);                            //Line 20
        System.out.println();                        //Line 21
    }

    public static <T> void print(T ... list)
    {
        for (T elem : list)
            System.out.print(elem + " ");
        System.out.println();
    }
}
```

Sample Run:
```
Line 2: intList: 2 13 4 18 21 11 5 10

Line 6: numList: 12.0 23.5 4.6 28.3 11.25
```

```
Line 10: strList: Java C++ Basic Perl

Line 19: clockList: 12:05:12 05:08:22 12:35:52 02:16:42 21:33:18
```

For the most part, the preceding output is self-explanatory. However, note that the statements in Lines 13 to 18 create the list `clockList` of `Clock` objects. The statement in Line 20 uses the generic method `print` to output the values of the list `clockList`.

Generic Methods and Bounded Type Parameters

The preceding section introduced generic methods and illustrated how a generic method is written and used. More specifically, we wrote the generic method `print` and used it to print lists of number, strings, and `Clock` objects, respectively. Recall that the definition of the method `print` is:

```
public static <T> void print(T ... list)
{
    for (T elem : list)
        System.out.print(elem + " ");
    System.out.println();
}
```

In this method definition, the type parameter `T` can refer to any Java class built-in, such as wrapper and `String`, and user-defined, such as the **class** `Clock`. In other words, there is no restriction on the type parameter `T`. However, there are situations when the type parameter `T` must be restricted. For example, consider the following.

In Chapter 7, when we introduced method overloading, the method `larger` was overloaded to find the larger of two integers, characters, floating-point numbers, or strings. To implement the method `larger`, we need to write four method definitions for the data type: one for `int`, one for `char`, one for `double`, and one for `String`. However, the body of each method is similar. Because a type parameter can represent only reference parameters, we will wrap primitive type values into their respective wrapper classes. Now each of the wrapper class and the **class** `String` contain the method `compareTo` to compare the value of two objects. Therefore, we can use the method `compareTo` when we write the definition of the generic method `larger` to compare the values of two objects (of the same class). Because our method `larger` will work on built-in classes as well as user-defined classes, and because there may be classes whose objects cannot be compared, the type parameter in the definition of the method `larger` must be restricted. In other words, we should allow the use of the method `larger` only for those classes that provide a definition of the method `compareTo`.

Next let us write a generic method to compare the values of two objects of the same type, such as `Integer`, `Double`, and `String`, and return the object with the larger value. Recall that the **interface** `Comparable` contains only one method—`compareTo`. Therefore, to ensure that a class provides an appropriate definition of the method `compareTo`, that class must implement the **interface** `Comparable`.

15

The definition of the generic method `larger` is as follows:

```
public static <T extends Comparable<T> > T larger(T x, T y)
{
    if (x.compareTo(y) >= 0)
        return x;
    else
        return y;
}
```

In the heading of the method `larger`, T represents a generic type. The formal parameters x and y are reference variables of the type T. Moreover, the return type of the method `larger` is T. Let us look at the expression:

```
<T extends Comparable<T> >
```

In this expression, T refers to any type, that is, **class**, that implements the **interface** `Comparable`. Here `Comparable` is known as the **upper bound** of the type parameter T. By default, `Object` is an upper bound. Note the use of the keyword **extends**. `Comparable` is an interface and we typically use the keyword **implements** when a **class** implements an **interface**. However, *when a type parameter declaration bounds a parameter, then we always use the keyword* **extends** *regardless of whether the type parameter extends a* **class** *or an* **interface**. The reason to bound the parameter T in the method `larger` is that the method definition uses the method `compareTo`, and not every **class** provides the method `compareTo`; that is, not all objects can be compared.

The program in Example 15-5 illustrates how to use the method `larger` in a program.

Example 15-5

```
public class GenericMethodLarger
{
    public static void main(String[] args)
    {
        Integer x, y;                                    //Line 1

        x = 45;                                          //Line 2
        y = 50;                                          //Line 3

        System.out.println("Line 4: " +
                            larger(x, y));               //Line 4

        System.out.println("Line 5: " +
                    larger(54, larger(13, 45)));         //Line 5

        System.out.println("Line 6: " +
                    larger(54.78,
                    larger(89.90, 44.34)));              //Line 6
```

```
            System.out.println("Line 7: " +
                      larger("Gym",
                      larger("Hi", "Here")));                //Line 7

            System.out.println("Line 8: " +
                      larger("There",
                      larger("Hi", "Here")));                //Line 8

        Clock myClock = new Clock(12, 34, 56);              //Line 9
        Clock yourClock = new Clock(8, 21, 45);             //Line 10

        System.out.println("Line 11: " +
                  larger(myClock, yourClock));              //Line 11

        System.out.println("Line 12: " +
                  larger(new Clock(6, 12, 34),
                         new Clock(16, 33, 55)));           //Line 12

        System.out.println("Line 13: " +
                  larger(new Clock(6, 12, 34),
                    larger(new Clock(18, 13, 44),
                           new Clock(11, 44, 11))));         //Line 13
    }

    public static <T extends Comparable<T> > T larger(T x, T y)
    {
        if (x.compareTo(y) >= 0)
            return x;
        else
            return y;
    }
}
```

Sample Run:
```
Line 4: 50
Line 5: 54
Line 6: 89.9
Line 7: Hi
Line 8: There
Line 11: 12:34:56
Line 12: 16:33:55
Line 13: 18:13:44
```

15

The preceding program works as follows. The statement in Line 1 declares the `Integer` reference variables x and y. The statement in Line 2 creates an `Integer` object with value 45 and assigns that object to x. Similarly, the statement in Line 3 creates an `Integer` object with value 50 and assigns that object to y. The statement in Line 4 outputs the larger of the values of x and y. The statement in Line 5 outputs the largest of 54, 13, and 45. Similarly, the statement in Line 6 outputs the largest of 54.78, 89.90, and 44.34.

The statement in Line 7 outputs the largest of the strings `"Gym"`, `"Hi"`, and `"Here"`. Similarly, the statement in Line 8 outputs the largest of the strings `"There"`, `"Hi"`, and `"Here"`.

The statements in Lines 9 and 10 create the `Clock` objects `myClock` and `yourClock`. The statement in Line 11 outputs the larger of the values of `myClock` and `yourClock`. The meaning of the remaining statements is similar.

 If you want to bound a type parameter by more than one class (or interface) than in the type parameter declaration, the class names are separated using the symbol &. For example, consider the following expression:

`<T extends Comparable<T> & Cloneable>`

In this declaration, the type parameter T is bounded by the **class**es Comparable and Cloneable.

Generic Classes

Just as you can define generic methods, you can also define generic classes. In this case, the type parameter(s) are enclosed in angular brackets (< and >) and placed after the name of the class. The type parameter may be bounded or unbounded. As before, a type parameter is used to declare variables and generic methods within the class. A typical form of a generic class is:

```
modifier(s) className<T> modifier(s)
{
    //class members
}
```

As in the case of generic methods, generic classes are used to write a single definition for a set of related classes. Later in this chapter we will define a generic class to process various types of lists. Note that generic classes are also known as **parametric classes**. Also, as with generic methods, you can declare reference variables using the type parameter T within the definition of the class. However, you cannot instantiate objects using the type parameter.

 This chapter introduces you to generics in Java. This is a new extension to the Java programming language. To increase the flexibility of generic code, Java also introduces wild card characters that can be used in place of type parameters. More information on generics in Java as well as how to use wild card characters can be found in the article "Generics in the Java Programming Languages," by Gilad Bracha. This article can be found on the Web at `http://java.sun.com/docs/books/tutorial/extra/generics/index.html`.

ARRAY-BASED LISTS

A local hardware store is about to open and needs to maintain a list of items sold. For each item sold, the list should contain the name of the item, an identification number, the price of the item, how many pieces of the item are currently in stock, and so on. Like the list of items sold by the hardware store, we come across various types of lists. For example, we might have a list consisting of employee's data, a list of student's data, a list of sales data, or a list of rental properties. One thing common to all lists is that all elements of a list are of the same type. More formally, we can define a list as follows:

List: A collection of elements of the same type.

The **length** of a list is the number of elements in the list.

Let us consider further the list of items sold by the hardware store. If a particular item is discontinued, it is removed from the list; if a new item is available for sale it is added to the list. Any time an item is sold, the remaining number of pieces in the stock must be updated. If an item goes on sale, its sale price must be updated. All these operations require you to access the elements of the list. As you can see, there are various types of operations performed on a list.

Typically, the operations performed on a list are as follows:

1. Create the list. The list is initialized to an empty state.

2. Determine whether the list is empty.

3. Determine whether the list is full.

4. Find the size of the list.

5. Destroy, or clear, the list.

6. Determine whether an item is the same as a given list element.

7. Insert an item in the list at the specified location.

8. Remove an item from the list at the specified location.

9. Replace an item at the specified location with another item.

10. Retrieve an item from the list from the specified location.

11. Search the list for a given item.

The following interface describes these operations:

```
public interface ArrayListADT<T> extends Cloneable
{
    public boolean isEmpty();
      //Method to determine whether the list is empty.
      //Postcondition: Returns true if the list is empty;
      //                otherwise, returns false.
```

15

```
public boolean isFull();
  //Method to determine whether the list is full.
  //Postcondition: Returns true if the list is full;
  //               otherwise, returns false.

public int listSize();
  //Method to return the number of elements in the list.
  //Postcondition: Returns the value of length.

public int maxListSize();
  //Method to return the maximum size of the list.
  //Postcondition: Returns the maximum number of elements
  //               that can be inserted in the list.

public void print();
  //Method to output the elements of the list.
  //Postcondition: Elements of the list are output on the
  //               standard output device.

public Object clone();
  //Returns a copy of objects data in store.
  //This method clones only the references stored in
  //the array. The objects that the array references
  //point to are not cloned.

public boolean isItemAtEqual(int location, T item);
  //Method to determine whether item is the same as the
  //item in the list at the position specified by location.
  //Postcondition: Returns true if the element in the list
  //               at the position specified by location is
  //               the same as item;
  //               otherwise, returns false.

public void insertAt(int location, T insertItem);
  //Method to insert insertItem in the list at the position
  //specified by location.
  //Postcondition: Starting at location, the elements of
  //               the list are shifted to make room for
  //               insertItem; insertItem is inserted at
  //               the position specified by location and
  //               the length of the list is incremented
  //               by 1. If the list is full or location
  //               is out of range, an appropriate message
  //               is output.

public void insertEnd(T insertItem);
  //Method to insert insertItem at the end of the list.
  //Postcondition: insertItem is inserted at the end of the
  //               list and the length of the list is
```

```
//                  incrmented by 1.
//                  If the list is full, an appropriate
//                  message is output.

public void removeAt(int location);
  //Method to remove the item from the list at the
  //position specified by location.
  //Postcondition: The element at the position specified by
  //               location is removed from the list and
  //               the length of the list is decremented by 1.
  //               If location is out of range, an
  //               appropriate message is output.

public T retrieveAt(int location);
  //Method to retrieve the element from the list at the
  //position specified by location.
  //Postcondition: A reference of the element at the
  //               position specified by location is
  //               returned. If location is out of range,
  //               an appropriate message is output and
  //               null is returned.

public void replaceAt(int location, T repItem);
  //Method to replace the element in the list at
  //the position specified by location with repItem.
  //Postcondition: repItem is inserted in the list at the
  //               position specified by location.
  //               If location is out of range, an
  //               appropriate message is output.

public void clearList();
  //Method to remove all the elements from the list.
  //Postcondition: The length of the list is 0.


public int seqSearch(T searchItem);
  //Method to determine whether searchItem is in the list.
  //Postcondition: If searchItem is found, returns the
  //               location in the array where searchItem
  //               is found; otherwise, returns -1.

public void remove(T removeItem);
  //Method to remove an item from the list.
  //The parameter removeItem specifies the item to
  //be removed.
  //Postcondition: If removeItem is found in the list, it
  //               is removed from the list and length is
  //               decremented by one.
}
```

15

Figure 15-1 shows a UML class diagram of the **interface** `ArrayListADT`. Note that in the UML class diagram of an **interface** the word interface is enclosed within the symbols **<<** and **>>** and placed on top of the interface shown in the first box of the UML class diagram.

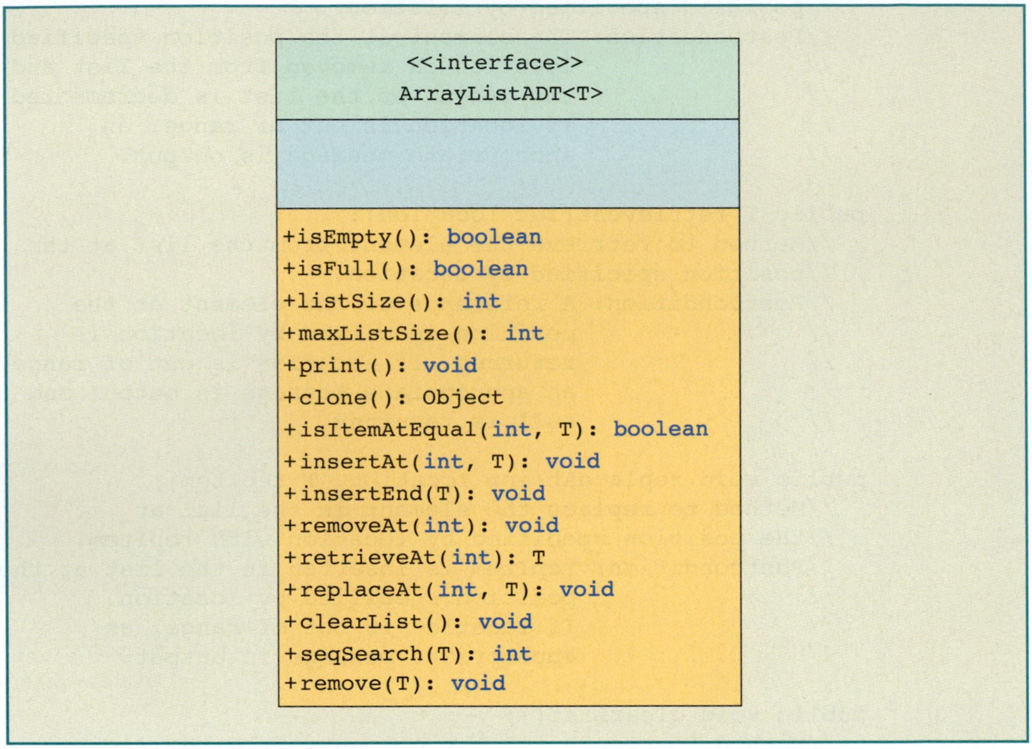

<<interface>>
ArrayListADT<T>

```
+isEmpty(): boolean
+isFull(): boolean
+listSize(): int
+maxListSize(): int
+print(): void
+clone(): Object
+isItemAtEqual(int, T): boolean
+insertAt(int, T): void
+insertEnd(T): void
+removeAt(int): void
+retrieveAt(int): T
+replaceAt(int, T): void
+clearList(): void
+seqSearch(T): int
+remove(T): void
```

Figure 15-1   UML class diagram of the **interface** `ArrayListADT`

Note that the **interface** `ArrayListADT` is generic. The type parameter `T` refers to the class whose objects need to be manipulated.

The list we create can be sorted or unsorted. However, the algorithms to implement certain operations are the same whether the list is sorted or unsorted. For example, a list, sorted or unsorted, is empty if the length of the list is 0. However, the search algorithms for sorted and unsorted lists are typically different. Therefore, next we create the abstract class that implements some of these operations. We will describe the classes to create sorted and unsorted lists separately.

Because all the elements of a list are of the same type, an effective, convenient, and common way to process a list is to store it in an array. Initially, the size of the array holding the list elements is usually larger than the number of elements in the list so that, at a later stage, the list can grow to a specific size. Thus, we must know how full the array is, that is, we must keep track of the number of list elements stored in the array. Java allows the programmer to create dynamic arrays. Therefore, we will leave it for the user to specify the size of the array. The size of the array can be specified when a list object is declared. It follows that, to maintain and process the list in an array, we need the following three variables:

1. The array, `list`, holding the list elements

2. A variable, `length`, to store the length of the list (that is, the number of list elements currently in the array)

3. A variable, `maxSize`, to store the size of the array (that is, the maximum number of elements that can be stored in the array)

The class `ArrayListClass`

In general, we deal with two types of lists—sorted and unsorted. Certain operations on these types of lists are implemented in the same way, while some are implemented differently. For example, the operation to determine whether a list is empty is implemented the same way for both types of lists. Both types of lists are empty if their lengths are `0`. On the other hand, items in an unsorted list can be inserted anywhere, while in a sorted list items must be inserted at the proper place. Therefore, this section describes the class that implements the operations whose implementations are the same for both types of lists. Let us call this **class** `ArrayListClass`. From this class we will derive two classes: one implementing unsorted lists and the other implementing sorted lists.

The **class** `ArrayListClass` does not implement all the operations of the **interface** `ArrayListADT`. We therefore do not want to instantiate objects of the **class** `ArrayListClass`, so we make this an **abstract** class. The following describes the heading, instance variables, constructors, and methods of the **class** `ArrayListClass`.

Class: `ArrayListClass`

```
public abstract class ArrayListClass<T> implements
                                    ArrayListADT<T>, Cloneable
```

Instance variables:

```
protected int length;   //to store the length of the list
protected int maxSize;  //to store the maximum size of
                        //the list
protected T[] list;     //array to hold the list elements
```

Constructors and instance methods:

```
public ArrayListClass()
    //Default constructor
    //Creates an array of size 100
    //Postcondition: list points to the array, length = 0,
    //                and maxSize = 100
```

15

```
public ArrayListClass(int size)
    //Constructor with a parameter
    //Creates an array of the size specified by the
    //parameter size.
    //Postcondition: list points to the array, length = 0,
    //                and maxSize = size

public boolean isEmpty()
    //Method to determine whether the list is empty.
    //Postcondition: Returns true if the list is empty;
    //                otherwise, returns false.

public boolean isFull()
    //Method to determine whether the list is full.
    //Postcondition: Returns true if the list is full;
    //                otherwise, returns false.

public int listSize()
    //Method to return the number of elements in the list.
    //Postcondition: Returns the value of length.

public int maxListSize()
    //Method to return the maximum size of the list.
    //Postcondition: Returns the value of maxSize.

public void print()
    //Method to output the elements of the list.
    //Postcondition: Elements of the list are output on the
    //                standard output device.

public Object clone()
    //Returns a copy of objects data in store.
    //This method clones only the references stored in
    //the array. The objects that the array references
    //point to are not cloned.

public boolean isItemAtEqual(int location, T item)
    //Method to determine whether item is the same as the item
    //in the list at the position specified by location.
    //Postcondition: Returns true if list[location] is the
    //                same as item; otherwise, returns false.

public abstract void insertAt(int location, T insertItem)
    //Method to insert insertItem in the list at the position
    //specified by location.
    //Postcondition: Starting at location, the elements of
    //                the list are shifted to make room for
    //                insertItem, list[location] = insertItem;,
    //                and length++;
```

```
//                      If the list is full or location is out
//                      of range, an appropriate message is
//                      output.

public abstract void insertEnd(T insertItem)
    //Method to insert insertItem at the end of the list.
    //Postcondition: list[length] = insertItem; and length++;
    //               If the list is full, an appropriate
    //               message is output.

public void removeAt(int location)
    //Method to remove the item from the list at the position
    //specified by location.
    //Postcondition: The list element at list[location] is
    //               removed and length is decremented by 1.
    //               If location is out of range, an
    //               appropriate message is output.

public T retrieveAt(int location)
    //Method to retrieve the element from the list at the
    //position specified by location.
    //Postcondition: A reference of the element at the
    //               position specified by location is
    //               returned. If location is out of range,
    //               an appropriate message is output and
    //               null is returned.

public abstract void replaceAt(int location, T repItem)
    //Method to replace the element in the list at
    //the position specified by location with repItem.
    //Postcondition: list[location] = repItem
    //               If location is out of range, an
    //               appropriate message is output.

public void clearList()
    //Method to remove all the elements from the list.
    //Postcondition: length = 0

public abstract int seqSearch(T searchItem);
    //Method to determine whether searchItem is in the list.
    //Postcondition: If searchItem is found, returns the
    //               location in the array where searchItem
    //               is found; otherwise, returns -1.

public abstract void remove(T removeItem);
    //Method to remove an item from the list.
    //The parameter removeItem specifies the item to
    //be removed.
    //Postcondition: If removeItem is found in the list, it is
    //               removed from the list and length is
    //               decremented by one.
```

15

Figure 15-2 shows the class diagram of the **class ArrayListClass**. Note that in the UML class diagram, typically, the name of the **abstract** class and **abstract** methods are shown in *italics*.

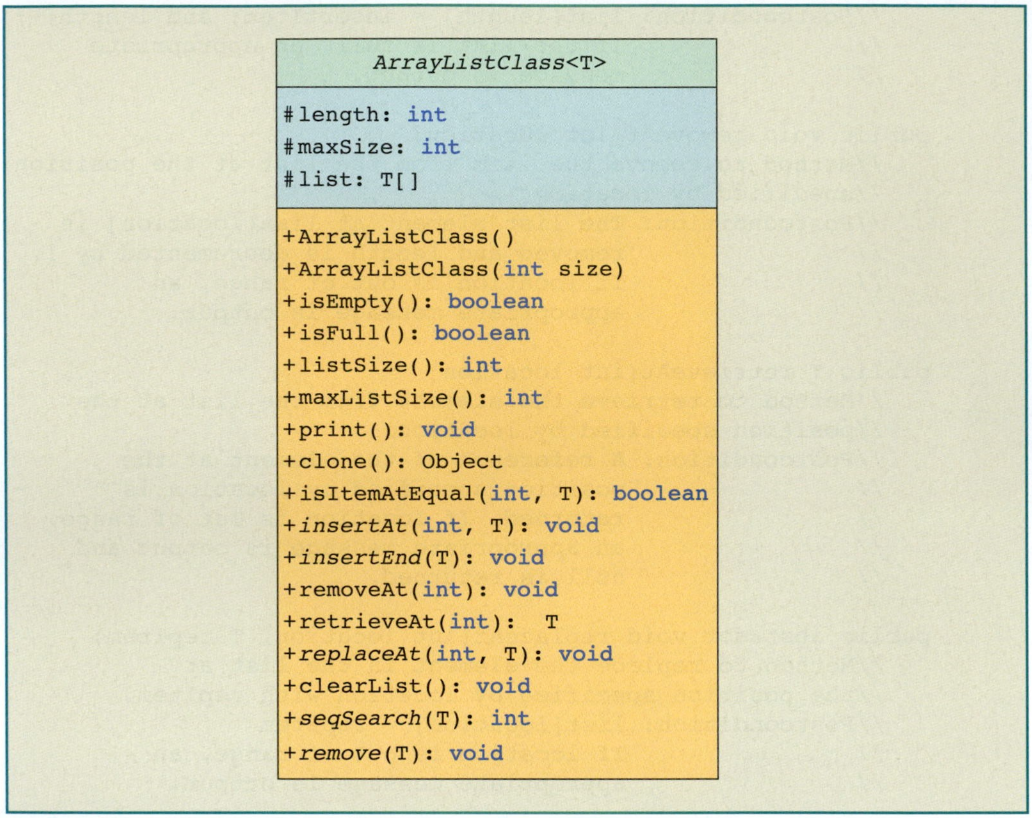

```
                    ArrayListClass<T>

    #length: int
    #maxSize: int
    #list: T[ ]

    +ArrayListClass()
    +ArrayListClass(int size)
    +isEmpty(): boolean
    +isFull(): boolean
    +listSize(): int
    +maxListSize(): int
    +print(): void
    +clone(): Object
    +isItemAtEqual(int, T): boolean
    +insertAt(int, T): void
    +insertEnd(T): void
    +removeAt(int): void
    +retrieveAt(int):   T
    +replaceAt(int, T): void
    +clearList(): void
    +seqSearch(T): int
    +remove(T): void
```

Figure 15-2　UML class diagram of the **class ArrayListClass**

Notice that the instance variables of the **class ArrayListClass** are declared as **protected**. Also notice that the methods **seqsearch**, **insertAt**, **insertEnd**, **insert**, **replaceAt**, and **remove** are declared as **abstract**. This is because, as remarked earlier, we will derive two classes, **class**es **OrderedArrayList** and **UnorderedArrayList**, from **class ArrayListClass**—the first to create sorted lists and the second to create unsorted lists. Because the algorithms to implement the operations search, insert, and remove differ slightly for sorted and unsorted lists, the **class**es **OrderedArrayList** and **UnorderedArrayList** will provide separate definitions for these operations. The **class ArrayListClass** does not need to provide the definitions of these operations. Therefore, it is declared as an **abstract** class. Furthermore, because each of the classes `UnorderedArrayList` and `OrderedArrayList` will provide separate definitions of the methods `seqsearch`, `insertAt`, `insertEnd`, `replaceAt`, and `remove`, and because these methods will access the instance variables, the instance variables of the **class** `ArrayListClass` are declared as **protected** to provide direct access to them.

Next we write the definitions of the nonabstract methods of the **class** `ArrayListClass`.

Constructors

The default constructor creates an array of 100 references. Its definition is:

```
public ArrayListClass()
{
    maxSize = 100;

    length = 0;
    list = (T[]) new Object[maxSize];
}
```

Let us take a look at the statement:

```
list = (T[]) new Object[maxSize];
```

This statement creates an array of references of the type `Object` and then type cast to an array of the type `T`. The obvious question is: Why cannot we instantiate an array of references of the type `T`? The answer is that Java *does not allow* you to instantiate generic type objects. That is why we first instantiate an array of references of the type `Object` and then type cast to an array of the type `T`.

Note that when you compile the preceding statement, you will get the following warning:

```
ArrayListClass.java:18: warning: [unchecked] unchecked cast
found   : java.lang.Object[]
required: T[]
        list = (T[]) new Object[maxSize];
```

The reason for this message is that at this point, the compiler cannot guarantee that the object `list` will not contain objects of the type other than `T`. Suppose `T` represents the type `Integer`. Then the `list` components should refer only to `Integer` objects. Next consider the following statement, which declares `myList` to be an array wherein each component is of the type `Object`:

```
Object[] myList;
```

The following statement makes `myList` refer to the array `list`:

```
myList = list;
```

Now it is possible to assign an object (for example, a `String` object) to the array by using a statement such as the following:

```
myList[0] = "Java";
```

15

However, during program execution, such a statement would result in run-time error. Therefore, if your program does not contain such statements, it should not encounter the run-time error.

The Web site accompanying this book contains the program `GenericMethodPrintAndRunTimeError.java` that shows such a run-time error.

 When you compile a generic class code, you may get warning messages similar to ones shown above. As long as your program does not do anything incompatible, the program should not have run-time errors.

The constructor with parameter uses the size specified by the formal parameter `size` to create an array of references. Its definition is:

```java
public ArrayListClass(int size)
{
    if (size <= 0)
    {
        System.err.println("The array size must be positive. "
                        + "Creating an array of size 100. ");
        maxSize = 100;
    }
    else
        maxSize = size;

    length = 0;
    list = (T[]) new Object[maxSize];
}
```

Note that the preceding code uses the object `System.err`, known as the standard error stream, to generate the output, rather than `System.out`, known as the standard output stream. Both `System.err` and `System.out` are streams, that is, sequences of bytes, and by default they display the output at the command prompt. Typically, `System.out` is used to display a program's output, while `System.err` is used to display a program's error. In fact, the output from these streams can be redirected to devices other than the command prompt. For example, we used file I/O to redirect the output of a program to a file. Using these two streams, a programmer can easily separate the error message from the output of the program. In subsequent chapters, we will use `System.err` to generate error messages.

The method `clone`

The method `clone` creates a copy of the array of references and returns a reference of the created array. Its definition is:

```java
public Object clone()
{
    ArrayListClass<T> copy;
```

```
    try
    {
        copy = (ArrayListClass<T>) super.clone();

    }
    catch (CloneNotSupportedException e)
    {
        return null;
    }

    copy.list = (T[]) list.clone();

    return copy;
}
```

Let us take a look at the definition of the `clone` method. First, the statement

```
copy = (ArrayListClass<T>) super.clone();
```

makes a bit-by-bit copy of the objects data in store. If no exception is thrown, then the statement

```
copy.list = (T[]) list.clone();
```

makes a copy of the references of the array `list`.

> **(Cloning)** We want to stress that the definition of the method `clone` makes only
> a copy of the references stored in the array. In other words, both `list[i]` and
> `copy.list[i]` point to the same object. Therefore, the object to which each
> array element (`list[i]`) points is not cloned. The obvious question is: Why
> didn't we clone each object to which each array element (`list[i]`) points? We
> don't because it is not possible to do so.
>
> To clone each object, we need the following statement before the **return** statement:
>
> ```
> for (int i = 0; i < length; i++)
>     copy.list[i] = (T) list[i].clone();
> ```
>
> However, this statement causes the following syntax error:
>
> `clone()` has protected access in `java.lang.Object`.
>
> The expression `list[i].clone()` is trying to invoke the method `clone()` of the
> **class** `Object`, which is **protected**, so it cannot be invoked. There are several rea-
> sons for making the method `clone` in the **class** `Object` **protected**. First, cloning
> objects can be very time-consuming and expensive. Second, there could be security con-
> cerns. Also, note that none of the wrapper classes or the `String` **class** contains the
> method `clone`. This is because wrapper classes and `String` objects are immutable. So
> there is no need to `clone` these objects. Moreover, if `list[i]` points to, say, a `String`
> object, then the expression `list[i].clone()` would cause a run-time error.

15

The definition of the method clone as given works fine as long as list[i] points to immutable objects. However, suppose list[i] points to a mutable object. Then the clone of list[i] and list[i] refer to the same object. If one of these references changes the value of the object, it affects the data of the other reference. In other words, we have a shallow copy of data. Unfortunately, this problem for mutable objects cannot be fixed within the definition of the method clone. However, with the help of an example, we will illustrate how to create a deep copy of each object's data in a user program.

Empty and Full

The list is empty if length is 0; it is full if length is equal to maxSize. Therefore, the definitions of the methods isEmpty and isFull are:

```java
public boolean isEmpty()
{
    return (length == 0);
}

public boolean isFull()
{
    return (length == maxSize);
}
```

length and maxSize

The instance variable length stores the number of elements currently in the list. Similarly, because the size of the array holding the list elements is stored in the instance variable maxSize, maxSize specifies the maximum size of the list. Therefore, the definitions of the methods listSize and maxListSize are:

```java
public int listSize()
{
    return length;
}

public int maxListSize()
{
    return maxSize;
}
```

print

The method print outputs the elements of the list. We assume that the output is sent to the standard output device.

```java
public void print()
{
    for (int i = 0; i < length; i++)
        System.out.println(list[i]);
    System.out.println();
}
```

isItemAtEqual

The definition of the method `isItemAtEqual` is given next.

```java
public boolean isItemAtEqual(int location, T item)
{
    if (location < 0 || location >= length)
    {
        System.err.println("The location of the item to "
                            + "be compared is out of range.");
        return false;
    }

    return (list[location].equals(item));
}
```

removeAt and retrieveAt

The method `removeAt` removes an item from a specific location in the list. The location of the item to be removed is passed as a parameter to this method. After removing the item from the list, the length of the list is reduced by 1. If the item to be removed is somewhere in the middle of the list, after removing the item we must move certain elements up one array slot because we cannot leave holes in the portion of the array containing the list. Figure 15-3 illustrates this concept.

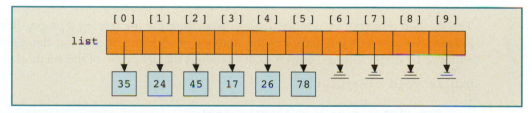

Figure 15-3   Array `list`

The number of elements currently in the list is **6**, so `length` is **6**. Thus, after removing an element, the `length` of the list is **5**. Suppose that the item to be removed is at location **3**. Clearly, we must move `list[4]` into `list[3]` and `list[5]` into `list[4]`, in this order.

The definition of the method `removeAt` is:

```java
public void removeAt(int location)
{
    if (location < 0 || location >= length)
        System.err.println("The location of the item to "
                            + "be removed is out of range.");
    else
```

15

```
    {
        for (int i = location; i < length - 1; i++)
            list[i] = list[i + 1];

        list[length - 1] = null;

        length--;
    }
} //end removeAt
```

The definition of the method `retrieveAt` is straightforward. The index of the item to be retrieved is passed as a parameter to this method. The definition of this method is:

```
public T retrieveAt(int location)
{
    if (location < 0 || location >= length)
    {
        System.err.println("The location of the item to be "
                        + "retrieved is out of range.");
        return null;
    }
    else
        return list[location];
} //end retrieveAt
```

clearList

The method `clearList` removes the elements from the list, leaving it empty. Because the instance variable `length` indicates the number of elements in the list, the elements are removed by simply setting `length` to 0. Therefore, the definition of this method is:

```
public void clearList()
{
    for (int i = 0; i < length; i++)
        list[i] = null;

    length = 0;

    System.gc();       //invoke garbage collector
} //end clearList
```

You can write the definition of the **class** ArrayListClass as follows:

```
public abstract class ArrayListClass<T> implements
                            ArrayListADT<T>, Cloneable
{
    protected int length;   //to store the length of the list
    protected int maxSize;  //to store the maximum size of the
                            //list
    protected T[] list;     //array to hold the list elements
```

```
    //Place the definitions of the instance methods and
    //abstract methods here
}
```

UNORDERED LISTS

As described in the preceding section, we derive the **class** UnorderedArrayList from the **abstract class** ArrayListClass and implement the operations insertAt, insertEnd, replaceAt, search, and remove.

The following describes the heading, instance variables (if any), constructors, and instance methods of the **class** UnorderedArrayList.

Class: UnorderedArrayList

```
public class UnorderedArrayList<T> extends ArrayListClass<T>
```

Instance Variables:

Same as the instance variables of the **class** ArrayListClass

Constructors and Instance Methods:

```
public UnorderedArrayList()
    //Default constructor

public UnorderedArrayList(int size)
    //Constructor with a parameter

public void insertAt(int location, T insertItem)
    //Method to insert insertItem in the list at the position
    //specified by location.
    //Postcondition: Starting at location, the elements of
    //                the list are shifted to make room for
    //                insertItem, list[location] = insertItem;,
    //                and length++;
    //                If the list is full or location is out
    //                of range, an appropriate message is
    //                output.

public void insertEnd(T insertItem)
    //Method to insert insertItem at the end of the list.
    //Postcondition: list[length] = insertItem; and length++;
    //                If the list is full, an appropriate
    //                message is output.
```

15

```
public void replaceAt(int location, T repItem)
   //Method to replace the element in the list at
   //the position specified by location with repItem.
   //Postcondition: list[location] = repItem
   //                If location is out of range, an
   //                appropriate message is output.

public int seqSearch(T searchItem)
   //Method to determine whether searchItem is in the list.
   //Postcondition: If searchItem is found, returns the location
   //                in the array where the searchItem is found;
   //                otherwise, returns -1.

public void remove(T removeItem)
   //Method to remove an item from the list.
   //The parameter removeItem specifies the item to
   //be removed.
   //Postcondition: If removeItem is found in the list, it is
   //                removed from the list and length is
   //                decremented by one.
```

Figure 15-4 shows the class diagram of the **class** UnorderedArrayList and the inheritance hierarchy.

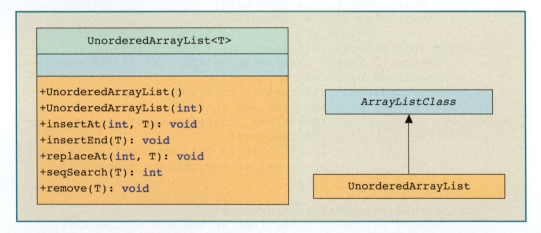

Figure 15-4 UML class diagram of the **class** UnorderedArrayList and the inheritance hierarchy

Next we discuss the definitions of the methods of the **class** UnorderedArrayList. First we describe the methods insertAt and insertEnd.

insertAt and insertEnd

The method **insertAt** inserts an item at a specific location in the list. The item to be inserted and the insert location in the array are passed as parameters to this method. To insert the item in the middle of the list, we must first make room for the new item. That is, we need to move certain elements down one array slot. Figure 15-5 illustrates this concept.

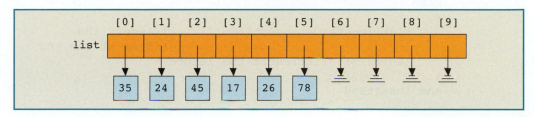

Figure 15-5   Array list

The number of elements currently in the list is 6, so **length** is 6. Thus, after inserting a new element, the **length** of the list is 7. If the item is to be inserted at, say, location 6, we can easily accomplish this by assigning the item in **list[6]**. On the other hand, if the item is to be inserted at, say, location 3, we first need to move elements **list[3]**, **list[4]**, and **list[5]** one array slot right to make room for the new item. Thus, we must first copy **list[5]** into **list[6]**, **list[4]** into **list[5]**, and **list[3]** into **list[4]**, in this order. Then we can copy the new item into **list[3]**.

Of course, special cases, such as trying to insert a full list, must be handled separately. The definition of the method **insertAt** is as follows:

```
public void insertAt(int location, T insertItem)
{
    if (location < 0 || location >= maxSize)
        System.err.println("The position of the item to "
                            + "be inserted is out of range.");
    else if (length >= maxSize)  //list is full
        System.err.println("Cannot insert in a full list.");
    else
    {
        for (int i = length; i > location; i--)
            list[i] = list[i - 1];  //move the elements down

        list[location] = insertItem;
        length++;   //increment the length
    }
} //end insertAt
```

15

The method `insertEnd` can be implemented by using the method `insertAt`. However, the method `insertEnd` does not require the shifting of elements. Therefore, its definition is the following:

```java
public void insertEnd(T insertItem)
{
    if (length >= maxSize)  //the list is full
        System.err.println("Cannot insert in a full list.");
    else
    {
        list[length] = insertItem;      //insert the
                                        //item at the end
        length++; //increment the length
    }
} //end insertEnd
```

replaceAt

The definition of the method `replaceAt` is straightforward:

```java
public void replaceAt(int location, T repItem)
{
    if (location < 0 || location >= length)
        System.err.println("The location of the item to be "
                            + "replaced is out of range.");
    else
        list[location] = repItem;
} //end replaceAt
```

Search

The search algorithm described next is called a **sequential**, or **linear**, search.

Consider the list of seven elements shown in Figure 15-6.

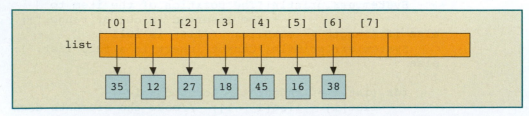

Figure 15-6   List of seven elements

Suppose that you want to determine whether 27 is in the list. The sequential search works as follows: First, you compare 27 with the element at `list[0]`—that is, compare 27 with 35.

Because the element at `list[0]` is not equal to 27, you then compare 27 with the element at `list[1]` (that is, with 12, the second item in the list). Because the element at `list[1]` is not equal to 27, you compare 27 with the next element in the list—that is, compare 27 with the element at `list[2]`. Because the element at `list[2]` is equal to 27, the search stops. This is a successful search.

Let us now search for 10. As before, the search starts with the first element in the list—that is, at `list[0]`. This time the search item, which is 10, is compared with every item in the list. Eventually, no more data is left in the list to compare with the search item. This is an unsuccessful search.

It now follows that, as soon as you find an element in the list that is equal to the search item, you must stop the search and report "success." (In this case, you usually also tell the location in the list where the search item was found.) Otherwise, after the search item is compared with every element in the list, you must stop the search and report "failure."

Suppose that the name of the array containing the list elements is `list`. The previous discussion translates into the following algorithm for the sequential search:

```
found is set to false;

for (loc = 0; loc < length; loc++)
    if (element at list[loc] is equal to searchItem)
    {
        found is set to true
        exit loop
    }

if (found)
    return loc;
else
    return -1;
```

The following method performs a sequential search on a list:

```java
public int seqSearch(T searchItem)
{
    int loc;
    boolean found = false;

    for (loc = 0; loc < length; loc++)
        if (list[loc].equals(searchItem))
        {
            found = true;
            break;
        }
```

15

```
    if (found)
        return loc;
    else
        return -1;
} //end seqSearch
```

Now that you know how to implement the sequential search algorithm, we can give the definition of the method **remove**.

remove

The method **remove** deletes an item from the list. The item to be deleted is passed as a parameter to this method. To delete the item, the method calls the method **seqSearch** to determine whether or not the item to be deleted is in the list. If the item to be deleted is found in the list, the item is removed from the list and the length of the list is decremented by 1. If the item to be removed is found in the list, the method **seqSearch** returns the **index** of the item in the list to be deleted. We can now use the **index** returned by the method **seqSearch** and use the method **removeAt** to remove the item from the list. Therefore, the definition of the method **remove** is:

```
public void remove(T removeItem)
{
    int loc;

    if (length == 0)
        System.err.println("Cannot delete from an "
                           + "empty list.");
    else
    {
        loc = seqSearch(removeItem);

        if (loc != -1)
            removeAt(loc);
        else
            System.out.println("The item to be deleted "
                               + "is not in the list.");
    }
} //end remove
```

The definitions of the constructors are given next.

```
    //Default constructor
public UnorderedArrayList()
{
    super();
}
```

```
    //Constructor with a parameter
public UnorderedArrayList(int size)
{
    super(size);
}
```

You can write the definition of the **class** `UnorderedArrayList` as follows:

```
public class UnorderedArrayList<T> extends ArrayListClass<T>

{
    //Place the definitions of the methods and the
    //constructors as described above here.
}
```

 (**Unordered Sets**) Recall that a list is a collection of elements of the same type. However, in a list an element may repeat. That is, the elements of the list need not be distinct. On the other hand, a **set** is also a collection of elements of the same type. However, the elements of a set are distinct. It follows that a set is a list with distinct elements. In this section, we designed the **class** `UnorderedArrayList` to process unordered lists. Note that the methods `insertAt` and `insertEnd` do not check whether the item to be inserted is already in the list. Similarly, the method `replaceAt` also does not check if the item to be replaced is already in the list. Just as you can design a class to manipulate lists, you can also design a class to manipulate sets. Programming Exercise 10 at the end of this chapter asks you to design the **class** `UnorderedSet`, derived from the **class** `UnorderedArrayList`, to manipulate sets.

Example 15-6

The following program tests various operations on a number list.

```
import java.util.*;

public class TestProgDoubleList
{
    static Scanner console = new Scanner(System.in);

    public static void main(String[] args)
    {
        UnorderedArrayList<Double> numList =
            new UnorderedArrayList<Double>(50);       //Line 1

        Double num;                                    //Line 2

        System.out.print("Line 3: Enter 8 "
                        + "numbers: ");                //Line 3

        for (int count = 0; count < 8; count++)        //Line 4
```

15

```java
    {
        num = console.nextDouble();              //Line 5
        numList.insertEnd(num);                  //Line 6
    }

    System.out.println();                        //Line 7
    System.out.println("Line 8: The list you "   //Line 8
                + "entered is: ");
    numList.print();                             //Line 9

    System.out.print("Line 10: Enter the num "
                + "to be deleted: ");            //Line 10
    num = console.nextDouble();                  //Line 11
    System.out.println();                        //Line 12

    numList.remove(num);                         //Line 13
    System.out.println("Line 14: After removing "
                + num
                + " the list is:");              //Line 14
    numList.print();                             //Line 15

    System.out.print("Line 16: Enter the "
                + "position of the num to "
                + "be deleted: ");               //Line 16
    int position = console.nextInt();            //Line 17
    System.out.println();                        //Line 18

    numList.removeAt(position);                  //Line 19
    System.out.println("Line 20: After removing "
                + "the element at the "
                + "position " + position
                + ", numList:");                 //Line 20

    numList.print();                             //Line 21

    System.out.print("Line 22: Enter the "
                +  "search item: ");             //Line 22

    num = console.nextDouble();                  //Line 23
    System.out.println();                        //Line 24

    if (numList.seqSearch(num) != -1)            //Line 25
        System.out.println("Line 26: Item "
                        + "found in the "
                        + "list");               //Line 26
    else                                         //Line 27
        System.out.println("Line 28: Item "
                        + "not in the list.");   //Line 28
    }
}
```

Sample Run: In this sample run, the user input is shaded.

```
Line 3: Enter 8 numbers:  12.46 34 62.98 21 81 67.45 72.34 87.11

Line 8: The list you entered is:
12.46
34.0
62.98
21.0
81.0
67.45
72.34
87.11

Line 10: Enter the num to be deleted: 67.45

Line 14: After removing 67.45 the list is:
12.46
34.0
62.98
21.0
81.0
72.34
87.11

Line 16: Enter the position of the num to be deleted: 2

Line 20: After removing the element at the position 2, numList:
12.46
34.0
21.0
81.0
72.34
87.11

Line 22: Enter the search item: 72.34

Line 26: Item found in the list
```

The preceding program works as follows. The statement in Line 1 creates the
`UnorderedArrayList` object `numList` to create a list of `Double` objects. The instance
variable `list` of `numList` is an array of 50 components. The statement in Line 2 declares `num`
to be a reference variable of the type `Double`. The statement in Line 3 prompts the user to
enter 8 numbers. The **for** loop in Lines 4 to 6 reads the numbers one-by-one and inserts them
in `numList`.

The statement in Line 9 uses the method `print` of `numList` to output the elements of
`numList` (see sample run Line marked 8). The statement in Line 10 prompts the user to
enter the number to be deleted from `numList` and the statement in Line 11 reads and stores
the number into the object `num`. The statement in Line 13 uses the method `remove` of
`numList` to remove the number from `numList`.

15

The statements in Lines 14 and 15 output the number that was deleted and `numList` after deleting this number, respectively.

The statement in Line 16 prompts the user to enter the position, in `numList`, of the item to be deleted. The statement in Line 17 stores the position of the item to be deleted into the variable `position`. The statement in Line 19 removes the desired item from `numList`. The statements in Lines 20 and 21 output the position of the item that was deleted and `numList` after deleting the item. The statements in Lines 22 through 28 prompt the user to enter the item to be searched and then output the result of the search.

The program in Example 15-7 illustrates that the `clone` method of the **class** `ArrayListClass` works for immutable objects.

Example 15-7

```java
//Test Program Array List

import java.util.*;

public class TestProgDoubleList
{
    static Scanner console = new Scanner(System.in);

    public static void main(String[] args)
    {
        UnorderedArrayList<Double> numList =
            new UnorderedArrayList<Double>(50);   //Line 1
        UnorderedArrayList<Double> temp;          //Line 2

        Double num;                               //Line 3

        System.out.print("Line 4: Enter 3 "
                    + "numbers: ");               //Line 4

        for (int count = 0; count < 3; count++)   //Line 5
        {
            num = console.nextDouble();           //Line 6
            numList.insertEnd(num);               //Line 7
        }

        System.out.println();                     //Line 8
        System.out.println("Line 9: The list "
                    + "you entered is: ");         //Line 9
        numList.print();                          //Line 10

        temp = (UnorderedArrayList<Double>)
                    numList.clone();              //Line 11
```

```
        System.out.println("List 12: temp: ");         //Line 12
        temp.print();                                    //Line 13

        temp.replaceAt(0, 58.39);                        //Line 14

        System.out.println("List 15: numList: ");        //Line 15
        numList.print();                                 //Line 16

        System.out.println("List 17: temp: ");           //Line 17
        temp.print();                                    //Line 18
    }
}
```

Sample Run: In this sample run, the user input is shaded.

```
Line 4: Enter 3 numbers: 12.46 34 62.98

Line 9: The list you entered is:
12.46
34.0
62.98

List 12: temp:
12.46
34.0
62.98

List 15: numList:
12.46
34.0
62.98

List 17: temp:
58.39
34.0
62.98
```

The preceding program works as follows. The statement in Line 1 creates the `UnorderedArrayList` object `numList` to create a list of `Double` objects. The instance variable `list` of `numList` is an array of `50` components. The statement in Line 2 declares the `UnorderedArrayList<Double>` reference variable `temp`. The statement in Line 3 declares `num` to be a reference variable of the type `Double`. The statement in Line 4 prompts the user to enter 3 numbers. The **for** loop in Lines 5 to 7 reads numbers one-by-one and inserts them in `numList`.

The `statement` in Line 10 uses the method `print` of `numList` to output the elements of `numList` (see sample run Line 9). The statement in Line 11 uses the `clone` method to create a clone of `numList` and assigns the clone to `temp`. The statement in Line 13 outputs the elements of `temp`.

15

The **statement** in Line 14 replaces the first component of **temp.list**. The statement in Line 16 outputs the elements of **numList** and the statement in Line 18 outputs the elements of **temp**. Note that the first element of **numList** and **temp** are different.

The program in Example 15-8 shows that the method **clone** of the **class ArrayListClass** does not work for mutable objects. This example also shows how to clone an **UnorderedArrayList** object whose elements refer to mutable objects.

Example 15-8

```java
public class TestProgUnorderedClockListWithClone
{
    public static void main(String[] args)
    {
        UnorderedArrayList<Clock> clockList
                = new UnorderedArrayList<Clock>(50);   //Line 1

        UnorderedArrayList<Clock> temp1;               //Line 2

        UnorderedArrayList<Clock> temp2;               //Line 3

        clockList.insertEnd(new Clock(12, 5, 32));     //Line 4
        clockList.insertEnd(new Clock(5, 8, 22));      //Line 5
        clockList.insertEnd(new Clock(8, 35, 11));     //Line 6

        System.out.println("Line 7: The list you "
                        + "entered is: ");             //Line 7
        clockList.print();                             //Line 8

        temp1 = (UnorderedArrayList<Clock>)
                            clockList.clone();          //Line 9

        temp2 = copyList(clockList);                   //Line 10

        Clock cl;                                      //Line 11

        cl = temp1.retrieveAt(0);                      //Line 12

        cl.setTime(15, 32, 44);                        //Line 13

        cl =  temp2.retrieveAt(0);                     //Line 14

        cl.setTime(10, 8, 55);                         //Line 15

        System.out.println("List 16: clockList: ");    //Line 16
        clockList.print();                             //Line 17
```

```java
        System.out.println("List 18: temp1: ");          //Line 18
        temp1.print();                                    //Line 19

        System.out.println("List 20: temp2: ");          //Line 20
        temp2.print();                                    //Line 21
    }

    public static UnorderedArrayList<Clock> copyList
                        (UnorderedArrayList<Clock> otherList)
    {
        UnorderedArrayList<Clock> tempList =
            new UnorderedArrayList<Clock>
                        (otherList.maxListSize());

        Clock cl;

        for (int k = 0; k <  otherList.listSize(); k++)
        {
            cl =  otherList.retrieveAt(k);

            tempList.insert((Clock) cl.clone());
        }

        return tempList;
    }
}
```

Sample Run:
```
Line 7: The list you entered is:
12:05:32
05:08:22
08:35:11

List 16: clockList:
15:32:44
05:08:22
08:35:11

List 18: temp1:
15:32:44
05:08:22
08:35:11

List 20: temp2:
10:08:55
05:08:22
08:35:11
```

15

The preceding program works as follows. This program contains the method `copyList`. This method takes as a parameter `otherList`, an `UnorderedArrayList` object wherein each component of the component list of `otherList` is a `Clock` object. Moreover, the **for** loop in this method creates a deep copy of the `otherList` and the method returns a reference of the clone.

The statement in Line 1 creates the `UnorderedArrayList` object `clockList` to create a list of `Clock` objects. The instance variable `list` of `clockList` is an array of 50 components. The statements in Lines 2 and 3 declare the `UnorderedArrayList<Clock>` reference variables `temp1` and `temp2`. The statements in Lines 3, 4, and 5 insert three `Clock` objects in `clockList`. The statement in Line 8 outputs the elements of `clockList`.

The statement in Line 9 uses the method `clone` of the **class** `ArrayListClass` to create a clone of `clockList` and assigns the reference of the clone to `temp1`. (Note that `temp1.list` is a shallow copy of `clockList.list`.) The statement in Line 10 uses the method `copyList` to create a copy of `clockList` and assigns the reference of the copy to `temp2`.

The statement in Line 11 declares `c1` to be a reference variable of the `Clock` type. The statement in Line 12 uses the method `retrieveAt` to retrieve the reference of the first element of `temp1.list`. The statement in Line 13 changes the value of the `Clock` object to which `c1` points. Note that the reference variables `c1`, `temp1.list[0]`, and `clockList.list[0]` point to the same `Clock` object. Therefore, the statement in Line 13 changes the value of the object to which `temp1.list[0]` and `clockList.list[0]` point.

The statement in Line 14 uses the method `retrieveAt` to retrieve the reference of the first element of `temp2.list`. The statement in Line 15 changes the value of the `Clock` object to which `c1` points. Because `c1` and `temp2.list[0]` point to the same `Clock` object, this statement also changes the value of `temp2.list[0]`.

The statements in Lines 17, 19, and 21 output the values of `clockList.list`, `temp1.list`, and `temp2.list`. The outputs of these statements show that `temp1` is a shallow copy of `clockList`, while `temp2` is a deep copy of `clockList`. It now follows that the `clone` method of the **class** `ArrayListClass` provides only a clone of the references of the instance variable `list` of `clockList`, not the clones of the objects to which the array references point.

ORDERED LIST

As described earlier, we will derive two classes from the **abstract class** `ArrayListClass`, which are `UnorderedArrayList` and `OrderedArrayList`. The preceding section described the **class** `UnorderedArrayList`. This section describes the **class** `OrderedArrayList`.

The **class** OrderedArrayList also contains the method **insert** to insert an item at the proper place in the list. The following describes the heading, instance variables (if any), constructors, and instance methods of the **class** OrderedArrayList:

Class: OrderedArrayList

```
public class OrderedArrayList <T> extends ArrayListClass<T>
```

Instance Variables:

Same as the instance variables of the **class** ArrayListClass

Constructors and Instance Methods:

```
public OrderedArrayList()
   //Default constructor

public OrderedArrayList(int size)
   //Constructor with a parameter

public int seqSearch(T searchItem)
   //Method to determine whether searchItem is in the list.
   //Postcondition: If searchItem is found, returns the
   //               location in the array where the
   //               searchItem is found;
   //               otherwise, returns -1.

public void insert(T insertItem)
   //Method to insert insertItem in the list.
   //Postcondition: The list is old list plus insertItem
   //               and length++.
   //               If the list is full, an appropriate
   //               message is output.

public void insertAt(int location, T insertItem)
   //Method to insert insertItem in the list at the
   //position specified by location. Because list is
   //sorted, insertItem is inserted at the proper place.
   //This method uses the method insert to insert
   //insertItem.
   //Postcondition: The list is old list plus insertItem
   //               and length++.
   //               If the list is full, an appropriate
   //               message is output.

public void insertEnd(T insertItem)
   //Method to insert insertItem in the list at the
   //end. Because list is sorted, insertItem is
   //inserted at the proper place. This method uses
```

15

```
        //the method insert to insert insertItem.
        //Postcondition: The list is old list plus insertItem
        //               and length++.
        //               If the list is full, an appropriate
        //               message is output.

public void replaceAt(int location, T repItem)
        //Method to replace the element in the list at the position
        //specified by location with repItem. Because the resulting
        //list should be in order, list item at location is removed
        //and repItem is inserted at the proper place.
        //Postcondition: If location is out of range, an
        //               appropriate message is output.
        //               Otherwise, the item at location is removed
        //               and repItem is inserted at the proper place
        //               in the list.

public void remove(T removeItem)
        //Method to remove an item from the list.
        //The parameter removeItem specifies the item to
        //be removed.
        //Postcondition: If removeItem is found in the list,
        //               it is removed from the list and
        //               length is decremented by one.
```

Figure 15-7 shows the UML class diagram of the **class** OrderedArrayList and the inheritance hierarchy.

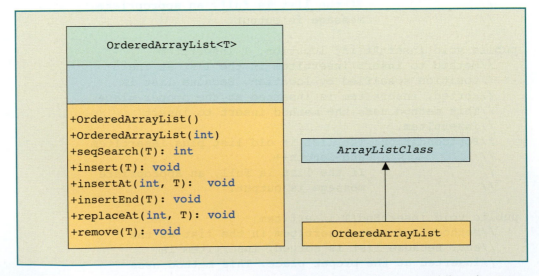

Figure 15-7 UML class diagram of the **class** OrderedArrayList and the inheritance hierarchy

Next we give the definitions of the methods of the **class** `OrderedArrayList`. The definitions of the constructors are similar to the definitions of the constructors of the **class** `UnorderedArrayList`. Their definitions are:

```java
    //Default constructor
public OrderedArrayList()
{
    super();
}

    //Constructor with a parameter
public OrderedArrayList(int size)
{
    super(size);
}
```

Search

Next we describe the sequential search algorithm. Because the list is sorted, we use a loop to search `searchItem` until we find an item in the list that is greater than or equal to the `searchItem` or until we have searched the entire list. Note that the loop does not make an explicit equality comparison to check if `searchItem` is in fact in the list, as it did for an unordered list. Therefore, after the loop terminates and we find an item in the list that is greater than or equal to `searchItem`, we make an equality comparison to ensure whether `searchItem` is in the list. The definition of the method `seqSearch` is:

```java
public int seqSearch(T searchItem)
{
    int loc;
    boolean found = false;

    for (loc = 0; loc < length; loc++)
    {
        Comparable<T> temp = (Comparable<T>) list[loc];
        if (temp.compareTo(searchItem) >= 0)
        {
            found = true;
            break;
        }
    }

    if (found)
    {
        if (list[loc].equals(searchItem))
            return loc;
        else
            return -1;
```

15

```
    }
    else
        return -1;
} //end seqSearch
```

Let us take a look at the following statement in the definition of the method `seqSearch`:

```
Comparable<T> temp = (Comparable<T>) list[loc];
```

Note that `list[loc]` is a reference of the `Object` type which was type cast to `T`. Now the **class** `Object` does not contain the method `compareTo`. So we first create a reference of the type `Comparable<T>` and then use the `compareTo` method. Also note that this method would work on the objects of only those classes that implement the **interface** `Comparable` and provide an appropriate definition of the method `compareTo`.

 Because the elements in the instance variable `list` of the **class** `OrderedArrayList` are ordered, you can use a more effective search algorithm, called binary search, to search the array `list`. In Chapter 18, Searching and Sorting Algorithms, we will describe a binary search algorithm and also explain how to include it in the **class** `OrderedArrayList`.

Insert

The method `insert` inserts a new item in the list. The new item is inserted at the proper place in the list and the length of the list is increased by 1. If the list is full, an appropriate message is output. The definition of this method is:

```
public void insert(T insertItem)
{
    int loc;

    boolean found = false;

    if (length == 0)            //list is empty
        list[length++] = insertItem;   //insert insertItem
                                        //and increment length
    else if (length == maxSize)
        System.err.println("Cannot insert in a full list.");
    else
    {
        for (loc = 0; loc < length; loc++)
        {
            Comparable<T> temp =
                        (Comparable<T>) list[loc];
            if (temp.compareTo(insertItem) >= 0)
            {
                found = true;
                break;
            }
        }
```

```
        }

        for (int i = length; i > loc; i--)
            list[i] = list[i - 1];   //move the
                                     //elements down

        list[loc] = insertItem;   //insert insertItem
        length++;    //increment the length
    }
} //end insert
```

insertAt and insertEnd

The method `insertAt` inserts an element at a specific position in the list. However, because we are implementing lists whose elements are ordered, the item must be inserted at the proper position. Similarly, the method `insertEnd` must insert the element at the proper position. In either case, we must determine the position in the list where the item should be inserted. To do so, we simply use the method `insert`, described in the preceding section. The definitions of the methods `insertAt` and `insertEnd` are:

```
public void insertAt(int location, T insertItem)
{
    if (location < 0 || location >= maxSize)
        System.err.println("The position of the item to be"
                            + "inserted is out of range.");
    else if (length == maxSize)   //list is full
        System.err.println("Cannot insert in a full list.");
    else
    {
        System.out.println("This is a sorted list. "
                            + "Inserting at the proper place.");
        insert(insertItem);
    }
} //end insertAt

public void insertEnd(T insertItem)
{
    if (length >= maxSize)   //the list is full
        System.err.println("Cannot insert in a full list.");
    else
    {
        System.out.println("This is a sorted list. "
                            + "Inserting at the proper "
                            + "place.");
        insert(insertItem);
    }
} //end insertEnd
```

15

Note that in reality the methods `insertAt` and `insertEnd` do not apply to ordered array lists because the new item must be inserted at the proper place in the list. However, you must provide the definitions as these methods are declared as `abstract` in the parent class.

remove

The definition of the method `remove` for the **class** `OrderedArrayList` is the same as the definition of the method `remove` of the **class** `UnorderedArrayList`. We therefore leave it as an exercise for you.

replaceAt

As in the case of the methods `insertAt` and `insertEnd`, we cannot arbitrarily replace an item in an ordered list because the resulting list must be ordered. Therefore, to replace an item at a specific position, we first remove the item at the given position and then insert the item at its proper place in the list. This is accomplished by using the methods `removeAt` and `insert`. The definition of the method `replaceAt` is:

```
public void replaceAt(int location, T repItem)
{
    if (location < 0 || location >= length)
        System.err.println("The location of the item "
                        + "to be replaced is out "
                        + "of range.");
    else
    {
        removeAt(location);
        insert(repItem);
    }
} //end replaceAt
```

You can write the definition of the **class** `OrderedArrayList` as follows:

```
public class OrderedArrayList <T> extends ArrayListClass<T>
{
    //Place the definitions of the methods as described above
    //and the definitions of the constructors here.
}
```

The Web site accompanying this book contains several programs that show how to use the **class** `OrderedArrayList`.

 (Ordered Sets) An ordered set is an ordered collection of distinct elements of the same type. Programming Exercise 11 at the end of this chapter asks you to design the **class** `OrderedSet`, derived from the **class** `OrderedArrayList`, to manipulate ordered sets.

 Chapter 10 discussed how to use the **class** `Vector` to create a list of objects.

PROGRAMMING EXAMPLE: POLYNOMIAL OPERATIONS

You learned in a college algebra or a calculus course that a polynomial $p(x)$, in one variable x, is an expression of the form:

$$p(x) = a_0 + a_1x + \ldots + a_{n-1}x^{n-1} + a_nx^n$$

where a_i are real (or complex) numbers and n is a nonnegative integer. If $p(x) = a_0$, then $p(x)$ is called a **constant** polynomial. If $p(x)$ is a nonzero constant polynomial, then the degree of $p(x)$ is defined to be 0. Even though in mathematics the degree of the zero polynomial is undefined, for the purpose of this program, we will consider the degree of such polynomials to be zero. If $p(x)$ is not constant and $a_n \ne 0$, then n is called the degree of $p(x)$, that is, the degree of a non-constant polynomial is defined to be the exponent of the highest power of x.

The basic operations performed on polynomials are evaluating a polynomial at a given value and adding, subtracting, multiplying, and dividing polynomials. For example, suppose that

$$p(x) = 1 + 2x + 3x^2,$$

and

$$q(x) = 4 + x.$$

The degree of $p(x)$ is 2 and the degree of $q(x)$ is 1. Moreover,

$$p(2) = 1 + 2 * 2 + 3 * 2^2 = 17$$
$$p(x) + q(x) = 5 + 3x + 3x^2$$
$$p(x) - q(x) = -3 + x + 3x^2$$
$$p(x) * q(x) = 4 + 9x + 14x^2 + 3x^3$$

The purpose of this programming example is to design and implement the **class Polynomial** to perform various polynomial operations in a program.

To be specific, in this program, we will implement the following operations on polynomials:

1. Evaluate a polynomial at a given value.
2. Add polynomials.
3. Subtract polynomials.
4. Multiply polynomials.

Moreover, we assume that the coefficients of polynomials are real numbers. You will be asked in the Programming Exercise 7 to generalize it so that the coefficients can also be complex numbers.

To store a polynomial, we use a dynamic array of objects as follows. Suppose $p(x)$ is a polynomial of degree $n \geq 0$. Let `list` be an array of objects of the size $n + 1$. Then `list[i]` refers to the coefficient a_i of x^i. See Figure 15-8.

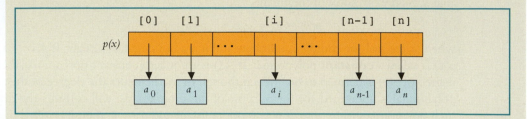

Figure 15-8   Polynomial $p(x)$

From Figure 15-8, it is clear that if $p(x)$ is a polynomial of degree n, then we need an array of the size $n + 1$ to store the coefficients of $p(x)$. Suppose that

$p(x) = 1 + 8x - 3x^2 + 5x^4 + 7x^8$.

Then the array storing the coefficient of $p(x)$ is shown in Figure 15-9.

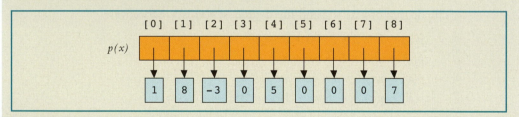

Figure 15-9   Polynomial $p(x)$ of degree 8 and its coefficients

Similarly, if

$q(x) = -5x^2 + 16x^5$,

then the array storing the coefficient of $q(x)$ is shown in Figure 15-10.

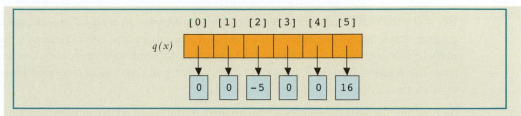

Figure 15-10 Polynomial $q(x)$ of degree 5 and its coefficients

Next we define the adding, subtracting, and multiplying operations. (Recall that this program does not implement the division operation on polynomials.)

Suppose that

$$p(x) = a_0 + a_1x + \ldots + a_{n-1}x^{n-1} + a_nx^n$$

and

$$q(x) = b_0 + b_1x + \ldots + b_{m-1}x^{m-1} + a_mx^m.$$

Let $t = max(n, m)$, that is, t is the larger of n and m. Then

$$p(x) + q(x) = c_0 + c_1x + \ldots + c_{t-1}x^{t-1} + c_tx^t$$

where $i = 0, 1, 2, \ldots, t$

$$c_i = \begin{cases} a_i + b_i & \text{if } i \leq min(n, m) \\ a_i & \text{if } i > m \\ b_i & \text{if } i > n \end{cases}$$

Here $min(n, m)$ denotes the smaller of n and m. The difference $p(x) - q(x)$ of $p(x)$ and $q(x)$ can be defined similarly. It follows that the degrees of the polynomials $p(x) + q(x)$ and $p(x) - q(x)$ are less than or equal to $max(n, m)$.

The product, $p(x) * q(x)$, of $p(x)$ and $q(x)$ is defined as follows:

$$p(x) * q(x) = d_0 + d_1x + \ldots + d_{n+m}x^{n+m},$$

The coefficient d_k for $k = 0, 1, 2, \ldots, n + m$, is given by the formula

$$d_k = a_0 * b_k + a_1 * b_{k-1} + \ldots + a_k * b_0,$$

where if either a_i or b_i does not exist, it is assumed to be 0. For example,

$$d_0 = a_0b_0$$
$$d_1 = a_0b_1 + a_1b_0$$

$\ldots$

$$d_{n+m} = a_nb_m$$

Because the coefficients of a polynomial are managed by an array of objects, we use the **class** `UnorderedArrayList` to store and manipulate the coefficients of a polynomial. In fact, we derive the **class** `Polynomial` to implement polynomial operations from the **class** `UnorderedArrayList`, which will requires us to implement only the operations needed to manipulate polynomials.

The following describes the heading, instance variables (if any), constructors, and instance methods of the **class** `Polynomial`.

Class: `Polynomial`

```
public class Polynomial extends UnorderedArrayList<Double>
```

Constructors and Instance Methods:

```
public Polynomial()
   //Default constructor
   //Postcondition: An array of the size 100, and
   //               length and maxSize are set to 100.

public Polynomial(int size)
   //Constructor with a parameter
   //Postcondition: An array of the size specified by
   //               the parameter size is created, length
   //               and maxSize are initialized to size.

public double evaluate(double x)
   //Method to evaluate a polynomial at a given value
   //Postcondition: The polynomial is evaluated at x and
   //               the value is returned.

public Polynomial add(Polynomial right)
   //Method to add two polynomials
   //Postcondition: This polynomial is added with the polynomial
   //               specified by the parameter right. A
   //               reference of the result is returned.

public Polynomial subtract(Polynomial right)
   //Method to subtract two polynomials
   //Postcondition: The polynomial specified by the
   //               parameter right is subtracted from this
   //               polynomial. A reference of the result
   //               is returned.

public Polynomial multiply(Polynomial right)
   //Method to multiply two polynomials
   //Postcondition: This polynomial is multiplied with the
   //               polynomial specified by the parameter right.
   //               A reference of the result is returned.
```

```
public int min(int x, int y)
   //Method to determine the smaller of x and y
   //Postcondition: The smaller of x and y is returned.

public int max(int x, int y)
   //Method to determine the larger of x and y
   //Postcondition: The larger of x and y is returned.

public void read()
   //Method to read the coefficients of a polynomial

public String toString()
   //Method to return the string containing the polynomial
```

In Exercise 14 at the end of the chapter, you are asked to draw the UML class diagram of the **class** **Polynomial**.

If $p(x)$ is a polynomial of degree 3, we create an object, say, p, of the type **Polynomial** and set the size of the array **list** to be 4. The following statement creates such an object p:

```
Polynomial p = new Polynomial(4);
```

The degree of the polynomial is stored in the instance variable **length**, which is inherited from the **class** **ArrayListClass**.

Next we discuss the definitions of the constructors and methods.

The definitions of the default constructor and the constructor with parameter are straightforward:

```
   //Default constructor
public Polynomial()
{
   super();
   length = 100;
}

   //Constructor with a parameter
public Polynomial(int size)
{
   super(size);
   length = size;
}
```

Next we consider the definition of the method **evaluate**. Suppose that you have the polynomial p, as shown in Figure 15-11.

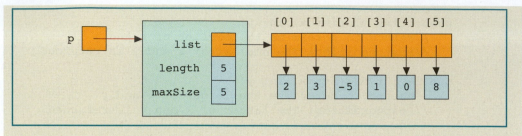

Figure 15-11 Polynomial $p(x)$

Suppose that we want to evaluate $p(4)$. Clearly:

$$p(4) = 2 + 3 * 4 - 5 * 4^2 + 1 * 4^3 + 0 * 4^4 + 8 * 4^5$$

It follows that we must retrieve the coefficients of the polynomial, multiply each coeffi-cient with an appropriate power of 4, and then add the numbers. Now the coefficients of the polynomial are stored into the array `list`. Each element `list[i]` is a reference to the object containing a coefficient. Moreover, `list[i]` is an object of the type `Double`. Suppose that we want to retrieve the coefficient of x. Now `list[1]` points the object containing the coefficient of x. To retrieve the coefficient of x we use the method `retrieveAt`:

```
Double coeff;

coeff = retrieveAt(1);
```

The last two statements are repeated for each list element. You can write the definition of the method `evaluate` as follows:

```
public double evaluate(Double x)
{
    double value = 0.0;

    Double coeff;

    for (int i = 0; i < length; i++)
    {
        coeff = retrieveAt(i);

        if (coeff != 0.0)
            value = value + coeff * Math.pow(x, i);
    }

    return value;
}
```

Suppose that $p(x)$ is a polynomial of degree n and $q(x)$ is a polynomial of degree m. If $n = m$, then the method **add** adds the corresponding coefficients of $p(x)$ and $q(x)$. If $n > m$, then the first m coefficients of $p(x)$ are added with the corresponding coefficients of $q(x)$. The remaining coefficients of $p(x)$ are copied into the polynomial containing the sum of $p(x)$ and $q(x)$. Similarly, if $n < m$, the first n coefficients of $q(x)$ are added with the corresponding coefficients of $p(x)$. The remaining coefficients of $q(x)$ are copied into the polynomial containing the sum. Consider the polynomials p and q as given in Figures 15-12 and 15-13.

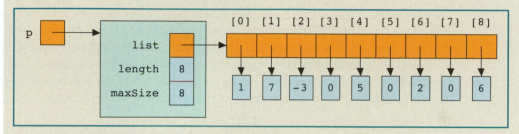

Figure 15-12 Polynomial $p(x)$

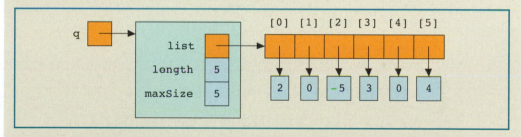

Figure 15-13 Polynomial $q(x)$

Suppose that the coefficients of $p(x) + q(x)$ will be stored in the polynomial **temp**. Then

$deg(temp) = max(deg(p), deg(q))$.

To add the corresponding coefficients of $p(x)$ and $q(x)$, we simultaneously retrieve the corresponding coefficients of $p(x)$ and $q(x)$ using techniques similar to one used in evaluating a polynomial. We declare two reference variables **coeffP** and **coeffQ** of the type

`Double`. Suppose that we want to retrieve the coefficients of x^2. Consider the following statements:

```
Double coeffP;                    //Line 1
Double coeffQ;                    //Line 2

coeffP = p.retrieveAt(2);        //Line 3
coeffQ = q.retrieveAt(2);        //Line 4

sumCoeff = coeffP + coeffQ;      //Line 5
temp.replaceAt(2, sumCoeff);     //Line 6
```

The statements in Lines 1 and 2 declare `coeffP` and `coeffQ` to be reference variables of the type `Double`. The statement in Line 3 makes `coeffP` point to the coefficient of x^2 of $p(x)$. Similarly, the statement in Line 4 makes `coeffQ` point to the coefficient of x^2 of $q(x)$. The statement in Line 5 adds the coefficients of x^2 and assigns the sum to `sumCoeff`. The statement in Line 6 inserts `sumCoeff` into the polynomial `temp`. We repeat this process for each corresponding coefficient of $p(x)$ and $q(x)$.

We can now write the definition of the method **add** as follows:

```
public Polynomial add(Polynomial right)
{
    int size = max(length, right.length);
    int i;
    Double sumCoeff;

    Double coeffP;
    Double coeffQ;

    Polynomial temp = new Polynomial(size);

    for (i = 0; i < min(length, right.length); i++)
    {
        coeffP = retrieveAt(i);
        coeffQ = right.retrieveAt(i);

        sumCoeff = coeffP + coeffQ;
        temp.replaceAt(i, sumCoeff);
    }

    if (size == length)
        for (i = min(length, right.length); i < length; i++)
            temp.replaceAt(i, retrieveAt(i));
    else
```

```
        for (i = min(length, right.length);
                            i < right.length; i++)
            temp.replaceAt(i, right.retrieveAt(i));

        return temp;
}
```

The definition of the method **subtract** is similar to the definition of the method **add** and is given next:

```
public Polynomial subtract(Polynomial right)
{
    int size = max(length, right.length);
    int i;
    Double diffCoeff;

    Double coeffP;
    Double coeffQ;

    Polynomial temp = new Polynomial(size);

    for (i = 0; i < min(length, right.length); i++)
    {
        coeffP = retrieveAt(i);
        coeffQ = right.retrieveAt(i);

        diffCoeff = coeffP - coeffQ;
        temp.replaceAt(i, diffCoeff);
    }

    if (size == length)
        for (i = min(length, right.length); i < length; i++)
            temp.replaceAt(i, retrieveAt(i));
    else
        for (i = min(length, right.length);
                            i < right.length; i++)
        {
            Double coeff;
            coeff = right.retrieveAt(i);
            coeff = -coeff;
            temp.replaceAt(i, coeff);
        }

    return temp;
}
```

The definition of the method `multiply` to multiply two polynomials is left as an exercise for you. See Programming Exercise 7 at the end of this chapter. The definitions of the remaining methods of the **class** `Polynomial` are:

```java
public int min(int x, int y)
{
    if (x <= y)
        return x;
    else
        return y;
}

public int max(int x, int y)
{
    if (x >= y)
        return x;
    else
        return y;
}

public void read()
{
    Scanner console = new Scanner(System.in);

    Double x;

    System.out.println("The degree of this polynomial is: "
                       + (length - 1));
    for (int i = 0; i < length; i++)
    {
        System.out.print("Enter the coefficient of x^"
                         + i + ": ");

        x = console.nextDouble();
        replaceAt(i, x);
    }
}

public String toString()
{
    int i;
    int firstNonzeroCoeff = 0;
    Double coeff = 0.0;
    String str = "";

    for (i = 0; i < length; i++)
    {
        coeff = retrieveAt(i);
```

```
        if (coeff != 0.0)
        {
            firstNonzeroCoeff = i;
            break;
        }
    }

    if (firstNonzeroCoeff < length)
    {
        if (firstNonzeroCoeff == 0)
            str = retrieveAt(firstNonzeroCoeff) + " ";
        else
            str = retrieveAt(firstNonzeroCoeff) + "x^"
                        + firstNonzeroCoeff + " ";

        for (i = firstNonzeroCoeff + 1; i < length; i++)
        {
            coeff = retrieveAt(i);

            if (coeff != 0.0)
                if (coeff > 0.0)
                    str += "+ " + coeff + "x^" + i + " ";
                else
                    str += "- " + (-coeff) + "x^" + i + " ";
        }
    }

    return str;
}
```

You can write the definition of the **class** `Polynomial` as follows:

```
import java.util.*;

public class Polynomial extends UnorderedArrayList<Double>
{
    //Place the definitions of the instance methods here.
}
```

The following program tests various polynomial operations:

```
//Test program: Polynomial Operations

public class ProgPolynomial
{
    public static void main(String[] args)
    {
        Polynomial p = new Polynomial(4);          //Line 1
        Polynomial q = new Polynomial(8);          //Line 2
```

```
        p.read();                                          //Line 3
        System.out.println();                              //Line 4

        System.out.println("Line 5: p(x): " + p);          //Line 5

        System.out.println("Line 6: p.evaluate(2): "
                        + p.evaluate(2.0));                 //Line 6
        System.out.println();                              //Line 7

        q.read();                                          //Line 8
        System.out.println("Line 9: q(x): " + q);          //Line 9

        System.out.println("Line 10: p(x) + q(x): "
                        + p.add(q));                        //Line 10

        System.out.println("Line 11: p(x) - q(x): "
                        + p.subtract(q));                   //Line 11
    }
}
```

Sample Run: In this sample run, the user input is shaded.

```
The degree of this polynomial is: 3
Enter the coefficient of x^0: 1
Enter the coefficient of x^1: 2
Enter the coefficient of x^2: 0
Enter the coefficient of x^3: 3

Line 5: p(x): 1.0 + 2.0x^1 + 3.0x^3
Line 6: p.evaluate(2): 29.0

The degree of this polynomial is: 7
Enter the coefficient of x^0: 0
Enter the coefficient of x^1: 1
Enter the coefficient of x^2: 4
Enter the coefficient of x^3: 0
Enter the coefficient of x^4: 0
Enter the coefficient of x^5: 0
Enter the coefficient of x^6: 0
Enter the coefficient of x^7: 6
Line 9: q(x): 1.0x^1 + 4.0x^2 + 6.0x^7
Line 10: p(x) + q(x): 1.0 + 3.0x^1 + 4.0x^2 + 3.0x^3 + 6.0x^7
Line 11: p(x) - q(x): 1.0 + 1.0x^1 - 4.0x^2 + 3.0x^3 - 6.0x^7
```

QUICK REVIEW

1. The method **clone of the class** Object is a protected method. So it is inherited, but it cannot be invoked by the object outside the class. For example, in a user program, an object cannot invoke the method clone of the **class** Object.

2. To force a class to provide an appropriate definition of the method **clone**, that class must implement the **interface** Cloneable.

3. The **interface** Cloneable has no method heading that needs to be implemented. Moreover, it has no defined constant.

4. When you define a class that implements the **interface** Cloneable, you must redefine the **clone** method (inherited from the super class or the **class** Object) in a particular way.

5. The default definition of the **clone** method provides a bit-by-bit copy of the object's data in storage. If the object's data is composed of only primitive type data or data of immutable objects, such as **Integer** or **String** objects, then the bit-by-bit copy works as required and has no unintended side effects. However, if the data in the object being cloned contains instance variables that refer to mutable objects, such as **Clock** objects, then the bit-by-bit copy would cause shallow copy of mutable objects data, as the instance variables of two different objects would refer to the same mutable object.

6. When writing the definition of the method **clone** in a class, first we invoke the **clone** method of the **class** Object (or whatever the super class is). If the class has instance variables whose type is a mutable class, then we change the values of those instance variables.

7. The method **clone** of the **class** Object throws CloneNotSupportedException, which must be handled.

8. The **interface** Comparable is used to force a **class** to provide an appropriate definition of the method **compareTo** so that the values of two objects of that **class** can be properly compared.

9. To force a class provide an appropriate definition of the method **compareTo**, that class implements the **interface** Comparable.

10. Generic methods are defined using type parameters.

11. Every generic method has a type parameters section that precedes the return type of the method, and the type parameters are separated by commas and enclosed in angular brackets (< and >).

12. Type parameters, also known as type variables, are identifiers that specify generic type names.

15

13. In a generic method, typically, type parameters are used to do the following:

    a. Declare the return type of the method.

    b. Declare formal parameters.

    c. Declare local variables.

14. A skeleton form of a generic method is:

    ```
    modifier(s) <T> methodType methodName(formal parameter list)
    {
         //method body
    }
    ```

    Here `T` is referred to as the type parameter.

15. Within a generic method, you can declare reference variables using the type parameter `T`. However, you cannot instantiate objects using the type parameter.

16. In the expression

    ```
    <T extends Comparable<T> >
    ```

    `T` refers to any type, that is, class, that implements the interface `Comparable`. Here `Comparable` is known as the upper bound of the type parameter `T`. By default, `Object` is an upper bound. Note the use of the keyword **extends**. `Comparable` is an interface and we typically use the keyword **implements** when a **class** implements an **interface**. However, when a type parameter declaration bounds a parameter, then we always use the keyword **extends** regardless of whether the type parameter extends a class or an interface. The reason to bound the parameter `T` is that the method definition uses the method `compareTo` and not every **class** provides the method `compareTo`, that is, not all objects can be compared.

17. If you want to bound a type parameter by more than one class (or interface), then in the type parameter declaration, the class names are separated using the symbol **&**. For example, consider the following expression:

    ```
    <T extends Comparable<T> & Cloneable>
    ```

    In this declaration, the type parameter `T` is bounded by the **class**es `Comparable` and `Cloneable`.

18. In a generic class, the type parameter(s) are enclosed in angular brackets and placed after the name of the class. The type parameter may be bounded or unbounded. As before, a type parameter is used to declare variables and generic methods within the class. A typical form of a generic class is:

    ```
    modifier(s) className<T> modifier(s)
    {
         //class members
    }
    ```

19. The generic classes are also known as parametric classes.

20. Within the definition of the class, you can declare reference variables using the type parameter **T**. However, you cannot instantiate objects using the type parameter.

21. A list is a collection of elements of the same type.

22. The length of a list is the number of elements in the list.

23. The commonly performed operations on a list are create the list, determine whether the list is empty, determine whether the list is full, find the size of the list, destroy or clear the list, determine whether an item is the same as a given list element, insert an item in the list at the specified location, remove an item from the list at the specified location, replace an item at the specified location with another item, retrieve an item from the list from the specified location, and search the list for a given item.

24. The **interface** `ArrayListADT<T>`, as described in this chapter, describes the basic operations on a list.

25. The **class** `ArrayListClass`, as described in this chapter, is an **abstract class**. It is the super class of the classes that implements a list.

26. The three instance variables of the **class** `ArrayListClass` are `length`, `maxSize`, and `list`. The instance variable `length` specifies the number elements currently in the list. The instance variable `maxSize` specifies the maximum number of elements that can be processed by the list. The instance variable `list` is an array of reference variables.

27. The **classes** `UnorderedArrayList` and `OrderedArrayList` are derived from the **class** `ArrayListClass`.

28. Objects of the **class** `UnorderedArrayList` arrange list elements in no particular order; that is, these lists are unsorted.

29. Objects of the **class** `OrderedArrayList` arrange list elements according to some comparison criteria, usually greater than or equal to.

30. The definition of the method `clone` of the **class** `ArrayListClass` makes only a copy of the references stored in the array.

EXERCISES

1. Suppose that `Mystery` is a user-defined class. Explain the meaning of the following statement:

   public class `Mystery` **implements** `Cloneable`

2. Suppose that you want to define the **class** `Secret`. Write the statement that ensures that the **class** `Secret` provides an appropriate definition of the method `compareTo` of the **interface** `Comparable`.

3. Within a generic method, list three things that you would normally do using its type parameter(s).

15

4. Write the definition of a generic method, `sumList`, which takes as parameter a list of numbers or an array of numbers and then returns the sum of the numbers. Also write a test program to test your method. Note that the type parameter must be appropriately bounded.

5. In a generic method, which keyword is used to bound a type parameter?

6. What is the effect of the following statements?

   a. `UnorderedArrayList<Integer> intList =`

   `new UnorderedArrayList<Integer>(50);`

   b. `UnorderedArrayList<String> stringList =`

   `new UnorderedArrayList<String>(1000);`

   c. `OrderedArrayList<Double> salesList =`

   `new OrderedArrayList<Double>(-10);`

7. Suppose that `stringList` is an `UnorderedArrayList<String>` object such that:

   `stringList = {"One", "Two", "Three", "Four"}`

   (The instance variable `list` of `stringList` is an array of 10 components.) What are the elements of list after the following statements execute?

   ```
   stringList.insertEnd("Five");
   stringList.insertAt(2, "Six");
   stringList.insertEnd("Three");
   ```

8. Suppose that `nameList` is an `UnorderedArrayList<String>` object such that:

   `nameList = {"Billy", "Johnny", "Sheila", "Peter", "Lisa"}`

   What are the elements of the object `nameList` after the following statements execute?

   ```
   nameList.removeAt(1);
   nameList.remove("Peter");
   ```

9. Suppose that you have the following declaration:

   ```
   UnorderedArrayList<Integer> numList =
                    new UnorderedArrayList <Integer>(100);
   ```

   What are the elements of `numList` after the following statements execute?

   ```
   numList.insertEnd(34);
   numList.insertEnd(18);
   numList.insertEnd(22);
   numList.insertEnd(4);
   numList.insertAt(1, 19);
   numList.insertEnd(12);
   numList.insertAt(2, 18);
   ```

10. Suppose that you have the following `UnorderedArrayList<String>`:

    ```
    studentLastName = ["Smith", "Shue", "Cox", "Jordan"]
    studentFirstName = ["James", "Sherly", "Chris", "Eliot"]
    ```

    a. Write a Java statement that will output the first name of the third student.

    b. Write a Java statement that will output the last name of the second student.

    c. Write a Java statement(s) that will output the first name followed by the last name separated by a single blank space of the first student.

    d. Write the necessary Java statements so that first and last names of `Eliot Jordan` are interchanged.

11. Assume that you have the `UnorderedArrayList<String>` objects defined in Exercise 10. Write a Java statement(s) that will change the names `James Smith` and `Sherly Shue` to `Sherly Smith` and `James Shue` by:

    a. changing the `UnorderedArrayList<String>` object `studentLastName`

    b. changing the `UnorderedArrayList<String>` object `studentFirstName`

12. What is the output of the following program?

    ```java
    public class TestProgExercise12
    {
        public static void main(String[] args)
        {
            UnorderedArrayList<Integer> numList =
                    new UnorderedArrayList<Integer>(50);

            numList.insertEnd(35);
            numList.insertEnd(28);
            numList.insertEnd(19);
            numList.insertAt(1, 12);
            numList.insertAt(4, 20);
            numList.insertAt(2, 28);
            numList.insertEnd(35);

            numList.print();
            System.out.println();

            numList.replaceAt(3, 44);

            numList.removeAt(5);
            numList.print();
            System.out.println();
        }
    }
    ```

15

13. What is the output of the following program?

```java
public class TestProgExercise13
{
    public static void main(String[] args)
    {
        OrderedArrayList<String> stringList =
                new OrderedArrayList<String>(50);

        stringList.insert("Jason");
        stringList.insert("Lisa");
        stringList.insert("Sheela");
        stringList.insertAt(1, "Kiran");
        stringList.insertAt(4, "Samual");
        stringList.insertAt(2, "Andy");
        stringList.insert("Billy");

        stringList.print();
        System.out.println();

        stringList.replaceAt(3, "Randy");

        stringList.removeAt(5);
        stringList.print();
        System.out.println();
    }
}
```

14. Draw the UML diagram of the **class** **Polynomial**. Also show the inheritance hierarchy.

PROGRAMMING EXERCISES

1. The method **removeAt**, which is inherited from the **class** **ArrayListClass**, of the **class** **UnorderedArrayList** removes an element from the list by shifting the elements of the list. However, if the element to be removed is at the beginning of the list and the list is fairly large, it could take a lot of computer time. Because the list elements are in no particular order, you could simply remove the element by copying the last element of the list at the position of the item to be removed and reducing the length of the list. Redefine the method **removeAt**, in the **class** **UnorderedArrayList**, using this technique. Also write a program to test your method

2. The method **remove** of the **class** **ArrayListClass** removes only the first occurrence of an element. Add the method **removeAll** to the **class** **ArrayListClass** as an **abstract** method that would remove all occurrences of a given element. Also, write the definition of the method **removeAll** in the **class** **UnorderedArrayList** and a program to test this method. (Note that you must add the method **removeAll** in the **interface** **ArrayListADT**.)

3. Add the method **min** to the **class** ArrayListClass, as an **abstract** method, to return the smallest element of the list. Also, write the definition of the method **min** in the **class** UnorderedArrayList and a program to test this method.

4. Add the method **max** to the **class** ArrayListClass, as an **abstract** method, to return the largest element of the list. Also, write the definition of the method **max** in the **class** UnorderedArrayList and a program to test this method.

5. Write the definition of the method **multiply** of the **class** Polynomial to multiply two polynomials. Also write a test program to test the method **multiply**.

6. Let $p(x) = a_0 + a_1x + \ldots + a_{n-1}x^{n-1} + a_nx^n$ be a polynomial of degree n, where a_i are real (or complex) numbers and n is a nonnegative integer. The derivative of $p(x)$, written $p'(x)$, is defined to be $p'(x) = a_1 + 2a_2x^2 + \ldots + na_nx^{n-1}$. If $p(x)$ is constant, then $p'(x) = 0$. Write the definition of the method **derivative** for the **class** Polynomial to determine and return the derivative of a polynomial.

7. The **class** Polynomial as given in the Programming Example Polynomial Operations processes polynomials with coefficients that are real numbers. Redesign this class so that it can also be used to process polynomials with complex numbers as coefficients. (Note that first you must design the **class** Complex to implement complex numbers.)

8. Using classes, design an online address book to keep track of the names, addresses, phone numbers, and dates of birth of family members, close friends, and certain business associates. Your program should be able to handle a maximum of 500 entries.

   a. Define the **class** Address that can store a street address, city, state, and ZIP code. Use the appropriate methods to print and store the address. Also, use constructors to automatically initialize the instance variables.

   b. Define the **class** ExtPerson using the **class** Person (as defined in this chapter), the **class** Date (as designed in this chapter), and the **class** Address. Add an instance variable to this class to classify the person as a family member, friend, or business associate. Also, add an instance variable to store the phone number. Add (or override) the methods to print and store the appropriate information. Use constructors to automatically initialize the instance variables.

   c. Define the **class** AddressBook using previously defined classes. An object of the type AddressBook should be able to process a maximum of 500 entries.

      The program should perform the following operations:

      (i)   Load the data into the address book from a disk.

      (ii) Search for a person by last name.

      (iii) Print the address, phone number, and date of birth (if it is in the list) of a given person.

15

(iv)   Print the names of the people whose birthdays are in a given month or between two given dates.

(v)   Print the names of all the people between two last names.

(vi)   For special occasions, such as birthdays, print three different messages: one for family members, one for friends, and one for business associates. Your program should be able to print the names of all family members, or the names of all friends, and so on.

9. The instance variable `list` of the **class** `ArrayListClass` is an array. Its default size is `100`. Include an overloaded method `resize`, without parameter and with parameter, which can be used to increase the size of the array `list`. (You also need to include this method in the **interface** `ArrayListADT`.) The method `resize` without parameters doubles the size of `list`. The method `resize`, with parameter, takes as a parameter an **int** value and increases the size of `list` by that value. Also write a program to test the method `resize`. (Use an object of the **class** `UnorderedArrayList` or the **class** `OrderedArrayList` to test the method `resize`.)

10. (**Unordered Sets**) As explained in this chapter, a set is a collection of distinct elements of the same type. Design the **class** `UnorderedSet`, derived from the **class** `UnorderedArrayList`, to manipulate sets. Note that you need to redefine only the methods `insertAt`, `insertEnd`, and `replaceAt`. If the item to be inserted is already in the list, the methods `insertAt` and `insertEnd` output an appropriate message. Similarly, if the item to be replaced is already in the list, the method `replaceAt` outputs an appropriate message. Also write a program to test your class.

11. (**Ordered Sets**) Programming Exercise 10 asks you to define the **class** `UnorderedSet` to manipulate sets. The elements of an `UnorderdSet` object are distinct, but in no particular order. Design the **class** `OrderedSet`, derived from the **class** `OrderedArrayList`, to manipulate ordered sets. The elements of an `OrderedSet` object are distinct and in ascending order. Note that you need to redefine only the methods `insert` and `replaceAt`. If the item to be inserted is already in the list, the method `insert` outputs an appropriate message. Similarly, if the item to be replaced is already in the list, the method `replaceAt` outputs an appropriate message. Also write a program to test your class.

12. Design a class to perform the various matrix operations. A matrix is a set of numbers arranged in rows and columns. Therefore, every element of a matrix has a row position and a column position. If A is a matrix of 5 rows and 6 columns, we say that the matrix A is of the size 5×6 and sometimes denote it as $A_{5 \times 6}$. Clearly, a convenient place to store a matrix is in a two-dimensional array. Two matrices can be added and subtracted if they have the same size. Suppose $A = [a_{ij}]$ and $B = [b_{ij}]$ are two matrices of the size $m \times n$, where a_{ij} denotes the element of A in the ith row and the jth column, and so on. The sum and difference of A and B is given by:

$A + B = [a_{ij} + b_{ij}]$

$A - B = [a_{ij} - b_{ij}]$

The multiplication of A and B, $(A * B)$, is defined only if the number of columns of A are the same as the number of rows of B. If A is of the size $m \times n$ and B is of the size $n \times t$, then $A * B = [c_{ik}]$ is of the size $m \times t$ and the element c_{ik} is given by the formula:

$$c_{ik} = a_{i1}b_{1k} + a_{i2}b_{2k} + \dots + a_{in}b_{nk}$$

Design and implement a **class** Matrix that can store a matrix of any size. Among others, provide the methods to perform the addition, subtraction, and multiplication operations; and a method to output a matrix. Also, write a test program to test the various operations on matrices.

13. (**Friendly Hardware Store Revisited**) Programming Exercise 2 in Chapter 10 asked you to write a program to keep track of a hardware store's inventory. In that program, you used seven parallel vectors to keep track of products sold by the store. In this program you redo that program using the **class** OrderedArrayList.

Define the **class** Product to implement the products (items) sold by the store. The **class** Product must store the information, as given in Chapter 10, about an item sold by the store. For example, some of the instance variables of this **class** are: productId, productName, and piecesOrdered. Add appropriate methods to manipulate a Product object. Note that this **class** must implement the **interfaces** Cloneable and Comparable. Two products are the same if they have the same productId.

Use the **class** OrderedArrayList to keep track of the products sold by the store. When printing the inventory, sort data according to productId.

15

LINKED LISTS

In this chapter, you will:

- ♦ Learn about linked lists
- ♦ Study the basic properties of linked lists
- ♦ Explore the insertion and deletion operations on linked lists
- ♦ Discover how to build and manipulate a linked list
- ♦ Learn how to construct a doubly linked list
- ♦ Become aware of circular linked lists

Y ou have already seen how you can organize data and process it sequentially using an array, called a **sequential list**. You have performed several operations on sequential lists, such as inserting, deleting, and searching. You also found that if data is not sorted, then searching for an item in the list can be very time-consuming, especially with large lists. Once the data is sorted, you can use another search algorithm, called the binary search (discussed in Chapter 18), and improve the search algorithm. However, if the list is sorted, insertion and deletion become time-consuming, especially with large lists, because these operations require data movement because the resulting list must also be sorted. Moreover, because the array size must be fixed during execution, new items can be added only if there is room. Thus, there are limitations when you organize data in an array.

This chapter helps you overcome some of these problems by introducing a data structure called linked lists. Recall that when data is stored in an array, memory for the components of the array is contiguous—that is, blocks are allocated one after the other. On the other hand, as you will see, the dynamically allocated components of a linked list are not necessarily contiguous.

LINKED LISTS

A **linked list** is a collection of components, called **nodes**. Every node (except the last node) contains the address of the next node. Thus, every node in a linked list has two components: one to store the relevant information (that is, the data); and one to store the address, called the **link**, of the next node in the list. The address of the first node in the list is stored in a separate location, called the **head** or **first**. Figure 16-1 shows a pictorial representation of a node.

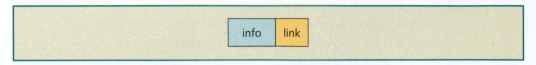

Figure 16-1   Structure of a node

In Java, there are two types of variables—variables of the primitive data types and reference variables. Therefore, in Figure 16-1, the `info` of the node can be either a value of a primitive type or a reference to an object.

<u>**Linked list:**</u> A list of items, called **nodes**, in which the order of the nodes is determined by the address, called the **link**, stored in each node.

The list in Figure 16-2 is an example of a linked list.

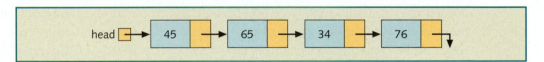

Figure 16-2   Linked list

The down arrow in the last node indicates that this link field is `null`. The arrow in each node indicates that the address of the node to which it is pointing is stored in that node. For a better understanding of this notation, suppose that the first node is at memory location `1200`, and the second node is at memory location `1575`. We thus have Figure 16-3.

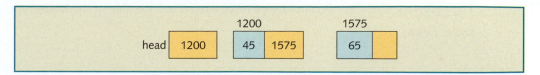

Figure 16-3   Linked list and the values of the links

The value of the head is **1200**, the data part of the first node is **45**, and the link component of the first node contains **1575**, the address of the second node. We will use the arrow notation whenever we draw the figure of a linked list.

In Figures 16-2 and 16-3, for illustration purposes we assume that the data type of the variable **info** is **int**. However, as remarked above, the **info** can be either a variable of a primitive data type or a reference variable. In fact, after describing the basic properties of linked lists and how to build a linked list, using generic classes we develop a generic code to process linked lists, which can be used in a variety of applications. Moreover, for simplicity and for the ease of understanding and clarity, Figures 16-3 through 16-6 use decimal integers as the values of memory addresses. However, in computer memory the memory addresses are in binary.

Because each node of a linked list has two components, we define **class** Node, with two instance variables, to create each node. The data type of each node depends on the specific application—that is, what kind of data is being processed; however, the **link** component of each node is a reference variable. In fact, **link** is a reference variable of the **Node** type. For the previous linked list, the definition of the node is as follows. (Suppose that the data type of **info** is **int**.)

```
public class Node
{
    public int info;
    public Node link;
}
```

Notice that we declare the **class** Node to implement the nodes of a linked list as **public**. Also notice that instance variables of the **class** Node are declared as **public**. We declared the instance variables as **public** for the simple reason that in the next few sections our focus is on the basic properties—such as traversing a linked list, item insertion and deletion—of a linked list. To directly access these instance variables, we have declared them **public**. If we declare them **private** or **protected**, then we will have to provide methods such as **set** and **get** to manipulate the data stored in the node. However, when we study linked list as an abstract data type ADT, then we will declare the **class** Node as **protected** and make it an inner class of the class that would implement linked lists as an ADT. Then the user would have direct access to the instance variables of the **class** Node. Furthermore, as remarked earlier, for illustration purposes, the data type of the instance variable **info** is **int**.

16

The following statement declares **head** to be a reference variable of the **Node** type:

```
Node head;
```

LINKED LISTS: SOME PROPERTIES

To help you better understand the concept of a linked list and a node, some important properties of linked lists are described next.

Consider the linked list in Figure 16-4.

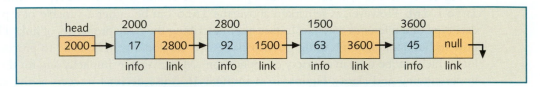

Figure 16-4   Linked list with four nodes

This linked list has four nodes. The address of the first node is stored in **head**. Each node has two components: **info**, to store the info; and **link**, to store the address of the next node.

Suppose that the first node is at location **2000**, the second node is at location **2800**, the third node is at location **1500**, and the fourth node is at location **3600**. Therefore, the value of **head** is **2000**, the value of the component **link** of the first node is **2800**, the value of the component **link** of the second node is **1500**, and so on. Also, the value **null** in the **link** of the last node means that this link does not point to anything, which we indicate by drawing a down arrow. The number at the top of each node is the address of the node.

Table 16-1 shows the values of head and some of the nodes of the linked list in Figure 16-4.

Table 16-1   Values of **head** and some of the nodes of the linked list in Figure 16-4

	Value	Explanation
head	2000	
head.info	17	Because head is 2000 and the info of the node at location 2000 is 17
head.link	2800	
head.link.info	92	Because head.link is 2800 and the info of the node at location 2800 is 92

Suppose that **current** is a reference variable of the same type as **head**. Then the statement

current = head;

copies the value of **head** into **current**. See Figure 16-5.

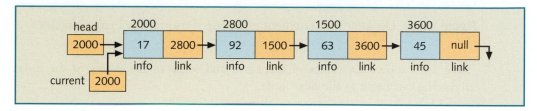

Figure 16-5   Linked list after **current = head;** executes

Table 16-2 shows the values of **current** and some of the nodes of the linked list in Figure 16-5.

Table 16-2   Values of **current** and some of the nodes of the linked list in Figure 16-5

	Value
current	2000
current.info	17
current.link	2800
current.link.info	92

Now consider the statement:

current = current.link;

This statement copies the value of **current.link**, which is **2800**, into **current**. There-fore, after this statement executes, **current** points to the second node in the list. (When working with linked lists, we typically use these types of statements to advance a reference variable to the next node in the list, such as when we traverse a linked list.) See Figure 16-6.

16

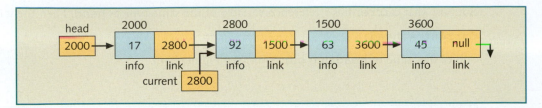

Figure 16-6 List after the statement `current = current.link;` executes

Table 16-3 shows the values of `current` and some of the nodes of the linked list after advancing `current` to the next node.

Table 16-3 Values of `current` and some of the nodes of the linked list in Figure 16-6

	Value
current	2800
current.info	92
current.link	1500
current.link.info	63

Finally, Table 16-4 shows the values of some other reference variables and nodes of the linked list in Figure 16-6.

Table 16-4 Values of various reference variables and nodes of the linked list in Figure 16-6

	Value
head.link.link	1500
head.link.link.info	63
head.link.link.link	3600
head.link.link.link.info	45
current.link.link	3600
current.link.link.info	45
current.link.link.link	null
current.link.link.link.info	Does not exist

From now on, we use only the arrow notation when we draw the figure of the linked list.

Traversing a Linked List

The basic operations of a linked list are:

- Search the list to determine whether a particular item is in the list.
- Insert an item in the list.
- Delete an item from the list.

These operations require the list to be traversed. Therefore, given a reference, that is, address of the first node of the list, we must step through the nodes of the list.

Suppose that **head** points to the first node in the list, and the link of the last node is **null**. We cannot use the variable **head** to traverse the list because if we use **head** to traverse the list we would lose the nodes of the list. This problem occurs because the links go in only one direction. The reference variable **head** contains the address of the first node, the first node contains the address of the second node, the second node contains the address of the third node, and so on. If we move **head** to the second node, the first node is lost (unless we save the address of this node). If we keep advancing **head** to the next node, we will lose all the nodes of the list (unless we save the address of each node before advancing **head**, which is impractical because it would require additional computer time and memory space to maintain the list).

Therefore, we always want **head** to point to the first node. It now follows that we must traverse the list using another reference variable of the same type as **head**. Suppose that **current** is a reference variable of the same type as **head**. The following code traverses the list:

```
current = head;
while (current != null)
{
    //Process current
    current = current.link;
}
```

For example, suppose that head points to a linked list. The following code outputs the data stored in each node:

```
current = head;
while (current != null)
{
    System.out.println(current.info + " ");
    current = current.link;
}
```

ITEM INSERTION AND DELETION

This section discusses how to insert an item in and delete an item from a linked list. Consider the following definition of a node. As before, for simplicity, we assume that the **info** type is **int**. The next section, which discusses linked lists as an abstract data type (ADT), uses the generic definition of a node:

```
public class Node
{
    public int info;
    public Node link;
}
```

We will use the following variable declaration, in which **head, p, q,** and **newNode** are reference variables of the **Node** type:

```
Node head, p, q, newNode;
```

Insertion

Consider the linked list shown in Figure 16-7.

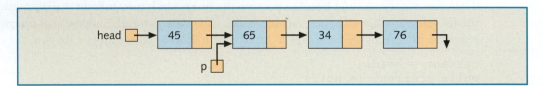

Figure 16-7   Linked list before item insertion

Suppose that **p** points to the node with **info 65**, and a new node with **info 50** is to be created and inserted after **p**. The following statements create and store **50** in the **info** field of a new node:

```
newNode = new Node();    //create newNode
newNode.info = 50;       //store 50 in the new node
```

The first statement, **newNode = new Node();**, creates a node somewhere in memory and stores the address of the newly created node in **newNode**. The second statement, **newNode.info = 50;**, stores **50** in the **info** field of the new node. See Figure 16-8.

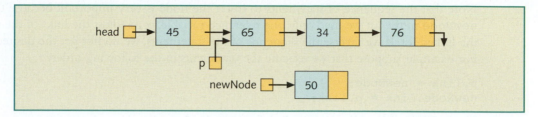

Figure 16-8 Create `newNode` and store `50` in it

The following statements insert the node in the linked list at the required place:

```
newNode.link = p.link;
p.link = newNode;
```

After the first statement, `newNode.link = p.link;`, executes, the resulting list is as shown in Figure 16–9.

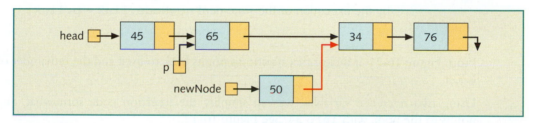

Figure 16-9 List after the statement `newNode.link = p.link;` executes

After the second statement, `p.link = newNode;`, executes, the resulting list is as shown in Figure 16–10.

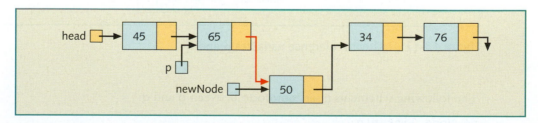

Figure 16-10 List after the statement `p.link = newNode;` executes

16

Note that the sequence of statements to insert the node is very important because to insert `newNode` in the list we used only one reference variable, `p`, to adjust the links of the node of the linked list. If we reverse the sequence of the statements, we do not get the desired result. For example, suppose that we execute the statements in the following order:

```
p.link = newNode;
newNode.link = p.link;
```

Figure 16–11 shows the resulting list after these statements execute.

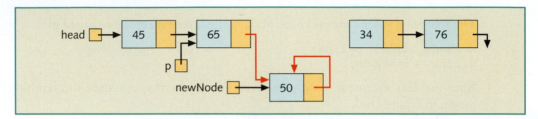

Figure 16-11   List after the execution of the statement `p.link = newNode;` followed by the execution of the statement `newNode.link = p.link;`

From Figure 16–11, it is clear that **newNode** points back to itself and the remainder of the list is lost.

Using two reference variables, we can simplify the insertion code somewhat. Suppose `q` points to the node with **info 34**. See Figure 16–12.

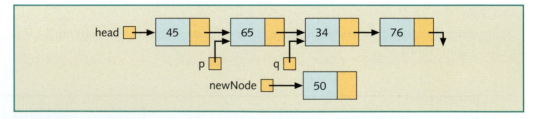

Figure 16-12   List with reference variables `p` and `q`

The following statements insert **newNode** between `p` and `q`:

```
newNode.link = q;
p.link = newNode;
```

The order in which these statements execute does not matter. To illustrate this, suppose that we execute the statements in the following order:

```
p.link = newNode;
newNode.link = q;
```

After the statement `p.link = newNode;` executes, the resulting list is as shown in Figure 16–13.

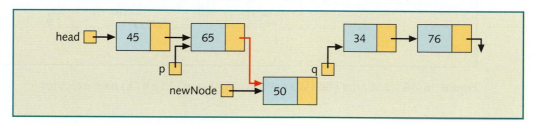

Figure 16-13   List after the statement `p.link = newNode;` executes

Because we have a reference variable, q, pointing to the remaining list, the remaining list is not lost. After the statement `newNode.link = q;` executes, the list is as shown in Figure 16–14.

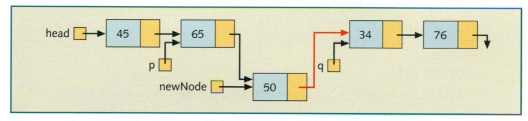

Figure 16-14   List after the statement `newNode.link = q;` executes

Deletion

Consider the linked list shown in Figure 16–15.

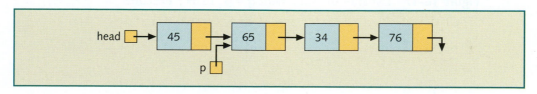

Figure 16-15   Node to be deleted is with `info` 34

16

Suppose that you need to delete the node with `info 34` from the list. The following statement removes the node from the list:

```
p.link = p.link.link;
```

Figure 16-16 shows the resulting list after the preceding statement executes.

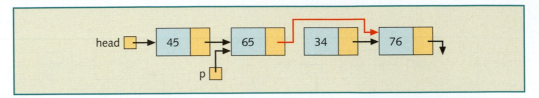

Figure 16-16   List after the statement `p.link = p.link.link;` executes

From Figure 16-16, it clear that the node with `info 34` is removed from the list. However, the memory may still be occupied by this node. That is, this node is dangling. When the system's automatic garbage collector runs and if no reference variable points to the node with `info 34`, then the memory occupied by this node will be reclaimed by the system. You can also issue the statement `System.gc();` to run the garbage collector.

With two reference variables, you can simplify the code somewhat to delete the node as follows (the code also shows how to include the statement `System.gc();`):

```
q = p.link;
p.link = q.link;
q = null;
System.gc();
```

After the statement `q = p.link;` executes, the list is as shown in Figure 16-17.

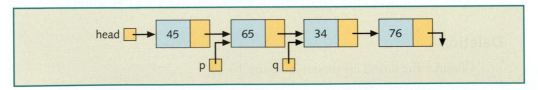

Figure 16-17   List after the statement `q = p.link;` executes

After the statement `p.link = q.link;` executes, the resulting list is as shown in Figure 16-18.

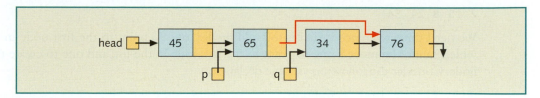

Figure 16-18 List after the statement `p.link = q.link;` executes

After the statements `q = null;` and `System.gc();` execute, the list is as shown in Figure 16-19.

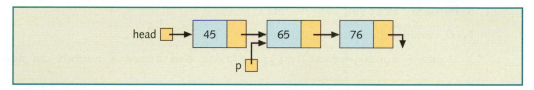

Figure 16-19 List after the statements `q = null;` and `System.gc();` execute

In general, from the preceding discussion it follows that to delete a node, as well as simplify the deletion, from a linked list you use two reference variables—one variable to traverse the list to find the node you want to delete, and another variable to adjust the `link` of node just before the node to be deleted. Of course, you must handle special cases separately, such as deleting the first node of the list. In this case, you make **head** point to the next node. This is accomplished by executing the statement **head** = **head.link**.

BUILDING A LINKED LIST

Now that you know how to insert a node in a linked list, next you can learn how to build a linked list. First, we consider a linked list in general. If the data we read is unsorted, the linked list need not be in order. You can build such a list in two ways: in the forward manner and in the backward manner. In the forward manner, a new node is always inserted at the end of the linked list; in the backward manner, a new node is always inserted at the beginning of the linked list. We consider both cases.

16

Building a Linked List Forward

Suppose that the nodes are in the usual `info-link` form and that `info` is of the type `int`. Let us assume that we process the following data:

```
2 15 8 24 34
```

We need three reference variables to build the list: one to point to the first node in the list, which cannot be moved; one to point to the last node in the list; and one to create the new node. Consider the following variable declaration:

```
Node first, last, newNode;
int num;
```

Assume that `console` is a `Scanner` object initialized to the standard input device. Suppose that `first` points to the first node in the list. Initially, the list is empty, so both `first` and `last` are `null`. Thus, we must have the statements

```
first = null;
last = null;
```

to initialize `first` and `last` to `null`.

Next, consider the following statements:

```
1    num = console.nextInt();    //read and store a number in num

2    newNode = new Node();       //allocate memory of the type
                                 //Node and store the address of
                                 //the allocated memory in newNode

3    newNode.info = num;         //copy the value of num into
                                 //the info field of newNode

4    newNode.link = null;        //initialize the link field
                                 //of newNode to null

5    if (first == null)          //if first is null, the list
                                 //is empty; make first
                                 //and last point to newNode
     {
5a       first = newNode;
5b       last = newNode;
     }
6    else                        //list is not empty
     {
6a       last.link = newNode;    //insert newNode at the end
                                 //of the list
6b       last = newNode;         //set last so that it points
                                 //to the actual last node
                                 //in the list
     }
```

Let us now execute these statements. Initially, both `first` and `last` are `null`. Therefore, we have the list as shown in Figure 16–20.

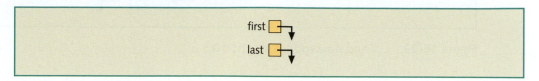

Figure 16-20 Empty list

After statement 1 executes, `num` is `2`. Statement 2 creates a node and stores the address of that node in `newNode`. Statement 3 stores `2` in the `info` field of `newNode`, and statement 4 stores `null` in the link field of `newNode`. See Figure 16-21.

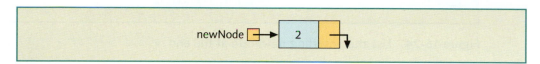

Figure 16-21 `newNode` with `info` 2

Because `first` is `null`, we execute statements 5a and 5b. Figure 16-22 shows the resulting list.

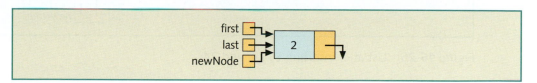

Figure 16-22 List after inserting `newNode`

We now repeat statements 1 through 6b. After statement 1 executes, `num` is `15`. Statement 2 creates a node and stores the address of the node in `newNode`. Statement 3 stores `15` in the `info` field of `newNode`, and statement 4 stores `null` in the link field of `newNode`. See Figure 16-23.

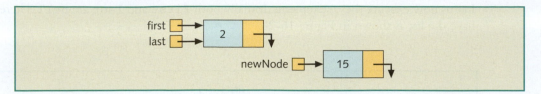

Figure 16-23   List and `newNode` with `info` 15

Because `first` is not `null`, we execute statements 6a and 6b. Figure 16-24 shows the resulting list.

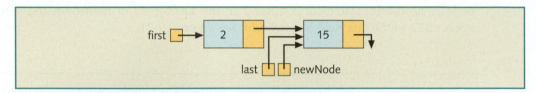

Figure 16-24   List after inserting `newNode` at the end

We now repeat statements 1 through 6b three more times. Figure 16-25 shows the resulting list.

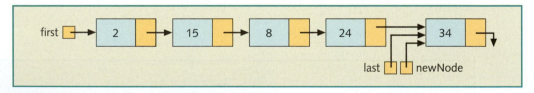

Figure 16-25   List after inserting 8, 24, and 34

To build the linked list more efficiently, we can put the previous statements in a loop, and execute the loop until certain conditions are met. We can, in fact, write a method to build a linked list.

Suppose that we read a list of integers ending with -999. The following method, **buildListForward**, builds a linked list in a forward manner and returns the reference, that is, the address of the first node of the built list:

```
Node buildListForward()
{
    Node first, newNode, last;
    int num;

    System.out.println("Enter integers ending with -999:");

    num = console.nextInt();

    first = null;

    while (num != -999)
    {
        newNode = new Node();

        newNode.info = num;
        newNode.link = null;

        if (first == null)
        {
            first = newNode;
            last = newNode;
        }
        else
        {
            last.link = newNode;
            last = newNode;
        }

        num = console.nextInt();
    }//end while

    return first;
}//end buildListForward
```

Building a Linked List Backward

We now consider the case of building a linked list backward. For the previously given data—2, 15, 8, 24, and 34—the linked list is as shown in Figure 16-26.

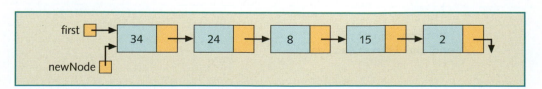

Figure 16-26 List after building it backward

Because the new node is always inserted at the beginning of the list, we do not need to know the end of the list, so the reference variable `last` is not needed. Also, after inserting the new node at the beginning, the new node becomes the first node in the list. Thus, we need to update the value `first` to correctly point to the first node in the list. We see, then, that we need only two reference variables to build the linked list: one to point to the list, and one to create the new node. Because initially the list is empty, `first` must be initialized to `null`. In pseudocode, the algorithm is:

1. Initialize `first` to `null`.

2. For each item in the list:

   a. Create the new node, `newNode`.

   b. Store the item in `newNode`.

   c. Insert `newNode` before `first`.

   d. Update the value of `first`.

The following Java method builds the linked list backward and returns the reference of the built list:

```java
Node buildListBackward()
{
    Node first, newNode;
    int num;

    System.out.println("Enter integers ending with -999:");

    num = console.nextInt();

    first = null;

    while (num != -999)
    {
        newNode = new Node();       //create a node
        newNode.info = num;         //store the data in newNode
        newNode.link = first;       //put newNode at the
                                    //beginning of the list
        first = newNode;            //update the head of the
                                    //list,
        num = console.nextInt();    //get the next number
    }

    return first;
}//end buildListBackward
```

LINKED LIST AS AN ADT

In the previous sections, you learned the basic properties of linked lists and how to construct and manipulate linked lists. Because a linked list is a very important data structure, rather than discuss specific lists such as a list of integers or a list of strings, this section discusses linked lists as an abstract data type (ADT). The programming example at the end of this chapter also uses this generic definition of linked lists.

The basic operations on linked lists are:

1. Initialize the list.

2. Check whether the list is empty.

3. Output the list.

4. Find the length of the list.

5. Destroy the list.

6. Retrieve the info contained in the first node.

7. Retrieve the info contained in the last node.

8. Search the list for a given item.

9. Insert an item in the list.

10. Delete an item from the list.

11. Make a copy of the linked list.

The following interface describes the basic operations of a linked list as an ADT:

```java
public interface LinkedListADT<T> extends Cloneable
{
    public Object clone();
       //Returns a copy of objects data in store.
       //This method clones only the references stored in
       //each node of the list. The objects that the
       //list nodes point to are not cloned.

    public boolean isEmptyList();
       //Method to determine whether the list is empty.
       //Postcondition: Returns true if the list is empty;
       //               false otherwise.

    public void initializeList();
       //Method to initialize the list to an empty state.
       //Postcondition: The list is initialized to an empty
       //               state.
```

16

```
    public void print();
        //Method to output the data contained in each node.

    public int length();
        //Method to return the number of nodes in the list.
        //Postcondition: The number of nodes in the list is
        //               returned.

    public T front();
        //Method to return a reference of the object containing
        //the data of the first node of the list.
        //Precondition: The list must exist and must not be empty.
        //Postcondition: The reference of the object that
        //               contains the info of the first node
        //               is returned.

    public T back();
        //Method to return a reference of object containing
        //the data of the last node of the list.
        //Precondition: The list must exist and must not be empty.
        //Postcondition: The reference of the object that
        //               contains the info of the last node
        //               is returned.

    public boolean search(T searchItem);
        //Method to determine whether searchItem is in the list.
        //Postcondition: Returns true if searchItem is found
        //               in the list; false otherwise.

    public void insertFirst(T newItem);
        //Method to insert newItem in the list.
        //Postcondition: newItem is inserted at the
        //               beginning of the list.

    public void insertLast(T newItem);
        //Method to insert newItem at the end of the list.
        //Postcondition: newItem is inserted at the end
        //               of the list.

    public void deleteNode(T deleteItem);
        //Method to delete deleteItem from the list.
        //Postcondition: If found, the node containing
        //               deleteItem is deleted from the
        //               list.
}
```

Figure 16-27 shows the UML class diagram of the **interface** `LinkedListADT`.

```
        <<interface>>
        LinkedListADT<T>


+clone(): Object
+isEmptyList(): boolean
+initializeList(): void
+print(): void
+length(): int
+front(): T
+back(): T
+search(T): boolean
+insertFirst(T): void
+insertLast(T): void
+deleteNode(T): void
```

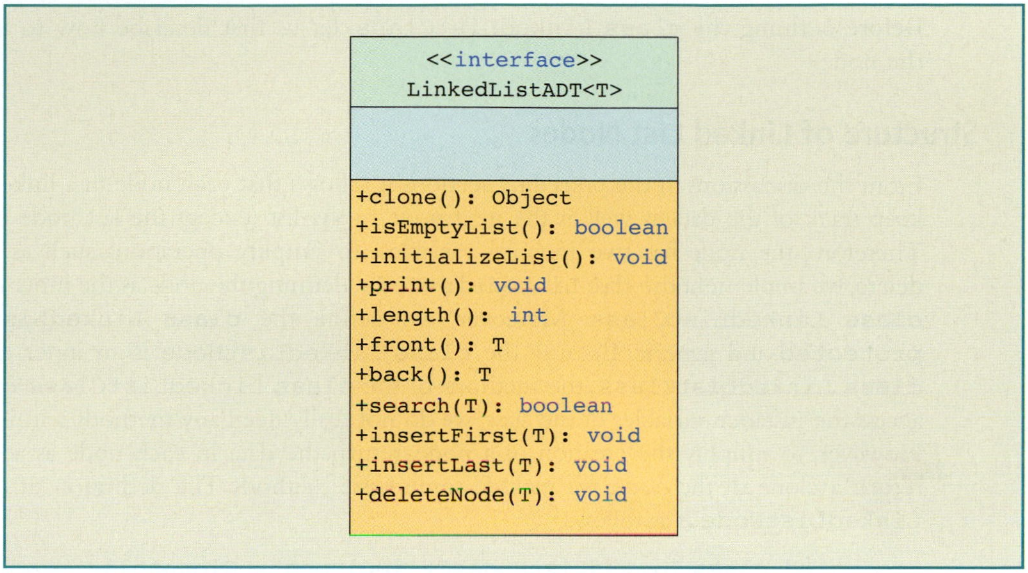

Figure 16-27   UML class diagram of the **interface** `LinkedListADT`

As in the case of array-based lists, there are two types of linked lists—sorted lists, whose elements are arranged according to some criteria, and unsorted lists, whose elements are in no particular order. The algorithms to implement the operations search, insert, and remove slightly differ for sorted and unsorted lists. Therefore, we will define the **class** `LinkedListClass` to implement the basic operations on a linked list as an **abstract class**. Using the principal of inheritance, we in fact will derive two **class**es—`UnorderedLinkedList` and `OrderedLinkedList`—from the **class** `LinkedListClass`.

Objects of the **class** `UnorderedLinkedList` would arrange list elements in no particular order, that is, these lists may not be sorted. On the other hand, objects of the **class** `OrderedLinkedList` would arrange elements according to some comparison criteria, usually less than or equal to. That is, these lists will be in ascending order. Moreover, after inserting an element into or removing an element from an ordered list, the resulting list will be ordered.

If a linked list is unordered, we can insert a new item at either the end or the beginning. Furthermore, you can build such a list in either a forward manner or a backward manner. The method `buildListForward` inserts the new item at the end, whereas the method `buildListBackward` inserts the new item at the beginning. To accommodate both operations, we will write two methods: `insertFirst`, to insert the new item at the beginning

16

of the list, and `insertLast`, to insert the new item at the end of the list. Also, to make the algorithms more efficient, we will use two reference variables in the list: `first`, which points to the first node in the list; and `last`, which points to the last node in the list.

Before defining the **class** `LinkedListClass`, let us first describe how to implement the node.

Structure of Linked List Nodes

From the discussions in the preceding sections it follows that each node of a linked list must keep track of the data as well as the next node in the list (except the last node of the list). Therefore, the node has two instance variables. To simplify operations such as insert and delete, we implement the class `LinkedListNode`, defining the node as the inner class of the **class** `LinkedListClass`. Moreover, we define the **class** `LinkedListNode` as **protected** and generic. Because the **class** `LinkedListNode` is an inner class of the **class** `LinkedListClass`, the methods of the **class** `LinkedListClass` can directly access the instance variables of the class; we do not really need any methods within this class. However, to simplify the creation of a node, return the data in each node as a string, and return a clone of the node, we include some basic methods. The definition of the **class** `LinkedListNode` is as follows

```
protected class LinkedListNode<T> implements Cloneable
{
    public T info;  //reference variable to store the data
    public LinkedListNode<T> link;  //reference variable to
                                    //store the reference of
                                    //the next node

        //Default constructor
        //Postcondition: info = null; link = null;
    public LinkedListNode()
    {
        info = null;
        link = null;
    }


        //Constructor with parameters
        //This method sets info pointing to the object to
        //which elem points and link is set to point to
        //the object to which ptr points.
        //Postcondition:  info = elem; link = ptr;
    public LinkedListNode(T elem, LinkedListNode<T> ptr)
    {
        info = elem;
        link = ptr;
    }
```

```
    //Returns a copy of objects data in store.
    //This method clones only the references stored in
    //the node. The objects that the nodes point to
    //are not cloned.
public Object clone()
{
    LinkedListNode<T> copy = null;

    try
    {
        copy = (LinkedListNode<T>) super.clone();
    }
    catch (CloneNotSupportedException e)
    {
        return null;
    }

    return copy;
}

    //Method to return the info as a string.
    //Postcondition: info as a String object is
    //                returned.
public String toString()
{
    return info.toString();
}
} //end class LinkedListNode
```

Figure 16–28 shows the UML class diagram of the **class** LinkedListNode and the outer-inner class relationship.

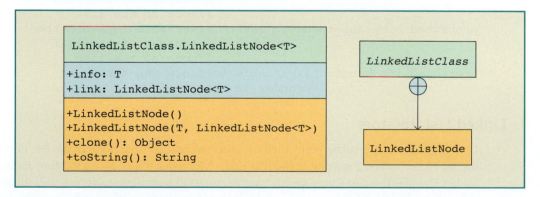

Figure 16-28   UML class diagram of the **class** LinkedListNode and the outer-inner class relationship

16

Let us look at the definition of the constructor with parameters of the **class** LinkedListNode. That is:

```
public LinkedListNode(T elem, LinkedListNode<T> ptr)
{
    info = elem;
    link = ptr;
}
```

Suppose that `temp` is a reference variable of the type `LinkedListNode` and `item` is a reference variable of the type `T`. Consider the following statement:

```
LinkedListNode<T> newNode = new LinkedListNode<T>(item, temp);
```

This statement allocates memory space of the type `LinkedListNode`, assigns the value of `item` to the instance variable `info` and the value of `temp` to the instance variable `link`. Finally, the address of the allocated node is stored in `newNode`. It follows that if `temp` is already pointing to a node, then the instance variable `link` of `newNode` contains the address of the node to which `temp` points. Therefore, you can use this constructor to create a node and insert the node before a given node in a linked list.

Instance Variables of the `class` `LinkedListClass`

To maintain a linked list we use two reference variables—`first` and `last`. The variable `first` points to the first node in the list, and `last` points to the last node in the list. We also keep a count of the number of nodes in the list. Therefore, the **class** `LinkedListClass` has three instance variables, as follows:

Instance variables:

```
protected LinkedListNode<T> first; //variable to store the
                                   //address of the first
                                   //node of the list
protected LinkedListNode<T> last;  //variable to store the
                                   //address of the last
                                   //node of the list
protected int count;  //variable to store the number of
                      //nodes in the list
```

Linked List Iterators

One of the basic operations performed on a list is to process each node of the list. This requires the list to be traversed starting at the first node. Moreover, a specific application requires each node to be processed in a very specific way. A common technique to accomplish this is to provide an iterator. So what is an iterator? An **iterator** is an object that produces each element of a collection, such as a linked list, one element at a time. An iterator typically has at least two methods, `hasNext` and `next`. The method `hasNext` determines whether there is a next element in the collection, and the method `next` gives access to the next element in the list. For example, a `Scanner` object such as `console`, as defined throughout this book, is an iterator.

Note that an iterator is an object. So we need to define a class, which we will call `LinkedListIterator`, to create iterators to objects of the **class** `LinkedListClass`. The iterator class would have two instance variables—one to refer to (the current) node and the other to refer to the node just before the (current node). Moreover, the **class** `LinkedListIterator` is generic, and is an inner class of the **class** `LinkedListClass` so that it can directly access the instance variables of a node. Also note that the **class** `LinkedListNode` is a **protected** inner class of the **class** `LinkedListClass`. Therefore, if we do not make **class** `LinkedListIterator` an inner class of the **class** `LinkedListClass`, then we would have to include methods that are necessary to access the instance variables of a node. The definition of the **class** `LinkedListIterator` is as follows:

```java
public class LinkedListIterator<T>
{
    protected LinkedListNode<T> current;    //variable to
                                            //point to the
                                            //current node in
                                            //list
    protected LinkedListNode<T> previous;   //variable to
                                            //point to the
                                            //node before the
                                            //current node

        //Default constructor
        //Sets current to point to the first node in the
        //list and sets previous to null.
        //Postcondition: current = first; previous = null;
    public LinkedListIterator()
    {
        current = (LinkedListNode<T>) first;
        previous = null;
    }

        //Method to reset the iterator to the first node
        //in the list.
        //Postcondition: current = first; previous = null;
    public void reset()
    {
        current = (LinkedListNode<T>) first;
        previous = null;
    }

        //Method to return a reference of the info of the
        //current node in the list and to advance iterator
        //to the next node.
```

16

```java
    //Postcondition: previous = current;
    //               current = current.link;
    //               A reference of the current node
    //               is returned.
public T next()
{
    if (!hasNext())
        throw new NoSuchElementException();

    LinkedListNode<T> temp = current;
    previous = current;
    current = current.link;

    return temp.info;
}

    //Method to determine whether there is a next
    //element in the list.
    //Postcondition: Returns true if there is a next
    //               node in the list; otherwise
    //               returns false.
public boolean hasNext()
{
    return (current != null);
}

    //Method to remove the node currently pointed to
    //by the iterator.
    //Postcondition: If iterator is not null, then the
    //               node that the iterator points to
    //               is removed. Otherwise the method
    //               throws NoSuchElementException.
public void remove()
{
    if (current == null)
        throw new NoSuchElementException();

    if (current == first)
    {
        first = first.link;
        current = (LinkedListNode<T>) first;
        previous = null;

        if (first == null)
            last = null;
    }
    else
```

```
        {
            previous.link = current.link;

            if (current == last)
            {
                last = first;

                while (last.link != null)
                    last = last.link;
            }
            current = current.link;
        }

        count--;
    }


    //Method to return the info as a string.
    //Postcondition: info as a String object is returned.
    public String toString()
    {
        return current.info.toString();
    }
} //end class LinkedListIterator
```

Figure 16-29 shows the UML class diagram of the **class** LinkedListIterator and the outer–inner class relationship.

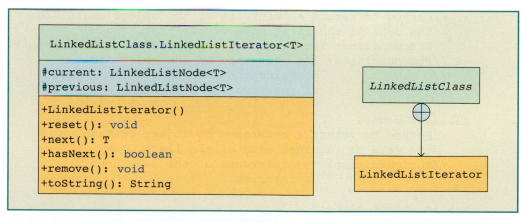

Figure 16-29 UML class diagram of the **class** LinkedListIterator and the outer-inner class relationship

16

Constructors and Instance Methods of the `class` `LinkedListClass`

This section describes the methods of the `class` `LinkedListClass`.

Constructors and Instance Methods:

```
public LinkedListClass()
   //Default constructor
   //Initializes the list to an empty state.
   //Postcondition: first = null, last = null,
   //               count = 0

public boolean isEmptyList()
   //Method to determine whether the list is empty.
   //Postcondition: Returns true if the list is empty;
   //               false otherwise.

public void initializeList()
   //Method to initialize the list to an empty state.
   //Postcondition: first = null, last = null,
   //               count = 0

public void print()
   //Method to output the data contained in each node.

public int length()
   //Method to return the number of nodes in the list.
   //Postcondition: The value of count is returned.

public T front()
   //Method to return a reference of the object containing
   //the data of the first node of the list.
   //Precondition: The list must exist and must not be empty.
   //Postcondition: The reference of the object that
   //               contains the info of the first node
   //               is returned.

public T back()
   //Method to return a reference of object containing
   //the data of the last node of the list.
   //Postcondition: The reference of the last node
   //               is returned.

public Object clone()
   //Returns a copy of objects data in store.
   //This method clones only the references stored in
   //each node of the list. The objects that the
   //list nodes point to are not cloned.
```

```
public LinkedListIterator<T> iterator()
    //Method to return an iterator of the list.
    //Postcondition: An iterator is instantiated and
    //                returned.

public abstract boolean search(T searchItem);
    //Method to determine whether searchItem is in
    //the list.
    //Postcondition: Returns true if searchItem is found
    //                in the list; false otherwise.

public abstract void insertFirst(T newItem);
    //Method to insert newItem in the list.
    //Postcondition: first points to the new list
    //                and newItem is inserted at the
    //                beginning of the list. Also,
    //                last points to the last node and
    //                count is incremented by 1.

public abstract void insertLast(T newItem);
    //Method to insert newItem at the end of the list.
    //Postcondition: first points to the new list and
    //                newItem is inserted at the end
    //                of the list. Also, last points to
    //                the last node and
    //                count is incremented by 1.

public abstract void deleteNode(T deleteItem);
    //Method to delete deleteItem from the list.
    //Postcondition: If found, the node containing
    //                deleteItem is deleted from the
    //                list. Also, first points to the first
    //                node, last points to the last
    //                node of the updated list, and count
    //                is decremented by 1.
```

Figure 16–30 shows the UML class diagram of the **class** LinkedListClass.

16

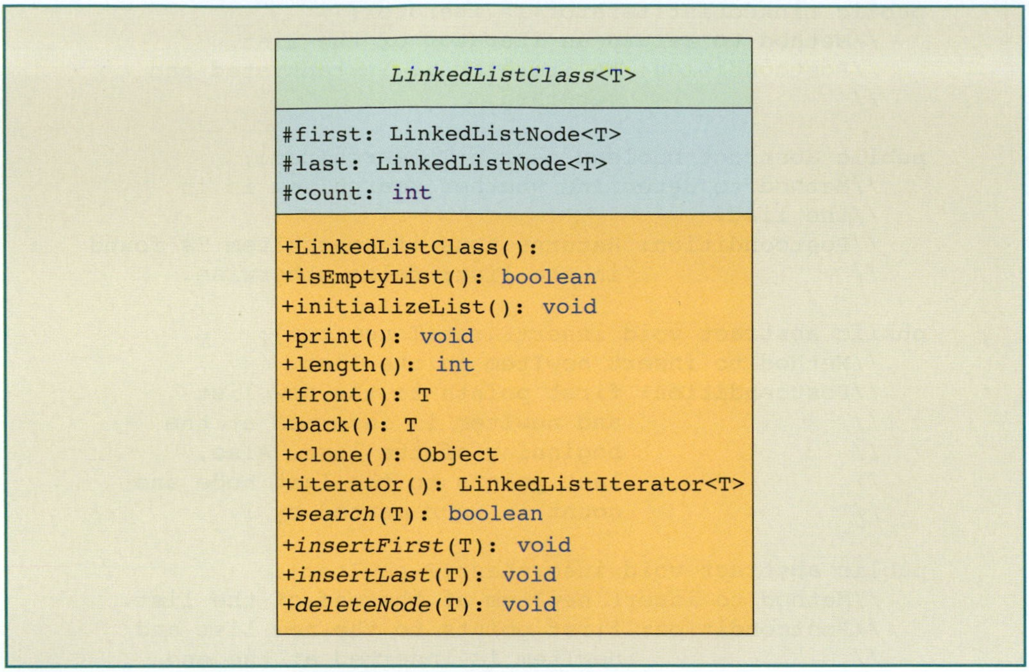

```
                    ┌─────────────────────────────────────────────┐
                    │            LinkedListClass<T>                │
                    ├─────────────────────────────────────────────┤
                    │ #first: LinkedListNode<T>                    │
                    │ #last: LinkedListNode<T>                     │
                    │ #count: int                                  │
                    ├─────────────────────────────────────────────┤
                    │ +LinkedListClass():                          │
                    │ +isEmptyList(): boolean                      │
                    │ +initializeList(): void                      │
                    │ +print(): void                               │
                    │ +length(): int                               │
                    │ +front(): T                                  │
                    │ +back(): T                                   │
                    │ +clone(): Object                             │
                    │ +iterator(): LinkedListIterator<T>           │
                    │ +search(T): boolean                          │
                    │ +insertFirst(T): void                        │
                    │ +insertLast(T): void                         │
                    │ +deleteNode(T): void                         │
                    └─────────────────────────────────────────────┘
```

Figure 16-30   UML class diagram of the **class** LinkedListClass

Notice that the instance variables `first` and `last`, as defined earlier, of the **class** LinkedListClass are **protected**, not **private**, because as noted previously, we will derive the **class**es UnorderedLinkedList and OrderedLinkedList from the **class** LinkedListClass. Because each of the **class**es UnorderedLinkedList and OrderedLinkedList will provide separate definitions of the methods `search`, `insertFirst`, `insertLast`, and `deleteNode`, and because these methods would access the instance variable, to provide direct access to the instance variables, the instance variables are declared as **protected**.

Next, we write the definitions of the nonabstract methods of the **class** LinkedListClass.

isEmptyList

The list is empty if `first` is `null`. Therefore, the definition of the method `isEmptyList` is:

```
public boolean isEmptyList()
{
    return (first == null);
}
```

Default Constructor

The default constructor initializes the list to an empty state. Recall that when an object of the type `LinkedListClass` is declared and no value is passed, the default constructor executes automatically. Its definition is:

```
public LinkedListClass()
{
    first = null;
    last = null;
    count = 0;
}
```

initializeList

The method `initializeList` initializes the list to an empty state. Note that the default constructor has already initialized the list when the list object was created. This operation, in fact, reinitializes the list to an empty state. Its definition is:

```
public void initializeList()
{
    first = null;
    last = null;
    count = 0;
}
```

print List

The method `print` outputs the data stored in the nodes of a linked list. To output the data contained in each node, we must traverse the list starting at the first node. Because `first` always points to the first node in the list, we need another reference variable to traverse the list. (If we use `first` to traverse the list, then the entire list is lost.) The definition of the method `print` is:

```
public void print()
{
    LinkedListNode<T> current; //variable to traverse
                               //the list

    current = first;     //set current so that it points to
                         //the first node
    while (current != null) //while more data to print
    {
        System.out.print(current + " ");
        current = current.link;
    }
}//end print
```

16

The method `print` assumes that the method `toString` is defined for the class that defines the type of `info`. For example, the wrapper classes, the **class** `String`, and the **class** `Clock` define the method `toString` to output the data stored in an object of their class.

Length of the List

The length of the linked list (that is, how many nodes are in the list) is stored in the variable `count`. Therefore, this method returns the value of this variable. Its definition is:

```java
public int length()
{
    return count;
}
```

Retrieve Data of the First and the Last Node

The method `front` returns the reference to the first node of the linked list and the method `back` returns the reference of the last node of the linked list. The definitions of these methods are:

```java
public T front()
{
    return first.info;
}
```

```java
public T back()
{
    return last.info;
}
```

Notice that if the list is empty, `first` and `last` are **null**. In this case, `first.info` and `last.info` do not exist. Therefore, if the list is empty, both the methods `front` and `back` would terminate the program with the error message, `NullPointerException`. So before calling any of these methods, verify that the list is nonempty.

clone

The method `clone` returns a clone of the list. Note that the method `clone` makes a shallow copy of the list. That is, it clones only the references in each node. This means that the reference in each node of the list and its clone points to the same object that stores the data. The definition of the method `clone` is:

```java
public Object clone()
{
    LinkedListClass<T> copy = null;
```

```java
    try
    {
        copy = (LinkedListClass<T>) super.clone();

    }
    catch (CloneNotSupportedException e)
    {
        return null;
    }

        //If the list is not empty, clone each node of
        //the list.
    if (first != null)
    {
            //Clone the first node
        copy.first = (LinkedListNode<T>) first.clone();
        copy.last = copy.first;

        LinkedListNode<T> current;

        if (first != null)
            current = first.link;
        else
            current = null;

            //Clone the remaining nodes of the list
        while (current != null)
        {
            copy.last.link =
                    (LinkedListNode<T>) current.clone();
            copy.last = copy.last.link;
            current = current.link;
        }
    }

    return copy;
}
```

Definition of the **class** LinkedListClass

In the preceding sections, we discussed how to implement the operations of the **class** LinkedListClass. You can write the definition of **class** LinkedListClass as follows:

16

```
public abstract class LinkedListClass<T> implements LinkedListADT<T>
{
    //Place the definition of the class LinkedListNode<T> here.

    //Place the definition of the class LinkedListIterator<T>
    //here.

    //Place the definition of the nonabstract methods and the
    //abstract methods here.
}
```

 Exercise 9 at the end of this chapter asks you to rewrite the definitions of the **class** LinkedListClass so that the **class** LinkedListNode is not an inner class. It is defined as a **public** class, outside every class definition, and the instance variables info and link are **private**. You will need to add appropriate methods to manipulate info and link.

UNORDERED LINKED LIST

As described in the preceding section, we derive the **class** UnorderedLinkedList from the **abstract class** LinkedListClass and implement the operations search, insertFirst, insertLast, and deleteNode.

The following defines the heading, instance variables, if any, constructors, and instance methods of the **class** UnorderedLinkedList.

Class: UnorderedLinkedList

```
public class UnorderedLinkedList<T> extends LinkedListClass<T>
```

Instance Variables:

Same as the instance variables of the **class** LinkedListClass

Constructors and Instance Methods:

```
public UnorderedLinkedList()
    //Default constructor

public boolean search(T searchItem)
    //Method to determine whether searchItem is in
    //the list.
    //Postcondition: Returns true if searchItem is found
    //              in the list; false otherwise.

public void insertFirst(T newItem)
    //Method to insert newItem in the list.
    //Postcondition: first points to the new list
    //              and newItem is inserted at the
```

```
    //              beginning of the list. Also,
    //              last points to the last node and
    //              count is incremented by 1.

public void insertLast(T newItem)
    //Method to insert newItem at the end of the list.
    //Postcondition: first points to the new list and
    //              newItem is inserted at the end
    //              of the list. Also, last points to
    //              the last node and
    //              count is incremented by 1.

public void deleteNode(T deleteItem)
    //Method to delete deleteItem from the list.
    //Postcondition: If found, the node containing
    //              deleteItem is deleted from the
    //              list. Also, first points to the first
    //              node, last points to the last
    //              node of the updated list, and count
    //              is decremented by 1.
```

Figure 16–31 shows the UML class diagram of the **class** UnorderedLinkedList and the inheritance hierarchy.

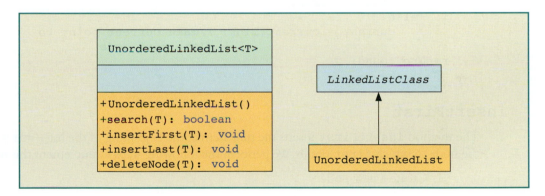

Figure 16-31   UML class diagram of the **class** UnorderedLinkedList and the inheritance hierarchy

search

16

The method **search** searches the list for a given item. If the item is found, it returns **true**; otherwise, it returns **false**. Because a linked list is not a random access data structure, we must sequentially search the list starting from the first node.

The following steps describe this method:

1. Compare the search item with the current node in the list. If the object to which `info` of the current node points contains the same data as the object to which the parameter `searchItem` points, stop the search; otherwise, make the next node the current node. To compare the objects we use the method `equals`.

2. Repeat Step 1 until either the item is found or no more data is left in the list to compare with the search item.

The definition of the method `search` is:

```
public boolean search(T searchItem)
{
    LinkedListNode<T> current; //variable to traverse
                               //the list
    boolean found;

    current = first;   //set current to point to the first
                       //node in the list

    found = false;     //set found to false

    while (current != null && !found) //search the list
        if (current.info.equals(searchItem)) //item is found
            found = true;
        else
            current = current.link; //make current point to
                                    //the next node
    return found;
}
```

insertFirst

The method `insertFirst` inserts the new item at the beginning of the list—that is, before the node to which `first` points. We perform the following steps to implement this method:

1. Create a new node.

2. Store the new item in the new node.

3. Insert the node before `first`.

4. Update the value of `first` and, if needed, the value of `last`.

As explained before, the first three steps are easily accomplished by using the constructor with parameters of the **class** `LinkedListNode` and passing appropriate parameters. For example, suppose that `newNode` is a reference variable of the type `LinkedListNode`. Then the following statement creates and inserts a node before `first`:

```
newNode = new LinkedListNode<T>(newItem, first);
```

Note that `newItem` is the new item that needs to be inserted in the linked list. It follows that the definition of the method `insertFirst` is:

```
public void insertFirst(T newItem)
{
    LinkedListNode<T> newNode;   //variable to create the
                                 //new node

    newNode =
        new LinkedListNode<T>(newItem, first); //create and
                                     //insert newNode before
                                     //first

    first = newNode;     //make first point to the
                         //actual first node

    if (last == null)    //if the list was empty, newNode is
                         //also the last node in the list
        last = newNode;

    count++;      //increment count
}
```

insertLast

The definition of the method `insertLast` is similar to the definition of the method `insertFirst`. Here we insert the new node after `last`. The definition of the method `insertLast` is:

```
public void insertLast(T newItem)
{
    LinkedListNode newNode; //variable to create the
                            //new node

    newNode =
        new LinkedListNode(newItem, null);   //create newNode

    if (first == null)  //if the list is empty, newNode is
                        //both the first and last node
    {
        first = newNode;
        last = newNode;
    }
    else      //if the list is not empty, insert
              //newNode after last
```

16

```
        {
            last.link = newNode; //insert newNode after last
            last = newNode;      //set last to point to the
                                 //actual last node
        }

        count++;
}//end insertLast
```

deleteNode

Next, we discuss the implementation of the method `deleteNode`. The reference of the object specifying the node to be deleted is passed as a parameter to this method. We need to consider several cases:

Case 1. The list is empty.

Case 2. The first node is the node to be deleted. In this case, we need to adjust the value of `first`.

Case 3. The node to be deleted is somewhere in the list. If the node to be deleted is the last node, we must adjust the value of `last`.

Case 4. The list does not contain the node to be deleted.

If the list is empty, we can simply print a message indicating that the list is empty. If the list is not empty, we search the list for the node with the given `info` and, if such a node is found, delete this node. In pseudocode, the algorithm is:

```
if the list is empty
    Output(cannot delete from an empty list);
else
{
    if the first node is the node to be deleted,
        adjust the value of first, and
        deallocate the memory;
    else
    {
        search the list for the node to be deleted
        if such a node is found, delete it
    }
}
```

Case 1: The list is empty.

If the list is empty, output an error message as shown in the pseudocode.

Case 2: The list is not empty. The node to be deleted is the first node.

This case has two scenarios: `list` has only one node, and `list` has more than one node, where `list` is an `UnorderedLinkedList` object. Consider the list of one node as shown in Figure 16-32.

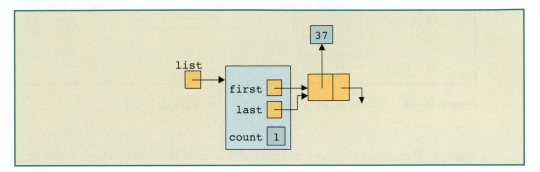

Figure 16-32 Linked `list` with one node

Suppose that we want to delete `37`. After deletion, the list becomes empty. Therefore, after deletion, both `first` and `last` are set to `null` and `count` is set to `0`.

Now consider the list of more than one node, as shown in Figure 16-33.

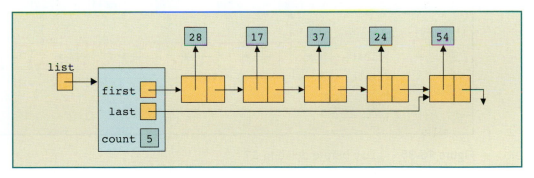

Figure 16-33 `list` with more than one node

Suppose that the node to be deleted is the node with data `28`. After deleting this node, the second node becomes the first node. Therefore, after deleting this node, the value of `first` changes; that is, after deletion, `first` contains the address of the node with data `17` and `count` is decremented by 1. Figure 16-34 shows the list after deleting `28`.

16

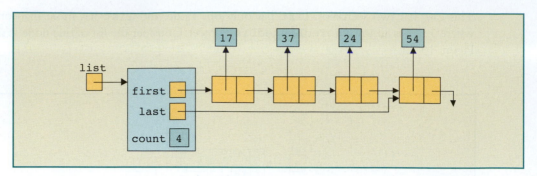

Figure 16-34 Linked `list` after deleting node with data `28`

Case 3: The node to be deleted is not the first node, but is somewhere in this list.

This case has two subcases: (a) the node to be deleted is not the last node, and (b) the node to be deleted is the last node. Let us illustrate both cases.

Case 3a: The node to be deleted is not the last node.

Consider the list shown in Figure 16-35.

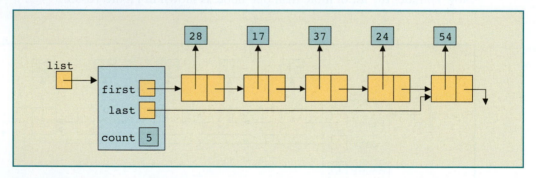

Figure 16-35 `list` before deleting `37`

Suppose that the node to be deleted is the node with data `37`. After deleting this node, the resulting list is as shown in Figure 16-36. Notice that the deletion of the node with data `37` does not require us to change the values of **first** and **last**. The link field of the previous node—that is, the node with **info 17**—changes. After deletion, the node with data `17` contains the address of the node with **info 24**.

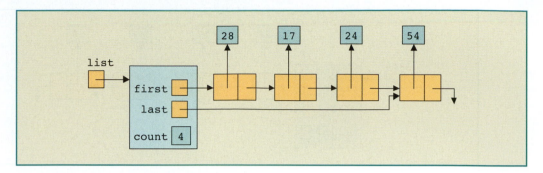

Figure 16-36   `list` after deleting 37

Case 3b: The node to be deleted is the last node.

Consider the list shown in Figure 16-37. Suppose that the node to be deleted is the node with data **54**.

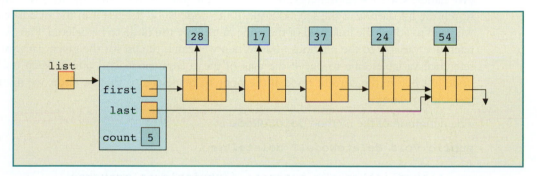

Figure 16-37   `list` before deleting 54

After deleting the node with data **54**, the node with data **24** becomes the last node. There-fore, the deletion of **54** requires us to change the value of **last**. After deleting **54**, last con-tains the address of the node with data **24**. Also, **count** is decremented by 1. Figure 16-38 shows the resulting list.

16

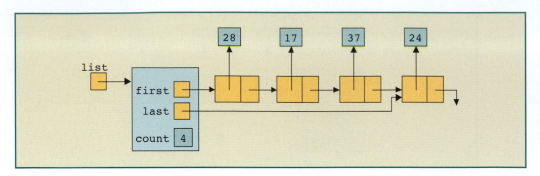

Figure 16-38 `list` after deleting `54`

Case 4: The node to be deleted is not in the list. In this case, the list requires no adjustment. We simply output an error message, indicating that the item to be deleted is not in the list.

From Cases 2, 3, and 4, it follows that the deletion of a node requires us to traverse the list. Because a linked list is not a random access data structure, we must sequentially search the list. (We handle Case 1 separately, because it does not require us to traverse the list.) We sequentially search the list starting at the second node. If the node to be deleted is in the middle of the list, we need to adjust the link field of the node just before the node to be deleted. Thus, we need a reference variable to the previous node. When we search the list for the given data, we use two reference variables: one to check the data of the current node, and one to keep track of the node just before the current node. If the node to be deleted is the last node, we must change the value of `last`.

The definition of the method `deleteNode` is:

```java
public void deleteNode(T deleteItem)
{
    LinkedListNode<T> current; //variable to traverse
                               //the list
    LinkedListNode<T> trailCurrent; //variable just
                                    //before current
    boolean found;

    if (first == null)    //Case 1; the list is empty
        System.err.println("Cannot delete from an empty "
                        + "list.");
    else
    {
        if (first.info.equals(deleteItem)) //Case 2
        {
            first = first.link;
```

```
            if (first == null)   //the list had only one node
                last = null;
            count--;
        }
        else  //search the list for the given info
        {
            found = false;
            trailCurrent = first;  //set trailCurrent to
                                   //point to the first node
            current = first.link;  //set current to point to
                                   //the second node

            while (current != null && !found)
            {
                if (current.info.equals(deleteItem))
                    found = true;
                else
                {
                    trailCurrent = current;
                    current = current.link;
                }
            }//end while

            if (found) //Case 3; if found, delete the node
            {
                count--;
                trailCurrent.link = current.link;

                if (last == current)   //node to be deleted
                                       //was the last node
                    last = trailCurrent;   //update the value
                                           //of last
            }
            else
                System.out.println("Item to be deleted is "
                                    + "not in the list.");
        }//end else
    }//end else
}//end deleteNode
```

You can write the definition of the **class** UnorderedLinkedList as follows:

```
public class UnorderedLinkedList<T> extends LinkedListClass<T>
{
    //Place the definitions of the default constructor and the
    //methods search, insertFirst, insertLast, and deleteNode
    //here.
}
```

The Web site accompanying this book contains several programs illustrating how to use the **class** UnorderedLinkedList.

ORDERED LINKED LISTS

The preceding section described the operations on an unordered linked list. This section deals with ordered linked lists. As noted earlier, we derive the **class** OrderedLinkedList from the **class** LinkedListClass and provide the definitions of the abstract methods insertFirst, insertLast, search, and deleteNode to take advantage of the fact that the elements of an ordered linked list are arranged using some ordering criteria. For simplicity, we assume that elements of an ordered linked list are arranged in ascending order.

Because the elements of an ordered linked list are in order, we include the method insert to insert an element in an ordered list at the proper place.

The following defines the heading, instance variables, if any, constructors, and instance methods of the **class** OrderedLinkedList:

Class: OrderedLinkedList

```
public class OrderedLinkedList<T> extends LinkedListClass<T>
```

Instance Variables:

Same as the instance variables of the **class** LinkedListClass

Instance Methods:

```
public OrderedLinkedList()
   //Default constructor

public boolean search(T searchItem)
   //Method to determine whether searchItem is in
   //the list.
   //Postcondition: Returns true if searchItem is found
   //               in the list; false otherwise.

public void insert(T insertItem)
   //Method to insert insertItem in the list.
   //Postcondition: first points to the new list,
   //       insertItem is inserted at the proper place
   //       in the list, and count is incremented by 1.

public void insertFirst(T newItem)
   //Method to insert newItem in the list.
   //Because the resulting list is sorted, newItem is
   //inserted at the proper place.
```

```
//This method uses the method insert to insert newItem.
//Postcondition: first points to the new list
//                and newItem is inserted at the
//                proper place. Also,
//                last points to the last node and
//                count is incremented by 1.

public void insertLast(T newItem)
    //Method to insert newItem in the list.
    //Because the resulting list is sorted, newItem is
    //inserted at the proper place.
    //This method uses the method insert to insert newItem.
    //Postcondition: first points to the new list
    //                and newItem is inserted at the
    //                proper place. Also,
    //                last points to the last node and
    //                count is incremented by 1.

public void deleteNode(T deleteItem)
    //Method to delete deleteItem from the list.
    //Postcondition: If found, the node containing
    //                deleteItem is deleted from the
    //                list. Also, first points to the first
    //                node, last points to the last
    //                node of the updated list, and count
    //                is decremented by 1.
```

Figure 16-39 shows the UML class diagram of the **class** OrderedLinkedList and the inheritance hierarchy.

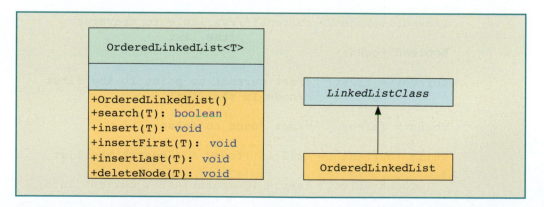

Figure 16-39   UML class diagram of the **class** OrderedLinkedList and the inheritance hierarchy

16

Next, we discuss how to implement the methods `search`, `insert`, `insertFirst`, `insertLast`, and `deleteNode` of the **class** OrderedLinkedList.

Search

First, we discuss the search operation. The algorithm to implement the search operation is similar to the search algorithm for general lists discussed earlier. Here, because the list is sorted, we can improve the search algorithm somewhat. As before, we start the search at the first node in the list. We stop the search as soon as we either find a node in the list with info greater than or equal to the search item, or we have searched the entire list. The parameter `searchItem` points to the object that contains the data to be compared with the data stored in the list.

This algorithm has the following steps:

1. Compare the search item with the current node in the list. If the data in the object to which `info` of the current node points is greater than or equal to the data of the object to which `searchItem` points, stop the search; otherwise, make the next node the current node. To compare the data stored in the objects, we use the method `compareTo`.

2. Repeat Step 1 until either an item in the list that is greater than or equal to the search item is found or no more data is left in the list to compare to the search item.

Note that the loop does not explicitly check whether the search item is equal to an item in the list. Thus, after the loop executes, we must check whether the search item is equal to the item in the list.

```java
public boolean search(T searchItem)
{
    LinkedListNode<T> current;   //variable to traverse
                                 //the list
    boolean found;

    current = first;   //set current to point to the first
                       //node in the list

    found = false;     //set found to false

    while (current != null && !found ) //search the list
    {
        Comparable<T> temp = (Comparable<T>) current.info;

        if (temp.compareTo(searchItem) >= 0)
            found = true;
```

```
        else
            current = current.link; //make current point to
                                     //the next node
    }

    if (found)
        found = current.info.equals(searchItem);

    return found;
}
```

Insert

To insert an item in an ordered linked list, we first find the place the new item is supposed to be inserted, and then we insert the item in the list. To find the place for the new item in the list, as before, we search the list. Here we use two reference variables, `current` and `trailCurrent`, to search the list. The variable `current` points to the node whose info is being compared to the item to be inserted, and `trailCurrent` points to the node just before `current`. Because the list is in order, the search algorithm is the same as before. The following cases arise:

Case 1: The list is initially empty. The node containing the new item is the only node and thus the first node in the list.

Case 2: The list is not empty and the new item is smaller than the smallest item in the list. The new item goes at the beginning of the list. In this case, we need to change the value of the variable to which the first node of the list points, which is `first`.

Case 3: The list is not empty, and the item to be inserted is larger than the first item in the list. The item is to be inserted somewhere in the list.

Case 3a: The new item is larger than all the items in the list. In this case, the new item is inserted at the end of the list. Thus, the value of `current` is `null` and the new item is inserted after `trailCurrent`.

Case 3b: The new item is to be inserted somewhere in the middle of the list. In this case, the new item is inserted between `trailCurrent` and `current`.

The following statements can accomplish both Cases 3a and 3b. Assume `newNode` points to the new node.

```
trailCurrent.link = newNode;
newNode.link = current;
```

Let us next illustrate these cases.

Case 1: The list is empty.

16

Consider the list shown in Figure 16-40.

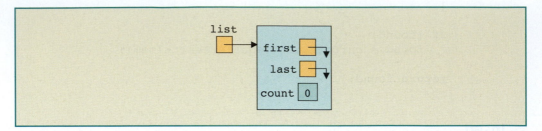

Figure 16-40 Empty `list`

Suppose that we want to insert **27** in the list. To accomplish this task, we create a node, make `info` point to an object with value **27**, set the link of the node to **null**, and have **first** point to the node. Figure 16-41 shows the resulting list.

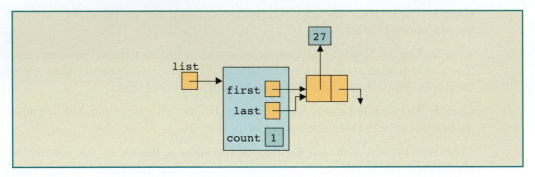

Figure 16-41 `list` after inserting 27

Notice that, after inserting **27**, the values of **first**, **last**, and **count** change.

Case 2: The list is not empty, and the item to be inserted is smaller than the smallest item in the list. Consider the list shown in Figure 16-42.

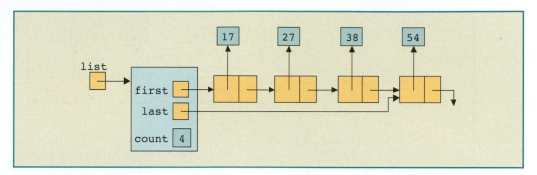

Figure 16-42 Nonempty `list` before inserting `10`

Suppose that `10` is to be inserted. After inserting `10` in the list, the node with data `10` becomes the first node of list. This requires us to change the value of **first**. Also, **count** is incremented by `1`. Figure 16-43 shows the resulting list.

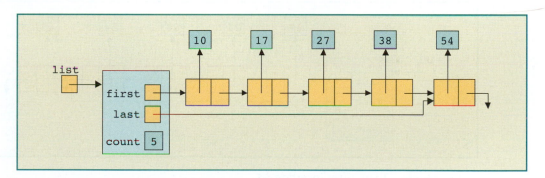

Figure 16-43 `list` after inserting `10`

Case 3: The list is not empty, and the item to be inserted is larger than the first item in the list. As indicated previously, this case has two scenarios.

16

Case 3a: The item to be inserted is larger than the largest item in the list; that is, it goes at the end of the list. Consider the list shown in Figure 16-44.

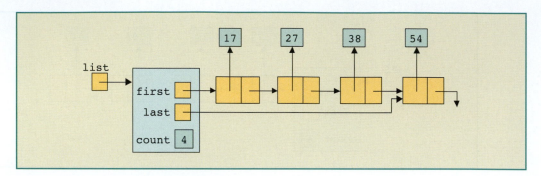

Figure 16-44 `list` before inserting 65

Suppose that we want to insert **65** in the list. After inserting **65**, the resulting list is as shown in Figure 16-45.

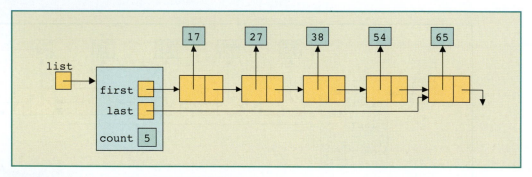

Figure 16-45 `list` after inserting 65

Case 3b: The item to be inserted goes somewhere in the middle of the list. Consider the list shown in Figure 16-46.

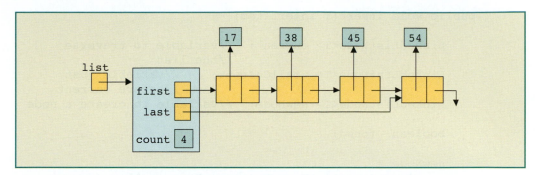

Figure 16-46 `list` before inserting 27

Suppose that we want to insert 27 in this list. Clearly, 27 goes between 17 and 38, which would require the link of the node with data 17 to be changed. After inserting 27, the resulting list is as shown in Figure 16-47.

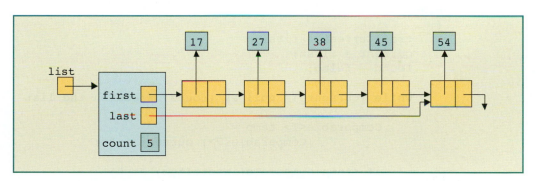

Figure 16-47 `list` after inserting 27

From Case 3, it follows that we must first traverse the list to find the place where the new item is to be inserted. As indicated previously, we traverse the list with two reference variables, say `current` and `trailCurrent`. The variable `current` traverses the list and compares the data of the node in the list with the item to be inserted. The variable `trailCurrent` points to the node just before `current`. For example, in Case 3b, when the search stops, `trailCurrent` points to node 17 and `current` points to node 38. The item is inserted after

16

trailCurrent. In Case 3a, after searching the list to find the place for 65, **trailCurrent** points to the node with data 54 and **current** is **null**.

Essentially, the method **insert** is:

```java
public void insert(T insertItem)
{
    LinkedListNode<T> current;    //variable to traverse
                                  //the list
    LinkedListNode<T> trailCurrent;    //variable just
                                       //before current
    LinkedListNode<T> newNode;    //variable to create a node

    boolean  found;

    newNode =
        new LinkedListNode<T>(insertItem, null); //create
                                                 //the node

    if (first == null)  //Case 1
    {
        first = newNode;
        last = newNode;
        count++;
    }
    else
    {
        trailCurrent = first;
        current = first;
        found = false;

        while (current != null && !found) //search the list
        {
            Comparable<T> temp =
                    (Comparable<T>) current.info;

            if (temp.compareTo(insertItem) >= 0)
                found = true;
            else
            {
                trailCurrent = current;
                current = current.link;
            }
        }

        if (current == first)    //Case 2
        {
            newNode.link = first;
```

```
                first = newNode;
                count++;
        }
        else                //Case 3
        {
                trailCurrent.link = newNode;
                newNode.link = current;

                if (current == null)
                        last = newNode;

                count++;
        }
    }//end else
}//end insert
```

 Notice that the method `insert` does not check whether the item to be inserted is already in the list, that is, it does not check for duplicates. Programming Exercise 8 at the end of this chapter asks you to revise the definition of the method `insert` so that before inserting the item, it checks whether it is already in the list. If the item to be inserted is already in the list, the method outputs an appropriate error message. In other words, duplicates are not allowed.

`insertFirst` Node

The method `insertFirst` inserts the new item at the beginning of the list. However, because the resulting list must be sorted, the new item must be inserted at the proper place. We therefore use the method `insert` to insert the new item at its proper place. The definition of the method `insertFirst` is:

```
public void insertFirst(T newItem)
{
    insert(newItem);
}
```

Note that in reality, the method `insertFirst` does not apply to ordered linked list because the new item must be inserted at the proper place in the list. However, you must provide its definition because this method is declared as **abstract** in the parent class.

`insertLast` Node

The method `insertLast` inserts the new item at the end of the list. However, because the resulting list must be sorted, the new item must be inserted at the proper place. We therefore

16

use the method `insert` to insert the new item at its proper place. The definition of the method `insertLast` is:

```
public void insertLast(T newItem)
{
    insert(newItem);
}//end insertLast
```

Note that in reality, as with the method `insertFirst`, the method `insertLast` does not apply to an ordered linked list because the new item must be inserted at the proper place in the list. However, you must provide its definition because this method is declared as **abstract** in the parent class.

deleteNode

To delete a given item from an ordered linked list, first we search the list to see whether the item to be deleted is in the list. The method to implement this operation is the same as the delete operation on general linked lists. Here, because the list is sorted, we can somewhat improve the algorithm for ordered linked lists.

As in the case of the method `insert`, we search the list with two reference variables, current and `trailCurrent`. Similar to the operation `insert`, several cases arise:

Case 1. The list is initially empty. We have an error because we cannot delete from an empty list.

Case 2. The item to be deleted is contained in the first node of the list. We must adjust the value of `first`.

Case 3 The item to be deleted is somewhere in the list. In this case, `current` points to the node containing the item to be deleted, and `trailCurrent` points to the node just before the node to which `current` points.

Case 4. The list is not empty, but the item to be deleted is not in the list.

The definition of the method `deleteNode` is:

```
public void deleteNode(T deleteItem)
{
    LinkedListNode<T> current;           //variable to traverse
                                         //the list
    LinkedListNode<T> trailCurrent;  //variable just before
                                         //current
    boolean found;

    if (first == null)    //Case 1; list is empty.
        System.err.println("Cannot delete from an "
                        + "empty list.");
    else
    {
        if (first.info.equals(deleteItem)) //Case 2
        {
            first = first.link;
```

```
        if (first == null)
            last = null;
        count--;
}
else  //search the list for the node with
      //the given info
{
    found = false;
    trailCurrent = first; //set trailCurrent to
                          //point to the first node
    current = first.link; //set current to point
                          //to the second node

    while (current != null && !found)
    {
        Comparable<T> temp =
                    (Comparable<T>) current.info;

        if (temp.compareTo(deleteItem) >= 0)
            found = true;
        else
        {
            trailCurrent = current;
            current = current.link;
        }
    }//end while

    if (current == null)    //Case 4
        System.out.println("Item to be deleted is "
                           + "not in the list.");
    else
        if (current.info.equals(deleteItem)) //item
                    //to be deleted is in the list
        {
            if (first == current)    //Case 2
            {
                first = first.link;

                if (first == null)
                    last = null;

                count--;
            }
            else                         //Case 3
            {
                trailCurrent.link = current.link;

                if (current == last)
                    last = trailCurrent;
```

16

```
                              count--;
                    }
            }
            else                        //Case 4
                System.out.println("Item to be deleted "
                                    + "is not in the list.");
        }
    }//end else
}//end deleteNode
```

You can write the definition of the **class** OrderedLinkedList as follows:

```
public class OrderedLinkedList<T> extends LinkedListClass<T>
{
    //Place the definitions of the default constructor and the
    //methods search, insert, insertFirst, insertLast, and
    //deleteNode here.
}
```

The following program tests various operations on an ordered linked list:

```
//Program to test various operations on an ordered linked list

import java.util.*;

public class TestProgOrderedLinkedList
{
    static Scanner console = new Scanner(System.in);

    public static void main(String[] args)
    {
        OrderedLinkedList<Integer> numList
                = new OrderedLinkedList<Integer>();   //Line 1

        Integer num;                                   //Line 2

        System.out.println("Line 3: Enter integers "
                            + "ending with -999");      //Line 3

        num = console.nextInt();                        //Line 4

        while (num != -999)                             //Line 5
        {
            numList.insert(num);                        //Line 6
            num = console.nextInt();                    //Line 7
        }
```

```
        System.out.println();                           //Line 8

        System.out.println("Line 9: numList: ");        //Line 9
        numList.print();                                //Line 10
        System.out.println();                           //Line 11

        System.out.println("Line 12: Length of "
                    + "numList: "
                    + numList.length());                //Line 12

        System.out.print("Line 13: Enter the number "
                    + "to be deleted: ");               //Line 13
        num = console.nextInt();                        //Line 14
        System.out.println();                           //Line 15

        numList.deleteNode(num);                        //Line 16

        System.out.println("Line 17: After deleting "
                    + num + ", numList: ");             //Line 17
        numList.print();                                //Line 18
        System.out.println();                           //Line 19

        System.out.println("Line 20: Length of "
                    + "numList: "
                    + numList.length());                //Line 20
    }
}
```

Sample Run: In this sample run, the user input is shaded.

```
Line 3: Enter integers ending with -999
32 76 34 89 86 12 190 21 5 55 -999

Line 9: numList:
5 12 21 32 34 55 76 86 89 190
Line 12: Length of numList: 10
Line 13: Enter the number to be deleted: 32

Line 17: After deleting 32, numList:
5 12 21 34 55 76 86 89 190
Line 20: Length of numList: 9
```

The details of how the preceding program works are left as an exercise for you.

16

The Web site accompanying this book contains additional programs illustrating how to use the **class** OrderedLinkedList.

DOUBLY LINKED LISTS

The preceding sections explained in detail how to create and manipulate single linked lists. In a single linked list, the links go in only one direction. This means that a single linked list is usually traversed in only one direction. This section describes another data structure related to linked lists, called doubly linked lists.

A **doubly linked** list is a linked list in which every node has a next pointer and a back pointer. In other words, every node contains the address of the next node (except the last node), and every node contains the address of the previous node (except the first node). See Figure 16-48.

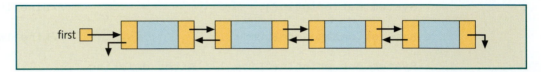

Figure 16-48   Doubly linked list

A doubly linked list can be traversed in either direction. That is, we can traverse the list starting at the first node or, if a reference variable to the last node is given, we can traverse the list starting at the last node.

As with a single linked list, the usual operations on a doubly linked list are:

1. Initialize the list.

2. Destroy the list.

3. Determine whether the list is empty.

4. Search the list for a given item.

5. Retrieve the first element of the list.

6. Retrieve the last element of the list.

7. Insert an item in the list.

8. Delete an item from the list.

9. Find the length of the list.

10. Output the list.

11. Make a copy of the list.

The following interface describes the operations on a doubly linked list as an ADT.

```
public interface DoublyLinkedListADT<T> extends Cloneable
{
    public Object clone();
        //Returns a copy of objects data in store.
        //This method clones only the references stored in
        //each node of the list. The objects that the
        //list nodes point to are not cloned.

    public boolean isEmptyList();
        //Method to determine whether the list is empty.
        //Postcondition: Returns true if the list is empty;
        //               false otherwise.

    public void initializeList();
        //Method to initialize the list to an empty state.
        //Postcondition: The list is initialized to an empty
        //               state.

    public int length();
        //Method to return the number of nodes in the list.
        //Postcondition: The number of nodes in the list is
        //               returned.

    public void print();
        //Method to output the info of each node.

    public void reversePrint();
        //Method to output the info of each node in the reverse
        //order.

    public boolean search(T searchItem);
        //Method to determine whether searchItem is in
        //the list.
        //Postcondition: Returns true if searchItem is found
        //               in the list; false otherwise.

    public T front();
        //Method to return the reference of the object containing
        //the data of the first node of the list.
        //Precondition: The list must exist and must not be empty.
        //Postcondition: The reference of the object that
        //               contains the info of the first node
        //               is returned.

    public T back();
        //Method to return the reference of the object containing
        //the data of the last node of the list.
        //Precondition: The list must exist and must not be empty.
```

16

```
                //Postcondition: The reference of the object that
                //               contains the info of the last node
                //               is returned.

    public void insertNode(T insertItem);
        //Method to insert insertItem in the list.
        //Precondition: If the list is nonempty, it must
        //              be in order.
        //Postcondition: insertItem is inserted at the
        //               proper place in the list.

    public void deleteNode(T deleteItem);
        //Method to delete deleteItem from the list.
        //Postcondition: If found, the node containing
        //               deleteItem is deleted from the list.
        //               Otherwise, an appropriate message
        //               is printed.
}
```

We leave the UML class diagram of the **interface** `DoublyLinkedListADT` as an exercise.

Next, we describe a generic class to implement the operations on an ordered doubly linked list. For simplicity, we assume that nodes of an ordered doubly linked list are arranged in ascending order.

Class: `DoublyLinkedList`

```
public class DoublyLinkedList<T> implements DoublyLinkedListADT<T>
```

Definition of the node:

```
public class DoublyLinkedListNode<T> implements Cloneable
{
    T info;
    DoublyLinkedListNode<T> next;
    DoublyLinkedListNode<T> back;

        //Default constructor
        //Postcondition: info = null;
        //               next = null; back = null;
    public DoublyLinkedListNode()
    {
        info = null;
        next = null;
        back = null;
    }
```

```
        //Returns a copy of objects data in store.
        //This method clones only the references stored in
        //the node. The objects that the nodes point to
        //are not cloned.
    public Object clone()
    {
        DoublyLinkedListNode<T> copy = null;

        try
        {
            copy = (DoublyLinkedListNode<T>) super.clone();
        }
        catch (CloneNotSupportedException e)
        {
            return null;
        }

        return copy;
    }

        //Method to return the info as a string.
        //Postcondition: info as a String object is
        //                returned.
    public String toString()
    {
        return info.toString();
    }
}
```

We leave as exercises the UML class diagram of the **class** DoublyLinkedListNode and the implementation of an iterator.

Instance variables:

```
protected int count;        //variable to store the
                            //number of nodes
protected DoublyLinkedListNode<T> first; //reference variable
                                         //to point to the
                                         //first node
protected DoublyLinkedListNode<T> last;  //reference variable
                                         //to point to the
                                         //last node
```

Constructors and Instance Methods

```
public DoublyLinkedList()
    //Default constructor
    //Initializes the list to an empty state.
    //Postcondition: first = null; last = null; count = 0
```

16

```java
public Object clone()
   //Returns a copy of objects data in store.
   //This method clones only the references stored in
   //each node of the list. The objects that the
   //list nodes point to are not cloned.

public boolean isEmptyList()
   //Method to determine whether the list is empty.
   //Postcondition: Returns true if the list is empty;
   //               false otherwise.

public void initializeList()
   //Method to initialize the list to an empty state.
   //Postcondition: first = null; last = null; count = 0

public int length()
   //Method to return the number of nodes in the list.
   //Postcondition: The value of count is returned.

public void print()
   //Method to output the info of each node.

public void reversePrint()
   //Method to output the info of each node in the reverse
   //order.

public boolean search(T searchItem)
   //Method to determine whether searchItem is in
   //the list.
   //Postcondition: Returns true if searchItem is found
   //               in the list; false otherwise.

public T front()
   //Method to return the reference of the object containing
   //the data of the first node of the list.
   //Precondition: The list must exist and must not be empty.
   //Postcondition: The reference of the object that
   //               contains the info of the first node
   //               is returned.

public T back()
   //Method to return the reference of the object containing
   //the data of the last node of the list.
   //Precondition: The list must exist and must not be empty.
   //Postcondition: The reference of the object that
   //               contains the info of the last node
   //               is returned.
```

```
public void insertNode(T insertItem)
    //Method to insert insertItem in the list.
    //Precondition: If the list is nonempty, it must
    //              be in order.
    //Postcondition: insertItem is inserted at the
    //         proper place in the list. Also, first points
    //         to the first node, last points to the
    //         last node of the new list, and count
    //         is incremented by 1.

public void deleteNode(T deleteItem)
    //Method to delete deleteItem from the list.
    //Postcondition: If found, the node containing
    //         deleteItem is deleted from the list. Also,
    //         first points to the first node of the new
    //         list, last points to the last node of the new
    //         list, and count is decremented by 1.
    //         Otherwise, an appropriate message
    //         is printed.
```

We leave the UML class diagram of the **class** DoublyLinkedList as an exercise.

The methods to implement the operations of a doubly linked list are similar to the ones discussed earlier for a single linked list. Here, because every node has two links, **back** and **next**, some of the operations require the adjustment of two links in each node. We will give the definition of each method here, except for the method **clone**, which we leave as Programming Exercise 11 at the end of this chapter.

Default Constructor

The default constructor initializes the doubly linked list to an empty state. It sets **first** and **last** to **null** and **count** to 0. Its definition is:

```
public DoublyLinkedList()
{
    first= null;
    last = null;
    count = 0;
}
```

isEmptyList

This operation returns **true** if the list is empty; otherwise, it returns **false**. The list is empty if **first** is **null**. Its definition is:

```
public boolean isEmptyList()
{
    return (first == null);
}
```

16

initializeList

This operation reinitializes the doubly linked list to an empty state. The definition of the method `initializeList` is:

```
public void initializeList()
{
    first = null;
    last = null;
    count = 0;
}
```

Length of the List

The length of a list is the number of nodes in the list. This operation returns the value of the instance variable **count**. Its definition is:

```
public int length()
{
    return count;
}
```

print

The method `print` outputs the data stored in the nodes of a doubly linked list. To output the data contained in each node, we must traverse the list starting at the first node. Because `first` always points to the first node in the list, we use another variable to traverse the list. The definition of the method `print` is:

```
public void print()
{
    DoublyLinkedListNode<T> current; //reference variable
                                     //to traverse the list

    current = first;   //set current to point to
                       //the first node

    while (current != null)
    {
        System.out.print(current + " ");
        current = current.next;
    }//end while
}//end print
```

reversePrint List

This method outputs the data contained in each node in reverse order. We traverse the list in reverse order starting from the last node. Its definition is:

```java
public void reversePrint()
{
    DoublyLinkedListNode<T> current; //reference variable to
                                     //traverse the list

    current = last;   //set current to point to the last node

    while (current != null)
    {
        System.out.print(current.info + "   ");
        current = current.back;
    }//end while
}//end reversePrint
```

search List

The method **search** returns **true** if the search item is in the list; otherwise, it returns **false**. The search algorithm for a doubly linked list is the same as the search algorithm for an ordered linked list. Its definition is:

```java
public boolean search(T searchItem)
{
    boolean found;
    DoublyLinkedListNode<T> current; //reference variable to
                                     //traverse the list

    found = false;

    current = first;

    while (current != null && !found)
    {
        Comparable<T> temp = (Comparable<T>) current.info;

        if (temp.compareTo(searchItem) >= 0)
            found = true;
        else
            current = current.next;
    }

    if (found)
        found = current.info.equals(searchItem); //test for
                                                 //equality

    return found;
}//end search
```

16

The First and the Last Element

The method `front` returns the reference of the first element of the list and the method `back` returns the reference of the last element. Their definitions are:

```
public T front()
{
    return first.info;
}

public T back()
{
    return last.info;
}
```

Note that if the list is empty, `first` and `last` are `null`. In this case, `first.info` and `last.info` do not exist. Therefore, if the list is empty, both the methods front and `back` would terminate the program with the error message, `NullPointerException`. Before calling any of these methods check to see whether the list is nonempty.

Insert

Because we are inserting an item in a doubly linked list, the insertion of a node in the list requires the adjustment of two links in certain nodes. As before, we find the place where the new item is supposed to be inserted, create the node, store the new item, and adjust the link fields of the new node and other specific nodes in the list. There are four cases:

Case 1: Insertion in an empty list

Case 2: Insertion at the beginning of a nonempty list

Case 3: Insertion at the end of a nonempty list

Case 4: Insertion somewhere in a nonempty list

Case 1 requires us to change the values of `first` and `last`. Case 2 requires us to change the value of `first`. Cases 3 and 4 are similar. Next, we show Case 4.

Consider the doubly linked list shown in Figure 16-49.

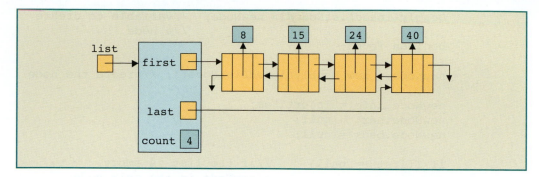

Figure 16-49   Doubly linked list before inserting 20

Suppose that 20 is to be inserted in the list. Figure 16-50 shows the list after inserting 20.

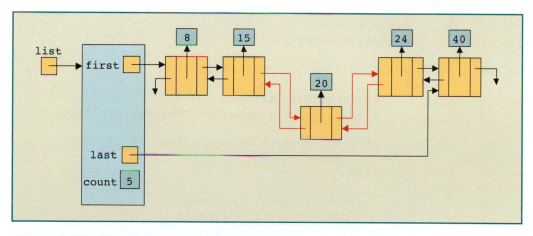

Figure 16-50   Doubly linked list after inserting 20

You can see from Figure 16-50 that the link **next** of the node with data **15**, the link **back** of the node with data **24**, and both the links **next** and **back** of the node with data **20** need to be adjusted. Also, **count** is incremented by **1**. The definition of the method **insertNode** is:

```
public void insertNode(T insertItem)
{
    DoublyLinkedListNode<T> current; //reference variable
                                     //to traverse the list
    DoublyLinkedListNode<T> trailCurrent = null; //reference
                                     //variable just before
                                     //current
```

16

```java
        DoublyLinkedListNode<T> newNode;   //variable to create
                                           //a node
    boolean found;

    newNode = new DoublyLinkedListNode(); //create the node

    newNode.info = insertItem;
    newNode.next = null;
    newNode.back = null;

    if (first == null)      //if the list is empty,
                            //newNode is the only node
    {
        first = newNode;
        last = newNode;
        count++;
    }
    else
    {
        found = false;
        current = first;

        while (current != null && !found)
        {
            Comparable<T> temp =
                        (Comparable<T>) current.info;

            if (temp.compareTo(insertItem) >= 0)
                found = true;
            else
            {
                trailCurrent = current;
                current = current.next;
            }
        } //end while

        if (current == first) //insert new node before first
        {
            first.back = newNode;
            newNode.next = first;
            first = newNode;
            count++;
        }
        else
        {
            //insert newNode between trailCurrent and current
            if (current != null)
            {
                trailCurrent.next = newNode;
                newNode.back = trailCurrent;
```

```
            newNode.next = current;
            current.back = newNode;
        }
        else
        {
            trailCurrent.next = newNode;
            newNode.back = trailCurrent;
            last = newNode;
        }
        count++;
    }//end else
 }//end else
}//end insertNode
```

Delete Node

This operation deletes a given item (if found) from the doubly linked list. As before, we first search the list to see whether the item to be deleted is in the list. The search algorithm is the same as before. Similar to the `insertNode` operation, this operation (if the item to be deleted is in the list) requires the adjustment of two links in certain nodes. The delete operation has several cases:

Case 1: The list is empty.

Case 2: The item to be deleted is in the first node of the list, which would require us to change the value of **first**.

Case 3: The item to be deleted is somewhere in the list.

Case 4: The item to be deleted is not in the list.

Let us demonstrate Case 3. Consider the list shown in Figure 16-51.

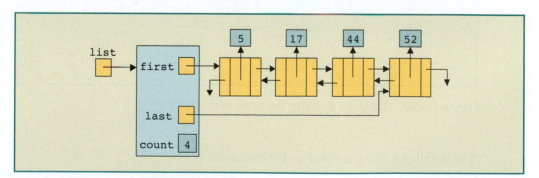

Figure 16-51　　Doubly linked list before inserting 17

16

Suppose that the item to be deleted is 17. We search the list, find the node with `info` 17, and then adjust the link field of the affected nodes. See Figure 16-52.

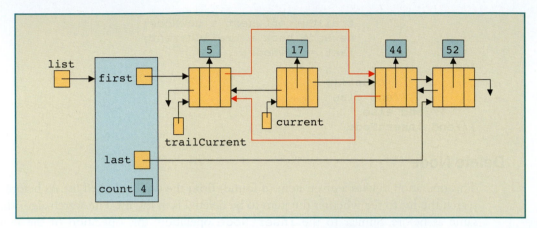

Figure 16-52   List after adjusting the links of the nodes before and after the node with data 17

After deleting the node to which **current** pointed, the resulting figure is Figure 16-53.

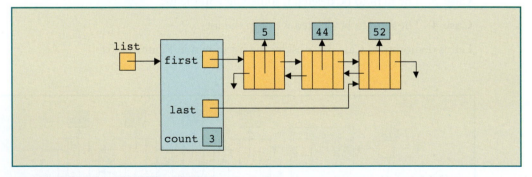

Figure 16-53   List after deleting the node with data 17

The definition of the method `deleteNode` is:

```java
public void deleteNode(T deleteItem)
{
    DoublyLinkedListNode<T> current; //reference variable
                                     //to traverse the list
    DoublyLinkedListNode<T> trailCurrent; //reference
                                          //variable just
                                          //before current

    boolean found;

    if (first == null)
        System.err.println("Cannot delete from an "
                         + "empty list.");
    else
        if (first.info.equals(deleteItem)) //node to be
                                   //deleted is the first node
        {
            current = first;
            first = first.next;

            if (first != null)
                first.back = null;
            else
                last = null;

            count--;
        }
        else
        {
            found = false;
            current = first;

                //search the list
            while (current != null && !found)
            {
                Comparable<T> temp =
                    (Comparable<T>) current.info;

                if (temp.compareTo(deleteItem) >= 0)
                    found = true;
                else
                    current = current.next;
            }

            if (current == null)
                System.out.println("The item to be deleted "
                                 + "is not in the list.");
            else
                if (current.info.equals(deleteItem))
                {
```

16

```
                    trailCurrent = current.back;
                    trailCurrent.next = current.next;

                    if (current.next != null)
                        current.next.back = trailCurrent;

                    if (current == last)
                        last = trailCurrent;

                    count--;
            }
            else
                System.out.println("The item to be "
                                    + "deleted is not in "
                                    + "list.");
        } //end else
} //end deleteNode
```

We leave the definition of the **class** DoublyLinkedList as an exercise. Also, Programming Exercise 12 at the end of this chapter asks you to write a program to test various operations of the **class** DoublyLinkedList.

CIRCULAR LINKED LISTS

A linked list in which the last node points to the first node is called a **circular linked list**. Figures 16-54 through 16-56 show various circular linked lists.

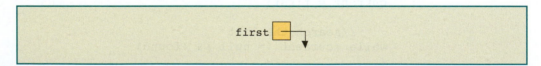

Figure 16-54   Empty circular linked list

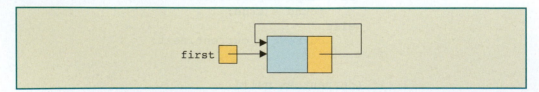

Figure 16-55   Circular linked list with one node

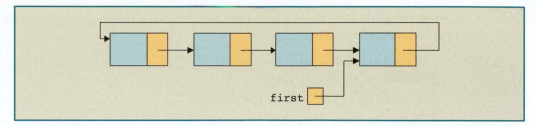

Figure 16-56   Circular linked list with more than one node

In a circular linked list with more than one node, as in Figure 16-56, it is convenient to make the reference variable `first` point to the last node of the list. Then, by using `first` you can access both the first and the last node of the list. For example, first points to the last node and `first.link` points to the first node.

As before, the usual operations on a circular list are:

1. Initialize the list (to an empty state).

2. Determine if the list is empty.

3. Destroy the list.

4. Print the list.

5. Find the length of the list.

6. Search the list for a given item.

7. Insert an item in the list.

8. Delete an item from the list.

9. Copy the list.

We leave it as an exercise for you to design a class to implement a sorted circular linked list. (See Programming Exercise 13 at the end of this chapter.)

PROGRAMMING EXAMPLE: VIDEO STORE

For a family or an individual, a favorite place to go on weekends or holidays is to a video store to rent movies. A new video store in your neighborhood is about to open. However, it does not have a program to keep track of its videos and customers. The store managers want someone to write a program for their system so that the video store can function efficiently both for employees and for customers. The program should be able to perform the following operations:

1. Rent a video; that is, check out a video.
2. Return, or check in, a video.
3. Create a list of videos owned by the store.
4. Show the details of a particular video.
5. Print a list of all the videos in the store.
6. Check whether a particular video is in the store.
7. Maintain a customer database.
8. Print a list of all the videos rented by each customer.

Let us write a program for the video store. This example further illustrates the object-oriented design methodology and, in particular, inheritance and polymorphism.

The programming requirement tells us that the video store has two major components: videos and customers. We will describe these two components in detail. We also need to maintain the following lists:

- A list of all the videos in the store
- A list of all the store's customers
- Lists of the videos currently rented by the customers

We will develop the program in two parts. In Part 1, we design, implement, and test the video component. In Part 2, we design, implement, and test the customer component, which is then added to the video component developed in part 1. That is, after completing Parts 1 and 2, we can perform all the operations listed previously.

We will use the generic **class** `UnorderedLinkedList` to maintain the list of videos owned by the store, the list of customers, and the lists of videos rented by the customers. We therefore first define the class to create a video object.

Part 1: The Video Component

The Video Object   This is the first stage, wherein we discuss the components of a video object. The common things associated with a video are the:

- Name of the movie
- Names of the stars
- Name of the producer
- Name of the director
- Name of the production company
- Number of copies in the store

From this list, we see that some of the operations to be performed on the video object are:

1. Set the video information—that is, the title, stars, production company, and so on.

2. Show the details of a particular video.

3. Check the number of copies in the store.

4. Check out (that is, rent) the video. In other words, if the number of copies is greater than zero, decrement the number of copies by one.

5. Check in (that is, return) the video. To check in a video, first we must check whether the store owns such a video and, if it does, increment the number of copies by one.

6. Check whether a particular video is available—that is, check whether the number of copies currently in the store is greater than zero.

To delete a video from the video list, the video list must be searched for the video to be deleted. Thus, we need to check the title of a video to find out which video is to be deleted. For simplicity, we assume that two videos are the same if they have the same title. We will include the methods `equals` and `compareTo` to compare two video objects in the class implementing video objects.

The following defines the heading, instance variables, if any, constructors, and instance methods of the **class** `Video`:

Class: `Video`

```
public class Video implements Cloneable, Comparable
```

Instance Variables:

```
private String videoTitle;    //variable to store the name
                              //of the movie
private String movieStar1;    //variable to store the name
                              //of the star
private String movieStar2;    //variable to store the name
                              //of the star
private String movieProducer;  //variable to store the name
                               //of the producer
private String movieDirector;  //variable to store the name
                               //of the director
private String movieProductionCo; //variable to store the
                                  //name of the production
                                  //company
private int copiesInStock;    //variable to store the number
                              //of copies in stock
```

Constructors and Instance Methods:

```java
public Video()
    //Default constructor
    //Instance variables are initialized to their
    //default values.
    //Postcondition: videoTitle = ""; movieStar1 = "";
    //          movieStar2 = ""; movieProducer = "";
    //          movieDirector = "";
    //          movieProductionCo = "";
    //          copiesInStock = 0;

public Video(String title, String star1,
             String star2, String producer,
             String director, String productionCo,
             int setInStock)
    //Constructor with parameters
    //Instance variables are set according to the parameters
    //Postcondition: videoTitle = title; movieStar1 = star1;
    //          movieStar2 = star2; movieProducer = producer;
    //          movieDirector = director;
    //          movieProductionCo = productionCo;
    //          copiesInStock = setInStock;

public Object clone()
    //Returns a copy of objects data in store.
    //Postcondition: A reference to a clone of video's
    //               data is returned.

public void setVideoInfo(String title, String star1,
                         String star2, String producer,
                         String director,
                         String productionCo,
                         int setInStock)
    //Method to set the details of a video.
    //Instance variables are set according to the
    //parameters.
    //Postcondition: videoTitle = title; movieStar1 = star1;
    //               movieStar2 = star2;
    //               movieProducer = producer;
    //               movieDirector = director;
    //               movieProductionCo = productionCo;
    //               copiesInStock = setInStock;

public int getNoOfCopiesInStock()
    //Method to check the number of copies in stock.
    //Postcondition: The value of the instance variable
    //               copiesInStock is returned.
```

```java
public void checkIn()
   //Method to check in a video.
   //Postcondition: The number of copies in stock is
   //               incremented by one.

public void checkOut()
   //Method to rent a video.
   //Postcondition: If there is a video in stock, its
   //               number of copies in stock is
   //               decremented by one; otherwise,
   //               an appropriate message is printed.

public void printTitle()
   //Method to print the title of a movie.

public void printInfo()
   //Method to print the details of a video.

public boolean checkTitle(String title)
   //Method to determine whether title is the same as the
   //title of the video.
   //Postcondition: Returns the value true if title is the
   //               same as the title of the video,
   //               false otherwise.

public void updateInStock(int num)
   //Method to increment the number of copies in stock by
   //adding the value of the parameter num.
   //Postcondition: copiesInStock = copiesInStock + num;

public void setCopiesInStock(int num)
   //Method to set the number of copies in stock.
   //Postcondition: copiesInStock = num;

public String getTitle()
   //Returns the title of the video
   //Postcondition: The value of the instance variable
   //               videoTitle is returned.

public boolean equals(Object otherVideo)
   //Method to compare the titles of two videos.
   //Postcondition: Returns true if this video's title is
   //               equal to the title of otherVideo;
   //               otherwise returns false.

public int compareTo(Object otherVideo)
   //Method to compare the titles of two videos.
   //Postconditition: Returns a negative value if the
   //                 title of this video is less than
```

```
//                    the title of otherVideo; zero if
//                    the title of this video is the
//                    same as the title of otherVideo;
//                    returns a positive value if the
//                    title of this video is greater
//                    than the title of otherVideo

public String toString()
   //Method to return the video info as a string.
```

We leave the UML class diagram of the **class** Video as an exercise for you.

Next, we write the definitions of each method in the **class** Video. The definitions of these methods are given next and are easy to follow:

```java
public void setVideoInfo(String title, String star1,
                         String star2, String producer,
                         String director,
                         String productionCo,
                         int setInStock)
{
    videoTitle = title;
    movieStar1 = star1;
    movieStar2 = star2;
    movieProducer = producer;
    movieDirector = director;
    movieProductionCo = productionCo;
    copiesInStock = setInStock;
}

public int getNoOfCopiesInStock()
{
    return copiesInStock;
}

public void checkIn()
{
    copiesInStock++;
}

public void checkOut()
{
    if (getNoOfCopiesInStock() > 0)
        copiesInStock--;
    else
        System.out.println("Currently out of stock.");
}
```

```java
public void printTitle()
{
    System.out.println("Video Title: " + videoTitle);
}

public void printInfo()
{
    System.out.println("Video Title: " + videoTitle);
    System.out.println("Stars: " + movieStar1 + " and "
                       + movieStar2);
    System.out.println("Producer: " + movieProducer);
    System.out.println("Director: " + movieDirector);
    System.out.println("Production Company: "
                       + movieProductionCo);
    System.out.println("Copies in stock: "
                       + copiesInStock);
    System.out.println();
}

public boolean checkTitle(String title)
{
    return (videoTitle.compareTo(title) == 0);
}

public void updateInStock(int num)
{
    copiesInStock += num;
}

public void setCopiesInStock(int num)
{
    copiesInStock = num;
}

public String getTitle()
{
    return videoTitle;
}

public Video()
{
    videoTitle = "";
    movieStar1 = "";
    movieStar2 = "";
    movieProducer = "";
    movieDirector = "";
    movieProductionCo = "";
    copiesInStock = 0;
}
```

```java
public Video(String title, String star1,
            String star2, String producer,
            String director, String productionCo,
            int setInStock)
{
    setVideoInfo(title, star1, star2, producer, director,
                productionCo, setInStock);
}

public boolean equals(Object otherVideo)
{
    Video temp = (Video) otherVideo;

    return (videoTitle.compareTo(temp.videoTitle) == 0);
}

public int compareTo(Object otherVideo)
{
    Video temp = (Video) otherVideo;

    return (videoTitle.compareTo(temp.videoTitle));
}

public String toString()
{
    String videoInfo;

    videoInfo = "Video Title: " + videoTitle + "\n"
                + "Stars: " + movieStar1 + " and "
                + movieStar2 + "\n"
                + "Producer: " + movieProducer + "\n"
                + "Director: " + movieDirector + "\n"
                + "Production Company: "
                + movieProductionCo + "\n"
                + "Copies in stock: " + copiesInStock
                + "\n\n";

    return videoInfo;
}
```

You can write the definition of the **class** Video as follows:

```java
public class Video implements Cloneable, Comparable
{
    //Place instance variables here
    //Place the definitions of the constructors and
    //instance methods here
}
```

The Video List   This program requires us to maintain a list of all the videos in the store, and we should be able to add a new video to and delete a video from our list. Typically, we would not know how many videos are in the store, and adding or deleting a video would change the number of videos in the store. Therefore, as remarked previously, we use a linked list to create a list of videos. See Figure 16-57.

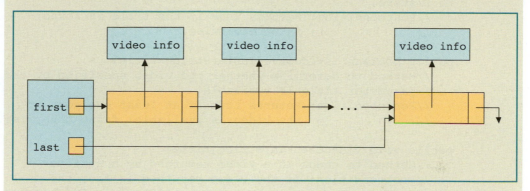

Figure 16-57   `videoList`

Earlier in this chapter, we defined the **class** `UnorderedLinkedList` to create a linked list of objects. We also defined the basic operations such as insertion and deletion of an item in the list. However, some operations are very specific to the video list, such as check out a video, check in a video, set the number of copies of a video, and so on. These operations are not available in the **class** `UnorderedLinkedList`. We will therefore derive the **class** `VideoList` from the **class** `UnorderedLinkedList` and add these operations.

The following defines the heading, instance variables, if any, constructors, and instance methods of the **class** `VideoList`.

Class: `VideoList`

```java
public class VideoList extends UnorderedLinkedList<Video>
```

Instance Variables:

Same as the instance variables of the **class** `UnorderedLinkedList`.

Constructors and Instance Methods:

```java
public VideoList()
   //Default constructor

private LinkedListNode<Video> searchVideoList(String title)
   //Method to search the video list for a
   //particular video, specified by the parameter title.
```

```
    //Postcondition: If the video is found, a reference to
    //              the node containing the video is returned;
    //              otherwise, the null reference is returned.

public boolean videoSearch(String title)
    //Method to search the list to see whether a particular
    //video, specified by the parameter title, is in the
    //store.
    //Postcondition: Returns true if the title is found;
    //              false otherwise.

public boolean isVideoAvailable(String title)
    //Method to determine whether the video specified by the
    //parameter title is available.
    //Postcondition: Returns true if at least one copy of
    //              the video is available; false otherwise.

public void videoCheckIn(String title)
    //Method to check in a video returned by a customer.
    //Postcondition: If the video returned is from the
    //              store, its copiesInStock is incremented
    //              by one; otherwise, an appropriate
    //              message is printed.

public void videoCheckOut(String title)
    //Method to check out a video, that is, rent a video.
    //Postcondition: If a video is available, its
    //              copiesInStock is decremented by one;
    //              otherwise, an appropriate message is
    //              printed.

public boolean videoCheckTitle(String title)
    //Method to determine whether the video specified by the
    //parameter title is in the store.
    //Postcondition: Returns true if the video is
    //              in the store; false otherwise.

public void videoUpdateInStock(String title, int num)
    //Method to update the number of copies of a video
    //by adding the value of the parameter num. The
    //parameter title specifies the name of the video
    //for which the number of copies is to be updated.
    //Postcondition: If video is found, then
    //              copiesInStock = copiesInStock + num;
    //              otherwise, an appropriate message is
    //              printed.
```

```
public void videoSetCopiesInStock(String title, int num)
   //Method to reset the number of copies of a video.
   //The parameter title specifies the name of the video
   //for which the number of copies is to be reset, and the
   //parameter num specifies the number of copies.
   //Postcondition: If video is found, then
   //                  copiesInStock = num;
   //               otherwise, an appropriate message
   //               is printed.

public void videoPrintTitle()
   //Method to print the titles of all the videos in
   //the store.

public void print()
   //Method to print the info of all the videos in the
   //store.
```

The definitions of the methods to implement the operations of the **class VideoList** are given next.

The primary operations on the video list are to check in a video and to check out a video. Both operations require the list to be searched, and the location of the video being checked in or checked out to be found in the video list. Other operations such as checking whether a particular video is in the store, updating the number of copies, and so on, also require the video list to be searched. To simplify the search process, we write a method that searches the video list for a particular video. If the video is found, it returns the reference, that is, address of the video, so that check–in, check–out, and other operations on the video object can be performed. Note that the method **searchVideoList** is a **private** member of the **class VideoList** because it is used only for internal manipulation. First, we describe the search procedure.

Consider the node of the video list shown in Figure 16-58.

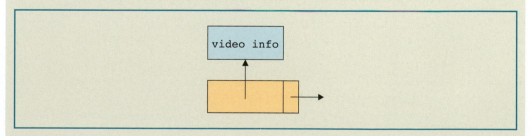

Figure 16-58   Node of a video list

The instance variable `info` points to an object of the **class** `Video` and the object contains the necessary information about a video. A `Video` object has seven instance variables: `videoTitle`, `movieStar1`, `movieStar2`, `movieProducer`, `movieDirector`, `movieProductionCo`, and `copiesInStock`. (See the definition of the **class** `Video`.) Therefore, the node of a video list has the form shown in Figure 16–59.

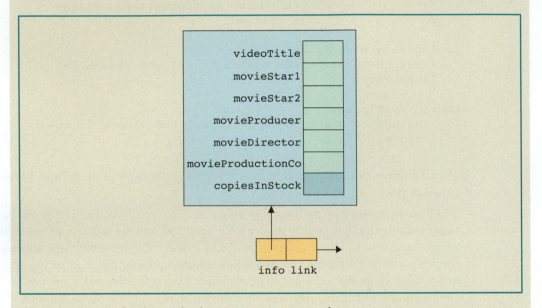

Figure 16-59   Video list node showing components of `info`

The instance variables of a `Video` object are all **private** and cannot be accessed directly. The methods of the **class** `Video` help us to check and/or set the value of a particular instance variable.

Suppose `current` points to a node in the video list. See Figure 16-60.

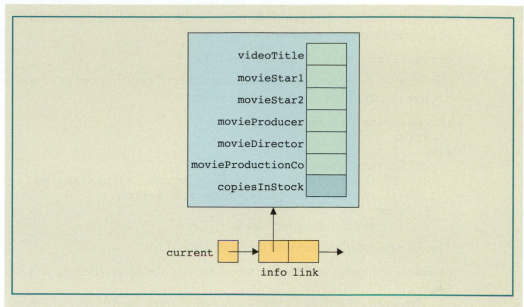

Figure 16-60   Variable `current` and a node of the video list

Now

```
current.info
```

refers to the `info` part of the node. Suppose that we want to know whether the title of the video stored in this node is the same as the title specified by the variable `title`. The expression

```
current.info.checkTitle(title)
```

is **true** if the title of the video stored in this node is the same as the title specified by the parameter `title`, and it is **false** otherwise. (Note that the method `checkTitle` is a value-returning method. See its declaration in the **class** `Video`.)

As another example, suppose that we want to set the value of the instance variable `copiesInStock` of this object to 10. Because `copiesInStock` is a **private** data member, it cannot be accessed directly. Therefore the statement

```
current.info.copiesInStock = 10;   //illegal
```

is incorrect and generates a compile-time error. We have to use the method
setCopiesInStock as follows:

```
current.info.setCopiesInStock(10);
```

Now that we know how to access a data member of a video stored in a node, let us
describe the algorithm to search the video list:

```
if video list is empty
    Error
else
    while (not found)
        if the title of the current video is the same as
            the desired title, stop the search
        else
            check the next node
```

The following method performs the desired search:

```
private LinkedListNode<Video> searchVideoList(String title)
{
    boolean found = false;    //set found to false
    LinkedListNode<Video> current = null;

    if (first == null)  //the list is empty
        System.out.println("Cannot search an empty list.");
    else
    {
        current = first;   //set current to point to first
                           //node in the list
        found = false;     //set found to false

        while (current != null && !found) //search the list
        {

            Video temp = (Video) current.info;

            if (temp.checkTitle(title)) //item is found
                found = true;
            else
                current = current.link; //advance current
                                        //to the next node
        }
    }//end else

    return current;
}//end searchVideoList
```

If the search is successful, the parameter `found` is set to `true` and the parameter `current` points to the node containing the video `info`. If it is unsuccessful, `found` is set to `false` and `current` is `null`.

The definitions of the other methods of the **class** `VideoList` are:

```java
public boolean videoSearch(String title)
{
    LinkedListNode<Video> location;

    location = searchVideoList(title);

    return (location != null);
}

public boolean isVideoAvailable(String title)
{
    LinkedListNode<Video> location;
    Video temp;

    location = searchVideoList(title);

    if (location != null)
    {
        temp = (Video) location.info;
        return (temp.getNoOfCopiesInStock() > 0);
    }
    else
        return false;
}

public void videoCheckIn(String title)
{
    LinkedListNode<Video> location;
    Video temp;

    location = searchVideoList(title);    //search the list

    if (location != null)
    {
        temp = (Video) location.info;
        temp.checkIn();
    }
    else
        System.out.println("The store does not carry "
                           + "this video.");
}
```

```java
public void videoCheckOut(String title)
{
    LinkedListNode<Video> location;
    Video temp;

    location = searchVideoList(title);  //search the list

    if (location != null)
    {
        temp = (Video) location.info;
        temp.checkOut();
    }
    else
        System.out.println("The store does not carry "
                         + "this video.");
}

public boolean videoCheckTitle(String title)
{
    LinkedListNode<Video> location;

    location = searchVideoList(title); //search the list

    return (location != null);
}

public void videoUpdateInStock(String title, int num)
{
    LinkedListNode<Video> location;
    Video temp;

    location = searchVideoList(title); //search the list

    if (location != null)
    {
        temp = (Video) location.info;
        temp.updateInStock(num);
    }
    else
        System.out.println("The store does not carry "
                         + "this video.");
}

public void videoSetCopiesInStock(String title, int num)
{
    LinkedListNode<Video> location;
    Video temp;

    location = searchVideoList(title);
```

```java
        if (location != null)
        {
            temp = (Video) location.info;
            temp.setCopiesInStock(num);
        }
        else
            System.out.println("The store does not carry "
                                + "this video");
    }

    public void videoPrintTitle()
    {
        LinkedListNode<Video> current;
        Video temp;

        current = first;
        while (current != null)
        {
            temp = (Video) current.info;
            temp.printTitle();
            current = current.link;
        }
    }

    public void print()
    {
        LinkedListNode<Video> current; //variable to
                                       //traverse the list
        Video temp;

        current = first;     //set current so that it points to
                             //the first node
        while (current != null) //while more data to print
        {
            temp = (Video) current.info;
            temp.printInfo();
            current = current.link;
        }
    }
}
```

You can write the definition of the **class** `VideoList` as follows:

```java
public class VideoList extends UnorderedLinkedList<Video>
{
    //Place instance variables here
    //Place the definitions of the constructors and the
    //instance methods here.
}
```

Part 2: The Customer Component

The Customer Object

The customer object stores information about a customer, such as the first name, last name, account number, and a list of videos rented by the customer. Thus, our video store program has two components:

1. A list of video objects wherein each video object contains the necessary information about a video, as described previously
2. A list of customer objects wherein each customer object contains the necessary information about a customer, which will be described soon

We create two lists that correspond to these two objects:

a. A list of all the videos in the store (as described earlier)
b. A list of all the customers

Next, we describe the customer object.

The primary characteristics of a customer are:

- The customer's first name
- The customer's last name
- The customer's account number
- The list of rented videos

Every customer is a person. We have already designed the **class** `Person` in Example 8-5 (Chapter 8) and described the necessary operations on the name of a person. Therefore, we can derive the **class** `Customer` from the **class** `Person` and add the additional members that we need.

The basic operations on `Customer` object are:

1. Print the name, account number, and number of rentals.
2. Set the name, account number, and number of rentals.
3. Rent a video; that is, add the video to the list of rented videos.
4. Return a video; that is, delete the video from the list of rented videos.
5. Show the account number.

The details of implementing the customer component are left as an exercise for you. (See Programming Exercise 14 at the end of this chapter.)

Main Program

We now write the main program to test the video object. We assume that the necessary data for the videos are stored in a file. We open the file and create the list of videos owned by the video store. The data in the input file is in the following form:

```
video title (the name of the movie)
movie star1
```

```
movie star2
movie producer
movie director
movie production company
number of copies
    .
    .
    .
```

We write a method, `createVideoList`, to read data from the input file and create the list of videos. We also write a method, `displayMenu`, to show the different choices—such as check in a movie or check out a movie—that the user can make. The algorithm of the method `main` is:

1. Open the input file.
2. If the input file does not exist, exit the program.
3. Create the list of videos (`createVideoList`).
4. Show the menu (`displayMenu`).
5. **while** not done
      Perform various operations.

Opening the input file and terminating the program if it does not exist is straightforward. Next, let us describe Steps 3 and 4, which are done by writing two separate methods: `createVideoList` and `displayMenu`.

createVideoList

This method reads the data from the input file and creates a linked list of videos. Because the data is read from a file and the input file was opened in the method `main`, we pass the appropriate input stream object to this method. We also pass the reference variable used to create the video list, declared in the method `main`, to this method. Next, we read the data for each video and then insert the video in the list. The general algorithm is:

a. Read the data and store it in a video object.
b. Insert the video in the list.
c. Repeat Steps a and b for each video's data in the file.

displayMenu

This method informs the user what to do. It contains the following output statements:

Select one of the following:

1: To check whether a particular video is in the store
2: To check out a video
3: To check in a video
4: To check whether a particular title is in stock

5: To print the titles of all the videos

6: To print a list of all the videos

9: To exit

In pseudocode, Step 5 of the main algorithm is:

```
get choice
while (choice != 9)
{
    switch (choice)
    {
    case 1:  a. get the movie name
             b. search the video list
             c. if found, report "success"
                else report "failure"
             d. break;
    case 2:  a. get the movie name
             b. search the video list
             c. if found, check out the video
                else report "failure"
             d. break;
    case 3:  a. get the movie name
             b. search the video list
             c. if found, check in the video
                else report "failure"
             d. break;
    case 4:  a. get the movie name
             b. search the video list
             c. if found
                    if number of copies > 0
                       report "success"
                    else
                       report "currently out of stock"
                else report "failure"
             d. break;
    case 5: print the titles of the videos
            break;
    case 6: print all the videos in the store
            break;
    default: invalid selection
    }//end switch

    displayMenu();
    get choice
}//end while
```

Main Program Listing

```java
import java.io.*;
import java.util.*;

public class mainProgVideoStore
{
    static Scanner console = new Scanner(System.in);

    public static void main(String[] args)
    {
        VideoList videoList = new VideoList();
        int choice;
        String title;

        try
        {
            Scanner infile =
                new Scanner(new FileReader("a:\\videoDat.txt"));

            createVideoList(infile, videoList);

            displayMenu();
            System.out.print("Enter the choice: ");
            choice = console.nextInt();
            console.nextLine();
            System.out.println();

            while (choice != 9)
            {
                switch (choice)
                {
                case 1: System.out.print("Enter the title: ");
                        title = console.nextLine();
                        System.out.println();

                        if (videoList.videoSearch(title))
                            System.out.println("The store "
                                  + "carries " + title);
                        else
                            System.out.println("The store does "
                                  + "not carry " + title);
                        break;
                case 2: System.out.print("Enter the title: ");
                        title = console.nextLine();
                        System.out.println();
```

```java
                    if (videoList.videoSearch(title))
                    {
                        if (videoList.isVideoAvailable(title))
                        {
                            videoList.videoCheckOut(title);
                            System.out.println("Enjoy your "
                                    + "movie: " + title);
                        }
                        else
                            System.out.println("Currently "
                                    + title
                                    + " is out of stock.");
                    }
                    else
                        System.out.println("The store does "
                                    + "not carry" + title);
                    break;
        case 3: System.out.print("Enter the title: ");
                    title = console.nextLine();
                    System.out.println();

                    if (videoList.videoSearch(title))
                    {
                        videoList.videoCheckIn(title);
                        System.out.println("Thanks for "
                                + "returning " + title);
                    }
                    else
                        System.out.println("The store does "
                                + " not carry " + title);
                    break;
        case 4: System.out.print("Enter the title: ");
                    title = console.nextLine();
                    System.out.println();

                    if (videoList.videoSearch(title))
                    {
                        if (videoList.isVideoAvailable(title))
                            System.out.println(title
                                        + " is currently "
                                        + "in stock.");
                        else
                            System.out.println(title
                                        + " is not in the "
                                        + "store.");
                    }
```

```java
                    else
                        System.out.println("The store does "
                                        + "not carry "
                                        + title);
                    break;
            case 5: videoList.videoPrintTitle();
                    break;
            case 6: videoList.print();
                    break;
            default: System.out.println("Invalid "
                                        + "selection");
            }//end switch

            displayMenu();
            System.out.print("Enter the choice: ");
            choice = console.nextInt();
            console.nextLine();
            System.out.println();
        }//end while
    }
    catch (FileNotFoundException fnfe)
    {
        System.out.println(fnfe.toString());
    }
} // end main

public static void createVideoList(Scanner infile,
                                   VideoList videoList)
{
    String vTitle;
    String mStar1;
    String mStar2;
    String mProducer;
    String mDirector;
    String mProductionCo;
    int vInStock;

    Video newVideo;

    while (infile.hasNext())
    {
        vTitle = infile.nextLine();
        mStar1 = infile.nextLine();
        mStar2 = infile.nextLine();
        mProducer = infile.nextLine();
        mDirector = infile.nextLine();
        mProductionCo = infile.nextLine();
        vInStock = infile.nextInt();
```

```
            infile.nextLine();
            newVideo = new Video();
            newVideo.setVideoInfo(vTitle, mStar1, mStar2,
                                  mProducer, mDirector,
                                  mProductionCo,vInStock);
            videoList.insertFirst(newVideo);
        }//end while
    }//end createVideoList

    public static void displayMenu()
    {
        System.out.println("Select one of the following: ");
        System.out.println("1: To check if a particular video "
                            + "is in the store");
        System.out.println("2: To check out a video");
        System.out.println("3: To check in a video");
        System.out.println("4: To see if a particular video "
                            + "is in the store");
        System.out.println("5: To print the titles of all "
                            + "the videos");
        System.out.println("6: To print a list of all the "
                            + "videos");
        System.out.println("9: To exit");
    }
}
```

QUICK REVIEW

1. A linked list is a list of items, called nodes, in which the order of the nodes is determined by the address, called a link, stored in each node.

2. The address of the first node of a linked list is stored in a separate location, called the head or first.

3. A linked list is a dynamic data structure.

4. The length of a linked list is the number of nodes in the list.

5. Item insertion and deletion from a linked list does not require data movement; only the links are adjusted.

6. A single linked list is traversed in only one direction.

7. The search on a linked list is sequential.

8. The variable first (or head) pointing to a linked list is always fixed, pointing to the first node in the list.

9. To traverse a linked list, the program must use a reference variable different from the reference variable that is pointing to the first node of the linked list.

10. In a doubly linked list, every node has two links: one points to the next node and one points to the previous node.

11. A doubly linked list can be traversed in either direction.

12. In a doubly linked list, item insertion and deletion requires the adjustment of two links in a node.

13. A circular linked list is a list in which, if the list is nonempty, the last node points to the first node.

EXERCISES

1. Mark the following statements as true or false.

   a. In a linked list, the order of the elements is determined by the order in which the nodes were created to store the elements.

   b. In a linked list, memory allocated for the nodes is sequential.

   c. A single linked list can be traversed in either direction.

   d. In a linked list, the nodes are always inserted either in the beginning or at the end because a linked link is not a random access data structure.

   e. The reference variable pointing to the first node of a linked list should be used to traverse the list.

Consider the linked list shown in Figure 16-61. Assume that the nodes are in the usual `info-link` form. Use this list to answer Exercises 2 through 7. If necessary, declare additional variables. (Assume that `list`, `p`, `s`, `A`, and `B` are reference variables of the type `Node`.)

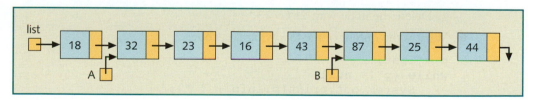

Figure 16-61   Linked list for Exercises 2 through 7

16

2. What is the output of the following Java statements?

   a. `System.out.println(list.info);`

   b. `System.out.println(A.info);`

   c. `System.out.println(B.link.info);`

   d. `System.out.println(list.link.link.info);`

3. What is the value of the following relational expressions?

   a. `list.info >= 18`

   b. `list.link == A`

   c. `A.link.info == 16`

   d. `B.link == null`

   e. `list.info == 18`

4. Mark each of the following statements as valid or invalid. If a statement is invalid, explain why.

   a. `A = B;`

   b. `list.link = A.link;`

   c. `list.link.info = 45;`

   d. `list = B;`

   e. `B = A.link.info;`

   f. `A.info = B.info;`

   g. `list = B.link.link;`

   h. `B = B.link.link.link;`

5. Write Java statements to do the following:

   a. Make A point to the node containing `info 23`.

   b. Make `list` point to the node containing `info 16`.

   c. Make `B` point to the last node in the list.

   d. Make `list` point to an empty list.

   e. Set the value of the node containing `25` to `35`.

   f. Create and insert the node with `info 10` after the node to which `A` points.

   g. Delete the node with `info 23`.

6. What is the output of the following Java code?

```
p = list;
while (p != null)
    System.out.print(p.info + " ");
    p = p.link;
System.out.println();
```

7. If the following Java code is valid, show the output. If it is invalid, explain why.

   a.
```
s = A;
p = B;
s.info = B;
p = p.link;
System.out.println(s.info + " " + p.info);
```

b.
```
p = A;
p = p.link;
s = p;
p.link = null;
s = s.link;
System.out.println(p.info + " " + s.info);
```

8. Show what is produced by the following Java code. Assume the node is in the usual info-link form with info of the type int. (Also, list and ptr are reference variables of the type Node.)

```
list = new Node();
list.info = 10;
ptr = new Node();
ptr.info = 13;
ptr.link = null;
list.link = ptr;
ptr = new Node();
ptr.info = 18;
ptr.link = list.link;
list.link = ptr;
System.out.print(list.info + "   " + ptr.info + " ");
ptr = ptr.link;
System.out.println(ptr.info);
```

9. Show what is produced by the following Java code. Assume the node is in the usual info-link form with info of the type int. (Also, list and ptr are reference variables of the type Node.)

```
list = new Node();
list.info = 20;
ptr = new Node();
ptr.info = 28;
ptr.link = null;
list.link = ptr;
ptr = new Node();
ptr.info = 30;
ptr.link = list;
list = ptr;
ptr = new Node();
ptr.info = 42;
ptr.link = list.link;
list.link = ptr;
ptr = list;
while (ptr != null)
{
    System.out.println(ptr.info);
    ptr = ptr.link;
}
```

16

10. Consider the following Java statements. (The **class** `UnorderedLinkedList` is as defined in this chapter.)

```
UnorderedLinkedList<Integer> list =
                   new UnorderedLinkedList<Integer>();
list.insertFirst(15);
list.insertLast(28);
list.insertFirst(30);
list.insertFirst(2);
list.insertLast(45);
list.insertFirst(38);
list.insertLast(25);
list.deleteNode(30);
list.insertFirst(18);
list.deleteNode(28);
list.deleteNode(12);
list.print();
System.out.println();
```

What is the output of this program segment?

11. Suppose the input is:

```
18  30  4  32  45  36  78  19  48  75
```

What is the output of the following Java code? (The **class** `UnorderedLinkedList` is as defined in this chapter.)

```
Scanner console = new Scanner(System.in);

UnorderedLinkedList<Integer> list =
                   new UnorderedLinkedList<Integer>();
UnorderedLinkedList<Integer> tempList;

Integer num;

while (console.hasNext())
{
    num = console.nextInt();

    if (num % 5 == 0 || num % 5 == 3)
        list.insertFirst(num);
    else
        list.insertLast(num);
}

System.out.print("List: ") ;
list.print() ;
System.out.println();

tempList = (UnorderedLinkedList<Integer>) list.clone();
```

```
tempList.deleteNode(78);

System.out.print("tempList: ");
tempList.print();
System.out.println();
```

12. Draw the UML diagram of the **class** Video of the Programming Example in this chapter.

13. Draw the UML diagram of the **class** VideoList of the Programming Example in this chapter.

PROGRAMMING EXERCISES

1. (**Online Address Book Revisited**) Programming Exercise 8 in Chapter 15 could handle a maximum of only 500 entries. Using linked lists, redo the program to handle as many entries as required. Add the following operations to your program:

   a. Add or delete a new entry to the address book.

   b. When the program terminates, write the data in the address book to a disk.

2. Extend the **class** LinkedListClass by adding the following operations:

   a. Find and delete the node with the smallest info in the list. (Delete only the first occurrence and traverse the list only once.)

   b. Find and delete all the occurrences of a given info from the list. (Traverse the list only once.)

   Add these as abstract methods in the **class** LinkedListClass and provide the definitions of these methods in the **class** UnorderedLinkedList. Also write a program to test these methods.

3. Extend the **class** LinkedListClass by adding the following operations:

   a. Write a method that returns the info of the kth element of the linked list. If no such element exists, terminate the program.

   b. Write a method that deletes the kth element of the linked list. If no such element exists, output an appropriate message.

   Provide the definitions of these methods in the **class** LinkedListClass. Also write a program to test these methods. (Use either the **class** UnorderedLinkedList or the **class** OrderedLinkedList to test your method.)

4. (**Printing a Single Linked List Backward**) Write and test a recursive method to print a (single) linked list backward. Add your method to the **interface** LinkedListADT and provide its definition in the **class** LinkedListClass. (Use either the **class** UnorderedLinkedList or the **class** OrderedLinkedList to test your method.)

16

5. **(Splitting a Linked List into Two Sublists of Almost Equal Sizes)**

   a. Add the method `splitMid` to the **class** `LinkedListClass` as follows:

```
public void splitMid(LinkedListClass<T> sublist);
    //This method splits the given list into two
    //sublists of (almost) equal sizes.
    //Precondition: The list must exist.
    //Postcondition: first points to the first node, and last
    //               points to the last node of the first
    //               sublist. sublist.first points to the
    //               first node, and sublist.last points to the
    //               last node of the second sublist.
```

   Consider the following statements:

```
UnorderedLinkedList<Integer> myList;
UnorderedLinkedList<Integer> subList;
```

   Suppose `myList` points to the list with elements 34, 65, 27, 89, and 12 (in this order). The statement

```
myList.splitMid(subList);
```

   splits `myList` into two sublists: `myList` points to the list with elements 34, 65, and 27, and `subList` points to the sublist with elements 89 and 12.

   b. Write the definition of the method `splitMid`. Also write a program to test your method. (Use either the **class** `UnorderedLinkedList` or the **class** `OrderedLinkedList` to test your method.)

6. **(Splitting a Linked List, at a Given Node, into Two Sublists)**

   a. Add the following as an **abstract method** to the **class** `LinkedListClass`:

```
public void splitAt(LinkedListClass<T> secondList, T item);
    //This method splits the list at the node with the
    //info item into two sublists.
    //Precondition: The list must exist.
    //Postcondition: first and last point to the first and last
    //               nodes of the first sublist, respectively.
    //               secondList.first and secondList.last
    //               point to the first and last nodes of
    //               the second sublist.
```

   Consider the following statements:

```
UnorderedLinkedList<Integer> myList;
UnorderedLinkedList<Integer> otherList;
```

   Suppose `myList` points to the list with the elements 34, 65, 18, 39, 27, 89, and 12 (in this order). The statement

```
myList.splitAt(otherList, 18);
```

splits `myList` into two sublists: `myList` points to the list with elements 34 and 65, and `otherList` points to the sublist with elements 18, 39, 27, 89, and 12.

b. Provide the definition of the method `splitAt` in the **class** `UnorderedLinkedList`. Also write a program to test your method.

7. **(Merge Sorted Linked Lists)**

a. Add the following method to the **class** `OrderedLinkedList`:

```
public void mergeLists(OrderedLinkedList<T> list1,
                       OrderedLinkedList<T> list2);
    //This operation creates a new list by merging the
    //elements of list1 and list2.
    //Precondition: Both lists, list1 and list2, are
    //              ordered.
    //Postcondition: first points to the merged list,
    //               and list1 and list2 are null.
```

Consider the following statements:

```
OrderedLinkedList<Integer> newList;
OrderedLinkedList<Integer> list1;
OrderedLinkedList<Integer> list2;
```

Suppose `list1` points to the list with elements 2, 6, and 7, and `list2` points to the list with elements 3, 5, and 8. The statement

```
newList.mergeLists(list1, list2);
```

creates a new linked list with the elements in the order 2, 3, 5, 6, 7, and 8, and the object `newList` points to this list. Also, after the preceding statement executes, `list1` and `list2` are empty.

b. Write the definition of the method `mergeLists` to implement the operation `mergeLists`. Also write a program to test your method.

8. The method `insert` of the **class** `OrderedLinkedList` does not check if the item to be inserted is already in the list; that is, it does not check for duplicates. Rewrite the definition of the method `insert` so that before inserting the item it checks whether the item to be inserted is already in the list. If the item to be inserted is already in the list, the method outputs an appropriate error message.

9. The **class** `LinkedListNode` to implement the nodes of a linked list is defined as an inner class of the **class** `LinkedListClass`. Rewrite the definitions of the **class** `LinkedListClass` so that the **class** `LinkedListNode` is not an inner class. It is a **public** class, defined outside of every class definition. Moreover, the instance variables `info` and `link` of the **class** `LinkedListNode` are **private**. Add appropriate methods to manipulate `info` and `link`.

16

10. Programming Exercise 9 asks you to redefine **class** LinkedListClass so that the **class** LinkedListNode is not an inner class. Therefore, the derived classes UnorderedLinkedList and OrderedLinkedList can no longer directly access the instance variables of the **class** LinkedListNode. Rewrite the definitions of the classes UnorderedLinkedList and OrderedLinkedList so that these classes are derived from the modified definition of the **class** LinkedListClass. Also write programs to test various operations of the **class**es UnorderedLinkedList and OrderedLinkedList.

11. Write the definition of the method clone of the **class** DoublyLinkedList. Also write a program to test your method.

12. Write a program to test various operations of the **class** DoublyLinkedList.

13. (**Circular Linked Lists**) This chapter defined and identified various operations on a circular linked list.

    a. Write the definition of the interface that describes the properties of a sorted circular linked list as described in this chapter.

    b. Write the definitions of the **class** CircularLinkedList and its methods. (You may assume that the elements of the circular linked list are in ascending order.)

    c. Write a program to test various operations of the class defined in (a).

14. (**Programming Example, Video Store**)

    a. Complete the design and implementation of the **class** Customer defined in the Programming Example Video Store.

    b. Design and implement the **class** CustomerList to create and maintain a list of customers for the video store.

15. (**Programming Example, Video Store**) Complete the design and implementation of the video store program.

STACKS AND QUEUES

In this chapter, you will:

- ♦ Learn about stacks
- ♦ Examine various stack operations
- ♦ Learn how to implement a stack as an array
- ♦ Learn how to implement a stack as a linked list
- ♦ Discover stack applications
- ♦ Learn how to use a stack to remove recursion
- ♦ Learn about queues
- ♦ Examine various queue operations
- ♦ Learn how to implement a queue as an array
- ♦ Discover queue applications

This chapter discusses two very useful data structures called stacks and queues. They have numerous applications in computer science.

STACKS

Suppose that you have a program with methods named A, B, C, and D. Now suppose that method A calls method B, method B calls method C, and method C calls method D. When method D terminates, control goes back to method C; when method C terminates, control goes back to method B; and when method B terminates, control goes back to method A. During program execution, how do you think the computer keeps track of the method calls? And how does the computer keep track of recursive calls?

This section discusses the data structure called the **stack**, which the computer uses to implement method calls. You can also use stacks to convert recursive algorithms into nonrecursive algorithms, especially recursive algorithms that are not tail recursive. Stacks have numerous other applications in computer science. After developing the tools necessary to implement a stack, we will examine some of these applications.

A stack is a list of homogeneous elements, wherein the addition and deletion of elements occurs only at one end, called the **top** of the stack. For example, in a cafeteria, the second tray in a stack of trays can be removed only if the first tray has been removed. For another example, to get to your favorite computer science book, which is underneath your math and history books, you must first remove the math and history books. After removing these books, the computer science book becomes the top book—that is, the top element of the stack. Figure 17-1 shows some examples of stacks.

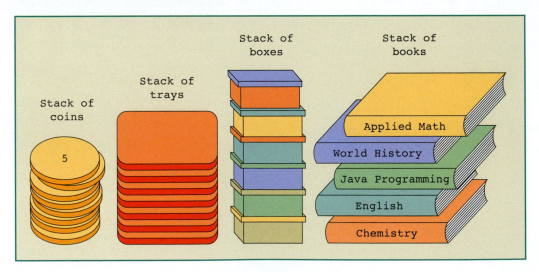

Figure 17-1 Various types of stacks

The elements at the bottom of the stack have been in the stack the longest. The top element of the stack is the last element added to the stack. Because elements are added and removed from one end (that is, the top), it follows that the item that is added last will be removed first. For this reason, a stack is also called a **Last In First Out (LIFO)** data structure.

Stack: A data structure in which the elements are added and removed from one end only; a Last In First Out (LIFO) data structure.

Now that you know what a stack is, let us see what kinds of operations can be performed on a stack. Because new items can be added to the stack, we can perform the add operation, called **push**, to add an element onto the stack. Similarly, because the top item can be retrieved and/or removed from the stack, we can perform the operation **peek** to look at the top element of the stack, and the operation **pop** to remove the top element from the stack. Note that the peek operation *does not* modify the stack.

The **push**, **peek**, and **pop** operations work as follows: Suppose there are boxes lying on the floor that need to be stacked on a table. Initially, all of the boxes are on the floor and the stack is empty. See Figure 17-2.

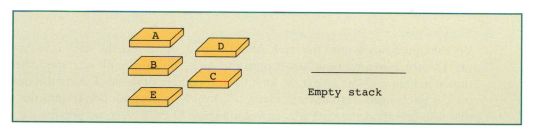

Figure 17-2   Empty stack

First we push box **A** onto the stack. After the push operation, the stack is as shown in Figure 17-3(a).

17

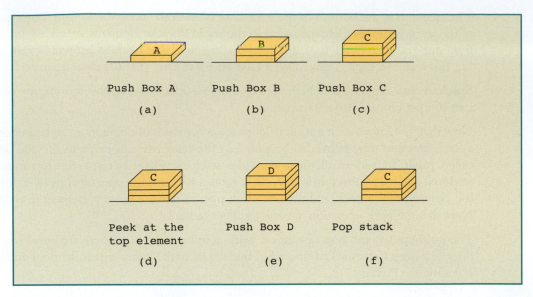

Figure 17-3 Stack operations

We then push box B onto the stack. After this push operation, the stack is as shown in Figure 17-3(b). Next, we push box C onto the stack. After this push operation, the stack is as shown in Figure 17-3(c). Next, we look the top element of the stack. After this operation, the stack is unchanged and shown in Figure 17-3(d). We then push box D onto the stack. After this push operation, the stack is as shown in Figure 17-3(e). Next, we pop the stack. After the pop operation, the stack is as shown in Figure 17-3(f).

An element can be removed and/or retrieved from the stack only if there is something in the stack, and an element can be added to the stack only if there is room. The two operations that immediately follow from **push**, **peek**, and **pop** are **isFullStack** (checks whether the stack is full) and **isEmptyStack** (checks whether the stack is empty). Because a stack keeps changing as we add and remove elements, the stack must be empty before we first start using it. Thus, we need another operation, called **initializeStack**, which initializes the stack to an empty state. Therefore, to successfully implement a stack, we need at least five operations, which are described in the next section. We might also need other operations on a stack, depending on the specific implementation.

Stack Operations

The basic operations on a stack are:

- **initializeStack**: Initializes the stack to an empty state.

- **isEmptyStack**: Checks whether the stack is empty. If the stack is empty, it returns the value **true**; otherwise, it returns the value **false**.

- **isFullStack**: Checks whether the stack is full. If the stack is full, it returns the value **true**; otherwise, it returns the value **false**.

- **push**: Adds a new element to the top of the stack. The input to this operation consists of the stack and the new element. Prior to this operation, the stack must exist and must not be full.

- **peek**: Look at the top element of the stack. Prior to this operation, the stack must exist and must not be empty.

- **pop**: Removes the top element of the stack Prior to this operation, the stack must exist and must not be empty.

The following interface defines these operations as an ADT:

```
public interface StackADT<T>
{
    public void initializeStack();
       //Method to initialize the stack to an empty state.
       //Postcondition: The stack is initialized.

    public boolean isEmptyStack();
       //Method to determine whether the stack is empty.
       //Postcondition: Returns true if the stack is empty;
       //               otherwise, returns false.

    public boolean isFullStack();
       //Method to determine whether the stack is full.
       //Postcondition: Returns true if the stack is full;
       //               otherwise, returns false.

    public void push(T newItem) throws StackOverflowException;
       //Method to add newItem to the stack.
       //Precondition: The stack exists and is not full.
       //Postcondition: The stack is changed and newItem
       //               is added to the top of the stack.
       //               If the stack is full, the method
       //               throws StackOverflowException.

    public T peek() throws StackUnderflowException;
       //Method to return a reference to the top element of
       //the stack.
       //Precondition: The stack exists and is not empty.
       //Postcondition: If the stack is empty, the method
       //               throws StackUnderflowException;
       //               otherwise, a reference to the top
       //               element of the stack is returned.
```

17

```
    public void pop() throws StackUnderflowException;
      //Method to remove the top element of the stack.
      //Precondition: The stack exists and is not empty.
      //Postcondition: The stack is changed and the top
      //                element is removed from the stack.
      //                If the stack is empty, the method
      //                throws StackUnderflowException.
}
```

Figure 17-4 shows the UML class diagram of the **interface** StackADT.

```
                <<interface>>
                StackADT<T>


+initializeStack(): void
+isEmptyStack(): boolean
+isFullStack(): boolean
+push(T): void
+peek(): T
+pop(): void
```

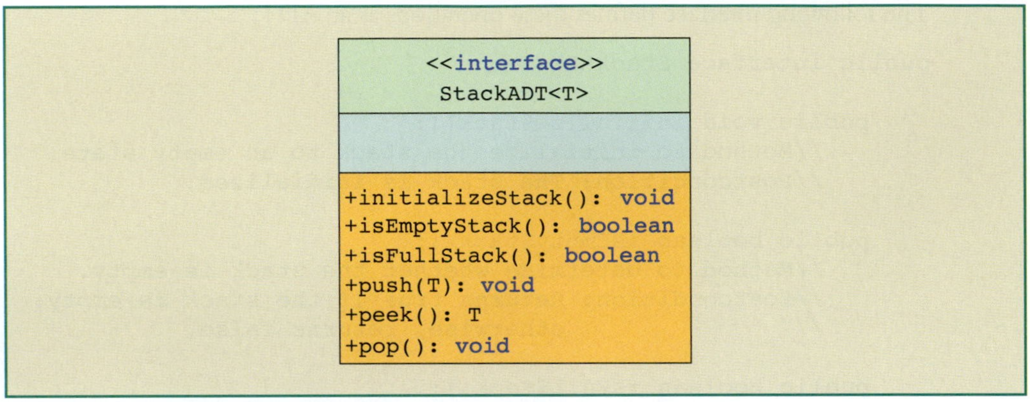

Figure 17-4   UML class diagram of the **interface** StackADT

We now consider the implementation of stacks as an ADT. To develop generic algorithms, just as we have done in Chapter 15 and 16, we will treat stack elements as references to objects where actual data is stored.

A stack can be implemented either as an array or as a linked list. If we implement a stack as an array, then a stack is an array of reference variables. Similarly, if we implement a stack as a linked list, then the info of each node is a reference to the object storing the data. Both implementations are useful and are discussed in this chapter.

StackException CLASS

The preceding section describes the basic operations on a stack: push, peek, and pop. Just as an element can be pushed into the stack if the stack is not full, so can an element be removed from the stack only if the stack is not empty. Adding an element to a full stack and removing an element from an empty stack would generate errors or exceptions called **stack overflow**

exception and **stack underflow exception**. To handle these exceptions we design exception classes as follows:

```java
public class StackException extends RuntimeException
{
    public StackException()
    {
    }

    public StackException(String msg)
    {
        super(msg);
    }
}

public class StackOverflowException extends StackException
{
    public StackOverflowException()
    {
        super("Stack Overflows");
    }

    public StackOverflowException(String msg)
    {
        super(msg);
    }
}

public class StackUnderflowException extends StackException
{
    public StackUnderflowException()
    {
        super("Stack Underflow");
    }

    public StackUnderflowException(String msg)
    {
        super(msg);
    }
}
```

When we write the method to implement the push operation, if the stack is full, then this method would throw the **StackOverflowException** exception. The method that implements the pop operation would throw a **StackUnderflowException** exception if we try to remove an item from an empty stack. Similarly, the method that implements the peek operation would throw a **StackUnderflowException** exception if we try to retrieve an item from an empty stack. Notice that the **class StackException** is derived from the **class** **RuntimeException**, so the stack overflow and underflow exceptions as we have defined them are unchecked exceptions. If you want to make these exceptions checked exceptions,

17

then you should derive the **class** StackException from the **class** Exception. Suppose that you make these checked exceptions. Then if a program uses the push, peek, and pop operations, the program either provides the code to handle these exceptions or explicitly throws these exceptions. For simplicity and to illustrate how to implement your own exception classes, we have made stack overflow and underflow unchecked exceptions.

IMPLEMENTATION OF STACKS AS ARRAYS

This section describes how to implement a stack using an array. As remarked previously, because we will design a generic class to implement stacks, the array implementing a stack is an array of reference variables.

The first element of the stack can be assigned to the first array slot, the second element of the stack to the second array slot, and so on. The top of the stack is the index of the last element added to the stack.

In this implementation of a stack, the stack elements are managed by an array of reference variables. An array is a random access data structure; that is, you can directly access any element of the array. However, remember that by definition, a stack is a data structure in which the elements are accessed (popped or pushed) at only one end—that is, it is a Last In First Out data structure. Thus, a stack element is accessed only through the top, not through the bottom or middle. This feature of a stack is extremely important and must be recognized from the beginning.

To keep track of the top position of the array, we can simply declare another variable, called **stackTop**.

Before we describe the class to implement stack operations, we note the following. In Chapters 15 and 16, we observed that while designing a generic class to implement a list in the definition of the class, we cannot include any method to produce a true clone of the list. (Recall that a generic class cannot produce a true clone of the list objects that are mutable.) Here our focus is on implementing a stack and its basic operations. Because cloning can be expensive, in this chapter we will not consider this operation. Therefore, we leave it as an exercise for you to modify the definition of the stack class that we design, so that the clone method can be included to clone a stack.

The following statements define the members of the class implementing a stack. Because we can specify the size of the array implementing the stack during program execution or at compile time, we will leave it for the user to specify the size of the array (that is, the stack size). We assume that the default stack size is 100.

Class: StackClass

```
public class StackClass<T> implements StackADT<T>
```

Instance variables:

```java
private int maxStackSize;   //variable to store the
                            //maximum stack size
private int stackTop;       //variable to point to
                            //the top of the stack
private T[] list;   //array of reference variables
```

Instance Methods and Constructors

```java
public StackClass()
   //Default constructor
   //Create an array of the size 100 to implement the stack.
   //Postcondition: The variable list contains the base
   //               address of the array, stackTop = 0,
   //               and maxStackSize = 100.

public StackClass(int stackSize)
   //Constructor with a parameter
   //Create an array of the size stackSize to implement the
   //stack.
   //Postcondition: The variable list contains the base
   //               address of the array, stackTop = 0,
   //               and maxStackSize = stackSize.

public void initializeStack()
   //Method to initialize the stack to an empty state.
   //Postcondition: stackTop = 0

public boolean isEmptyStack()
   //Method to determine whether the stack is empty.
   //Postcondition: Returns true if the stack is empty;
   //               otherwise, returns false.

public boolean isFullStack()
   //Method to determine whether the stack is full.
   //Postcondition: Returns true if the stack is full;
   //               otherwise, returns false.

public void push(T newItem) throws StackOverflowException
   //Method to add newItem to the stack.
   //Precondition: The stack exists and is not full.
   //Postcondition: The stack is changed and newItem
   //               is added to the top of stack.
   //               If the stack is full, the method
   //               throws StackOverflowException.
```

17

```
public T peek() throws StackUnderflowException
    //Method to return a reference to the top element of
    //the stack.
    //Precondition: The stack exists and is not empty.
    //Postcondition: If the stack is empty, the method
    //                throws StackUnderflowException;
    //                otherwise, a reference to the top
    //                element of the stack is returned.

public void pop() throws StackUnderflowException
    //Method to remove the top element of the stack.
    //Precondition: The stack exists and is not empty.
    //Postcondition: The stack is changed and the top
    //                element is removed from the stack.
    //                If the stack is empty, the method
    //                throws StackUnderflowException.
```

Figure 17-5 shows the UML class diagram of the **class StackADT**.

```
                    StackClass<T>

            -maxStackSize: int
            -stackTop: int
            -list: T[]

            +StackClass()
            +StackClass(int)
            +initializeStack(): void
            +isEmptyStack(): boolean
            +isFullStack(): boolean
            +push(T): void
            +peek(): T
            +pop(): void
```

Figure 17-5   UML class diagram of the **class** StackClass

Because Java arrays begin with the index 0, we need to distinguish between the value of stackTop and the array position indicated by stackTop. If stackTop is 0, the stack is empty; if stackTop is nonzero, then the stack is nonempty and the top element of the stack is given by stackTop – 1.

Figure 17-6 shows this data structure, wherein **stack** is an object of the type **StackClass**. Note that **stackTop** can range from 0 to **maxStackSize**. If **stackTop** is nonzero, then `stackTop - 1` is the index of the `stackTop` element of the stack. Suppose that `maxStackSize = 100`.

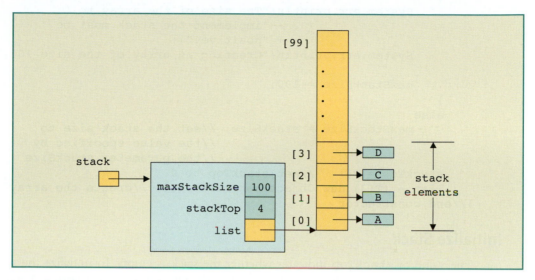

Figure 17-6   Example of a stack

Note that the instance variable `list` contains the base address of the array (holding the stack elements)—that is, the address of the first array component. The next seven sections of this chapter define the methods of the **class** `StackClass` that implement the stack operations.

Next we give the definitions of the methods of the **class** `StackClass`.

Constructors

The definitions of the constructors are straightforward. The constructor with a parameter sets the stack size to the size specified by the user, sets `stackTop` to 0, and creates an appropriate array in which to store the stack elements. The default constructor creates an array of the size 100. The definitions of the constructors are:

```
public StackClass()
{
    maxStackSize = 100;
    stackTop = 0;              //set stackTop to 0
    list = (T[]) new Object[maxStackSize]; //create the array
}//end default constructor
```

17

```java
public StackClass(int stackSize)
{
    if (stackSize <= 0)
    {
        System.err.println("The size of the array to "
                        + "implement the stack must be "
                        + "positive.");
        System.err.println("Creating an array of the size 100.");

        maxStackSize = 100;
    }
    else
        maxStackSize = stackSize; //set the stack size to
                                  //the value specified by
                                  //the parameter stackSize
    stackTop = 0;     //set stackTop to 0
    list = (T[]) new Object[maxStackSize]; //create the array
}//end constructor
```

Initialize Stack

The value of **stackTop** indicates whether the stack is empty. To initialize the stack to an empty state, we set the elements of the stack in the range 0...**stackTop** – 1 to **null** and then set **stackTop** to 0. See Figure 17-7.

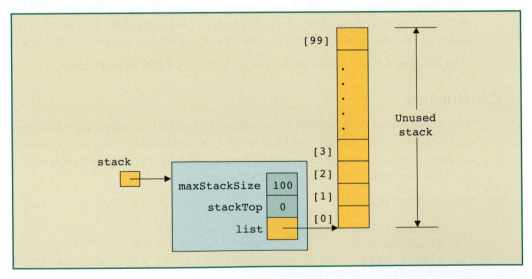

Figure 17-7 Empty stack

The definition of the method `initializeStack` is:

```
public void initializeStack()
{
    for (int i = 0; i < stackTop; i++)
        list[i] = null;

    stackTop = 0;
}//end initializeStack
```

Empty Stack

We have seen that the value of `stackTop` indicates whether the stack is empty. If `stackTop` is 0, the stack is empty; otherwise, the stack is not empty. The definition of the method `isEmptyStack` is:

```
public boolean isEmptyStack()
{
    return (stackTop == 0);
}//end isEmptyStack
```

Full Stack

Next, we consider the operation `isFullStack`. It follows that the stack is full if `stackTop` is equal to `maxStackSize`. The definition of the method `isFullStack` is:

```
public boolean isFullStack()
{
    return (stackTop == maxStackSize);
}//end isFullStack
```

Push

Adding, or pushing, an element onto the stack is a two-step process. Recall that the value of `stackTop` indicates the number of elements in the stack, and `stackTop - 1` gives the position of the `stackTop` element of the stack. Therefore, the push operation is as follows:

    a. Assign `newItem` to the array component indicated by `stackTop`.

    b. Increment `stackTop`.

Figures 17-8 and 17-9 illustrate the push operation.

Suppose that before the push operation, the stack is as shown in Figure 17-8.

17

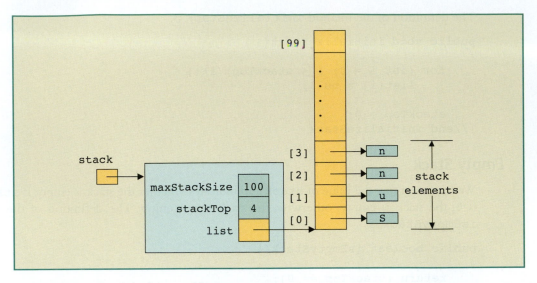

Figure 17-8 Stack before pushing y

Assume `newItem` is `'y'`. After the push operation, the stack is as shown in Figure 17-9.

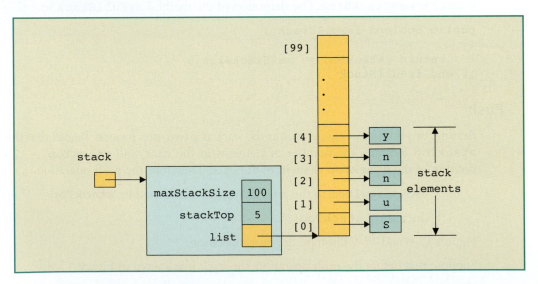

Figure 17-9 Stack after pushing y

If the stack is full, of course, we cannot add any elements to the stack. Therefore, before adding an element to the stack, the method **push** checks whether the stack is full. The definition of the method **push** is:

```
public void push(T newItem) throws StackOverflowException
{
    if (isFullStack())
        throw new StackOverflowException();

    list[stackTop] = newItem;  //add newItem at the
                               //top of the stack
    stackTop++;                //increment stackTop
}//end push
```

Peek

The method **peek** returns a reference to the top element of the stack. If the stack is empty, this method throws **StackUnderflowException**. Its definition is:

```
public T peek() throws StackUnderflowException
{
    if (isEmptyStack())
        throw new StackUnderflowException();

    return (T) list[stackTop - 1];
}//end peek
```

Pop

To remove, or pop, an element from the stack, we decrement **stackTop** by 1 and set the array element indicated by **stackTop** to **null**.

Figures 17-10 and 17-11 illustrate the **pop** operation.

Suppose that before the **pop** operation, the stack is as shown in Figure 17-10.

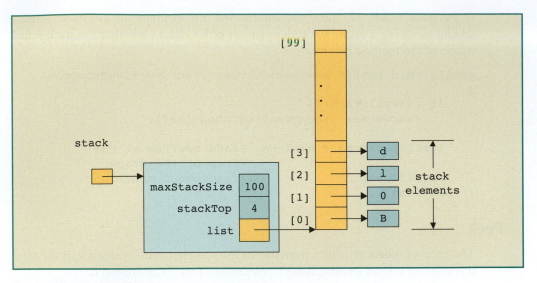

Figure 17-10 Stack before popping d

After the **pop** operation, the stack is as shown in Figure 17-11.

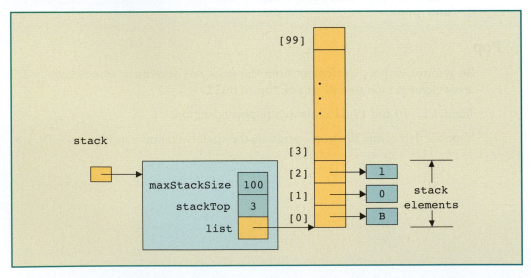

Figure 17-11 Stack after popping d

If the stack is empty, of course, we cannot remove any element from the stack. Therefore, before removing the top element from the stack, the method **pop** checks whether the stack is empty. Using the previous algorithm, the definition of the method **pop** is:

```java
public void pop() throws StackUnderflowException
{
    if (isEmptyStack())
        throw new StackUnderflowException();

    stackTop--;          //decrement stackTop
    list[stackTop] = null;
}//end pop
```

We leave it as an exercise for you to write the complete definition of the **class** **StackClass**.

Example 17-1

The following program tests various operations on a stack:

```java
public class StackProgram
{
    public static void main(String[] args)
    {
        StackClass<Integer> intStack =
                    new StackClass<Integer>(50);     //Line 1

        try                                          //Line 2
        {
            intStack.push(23);                       //Line 3
            intStack.push(45);                       //Line 4
            intStack.push(38);                       //Line 5
        }
        catch (StackOverflowException sofe)          //Line 6
        {
            System.out.println(sofe.toString());     //Line 7
            System.exit(0);                          //Line 8
        }

        System.out.print("intStack elements: ");     //Line 9

        while (!intStack.isEmptyStack())             //Line 10
        {
            System.out.print(intStack.peek()
                            + " ");                  //Line 11
            intStack.pop();
        }

        System.out.println();                        //Line 12
    }
}
```

17

Sample Run:

```
intStack elements: 38 45 23
```

It is recommended that you do a walk-through of this program.

PROGRAMMING EXAMPLE: HIGHEST GPA

In this example, we write a Java program that reads a data file consisting of each student's GPA followed by the student's name. The program then prints the highest GPA and the names of all the students who received that GPA. The program scans the input file only once. Moreover, we assume that there are a maximum of 100 students in the class.

Input

The program reads an input file consisting of the student's GPA, followed by the student's name. Some sample data is as follows:

```
3.8 Lisa
3.6 John
3.9 Susan
3.7 Kathy
3.4 Jason
3.9 David
3.4 Jack
```

Output

The highest GPA and all the names associated with the highest GPA will be the output. For example, for the above data, the highest GPA is **3.9** and the students with that GPA are **Susan** and **David**.

Program Analysis and Algorithm Design

To store the highest GPA, we use the variable **highestGPA** of the type **double** initialized to **0**. For each line in the input file, we need to do the following:

1. Retrieve the GPA and the name of the student associated with this GPA.
2. Compare this GPA with **highestGPA**. Three cases arise:
   a. The new GPA is greater than the highest GPA so far. In this case, we:
      i.   Update the value of the highest GPA so far.
      ii. Initialize the stack, that is, remove the names of the students from the stack.
      iii. Save the name of the student having the highest GPA so far in the stack.

b. The new GPA is equal to the highest GPA so far. In this case, we add the name of the new student to the stack.

c. The new GPA is less than the highest GPA so far. In this case, we discard the name of the student having this grade.

From this discussion, it is clear that we need the following variables:

```java
double gpa; //variable to hold the current GPA
double highestGpa = 0.0; //variable to hold the highest GPA

String name; //object to hold name

StackClass<String> nameStack =
         new StackClass<String>(100); //stack to hold
                                      //names that have the
                                      //highest GPA

Scanner infile;
```

The preceding discussion translates into the following algorithm:

1. Declare and initialize the variables.
2. Open the input file.
3. If the input file does not exist, exit the program.
4. If the input file does exist, then:

```java
        while (data to process)
        {
            Get the next GPA;
            Get the next name;
            if (GPA > highestGPA);
            {
                initialize stack;
                push(stack, student name);
                highestGPA = GPA;
            }
            else if (GPA is equal to highestGPA)
                push(stack, student name);
        }
```

5. Output the highest GPA.
6. Output the names of the students having the highest GPA.

Complete Program Listing

```java
//Program highest gpa.

import java.io.*;
import java.util.*;
```

```java
public class HighestGPA
{
    public static void main(String[] args)
    {
                //Step 1
        double gpa;
        double highestGpa = 0.0;
        String name;

        StackClass<String> nameStack =
                new StackClass<String>(100);

        try
        {
            Scanner infile = new Scanner
                (new FileReader
                    ("a:\\HighestGPAData.txt"));      //Step 2

            while (infile.hasNext())                  //Step 4
            {
                gpa = infile.nextDouble();
                name = infile.next();

                if (gpa > highestGpa)
                {
                    nameStack.initializeStack();

                    try
                    {
                        nameStack.push(name);
                    } //end try
                    catch (StackOverflowException sofe)
                    {
                        System.out.println(sofe.toString());
                        System.exit(0);
                    }

                    highestGpa = gpa;
                }
                else if (gpa == highestGpa)
                    try
                    {
                        nameStack.push(name);
                    } //end try
                    catch (StackOverflowException sofe)
                    {
```

```
                                System.out.println(sofe.toString());
                                System.exit(0);
                            }
                    }

                    System.out.printf("Highest GPA = %.2f%n",
                                      highestGpa);              //Step 5
                    System.out.println("The students holding "
                                    + "the highest GPA are:"); //Step 6

                    while (!nameStack.isEmptyStack())
                    {
                        System.out.println(nameStack.peek());
                        nameStack.pop();
                    }

                    System.out.println();
                } //end try
                catch (FileNotFoundException fnfe)      //Step 3
                {
                    System.out.println(fnfe.toString());
                }
            }
        }
```

Sample Run

Input File (`HighestGPAData.txt`)

```
3.4 Randy
3.2 Kathy
2.5 Colt
3.4 Tom
3.8 Ron
3.8 Mickey
3.6 Peter
3.5 Donald
3.8 Cindy
3.7 Dome
3.9 Andy
3.8 Fox
3.9 Minnie
2.7 Gilda
3.9 Vinay
3.4 Danny
```

> **Output**
>
> ```
> Highest GPA = 3.90
> The students holding the highest GPA are:
> Vinay
> Minnie
> Andy
> ```
>
> Note that the names of the students with the highest GPA are output in the reverse order, relative to the order they appear in the input, because the top element of the stack is the last element added to the stack.

LINKED IMPLEMENTATION OF STACKS

Because an array size is fixed, in the array (linear) representation of a stack, only a fixed number of elements can be pushed onto the stack. If in a program the number of elements to be pushed exceeds the size of the array, the program might terminate in an error. We must overcome these problems.

We have seen that by using reference variables we can dynamically allocate memory, and by using linked lists we can dynamically organize data (such as an ordered list). We can use these concepts to implement a stack dynamically.

Recall that in the array representation of a stack, the value of **stackTop** indicates the number of elements in the stack, and the value of **stackTop – 1** indicates where the top item is in the stack. With the help of **stackTop**, we can find the top element, check whether the stack is empty, and so on.

Similar to the array representation, in a linked representation, **stackTop** is used to locate the top element of the stack. However, there is a slight difference. In the former case, **stackTop** gives the index of the array; in the latter case, **stackTop** gives the reference of node whose info contains the reference of the top element of the stack.

The following statements define the members of a linked stack:

Class: LinkedStackClass

```
public class LinkedStackClass<T> implements StackADT<T>
```

Definition of the class defining the node of the linked stack

```
private class StackNode<T>
{
    public T info;
    public StackNode<T> link;
```

```java
    //Default constructor
    //Postcondition: info = null; link = null;
public StackNode()
{
    info = null;
    link = null;
}


    //Constructor with parameters
    //Sets info point to the object elem points to
    //and link is set to point to the object ptr
    //points to.
    //Postcondition:  info = elem; link = ptr
public StackNode(T elem, StackNode<T> ptr)
{
    info = elem;
    link = ptr;
}


    //Method to return the info as a string.
    //Postcondition: info as a String object is
    //                      returned.
public String toString()
{
    return info.toString();
}
}
```

Instance variables:

```java
private StackNode<T> stackTop;   //reference variable to the
                                 //top element of the stack
```

Instance Methods and Constructors

```java
public LinkedStackClass()
   //Default constructor
   //Postcondition: stackTop = null

public void initializeStack()
   //Method to initialize the stack to an empty state.
   //Postcondition: stackTop = null

public boolean isEmptyStack()
   //Method to determine whether the stack is empty.
   //Postcondition: Returns true if the stack is empty;
   //                      otherwise, returns false.
```

17

```
public boolean isFullStack()
    //Method to determine whether the stack is full.
    //Postcondition: Returns true if the stack is full;
    //               otherwise, returns false.

public void push(T newElement)
    //Method to add newItem to the stack.
    //Postcondition: The stack is changed and newItem
    //               is added to the top of stack.

public T peek() throws StackUnderflowException
    //Method to return a reference to the top element of
    //the stack.
    //Precondition: The stack exists and is not empty.
    //Postcondition: If the stack is empty, the method throws
    //               StackUnderflowException; otherwise, a
    //               reference to the top element of the stack
    //               is returned.

public void pop()throws StackUnderflowException
    //Method to remove the top element of the stack.
    //Precondition: The stack exists and is not empty.
    //Postcondition: The stack is changed and the top
    //               element is removed from the stack.
    //               If the stack is empty, the method throws
    //               StackUnderflowException.
```

 In this linked implementation of stacks, the memory to store the stack elements is allocated dynamically. Therefore, logically, the stack is never full. The stack is full only if we run out of memory space. Thus, it is not necessary to implement the operation `isFullStack` to determine whether the stack is full. However, because the **class** `LinkedStackClass` implements the **interface** `StackADT`, which includes the method `isFullStack`, the **class** `LinkedStackClass` must provide a definition of this method.

The following example shows how both empty and nonempty linked stacks appear.

Example 17-2

Empty linked stack: The empty linked stack is shown in Figure 17–12.

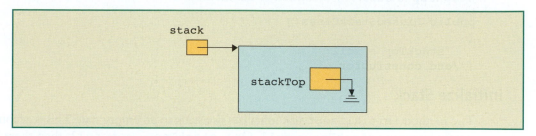

Figure 17-12   Empty linked stack

Nonempty stack: The nonempty stack is shown in Figure 17–13.

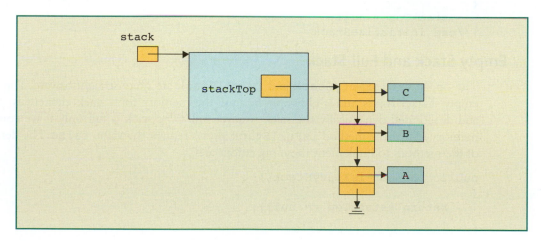

Figure 17-13   Nonempty linked stack

In Figure 17–13, the top element of the stack is C; that is, the last element pushed onto the stack is C.

Next, we discuss the definitions of the methods to implement the operations of a linked stack.

Default Constructor

The first operation that we consider is the default constructor. The default constructor initializes the stack to an empty state when a stack object is declared. Thus, this method sets `stackTop` to `null`. The definition of this method is:

```java
public LinkedStackClass()
{
    stackTop = null;
}//end constructor
```

Initialize Stack

The method `initializeStack` initializes the stack to an empty state. This is accomplished simply by setting `stackTop` to `null`. Once `stackTop` is set to `null`, then there will not be any reference variable pointing to the first element of the stack. The system's garbage collector will eventually reclaim the memory occupied by the stack elements. The definition of this method is:

```java
public void initializeStack()
{
    stackTop = null;
}//end initializeStack
```

Empty Stack and Full Stack

The operations `isEmptyStack` and `isFullStack` are quite straightforward. The stack is empty if stackTop is `null`. However, because the memory for a stack element is allocated and deallocated dynamically, the stack is never full. (The stack is full only if we run out of memory.) Thus, the method `isFullStack` always returns the value **false**. The definitions of the methods to implement these operations are:

```java
public boolean isEmptyStack()
{
    return (stackTop == null);
}

public boolean isFullStack()
{
    return false;
}
```

Next, we consider the `push`, `peek`, and `pop` operations. From Figure 17-13, it is clear that the `newElement` is added (in the case of `push`) at the beginning of the linked list to which `stackTop` points. In the case of `pop`, the node to which `stackTop` points is removed. In both cases, the value of `stackTop` is updated.

Push

Consider the stack shown in Figure 17-14.

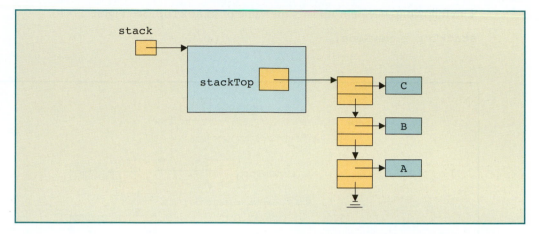

Figure 17-14   Stack before `push` operation

Assume that the new element to be pushed is `'D`. Creating a node to store this element and then adding this node to the top of the stack is accomplished by calling the constructor with parameter of the **class** `StackNode`. Thus we need only the following statement:

`newNode = `**`new`**` StackNode<T>(newElement, stackTop);`

After executing this statement, the resulting stack is shown in Figure 17-15.

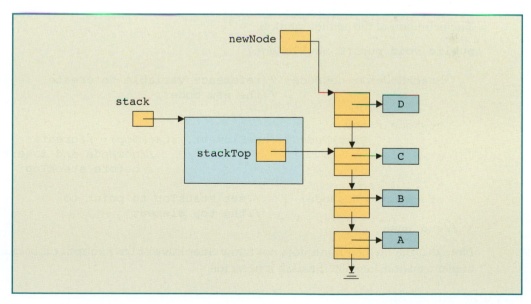

Figure 17-15   Stack after the statement `newNode = `**`new`**` StackNode<T>(newElement, stackTop);` executes

The following statement updates the value of **stackTop**. See Figure 17-16.

```
stackTop = newNode;
```

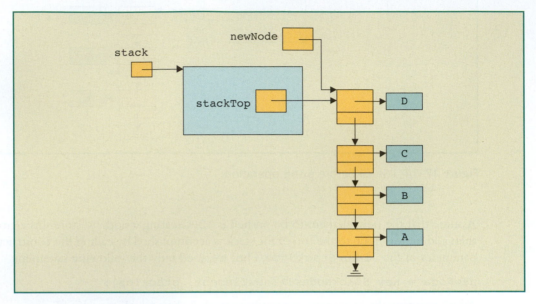

Figure 17-16 Stack after the statement **stackTop = newNode;** executes

The definition of the method **push** is:

```
public void push(T newElement)
{
    StackNode<T> newNode;  //reference variable to create
                           //the new node

    newNode = new
             StackNode<T>(newElement, stackTop); //create
                                    //newNode and insert
                                    //before stackTop

    stackTop = newNode;        //set stackTop to point to
                               //the top element
} //end push
```

Note that the method **push** does not throw **StackOverflowException** because in this implementation, logically, the stack is never full.

Peek

The method **peek** returns a reference to the top element of the stack. However, if the stack is empty, it throws `StackUnderflowException`. Its definition is:

```java
public T peek() throws StackUnderflowException
{
    if (stackTop == null)
        throw new StackUnderflowException();

    return stackTop.info;
}//end top
```

Pop

Now we consider the **pop** operation. Consider the stack shown in Figure 17-17.

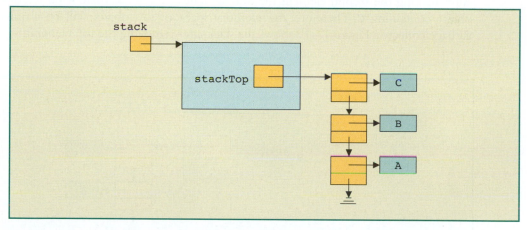

Figure 17-17   Stack before the pop operation

The statement

```java
stackTop = stackTop.link;
```

makes the second element of the stack become the top element of the stack. We then have the situation shown in Figure 17-18.

17

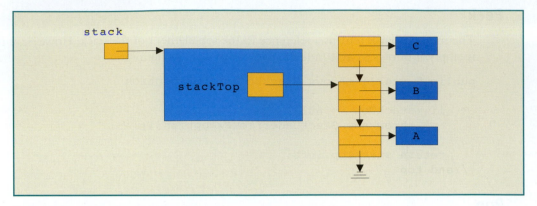

Figure 17-18   Stack after the statement `stackTop = stackTop.link;` executes

After making the second element the top element of the stack, there is no reference to the object containing C. Therefore, the memory space of this object will be claimed by the garbage collector. Figure 17–19 shows the stack after removing the top element.

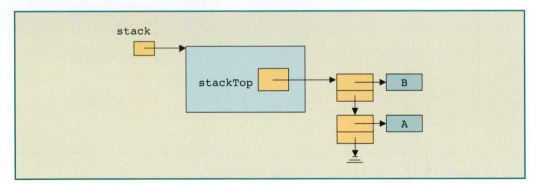

Figure 17-19   Stack after popping the top element

The definition of the method **pop** is:

```
public void pop() throws StackUnderflowException
{
    if (stackTop == null)
        throw new StackUnderflowException();

    stackTop = stackTop.link;   //advance stackTop to the
                                //next node
}//end pop
```

We leave it as an exercise for you to write the complete definition of the **class** LinkedStackClass.

Stack as Derived from the **class** UnorderedLinkedList

If we compare the push method of the stack with the insertFirst method discussed for general lists in Chapter 16, we see that the algorithms to implement these operations are similar. A comparison of other methods, such as initializeStack and initializeList, isEmptyList and isEmptyStack, and so on, suggests that the **class** LinkedStackClass can be derived from the **class** LinkedListClass. Moreover, the methods isFullStack, top, and pop can be implemented as in the previous section.

Because the **class** LinkedListClass is an abstract class and because we do not provide the definition of the abstract methods of this class, we can derive the **class** LinkedStackClass from the **class** UnorderedLinkedList, which was designed in Chapter 16.

Next, we define the **class** LinkedStackClass that is derived from the **class** UnorderedLinkedList. The definitions of the methods to implement the stack operations are also given.

```java
public class LinkedStackClass<T> extends UnorderedLinkedList<T>
{
    public LinkedStackClass()
    {
        super();
    }

    public void initializeStack()
    {
        initializeList();
    }

    public boolean isEmptyStack()
    {
        return isEmptyList();
    }

    public boolean isFullStack()
    {
        return false;
    }

    public void push(T newElement)
    {
        insertFirst(newElement)
    } //end push
```

17

```
public T peek() throws StackUnderflowException
{
    if (first == null)
        throw new StackUnderflowException();

    return front();
} //end peek

public void pop()throws StackUnderflowException
{
    if (first == null)
        throw new StackUnderflowException();

    first = first.link;

    count--;

    if (first == null)
        last = null;
}//end pop
}
```

APPLICATION OF STACKS: POSTFIX EXPRESSION CALCULATOR

The usual notation for writing arithmetic expressions (the notation we learned in elementary school) is called **infix** notation, in which the operator is written between the operands. For example, in the expression $a + b$, the operator + is between the operands a and b. In infix notation, the operators have precedence. That is, we evaluate expressions from left to right, and multiplication and division have higher precedence than addition and subtraction. If we want to evaluate an expression in a different order, we must include parentheses. For example, in the expression $a + b * c$, we first evaluate * using the operands b and c, and then we evaluate + using the operand a and the result of $b * c$.

In the early 1920s, the Polish mathematician Jan Lukasiewicz discovered that if operators were written before the operands (**prefix** or **Polish** notation; for example, + a b) the parentheses can be omitted. In the late 1950s, the Australian philosopher and early computer scientist Charles L. Hamblin proposed a scheme in which the operators *follow* the operands (postfix operators), resulting in the **Reverse Polish** notation. This has the advantage that the operators appear in the order required for computation.

For example, the expression

$a + b * c$

in a postfix expression is

a b c * +

The following example shows infix expressions and their equivalent postfix expressions:

Example 17-3

Table 17-1 shows various infix expressions and their equivalent postfix expressions.

Table 17-1 Infix expressions and their equivalent postfix expressions

Infix Expression	Equivalent Postfix Expression
$a + b$	$a\ b\ +$
$a + b * c$	$a\ b\ c\ *\ +$
$a * b + c$	$a\ b\ *\ c\ +$
$(a + b) * c$	$a\ b\ +\ c\ *$
$(a - b) * (c + d)$	$a\ b\ -\ c\ d\ +\ *$
$(a + b) * (c - d / e) + f$	$a\ b\ +\ c\ d\ e\ /\ -\ *\ f\ +$

It was realized that postfix notation had important applications in computer science. In fact, many compilers now first translate arithmetic expressions into some form of postfix notation and then translate this postfix expression into machine code. Postfix expressions can be evaluated using the following algorithm:

Scan the expression from left to right. When an operator is found, back up to get the required number of operands, perform the operation, and continue.

Next, we clarify how this algorithm works. Consider the following postfix expression:

6 3 + 2 * =

Let us evaluate this expression using a stack and the previous algorithm. (In the following discussion, we list the postfix expression after each step. The shading indicates the part of the expression that has been processed.)

6 3 + 2 * =

1. Read the first symbol, **6**, which is a number. Push the number onto the stack. See Figure 17-20.

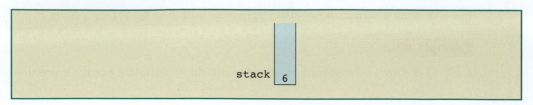

Figure 17-20   Stack after pushing 6

6 3 + 2 * =

2. Read the next symbol, 3, which is a number. Push the number onto the stack. See Figure 17-21.

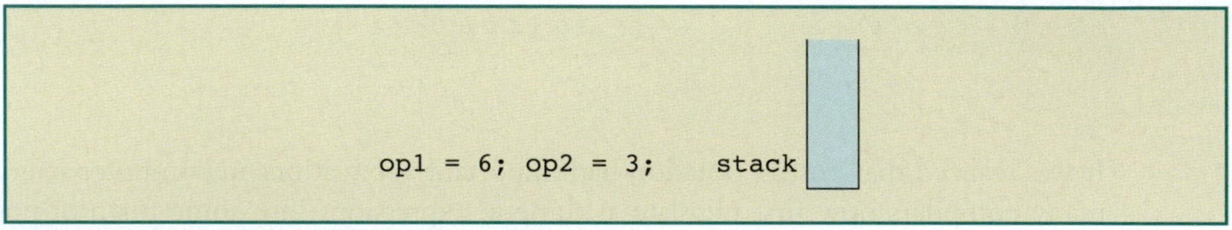

```
                              opl = 6; op2 = 3;      stack
```

Figure 17-21   Stack after popping twice

6 3 + 2 * =

3. Read the next symbol, +, which is an operator. Because an operator requires two operands to be evaluated, pop the stack twice. Perform the operation and put the result back onto the stack. See Figure 17-22.

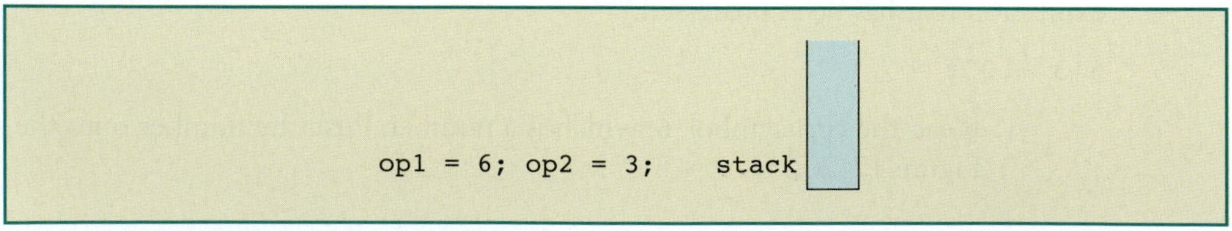

```
                              opl = 6; op2 = 3;      stack
```

Figure 17-22   Stack after popping twice

Perform the operation: `op1 + op2 = 6 + 3 = 9`

Push the result onto the stack. See Figure 17-23.

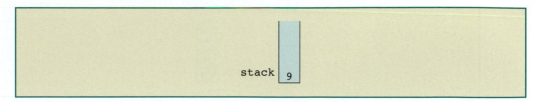

Figure 17-23   Stack after pushing the result of op1 + op2, which is 9

6 3 + 2 * =

4. Read the next symbol, 2, which is a number. Push the number onto the stack. See Figure 17-24.

Figure 17-24   Stack after pushing 2

6 3 + 2 * =

5. Read the next symbol, *, which is an operator. Because an operator requires two operands to be evaluated, pop the stack twice. Perform the operation and put the result back onto the stack. See Figures 17-25 and 17-26.

Figure 17-25   Stack after popping twice

Perform the operation: op1 * op2 = 9 * 2 = 18

Push the result onto the stack. See Figure 17-26.

17

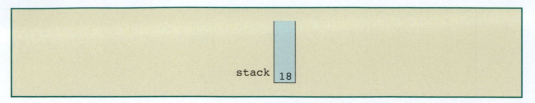

Figure 17-26 Stack after pushing the result of op1 * op2, which is 18

6 3 + 2 * =

6. Scan the next symbol, =, which is the equal sign, indicating the end of the expression. Therefore, print the result. The result of the expression is in the stack, so pop and print are as shown in Figure 17-27.

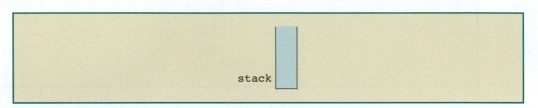

Figure 17-27 Stack after popping the element

The value of the expression 6 3 + 2 * = 18.

From this discussion, it is clear that when we read a symbol other than a number, the following cases arise:

1. The symbol we read is one of the following: +, −, *, /, or =.

   a. If the symbol is +, −, *, or /, the symbol is an operator, so we must evaluate it. Because an operator requires two operands, the stack must have at least two elements; otherwise, the expression has an error.

   b. If the symbol is = (an equal sign), the expression ends and we must print the answer. At this step, the stack must contain exactly one element; otherwise, the expression has an error.

2. The symbol we read is something other than +, −, *, /, or =. In this case, the expression contains an illegal operator.

   It is also clear that when an operand (number) is encountered in an expression, it is pushed onto the stack because the operators come after the operands.

Consider the following expressions:

(i)   7 6 + 3 ; 6 – =

(ii) 14 + 2 3 * =

(iii) 14 2 3 + =

Expression (i) has an illegal operator, expression (ii) does not have enough operands for +, and expression (iii) has too many operands. In the case of expression (iii), when we encounter the equal sign (=), the stack has two elements and this error cannot be discovered until we are ready to print the value of the expression.

We assume that each expression contains only the +, –, *, and / operators.

This program that we design outputs the entire postfix expression together with the answer. If the expression has an error, the expression is discarded. In this case, the program outputs the expression together with an appropriate error message. Because an expression may contain an error, we must clear the stack before processing the next expression. Also, the stack must be initialized; that is, the stack must be empty.

Main Algorithm

Pursuant to the previous discussion, the main algorithm in pseudocode is:

```
Get the next expression
while more data to process
{
    a. initialize the stack
    b. process the expression
    c. output result
    d. get the next expression
}
```

To simplify the complexity of the method **main**, we write three methods— **evaluateExpression**, **evaluateOpr**, and **printResult**. The method **evaluateExpression**, if possible, evaluates the expression and leaves the result in the stack. If the postfix expression is error free, the method **printResult** outputs the result. To simplify the program, we use two instance variables: **strToken** to store a token from the postfix expression, and **expressionOk** to indicate whether the expression is error free. Next, we describe each of these methods.

Method **evaluateExpression**

The method **evaluateExpression** evaluates each postfix expression. Each expression ends with the symbol =. The general algorithm is:

17

```
get the next token

while (token != '=')
{
    if (token is a number)
    {
        output number
        push number into stack
    }
    else
    {
        token is an operation
        call method evaluateOpr to evaluate the operation
    }

    if (no error in the expression)
        get next token
    else
        discard the expression
}
```

From this algorithm it follows that this method has three parameters—a parameter to access the stack, a parameter to access the output file, and a parameter to access the input line. The definition of this method is:

```
public static void evaluateExpression
                        (StackClass<Double> pStack,
                         PrintWriter outp, Scanner inpF)
{
    Double num;

    strToken = inpF.next();

    while (strToken.charAt(0) != '=')
    {
        if (Character.isDigit(strToken.charAt(0)))
        {
            num = Double.parseDouble(strToken);
            outp.print(num + " ");

            if (!pStack.isFullStack())
                pStack.push(num);
            else
            {
                System.out.print("Stack overflow. "
                                + "Program terminates!");
                System.exit(0);
            }
        }
        else
```

```
        {
            outp.print(strToken + " ");
            evaluateOpr(pStack, outp);
        }

        if (expressionOk) //if no error
            strToken = inpF.next();
        else
        {
            strToken = inpF.next();

            while (strToken.charAt(0) != '=')
            {
                    outp.print(strToken + " ");
                    strToken = inpF.next();
            }

            outp.print(strToken + " ");
        }
    } //end while (!= '=')
} //end evaluateExpression
```

Method evaluateOpr

This method (if possible) evaluates an operation. Two operands are needed to evaluate an operation and operands are saved in the stack. Therefore, the stack must contain at least two numbers. If the stack contains fewer than two numbers, then the expression has an error. In this case, the entire expression is discarded and an appropriate message is printed. This method also checks for any illegal operations. In pseudocode, this method is:

```
if stack is empty
{
   error in the expression
   set expressionOk to false
}
else
{
    retrieve the top element of stack into op2
    pop stack
    if stack is empty
    {
       error in the expression
       set expressionOk to false
    }
    else
    {
        retrieve the top element of stack into op1
        pop stack
```

17

```
                    //if the operation is legal, perform the
                    //operation and push the result onto the stack
                switch (operator)
                {
                case '+': //perform the operation and push the result
                          //onto the stack
                          stack.push(op1 + op2);
                          break;
                case '-': //perform the operation and push the result
                          //onto the stack
                          stack.push(op1 - op2);
                          break;
                case '*': //perform the operation and push the result
                          //onto the stack
                          stack.push(op1 * op2);
                          break;
                case '/': //if(op2 != 0), perform the operation and
                          //push the result onto the stack
                          stack.push(op1 / op2);

                          //otherwise, report error
                          //set expressionOk to false
                          break;
                 otherwise operation is illegal
                    {
                        output an appropriate message;
                        set expressionOk to false
                    }
                } //end switch
        }
    }
```

To evaluate an operation, the method **evaluateOpr** must have access to the stack and the output file. If an error in the postfix expression is found, the instance variable **expressionOk** is set to **false**. This method has two parameters—a parameter to access the stack and another parameter to access the output file. The definition of this method is:

```
public static void evaluateOpr(StackClass<Double> pStack,
                               PrintWriter outp)
{
    Double op1;
    Double op2;
    Double answer;
    Double temp;

    if (pStack.isEmptyStack())
    {
        outp.print(" (Not enough operands) ");
        expressionOk = false;
    }
    else
```

```
        {
            op2 = (Double) pStack.peek();
            pStack.pop();

            if (pStack.isEmptyStack())
            {
                outp.print(" (Not enough operands) ");
                expressionOk = false;
            }
            else
            {
                op1 = (Double) pStack.peek();
                pStack.pop();

                switch (strToken.charAt(0))
                {
                case '+': answer = op1 + op2;
                          pStack.push(answer);
                          break;
                case '-': answer = op1 - op2;
                          pStack.push(answer);
                          break;
                case '*': answer = op1 * op2;
                          pStack.push(answer);
                          break;
                case '/': if (op2 != 0)
                          {
                              answer = op1 / op2;
                              pStack.push(answer);
                          }
                          else
                          {
                              outp.print(" Division by 0 ");
                              expressionOk = false;
                          }
                          break;
                default: outp.print(" (Illegal operator) ");
                         expressionOk = false;
                } //end switch
            } //end else
        } //end else
} //end evaluateOpr
```

Method `printResult`

If the postfix expression contains no errors, the method `printResult` prints the result; otherwise it outputs an appropriate message. The result of the expression is in the stack and the output is sent to a file. Therefore this method must have access to the stack and the output file. Suppose that no errors were encountered by the method `evaluateExpression`.

17

If the stack has only one element, then the expression is error free and the top element of the stack is printed. If either the stack is empty or it has more than one element, then there is error in the postfix expression. In this, case this method outputs an appropriate error message. The definition of this method is:

```java
public static void printResult(StackClass<Double> pStack,
                               PrintWriter outp)
{
    Double result;
    Double temp;

    if (expressionOk) //if no error, print the result
    {
        if (!pStack.isEmptyStack())
        {
            result = (Double) pStack.peek();

            pStack.pop();

            if (pStack.isEmptyStack())
                outp.printf("%s %.2f %n", strToken, result);
            else
                outp.println(strToken
                        + " (Error: Too many operands)");
        }//end if
        else
            outp.println(" (Error in the expression)");
    }
    else
        outp.println(" (Error in the expression)");

    outp.println("_____");
}//end printResult
```

Program Listing

```java
//Postfix Calculator

import java.io.*;
import java.util.*;

public class PostfixCalculator
{
    static String strToken;
    static boolean expressionOk;

    public static void main(String[] args)
    {
```

```
          StackClass<Double> postfixStack =
                        new StackClass<Double>(100);

          try
          {
              Scanner inputStream = new
                      Scanner(new FileReader("a:\\RpnData.txt"));
              PrintWriter outfile = new
                      PrintWriter("a:\\RpnOutput.out");

              while (inputStream.hasNext())
              {
                  postfixStack.initializeStack();
                  expressionOk = true;

                  evaluateExpression(postfixStack, outfile,
                                  inputStream);
                  printResult(postfixStack, outfile);
              }//end while

              outfile.close();
          }
          catch (FileNotFoundException fnfe)      //Step 3
          {
              System.out.println(fnfe.toString());
          }

     }//end main

     //Place the definitions of the methods evaluateExpression,
     //evaluateOpr, and printResult as described previously here.
}
```

Sample Run

Input File: (RpnData.txt)

```
35  27 + 3 * =
26  28 + 32 2 ; - 5 / =
23  30 15 * / =
2  3 4 + =
23  0 / =
20  29 9 * ; =
25  23 - + =
34  24 12 7 / * + 23 - =
```

Output File: (RpnOutput.out)

```
35.0 27.0 + 3.0 * = 186.00
```

```
26.0 28.0 + 32.0 2.0 ;  (Illegal operator) - 5 / =  (Error in the expression)
```

17

```
23.0 30.0 15.0 * / = 0.05
```

```
2.0 3.0 4.0 + = (Error: Too many operands)
```

```
23.0 0.0 /  Division by 0 =  (Error in the expression)
```

```
20.0 29.0 9.0 * ;  (Illegal operator) =  (Error in the expression)
```

```
25.0 23.0 - +  (Not enough operands) =  (Error in the expression)
```

```
34.0 24.0 12.0 7.0 / * + 23.0 - = 52.14
```

Postfix Expression Calculator: Graphical User Interface (GUI)

In the preceding section, we designed a Java application program to evaluate postfix expressions. In this section, we redo that program to create the graphical user interface (GUI) shown in Figure 17-28.

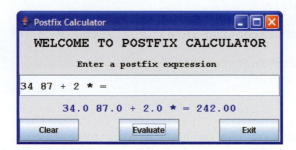

Figure 17-28 GUI for the postfix calculator

In this user interface, the use can enter the expression in the white area. After entering the expression, the user can either press the **Enter** key or click the **Evaluate** button to evaluate the expression. The result is displayed below the white area. To evaluate a new expression, the user can click the **Clear** button and type the new expression in the white area.

For the most part, the GUI version of the postfix calculator is the same as before. The methods **evaluateExpression**, **evaluateOpr**, and **printResult** need minor modifications. Because the data are no longer coming from a file and the output is no longer stored in a file, we no longer need file stream objects. Moreover, to simplify the accessing of the stack, we will declare it as the instance variable of the class containing the GUI program. To be specific, we use the following instance variables:

```
private String strToken;
private boolean expressionOk;
```

```java
private String inputLine;
private String outputLine = "";

private StackClass<Double> postfixStack =
                new StackClass<Double> (100);
```

Before describing the GUI parts, let us first give the modified definitions of the methods evaluateExpression, evaluateOpr, and printResult. (Notice that because the StackClass object postfixStack is declared as an instance variable, it no longer needs to be passed as a parameter to these methods.)

```java
public void evaluateExpression()
{
    postfixStack.initializeStack();
    expressionOk = true;
    Double num;

    String[] postFixExp;

        //split post expression into individual tokens
    postFixExp = inputLine.split(" ");

    int index = 0;

    strToken = postFixExp[index++];

    while (strToken.charAt(0) != '=')
    {
        if (Character.isDigit(strToken.charAt(0)))
        {
            num = Double.parseDouble(strToken);

            outputLine += num + " ";

            if (!postfixStack.isFullStack())
                postfixStack.push(num);
            else
            {
                outputLine = "Stack overflow. "
                            + "Program terminates!";
                System.exit(0);
            }
        }
        else
        {
            outputLine += strToken + " ";
            evaluateOpr();
        }
    }
```

17

```
            if (expressionOk) //if no error
                strToken = postFixExp[index++];
            else
            {
                while (index < postFixExp.length)
                    outputLine = outputLine +
                                    postFixExp[index++] + " ";

                strToken = "=";
            }
    } //end while (!= '=')
} //end evaluateExpression

public void evaluateOpr()
{
    Double op1;
    Double op2;
    Double answer;
    Double temp;

    if (postfixStack.isEmptyStack())
    {
        outputLine = outputLine + " (Not enough operands) ";
        expressionOk = false;
    }
    else
    {
        op2 = (Double) postfixStack.peek();
        postfixStack.pop();

        if (postfixStack.isEmptyStack())
        {
            outputLine = outputLine +
                        " (Not enough operands) ";
            expressionOk = false;
        }
        else
        {
            op1 = (Double) postfixStack.peek();
            postfixStack.pop();

            switch (strToken.charAt(0))
            {
            case '+': answer = op1 + op2;
                    postfixStack.push(answer);
                    break;
            case '-': answer = op1 - op2;
                    postfixStack.push(answer);
                    break;
```

```
            case '*': answer = op1 * op2;
                      postfixStack.push(answer);
                      break;
            case '/': if (op2 != 0)
                      {
                          answer = op1 / op2;
                          postfixStack.push(answer);
                      }
                      else
                      {
                          outputLine = outputLine +
                                    " Division by 0 ";
                          expressionOk = false;
                      }
                      break;
            default:  outputLine = outputLine +
                      " (Illegal operator) ";
                      expressionOk = false;
            }//end switch
        }//end else
    }//end else
}//end evaluateOpr

public void printResult()
{
    Double result;

    if (expressionOk) //if no error, print the result
    {
        if (!postfixStack.isEmptyStack())
        {
            result = (Double) postfixStack.peek();
            postfixStack.pop();

            if (postfixStack.isEmptyStack())
                outputLine += strToken + " " +
                              String.format("%.2f", result);
            else
                outputLine += strToken +
                              " (Error: Too many operands)";
        }//end if
        else
            outputLine += " (Error in the expression)";
    }
    else
        outputLine += " (Error in the expression)";
}//end printResult
```

17

Next, we discuss how to create the GUI. To create the GUI, we make the class containing the postfix calculator program extend the definition of the **class** JFrame. Suppose that the name of the class containing the application program to create the preceding GUI is PostfixCalculator.

The GUI interface contains several labels, three buttons, and a text field. We therefore use the following reference variables to create these GUI components:

```
private JTextField inputTF;
private JLabel outputLabel;
private JButton clearB, evaluateB, exitB;
```

When the user clicks a button, it should generate an action event. We therefore need to write the definition of the method **actionPerformed**, and then instantiate and register the listener object to these buttons. The definition of the method **actionPerformed** is as follows:

```
public void actionPerformed(ActionEvent e)
{
    if ((e.getSource().equals(inputTF)) ||
        (e.getSource().equals(evaluateB)))
    {
        inputLine = inputTF.getText();

        if (inputLine != null)
        {
            evaluateExpression();
            printResult();
        }
        else
        {
            System.out.println("No expression. "
                        + "Program terminates!");
            System.exit(0);
        }

        if (!expressionOk)
            outputLabel.setForeground(Color.red);
        else
            outputLabel.setForeground(Color.blue);

        outputLabel.setText(outputLine);
        outputLine = "";
        inputLine="";
    }
    else
        if (e.getSource().equals(clearB))
        {
            inputTF.setText("");
            outputLabel.setText("");
```

```
                outputLine = "";
                inputLine = "";
        }
        else
            if (e.getSource().equals(exitB))
                System.exit(0);
}
```

Next, we write the definition of the constructor `PostfixCalculator` to create the GUI components. The constructor gets access to the content pane; sets the title and size of the window; instantiates the labels, text field, and buttons; and creates and registers the listener object to the labels. The definition of the constructor is:

```
PostfixCalculator()
{
        //Setting up the GUI
    super("Postfix Calculator");
    setSize(400, 200);
    Container pane = getContentPane();
    pane.setLayout(new GridLayout(5, 1));

    JLabel welcomeLabel = new
                    JLabel("WELCOME TO POSTFIX CALCULATOR",
                            SwingConstants.CENTER);
    welcomeLabel.setForeground(Color.black);
    welcomeLabel.setFont(new Font("Courier", Font.BOLD, 20));

    JLabel inputLabel = new
                      JLabel("Enter a postfix expression ",
                            SwingConstants.CENTER);
    inputLabel.setForeground(Color.black);
    inputLabel.setFont(new Font("Courier", Font.BOLD, 14));

    inputTF = new JTextField(10);
    inputTF.setFont(new Font("Courier", Font.BOLD, 16));

    outputLabel = new JLabel("", SwingConstants.CENTER);
    outputLabel.setFont(new Font("Courier", Font.BOLD, 16));
    outputLabel.setForeground(Color.black);

    Panel buttonPanel = new Panel();
    clearB = new JButton("Clear");
    evaluateB = new JButton("Evaluate");
    exitB = new JButton("Exit");

    inputTF.addActionListener(this);
    clearB.addActionListener(this);
    evaluateB.addActionListener(this);
    exitB.addActionListener(this);
```

17

```
        pane.add(welcomeLabel);
        pane.add(inputLabel);
        pane.add(inputTF);
        pane.add(outputLabel);
        pane.add(buttonPanel);
        buttonPanel.setLayout(new GridLayout(1, 3, 60, 10));
        buttonPanel.add(clearB);
        buttonPanel.add(evaluateB);
        buttonPanel.add(exitB);

        setVisible(true);
        setDefaultCloseOperation(EXIT_ON_CLOSE);
    }
```

Next, we outline the definition of the **class** PostfixCalculator to create the complete program:

```
import java.awt.*;
import java.awt.event.*;
import javax.swing.*;
import java.io.*;
import java.util.*;

public class PostfixCalculator extends JFrame
                               implements ActionListener
{
    private String strToken;
    private boolean expressionOk;

    private String inputLine;
    private String outputLine = "";

    private StackClass<Double> postfixStack =
                        new StackClass<Double>(100);

    private JTextField inputTF;
    private JLabel outputLabel;
    private JButton clearB, evaluateB, exitB;

      //Place the definition of the constructor
      //PostfixCalculator here.

      //Place the definition of the method actionPerformed here.

      //Place the definition of the methods evaluateExpression,
      //evaluateOpr, and printExpression here.

    public static void main(String[] args)
```

```
    {
        PostfixCalculator pc = new PostfixCalculator();
    }
} //end PostfixCalculator
```

Sample Run1: Figure 17-29 shows a sample run of this program.

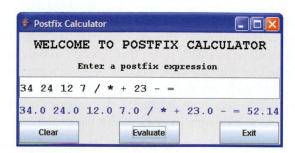

Figure 17-29   Sample run of `PostfixCalculator` program

Sample Run2: Figure 17-30 shows a sample run of this program.

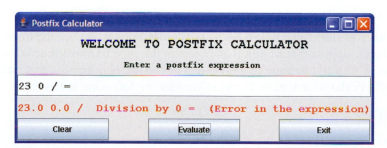

Figure 17-30   Sample run of `PostfixCalculator` program

REMOVING RECURSION: NONRECURSIVE ALGORITHM TO PRINT A LINKED LIST BACKWARD

Programming Exercise 4 in Chapter 16 asks you to write a recursive method to print a linked list backward. In this section, you learn how a stack can be used to design a nonrecursive algorithm to print a linked list backward.

Consider the linked list shown in Figure 17-31.

17

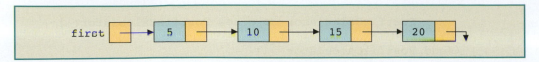

Figure 17-31 Linked list

To print the list backward, first we need to get to the last node of the list, which we can do by traversing the linked list starting at the first node. However, once we are at the last node, how do we get back to the previous node, especially given that links go in only one direction? You can again traverse the linked list with the appropriate loop termination condition, but this approach might waste a considerable amount of computer time, especially if the list is very large. Moreover, if we do this for every node in the list, the program might execute very slowly. Let us see how to use a stack effectively to print the list backward.

After printing the `info` of a particular node, we need to move to the node immediately behind this node. For example, in Figure 17-31, after printing `20`, we need to move to the node with `info 15`. Thus, while initially traversing the list to move to the last node, we must save references to each node. For example, for the list in Figure 17-31, we must save references to each of the nodes with `info 5, 10`, and `15`. After printing `20`, we go back to the node with `info 15`; after printing `15`, we go back to the node with `info 10`, and so on. From this, it follows that we must save references to each node in a stack, so as to implement the Last In First Out principle.

Because the number of nodes in a linked list is usually not known, we use the linked implementation of a stack. Suppose that `stack` is an object of the type `LinkedStackClass` such that each element in `stack` can point to a node of a linked list. Also suppose that `current` is a reference variable of the same type as `first`. Consider the following statements:

```
current = first;                    //Line 1

while (current != null)             //Line 2
{
    stack.push(current);           //Line 3
    current = current.link;        //Line 4
}
```

After the statement in Line 1 executes, `current` points to the first node. See Figure 17-32.

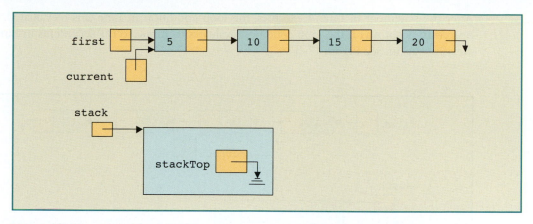

Figure 17-32 List after the statement `current = first;` executes

Because **current** is not **null**, the statements in Lines 3 and 4 execute. See Figure 17-33.

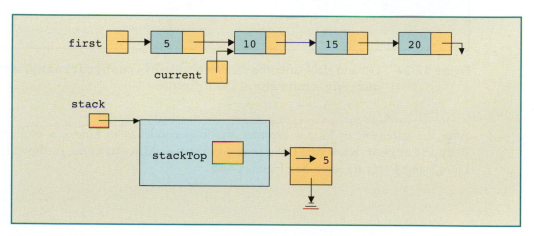

Figure 17-33 List and stack after the statements `stack.push(current);` and `current = current.link;` execute

17

After the statement in Line 4 executes, the loop condition in Line 2 is reevaluated. Because `current` is not **null**, the loop condition evaluates to **true**, so the statements in Lines 3 and 4 execute again. See Figure 17-34.

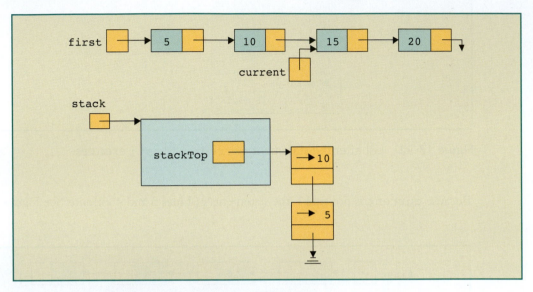

Figure 17-34   List and stack after the statements `stack.push(current);` and `current = current.link;` execute

After the statement in Line 4 executes, the loop condition in Line 2 is evaluated again. Because **current** is not **null**, the loop condition evaluates to **true**, so the statements in Lines 3 and 4 execute again. See Figure 17-35.

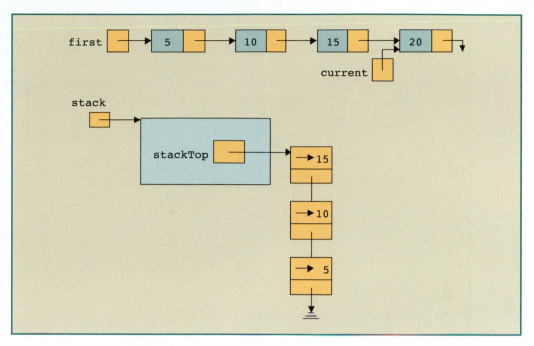

Figure 17-35   List and stack after the statements `stack.push(current);` and `current = current.link;` execute

After the statement in Line 4 executes, the loop condition in Line 2 is evaluated again. Because `current` is not `null`, the loop condition evaluates to `true`, so the statements in Lines 3 and 4 execute again. See Figure 17-36.

17

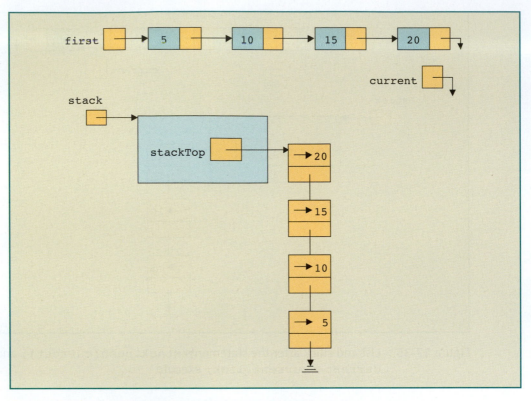

Figure 17-36 List and stack after the statements `stack.push(current);` and `current = current.link;` execute

After the statement in Line 4 executes, the loop condition in Line 2 is evaluated again. Because `current` is **null**, the loop condition evaluates to **false** and the **while** loop in Line 2 terminates. From Figure 17-36, it follows that a reference to each node in the linked list is saved in the stack. The top element of the stack contains a reference to the last node in the list, and so on. Let us now execute the following statements:

```
while (!stack.isEmptyStack())              //Line 5
{
    current = stack.peek();                //Line 6
    stack.pop();                           //Line 7
    System.out.println(current + " ");     //Line 8
}
```

The loop condition in Line 5 evaluates to **true** because the stack is nonempty. Therefore, the statements in Lines 6, 7, and 8 execute. After the statement in Line 6 executes, `current` points to the last node and after the statement in Line 7 executes, the top element of the stack is removed. See Figure 17-37.

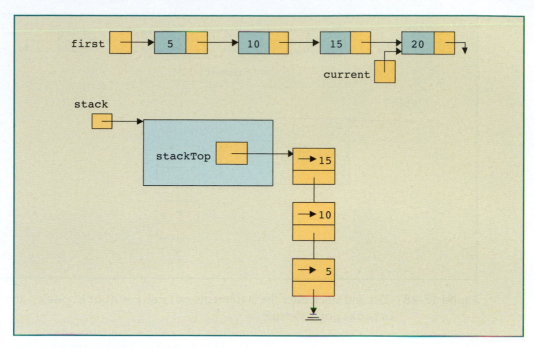

Figure 17-37 List and stack after the statements `current = stack.peek;` and `stack.pop;` execute

The statement in Line 8 outputs the info of the object to which `current.info` points, which is **20**. Next, the loop condition in Line 5 is evaluated. Because the loop condition evaluates to **true**, the statements in Lines 6, 7, and 8 execute. After the statements in Lines 6 and 7 execute, Figure 17–38 results.

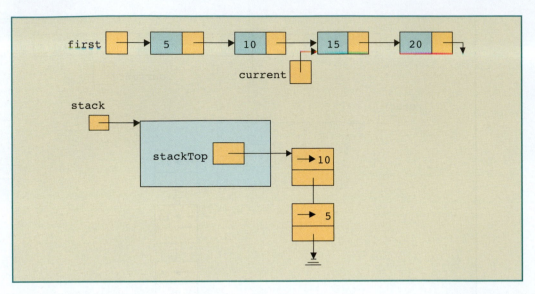

Figure 17-38 List and stack after the statements `current = stack.peek;` and `stack.pop;` execute

The statement in Line 8 outputs the info of the object to which `current.info` points, which is **15**. Next, the loop condition in Line 5 is evaluated. Because the loop condition evaluates to **true**, the statements in Lines 6, 7, and 8 execute. After the statements in Lines 6 and 7 execute, Figure 17-39 results.

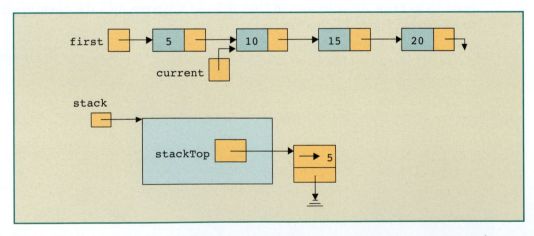

Figure 17-39 List and stack after the statements `current = stack.peek;` and `stack.pop;` execute

The statement in Line 8 outputs the info of the object to which `current.info` points, which is `10`. Next, the loop condition in Line 5 is evaluated. Because the loop condition evaluates to **true**, the statements in Lines 6, 7 and 8 execute. After the statements in Lines 6 and 7 execute, Figure 17-40 results.

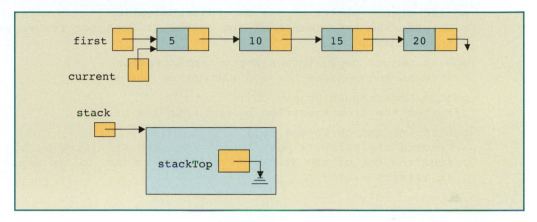

Figure 17-40   List and stack after the statements `current = stack.peek;` and `stack.pop;` execute

The statement in Line 8 outputs the info of the object to which `current.info` points, which is **5**. Next, the loop condition in Line 5 is evaluated. Because the loop condition evaluates to **false**, the **while** loop terminates. The **while** loop in Line 5 produces the following output:

```
20 15 10 5
```

Programming Exercise 6 at the end of this chapter asks you to add the method `revPrint` in the **inteface** `LinkedListADT`, provide its definition in the **class** `LinkedListClass`, and then write a program to test this method.

THE class Stack

The preceding sections discussed the data structure stack in detail. Because a stack is an important data structure, Java provides a class to implement a stack in a program. The name of the **class** defining a stack is `Stack`. Moreover, the **class** `Stack` is contained in the package `java.util`. Table 17-2 lists the members of the **class** `Stack`.

17

Table 17-2 Members of the **class** Stack

```
public Stack()
//Creates an empty Stack object.
```

```
public boolean empty()
//Returns true is the stack is empty; otherwise returns false.
```

```
public Object peek() throws EmptyStackException
//Returns the top element of the stack. It does not remove the
//top element.
```

```
public Object pop() throws EmptyStackException
//Returns and removes the top element of the stack.
```

```
public Object push(Object obj)
//Pushes the item specified by obj onto the stack.
```

```
public int search(Object obj)
//Returns the relative position of the item specified by obj
//from the top of the stack. If the item is not in the stack,
//it returns -1.
```

Notice that the formal parameter of the method **push** is a reference to an object. Therefore, to use a **Stack** object to manipulate values of primitive types they must be wrapped in an appropriate class. For example, to manipulate **int** values, we can use the wrapper **class** Integer provided by Java. As with other generic classes, when you declare a **Stack** object, you specify the type of the objects the **Stack** object will maintain.

The program in Example 17-4 illustrates how to use the **class** Stack. (In this example, we use the **class** Integer to wrap **int** values.)

Example 17-4

```java
//Program to illustrate how to use the class Stack.

import java.util.*;

public class Example_17_4
{
    public static void main(String[] args)
    {
        Stack<Integer> myStack =
                new Stack<Integer>();            //Line 1

        myStack.push(16);                        //Line 2
        myStack.push(8);                         //Line 3
        myStack.push(20);                        //Line 4
        myStack.push(3);                         //Line 5
```

```
        System.out.println("Line 6: The top "
                        + "element of myStack: "
                        + myStack.peek());              //Line 6

    myStack.pop();                                       //Line 7

        System.out.println("Line 8: After the "
                        + "pop operation, the "
                        + "top element of "
                        + "myStack: "
                        + myStack.peek());              //Line 8

        System.out.print("Line 9: myStack "
                        + "elements: ");                //Line 9

        while (!myStack.empty())                        //Line 10
        {
            System.out.print(myStack.peek() + " ");    //Line 11
            myStack.pop();                              //Line 12
        }

        System.out.println();                           //Line 13
    }
}
```

Sample Run:

```
Line 6: The top element of myStack: 3
Line 8: After the pop operation, the top element of myStack: 20
Line 9: myStack elements: 20 8 16
```

The preceding output is self-explanatory. The details are left as an exercise for you.

QUEUES

This section discusses another important data structure, called a *queue*. The notion of a **queue** in computer science is the same as the notion of the queues to which you are accustomed in everyday life. There are queues of customers in a bank or in a grocery store, and queues of cars waiting to pass through a tollbooth. Similarly, because a computer can send a print request faster than a printer can print, a queue of documents is often waiting to be printed at a printer. The general rule to process elements in a queue is that the customer at the front of the queue is served next and that when a new customer arrives, he or she stands at the end of the queue. That is, a queue is a First In First Out data structure.

Queues have numerous applications in computer science. Whenever a system is modeled on the First In First Out principle, queues are used. This chapter discusses one of the most widely used applications of queues, computer simulation. First, however, we need to develop

17

the tools necessary to implement a queue. The next few sections discuss how to design classes to implement queues as an abstract data type (ADT).

A queue is a set of elements of the same type in which the elements are added at one end, called the **back** or **rear**, and deleted from the other end, called the **front**. For example, consider a line of customers in a bank, wherein customers are waiting to withdraw/deposit money or to conduct some other business. Each new customer gets in the line at the rear. Whenever a teller is ready for a new customer, the customer at the front of the line is served.

The rear of the queue is accessed whenever a new element is added to the queue, and the front of the queue is accessed whenever an element is deleted from the queue. As in a stack, the middle elements of the queue are inaccessible, even if the queue elements are stored in an array.

Queue: A data structure in which the elements are added at one end, called the rear, and deleted from the other end, called the front; it is a First In First Out (FIFO) data structure.

Queue Operations

From the definition of queues, we see that the two key operations are add and delete. We call the add operation **addQueue** and the delete operation **deleteQueue**. Because elements can be neither deleted from an empty queue nor added to a full queue, we need two more operations to successfully implement the **addQueue** and **deleteQueue** operations: **isEmptyQueue** (checks whether the queue is empty) and **isFullQueue** (checks whether the queue is full).

We also need an operation, **initializeQueue**, to initialize the queue to an empty state. Moreover, to retrieve the first and last element of the queue, we include the operations **front** and **back** as described in the following list. Therefore, some of the queue operations are:

- **initializeQueue:** Initializes the queue to an empty state.

- **isEmptyQueue:** Determines whether the queue is empty. If the queue is empty, it returns the value **true**; otherwise, it returns the value **false**.

- **isFullQueue:** Determines whether the queue is full. If the queue is full, it returns the value **true**; otherwise, it returns the value **false**.

- **front:** Returns a reference to the front, that is, the first element of the queue. Input to this operation consists of the queue. Prior to this operation, the queue must exist and must not be empty.

- **back:** Returns a reference to the last element of the queue. Input to this operation consists of the queue. Prior to this operation, the queue must exist and must not be empty.

- **addQueue:** Adds a new element to the rear of the queue. Input to this operation consists of the queue and the new element. Prior to this operation, the queue must exist and must not be full.

- **deleteQueue:** Removes the front element from the queue. Input to this operation consists of the queue. Prior to this operation, the queue must exist and must not be empty.

The following interface defines these operations as ADT:

```java
public interface QueueADT<T>
{
    public void initializeQueue();
        //Method to initialize the queue to an empty state.
        //Postcondition: The queue is initialized.

    public boolean isEmptyQueue();
        //Method to determine whether the queue is empty.
        //Postcondition: Returns true if the queue is empty;
        //               otherwise, returns false.

    public boolean isFullQueue();
        //Method to determine whether the queue is full.
        //Postcondition: Returns true if the queue is full;
        //               otherwise, returns false.

    public T front() throws QueueUnderflowException;
        //Method to return the first element of the queue.
        //Precondition: The queue exists and is not empty.
        //Postcondition: If the queue is empty, the method throws
        //               QueueUnderflowException; otherwise, a
        //               reference to the first element of the
        //               queue is returned.

    public T back() throws QueueUnderflowException;
        //Method to return the last element of the queue.
        //Precondition: The queue exists and is not empty.
        //Postcondition: If the queue is empty, the method throws
        //               QueueUnderflowException; otherwise, a
        //               reference to the last element of the
        //               queue is returned.

    public void addQueue(T queueElement)
                            throws QueueOverflowException;
        //Method to add queueElement to the queue.
        //Precondition: The queue exists and is not full.
        //Postcondition: The queue is changed and queueElement
        //               is added to the queue.

    public void deleteQueue() throws QueueUnderflowException;
        //Method to remove the first element of the queue.
        //Precondition: The queue exists and is not empty.
        //Postcondition: The queue is changed and the first
        //               element is removed from the queue.
}
```

17

We leave it as exercise for you to draw the UML class diagram of the **interface** QueueADT. Next, we consider the implementation of the queue operations.

As in the case of a stack, a queue can be stored either in an array or in a linked list. We will consider both implementations. Because the elements are added at one end and removed from the other end, we need two variables to keep track of the front and rear of the queue, called **queueFront** and **queueRear**.

QueueException CLASS

The preceding section describes the basic operations on a queue. Note that the methods front, back, addQueue, and deleteQueue throw certain exceptions. As in the case of a stack, the two main operations on a queue are addQueue and deleteQueue. Remember that an element can be added to the queue if the queue is not full and that an element can be removed from the queue only if the queue is not empty. Adding an element to a full queue and removing an element from an empty queue would generate errors or exceptions called **queue overflow exception** and **queue underflow exception**. As in the case of stacks, to handle these exceptions we design exception classes as follows:

```java
public class QueueException extends RuntimeException
{
    public QueueException()
    {
    }

    public QueueException(String msg)
    {
        super(msg);
    }
}

public class QueueOverflowException extends QueueException
{
    public QueueOverflowException()
    {
        super("Queue Overflows");
    }

    public QueueOverflowException(String msg)
    {
        super(msg);
    }
}
```

```java
public class QueueUnderflowException extends QueueException
{
    public QueueUnderflowException()
    {
        super("Queue Underflow");
    }

    public QueueUnderflowException(String msg)
    {
        super(msg);
    }
}
```

When we write the method to implement the **addQueue** operation, if the queue is full, then this method would throw **QueueOverflowException** exception. Similarly, the method that implements **deleteQueue** operation would throw **QueueUnderflowException** exception if we try to remove an item from an empty queue. Also, the methods that implement the operations **front** and **back** would throw **QueueUnderflowException** exception if we try to retrieve an item from an empty queue. As in the case of stacks, notice that the **class QueueException** is derived from the **class RuntimeException**, so the queue overflow and underflow exceptions as we have defined them are unchecked exceptions.

IMPLEMENTATION OF QUEUES AS ARRAYS

Before giving the definition of the class to implement a queue as an ADT, we need to decide how many instance variables are needed to implement the queue. Of course, we need an array to store the queue elements, the variables **queueFront** and **queueRear** to keep track of the first and last elements of the queue, and the variable **maxQueueSize** to specify the maximum size of the queue. Thus, we need at least four instance variables.

Before writing the algorithms to implement the queue operations, we need to decide how to use **queueFront** and **queueRear** to access the queue elements. How do **queueFront** and **queueRear** indicate that the queue is empty or full? Suppose that **queueFront** gives the index of the first element of the queue, and **queueRear** gives the index of the last element of the queue. To add an element to the queue, we first advance **queueRear** to the next array position and then add the element at the position to which **queueRear** is pointing. To delete an element from the queue, we advance **queueFront** to the next element of the queue. (We add the operation **front** that returns the front element of the queue.) Thus, **queueFront** changes after each **deleteQueue** operation and **queueRear** changes after each **addQueue** operation.

Let us see what happens when **queueFront** changes after a **deleteQueue** operation and **queueRear** changes after an **addQueue** operation. Assume that the array to hold the queue elements is the size **100**.

Initially, the queue is empty. Assume that **queueFront** and **queueRear** point directly to the first and last elements of the queue, respectively. After the operation

17

```
addQueue('A');
```

the array is as shown in Figure 17-41.

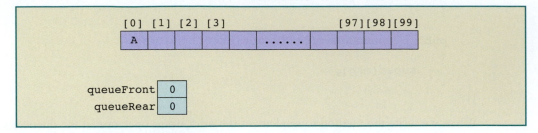

Figure 17-41 Queue after the first `addQueue` operation

After two more `addQueue` operations,

```
addQueue('B');
addQueue('C');
```

the array is as shown in Figure 17-42.

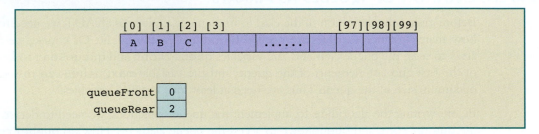

Figure 17-42 Queue after two more `addQueue` operations

Now consider the `deleteQueue` operation:

```
deleteQueue();
```

After this operation, the array containing the queue is as shown in Figure 17-43.

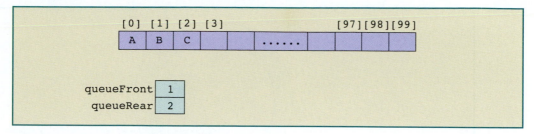

Figure 17-43   Queue after the `deleteQueue` operation

Will this queue design work? Suppose A stands for add (that is, `addQueue`) an element to the queue, and D stands for delete (that is, `deleteQueue`) an element from the queue. Consider the following sequence of operations:

AAADADADADADADADA...

This sequence of operations would eventually set the index `queueRear` to point to the last array position, giving the impression that the queue is full. However, the queue has only two or three elements and the front of the array is empty. See Figure 17-44.

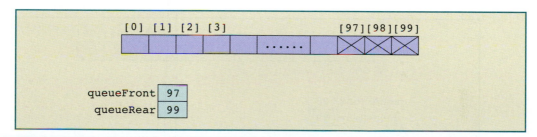

Figure 17-44   Queue after the sequence of operations `AAADADADADADA...`

One solution to this problem is that when the queue overflows to the rear (that is, `queueRear` points to the last array position), we can check the value of the index `queueFront`. If the value of `queueFront` indicates that there is room in the front of the array, then when the rear gets to the last array position, we can slide all of the queue elements toward the first array position. This solution is good if the queue size is very small; otherwise, the program may execute more slowly.

Another solution to this problem is to assume that the array is circular—that is, the first array position immediately follows the last array position, as in Figure 17-45.

17

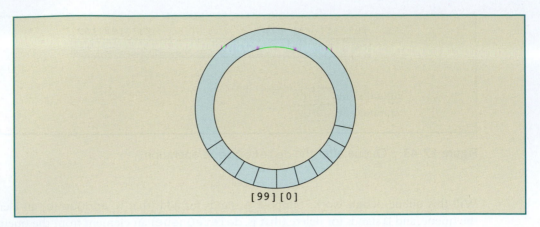

Figure 17-45 Circular queue

We consider the array containing the queue to be circular, although we draw the figures of the array holding the queue elements as before.

Suppose that we have the queue shown in Figure 17–46.

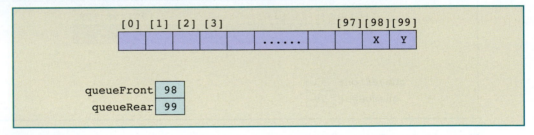

Figure 17-46 Queue with two elements at positions 98 and 99

After the operation

```
addQueue('Z');
```

the queue is as shown in Figure 17–47.

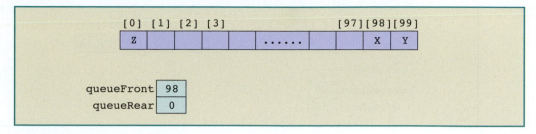

Figure 17-47   Queue after one more `addQueue` operation

Because the array containing the queue is circular, we can use the following statement to advance `queueRear` to the next array position:

```
queueRear = (queueRear + 1) % maxQueueSize;
```

If `queueRear < maxQueueSize - 1`, then `queueRear + 1 <= maxQueueSize - 1` and so `(queueRear + 1) % maxQueueSize = queueRear + 1`. If `queueRear == maxQueueSize - 1` (that is, `queueRear` points to the last array position), then `queueRear + 1 == maxQueueSize`, so `(queueRear + 1) % maxQueueSize == 0`. In this case, `queueRear` is set to 0, which is the first array position. We can use a statement similar to the previous statement to advance `queueFront` to the next array position.

This queue design seems to work well. Before we write the algorithms to implement the queue operations, consider the following two cases.

Case 1: Suppose that after certain operations, the array containing the queue is as shown in Figure 17-48.

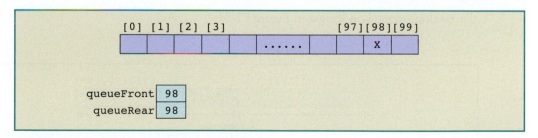

Figure 17-48   Queue with one element

After the operation

```
deleteQueue();
```

the resulting array is as shown in Figure 17-49.

17

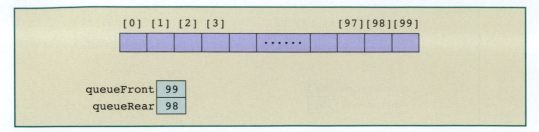

Figure 17-49   Queue after the `deleteQueue` operation

Case 2: Let us now consider the queue shown in Figure 17-50.

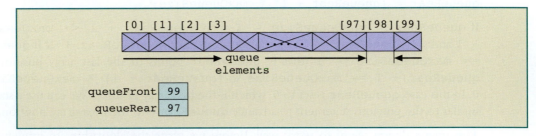

Figure 17-50   Queue with 99 elements

After the operation

`addQueue('Z');`

the resulting array is as shown in Figure 17-51.

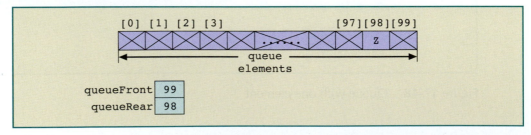

Figure 17-51   Queue after the `addQueue` operation; it is full

The arrays in Figures 17-49 and 17-51 have identical values for `queueFront` and `queueRear`. However, the resulting array in Figure 17-49 represents an empty queue, whereas the resulting array in Figure 17-51 represents a full queue. This latest queue design poses another problem: distinguishing between an empty and a full queue.

This problem has several possible solutions. One possible solution is to keep a count. In addition to the instance variables `queueFront` and `queueRear`, we need another variable, `count`, to implement the queue. The value of `count` is incremented whenever a new element is added to the queue, and decremented whenever an element is removed from the queue. In this case, the methods `initializeQueue` and `destroyQueue` initialize `count` to 0. This solution is useful if the queue user frequently needs to know the number of elements in the queue.

Another possible solution is to let `queueFront` indicate the index of the array position *preceding* the first element of the queue, rather than the index of the (actual) first element itself. In this case, assuming `queueRear` still indicates the index of the last element in the queue, the queue is empty if `queueFront == queueRear`. In this solution, the slot indicated by the index `queueFront` (that is, the slot preceding the first true element) is reserved. The queue is full if the next available space is this special reserved slot indicated by `queueFront`. Finally, because the array position indicated by `queueFront` is to be kept empty, if the array size is, say 100, then 99 elements can be stored in the queue. See Figure 17-52.

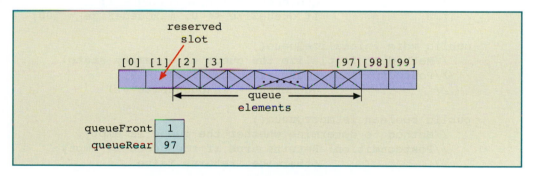

Figure 17-52   Array to store the queue elements with a reserved slot

Let us implement the queue using the first solution. That is, we'll use the variable `count` to indicate whether the queue is empty or full.

The following describes the heading, instance variables, constructors, and method of the **class** `QueueClass`. (Because arrays can be allocated dynamically, we leave it for the user to specify the size of the array to implement the queue. The default size of the array is 100.)

Class: `QueueClass`

```
public class QueueClass<T> implements QueueADT<T>
```

17

Instance variables:

```
private int maxQueueSize;
private int count;
private int queueFront;
private int queueRear;
private T[] list;  //Array of references to the
                   //objects that store queue elements
```

Instance methods:

```
public QueueClass()
   //Default constructor
   //Postcondition: Creates the array of references to the
   //               objects that store queue elements.
   //               maxQueueSize = 100;
   //               count = 0; queueFront = 0;
   //               queueRear = maxQueueSize - 1;

public QueueClass(int queueSize)
   //Constructor with a parameter
   //Postcondition: Creates the array of references to the
   //               objects that store queue elements.
   //               maxQueueSize = queueSize;
   //               count = 0; queueFront = 0;
   //               queueRear = maxQueueSize - 1;
   //               If queueSize <= 0, maxQueueSize = 100;

public void initializeQueue()
   //Method to initialize the queue to an empty state.
   //Postcondition: count = 0; queueFront = 0;
   //               queueRear = maxQueueSize - 1

public boolean isEmptyQueue()
   //Method to determine whether the queue is empty.
   //Postcondition: Returns true if the queue is empty;
   //               otherwise, returns false.

public boolean isFullQueue()
   //Method to determine whether the queue is full.
   //Postcondition: Returns true if the queue is full;
   //               otherwise, returns false.

public T front() throws QueueUnderflowException
   //Method to return the first element of the queue.
   //Precondition: The queue exists and is not empty.
   //Postcondition: If the queue is empty, the method throws
   //               QueueUnderflowException; otherwise, a
   //               reference to the first element of the
   //               queue is returned.
```

```
public T back() throws QueueUnderflowException
   //Method to return the last element of the queue.
   //Precondition: The queue exists and is not empty.
   //Postcondition: If the queue is empty, the method throws
   //               QueueUnderflowException; otherwise, a
   //               reference to the last element of the
   //               queue is returned.

public void addQueue(T queueElement)
                     throws QueueOverflowException
   //Method to add queueElement to the queue.
   //Precondition: The queue exists and is not full.
   //Postcondition: The queue is changed and queueElement
   //               is added to the queue.

public void deleteQueue() throws QueueUnderflowException
   //Method to remove the first element of the queue.
   //Precondition: The queue exists and is not empty.
   //Postcondition: The queue is changed and the first
   //               element is removed from the queue.
```

We leave it as exercise for you to draw the UML class diagram of the **class** QueueClass. Next, we consider the implementation of the queue operations.

Constructors

First we consider the implementation of the constructors. The default constructor creates an array of the size 100 and sets the variable maxQueueSize to the size of the array. The constructor with a parameter creates an array of the size specified by the user and sets the variable maxQueueSize to the size of the array. The constructors also initialize queueFront and queueRear to indicate that the queue is empty. The definition of the constructors is:

```
    //Default constructor
public QueueClass()
{
    maxQueueSize = 100;
    queueFront = 0;                        //initialize queueFront
    queueRear = maxQueueSize - 1;    //initialize queueRear
    count = 0;
    list = (T[]) new Object[maxQueueSize];   //create the
                                //array to implement the queue

}
```

```java
    //Constructor with a parameter
public QueueClass(int queueSize)
{
    if (queueSize <= 0)
    {
        System.err.println("The size of the array to "
                        + "implement the queue must be "
                        + "positive.");
        System.err.println("Creating an array of the "
                        + "size 100.");

        maxQueueSize = 100;
    }
    else
        maxQueueSize = queueSize;  //set maxQueueSize to
                                   //queueSize

    queueFront = 0;                   //initialize queueFront
    queueRear = maxQueueSize - 1;     //initialize queueRear
    count = 0;
    list = (T[]) new Object[maxQueueSize]; //create the
                                //array to implement the queue
}
```

initializeQueue

The next operation that we consider is `initializeQueue`. This operation initializes a queue to an empty state, and the first element is added at the first array position. Therefore, we initialize `queueFront` to 0, `queueRear` to `maxQueueSize - 1`, and `count` to 0. See Figure 17-53.

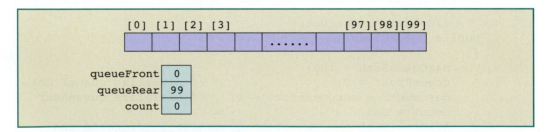

Figure 17-53 Empty queue

The definition of the method `initializeQueue` is:

```java
public void initializeQueue()
{
    for (int i = queueFront; i < queueRear;
```

```
                              i = (i + 1) % maxQueueSize)
            list[i] = null;

        queueFront = 0;
        queueRear = maxQueueSize - 1;
        count = 0;
    }
```

Empty Queue and Full Queue

As discussed earlier, the queue is empty if count is 0, and the queue is full if count is maxQueueSize. So the methods to implement isEmptyQueue and isFullQueue are:

```
public boolean isEmptyQueue()
{
    return (count == 0);
}

public boolean isFullQueue()
{
    return (count == maxQueueSize);
}
```

Front

This operation returns a reference to the first element of the queue. If the queue is nonempty, a reference to the first element of the queue is returned; otherwise, it throws QueueUnderflowException.

```
public T front() throws QueueUnderflowException
{
    if (isEmptyQueue())
        throw new QueueUnderflowException();

    return (T) list[queueFront];
}
```

Back

This operation returns a reference to the last element of the queue. If the queue is non-empty, a reference to the last element of the queue is returned; otherwise, it throws QueueUnderflowException.

```
public T back() throws QueueUnderflowException
{
    if (isEmptyQueue())
        throw new QueueUnderflowException();

    return (T) list[queueRear];
}
```

17

addQueue

Next, we implement the **addQueue** operation. Because **queueRear** directly points to the last element of the queue, to add a new element to the queue we first advance **queueRear** to the next array position and then add the new element to the array position to which **queueRear** is pointing. We also increment **count** by 1. If the queue is full, this method throws QueueOverflowException. So the definition of the method **addQueue** is:

```java
public void addQueue(T queueElement)
                         throws QueueOverflowException
{
    if (isFullQueue())
        throw new QueueOverflowException();

    queueRear = (queueRear + 1) % maxQueueSize; //use the
                         //mod operator to advance queueRear
                         //because the array is circular
    count++;
    list[queueRear] = queueElement;
}
```

deleteQueue

To implement the **deleteQueue** operation, we advance **queueFront** to the next queue element and decrement **count** by 1. If the queue is empty, this method throws QueueUnderflowException. So the method **deleteQueue** is:

```java
public void deleteQueue() throws QueueUnderflowException
{
    if (isEmptyQueue())
        throw new QueueUnderflowException();

    count--;
    list[queueFront] = null;
    queueFront = (queueFront + 1) % maxQueueSize; //use the
                         //mod operator to advance queueFront
                         //because the array is circular
}
```

We leave it as an exercise for you to write the complete definition of the **class QueueClass**.

The program in Example 17-5 tests various operations on a queue.

Example 17-5

```java
public class Example_17_5
{
    public static void main(String[] args)
```

```
    {
        QueueClass<Integer> intQueue =
                             new QueueClass<Integer>();

        intQueue.addQueue(23);
        intQueue.addQueue(45);
        intQueue.addQueue(38);

        System.out.print("intQueue elements: ");

        while (!intQueue.isEmptyQueue())
        {
            System.out.print(intQueue.front() + " ");
            intQueue.deleteQueue();
        }

        System.out.println();
    }
}
```

Sample Run:

```
intQueue elements: 23 45 38
```

The preceding output is self-explanatory. We leave the details as an exercise.

LINKED IMPLEMENTATION OF QUEUES

Because the size of the array to store the queue elements is fixed, only a finite number of queue elements can be stored in the array. Also, the array implementation of the queue requires the array to be treated in a special way together with the values of the indices queueFront and queueRear. The linked implementation of a queue simplifies many of the special cases of the array implementation and, because the memory to store a queue element is allocated dynamically, the queue is never full. This section discusses the linked implementation of a queue.

Because elements are added at one end, queueRear, and removed from the other end, queueFront, we need to know the front of the queue and the rear of the queue. Thus, we need two reference variables, **queueFront** and **queueRear**, to maintain the queue. The following describes the heading, instance variables, constructors, and method of the **class** LinkedQueueClass as an ADT.

Class: LinkedQueueClass

```
public class LinkedQueueClass<T> implements QueueADT<T>
```

17

Class: `QueueNode`

```
protected class QueueNode<T>
{
    T info;
    QueueNode<T> link;

        //Default constructor
        //Postcondition: info = null; link = null;
    public QueueNode()
    {
        info = null;
        link = null;
    }

        //Constructor with parameters
        //Sets info to point to the object elem points to
        //and link is set to point to the object ptr
        //points to.
        //Postcondition:  info = elem; link = ptr
    public QueueNode(T elem, QueueNode<T> ptr)
    {
        info = elem;
        link = ptr;
    }

        //Method to return the info as a string.
        //Postcondition: info as a String object is
        //                      returned.
    public String toString()
    {
        return info.toString();
    }
}
```

Instance variables:

```
private QueueNode<T> queueFront;  //reference variable to
                                  //the first element of
                                  //the queue
private QueueNode<T> queueRear;   //reference variable to
                                  //the last element of
                                  //the queue
```

Constructors and Instance methods:

```
public LinkedQueueClass()
    //Default constructor
    //Postcondition: queueFront = null; queueRear = null;

public void initializeQueue()
    //Method to initialize the queue to an empty state.
    //Postcondition: queueFront = null; queueRear = null;
```

```
public boolean isEmptyQueue()
    //Method to determine whether the queue is empty.
    //Postcondition: Returns true if the queue is empty;
    //                otherwise, returns false.

public boolean isFullQueue()
    //Method to determine whether the queue is full.
    //Postcondition: Returns true if the queue is full;
    //                otherwise, returns false.

public T front() throws QueueUnderflowException
    //Method to return the first element of the queue.
    //Precondition: The queue exists and is not empty.
    //Postcondition: If the queue is empty, the method throws
    //                QueueUnderflowException; otherwise, a
    //                reference to the first element of the
    //                queue is returned.

public T back() throws QueueUnderflowException
    //Method to return the last element of the queue.
    //Precondition: The queue exists and is not empty.
    //Postcondition: If the queue is empty, the method throws
    //                QueueUnderflowException; otherwise, a
    //                reference to the first element of the
    //                queue is returned.

public void addQueue(T newElement)
    //Method to add queueElement to the queue.
    //Precondition: The queue exists.
    //Postcondition: The queue is changed and queueElement
    //                is added to the queue.

public void deleteQueue() throws QueueUnderflowException
    //Method to remove the first element of the queue.
    //Precondition: The queue exists and is not empty.
    //Postcondition: The queue is changed and the first
    //                element is removed from the queue.
```

The UML class diagram of the **class** LinkedQueueClass is left as an exercise for you.

Notice that the method addQueue does not throw QueueOverflowException because in the linked implementation of queues, logically, the queue is never full.

The definitions of the methods to implement the queue operations are given next.

The operation initializeQueue initializes the queue to an empty state. The queue is empty if there are no elements in the queue. This is easily accomplished by setting queueFront and queueRear to null. The definition of this method is:

```
public void initializeQueue()
{
    queueFront = null;
```

17

```
        queueRear = null;
}
```

The queue is empty if `queueFront` is `null`. Memory to store the queue elements is allocated dynamically. Therefore, the queue is never full, so the method to implement the `isFullQueue` operation returns the value **false**. (The queue is full only if we run out of memory.) The definitions of the methods to implement the operations `isEmptyQueue` and `isFullQueue` are:

```
public boolean isEmptyQueue()
{
    return (queueFront == null);
}

public boolean isFullQueue()
{
    return false;
}
```

Note that in reality, in the linked implementation of queues, the method `isFullQueue` does not apply because logically the queue is never full. However, you must provide its definition because the **class** LinkedQueueClass implements the **interface** QueueADT, which includes the method `isFullQueue`.

addQueue, front, back, and deleteQueue Operations

The `addQueue` operation adds a new element at the end of the queue. To implement this operation, we use the instance variable `queueRear`.

If the queue is nonempty, the operation **front** returns a reference to the first element of the queue; that is, a reference to the element of the queue indicated by `queueFront` is returned. If the queue is empty, the method **back** throws QueueUnderflowException.

If the queue is nonempty, the operation **back** returns a reference to the last element of the queue; that is, a reference to the element of the queue indicated by `queueRear` is returned. If the queue is empty, the method **back** throws QueueUnderflowException.

Similarly, if the queue is nonempty, the operation `deleteQueue` removes the first element of the queue, so we use the instance variable `queueFront`. If the queue is empty, the method `deleteQueue` throws QueueUnderflowException.

The definitions of the methods to implement these operations are:

```
public void addQueue(T newElement)
{
    QueueNode<T> newNode;

    newNode = new QueueNode<T>(newElement, null); //create
                            //newNode and assign newElement
                            //to newNode
```

```
      if (queueFront == null) //if initially the queue is empty
      {
          queueFront = newNode;
          queueRear = newNode;
      }
      else    //add newNode at the end
      {
          queueRear.link = newNode;
          queueRear = queueRear.link;
      }
}//end addQueue

public T front() throws QueueUnderflowException
{
    if (isEmptyQueue())
        throw new QueueUnderflowException();

    return queueFront.info;
}

public T back() throws QueueUnderflowException
{
    if (isEmptyQueue())
        throw new QueueUnderflowException();

    return queueRear.info;
}

public void deleteQueue() throws QueueUnderflowException
{
    if (isEmptyQueue())
        throw new QueueUnderflowException();

    queueFront = queueFront.link; //advance queueFront

    if (queueFront == null)  //if after deletion the queue
        queueRear = null;   //is empty, set queueRear to null
} //end deleteQueue
```

The definition of the method to implement the default constructor is similar to the definition of the method `initializeQueue` and is therefore left as an exercise for you.

We also leave it as an exercise for you to write the complete definition of the **class** QueueClass.

17

QUEUE DERIVED FROM THE `class UnorderedLinkedList`

From the definitions of the methods to implement the queue operations, it is clear that the linked implementation of a queue is similar to the implementation of a linked list created in a forward manner. (See Chapter 16.) The `addQueue` operation is similar to the operation `insertFirst`. Likewise, the operations `initializeQueue`, `initializeList`, `isEmptyQueue`, and `isEmptyList` are similar. The operations `deleteQueue` and `isFullQueue` can be implemented as in the previous section. The reference variable `queueFront` is the same as the reference variable `first`, and the reference variable `queueRear` is the same as the reference variable `last`. This correspondence suggests that we can derive the class to implement the queue from the **class** `UnorderedLinkedList`. (See Chapter 16.) We leave it as an exercise for you to design a class that implements a queue as a linked list derived from the **class** `UnorderedLinkedList`. (See Programming Exercise 20 at the end of this chapter.)

APPLICATION OF QUEUES: SIMULATION

A technique in which one system models the behavior of another system is called **simulation**. For example, physical simulators include wind tunnels used to experiment with the design of car bodies and flight simulators are used to train airline pilots. Simulation techniques are used when it is too expensive or dangerous to experiment with real systems. You can also design computer models to study the behavior of real systems. (Some real systems modeled by computers will be described in this section.) Simulating the behavior of an expensive or dangerous experiment using a computer model is usually less expensive than using the real system, and is a good way to gain insight without putting human life in danger. Moreover, computer simulations are particularly useful for complex systems where it is difficult to construct a mathematical model. For such systems, computer models can retain descriptive accuracy. In mathematical simulations, the steps of a program are used to model the behavior of a real system. Let us consider one such problem.

The manager of a local movie theater is hearing complaints from customers about the time they have to wait in line to buy tickets. The theater currently has only one cashier. Another theater is preparing to open in the neighborhood and the manager is afraid of losing customers. The manager wants to hire enough cashiers so that a customer does not have to wait too long to buy a ticket, but does not want to hire extra cashiers on a trial basis and potentially waste time and money. One thing that the manager would like to know is the average time a customer has to wait for service. The manager wants someone to write a program to simulate what happens at the theater.

In computer simulation, the objects being studied are usually represented as data. For the theater problem, some of the objects are the customers and the cashier. The cashier serves the customers and we want to determine a customer's average waiting time. Actions are implemented by writing algorithms, which in a programming language are implemented with the help of methods. Thus, methods are used to implement the actions of the objects.

In Java, we can combine the data and the operations on that data into a single unit with the help of classes. Thus, objects can be represented as classes. The data members of the class describe the properties of the objects, and the methods describe the actions on that data. This change in simulation results can also occur if we change the values of the data or modify the definitions of the methods (that is, modify the algorithms implementing the actions). The main goal of a computer simulation is to either generate results showing the performance of an existing system or predict the performance of a proposed system.

In the theater problem, when the cashier is serving a customer, the other customers must wait. Because customers are served on a first-come, first-served basis and queues are an effective way to implement a First In First Out system, queues are important data structures for use in computer simulations. This section examines computer simulations in which queues are the basic data structure. These simulations model the behavior of systems, called **queuing systems**, in which queues of objects are waiting to be served by various servers. In other words, a queuing system consists of servers and queues of objects waiting to be served.

We deal with a variety of queuing systems on a daily basis. For example, a grocery store and a bank are both queuing systems. Furthermore, when you send a print request to a net-worked printer that is shared by many people, your print request goes in a queue. Print requests that arrived before your print request are usually completed before yours. Thus, the printer acts as the server when a queue of documents is waiting to be printed.

Designing a Queuing System

We now describe a queuing system that can be used in a variety of applications, such as a grocery store, bank, movie theater, printer, or a mainframe environment in which several people are trying to use the same processors to execute their programs. To describe a queuing system, we use the term **server** for the object that provides the service. For example, in a bank, a teller is a server; in a grocery store or movie theater, a cashier is a server. We call the object receiving the service the **customer**, and the time it takes to serve a customer the **transaction time**.

Because a queuing system consists of servers and a queue of waiting objects, we model a system that consists of a list of servers and a waiting queue holding the customers to be served. The customer at the front of the queue waits for the next available server. When a server becomes free, the customer at the front of the queue moves to the free server to be served.

When the first customer arrives, all servers are free and the customer moves to the first server. When the next customer arrives, if a server is available, the customer immediately moves to the available server; otherwise, the customer waits in the queue. To model a queuing system, we need to know the number of servers, the expected arrival time of a customer, the time between the arrivals of customers, and the number of events affecting the system.

Let us again consider the movie theater system. The performance of the system depends on how many servers are available, how long it takes to serve a customer, and how often a customer arrives. If it takes too long to serve a customer and customers arrive frequently, then

17

more servers are needed. This system can be modeled as a time-driven simulation. In a **time-driven simulation**, the clock is implemented as a counter and the passage of, say, one minute can be implemented by incrementing the counter by one. The simulation is run for a fixed amount of time. If the simulation needs to be run for 100 minutes, the counter starts at one and goes up to 100, which can be implemented by using a loop.

For the simulation described in this section, we want to determine the average wait time for a customer. To calculate the average wait time for a customer, we need to add the waiting time of each customer, and then divide the sum by the number of customers who have arrived. When a customer arrives, he or she goes to the end of the queue and the customer's waiting time starts. If the queue is empty and a server is free, the customer is served immediately, so this customer's waiting time is zero. On the other hand, when the customer arrives and if the queue is nonempty or all the servers are busy, the customer must wait for the next available server and, therefore, this customer's waiting time starts. We can keep track of the customer's waiting time by using a timer for each customer. When a customer arrives, the timer is set to 0, which is incremented after each clock unit.

Suppose that, on average, it takes five minutes for a server to serve a customer. When a server becomes free and the waiting customers' queue is nonempty, the customer at the front of the queue proceeds to begin the transaction. Thus, we must keep track of the time a customer is with a server. When the customer arrives at a server, the transaction time is set to five and is decremented after each clock unit. When the transaction time becomes zero, the server is marked as free. Hence, the two objects needed to implement a time-driven computer simulation of a queuing system are the customer and the server.

Next, before designing the main algorithm to implement this simulation, we design the classes to implement each of the two objects: `customer` and `server`.

Customer

Every customer has a customer number, arrival time, waiting time, transaction time, and departure time. If we know the arrival, waiting, and transaction times, we can determine the departure time by adding the arrival time, waiting time, and transaction time. Let us call the class to implement the customer object `Customer`. It follows that the **class** `Customer` has four instance variables: the `customerNumber`, `arrivalTime`, `waitingTime`, and `transactionTime`, each of the data type `int`. The basic operations that must be performed on an object of the type `Customer` are as follows: set the customer's number, arrival time, and waiting time; increment the waiting time by one clock unit; return the waiting time; return the arrival time; return the transaction time; and return the customer number.

The following defines the heading, instance variables, constructors, and instance methods of the **class** `Customer`. See Figure 17-54.

Class: `Customer`

```
public class Customer implements Cloneable
```

Instance variables:

```java
private int customerNumber;
private int arrivalTime;
private int waitingTime;
private int transactionTime;
```

Instance methods:

```java
public Customer()
   //Default constructor
   //Instance variables are initialized to the default
   //values
   //Postcondition: customerNumber = 0; arrivalTime = 0;
   //               waitingTime = 0; transactionTime = 0;

public Customer(int customerN, int arrvTime, int wTime,
               int tTime)
   //Constructor with parameters.
   //Instance variables are initialized according to the
   //parameters
   //Postcondition: customerNumber = customerN;
   //               arrivalTime = arrvTime;
   //               waitingTime = wTime;
   //               transactionTime = tTime;

public void setCustomerInfo(int customerN, int arrvTime,
                            int wTime, int tTime)
   //Method to set the instance variable according to the
   //parameters.
   //Postcondition: customerNumber = customerN;
   //               arrivalTime = arrvTime;
   //               waitingTime = wTime;
   //               transactionTime = tTime;

public int getWaitingTime()
    //Method to return the waiting time of a customer.
    //Postcondition: The value of waitingTime is returned.

public void setWaitingTime(int time)
    //Method to set the waiting time of a customer.
    //Postcondition: waitingTime = time;

public void incrementWaitingTime()
    //Method to increment the waiting time.
    //Postcondition: waitingTime++;

public int getArrivalTime()
    //Method to return the arrival time of a customer.
    //Postcondition: The value of arrivalTime is returned.
```

17

```java
public int getTransactionTime()
    //Method to return the transaction time of a customer.
    //Postcondition: The value of transactionTime is returned.

public int getCustomerNumber()
    //Method to return the customer number.
    //Postcondition: The value of customerNumber is returned.

public boolean equals(Object otherElement)
    //Method to determine if two customers are the same.
    //Postcondition: Returns true if this customer is the
    //               same as otherCustomer; otherwise it
    //               returns false.

public Object clone()
    //Method to return a clone of this customer object.
    //Postcondition: A clone of this customer's object
    //               is returned.
```

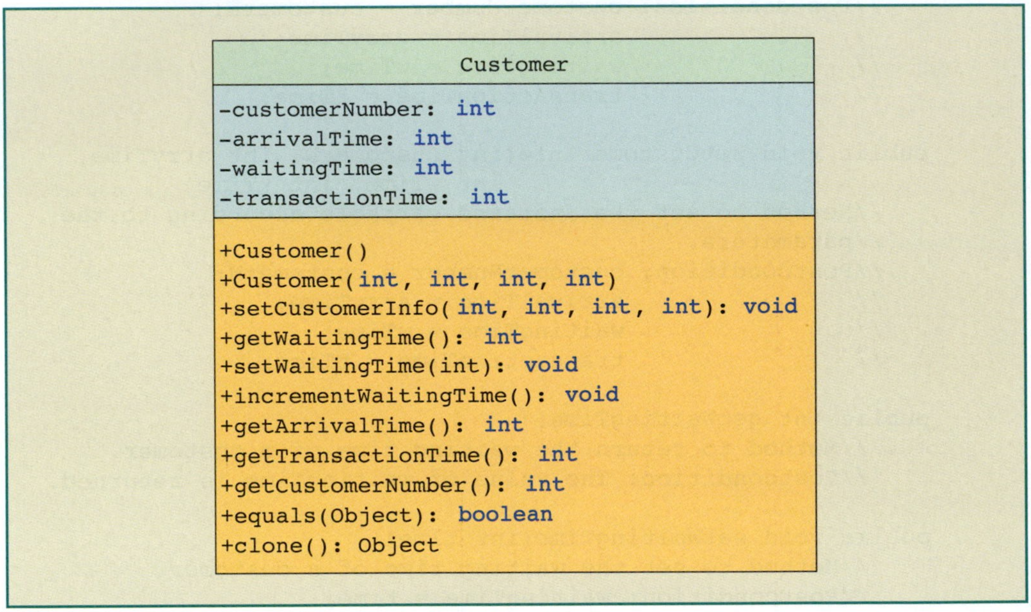

```
                        Customer

        -customerNumber: int
        -arrivalTime: int
        -waitingTime: int
        -transactionTime: int

        +Customer()
        +Customer(int, int, int, int)
        +setCustomerInfo(int, int, int, int): void
        +getWaitingTime(): int
        +setWaitingTime(int): void
        +incrementWaitingTime(): void
        +getArrivalTime(): int
        +getTransactionTime(): int
        +getCustomerNumber(): int
        +equals(Object): boolean
        +clone(): Object
```

Figure 17-54   UML class diagram of the **class** Customer

Next, we give the definitions of the member methods of the **class** Customer.

The method `setCustomerInfo` uses the values of the parameters to initialize `customerNumber`, `arrivalTime`, `waitingTime`, and `transactionTime`. Its definition is:

```java
public void setCustomerInfo(int customerN, int arrvTime,
                            int wTime, int tTime)
{
    customerNumber = customerN;
    arrivalTime = arrvTime;
    waitingTime = wTime;
    transactionTime = tTime;
}
```

The definitions of the constructors are similar to the definition of the method `setCustomerInfo`. The default constructor initializes the instance variables to 0. The constructor with parameters uses the values of the parameters to initialize `customerNumber`, `arrivalTime`, `waitingTime`, and `transactionTime`. To make debugging easier, we use the method `setCustomerInfo` to write the definition of the constructors, which is given next:

```java
public Customer()
{
    setCustomerInfo(0, 0, 0, 0);
}

public Customer(int customerN, int arrvTime, int wTime,
                int tTime)
{
    setCustomerInfo(customerN, arrvTime, wTime, tTime);
}
```

The method `getWaitingTime` returns the current waiting time. Because the waiting time is stored in `waitingTime`, the method `getWaitingTime` returns the value of `waitingTime`. The definition of the method `getWaitingTime` is:

```java
public int getWaitingTime()
{
    return waitingTime;
}
```

The method `incrementWaitingTime` increments the value of `waitingTime`. Its definition is:

```java
public void incrementWaitingTime()
{
    waitingTime++;
}
```

The definitions of the methods `setWaitingTime`, `getArrivalTime`, `getTransactionTime`, `getCustomerNumber`, `equals`, and `clone` are left as an exercise for you.

17

Server

At any given time unit, the server is either busy serving a customer or is free. We use the string variable status to set the status of the server. Every server has a timer, and, because the program might need to know which server serves which customer, the server also stores the information of the customer being served. Thus, three instance variables are associated with a server: the **status** of the type **String**, the **transactionTime** of the type **int**, and the **currentCustomer** of the type **Customer**. Some of the basic operations that must be performed on a server are as follows: check whether the server is free; set the server as free; set the server as busy; set the transaction time (that is, how long it takes to serve the customer); return the remaining transaction time (to determine whether the server should be set to free); if the server is busy after each time unit, decrement the transaction time by one time unit; and so on. The following defines the heading, instance variables, constructors, and instance methods of the **class Server**. See Figure 17-55.

Class: Server

```
public class Server
```

Instance variables:

```
private Customer currentCustomer;
private String status;
private int transactionTime;
```

Instance methods

```
public Server()
   //Default constructor
   //Set the values of the instance variables to their
   //default values.
   //Postcondition: currentCustomer is initialized by its
   //               default constructor; status = "free";
   //               the transaction time is initialized
   //               to 0.

public boolean isFree()
   //Method to determine whether a server is free.
   //Postcondition: Returns true if the server is free;
   //               otherwise, returns false.

public void setBusy()
   //Method to set the status of a server to "busy".
   //Postcondition: status = "busy";

public void setFree()
   //Method to set the status of a server to "free".
   //Postcondition: status = "free";

public void setTransactionTime(int t)
     //Method to set the transaction time according
     //to the parameter t.
     //Postcondition: transactionTime = t;
```

```
public void setTransactionTime()
   //Method to set the transaction time according
   //to the transaction time of the current customer.
   //Postcondition:
   //   transactionTime = currentCustomer.transactionTime;

public int getRemainingTransactionTime()
   //Method to return the remaining transaction time.
   //Postcondition: The value of the instance variable
   //               transactionTime is returned.

public void decreaseTransactionTime()
   //Method to decrease the transaction time by 1.
   //Postcondition: transactionTime--;

public void setCurrentCustomer(Customer cCustomer)
   //Method to set the info of the current customer
   //according to the parameter cCustomer.
   //Postcondition: currentCustomer = cCustomer;

public int getCurrentCustomerNumber()
   //Method to return the customer number of the
   //current customer.
   //Postcondition: The value of the instance variable
   //               customerNumber of the current customer
   //               is returned.

public int getCurrentCustomerArrivalTime()
   //Method to return the arrival time of the current
   //customer.
   //Postcondition: The value of the instance variable
   //               arrivalTime of the current customer
   //               is returned.

public int getCurrentCustomerWaitingTime()
   //Method to return the current waiting time of the
   //current customer.
   //Postcondition: The value of the instance variable
   //               waitingTime of the current
   //               customer is returned.

public int getCurrentCustomerTransactionTime()
   //Method to return the transaction time of the
   //current customer.
   //Postcondition: The value of the instance variable
   //               transactionTime of the current
   //               customer is returned.
```

17

Figure 17-55 UML class diagram of the **class** Server

The definitions of the methods of the **class** Server are as follows:

```
public Server()
{
    status = "free";
    transactionTime = 0;
    currentCustomer = new Customer();
}

public boolean isFree()
{
    return (status.equals("free"));
}

public void setBusy()
{
    status = "busy";
}

public void setFree()
{
    status = "free";
}
```

```java
public void setTransactionTime(int t)
{
    transactionTime = t;
}

public void setTransactionTime()
{
    transactionTime = currentCustomer.getTransactionTime();
}

public void decreaseTransactionTime()
{
    transactionTime--;
}
```

We leave the definitions of the methods `getRemainingTransactionTime`, `setCurrentCustomer`, `getCurrentCustomerNumber`, `getCurrentCustomerArrivalTime`, `getCurrentCustomerWaitingTime`, and `getCurrentCustomerTransactionTime` as an exercise for you.

Because we are designing a simulation program that can be used in a variety of applications, we need to design two more classes: a class to create and process a list of servers, and a class to create and process a queue of waiting customers. The next two sections describe each of these classes.

Server List

A server list is a set of servers, like a row of bank tellers. At any given time, a server is either free or busy. For the customer at the front of the queue, we need to find a server in the list that is free. If all the servers are busy, then the customer must wait until one of the servers becomes free. Thus, the class that implements a list of servers has two instance variables: one to store the number of servers, and one to maintain a list of servers. Using dynamic arrays, depending on the number of servers specified by the user, a list of servers is created during program execution. Some of the operations that must be performed on a server list are as follows: return the server number of a free server; when a customer gets ready to conduct business and a server is available, set the server to `"busy"`; when the simulation ends, some of the servers might still be busy, so return the number of busy servers; after each time unit, reduce the `transactionTime` of each busy server by one time unit; and if the `transactionTime` of a server becomes zero, set the server to `"free"`. The following defines the heading, instance variables, constructors, and instance methods of the **class** `ServerList`. See Figure 17-56.

Class: `ServerList`

`public class ServerList`

17

Instance variables:

```
private int numOfServers;
private Server[] servers;
```

Constructors and Instance methods

```
public ServerList()
   //Default constructor to initialize a list of servers
   //Postcondition: numOfServers = 1
   //                A server is created.

public ServerList(int num)
   //Constructor with a parameter
   //Creates a list of servers. The number of servers are
   //specified by the parameter num.
   //Postcondition: numOfServers = num
   //    A list of servers, specified by num, is created.

public int getFreeServerID()
   //Method to search the list of servers.
   //Postcondition: If a free server is found, return its ID;
   //    otherwise, return -1.

public int getNumberOfBusyServers()
   //Method to return the number of busy servers.
   //Postcondition: The number of busy servers is returned.

public void setServerBusy(int serverID,  Customer cCustomer,
                          int tTime)
   //Method to set a server to "busy".
   //Postcondition: To serve the customer specified by
   //    cCustomer the server specified by serverID is set
   //    to "busy", and the transaction time is set according
   //    to the parameter tTime.

public void setServerBusy(int serverID, Customer cCustomer)
   //Method to set a server to busy.
   //Postcondition: To serve the customer specified by
   //    cCustomer, the server specified by serverID is set
   //    to "busy", and the transaction time is set according
   //    to the customer's transaction time.

public void  updateServers()
   //Method to update the transaction time of each busy
   //server.
   //Postcondition: The transaction time of each busy server
   //    is decremented by one time unit. If the transaction
   //    time of a busy server is reduced to zero, the
```

```
//      server is set to "free" and a message indicating which
//      customer was served, together with the customer's
//      departing time, is printed on the screen.

public void  updateServers(PrintWriter outF)
   //Method to update the transaction time of each
   //busy server.
   //Postcondition: The transaction time of each busy
   //      server is decremented by one time unit. If the
   //      transaction time of a busy server is reduced to
   //      zero, the server is set to "free" and a message
   //      indicating which customer was served, together
   //      with the customer's departing time, is sent to
   //      the file specified by outF.
```

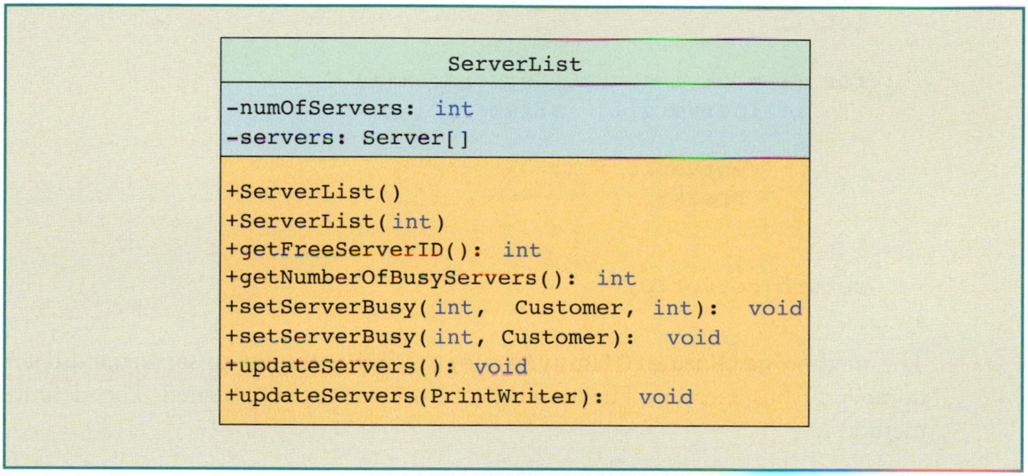

Figure 17-56   UML class diagram of the **class** ServerList

Following are the definitions of the methods of the **class** ServerList. The definitions of the constructors are as follows:

```
public ServerList()
{
    numOfServers = 1;
    servers = new Server[1];
    servers[0] = new Server();
}
```

17

```
public ServerList(int num)
{
    numOfServers = num;
    servers = new Server[num];

    for (int i = 0; i < num; i++)
        servers[i] = new Server();
}
```

The method `getFreeServerID` searches the list of servers. If a free server is found, it returns the server's ID; otherwise, the value `-1` is returned, which indicates that all of the servers are busy. The definition of this method is:

```
public int getFreeServerID()
{
    int serverID = -1;

    int i;

    for (i = 0; i < numOfServers; i++)
        if (servers[i].isFree())
        {
            serverID = i;
            break;
        }

    return serverID;
}
```

The method `getNumberOfBusyServers` searches the list of servers and determines the number of busy servers. The number of busy servers is returned. The definition of this method is:

```
public int getNumberOfBusyServers()
{
    int busyServers = 0;

    int i;

    for (i = 0; i < numOfServers; i++)
        if (!servers[i].isFree())
            busyServers++;

    return busyServers;
}
```

The method `setServerBusy` sets a server to `"busy"`. This method is overloaded. The `serverID` of the server that is set to `"busy"` is passed as a parameter to this method. One method sets the server's transaction time according to the parameter `tTime`; the other method sets it by using the transaction time stored in the object `cCustomer`. The transaction time is later needed to determine the average wait time. The definitions of these methods are as follows:

```java
public void setServerBusy(int serverID,  Customer cCustomer,
                          int tTime)
{
    servers[serverID].setBusy();
    servers[serverID].setTransactionTime(tTime);
    servers[serverID].setCurrentCustomer(cCustomer);
}

public void setServerBusy(int serverID, Customer cCustomer)
{
    int time;

    time = cCustomer.getTransactionTime();

    servers[serverID].setBusy();
    servers[serverID].setTransactionTime(time);
    servers[serverID].setCurrentCustomer(cCustomer);
}
```

Next, we consider the definition of the method `updateServers`. Starting at the first server, it searches the list of servers for busy servers. When a busy server is found, its `transactionTime` is decremented by one. If the `transactionTime` reduces to zero, the server is set to `"free"`. If the `transactionTime` of a busy server reduces to zero, then the transaction of the customer being served by this server is completed. A message indicating the customer's server number, customer number, and departure time is then printed. The method `updateServers` is overloaded. One method sends the output to the screen; the other sends the output to a file. We give the definition of the method that sends output to the screen and leave the other method as an exercise for you.

```java
public void  updateServers()
{
    int i;

    for (i = 0; i < numOfServers; i++)
        if (!servers[i].isFree())
        {
            servers[i].decreaseTransactionTime();

            if (servers[i].getRemainingTransactionTime() == 0)
            {
                System.out.println("From server number "
                  + (i + 1) + ", customer number "
                  + servers[i].getCurrentCustomerNumber()
                  + "\n       departed at clock unit "
                  + (servers[i].getCurrentCustomerArrivalTime()
```

17

```
                        + servers[i].getCurrentCustomerWaitingTime()
                        + servers[i].
                              getCurrentCustomerTransactionTime()));

                  servers[i].setFree();
              }
           }
    }
```

Waiting Customers Queue

When a customer arrives, he or she goes to the end of the queue. When a server becomes available, the customer at the front of the queue leaves to conduct the transaction. After each time unit, the waiting time of each customer in the queue is incremented by 1. The **class** QueueClass designed in this chapter has all the operations needed to implement a queue, except the operation of incrementing the waiting time of each customer in the queue by one time unit. Thus, we derive the **class** WaitingCustomerQueue from the **class** QueueClass and add the additional operations to implement the customers' queue. The definition of the **class** WaitingCustomerQueue is:

```
class WaitingCustomerQueue extends QueueClass
{
        //Default constructor
    public WaitingCustomerQueue()
    {
        super();
    }

        //Constructor with a parameter
    public WaitingCustomerQueue(int size)
    {
        super(size);
    }

        //Method to increment the waiting time of each
        //customer in the queue by one time unit.
        //Postcondition: The waiting time of each customer in
        //    the queue is incremented by one time unit.
    public void updateWaitingQueue()
    {
        //Definition as given below.
    }
}
```

Notice that the **class** WaitingCustomerQueue is derived from the **class** QueueClass, which implements the queue in an array. You can also derive the **class** WaitingCustomerQueue from the **class** LinkedQueueClass, which implements the queue in a linked list. We leave the details as an exercise for you.

The method `updateWaitingQueue` increments the waiting time of each customer in the queue by one time unit. The **class** `WaitingCustomerQueue` is derived from the **class** `QueueClass`. Because the instance variables of `QueueClass` are **private**, the method `updateWaitingQueue` cannot directly access the elements of the queue. The only way to access the elements of the queue is to use the `deleteQueue` operation. After incrementing the waiting time, the element can be put back into the queue by using the `addQueue` operation.

The `addQueue` operation inserts the element at the end of the queue. If we perform the `front` and `deleteQueue` operations followed by the `addQueue` operation for each element of the queue, then eventually the front element again becomes the first element. Given that each `front` and `deleteQueue` operation is followed by an `addQueue` operation, how do we determine that all the elements of the queue have been processed? We cannot use the `isEmptyQueue` or `isFullQueue` operations on the queue, because the queue will never be empty or full.

One solution to this problem is to create a temporary queue. Every element of the original queue is removed, processed, and inserted into the temporary queue. When the original queue becomes empty, all of the elements in the queue are processed. We can then copy the elements from the temporary queue back into the original queue. However, this solution requires us to use extra memory space, which could be significant. Also, if the queue is large, extra computer time is needed to copy the elements from the temporary queue back into the original queue. Let us look into another solution.

Before starting to update the elements of the queue, we can insert a dummy customer with a waiting time of, say, –1. During the update process, when we arrive at the customer with the waiting time of –1, we can stop the update process without processing this customer. If we do not process the customer with the waiting time of –1, this customer is removed from the queue and, after processing all the elements of the queue, the queue contains no extra elements. This solution does not require us to create a temporary queue, so we do not need extra computer time to copy the elements back into the original queue. We will use this solution to update the queue. Therefore, the definition of the method `updateWaitingQueue` is:

```java
public void updateWaitingQueue()
{
    Customer cust = new Customer();

    cust.setWaitingTime(-1);
    int wTime = 0;

    addQueue(cust);

    while (wTime != -1)
    {
        cust = (Customer) front();
        deleteQueue();
        wTime = cust.getWaitingTime();
```

17

```
            if (wTime == -1)
                break;

            cust.incrementWaitingTime();
            addQueue(cust);
        }
    }
```

Main Program

To run the simulation, we first need to get the following information:

■ The number of time units the simulation should run. Assume that each time unit is one minute.

■ The number of servers.

■ The amount of time it takes to serve a customer—that is, the transaction time.

■ The approximate time between customer arrivals.

These pieces of information are called simulation parameters. By changing the values of these parameters, we can observe the changes in the performance of the system. The program that we write uses the following instance variables to store this information:

```
private static int simulationTime;
private static int numberOfServers;
private static int transactionTime;
private static int timeBetweenCustomerArrival;
```

We can write a method, setSimulationParameters, to prompt the user to specify these values. The definition of this method is:

```
public static void setSimulationParameters()
{
    System.out.print("Enter the simulation time: ");
    simulationTime = console.nextInt();
    System.out.println();

    System.out.print("Enter the number of servers: ");
    numberOfServers = console.nextInt();
    System.out.println();

    System.out.print("Enter the transaction time: ");
    transactionTime = console.nextInt();
    System.out.println();

    System.out.print("Enter the time between customer arrivals: ");
    timeBetweenCustomerArrival = console.nextInt();
    System.out.println();
}
```

When a server becomes free and the customer queue is nonempty, we can move the customer at the front of the queue to the free server to be served. Moreover, when a customer starts the transaction, the waiting time ends. The waiting time of the customer is added to the total waiting time. The general algorithm to start the transaction (supposing that `serverID` denotes the ID of the free server) is:

1. Retrieve and remove the customer from the front of the queue.

   ```
   customer = (Customer) customerQueue.front();
   customerQueue.deleteQueue();
   ```

2. Update the total waiting time by adding the current customer's waiting time to the previous total waiting time.

   ```
   totalWaitTimeServedCustomers = totalWaitTimeServedCustomers
                                + customer.getWaitingTime();
   ```

3. Set the free server to begin the transaction.

   ```
   serverList.setServerBusy(serverID, customer, transTime);
   ```

To run the simulation, we need to know the number of customers arriving at a given time unit and how long it takes to serve the customer. We use the Poisson distribution from statistics, which says that the probability of y events occurring at a given time is given by the formula:

$$P(y) = \frac{\lambda^y e^{-\lambda}}{y!}, y = 0,1,2,\ldots,$$

where λ is the expected value that y events occur at that time. Suppose that, on average, a customer arrives every four minutes. During this four-minute period, the customer can arrive at any one of the four minutes. Assuming an equal likelihood of each of the four minutes, the expected value that a customer arrives in each of the four minutes is therefore, $1/4 = .25$. Next, we need to determine whether or not the customer actually arrives at a given minute.

Now $P(0) = e^{-\lambda}$ is the probability that no event occurs at a given time. One of the basic assumptions of the Poisson distribution is that the probability of more than one outcome occurring in a short time interval is negligible. For simplicity, we assume that only one customer arrives at a given time unit. Thus, we use $e^{-\lambda}$ as the cutoff point to determine whether a customer arrives at a given time unit. Suppose that, on average, a customer arrives every four minutes. Then $\lambda = 0.25$. We can use an algorithm to generate a number between 0 and 1. If the value of the number generated is $> e^{-0.25}$, we can assume that the customer arrived at a particular time unit. For example, suppose that $rNum$ is a random number such that $0 \leq rNum \leq 1$. If $rNum > e^{-0.25}$, the customer arrived at the given time unit.

17

We now describe the method `runSimulation` to implement the simulation. Suppose that we run the simulation for 100 time units and customers arrive at time units 93, 96, and 100. The average transaction time is 5 minutes—that is, 5 time units. For simplicity, assume that we have only one server and the server becomes free at time unit 97, and that all customers arriving before time unit 93 have been served. When the server becomes free at time unit 97, the customer who arrived at time unit 93 starts the transaction. Because the transaction of the customer arriving at time unit 93 starts at time unit 97 and it takes 5 minutes to complete a transaction, when the simulation loop ends, this customer is still at the server. Moreover, customers who arrive at time units 96 and 100 are still in the queue. For simplicity, we assume that when the simulation loop ends, the customers at the servers are considered served. The general algorithm for this method is:

1. Declare and initialize the variables, such as the simulation parameters, customer number, clock, total and average waiting times, number of customers arrived, number of customers served, number of customers left in the waiting queue, number of customers left with the servers, `waitingCustomersQueue`, and a list of servers.

2. The main loop is:

```
for (clock = 1; clock <= simulationTime; clock++)
{
```

   a. Update the server list to decrement the transaction time of each busy server by one time unit.

   b. If the customers' queue is nonempty, increment the waiting time of each customer by one time unit.

   c. If a customer arrives, increment the number of customers by 1 and add the new customer to the queue.

   d. If a server is free and the customers' queue is nonempty, remove a customer from the front of the queue and send the customer to the free server.

```
}
```

3. Print the appropriate results. Your results must include the number of customers left in the queue, the number of customers still with servers, the number of customers arrived, and the number of customers who actually completed a transaction.

Once you have designed the method `runSimulation`, the definition of the method `main` is simple and straightforward because the method `main` calls only the method `runSimulation`.

When we tested our version of the simulation program, we generated the following results. We assumed that the average transaction time is 5 minutes and that, on average, a customer arrives every 4 minutes. We used a random number generator to generate a number between 0 and 1 to decide whether a customer arrived at a given time unit.

Sample Runs:

Sample Run 1:

```
Enter the simulation time: 100

Enter the number of servers: 1

Enter the transaction time: 5

Enter the time between customer arrivals: 4

Customer number 1 arrived at time unit 6
Customer number 2 arrived at time unit 7
From server number 1, customer number 1
      departed at clock unit 11
Customer number 3 arrived at time unit 11
From server number 1, customer number 2
      departed at clock unit 16
From server number 1, customer number 3
      departed at clock unit 21
Customer number 4 arrived at time unit 30
From server number 1, customer number 4
      departed at clock unit 35
Customer number 5 arrived at time unit 36
Customer number 6 arrived at time unit 37
Customer number 7 arrived at time unit 39
From server number 1, customer number 5
      departed at clock unit 41
From server number 1, customer number 6
      departed at clock unit 46
From server number 1, customer number 7
      departed at clock unit 51
Customer number 8 arrived at time unit 53
Customer number 9 arrived at time unit 54
Customer number 10 arrived at time unit 57
From server number 1, customer number 8
      departed at clock unit 58
From server number 1, customer number 9
      departed at clock unit 63
Customer number 11 arrived at time unit 64
Customer number 12 arrived at time unit 65
Customer number 13 arrived at time unit 67
From server number 1, customer number 10
      departed at clock unit 68
Customer number 14 arrived at time unit 71
From server number 1, customer number 11
      departed at clock unit 73
From server number 1, customer number 12
      departed at clock unit 78
```

17

```
Customer number 15 arrived at time unit 82
From server number 1, customer number 13
     departed at clock unit 83
From server number 1, customer number 14
     departed at clock unit 88
Customer number 16 arrived at time unit 89
Customer number 17 arrived at time unit 92
From server number 1, customer number 15
     departed at clock unit 93
Customer number 18 arrived at time unit 93
From server number 1, customer number 16
     departed at clock unit 98

Simulation ran for 100 time units
Number of servers: 1
Average transaction time: 5
Average arrival time difference between customers: 4
Total wait time: 88
Number of customers who completed a transaction: 16
Number of customers left in the servers: 1
Number of customers left in the queue: 1
Average wait time: 4.89
************** END SIMULATION *************
```

Sample Run 2:

```
Enter the simulation time: 100

Enter the number of servers: 2

Enter the transaction time: 5

Enter the time between customer arrivals: 4

Customer number 1 arrived at time unit 1
Customer number 2 arrived at time unit 5
From server number 1, customer number 1
     departed at clock unit 6
From server number 2, customer number 2
     departed at clock unit 10
Customer number 3 arrived at time unit 14
From server number 1, customer number 3
     departed at clock unit 19
Customer number 4 arrived at time unit 21
From server number 1, customer number 4
     departed at clock unit 26
Customer number 5 arrived at time unit 29
From server number 1, customer number 5
     departed at clock unit 34
Customer number 6 arrived at time unit 47
```

```
From server number 1, customer number 6
      departed at clock unit 52
Customer number 7 arrived at time unit 57
From server number 1, customer number 7
      departed at clock unit 62
Customer number 8 arrived at time unit 62
From server number 1, customer number 8
      departed at clock unit 67
Customer number 9 arrived at time unit 70
From server number 1, customer number 9
      departed at clock unit 75
Customer number 10 arrived at time unit 75
From server number 1, customer number 10
      departed at clock unit 80
Customer number 11 arrived at time unit 82
Customer number 12 arrived at time unit 85
From server number 1, customer number 11
      departed at clock unit 87
From server number 2, customer number 12
      departed at clock unit 90
Customer number 13 arrived at time unit 92
Customer number 14 arrived at time unit 94
From server number 1, customer number 13
      departed at clock unit 97
From server number 2, customer number 14
      departed at clock unit 99

Simulation ran for 100 time units
Number of servers: 2
Average transaction time: 5
Average arrival time difference between customers: 4
Total wait time: 0
Number of customers who completed a transaction: 14
Number of customers left in the servers: 0
Number of customers left in the queue: 0
Average wait time: 0.00
************** END SIMULATION **************
```

QUICK REVIEW

1. A stack is a data structure wherein the items are added and deleted from one end only.

2. A stack is a Last In First Out (LIFO) data structure.

3. The basic operations on a stack are: push an item onto the stack, pop an item from the stack, return the top element of the stack, initialize the stack, destroy the stack, check whether the stack is empty, and check whether the stack is full.

17

4. A stack can be implemented either as an array or as a linked list.

5. The middle elements of a stack should not be accessed directly.

6. Stacks are restricted versions of arrays and linked lists.

7. The postfix notation does not require the use of parentheses to enforce operator precedence.

8. In postfix notation, the operators are written after the operands.

9. Postfix expressions are evaluated according to the following rules:

   a. Scan the expression from left to right.

   b. If an operator is found, back up to get the required number of operands, evaluate the operator, and continue.

10. A queue is a data structure wherein the items are added at one end and removed from the other end.

11. A queue is a First In First Out (FIFO) data structure.

12. The basic operations on a queue are: initialize the queue, destroy the queue, check whether the queue is empty, check whether the queue is full, add an item to the queue, and remove an item from the queue.

13. A queue can be implemented either as an array or as a linked list.

14. The middle elements of a queue should not be accessed directly.

15. If the queue is nonempty, the method **front** returns the front element of the queue, and the method **back** returns the last element of the queue.

16. Queues are restricted versions of arrays and linked lists.

EXERCISES

1. Consider the following statements:

```
StackClass<Integer> stack = new StackClass<Integer>();
Integer x, y;
```

Show what is output by the following segment of code:

```
stack.initializeStack();

x = 4;
y = 0;
stack.push(y);
stack.push(x);
stack.push( x + 5);
y = stack.peek();
stack.pop();
stack.push(9);
stack.push(y - 2);
stack.push(3);
```

```
x = stack.peek();
stack.pop();
System.out.println("x = " + x);
System.out.println("y = " + y);

while (!stack.isEmptyStack())
{
    y = stack.peek();
    System.out.println(y);
    stack.pop();
}
```

2. Consider the following statements:

```
StackClass<Integer> stack = new StackClass<Integer>();
Integer x, y;
```

Suppose that the input is:

```
14 45 34 23 10 5 -999
```

Show what is output by the following segment of code. (Assume that **console** is a **Scanner** object initialized to the standard input device.)

```
stack.initializeStack();

stack.push(5);

x = console.nextInt();

while (x != -999)
{
    if (x % 2 == 0)
    {
        if (!stack.isFullStack())
            stack.push(x);
    }
    else
        System.out.println("x = " + x);

    x = console.nextInt();
}

System.out.println("Stack Elements: ");

while (!stack.isEmptyStack())
{
    y = stack.peek();
    System.out.println(y);
    stack.pop();
}
System.out.println();
```

17

3. Evaluate the following postfix expressions:

   a. 6 4 + 3 * 16 4 / - =

   b. 12 25 5 1 / / * 8 7 + - =

   c. 70 14 4 5 15 3 / * - - / 6 + =

4. Convert the following infix expressions to postfix notations. (For an algorithm to convert an infix expression into an equivalent postfix expression, see Programming Exercise 11 of this chapter.)

   a. (A + B) * (C + D) - E

   b. A - (B + C) * D + E / F

   c. ((A + B) / (C - D) + E) * F - G

   d. A + B * (C + D) - E / F * G + H

5. Write the equivalent infix expression for the following postfix expressions:

   a. A B * C +

   b. A B + C D - *

   c. A B - C - D *

6. What is the output of the following program?

```java
public class Exercise6
{
    public static void main(String[] args)
    {
        StackClass<String> s1 =  new StackClass<String> ();
        StackClass<String> s2 = new StackClass<String> ();

        String list[] = {"Winter", "Spring", "Summer", "Fall",
                         "Cold", "Warm", "Hot"};

        for (int i = 0; i < 7; i++)
            s1.push(list[i]);

        mystery(s1, s2);

        while (!s2.isEmptyStack())
        {
            System.out.print(s2.peek() + " ");
            s2.pop();
        }
        System.out.println();
    }
}
```

```java
    public static <T> void mystery(StackClass<T> s,
                                   StackClass<T> t)
    {
        while (!s.isEmptyStack())
        {
            t.push(s.peek());
            s.pop();
        }
    }
}
```

7. What is the output of the following program?

```java
public class Exercise7
{
    public static void main(String[] args)
    {
        int list[] = {5, 10, 15, 20, 25};

        StackClass<Integer> s1 = new StackClass<Integer>();
        StackClass<Integer> s2 = new StackClass<Integer>();

        for (int i = 0; i < 5; i++)
            s1.push(list[i]);

        mystery(s1, s2);

        while (!s2.isEmptyStack())
        {
            System.out.print(s2.peek() + " ");
            s2.pop();
        }
        System.out.println();
    }

    public static void mystery(StackClass<Integer> s,
                               StackClass<Integer> t)
    {
        Integer num;

        while (!s.isEmptyStack())
        {

            num = (Integer) s.peek();

            t.push(2 * num);

            s.pop();
        }
    }
}
```

17

8. Write the definition of the method **second** that takes as a parameter a stack object and returns the second element of the stack. The original stack remains unchanged.

9. Write the definition of the method **clear** that takes as a parameter a stack object of the type **Stack** (the class provided by Java) and removes all the elements from the stack.

10. What is the output of the following program segment?

```
QueueClass<Integer> q = new QueueClass<Integer>();
Integer x, y;

x = 2;
q.addQueue(8);
q.addQueue(x + 3);
y = q.front();
q.addQueue(2 * y);
q.deleteQueue();
x = q.front();
q.addQueue(q.front());

while (!q.isEmptyQueue())
{
    System.out.print(q.front() + " ");
    q.deleteQueue();
}

System.out.println();
```

11. Consider the following statements:

```
QueueClass<Integer> queue = new QueueClass<Integer>();
Integer x, y;
```

Show what is output by the following segment of code:

```
queue.initializeQueue();
x = 4;
y = 5;
queue.addQueue(x);
queue.addQueue(y);
x = queue.front();
queue.deleteQueue();
queue.addQueue(x + 5);
queue.addQueue(16);
queue.addQueue(x);
queue.addQueue(y - 3);

System.out.println("Queue Elements: ");
```

```
while (!queue.isEmptyQueue())
{
    System.out.print(queue.front() + " ");
    queue.deleteQueue();
}

System.out.println();
```

12. Consider the following statements:

```
StackClass<Integer> stack = new StackClass<Integer>();
QueueClass<Integer> queue = new QueueClass<Integer>();

Integer x;
```

Suppose the input is:

```
15 28 14 22 64 35 19 32 7 11 13 30 -999
```

Show what is written by the following segment of code. (Assume that `console` is a `Scanner` object initialized to the standard input device.)

```
stack.initializeStack();
queue.initializeQueue();
stack.push(0);
queue.addQueue(0);

x = console.nextInt();

while (x != -999)
{
    switch (x % 4)
    {
    case 0: stack.push(x);
            break;
    case 1: if (!stack.isEmptyStack())
            {
                System.out.println("Stack Element = "
                                    + stack.peek());
                stack.pop();
            }
            else
                System.out.println("Sorry, the stack is empty");
            break;
    case 2: queue.addQueue(x);
            break;
    case 3: if (!queue.isEmptyQueue())
            {
                System.out.println("Queue Element = "
                                    + queue.front());
                queue.deleteQueue();
            }
```

17

```
                        else
                            System.out.println("Sorry, the queue is empty");
                        break;
                }//end switch

            x = console.nextInt();
        }//end while

    System.out.print("Stack Elements: ");

    while (!stack.isEmptyStack())
    {
        System.out.print(stack.peek() + " ");
        stack.pop();
    }

    System.out.println();

    System.out.print("Queue Elements: ");

    while (!queue.isEmptyQueue())
    {
        System.out.print(queue.front() + " ");
        queue.deleteQueue();
    }

    System.out.println();
```

13. What does the following method do?

```
public static void mystery(QueueClass<Integer> q)
{
    StackClass<Integer> s = new StackClass<Integer>();

    while (!q.isEmptyQueue())
    {
        s.push(q.front());
        q.deleteQueue();
    }

    while (!s.isEmptyStack())
    {
        q.addQueue(2 * s.peek());
        s.pop();
    }
}
```

14. Suppose that queue is a `QueueClass` object and the size of the array implementing queue is `100`. Also suppose that the value of `queueFront` is `50` and the value of `queueRear` is `99`.

    a. What are the values of `queueFront` and `queueRear` after adding an element to queue?

    b. What are the values of `queueFront` and `queueRear` after removing an element from queue?

15. Suppose that queue is a `QueueClass` object and the size of the array implementing queue is `100`. Also suppose that the value of `queueFront` is `99` and the value of `queueRear` is `25`.

    a. What are the values of `queueFront` and `queueRear` after adding an element to queue?

    b. What are the values of `queueFront` and `queueRear` after removing an element from queue?

16. Suppose that queue is a `QueueClass` object and the size of the array implementing queue is `100`. Also suppose that the value of `queueFront` is `25` and the value of queueRear is `75`.

    a. What are the values of `queueFront` and `queueRear` after adding an element to queue?

    b. What are the values of `queueFront` and `queueRear` after removing an element from queue?

17. Suppose that queue is a `QueueClass` object and the size of the array implementing queue is `100`. Also suppose that the value of `queueFront` is `99` and the value of `queueRear` is `99`.

    a. What are the values of `queueFront` and `queueRear` after adding an element to queue?

    b. What are the values of `queueFront` and `queueRear` after removing an element from queue?

18. Suppose that queue is implemented as an array with the special reserved slot, as described in this chapter. Also suppose that the size of the array implementing queue is `100`. If the value of `queueFront` is `50`, what is the position of the first queue element?

19. Suppose that queue is implemented as an array with the special reserved slot, as described in this chapter. Suppose that the size of the array implementing queue is `100`. Also suppose that the value of `queueFront` is `74` and the value of `queueRear` is `99`.

    a. What are the values of `queueFront` and `queueRear` after adding an element to queue?

    b. What are the values of `queueFront` and `queueRear` after removing an element from queue? Also, what is the position of the removed queue element?

20. Write the method **reverseStack** that takes as a parameter a stack object and a queue object whose elements are of the same type. The method **reverseStack** uses the queue to reverse the elements of the stack.

21. Write the method **reverseQueue** that takes as a parameter a stack object and a queue object whose elements are of the same type. The method **reverseQueue** uses the stack to reverse the elements of the queue.

22. Add the operation **queueCount** to the **class** QueueClass (the array implementation of queues), which returns the number of elements in the queue. Write the definition of the method to implement this operation.

PROGRAMMING EXERCISES

1. Write the definitions of the method **clone** for the **class** StackClass.

2. Two stacks are the same if they have the same size and their elements at the corresponding positions are the same. Add the method **equalStack** to the **class** StackClass that takes as a parameter a **StackClass** object, say **otherStack**, and returns **true** if this stack is the same as **otherStack**. Also write the definition of the method **equalStack** and a program to test your method.

3. Repeat Exercise 2 for the **class** LinkedStackClass.

4. a. Add the following operation to the **class** StackClass:

   ```
   void reverseStack(StackClass<T> otherStack);
   ```

   This operation copies the elements of a stack in reverse order onto another stack.

   Consider the following statements:

   ```
   StackClass<T> stack1;
   StackClass<T> stack2;
   ```

   The statement

   ```
   stack1.reverseStack(stack2);
   ```

   copies the elements of **stack1** onto **stack2** in the reverse order. That is, the top element of **stack1** is the bottom element of **stack2**, and so on. The old contents of **stack2** are destroyed and **stack1** is unchanged.

   b. Write the definition of the method to implement the operation **reverseStack**. Also write a program to test the method **reverseStack**.

5. Repeat Exercises 4a and 4b for the **class** LinkedStackClass. Also write the program to test your method.

6. Write the definition of the method **revPrint**, as explained in the section "Removing Recursion" of this chapter, that uses a stack to print a (single) linked list backward. Add the method **revPrint** in the **interface** LinkedListADT, provide its definition in the **class** LinkedListClass, and then write a program to test this method.

7. Write a program that takes as input an arithmetic expression. The program outputs whether the expression conatins matching grouping symbols. For example, the arithmetic expressions {25 + (3 - 6) * 8} and 7 + 8 * 2 contains matching grouping symbols. However, the expression 5 + {(13 + 7) / 8 - 2 * 9 does not contain matching grouping symbols.

8. Write a program that uses a stack to print the prime factors of a positive integer in descending order.

9. Programming Exercise 14 in Chapter 14, Converting a Number from Binary to Decimal, uses recursion to convert a binary number into an equivalent decimal number. Write a program that uses a stack to convert a binary number into an equivalent decimal number.

10. Programming Example: Converting a Number from Decimal to Binary (in Chapter 14), contains a program that uses recursion to convert a decimal number into an equivalent binary number. Write a program that uses a stack to convert a decimal number into an equivalent binary number.

11. **Infix to Postfix:** Write a program that converts an infix expression into an equivalent postfix expression.

    The rules to convert an infix expression into an equivalent postfix expression are as follows:

    a. Scan the expression from left to right. One pass is sufficient.

    b. If the next scanned symbol is an operand, append it to the postfix expression.

    c. If the next scanned symbol is a left parenthesis, push it onto the stack.

    d. If the next scanned symbol is a right parenthesis, pop and append all the symbols from the stack until the most recent left parenthesis. Pop and discard the left parenthesis.

    e. If the next scanned symbol is an operator:

       i. Pop and append to the postfix expression every operator from the stack that is above the most recently scanned left parenthesis, and that has precedence greater than or equal to the new operator.

       ii. Push the new operator onto the stack.

    f. After the infix string is completely processed, pop and append to the postfix string everything from the stack.

    In this program, you are to consider the following (binary) arithmetic operators: +, -, *, and /. You may assume that the expressions you process are error-free.

    Design a class that stores the infix and postfix strings. The class must include the following operations:

    getInfix: Stores the infix expression.

    showInfix: Outputs the infix expression.

    showPostfix: Outputs the postfix expression.

17

Some other operations that you might need are the following:

`convertToPostfix:` Converts the infix expression into a postfix expression. The resulting postfix expression is stored in `postfixString`.

`precedence:` Determines the precedence between two operators. If the first operator is of higher or equal precedence than the second operator, it returns the value **true**; otherwise, it returns the value **false**.

Test your program on the following expressions:

1. `A + B - C;`

2. `(A + B) * C;`

3. `(A + B) / (C - D);`

4. `A + ((B + C) * (E - F) - G) / (H - I);`

5. `A + B * (C + D ) - E / F * G + H;`

For each expression, your answer must be in the following form:

```
Infix Expression: A + B - C;
Postfix Expression: AB+C-
```

12. Redo the program in the section "Application of Stacks: Postfix Expressions Calculator" from this chapter so that it uses the Java **class** Stack to evaluate the postfix expressions.

13. Redo Programming Exercise 11 so that it uses the Java **class** Stack to convert the infix expressions to postfix expressions.

14. Write a program to test various operations of the **class** LinkedStackClass, which is derived from the **class** UnorderedLinkedList.

15. The array implementation of queues given in this chapter uses a special array slot—a reserved slot—to distinguish between an empty queue and a full queue. Write the array implementation of queues as an ADT, in which a variable count is used to keep track of the number of elements in the queue. Write the definitions of the methods of this queue design. Also, write a program to test various operations on the queue.

16. Write the definition of the method `moveNthFront` that takes as a parameter a positive integer, *n*. The method moves the *n*th element of the queue to the front. The order of the remaining elements remains unchanged. For example, suppose:

    queue = {5, 11, 34, 67, 43, 55} and *n* = 3.

    After a call to the method `moveNthFront`

    queue = {34, 5, 11, 67, 43, 55}.

    Add this method to the **interface** QueueADT and the **class** QueueClass. Also write a program to test your method.

17. Write a program that reads a line of text, changes each uppercase letter to lowercase, and places each letter both in a queue and onto a stack. The program should then verify whether the line of text is a palindrome (a set of letters or numbers that reads the same forward and backward).

18. The implementation of queue in an array, as given in this chapter, uses the variable count to determine whether the queue is empty or full. You can also use the variable count to return the number of elements in the queue; see Exercise 17 of this chapter. On the other hand, the **class** LinkedQueueClass does not use such a variable to keep track of the number of elements in the queue. Redefine the **class** LinkedQueueClass by addding the instance variable count to keep track of the number of elements in the queue. Modify the definitions of the methods addQueue and deleteQueue as necessary, and add the method queueCount to return the number of elements in the queue. Also write a program to test the various operations of the class you defined.

19. Write a program to test various operations of the **class** LinkedQueueClass.

20. Write the definition of the **class** LinkedQueueClass, which is derived from the **class** UnorderedLinkedList, as explained in this chapter. Also write a program to test various operations of this class.

21. a. Write the definitions of the methods setWaitingTime, getArrivalTime, getTransactionTime, and getCustomerNumber of the **class** Customer defined in the section "Application of Queues: Simulation."

    b. Write the definitions of the methods getRemainingTransactionTime, setCurrentCustomer, getCurrentCustomerNumber, getCurrentCustomerArrivalTime, getCurrentCustomerWaitingTime, and getCurrentCustomerTransactionTime of the **class** Server defined in the section "Application of Queues: Simulation."

    c. Write the definition of the method runSimulation to complete the design of the computer simulation program in the section "Application of Queues: Simulation." Test run your program for a variety of data. Also use a random number generator to decide whether a customer arrived at a given time unit.

17

SEARCHING AND SORTING ALGORITHMS

> **In this chapter, you will:**
>
> ♦ Learn the various search algorithms
> ♦ Explore how to implement the sequential and binary search algorithms
> ♦ Discover how the sequential and binary search algorithms perform
> ♦ Learn about asymptotic and big-O notation
> ♦ Become aware of the lower bound on comparison-based search algorithms
> ♦ Learn the various sorting algorithms
> ♦ Explore how to implement the selection, insertion, quick, merge, and heap sorting algorithms
> ♦ Discover how the sorting algorithms discussed in this chapter perform

Chapter 15 described how to organize data into computer memory using an array and how to perform basic operations on that data. Chapter 16 then described how to organize data using linked lists. The most important operation performed on a list is the search algorithm. Using the search algorithm, you can:

- Determine whether a particular item is in the list.

- If the data is specially organized (for example, sorted), find the location in the list where a new item can be inserted.

- Find the location of an item to be deleted.

The search algorithm's performance, therefore, is crucial. If the search is slow, it takes a large amount of computer time to accomplish your task; if the search is fast, you can accomplish your task quickly.

In the first part of this chapter, we describe the search algorithms sequential search and binary search. Certain search algorithms work only on sorted data. Therefore, the second half of this chapter discusses various sorting algorithms.

SEARCHING AND SORTING ALGORITHMS INTERFACE

The searching and sorting algorithms that we describe are generic. Because searching and sorting require comparisons of data, they should work on the type of data that provide appropriate methods to compare data items. Now data can be organized with the help of an array or a linked list. You can create an array of data items, or you can use the classes `UnorderedArrayList` or `OrderedArrayList` to organize data. However, the algorithms that we describe should work on either organization. We therefore, create the interface that describes the searching and sorting algorithms discussed in this section. All the algorithms except the merge sort algorithms that we describe are for array-based lists. Because of the storage and some other overheads, merge sort works better for linked list. Therefore, after describing the merge sort algorithm, we will add it as a method to the **class** `UnorderedLinkedList`.

The definition of the **interface** `SearchSortADT` is as follows:

```
//Generic interface that describes various searching and sorting
//algorithms. Note that the type parameter is unbounded. However,
//for these algorithms to work correctly, the data objects must
//be compared using the method compareTo and equals.
//In other words, the classes implementing the list objects
//must implement the interface Comparable. The type parameter T
//is unbounded because we would like to use these algorithms to
//work on an array of objects as well as on objects of the
//classes UnorderedArrayList and OrderedArrayList.

public interface SearchSortADT<T>
{
    public int seqSearch(T[] list, int length, T searchItem);
       //Sequential search algorithm.
       //Postcondition: If searchItem is found in the list,
       //               it returns the location of searchItem;
       //               otherwise it returns -1.

    public int binarySearch(T[] list, int length, T item);
       //Binary search algorithm.
       //Precondition: The list must be sorted.
```

```
                  //Postcondition: If searchItem is found in the list,
                  //                it returns the location of searchItem;
                  //                otherwise it returns -1.

      public void bubbleSort(T list[], int length);
         //Bubble sort algorithm.
         //Postcondition: list objects are in ascending order.

      public void selectionSort(T[] list, int length);
         //Selection sort algorithm.
         //Postcondition: list objects are in ascending order.

      public void insertionSort(T[] list, int length);
         //Insertion sort algorithm.
         //Postcondition: list objects are in ascending order.

      public void quickSort(T[] list, int length);
         //Quick sort algorithm.
         //Postcondition: list objects are in ascending order.

      public void heapSort(T[] list, int length);
         //Heap sort algorithm.
         //Postcondition: list objects are in ascending order.
}
```

To implement the searching and sorting algorithms described in the **interface** SearchSortADT, we will design the **class** SearchSortAlgorithms. The **class** SearchSortAlgorithms will implement the **interface** SearchSortADT and provide the definitions of the methods of this **interface**. After developing a particular algorithm, we will add that algorithm to the **class** SearchSortAlgorithms.

SEARCH ALGORITHMS

Chapters 15 and 16 described how to implement the sequential search algorithm. This chapter discusses other search algorithms and also analyzes the algorithms. Analysis of the algorithms enables programmers to decide which algorithm to use for a specific application. Before exploring these algorithms, let us make the following observations.

Associated with each item in a data set is a special member that uniquely identifies the item in the data set. For example, if you have a data set consisting of student records, then the student ID uniquely identifies each student in a particular school. This unique member of the item is called the **key** of the item. The keys of the items in the data set are used in operations such as searching, sorting, inserting, and deleting. For instance, when we search the data set for a particular item, we compare the key of the item for which we are searching with the keys of the items in the data set.

18

As previously remarked, this chapter, in addition to describing the searching and sorting algorithms, analyzes these algorithms. In the analysis of an algorithm, the key comparisons refer to comparing the key of the search item with the key of an item in the list. The number of key comparisons refers to the number of times the key of the search item (in algorithms such as searching and sorting) is compared with the keys of the items in the list.

Sequential Search

The sequential search (also called the linear search) on array-based lists was described in Chapter 15, and the sequential search on linked lists was covered in Chapter 16. The sequential search works the same for array-based and linked lists. The search always starts at the first element in the list and continues until either the item is found in the list or the entire list is searched.

Because we are interested in the performance of the sequential search (that is, the analysis of this type of search), for easy reference and the sake of completeness, next we give the sequential search algorithm for array-based lists (as described in Chapter 15). If the search item is found, its index (that is, its location in the array) is returned. If the search is unsuccessful, -1 is returned. Note that the following sequential search does not require the list elements to be in any particular order:

```java
public int seqSearch(T[] list, int length, T searchItem)
{
    int loc;
    boolean found = false;

    for (loc = 0; loc < length; loc++)
    {
        if (list[loc].equals(searchItem))
        {
            found = true;
            break;
        }
    }

    if (found)
        return loc;
    else
        return -1;
} //end seqSearch
```

The sequential search algorithm, as given here, uses an iterative control structure (the **for** loop) to compare the search item with the list elements. You can also write a recursive algorithm to implement the sequential search algorithm. (See Programming Exercise 1 at the end of this chapter.)

Sequential Search Analysis

This section analyzes the performance of the sequential search algorithm in both the worst case and the average case.

The statements before and after the loop are executed only once, and hence require very little computer time. The statements in the **for** loop are the ones that are repeated several times. For each iteration of the loop, the search item is compared with an element in the list, and a few other statements are executed, including some other comparisons. Clearly, the loop terminates as soon as the search item is found in the list. Therefore, the execution of the other statements in the loop is directly related to the outcome of the key comparison. Also, different programmers might implement the same algorithm differently, although the number of key comparisons would typically be the same. The speed of a computer can also affect the time an algorithm takes to perform, but it does not affect the number of key comparisons required.

Therefore, when analyzing a search algorithm, we count the number of key comparisons because this number gives us the most useful information. Furthermore, the criteria for counting the number of key comparisons can be applied equally well to other search algorithms.

Suppose that L is a list of length n. We want to determine the number of key comparisons made by the sequential search when the list L is searched for a given item.

If the search item is not in the list, we then compare the search item with every element in the list, making n comparisons. This is an unsuccessful case.

Suppose that the search item is in the list. Then the number of key comparisons depends on where in the list the search item is located. If the search item is the first element of L, we make only one key comparison. This is the best case. On the other hand, if the search item is the last element in the list, the algorithm makes n comparisons. This is the worst case. The best and worst cases are not likely to occur every time we apply the sequential search on L, so it would be more helpful if we could determine the average behavior of the algorithm. That is, we need to determine the average number of key comparisons the sequential search algorithm makes in the successful case.

To determine the average number of comparisons in the successful case of the sequential search algorithm:

1. Consider all possible cases.

2. Find the number of comparisons for each case.

3. Add the number of comparisons and divide by the number of cases.

If the search item, called the **target**, is the first element in the list, one comparison is required. If the target is the second element in the list, two comparisons are required. Similarly, if the target is the kth element in the list, k comparisons are required. We assume that the target can be any element in the list; that is, all list elements are equally likely to be

18

the target. Suppose that there are n elements in the list. The following expression gives the average number of comparisons:

$$\frac{1+2+\ldots+n}{n}$$

It is known that

$$1+2+\ldots+n = \frac{n(n+1)}{2}$$

Therefore, the following expression gives the average number of comparisons made by the sequential search in the successful case:

$$\frac{1+2+\ldots+n}{n} = \frac{1}{n}\frac{n(n+1)}{2} = \frac{n+1}{2}$$

This expression shows that, on average, a successful sequential search searches half the list. It thus follows that if the list size is 1,000,000, on average, the sequential search makes 500,000 comparisons. As a result, the sequential search is not efficient for large lists.

Binary Search

As you can see, the sequential search is not efficient for large lists because, on average, the sequential search searches half the list. We therefore describe another search algorithm, called the **binary search**, which is very fast. However, a binary search can be performed only on sorted lists. We therefore assume that the list is sorted. Later in this chapter, we describe several sorting algorithms.

The binary search algorithm uses the "divide and conquer" technique to search the list. First, the search item is compared with the middle element of the list. If the search item is less than the middle element of the list, we restrict the search to the first half of the list; otherwise, we search the second half of the list.

Consider the sorted list of `length` = 12 in Figure 18-1.

	[0]	[1]	[2]	[3]	[4]	[5]	[6]	[7]	[8]	[9]	[10]	[11]
list	4	8	19	25	34	39	45	48	66	75	89	95

Figure 18-1 List of length 12

Suppose that we want to determine whether 75 is in the list. Initially, the entire list is the search list (see Figure 18-2).

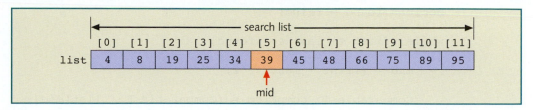

Figure 18-2 Search list, `list[0]...list[11]`

First, we compare 75 with the middle element in this list, `list[5]` (which is 39). Because 75 ≠ `list[5]` and 75 > `list[5]`, we then restrict our search to the list `list[6]...list[11]`, as shown in Figure 18-3.

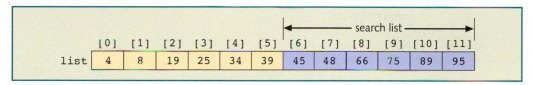

Figure 18-3 Search list, `list[6]...list[11]`

This process is now repeated on the list `list[6]...list[11]`, which is a list of `length = 6`.

Because we need to determine the middle element of the list frequently, the binary search algorithm is typically implemented for array-based lists. To determine the middle element of the list, we add the starting index, `first`, and the ending index, `last`, of the search list and then divide by 2 to calculate its index. That is:

$$mid = \frac{first + last}{2}$$

Initially, `first = 0` and `last = length - 1` (this is because an array index in Java starts at 0 and `length` denotes the number of elements in the list).

The following Java method implements the binary search algorithm. If the item is found in the list, its location is returned; if the search item is not in the list, -1 is returned.

```java
public int binarySearch(T[] list, int length, T searchItem)
{
    int first = 0;
    int last = length - 1;
    int mid = -1;
```

18

```
            boolean found = false;

            while (first <= last && !found)
            {
                mid = (first + last) / 2;

                Comparable<T> compElem = (Comparable<T>) list[mid];

                if (compElem.compareTo(searchItem) == 0)
                    found = true;
                else
                    if (compElem.compareTo(searchItem) > 0)
                        last = mid - 1;
                    else
                        first = mid + 1;
            }
            if (found)
                return mid;
            else
                return -1;
}//end binarySearch
```

In the binary search algorithm, each time through the loop we make two key comparisons. The only exception is in the successful case; the last time through the loop only one key comparison is made.

 The binary search algorithm, as given in this chapter, uses an iterative control structure (the `while` loop) to compare the search item with the list elements. You can also write a recursive algorithm to implement the binary search algorithm. (See Programming Exercise 2 at the end of this chapter.)

Example 18-1 further illustrates how the binary search algorithm works.

Example 18-1

Consider the list given in Figure 18-4.

	[0]	[1]	[2]	[3]	[4]	[5]	[6]	[7]	[8]	[9]	[10]	[11]
list	4	8	19	25	34	39	45	48	66	75	89	95

Figure 18-4   Sorted list for a binary search

The size of this list is 12; that is, the length is 12. Suppose that we are searching for item 89. Table 18-1 shows the values of first, last, and middle each time through the loop. It also shows the number of times the item is compared with an element in the list each time through the loop.

Table 18-1 Values of first, last, and middle and the Number of Comparisons for Search Item 89

Iteration	first	last	mid	list[mid]	Number of Comparisons
1	0	11	5	39	2
2	6	11	8	66	2
3	9	11	10	89	1(found is **true**)

The item is found at location 10, and the total number of comparisons is 5.

Next, let us search the list for item 34. Table 18-2 shows the values of first, last, and middle each time through the loop. It also shows the number of times the item is compared with an element in the list each time through the loop.

Table 18-2 Values of first, last, and middle and the Number of Comparisons for Search Item 34

Iteration	first	last	mid	list[mid]	Number of Comparisons
1	0	11	5	39	2
2	0	4	2	19	2
3	3	4	3	25	2
4	4	4	4	34	1 (found is **true**)

The item is found at location 4, and the total number of comparisons is 7.

Let us now search for item 22, as shown in Table 18-3.

18

Table 18-3 Values of `first`, `last`, and `middle` and the Number of Comparisons for Search Item 22

Iteration	`first`	`last`	`mid`	`list[mid]`	Number of Comparisons
1	0	11	5	39	2
2	0	4	2	19	2
3	3	4	3	25	2
4	3	2		the loop stops (because `first > last`)	

This is an unsuccessful search. The total number of comparisons is 6.

Example 18-2 illustrates how to use the binary search algorithm in a program.

Example 18-2

```java
public class TestBinarySearch
{
    public static void main(String[] args)
    {
        Integer[] intList = {2, 16, 34, 45, 53, 56,
                             69, 70, 75, 96};            //Line 1

        SearchSortAlgorithms<Integer> intSearchObject
            = new SearchSortAlgorithms<Integer>();       //Line 2

        int pos;                                         //Line 3

        pos = intSearchObject.binarySearch(intList,
                               intList.length, 45);      //Line 4

        if (pos != -1)                                   //Line 5
            System.out.println("Line 6: " + 45
                              + " found at position "
                              + pos);                    //Line 6
        else                                             //Line 7
            System.out.println("Line 8: " + 45
                              + " is not in intList "); //Line 8
    }
}
```

Sample Run:
```
Line 6: 45 found at position 3
```

The preceding program works as follows. The statement in Line 1 creates the array `intList`. (Note the array `intList` is sorted.) The statement in Line 2 creates the

SearchSortAlgorithms object intSearchObject. The statement in Line 3 declares pos to be an **int** variable. The statement in Line 4 uses the binary search algorithm to determine whether 45 is in intList. Note that the array intList, its lengths, and the search item, which is 45, are passed as parameters to the method binarySearch. The statements in Lines 5 to 8 output the result of the search. Note that this is a successful search.

Performance of Binary Search

Suppose that L is a sorted list of 1000 elements, and you want to determine whether x is in L. Because L is sorted, you can apply the binary search algorithm to search for x. Suppose that L is as shown in Figure 18-5.

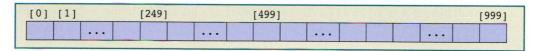

Figure 18-5 List L

The first iteration of the **while** loop searches for x in L[0]...L[999], which is a list of 1000 items. This iteration of the **while** loop compares x with L[499] (see Figure 18-6).

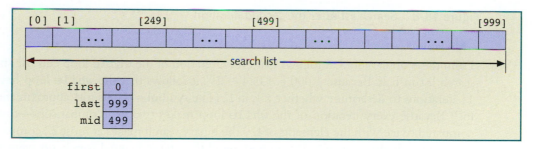

Figure 18-6 Search list

Suppose that x ≠ L[499]. If x < L[499], then the next iteration of the **while** loop looks for x in L[0]...L[498]; otherwise, the **while** loop looks for x in L[500]...L[999]. Suppose that x < L[499]. Then the next iteration of the **while** loop looks for x in L[0]...L[498], which is a list of 499 items, as shown in Figure 18-7.

18

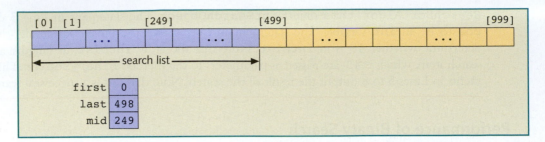

Figure 18-7   Search list after the first iteration

The second iteration of the **while** loop compares **x** with **L[249]**. Once again, suppose that **x** ≠ **L[249]**. Further suppose that **x** > **L[249]**. The next iteration of the **while** loop searches for **x** in **L[250]...L[498]**, which is a list of **249** items, as shown in Figure 18-8.

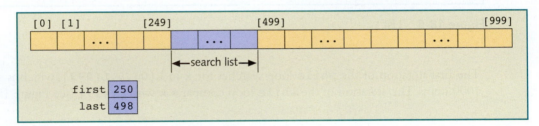

Figure 18-8   Search list after the second iteration

From these observations, it follows that every iteration of the **while** loop cuts the size of the search list in half. Because $1,000 \approx 1,024 = 2^{10}$, it follows that the **while** loop has at most 11 iterations to determine whether **x** is in **L**. (The symbol ≈ stands for "approximately equal to.") Because every iteration of the **while** loop makes two key comparisons—that is, **x** is compared twice with the elements of **L**—the binary search makes at most 22 comparisons to determine whether **x** is in **L**. By contrast, recall that the sequential search, on average, makes 500 comparisons to determine whether **x** is in **L**.

To have a better idea of how fast a binary search is compared to a sequential search, suppose that **L** is of size 1,000,000. Because $1,000,000 \approx 1,048,576 = 2^{20}$, it follows that the **while** loop in a binary search has at most 21 iterations to determine whether an element is in **L**. Every iteration of the **while** loop makes two item (that is, key) comparisons. Therefore, to determine whether an element is in **L**, a binary search makes at most 42 item comparisons. By contrast, the sequential search, on average, makes 500,000 item (key) comparisons to determine whether an element is in **L**.

Note that:

$$40 = 2 * 20 = 2 * \log_2 2^{20} = 2 * \log_2(1048576) \quad 2 * \log_2(1000000)$$

In general, suppose that L is a sorted list of size n. Moreover, suppose that n is a power of 2, that is, $n = 2^m$, for some nonnegative integer m. After each iteration of the **for** loop, about half the elements are left to search, that is, the search sublist for the next iteration is half the size of the current sublist. For example, after the *first* iteration, the search sublist is of the size about $n/2 = 2^{m-1}$. It is easy to see that the maximum number of the iteration of the **for** loop is about $m + 1$. Also $m = \log_2 n$. Each iteration makes two key comparisons. Thus, the maximum number of comparisons to determine whether an element x is in L is $2(m + 1) = 2(\log_2 n + 1) = 2\log_2 n + 2$.

In the case of a successful search, it can be shown that for a list of length n, on average, a binary search makes $2\log_2 n - 3$ key comparisons. In the case of an unsuccessful search, it can be shown that for a list of length n, a binary search makes approximately $2\log_2 n$ key comparisons.

Binary Search Algorithm and the **class** OrderedArrayList

The **class** OrderedArrayList, designed in Chapter 15, does not contain the binary search algorithm. Now that you know how to implement the binary search algorithm, you can learn how to use it in the **class** OrderedArrayList.

To use the binary search algorithm within the **class** OrderedArrayList, we create a SearchSortAlgorithms object and then use the binarySearch algorithm with appropriate parameters, as shown in the following:

```
public class OrderedArrayList<T> extends ArrayListClass<T>
{
    //The definitions of the constructors and other methods is the
    //same as before.
    //We only show how to include the binary search algorithm.
    // .
    // .
    // .

    public int binarySearch(T searchItem)
    {
        SearchSortAlgorithms<T> searchObject
                    = new SearchSortAlgorithms<T>();

        return searchObject.binarySearch(list, length,
                                    searchItem);
    }
}
```

The program in Example 18-3 illustrates how to use the binary search algorithm on objects of the **class** OrderedArrayList.

18

Example 18-3

```java
import java.util.*;

public class Example_18_3
{
    static Scanner console = new Scanner(System.in);

    public static void main(String[] args)
    {
        OrderedArrayList<Integer> intList =
            new OrderedArrayList<Integer>(50);        //Line 1

        Integer num;                                  //Line 2

        System.out.print("Line 3: Enter 8 "
                    + "integers: ");                  //Line 3

        for (int count = 0; count < 8; count++)       //Line 4
        {
            num = console.nextInt();                  //Line 5
            intList.insert(num);                      //Line 6
        }

        System.out.println();                         //Line 7

        System.out.println("Line 8: intList: ");      //Line 8
        intList.print();                              //Line 9

        System.out.print("Line 10: Enter the "
                    + "search item: ");               //Line 10

        num = console.nextInt();                      //Line 11
        System.out.println();                         //Line 12

        int pos;                                      //Line 13

        pos = intList.binarySearch(num);              //Line 14

        if ( pos != -1)                               //Line 15
            System.out.println("Line 16: " + num
                        + " found at position "
                        + pos);                       //Line 16
        else                                          //Line 17
            System.out.println("Line 18: " + num
                        + "is not in "
                        + "intList.");                //Line 18
    }
}
```

Sample Run: In this sample run, the user input is shaded.
```
Line 3: Enter 8 integers: 2 56 34 25 73 46 89 10

Line 8: intList:
2
10
25
34
46
56
73
89

Line 10: Enter the search item: 56

Line 16: 56 found at position 5
```

The preceding program works as follows. The statement in Line 1 creates the `OrderedArrayList` object `intList`. The statement in Line 2 declares num be a variable of type `Integer`. The statement in Line 3 prompts the user to enter 8 integers. The **for** loop in Lines 4 to 6 stores those numbers into `intList`. The statement in Line 8 outputs `intList`. The statement in Line 10 prompts the user to enter the number to be searched. The statement in Line 11 stores that number in the object `num`. The statement in Line 13 declares `pos` to be an **int** variable. The statement in Line 14 uses the binary search algorithm to determine whether `num` is in `intList`. The statements in Lines 15 to 18 output the result of the search. Note that this is a successful search.

ASYMPTOTIC NOTATION: BIG-O NOTATION

Just as a problem is analyzed before writing the algorithm and the computer program, after an algorithm is designed it should also be analyzed. Usually, there are various ways to design a particular algorithm. Certain algorithms take very little computer time to execute, while others take a considerable amount of time. Consider the following examples:

Example 18-4

Consider the following algorithm (assume that all variables are properly declared):

```
System.out.print("Enter the first number: ");      //Line 1
num1 = console.nextInt();                           //Line 2
System.out.println();                               //Line 3

System.out.print("Enter the second number: ");     //Line 4
num2 = console.nextInt();                           //Line 5
System.out.println();                               //Line 6
```

18

```
if   (num1 >= num2)                                    //Line 7
     max = num1;                                       //Line 8
else                                                   //Line 9
     max = num2;                                       //Line 10

System.out.println("The maximum number is: "
                   + max);                             //Line 11
```

Lines 2 and 5 each have 1 operation, =. Line 7 has 1 operation, >=. Either Line 8 or Line 9 executes; each has 1 operation. There is 1 operation, +, in Line 11. Therefore, the total number of operations executed in the preceding code is $1 + 1 + 1 + 1 + 1 = 5$. In this algorithm, the number of operations executed is fixed.

Example 18-5

Consider the following algorithm (assume that all variables are properly declared):

```
System.out.println("Enter positive integers "
                   + "ending with -1");               //Line 1

count = 0;                                             //Line 2
sum = 0;                                               //Line 3

num = console.nextInt();                               //Line 4

while (num != -1)                                      //Line 5
{
    sum = sum + num;                                   //Line 6
    count++;                                           //Line 7
    num = console.nextInt();                           //Line 8
}

System.out.println("The sum of the numbers is: "
                   + sum);                             //Line 9

if (count != 0)                                        //Line 10
    average = sum / count;                             //Line 11
else                                                   //Line 12
    average = 0;                                       //Line 13

System.out.println("The average is: "
                   + average);                         //Line 14
```

This algorithm has 4 operations (Lines 1 through 4) before the **while** loop. Similarly, there are 5 or 6 operations after the **while** loop, depending on whether Line 11 or Line 13 executes.

Line 5 has 1 operation, and 4 operations within the while loop (Lines 6 through 8). Thus, Lines 5 through 8 have 5 operations. If the `while` loop executes 10 times, these 5 operations execute 10 times, plus one extra operation is executed at Line 5 to terminate the loop. Therefore, the number of operations executed is 51 from Lines 5 through 8.

If the `while` loop executes 10 times, the total number of operations executed is:

$10 * 5 + 1 + 4 + 6$ or $10 * 5 + 1 + 4 + 5$

that is,

$10 * 5 + 11$ or $10 * 5 + 10$

We can generalize it to the case when the `while` loop executes n times. If the `while` loop executes n times, the number of operations executed is:

$5n + 11$ or $5n + 10$

In these expressions, for very large values of n, the term $5n$ becomes the dominating term, and the terms 11 and 10 become negligible.

Usually, in an algorithm, certain operations are dominant. For example, in the algorithm in Example 18-5, to add numbers, the dominant operation is in Line 6. Similarly, in a search algorithm, because the search item is compared with the items in the list, the dominant operations would be comparisons, that is, the relational operations. Therefore, in the case of a search algorithm, we count the number of comparisons.

Suppose that an algorithm performs $f(n)$ basic operations to accomplish a task, where n is the size of the problem. Suppose that you want to determine whether an item is in a list and that the size of the list is n. To determine whether the item is in the list, there are various algorithms. However, the basic method is to compare the item with the items in the list. Therefore, the performance of the algorithm depends on the number of comparisons.

Thus, in the case of a search, n is the size of the list and $f(n)$ becomes the count function, that is, $f(n)$ gives the number of comparisons done by the search algorithm. Suppose that, on a particular computer, it takes c units of computer time to execute one operation. Thus, the computer time it would take to execute $f(n)$ operations is $cf(n)$. Clearly, the constant c depends on the speed of the computer, and therefore varies from computer to computer. However, $f(n)$, the number of basic operations, is the same on each computer. If we know how the function $f(n)$ grows as the size of the problem grows, we can determine the efficiency of the algorithm. Consider Table 18-4.

18

Table 18-4   Growth Rate of Various Functions

n	$log_2 n$	$nlog_2 n$	n^2	2^n
1	0	0	1	2
2	1	2	2	4
4	2	8	16	16
8	3	24	64	256
16	4	64	256	65536
32	5	160	1024	4294967296

Table 18-4 shows how certain functions grow as the parameter n (the problem size) grows. Suppose that the problem size is doubled. From Table 18-4, it follows that if the number of basic operations is a function of $f(n) = n^2$; the number of basic operations is quadrupled. If the number of basic operations is a function of $f(n) = 2^n$, then the number of basic operations is squared. However, if the number of operations is a function of $f(n) = log_2 n$, the change in the number of basic operations is insignificant.

Suppose that a computer can execute one billion steps per second. Table 18-5 shows the time that computer takes to execute $f(n)$ steps.

Table 18-5   Time for $f(n)$ Instructions on a Computer that Executes One Billion Instructions Per Second

n	$f(n) = n$	$f(n) = log_2 n$	$f(n) = nlog_2 n$	$f(n) = n^2$	$f(n) = 2^n$
10	0.01µs	0.003µs	0.033µs	0.1µs	1µs
20	0.02µs	0.004µs	0.086µs	0.4µs	1ms
30	0.03µs	0.005µs	0.147µs	0.9µs	1s
40	0.04µs	0.005µs	0.213µs	1.6µs	18.3min
50	0.05µs	0.006µs	0.282µs	2.5µs	13 days
100	0.10µs	0.007µs	0.664µs	10µs	4×10^{13} years
1000	1.00µs	0.010µs	9.966µs	1ms	
10000	10µs	0.013µs	130µs	100ms	
100000	0.10ms	0.017µs	1.67ms	10s	
1000000	1 ms	0.020µs	19.93ms	16.7m	
10000000	0.01s	0.023µs	0.23s	1.16 days	
100000000	0.10s	0.027µs	2.66s	115.7 days	

In Table 18-5, $1µs = 10^{-6}$ seconds and $1ms = 10^{-3}$ seconds.

Figure 18-9 shows the growth rate of functions in Table 18-5.

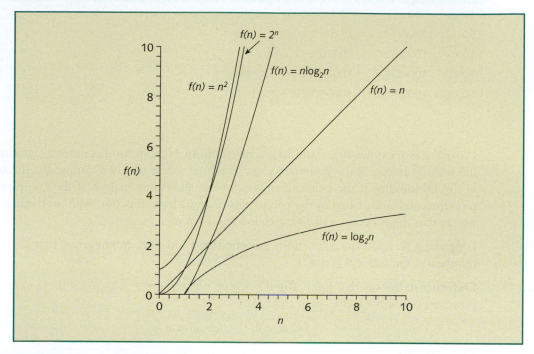

Figure 18-9 Growth rate of various functions

The remainder of this section develops a notation that shows how a function $f(n)$ grows as n increases without bound. That is, we develop a notation that is useful in describing the behavior of the algorithm, which gives us the most useful information about the algorithm. First, we define the term "asymptotic."

Let f be a function of n. By the term **asymptotic** we mean the study of the function f as n becomes larger and larger without bound.

Consider the functions $g(n) = n^2$ and $f(n) = n^2 + 4n + 20$. Clearly, the function g does not contain any linear term, that is, the coefficient of n in g is zero. Consider Table 18-6.

18

Table 18-6 Growth Rate of n^2 and $n^2 + 4n + 20$

n	$g(n) = n^2$	$f(n) = n^2 + 4n + 20$
10	100	160
50	2500	2720
100	10000	10420
1000	1000000	1004020
10000	100000000	100040020

Clearly, as n becomes larger and larger, the term $4n + 20$ in $f(n)$ becomes insignificant, and the term n^2 becomes the dominant term. For large values of n, we can predict the behavior of $f(n)$ by looking at the behavior of $g(n)$. In the algorithm analysis, if the complexity of a function can be described by the complexity of a quadratic function without the linear term, we say that the function is of $O(n^2)$, called Big-O of n^2.

Let f and g be real-valued functions. Assume that f and g are nonnegative, that is, for all real numbers n, $f(n) \geq 0$ and $g(n) \geq 0$.

Definition: We say that $f(n)$ is **Big-O** of $g(n)$, written $f(n) = O(g(n))$, if there exist positive constants c and n_0 such that:

$$f(n) \leq cg(n) \qquad \text{for all } n \geq n_0.$$

Example 18-6

Let $f(n) = a$, where a is a nonnegative real number and $n \geq 0$. Note that f is a constant function. Now:

$$f(n) = a \leq a \cdot 1 \text{ for all } n \geq a.$$

Let $c = a$, $n_0 = a$, and $g(n) = 1$. Then $f(n) \leq cg(n)$ for all $n \geq n_0$. It now follows that $f(n) = O(g(n)) = O(1)$.

From Example 18-6, it follows that if f is a nonnegative constant function, then f is $O(1)$.

Example 18-7

Let $f(n) = 2n + 5$, $n \geq 0$. Note that:

$$f(n) = 2n + 5 \leq 2n + n = 3n \text{ for all } n \geq 5.$$

Let $c = 3$, $n_0 = 5$, and $g(n) = n$. Then $f(n) \leq cg(n)$ for all $n \geq 5$. It now follows that $f(n) = O(g(n)) = O(n)$.

Example 18-8

Let $f(n) = n^2 + 3n + 2$, $g(n) = n^2$, $n \geq 0$. Note that:

$3n + 2 \leq n^2$ for all $n \geq 4$.

This implies that:

$f(n) = n^2 + 3n + 2 \leq n^2 + n^2 \leq 2n^2 = 2g(n)$ for all $n \geq 4$.

Let $c = 2$ and $n_0 = 4$. Then $f(n) \leq cg(n)$ for all $n \geq 4$. It now follows that $f(n) = O(g(n)) = O(n^2)$.

In general, we can prove the following theorem. We state the theorem without proof.

Theorem: Let $f(n)$ be a nonnegative real-valued function such that

$$f(n) = a_m n^m + a_{m-1} n^{m-1} + \cdots + a_1 n + a_0,$$

where a_i's are real numbers, $a_m \neq 0$, $n \geq 0$, and m is a nonnegative integer. Then $f(n) = O(n^m)$.

In Example 18-9, we use the preceding theorem to establish the Big-O of certain functions.

Example 18-9

In the following, $f(n)$ is a nonnegative real-valued function.

Function	Big-O
$f(n) = an + b$, where a and b are real numbers and a is nonzero.	$f(n) = O(n)$
$f(n) = n^2 + 5n + 1$	$f(n) = O(n^2)$
$f(n) = 4n^6 + 3n^3 + 1$	$f(n) = O(n^6)$
$f(n) = 10n^7 + 23$	$f(n) = O(n^7)$
$f(n) = 6n^{15}$	$f(n) = O(n^{15})$

Example 18-10

Suppose that $f(n) = 2\log_2 n + a$, where a is a real number. It can be shown that $f(n) = O(\log_2 n)$.

18

Example 18-11

Consider the following code, where m and n are **int** variables and their values are nonnegative:

```
for (int i = 0; i < m; i++)          //Line 1
    for (int j = 0; j < n; j++)      //Line 2
        System.out.println(i * j);   //Line 3
```

This code contains nested **for** loops. The outer **for** loop, at Line 1, executes m times. For each iteration of the outer loop, the inner loop, at Line 2, executes n times. For each iteration of the inner loop, the output statement in Line 3 executes. It follows that the total number of iterations of the nested **for** loop is mn. So the number of times the statement in Line 3 executes is mn. It follows that this algorithm is $O(mn)$. Note that if $m = n$, then this algorithm is $O(n^2)$.

Table 18-7 shows some common Big-O functions that appear in the algorithm analysis. Let $f(n) = O(g(n))$, where n is the problem size.

Table 18-7 Some Big-O Functions That Appear in Algorithm Analysis

Function $g(n)$	Growth rate of $f(n)$
$g(n) = 1$	The growth rate is constant and so does not depend on n, the size of the problem.
$g(n) = \log_2 n$	The growth rate is a function of $\log_2 n$. Because a logarithm function grows slowly, the growth rate of the function f is also slow.
$g(n) = n$	The growth rate is linear. The growth rate of f is directly proportional to the size of the problem.
$g(n) = n\log_2 n$	The growth rate is faster than the linear algorithm.
$g(n) = n^2$	The growth rate of such functions increases rapidly with the size of the problem. The growth rate is quadrupled when the problem size is doubled.
$g(n) = 2^n$	The growth rate is exponential. The growth rate is squared when the problem size is doubled.

It can be shown that:

$$O(1) \leq O(\log_2 n) \leq O(n) \leq O(n\log_2 n) \leq O(n^2) \leq O(2^n).$$

Using the notations developed in this section, we can conclude that the algorithm in Example 18-4 is of order $O(1)$, and the algorithm in Example 18-5 is of $O(n)$. Table 18-8 summarizes the algorithm analysis of the search algorithms discussed earlier.

Table 18-8 Number of Comparisons for a List of Length n

Algorithm	Successful Search	Unsuccessful Search
Sequential search	$\dfrac{n+1}{2} = \dfrac{1}{2}n + \dfrac{1}{2} = O(n)$	$n = O(n)$
Binary search	$2\log_2 n - 3 = O(\log_2 n)$	$2\log_2 n = O(\log_2 n)$

Lower Bound on Comparison-Based Search Algorithms

Sequential and binary search algorithms search the list by comparing the target element with the list elements. For this reason, these algorithms are called **comparison-based search algorithms**. Earlier sections of this chapter showed that a sequential search is of the order n, and a binary search is of the order $\log_2 n$, where n is the size of the list. The obvious question is: can we devise a search algorithm that has an order less than $\log_2 n$? Before we answer this question, first we obtain the lower bound on the number of comparisons for the comparison-based search algorithms.

Theorem: Let L be a list of size $n > 1$. Suppose that the elements of L are sorted. If $SRH(n)$ denotes the minimum number of comparisons needed, in the worst case, by using a comparison-based algorithm to recognize whether an element x is in L, then $SRH(n) \geq \log_2(n + 1)$.

Corollary: The binary search algorithm is an optimal worst-case algorithm for solving search problems by the comparison method.

From these results, it follows that if we want to design a search algorithm that is of an order less than $\log_2 n$, then it cannot be comparison-based.

SORTING ALGORITHMS

There are several sorting algorithms in the literature. In this chapter, we discuss some of the commonly used sorting algorithms that are listed in the **interface SearchSortADT**. To compare the performance of these algorithms, we also provide some analysis of these algorithms. These sorting algorithms can be applied to either array-based lists or linked lists. We will specify whether the algorithm being developed is for array-based lists or linked lists.

For simplicity and for the ease of understanding, when we draw figures to illustrate a particular algorithm, for array-based lists we show that the data is stored in the array and for linked lists the data is stored in the node. When we write a Java method to implement a particular algorithm, we use the fact that for array-based lists, an array component is a reference to the object storing the data. Similarly, for linked lists, the info of a node is also a reference to the object storing the data.

18

SORTING A LIST: BUBBLE SORT

Many sorting algorithms are available in the literature. This section describes the sorting algorithm called the **bubble sort** to sort a list.

Suppose `list[0...n – 1]` is a list of n elements, indexed 0 to n – 1. We want to rearrange, that is, sort, the elements of `list` in increasing order. The bubble sort algorithm works as follows:

In a series of n – 1 iterations, the successive elements `list[index]` and `list[index + 1]` of the list are compared. If `list[index]` is greater than `list[index + 1]`, then the elements `list[index]` and `list[index + 1]` are swapped.

It follows that the smaller elements move toward the top, and the larger elements move toward the bottom.

In the first iteration, we consider `list[0...n – 1]`. As you will see after the first iteration, the largest element of the list is moved to the last position, which is position n − 1, in the list. In the second iteration, we consider the `list[0...n – 2]`. After the second iteration, the second largest element in the list is moved to the position n − 2, which is second to the last position in the list. In the third iteration, we consider the `list[0...n – 3]`, and so on. As you will see, after each iteration, the size of the unsorted portion of the list shrinks.

Consider the `list[0...4]` of five elements, as shown in Figure 18-10.

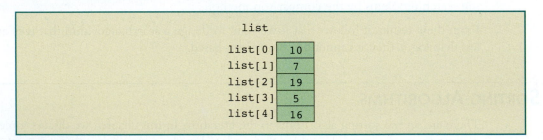

Figure 18-10   List of five elements

Iteration 1: Sort `list[0...4]`. Figure 18-11 shows how the elements of `list` get rearranged in the first iteration.

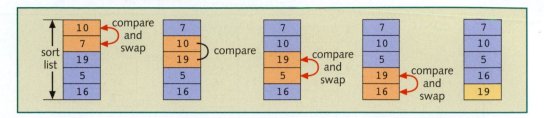

Figure 18-11   Elements of list during the first iteration

Notice that in the first diagram of Figure 18-11, list[0] > list[1]. Therefore, list[0] and list[1] are swapped. In the second diagram, list[1] and list[2] are compared. Because list[1] < list[2], they do not get swapped. The third diagram of Figure 18-11 compares list[2] with list[3]; because list[2] > list[3], list[2] is swapped with list[3]. Then, in the fourth diagram, we compare list[3] with list[4]. Because list[3] > list[4], list[3] and list[4] are swapped.

After the first iteration, the largest element is at the last position. Therefore, in the next iteration, we consider the list[0...3].

Iteration 2: Sort list[0...3]. Figure 18-12 shows how the elements of list get rearranged in the second iteration.

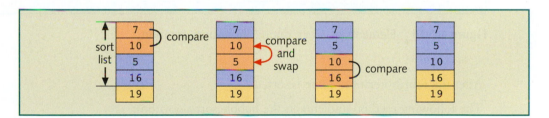

Figure 18-12   Elements of list during the second iteration

The elements are compared and swapped as in the first iteration. Here, only the list elements list[0] through list[3] are considered. After the second iteration, the last two elements are in the right place. Therefore, in the next iteration, we consider list[0...2].

Iteration 3: Sort list[0...2]. Figure 18-13 shows how the elements of list get rearranged in the third iteration.

18

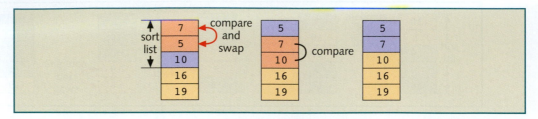

Figure 18-13 Elements of `list` during the third iteration

After the third iteration, the last three elements are in the right place. Therefore, in the next iteration, we consider `list[0...1]`.

Iteration 4: Sort `list[0...1]`. Figure 18-14 shows how the elements of `list` get rearranged in the fourth iteration.

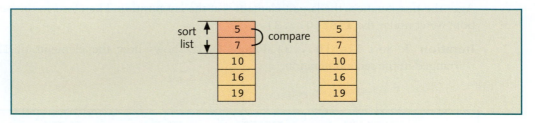

Figure 18-14 Elements of `list` during the fourth iteration

After the fourth iteration, `list` is sorted.

The following method implements the bubble sort algorithm:

```
public void bubbleSort(T list[], int length)
{
    for (int iteration = 1; iteration < length; iteration++)
    {
        for (int index = 0; index < length - iteration;
                            index++)
        {
            Comparable<T> compElem =
                        (Comparable<T>) list[index];

            if (compElem.compareTo(list[index + 1]) > 0)
            {
                T temp = list[index];
                list[index] = list[index + 1];
```

```
                    list[index + 1] = temp;
            }
        }
    }
}//end bubble sort
```

Example 18-12 illustrates how to use the bubble sort algorithm in a program.

Example 18-12 (Bubble Sort)

```
public class TestBubbleSort
{
    public static void main(String[] args)
    {
        Integer[] intList = {2, 56, 34, 25, 73, 46,
                            89, 10, 5, 16};          //Line 1

        SearchSortAlgorithms<Integer> intSortObject
            = new SearchSortAlgorithms<Integer>();   //Line 2

        System.out.println("Line 3: Before "
                        + "sorting, intList:");       //Line 3

        print(intList, intList.length);              //Line 4
        System.out.println();                        //Line 5

        intSortObject.bubbleSort(intList,
                            intList.length);          //Line 6

        System.out.println("Line 7: After "
                        + "sorting, intList: ");      //Line 7

        print(intList, intList.length);              //Line 8
    }

    public static <T> void print(T[] list, int length)
    {
        for (int i = 0; i < length; i++)
            System.out.print(list[i] + " ");

        System.out.println();
    }
}
```

Sample Run:
```
Line 3: Before sorting, intList:
2 56 34 25 73 46 89 10 5 16

Line 7: After sorting, intList:
2 5 10 16 25 34 46 56 73 89
```

18

The statement in Line 1 declares and initializes `intList` to be an array of 10 components of the type `Integer`. The statement in Line 2 creates the `SearchSortAlgorithms` object `intSortObject` to sort arrays of integer values. The statement in Line 4 outputs the values of the array `intList` before sorting this array. The statement in Line 6 uses the method `bubbleSort` to sort `list`. Notice that both `intList` and its length (the number of elements in it, which is `intList.length`) are passed as parameters to the method `bubbleSort`. The statement in Line 8 outputs the sorted `intList`.

Analysis: Bubble Sort

In the case of search algorithms, our only concern was with the number of key (item) comparisons. A sorting algorithm makes key comparisons and also moves the data. Therefore, in analyzing the sorting algorithm, we look at the number of key comparisons as well as the number of data movements.

Suppose a list L of length n is to be sorted using bubble sort. Consider the method `bubbleSort` as given in this chapter. This method contains nested **for** loops. Because L is of length n, the outer loop executes $n - 1$ times. For each iteration of the outer loop, the inner loop executes a certain number of times. Let us consider the first iteration of the outer loop. During the first iteration of the outer loop, the number of iterations of the inner loop is $n - 1$. So there are $n - 1$ comparisons. Similarly, during the second iteration of the outer loop, the number of iterations of the inner loop is $n - 2$, and so on. Thus, the total number of comparisons is:

$$(n-1)+(n-2)+\cdots+2+1=\frac{n(n-1)}{2}=\frac{1}{2}n^2-\frac{1}{2}n=O(n^2).$$

In the worst case, the body of the **if** statement always executes. So in the worst case, the number of assignments is:

$$3\frac{n(n-1)}{2}=\frac{3}{2}n^2-\frac{3}{2}n=O(n^2).$$

If the list is already sorted, which is the best case, the number of assignments is 0. It can be shown that on average, bubble sort makes about:

$$\frac{n(n-1)}{4}$$

item assignments. However, the number of comparisons for the bubble sort, as given in this chapter, is always:

$$\frac{n(n-1)}{4}.$$

Therefore, to sort a list of size 1000, bubble sort makes about 500,000 key comparisons and about 250,000 item assignments. The next section presents the selection sort algorithm that reduces the number of item assignments.

 Exercise 5 at the end of this chapter gives a version of the bubble sort algorithm, in which the number of comparisons in the best case is $O(n)$.

SELECTION SORT: ARRAY-BASED LISTS

The selection sort algorithm sorts a list by selecting the smallest element in the (unsorted portion of the) list, and then moving this smallest element to the top of the (unsorted) list. The first time we locate the smallest item in the entire list; the second time we locate the smallest item in the list starting from the second element in the list, and so on. The selection sort algorithm described here is designed for array-based lists.

For example, suppose that you have the list as shown in Figure 18-15.

	[0]	[1]	[2]	[3]	[4]	[5]	[6]	[7]	[8]	[9]
list	16	30	24	7	25	62	45	5	65	50

Figure 18-15   List of 10 elements

Initially, the entire list is unsorted. So we find the smallest item in the list, which is at position 7, as shown in Figure 18-16.

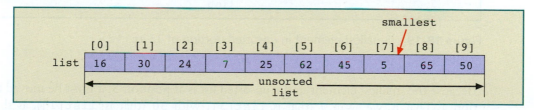

Figure 18-16   Smallest element of the unsorted list

Because this is the smallest item, it must be moved to position 0. We therefore swap 16 (that is, list[0]) with 5 (that is, list[7]), as shown in Figure 18-17.

18

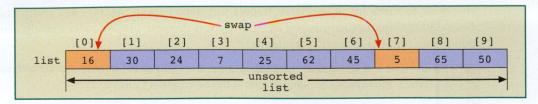

Figure 18-17   Swap elements `list[0]` and `list[7]`

Figure 18–18 shows the list after swapping these elements.

Figure 18-18   List after swapping `list[0]` and `list[7]`

Now the unsorted list is `list[1]...list[9]`. Next, we find the smallest element in the unsorted portion of the list. The smallest element is at position 3, as shown in Figure 18-19.

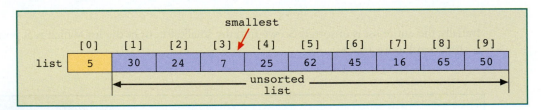

Figure 18-19   Smallest element in unsorted portion of `list`

Because the smallest element in the unsorted list is at position 3, it must be moved to position 1. That is, we swap 7 (that is, `list[3]`) with 30 (that is, `list[1]`), as shown in Figure 18-20.

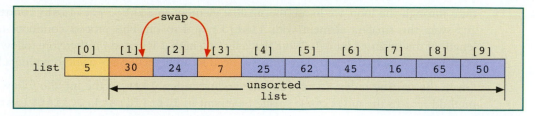

Figure 18-20   Swap `list[1]` with `list[3]`

After swapping `list[1]` with `list[3]`, Figure 18-21 shows the resulting list.

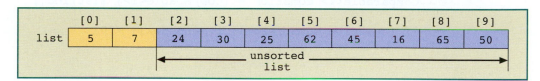

Figure 18-21   `list` after swapping `list[1]` with `list[3]`

Now the unsorted list is `list[2]...list[9]`. We repeat this process of finding the position of the smallest element in the unsorted portion of the list and moving it to the beginning of the unsorted portion of the list. The selection sort algorithm thus involves the following steps in the unsorted portion of the list:

a. Find the location of the smallest element.

b. Move the smallest element to the beginning of the unsorted list.

Initially, the entire list, `list[0]...list[length – 1]`, is the unsorted list. After executing Steps a and b once, the unsorted list is `list[1]...list[length – 1]`. After executing Steps a and b a second time, the unsorted list is `list[2]...list[length – 1]`, and so on. We can keep track of the unsorted portion of the list and repeat Steps a and b with the help of a **for** loop as follows:

```
for (int index = 0; index < length - 1; index++)
{
    a. Find the location, smallestIndex, of the smallest element in
       list[index]...list[length - 1].
    b. Swap the smallest element with list[index]. That is, swap
       list[smallestIndex] with list[index].
}
```

The first time through the loop, we locate the smallest element in `list[0]...list[length – 1]` and swap this smallest element with `list[0]`. The second

18

time through the loop, we locate the smallest element in `list[1]...list[length - 1]` and swap this smallest element with `list[1]`, and so on. This process continues until the length of the unsorted list is 1. (Note that a list of length 1 is sorted.) It therefore follows that to implement the selection sort algorithm, we need to implement Steps a and b within a loop.

Given the starting index, `first`, and the ending index, `last`, of the list, the following Java method returns the index of the smallest element in `list[first]...list[last]`:

```
private int minLocation(T[] list, int first, int last)
{
    int minIndex = first;

    for (int loc = first + 1; loc <= last; loc++)
    {
        Comparable<T> compElem = (Comparable<T>) list[loc];

        if (compElem.compareTo(list[minIndex]) < 0)
            minIndex = loc;
    }

    return minIndex;
}//end minLocation
```

Given the locations in the list of the elements to be swapped, the following Java method, `swap`, swaps those elements:

```
private void swap(T[] list, int first, int second)
{
    T temp;

    temp = list[first];
    list[first] = list[second];
    list[second] = temp;
}//end swap
```

We can now complete the definition of the method `selectionSort`:

```
public void selectionSort(T[] list, int length)
{
    for (int index = 0; index < length - 1; index++)
    {
        int minIndex = minLocation(list, index, length - 1);

        swap(list, index, minIndex);
    }
}//end selectionSort
```

The definition of the **class** SearchSortAlgorithms to implement the selection sort algorithm is as follows:

```
public class SearchSortAlgorithms<T> implements SearchSortADT<T>
{
    //Place the definitions of the methods seqSearch and
    //binarySearch here.

    //Place the definition of the method selectionSort as
    //described above here.
    //Place the definition of the method swap as described
    //above here.
    //Place the definition of the method minLocation as
    //described above here.

}
```

We leave it as an exercise for you to write a program to test the selection sort algorithm. (See Programming Exercise 6 at the end of this chapter.)

1. A selection sort can also be implemented by selecting the largest element in the unsorted portion of the list and moving it to the bottom of the list. You can easily implement this form of selection sort by altering the **if** statement in the method minLocation and passing the appropriate parameters to the corresponding method and to the method swap (when these methods are called in the method selectionSort).

2. A selection sort can also be applied to linked lists. The general algorithm is the same, and the details are left as an exercise for you. See Programming Exercise 7 at the end of this chapter.

Analysis: Selection Sort

Suppose that the length of the list is n. The method **swap** does three item assignments and is executed $n - 1$ times. Hence, the number of item assignments is $3(n - 1) = O(n)$.

The key comparisons are made by the method **minLocation**. For a list of length k, the method **minLocation** makes $k - 1$ key comparisons. Also, the method **minLocation** is executed $n - 1$ times (by the method **selectionSort**). The first time, the method **minLocation** finds the index of the smallest key item in the entire list and therefore makes $n - 1$ comparisons. The second time, the method **minLocation** finds the index of the

18

smallest element in the sublist of length $n - 1$ and so makes $n - 2$ comparisons, and so on. Hence the number of key comparisons is as follows:

$$
\begin{aligned}
(n-1)+(n-2)+\ldots+2+1 &= \frac{n(n-1)}{2} \\
&= \frac{1}{2}n^2 - \frac{1}{2}n \\
&= \frac{1}{2}n^2 + O(n) \\
&= O(n^2).
\end{aligned}
$$

It thus follows that if $n = 1000$, the number of key comparisons the selection sort algorithm makes is:

$$
\frac{1}{2}(1000)^2 - \frac{1}{2}(1000) = 499500 \approx 500000.
$$

Note that the selection sort algorithm does not depend on the initial arrangement of the data. The number of comparisons is always $O(n^2)$ and the number of assignments is $O(n)$. In general, this algorithm is good only for small size lists because $O(n^2)$ grows rapidly as n grows. However, if data movement is expensive and the number of comparisons is not, then this algorithm could be a better choice over other algorithms.

INSERTION SORT: ARRAY-BASED LISTS

The previous section described and analyzed the selection sort algorithm. It was shown that if $n = 1000$, the number of key comparisons is approximately 500,000, which is quite high. This section describes the sorting algorithm called the **insertion sort**, which tries to improve—that is, reduce—the number of key comparisons.

The insertion sort algorithm sorts the list by moving each element to its proper place in the sorted portion of the list. Consider the list given in Figure 18-22.

	[0]	[1]	[2]	[3]	[4]	[5]	[6]	[7]
list	10	18	25	30	23	17	45	35

Figure 18-22 `list`

The length of the list is 8. In this list, the elements `list[0]`, `list[1]`, `list[2]`, and `list[3]` are in order. That is, `list[0]...list[3]` is sorted (see Figure 18-23).

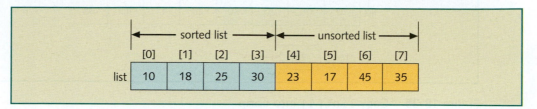

Figure 18-23   Sorted and unsorted portion of `list`

Next, we consider the element `list[4]`, the first element of the unsorted list. Because `list[4] < list[3]`, we need to move `list[4]` to its proper location. It thus follows that `list[4]` should be moved to `list[2]` (see Figure 18-24).

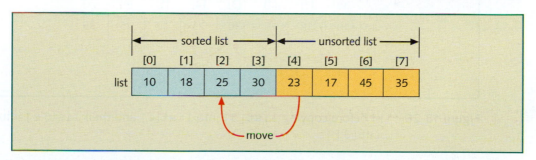

Figure 18-24   Move `list[4]` into `list[2]`

To move `list[4]` into `list[2]`, first we copy `list[4]` into `temp`, a temporary memory space (see Figure 18-25).

18

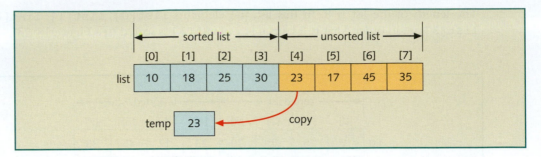

Figure 18-25 Copy `list[4]` into `temp`

Next, we copy `list[3]` into `list[4]`, and then `list[2]` into `list[3]` (see Figure 18-26).

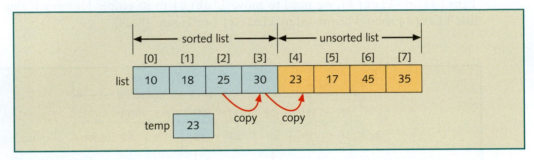

Figure 18-26 List before copying `list[3]` into `list[4]` and then `list[2]` into `list[3]`

After copying `list[3]` into `list[4]` and `list[2]` into `list[3]`, the list is as shown in Figure 18-27.

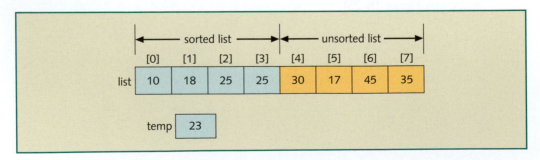

Figure 18-27 List after copying `list[3]` into `list[4]` and then `list[2]` into `list[3]`

We now copy temp into list[2]. Figure 18-28 shows the resulting list.

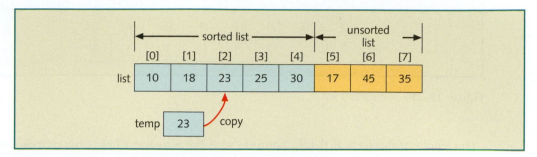

Figure 18-28   List after copying temp into list[2]

Now list[0]...list[4] is sorted and list[5]...list[7] is unsorted. We repeat this process on the resulting list by moving the first element of the unsorted list into the sorted list in the proper place.

From this discussion, we see that during the sorting phase the array containing the list is divided into two sublists, *sorted* and *unsorted*. Elements in the sorted sublist are in order; elements in the unsorted sublist are to be moved one at a time to their proper places in the sorted sublist. We use an index—say, firstOutOfOrder—to point to the first element in the unsorted sublist; that is, firstOutOfOrder gives the index of the first element in the unsorted portion of the array. Initially, firstOutOfOrder is initialized to 1.

This discussion translates into the following pseudo-code algorithm:

```
for (firstOutOfOrder = 1; firstOutOfOrder < length; firstOutOfOrder++)
  if (list[firstOutOfOrder] is less than list[firstOutOfOrder - 1])
  {
      copy list[firstOutOfOrder] into temp

      initialize location to firstOutOfOrder

      do
      {
         a. copy list[location - 1] into list[location]
         b. decrement location by 1 to consider the next element
            of the sorted portion of the array
      }
      while (location > 0 && the list element at location - 1 is
                            greater than temp)
  }
copy temp into list[location]
```

18

Let us trace the execution of this algorithm on the list given in Figure 18-29.

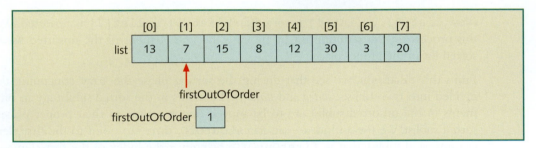

Figure 18-29 Unsorted list

The length of this list is 8; that is, `length` = 8. We initialize `firstOutOfOrder` to 1 (see Figure 18-30).

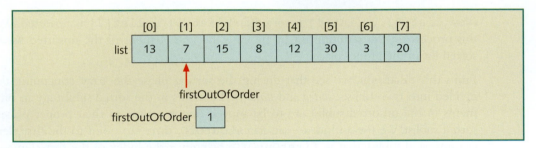

Figure 18-30 `firstOutOfOrder = 1`

Because `list[firstOutOfOrder]` = 7, `list[firstOutOfOrder - 1]` = 13, and 7 < 13, the expression in the `if` statement evaluates to **true**. So we execute the body of the `if` statement:

```
temp = list[firstOutOfOrder] = 7
location = firstOutOfOrder = 1
```

Next, we execute the **do...while** loop:

```
list[1] = list[0] = 13      (copy list[0] into list[1])
location = 0                (decrement location)
```

The **do...while** loop terminates because `location` is 0. We copy `temp` into `list[location]`—that is, into `list[0]`.

Figure 18-31 shows the resulting list.

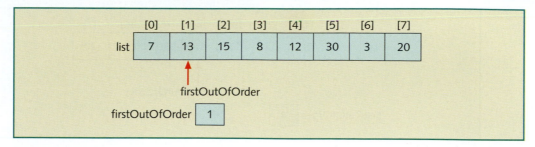

Figure 18-31   List after the first iteration of the insertion sort algorithm

Now suppose that we have the list given in Figure 18–32.

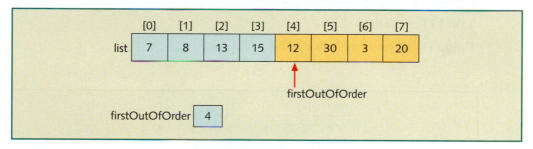

Figure 18-32   First out-of-order element is at position 4

Here `list[0]...list[3]`, that is, the elements `list[0]`, `list[1]`, `list[2]`, and `list[3]`, are in order. Now `firstOutOfOrder` = 4. Because `list[4]` < `list[3]`, the element `list[4]`, which is 12, needs to be moved to its proper location.

As before,

```
temp = list[firstOutOfOrder] = 12
location = firstOutOfOrder = 4
```

First, we copy `list[3]` into `list[4]` and decrement `location` by 1. Then we copy `list[2]` into `list[3]` and again decrement `location` by 1. Now the value of `location` is 2. At this point, the list is as shown in Figure 18-33.

18

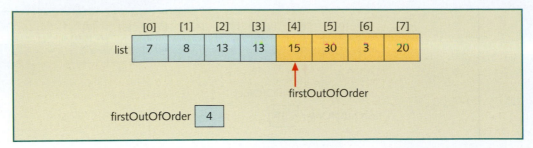

Figure 18-33   List after copying `list[3]` into `list[4]` and then `list[2]` into `list[3]`

Because `list[1] < temp`, the **do ...while** loop terminates. At this point `location` is 2, so we copy `temp` into `list[2]`. That is:

`list[2] = temp = 12`

Figure 18–34 shows the resulting list.

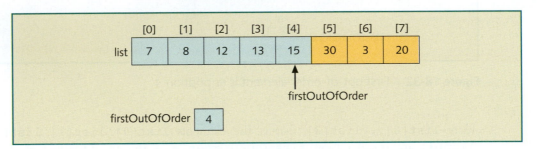

Figure 18-34   List after copying `temp` into `list[2]`

Next suppose that we have the list given in Figure 18–35.

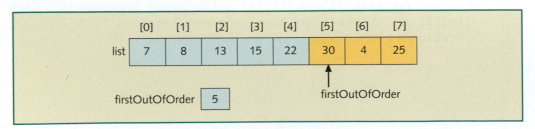

Figure 18-35   First out-of-order element is at position 5

Here `list[0]`...`list[4]`, or the elements `list[0]`, `list[1]`, `list[2]`, and `list[4]`, are in order. Now `firstOutOfOrder = 5`. Because `list[5] > list[4]`, the `if` statement evaluates to `false`. So the body of the `if` statement does not execute and the next iteration of the `for` loop, if any, takes place. Note that this is case when the `firstOutOfOrder` element is already at the proper place. So we simply we need to advance `firstOutOfOrder` to the next array element, if any.

We can repeat this process for the remaining elements of `list` to sort `list`.

The following Java method implements the previous algorithm:

```java
public void insertionSort(T[] list, int length)
{
    for (int firstOutOfOrder = 1; firstOutOfOrder < length;
                              firstOutOfOrder ++)
    {
        Comparable<T> compElem =
                (Comparable<T>) list[firstOutOfOrder];

        if (compElem.compareTo(list[firstOutOfOrder - 1]) < 0)
        {
            Comparable<T> temp =
                    (Comparable<T>) list[firstOutOfOrder];

            int location = firstOutOfOrder;

            do
            {
                list[location] = list[location - 1];
                location--;
            }
            while (location > 0 &&
                    temp.compareTo(list[location - 1]) < 0);

            list[location] = (T) temp;
        }
    }
}//end insertionSort
```

We leave it as an exercise for you to write a program to test the insertion sort algorithm. (See Programming Exercise 8 at the end of this chapter.)

 An insertion sort can also be applied to linked lists. The general algorithm is the same, and the details are left as an exercise for you. See Programming Exercise 9 at the end of this chapter.

Analysis: Insertion Sort

Let L be a list of length n. Suppose L is to be sorted using insertion sort. The **for** loop executes $n - 1$ times. In the best case, when the list is already sorted, for each iteration of the **for** loop the **if** statement evaluates to **false**, so there are $n - 1$ key comparisons. Thus, in the best case, the number of key comparisons is $n - 1 = O(n)$. Let us consider the worst case. In this case, for each iteration of the **for** loop, the **if** statement evaluates to **true**. Moreover, in the worst case, for each iteration of the **for** loop, the **do...while** loop executes **firstOutOfOrder - 1** times. It follows that in the worst case, the number of key comparisons is:

$$1 + 2 + \ldots + (n - 1) = n(n - 1) / 2 = O(n^2).$$

It can be shown that the average number of key comparisons and the average number of item assignments in an insertion sort algorithm are:

$$\frac{1}{4}n^2 + O(n) = O(n^2)$$

Table 18-9 summarizes the behavior of the bubble sort, selection sort, and insertion sort algorithms.

Table 18-9 Average Case Behavior of the Bubble Sort, Selection Sort, and Insertion Sort Algorithms for a List of Length n

Algorithm	Number of Comparisons	Number of Swaps
Bubble sort	$\dfrac{n(n-1)}{2} = O(n^2)$	$\dfrac{n(n-1)}{4} = O(n^2)$
Selection sort	$\dfrac{n(n-1)}{2} = O(n^2)$	$3(n-1) = O(n)$
Insertion sort	$\dfrac{1}{4}n^2 + O(n) = O(n^2)$	$\dfrac{1}{4}n^2 + O(n) = O(n^2)$

LOWER BOUND ON COMPARISON-BASED SORT ALGORITHMS

In the previous sections, we discussed the selection and insertion sort algorithms, and noted that the average-case behavior of these algorithms is $O(n^2)$. Both of these algorithms are comparison-based algorithms; that is, the lists are sorted by comparing their respective keys. Before discussing any additional sorting algorithms, let us discuss the best-case scenario for the comparison-based sorting algorithms.

We can trace the execution of a comparison-based algorithm by using a graph called a **comparison tree**. Let L be a list of n distinct elements, where $n > 0$. For any j and k, where

$1 \leq j \leq n$, $1 \leq k \leq n$, either $L[j] < L[k]$ or $L[j] > L[k]$. Because each comparison of the keys has two outcomes, the comparison tree is a **binary tree**. While drawing this figure, we draw each comparison as a circle, called a **node**. The node is labeled as $j{:}k$, representing the comparison of $L[j]$ with $L[k]$. If $L[j] < L[k]$, follow the left branch; otherwise, follow the right branch. Figure 18-36 shows the comparison tree for a list of length 3. (In Figure 18-36, the rectangle, called a **leaf**, represents the final ordering of the nodes.)

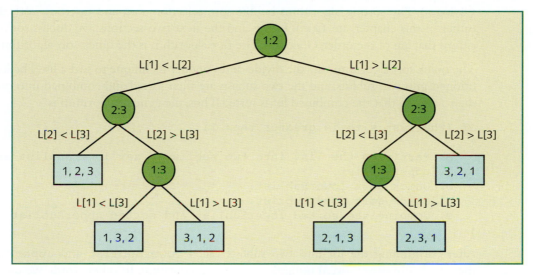

Figure 18-36   Comparison tree for sorting three items

We call the top node in the figure the **root** node. The straight line that connects the two nodes is called a **branch**. A sequence of branches from a node, x, to another node, y, is called a **path** from x to y.

Associated with each path from the root to a leaf is a unique permutation of the elements of L. This uniqueness follows because the sort algorithm only moves the data and makes comparisons. Furthermore, the data movement on any path from the root to a leaf is the same regardless of the initial inputs. For a list of n elements, $n > 0$, there are $n!$ different permutations. Any one of these $n!$ permutations might be the correct ordering of L. Thus, the comparison tree must have at least $n!$ leaves.

Let us consider the worst case for all comparison-based sorting algorithms. We state the following result without proof.

Theorem: Let L be a list of n distinct elements. Any sorting algorithm that sorts L by comparison of the keys only, in its worst case, makes at least $O(n\log_2 n)$ key comparisons.

18

As analyzed in the previous sections, both the selection and insertion sort algorithms are of the order $O(n^2)$. The remainder of this chapter discusses sorting algorithms that, on average, are of the order $O(n\log_2 n)$.

QUICK SORT: ARRAY-BASED LISTS

In the previous section, we noted that the lower bound on comparison-based algorithms is $O(n\log_2 n)$. The sorting algorithms bubble sort, selection sort, and insertion sort, discussed earlier in this chapter, are $O(n^2)$. In this and the next two sections, we discuss sorting algorithms that are of the order $O(n\log_2 n)$. The first algorithm is the quick sort algorithm.

The quick sort algorithm uses the divide-and-conquer technique to sort a list. The list is partitioned into two sublists, and the two sublists are then sorted and combined into one list in such a way so that the combined list is sorted. Thus, the general algorithm is:

```
if (the list size is greater than 1)
{
    a. Partition the list into two sublists, say lowerSublist and
       upperSublist.
    b. Quick sort lowerSublist.
    c. Quick sort upperSublist.
    d. Combine the sorted lowerSublist and sorted upperSublist.
}
```

After partitioning the list into two sublists called `lowerSublist` and `upperSublist`, these two sublists are sorted using the quick sort algorithm. In other words, we use *recursion* to implement the quick sort algorithm.

The quick sort algorithm described here is for array-based lists. The algorithm for linked lists can be developed in a similar manner and is left as an exercise for you.

In the quick sort algorithm, the list is partitioned in such way that combining the sorted `lowerSublist` and `upperSublist` is trivial. Therefore, in a quick sort, all the sorting work is done in partitioning the list. Because all the sorting work occurs during the partitioning of the list, we first describe the partition procedure in detail.

To partition the list into two sublists, first we choose an element of the list called **pivot**. The **pivot** is used to divide the list into two sublists: `lowerSublist` and `upperSublist`. The elements in `lowerSublist` are smaller than **pivot**, and the elements in `upperSublist` are greater than or equal to **pivot**. For example, consider the list in Figure 18-37.

	[0]	[1]	[2]	[3]	[4]	[5]	[6]	[7]	[8]
list	45	82	25	94	50	60	78	32	92

Figure 18-37 `list` before the partition

There are several ways to determine `pivot`. However, `pivot` is chosen so that, it is hoped, `lowerSublist` and `upperSublist` are of nearly equal size. For illustration purposes, let us choose the middle element of the list as `pivot`. The partition procedure that we describe partitions this list using `pivot` as the middle element, in our case 50, as shown in Figure 18-38.

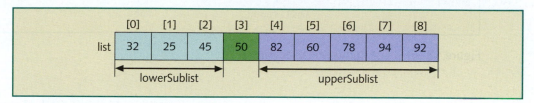

Figure 18-38 `list` after the partition

From Figure 18-38, it follows that after partitioning `list` into `lowerSublist` and `upperSublist`, pivot is in the right place. Thus, after sorting `lowerSublist` and `upperSublist`, combining the two sorted sublists is trivial.

The partition algorithm is as follows (we assume that `pivot` is chosen as the middle element of the list):

1. Determine `pivot`, and swap `pivot` with the first element of the list.

Suppose that the index `smallIndex` points to the last element less than `pivot`. The index `smallIndex` is initialized to the first element of the list.

2. For the remaining elements in the list (starting at the second element):

   If the current element is less than pivot

   a. Increment `smallIndex`.

   b. Swap the current element with the array element to which `smallIndex` points.

3. Swap the first element, that is, `pivot`, with the array element to which `smallIndex` points.

Step 2 can be implemented using a **for** loop, with the loop starting at the second element of the list.

Step 1 determines the pivot and moves `pivot` to the first array position. During the execution of Step 2, the list elements get arranged as shown in Figure 18-39. (Suppose the name of the array containing the list elements is list.)

18

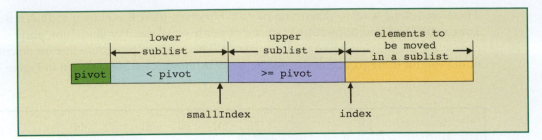

Figure 18-39 List during the execution of Step 2

As shown in Figure 18-39, `pivot` is in the first array position. Elements in the lower sublist are less than `pivot`; elements in the upper sublist are greater than or equal to `pivot`. The variable `smallIndex` contains the index of the last element of the lower sublist; the variable `index` contains the index of the next element that needs to be moved either in the lower sublist or in the upper sublist. As explained in Step 2, if the next element of the list (that is, `list[index]`) is less than `pivot`, we advance `smallIndex` to the next array position and swap `list[index]` with `list[smallIndex]`. Next we illustrate Step 2.

Suppose that the list is as given in Figure 18-40.

[0]	[1]	[2]	[3]	[4]	[5]	[6]	[7]	[8]	[9]	[10]	[11]	[12]	[13]
32	55	87	13	78	96	52	48	22	11	58	66	88	45

Figure 18-40 List before sorting

Step 1 requires us to determine the `pivot` and swap it with the first array element. For the list in Figure 18-40, the middle element is at the position `(0 + 13) / 2 = 6`. That is, `pivot` is at position 6. Therefore, after swapping `pivot` with the first array element, the list is as shown in Figure 18-41. (Notice that in Figure 18-41, 52 is swapped with 32.)

[0]	[1]	[2]	[3]	[4]	[5]	[6]	[7]	[8]	[9]	[10]	[11]	[12]	[13]
52	55	87	13	78	96	32	48	22	11	58	66	88	45

pivot

Figure 18-41 List after moving `pivot` to the first array position

Suppose that after executing Step 2 a few times, the list is as shown in Figure 18-42.

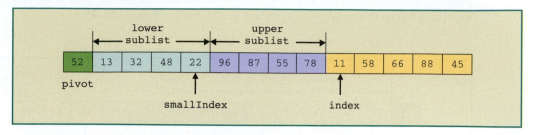

Figure 18-42   List after a few iterations of Step 2

As shown in Figure 18-42, the next element of the list that needs to be moved into a sublist is indicated by `index`. Because `list[index] < pivot`, we need to move the element `list[index]` into the lower sublist. To do so, we first advance `smallIndex` to the next array position and then swap `list[smallIndex]` with `list[index]`. The resulting list is as shown in Figure 18-43. (Notice that **11** is swapped with **96**.)

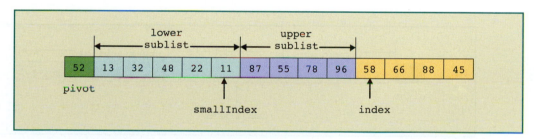

Figure 18-43   List after moving 11 into the lower sublist

Now consider the list in Figure 18-44.

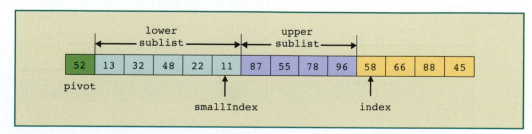

Figure 18-44   List before moving 58 into a sublist

18

For the list in Figure 18-44, `list[index]` is `58`, which is greater than `pivot`. Therefore, `list[index]` is to be moved in the upper sublist. This is accomplished by leaving `58` at its position and increasing the size of the upper sublist by one, to the next array position. After moving `58` into the upper sublist, the list is as shown in Figure 18-45.

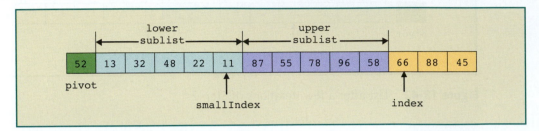

Figure 18-45 List after moving `58` into the upper sublist

After moving the elements that are less than pivot into the lower sublist and elements that are greater than pivot into the upper sublist (that is, after completely executing Step 2), Figure 18-46 shows the resulting list.

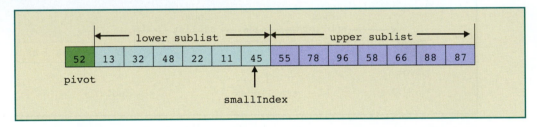

Figure 18-46 List elements after arranging elements into the lower sublist and upper sublist

Next we execute Step 3 and move `52`, `pivot`, to the proper position in the list. This is accomplished by swapping `52` with `45`. The resulting list is as shown in Figure 18-47.

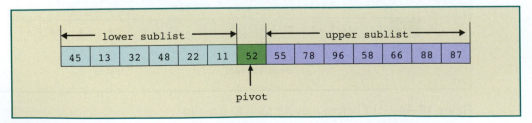

Figure 18-47 List after swapping `52` with `45`

As shown in Figure 18-47, Steps 1, 2, and 3 in the preceding algorithm partition the list into two sublists. The elements less than pivot are in the lower sublist; the elements greater than or equal to `pivot` are in the upper sublist.

To partition the list into the lower and upper sublists, we need to keep track of only the last element of the lower sublist and the next element of the list that needs to be moved into either the lower sublist or the upper sublist. In fact, the upper sublist is between the two indices `smallIndex` and `index`.

We now write the method, `partition`, to implement the preceding partition algorithm. After rearranging the elements of the list, the method `partition` returns the location of `pivot` so that we can determine the starting and ending locations of the sublists. The definition of the method `partition` is:

```
private int partition(T[] list, int first, int last)
{
    T pivot;

    int smallIndex;

    swap(list, first, (first + last) / 2);

    pivot = list[first];
    smallIndex = first;

    for (int index = first + 1; index <= last; index++)
    {
        Comparable<T> compElem = (Comparable<T>) list[index];

        if (compElem.compareTo(pivot) < 0)
        {
            smallIndex++;
            swap(list, smallIndex, index);
        }
    }

    swap(list, first, smallIndex);

    return smallIndex;
}//end partition
```

Note that the formal parameters `first` and `last` specify the starting and ending indices, respectively, of the sublist of the `list` to be partitioned. If `first = 0` and `last = list.length - 1`, the entire list is partitioned.

As you can see from the definition of the method `partition`, certain elements of the list need to be swapped. The following method, `swap`, accomplishes this task. (Notice that this `swap` method is the same as the one given earlier in this chapter for the selection sort algorithm.)

18

```
private void swap(T[] list, int first, int second)
{
    T temp;

    temp = list[first];
    list[first] = list[second];
    list[second] = temp;
}//end swap
```

Once the list is partitioned into `lowerSublist` and `upperSublist`, we again apply the quick sort method to sort the two sublists. Because both sublists are sorted using the same quick sort algorithm, the easiest way to implement this algorithm is to use recursion. Therefore, this section gives the recursive version of the quick sort algorithm. As explained previously, after rearranging the elements of the list, the method `partition` returns the index of `pivot` so that the starting and ending indices of the sublists can be determined.

Given the starting and ending indices of a list, the following method, `recQuickSort`, implements the recursive version of the quick sort algorithm:

```
private void recQuickSort(T[] list, int first, int last)
{
    if (first < last)
    {
        int pivotLocation = partition(list, first, last);
        recQuickSort(list, first, pivotLocation - 1);
        recQuickSort(list, pivotLocation + 1, last);
    }
}//end recQuickSort
```

Finally, we write the quick sort method, `quickSort`, that calls the method `recQuickSort` on the original list.

```
public void quickSort(T[] list, int length)
{
    recQuickSort(list, 0, length - 1);
}//end quickSort
```

We leave it as an exercise for you to write a program to test the quick sort algorithm. See Programming Exercise 10 at the end of this chapter.

Analysis: Quick Sort

The general analysis of the quick sort algorithm is beyond the scope of this book. However, let us determine the number of comparisons in the worst case. Suppose that L is a list of n elements, and n 0. In quick sort, all the sorting work is done by the method `partition`. From the definition of the method `partition`, it follows that to partition a list of length k, the method `partition` makes $k - 1$ key comparisons. Also, in the worst case, after partition one of the sublist is of length $k - 1$ and the other sublist is of length 0.

It follows that in the worst case, the first call of the method `partition` makes $n - 1$ key comparisons. In the second call, the method `partition` partitions a list of length $n - 1$, so it makes $n - 2$ key comparisons, and so on. We can now conclude that to sort a list of length n, in the worst case, the total number of key comparisons made by quick sort is:

$(n - 1) + (n - 2) + ... + 2 + 1 = n(n - 1) / 2 = O(n^2)$.

Table 18-10 summarizes the behavior of the quick sort algorithm for a list of length n.

Table 18-10 Analysis of the Quick Sort Algorithm for a List of Length n

	Number of Comparisons	Number of Swaps
Average case	$(1.39)n\log_2 n + O(n) = O(n\log_2 n)$	$(0.69)n\log_2 n + O(n) = O(n\log_2 n)$
Worst case	$\dfrac{n^2}{2} - \dfrac{n}{2} = O(n^2)$	$\dfrac{n^2}{2} + \dfrac{3n}{2} - 2 = O(n^2)$

MERGE SORT: LINKED LIST-BASED LISTS

In the previous section, we described the quick sort algorithm and stated that the average-case behavior of a quick sort is $O(n\log_2 n)$. However, the worst-case behavior of a quick sort is $O(n^2)$. This section describes the sorting algorithm whose behavior is always $O(n\log_2 n)$.

Like the quick sort algorithm, the merge sort algorithm uses the divide-and-conquer technique to sort a list. A merge sort algorithm also partitions the list into two sublists, sorts the sublists, and then combines the sorted sublists into one sorted list. This section describes the merge sort algorithm for linked list-based lists. We leave it for you to develop the merge sort algorithm for array-based lists, which can be done by using the techniques described for linked lists.

The merge sort and the quick sort algorithms differ in how they partition the list. As discussed earlier, a quick sort first selects an element in the list, called `pivot`, and then partitions the list so that the elements in one sublist are less than `pivot` and the elements in the other sublist are greater than or equal to `pivot`. By contrast, a merge sort divides the list into two sublists of nearly equal size. For example, consider the list whose elements are as follows:

```
list: 35 28 18 45 62 48 30 38
```

The merge sort algorithm partitions this list into two sublists as follows:

```
first sublist: 35 28 18 45
second sublist: 62 48 30 38
```

The two sublists are sorted using the same algorithm (that is, a merge sort) used on the original list. Suppose that we have sorted the two sublists. That is, suppose that the lists are now as follows:

```
first sublist: 18 28 35 45
second sublist: 30 38 48 62
```

18

Next, the merge sort algorithm combines, that is, merges, the two sorted sublists into one sorted list.

Figure 18-48 further illustrates the merge sort process.

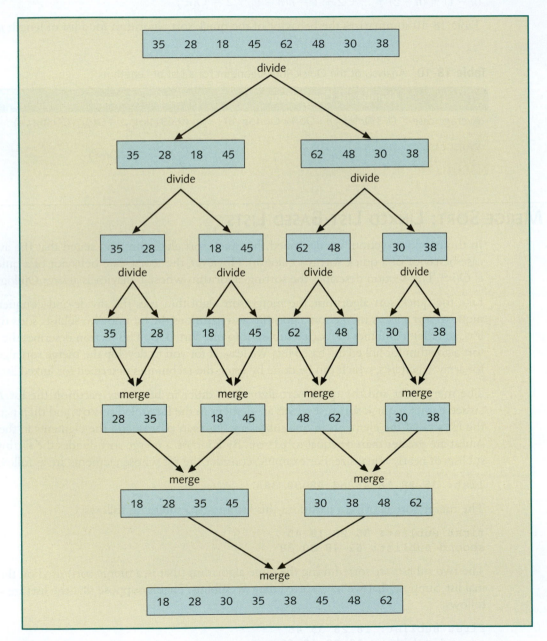

Figure 18-48   Merge sort algorithm

From Figure 18-48, it is clear that in the merge sort algorithm, most of the sorting work is done in merging the sorted sublists.

The general algorithm for the merge sort is as follows:

```
if the list is of size greater than 1
{
    a. Divide the list into two sublists.
    b. Merge sort the first sublist.
    c. Merge sort the second sublist.
    d. Merge the first sublist and the second sublist.
}
```

As remarked previously, after dividing the list into two sublists—the first sublist and the second sublist—these two sublists are sorted using the merge sort algorithm. In other words, we use recursion to implement the merge sort algorithm.

We next describe the necessary algorithm to:

- Divide the list into two sublists of nearly equal size.

- Merge sort both sublists.

- Merge the sorted sublists.

Divide

Because data is stored in a linked list, we do not know the length of the list. Furthermore, a linked list is not a random access data structure. Therefore, to divide the list into two sublists, we need to find the middle node of the list.

Consider the list in Figure 18-49.

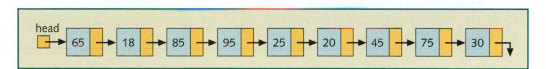

Figure 18-49 Unsorted linked list

To find the middle of the list, we traverse the list with two reference variables—say, `middle` and `current`. The reference variable `middle` is initialized to the first node of the list. Because this list has more than two nodes, we initialize `current` to the third node. (Recall that we sort the list only if it has more than one element because a list of size 1 is already sorted. Also, if the list has only two nodes, we set `current` to `null`.) Consider the list shown in Figure 18-50.

18

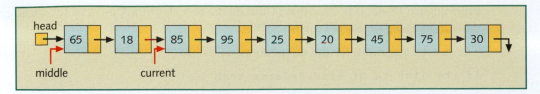

Figure 18-50 `middle` and `current` before traversing the list

Every time we advance `middle` by one node, we advance `current` by one node. After advancing `current` by one node, if `current` is not `null`, we again advance `current` by one node. That is, for the most part, every time `middle` advances by one node, `current` advances by two nodes. Eventually, `current` becomes `null` and `middle` points to the last node of the first sublist. For example, for the list in Figure 18-50, when `current` becomes `null`, `middle` points to the node with `info 25` (see Figure 18-51).

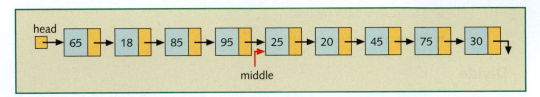

Figure 18-51 `middle` after traversing the list

It is now easy to divide the list into two sublists. First, using the link of `middle`, we assign a reference variable to the node following `middle`. Then we set the link of `middle` to `null`. Figure 18-52 shows the resulting sublists.

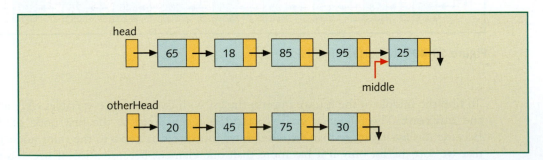

Figure 18-52 List after dividing it into two lists

This discussion translates into the following Java method, `divideList`. Notice that the method `divideList` divides the list that `head` points to and returns the reference of the first node of the second sublist.

```java
private LinkedListNode<T> divideList(LinkedListNode<T> head)
{
    LinkedListNode<T> middle;
    LinkedListNode<T> current;

    LinkedListNode<T> secondListHead;

    if (head == null)    //list is empty
        secondListHead = null;
    else
        if (head.link == null)   //list has only one node
            secondListHead = null;
        else
        {
            middle = head;
            current = head.link;

            if (current != null) //list has more than two nodes
                current = current.link;

            while (current != null)
            {
                middle = middle.link;
                current = current.link;

                if (current != null)
                    current = current.link;
            } //end while

            secondListHead = middle.link;  //secondListHead
                                           //points to the first node
                                           //of the second sublist
            middle.link = null;     //set the link of the last
                                    //node of the first sublist
                                    //to null
        } //end else

    return secondListHead;
}//end divideList
```

Now that we know how to divide a list into two sublists of nearly equal size, next we focus on merging the sorted sublists. Recall that, in a merge sort, most of the sorting work is done in merging the sorted sublists.

18

Merge

Once the sublists are sorted, the next step in the merge sort algorithm is to merge the sorted sublists. Sorted sublists are merged into a sorted list by comparing the elements of the sublists, and then adjusting the references of the nodes with the smaller `info`. Let us illustrate this procedure on the sublists shown in Figure 18-53. Suppose that `first1` points to the first node of the first sublist, and `first2` points to the first node of the second sublist.

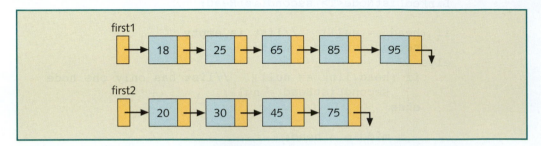

Figure 18-53   Sublists before merging

We first compare the `info` of the first node of each of the two sublists to determine the first node of the merged list. We set `newHead` to point to the first node of the merged list. We also use the reference variable `lastMerged` to keep track of the last node of the merged list. The reference variable of the first node of the sublist with the smaller node then advances to the next node of that sublist. Figure 18-54 shows the sublist of Figure 18-53 after setting `newHead` and `lastMerged` and advancing `first1`.

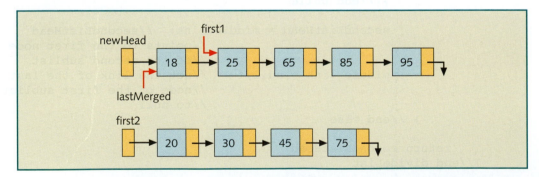

Figure 18-54   Sublists after setting `newHead` and `lastMerged` and advancing `first1`

In Figure 18-54, `first1` points to the first node of the first sublist that is yet to be merged with the second sublist. So we again compare the nodes to which `first1` and `first2` point, and adjust the link of the smaller node and the last node of the merged list to move the smaller node to the end of the merged list. For the sublists shown in Figure 18-54, after adjusting the necessary links, we have Figure 18-55.

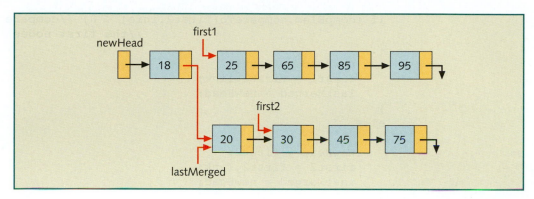

Figure 18-55   Merged list after putting node with `info` 20 at end of merged list

We continue this process for the remaining elements of both sublists. Every time we move a node to the merged list, we advance either `first1` or `first2` to the next node. Eventually, either `first1` or `first2` becomes `null`. If `first1` becomes `null`, the first sublist is exhausted first, and so we attach the remaining nodes of the second sublist at the end of the partially merged list. If `first2` becomes `null`, the second sublist is exhausted first, and so we attach the remaining nodes of the first sublist at the end of the partially merged list.

Following this discussion, we can now write the Java method, `mergeList`, to merge the two sorted sublists. The references, that is, addresses, of the first nodes of the sublists are passed as parameters to the method `mergeList`.

```
private LinkedListNode<T> mergeList(LinkedListNode<T> first1,
                                    LinkedListNode<T> first2)
{
    LinkedListNode<T> lastMerged;   //reference variable to the
                                    //last node of the merged list
    LinkedListNode<T> newHead;  //reference variable to the
                                //merged list

    if (first1 == null)             //the first sublist is empty
        return first2;
```

18

```
        else
            if (first2 == null)     //the second sublist is empty
                return first1;
        else
        {
            Comparable<T> compElem =
                        (Comparable<T>) first1.info;

            if (compElem.compareTo(first2.info) < 0) //compare
                                            //the first nodes
            {
                newHead = first1;
                first1 = first1.link;
                lastMerged = newHead;
            }
            else
            {
                newHead = first2;
                first2 = first2.link;
                lastMerged = newHead;
            }

            while (first1 != null && first2 != null)
            {
                Comparable<T> compElement =
                        (Comparable<T>) first1.info;

                if (compElement.compareTo(first2.info) < 0)
                {
                    lastMerged.link = first1;
                    lastMerged = lastMerged.link;
                    first1 = first1.link;
                }
                else
                {
                    lastMerged.link = first2;
                    lastMerged = lastMerged.link;
                    first2 = first2.link;
                }
            } //end while

            if (first1 == null)  //first sublist is exhausted
                                        //first
                lastMerged.link = first2;
            else                    //second sublist is exhausted
                                        //first
                lastMerged.link = first1;
```

```
            return newHead;
        }
}//end mergeList
```

Finally, we write the recursive merge sort method, `recMergeSort`, which uses the `divideList` and `mergeList` methods to sort a list. The reference of the first node of the list to be sorted is passed as a parameter to the method `recMergeSort`.

```
private LinkedListNode<T> recMergeSort(LinkedListNode<T> head)
{
    LinkedListNode<T> otherHead;

    if (head != null)  //if the list is not empty
        if (head.link != null) //if the list has more
                               //than one node
        {
            otherHead = divideList(head);
            head = recMergeSort(head);
            otherHead = recMergeSort(otherHead);
            head = mergeList(head, otherHead);
        }

    return head;
}//end recMergeSort
```

We can now give the definition of the method `mergeSort`, which should be included as a **public** member of the **class** `UnorderedLinkedList`. (Note that the methods `divideList`, `merge`, and `recMergeSort` can be included as **private** members of the **class** `UnorderedLinkedList` because these methods are used only to implement the method `mergeSort`.) The method `mergeSort` calls the method `recMergeSort` and passes `first` to this method. It also sets `last` to point to the last node of the list. The definition of the method `mergeSort` is:

```
public void mergeSort()
{
    first = recMergeSort(first);

    if (first == null)
        last = null;
    else
    {
        last = first;
        while (last.link != null)
            last = last.link;
    }
} //end mergeSort
```

We leave it as an exercise for you to write a program to test the merge sort algorithm. See Programming Exercise 13 at the end of this chapter.

18

Analysis: Merge Sort

Suppose that L is a list of n elements, where $n > 0$. Suppose that n is a power of 2, that is, $n = 2^m$ for some nonnegative integer m. So that we can divide the list into two sublists, each of the size $n / 2 = 2^m / 2 = 2^{m-1}$. Moreover, each sublist can also be divided into two sublists of the same size. Each call to the method `recMergeSort` makes two recursive calls to the method `recMergeSort` and each call divides the sublist into two sublists of the same size. Suppose that $m = 3$, that is, $n = 2^3 = 8$. So the length of the original list is 8. The first call to the method `recMergeSort` divides the original list into two sublists, each of the size 4. The first call then makes two recursive calls to the method `recMergeSort`. Each of these recursive calls divides each sublist, of the size 4, into two sublists, each of the size 2. We now have 4 sublists, each of the size 2. The next set of recursive calls divides each sublist, of the size 2, into sublists of the size 1. So we now have 8 sublists, each of the size 1. It follows that the exponent 3 in 2^3 indicates the level of the recursion. See Figure 18-56.

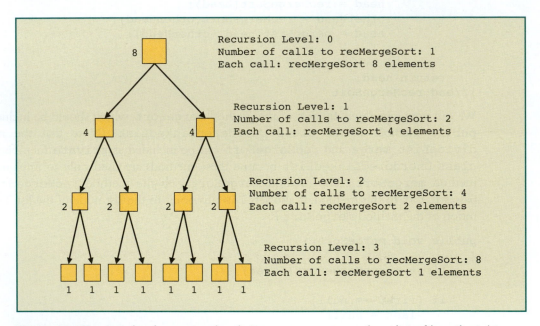

Figure 18-56   Levels of recursion levels to `recMergeSort` for a list of length eight

Let us consider the general case when $n = 2^m$. Note that the number of recursion levels is m. Also, note that to merge a sorted list of the size s with a sorted list of the size t, the maximum number of comparisons is $s + t - 1$.

Consider the method `mergeList`, which merges two sorted lists into a sorted list. Note that this is where the actual work, comparisons and assignments, is done. The initial call to the method `recMergeSort`, at level 0, produces two sublists, each of the size $n / 2$. To merge these two lists, after they are sorted, the maximum number of comparisons is $n / 2 + n / 2 - 1$ $= n - 1 = O(n)$. At level 1, we merge two sets of sorted lists, where each sublist is of the size $n / 4$. To merge two sorted sublists, each of the size $n / 4$, we need at most $n / 4 + n / 4 - 1$ $= n / 2 - 1$ comparisons. Thus, at level 1 of the recursion, the number of comparisons is $2(n / 2 - 1) = n - 2 = O(n)$. In general, at level k of the recursion, there are a total of 2^k calls to the method `mergeList`. Each of these calls merge two sublists, each of the size $n / 2^{k + 1}$, which requires a maximum of $n / 2^k - 1$ comparisons. Thus at level k of the recursion, the maximum number of comparisons is $2^k (n / 2^k - 1) = n - 2^k = O(n)$. It now follows that the maximum number of comparisons at each level of the recursion is $O(n)$. Because the number of levels of the recursion is m, the maximum number of comparisons made by the merge sort algorithms is $O(nm)$. Now $n = 2^m$ implies that $m = \log_2 n$. Hence, the maximum number of comparisons made by the merge sort algorithm is $O(n \log_2 n)$.

If $W(n)$ denotes the number of key comparisons in the worst case to sort L, then $W(n) = O(n \log_2 n)$.

Let $A(n)$ denote the number of key comparisons in the average case. In the average case, during merge one of the sublists will exhaust before the other list. From this, it follows that on average, when merging two sorted sublists of combined size n, the number of comparisons will be less than $n - 1$. On average it can be shown that the number of comparison for merge sort is given by the following equation: If n is a power of 2, $A(n) = n \log_2 n - 1.25n = O(n \log_2 n)$. This is also a good approximation when n is not a power of 2.

 We can also obtain an analysis of the merge sort algorithm by constructing and solving certain equations as follows. As noted before, in merge sort, all the comparisons are made in the procedure mergeList, which merges two sorted sublists. If one sublist is of size s and the other sublist is of size t, then merging these lists would require at most $s + t - 1$ comparisons in the worst case. Hence:

$$W(n) = W(s) + W(t) + s + t - 1$$

Note that $s = n / 2$ and $t = n / 2$. Suppose that $n = 2^m$. Then $s = 2^{m-1}$ and $t = 2^{m-1}$. It follows that $s + t = n$. Hence:

$$W(n) = W(n / 2) + W(n / 2) + n - 1 = 2 W(n / 2) + n - 1, n > 0.$$

Also:

$$W(1) = 0.$$

It is known that when n is a power of 2, $W(n)$ is given by the following equation:

$$W(n) = n \log_2 n - (n - 1) = O(n \log_2 n).$$

HEAP SORT: ARRAY-BASED LISTS

In an earlier section, we described the quick sort algorithm for contiguous lists, that is, array-based lists. We remarked that, on average, the quick sort is of the order $O(n\log_2 n)$. However, in the worst case, the quick sort is of the order $O(n^2)$. This section describes another algorithm, the heap sort, for array-based lists. This algorithm is of the order $O(n\log_2 n)$ even in the worst case, therefore overcoming the worst case of the quick sort.

Definition: A **heap** is a list in which each element contains a key, such that the key in the element at position k in the list is at least as large as the key in the element at position $2k + 1$ (if it exists), and $2k + 2$ (if it exists).

Recall that in Java the array index starts at 0. Therefore, the element at position k is in fact the $k + 1$th element of the list.

Consider the list in Figure 18-57.

[0]	[1]	[2]	[3]	[4]	[5]	[6]	[7]	[8]	[9]	[10]	[11]	[12]
85	70	80	50	40	75	30	20	10	35	15	62	58

Figure 18-57 A list that is a heap

It can be checked that the list in Figure 18-57 is a heap.

Given a heap, we can construct a complete binary tree as follows: The root node of the tree is the first element of the list. The left child of the root is the second element of the list, and the right child of the root node is the third element of the list. Thus, in general, for the node k, which is the $k - 1$th element of the list, its left child is the $2k$th element of the list (if it exists), which is at position $2k - 1$ in the list, and the right child is the $(2k+1)$th element of the list (if it exists), which is at position $2k$ in the list.

The diagram in Figure 18-58 represents the complete binary tree corresponding to the list in Figure 18-57.

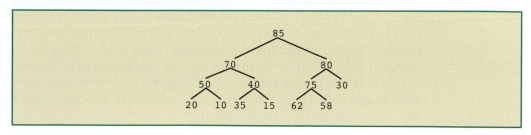

Figure 18-58   Complete binary tree corresponding to the list in Figure 18-57

Figure 18-58 shows that the list in Figure 18-57 is a heap. In fact, to demonstrate the heap sort algorithm, we will always draw the complete binary tree corresponding to a list.

We now describe the heap sort algorithm.

The first step in the heap sort algorithm is to convert the list into a heap, called `buildHeap`. After we convert the array into a heap, the sorting phase begins.

Build Heap

This section describes the build heap algorithm.

The general algorithm is as follows: suppose `length` denotes the length of the list. Let `index = length / 2 - 1`. Then `list[index]` is the last element in the list that is not a leaf; that is, this element has at least one child. Thus, elements `list[index + 1]...list[length - 1]` are leaves.

First, we convert the subtree with the root node `list[index]` into a heap. Note that this subtree has at most three nodes. We then convert the subtree with the root node `list[index - 1]` into a heap, and so on.

To convert a subtree into a heap, we perform the following steps: suppose that `list[a]` is the root node of the subtree, `list[b]` is the left child of `list[a]`, and `list[c]`, if it exists, is the right child of `list[a]`.

Compare `list[b]` with `list[c]` to determine the larger child. If `list[c]` does not exist, then `list[b]` is the larger child. Suppose that `largerIndex` indicates the larger child. (Notice that `largerIndex` is either b or c.)

1. Compare `list[a]` with `list[largerIndex]`. If `list[a]` < `list[largerIndex]`, then swap `list[a]` with `list[largerIndex]`; otherwise, the subtree with the root node `list[a]` is already in a heap.

18

2. Suppose that list[a] < list[largerIndex] and we swap the elements list[a] and list[largerIndex]. After making this swap, the subtree with the root node list[largerIndex] might not be in a heap. If this is the case, then we repeat Steps 1 and 2 at the subtree with the root node list[largerIndex], and continue this process until either the heaps in the subtrees are restored or we arrive at an empty subtree. This step is implemented using a loop, which is described when we write the algorithm.

Consider the list in Figure 18-59. Let us call this list.

	[0]	[1]	[2]	[3]	[4]	[5]	[6]	[7]	[8]	[9]	[10]
list	15	60	72	70	56	32	62	92	45	30	65

Figure 18-59 Array list

Figure 18-60 shows the complete binary tree corresponding to the list in Figure 18-59.

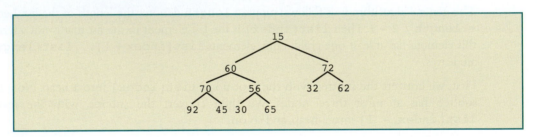

Figure 18-60 Complete binary tree corresponding to the list in Figure 18-59

To facilitate this discussion, when we say node 56 we mean the node with info 56.

This list has 11 elements, so the length of the list is 11. To convert the array into a heap, we start at the list element n / 2 – 1 = 11 / 2 – 1 = 5 – 1 = 4, which is the fifth element of the list.

Now list[4] = 56. The children of list[4] are list[4 * 2 + 1] and list[4 * 2 + 2], that is, list[9] and list[10]. In the previous list, both list[9] and list[10] exist. To convert the tree with root node list[4], we perform the following three steps:

1. Find the larger of list[9] and list[10], that is, the largest child of list[4]. In this case, list[10] is larger than list[9].

2. Compare the larger child with the parent node. If the larger child is larger than the parent, swap the larger child with the parent. Because list[4] < list[10], we swap list[4] with list[10].

3. Because list[10] does not have a subtree, Step 3 does not execute.

Figure 18-61 shows the resulting binary tree.

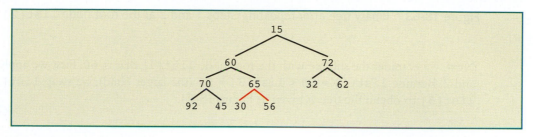

Figure 18-61   Binary tree after swapping list[4] with list[10]

Next, we consider the subtree with root node list[3], that is 70, and repeat the three steps given earlier to obtain the complete binary tree as given in Figure 18-62. (Notice that here also Step 3 does not execute.)

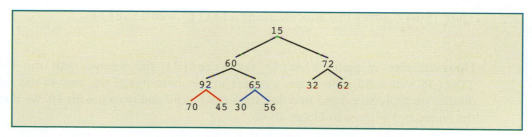

Figure 18-62   Binary tree after repeating Steps 1, 2, and 3 at the root node list[3]

Now we consider the subtree with the root node list[2], that is, 72, and apply the three steps given earlier. Figure 18-63 shows the resulting binary tree. (Note that in this case, because the parent is larger than both children, this subtree is already in a heap.)

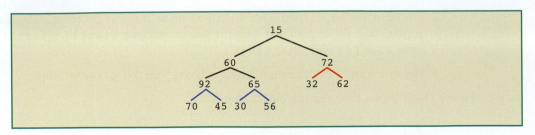

Figure 18-63 Binary tree after repeating Steps 1 and 2 at the root node `list[2]`

Next, we consider the subtree with the root node `list[1]`, that is, `60`. First we apply Steps 1 and 2. Because `list[1] = 60 < list[3] = 92` (the larger child), we swap `list[1]` with `list[3]` to obtain the tree as given in Figure 18-64.

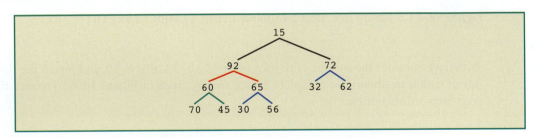

Figure 18-64 Binary tree after swapping `list[1]` with `list[3]`

However, after swapping `list[1]` with `list[3]`, the subtree with the root node `list[3]`, that is, `60`, is no longer a heap. Thus, we must restore the heap in this subtree. To do this, we apply Step 3 and find the larger child of `60` and swap it with `60`. We then obtain the binary tree as given in Figure 18-65.

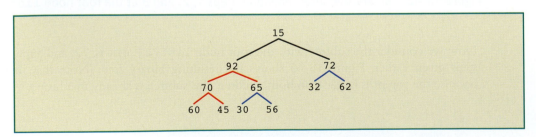

Figure 18-65 Binary tree after restoring the heap at `list[3]`

Once again, the subtree with the root node `list[1]`, that is, `92`, is a heap (see Figure 18-65).

Finally, we consider the tree with the root node `list[0]`, that is, `15`. We repeat the previous three steps to obtain the binary tree as given in Figure 18-66.

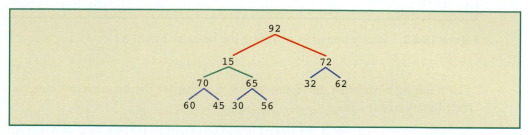

Figure 18-66   Binary tree after applying Steps 1 and 2 at `list[0]`

We see that the subtree with the root node `list[1]`, that is, `15`, is no longer in a heap. So we must apply Step 3 to restore the heap in this subtree. (This requires us to repeat Steps 1 and 2 at the subtree with root node `list[1]`.) We swap `list[1]` with the larger child, `list[3]` (that is, `70`). We then get the binary tree as shown in Figure 18-67.

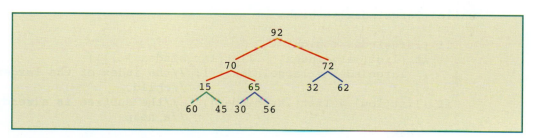

Figure 18-67   Binary tree after applying Steps 1 and 2 at `list[1]`

The subtree with the root node `list[3]` = 15 is not in a heap, and so we must restore the heap in this subtree. To do so, we apply Steps 1 and 2 at the subtree with the root node `list[3]`. We swap `list[3]` with the larger child, `list[7]` (that is, `60`). Figure 18-68 shows the resulting binary tree.

18

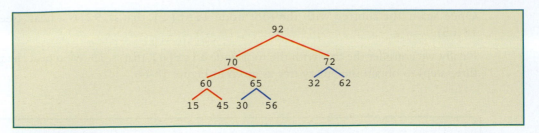

Figure 18-68   Binary tree after restoring the heap at `list[3]`

The resulting binary tree (in Figure 18-68) is a heap, so the list corresponding to this complete binary tree is a heap.

Thus, in general, starting at the lowest level from right to left, we look at a subtree and convert the subtree into a heap as follows: If the root node of the subtree is smaller than the larger child, we swap the root node with the larger child; after swapping the root node with the larger child, we must restore the heap in the subtree whose root node was swapped.

Suppose `low` contains the index of the root node of the subtree, and `high` contains the index of the last item in the list. The heap is to be restored in the subtree rooted at `list[low]`. The preceding discussion translates into the following Java algorithm:

```
int largeIndex = 2 * low + 1;    //the index of the left child

while (largeIndex <= high)
{
    if (largeIndex < high)
        if (list[largeIndex] < list[largeIndex + 1]))
            largeIndex = largeIndex + 1; //the index of the larger
                                         //child
    if (list[low] > list[largeIndex])    //the subtree is already in
                                         //a heap

        break;
    else
    {
        swap(list[low], list[largeIndex]);    //Line **
        low = largeIndex;   //go to the subtree to further
                            //restore the heap
        largeIndex = 2 * low + 1;
    } //end else
}//end while
```

The **swap** statement at the line marked **Line **** swaps the parent with the larger child. Because a **swap** statement makes three item assignments to swap the contents of two variables, each time through the loop three item assignments are made. The **while** loop moves the parent node to a place in the tree so that the resulting subtree with the root node `list[low]` is a heap. We can easily reduce the number of assignments each time through the loop from three to one by first storing the root node in a temporary location, say `temp`. Then each time through the loop, the larger child is compared with `temp`. If the larger child is larger than `temp`, we move the larger child to the root node of the subtree under consideration. Next, we describe the method `heapify`, which restores the heap in a subtree by making one item assignment each time through the loop. The index of the root node of the list and the index of the last element of the list are passed as parameters to this method.

```
private void heapify(T[] list, int low, int high)
{
    int largeIndex;

    Comparable<T> temp =
            (Comparable<T>) list[low];    //copy the root
                                          //node of
                                          //the subtree

    largeIndex = 2 * low + 1;  //index of the left child

    while (largeIndex <= high)
    {
        if (largeIndex < high)
        {
            Comparable<T> compElem =
                    (Comparable<T>) list[largeIndex];

            if (compElem.compareTo(list[largeIndex + 1]) < 0)
                largeIndex = largeIndex + 1; //index of the
                                             //largest child
        }

        if (temp.compareTo(list[largeIndex]) > 0) //subtree
                                      //is already in a heap
            break;
        else
        {
            list[low] = list[largeIndex]; //move the larger
                                          //child to the root
            low = largeIndex;    //go to the subtree to
                                 //restore the heap
            largeIndex = 2 * low + 1;
        }
    }//end while

    list[low] = (T) temp; //insert temp into the tree,
                          //that is, list
}//end heapify
```

18

Next, we use the method `heapify` to implement the `buildHeap` method to convert the list into a heap.

```
private void buildHeap(T[] list, int length)
{
    for (int index = length / 2 - 1; index >= 0; index--)
        heapify(list, index, length - 1);
}//end buildHeap
```

We now describe the heap sort algorithm.

Suppose the list is a heap. Consider the complete binary tree representing the list as given in Figure 18-69.

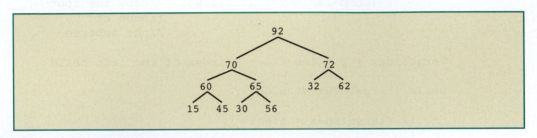

Figure 18-69   A heap

Because this is a heap, the root node is the largest element of the tree (or the list). This means that it must be moved to the end of the list. We swap the root node of the tree (which is the first element of the list) with the last node in the tree (which is the last element of the list). We then obtain the binary tree as shown in Figure 18-70.

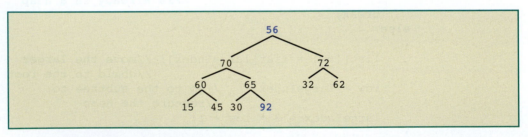

Figure 18-70   Binary tree after moving the root node to the end

Because the largest element is now in its proper place, we consider the remaining elements of the list, that is, elements `list[0]...list[9]`. The complete binary tree representing this list is no longer a heap, so we must restore the heap in this portion of the complete binary tree. We use the method `heapify` to restore the heap. A call to this method is:

```
heapify(list, 0, 9);
```

We thus obtain the binary tree as shown in Figure 18-71.

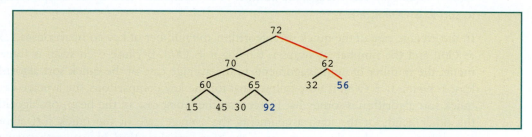

Figure 18-71   Binary tree after the statement `heapify(list, 0, 9);` executes

We repeat this process for the complete binary tree corresponding to the list elements `list[0]...list[9]`. We swap `list[0]` with `list[9]` and then restore the heap in the complete binary tree corresponding to the list elements `list[0]...list[8]`. We continue this process.

The following Java method describes this algorithm:

```java
public void heapSort(T[] list, int length)
{
    buildHeap(list, length);

    for (int lastOutOfOrder = length - 1; lastOutOfOrder >= 0;
                        lastOutOfOrder--)
    {
        T temp = list[lastOutOfOrder];
        list[lastOutOfOrder] = list[0];
        list[0] = temp;
        heapify(list, 0, lastOutOfOrder - 1);
    }//end for
}//end heapSort
```

We leave it as an exercise for you to write a program to test the heap sort algorithm. See Programming Exercise 15 at the end of this chapter.

18

Analysis: Heap Sort

Suppose that L is a list of n elements, where $n > 0$. In the worst case, the number of key comparisons in the heap sort algorithm to sort L (the number of comparisons in `heapSort` and the number of comparisons in `buildHeap`) is $2n\log_2 n + O(n) = O(n\log_2 n)$. Also, in the worst case, the number of item assignments in the heap sort algorithm to sort L is $n\log_2 n + O(n) = O(n\log_2 n)$. On average, the number of comparisons made by the heap sort algorithm to sort L is $O(n\log_2 n)$.

In the average case of the quick sort algorithm, the number of key comparisons is $1.39n\log_2 n + O(n)$ and the number of swaps is $0.69\log_2 n + O(n)$. Because each swap is three assignments, the number of item assignments in the average case of the quick sort algorithm is at least $1.39n\log_2 n + O(n)$. It now follows that for the key comparisons, the average case of the quick sort algorithm is somewhat better than the worst case of the heap sort algorithm. On the other hand, for the item assignments, the average case of the quick sort algorithm is somewhat poorer than the worst case of the heap sort algorithm. However, the worst case of the quick sort algorithm is $O(n^2)$. Empirical studies have shown that the heap sort algorithm usually takes twice as long as the quick sort algorithm, but avoids the slight possibility of poor performance.

In this chapter, we discussed various sorting and searching algorithms. For array-based lists, the searching and sorting algorithms that we described are part of the **class** `SearchSortAlgorithms<T>`, which implements the **interface** `SearchSortADT<T>`. Note that we kept the type parameter T unbounded so that we can use these algorithms for array-based lists whose objects implement the **interface** `Comparable` as well objects of the **class**es `UnorderedArrayList` and `OrderedArrayList`, which we developed in Chapter 15. Because the type parameter T is unbounded, to compare two list elements, using the method `compareTo`, one of the list elements was type cast to an object of the type `Comparable`. For example, we used statements such as the following bubble sort algorithm:

```
Comparable<T> compElem = (Comparable<T>) list[index];
```

If you bound the type parameter T in the **class** `SearchSortAlgorithms<T>`, then you could directly compare two list elements. However, in that case, you may not able to use these algorithms for objects of the **class**es `UnorderedArrayList` and `OrderedArrayList`. In this case, you can directly provide the codes of these algorithms in these classes. The definition of the **class** `SearchSortAlgorithms<T>` that bound the type parameter T is available at the Web site accompanying this book. You might like to look at those algorithms to see how they are written. We have also included some test programs. These classes are in the folder `SearchSortAlgorithmsWithBoundTypeParameter`.

PROGRAMMING EXAMPLE: ELECTION RESULTS

The presidential election for the student council of your local university is about to be held. Due to confidentiality, the chair of the election committee wants to computerize the voting. The chair has asked you to write a program to analyze the data and report the winner.

The university has four major divisions, and each division has several departments. For the election, the four divisions are labeled as region 1, region 2, region 3, and region 4. Each department in each division handles its own voting and directly reports the votes received by each candidate to the election committee. The voting is reported in the following form:

```
firstName lastName regionNumber numberOfVotes
```

The election committee wants the output in the following tabular form:

```
--------------------Election Results-----------------

                       Votes By Region
Candidate Name   Rgn#1   Rgn#2   Rgn#3   Rgn#4   Total
--------------   -----   -----   -----   -----   -----
Sheila Bower        23      70     133     267     493
Danny Dillion       25      71     156      97     349
 .
 .
 .

Winner: ???,  Votes Received: ???
Total votes polled: ???
```

The names of the candidates must be in alphabetical order in the output.

For this program, we assume that six candidates are seeking the student council's president post. This program can be enhanced to handle any number of candidates.

The data are provided in two files. One file, `candData.txt`, consists of the names of the candidates seeking the president's post. The names of the candidates in this file are in no particular order. In the second file, `voteData.txt`, each line consists of the voting results in the following form:

```
firstName lastName regionNumber numberOfVotes
```

That is, each line in the file `voteData.txt` consists of the candidate's name, the region number, and the number of votes received by the candidate in that region.

There is one entry per line. For example, the input file containing the voting data looks like the following:

```
Greg Goldy 2 34
Mickey Miller 1 56
Lisa Fisher 2 56
Peter Lamba 1 78
Danny Dillion 4 29
Sheila Bower 4 78
    .
    .
    .
```

The first line indicates that `Greg Goldy` received `34` votes from region `2`.

Input

Two files: One containing the candidates' names, and the other containing the voting data as described previously

Output

The election results in a tabular form as described previously, and the winner's name

Problem Analysis and Algorithm Design

From the output, it is clear that the program must organize the voting data by region, and calculate the total votes received by each candidate and polled for the election. Furthermore, the names of the candidates must appear in alphabetical order.

The main component of this program is a candidate. Therefore, first we will design the **class** `Candidate` to implement a candidate object. Moreover, in this program, we use an `OrderedArrayList` object to implement the list of candidates.

Candidate

As remarked previously, the main component of this program is candidate. Every candidate has a name and can receive votes. Because there are four regions, we can use an array of four components to store the votes received. In Chapter 15, we redesigned the **class** `Person` to implement the name of a person as well as implement the **interface**s `Cloneable` and `Comparable`. Recall that an object of the type `Person` can store the first name and the last name. Because every candidate is a person, we derive the **class** `Candidate` from the **class** `Person`. We also need a data member to store the total number of votes received by each candidate.

There are six candidates. Therefore, we declare a list of six candidates of the type `Candidate`. Chapter 15 defined and implemented the generic **class** `OrderedArrayList` to implement a sorted list; we use this class to maintain the list of candidates. Because objects in an `OrderedArrayList` are in ascending order, we will use the binary search algorithm to search an `OrderedArrayList` object. Therefore, we must provide the definitions of the methods `equals` and `compareTo` for the **class** `Candidate` because some of these methods are used by the sorting and searching algorithms.

The following statements define `Candidate` as an ADT.

Class: `Candidate`

```
public class Candidate extends Person
```

Instance Variables and Constants

```
private final int NO_OF_REGIONS = 4;

private int[] votesByRegion;
private int totalVotes;
```

Constructors and Instance Methods

```
Candidate()
   //Default constructor
   //Postcondition: Creates the array votesByRegion and
   //               sets totalVotes to zero.

public void setVotes(int region, int votes)
   //Method to set the votes of a candidate for a
   //particular region.
   //Postcondition: The votes specified by the parameter votes
   //               are assigned to the region specified by the
   //               parameter region.

public void updateVotesByRegion(int region, int votes)
   //Method to update the votes of a candidate for a
   //particular region.
   //Postcondition: The votes specified by the parameter votes
   //               are added to the region specified by the
   //               parameter region.

public void calculateTotalVotes()
   //Method to calculate the total votes received by a
   //candidate.
   //Postcondition: The votes received in each region are added.

public int getTotalVotes()
   //Method to return the total votes received by a
   //candidate.
   //Postcondition: The total votes received by the candidate
   //               are returned.
```

```
public void printData()
    // Method to output the candidate's name, the votes
    //received in each region, and the total votes received.

public boolean equals(Object otherElement)
public int compareTo(Object otherElement)
```

Figure 18-72 shows the UML diagram of the **class** Candidate and the inheritance hierarchy.

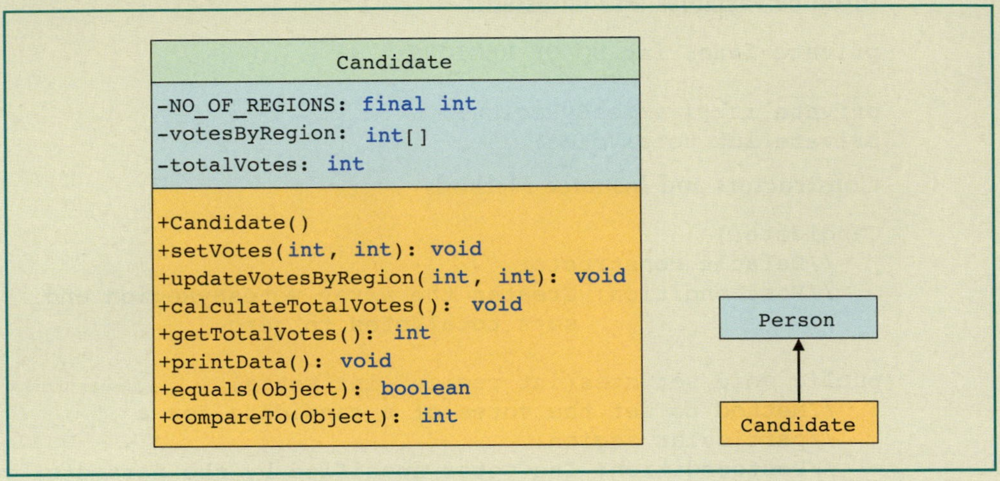

Figure 18-72 UML class diagram of **class** Candidate and the inheritance hierarchy

The definitions of the methods of the **class** Candidate are given next.

To set the votes of a particular region, the region number and the number of votes are passed as parameters to the method **setVotes**. Because an array index starts at **0**, region 1 corresponds to the array component at position **0**, and so on. Therefore, to set the value of the correct array component, **1** is subtracted from the region. The definition of the method **setVotes** is:

```
public void setVotes(int region, int votes)
{
    votesByRegion[region - 1] = votes;
}
```

To update the votes for a particular region, the region number and the number of votes for that region are passed as parameters. The votes are then added to the region's previous value. The definition of the method **updateVotesByRegion** is:

```java
public void updateVotesByRegion(int region, int votes)
{
    votesByRegion[region - 1] = votesByRegion[region - 1]
                                + votes;
}
```

The definitions of the methods `calculateTotalVotes`, `getTotalVotes`, `printData`, and the default constructor are given next.

```java
public void calculateTotalVotes()
{
    totalVotes = 0;

    for (int i = 0; i < NO_OF_REGIONS; i++)
        totalVotes += votesByRegion[i];
}

public int getTotalVotes()
{
    return totalVotes;
}

public void printData()
{
    System.out.printf("%-14s ", super.toString());

    for (int i = 0; i < NO_OF_REGIONS; i++)
        System.out.printf("%6d  ", votesByRegion[i]);

    System.out.printf("%5d%n", totalVotes);
}

Candidate()
{
    super();
    totalVotes = 0;
    votesByRegion = new int[NO_OF_REGIONS];
}
```

Next, we give the definition of the method `equals` and leave the others as an exercise for you. See Programming Exercise 16.

```java
public boolean equals(Object otherElement)
{
    Candidate temp = (Candidate) otherElement;

    return (this.getFirstName().equals(temp.getFirstName())
            && this.getLastName().equals(temp.getLastName()));
}
```

Main Program

Now that the **class** `Candidate` has been designed, we focus on designing the main program.

Because there are six candidates, we create a list, `candidateList`, containing six components of the type `Candidate`. The first thing that the program should do is read each candidate's name from the file `candData.txt` into the list `candidateList`. Because `candidateList` is an `OrderedArrayList` object, the names of the candidates are inserted into ascending order.

The next step is to process the voting data from the file **voteData.txt**, which holds the voting data. After processing the voting data, the program should calculate the total votes received by each candidate and then print the data as shown previously. Thus, the general algorithm is:

1. Read each candidate's name into `candidateList`.
2. Process the voting data.
3. Calculate the total votes received by each candidate.
4. Print the results.

The following statement creates the object `candidateList` of the type `OrderedArrayList`:

```
OrderedArrayList<Candidate> candidateList = new
            OrderedArrayList<Candidate>(NO_OF_CANDIDATES);
```

Figure 18-73 shows the object `candidateList`. Every component of the array list is an object of the `Candidate` type.

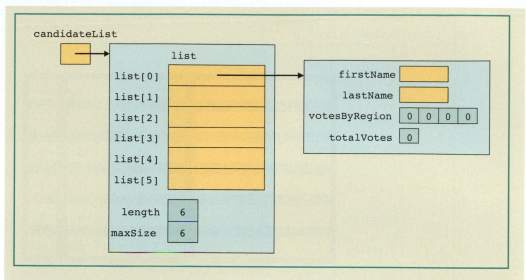

Figure 18-73 `candidateList`

In Figure 18-73, the array `votesByRegion` and the variable `totalVotes` are initial-ized to 0 by the default constructor of the **class** `Candidate`. To save space, whenever needed, we will draw the object `candidateList` as shown in Figure 18-74.

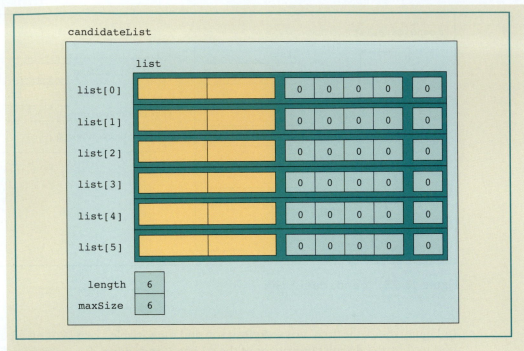

Figure 18-74 Object `candidateList`

fillNames

The first thing that the program must do is to read the candidates' names into `candidateList`. Therefore, we write a method to accomplish this task. The file `candData.txt` is opened in the method `main`. The name of the input file and `candidateList` are therefore passed as parameters to the method `fillNames`. Because the instance variable `list` of the object `candidateList` is **protected**, it cannot be accessed directly. We therefore create a `Candidate` object `temp` to store the candidates' names, and use the method `insert` (of the **class** `OrderedArrayList`) to store each candidate's name in the object `candidateList`. The definition of the method `fillNames` is as follows:

```
public static void fillNames(Scanner inFile,
                             OrderedArrayList<Candidate> cList)
{
    String firstN;
    String lastN;

    Candidate temp;
```

```
    for (int i = 0; i < NO_OF_CANDIDATES; i++)
    {
        firstN = inFile.next();
        lastN = inFile.next();
        temp   = new Candidate();
        temp.setName(firstN, lastN);
        cList.insert(temp);
    }
}
```

Figure 18-75 shows the object `candidateList` after a call to the method `fillNames`.

candidateList

list						
list[0]	Sheila	Bower	0	0	0	0	0
list[1]	Danny	Dillion	0	0	0	0	0
list[2]	Lisa	Fisher	0	0	0	0	0
list[3]	Greg	Goldy	0	0	0	0	0
list[4]	Peter	Lamba	0	0	0	0	0
list[5]	Mickey	Miller	0	0	0	0	0

length   6
maxSize 6

Figure 18-75   Object `candidateList` after a call to the method `fillNames`

Process Voting Data

We now discuss how to process the voting data. Each entry in the file **voteData.txt** is of the form:

```
firstName lastName regionNumber numberOfVotes
```

After reading an entry from the file `voteData.txt`, we locate the row in the array list (of the object `candidateList`) corresponding to the specific candidate, and update the entry specified by `regionNumber`.

The field `votesByRegion` is a **private** data member of each component of the array list. Moreover, `list` is a **private** data member of `candidateList`. We use the method `retrieveAt` to access the candidate whose votes need to be updated. Suppose the next entry read is:

```
Lisa Fisher 2 35
```

This entry says that `Lisa Fisher` received `35` votes from region `2`. Suppose that before processing this entry, `candidateList` is as shown in Figure 18-76.

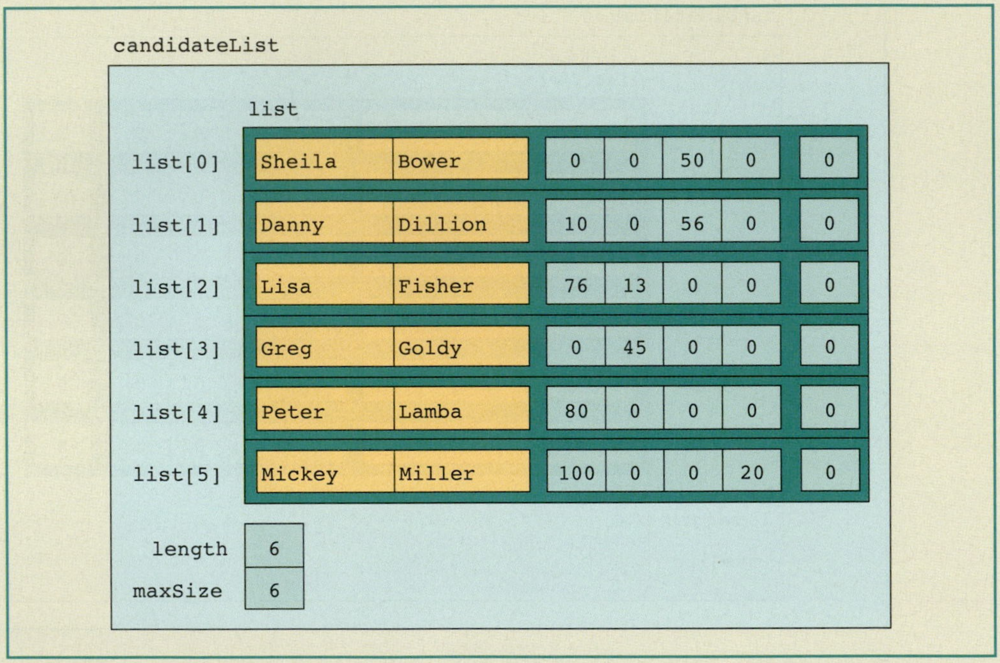

Figure 18-76 Object `candidateList` before processing the entry Lisa Fisher 2 35

Next, the following statement updates the voting data for region 2 (here **region = 2** and **votes = 35**):

```
temp.updateVotesByRegion(region, votes);
```

where `temp` is reference to the object `Lisa Fisher`. After this statement executes, the object `candidateList` is as shown in Figure 18-77.

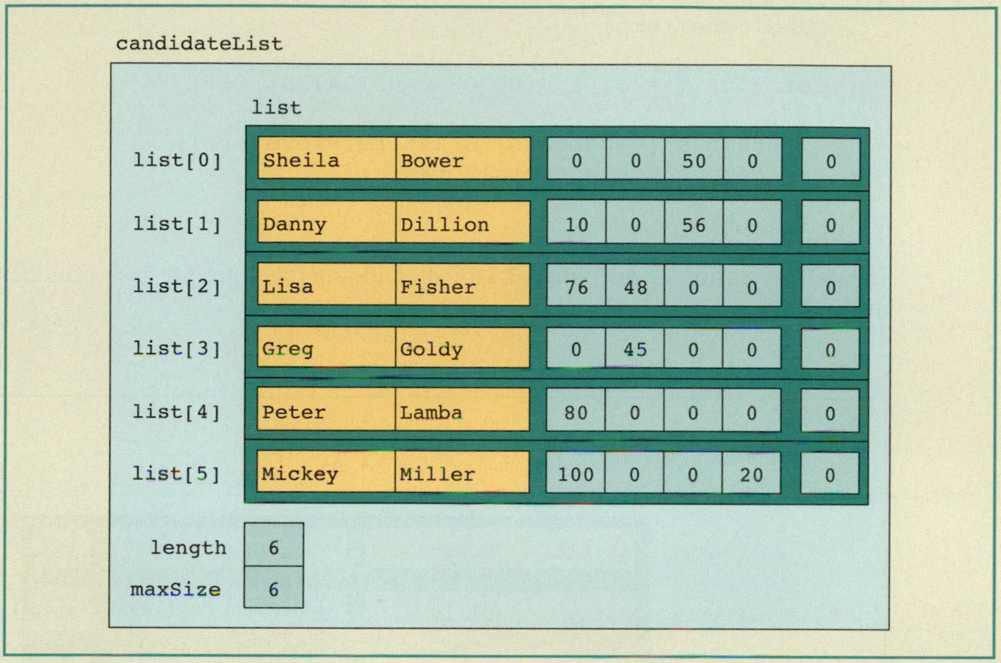

candidateList

list

	list						
list[0]	Sheila	Bower	0	0	50	0	0
list[1]	Danny	Dillion	10	0	56	0	0
list[2]	Lisa	Fisher	76	48	0	0	0
list[3]	Greg	Goldy	0	45	0	0	0
list[4]	Peter	Lamba	80	0	0	0	0
list[5]	Mickey	Miller	100	0	0	20	0

length 6
maxSize 6

Figure 18-77   `candidateList` after copying `temp`

Because the instance variable `list` of `candidateList` is sorted, we can use the binary search algorithm to find the row position in list corresponding to the candidate whose votes need to be updated. We use the method `binarySearch` of the **class** `OrderedArrayList`, which in fact uses the method `binarySearch` of the **class** `SearchSortAlgorithms`. We leave the definition of the method `processVotes` to process the voting data as an exercise for you. See Programming Exercise 16 at the end of this chapter.

Add Votes

After processing the voting data, the next step is to find the total votes received by each candidate. This is done by adding the votes received in each region. Now `votesByRegion` is a **private** member of `Candidate` and `list` is a **protected** member of `candidateList`. Therefore, to add the votes for each candidate, we use the `retrieveAt` method to access each candidate's data and add the votes. The following method does this:

```
public static void addVotes(OrderedArrayList<Candidate> cList)
{
    Candidate temp;

    for (int i = 0; i < NO_OF_CANDIDATES; i++)
    {
        temp = (Candidate) cList.retrieveAt(i);
        temp.calculateTotalVotes();
    }
}
```

Figure 18-78 shows `candidateList` after adding the votes for each candidate—that is, after a call to the method `addVotes`.

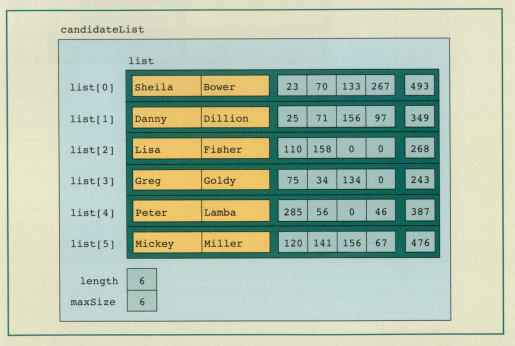

Figure 18-78   `candidateList` after a call to the method `addVotes`

Print Heading and Print Results

To complete the program, we include a method to `print` the heading, which is the first four lines of the output. The following method accomplishes this task:

```
public static void printHeading()
{
    System.out.println("--------------------Election Results"
                  + "-----------------\n");
    System.out.println("                                      "
                  + "Votes By Region");
    System.out.println("Candidate Name  Rgn#1 \tRgn#2 \t"
                  + "Rgn#3 \tRgn#4 \tTotal");
    System.out.println("--------------  ----- \t----- "
                  + "\t----- \t----- \t-----");
}
```

We now describe the method `printResults`, which prints the results. Suppose that the variable `sumVotes` holds the total votes polled for the election, the variable `largestVotes` holds the largest number of votes received by a candidate, and the variable `winLoc` holds the index of the winning candidate in the array list. Further suppose that `temp` is a reference variable of the `Candidate` type. The algorithm for this method is:

1. Initialize `sumVotes`, `largestVotes`, and `winLoc` to 0.
2. For each candidate:
   a. Access the candidate's data using `temp`.
   b. Print the candidate's name and relevant data.
   c. Retrieve the total votes received by the candidate and update `sumVotes`.

```
if (largestVotes < temp.getTotalVotes())
{
    largestVotes = temp.getTotalVotes();
    winLoc = i;
}
```
3. Output the final lines of the output.

We leave the definition of the method `printResults` to print the results as an exercise for you. See Programming Exercise 16 at the end of this chapter.

Program Listing (Main Program)

```
import java.io.*;

import java.util.*;

public class ElectionResult
```

```
{
    static final int NO_OF_CANDIDATES = 6;

    public static void main(String[] args)
    {
        OrderedArrayList<Candidate> candidateList =
                new OrderedArrayList<Candidate>(NO_OF_CANDIDATES);

        Candidate temp;

        try
        {
            Scanner inFile = new Scanner
                        (new FileReader("a:\\candData.txt"));

            fillNames(inFile, candidateList);

            inFile = null;

            inFile = new Scanner
                        (new FileReader("a:\\voteData.txt"));

            processVotes(inFile, candidateList);

            addVotes(candidateList);

            printHeading();
            printResults(candidateList);
        }
        catch (FileNotFoundException fnfe)
        {
            System.out.println(fnfe.toString());
        }
        catch (IOException ioe)
        {
            System.out.println(ioe.toString());
        }
    }

    //Place the definitions of the methods fillNames,
    //addVotes, and printHeading here. Also, write and place
    //the definitions of the methods processVotes and
    //printResults here.
}
```

Sample Run: After you have written the definitions of the methods of the **class**es Person and Candidate and of the methods processVotes and printResults, and then run your program, it should produce the following output. See Programming Exercise 16.

```
--------------------Election Results----------------

                       Votes By Region
Candidate Name  Rgn#1   Rgn#2   Rgn#3   Rgn#4   Total
--------------  -----   -----   -----   -----   -----
Sheila Bower       23      70     133     267     493
Danny Dillion      25      71     156      97     349
Lisa Fisher       110     158       0       0     268
Greg Goldy         75      34     134       0     243
Peter Lamba       285      56       0      46     387
Mickey Miller     112     141     156      67     476

Winner: Sheila Bower,  Votes Received: 493

Total votes polled: 2216
```

Input Files

```
 candData.txt
Greg Goldy
Mickey Miller
Lisa Fisher
Peter Lamba
Danny Dillion
Sheila Bower

 voteData.txt
Greg Goldy 2 34
Mickey Miller 1 56
Lisa Fisher 2 56
Peter Lamba 1 78
Danny Dillion 4 29
Sheila Bower 4 78
Mickey Miller 2 63
Lisa Fisher 1 23
Peter Lamba 2 56
Danny Dillion 1 25
Sheila Bower 2 70
Peter Lamba 4 23
Danny Dillion 4 12
Greg Goldy 3 134
Sheila Bower 4 100
Mickey Miller 3 67
Lisa Fisher 2 67
Danny Dillion 3 67
Sheila Bower 1 23
Mickey Miller 1 56
```

```
Lisa Fisher 2 35
Sheila Bower 3 78
Peter Lamba 1 27
Danny Dillion 2 34
Greg Goldy 1 75
Peter Lamba 4 23
Sheila Bower 3 55
Mickey Miller 4 67
Peter Lamba 1 23
Danny Dillion 3 89
Mickey Miller 3 89
Peter Lamba 1 67
Danny Dillion 2 37
Sheila Bower 4 89
Mickey Miller 2 78
Lisa Fisher 1 87
Peter Lamba 1 90
Danny Dillion 4 56
```

QUICK REVIEW

1. The sequential search algorithm searches the list for a given item, starting with the first element in the list. It continues to compare the search item with the elements in the list until either the item is found or no more elements with which it can be compared are left in the list.

2. On average, the sequential search algorithm searches half the list.

3. For a list of length n, in a successful search, on average, the sequential search makes

$$\frac{n+1}{2} = O(n)$$

comparisons.

4. A sequential search is not efficient for large lists.

5. A binary search is much faster than a sequential search.

6. A binary search requires the list elements to be in order—that is, sorted.

7. To search for an item in a list of length 1024, a binary search requires no more than 11 iterations of the loop, and so no more than 22 comparisons.

8. For a list of length n, in a successful search, on average, the binary search makes $2\log_2 n - 3$ key comparisons.

9. Let f be a function of n. By the term asymptotic we mean the study of the function f as n becomes larger and larger without bound.

10. Let f and g be nonnegative real-valued functions. Assume that f and g are nonnegative, that is, for all real numbers n, $f(n) \geq 0$, and $g(n) \geq 0$. We say that $f(n)$ is Big-O of $g(n)$, written $f(n) = O(g(n))$, if there exists positive constants c and n_0 such that $f(n) \leq cg(n)$ for all $n \geq n_0$.

11. Let $f(n)$ be a nonnegative real-valued function such that $f(n) = a_m n^m + a_{m-1} n^{m-1} + \cdots + a_1 n + a_0$, where a_i's are real numbers, $a_m \neq 0$, $n \geq 0$, and m is a nonnegative integer. Then $f(n) = O(n^m)$.

12. Let L be a list of size $n > 1$. Suppose that the elements of L are sorted. If $SRH(n)$ is the minimum number of comparisons needed, in the worst case, by using a comparison-based algorithm to recognize whether an element x is in L, then $SRH(n) \geq \log_2(n + 1)$.

13. The binary search algorithm is the optimal worst-case algorithm for solving search problems by using the comparison method.

14. To construct a search algorithm of the order less than $\log_2 n$, it cannot be comparison based.

15. For a list of length n, on average, a bubble sort makes

$$\frac{n(n-1)}{2}$$

key comparisons and about

$$\frac{n(n-1)}{4}$$

item assignments.

16. The selection sort algorithm sorts a list by finding the smallest (or equivalently largest) element in the list, and then moving it to the beginning (or end) of the list.

17. For a list of length n, where $n > 0$, the selection sort algorithm makes

$$\frac{1}{2}n^2 - \frac{1}{2}n$$

key comparisons and $3(n-1)$ item assignments.

18. For a list of length n, where $n > 0$, on average, the insertion sort algorithm makes

$$\frac{1}{4}n^2 + O(n)$$

key comparisons and

$$\frac{1}{4}n^2 + O(n)$$

item assignments.

18

19. Let L be a list of n distinct elements. Any sorting algorithm that sorts L by comparison of the keys only, in its worst case, makes at least $O(n\log_2 n)$ key comparisons.

20. Both the quick sort and merge sort algorithms sort a list by partitioning it.

21. To partition a list, the quick sort algorithm first selects an item from the list, called `pivot`. The algorithm then rearranges the elements so that the elements in one of the sublists are less than `pivot` and the elements in the other sublist are greater than or equal to `pivot`.

22. In a quick sort, the sorting work is done in partitioning the list.

23. On average, the number of key comparisons in a quick sort is $O(n\log_2 n)$. In the worst case, the number of key comparisons in a quick sort is $O(n^2)$.

24. The merge sort algorithm partitions the list by dividing it in the middle.

25. In a merge sort, the sorting work is done in merging the list.

26. The number of key comparisons in a merge sort is $O(n\log_2 n)$.

27. A heap is a list in which each element contains a key, such that the key in the element at position k in the list is at least as large as the key in the element at position $2k + 1$ (if it exists), and $2k + 2$ (if it exists).

28. The first step in the heap sort algorithm is to convert the list into a heap, called `buildHeap`. After we convert the array into a heap, the sorting phase begins.

29. Suppose that L is a list of n elements, where $n > 0$. In the worst case, the number of key comparisons in the heap sort algorithm to sort L is $2n\log_2 n + O(n) = O(n\log_2 n)$. Also, in the worst case, the number of item assignments in the heap sort algorithm to sort L is $n\log_2 n + O(n) = O(n\log_2 n)$.

EXERCISES

1. Mark the following statements as true or false.

   a. A sequential search of a list assumes that the list is in ascending order.

   b. A binary search of a list assumes that the list is sorted.

   c. A binary search is faster on ordered lists and slower on unordered lists.

   d. A binary search is faster on large lists, but a sequential search is faster on small lists.

2. Consider the following list:

   ```
   63, 45, 32, 98, 46, 57, 28, 100
   ```

   Using the sequential search as described in this chapter, how many comparisons are required to find whether the following items are in the list? (Recall that by comparisons we mean item comparisons, not index comparisons.)

   a. 90

   b. 57

   c. 63

   d. 120

3. Consider the following list:

   2, 10, 17, 45, 49, 55, 68, 85, 92, 98, 110

   Using the binary search as described in this chapter, how many comparisons are required to find whether the following items are in the list? Show the values of `first`, `last`, and `middle` and the number of comparisons after each iteration of the loop.

   a. 15

   b. 49

   c. 98

   d. 99

4. Sort the following list using the bubble sort algorithm as discussed in this chapter. Show the list after each iteration of the outer **for** loop.

   26, 45, 17, 65, 33, 55, 12, 18

5. The number of comparisons in the best case of a bubble sort algorithm, as given in this chapter, is $O(n^2)$. Show that the following version of the bubble sort algorithm reduces the number of comparisons in the best case of the bubble sort algorithm to $O(n)$.

```
//list - list to be sorted
//T - type of the list elements
//length - length of the list

boolean isSorted = false;

for (int iteration = 1; (iteration < length) && !isSorted;
                        iteration++)
{
    isSorted = true;   //assume that the sublist is sorted

    for (int index = 0; index < length - iteration; index++)
    {
        Comparable<T> compElem = (Comparable<T>) list[index];

        if (compElem.compareTo(list[index + 1]) > 0)
        {
            T temp = list[index];
            list[index] = list[index + 1];
            list[index + 1] = temp;
            isSorted = false;
        }
    }
}
```

6. Sort the following list using the selection sort algorithm as discussed in this chapter. Show the list after each iteration of the outer **for** loop.

   36, 55, 17, 35, 63, 85, 12, 48, 3, 66

18

7. Assume the following list of keys:

   5, 18, 21, 10, 55, 20

   The first three keys are in order. To move 10 to its proper position using the insertion sort algorithm as described in this chapter, exactly how many key comparisons are executed?

8. Assume the following list of keys:

   7, 28, 31, 40, 5, 20

   The first four keys are in order. To move 5 to its proper position using the insertion sort algorithm as described in this chapter, exactly how many key comparisons are executed?

9. Assume the following list of keys:

   28, 18, 21, 10, 25, 30, 12, 71, 32, 58, 15

   This list is to be sorted using the insertion sort algorithm as described in this chapter for array-based lists. Show the resulting list after 6 passes of the sorting phase—that is, after 6 iterations of the **for** loop.

10. Recall the insertion sort algorithm (contiguous version) as discussed in this chapter. Assume the following list of keys:

    18, 8, 11, 9, 15, 20, 32, 61, 22, 48, 75, 83, 35, 3

    Exactly how many key comparisons are executed to sort this list using the insertion sort algorithm?

11. Both the merge sort and quick sort algorithms sort a list by partitioning it. Explain how the merge sort algorithm differs from the quick sort algorithm in partitioning the list.

12. Assume the following list of keys:

    16, 38, 54, 80, 22, 65, 55, 48, 64, 95, 5, 100, 58, 25, 36

    This list is to be sorted using the quick sort algorithm as discussed in this chapter. Use **pivot** as the middle element of the list.

    a. Give the resulting list after one call to the partition procedure.

    b. Give the resulting list after two calls to the partition procedure.

13. Assume the following list of keys:

    18, 40, 16, 82, 64, 67, 57, 50, 37, 47, 72, 14, 17, 27, 35

    This list is to be sorted using the quick sort algorithm as discussed in this chapter. Use **pivot** as the median of the **first**, **last**, and **middle** elements of the list.

    a. What is the pivot?

    b. Give the resulting list after one call to the partition procedure.

14. Use the method `buildHeap` as given in this chapter to convert the following array into a heap. Show the final form of the array.

    47, 78, 81, 52, 50, 82, 58, 42, 65, 80, 92, 53, 63, 87, 95, 59, 34, 37, 7, 20

15. Suppose that the following list was created by the method `buildHeap` during the heap creation phase of the heap sort algorithm:

    100, 85, 94, 47, 72, 82, 76, 30, 20, 60, 65, 50, 45, 17, 35, 14, 28, 5

    Show the resulting array after two passes of the heap sort algorithm. (Use the `heapify` procedure as given in this chapter.) Exactly how many key comparisons are executed during the first pass?

PROGRAMMING EXERCISES

1. **(Recursive sequential search)** The sequential search algorithm given in this chapter is nonrecursive. Write and implement a recursive version of the sequential search algorithm.

2. **(Recursive binary search)** The binary search algorithm given in this chapter is non-recursive. Write and implement a recursive version of the binary search algorithm. Also write a program to test your algorithm.

3. Write the definition of the method `seqOrdSearch` to implement a version of the sequential search algorithm for ordered lists. Also write a program to test it.

4. Write a program to find the number of comparisons using `binarySearch` and the sequential search algorithm as follows:

   Suppose `list` is an array of 1000 elements.

   a. Use a random number generator to fill `list`.

   b. Use any sorting algorithm to sort `list`.

   c. Search `list` for some items as follows:

      i. Use the binary search algorithm to search `list`. (You may need to modify the algorithm given in this chapter to count the number of comparisons.)

      ii. Use the binary search algorithm to search `list`, switching to a sequential search when the size of the search list reduces to less than 15. (Use the sequential search algorithm for a sorted list.)

   d. Print the number of comparisons for Steps c.i and c.ii. If the item is found in the list, then print its position.

18

5. (**Modified Bubble Sort**) Write a complete Java method to implement the modified bubble sort algorithm given in Exercise 5 of this chapter. Call this method `modifiedBubbleSort`. Also add this method to the **interface** `SearchSortADT`, provide its definition in the **class** `SearchSortAlgorithms`, and write a program to test your method.

6. Write a program to test the selection sort algorithm for array-based lists as given in this chapter.

7. Write and test a version of the selection sort algorithm for linked lists.

8. Write a program to test the insertion sort algorithm for array-based lists as given in this chapter.

9. Write and test a version of the insertion sort algorithm for linked lists.

10. Write a program to test the quick sort algorithm for array-based lists as given in this chapter.

11. (**C. A. R. Hoare**) Let L be a list of size n. The quick sort algorithm can be used to find the kth smallest item in L, where $0 \le k \le n - 1$, without completely sorting L. Write and implement a Java method, `kThSmallestItem`, that uses a version of the quick sort algorithm to determine the kth smallest item in L without completely sorting L.

12. Sort an array of 10,000 elements using the quick sort algorithm as follows:

    a. Sort the array using `pivot` as the middle element of the array.

    b. Sort the array using `pivot` as the median of the first, last, and middle elements of the array.

    c. Sort the array using `pivot` as the middle element of the array. However, when the size of any sublist reduces to less than 20, sort the sublist using an insertion sort.

    d. Sort the array using `pivot` as the median of the first, last, and middle elements of the array. When the size of any sublist reduces to less than 20, sort the sublist using an insertion sort.

    e. Calculate and print the CPU time for each of the preceding four steps. (You can use the method `currentTimeMillis` of the **class** `System` to find the current time of the system in millisecond as a **long** value. Note that the method `currentTimeMillis` is a **static** method. Therefore, the expression `System.currentTimeMillis()` returns the time as a **long** value. Also note that the **class** `System` is part of the **package** `java.lang`.)

13. Write a program to test the merge sort algorithm for linked lists as given in this chapter.

14. Write and test a version of the merge sort algorithm for array-based lists.

15. Write a program to test the heap sort algorithm for linked lists as given in this chapter.

16. a. Write the definitions of the methods of the **class** Candidate in the Programming Example Election Results that were not given in the programming example.

   b. Write the definitions of the methods `processVotes` and `printResults` of the Programming Example Election Results.

   c. After completing a and b, write a program to produce the output shown in the Sample Run of the Programming Example Election Results.

17. In the Programming Example Election Results, the **class** Candidate contains the method `calculateTotalVotes`. After processing the voting data, this method calculates the total number of votes received by a candidate. The method `updateVotesByRegion` (of the **class** Candidate) updates only the number of votes for a particular region. Modify the definition of this method so that it also updates the total number of votes received by the candidate. By doing so, the method `addVotes` in the main program is no longer needed. Modify and run your program with the modified definition of the method `updateVotesByRegion`.

18

BINARY TREES

> **In this chapter, you will:**
>
> ♦ Learn about binary trees
> ♦ Explore various binary tree traversal algorithms
> ♦ Learn how to organize data in a binary search tree
> ♦ Discover how to insert and delete items in a binary search tree
> ♦ Explore nonrecursive binary tree traversal algorithms
> ♦ Learn about AVL (height-balanced) trees

When data is being organized, a programmer's highest priority is to organize it in such a way that insertions, deletions, and lookups (searches) are fast. You have already seen how to store and process data in an array. Because an array is a random access data structure, if the data is properly organized (say, sorted), then we can use a search algorithm, such as a binary search, to effectively find and retrieve an item from the list. However, we know that storing data in an array has its limitations. For example, item insertion (especially if the array is sorted) and item deletion can be very time consuming, especially if the list size is very large, because each of these operations requires data movement. To speed up item insertion and deletion, we used linked lists. Item insertion and deletion in a linked list do not require any data movement; we simply adjust some of the links in the list. However, one of the drawbacks of linked lists is that they must be processed sequentially. That is, to insert or delete an item, or simply search the list for a particular item, we must begin our search at the first node in the list. As you know, a sequential search is good for only very small lists because the average search length of a sequential search is half the size of the list.

Binary Trees

This chapter discusses how to organize data dynamically so that insertions, deletions, and lookups are more efficient.

We first introduce some definitions to facilitate our discussion.

Definition: A **binary tree**, T, is either empty or:

    i. T has a special node called the root node;

    ii. T has two sets of nodes, L_T and R_T, called the **left subtree** and **right subtree** of T, respectively; and

    iii. L_T and R_T are binary trees.

A binary tree can be shown pictorially. Suppose that T is a binary tree with the root node A. Let L_A denote the left subtree of A, and R_A denote the right subtree of A. L_A and R_A are also binary trees. Suppose that B is the root node of L_A and C is the root node of R_A. B is called the **left child** of A, C is called the **right child** of A, and A is called the **parent** of B and C.

In the diagram of a binary tree, each node of the binary tree is represented as a circle and the circle is labeled by the node. The root node of the binary tree is drawn at the top. The left child of the root node (if any) is drawn below and to the left of the root node. Similarly, the right child of the root node (if any) is drawn below and to the right of the root node. Children are connected to the parent by an arrow from the parent to the child. An arrow is usually called a **directed edge** or a **directed branch** (or simply a **branch**). After drawing the root node, B, of L_A, we apply the same (recursive) procedure to draw the remaining parts of L_A. R_A is drawn similarly. If a node has no left child, for example, when we draw an arrow from the node to the left, we end the arrow with three lines. That is, three lines at the end of an arrow indicate that the subtree is empty.

The diagram in Figure 19-1 is an example of a binary tree. The root node of this binary tree is A. The left subtree of the root node, which we denote by L_A, is the set $L_A = \{B, D, E, G\}$ and the right subtree of the root node, which we denote by R_A, is the set $R_A = \{C, F, H\}$. The root node of the left subtree of A—that is, the root node of L_A—is node B. The root node of R_A is C, and so on. Clearly, L_A and R_A are also binary trees. Because three lines at the end of an arrow mean that the subtree is empty, it follows that the left subtree of D is empty.

In Figure 19-1, the left child of A is B and the right child of A is C. Similarly, for node F, the left child is H, and node F has no right child.

Examples 19-1 to 19-5 show nonempty binary trees.

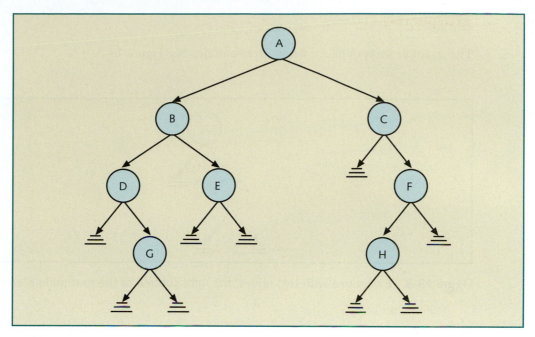

Figure 19-1   Binary tree

Example 19-1

This example shows a binary tree with one node. See Figure 19-2.

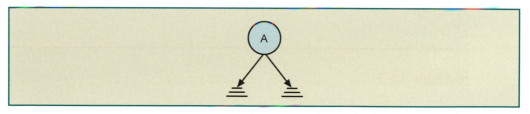

Figure 19-2   Binary tree with one node

In the binary tree of Figure 19-2:

The root node of the binary tree = A.

L_A = empty

R_A = empty

This example shows a binary tree with two nodes. See Figure 19-3.

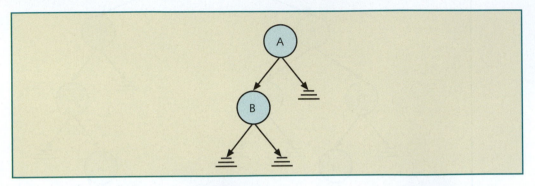

Figure 19-3   Binary tree with two nodes; the right subtree of the root node is empty

In the binary tree of Figure 19-3:

The root node of the binary tree = **A**.

$L_A = \{B\}$

$R_A = $ empty

The root node of $L_A = $ **B**.

$L_B = $ empty

$R_B = $ empty

This example shows a binary tree with two nodes. See Figure 19-4.

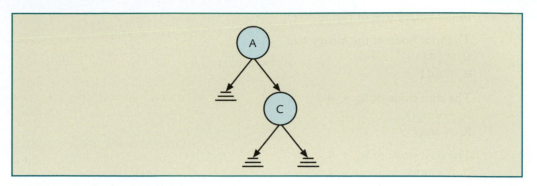

Figure 19-4   Binary tree with two nodes; the left subtree of the root node is empty

In the binary tree of Figure 19-4:

The root node of the binary tree = A.

L_A = empty

$R_A = \{C\}$

The root node of R_A = C.

L_C = empty

R_C = empty

Example 19-4

This example shows a binary tree with three nodes. See Figure 19-5.

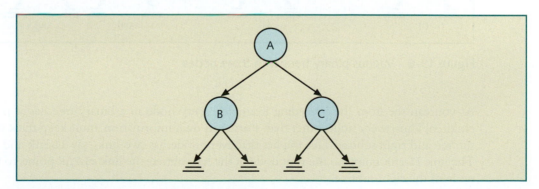

Figure 19-5   Binary tree with three nodes

In the binary tree of Figure 19-5:

The root node of the binary tree = A.
$L_A = \{B\}$
$R_A = \{C\}$

The root node of L_A = B.
L_B = empty
R_B = empty

The root node of R_A = C.
L_C = empty
R_C = empty

Example 19-5

This example shows other cases of nonempty binary trees with three nodes. See Figure 19-6.

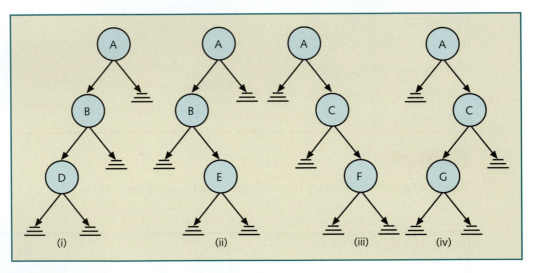

Figure 19-6   Various binary trees with three nodes

As you can see from the preceding examples, every node in a binary tree has at most two children. Thus, every node, other than storing its own information, must keep track of its left subtree and right subtree. This implies that every node has two links, say lLink and rLink. The link lLink points to the root node of the left subtree; the link rLink points to the root node of the right subtree.

The following class defines the node of a binary tree:

```java
    //Definition of the class implementing binary nodes
protected class BinaryTreeNode<T>
{
    public T info;
    public BinaryTreeNode<T> lLink;
    public BinaryTreeNode<T> rLink;

       //Default constructor
       //Postcondition: info = null; lLink = null; rLink = null;
    public BinaryTreeNode()
    {
        info = null;
        lLink = null;
        rLink = null;
    }

       //Constructor with parameters
       //Sets info to point to the object elem points to and
       //lLink and rLink are set to point to the objects left
       //and right, respectively.
       //Postcondition:  info = elem; lLink = left;
       //                      rLink = right;
    public BinaryTreeNode(T elem, BinaryTreeNode<T> left,
                                  BinaryTreeNode<T> right)
    {
        info = elem;
        lLink = left;
        rLink = right;
    }

       //Returns a clone of this binary tree.
       //This method clones only the references stored in the
       //nodes of the binary tree. The objects that binary tree
       //nodes point to are not cloned.
    public Object clone()
    {
        BinaryTreeNode<T> copy = null;

        try
        {
            copy = (BinaryTreeNode<T>) super.clone();

        }
        catch (CloneNotSupportedException e)
        {
            return null;
        }
```

```
            return copy;
        }


        //Method to return the info as a string.
        //Postcondition: info as a String object is returned.
    public String toString()
    {
        return info.toString();
    }
}
```

Note that the **class** `BinaryTreeNode` is declared **protected** and its instance variables are **public**. This is because, as in the case of linked list, this class will be an inner class of the **class** `BinaryTree`, discussed later in this chapter, which implements a binary tree. The methods of the **class** `BinaryTree` can directly access the instance variables of **class** `BinaryTreeNode`.

Figure 19-7 shows a UML class diagram of the **class** `BinaryTreeNode`.

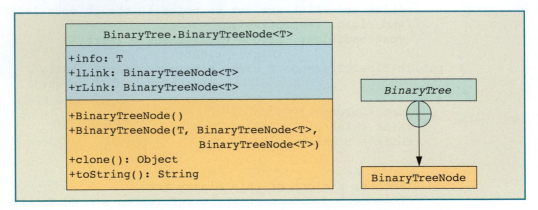

Figure 19-7 UML class diagram of the **class** `BinaryTreeNode` and the outer-inner class relationship

From the definition of the `BinaryTreeNode` it is clear that for each node:

- The data is stored in the object to which `info` points.

- The reference of the left child is stored in `lLink`.

- The reference of the right child is stored in `rLink`.

Furthermore, the reference of the root node of a binary tree is stored outside the binary tree in a reference variable, usually called the **root**, of the type `BinaryTreeNode`. Thus, in general, a binary tree looks like the diagram in Figure 19-8.

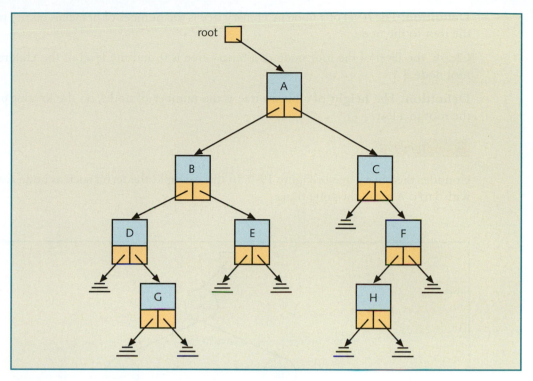

Figure 19-8   Binary tree

For simplicity, we will continue to draw binary trees as before. That is, we will use circles to represent nodes, and left and right arrows to represent links. As before, three lines at the end of an arrow mean that the subtree is empty.

Before we leave this section, let us define a few more terms.

A node in a binary tree is called a **leaf** if it has no left and right children. Let U and V be two nodes in the binary tree T. U is called the **parent** of V if there is a branch from U to V. A **path** from a node X to a node Y in a binary tree is a sequence of nodes $X_0, X_1, ..., X_n$ such that:

    i. $X = X_0, X_n = Y$

    ii. X_{i-1} is the parent of X_i for all $i = 1, 2, ..., n$. That is, there is a branch from X_0 to X_1, X_1 to $X_2, ..., X_{i-1}$ to $X_i, ..., X_{n-1}$ to X_n.

If $X_0, X_1, ..., X_n$ is a path from node X to node Y, sometimes we denote it by $X = X_0 - X_1 - \cdots - X_{n-1} - X_n = Y$ or simply $X - X_1 - \cdots - X_{n-1} - Y$.

Because the branches go only from a parent to its children, from the previous discussion it is clear that in a binary tree, there is a unique path from the root to every node in the binary tree.

Definition: The **length** of a path in a binary tree is the number of branches on that path.

Definition: The **level** of a node in a binary tree is the number of branches on the path from the root to the node.

Clearly, the level of the root node of a binary tree is 0, and the level of the children of the root node is 1.

Definition: The **height** of a binary tree is the number of nodes on the longest path from the root to a leaf.

Example 19-6

Consider the binary tree of Figure 19-9. In this example, the terms such as node **A** and node with `info` **A** mean the same thing.

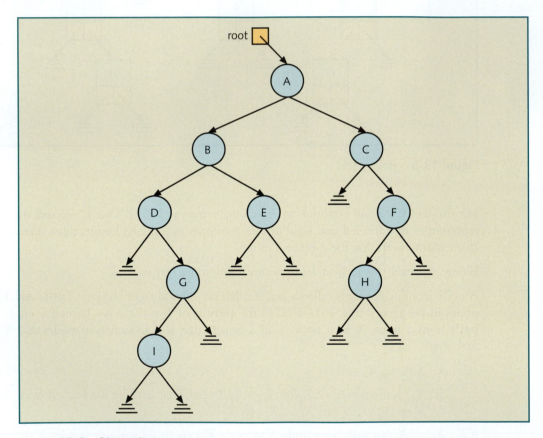

Figure 19-9 Binary tree

In this binary tree, the nodes **I**, **E**, and **H** have no left and right children. So the nodes **I**, **E**, and **H** are leaves.

There is branch from the node A to the node B. So the node A is the parent of the node B. Similarly, the node A is the parent of the node C, the node B is the parent of the nodes D and E, the node C is the parent of the node F, the node D is the parent of the node G, and so on.

A–B–D–G is a path from the node A to the node G. Because there are three branches on this path, the length of this path is 3. Similarly, B–D–G–I is a path from the node B to the node I.

There are three leaves in this binary tree, which are I, E, and H. Also, the paths from the root to these leaves are: A–B–D–G–I, A–B–E, and A–C–F–H. Clearly, the longest path from root to a leaf is A–B–D–G–I. The number of nodes on this path is 5. Hence, the height of the given binary tree is 5.

Suppose that a reference, p, of the root node of a binary tree is given. We next describe the Java method **height** to find the height of the binary tree. The reference of the root node is passed as a parameter to the method **height**.

If the binary tree is empty, then the **height** is 0. Suppose that the binary tree is nonempty. To find the height of the binary tree, we first find the height of the left subtree and the height of the right subtree. We then take the maximum of these two heights and add 1 to find the height of the binary tree. To find the height of the left (right) subtree, we apply the same procedure because the left (right) subtree is a binary tree. Therefore, the general algorithm to find the height of a binary tree is as follows (suppose **height(p)** denotes the height of the binary tree with root p):

```
if (p is null)
    height(p) =  0
else
    height(p) = 1 + maximum(height(p.lLink), height(p.rLink))
```

Clearly, this is a recursive algorithm. The following method implements this algorithm:

```
private int height(BinaryTreeNode<T> p)
{
    if (p == null)
        return 0;
    else
        return 1 + Math.max(height(p.lLink), height(p.rLink));
}
```

The definition of the method **height** uses the method **max**, of the Java **class** Math, to determine the larger of two integers. Recall that **max** is a **public static** member of the **class** Math. So you can use this method using the name of the class and the dot operator, as shown in the code. You can also write your own method **max** to determine the larger of two integers. Also note that the method **height** is declared as **private**. This is because this method will be used to implement the method to find the height of a binary tree, as described later in this chapter.

Similarly, we can implement algorithms to find the number of nodes and number of leaves in a binary tree.

Clone Tree

One useful operation on binary trees is to make an identical copy of a binary tree. A binary tree is a dynamic data structure; that is, memory for its nodes is allocated and deallocated during program execution. Therefore, if we use just the value of the reference variable of the root node to make a copy of a binary tree, we get a shallow copy of the data. To make an identical copy of a binary tree, we need to create as many nodes as there are in the binary tree to be copied. Also, in the copied tree, these nodes must appear in the same order as they are in the original binary tree.

Given the reference of the root node of a binary tree, we next describe the method `copyTree`, which makes a copy of a given binary tree and returns the reference of the root node of the copied tree. This method is also useful in implementing the method `clone`, as described later in this chapter (see the section "Implementing Binary Trees").

```java
private BinaryTreeNode<T> copyTree
                   (BinaryTreeNode<T> otherTreeRoot)
{
    BinaryTreeNode<T> temp;

    if (otherTreeRoot == null)
        temp = null;
    else
    {
        temp = (BinaryTreeNode<T>) otherTreeRoot.clone();
        temp.lLink = copyTree(otherTreeRoot.lLink);
        temp.rLink = copyTree(otherTreeRoot.rLink);
    }

    return temp;
}//end copyTree
```

Note that the method `copyTree` clones only the nodes of a binary tree. It does not clone the objects to which the references `info` point. This is because this is a generic method and, as explained in Chapter 15, it is not possible to produce true clones of the objects to which the reference `info` points. If these objects are immutable, then the method `copyTree` would work as desired.

BINARY TREE TRAVERSAL

The item insertion, deletion, and lookup operations require that the binary tree be traversed. Thus, the most common operation performed on a binary tree is to traverse the binary tree, or visit each node of the binary tree. As you can see from the diagram of a binary tree (for example, Figure 19-9), the traversal must start at the root node because we have the reference of the root node. For each node, we have two choices:

- Visit the node first.
- Visit the subtrees first.

These choices lead to three commonly used traversals of a binary tree, as described in the ensuing three sections:

- Inorder traversal

- Preorder traversal

- Postorder traversal

Inorder Traversal

In an **inorder traversal**, the binary tree is traversed as follows:

1. Traverse the left subtree.

2. Visit the node.

3. Traverse the right subtree.

Preorder Traversal

In a **preorder traversal**, the binary tree is traversed as follows:

1. Visit the node.

2. Traverse the left subtree.

3. Traverse the right subtree.

Postorder Traversal

In a **postorder traversal**, the binary tree is traversed as follows:

1. Traverse the left subtree.

2. Traverse the right subtree.

3. Visit the node.

Clearly, each of these traversal algorithms is recursive.

The listing of the nodes produced by the inorder traversal of a binary tree is called the **inorder sequence**. The listing of the nodes produced by the preorder traversal of a binary tree is called the **preorder sequence**. The listing of the nodes produced by the postorder traversal of a binary tree is called the **postorder sequence**.

Before giving the Java code for each of these traversals, let us illustrate the inorder traversal of the binary tree in Figure 19-10. For simplicity, we assume that visiting a node means to output the data stored in the node.

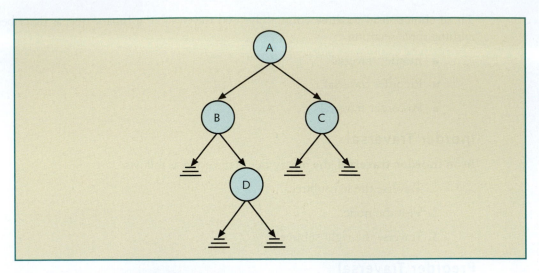

Figure 19-10 Binary tree for an inorder traversal

The reference of the root node of the binary tree in Figure 19-10 is stored in **root** (which points to the node with info **A**). Therefore, we start the traversal at **A**.

1. Traverse the left subtree of **A**; that is, traverse L_A = {**B,D**}.

2. Visit **A**.

3. Traverse the right subtree of **A**; that is, traverse R_A = {**C**}.

We cannot do Step 2 until we have finished Step 1.

1. Traverse the left subtree of **A**; that is, traverse L_A = {**B,D**}. Now L_A is a binary tree with the root node **B**. Because L_A is a binary tree, we apply the inorder traversal criteria to L_A.

    1.1 Traverse the left subtree of **B**; that is, traverse L_B = empty.

    1.2 Visit **B**.

    1.3 Traverse the right subtree of **B**; that is, traverse R_B = {**D**}.

As before, first we must complete Step 1.1 before going to Step 1.2.

1.1. Because the left subtree of **B** is empty, there is nothing to traverse. Step 1.1 is completed, so we proceed to Step 1.2.

1.2. Visit **B**. That is, output **B** on an output device. Clearly, the first node printed is **B**. This completes Step 1.2, so we proceed to Step 1.3.

1.3. Traverse the right subtree of **B**; that is, traverse R_B = {**D**}. Now R_B is a binary tree with the root node **D**. Because R_B is a binary tree, we apply the inorder traversal criteria to R_B.

19

1.3.1. Traverse the left subtree of D; that is, traverse L_D = empty.

1.3.2. Visit D.

1.3.3. Traverse the right subtree of D; that is, traverse R_D = empty.

1.3.1. Because the left subtree of D is empty, there is nothing to traverse. Step 1.3.1 is completed, so we proceed to Step 1.3.2.

1.3.2. Visit D. That is, output D on an output device. This completes Step 1.3.2, so we proceed to Step 1.3.3.

1.3.3. Because the right subtree of D is empty, there is nothing to traverse. Step 1.3.3 is completed.

This completes Step 1.3. Because Steps 1.1, 1.2, and 1.3 are completed, Step 1 is completed, so we go to Step 2.

2. Visit A. That is, output A on an output device. This completes Step 2, so we proceed to Step 3.

3. Traverse the right subtree of A; that is, traverse R_A = {C}. Now R_A is a binary tree with the root node C. Because R_A is a binary tree, we apply the inorder traversal criteria to R_A.

3.1 Traverse the left subtree of C; that is, traverse L_C = empty.

3.2 Visit C.

3.3 Traverse the right subtree of C; that is, traverse R_C = empty.

3.1. Because the left subtree of C is empty, there is nothing to traverse. Step 3.1 is completed, so we proceed to Step 3.2.

3.2. Visit C. That is, output C on an output device. This completes Step 3.2, so we proceed to Step 3.3.

3.3. Because the right subtree of C is empty, there is nothing to traverse. Step 3.3 is completed.

This completes Step 3, which in turn completes the traversal of the binary tree.

Clearly, the inorder traversal of the previous binary tree outputs the nodes in the following order:

Inorder sequence: B D A C

Similarly, the preorder and postorder traversals output the nodes in the following order:

Preorder sequence: A B D C

Postorder sequence: D B C A

As you can see from the walk-through of the inorder traversal, after visiting the left subtree of a node, we must come back to the node itself. The links are in only one direction; that is, the parent node points to the left and right children, but there is no link from each child to the parent. Therefore, before going to a child, we must somehow save the reference of the parent node. A convenient way to do this is to write a recursive inorder method; this is because in a recursive call, after completing a particular call, the control goes back to the caller. (Later we discuss how to write nonrecursive traversal methods.) The recursive definition of the method to implement the inorder traversal algorithm is:

```
private void inorder(BinaryTreeNode<T> p)
{
    if (p != null)
    {
        inorder(p.lLink);
        System.out.print(p + " ");
        inorder(p.rLink);
    }
}
```

To do the inorder traversal of a binary tree, the root node of the binary tree is passed as a parameter to the method **inorder**. For example, if the root points to the root node of the binary tree, a call to the method **inorder** is:

```
inorder(root);
```

Similarly, we can write the methods to implement the preorder and postorder traversals. The definitions of these methods are:

```
private void preorder(BinaryTreeNode<T> p)
{
    if (p != null)
    {
        System.out.print(p + " ");
        preorder(p.lLink);
        preorder(p.rLink);
    }
}
```

```
private void postorder(BinaryTreeNode<T> p)
{
    if (p != null)
    {
        postorder(p.lLink);
        postorder(p.rLink);
        System.out.print(p + " ");
    }
}
```

This section described the binary tree traversal algorithms inorder, preorder, and postorder. If you want to make a copy of a binary tree while preserving the structure of the binary tree, you can use preorder traversal. To delete all the nodes of a binary tree, you can use the postorder traversal. Later in this chapter, we discuss the binary search tree. The inorder traversal of a binary search tree visits the nodes in sorted order.

 In addition to the inorder, preorder, and postorder traversals, a binary tree can also be traversed **level-by-level**, also known as **breadth-first traversal**. In Chapter 20, we discuss graphs. A binary tree is also a graph. We discuss how to implement breadth-first traversal algorithms for graphs. You can modify that algorithm to do a breadth-first traversal of binary trees.

Implementing Binary Trees

The preceding sections described various operations that can be performed on a binary tree, as well as the methods to implement these operations. This section describes binary trees as an ADT. Before designing the class to implement a binary tree as an ADT, let us list various operations that are typically performed on a binary tree.

- Determine whether the binary tree is empty.
- Search the binary tree for a particular item.
- Insert an item in the binary tree.
- Delete an item from the binary tree.
- Find the height of the binary tree.
- Find the number of nodes in the binary tree.
- Find the number of leaves in the binary tree.
- Traverse the binary tree.
- Copy the binary tree.

The following interface defines the operations on a binary tree as an ADT:

```
public interface BinaryTreeADT<T> extends Cloneable
{
    public Object clone();
        //Returns a clone of this binary tree.
        //This method clones only the references stored in the
        //nodes of the binary tree. The objects that binary tree
        //nodes point to are not cloned.
```

```
public boolean isEmpty();
    //Method to determine whether the binary tree is empty.
    //Postcondition: Returns true if the binary tree is
    //               empty; otherwise, returns false.

public void inorderTraversal();
    //Method to do an inorder traversal of the binary tree.
    //Postcondition: The nodes of the binary tree are
    //               output in the inorder sequence.

public void preorderTraversal();
    //Method to do a preorder traversal of the binary tree.
    //Postcondition: The nodes of the binary tree are output
    //               in the preorder sequence.

public void postorderTraversal();
    //Method to do a postorder traversal of the binary tree.
    //Postcondition: The nodes of the binary tree are output
    //               in the postorder sequence.

public int treeHeight();
    //Method to determine the height of the binary tree.
    //Postcondition: The height of the binary tree is
    //               returned.

public int treeNodeCount();
    //Method to determine the number of nodes in the
    //binary tree.
    //Postcondition: The number of nodes in the binary
    //               tree is returned.

public int treeLeavesCount();
    //Method to determine the number of leaves in the binary
    //tree.
    //Postcondition: The number of leaves in the binary tree
    //               is returned.

public void destroyTree();
    //Method to destroy the binary tree.
    //Postcondition: The root of the binary tree is null.

public boolean search(T searchItem);
    //Method to determine whether searchItem is in the binary
    //tree.
    //Postcondition: Returns true if searchItem is found
    //               in the binary tree;
    //               otherwise, returns false.
```

```
    public void insert(T insertItem);
        //Method to insert insertItem in the binary tree.
        //Postcondition: If no node in the binary tree has the
        //               same info as insertItem, a node with the
        //               info insertItem is created and inserted
        //               in the binary search tree.

    public void deleteNode(T deleteItem);
        //Method to delete deleteItem from the binary tree.
        //Postcondition: If a node with the same info as
        //               deleteItem is found, it is deleted from
        //               the binary tree.
}
```

Figure 19-11 shows a UML class diagram of the **interface** BinaryTreeADT.

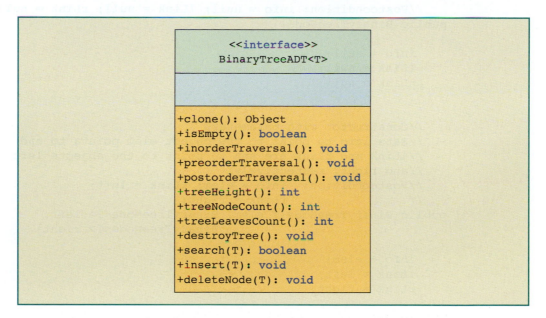

Figure 19-11   UML class diagram of the **interface** BinaryTreeADT

The item search, insertion, and deletion operations all require the binary tree to be traversed. However, because the nodes of a binary tree are in no particular order, these algorithms are not very efficient on arbitrary binary trees. That is, no criteria exist to guide the search on these binary trees, as we will see in the next section. Therefore, the **class** BinaryTree, which we describe next, is declared **abstract** because this class does not provide the definitions of the methods search, insert, and deleteNode. We will discuss these algorithms when we discuss special types of binary trees later in this chapter.

The following defines the heading, instance variables, constructors, and method of the **class** BinaryTree. Note that the definition of the node is the same as before. For the sake of completeness and easy reference, the definition of the node follows:

Class: BinaryTree

```
public abstract class BinaryTree<T> implements BinaryTreeADT<T>
```

Binary Tree Node: The following class implements the nodes of a binary tree

```
protected class BinaryTreeNode<T> implements Cloneable
{
    public T info;
    public BinaryTreeNode<T> lLink;
    public BinaryTreeNode<T> rLink;

        //Default constructor
        //Postcondition: info = null; lLink = null; rLink = null;
    public BinaryTreeNode()
    {
        info = null;
        lLink = null;
        rLink = null;
    }

        //Constructor with parameters
        //Sets info to point to the object elem points to and
        //lLink and rLink are set to point to the objects left
        //and right, respectively.
        //Postcondition:  info = elem; lLink = left;
        //                      rLink = right;
    public BinaryTreeNode(T elem, BinaryTreeNode<T> left,
                                  BinaryTreeNode<T> right)
    {
        info = elem;
        lLink = left;
        rLink = right;
    }

        //Returns a clone of this binary tree.
        //This method clones only the references stored in the
        //nodes of the binary tree. The objects that binary tree
        //nodes point to are not cloned.
    public Object clone()
    {
        BinaryTreeNode<T> copy = null;

        try
        {
```

```
            copy = (BinaryTreeNode<T>) super.clone();
        }
        catch (CloneNotSupportedException e)
        {
            return null;
        }

        return copy;
    }

        //Method to return the info as a string.
        //Postcondition: info as a String object is returned.
    public String toString()
    {
        return info.toString();
    }
}
```

Instance Variable

```
protected BinaryTreeNode<T> root;
```

Constructor and Instance Methods

```
public BinaryTree()
    //Default constructor
    //Postcondition: root = null;

public Object clone()
    //Returns a clone of this binary tree.
    //This method clones only the references stored in the nodes
    //of the binary tree. The objects that binary tree nodes
    //point to are not cloned.

public boolean isEmpty()
    //Method to determine whether the binary tree is empty.
    //Postcondition: Returns true if the binary tree is
    //               empty; otherwise, returns false.

public void inorderTraversal()
    //Method to do an inorder traversal of the binary tree.
    //Postcondition: The nodes of the binary tree are output
    //               in the inorder sequence.

public void preorderTraversal()
    //Method to do a preorder traversal of the binary tree.
    //Postcondition: The nodes of the binary tree are output
    //               in the preorder sequence.
```

```java
public void postorderTraversal()
    //Method to do a postorder traversal of the binary tree.
    //Postcondition: The nodes of the binary tree are output
    //                in the postorder sequence.

public int treeHeight()
    //Method to determine the height of the binary tree.
    //Postcondition: The height of the binary tree is
    //                returned.

public int treeNodeCount()
    //Method to determine the number of nodes in the
    //binary tree.
    //Postcondition: The number of nodes in the binary tree
    //                is returned.

public int treeLeavesCount()
    //Method to determine the number of leaves in the
    //binary tree.
    //Postcondition: The number of leaves in the binary tree
    //                is returned.

public void destroyTree()
    //Method to destroy the binary tree.
    //Postcondition: root = null

public abstract boolean search(T searchItem);
    //Method to determine whether searchItem is in the binary
    //tree.
    //Postcondition: Returns true if searchItem is found
    //                in the binary tree;
    //                otherwise, returns false.

public abstract void insert(T insertItem);
    //Method to insert insertItem in the binary tree.
    //Postcondition: If no node in the binary tree has the same
    //                info as insertItem, a node with the info
    //                insertItem is created and inserted
    //                in the binary tree.

public abstract void deleteNode(T deleteItem);
    //Method to delete deleteItem from the binary tree.
    //Postcondition: If a node with the same info as
    //                deleteItem is found, it is deleted
    //                from the binary tree.
```

```
private void inorder(BinaryTreeNode<T> p)
    //Method to do an inorder traversal of the binary
    //tree to which p points.
    //Postcondition: The nodes of the binary tree to which
    //               p points are output in the inorder
    //               sequence.

private void preorder(BinaryTreeNode<T> p)
    //Method to do a preorder traversal of the binary
    //tree to which p points.
    //Postcondition: The nodes of the binary tree to which p
    //               points are output in the preorder
    //               sequence.

private void postorder(BinaryTreeNode<T> p)
    //Method to do a postorder traversal of the binary
    //tree to which p points.
    //Postcondition: The nodes of the binary tree to which p
    //               points are output in the postorder
    //               sequence.

private int height(BinaryTreeNode<T> p)
    //Method to determine the height of the binary tree
    //to which p points.
    //Postcondition: The height of the binary tree to
    //               which p points is returned.

private int nodeCount(BinaryTreeNode<T> p)
    //Method to determine the number of nodes in the binary
    //tree to which p points.
    //Postcondition: The number of nodes in the binary tree
    //               to which p points is returned.

private int leavesCount(BinaryTreeNode<T> p)
    //Method to determine the number of leaves in the binary
    //tree to which p points.
    //Postcondition: The number of leaves in the binary tree
    //               to which p points is returned.

private BinaryTreeNode<T> copyTree
                     (BinaryTreeNode<T> otherTreeRoot)
    //Method to make a copy of the binary tree to which
    //otherTreeRoot points.
    //Postcondition: A copy of the binary tree to which
    //               otherTreeRoot is created and the reference of
    //               the root node of the copied binary tree
    //               is returned.
```

Figure 19-12 shows a UML class diagram of the **class** BinaryTree.

```
+---------------------------------------------------+
|                 BinaryTree<T>                     |
+---------------------------------------------------+
| #root: BinaryTreeNode<T>                          |
+---------------------------------------------------+
| +BinaryTree()                                     |
| +clone(): Object                                  |
| +isEmpty(): boolean                               |
| +inorderTraversal(): void                         |
| +preorderTraversal(): void                        |
| +postorderTraversal(): void                       |
| +treeHeight(): int                                |
| +treeNodeCount(): int                             |
| +treeLeavesCount(): int                           |
| +destroyTree():void                               |
| +search(T): boolean                               |
| +insert(T): void                                  |
| +deleteNode(T): void                              |
| -inorder(BinaryTreeNode<T>): void                 |
| -preorder(BinaryTreeNode<T>): void                |
| -postorder(BinaryTreeNode<T>): void               |
| -height(BinaryTreeNode<T>): int                   |
| -nodeCount(BinaryTreeNode<T>): int                |
| -leavesCount(BinaryTreeNode<T>): int              |
| -copyTree(BinaryTreeNode<T>): BinaryTreeNode<T>   |
+---------------------------------------------------+
```

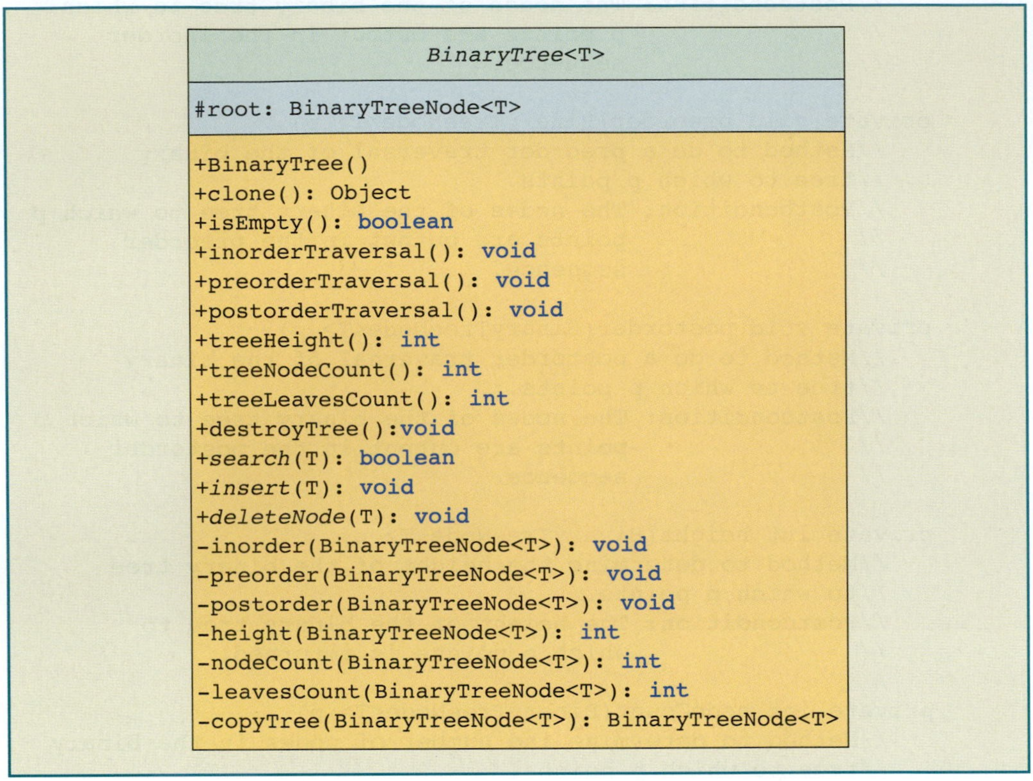

Figure 19-12   UML class diagram of the **class** BinaryTree

The definition of the **class** BinaryTree contains several methods that are **private** members of the class. These methods are used to implement the **public** member methods of the class and the user need not know of their existence. For example, to do an inorder traversal, the method inorderTraversal calls the method inorder and passes root as a parameter to this method. Suppose that you have the following statement:

BinaryTree<String> myTree;

Also assume that the object myTree has been created. The following statement performs an inorder traversal of myTree:

myTree.inorderTraversal();

Also, note that in the definition of the **class** BinaryTree, root is declared as a **protected** member so that we can later derive special binary trees.

Next, we give the definitions of the nonabstract methods of the **class** BinaryTree.

The binary tree is empty if `root` is `null`. So the definition of the method `isEmpty` is:

```java
public boolean isEmpty()
{
    return (root == null);
}
```

The default constructor initializes the binary tree to an empty state; that is, it sets `root` to `null`. Therefore, the definition of the default constructor is:

```java
public BinaryTree()
{
    root = null;
}
```

The definitions of the other methods are:

```java
public void inorderTraversal()
{
    inorder(root);
}

public void preorderTraversal()
{
    preorder(root);
}

public void postorderTraversal()
{
    postorder(root);
}

public int treeHeight()
{
    return height(root);
}

public int treeNodeCount()
{
    return nodeCount(root);
}

public int treeLeavesCount()
{
    return leavesCount(root);
}

private void inorder(BinaryTreeNode<T> p)
```

```java
{
    if (p != null)
    {
        inorder(p.lLink);
        System.out.print(p + " ");
        inorder(p.rLink);
    }
}

private void preorder(BinaryTreeNode<T> p)
{
    if (p != null)
    {
        System.out.print(p + " ");
        preorder(p.lLink);
        preorder(p.rLink);
    }
}

private void postorder(BinaryTreeNode<T> p)
{
    if (p != null)
    {
        postorder(p.lLink);
        postorder(p.rLink);
        System.out.print(p + " ");
    }
}

private int height(BinaryTreeNode<T> p)
{
    if (p == null)
        return 0;
    else
        return 1 + Math.max(height(p.lLink),
                            height(p.rLink));
}
```

The definitions of the methods **nodeCount** and **leavesCount** are left as exercises for you. (See Programming Exercises 1 and 2 at the end of this chapter.)

Next, we give the definitions of the methods **copyTree**, **clone**, and **destroyTree**.

The definition of the method **copyTree** is the same as given earlier in this chapter. We include it again here for easy reference:

```java
private BinaryTreeNode<T> copyTree
                    (BinaryTreeNode<T> otherTreeRoot)
{
    BinaryTreeNode<T> temp;
```

```
        if (otherTreeRoot == null)
        {
            temp = null;
        }
        else
        {
            temp = (BinaryTreeNode<T>) otherTreeRoot.clone();
            temp.lLink = copyTree(otherTreeRoot.lLink);
            temp.rLink = copyTree(otherTreeRoot.rLink);
        }

        return temp;
    }//end copyTree
```

The definition of the method **clone** is:

```
public Object clone()
{
    BinaryTree<T> copy = null;

    try
    {
        copy = (BinaryTree<T>) super.clone();

    }
    catch (CloneNotSupportedException e)
    {
        return null;
    }

    if (root != null)
        copy.root = copyTree(root);

    return copy;
}
```

To destroy a binary tree, we simply set **root** to **null**. The definition of the method **destroyTree** is:

```
public void destroyTree()
{
    root = null;
}
```

BINARY SEARCH TREES

Now that you know the basic operations on a binary tree, you can study a special type of binary tree, called a binary search tree.

Consider the binary tree in Figure 19-13.

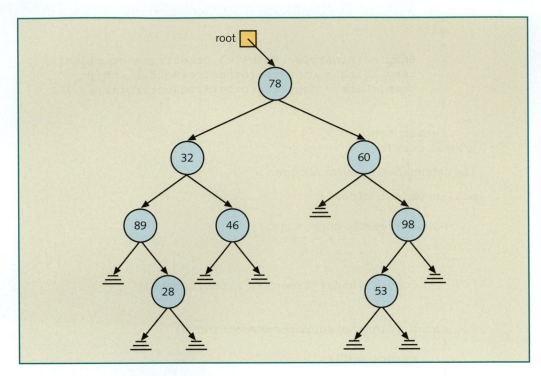

Figure 19-13 Arbitrary binary tree

Suppose that we want to determine whether **50** is in the binary tree in Figure 19-13. To do so, we can use any of the previous traversal algorithms to visit each node and compare the search item with the data stored in the node. However, this could require us to traverse a large part of the binary tree, so the search would be slow. Because no criteria exist to guide our search, we would need to visit each node in the binary tree until either the item is found or we have traversed the entire binary tree. This case is like an arbitrary linked list where we must start our search at the first node, and continue looking at each node until either the item is found or the entire list is searched.

On the other hand, consider the binary tree in Figure 19-14.

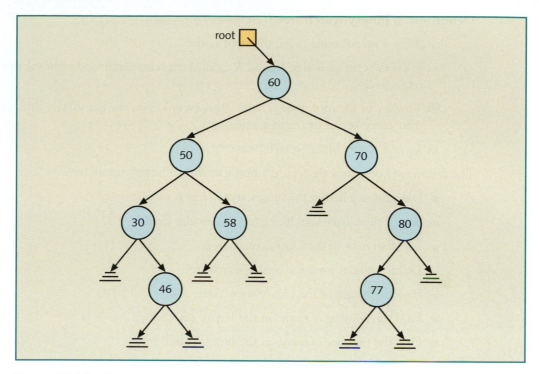

Figure 19-14   Binary search tree

The binary tree in Figure 19-14 has some order to its nodes. The data in each node is larger than the data in its left child and smaller than the data in its right child.

Suppose that we want to determine whether 58 is in this binary tree. As before, we must start our search at the root node. We compare 58 with the data in the root node; that is, we compare 58 with 60. Because 58 ≠ 60 and 58 < 60, it is guaranteed that 58 is not in the right subtree of the root node. Therefore, if 58 is in the binary tree, then it must be in the left subtree of the root node. We follow the left link of the root node and go to the node with info 50. We now apply the same criteria at this node. Because 58 > 50, we must follow the right link of this node and go to the node with info 58. At this node we find item 58.

This example shows that every time we move down to a child, we eliminate one of the subtrees of the node from our search. If the binary tree is nicely constructed, then the search is very similar to the binary search on arrays.

The binary tree given in Figure 19-14 is a special type of binary tree, called a binary search tree. (In the following definition, by the term key of a node, we mean the key of the data item that uniquely identifies the item.)

Definition: A **binary search tree**, T, is either empty or:

   i. T has a special node called the **root** node;

   ii. T has two sets of nodes, L_T and R_T, called the left subtree and right subtree of T, respectively;

   iii. The key in the root node is larger than every key in the left subtree and smaller than every key in the right subtree; and

   iv. L_T and R_T are binary search trees.

The following operations are typically performed on a binary search tree:

- Determine whether the binary search tree is empty.

- Search the binary search tree for a particular item.

- Insert an item in the binary search tree.

- Delete an item from the binary search tree.

- Find the height of the binary search tree.

- Find the number of nodes in the binary search tree.

- Find the number of leaves in the binary search tree.

- Traverse the binary search tree.

- Copy the binary search tree.

Clearly, every binary search tree is a binary tree. The height of a binary search tree is determined the same way as the height of a binary tree. Similarly, the operations to find the number of nodes, find the number of leaves, and to do inorder, preorder, and postorder traversals of a binary search tree are the same as those for a binary tree. Therefore, we can inherit all of these operations from the binary tree. That is, we can extend the definition of the binary tree by using the principle of inheritance, and hence define the binary search tree. Note that we need to implement only the abstract methods of the **class** BinaryTree.

The following described the heading, constructors, and instance methods of the **class** BinarySearchTree by extending the definition of the binary tree:

Class: BinarySearchTree

```
public class BinarySearchTree<T> extends BinaryTree<T>
```

Constructor and Instance Methods:

```
public BinarySearchTree()
    //Default constructor
    //Postcondition: root = null;

public boolean search(T searchItem)
    //Method to determine whether searchItem is in the
```

```
   //binary search tree.
   //Postcondition: Returns true if searchItem is found
   //                in the binary search tree;
   //                otherwise, returns false.

public void insert(T insertItem)
   //Method to insert insertItem in the binary search tree.
   //Postcondition: If no node in the binary search tree has
   //               the same info as insertItem, a node with
   //               the info insertItem is created and inserted
   //               in the binary search tree.

public void deleteNode(T deleteItem)
   //Method to delete deleteItem from the binary search tree
   //Postcondition: If a node with the same info as
   //               deleteItem is found, it is deleted from
   //               the binary search tree.

private BinaryTreeNode<T> deleteFromTree(BinaryTreeNode<T> p)
   //Method to delete the node to which p points, from
   //the binary search tree.
   //Postcondition: The node to which p points is deleted
   //               from the binary search tree. The
   //               reference of the root node of the binary
   //               search tree after deletion is returned.
```

Figure 19-15 shows a UML class diagram of the **class** BinarySearchTree and the inheritance hierarchy.

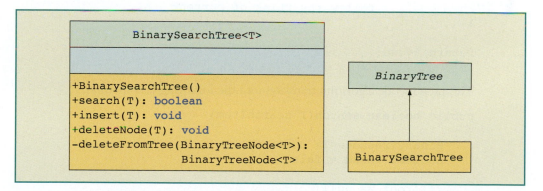

Figure 19-15   UML class diagram of the **class** BinarySearchTree and the inheritance hierarchy

Next, we describe each of these operations.

Search

The method **search** searches the binary search tree for a given item. If the item is found in the binary search tree, it returns **true**; otherwise, it returns **false**. We use a **boolean** variable **found** to keep track of our search result. Because **root** points to the root node of the binary search tree, we must begin our search at the root node. Furthermore, because **root** must always point to the root node, we need a reference variable, say **current**, to traverse the binary search tree. The reference variable **current** is initialized to **root**.

If the binary search tree is nonempty, we first compare the search item with the info in the root node. If they are the same, we stop the search and return **true**. Otherwise, if the search item is smaller than the info in the node, we follow **lLink** to go to the left subtree; otherwise, we follow **rLink** to go to the right subtree. We repeat this process for the next node. If the search item is in the binary search tree, our search ends at the node containing the search item; otherwise, the search ends at an empty subtree. Thus, the general algorithm is:

```
found = false;   //initialize found to false
if root is null
    Cannot search an empty tree.
else
{
    current = root;

    while (current is not null and not found)
        if (current.info is the same as the search item)
            set found to true;
        else if (current.info is greater than the search item)
            follow the lLink of current
        else
            follow the rLink of current
}

return found;
```

This pseudocode algorithm translates into the following Java method:

```java
public boolean search(T searchItem)
{
    BinaryTreeNode<T> current;
    boolean found = false;

    if (root == null)
        System.out.println("Cannot search an empty tree.");
    else
    {
        current = root;
```

```
        while (current != null && !found)
        {
            Comparable<T> temp =
                    (Comparable<T>) current.info;

            if (temp.compareTo(searchItem) == 0)
                found = true;
            else if (temp.compareTo(searchItem) > 0)
                current = current.lLink;
            else
                current = current.rLink;
        }//end while
    }//end else

    return found;
}//end search
```

Insert

The method **insert** inserts a new item into a binary search tree. After inserting an item in a binary search tree, the resulting binary tree must also be a binary search tree. To insert a new item, first we search the binary search tree and find the place where the new item is to be inserted. The search algorithm is similar to the search algorithm of the method **search**. Here we traverse the binary search tree with two reference variables—**current**, to check the current node, and **trailCurrent**, pointing to the parent of **current**. Because duplicate items are not allowed, our search must end at an empty subtree. We can then use **trailCurrent** to insert the new item at the proper place. The item to be inserted, **insertItem**, is passed as a parameter to the method **insert**. The general algorithm is:

  a. Create a new node and assign **insertItem** to the **info** field of this node. Also set **lLink** and **rLink** of the new node to **null**. (This is accomplished by using the constructor with parameters of the **class** **BinaryTreeNode** and passing appropriate parameters.)

  b. **if** root is **null**,

the tree is empty, so make **root** point to the new node.

```
else
{
    current = root;
    while (current is not null)     //search the binary tree
    {
        trailCurrent = current;
        if (current.info is the same as insertItem)
            Error: Cannot insert duplicate items.
            exit
        else
```

```
                    if (current.info is greater than insertItem)
                        Follow lLink of current
                    else
                        Follow rLink of current
            }

        //insert the new node in the binary tree

        if (trailCurrent.info is greater than insertItem)
            make the new node the left child of trailCurrent
        else
            make the new node the left child of trailCurrent
    }
```

This pseudocode algorithm translates into the following Java method:

```java
public void insert(T insertItem)
{
    BinaryTreeNode<T> current;       //reference variable to
                                     //traverse the tree
    BinaryTreeNode<T> trailCurrent = null; //reference variable
                                           //behind current
    BinaryTreeNode<T> newNode;       //reference variable to
                                     //create the node

    newNode = new BinaryTreeNode<T>(insertItem, null, null);

    if (root == null)
        root = newNode;
    else
    {
        current = root;

        while (current != null)
        {
            trailCurrent = current;

            Comparable<T> temp1 =
                    (Comparable<T>) current.info;

            if (temp1.compareTo(insertItem) == 0)
            {
                System.err.print("The insert item is "
                            + "already in the tree -- "
                            + "duplicates are not "
                            + "allowed.");
                return;
            }
```

```
            else if (temp1.compareTo(insertItem) > 0)
                current = current.lLink;
            else
                current = current.rLink;
        }//end while

        Comparable<T> temp2 =
                    (Comparable<T>) trailCurrent.info;

        if (temp2.compareTo(insertItem) > 0)
            trailCurrent.lLink = newNode;
        else
            trailCurrent.rLink = newNode;
    }
}//end insert
```

Delete

The method `deleteNode` deletes an item from the binary search tree. After deleting the item, the resulting binary tree must be a binary search tree. As before, first we search the binary search tree to find the node to be deleted. To help you better understand the delete operation, before describing the method to delete an item from the binary search tree, let us consider the binary search tree given in Figure 19-16.

After deleting the desired item (if it exists in the binary search tree), the resulting tree must be a binary search tree. The delete operation has four cases:

Case 1: The node to be deleted has no left and right subtrees; that is, the node to be deleted is a leaf. For example, the node with info **45** is a leaf.

Case 2: The node to be deleted has no left subtree; that is, the left subtree is empty, but it has a nonempty right subtree. For example, the left subtree of the node with info **40** is empty, and its right subtree is nonempty.

Case 3: The node to be deleted has no right subtree; that is, the right subtree is empty, but it has a nonempty left subtree. For example, the right subtree of the node with info **80** is empty and its left subtree is nonempty.

Case 4: The node to be deleted has nonempty left and right subtrees. For example, the left and right subtrees of the node with info **50** are nonempty.

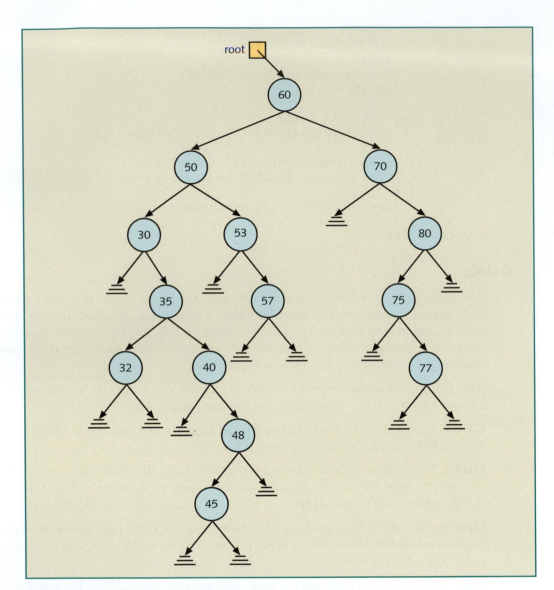

Figure 19-16 Binary search tree before deleting a node

For Case 1, suppose that we want to delete **45** from the binary search tree in Figure 19-16. We search the binary search tree and arrive at the node containing **45**. Because this node is a leaf and is the left child of its parent, we can simply set the **lLink** of the parent node, of **45**, to **null**. After deleting this node, Figure 19-17 shows the resulting binary search tree.

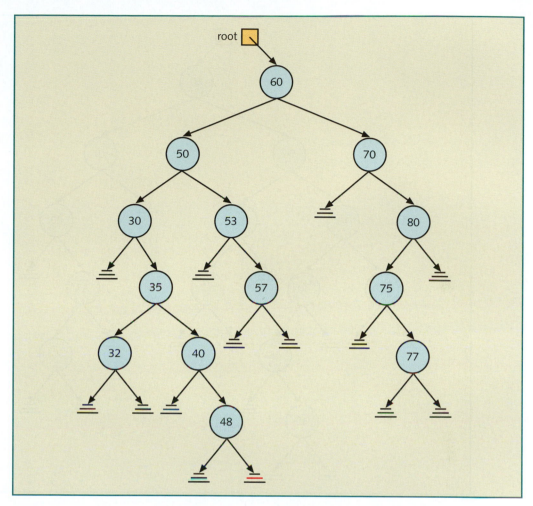

Figure 19-17 Binary search tree after deleting 45

For Case 2, suppose that we want to delete 30 from the binary search tree in Figure 19-16. In this case, the node to be deleted has no left subtree. Because 30 is the left child of its parent node, we make the `lLink` of the parent node, of 30, point to the right child of 30. The parent node of 30 is 50 and the right child of 30 is 35. So we make the `lLink` of 50 point to the node 35. Figure 19-18 shows the resulting binary search tree.

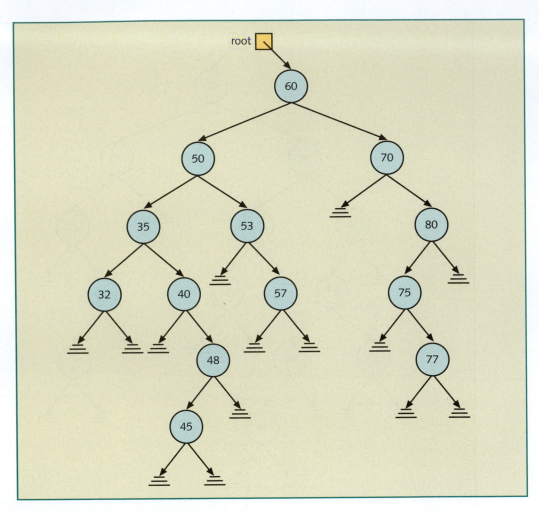

Figure 19-18 Binary search tree after deleting 30

For Case 3, suppose that we want to delete 80 from the binary search tree in Figure 19-16. The node containing 80 has no right child and is the right child of its parent. Thus, we make the `rLink` of the parent of 80—that is, 70—point to the left child of 80. Figure 19-19 shows the resulting binary search tree.

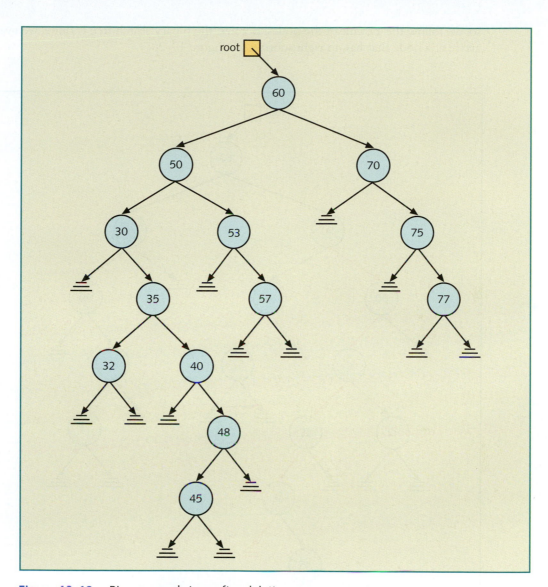

Figure 19-19   Binary search tree after deleting 80

For Case 4, suppose that we want to delete 50 from the binary search tree in Figure 19-16. The node with info 50 has a nonempty left subtree and a nonempty right subtree. Here, we first reduce this case to either Case 2 or Case 3 as follows. To be specific, suppose that we reduce it to Case 3—that is, the node to be deleted has no right subtree. For this case, we find the immediate predecessor of 50 in this binary tree, which is 48. This is done by first going to the left child of 50, and then locating the rightmost node of the left subtree of 50. To do so, we follow the `rLink` of the nodes. Because the binary search tree is finite, we eventually arrive at a node that has no right subtree; see Figure 19-20.

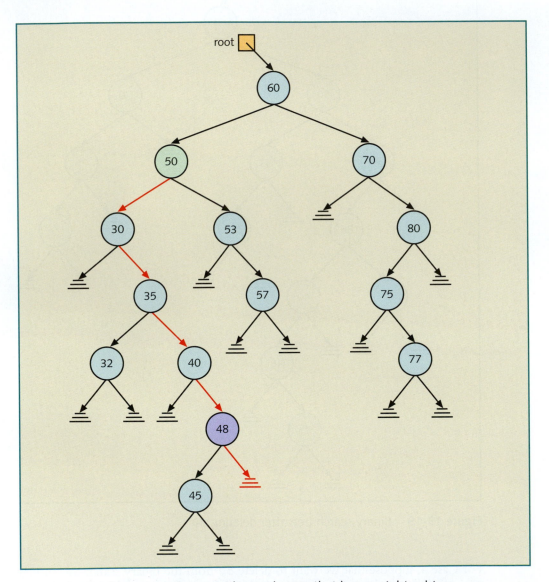

Figure 19-20 Binary search tree with a node, 48, that has no right subtree

Next, we swap the info of the node to be deleted with the info of its immediate predecessor. In this case, we swap 48 with 50. This reduces to the case wherein the node to be deleted has no right subtree. We now apply Case 3 to delete the node. (Note that because we delete the immediate predecessor from the binary search tree, we, in fact, copy only the info of the immediate predecessor into the node to be deleted.) After deleting 50 from the binary search tree in Figure 19-16, the resulting binary tree is as shown in Figure 19-21.

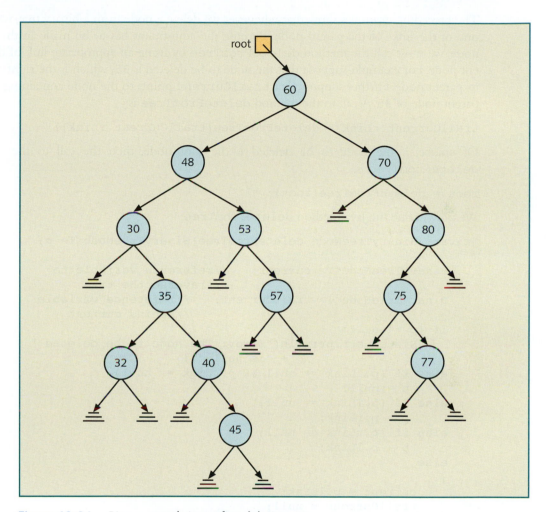

Figure 19-21   Binary search tree after deleting 50

In each case, we see that the resulting binary tree is again a binary search tree.

From this discussion, it follows that to delete an item from a binary search tree, we must do the following:

1. Find the node containing the item (if any) to be deleted.

2. Delete the node.

We accomplish the second step by a separate method, which we call `deleteFromTree`. Given a reference of the node to be deleted, this method deletes the node by taking into account the previous four cases. After deleting the node, it returns the reference of the root node of the binary search subtree.

The preceding examples show that whenever we delete a node from a binary tree, we adjust one of the links of the parent node. Because the adjustment has to be made in the parent node, we must call the method `deleteFromTree` by using an appropriate link of the parent node. For example, suppose that the node to be deleted is 35, which is the right child of its parent node. Further suppose that `trailCurrent` points to the node containing 30, the parent node of 35. A call to the method `deleteFromTree` is:

```
trailCurrent.rLink = deleteFromTree(trailCurrent.rLink);
```

Of course, if the node to be deleted is the root node, then the call to the method `deleteFromTree` is:

```
root = deleteFromTree(root);
```

We now define the Java method `deleteFromTree`:

```java
private BinaryTreeNode deleteFromTree(BinaryTreeNode<T> p)
{
    BinaryTreeNode<T> current;     //reference variable to
                                   //traverse the tree
    BinaryTreeNode<T> trailCurrent;  //reference variable
                                     //behind current

    if (p == null)
        System.err.println("Error: The node to be deleted "
                        + "is null.");
    else if (p.lLink == null && p.rLink == null)
        p = null;
    else if (p.lLink == null)
        p = p.rLink;
    else if (p.rLink == null)
        p = p.lLink;
    else
    {
        current = p.lLink;
        trailCurrent = null;

        while (current.rLink != null)
        {
            trailCurrent = current;
            current = current.rLink;
        }//end while

        p.info = current.info;
```

```
        if (trailCurrent == null) //current did not move;
                                  //current == p.lLink;
                                  //adjust p
            p.lLink = current.lLink;
        else
            trailCurrent.rLink = current.lLink;
    }//end else

    return p;
}//end deleteFromTree
```

Next, we describe the method `deleteNode`. The method `deleteNode` first searches the binary search tree to find the node containing the item to be deleted. The item to be deleted, `deleteItem`, is passed as a parameter to the method. If the node containing `deleteItem` is found in the binary search tree, the method `deleteNode` calls the method `deleteFromTree` to delete the node. The definition of the method `deleteNode` is given next.

```
public void deleteNode(T deleteItem)
{
    BinaryTreeNode<T> current;   //reference variable to
                                 //traverse the tree
    BinaryTreeNode<T> trailCurrent; //reference variable
                                 //behind current
    boolean found = false;

    if (root == null)
        System.err.println("Cannot delete from an "
                    + "empty tree.");
    else
    {
        current = root;
        trailCurrent = root;

        while (current != null && !found)
        {
            if (current.info.equals(deleteItem))
                found = true;
            else
            {
                trailCurrent = current;

                Comparable<T> temp =
                        (Comparable<T>) current.info;

                if (temp.compareTo(deleteItem) > 0)
                    current = current.lLink;
                else
                    current = current.rLink;
            }
        }
```

```
          }//end while

      if (current == null)
          System.out.println("The delete item is not in "
                             + "the tree.");
      else if (found)
      {
          if (current == root)
              root = deleteFromTree(root);
          else
          {
              Comparable<T> temp =
                      (Comparable<T>) trailCurrent.info;

              if (temp.compareTo(deleteItem) > 0)
                  trailCurrent.lLink =
                          deleteFromTree(trailCurrent.lLink);
              else
                  trailCurrent.rLink =
                          deleteFromTree(trailCurrent.rLink);
          }
      }//end else-if
  }

}//end deleteNode
```

BINARY SEARCH TREE: ANALYSIS

This section provides an analysis of the performance of binary search trees. Let T be a binary search tree with n nodes, where $n > 0$. Suppose that we want to determine whether an item, x, is in T. The performance of the search algorithm depends on the shape of T. Let us first consider the worst case. In the worst case, T is linear. That is, T is one of the forms shown in Figure 19-22.

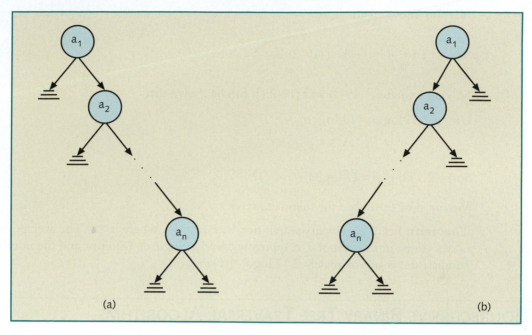

Figure 19-22   Linear binary search trees

Because T is linear, the performance of the search algorithm on T is the same as its performance on a linked list. Therefore, in the successful case, on average, the search algorithm makes $\frac{n+1}{2} = O(n)$ key comparisons. In the unsuccessful case, it makes n comparisons.

Let us now consider the average-case behavior. In the successful case, the search would end at a node. Because there are n items, there are $n!$ possible orderings of the keys. We assume that all $n!$ orderings of the keys are possible. Let $S(n)$ denote the number of comparisons in the average successful case, and $U(n)$ denote the number of comparisons in the average unsuccessful case.

The number of comparisons required to determine whether x is in T is one more than the number of comparisons required to insert x in T. Furthermore, the number of comparisons required to insert x in T is the same as the number of comparisons made in the unsuccessful search, reflecting that x is not in T. From this, it follows that:

$$S(n) = 1 + \frac{U(0) + U(1) + \ldots + U(n-1)}{n} \qquad (19\text{-}1)$$

It is also known that:

$$S(n) = \left(1 + \frac{1}{n}\right) U(n) - 3 \quad (19\text{-}2)$$

Solving Equations (19-1) and (19-2), it can be shown that

$$U(n) \approx 2.77 \log_2 n = O(\log_2 n)$$

and

$$S(n) \approx 2.77 \log_2 n = O(\log_2 n)$$

We can now formulate the following result.

Theorem: Let T be a binary search tree with n nodes, where $n > 0$. The average number of nodes visited in a search of T is approximately $1.39 \log_2 n = O(\log_2 n)$, and the number of key comparisons is approximately $2.77 \log_2 n = O(\log_2 n)$.

NONRECURSIVE BINARY TREE TRAVERSAL ALGORITHMS

The previous sections described how to do the following:

- Traverse a binary tree using the inorder, preorder, and postorder methods.

- Construct a binary search tree.

- Insert an item in a binary search tree.

- Delete an item from a binary search tree.

The traversal algorithms—inorder, preorder, and postorder—discussed earlier are recursive. Because traversing a binary tree is a fundamental operation and recursive methods are somewhat less efficient than their iterative versions, this section discusses the nonrecursive inorder, preorder, and postorder traversal algorithms.

Nonrecursive Inorder Traversal

In an inorder traversal of a binary tree, for each node, the left subtree is visited first, then the node, and then the right subtree. It follows that in an inorder traversal, the first node visited is the leftmost node of the binary tree. For example, in the binary tree in Figure 19-23, the leftmost node is the node with info 28.

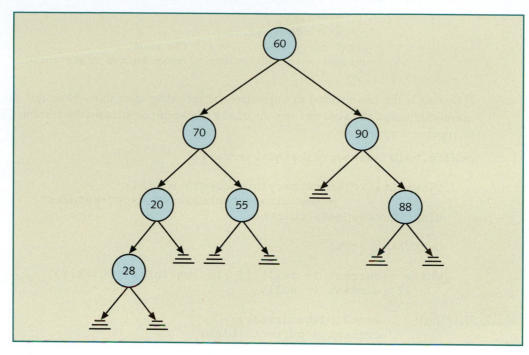

Figure 19-23   Binary tree; the leftmost node is 28

To get to the leftmost node of the binary tree, we start by traversing the binary tree at the root node, and then we follow the left link of each node until the left link of a node becomes **null**. We then back up to the parent node, visit the node, and then move to the right node. Because links go in only one direction, to get back to a node we must save the reference of the node before moving to the child node. Moreover, the nodes must be backtracked in the order they were traversed. It follows that while backtracking, the nodes must be visited in a Last In First Out manner. This can be done by using a stack. We therefore save reference of a node in a stack. The general algorithm is as follows:

1. Create stack.

2. `current = root;` `//start traversing the binary tree at the root node`

3. `while` `(current is not null or stack is nonempty)`
       `if` `(current is not null)`
       `{`
           `push current onto the stack;`
           `current = current.lLink;`
       `}`
       `else`

```
        {
            pop stack into current;
            visit current;        //visit the node
            current = current.rLink;   //move to the right child
        }
```

Following is the Java method to implement the preceding algorithm. (Note that the method nonRecursiveInTraversal uses the **class** LinkedStackClass described in Chapter 17 to implement a stack.)

```
public void nonRecursiveInTraversal()
{
    LinkedStackClass<BinaryTreeNode<T> > stack
                = new LinkedStackClass<BinaryTreeNode<T> >();
    BinaryTreeNode<T> current;

    current = root;

    while ((current != null) || (!stack.isEmptyStack()))
        if (current != null)
        {
            stack.push(current);
            current = current.lLink;
        }
        else
        {
            current = (BinaryTreeNode<T>) stack.peek();
            stack.pop();
            System.out.print(current.info + " ");
            current = current.rLink;
        }

    System.out.println();
}
```

Nonrecursive Preorder Traversal

In a preorder traversal of a binary tree, for each node, first the node is visited, then its left subtree is visited, and then its right subtree is visited. As in the case of an inorder traversal, after visiting a node and before moving to the left subtree, we must save the reference of the node so that after visiting the left subtree, we can visit the right subtree. The general algorithm is as follows:

1. Create stack.

2. current = root;   //start the traversal at the root node

3. **while** (current is not **null** or stack is nonempty)
       if (current is not **null**)
       {
           visit current;
```
```

```
        push current onto stack;
        current = current.lLink;
    }
    else
    {
        pop stack into current;
        current = current.rLink;    //prepare to visit the
                                    //right subtree
    }
```

We leave it as an exercise for you to write a Java method to implement the preceding algorithm. (See Programming Exercise 6.)

Nonrecursive Postorder Traversal

In a postorder traversal of a binary tree, for each node, first the left subtree is visited, then the right subtree is visited, and then the node is visited. As in the case of an inorder traversal, in a postorder traversal, the first node visited is the leftmost node of the binary tree. Because—for each node—the left and right subtrees are visited before visiting the node, we must indicate to the node whether the left and right subtrees have been visited. After visiting the left subtree of a node and before visiting the node, we must visit its right subtree. Therefore, after returning from a left subtree, we must tell the node that the right subtree needs to be visited, and after visiting the right subtree, we must tell the node that it can now be visited. To do this, other than saving the reference of the node (to get back to the right subtree and to the node itself), we also save an integer value of 1 before moving to the left subtree, and an integer value of 2 before moving to the right subtree. Whenever the stack is popped, the integer value associated with that reference is popped as well. This integer value tells whether the left and right subtrees of a node have been visited.

The general algorithm is:

1. Create stack(s).

2. `current = root;`   `//start the traversal at the root node`

3. `v = 0;`

4. `if` (current is `null`)

    the binary tree is empty

5. `if` (current is not `null`)

   a. `push current onto stack;`

   b. `push 1 onto stack;`

   c. `current = current.lLink;`

```
d. while (stack is not empty)
       if (current is not null and v is 0)
       {
           push current and 1 onto stack;
           current = current.lLink;
       }
       else
       {
           pop stack into current and v;
           if (v == 1)
           {
               push current and 2 onto stack;
               current = current.rLink;
               v = 0;
           }
           else
               visit current;
       }
```

We use two (parallel) stacks: one to save the reference to a node, and another to save the integer value (1 or 2). We leave it as an exercise for you to write the definition of a Java method to implement the preceding postorder traversal algorithm. (See Programming Exercise 6 at the end of this chapter.)

AN ITERATOR TO A BINARY TREE

In Chapter 16, we described how to implement an iterator to a linked list. Just as we can create and use an iterator to a linked list, we can also create and use an iterator to a binary tree. As described earlier in this chapter, typically, there are three ways a binary tree can be traversed—inorder, preorder, and postorder. We can implement an iterator to a binary tree using these same three ways. In this section, we discuss how to implement an iterator to a binary tree that traverses the nodes of the binary tree in the inorder sequence. To accomplish this, we use the non-recursive inorder traversal algorithm discussed in the preceding section. Moreover, the class that implements an inorder iterator to a binary tree is an *inner class* of the **class** BinaryTree.

The following describes the heading, instance variables, constructors, and instance methods of the class that implements an inorder iterator to a binary tree:

Class: BinaryTreeInorderIterator
public class BinaryTreeInorderIterator<T>

Instance Variable:

```
protected BinaryTreeNode<T> current;   //variable to
                                       //point to the
                                       //current node in
                                       //tree
LinkedStackClass<BinaryTreeNode<T> > stack;
```

Constructor and Instance methods:

```
public BinaryTreeInorderIterator()
    //Default constructor
    //Creates an iterator to a binary tree.
    //Postcondition: create stack, and current = root;

public void reset()
    //Method to reset the iterator to the root node of
    //the binary tree.
    //Postcondition: current = first;

public BinaryTreeNode<T> next()
    //Method to return a reference of the current node
    //in the tree and also to advance iterator to the
    //next node in inorder traversal.
    //Postcondition: A reference of the current node is
    //               returned and current is advanced to
    //               the next node in inorder traversal.

public boolean hasNext()
    //Method to determine whether there is a next
    //node in the tree.
    //Postcondition: Returns true, if there is a next node
    //               in the tree; otherwise returns false.

public T getCurrent()
    //Method to return a reference of the object to which
    //the info field of current node points.
    //Postcondition: If there is a next node,
    //               return current.info.
```

We leave the UML class diagram of the **class** `BinaryTreeInorderIterator` and the outer–inner class relationship as an exercise for you.

Next, we give the definition of the constructors and instance methods.

```
public BinaryTreeInorderIterator()
{
    stack = new LinkedStackClass<BinaryTreeNode<T> >();

    current = (BinaryTreeNode<T>) root;
}

public void reset()
{
    stack = new LinkedStackClass<BinaryTreeNode<T> >();

    current = (BinaryTreeNode<T>) root;
}
```

```java
public BinaryTreeNode<T> next()
{
    BinaryTreeNode<T> nextNode = null;

    while (current != null)
    {
        stack.push(current);
        current = current.lLink;
    }

    if (!stack.isEmptyStack())
    {
        nextNode = stack.peek();
        current = stack.peek();
        stack.pop();

        current = current.rLink;
    }
    else
        throw new NoSuchElementException();

    return nextNode;
}

public boolean hasNext()
{
    return (!stack.isEmptyStack()) || (current != null);
}

public T getCurrent()
{
    if (!hasNext())
        throw new NoSuchElementException();

    return current.info;
}
```

The complete definition of the **class** `BinaryTree`, which includes the **class** `BinaryTreeInorderIterator`, is available at the Web site accompanying this book. The Web site also contains the program `TestProgInorderIterator.java`, which illustrates how to use an inorder iterator in a program.

AVL (Height-Balanced) Trees

In the previous sections, you learned how to build and manipulate a binary search tree. The performance of the search algorithm on a binary search tree depends on how the binary tree is built. The shape of the binary search tree depends on the data set. If the data set is sorted, then the binary search tree is linear, and the search algorithm would not be efficient. On the other hand, if the tree is nicely built, then the search would be fast. In fact, the smaller the height of the tree, the faster the search. Therefore, we want the height of the binary search tree to be as small as possible. This section describes a special type of binary search tree, called the **AVL tree** (also called the **height-balanced tree**), in which the resulting binary search tree is nearly balanced. AVL trees were introduced by the mathematicians G. M. Adel'son-Vel'skii and E.M. Landis in 1962 and are named in their honor.

We begin with the following definition:

Definition: A **perfectly balanced** binary tree is a binary tree such that:

    i. The heights of the left and right subtrees of the root are equal.

    ii. The left and right subtrees of the root are perfectly balanced binary trees.

Figure 19-24 shows a perfectly balanced binary tree.

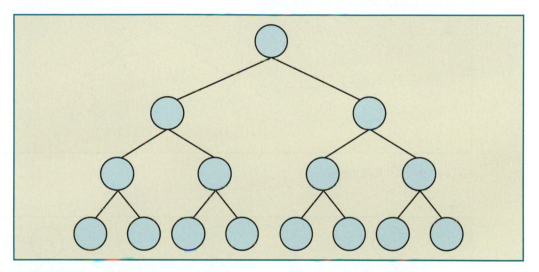

Figure 19-24   Perfectly balanced binary tree

Let T be a binary tree and x be a node in T. If T is perfectly balanced, then, from the definition of the perfectly balanced tree, it follows that the height of the left subtree of x is the same as the height of the right subtree, of x.

It can be proved that if T is a perfectly balanced binary tree of height h, then the number of nodes in T is $2^h - 1$. From this it follows that if the number of items in the data set is not equal to $2^h - 1$, for some nonnegative integer h, then we cannot construct a perfectly balanced binary tree. Moreover, perfectly balanced binary trees are a too-stringent refinement.

Definition: An **AVL tree** (or **height–balanced tree**) is a binary search tree such that:

   i. The height of the left and right subtrees of the root differs by at most 1.

  ii. The left and right subtrees of the root are AVL trees.

Figures 19-25 and 19-26 give examples of AVL and non-AVL trees.

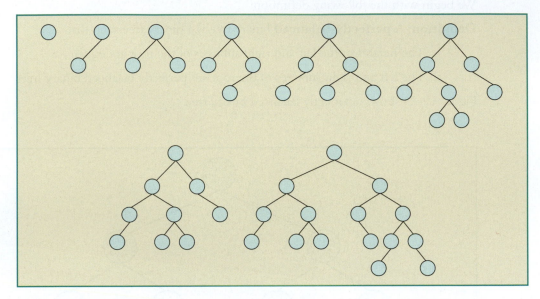

Figure 19-25   AVL trees

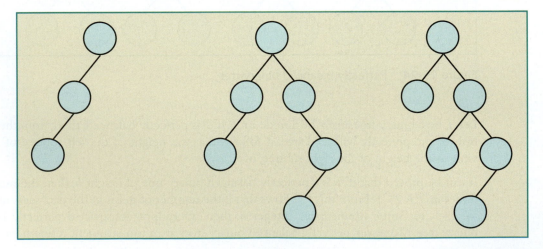

Figure 19-26   Non-AVL trees

Let x be a node in a binary tree. Let x_l denote the height of the left subtree of x, and x_r denote the height of the right subtree of x.

Theorem: Let T be an AVL tree and x be a node in T. Then $|x_r - x_l|$ 1, where $|x_r - x_l|$ denotes the absolute value of $x_r - x_l$.

Let x be a node in the AVL tree T.

 1. If $x_l > x_r$, we say that x is **left high**. In this case, $x_l = x_r + 1$.

 2. If $x_l = x_r$, we say that x is **equal high**.

 3. If $x_r > x_l$, we say that x is **right high**. In this case, $x_r = x_l + 1$.

Definition: The **balance factor** of x, written $bf(x)$, is defined by $bf(x) = x_r - x_l$.

Let x be a node in the AVL tree T. Then:

 1. If x is left high, then $bf(x) = -1$.

 2. If x is equal high, then $bf(x) = 0$.

 3. If x is right high, then $bf(x) = 1$.

Definition: Let x be a node in a binary tree. We say that the node x **violates the balance criteria** if $|x_r - x_l| > 1$, that is, if the height of the left and right subtrees of x differ by more than 1.

From the previous discussion, it follows that in addition to the data and references of the left and right subtrees, one more thing associated with each node x in the AVL tree T is the balance factor of x. Thus, every node must keep track of its balance factor. To make the algorithms efficient, we store the balance factor of each node in the node itself. The following class defines the node of an AVL tree. (Note that the **class** AVLNode is **protected** and its instance variables are **public**. This is because this will be an inner class of the class that implements an AVL tree.)

```
protected class AVLNode<T>
{
    public T info;
    public int bfactor;
    public AVLNode<T> lLink;
    public AVLNode<T> rLink;

        //Default constructor
        //Postcondition: info = null; bfactor = 0;
        //               lLink = null; rLink = null;
    public AVLNode()
    {
        info = null;
        bfactor = 0;
        lLink = null;
        rLink = null;
    }
}
```

```
          //Constructor with parameters.
          //Sets info to point to the object elem points to,
          //bfactor is set to bf; lLink is set to point to the
          //object left points to, and rLink is set to point to
          //the object right points to.
          //Postcondition: info = elem; bfactor = bf;
          //                lLink = left; rLink = right;
      public AVLNode(T elem, int bf, AVLNode<T> left,
                  AVLNode<T> right)
      {
          info = elem;
          bfactor = bf;
          lLink = left;
          rLink = right;
      }


          //Method to return the info as a string.
          //Postcondition: info as a String object is returned.
      public String toString()
      {
          return info.toString();
      }
}
```

We leave the UML class diagram of the **class** AVLNode as an exercise for you.

Because an AVL tree is a binary search tree, the search algorithm for an AVL tree is the same as the search algorithm for a binary search tree. Other operations, such as finding the height, determining the number of nodes, checking whether the tree is empty, tree traversal, and so on, can be implemented exactly the same way they are implemented on binary trees. However, item insertion and deletion operations on AVL trees are somewhat different from the ones discussed for binary search trees. This is because after inserting (or deleting) a node from an AVL tree, the resulting binary tree must be an AVL tree. Next, we describe these operations.

Insertion into AVL Trees

To insert an item in an AVL tree, first we search the tree and find the place where the new item is to be inserted. Because an AVL tree is a binary search tree, to find the place for the new item, we can search the AVL tree using a search algorithm similar to the search algorithm designed for binary search trees. If the item to be inserted is already in the tree, then the search ends at a nonempty subtree. Because duplicates are not allowed, in this case, we can output an appropriate error message. Suppose that the item to be inserted is not in the

AVL tree. Then the search ends at an empty subtree and we insert the item in that subtree. After inserting the new item in the tree, the resulting tree might not be an AVL tree. Thus, we must restore the tree's balance criteria. This is accomplished by traveling the same path, back to the root node, which was followed when the new item was inserted in the AVL tree. The nodes on this path (back to the root node) are visited, and either their balance factors are changed, or we might have to reconstruct part of the tree. We illustrate these cases with the help of the following examples.

 In Figures 19-27 through 19-38, for each node, we show only the data stored in the node. An equal sign (=) on the top of a node indicates that the balance factor of this node is 0; the less than symbol (<) indicates that the balance factor of this node is −1; and the greater than symbol (>) indicates that the balance factor of this node is 1.

Consider the AVL tree of Figure 19-27.

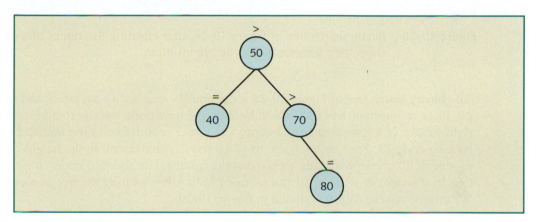

Figure 19-27   AVL tree before inserting 90

Let us insert 90 into this AVL tree. We search the tree starting at the root node to find the place for 90. The dotted arrow shows the path traversed. We insert the node with info 90 and obtain the binary search tree shown in Figure 19-28.

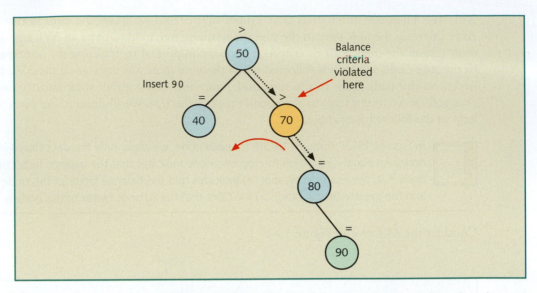

Figure 19-28 Binary search tree of Figure 19-26 after inserting 90; nodes other than 90 show their balance factors before insertion

The binary search tree of Figure 19-28 is not an AVL tree. So we backtrack and go to node 80. Prior to insertion, bf(80) was 0. Because the new node was inserted into the (empty) right subtree of 80, we change its balance factor to 1 (not shown in the figure). Now we go back to node 70. Prior to insertion, bf(70) was 1. After insertion, the height of the right subtree of 70 is increased; thus, we see that the subtree with the root node 70 is not an AVL tree. In this case, we reconstruct this subtree (this is called rotating the tree at root node 70). We thus obtain the AVL tree shown in Figure 19-29.

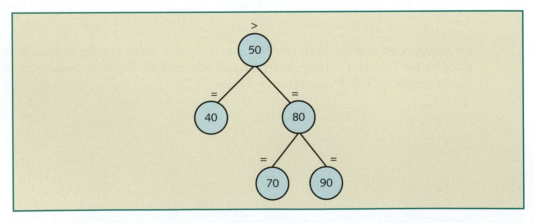

Figure 19-29 AVL tree of Figure 19-26 after inserting 90 and adjusting the balance factors

The binary search tree of Figure 19-29 is an AVL tree.

Now consider the AVL tree of Figure 19-30.

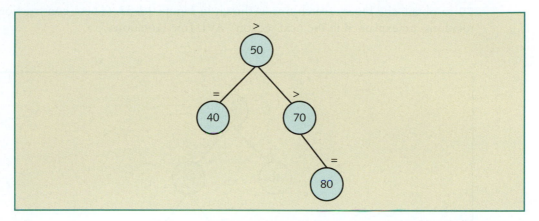

Figure 19-30   AVL tree before inserting 75

Let us insert 75 into the AVL tree of Figure 19-30.

As before, we search the tree starting at the root node. The dotted arrows show the path traversed. After inserting 75, the resulting binary search tree is as shown in Figure 19-31.

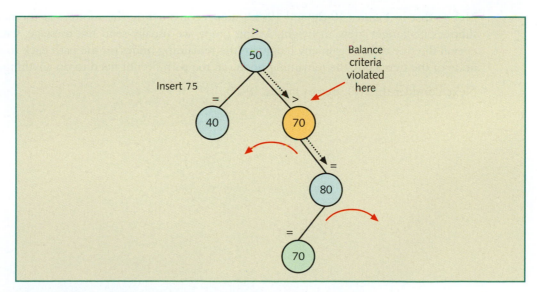

Figure 19-31   Binary search tree of Figure 19-30 after inserting 75; nodes other than 75 show their balance factors before insertion

After inserting 75, we backtrack. First we go to node 80 and change its balance factor to –1. The subtree with the root node 80 is an AVL tree. Now we go back to 70. Clearly, the subtree with the root node 70 is not an AVL tree. So we reconstruct this subtree. In this case, we first reconstruct the subtree at root node 80, and then reconstruct the subtree at root node 70 to obtain the binary search tree as shown in Figure 19-32. (These constructions, called rotations, are explained in the next section, "AVL Tree Rotations.")

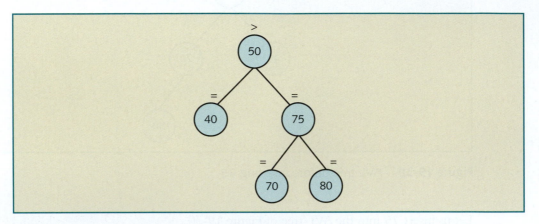

Figure 19-32   AVL tree of Figure 19-30 after inserting 75 and adjusting the balance factors

After reconstruction, the root of the constructed subtree is 75.

Notice that in Figures 19-29 and 19-32, after reconstructing the subtrees at the nodes, the subtrees no longer grew in height. At this point, we usually send the message, stating that overall the tree did not gain any height, to the remaining nodes on the path back to the root node of the tree. Thus, the remaining nodes on the path do not need to do anything.

Next, consider the AVL tree of Figure 19-33.

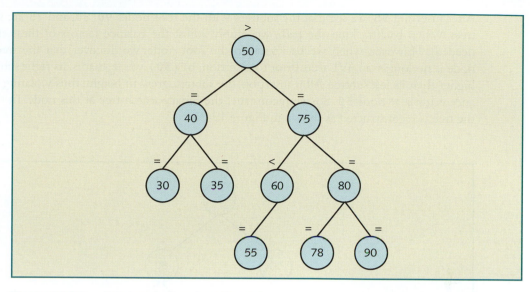

Figure 19-33   AVL tree before inserting 95

Let us insert 95 into this AVL tree. We search the tree and insert 95, as shown in Figure 19–34.

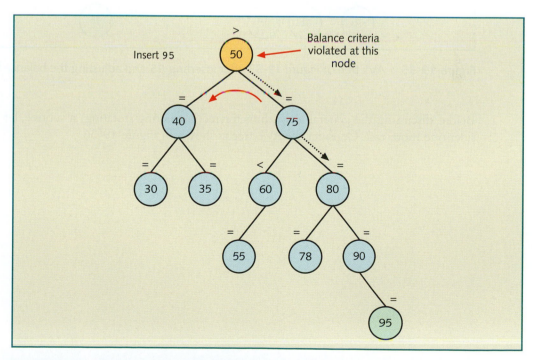

Figure 19-34   Binary search tree of Figure 19-33 after inserting 95; nodes other than 95 show their balance factors before insertion

After inserting 95, we see that the subtrees with the root nodes 90, 80, and 75 are still AVL trees. When backtracking the path, we simply adjust the balance factors of these nodes (if needed). However, when we backtrack to the root node, we discover that the tree at this node is no longer an AVL tree. Prior to insertion, bf(50) was 1, that is, its right subtree was higher than its left subtree. After insertion, the subtree grew in height, thus violating the balance criteria at node 50. So, we reconstruct the binary search tree at this node. In this case, the tree is reconstructed as shown in Figure 19-35.

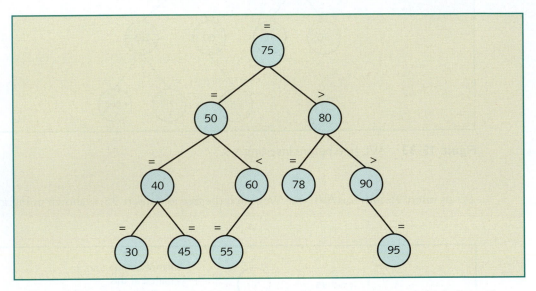

Figure 19-35   AVL tree of Figure 19-33 after inserting 95 and adjusting the balance factors

Before discussing the general algorithms for reconstructing (rotating) a subtree, let us consider one more case. Consider the AVL tree as shown in Figure 19-36.

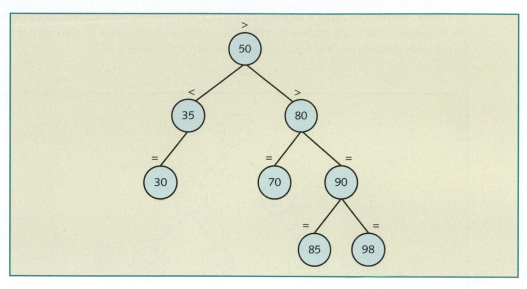

Figure 19-36   AVL tree before inserting 88

Let us insert 88 into the tree of Figure 19-36. Following the insertion procedure described previously, we obtain the binary search tree as shown in Figure 19-37.

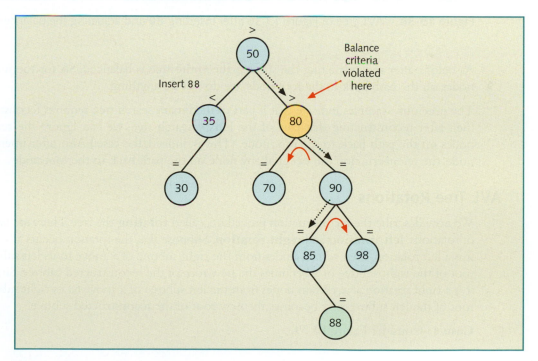

Figure 19-37   Binary search tree of Figure 19-36 after inserting 88; nodes other than 88 show their balance factors before insertion

As before, we now backtrack to the root node. We adjust the balance factors of nodes 85 and 90. When we visit node 80, we discover that at this node we need to reconstruct the subtree. In this case, the subtree is reconstructed as shown in Figure 19-38.

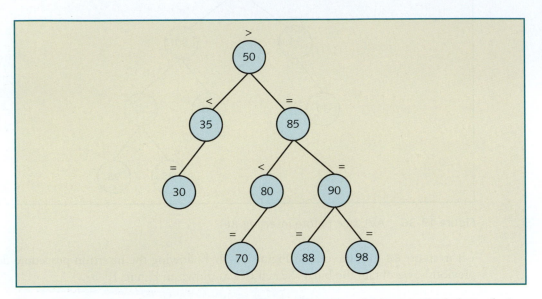

Figure 19-38 AVL tree of Figure 19-36 after inserting 88 and adjusting the balance factors

As before, after reconstructing the subtree, the entire tree is balanced. So, for the remaining nodes on the path back to the root node, we do not do anything.

The previous examples indicate that if part of the binary search tree requires reconstruction, then after reconstructing that part of the binary search tree, we can ignore the remaining nodes on the path back to the root node. (This is, indeed, the case.) Also, after inserting the node, the reconstruction can occur at any node on the path back to the root node.

AVL Tree Rotations

We now describe the reconstruction procedure, called **rotating** the tree. There are two types of rotations: **left rotation** and **right rotation**. Suppose that the rotation occurs at node *x*. If it is a left rotation, then certain nodes from the right subtree of *x* move to its left subtree; the root of the right subtree of *x* becomes the new root of the reconstructed subtree. Similarly, if it is a right rotation at *x*, certain nodes from the left subtree of *x* move to its right subtree; the root of the left subtree of *x* becomes the new root of the reconstructed subtree.

Case 1: Consider Figure 19-39.

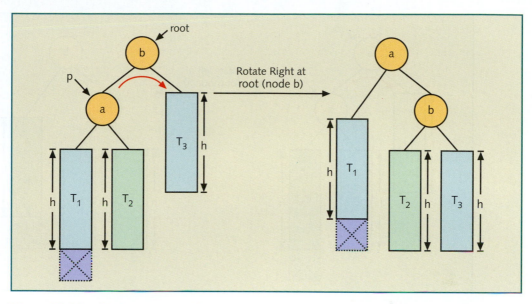

Figure 19-39   Right rotation at *b*

In Figure 19-39, subtrees T_1, T_2, and T_3 are of equal height—*h*. The dotted rectangle shows an item insertion in T_1, causing the height of the subtree T_1 to increase by 1. The subtree at node *a* is still an AVL tree, but the balance criteria is violated at the root node. We note the following in this binary search tree:

- Every key in T_1 is smaller than the key in node *a*.

- Every key in T_2 is larger than the key in node *a*.

- Every key in T_2 is smaller than the key in node *b*.

Therefore:

1. We make T_2 (the right subtree of node *a*) the left subtree of node *b*.

2. We make node *b* the right child of node *a*.

3. Node *a* becomes the root node of the reconstructed tree, as shown in Figure 19-39.

Case 2: This case is a mirror image of Case 1. See Figure 19-40.

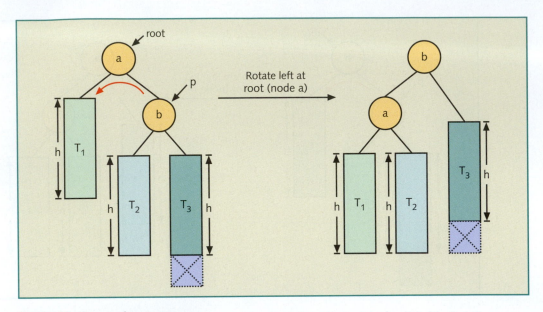

Figure 19-40   Left rotation at *a*

Case 3: Consider Figure 19–41.

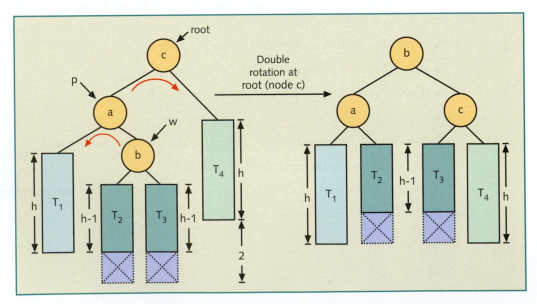

Figure 19-41   Double rotation: first rotate left at *a*, then rotate right at *c*. New item is inserted in either the subtree T_2 or T_3

In Figure 19-41, the tree on the left is the tree prior to the reconstruction. The heights of the subtrees are shown in the figure. The dotted rectangle shows that a new item is inserted in the subtree, T_2 or T_3, causing the subtree to grow in height. We note the following in the tree prior to reconstruction:

- All keys in T_3 are smaller than the key in node c.

- All keys in T_3 are larger than the key in node b.

- All keys in T_2 are smaller than the key in node b.

- All keys in T_2 are larger than the key in node a.

- After insertion, the subtrees with root nodes a and b are still AVL trees.

- The balance criteria is violated at the root node, c, of the tree.

- The balance factors of node c, $bf(c) = -1$, and node a, $bf(a) = 1$, are opposite.

This is an example of double rotation. One rotation is required at node a, and another rotation is required at node c. If the balance factor of the node where the tree is to be reconstructed and the balance factor of the higher subtree are opposite, that node requires a double rotation. First we rotate the tree at node a and then at node c. Now the tree at node a is right high and so we make a left rotation at a. Next, because the tree at node c is left high, we make a right rotation at c. Figure 19-41 shows the resulting tree (which is to the right of the tree after insertion). Figure 19-42 shows both rotations in sequence.

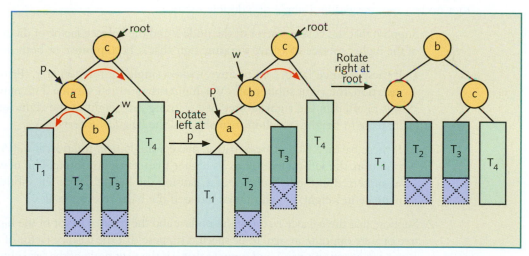

Figure 19-42   Left rotation at a followed by a right rotation at c

Case 4: This is a mirror image of Case 3. We illustrate this with the help of Figure 19-43.

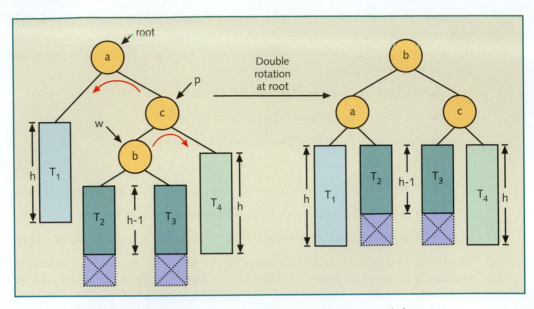

Figure 19-43   Double rotation: first rotate right at *c*, then rotate left at *a*

Using these four cases, we now describe what type of rotation might be required at a node.

Suppose that the tree is to be reconstructed, by rotation, at node *x*. Then the subtree with the root node *x* requires either a single or a double rotation.

1. Suppose that the balance factor of the node *x* and the balance factor of the root node of the higher subtree of *x* have the same sign, that is, both positive or both negative.

    a. If these balance factors are positive, make a single *left* rotation at *x*. (Prior to insertion, the right subtree of *x* was higher than its left subtree. The new item was inserted in the right subtree of *x*, causing the height of the right subtree to increase in height, which in turn violated the balance criteria at *x*.)

    b. If these balance factors are negative, make a single *right* rotation at *x*. (Prior to insertion, the left subtree of *x* was higher than its right subtree. The new item was inserted in the left subtree of *x*, causing the height of the left subtree to increase in height, which in turn violated the balance criteria at *x*.)

2. Suppose that the balance factor of the node *x* and the balance factor of the higher subtree of *x* are opposite in sign. To be specific, suppose that the balance factor of the node *x* prior to insertion was -1 and suppose that *y* is the root node of the left subtree of *x*. After insertion, the balance factor of the node *y* is 1. That is, after insertion, the right subtree of node *y* grew in height. In this case, we require a *double* rotation at *x*. First we make a left rotation at *y* (because *y* is right high). Then we make a right rotation at *x*. The other case, which is a mirror image of this case, is handled similarly.

The following Java methods implement the left and right rotations of a node. The reference of the node requiring the rotation is passed as a parameter to the method.

```java
private AVLNode<T> rotateToLeft(AVLNode<T> root)
{
    AVLNode<T> p; //reference variable to the root of
                  //the right subtree of root
    if (root == null)
        System.err.println("Error in the tree.");
    else
        if (root.rLink == null)
            System.err.println("Error in the tree: "
                                + "No right subtree to rotate.");
        else
        {
            p = root.rLink;
            root.rLink = p.lLink; //the left subtree of p
                                  //becomes the right
                                  //subtree of root
            p.lLink = root;
            root = p;    //make p the new root node
        }

    return root;
}//end rotateToLeft

private AVLNode<T> rotateToRight(AVLNode<T> root)
{
    AVLNode<T> p;   //reference variable to the root of the
                    //left subtree of root

    if (root == null)
        System.err.println("Error in the tree.");
    else
        if (root.lLink == null)
            System.err.println("Error in the tree: "
                                + "No left subtree to rotate.");
        else
        {
            p = root.lLink;
            root.lLink = p.rLink; //the right subtree of p
                                  //becomes the left subtree of root
            p.rLink = root;
            root = p;    //make p the new root node
        }

    return root;
}//end rotateToRight
```

Now that we know how to implement both rotations, we next write the Java methods, `balanceFromLeft` and `balanceFromRight`, which are used to reconstruct the tree at a particular node. The reference of the node where the reconstruction occurs is passed as a parameter to this method. These methods use the methods `rotateToLeft` and `rotateToRight` to reconstruct the tree, and also adjust the balance factors of the nodes affected by the reconstruction. The method `balanceFromLeft` is called when the subtree is left double high and certain nodes need to be moved to the right subtree. The method `balanceFromRight` has similar conventions.

```java
private AVLNode<T> balanceFromLeft(AVLNode<T> root)
{
    AVLNode<T> p;
    AVLNode<T> w;

    p = root.lLink;    //p points to the left subtree
                       //of root

    switch (p.bfactor)
    {
    case -1: root.bfactor = 0;
             p.bfactor = 0;
             root = rotateToRight(root);
             break;
    case 0:  System.err.println("Error: Cannot balance "
                                + "from the left.");
             break;
    case 1:  w = p.rLink;
             switch (w.bfactor)  //adjust the balance factors
             {
             case -1: root.bfactor = 1;
                      p.bfactor = 0;
                      break;
             case 0:  root.bfactor = 0;
                      p.bfactor = 0;
                      break;
             case 1:  root.bfactor = 0;
                      p.bfactor = -1;
             }//end switch

             w.bfactor = 0;
             p = rotateToLeft(p);
             root.lLink = p;
             root = rotateToRight(root);
    }//end switch;

    return root;
}//end balanceFromLeft
```

For completeness, we also give the definition of the method `balanceFromRight`:

```java
private AVLNode<T> balanceFromRight(AVLNode<T> root)
{
    AVLNode<T> p;
    AVLNode<T> w;

    p = root.rLink;    //p points to the right
                       //subtree of root

    switch (p.bfactor)
    {
    case -1: w = p.lLink;
            switch (w.bfactor) //adjust the balance factors
            {
            case -1: root.bfactor = 0;
                    p.bfactor = 1;
                    break;
            case 0:  root.bfactor = 0;
                    p.bfactor = 0;
                    break;
            case 1:  root.bfactor = -1;
                    p.bfactor = 0;
            }//end switch

            w.bfactor = 0;
            p = rotateToRight(p);
            root.rLink = p;
            root = rotateToLeft(root);
            break;
    case 0: System.err.println("Error: Cannot balance "
                                + "from the right.");
            break;
    case 1: root.bfactor = 0;
            p.bfactor = 0;
            root = rotateToLeft(root);
    }//end switch;

    return root;
}//end balanceFromRight
```

We now focus our attention on the method `insertIntoAVL`. The method `insertIntoAVL` inserts a new item into an AVL tree. The item to be inserted and the reference of the root node of the AVL tree are passed as parameters to this method.

The following steps describe the method `insertIntoAVL`:

1. Create a node and assign the item to be inserted to the `info` field of this node.

2. Search the tree and find the place for the new node in the tree.

3. Insert the new node in the tree.

4. Backtrack the path, which was constructed to find the place for the new node in the tree, to the root node. If necessary, adjust the balance factors of the nodes, or reconstruct the tree at a node on the path.

Because Step 4 requires us to backtrack the path to the root node, and in a binary tree we have links only from the parent to the children, the easiest way to implement the method `insertIntoAVL` is to use recursion. (Recall that recursion takes care of the backtracking automatically.) This is exactly what we do. The method `insertIntoAVL` also uses a `boolean` instance variable, `isTaller`, to indicate to the parent whether the subtree grew in height or not.

```java
private AVLNode<T> insertIntoAVL(AVLNode<T> root,
                                 AVLNode<T> newNode)
{
    if (root == null)
    {
        root = newNode;
        isTaller = true;
    }
    else
        if (root.info.equals(newNode.info))
            System.err.println("No duplicates are allowed.");
        else
        {
            Comparable<T> temp = (Comparable<T>) root.info;

            if (temp.compareTo(newNode.info) > 0) //newNode
                                                  //goes in the left subtree
            {
                root.lLink = insertIntoAVL(root.lLink,
                                           newNode);

                if (isTaller)     //after insertion, the
                                  //subtree grew in height
                    switch (root.bfactor)
                    {
                    case -1: root = balanceFromLeft(root);
                             isTaller = false;
                             break;
                    case 0:  root.bfactor = -1;
                             isTaller = true;
                             break;
                    case 1:  root.bfactor = 0;
                             isTaller = false;
                    }//end switch
            }//end if
            else
            {
```

```
            root.rLink = insertIntoAVL(root.rLink,
                                       newNode);

        if (isTaller)          //after insertion, the
                               //subtree grew in height
            switch (root.bfactor)
            {
            case -1: root.bfactor = 0;
                     isTaller = false;
                     break;
            case 0:  root.bfactor = 1;
                     isTaller = true;
                     break;
            case 1:  root = balanceFromRight(root);
                     isTaller = false;
            }//end switch
        }//end else
    }

    return root;
}//end insertIntoAVL
```

Next, we illustrate how the method `insertIntoAVL` works and build an AVL tree from scratch. Initially the tree is empty. Each figure (Figures 19-44 through 19-52) shows the item to be inserted as well as the balance factor of each node. Again, an equal sign (=) on the top of a node indicates that the balance factor of this node is 0; the less-than symbol (<) indicates that the balance factor of this node is –1; and the greater-than symbol (>) indicates that the balance factor of this node is 1.

Initially, the AVL tree is empty. Let us insert 40 into the empty AVL tree. See Figure 19-44.

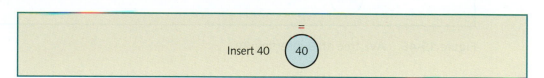

Figure 19-44   AVL tree after inserting 40

Next, we insert 30 into the AVL tree. See Figure 19-45.

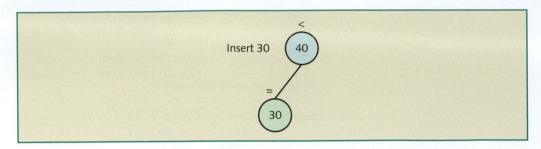

Figure 19-45   AVL tree after inserting 30

Item 30 is inserted into the left subtree of node 40, causing the left subtree of 40 to grow in height. After insertion, the balance factor of node 40 is −1.

Next, we insert 20 into the AVL tree. See Figure 19-46.

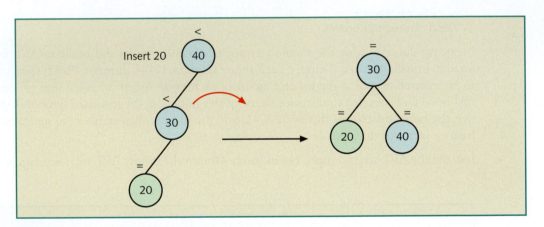

Figure 19-46   AVL tree after inserting 20

The insertion of 20 violates the balance criteria at node 40. The tree is reconstructed at node 40 by making a single right rotation.

Next, we insert 60 into the AVL tree. See Figure 19-47.

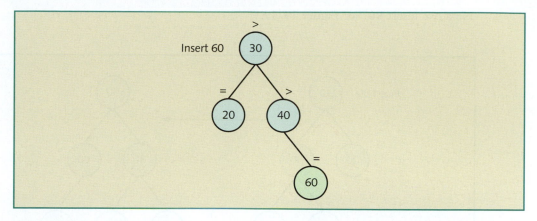

Figure 19-47   AVL tree after inserting 60

The insertion of 60 does not require reconstruction; only the balance factors are adjusted at nodes 40 and 30.

Next, we insert 50. See Figure 19-48.

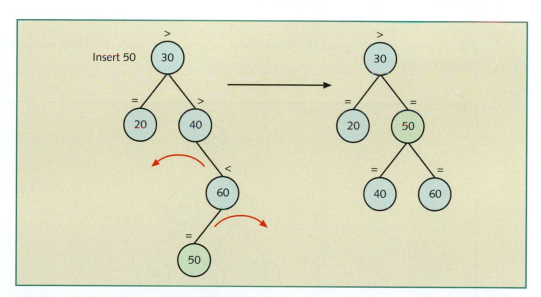

Figure 19-48   AVL tree after inserting 50

The insertion of 50 requires the tree to be reconstructed at 40. Notice that a double rotation is made at node 40.

Next, we insert 80. See Figure 19-49.

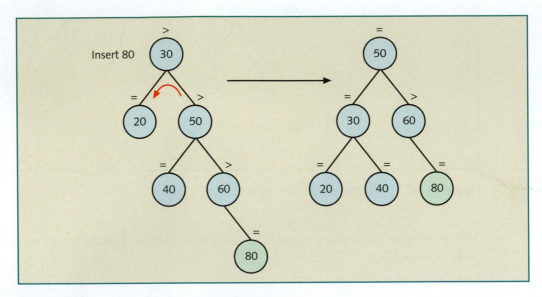

Figure 19-49 AVL tree after inserting 80

The insertion of 80 requires the tree to be reconstructed at node 30. Next, we insert 15. See Figure 19-50.

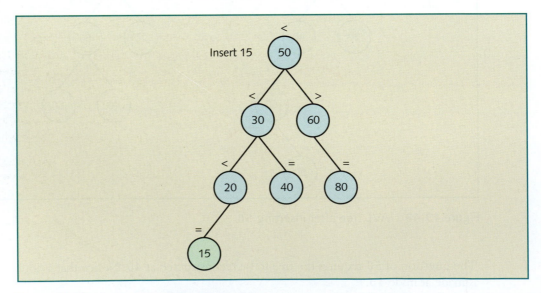

Figure 19-50 AVL tree after inserting 15

The insertion of node 15 does not require any part of the tree to be reconstructed. We need only to adjust the balance factors of nodes 20, 30, and 50.

Next, we insert 28. See Figure 19-51.

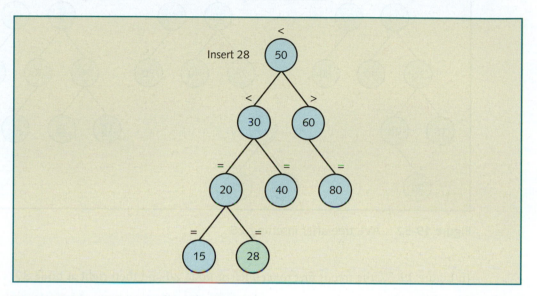

Figure 19-51 AVL tree after inserting 28

The insertion of node 28 also does not require any part of the tree to be reconstructed. We need only to adjust the balance factor of node 20.

Next, we insert 25. The insertion of 25 requires a double rotation at node 30. Figure 19-52 shows both rotations in sequence.

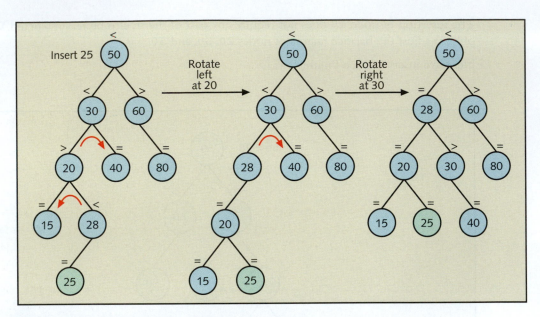

Figure 19-52 AVL tree after inserting 25

In Figure 19-52, the tree is first rotated left at node 20 and then right at node 30.

The following method creates a node, stores the information in the node, and calls the method `insertIntoAVL` to insert the new node into the AVL tree.

```
public void insert(T newItem)
{
    isTaller = false;
    AVLNode<T> newNode;

    newNode = new AVLNode<T>(newItem, 0, null, null);

    root = insertIntoAVL(root, newNode);
}
```

We leave it as an exercise for you to design the class to implement AVL trees as an ADT. (See Programming Exercise 9 at the end of this chapter.) Notice that because the structure of the node of an AVL tree is different from the structure of the node of a binary tree discussed in the beginning of this chapter, you cannot use inheritance to derive the class to implement AVL trees from the **class** `BinaryTree`.

Deletion from AVL Trees

To delete an item from an AVL tree, first we find the node containing the item to be deleted. The following four cases arise:

Case 1: The node to be deleted is a leaf.

Case 2: The node to be deleted has no right child, that is, its right subtree is empty.

Case 3: The node to be deleted has no left child, that is, its left subtree is empty.

Case 4: The node to be deleted has a left child and a right child.

Cases 1 through 3 are easier to handle than Case 4. Let us first discuss Case 4.

Suppose that the node to be deleted, say x, has a left and a right child. As in the case of deletion from a binary search tree, we reduce Case 4 to Case 2. That is, we find the immediate predecessor, say y of x. Then the data of y is copied into x and now the node to be deleted is y. Clearly, y has no right child.

To delete the node, we adjust one of the links of the parent node. After deleting the node, the resulting tree may no longer be an AVL tree. As in the case of insertion into an AVL tree, we traverse the path (from the parent node) back to the root node. For each node on this path, sometimes we need to change only the balance factor, while other times the tree at a particular node is reconstructed. The following steps describe what to do at a node on the path back to the root node. (As in the case of insertion, we use the **boolean** variable **shorter** to indicate whether the height of the subtree is reduced.) Let p be a node on the path back to the root node. We look at the current balance factor of p.

1. If the current balance factor of p is equal high, then the balance factor of p is changed according to whether the left subtree of p was shortened or the right subtree of p was shortened. The variable **shorter** is set to **false**.

2. Suppose that the balance factor of p is not equal high and the taller subtree of p is shortened. The balance factor of p is changed to equal high, and the variable **shorter** is left as **true**.

3. Suppose that the balance factor of p is not equal high and the shorter subtree of p is shortened. Further suppose that q points to the root of the taller subtree of p.

   a. If the balance factor of q is equal high, a single rotation is required at p and **shorter** is set to **false**.

   b. If the balance factor of q is the same as p, a single rotation is required at p and **shorter** is set to **true**.

   c. Suppose that the balance factors of p and q are opposite. A double rotation is required at p (a single rotation at q and then a single rotation at p). We adjust the balance factors and set **shorter** to **true**.

We leave it as an exercise for you to develop and implement an algorithm to delete a node from an AVL tree.

Analysis: AVL Trees

Consider all the possible AVL trees of height h. Let T_h be an AVL tree of height h such that T_h has the fewest number of nodes. Let T_{hl} denote the left subtree of T_h and T_{hr} denote the right subtree of T_h. Then

$$|T_h| = |T_{hl}| + |T_{hr}| + 1$$

where $|T_h|$ denotes the number of nodes in T_h.

Because T_h is an AVL tree of height h such that T_h has the fewest number of nodes, it follows that one of the subtrees of T_h is of height $h-1$ and the other is of height $h-2$. To be specific, suppose that T_{hl} is of height $h-1$ and T_{hr} is of height $h-2$. From the definition of T_h, it follows that T_{hl} is an AVL tree of height $h-1$ such that T_{hl} has the fewest number of nodes among all AVL trees of height $h-1$. Similarly, T_{hr} is an AVL tree of height $h-2$ that has the fewest number of nodes among all AVL trees of height $h-2$. Thus, T_{hl} is of the form T_{h-1} and T_{hr} is of the form T_{h-2}. Hence:

$$|T_h| = |T_{h-1}| + |T_{h-2}| + 1$$

Clearly:

$$|T_0| = 1$$
$$|T_1| = 2$$

Let $F_{h+2} = |T_h| + 1$. Then:

$$F_{h+2} = F_{h+1} + F_h$$
$$F_2 = 2$$
$$F_3 = 3.$$

This is called a Fibonacci sequence. The solution to F_h is given by:

$$F_h \approx \frac{\phi^h}{\sqrt{5}}, \quad where \quad \phi = \frac{1+\sqrt{5}}{2}.$$

Hence:

$$|T_h| \approx \frac{\phi^{h+2}}{\sqrt{5}} = \frac{1}{\sqrt{5}}\left[\frac{1+\sqrt{5}}{2}\right]^{h+2}$$

From this it can be concluded that:

$$h \approx (1.44)\log_2 |T_h|$$

This implies that, in the worst case, the height of an AVL tree with n nodes is approximately $1.44\log_2 n = O(\log_2 n)$. Because the height of a perfectly balanced binary tree with n nodes is $\log_2 n$, it follows that, in the worst case, the time to manipulate an AVL tree is no more than 44% of the optimum time. However, in general, AVL trees are not as sparse as in the worst case. It can be shown that the average search time of an AVL tree is about 4% more than the optimum.

PROGRAMMING EXAMPLE: VIDEO STORE (REVISITED)

In Chapter 16, we designed a program to help a video store automate its video rental process. That program used an (unordered) linked list to keep track of the video inventory in the store. Because the search algorithm on a linked list is sequential and the list is fairly large, the search could be time consuming. In this chapter, you learned how to organize data into a binary tree. If the binary tree is nicely constructed (that is, it is not linear), then the search algorithm can be improved considerably. Moreover, in general, item insertion and deletion in a binary search tree is faster than in a linked list. We will, therefore, redesign the video store program so that the video inventory can be maintained in a binary tree. As in Chapter 16, we leave the design of the customer list as a binary tree as an exercise for you.

Video Object

The **class** Video is the same as in Chapter 16.

Video Binary Tree

The video list is maintained in a binary search tree. Therefore, we derive the **class** VideoBinaryTree from the **class** BinarySearchTree.

```
public class VideoBinaryTree extends BinarySearchTree<Video>
```

The following statements describe the members of the **class** VideoBinaryTree:

```
public VideoBinaryTree()
    //Default constructor
    //Postcondition: root = null;
```

```
private BinaryTreeNode<Video> searchVideoList(String title)
    //Method to search the video list for a
    //particular video, specified by the parameter title.
    //Postcondition: If the video is found, a reference to
    //               the node containing the video is returned;
    //               otherwise, the value null is returned.

public boolean videoSearch(String title)
    //Method to search the list to see if a particular
    //title, specified by the parameter title, is in the store.
    //Postcondition: Returns true if the title is found;
    //               false otherwise.

public boolean isVideoAvailable(String title)
    //Method to determine if the video specified by the
    //parameter title is available.
    //Postcondition: Returns true if at least one copy of the
    //               video is available, false otherwise.

public void videoCheckIn(String title)
    //Method to check in a video returned by a customer.
    //The parameter title specifies the video to be checked in.
    //Postcondition: If the video returned is from the
    //               store, its copiesInstock is incremented
    //               by one; otherwise, an appropriate message
    //               is output.

public void videoCheckOut(String title)
    //Method to check out a video, that is, rent a video.
    //The parameter title specifies the video to be checked out.
    //Postcondition: If a video is available, its copiesInStock
    //               is decremented by one; otherwise, an
    //               appropriate message is output.

public void videoUpdateInStock(String title, int num)
    //Method to update the number of copies of a video
    //by adding the value of the parameter num. The
    //parameter title specifies the name of the video
    //for which the number of copies is to be updated.
    //Postcondition: If video is found; then
    //               copiesInStock = copiesInStock + num;
    //               otherwise, an appropriate message is
    //               output.

public void videoSetCopiesInStock(String title, int num)
    //Method to reset the number of copies of a video.
    //The parameter title specifies the name of the video
```

```
        //for which the number of copies is to be reset and the
        //parameter num specifies the number of copies.
        //Postcondition: If video is found, then
        //                copiesInStock = num;
        //                otherwise, an appropriate message
        //                is output.

public void videoPrintTitle()
    //Method to print the titles of all the videos in stock.

private void inorderTitle(BinaryTreeNode<Video> p)
    //Method to print the titles of all the videos in
    //the tree pointed to by p.
```

The definitions of the methods of the **class** `VideoBinaryTree` are similar to the ones given in Chapter 16. We give the definitions of only the methods `searchVideoList`, `videoCheckOut`, `inorderTitle`, and `videoPrintTitle`. (See Programming Exercise 8 at the end of the chapter.)

The method `searchVideoList` uses a search algorithm similar to the search algorithm for a binary search tree given earlier in this chapter. If the search item is found in the list, it returns the reference of the node containing the search item; otherwise it returns the value `null`. Note that the method `searchVideoList` is a **private** member of the **class** `VideoBinaryTree`. So the user cannot directly use this method in a program. Therefore, even though this method returns a reference of a node in the tree, the user cannot directly access the node. The method `searchVideoList` is used only to implement the other methods of the **class** `VideoBinaryTree`. The definition of this method is as follows:

```
private BinaryTreeNode<Video> searchVideoList(String title)
{
    boolean found = false;    //set found to false
    BinaryTreeNode<Video> current = null;
    Video temp = new Video();

    temp.setVideoInfo(title, "", "", "", "", "", 0);

    if (root == null)  //the tree is empty
        System.out.println("Cannot search an empty list. ");
    else
    {
        current = root;    //set current point to the root node
                           //of the binary tree
        found = false;     //set found to false
```

```
        while (current != null && !found) //search the tree
            if (current.info.equals(temp)) //the item is found
                found = true;
            else
                if (current.info.compareTo(temp) > 0)
                    current = current.lLink;
                else
                    current = current.rLink;
    } //end else

    return current;
}//end searchVideoList
```

The definition of the method `videoCheckOut` is:

```
public void videoCheckOut(String title)
{
    BinaryTreeNode<Video> location;
    Video temp;

    location = searchVideoList(title);  //search the list

    if (location != null)
    {
        temp = (Video) location.info;
        temp.checkOut();
    }
    else
        System.out.println("The store does not carry "
                            + "this video.");
}
```

Given a reference of the root node of the binary tree containing the videos, the method `inorderTitle` uses the inorder traversal algorithm to print the titles of the videos. Notice that this method outputs only the video titles. The definition of this method is as follows:

```
private void inorderTitle(BinaryTreeNode<Video> p)
{
    Video temp;

    if (p != null)
    {
        inorderTitle(p.lLink);
        temp = (Video) p.info;
        temp.printTitle();
        inorderTitle(p.rLink);
    }
}
```

The method `videoPrintTitle` uses the method `inorderTitle` to print the titles of all the videos in the store. The definition of this method is:

```
public void videoPrintTitle()
{
      inorderTitle(root);
}
```

Main Program

For most parts, the main program is the same as in Chapter 16. Here we give only the listing of this program:

```
import java.io.*;
import java.util.*;

public class MainProgVideoStore
{
    static Scanner console = new Scanner(System.in);

    public static void main(String[] args)
    {
        VideoBinaryTree videoList = new VideoBinaryTree();
        int choice;
        String title;

        try
        {
            Scanner infile =
                new Scanner(new FileReader("a:\\videoDat.txt"));

            createVideoList(infile, videoList);

            displayMenu();
            System.out.print("Enter your choice: ");
            choice = console.nextInt();
            console.nextLine();
            System.out.println();

            while (choice != 9)
            {
                switch (choice)
                {
                case 1: System.out.print("Enter the title: ");
                        title = console.nextLine();
                        System.out.println();
                        if (videoList.videoSearch(title))
                            System.out.println("Title found.");
```

```
                else
                    System.out.println("This video is not "
                                    + "in the store.");
            break;
    case 2: System.out.print("Enter the title: ");
            title = console.nextLine();
            System.out.println();
            if (videoList.videoSearch(title))
            {
                if (videoList.isVideoAvailable(title))
                {
                    videoList.videoCheckOut(title);
                    System.out.println("Enjoy your "
                                    + "movie: " + title);
                }
                else
                    System.out.println("Currently
                                    + title + " is out "
                                    + " of stock.");
            }
            else
                System.out.println("The store does "
                                    + "not carry "
                                    + title);
            break;
    case 3: System.out.print("Enter the title: ");
            title = console.nextLine();
            System.out.println();
            if (videoList.videoSearch(title))
            {
                videoList.videoCheckIn(title);
                System.out.println("Thanks for "
                                    + "returning "
                                    + title);
            }
            else
                System.out.println("This video is "
                                    + "not from our store.");
            break;
    case 4: System.out.print("Enter the title: ");
            title = console.nextLine();
            System.out.println();
            if (videoList.videoSearch(title))
            {
                if (videoList.isVideoAvailable(title))
                    System.out.println(title + " is "
                        + "currently in stock.");
```

```java
                    else
                        System.out.println(title +
                                " is not in the store.");
                }
                else
                    System.out.println(title + " is "
                            + "not from this store.");
                break;
        case 5: videoList.videoPrintTitle();
                break;
        case 6: videoList.inorderTraversal();
                break;
        default: System.out.println("Invalid "
                                    + "selection!!!");
        }//end switch

        displayMenu();
        System.out.print("Enter your choice: ");
        choice = console.nextInt();
        console.nextLine();
        System.out.println();
    }//end while
}
catch (FileNotFoundException fnfe)
{
    System.out.println(fnfe.toString());
}
catch (IOException ioe)
{
    System.out.println(ioe.toString());
}
}

public static void createVideoList(Scanner infile,
                                VideoBinaryTree videoList)
{
    String vTitle;
    String mStar1;
    String mStar2;
    String mProducer;
    String mDirector;
    String mProductionCo;
    int vInStock;

    Video newVideo;

    while (infile.hasNext())
```

```java
        {
            vTitle = infile.nextLine();
            mStar1 = infile.nextLine();
            mStar2 = infile.nextLine();
            mProducer = infile.nextLine();
            mDirector = infile.nextLine();
            mProductionCo = infile.nextLine();
            vInStock = infile.nextInt();
            infile.nextLine();
            newVideo = new Video();
            newVideo.setVideoInfo(vTitle, mStar1, mStar2,
                                  mProducer, mDirector,
                                  mProductionCo, vInStock);
            videoList.insert(newVideo);
        }//end while
    }//end createVideoList

    public static void displayMenu()
    {
        System.out.println("Select one of the following: ");
        System.out.println("1: To check whether a particular "
                            + "video is in the store");
        System.out.println("2: To check out a video");
        System.out.println("3: To check in a video");
        System.out.println("4: Check whether a particular "
                            + "video is in stock");
        System.out.println("5: To print the titles of all "
                            + "the videos");
        System.out.println("6: To print a list of all "
                            + "the videos");
        System.out.println("9: To exit");
    }
}
```

QUICK REVIEW

1. A binary tree is either empty or it has a special node called the root node. If the tree is nonempty, the root node has two sets of nodes, called the left and right subtrees, such that the left and right subtrees are also binary trees.

2. The node of a binary tree has two links in it.

3. A node in a binary tree is called a leaf if it has no left and right children.

4. A node U is called the parent of a node V if there is a branch from U to V.

5. A path from a node X to a node Y in a binary tree is a sequence of nodes $X_0, X_1, ..., X_n$ such that (a) $X = X_0$, $X_n = Y$, and (b) X_{i-1} is the parent of X_i for all $i = 1, 2, ..., n$. That is, there is a branch from X_0 to X_1, X_1 to X_2, ..., X_{i-1} to X_i, ..., X_{n-1} to X_n.

6. The length of a path in a binary tree is the number of branches on that path.

7. The level of a node in a binary tree is the number of branches on the path from the root to the node.

8. The level of the root node of a binary tree is 0; the level of the children of the root node is 1.

9. The height of a binary tree is the number of nodes on the longest path from the root to a leaf.

10. In an inorder traversal, the binary tree is traversed as follows:
    a. Traverse the left subtree.
    b. Visit the node.
    c. Traverse the right subtree.

11. In a preorder traversal, the binary tree is traversed as follows:
    a. Visit the node.
    b. Traverse the left subtree.
    c. Traverse the right subtree.

12. In a postorder traversal, the binary tree is traversed as follows:
    a. Traverse the left subtree.
    b. Traverse the right subtree.
    c. Visit the node.

13. A binary search tree T is either empty or:
    i. T has a special node called the root node;
    ii. T has two sets of nodes, L_T and R_T, called the left subtree and the right subtree of T, respectively;
    iii. The key in the root node is larger than every key in the left subtree and smaller than every key in the right subtree; and
    iv. L_T and R_T are binary search trees.

14. To delete a node from a binary search tree that has both left and right nonempty subtrees, first its immediate predecessor is located, then the predecessor's `info` is copied into the node, and finally the predecessor is deleted.

15. A perfectly balanced binary tree is a binary tree such that:

    (i) The height of the left and right subtrees of the root are equal.

    (ii) The left and right subtrees of the root are perfectly balanced binary trees.

16. An AVL (or height-balanced) tree is a binary search tree such that:

    (i) The height of the left and right subtrees of the root differ by at most 1.

    (ii) The left and right subtrees of the root are AVL trees.

17. Let x be a node in a binary tree. Then x_l denotes the height of the left subtree of x, and x_r denotes the height of the right subtree of x.

18. Let T be an AVL tree and x be a node in T. Then $|x_r - x_l|$ 1, where $|x_r - x_l|$ denotes the absolute value of $x_r - x_l$.

19. Let x be a node in the AVL tree T.

    a. If $x_l > x_r$, we say that x is left high. In this case, $x_l = x_r + 1$.

    b. If $x_l = x_r$, we say that x is equal high.

    c. If $x_r > x_l$, we say that x is right high. In this case, $x_r = x_l + 1$.

20. The balance factor of x, written $bf(x)$, is defined as $bf(x) = x_r - x_l$.

21. Let x be a node in the AVL tree T. Then:

    a. If x is left high, then $bf(x) = -1$.

    b. If x is equal high, then $bf(x) = 0$.

    c. If x is right high, then $bf(x) = 1$.

22. Let x be a node in a binary tree. We say that node x violates the balance criteria if $|x_r - x_l| > 1$, that is, the height of the left and right subtrees of x differ by more than 1.

23. Every node x in the AVL tree T, in addition to the data and references of the left and right subtrees, must keep track of its balance factor.

24. In an AVL tree, there are two types of rotations: left rotation and right rotation. Suppose that the rotation occurs at node x. If it is a left rotation, then certain nodes from the right subtree of x move to its left subtree; the root of the right subtree of x becomes the new root of the reconstructed subtree. Similarly, if it is a right rotation at x, certain nodes from the left subtree of x move to its right subtree; the root of the left subtree of x becomes the new root of the reconstructed subtree.

1. Mark the following statements as true or false.

   a. A binary tree must be nonempty.

   b. The level of the root node is 0.

   c. If a tree has only one node, the height of the tree is 0 because the number of levels is 0.

   d. The inorder traversal of a binary tree always outputs the data in ascending order.

2. There are 14 different binary trees that have four nodes. Draw all of them.

The binary tree of Figure 19-53 is to be used for Exercises 3 to 8.

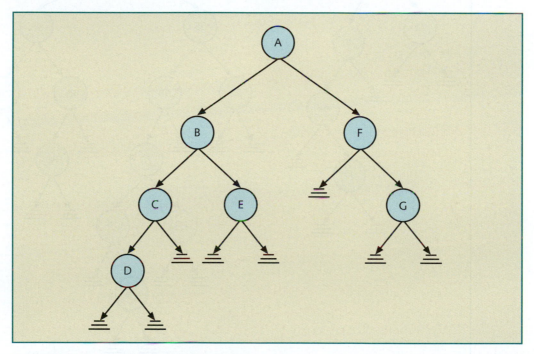

Figure 19-53   Figure for Exercises 3 to 8

3. Find L_A, the node in the left subtree of A.

4. Find R_A, the node in the right subtree of A.

5. Find R_B, the node in the right subtree of B.

6. List the nodes of this binary tree in an inorder sequence.

7. List the nodes of this binary tree in a preorder sequence.

8. List the nodes of this binary tree in a postorder sequence.

The binary tree of Figure 19-54 is to be used for Exercises 9 to 13.

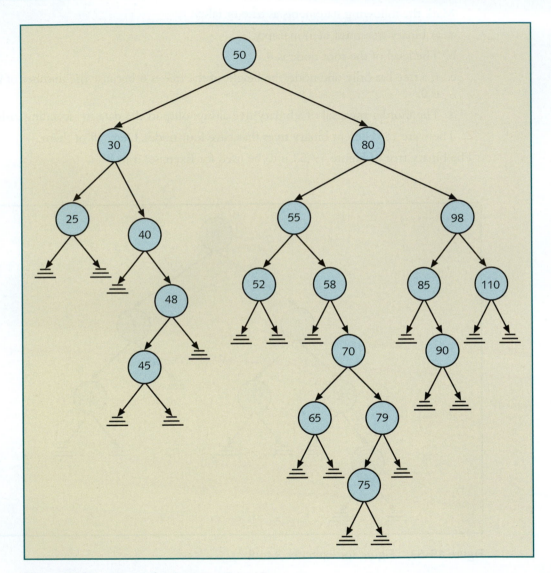

Figure 19-54   Figure for Exercises 9 to 13

9. List the path from the node with `info` 80 to the node with `info` 79.

10. A node with `info` 35 is to be inserted in the tree. List the nodes that are visited by the method `insert` to insert 35. Redraw the tree after inserting 35.

11. Delete node 52 and redraw the binary tree.

12. Delete node 40 and redraw the binary tree.

13. Delete nodes 80 and 58 in that order. Redraw the binary tree after each deletion.

14. Suppose that you are given two sequences of elements corresponding to the inorder sequence and the preorder sequence. Prove that it is possible to reconstruct a unique binary tree.

15. The following code lists the nodes in a binary tree in two different orders:

    preorder: ABCDEFGHIJKLM

    inorder: CEDFBAHJIKGML

    Draw the binary tree.

16. Given the preorder sequence and the postorder sequence, show that it may not be possible to reconstruct the binary tree.

17. Insert 100 in the AVL tree in Figure 19-55. The resulting tree must be an AVL tree. What is the balance factor at the root node after the insertion?

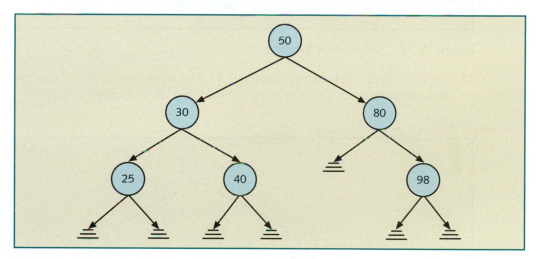

Figure 19-55   AVL tree for Exercise 17

18. Insert 45 in the AVL tree shown in Figure 19-56. The resulting tree must be an AVL tree. What is the balance factor at the root node after the insertion?

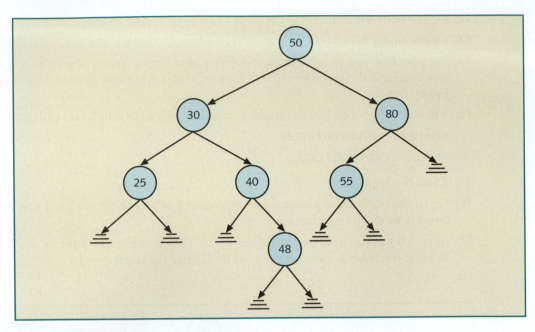

Figure 19-56   AVL tree for Exercise 18

19. Insert **42** in the AVL tree of Figure 19-57. The resulting tree must be an AVL tree. What is the balance factor at the root node after the insertion?

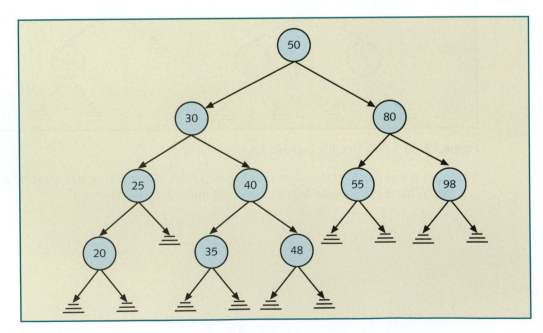

Figure 19-57   AVL tree for Exercise 19

20. The following keys are inserted (in the order given) into an initially empty AVL tree. Show the AVL tree after each insertion.

```
24, 39, 31, 46, 48, 34, 19, 5, 29
```

PROGRAMMING EXERCISES

1. Write the definition of the method `nodeCount` that returns the number of nodes in a binary tree. Add this method to the **class** `BinaryTree` and create a program to test this method. (*Note:* To test your algorithm, first create a binary search tree.)

2. Write the definition of the method `leavesCount` that takes as a parameter a reference of the root node of a **binary** tree and returns the number of leaves in a binary tree. Add this method to the **class** `BinaryTree` and create a program to test this method. (*Note:* To test your algorithm, first create a binary search tree.)

3. Write a method, `swapSubtrees`, that swaps all of the left and right subtrees of a binary tree. Add this method to the **class** `BinaryTree` and create a program to test this method. (*Note:* To test your algorithm, first create a binary search tree.)

4. Write a method, `singleParent`, that returns the number of nodes in a binary tree that have only one child. Add this method to the **class** `BinaryTree` and create a program to test this method. (*Note:* To test your algorithm, first create a binary search tree.)

5. Write a program to test various operations on a binary search tree.

6. a. Write the definition of the method to implement the nonrecursive preorder traversal algorithm.

b. Write the definition of the method to implement the nonrecursive postorder traversal algorithm.

c. Write a program to test the nonrecursive inorder, preorder, and postorder traversal algorithms. (*Note:* First create a binary search tree.)

7. a. Write the definition of the class that implements an AVL tree as an ADT. In addition to the methods to implement the operation to insert an item in an AVL tree, your class must, at least, contain the constructors, the methods `clone`, `copyTree`, and traversal algorithms. (You do not need to implement the delete operation.)

b. Write the definitions of the constructors and the methods of the class that you defined in (a).

c. Write a program to test various operations of an AVL tree.

8. Write the definitions of the methods of the **class** `VideoBinaryTree` not given in the Programming Example Video Store.

9. **(Video Store Program)**

   a. Redo Programming Exercise 14 (a) in Chapter 16 so that the videos rented by a customer are maintained in a binary search tree.

   b. In Programming Exercise 14 (b) in Chapter 16, you were asked to design and implement a class to maintain customer data in a linked list. Because the search on a linked list is sequential and therefore can be time consuming, design and implement the **class** `CustomerBinaryTree` so that the customers' data can be stored in a binary search tree. The **class** `CustomerBinaryTree` must be derived from the **class** `BinarySearchTree` as designed in this chapter.

   c. Write a program to test the customer component. Also write the definition of the method `nodeCount` of the **class** `BinaryTree` before executing the program.

10. **(Video Store Program)** Using classes to implement the video data, video list data, customer data, and customer list data, as designed in this chapter and in Programming Exercises 8 and 9, design and complete the program to put the video store into operation. Write the definition of the method `nodeCount` of the **class** `BinaryTree` before executing the program.

20

GRAPHS

In this chapter, you will:

♦ Learn about graphs

♦ Become familiar with the basic terminology of graph theory

♦ Discover how to represent graphs in computer memory

♦ Explore graphs as ADTs

♦ Examine and implement various graph traversal algorithms

♦ Learn how to implement the shortest path algorithm

♦ Examine and implement the minimal spanning tree algorithm

In previous chapters, you learned various ways to represent and manipulate data. This chapter discusses how to implement and manipulate graphs, which have numerous applications in computer science.

INTRODUCTION

In 1736, the following problem was posed. In the town of Königsberg (now called Kaliningrad), the river Pregel (Pregolya) flows around the island Kneiphof and then divides into two. See Figure 20-1.

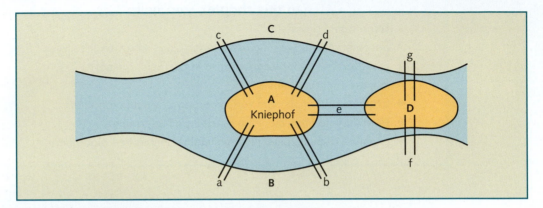

Figure 20-1   Königsberg bridge problem

The river has four land areas (*A*, *B*, *C*, and D), as shown in the figure. These land areas are connected using seven bridges, as shown in Figure 20-1. The bridges are labeled *a*, *b*, *c*, *d*, *e*, *f*, and *g*. The Königsberg bridge problem is as follows: Starting at one land area, is it possible to walk across all the bridges exactly once and return to the starting land area? In 1736, Euler represented the Königsberg bridge problem as a graph, as shown in Figure 20-2, and answered the question in the negative. This marked (as recorded) the birth of graph theory.

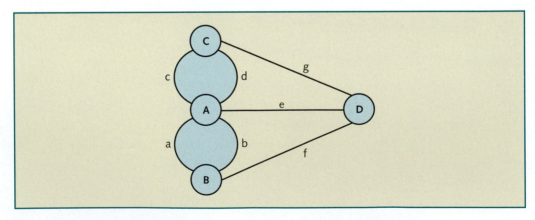

Figure 20-2   Graph representation of Königsburg bridge problem

A solution to the Königsberg bridge problem is given in the book *Discrete Mathematical Structures: Theory and Applications,* listed in Appendix F.

Over the past 200 years, graph theory has been applied to a variety of applications. Graphs are used to model electrical circuits, chemical compounds, highway maps, and so on. They are also used in the analysis of electrical circuits, finding the shortest route, project planning, linguistics, genetics, social science, and so forth. In this chapter, you learn about graphs and their applications in computer science.

GRAPH DEFINITIONS AND NOTATIONS

To facilitate and simplify our discussion, we borrow a few definitions and terminology from set theory. Let X be a set. If a is an element of X, then we write $a \in X$. (The symbol $\in$ means "belongs to.") A set Y is called a **subset** of X if every element of Y is also an element of X. If Y is a subset of X, we write $Y \subseteq X$. (The symbol $\subseteq$ means "is a subset of.") The **intersection** of sets A and B, written $A \cap B$, is the set of all the elements that are in A and B; that is, $A \cap B = \{x \mid x \in A \text{ and } x \in B\}$. (The symbol $\cap$ means "intersection," and the symbol $\mid$ is read as "such that.") The **union** of sets A and B, written $A \cup B$, is the set of all the elements that are in A or in B; that is, $A \cup B = \{x \mid x \in A \text{ or } x \in B\}$. (The symbol $\cup$ means "union.") So $x \in A \cup B$ means x is in A or x is in B or x is in both A and B.

For sets A and B, the set $A \times B$ is the set of all the ordered pairs of elements of A and B; that is, $A \times B = \{(a, b) \mid a \in A, b \in B\}$.

A **graph** G is a pair, $G = (V, E)$, where V is a finite nonempty set, called the set of **vertices** of G, and $E \subseteq V \times V$. That is, the elements of E are the pair of elements of V. E is called the set of **edges**.

Let $V(G)$ denote the set of vertices, and $E(G)$ denote the set of edges of a graph G. If the elements of $E(G)$ are ordered pairs, G is called a **directed graph** or **digraph**; otherwise, G is called an **undirected graph**. In an undirected graph, the pairs (u, v) and (v, u) represent the same edge. If (u, v) is an edge in a directed graph, then sometimes the vertex u is called the **origin** of the edge, and the vertex v is called the **destination**.

Let G be a graph. A graph H is called a **subgraph** of G if $V(H) \subseteq V(G)$ and $E(H) \subseteq E(G)$; that is, every vertex of H is a vertex of G, and every edge in H is an edge in G.

To learn more about sets and graph terminology, the interested reader is referred to the book *Discrete Mathematical Structures: Theory and Applications,* listed in Appendix F.

A graph can be shown pictorially. The vertices are drawn as circles, and a label inside the circle represents the vertex. In an undirected graph, the edges are drawn using lines. In a directed graph, the edges are drawn using arrows. Moreover, in a directed graph, the tail of a pictorial directed edge is the origin, and the head is the destination.

Example 20-1

Figure 20-3 shows some examples of undirected graphs.

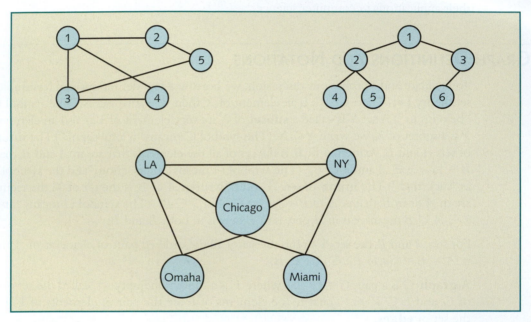

Figure 20-3 Various undirected graphs

Example 20-2

Figure 20-4 shows some examples of directed graphs.

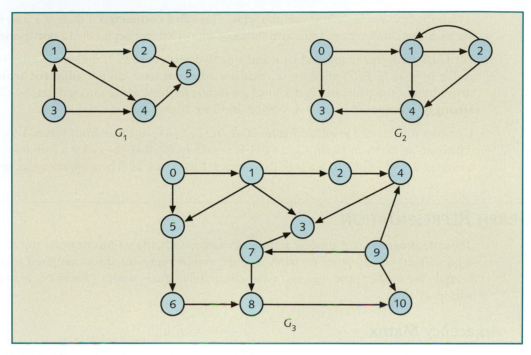

Figure 20-4   Various directed graphs

For the graphs of Figure 20–4, we have:

$V(G_1) = \{1, 2, 3, 4, 5\}$	$E(G_1) = \{(1, 2), (1, 4), (2, 5), (3, 1), (3, 4), (4, 5)\}$
$V(G_2) = \{0, 1, 2, 3, 4,\}$	$E(G_2) = \{(0, 1), (0, 3), (1, 2), (1, 4), (2, 1), (2, 4), (4, 3)\}$
$V(G_3) = \{0, 1, 2, 3, 4, 5, 6, 7, 8, 9, 10\}$	$E(G_3) = \{(0, 1), (0, 5), (1, 2), (1, 3), (1, 5), (2, 4), (4, 3),$ $(5, 6), (6, 8), (7, 3), (7, 8), (8, 10), (9, 4), (9, 7), (9, 10)\}$

Let G be an undirected graph. Let u and v be two vertices in G. Then u and v are called **adjacent** if there is an edge from one to the other; that is, $(u, v) \in E(G)$. Let $e = (u, v)$ be an edge in G. We then say that edge e is **incident** on the vertices u and v. An edge incident on a single vertex is called a **loop**. If two edges, e_1 and e_2, are associated with the same pair of vertices, then e_1 and e_2 are called **parallel edges**. A graph is called a **simple graph** if it has no loops and no parallel edges. There is a **path** from u to v if there is a sequence of vertices $u_1, u_2,$ ..., u_n such that $u = u_1, u_n = v$, and (u_i, u_{i+1}) is an edge for all $i = 1, 2, ..., n - 1$. Vertices u and v are called **connected** if there is a path from u to v. A **simple path** is a path in which all the vertices, except possibly the first and last vertices, are distinct. A **cycle** in G is a simple path in which the first and last vertices are the same. G is called **connected** if there is a path from any vertex to any other vertex. A maximal subset of connected vertices is called a **component** of G.

Let G be a directed graph, and let u and v be two vertices in G. If there is an edge from u to v, that is, $(u, v) \in E(G)$, then we say that u is **adjacent to** v and v is **adjacent from** u. The definitions of the paths and cycles in G are similar to those for undirected graphs. G is called **strongly connected** if any two vertices in G are connected.

Consider the directed graphs of Figure 20-4. In G_1, 1–4–5 is a path from vertex 1 to vertex 5. There are no cycles in G_1. In G_2, 1–2–1 is a cycle. In G_3, 0–1–2–4–3 is a path from vertex 0 to vertex 3; 1–5–6–8–10 is a path from vertex 1 to vertex 10. There are no cycles in G_3.

GRAPH REPRESENTATION

To write programs that process and manipulate graphs, the graphs must be stored—that is, represented—in computer memory. A graph can be represented (in computer memory) in several ways. We now discuss two commonly used ways: adjacency matrices and adjacency lists.

Adjacency Matrix

Let G be a graph with n vertices, where $n > 0$. Let $V(G) = \{v_1, v_2, ..., v_n\}$. The **adjacency matrix** A_G of G is a two-dimensional $n \times n$ matrix such that the (i, j)th entry of A_G is 1 if there is an edge from v_i to v_j; otherwise, the (i, j)th entry is zero. That is:

$$A_G(i, j) = \begin{cases} 1 & \text{if } \left(v_i, v_j\right) \in E(G) \\ 0 & \text{otherwise} \end{cases}$$

In an undirected graph, if $(v_i, v_j) \in E(G)$, then $(v_j, v_i) \in E(G)$, so $A_G(i, j) = 1 = A_G(j, i)$. It follows that the adjacency matrix of an undirected graph is symmetric.

Example 20-3

Consider the directed graphs of Figure 20-4. The adjacency matrices of the directed graphs G_1, G_2, and G_3 are as follows:

$$A_{G_1} = \begin{bmatrix} 0 & 1 & 0 & 1 & 0 \\ 0 & 0 & 0 & 0 & 1 \\ 1 & 0 & 0 & 1 & 0 \\ 0 & 0 & 0 & 0 & 1 \\ 0 & 0 & 0 & 0 & 0 \end{bmatrix}$$

$$A_{G_2} = \begin{bmatrix} 0 & 1 & 0 & 1 & 0 \\ 0 & 0 & 1 & 0 & 1 \\ 0 & 1 & 0 & 0 & 1 \\ 0 & 0 & 0 & 0 & 0 \\ 0 & 0 & 0 & 1 & 0 \end{bmatrix}$$

$$A_{G_3} = \begin{array}{c} 0 \\ 1 \\ 2 \\ 3 \\ 4 \\ 5 \\ 6 \\ 7 \\ 8 \\ 9 \\ 10 \end{array} \begin{bmatrix} 0 & 1 & 0 & 0 & 0 & 1 & 0 & 0 & 0 & 0 & 0 \\ 0 & 0 & 1 & 1 & 0 & 1 & 0 & 0 & 0 & 0 & 0 \\ 0 & 0 & 0 & 0 & 1 & 0 & 0 & 0 & 0 & 0 & 0 \\ 0 & 0 & 0 & 0 & 0 & 0 & 0 & 0 & 0 & 0 & 0 \\ 0 & 0 & 0 & 1 & 0 & 0 & 0 & 0 & 0 & 0 & 0 \\ 0 & 0 & 0 & 0 & 0 & 0 & 1 & 0 & 0 & 0 & 0 \\ 0 & 0 & 0 & 0 & 0 & 0 & 0 & 0 & 1 & 0 & 0 \\ 0 & 0 & 0 & 1 & 0 & 0 & 0 & 0 & 1 & 0 & 0 \\ 0 & 0 & 0 & 0 & 0 & 0 & 0 & 0 & 0 & 0 & 1 \\ 0 & 0 & 0 & 0 & 1 & 0 & 0 & 1 & 0 & 0 & 1 \\ 0 & 0 & 0 & 0 & 0 & 0 & 0 & 0 & 0 & 0 & 0 \end{bmatrix}$$

Adjacency Lists

Let G be a graph with n vertices, where $n > 0$. Let $V(G) = \{v_1, v_2, ..., v_n\}$. In the adjacency list representation, corresponding to each vertex, v, there is a linked list such that each node of the linked list contains the vertex, u, such that $(v, u) \in E(G)$. Because there are n nodes, we use an array, A, of size n, such that $A[i]$ is a reference variable pointing to the first node of the linked list containing the vertices to which v_i is adjacent. Clearly, each node has two components, say **vertex** and **link**. The component **vertex** contains the index of the vertex adjacent to vertex i.

Example 20-4

Consider the directed graphs of Figure 20-4. Figure 20-5 shows the adjacency list of the directed graph G_2.

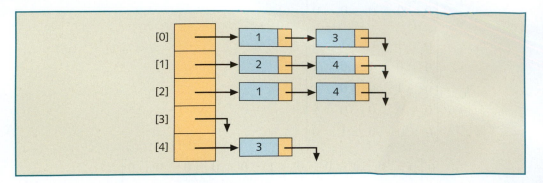

Figure 20-5   Adjacency list of graph G_2 of Figure 20-4

Figure 20-6 shows the adjacency list of the directed graph G_3.

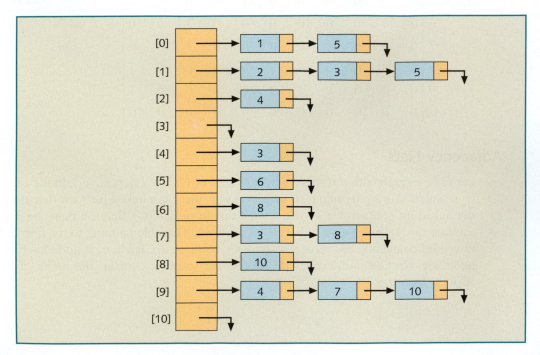

Figure 20-6   Adjacency list of graph G_3 of Figure 20-4

OPERATIONS ON GRAPHS

Now that you know how to represent graphs in computer memory, the next obvious step is to learn the basic operations on a graph. The operations commonly performed on a graph are as follows:

1. Create the graph. That is, store the graph in computer memory using a particular graph representation.

2. Clear the graph. This operation makes the graph empty.

3. Determine whether the graph is empty.

4. Traverse the graph.

5. Print the graph.

We will add more operations on a graph when we discuss a specific application or a particular graph later in this chapter.

The following interface defines basic operations on a graph as an ADT:

```
public interface GraphADT
{
    public boolean isEmpty();
      //Method to determine if the graph is empty.
      //Postcondition: Returns true if the graph is empty;
      //               otherwise, returns false.

    public void createGraph();
      //Method to create the graph.
      //Postcondition: The graph is created using the
      //               adjacency list representation.

    public void clearGraph();
      //Method to clear the graph.
      //Postcondition: Graph is empty.

    public void printGraph();
      //Method to print the graph.
      //Postcondition: For each vertex, the vertex and the
      //               vertices adjacent to the vertex are
      //               output.

    public void depthFirstTraversal();
      //Method to perform a depth first traversal of the
      //entire graph.
      //Postcondition: The vertices of the graph in the depth
      //               first traversal order are output.
```

```
public void dftAtVertex(int vertex);
    //Method to perform a depth first traversal at a
    //given vertex.
    //Postcondition: The vertices of the graph in the depth
    //               first traversal order are output.

public void breadthFirstTraversal();
    //Method to perform a breadth first traversal of the
    //graph.
    //Postcondition: The vertices of the graph in the breadth
    //               first traversal order are output.
}
```

We leave the UML class diagram of the **interface** GraphADT as an exercise.

IMPLEMENTING GRAPH OPERATIONS

In this section, we describe the class to implement the operations on graphs.

How a graph is represented in computer memory depends on the specific application. For illustration purposes, we use the adjacency list (linked list) representation of graphs. Therefore, for each vertex, v, the vertices adjacent to v (in a directed graph, also called the **immediate successors**) are stored in the linked list associated with v.

To manage the data in a linked list, we use the **class** UnorderedLinkedList, discussed in Chapter 16.

We design the **class** Graph implementing the **interface** GraphADT.

Class: Graph

```
public class Graph implements GraphADT
```

Instance Variables:

```
protected int maxSize;          //maximum number of vertices
protected int gSize;            //current number of vertices
protected UnorderedLinkedList[] graph; //array of references
                                       //to create adjacency lists
```

Instance Methods:

```
public Graph()
    //Default constructor
    //Postcondition: The graph size is set to 0, that is,
    //               gSize = 0; maxSize = 100

public Graph(int size)
    //Constructor
    //Postcondition: The graph size is set to 0, that is,
    //               gSize = 0; maxSize = size
```

```java
public boolean isEmpty()
    //Method to determine if the graph is empty.
    //Postcondition: Returns true if the graph is empty;
    //               otherwise, returns false.

public void createGraph()
    //Method to create the graph.
    //Postcondition: The graph is created using the
    //               adjacency list representation.

public void clearGraph()
    //Method to clear the graph.
    //Postcondition: Each entry of the array graph is set
    //               to null and gSize = 0;

public void printGraph()
    //Method to print the graph.
    //Postcondition: For each vertex, the vertex and the
    //               vertices adjacent to the vertex are
    //               output.

private void dft(int v, boolean[] visited)
    //Method to perform a depth first traversal at a
    //given vertex.
    //This method is used by the method, depthFirstTraversal
    //and the method dftAtVertex.
    //Postcondition: A depth first search starting at the
    //                vertex v is performed.

public void depthFirstTraversal()
    //Method to perform a depth first traversal of the
    //entire graph.
    //Postcondition: The vertices of the graph in the depth
    //               first traversal order are output.

public void dftAtVertex(int vertex)
    //Method to perform a depth first traversal at a
    //given vertex.
    //Postcondition: The vertices of the graph in the depth
    //               first traversal order are output.

public void breadthFirstTraversal()
    //Method to perform a breadth first traversal of the
    //graph.
    //Postcondition: The vertices of the graph in the breadth
    //               first traversal order are output.
```

We leave the UML class diagram of the **class** Graph as an exercise for you.

In the rest of this chapter, whenever we write graph algorithms in Java, we assume that the *n* vertices of the graphs are numbered 0, 1, ..., *n* – 1. Therefore, the vertex type is an integer. Moreover, because the `info` of a node is a reference to the object holding the data, we will use the **class** `Integer` to create the adjacency lists.

The definitions of the methods of the **class** `Graph` are discussed next.

A graph is empty if the number of vertices is zero—that is, if `gSize` is zero. Therefore, the definition of the method `isEmpty` is:

```
public boolean isEmpty()
{
    return (gSize == 0);
}
```

The definition of the method `createGraph` depends on how the data is input into the program. For illustration purposes, we assume that the data to the program is input from a file. The user is prompted for the input file. The data in the file appears in the following form:

```
5
0  2  4 ... -999
1  3  6  8 ... -999
...
```

The first line of input specifies the number of vertices in the graph. The first entry in the remaining lines specifies the vertex, and all of the remaining entries in the line (except the last) specify the vertices that are adjacent to the vertex. Each line ends with the number –999.

Using these conventions, the definition of the method `createGraph` is:

```
public void createGraph()
{
    Scanner console = new Scanner(System.in);

    String fileName;

    if (gSize != 0)
        clearGraph();

    Scanner infile = null;

    try
    {
        System.out.print("Enter input file name: ");
        fileName = console.nextLine();
        System.out.println();
```

```
        infile = new Scanner(new FileReader(fileName));
    }
    catch (FileNotFoundException fnfe)
    {
        System.out.println(fnfe.toString());
        System.exit(0);
    }

    gSize = infile.nextInt(); //get the number of vertices

    for (int index = 0; index < gSize; index++)
    {
        int vertex = infile.nextInt();
        int adjacentVertex = infile.nextInt();

        while (adjacentVertex != -999)
        {
            graph[vertex].insertLast(adjacentVertex);
            adjacentVertex = infile.nextInt();
        } //end while
    } // end for
}//end createGraph
```

The method **clearGraph** empties the graph by setting each array reference to null and then setting the number of vertices to zero.

```
public void clearGraph()
{
    int index;

    for (index = 0; index < gSize; index++)
        graph[index] = null;

    gSize = 0;
}
```

The definition of the method **printGraph** is given next.

```
public void printGraph()
{
    for (int index = 0; index < gSize; index++)
    {
        System.out.print(index + " ");
        graph[index].print();
        System.out.println();
    }

    System.out.println();
}
```

The definitions of the constructors are given next.

```java
public Graph()
{
    maxSize = 100;
    gSize = 0;
    graph = new UnorderedLinkedList[maxSize];

    for (int i = 0; i < maxSize; i++)
        graph[i] = new UnorderedLinkedList<Integer>();
}

public Graph(int size)
{
    maxSize = size;
    gSize = 0;
    graph  = new UnorderedLinkedList[maxSize];

    for (int i = 0; i < maxSize; i++)
        graph[i] = new UnorderedLinkedList<Integer>();
}
```

GRAPH TRAVERSALS

Processing a graph requires the ability to traverse the graph. This section discusses the graph traversal algorithms.

Traversing a graph is similar to traversing a binary tree, except that traversing a graph is a bit more complicated. Recall that a binary tree has no cycles. Also, starting at the root node, we can traverse the entire tree. On the other hand, a graph might have cycles and we might not be able to traverse the entire graph from a single vertex (for example, if the graph is not connected). Therefore, we must keep track of the vertices that have been visited. We must also traverse the graph from each vertex (that has not been visited) of the graph. This ensures that the entire graph is traversed.

The two most common graph traversal algorithms are the **depth first traversal** and **breadth first traversal**, which are described next. For simplicity, we assume that when a vertex is visited, its index is output. Moreover, each vertex is visited only once. We use a Boolean array, `visited`, to keep track of the visited vertices.

Depth First Traversal

The **depth first traversal** is similar to the preorder traversal of a binary tree. The general algorithm is:

```
for each vertex, v, in the graph
    if v is not visited
        start the depth first traversal at v
```

Consider the graph G₃ of Figure 20–4. It is shown here again as Figure 20-7 for easy reference.

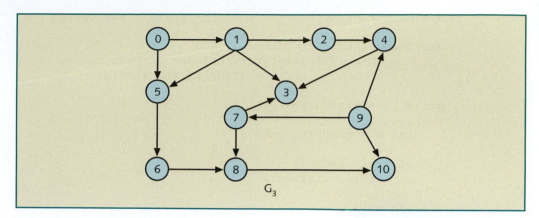

Figure 20-7   Directed graph G_3

A depth first ordering of the vertices of the graph G_3 in Figure 20-7 is:

0 1 2 4 3 5 6 8 10 7 9

For the graph of Figure 20-7, the depth first search starts at the vertex 0. After visiting all the vertices that can be reached starting at the vertex 0, the depth first search starts at the next vertex that has not been visited. In this graph, there is a path from the vertex 0 to every other vertex except the vertices 7 and 9. Therefore, when the depth first search starts at the vertex 0, all the vertices except 7 and 9 are visited before these vertices. After completing the depth first search that started at the vertex 0, the depth first search starts at the vertex 7 and then at the vertex 9. Note that there is no path from the vertex 7 to the vertex 9 or from the vertex 9 to the vertex 7. Therefore, after completing the depth first search that started at the vertex 7, the depth first search starts at the vertex 9.

The general algorithm to do a depth first traversal at a given node, *v*, is:

1. Mark node **v** as visited.

2. Visit the node.

3. **for** each vertex u adjacent to **v**,
      if u is not visited
         start the depth first traversal at u

Clearly, this is a recursive algorithm. We use a recursive method, **dft**, to implement this algorithm. The vertex at which the depth first traversal is to be started and the **boolean** array **visited** are passed as parameters to this method.

```
private void dft(int v, boolean[] visited)
{
    visited[v] = true;
```

```
        System.out.print(" " + v + " ");   //visit the vertex

        UnorderedLinkedList<Integer>.
                LinkedListIterator<Integer> graphIt
                                = graph[v].iterator();

        while (graphIt.hasNext())
        {
            int w = graphIt.next();

            if (!visited[w])
                dft(w, visited);

        } //end while
} //end dft
```

In the preceding code, note that the statement

```
UnorderedLinkedList<Integer>.
        LinkedListIterator<Integer> graphIt
                        = graph[v].iterator();
```

creates the iterator, `graphIt`, to the linked list to which the reference variable `graph[v]` points. Using this iterator, we can traverse this linked list. Next, let us look at the statement:

```
int w = graphIt.next();
```

The expression `graphIt.next()` returns the reference of the `info` of the current node; this is, the label of a vertex adjacent to the vertex `v` to which `graphIt` points. The returned reference is of the `Integer` type. The auto-unboxing feature of Java stores the label of the node in `w`. Therefore, after this statement executes, the value of `w` is a vertex that is adjacent to the vertex `v`. Note that the expression `graphIt.next()` also advances the iterator `graphIt` to the next node in the list.

Next, we give the definition of the method `depthFirstTraversal` to implement the depth first traversal of the graph.

```
public void depthFirstTraversal()
{
    boolean[] visited;   //array to keep track of the
                         //visited vertices
    visited = new boolean[gSize];

    for (int index = 0; index < gSize; index++)
        visited[index] = false;
```

```
    for (int index = 0; index < gSize; index++) //for each
                                                 //vertex that
        if (!visited[index])                //has not been visited
            dft(index, visited);            //do a depth first
                                            //traversal
} //end depthFirstTraversal
```

The method `depthFirstTraversal` performs a depth first traversal of the entire graph. The definition of the method `dftAtVertex`, which performs a depth first traversal at a given vertex, is as follows:

```
public void dftAtVertex(int vertex)
{
    boolean[] visited;
    visited = new boolean[gSize];

    for (int index = 0; index < gSize; index++)
        visited[index] = false;

    dft(vertex,visited);
} //end dftAtVertex
```

Breadth First Traversal

The **breadth first traversal** of a graph is similar to traversing a binary tree level by level (in which the nodes at each level are visited from left to right). All the nodes at any level, i, are visited before visiting the nodes at level $i + 1$.

A breadth first ordering of the vertices of the graph G_3 (Figure 20-7) is:

```
0   1   5   2   3   6   4   8   10   7   9
```

For the graph G_3, we start the breadth traversal at vertex 0. After visiting the vertex 0, next we visit the vertices that are directly connected to it and have not been visited, which in this case are 1 and 5. Next, we visit the vertices that are directly connected to 1 and have not been visited, which are 2 and 3. After this, we visit the vertex that is directly connected to 5 and has not been visited, which is 6. After this, we visit the vertices that are directly connected to 2 and have not been visited, and so on.

As in the case of the depth first traversal, because it might not be possible to traverse the entire graph from a single vertex, the breadth first traversal also traverses the graph from each vertex that has not been visited. Starting at the first vertex, the graph is traversed as much as possible; we then go to the next vertex that has not been visited. To implement the breadth first search algorithm, we use a queue. The general algorithm is:

1. **for** each vertex **v** in the graph
           if **v** is not visited
                     add **v** to the `queue` //**start the breadth first search at v**

2. Mark **v** as `visited`

3. **while** the queue is not empty

    3.1.   Remove vertex u from the queue

    3.2.   Retrieve the vertices adjacent to u

    3.3.   **for** each vertex w that is adjacent to u

           if w is not visited

        3.3.1. Add w to the queue

        3.3.2. Mark w as **visited**

The following Java method, `breadthFirstTraversal`, implements this algorithm:

```java
public void breadthFirstTraversal()
{
    LinkedQueueClass<Integer> queue =
                new LinkedQueueClass<Integer>();

    boolean[] visited;
    visited = new boolean[gSize];

    for (int ind = 0; ind < gSize; ind++)
        visited[ind] = false;    //initialize the array
                                 //visited to false

    for (int index = 0; index < gSize; index++)
        if (!visited[index])
        {
            queue.addQueue(index);
            visited[index] = true;
            System.out.print(" " + index + " ");

            while (!queue.isEmptyQueue())
            {
                int u = queue.front();

                queue.deleteQueue();

                UnorderedLinkedList<Integer>.
                    LinkedListIterator<Integer> graphIt
                                = graph[u].iterator();

                while (graphIt.hasNext())
                {
                    int w1 = graphIt.next();

                    if (!visited[w1])
                    {
```

```
                                queue.addQueue(w1);
                                visited[w1] = true;
                                System.out.print(" " + w1 + " ");
                        }
                }
            } //end while
        } //end if
} //end breadthFirstTraversal
```

After including the previous graph traversal algorithms, you can write the definition of the **class** Graph as follows:

```java
import java.io.*;
import java.util.*;

public class Graph implements GraphADT
{
    //Put constants and instance variables here.
    //Put the definitions of the constructors and the methods
    //described above here.
}
```

As we continue to discuss graph algorithms, we will be writing Java methods to implement specific algorithms, and so we will derive (using inheritance) new classes from the **class** Graph.

SHORTEST PATH ALGORITHM

The graph theory has many applications. For example, we can use graphs to show how different chemicals are related or to show airline routes. They can also be used to show the highway structure of a city, state, or country. The edges connecting two vertices can be assigned a nonnegative real number, called the **weight of the edge**. If the graph represents a highway structure, the weight can represent the distance between two places, or the travel time from one place to another. Such graphs are called **weighted graphs**.

Let *G* be a weighted graph. Let *u* and *v* be two vertices in *G*, and let *P* be a path in *G* from *u* to *v*. The **weight of the path** *P* is the sum of the weights of all the edges on the path *P*, which is also called the **weight** of *v* from *u* via *P*.

Let *G* be a weighted graph representing a highway structure. Suppose that the weight of an edge represents the travel time. For example, to plan monthly business trips, salespeople want to find the **shortest path** (that is, the path with the smallest weight) from their home cities to every other city in the graph. Many such problems exist in which we want to find the shortest path from a given vertex, called the **source**, to every other vertex in the graph.

This section describes the **shortest path algorithm**, also called a **greedy algorithm**, developed by Dijkstra.

Let G be a graph with n vertices, where $n > 0$. Let $V(G) = \{v_1, v_2, ..., v_n\}$. Let W be a two-dimensional $n \times n$ matrix such that:

$$W(i,j) = \begin{cases} w_{ij} \text{ if } (v_i, v_j) \text{ is an edge in G and } w_{ij} \text{ is the weight of the edge } (v_i, v_j) \\ \infty \text{ if there is no edge from } v_i \text{ to } v_j \end{cases}$$

The input to the program is the graph and the weight matrix associated with the graph. To make inputting the data easier, we extend the definition of the **class** Graph (using inheritance), and we add the method `createWeightedGraph` to create the graph and the weight matrix associated with the graph. Let us call this **class** WeightedGraph. The methods to implement the shortest path algorithm will also be added to this class.

Class: `WeightedGraph`

```
public class WeightedGraph extends Graph
```

Instance Variables:

```
protected double[][] weights;          //weight matrix
protected double[] smallestWeight;     //smallest weight from
                                       //source to vertices
```

Constructors and Instance Methods

```
public WeightedGraph()
   //Default constructor

public WeightedGraph(int size)
   //Constructor with a parameter

public void createWeightedGraph()
   //Method to create the graph and the weight matrix.

public void shortestPath(int vertex)
   //Method to determine the smallest weight from,
   //vertex, that is, the source to every other vertex
   //in the graph.

public void printShortestDistance(int vertex)
   //Method to print the shortest weight from the
   //source to the other vertices in the graph.
```

We leave the UML class diagram of the **class** WeightedGraph and the inheritance hierarchy as an exercise for you, as well as the definition of the method `createWeightedGraph`. Next, we describe the shortest path algorithm.

Shortest Path

Given a vertex, say `vertex` (that is, a source), this section describes the shortest path algorithm.

The general algorithm is:

1. Initialize the array `smallestWeight` so that

   `smallestWeight[u] = weights[vertex, u]`

2. Set `smallestWeight[vertex] = 0`.

3. Find the vertex `v`, that is closest to `vertex` for which the shortest path has not been determined.

4. Mark `v` as the (next) vertex for which the smallest weight is found.

5. For each vertex `w` in `G`, such that the shortest path from `vertex` to `w` has not been determined and an edge `(v, w)` exists, if the weight of the path to `w` via `v` is smaller than its current weight, update the weight of `w` to the weight of `v` + the weight of the edge `(v, w)`.

Because there are `n` vertices, repeat Steps 3 through 5 $n - 1$ times.

Example 20-5 illustrates the shortest path algorithm. We use the Boolean array `weightFound` to keep track of the vertices for which the smallest weight from the source vertex has been found. If the smallest weight for a vertex from the source has been found, then this vertex's corresponding entry in the array `weightFound` is set to **true**; otherwise, the corresponding entry is **false**.

Example 20-5

Let G be the graph shown in Figure 20-8.

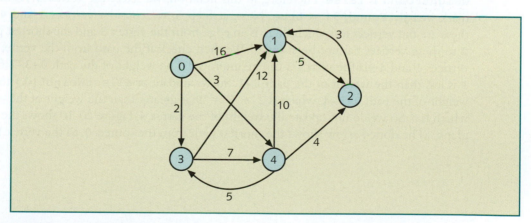

Figure 20-8   Weighted graph G

Suppose that the source vertex of G is 0. The graph shows the weight of each edge. After Steps 1 and 2 execute, the resulting graph is as shown in Figure 20-9.

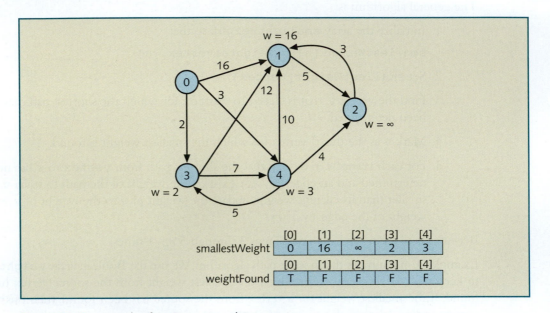

smallestWeight

	[0]	[1]	[2]	[3]	[4]
	0	16	∞	2	3

weightFound

	[0]	[1]	[2]	[3]	[4]
	T	F	F	F	F

Figure 20-9   Graph after Steps 1 and 2 execute

Iteration 1 of Steps 3 to 5: At Step 3, we select a vertex that is closest to the vertex 0 and for which the shortest path has not been found. We do this by finding a vertex in the array `smallestWeight` that has the smallest weight and whose corresponding entry in the array `weightFound` is **false**. Therefore, in this iteration, we select the vertex 3. At Step 4, we mark `weightFound[3]` as **true**. Next, at Step 5, we consider vertices 1 and 4 because these are the vertices for which there is an edge from the vertex 3 and the shortest part from 0 to these vertices has not been found. We then check if the path from the vertex 0 to the vertices 1 and 4 via the vertex 3 can be improved. The weight of the path 0-3-1 from 0 to 1 is less than the weight of the path 0-1. So we update `smallestWeight[1]` to 14. The weight of the path 0-3-4, which is 2 + 7 = 9, is greater than the weight of the path 0-4, which is 3. So we do not update the weight of the vertex 4. Figure 20-10 shows the resulting graph. (The dotted arrow shows the shortest path from the source, 0, to the vertex.)

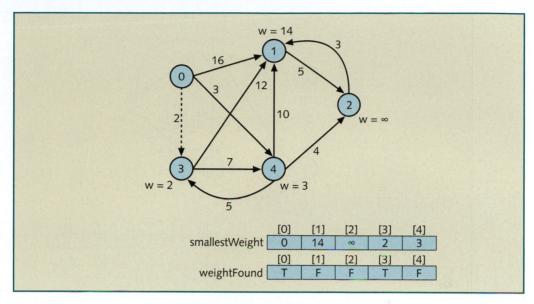

Figure 20-10   Graph after the first iteration of Steps 3, 4, and 5

Iteration 2 of Steps 3 to 5: At Step 3, we select vertex 4 because this is the vertex in the array `smallestWeight` that has the smallest weight and whose corresponding entry in the array `weightFound` is **false**. Next we execute Steps 4 and 5. At Step 4, we set `weightFound[4]` to **true**. At Step 5, we consider vertices 1 and 2 because these are the vertices for which there is an edge from vertex 4 and the shortest part from 0 to these vertices has not been found. We then check if the path from the vertex 0 to the vertices 1 and 2 via the vertex 4 can be improved. Clearly, the weight of the path 0–4–1, which is 13, is smaller than the current weight of 1, which is 14. So we update `smallestWeight[1]`. Similarly, we update `smallestWeight[2]`. Figure 20-11 shows the resulting graph.

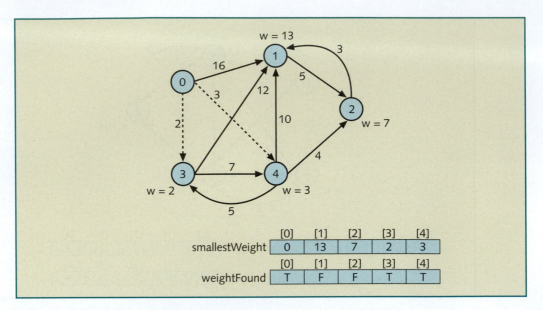

Figure 20-11 shows the following data:

	[0]	[1]	[2]	[3]	[4]
smallestWeight	0	13	7	2	3

	[0]	[1]	[2]	[3]	[4]
weightFound	T	F	F	T	T

Figure 20-11   Graph after the second iteration of Steps 3, 4, and 5

Iteration 3 of Steps 3 to 5: At Step 3, the vertex selected is **2**. At Step 4, we set
`weightFound[2]` to **true**. Next, at Step 5, we consider the vertex **1** because this is the vertex for which there is an edge from the vertex **2**, and the shortest path from **0** to this vertex
has not been found. We then check if the path from the vertex **0** to the vertex **1** via the vertex **2** can be improved. Clearly, the weight of the path **0-4-2-1**, which is **10**, is smaller than
the current weight of **1** (which is **13**). So we update `smallestWeight[1]`. Figure 20-12
shows the resulting graph.

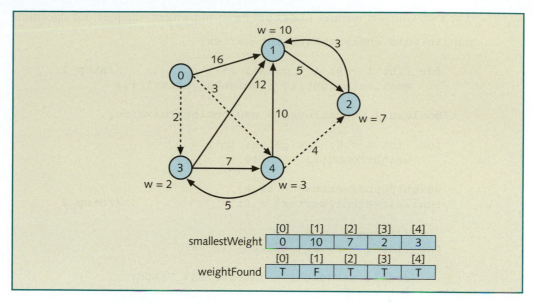

Figure 20-12   Graph after the third iteration of Steps 3, 4, and 5

Iteration 4 of Steps 3 to 5: At Step 3, the vertex 1 is selected, and at Step 4 `weightFound[1]` is set to **true**. In this iteration, the action of Step 5 is null because the shortest path from the vertex 0 to every other vertex in the graph has been determined. Figure 20–13 shows the final graph.

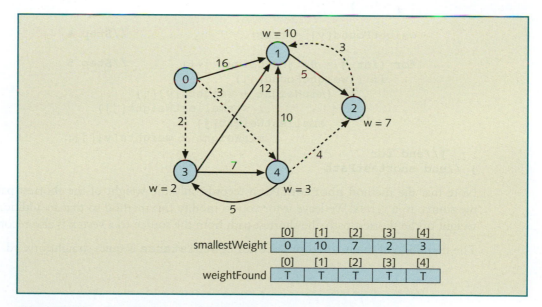

Figure 20-13   Graph after the fourth iteration of Steps 3, 4, and 5

The following Java method, `shortestPath`, implements the previous algorithm:

```java
public void shortestPath(int vertex)
{
    for (int i = 0; i < gSize; i++)              //Step 1
        smallestWeight[i] = weights[vertex][i];

    boolean[] weightFound = new boolean[maxSize];

    for (int i = 0; i < gSize; i++)
        weightFound[i] = false;

    weightFound[vertex] = true;
    smallestWeight[vertex] = 0;                  //Step 2

        //Steps 3 to 5
    for (int i = 0; i < gSize - 1; i++)
    {
        double minWeight = Integer.MAX_VALUE;
        int v = 0;

        for (int j = 0; j < gSize; j++)          //Step 3
            if (!weightFound[j])
                if (smallestWeight[j] < minWeight)
                {
                    v = j;
                    minWeight = smallestWeight[v];
                }

        weightFound[v] = true;                   //Step 4

        for (int j = 0; j < gSize; j++)          //Step 5
            if (!weightFound[j])
                if (minWeight + weights[v][j]
                            < smallestWeight[j])
                    smallestWeight[j] =
                            minWeight + weights[v][j];
    }//end for
} //end shortestPath
```

Note that the method `shortestPath` records only the weight of the shortest path from the source to a vertex. We leave it for you to modify this method so that in addition to the weight of the shortest path, the shortest path from the source to a vertex is also recorded.

The definition of the method `printShortestDistance` is quite straightforward.

```java
public void printShortestDistance(int vertex)
{
    System.out.println("Source Vertex: " + vertex);
    System.out.println("Shortest Distance from Source "
                    + "to each Vertex");
    System.out.println("Vertex   Shortest_Distance");

    for (int j = 0; j < gSize; j++)
    {
        System.out.print("    " + j + " \t\t");
        System.out.printf("%.2f \n", smallestWeight[j]);
    }

    System.out.println();
}
```

MINIMAL SPANNING TREE

Consider the graph of Figure 20-14, which represents the airline connections of a company between seven cities. The number on each edge represents some cost factor of maintaining the connection between the cities.

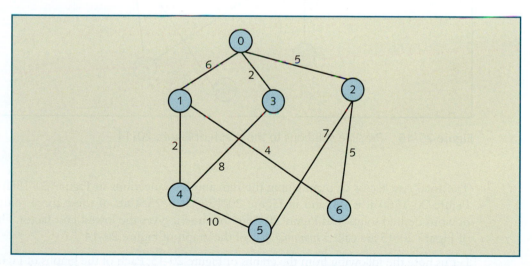

Figure 20-14   Airline connections between cities and the cost factor of maintaining the connections

Due to financial hardship, the company needs to shut down the maximum number of connections and still be able to fly from one city to another (even if not directly). The graphs of Figure 20-15(a), (b), and (c) shows three different solutions.

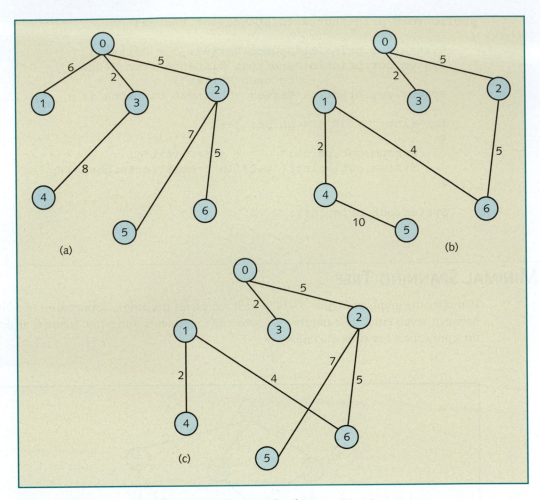

Figure 20-15 Possible solutions to the graph of Figure 20-14

The total cost factor of maintaining the remaining connections in Figure 20-15(a) is **33**, in Figure 20-15(b) it is **28**, and in Figure 20-15(c) it is **25**. Out of these three solutions, the obvious desired solution is Figure 20-15(c) because it gives the lowest cost factor. The graphs of Figure 20-15 are called *spanning trees* of the graph of Figure 20-14.

Let us note the following from the graphs of Figure 20-15. Each of the graphs of Figure 20-15 is a subgraph of the graph of Figure 20-14, and in each one there is a unique path from a node to any other node. Such graphs are called trees. There are many other situations where, given a weighted graph, we need to determine a graph such as in Figure 20-15 with the smallest weight. In this section, we give an algorithm to determine such graphs. However, first we introduce some terminology.

A (**free**) **tree** T is a simple graph such that if u and v are two vertices in T, then there is a unique path from u to v. A tree in which a particular vertex is designated as a root is called a **rooted tree**. If a weight is assigned to the edges in T, T is called a **weighted tree**. If T is a weighted tree, the **weight** of T, denoted by $W(T)$, is the sum of the weights of all the edges in T.

A tree T is called a **spanning tree** of graph G if T is a subgraph of G, such that $V(T) = V(G)$; that is, if all the vertices of G are in T.

Suppose G denotes the graph of Figure 20-14. Then the graphs of Figure 20-15 show three spanning trees of G. Let us note the following theorem.

Theorem: A graph G has a spanning tree if and only if G is connected.

From this theorem, it follows that to determine a spanning tree of a graph, the graph must be connected.

Let G be a weighted graph. A **minimal spanning tree** of G is a spanning tree with the minimum weight.

There are two well-known algorithms, Prim's algorithm and Kruskal's algorithm, to find the minimal spanning tree of a graph. This section discusses Prim's algorithm to find a minimal spanning tree. The interested reader can find the Kruskal's algorithm in the discrete structures book or a data structures book listed in Appendix F.

Prim's algorithm builds the tree iteratively by adding edges until a minimal spanning tree is obtained. We start with a designated vertex, which we call the source vertex. At each iteration, a new edge that does not complete a cycle is added to the tree.

Let G be a weighted graph such that $V(G) = \{v_0, v_1, ..., v_{n-1}\}$, where n, the number of vertices, is positive. Let v_0 be the source vertex. Let T be the partially built tree. Initially, $V(T)$ contains the source vertex and $E(T)$ is empty. At the next iteration, a new vertex that is not in $V(T)$ is added to $V(T)$, such that an edge exists from a vertex in T to the new vertex so that the corresponding edge has the smallest weight. The corresponding edge is added to $E(T)$.

The general form of Prim's algorithm is as follows. (Let n be the number of vertices in G.)

1. Set $V(T) = \{source\}$.

2. Set $E(T) = empty$.

3. **for** i = 1 to n

```
   3.1 minWeight = infinity;
   3.2 for j = 1 to n
           if v_j is in V(T)
              for k = 1 to n
                 if v_k is not in T and weight[v_j, v_k] < minWeight
                 {
                     endVertex = v_k;
                     edge = (v_j, v_k);
                     minWeight = weight[v_j, v_k];
                 }
```

```
3.3 V(T) = V(T) ∪ {endVertex};
3.4 E(T) = E(T) ∪ {edge};
```

Let us illustrate Prim's algorithm using the graph G of Figure 20-16 (which is same as the graph of Figure 20-14).

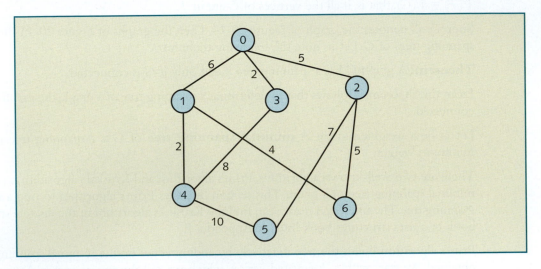

Figure 20-16 Weighted graph G

Let N denote the set of vertices of G that are not in T. Suppose that the source vertex is 0. After Steps 1 and 2 execute, $V(T)$, $E(T)$, and N are as shown in Figure 20-17.

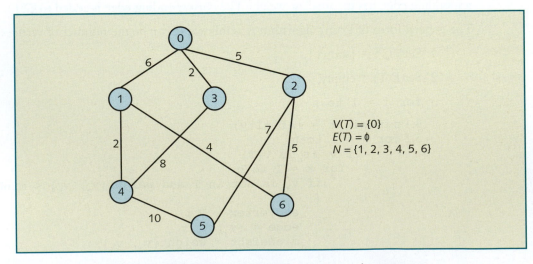

Figure 20-17 Graph G, $V(T)$, $E(T)$, and N after Steps 1 and 2 execute

Step 3.2 checks the following edges:

Edge	Weight of the Edge
(0,1)	6
(0,2)	5
(0,3)	2

Clearly, the edge (0,3) has the smallest weight. Therefore, vertex 3 is added to $V(T)$ and the edge (0,3) is added to $E(T)$. Figure 20-18 shows the resulting graph, $V(T)$, $E(T)$, and N. (The dotted line shows the edge in T.)

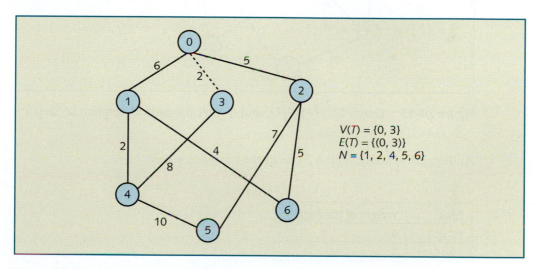

Figure 20-18   Graph G, $V(T)$, $E(T)$, and N after the first iteration of Step 3

Next, Step 3.2 checks the following edges:

Edge	Weight of the Edge
(0,1)	6
(0,2)	5
(3,4)	8

Clearly, the edge (0,2) has the smallest weight. Therefore, vertex 2 is added to $V(T)$ and the edge (0,2) is added to $E(T)$. Figure 20-19 shows the resulting graph, $V(T)$, $E(T)$, and N. (The dotted line shows the edge in T.)

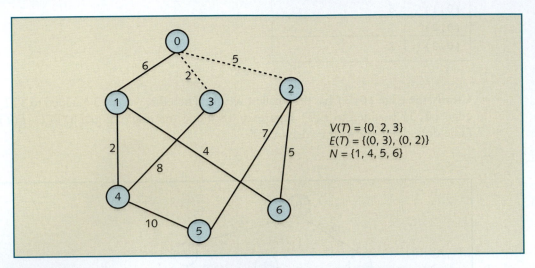

$V(T) = \{0, 2, 3\}$
$E(T) = \{(0, 3), (0, 2)\}$
$N = \{1, 4, 5, 6\}$

Figure 20-19   Graph G, $V(T)$, $E(T)$, and N after the second iteration of Step 3

At the next iteration, Step 3.2 checks the following edges:

Edge	Weight of the Edge
(0,1)	6
(2,5)	7
(2,6)	5
(3,4)	8

Clearly, the edge (2,6) has the smallest weight. Therefore, vertex 6 is added to $V(T)$ and the edge (2,6) is added to $E(T)$. Figure 20-20 shows the resulting graph, $V(T)$, $E(T)$, and N. (The dotted lines show the edges in T.)

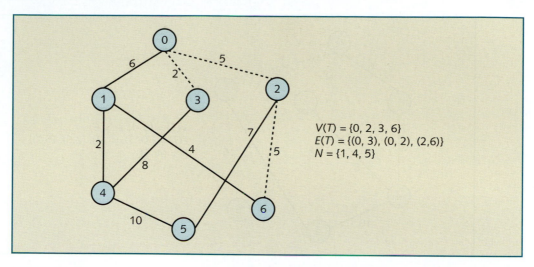

$V(T) = \{0, 2, 3, 6\}$
$E(T) = \{(0, 3), (0, 2), (2,6)\}$
$N = \{1, 4, 5\}$

Figure 20-20   Graph G, $V(T)$, $E(T)$, and N after the third iteration of Step 3

At the next iteration, Step 3.2 checks the following edges:

Edge	Weight of the Edge
(0,1)	6
(2,5)	7
(3,4)	8
(6,1)	4

Clearly, the edge (6,1) has the smallest weight. Therefore, vertex 1 is added to $V(T)$ and the edge (6,1) is added to $E(T)$. Figure 20-21 shows the resulting graph, $V(T)$, $E(T)$, and N. (The dotted lines show the edges in T.)

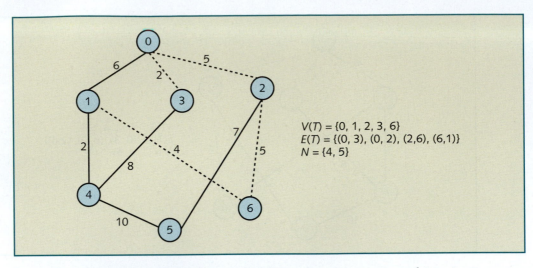

$V(T) = \{0, 1, 2, 3, 6\}$
$E(T) = \{(0, 3), (0, 2), (2,6), (6,1)\}$
$N = \{4, 5\}$

Figure 20-21   Graph G, $V(T)$, $E(T)$, and N after the fourth iteration of Step 3

At the next iteration, Step 3.2 checks the following edges:

Edge	Weight of the Edge
(1,4)	2
(2,5)	7
(3,4)	8

Clearly, the edge (1,4) has the smallest weight. Therefore, vertex 4 is added to $V(T)$ and the edge (1,4) is added to $E(T)$. Figure 20-22 shows the resulting graph, $V(T)$, $E(T)$, and N. (The dotted lines show the edges in T.)

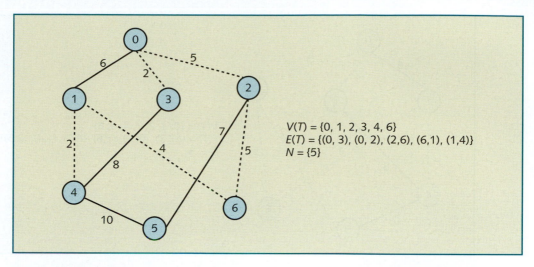

$V(T) = \{0, 1, 2, 3, 4, 6\}$
$E(T) = \{(0, 3), (0, 2), (2,6), (6,1), (1,4)\}$
$N = \{5\}$

Figure 20-22 Graph G, $V(T)$, $E(T)$, and N after the fifth iteration of Step 3

At the next iteration, Step 3.2 checks the following edges:

Edge	Weight of the Edge
(2,5)	7
(4,5)	10

Clearly, the edge (2,5) has the smallest weight. Therefore, vertex 5 is added to $V(T)$ and the edge (2,5) is added to $E(T)$. Figure 20-23 shows the resulting graph, $V(T)$, $E(T)$, and N. (The dotted lines show the edges in T.)

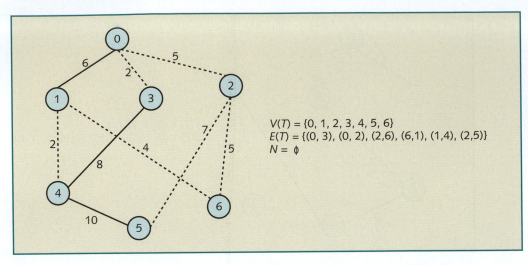

$V(T) = \{0, 1, 2, 3, 4, 5, 6\}$
$E(T) = \{(0, 3), (0, 2), (2,6), (6,1), (1,4), (2,5)\}$
$N = \phi$

Figure 20-23 Graph G, $V(T)$, $E(T)$, and N after the sixth iteration of Step 3

The dotted lines show a minimal spanning tree of G of weight **25**.

Before we give the definition of the method to implement Prim's algorithm, let us first define the spanning tree as an ADT.

Let `mstv` be a **boolean** array such that `mstv [j]` is **true** if the vertex v_i is in T, and **false** otherwise. Let `edges` be an array such that `edges[j] = k` if there is an edge connecting vertices v_j and v_k. Suppose that the edge (v_i, v_j) is in the minimal spanning tree. Let `edgeWeights` be an array such that `edgeWeights[j]` is the weight of the edge (v_i, v_j).

Using these conventions, the following class defines a spanning tree as an ADT:

Class: `MSTree`

```
public MSTree extends Graph
```

Instance Variables:

```
protected int source;
protected double[][] weights;
protected int[] edges;
protected double[] edgeWeights;
```

Constructors and Instance Methods:

```
public MSTree()
    //Default constructor

public MSTree(int size)
    //Constructor with a parameter

public void createSpanningGraph()
    //Method to create the graph and the weight matrix
```

```java
public void minimalSpanning(int sVertex)
   //Method to create the edges of the minimal
   //spanning tree. The weight of the edges is also
   //saved in the array edgeWeights.

public void printTreeAndWeight()
   //Method to output the edges of the minimal spanning
   //tree and the weight of the minimal spanning tree
```

We leave the UML class diagram of the **class MSTree** and the inheritance hierarchy as an exercise for you, as well as the definition of the method **createSpanningGraph**. This method creates the graph and the weight matrix associated with the graph.

The following Java method, **minimalSpanning**, implements Prim's algorithm, as described previously:

```java
public void minimalSpanning(int sVertex)
{
    source = sVertex;

    boolean[] mstv = new boolean[maxSize];

    for (int j = 0; j < gSize; j++)
    {
        mstv[j] = false;
        edges[j] = source;
        edgeWeights[j] = weights[source][j];
    }

    mstv[source] = true;
    edgeWeights[source] = 0;

    for (int i = 0; i < gSize - 1; i++)
    {
        double minWeight = Integer.MAX_VALUE;
        int startVertex = 0;
        int endVertex = 0;

        for (int j = 0; j < gSize; j++)
            if (mstv[j])
                for (int k = 0; k < gSize; k++)
                    if (!mstv[k] && weights[j][k] < minWeight)
                    {
                        endVertex = k;
                        startVertex = j;
                        minWeight = weights[j][k];
                    }
        mstv[endVertex] = true;
        edges[endVertex] = startVertex;
        edgeWeights[endVertex] = minWeight;
    } //end for
} //end minimalSpanning
```

The definition of the method `minimalSpanning` contains three nested **for** loops. Therefore, in the worst case, Prim's algorithm given in this section is of the order $O(n^3)$. It is possible to design Prim's algorithm so that it is of the order $O(n^2)$; Programming Exercise 5 at the end of this chapter asks you to do so.

The definition of the method `printTreeAndWeight` is straightforward and is given next:

```java
public void printTreeAndWeight()
{
    double treeWeight = 0;

    System.out.println("Source Vertex: " + source);
    System.out.println("Edges    Weight");

    for (int j = 0; j < gSize; j++)
    {
        if (edges[j] != j)
        {
            treeWeight = treeWeight + edgeWeights[j];
            System.out.print("(" + edges[j] + ", " + j
                              + ")      ");
            System.out.printf("%.2f \n", edgeWeights[j]);
        }
    }

    System.out.println();
    System.out.print("Minimal Spanning Tree Weight: ");
    System.out.printf("%.2f \n", treeWeight);
} //end printTreeAndWeight
```

The definitions of the constructors are as follows:

```java
    //Default constructor
public MSTree()
{
    super();
    weights = new double[maxSize][maxSize];
    edges = new int[maxSize];
    edgeWeights = new double[maxSize];
}


    //Constructor with a parameter
public MSTree(int size)
{
    super(size);

    weights = new double[maxSize][maxSize];
    edges = new int[maxSize];
    edgeWeights = new double[maxSize];
}
```

(Topological Ordering) This chapter also discusses topological ordering. The necessary material is in the file Topological Order.pdf. This file is on the CD that is included with this book.

SOME WELL-KNOWN GRAPH THEORY PROBLEMS

The beginning of this chapter described the well-known Königsberg bridge problem. There are several other well-known graph theory problems. Before we close this chapter, we describe some of the problems.

Three Utilities Problem: Suppose there are three houses, which are to be connected to three services, water, telephone, and electricity, by the means of underground pipelines. The services are to be connected subject to the following condition: The pipes must be laid so that they do not cross each other. Consider three distinct points A, B, and C as three houses, and three other distinct points W, T, and E, which represent water source, telephone's connection point, and electricity's connection point. Try to join W, T, and E with each of A, B, and C by drawing lines (they might not be straight lines) so that no two lines intersect each other. This is known as the **three utilities problem**. The answer to this problem is no.

Traveling Salesperson Problem: A **cycle** in a graph is a path that starts at a vertex and ends at the same vertex such that each vertex and each edge on the path appear exactly once. A cycle in a graph G is called a **Hamiltonian cycle** if it contains each vertex of G. Consider the following question: Is it possible to determine whether a graph has a Hamiltonian cycle? The answer to this question has not been completely obtained. However, a well-known variation of this is the traveling salesperson problem, which involves a weighted graph in which the vertices represent cities and edges represent roadways. The weight of each edge represents, say, the distance or the traveling time between the cities. The objective of the salesperson is to start from the home city, drive from one city to another, return to the home city, and visit each city exactly once so that the total cost factor is smallest. A solution to this problem exists. However, the solution is quite slow.

Four Color Problem: A graph G is called a **planar** graph if it can be drawn in the plane such that no two edges intersect except at the vertices, which may be the common end vertices of the edges. A graph drawn in the plane (on paper or a chalkboard) is called a **plane** graph if no two edges meet at a point except the common vertex, if they meet at all. Given a planer graph, is it possible to color the vertices, using only, say, four colors, so that no two adjacent vertices have the same color? This problem was first proposed more than a century ago. In 1976, the problem was finally solved by two American mathematicians, Kenneth Apple and Wolfgang Haken. The proof used 1000 hours of computer time with fast, large computers. Apple and Haken worked on this problem for 10 years.

Some of the problems, such as the three utility problem, Hamiltonian cycle, and the graph coloring are discussed in the book *Discrete Mathematical Structures: Theory and Applications* listed in Appendix F.

QUICK REVIEW

1. A graph G is a pair, $G = (V, E)$, where V is a finite nonempty set, called the set of vertices of G, and $E \subseteq V \times V$, called the set of edges.

2. In an undirected graph $G = (V, E)$, the elements of E are unordered pairs.

3. In a directed graph $G = (V, E)$, the elements of E are ordered pairs.

4. Let G be a graph. A graph H is called a subgraph of G if every vertex of H is a vertex of G and every edge in H is an edge in G.

5. Two vertices u and v in an undirected graph are called adjacent if there is an edge from one to the other.

6. Let $e = (u, v)$ be an edge in an undirected graph G. Then the edge e is said to be incident on the vertices u and v.

7. An edge incident on a single vertex is called a loop.

8. In an undirected graph, if two edges e_1 and e_2 are associated with the same pair of vertices, then e_1 and e_2 are called parallel edges.

9. A graph is called a simple graph if it has no loops and no parallel edges.

10. A path from a vertex u to a vertex v is a sequence of vertices $u_1, u_2, ..., u_n$ such that $u = u_1$, $u_n = v$, and (u_i, u_{i+1}) is an edge for all $i = 1, 2, ..., n - 1$.

11. The vertices u and v are called connected if there is a path from u to v.

12. A simple path is a path in which all the vertices, except possibly the first and last vertices, are distinct.

13. A cycle in G is a simple path in which the first and last vertices are the same.

14. An undirected graph G is called connected if there is a path from any vertex to any other vertex.

15. A maximal subset of connected vertices is called a component of G.

16. Suppose that u and v are vertices in a directed graph G. If there is an edge from u to v, that is, $(u, v) \in E$, we say that u is adjacent to v and v is adjacent from u.

17. A directed graph G is called strongly connected if any two vertices in G are connected.

18. Let G be a graph with n vertices, where $n > 0$. Let $V(G) = \{v_1, v_2, ..., v_n\}$. The adjacency matrix A_G is a two-dimensional $n \times n$ matrix such that the (i, j)th entry of A_G is 1 if there is an edge from v_i to v_j; otherwise, the (i, j)th entry is zero.

19. In an adjacency list representation, corresponding to each vertex v is a linked list such that each node of the linked list contains the vertex u, and $(v, u) \in E(G)$.

20. The depth first traversal of a graph is similar to the preorder traversal of a binary tree.

21. The breadth first traversal of a graph is similar to the level-by-level traversal of a binary tree.

22. The shortest path algorithm gives the shortest distance for a given node to every other node in the graph.

20

23. In a weighted graph, every edge has a nonnegative weight.

24. The weight of the path P is the sum of the weights of all the edges on the path P, which is also called the weight of v from u via P.

25. A (free) tree T is a simple graph such that if u and v are two vertices in T, there is a unique path from u to v.

26. A tree in which a particular vertex is designated as a root is called a rooted tree.

27. Suppose T is a tree. If a weight is assigned to the edges in T, T is called a weighted tree.

28. If T is a weighted tree, the weight of T, denoted by $W(T)$, is the sum of the weights of all the edges in T.

29. A tree T is called a spanning tree of graph G if T is a subgraph of G such that $V(T) = V(G)$, that is, if all the vertices of G are in T.

EXERCISES

Use the graph in Figure 20-24 for Exercises 1 through 4.

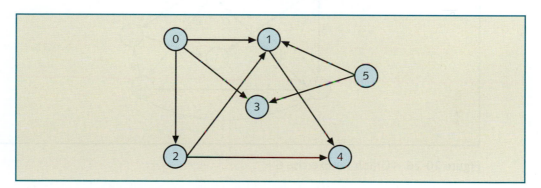

Figure 20-24   Graph for Exercises 1 through 4

1. Find the adjacency matrix of the graph.

2. Draw the adjacency list of the graph.

3. List the nodes of the graph in a depth first traversal.

4. List the nodes of the graph in a breadth first traversal.

5. Find the weight matrix of the graph in Figure 20-25.

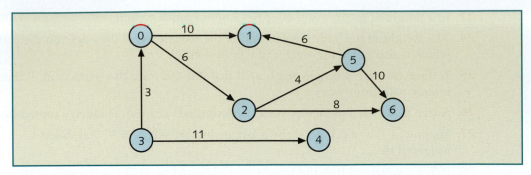

Figure 20-25   Graph for Exercise 5

6. Consider the graph in Figure 20-26. Find the shortest distance from node 0 to every other node in the graph.

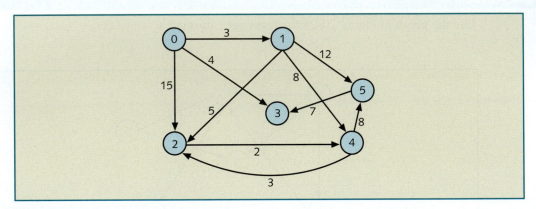

Figure 20-26   Graph for Exercise 6

7. Find a spanning tree in the graph in Figure 20-27.

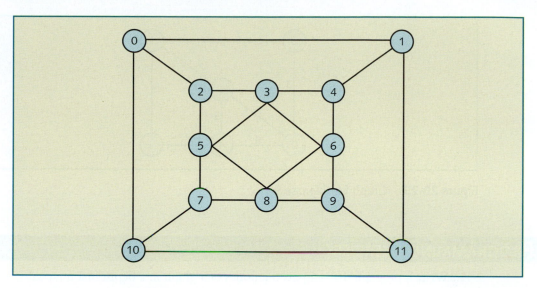

Figure 20-27   Graph for Exercise 7

8. Find a spanning tree in the graph in Figure 20-28.

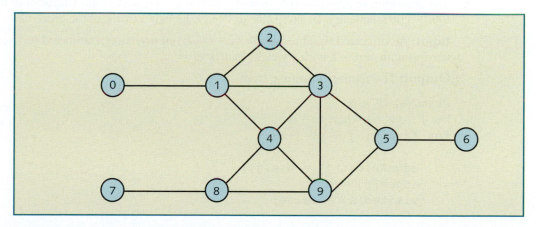

Figure 20-28   Graph for Exercise 8

9. Find the minimal spanning tree for the graph in Figure 20-29 using the algorithm given in this chapter.

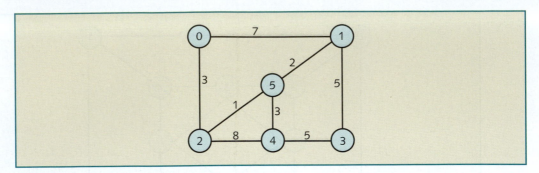

Figure 20-29 Graph for Exercise 9

PROGRAMMING EXERCISES

1. Write a program that outputs the nodes of a graph in a depth first traversal.

2. Write a program that outputs the nodes of a graph in a breadth first traversal.

3. Write a program that outputs the shortest distance from a given node to every other node in the graph.

4. Write a program that outputs the minimal spanning tree for a given graph.

5. The algorithm to determine the minimal spanning tree given in this chapter is of the order $O(n^3)$. The following is an alternative to Prim's algorithm that is of the order $O(n^2)$.

Input: A connected weighted graph $G = (V, E)$ of n vertices, numbered $0, 1, ..., n-1$; starting with vertex s, with a weight matrix of W

Output: The minimal spanning tree

```
Prim2(G, W, n, s)
Let T = (V, E), where E = φ.
for (j = 0; j < n; j++)
{
    edgeWeight[j] = W(s,j);
    edges[j] = s;
    visited[s] = false;
}
edgeWeight[s] = 0;
visited[s] = true;
while (not all nodes have been visited)
{
    Choose the node that has not been visited and has the smallest weight, and call it k.
    visited[k] = true;
    E = E ∪ {(k, edges[k])}
    V = V ∪ {k}
```

```
    for each node j that has not been visited
        if (W(k,j) < edgeWeight[k])
        {
            edgeWeight[k] = W(k,j);
            edges[j] = k;
        }
}
return T.
```

Write a definition of the method **Prim2** to implement this algorithm, and also add this method to the **class** **MsTree**. Also write a program to test this version of Prim's algorithm.

COLLECTIONS

In this chapter, you will:

♦ Learn about the Java `class` `LinkedList` and how to use various operations of this class

♦ Explore iterators and how they work

♦ Learn about the `interface` `Collection` and its framework

♦ Examine the `interface` `Set`

♦ Learn about the `class`es `HashSet` and `TreeSet` and how they are used in a program

♦ Explore the `interface` `Map`

♦ Examine the `class` `HashMap`

♦ Learn about various collection algorithms

In Chapters 15, 16, 17, and 19, we discussed various data structures such as lists and binary trees. In some of these chapters, we also discussed Java's built-in classes to do the same thing. For example, the `class` `Vector`, discussed in Chapter 10, can be used to implement array-based lists, and the `class` `Stack`, discussed in Chapter 17, can be used to implement a stack. Does this mean that all the work that we did in earlier chapters to design our own classes was unnecessary? The simple answer is no. Even though Java has provided a good number of classes, there might be situations where you need to design your own classes. As a computer science student or a programmer, it is important not only to learn how to use what is available, but also to learn the internal structures of the code so you can create your own code.

Java classes such as `Vector` and `Stack` are known as collection classes or simply collections. The main objective of this chapter is to discuss in some detail Java's collection classes and how to use them in a program.

As remarked in the preceding paragraphs, Java provides the `class` `Vector` to implement array-based lists and the `class` `Stack` to implement a stack. Similarly to these classes, Java provides the `class` `LinkedList` to implement a linked list. Before discussing collections in general, in the next section we describe the `class` `LinkedList` and explain how to use it in a program.

THE class LinkedList

This section describes the **class** LinkedList. The objects of the **class** LinkedList are implemented as doubly linked lists. Thus, every element in a LinkedList object points to both its immediate predecessor and its immediate successor (except the first and last elements). The definition of the **class** LinkedList and the definitions of the methods to implement various operations on a list are contained in the package java.util. Therefore, to use a LinkedList object in a program, the program should include either the statement

```
import java.util.*;
```

or the statement

```
import java.util.LinkedList;
```

The **class** LinkedList contains two constructors. These two constructors and other methods of the **class** LinkedList are described in Table 21-1. (Appendix E lists the exceptions, if any, thrown by the methods.)

Table 21-1 The **class** LinkedList, its Constructors, and Some of its Methods

public class LinkedList<E> extends AbstractSequentialList<E>
Constructors
public LinkedList() //Constructs an empty list.

public LinkedList(Collection<? extends E> coll)
//Constructs a list containing the elements of the collection
//specified by the parameter coll, in the order they are
//returned by the collection's iterator. If the collection coll
//is null, it throws NullPointerException.

Methods

public boolean add(E obj)
//Appends the element specified by the parameter obj to the
//end of this list. It returns true if this collection changed
//as a result of the call; false otherwise.

public void add(int index, E elem)
//Inserts the element specified by the parameter elem at
//the position index in this list. The element currently at
//that position (if any) and any subsequent elements are
//shifted to the right.

Table 21-1 The **class** LinkedList, its Constructors, and Some of its Methods
(continued)

```
public boolean addAll(Collection<? extends E> coll)
    //Appends all of the elements in the collection coll to the
    //end of this list, in the order that they are returned by
    //the iterator of coll. It returns true if this list is
    //changed as a result of the call. If the collection coll
    //is modified while this operation is in progress, then the
    //behavior of this operation is undefined. It returns true if
    //this list changed as a result of the call.
```

```
public boolean addAll(int index, Collection<? extends E> coll)
    //Inserts all of the elements of the collection coll into this
    //list, starting at the position index. The element currently
    //at that position (if any) and any subsequent elements are
    //shifted to the right (increases their indices). The new
    //elements appear in the list in the order that they are
    //returned by the iterator of coll. It returns true if this
    //list changed as a result of the call.
```

```
public void addFirst(E obj)
    //Inserts the element specified by the parameter obj at the
    //beginning of this list.
```

```
public void addLast(E obj)
    //Appends the element specified by the parameter obj to the
    //end of this list.
```

```
public void clear()
    //Removes all of the elements from this list.
```

```
public Object clone()
    //Returns a shallow copy of this LinkedList. (The elements
    //themselves are not cloned.)
```

```
public boolean contains(Object obj)
    //Returns true if this list contains the element specified
    //by the parameter obj. Otherwise it returns false.
```

```
public E element()
    //Retrieves, but does not remove, the first element of this
    //list.
```

```
public E get(int index)
    //Returns the element at the position specified by index in
    //this list.
```

```
public E getFirst()
    //Returns the first element in this list.
```

```
public E getLast()
    //Returns the last element in this list.
```

```
public int indexOf(Object obj)
    //Returns the index in this list of the first occurrence of
    //the element specified by the parameter obj. If this list
    //does not contain the specified element, it returns -1.
```

Table 21-1 The **class** LinkedList, its Constructors, and Some of its Methods (continued)

```
public int lastIndexOf(Object obj)
   //Returns the index, in this list, of the last occurrence of
   //the element specified by the parameter obj. If this list
   //does not contain the specified element, it returns -1.
```

```
public ListIterator<E> listIterator(int index)
   //Returns a list-iterator of the elements in this list (in
   //proper sequence), starting at the position specified by
   //index in the list.
```

```
public boolean offer(E obj)
   //Adds the element specified by the parameter obj as the tail
   //(last element) of this list. It returns true if it was
   //possible to add the element to this list; false otherwise.
```

```
public E peek()
   //Retrieves, but does not remove, the first element of this
   //list. If this list is empty it returns null.
```

```
public E poll()
   //Retrieves and removes the first element of this list. If
   //this list is empty it returns null.
```

```
public E remove(int index)
   //Removes the element at the position specified by index in
   //this list. Any subsequent elements are shifted to the left
   //(subtracts one from their indices). It also returns the
   //element that was removed from the list.
```

```
public E remove()
   //Retrieves and removes the first element of this list.
```

```
public boolean remove(Object obj)
   //Removes the first occurrence of the element specified by
   //the parameter obj in this list. If the list does not contain
   //the element, it is unchanged. It returns true if the list
   //contained the element obj.
```

```
public E removeFirst()
   //Removes and returns the first element from this list.
```

```
public E removeLast()
   //Removes and returns the last element from this list.
```

```
public E set(int index, E element)
   //Replaces the element at the position specified by index, in
   //this list, with the element specified by the parameter
   //element. It also returns the element previously at the
   //position index.
```

```
public int size()
   //Returns the number of elements in this list.
```

```
public Object[] toArray()
   //Returns an array containing all of the elements in this
   //list in the correct order.
```

Note the question mark in one of the constructors of the **class** LinkedList, that is:

Collection<? **extends** E>

Here, **?** represents an unknown type. The type parameter **?** is called a **wildcard**. In the previous statement, the wildcard **extends** the type E. The type E is an upperbound of the wildcard. The unknown type can be either the type E or any subclass of the type E.

The program in Example 21-1 Illustrates how various methods of the **class** LinkedList work.

Example 21-1

```
//Various operations of the class LinkedList

import java.util.*;

public class LinkedListExp1
{
    public static void main(String[] args)
    {
        LinkedList<String> strList =
                new LinkedList<String>();            //Line 1

        strList.add("Fall");                         //Line 2
        strList.add("Winter");                       //Line 3
        strList.add("Spring");                       //Line 4
        strList.add("Summer");                       //Line 5
        strList.add("Cold");                         //Line 6
        strList.add("Warm");                         //Line 7
        strList.add("Sunny");                        //Line 8
        strList.add("Cold");                         //Line 9
        strList.add("Cloudy");                       //Line 10

        System.out.print("Line 11: strList:\n"
                + "     ");                           //Line 11
        print(strList);                              //Line 12

        System.out.println("Line 13: The size of "
                + "strList: "
                + strList.size());                   //Line 13

        System.out.println("Line 14: The index of "
                + "Sunny in strList: "
                + strList.indexOf("Sunny"));         //Line 14

        System.out.println("Line 15: The last index "
                + "of Cold in strList: "
                + strList.lastIndexOf ("Cold"));     //Line 15
```

```java
        System.out.println("Line 16: In strList, "
                     + "the string at position "
                     + "6: "
                     + strList.get(6));              //Line 16

        System.out.println("Line 17: The first "
                     + "element of strList: "
                     + strList.peek());              //Line 17

        strList.add(2, "Windy");                     //Line 18

        System.out.print("Line 19: After adding "
                     + "Windy at position 2 "
                     + "strList: \n"
                     + "         ");                  //Line 19
        print(strList);                              //Line 20

        if (strList.contains("Snow"))                //Line 21
            System.out.println("Line 22: strList "
                         + "contains Snow.");         //Line 22
        else                                         //Line 23
            System.out.println("Line 24: strList "
                         + "does not contain "
                         + "Snow.");                  //Line 24

        strList.remove("Warm");                      //Line 25

        System.out.print("Line 26: After removing "
                     + "Warm strList:\n"
                     + "         ");                  //Line 26
        print(strList);                              //Line 27

    }

    public static <T> void print(Collection<T> c)
    {
        for (T obj : c)
            System.out.print(obj + " ");

        System.out.println();
    }
}
```

Sample Run:

```
Line 11: strList:
     Fall Winter Spring Summer Cold Warm Sunny Cold Cloudy
Line 13: The size of strList: 9
Line 14: The index of Sunny in strList: 6
```

```
Line 15: The last index of Cold in strList: 7
Line 16: In strList, the string at position 6: Sunny
Line 17: The first element of strList: Fall
Line 19: After adding Windy at position 2 strList:
    Fall Winter Windy Spring Summer Cold Warm Sunny Cold Cloudy
Line 24: strList does not contain Snow.
Line 26: After removing Warm strList:
    Fall Winter Windy Spring Summer Cold Sunny Cold Cloudy
```

The preceding program works as follows. The statement in Line 1 creates **strList** to be a **LinkedList** object to create a linked list of **String** objects. The statements in Lines 2 to 10 use the method **add** to add the strings **"Fall"**, **"Winter"**, **"Spring"**, **"Summer"**, **"Cold"**, **"Warm"**, **"Sunny"**, **"Cold"**, and **"Cloudy"** in **strList**.

Note that the preceding program contains the generic method **print** to print the elements of a collection. This method uses a foreach statement to iterate through the elements of the collection.

The statement in Line 12 uses the method **print** to output the elements of **strList**. The statement in Line 13 outputs the size (the number of elements) of **strList**. The statement in Line 14 outputs the position of the string **"Sunny"** in **strList**. The statement in Line 15 outputs the position of the last occurrence of the string **"Cold"** in **strList**.

The statement in Line 16 uses the method **get** to output the element at position 6 in **strList**. The statement in Line 17 uses the method **peek** to output the first element of **strList**. (Note that the method returns a reference of the first element of **strList**.)

The statement in Line 18 adds the string **"Windy"** at position 2 in **strList**. The statement in Line 20 outputs the elements of the modified **strList**. The statements in Lines 21 to 24 determine and output whether the string **"Snow"** is in **strList**.

The statement in Line 25 uses the method **remove** to find and remove the string **"Warm"** from **strList**. The statement in Line 27 outputs the elements of the modified **strList**.

Note that in the preceding program the statements

```
strList.add("Fall");
strList.add("Winter");
strList.add("Spring");
strList.add("Summer");
strList.add("Cold");
strList.add("Warm");
strList.add("Sunny");
strList.add("Cold");
strList.add("Cloudy");
```

can be replaced with the following statements:

```
String[] strArray = {"Fall", "Winter", "Spring", "Summer",
                     "Cold", "Warm", "Sunny", "Cold",
                     "Cloudy"};

for (String str: strArray)
    strList.add(str);
```

It follows that if you have a sequence of statements to add elements in a list, you could first create an array of elements to be added and then use a foreach statement, as shown above, to add the elements in the list.

Iterators

Sometimes it is necessary to process all the elements of a collection one by one. One way to iterate over the elements of a `LinkedList` object is to use a foreach loop. In fact, the for-each loop is a new feature of Java and is introduced with the release of JDK 5.0. Another way to iterate over the elements of a collection is to use iterators. Recall that an iterator is an object that produces the elements in a collection one after the other. Chapter 16 explains how to design a class to implement an iterator. Here we discuss the Java class that allows us to create an iterator to a `LinkedList` object.

Note that one of the methods of the **class** `LinkedList` has the following heading and description:

```
public ListIterator<E> listIterator(int index)
    //Returns a list-iterator of the elements in this list (in
    //proper sequence), starting at the position specified by
    //index in the list. If index is out of range, that is,
    //(index < 0 or index > size()), it throws
    //IndexOutOfBoundsException.
```

From the description of this method, it follows that a call to this method produces an iterator which is an object of the **interface** `ListIterator`. The **interface** `ListIterator` implements the **interface** `Iterator` and provides methods such as **next** and **previous** to iterate over the elements of a `LinkedList` object.

Before giving an example to show how an iterator works, we describe the **interface**s `Iterator` and `ListIterator`.

The `Iterator` **interface** has only three methods, which are described in Table 21-2. (Appendix E lists the exceptions, if any, thrown by the methods.)

Table 21-2 Methods of the **interface** Iterator

public interface Iterator<E>
Methods
boolean hasNext() //Returns true if the iteration has more elements.

E next()
//Returns the next element in the iteration.
//If this method is called repeatedly until the method
//hasNext() returns false, it will return each element in the
//underlying collection exactly once.

void remove()
//Removes from the underlying collection the last element
//returned by the iterator (optional operation). This method
//can be called only once per call to next. The behavior of
//an iterator is unspecified if the underlying collection is
//modified while the iteration is in progress in any way other
//than by calling this method.

Typically, an iterator moves only in one direction, starting at the first element of the collection. The objects of the **class** LinkedList are implemented as doubly linked lists. Therefore, an iterator to a LinkedList object should be able to move in both directions. In order to move in both directions of a LinkedList object, Java provides the **interface** ListInterface, which extends the Iterator **interface**. ListIterator **interface** has all the methods of the **interface** Iterator and the methods that make it possible for a list iterator to move backward and forward. A list iterator can also be used to add an element at a specific location and replace an element at a specific location. Table 21-3 describes the methods of the ListIterator **interface**. (Appendix E lists the exceptions, if any, thrown by the methods.)

Table 21-3 The **interface** ListIterator and its Methods

public interface ListIterator<E> extends Iterator<E>
Methods

void add(E obj)
//Inserts the element specified by the parameter obj into the
//list. It is an optional operation. The element is inserted
//immediately before the next element that would be returned
//by next, if any, and after the next element that would be
//returned by previous, if any. (If the list was empty, the
//new element becomes the sole element on the list.) The new
//element is inserted before the implicit cursor: a
//subsequent call to next would be unaffected, and a subsequent
//call to previous would return the new element.

Table 21-3 The **interface** ListIterator and its Methods (continued)

```
boolean hasNext()
   //Returns true if this list iterator has more elements when
   //traversing the list in the forward direction.
```

```
boolean hasPrevious()
   //Returns true if this list iterator has more elements when
   //traversing the list in the reverse direction.
```

```
E next()
   //Returns the next element in the list. This method may be
   //called repeatedly to iterate through the list, or it may be
   //intermixed with calls to previous to go back and forth.
```

```
int nextIndex()
   //Returns the index of the element that would be returned by
   //a subsequent call to next. It returns list-size if the list
   //iterator is at the end of the list.
```

```
E previous()
   //Returns the previous element in the list. This method may
   //be called repeatedly to iterate through the list backward,
   //or it may be intermixed with calls to next to go back and forth.
```

```
int previousIndex()
   //Returns the index of the element that would be returned by
   //a subsequent call to previous. If the list iterator is at
   //the beginning of the list, it returns -1.
```

```
void remove()
   //Removes from the list the last element that was returned by
   //the method next or previous (optional operation). This
   //method can be called once per call to next or previous. It
   //can be made only if ListIterator.add has not been called
   //after the last call to next or previous.
```

```
void set(E obj)
   //Replaces the last element returned by the method next or
   //previous with the element specified by the parameter obj. It
   //is an optional operation. This method can be called only if
   //neither ListIterator.remove nor ListIterator.add have been
   //called after the last call to next or previous.
```

Consider the following statements:

```
LinkedList<Integer> intList =
                new LinkedList<Integer>();          //Line 1

Integer[] intArray = {23, 12, 33, 89, 54, 9, 77,
                55, 8, 19, 30, 15, 62};             //Line 2

for (Integer num : intArray)                        //Line 3
    intList.add(num);                               //Line 4
```

The statement in Line 1 creates the `LinkedList` object `intList` to create a list of `Integer` objects. The statement in Line 2 creates the `Integer` array `intArray` with the values as shown in Line 2. The foreach loop in Lines 3 and 4 adds the elements of `intArray` into `intList`. Therefore, after the foreach loop in Line 3 executes, `intList` is:

```
intList = {23, 12, 33, 89, 54, 9, 77, 55, 8, 19, 30, 15, 62};
```

Consider the following statement:

```
ListIterator<Integer> listIt = intList.listIterator(0);
```

This statement creates `listIt` to be an iterator and initializes `listIt` to point to the first element of `intList`.

Now consider the following statement:

```
System.out.println(listIt.next());
```

This statement outputs the next element in the list, which is the first element of `intList`. Therefore, this statement outputs **23**. Note that the expression `listIt.next()` returns the reference of the current element and also moves `listIt` to the next element in `intList`, which is **12**. Therefore, after the expression `listIt.next()` executes, `listIt` points to the element **12** in `intList`.

Next, consider the statement:

```
System.out.println(listIt.next());
```

Because `listIt` was pointing to **12**, this statement outputs **12** and then moves `listIt` to the next element in `intList`, which is **33**. Therefore, after the expression `listIt.next()` executes, `listIt` points to the element **33** in `intList`.

Next, consider the statement:

```
listIt.set(999);
```

This statement replaces the last element returned, which is **12**, with **999**. Therefore, after this statement executes, `intList` is:

```
intList = {23, 999, 33, 89, 54, 9, 77, 55, 8, 19, 30, 15, 62};
```

Next, consider the statement:

```
listIt.add(1111);
```

This statement adds **1111** immediately before the next element that would be returned by the method **next** and after the next element that would be returned by the method **previous** (the last element returned). Prior to executing the preceding statement, `listIt` was pointing to **33**. Therefore, **1111** is inserted before **33** and after **999** in `intList`. After this statement executes, `intList` is:

```
intList = {23, 999, 1111, 33, 89, 54, 9, 77, 55, 8, 19, 30, 15, 62};
```

The program in Example 21-2 further illustrates how the preceding statements work.

Example 21-2

```java
//This program illustrates how an iterator works with a
//LinkedList object.

import java.util.*;

public class LinkedListAndIterator
{
    public static void main(String[] args)
    {
        LinkedList<Integer> intList =
                new LinkedList<Integer>();              //Line 1

        Integer[] intArray = {23, 12, 33, 89, 54,
                        9, 77, 55, 8, 19, 30,
                        15, 62};                        //Line 2

        for (Integer num : intArray)                    //Line 3
            intList.add(num);                           //Line 4

        System.out.print("Line 5: intList:\n"
                    + "        ");                       //Line 5
        print(intList);                                 //Line 6

        ListIterator<Integer> listIt
                = intList.listIterator(0);              //Line 7

        System.out.println("Line 8: listIt points "
                    + "to: " + listIt.next());          //Line 8

        System.out.println("Line 9: listIt points "
                    + "to: " + listIt.next());          //Line 9

        listIt.set(999);                                //Line 10

        System.out.print("Line 13: intList:\n"
                      + "        ");                     //Line 13
        print(intList);                                 //Line 14

        listIt.add(1111);                               //Line 15

        System.out.print("Line 16: After adding "
                    + "1111 intList:\n"
                    + "        ");                       //Line 16
        print(intList);                                 //Line 17
    }
```

```
    public static <T> void print(Collection<T> c)
    {
        for (T obj : c)
            System.out.print(obj + " ");

        System.out.println();
    }
}
```

Sample Run:

```
Line 5: intList:
    23 12 33 89 54 9 77 55 8 19 30 15 62
Line 8: listIt points to: 23
Line 9: listIt points to: 12
Line 13: intList:
    23 999 33 89 54 9 77 55 8 19 30 15 62
Line 16: After adding 1111 intList:
    23 999 1111 33 89 54 9 77 55 8 19 30 15 62
```

The preceding output is self-explanatory. We leave the details as an exercise for you.

COLLECTIONS

A **collection** is a data structure, in fact, an object, that can hold references to other objects. For example, a **Vector** object is a collection, and so is an array. Similarly, **ArrayListClass** objects (from Chapter 15), **UnorderedLinkedList** and **OrderedLinkedList** objects (from Chapter 16), and binary tree objects (from Chapter 19) are also collections. A **collection class** is a class whose objects are collections. For example, **class Vector** is a collection class.

Java provides a number of interfaces and classes to systematically implement collections. These classes and interfaces have a hierarchical structure. For example, the **interface Collection** is the super class (interface) of all Java collection classes. Figure 21-1 shows the **interface Collection** and its subinterfaces and collection classes in the hierarchy.

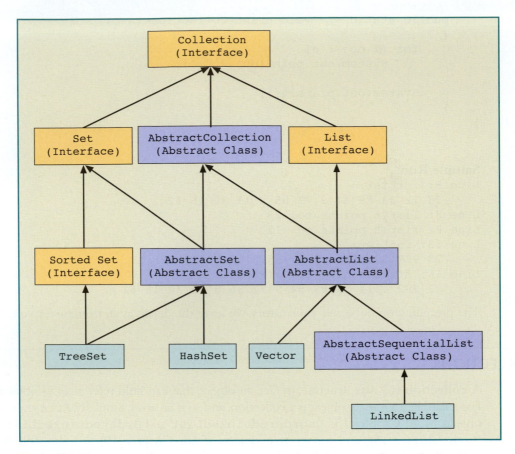

Figure 21-1 Some Java Collection classes and the inheritance hierarchy

 Another set of collection classes is derived from the **interface** Map. We will discuss this **interface** and its subclasses later in this chapter.

From Figure 21-1, it follows that the **class** Vector extends the **abstract class** AbstractList, and the **class** LinkedList extends the **abstract class** AbstractSequentialList. The **abstract class** AbstractList implements the **interface** List and extends the **abstract** class AbstractCollection. The **interface**s Set and List extend the **interface** Collection, and the **abstract class** AbstractCollection implements the **interface** Collection.

 As of Java 5.0, all collection classes, such as Vector, are also parameterized. This means that when you declare a reference variable of a collection class, you need to specify the type of objects to which the reference variable would point. Otherwise, the compiler will give warning messages such as unsafe type check.

The **interface** Collection is at the highest level of the Java collection classes TreeSet, HashSet, Vector, and LinkedList. This interface describes the basic operations that should be implemented by all collection classes. Table 21-4 describes the method headings contained in the **Collection** **interface**. (Appendix E lists the exceptions, if any, thrown by the methods.)

Table 21-4 The **interface** Collection and its Methods

public interface **Collection<E>** extends Iterable<E>
Methods

boolean **add**(E obj)
 //This method ensures that this collection contains the
 //element specified by obj (optional operation). Returns true
 //if this collection changed as a result of the call. Returns
 //false if this collection does not permit duplicates and
 //already contains the specified element.

boolean **addAll**(Collection<? extends E> coll)   //Adds all of the elements of coll to this collection   //(optional operation).
void **clear**()   //Removes all of the elements from this collection   //(optional operation).

boolean **contains**(Object obj)
 //Returns true if this collection contains the element
 //specified by obj.

boolean **containsAll**(Collection<?> coll)
 //Returns true if this collection contains all of the elements
 //of coll.

boolean **equals**(Object obj)
 //Compares the object specified by obj with this collection for
 //equality.

int **hashCode**()   //Returns the hash code value for this collection.
boolean **isEmpty**()   //Returns true if this collection contains no elements.
Iterator<E> **iterator**()   //Returns an iterator over the elements in this collection.

boolean **remove**(Object obj)
 //Removes a single instance of obj from this collection, if
 //it is present (optional operation). Returns true if this
 //collection contained the specified element.

Table 21-4 The `interface` `Collection` and its Methods (continued)

```
boolean removeAll(Collection<?> coll)
  //Removes all this collection's elements that are also
  //contained in coll (optional operation).

boolean retainAll(Collection<?> coll)
  //Retains only the elements in this collection that are
  //contained in coll. In other words, all elements in this
  //collection that are not contained in the collection coll are
  //removed. It returns true if this collection is changed as a
  //result of the call.

int size()
  //Returns the number of elements in this collection. If
  //this collection contains more than Integer.MAX_VALUE
  //elements, it returns Integer.MAX_VALUE.

Object [] toArray()
  //Returns an array containing all of the elements in this
  //collection. If this collection makes any guarantees as to
  //what order its elements are returned by its iterator, this
  //method must return the elements in the same order.

<T> T[] toArray(T[] a)
  //Returns an array containing all of the elements in this
  //collection; the runtime type of the returned array is that
  //of the specified array. If the collection fits in the
  //specified array, it is returned therein. Otherwise, a new
  //array is allocated with the runtime type of the specified
  //array and the size of this collection.
```

 Some of the operations in Table 21-4 are marked optional. These methods still must be implemented. However, if for some reason we do want to give a real implementation, we can simply throw `UnsupportedOperationException`. `UnsupportedOperationException` exception is a `RunTimeException` and is not required to be caught or declared in a throw clause.

The two main interfaces that extend the `Collection` `interface` are `Set` and `List`. Classes that implement the `Set` `interface` do not allow duplicates, that is, an element in a collection occurs only once. On the other hand, classes that implement the `List` `interface` allow elements to occur more than once. Moreover, elements of the objects of classes that implement the `List` `interface` are ordered in the sense that there is a zeroth element, a first element, a second element, and so on. We will describe these interfaces separately later in this chapter.

The **abstract class** `AbstractCollection` implements the `Collection` `interface`. It is the base class of the **abstract classes** `AbstractSet` and `AbstractList`. Note that the **class** `Vector` is derived from the **class** `AbstractList`.

The `interface` List and its Subclasses

In this section, we discuss the `interface` List and its subclasses. The `class`es Vector and `LinkedList` that you have encountered are the descendents of this interface. In addition to the methods listed in Table 21-4, Table 21-5 describes the methods of the `interface` List. (Appendix E lists the exceptions, if any, thrown by the methods.)

Table 21-5 The `interface` List and its Additional Methods

`public interface List<E> extends Collection<E>`
Methods

`void add(int index, E element)`
`//Inserts the element at the position specified by index in`
`//this list (optional operation). Shifts the element`
`//currently at that position (if any) and any subsequent`
`//elements to the right (adds one to their indices).`

`boolean addAll(int index, Collection<? extends E> coll)`
`//Inserts all of the elements of coll into this list at the`
`//position specified by index (optional operation). Shifts`
`//the element currently at that position (if any) and any`
`//subsequent elements to the right (increases their indices).`
`//The new elements will appear in this list in the order that`
`//they are returned by the iterator of coll.`

`E get(int index)`
`//Returns the element in the list at the position specified`
`//by index.`

`int indexOf(Object obj)`
`//Returns the index in this list of the first occurrence of`
`//Obj. If this list does not contain obj, it returns -1.`

`boolean isEmpty()` `//Returns true if this list contains no elements.`

`Iterator<E> iterator()`
`//Returns an iterator over the elements in this list in`
`//proper sequence.`

`int lastIndexOf(Object obj)`
`//Returns the index in this list of the last occurrence of obj.`
`//If this list does not contain obj, it returns -1.`

`ListIterator<E> listIterator()`
`//Returns a list iterator of the elements in this list (in`
`//proper sequence).`

`ListIterator<E> listIterator(int index)`
`//Returns a list iterator of the elements in this list (in`
`//proper sequence), starting at index in this list. The`
`//value of index indicates the first element that would be`
`//returned by an initial call to the next method. An initial`
`//call to the previous method would return the element with`
`//the specified index minus one.`

Table 21-5 The **interface** List and its Additional Methods (continued)

```
E remove(int index)
  //Removes the element at the position index in this list
  //(optional operation). Shifts any subsequent elements to the
  //left (subtracts one from their indices). It also returns
  //the element that was removed from the list.
```

```
E set(int index, E elem)
  //Replaces the element at index in this list with the element
  //specified by elem (optional operation).
```

```
List<E> subList(int fromIndex, int toIndex)
  //Returns a view of this list between the indices fromIndex,
  //inclusive, and toIndex, exclusive. (If fromIndex and
  //toIndex are equal, the returned list is empty.)
```

The **abstract class** AbstractList extends the **abstract class** AbstractCollection and implements the **interface** List. In addition to the methods of the **abstract class** AbstractCollection, the members of this class are given in Table 21-6.

Table 21-6 Additional Members of the **abstract class** AbstractList

```
public abstract class AbstractList<E> extends AbstractCollection<E>
                                      implements List<E>
```

```
protected transient int modCount
```

```
protected AbstractList()
  //Default constructor
```

```
protected void removeRange(int fromIndex, int toIndex)
  //Removes from this list all of the elements whose index is
  //between fromIndex, inclusive, and toIndex, exclusive. Shifts
  //any succeeding elements to the left (reduces their index).
```

The **class** Vector is derived from the **abstract class** AbstractList. We studied this class in detail in Chapter 10. The **class** LinkedList is derived from the **abstract class** AbstractSequentialList, which extends the **abstract class** AbstractList. The **abstract class** AbstractSequentialList overrides some methods inherited from the **class** AbstractList; there are no completely new methods in this class. The purpose of the **class** AbstractSequentialList is to provide efficient algorithms to sequentially move through the list. The first section of this chapter described the **class** LinkedList and showed how to use this class in a program. That section also described and discussed iterators.

SETS

As remarked earlier in this chapter, the two main interfaces that extend the `Collection` `interface` are `Set` and `List`. The preceding sections described in some detail the `interface` `List` and some of the classes that implement this interface. This section describes the `interface` `Sets` and some of the classes that implement this interface.

Classes that implement the `Set` `interface` do not allow duplicates, that is, an element in a collection occurs only once. Some of the methods of the `interface` `Set` are: `add`, `addAll`, `clear`, `contains`, `containsAll`, `equals`, `hashCode`, `isEmpty`, `iterator`, `remove`, `removeAll`, `retainAll`, `size`, and `toArray`. The descriptions of these methods are similar to the methods listed in Table 21-4. The `interface` `Set` is also described in Appendix E.

The `class` `HashSet`

The `class` `HashSet` extends the `class` `AbstractSet` and implements the `interface` `Set`. The `class` `AbstractSet` implements the methods `equals`, `hashCode`, and `removeAll` of the `interface` `Set`. Table 21-7 describes the constructors of the `class` `HashSet`.

Table 21-7 Constructors of the `class` `HashSet`

```
public HashSet()
  //Constructs a new empty set with the default initial
  //capacity (16) and load factor (0.75).

public HashSet(int initialCapacity)
  //Constructs a new empty set with the initial capacity
  //specified by the parameter initialCapacity and load factor
  //of 0.75. If the initial capacity is less than zero, it
  //throws IllegalArgumentException.

public HashSet(int initialCapacity, float loadFactor)
  //Constructs a new empty set with the initial capacity
  //specified by the parameter initialCapacity and load factor
  //specified by the parameter loadFactor. If the initial
  //capacity is less than zero, or if the load factor is
  //nonpositive, it throws IllegalArgumentException.

public HashSet(Collection<? extends E> c)
  //Constructs a new set containing the elements of the
  //collection c. The load factor is 0.75 and the initial
  //capacity is sufficient to contain the elements of the
  //collection c. If the collection c is null, it throws
  //NullPointerException.
```

21

The **class** HashSet implements the methods iterator, size, isEmpty, contains, remove, and clear of the **interface** Set. It also contains the **public** method clone.

Note that the parameters of some of the constructors of the **class** HashSet are initialCapacity and loadFactor. To explain the meanings of the parameters initialCapacity and loadFactor, we next briefly explain how data is organized using hashing.

Hashing

In hashing, the data are organized with the help of a table, called the **hash table**, and the hash table is stored in an array. For the sake of discussion, let **HT** denote the hash table. To determine whether a particular item with a key, say X, is in the table, we apply a function h, called the **hash function**, to the key X; that is, we compute $h(X)$ (read as "h of X"). The function h is an arithmetic function, and $h(X)$ gives the address of the item in the hash table. Suppose that the size of the hash table HT is m. Then $0 \leq h(X) < m$. Thus, to determine whether the item with key X is in the table, we look at the entry $HT[h(X)]$ in the hash table. Because the address of an item is computed with the help of a function, it follows that the items are stored in no particular order.

There are two ways that data are organized with the help of the hash table. In the first approach, the data are stored within the hash table, that is, in an array. In the second approach, the data are stored in linked lists, and the hash table is an array of reference variables to those linked lists. Each approach has its own advantages and disadvantages, and we discuss both approaches in detail. The hash table HT is usually divided into, say, b buckets $HT[0]$, $HT[1]$, ..., $HT[b-1]$. Each bucket is capable of holding, say, r items. It thus follows that $br = m$, where m is the size of HT. Generally, $r = 1$, and so each bucket can hold one item. The hash function h maps the key X onto an integer t, that is, $h(X) = t$, such that $0 \leq h(X) \leq b - 1$. Two keys, X_1 and X_2, such that $X_1 \neq X_2$, are called **synonyms** if $h(X_1) = h(X_2)$. Let X be a key and $h(X) = t$. If bucket t is full, we say that an **overflow** occurs. Let X_1 and X_2 be two nonidentical keys, that is, $X_1 \neq X_2$. If $h(X_1) = h(X_2)$, we say that a **collision** occurs. If $r = 1$, that is, if the bucket size is 1, an overflow and a collision occur at the same time.

When choosing a hash function, the main objectives are: Choose a hash function that is easy to compute and that will minimize the number of collisions. There are various ways to select the hash function and also to resolve collision. To learn about these, you may consult the book *Discrete Mathematical Structures: Theory and Applications*, as well as the data structures books listed in Appendix F.

The capacity is the number of buckets in the hash table, and the initial capacity is simply the capacity at the time the hash table is created. Suppose *HTSize* denotes the size of the hash table. Then the load factor of the hash table is (number of items in the hash table) / *HTSize*. Therefore, if the load factor is 1, then the table is full; if the load factor is 0.75, then the table is 75% full. Thus, the load factor is a measure of how full the hash table is allowed to get.

Note that when a **HashSet** object's hash table is full, its capacity is automatically increased. Moreover, when the number of entries in the hash table exceeds the product of the load factor and the current capacity, the capacity is roughly doubled.

The program in Example 21-3 illustrates how various methods of the **class** HashSet work.

Example 21-3

```java
//Various operations of the class HashSet

import java.util.*;

public class HashSetExp
{
    public static void main(String[] args)
    {
        HashSet<String> strSet =
                    new HashSet<String>();              //Line 1

        String[] strArray = {"Fall", "Winter",
                             "Spring", "Summer",
                             "Cold", "Warm",
                             "Sunny", "Cold",
                             "Cloudy"};                 //Line 2

        for (String str: strArray)                      //Line 3
            strSet.add(str);                            //Line 4

        System.out.print("Line 5: strSet:\n"
                    + "    ");                           //Line 5
        print(strSet);                                  //Line 6

        System.out.println("Line 7: The size of "
                    + "strSet: "
                    + strSet.size());                   //Line 7

        strSet.add("Windy");                            //Line 8

        System.out.print("Line 9: After adding "
                    + "Windy strSet: \n"
                    + "    ");                           //Line 9
        print(strSet);                                  //Line 10

        if (strSet.contains("Fall"))                    //Line 11
            System.out.println("Line 12: strSet "
                        + "contains Fall.");            //Line 12
```

```
        else                                              //Line 13
            System.out.println("Line 14: strSet "
                              + "does not contain "
                              + "Fall.");                   //Line 14

        strSet.remove("Warm");                             //Line 15

        System.out.print("Line 16: After removing "
                        + "Warm strSet:\n"
                        + "        ");                      //Line 16
        print(strSet);                                     //Line 17

    }

    public static <T> void print(Collection<T> c)
    {
        for (T obj : c)
            System.out.print(obj + " ");

        System.out.println();
    }
}
```

Sample Run:
```
Line 5: strSet:
    Warm Cloudy Summer Fall Sunny Winter Spring Cold
Line 7: The size of strSet: 8
Line 9: After adding Windy strSet:
    Warm Cloudy Summer Fall Sunny Winter Windy Spring Cold
Line 12: strSet contains Fall.
Line 16: After removing Warm strSet:
    Cloudy Summer Fall Sunny Winter Windy Spring Cold
```

Note that the preceding program contains the generic method **print** to output the elements of a collection.

The preceding program works as follows. The statement in Line 1 creates the **HashSet** object **strSet**, with the default initial capacity and load factor, to create a set of **String** objects. The statement in Line 2 creates the array **strArray** of **String** objects. The foreach loop in Lines 3 and 4 inserts the elements of **strArray** into **strSet**. The statement in Line 6 uses the generic method **print** to output the elements of **strSet**. The statement in Line 7 outputs the number of elements in **strSet**.

The statement in Line 8 adds the string **"Windy"** into **strSet**, and the statement in Line 10 outputs the modified **strSet**. The statements in Lines 11 to 14 use the method **contains** to determine if **strSet** contains the string **"Fall"** and then outputs the appropriate message.

The statement in Line 15 uses the method **remove** to remove the string from **strSet**, and the statement in Line 17 outputs the modified **strSet**.

The class TreeSet

The **class** TreeSet extends the **class AbstractSet** and implements the **interface** Set. Objects of the **class** TreeSet organize data in a binary tree. Table 21-8 describes some of the constructors of the **class** TreeSet.

Table 21-8 Some Constructors of the **class** TreeSet

```
public TreeSet()
   //Constructs a new, empty set. Elements are sorted according
   //to the elements' natural order.
```

```
public TreeSet(Comparator<? super E> coll)
   //Constructs a new, empty set. Elements are sorted according
   //to the comparator specified by the parameter coll.
```

```
public TreeSet(Collection<? extends E> coll)
   //Constructs a new set containing the elements of the
   //collection, specified by the parameter coll. The elements are
   //sorted according to the elements' natural order.
```

The **class** TreeSet also implements the methods add, addAll, clear, contains, isEmpty, iterator, remove, and size. This class contains the method clone and the methods first and last to return the first and last elements of the set, respectively. To return a subset of a given set, this class contains the methods subSet, headSet, and tailSet. Example 21-4 shows how to use the **class** TreeSet in a program.

Example 21-4

```java
//Various operations of the class TreeSet

import java.util.*;

public class TreeSetExp
{
    public static void main(String[] args)
    {
        TreeSet<String> strSet =
                    new TreeSet<String>();          //Line 1

        String[] strArray = {"Fall", "Winter",
                            "Spring", "Summer",
                            "Cold", "Warm",
                            "Sunny", "Cold",
                            "Cloudy"};              //Line 2

        for (String str: strArray)                  //Line 3
            strSet.add(str);                        //Line 4
```

```
            System.out.print("Line 5: strSet:\n"
                        + "      ");                          //Line 5
            print(strSet);                                   //Line 6

            System.out.println("Line 7: The size of "
                        + "strSet: "
                        + strSet.size());                    //Line 7

            strSet.add("Windy");                             //Line 8

            System.out.print("Line 9: After adding "
                        + "Windy strSet: \n"
                        + "      ");                          //Line 9
            print(strSet);                                   //Line 10

            if (strSet.contains("Fall"))                     //Line 11
                System.out.println("Line 12: strSet "
                            + "contains Fall.");             //Line 12
            else                                             //Line 13
                System.out.println("Line 14: strSet "
                            + "does not contain "
                            + "Fall.");                      //Line 14

            strSet.remove("Warm");                           //Line 15

            System.out.print("Line 16: After removing "
                        + "Warm strSet:\n"
                        + "      ");                          //Line 16
            print(strSet);                                   //Line 17

    }

    public static <T> void print(Collection<T> c)
    {
        for (T obj : c)
            System.out.print(obj + " ");

        System.out.println();
    }
}
```

Sample Run:
```
Line 5: strSet:
    Cloudy Cold Fall Spring Summer Sunny Warm Winter
Line 7: The size of strSet: 8
Line 9: After adding Windy strSet:
    Cloudy Cold Fall Spring Summer Sunny Warm Windy Winter
Line 12: strSet contains Fall.
```

```
Line 16: After removing Warm strSet:
        Cloudy Cold Fall Spring Summer Sunny Windy Winter
```

This program is the same as the program in Example 21-3. Here the string objects are stored in a `TreeSet` object. Recall that a `TreeSet` object organizes data in a binary tree. Also note that the elements of `strSet` are output in ascending order. We leave the details as an exercise for you.

MAPS

As remarked earlier in this chapter, another set of collections classes are derived from the `interface` Map. Objects of the collection `Map` manage its elements in the form of key/value pairs. Table 21-9 shows some of the methods of this interface. (Appendix E lists the exceptions, if any, thrown by the methods.)

Table 21-9 The `interface` Map and Some of its Methods

`interface Map<K, V>`
Methods

`public void clear()`
`//Removes all the mappings from this map. It is an optional`
`//operation.`

`public boolean containsKey(Object key)`
`//Returns true if this map contains a mapping for the`
`//specified key.`

`public boolean containsValue(Object value)`
`//Returns true if this map maps one or more keys to the`
`//value specified by the parameter value.`

`public boolean equals(Object obj)`
`//Compares the object specified by the parameter obj with this`
`//map for equality. Returns true if the given object is also`
`//a map and the two Maps represent the same mappings.`

`public V get(Object key)`
`//Returns the value to which this map maps the key specified`
`//by the parameter key. Returns null if the map contains no`
`//mapping for this key. Note that a return value of null does`
`//not necessarily indicate that the map contains no mapping`
`//for the key; it's also possible that the map explicitly`
`//maps the key to null.`

`boolean isEmpty()`
`//Returns true if this map does not contain any key/value`
`//mappings.`

Table 21-9 The `interface` Map and Some of its Methods (continued)

```
public Set<K> keySet()
  //This method returns the keys contained in the map as a Set
  //object.
```
```
public V put(K key, V value)
  //This method associates the value specified by the parameter
  //value with the key specified by the parameter key in this
  //map. It is an optional operation. If the map previously
  //contained a mapping for this key, the old value is replaced
  //by the specified value. This method also returns the
  //previous value associated with the specified key, or null if
  //there was no mapping for key.
```
```
public V remove(Object key)
  //Removes the mapping for the key specified by the parameter
  //key from this map if it is present. It is an optional
  //operation. This method also returns the previous value
  //associated with the specified key, or null if there was no
  //mapping for the key.
```
```
public int size()
  //Returns the number of key/value mappings in this map. If the
  //number of elements in the map is more than Integer.MAX_VALUE
  //elements, it returns Integer.MAX_VALUE.
```
```
public Collection<V> values()
  //Returns a collection view of the values contained in this
  //map.
```

Some of the classes that implement the **interface** Map are `HashTable`, `HashMap`, and `TreeMap`. In the next section, we describe the **class** `HashMap`.

The **class** `HashMap`

The **class** `HashMap` extends the **class** `AbstractMap` and implements the **interface** Map. The **class** `AbstractMap` extends the **class** `Object` and implements the **interface** Map. Table 21-10 describes some of the constructors of the **class** `HashMap`.

Table 21-10 Constructors of the **class** `HashMap`

```
public HashMap()
  //Constructs a new empty map with the default initial
  //capacity (16) and load factor (0.75).
```
```
public HashMap(int initialCapacity)
  //Constructs a new empty map with the initial capacity
  //specified by the parameter initialCapacity and load factor
  //of 0.75. If the initial capacity is less than zero, it
  //throws IllegalArgumentException.
```

Table 21-10 Constructors of the **class** HashMap (continued)

```
public HashMap(int initialCapacity, float loadFactor)
   //Constructs a new empty map with the initial capacity
   //specified by the parameter initialCapacity and load factor
   //specified by the parameter loadFactor. If the initial
   //capacity is less than zero, or if the load factor is
   //nonpositive, it throws IllegalArgumentException.

public HashMap (Collection<? extends E> c)
   //Constructs a new map containing the elements of the
   //collection c. The load factor is 0.75 and the initial
   //capacity is sufficient to contain the elements of the
   //collection c. If the collection c is null, it throws
   //NullPointerException.
```

Example 21-5 illustrates how some of the operations of the **class** HashMap work.

Example 21-5

```java
//Various operations of the class HashMap

import java.util.*;

public class HashMapExp
{
    public static void main(String[] args)
    {
        HashMap<Integer, String> strMap =
            new HashMap<Integer, String>();          //Line 1

        String[] strArray = {"Fall", "Winter",
                             "Spring", "Summer",
                             "Cold", "Warm",
                             "Sunny", "Cold",
                             "Cloudy", "One",
                             "Two", "Three",
                             "Four", "Five",
                             "Six", "Seven",
                             "Eight", "Nine",
                             "Ten"};                   //Line 2

        Integer index = 0;                            //Line 3

        for (String str : strArray)                   //Line 4
        {
            strMap.put(index, str);                   //Line 5
            index++;                                  //Line 6
        }
```

```
            System.out.println("Line 7: strMap:\n"
                            + "        ");                 //Line 7
            print(strMap);                                //Line 8

            System.out.println("Line 9: The size of "
                            + "strMap: "
                            + strMap.size());             //Line 9

            strMap.put(9, "Windy");                       //Line 10

            System.out.println("Line 11: After adding "
                            + "Windy strMap: \n"
                            + "        ");                 //Line 11
            print(strMap);                                //Line 12

            if (strMap.containsValue("Fall"))             //Line 13
                System.out.println("Line 14: strMap "
                                + "contains Fall.");       //Line 14
            else                                          //Line 15
                System.out.println("Line 16: strMap "
                                + "does not contain "
                                + "Fall.");                //Line 16

        }

    public static <K, V> void print(Map<K, V> hMap)
    {
        Set<K> mapKeys = hMap.keySet();

        for (K key: mapKeys)
            System.out.println(key + " " +
                                hMap.get(key) + " ");

        System.out.println();
    }
}
```

Sample Run:
```
Line 7: strMap:

15 Seven
4 Cold
8 Cloudy
11 Three
16 Eight
18 Ten
3 Summer
7 Cold
```

```
12 Four
17 Nine
2 Spring
13 Five
9 One
6 Sunny
1 Winter
14 Six
10 Two
5 Warm
0 Fall

Line 9: The size of strMap: 19
Line 11: After adding Windy strMap:

15 Seven
4 Cold
8 Cloudy
11 Three
16 Eight
18 Ten
3 Summer
7 Cold
12 Four
17 Nine
2 Spring
13 Five
9 Windy
6 Sunny
1 Winter
14 Six
10 Two
5 Warm
0 Fall

Line 14: strMap contains Fall.
```

Note that this program contains the generic method **print** to output the elements of a **HashMap** object. In the method **print**, first the method **keySet** is used to retrieve all the keys of a **HashMap** as a set. The object **mapKeys** contains all the keys of the **HashMap** object **hMap**. The foreach loop then uses the method **get** and the keys to retrieve the corresponding values.

This program works as follows. The statement in Line 1 creates the **HashMap** object **strMap** with the default initial capacity and load factor. The key of the object **strMap** is of the type **Integer** and the values are **String** objects. The statement in Line 2 creates the **String** array **strArray**. The statement in Line 3 creates the **Integer** object **index** and initializes it to 0.

The foreach loop in Lines 4 to 6 inserts the `String` objects as values with `Integer` objects as the keys into `strMap`. The statement in Line 8 uses the method `print` to output the elements of `strMap`.

The statement in Line 9 outputs the number of elements in `strMap`. The statement in Line 10 uses the method `put` to insert the string `"Windy"` with the key `9` into `strMap`. Because there is already an element with the key 9 in `strMap`, this statement, in fact, replaces the element with the key 9. The statement in Line 12 outputs the modified `strMap`.

The statements in Line 13 to 16 use the method `containsValue` to determine whether the string `"Fall"` is in `strMap` and then output the appropriate message.

COLLECTION ALGORITHMS

Several operations can be defined on a collection. Some of the operations are very specific to a collection and are therefore provided as part of the collection definition (that is, as methods of the class implementing the collection objects). However, several operations, such as `search` and `sort`, are common to all the collections. These common operations are therefore provided as generic algorithms, and can be applied to all the collections.

The generic algorithms are designed as **static** methods of the **class** Collections, which extends the **class** Object. Table 21-11 lists the methods of Collections **class**.

Table 21-11 Methods of Collections **class**

addAll	frequency	sort
binarySearch	indexOfSubList	swap
checkedCollection	lastIndexOfSubList	synchronizedCollection
checkedList	list	synchronizedList
checkedMap	max	synchronizedMap
checkedSet	min	synchronizedSet
checkedSortedMap	nCopies	synchronizedSortedMap
checkedSortedSet	replaceAll	synchronizedSortedSet
copy	reverse	unmodifiableCollection
disjoint	reverseOrder	unmodifiableList
emptyList	rotate	unmodifiableMap
emptyMap	shuffle	unmodifiableSet
emptySet	singleton	unmodifiableSortedMap
enumeration	singletonList	unmodifiableSortedSet
fill	singletonMap	

In the subsequent subsections, we illustrate how some of these algorithms work. While describing these algorithms, we also give the headings of the methods implementing these algorithms. Moreover, because algorithms are implemented with the help of methods, in these sections, the terms "method" and "algorithm" mean the same thing.

The Method `addAll`

The method `addAll` adds all the elements of a collection into another collection. Its heading is:

```
public static <T> boolean addAll(Collection<? super T> coll,
                                 T... list)
  //Adds all of the elements specified by the parameter list
  //into the collection coll. Note that list is a variable
  //length parameter. Therefore, elements to be added may be
  //specified individually or as an array. If the collection
  //coll does not support this method, it throws
  //UnsupportedOperationException. If the elements contain one
  //or more null values and coll does not support null elements,
  //or if coll or elements are null, it throws NullPointerException.
  //If some aspect of a value in elements prevents it from
  //being added to coll, it throws IllegalArgumentException.
```

Suppose that we have the following statement:

```
Vector<String> strList = new Vector<String>();
```

Suppose we want to add the strings `"Fall"`, `"Winter"`, `"Spring"`, and `"Summer"` to `strList`. This is accomplished by the following statement:

```
Collections.addAll(strList, "Fall", " Winter", "Spring", "Summer");
```

Example 21-6 further explains how the method `addAll` works.

Example 21-6

```
//Collections algorithm addAll.

import java.util.*;

public class AddAllExample
{
    public static void main(String[] args)
    {
        Vector<String> strList =
                new Vector<String>();                      //Line 1

        Collections.addAll(strList, "Fall",
                           "Winter", "Spring",
                           "Summer");                      //Line 2
```

```
        System.out.print("Line 3: strList: ");        //Line 3
        print(strList);                                //Line 4

        Collections.addAll(strList, "Sunny", "Snow",
                           "Rain");                     //Line 5

        System.out.print("Line 6: new strList: ");     //Line 6
        print(strList);                                //Line 7

        LinkedList<Double> numList =
                   new LinkedList<Double>();            //Line 8

        Double[] decimalNumbers = {12.46, 34.0,
                           62.98, 21.0, 67.45,
                           92.34, 11.0};                //Line 9

        Collections.addAll(numList, decimalNumbers);   //Line 10

        System.out.print("Line 11: numList: ");        //Line 11
        print(numList);                                //Line 12

        HashSet<Double> numHashSetList =
                   new HashSet<Double>();               //Line 13

        Collections.addAll(numHashSetList,
                           decimalNumbers);             //Line 14

        System.out.print("Line 15: "
                   + "numHashSetList: ");               //Line 15
        print(numHashSetList);                         //Line 16

        TreeSet<Double> numTreeSetList =
                   new TreeSet<Double>();               //Line 17

        Collections.addAll(numTreeSetList,
                           decimalNumbers);             //Line 18

        System.out.print("Line 19: "
                   + "numTreeSetList: ");               //Line 19
        print(numTreeSetList);                         //Line 20
    }

    public static <T> void print(Collection<T> c)
    {
        for (T obj : c)
            System.out.print(obj + " ");

        System.out.println();
    }
}
```

Sample Run:
```
Line 3: strList: Fall Winter Spring Summer
Line 6: new strList: Fall Winter Spring Summer Sunny Snow Rain
Line 11: numList: 12.46 34.0 62.98 21.0 67.45 92.34 11.0
Line 15: numHashSetList: 62.98 92.34 21.0 67.45 11.0 34.0 12.46
Line 19: numTreeSetList: 11.0 12.46 21.0 34.0 62.98 67.45 92.34
```

21

Note that this program contains the generic method `print` to output the elements of a collection.

This program works as follows. The statement in Line 1 creates the empty `Vector` object `strList`. The statement in Line 2 uses the method `addAll` to insert the strings `"Fall"`, `"Winter"`, `"Spring"`, and `"Summer"` into `strList`. The statement in Line 4 uses the method `print` to output the elements of `strList`. The statement in Line 5 uses the method `addAll` to insert the strings `"Sunny"`, `"Snow"`, and `"Rain"` into `strList`. The statement in Line 7 outputs the modified `strList`.

The statement in Line 8 creates the `LinkedList` object `numList` to create a list of `Double` objects. The statement in Line 9 creates the array `decimalNumbers` of `Double` objects. The statement in Line 10 uses the method `addAll` to add all the elements of the array `decimalNumbers` into `numList`. The statement in Line 12 outputs the elements of `numList`.

The statement in Line 13 creates the `HashSet` object `numHashSetList`, and the statement in Line 14 uses the method `addAll` to insert the elements of the array `decimalNumbers` into `numHashSetList`. The statement in Line 16 outputs the elements of `numHashSetList`.

The statement in Line 17 creates the `TreeSet` object `numTreeSetList`, and the statement in Line 18 uses the method `addAll` to insert the elements of the array `decimalNumbers` into `numTreeSetList`. The statement in Line 20 outputs the elements of `numTreeSetList`. Notice that the elements of `numTreeSetList` are output in ascending order.

The Methods `binarySearch`, `sort`, and `reverseOrder`

The method `binarySearch` searches a list for a given element. Because the binary search algorithm requires the list to be sorted, in this section we also discuss the method `sort`. Moreover, a list can be sorted in ascending (natural) order or descending order. To specify that the list be sorted in descending order, we use the method `reverseOrder` of the `class` `Collections`. Therefore, we also describe the method `reverseOrder`.

Let us first describe the method `reverseOrder`. It is an overloaded method. Its headings are:

```
public static <T> Comparator<T> reverseOrder()
  //Returns a comparator that imposes the reverse of the natural
  //ordering on a collection of objects that implement the
```

```
//Comparable interface. Note that the natural ordering is
//the ordering imposed by the objects' own compareTo method.
```

```
public static <T> Comparator<T> reverseOrder(Comparator<T> cmp)
    //Returns a comparator that imposes the reverse ordering of
    //the specified comparator. If the specified comparator is null,
    //this method is equivalent to reverseOrder().
```

The method **sort** is an overloaded method. The first method heading is:

```
public static <T extends Comparable<? super T>> void sort(List<T> list)
```

This method sorts the specified list into ascending order according to the natural ordering of its elements. Note that the type parameter **T** is bounded. This means that the class of the list elements must implement the **interface** Comparable. Furthermore, all elements in the list must be mutually comparable; that is, **elem1.compareTo(elem2)** must not throw a **ClassCastException** for any elements **elem1** and **elem2** in the list.

The second heading of the **sort** method is:

```
public static <T> void sort(List<T> list,
                            Comparator<? super T> coll)
```

This method sorts the specified list according to the order induced by the comparator **coll**. All elements in the list must be mutually comparable using the specified comparator; that is, **coll.compare(elem1, elem2)** must not throw a **ClassCastException** for any elements **elem1** and **elem2** in the list.

Both forms of the **sort** method throw the following exceptions:

- **ClassCastException** is thrown if the list contains elements that are not mutually comparable using the specified comparator.

- **UnsupportedOperationException** is thrown if the specified list's list–iterator does not support the set operation.

The method **binarySearch** is an overloaded method. The headings of this method are:

```
public static <T> int binarySearch(
            List<? extends Comparable<? super T>> list, T key)
public static <T> int binarySearch(List<? extends T> list,
                            T key, Comparator<? super T> coll)
```

Both forms of **binarySearch** search the list, specified by the parameter **list**, for the object, specified by the parameter, **key**. To use the form, the **list** must be sorted into ascending order according to the natural ordering of its elements prior to making this call. To use the second form, the list must be sorted into ascending order according to the specified comparator prior to making this call. If the list is not sorted, the results are undefined. If the list contains multiple elements equal to the specified object, there is no guarantee which one will be found.

The method returns an **int** value as follows: If **key** is in **list**, it returns the index of **key** in **list**; otherwise, it returns (–(*insertion point*) – 1). Note that the *insertion point* is the point at which the **key** would be inserted into the list, that is, the index of the first element greater than the **key**, or **list.size()**, if all elements in the list are less than the specified key.

Both forms of **binarySearch** throw **ClassCastException** if **list** contains elements that are not *mutually comparable* (for example, strings and integers), or if the search key is not mutually comparable with the elements of the list.

Example 21-7 further clarifies how the methods **binarySearch**, **sort**, and **reverseOrder** work.

21

Example 21-7

```
//Collections algorithms binarySearch, sort, and reverseOrder.

import java.util.*;

public class SearchSortExample1
{
    public static void main(String[] args)
    {
        Vector<String> strList =
                    new Vector<String>();              //Line 1

        Collections.addAll(strList,
                        "Fall", "Winter",
                        "Spring", "Summer",
                        "Cold", "Icy",
                        "Bright");                     //Line 2

        System.out.println("Line 3: strList before "
                    + "sorting: ");                    //Line 3
        print(strList);                                //Line 4

            //sort strList
        Collections.sort(strList);                     //Line 5

        System.out.println("Line 6: After sorting "
                    + "strList: ");                    //Line 6
        print(strList);                                //Line 7

            //search strList using binary search
        int pos = Collections.binarySearch(strList,
                                    "Summer"); //Line 8
```

```
    if (pos >= 0)                                      //Line 9
        System.out.println("Line 10: "
                        + "Summer found in "
                        + "strList at "
                        + "position " + pos);          //Line 10
    else                                               //Line 11
        System.out.println("Line 12: "
                        + "Summer is "
                        + "not in strList.");           //Line 12

    LinkedList<Double> numList =
                new LinkedList<Double>();               //Line 13

    Double[] decimalNumbers = {12.46, 34.0,
                        62.98, 21.0, 67.45,
                        92.34, 11.0};                   //Line 14

    Collections.addAll(numList, decimalNumbers);       //Line 15

    System.out.println("Line 16: numList "
                        + "before sorting: ");          //Line 16
    print(numList);                                     //Line 17

        //sort numList in reverse order
    Collections.sort(numList,
                Collections.reverseOrder());            //Line 18

    System.out.println("Line 19: numList "
                        + "after sorting in "
                        + "reverse order: ");           //Line 19
    print(numList);                                     //Line 20

        //search numList
    pos = Collections.binarySearch(numList,
                67.45,
                Collections.reverseOrder());            //Line 21

    if (pos >= 0)                                       //Line 22
        System.out.println("Line 23: "
                        + 67.45 + " found in "
                        + "numList at position "
                        + pos);                         //Line 23
    else                                                //Line 24
        System.out.println("Line 25: "
                        + 67.45 + " is not "
                        + "in numList.");               //Line 25

        //search numList
```

```
            pos = Collections.binarySearch(numList,
                        13.45,
                        Collections.reverseOrder());     //Line 26

        if (pos >= 0)                                     //Line 27
            System.out.println("Line 28: "
                        + 13.45 + " found "
                        + "at position "
                        + pos);                           //Line 28
        else                                              //Line 29
            System.out.println("Line 30: "
                        + 13.45 + " is not "
                        + "in numList.");                 //Line 30
    }

    public static <T> void print(Collection<T> c)
    {
        for (T obj : c)
            System.out.print(obj + " ");

        System.out.println();
    }
}
```

Sample Run:
```
Line 3: strList before sorting:
Fall Winter Spring Summer Cold Icy Bright
Line 6: After sorting strList:
Bright Cold Fall Icy Spring Summer Winter
Line 10: Summer found in strList at position 5
Line 16: numList before sorting:
12.46 34.0 62.98 21.0 67.45 92.34 11.0
Line 19: numList after sorting in reverse order:
92.34 67.45 62.98 34.0 21.0 12.46 11.0
Line 23: 67.45 found in numList at position 1
Line 30: 13.45 is not in numList.
```

The preceding program works as follows. The statement in Line 1 creates the empty **Vector** object **strList** and the statement in Line 2 uses the method **addAll** to add the strings **"Fall"**, **"Winter"**, **"Spring"**, **"Summer"**, **"Cold"**, **"Icy"**, and **"Bright"** into **strList**. The statement in Line 4 outputs the elements of **strList** before sorting them. The statement in Line 5 uses the method **sort** to sort the elements of **strList**, and the statement in Line 7 outputs the elements of **strList** after sorting them.

The statement in Line 8 uses the method **binarySearch** to find the position of the string **"Summer"** in **strList** and stores the position into the variable **pos**. The statements in Lines 9 to 12 use the value of **pos** to output the message of whether the string **"Summer"** is in **strList**.

The statement in Line 13 creates the `LinkedList` object `numList` to create a list of `Double` objects. The statement in Line 14 creates the `Double` array `decimalNumbers`. The statement in Line 15 uses the method `addAll` to add all the elements of the array `decimalNumbers` into `numList`. The statement in Line 17 outputs the elements of `numList` before sorting them. The statement in Line 18 use the method `sort` to sort the elements of `numList` in the reverse order. Note that the second parameter `Collections.reverseOrder()` specifies that the elements be sorted in the reverse order.

The statements in Lines 22 to 30 use the `binarySearch` method to determine whether certain elements are in `numList` and then output the appropriate message. Note that the third parameter of the `binarySearch` method in the statements in Lines 21 and 26 is `Collections.reverseOrder()` because `numList` was sorted using the `reveseOrder` criteria. We leave the other details as an exercise for you.

Note that the last parameter of the second heading of the methods `binarySearch`, `sort`, and `reverseOrder` is a `Comparator` object. So what is `Comparator`? `Comparator` is an **interface** that allows us to define a comparison function, which imposes a *total ordering* on a collection of objects. Comparators can be passed to a sort method (such as `Collections.sort`) to allow precise control over the sort order.

The **interface** `Comparator` has only two methods, shown in Table 21-12.

Table 21-12 Methods of the **interface** `Comparator`

`public interface Comparator<T>`

`int compare(T obj1,  T obj2)`
`  //Compares the objects specified by obj1 and obj2 for order.`
`  //Returns a negative integer, zero, or a positive integer as`
`  //the first argument is less than, equal to, or greater than`
`  //the second.`

`boolean equals(Object obj)`
`  //Indicates whether the object specified by obj is equal to`
`  //this Comparator.`

In Chapter 8 we defined the **class** `Clock`. Next, let us define a `Comparator` for the **class** `Clock`. The following class defines a `Comparator` for `Clock` Objects:

```
import java.util.Comparator;

public class ClockComparator implements Comparator<Clock>
{
    public int compare(Clock cl1, Clock cl2)
    {
```

```
        int hrDiff = cl1.getHours() - cl2.getHours();
        int minDiff = cl1.getMinutes() - cl2.getMinutes();
        int secDiff = cl1.getSeconds() - cl2.getSeconds();

        if (hrDiff != 0)   //Hours of cl1 and cl2 are
                           //different.
            return hrDiff;
        else if (minDiff != 0) //Hours of cl1 and cl2 are the
                               //same. So compare cl1 and cl2
                               //according to the minutes.
            return minDiff;
        else                      //hours and minutes of cl1 and cl2
                                  //are the same. So compare cl1 and
                                  //cl2 according to the seconds.
            return secDiff;
    }
}
```

Note that the ordering imposed by a `Comparator` `comp` on a set of elements `S` is said to be *consistent with equals* if and only if (`compare((Object) elem1, (Object) elem2)== 0`) has the same `boolean` value as `elem1.equals((Object) elem2)` for every `elem1` and `elem2` in `S`.

The program in Example 21-8 illustrates how to use `ClockComparator` in conjunction with the methods `binarySearch` and `sort`.

Example 21-8

```
/Collections algorithms binarySearch, and sort
//with a comparator.

import java.util.*;

public class SearchSortExample2
{
    public static void main(String[] args)
    {
        LinkedList<Clock> clockList =
                new LinkedList<Clock>();              //Line 1

        Collections.addAll(clockList,
                    new Clock(12, 5,32),
                    new Clock(5, 8, 22),
                    new Clock(12, 35, 52),
                    new Clock(2, 16, 42),
                    new Clock(21, 33, 18),
                    new Clock(19, 15, 47));     //Line 2
```

```
System.out.println("Line 3: clockList "
                    + "before sorting: ");          //Line 3
print(clockList);                                    //Line 4

    //sort clockList
Collections.sort(clockList,
                new ClockComparator());              //Line 5

System.out.println("Line 6: clockList "
                    + "after sorting: ");            //Line 6
print(clockList);                                    //Line 7

Clock myClock = new Clock(12, 35, 52);              //Line 8

    //search strList using binary search
int pos = Collections.binarySearch
                    (clockList, myClock,
                     new ClockComparator());         //Line 9

if (pos >= 0)                                        //Line 10
    System.out.println("Line 11: " + myClock
                     + " found in "
                     + "clockList at "
                     + "position " + pos);           //Line 11
else                                                 //Line 12
    System.out.println("Line 13: "
                     +  myClock + " not "
                     + "in clockList.");             //Line 13

    //sort clockList in reverse order
Collections.sort(clockList,
                Collections.reverseOrder
                    (new ClockComparator()));        //Line 14

System.out.println("Line 15: clockList "
                     + "after sorting in "
                     + "reverse order: ");           //Line 15
print(clockList);                                    //Line 16

    //search strList using binary search
pos = Collections.binarySearch(clockList,
                    new Clock(19, 15, 47),
                    Collections.reverseOrder
                    (new ClockComparator()));        //Line 17
```

```
        if (pos >= 0)                                    //Line 18
            System.out.println("Line 19: "
                              + new Clock(19, 15, 47)
                              + " found in "
                              + "clockList at "
                              + "position " + pos);      //Line 19
        else                                             //Line 20
            System.out.println("Line 21: "
                              + new Clock(19, 15, 47)
                              + " not in clockList.");   //Line 21
    }

    public static <T> void print(Collection<T> c)
    {
        for (T obj : c)
            System.out.print(obj + " ");

        System.out.println();
    }
}
```

Sample Run:
```
Line 3: clockList before sorting:
12:05:32 05:08:22 12:35:52 02:16:42 21:33:18 19:15:47
Line 6: clockList after sorting:
02:16:42 05:08:22 12:05:32 12:35:52 19:15:47 21:33:18
Line 11: 12:35:52 found in clockList at position 3
Line 15: clockList after sorting in reverse order:
21:33:18 19:15:47 12:35:52 12:05:32 05:08:22 02:16:42
Line 19: 19:15:47 found in clockList at position 1
```

The preceding program works as follows. The statement in Line 1 creates the `LinkedList` object `clockList` to create a list of `Clock` objects. The statement in Line 2 uses the method `addAll` to add various `Clock` objects into `clockList`. The statement in Line 4 outputs the elements of `clockList` before sorting them.

The statement in Line 5 uses the sort algorithm to sort the elements of `clockList` using the comparison criteria specified by the **class** `ClockComparator`. The statement in Line 7 outputs the elements of `clockList` after sorting them.

The statement in Line 8 creates the `Clock` object `myClock`. The hours, minutes, and seconds of `myClock` are set to 12, 35, and 52, respectively. The statement in Line 9 uses the method `binarySearch` to determine the position of `myClock` in `clockList`. Note that the comparison criteria, specified by **class** `ClockComparator`, is also passed as a parameter.

The statements in Lines 10 to 13 output whether `myClock` is in `clockList`.

The statements in Lines 14 to 21 work the same way as the statements in Lines 5 to 13, except that the `clockList` is sorted in the reverse order. Note how, in the statements in

Lines 14 and 17, the **class ClockComparator** object is passed as a parameter to the **Collection** method **reverseOrder**.

Note that in the preceding program, the statement in Line 2, that is,

```
Collections.addAll(clockList,
                new Clock(12, 5,32),
                new Clock(5, 8, 22),
                new Clock(12, 35, 52),
                new Clock(2, 16, 42),
                new Clock(21, 33, 18),
                new Clock(19, 15, 47));     //Line 2
```

can be replaced with the following statements:

```
clockList.add(new Clock(12, 5,32));
clockList.add(new Clock(5, 8, 22));
clockList.add(new Clock(12, 35, 52));
clockList.add(new Clock(2, 16, 42));
clockList.add(new Clock(21, 33, 18));
clockList.add(new Clock(19, 15, 47));
```

That is, you can use the method **add** of the **class** **LinkedList** to add **Clock** objects into **clockList**.

The Method copy

The method **copy** is used to copy the elements of one collection object into another collection object (of the same type). Its heading is:

```
public static <T> void copy(List<? super T> destList,
                    List<? extends T> srcList)
```

The **copy** method copies all of the elements (references) of **srcList** into **destList**. After the **copy** operation, the index of each copied element in **destList** list is identical to its index in **srcList**. The destination list must be at least as long as the source list. If **destList** is longer, then the remaining elements in **destList** are unaffected. If **destList** is too small to contain the entire **srcList**, the **copy** method throws **IndexOutOfBoundsException**.

Consider the following statements:

```
Vector<String> strList = new Vector<String>();     //Line 1
```

```
Collections.addAll(strList, "Fall", "Winter",
                "Spring", "Summer");     //Line 2
```

The statement in Line 1 creates the empty **Vector** object **strList**. The statement in Line 2 adds four **String** objects into **strList**. Next, consider the following statement:

```
Vector<String> tempStrList = new Vector<String>
```

This statement creates the empty **Vector** object **tempStrList**. Note that the size of **tempStrList** is 0.

Suppose that you want to copy the elements of **strList** into **tempStrList** using the method **copy**. Because the size of **tempStrList** is 0, the statement

```
Collections.copy(tempStrList, strList);
```

throws **IndexOutOfBoundsException**.

One way to copy the elements of **strList** into **tempStrList** is to first insert at least four **null** references into **tempStrList**. So consider the following statements:

```
String[] strArray = new String[5];

Vector<String> tempStrList = new Vector<String>
                                (Arrays.asList(strArray));

Collections.copy(temp, strList);
```

The first statement creates an empty **String** array **strArray** of the size 5. In the second statement, the expression **Arrays.asList(strArray)** uses the method **asList** of the Java **class** **Arrays** to return the elements of **strArray** as a **List** object. The returned **List** object is used to initialize the **Vector** object **tempStrList**. Finally, the third statement copies the elements of **strList** into **tempStrList**. Because the size of **strList** is 4 and the size of **tempStrList** is 5, the last element of **tempStrList** is unchanged. How the preceding statements work is further illustrated in Example 21-9. Also, additional information for the Java **class** **Arrays** can be found at the Web site **www.sun.com**.

Note that the **copy** method copies only the references of the objects in **srcList**. In other words, the elements of **srcList** that are copied in **destList** refer to the same objects. Therefore, if the objects in **srcList** are mutable, changing the value of an object using **srcList** changes the value of the corresponding object in **destList** and vice versa. This is further illustrated by the program in Example 21-9.

Example 21-9

```
//Collections algorithm copy.

import java.util.*;

public class CopyMethod
{
    public static void main(String[] args)
    {
        Vector<String> strList =
                new Vector<String>();                    //Line 1
```

```
Collections.addAll(strList, "Fall",
                    "Winter", "Spring",
                    "Summer");                          //Line 2

System.out.print("Line 3: strList: ");                 //Line 3
print(strList);                                         //Line 4

String[] strArray = new String[5];                     //Line 5

Vector<String> tempStrList =
        new Vector<String>
        (Arrays.asList(strArray));                      //Line 6

Collections.copy(tempStrList, strList);                //Line 7

System.out.print("Line 8: tempStrList: ");             //Line 8
print(tempStrList);                                     //Line 9

    //replace the element at position 0
strList.set(0, "*****");                               //Line 10
System.out.print("Line 11: new strList: ");            //Line 11
print(strList);                                         //Line 12

System.out.print("Line 13: tempStrList: ");            //Line 13
print(tempStrList);                                     //Line 14

LinkedList<Clock> clockList =
        new LinkedList<Clock>();                        //Line 15

Collections.addAll(clockList,
                new Clock(12, 5, 32),
                new Clock(5, 8, 22),
                new Clock(12, 35, 52),
                new Clock(2, 16, 42),
                new Clock(21, 33, 18),
                new Clock(19, 15, 47));                 //Line 16

System.out.println("Line 17: "
                + "clockList: ");                       //Line 17
print(clockList);                                       //Line 18

Clock[] clockArray = new Clock[7];                      //Line 19

LinkedList<Clock> tempClockList =
            new LinkedList<Clock>
            (Arrays.asList(clockArray));                //Line 20

Collections.copy(tempClockList, clockList);            //Line 21
```

```
        System.out.println("Line 22: "
                        + "tempClockList ");          //Line 22
        print(tempClockList);                         //Line 23

        ListIterator<Clock> it =
                clockList.listIterator(0);            //Line 24

        it.next().setTime(8, 8, 8);                   //Line 25

        System.out.println("Line 26: "


                        + "clockList: ");             //Line 26
        print(clockList);                             //Line 27

        System.out.println("Line 28: "
                        + "tempClockList ");          //Line 28
        print(tempClockList);                         //Line 29
    }

    public static <T> void print(Collection<T> c)
    {
        for (T obj : c)
            System.out.print(obj + " ");

        System.out.println();
    }
}
```

Sample Run:
```
Line 3: strList: Fall Winter Spring Summer
Line 8: tempStrList: Fall Winter Spring Summer null
Line 11: new strList: ***** Winter Spring Summer
Line 13: tempStrList: Fall Winter Spring Summer null
Line 17: clockList:
12:05:32 05:08:22 12:35:52 02:16:42 21:33:18 19:15:47
Line 22: tempClockList
12:05:32 05:08:22 12:35:52 02:16:42 21:33:18 19:15:47 null
Line 26: clockList:
08:08:08 05:08:22 12:35:52 02:16:42 21:33:18 19:15:47
Line 28: tempClockList
08:08:08 05:08:22 12:35:52 02:16:42 21:33:18 19:15:47 null
```

The preceding program works as follows. The statement in Line 1 creates the empty `Vector` object `strList`. The statement in Line 2 uses the method `addAll` to add various strings into `strList`. The statement in Line 4 outputs `strList`.

The statements in Lines 5 to 9 copy the elements, as explained before this example, into the `Vectors` object `tempStrList`. The statement in Line 10 replaces the element of strList at position 0 with the string "*****". The statements in Lines 12 and 14 output strList and tempStrList, respectively. Note that the statement in Line 10 affects only strList. The object tempStrList is unaffected because String objects are immutable.

The statements in Lines 15 to 29 work similarly as the statements in Lines 1 to 14. Note that the Clock objects are mutable. Therefore, the statement in Line 25 changes the first object of clockList as well as of tempClockList; see the outputs of the statements in Lines 27 and 29.

The Method disjoint

The method disjoint is used to determine whether two collections have any elements in common. Its heading is:

```
public static boolean disjoint(Collection<?> coll1,
                               Collection<?> coll2)
```

The method disjoint returns **true** if collections coll1 and coll2 have no elements in common; otherwise it returns **false**. If both the collections coll1 and coll2 are the same, then this method returns **true** if and only if coll1 is empty.

Suppose that strList1 and strList2 are **Vector** objects such that

```
strList1 = {"Fall", "Winter", "Spring", "Summer"}
```

and

```
strList2 = {"Java", "C++", "Fall");
```

Because the string "Fall" is in strList1 and strList2, it follows that the expression

```
Collections.disjoint(strList1, strList2)
```

evaluates to **false**.

Now suppose that clockList1 and clockList2 are linked lists of Clock objects such that

```
clockList1 = {(12, 5, 32); (5, 8, 22); (12, 35, 52);
              (2, 16, 42); (21, 33, 18); (19, 15, 47)}
```

and

```
clockList2 = {(10, 25, 52); (11, 46, 32); (5, 18, 22);
              (19, 25, 47)}
```

where expressions such as (12, 5, 32) represent a Clock object with hours, minutes, and seconds as 12, 5, and 32, respectively. Because clockList1 and clockList2 have no Clock objects in common, it follows that the expression

```
Collections.disjoint(clockList1, clockList2)
```

evaluates to **true**.

The Web site accompanying this book contains the program `DisjointMethod.java`, which illustrates how the method `disjoint` is used in a program.

The Methods `max` and `min`

The methods `max` and `min` are used to determine the maximum and minimum elements in a collection. Both these methods are overloaded. Their headings are:

```
public static <T extends Object & Comparable<? super T>> T
                max(Collection<? extends T> coll)
```

This method returns the maximum element of the collection `coll`, according to the natural ordering of its elements. Because the parameter `T` is bounded by the **interface** `Comparable`, all elements in the collection must implement the `Comparable` **interface**.

```
public static <T> T max(Collection<? extends T> coll,
                Comparator<? super T> comp)
```

This method returns the maximum element of the collection `coll`, according to the order induced by the comparator `comp`. All elements in `coll` must be mutually comparable by the comparator `comp`, that is, for any elements `elem1` and `elem2` in the collection, `comp.compare(elem1, elem2)` must not throw a `ClassCastException`. If **null** value is specified for `comp`, then the elements' natural ordering is used.

```
public static <T extends Object & Comparable<? super T>> T
                min(Collection<? extends T> coll)
```

This method returns the smallest element of the collection `coll`, according to the natural ordering of its elements. Because the parameter `T` is bounded by the **interface** `Comparable`, elements in the collection must implement the `Comparable` **interface**.

```
public static <T> T min(Collection<? extends T> coll,
                Comparator<? super T> comp)
```

This method returns the minimum element of the collection `coll`, according to the order induced by the comparator `comp`. All elements in `coll` must be mutually comparable by the comparator `comp`, that is, any elements `elem1` and `elem2` in the collection `comp.compare(elem1, elem2)` must not throw a `ClassCastException`. If **null** value is specified for `comp`, then the elements' natural ordering is used.

These methods throw the following exceptions:

`ClassCastException` is thrown if the collection contains elements that are not mutually comparable using the specified comparator.

`NoSuchElementException` is thrown if the collection is empty.

Example 21-10

```java
//Collections algorithms max and min.

import java.util.*;

public class MaxAndMinMethods
{
    public static void main(String[] args)
    {
        Vector<String> strList =
                new Vector<String>();                       //Line 1

        Collections.addAll(strList, "Math",
                           "Computer Science",
                           "Physics", "History",
                           "Arts");                          //Line 2

        System.out.print("Line 3: strList: ");              //Line 3
        print(strList);                                     //Line 4

            //Output the largest element in strList
        System.out.println("Line 5: max element "
                    + "of strList: "
                    + Collections.max(strList));   //Line 5

            //Output the smallest element in strList
        System.out.println("Line 6: min element "
                    + "of strList: "
                    + Collections.min(strList));   //Line 6

        LinkedList<Double> numList =
                new LinkedList<Double>();            //Line 7

        Double[] decimalNumbers = {12.46, 34.0,
                        62.98, 21.0, 67.45,
                        92.34, 11.0};                //Line 8

        Collections.addAll(numList, decimalNumbers); //Line 9

        System.out.print("Line 10: numList: ");         //Line 10
        print(numList);                                 //Line 11

            //Output the largest element in numList
        System.out.println("Line 12: max element "
                    + "of numList: "
                    + Collections.max(numList));   //Line 12
```

```
                    //Output the smallest element in numList
        System.out.println("Line 13: min element "
                        + "of numList: "
                        + Collections.min(numList));   //Line 13

        LinkedList<Clock> clockList =
                    new LinkedList<Clock>();           //Line 14

        Collections.addAll(clockList,
                        new Clock(12, 5,32),
                        new Clock(5, 8, 22),
                        new Clock(12, 35, 52),
                        new Clock(2, 16, 42),
                        new Clock(21, 33, 18),
                        new Clock(19, 15, 47));    //Line 15

        System.out.println("Line 16: "
                        + "clockList: ");              //Line 16
        print(clockList);                              //Line 17

            //Output the largest element in clockList
        System.out.println("Line 18: max element "
                        + "of clockList: "
                        + Collections.max(clockList,
                            new ClockComparator()));   //Line 18

            //Output the smallest element in clockList
        System.out.println("Line 19: min element "
                        + "of clockList: "
                        + Collections.min(clockList,
                            new ClockComparator()));   //Line 19
    }

    public static <T> void print(Collection<T> c)
    {
        for (T obj : c)
            System.out.print(obj + " ");

        System.out.println();
    }
}
```

Sample Run:
```
Line 3: strList: Math Computer Science Physics History Arts
Line 5: max element of strList: Physics
Line 6: min element of strList: Arts
Line 10: numList: 12.46 34.0 62.98 21.0 67.45 92.34 11.0
Line 12: max element of numList: 92.34
```

```
Line 13: min element of numList: 11.0
Line 16: clockList:
12:05:32 05:08:22 12:35:52 02:16:42 21:33:18 19:15:47
Line 18: max element of clockList: 21:33:18
Line 19: min element of clockList: 02:16:42
```

The preceding program works as follows. The statement in Line 1 creates the empty `Vector` object `strList` to create a list of `String` objects. The statement in Line 2 inserts various strings into `strList`. The statement in Line 4 outputs `strList`. The statement in Line 5 uses the `Collections` method `max` to output the largest string in `strList`, and the statement in Line 6 uses the `Collections` method `min` to output the smallest string in `strList`.

The statement in Line 7 creates the empty `LinkedList` object `numList` to create a list of `Double` objects. The statement in Line 8 creates the `Double` array `decimalNumbers`. The statement in Line 9 inserts the elements of the array `decimalNumbers` into `numList`. The statement in Line 11 outputs `numList`. The statement in Line 12 uses the `Collections` method `max` to output the largest number in `numList`, and the statement in Line 13 uses the `Collections` method `min` to output the smallest number in `numList`.

The statement in Line 14 creates the empty `LinkedList` object `clockList` to create a list of `Clock` objects. The statement in Line 15 inserts various `Clock` objects into `clockList`. The statement in Line 17 outputs `clockList`. The statement in Line 18 uses the `Collections` method `max` to output the largest clock in `clockList`, and the statement in Line 19 uses the `Collections` method `min` to output the smallest clock in `clockList`. Note that in these statements, the comparison criteria are specified by the `ClockComparator` object, which is passed as a parameter to the methods `max` and `min`.

The Methods `fill` and `frequency`

The method `fill` is used to replace all the elements of a given list with a given element. Its heading is:

```java
public static <T> void fill(List<? super T> list, T obj)
```

The method `fill` replaces all of the elements of `list` with the element specified by `obj`. The type parameter `T` specifies the type of `list` elements as well as the type of the element with which it is being replaced. If `list` or its list-iterator does not support the set operation, then the method `fill` throws `UnsupportedOperationException`.

The method `frequency` finds the number of times a specific object appears in a collection. Its heading is:

```java
public static int frequency(Collection<?> coll, Object obj)
```

The method `frequency` returns the number of times `obj` appears in the collection `coll`. If the collection `coll` is `null`, the method `frequency` throws `NullPointerException`.

Example 21-11

```java
//Collections algorithms fill and frequency.

import java.util.*;

public class FillAndFrequencyMethods
{
    public static void main(String[] args)
    {
        Vector<String> strList =
                new Vector<String>();                   //Line 1

        Collections.addAll(strList, "Math", "CSC",
                        "English", "History",
                        "Arts", "CSC");                 //Line 2

        System.out.print("Line 3: strList: ");          //Line 3
        print(strList);                                 //Line 4

            //Determine the number of times the string
            //"CSC" appears in strList
        int freqWord =
            Collections.frequency(strList, "CSC");      //Line 5

            //Output the number of times the string
            //"CSC" appears in strList
        System.out.println("Line 6: CSC appears "
                        + freqWord
                        + " times in strList.");        //Line 6

            //Replace each string in strList with the
            //string "***"
        Collections.fill(strList, "***");               //Line 7

        System.out.println("Line 8: strList after "
                        + " replacing all the "
                        + "elemnts with ***: ");        //Line 8

        print(strList);                                 //Line 9

        LinkedList<Double> numList =
                new LinkedList<Double>();               //Line 10

        Collections.addAll(numList, 12.46, 34.0,
                        12.46, 21.0, 67.45,
                        92.34, 11.0, 12.46);            //Line 11
```

```
        System.out.print("Line 12: numList: ");        //Line 12
        print(numList);                                 //Line 13

            //Output the number of times the number
            //12.46 appears in strList
        System.out.println("Line 14: 12.46 appears "
                + Collections.frequency(numList, 12.46)
                + " times in numList.");                //Line 14

            //Replace each number in numList with the
            //number 0.0
        Collections.fill(numList, 0.0);                 //Line 15

        System.out.println("Line 16: numList after "
                        + " replacing all the "
                        + "elements with 0.0: ");        //Line 16

        print(numList);                                 //Line 17
    }


    public static <T> void print(Collection<T> c)
    {
        for (T obj : c)
            System.out.print(obj + " ");

        System.out.println();
    }

}
```

Sample Run:
```
Line 3: strList: Math CSC English History Arts CSC
Line 6: CSC appears 2 times in strList.
Line 8: strList after replacing all the elemnts with ***:
*** *** *** *** *** ***
Line 12: numList: 12.46 34.0 12.46 21.0 67.45 92.34 11.0 12.46
Line 14: 12.46 appears 3 times in numList.
Line 16: numList after replacing all the elemnts with 0.0:
0.0 0.0 0.0 0.0 0.0 0.0 0.0 0.0
```

The preceding program works as follows. The statement in Line 1 creates the empty `Vector` object `strList` to create a list of `String` objects. The statement in Line 2 inserts various strings into `strList`. The statement in Line 4 outputs `strList`. The statement in Line 5 uses the `Collections` method `frequency` to determine the number of times the string `"CSC"` appears in `strList` and stores that number into the variable `freqWord`. The statement in Line 6 outputs the frequency of the string `"CSC"` in `strList`. The statement in Line 7 uses the `Collections` method `fill` to replace each string in `strList` with the string `"***"`. The statement in Line 9 outputs the modified `strList`.

The meaning of the statements in Lines 10 to 17 is similar to the statements in Lines 1 to 9. In these statements, we use a number list to illustrate the methods **frequency** and **fill**. We leave the details as an exercise for you.

The Method nCopies

The method **nCopies** creates a list of **n** copies of a given object and returns a reference of the created list. The list created is immutable, that is, it cannot be modified. The heading of the method **nCopies** is:

```
public static <T> List<T> nCopies(int n, T obj)
```

The method **nCopies** returns a reference of an immutable list containing **n** copies of the object specified by **obj**. The type parameter **T** specifies the type of **obj**. Note that the newly allocated data object is tiny; that is, it contains a single reference to **obj**. This method is especially useful in combination with the **List.addAll** method to grow lists. If **n < 0**, this method throws **IllegalArgumentException**.

The program in Example 21-12 illustrates how the method **nCopies** works.

Example 21-12

```java
//Collections algorithm nCopies.

import java.util.*;

public class NCopiesMethod
{
    public static void main(String[] args)
    {
        List<String> strList;                       //Line 1

            //Create a list of 5 copies of the string
            //"Java" and assign the reference of the
            //list to strList.
        strList = Collections.nCopies(5, "Java");   //Line 2

        System.out.print("Line 3: strList: ");      //Line 3
        print(strList);                             //Line 4

            //Determine the number of times the string
            //"Java" appears in strList.
        int freqWord =
            Collections.frequency(strList, "Java"); //Line 5

            //Output the frequency of the string "Java"
            //in strList.
```

```
                System.out.println("Line 6: Java appears "
                            + freqWord
                            + " times in strList.");      //Line 6
    }

    public static <T> void print(Collection<T> c)
    {
        for (T obj : c)
            System.out.print(obj + " ");

        System.out.println();
    }
}
```

Sample Run:
```
Line 3: strList: Java Java Java Java Java
Line 6: Java appears 5 times in strList.
```

The preceding program is self-explanatory. We leave the details as an exercise for you.

The Method `replaceAll`

The method `replaceAll` is used to replace all the occurrences of a given element with another. Its heading is:

```
public static <T> boolean replaceAll(List<T> list,
                                     T oldVal,
                                     T newVal)
```

All occurrences of `oldVal` in `list` are replaced with `newVal`. The type parameter `T` specifies the type of list elements. Moreover, the method `replaceAll` returns `true` if `list` contained one or more elements `obj` such that (`oldVal == null ? obj == null : oldVal.equals(obj)`). If `list` or its list-iterator does not support the `set` method, this method throws `UnsupportedOperationException`.

Example 21-13 illustrates how the method `replaceAll` works.

Example 21-13

```
//Collections algorithm replaceAll.

import java.util.*;

public class ReplaceAllMethod
{
    public static void main(String[] args)
    {
        Vector<String> strList =
                new Vector<String>();                      //Line 1
```

```
      Collections.addAll(strList, "Math",
                         "CSC", "Physics",
                         "History", "CSC");        //Line 2

      System.out.print("Line 3: strList: ");       //Line 3
      print(strList);                               //Line 4

         //In strList, replace all occurrences of
         //the string "CSC" with the string
         //"Computer Science".
      Collections.replaceAll(strList, "CSC",
                            "Computer Science");    //Line 5

      System.out.println("Line 6: Modified "
                        + "strList: ");             //Line 6
      print(strList);                               //Line 7

      LinkedList<Double> numList =
               new LinkedList<Double>();            //Line 8

      Collections.addAll(numList, 12.46, 34.0,
                        12.46, 21.0, 12.46,
                        92.34, 11.0);               //Line 9

      System.out.print("Line 10: numList: ");       //Line 10
      print(numList);                               //Line 11

         //In numList, replace all occurrences of
         //the number 12.46 with the number
         //8.5.
      Collections.replaceAll(numList, 12.46,
                        8.5);                       //Line 12

      System.out.print("Line 13: Modified "
                      + "numList: ");               //Line 13
      print(numList);                               //Line 14

   }

   public static <T> void print(Collection<T> c)
   {
      for (T obj : c)
         System.out.print(obj + " ");

      System.out.println();
   }
}
```

Sample Run:
```
Line 3: strList: Math CSC Physics History CSC
Line 6: Modified strList:
Math Computer Science Physics History Computer Science
Line 10: numList: 12.46 34.0 12.46 21.0 12.46 92.34 11.0
Line 13: Modified numList: 8.5 34.0 8.5 21.0 8.5 92.34 11.0
```

The preceding program works as follows. The statement in Line 1 creates the empty **Vector** object **strList** to create a list of **String** objects. The statement in Line 2 inserts various strings into **strList**. The statement in Line 4 outputs **strList**. The statement in Line 5 uses the **Collections** method **replaceAll** to replace, in **strList**, all occurrences of the **"CSC"** with the string **"Computer Science"**. The statement in Line 7 outputs the modified **strList**.

The statement in Line 8 creates the empty **LinkedList** object **numList** to create a list of **Double** objects. The statement in Line 9 inserts various numbers into **numList**. The statement in Line 11 outputs **numList**. The statement in Line 12 uses the **Collections** method **replaceAll** to replace, in **numList**, all occurrences of **12.46** with **8.5**. The statement in Line 14 outputs the modified **numList**.

The Methods reverse and rotate

The method **reverse** reverses the order of the elements in a list. Its heading is:

public static void reverse(List<?> list)

After a call to the method **reverse**, the elements in **list** are in reverse order. If **list** or its list-iterator does not support the set method, this method throws **UnsupportedOperationException**.

The method **rotate** is used to rotate the elements of a list in a specific manner. Its heading is:

public static void rotate(List<?> list, **int** dist)

The method **rotate** rotates the elements in **list** by the distance specified by the parameter **dist**. After a call to this method, the element at index i, in **list**, is the element previously at index $(i - dist) \bmod list.size()$, for all values of i, $0 <= i <= list.size()-1$. If **list** or its list-iterator does not support the set method, this method throws **UnsupportedOperationException**.

Suppose:

list = [p, l, a, n, e]

After invoking

Collections.rotate(list, 1)

or

```
Collections.rotate(list, -4))

list = [e, p, l, a, n]
```

Note that this method can be applied to sublists to move one or more elements within a list, while preserving the order of the remaining elements. For example, the following statement moves the element at index j forward to position k. (Note that k must be greater than or equal to j):

```
Collections.rotate(list.subList(j, k + 1), -1);
```

To be specific, suppose:

```
list = [a, b, c, d, e, f, g].
```

The following statement moves the element at index 1, which is b, forward four positions:

```
Collections.rotate(list.subList(1, 6), -1);
```

The resulting list is:

```
list = [a, c, d, e, f, b, g].
```

The program in Example 21-14 further illustrates how the methods reverse and rotate work.

Example 21-14

```java
//Collections algorithms reverse and rotate.

import java.util.*;

public class ReverseAndRotateMethods
{
    public static void main(String[] args)
    {
        Vector<Character> charList =
                new Vector<Character>();                 //Line 1

        Character[] charArray = {'A', 'B', 'C',
                                 'D', 'E', 'F',
                                 'G', 'H', 'I',
                                 'J'};                   //Line 2

        Collections.addAll(charList, charArray);         //Line 3

        System.out.print("Line 4: charList: ");          //Line 4
        print(charList);                                 //Line 5

            //Reverse the elements of charList.
        Collections.reverse(charList);                   //Line 6

        System.out.print("Line 7: Reversed "
                         + "charList: ");                //Line 7
```

21

```
    print(charList);                                  //Line 8

        //Delete all the elements of charList.
    charList.clear();                                 //Line 9
        //Add elements of charArray into charList.
    Collections.addAll(charList, charArray);          //Line 10
        //Rotate the elements of charList at a
        //distance of 1.
    Collections.rotate(charList, 1);                  //Line 11

    System.out.print("Line 12: Rotated "
                + "charList at a "
                + "distance of 1: \n"
                + "            ");                     //Line 12
    print(charList);                                  //Line 13

    LinkedList<Integer> numList =
                new LinkedList<Integer>();            //Line 14

    Integer[] intArray = {2, 4, 6, 8, 10, 12,
                        14, 16, 18, 20};              //Line 15

    Collections.addAll(numList, intArray);            //Line 16

    System.out.print("Line 17: numList: ");           //Line 17
    print(numList);                                   //Line 18

        //Reverse the elements of numList.
    Collections.reverse(numList);                     //Line 19

    System.out.print("Line 20: Reversed "
                + "numList: \n"
                + "              ");                   //Line 20
    print(numList);                                   //Line 21

        //Delete all the elements of numList.
    numList.clear();                                  //Line 22
        //Add all the elements of intArray into
        //numList.
    Collections.addAll(numList, intArray);            //Line 23

        //Rotate the elements of numList at a
        //distance of 3.
    Collections.rotate(numList, 3);                   //Line 24
    System.out.print("Line 25: Rotated "
                + "numList at a "
                + "distance of 3: \n"
                + "            ");                     //Line 25
    print(numList);                                   //Line 26
```

```
            //Delete all the elements of numList.
        numList.clear();                                   //Line 27
            //Add all the elements of intArray into
            //numList.
        Collections.addAll(numList, intArray);             //Line 28

            //Rotate the elements of the sublist of
            //numList at a distance of 2.
        Collections.rotate(numList.subList(3, 7), 2); //Line 29

        System.out.print("Line 30: numList after "
                    + "rotating its "
                    + "sublist(3, 7) at \n"
                    + "          a distance of 2: ");   //Line 30
        print(numList);                                    //Line 31
    }

    public static <T> void print(Collection<T> c)
    {
        for (T obj : c)
            System.out.print(obj + " ");

        System.out.println();
    }
}
```

Sample Run:
```
Line 4: charList: A B C D E F G H I J
Line 7: Reversed charList: J I H G F E D C B A
Line 12: Rotated charList at a distance of 1:
        J A B C D E F G H I
Line 17: numList: 2 4 6 8 10 12 14 16 18 20
Line 20: Reversed numList:
        20 18 16 14 12 10 8 6 4 2
Line 25: Rotated numList at a distance of 3:
        16 18 20 2 4 6 8 10 12 14
Line 30: numList after rotating its sublist(3, 7) at
        a distance of 2: 2 4 6 12 14 8 10 16 18 20
```

The preceding program works as follows. The statement in Line 1 creates the empty **Vector** objects **charList** to create a list of **Character** objects. The statement in Line 2 creates the **Character** array **charArray**. The statement in Line 3 inserts all the elements of **charArray** into **charList**. The statement in Line 5 outputs **charList**. The statement in Line 6 reverses the order of the elements of **charList**. The statement in Line 7 outputs the modified **charList**.

The statement in Line 9 deletes all the elements of **charList**, and the statement in Line 10 inserts all the elements of **charArray** into **charList**. The statement in Line 11 rotates the elements of `charList` at a distance of 1. After the execution of this statement, the element at position 0 becomes the element at position 1, the element at position 1 becomes the element at position 2, and so on. Note that the last element becomes the first element. The statement in Line 13 outputs the modified `charList`.

The statement in Line 14 creates the empty `LinkedList` objects `numList` to create a list of `Integer` objects. The statement in Line 15 creates the `Integer` array `intArray`. The statement in Line 16 inserts all the elements of `intArray` into `numList`. The statement in Line 18 outputs `numList`. The statement in Line 19 reverses the order of the elements of `numList`. The statement in Line 21 outputs the modified `numList`.

The statement in Line 22 deletes all the elements of `numList`, and the statement in Line 23 inserts all the elements of `intArray` into `numList`. The statement in Line 24 rotates the elements of `numList` at a distance of 3. After the execution of this statement, the element at position 0 becomes the element at position 3, the element at position 1 becomes the element at position 4, and so on. Note that the last element becomes the element at position 3.

The statement in Line 29 rotates the elements of the sublist within the indices 3 and 7 of `numList` at a distance of 2. The statement in Line 31 outputs the modified `numList`.

The Methods `shuffle` and `swap`

The method `shuffle` randomly shuffles the elements of a list. This is an overloaded method. Its headings are:

```
public static void shuffle(List<?> list)
```

```
public static void shuffle(List<?> list, Random rnd)
```

The first form randomly permutes the elements of `list` using a default source of randomness. All permutations occur with approximately equal likelihood. The second form randomly permutes the elements of `list` using the source of randomness specified by `rnd`. All permutations occur with equal likelihood, assuming that the source of randomness is fair. If `list` or its list-iterator does not support the set operation, then this method throws `UnsupportedOperationException`.

The method `swap` swaps any two elements of a list. Its heading is:

```
public static void swap(List<?> list, int i, int j)
```

After a call to the method `swap`, elements of `list` at the positions `i` and `j` are swapped. If either `i` or `j` is out of range, that is, if `i < 0` or `i >= list.size()` or `j < 0` or `j >= list.size()`, then this method throws `IndexOutOfBoundsException`.

Example 21-15

```java
//Collections algorithm shuffle and swap.

import java.util.*;

public class ShuffleAndSwapMethods
{
    public static void main(String[] args)
    {
        Vector<Character> charList =
                new Vector<Character>();                //Line 1

        Character[] charArray = {'A', 'B', 'C',
                                 'D', 'E', 'F',
                                 'G', 'H', 'I',
                                 'J'};                  //Line 2

        Collections.addAll(charList, charArray);        //Line 3

        System.out.print("Line 3: charList: ");         //Line 4
        print(charList);                                //Line 5
            //Shuffle chatList
        Collections.shuffle(charList);                  //Line 6

        System.out.print("Line 7: After shuffling "
                    + "charList: ");                    //Line 7
        print(charList);                                //Line 8


            //Delete all the elements of charList
        charList.clear();                               //Line 9
            //Add elements of charArray into charList.
        Collections.addAll(charList, charArray);        //Line 10
            //Swap the elements of charList,
            //at the positions 2 and 7
        Collections.swap(charList, 2, 7);               //Line 11
        System.out.print("Line 12: charList after "
                    + "swapping elements "
                    + "at the positions \n"
                    + "        2 and 7: ");             //Line 12
        print(charList);                                //Line 13

        LinkedList<Integer> numList =
                new LinkedList<Integer>();              //Line 14

        Integer[] intArray = {2, 4, 6, 8, 10, 12,
                    14, 16, 18, 20};                    //Line 15
```

```
        Collections.addAll(numList, intArray);              //Line 16

        System.out.print("Line 17: numList: ");             //Line 17
        print(numList);                                     //Line 18

            //Shuffle numList
        Collections.shuffle(numList);                       //Line 19

        System.out.print("Line 20: After shuffling "
                        + "numList: \n"
                        + "              ");                 //Line 20
        print(numList);                                     //Line 21
    }

    public static <T> void print(Collection<T> c)
    {
        for (T obj : c)
            System.out.print(obj + " ");

        System.out.println();
    }
}
```

Sample Run:
```
Line 3: charList: A B C D E F G H I J
Line 7: After shuffling charList: F E C H I G J A B D
Line 12: charList after swapping elements at the positions
        2 and 7: A B H D E F G C I J
Line 17: numList: 2 4 6 8 10 12 14 16 18 20
Line 20: After shuffling numList:
        2 14 12 20 4 16 8 6 18 10
```

The preceding program works as follows. The statement in Line 1 creates the empty **Vector** objects **charList** to create a list of **Character** objects. The statement in Line 2 creates the **Character** array **charArray**. The statement in Line 3 inserts all the elements of **charArray** into **charList**. The statement in Line 5 outputs **charList**. The statement in Line 6 shuffles the elements of **charList**. The statement in Line 8 outputs the modified **charList**.

The statement in Line 9 deletes all the elements of **charList**, and the statement in Line 10 inserts all the elements of **charArray** into **charList**. The statement in Line 11 swaps the elements at the positions 2 and 7, which are the third and the eighth elements of **charList**. The statement in Line 13 outputs the modified **charList**.

The statement in Line 14 creates the empty **LinkedList** objects **numList** to create a list of **Integer** objects. The statement in Line 15 creates the **Integer** array **intArray**. The statement in Line 16 inserts all the elements of **intArray** into **numList**. The statement in

Line 18 outputs `numList`. The statement in Line 19 shuffles the elements of `numList`. The statement in Line 21 outputs the modified `numList`.

PROGRAMMING EXAMPLE: VIDEO STORE (REVISTED)

In Chapter 16, we designed a program to make a video store operational. In that chapter, the **class** `VideoList` to implement a list of video objects was derived from the **class** `UnorderedLinkedList`. In this chapter, we discussed the Java **class** `LinkedList` to implement a linked list. Therefore, in this programming example, we redesign the **class** `VideoList` so that it uses a `LinkedList` object to implement a list of video objects. Note that we do not need to modify the **class** `Video` to implement a video object.

Class `VideoList`   To implement a list of video objects, we use a `LinkedList` object, which is declared as a **private** instance variable of the **class** `VideoList`. The following describes the instance variable(s), constructor, and instance methods of the **class** `VideoList`.

Class: VideoList

```java
public class VideoList
```

Instance Variable:

```java
private LinkedList<Video> videosList; //object to create a
                                      //list of video objects
```

Constructor and Instance Methods:

```java
public VideoList()
   //Default constructor
   //Postcondition: videosList is instantiated and
   //               initialized to an empty state.

public void insert(Video vidObj)
   //Method to insert a video object in videosList.
   //Postconditon: The video object specified by the
   //              parameter vidObj is inserted at the
   //              end of videosList.

public void delete(Video vidObj)
   //Method to delete a video object from videosList.
   //Postconditon: If found, the video object specified
   //              by the parameter vidObj is removed from
   //              videosList.
```

```
public boolean videoSearch(String title)
    //Method to search videosList to see whether a particular
    //video, specified by the parameter title, is in the
    //store.
    //Postcondition: Returns true if the title is found;
    //               false otherwise.

public boolean isVideoAvailable(String title)
    //Method to determine whether the video specified by the
    //parameter title is available.
    //Postcondition: Returns true if at least one copy of
    //               the video is available; false otherwise.

public void videoCheckIn(String title)
    //Method to check in a video returned by a customer.
    //Postcondition: If the video returned is from the
    //               store, its copiesInstock is incremented
    //               by one; otherwise, an appropriate
    //               message is printed.

public void videoCheckOut(String title)
    //Method to check out a video, that is, rent a video.
    //Postcondition: If a video is available, its
    //               copiesInStock is decremented by one;
    //               otherwise, an appropriate message is
    //               printed.

public boolean videoCheckTitle(String title)
    //Method to determine whether the video specified by the
    //parameter title is in the store.
    //Postcondition: Returns true if the video is
    //               in the store; false otherwise.

public void videoUpdateInStock(String title, int num)
    //Method to update the number of copies of a video
    //by adding the value of the parameter num. The
    //parameter title specifies the name of the video
    //for which the number of copies is to be updated.
    //Postcondition: If video is found, then
    //               copiesInStock = copiesInStock + num;
    //               otherwise, an appropriate message is
    //               printed.

public void videoSetCopiesInStock(String title, int num)
    //Method to reset the number of copies of a video.
    //The parameter title specifies the name of the video
    //for which the number of copies is to be reset, and the
    //parameter num specifies the number of copies.
```

```
   //Postcondition: If video is found, then
   //               copiesInStock = num;
   //               otherwise, an appropriate message
   //               is printed.

public void videoPrintTitle()
   //Method to print the titles of all the videos in
   //the store.

public void print()
   //Method to print the info of all the videos in the
   //store.
```

Before giving the definitions of the methods of the **class** `VideoList`, let us note the following. In addition to the methods of the **class** `VideoList`, given in Chapter 16, this class contains the methods **insert** and **delete**. The instance variable `videosList` is a `LinkedList` object. To insert a video object in `videosList`, the method **insert** uses the method **add** of the **class** `LinkedList`. The video object is inserted at the end of the list. Similarly, the method **delete** uses the method **remove** of the **class** `LinkedList` to find and delete a particular video from `videosList`.

To determine whether a particular video is in the store, we use the method `indexOf` of the **class** `LinkedList`. Recall that if a particular video is in `videosList`, the method `indexOf` returns the index of the video in `videosList`; otherwise it returns −1. For example, consider the following statement:

```
Video temp = new Video("Alice in WonderLand", "",
                  "", "", "", "", 0);            //Line 1
int index = videosList.indexOf(temp);           //Line 2
```

The statement in Line 1 creates the `Video` object `temp` with the title `"Alice in WonderLand"`. The statement in Line 2 uses the method `indexOf` to determine if there is a video with the title `"Alice in WonderLand"` in `videosList`. The value returned by the method `indexOf` is stored in the variable `index`. Next, consider the following statement:

```
if (index != -1)                                //Line 3
    temp = videosList.get(index);               //Line 4
```

The **if** statement in Line 3 checks whether `index` is −1. If `index` is not −1, the statement in Line 4 assigns the reference of the `Video` object returned by the method **get** of the **class** `LinkedList` to `temp`.

We now give the definitions of the methods of the **class** `VideoList`:

```
public VideoList()
{
    videosList = new LinkedList<Video>();
}
```

```
public void insert(Video vidObj)
{
    videosList.add(vidObj);
}

public void delete(Video vidObj)
{
    videosList.remove(vidObj);
}

public boolean videoSearch(String title)
{
    Video temp = new Video(title, "", "", "", "", "", 0);

    int index = videosList.indexOf(temp);

    return (index != -1);
}

public boolean isVideoAvailable(String title)
{
    Video temp = new Video(title, "", "", "", "", "", 0);

    int index = videosList.indexOf(temp);

    if (index != -1)
    {
        temp = videosList.get(index);
        return (temp.getNoOfCopiesInStock() > 0);
    }
    else
        return false;
}

public void videoCheckIn(String title)
{
    Video temp = new Video(title, "", "", "", "", "", 0);

    int index = videosList.indexOf(temp);

    if (index != -1)
    {
        temp = videosList.get(index);
        temp.checkIn();
    }
    else
        System.out.println("The store does not carry "
                         + "this video.");
```

```java
}

public void videoCheckOut(String title)
{
    Video temp = new Video(title, "", "", "", "", "", 0);

    int index = videosList.indexOf(temp);

    if (index != -1)
    {
        temp = videosList.get(index);
        temp.checkOut();
    }
    else
        System.out.println("The store does not carry "
                          + "this video.");
}

public boolean videoCheckTitle(String title)
{
    Video temp = new Video(title, "", "", "", "", "", 0);

    int index = videosList.indexOf(temp);

    return (index != -1);
}

public void videoUpdateInStock(String title, int num)
{
    Video temp = new Video(title, "", "", "", "", "", 0);

    int index = videosList.indexOf(temp);

    if (index != -1)
    {
        temp = videosList.get(index);
        temp.updateInStock(num);
    }
    else
        System.out.println("The store does not carry "
                          + "this video.");
}

public void videoSetCopiesInStock(String title, int num)
{
    Video temp = new Video(title, "", "", "", "", "", 0);

    int index = videosList.indexOf(temp);
```

```
        if (index != -1)
        {
            temp = videosList.get(index);
            temp.setCopiesInStock(num);
        }
        else
            System.out.println("The store does not carry "
                                   + "this video");
    }

    public void videoPrintTitle()
    {
        for (Video obj: videosList)
            obj.printTitle();
    }

    public void print()
    {
        for (Video obj: videosList)
            obj.printInfo();
    }
```

The main program to test the **class VideoList** as well as implement the video component is the same as in Chapter 16. The complete definitions of the classes and the main program are available at the Web site accompanying this book.

QUICK REVIEW

1. The objects of the **class LinkedList** are implemented as doubly linked lists.

2. The definition of the **class LinkedList** is contained in the package java.util.

3. Some of the methods of the **class LinkedList** are add, addAll, addFirst, addLast, clear, clone, contains, element, get, getFirst, getLast, indexOf, lastIndexOf, listIterator, offer, peek, poll, remove, removeFirst, removeLast, set, size, and toArray.

4. One way to iterate over the elements of a **LinkedList** object is to use a foreach loop. Another way to iterate over the elements of a collection is to use iterators.

5. The **interface ListIterator** implements the **interface Iterator** and provides methods such as **next** and **previous** to iteratate over the elements of a **LinkedList** object.

6. A collection is a data structure, in fact, an object, that can hold references to other objects.

7. A collection class is a class whose objects are collections.

8. The **interface** `Collection` is the super class (interface) of all Java collection classes.

9. The **class** `Vector` extends the **abstract class** `AbstractList`, and the **class** `LinkedList` extends the **abstract class** `AbstractSequentialList`.

10. The **abstract class** `AbstractList` implements the **interface** `List` and extends the **abstract class** `AbstractCollection`.

11. The **interface**s `Set` and `List` extend the **interface** `Collection`.

12. The **interface** `Collection` describes the basic operations that should be implemented by all collection classes.

13. Some of the methods of the **interface** `Collection` are `add`, `addAll`, `clear`, `contains`, `containsAll`, `equals`, `hashCode`, `isEmpty`, `iterator`, `remove`, `removeAll`, `retainAll`, `size`, and `toArray`.

14. The two main interfaces that extend the `Collection` **interface** are `Set` and `List`.

15. Classes that implement the `Set` **interface** do not allow duplicates; that is, an element in a collection occurs only once.

16. Classes that implement the `List` **interface** allow elements to occur more than once.

17. The **abstract class AbstractCollection** implements the `Collection` **interface**. It is the base class of the **abstract class**es `AbstractSet` and `AbstractList`.

18. The **abstract class** `AbstractList` extends the **abstract class** `AbstractCollection` and implements the **interface** `List`.

19. The **class** `Vector` is derived from the **abstract class** `AbstractList`.

20. The **class** `LinkedList` is derived from the **abstract class** `AbstractSequentialList`, which extends the **abstract class** `AbstractList`.

21. The **abstract class** `AbstractSequentialList` overrides some methods inherited from the **class** `AbstractList`; there are no completely new methods in this class. The purpose of the **class** `AbstractSequentialList` is to provide efficient algorithms to sequentially move through the list.

22. Some of the methods of the **interface** `Set` are `add`, `addAll`, `clear`, `contains`, `containsAll`, `equals`, `hashCode`, `isEmpty`, `iterator`, `remove`, `retainAll`, `removeAll`, `size`, and `toArray`.

23. The **class** `HashSet` extends the **class** `AbstractSet` and implements the **interface** `Set`.

24. The **class** AbstractSet implements the methods equals, hashCode, and removeAll of the **interface** Set.

25. The **class** HashSet implements the methods iterator, size, isEmpty, contains, remove, and clear of the **interface** Set. It also contains the **public** method clone.

26. In hashing, the data are organized with the help of a table called the hash table, and the hash table is stored in an array.

27. To determine whether a particular item with a key, say X, is in the table, we apply a function h, called the hash function, to the key X; that is, we compute $h(X)$, read as "h of X."

28. The function h is an arithmetic function and $h(X)$ gives the address of the item in the hash table. Because the address of an item is computed with the help of a function, it follows that the items are stored in no particular order.

29. There are two ways that data are organized with the help of the hash table. In the first approach, the data are stored within the hash table, that is, in an array. In the second approach, the data are stored in linked lists and the hash table is an array of reference variables to those linked lists.

30. Two keys, X_1 and X_2, such that $X_1 \neq X_2$, are called synonyms if $h(X_1) = h(X_2)$.

31. Let X_1 and X_2 be two nonidentical keys, that is, $X_1 \neq X_2$. If $h(X_1) = h(X_2)$, we say that a collision occurs.

32. When choosing a hash function, the main objectives are: Choose a hash function that is easy to compute and minimize the number of collisions.

33. The capacity of a hash table is the number of buckets in the hash table, and the initial capacity is simply the capacity at the time the hash table is created.

34. Suppose *HTSize* denotes the size of the hash table. Then the load factor of the hash table is (number of items in the hash table) / *HTSize*.

35. The load factor is a measure of how full the hash table is allowed to get.

36. When a **HashSet** object's hash table is full, its capacity is automatically increased. Moreover, when the number of entries in the hash table exceeds the product of the load factor and the current capacity, the capacity is roughly doubled.

37. The **class** TreeSet extends the **class** AbstractSet and implements the **interface** Set. Objects of the **class** TreeSet organize data in a binary tree.

38. The **class** TreeSet also implements the methods add, addAll, clear, contains, isEmpty, iterator, remove, and size. This class contains the method clone and the methods **first** and **last** to return the first and last element of the set, respectively. To return a subset of a given set, this class contains the methods subSet, headSet, and tailSet.

39. Objects of the collection **Map** manage its elements in the form key/pair.

40. Some of the classes that implement the **interface** Map are HashTable, HashMap, and TreeMap.

41. The **class** HashMap extends the **class** AbstractMap and implements the **interface** Map.

42. The generic algorithms are designed as **static** methods of the **class** Collections, which extends the **class** Object.

43. Some of the methods of **class** Collections are addAll, binarySearch, copy, disjoint, fill, frequency, max, min, nCopies, replaceAll, reverse, reverseOrder, rotate, shuffle, sort, and swap.

44. The method addAll adds all the elements of a collection into another collection.

45. The method binarySearch searches a list for a given element. The binary search algorithm requires the list to be sorted.

46. The method sort sorts a list.

47. To specify that the list be sorted in descending order, the method reverseOrder of the **class** Collections is used.

48. The **interface** Comparator allows us to define a comparison function, which imposes a total ordering on some collection of objects.

49. The method copy is used to copy the elements of one collection object into another collection object (of the same type).

50. The method disjoint is used to determine whether two collections have any elements in common.

51. The methods max and min are used to determine the maximum and minimum elements in a collection.

52. The method fill is used to replace all the elements of a given list with a given element.

53. The method frequency finds the number of times a specific object appears in a collection.

54. The method nCopies creates a list of n copies of a given object and returns a reference of the created list. The list created is immutable, that is, it cannot be modified.

55. The method replaceAll is used to replace all the occurrences of a given element with another.

56. The method reverse reverses the order of the elements in a list.

57. The method rotate is used to rotate the elements of a list in a specific manner.

58. The method shuffle randomly shuffles the elements of a list.

59. The method swap swaps any two elements of a list.

21

EXERCISES

1. What is the difference between an `Iterator` object and a `ListIterator` object?

2. Name three interfaces that directly extend the **interface** `Collection`.

3. a. Write a Java statement that creates the empty `LinkedList` object `numList` to create a linked list of `Double` objects.

   b. Write a single Java statement that inserts the numbers `34.56`, `78.32`, `45.00`, `23.78`, `90.00`, and `12.50` into the object `numList` created in (a).

   c. Write a Java statement that creates the `ListIterator` object to iterate over the elements of `numList`.

4. What is the difference between a `HashSet` object and a `TreeSet` object?

5. What is the output of the following statements?

```
TreeSet<Integer> intSet = new TreeSet<Integer>();
Collections.addAll(intSet, 12, 20, 15, 27, 45,
                           20, 35, 12);

for (Integer num : intSet)
     System.out.print(num + " ");
System.out.println();

System.out.println("The size of intSet: "
                   + intSet.size());
```

6. Suppose that `list1`, `list2`, and `list3` are `Vector<Integer>` objects such that:

```
list1 = {2, 4, 6, 8};
list2 = {1, 2, 3, 5, 7};
list3 = {1, 5, 9};
```

   What are the values of the following expressions?

   a. `Collections.disjoint(list1, list2);`

   b. `Collections.disjoint(list2, list3);`

   c. `Collections.disjoint(list1, list3);`

7. Suppose `intList` is a `Vector<Integer>` object such that:

```
intList = {2, 4, 6, 8, 10, 12};
```

   What are elements of `intList` after the following statement executes?

```
Collections.rotate(intList, 3);
```

PROGRAMMING EXERCISES

1. Redo Programming Exercise 14 of Chapter 16 so that it uses the `Collection` **class** `LinkedList` to process the list of videos rented by the customer and the list of store members.

2. Redo Programming Exercise 15 of Chapter 16 so that it uses the `Collection` **class** `LinkedList` to process the list of videos owned by the store, the list of videos rented by each customer, and the list of store members.

3. Write a program to play the Card Guessing Game. Your program must give the user the following choices:

   a. Guess only the face value of the card.

   b. Guess only the suit of the card.

   c. Guess both the face value and suit of the card.

   Before the start of the game, create a deck of cards. Before each guess, use the method `shuffle` to randomly shuffle the deck.

Index